Boatowner's Mechanical and Electrical Manual

Second Edition

How to Maintain, Repair, and Improve Your Boat's Essential Systems

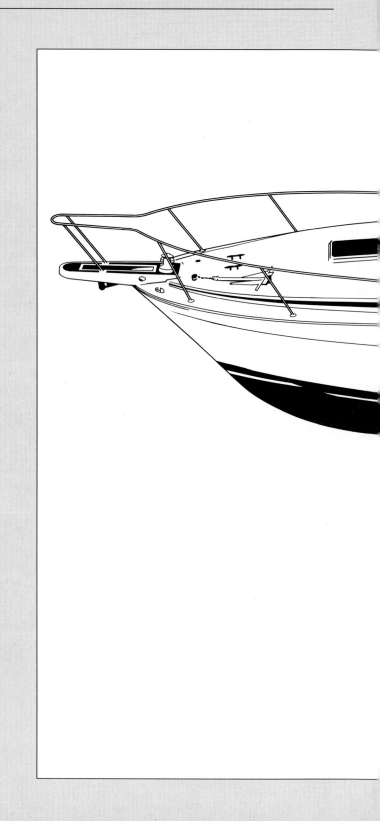

Other Books by Nigel Calder

Marine Diesel Engines, Second Edition
Refrigeration for Pleasureboats
Repairs at Sea
Cruising Guide to the Northwest Caribbean

International Marine/
Ragged Mountain Press
A Division of The McGraw-Hill Companies

1112131415 KGP KGP 098765432

Copyright © 1996 by International Marine, a division of
The McGraw-Hill Companies.

Library of Congress Cataloging-in-Publication Data
Calder, Nigel.
    Boatowner's mechanical and electrical manual / Nigel Calder.—2nd ed.
        p. cm
    ISBN 0-07-009618-X (alk. paper)
    1. Boats and boating—Maintenance and repair—Handbooks, manuals,
etc. 2. Boats and boating—Electric equipment—Maintenance and
repair—Handbooks, manuals, etc. I. Title.
VM322.C35 1995   95-25808
623.8'50028'8—dc20   CIP

Questions regarding the content of this book should be addressed to:

International Marine
P.O. Box 220
Camden, ME 04843

Questions regarding the ordering of this book should be addressed to:

The McGraw-Hill Companies
Customer Service Department
P.O. Box 547
Blacklick, OH 43004
Retail customers: 1-800-822-8158
Bookstores: 1-800-722-4726

Printed by Quebecor
Production by Mary Ann Hensel, Deborah Krampf, and Molly Mulhern
Edited by Jonathan Eaton, Tom McCarthy, Sydne Matus

Second Edition

Boatowner's Mechanical and Electrical Manual
Nigel Calder

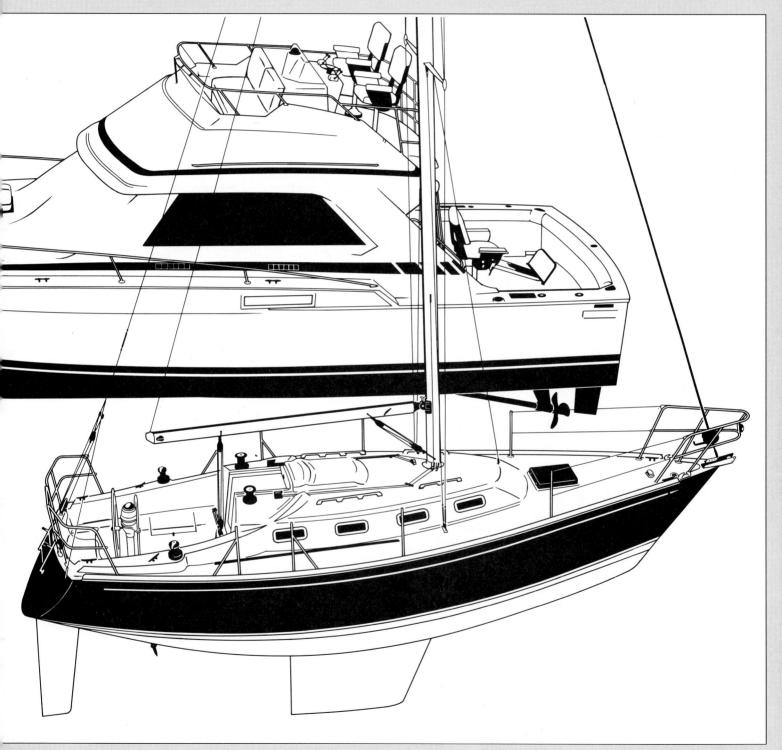

International Marine
Camden, Maine

McGraw Hill

FLO

DEDICATION

To Pippin and Paul;
may this book hasten the day when they
take over the maintenance of the boat.

Contents

List of Troubleshooting Charts

List of Tables

Acknowledgments/Preface to the Second Edition

In the six years since I wrote the first edition of this book there have been significant changes in boat systems, particularly electrical systems, which would, in themselves, have been justification for a second edition. But in addition to this, the success of the first edition has established me as a professional technical writer. This has not only afforded me the luxury of studying the subjects covered in this book full time, but has also brought me into contact with many of the smartest and most innovative people in the boating equipment world, which has greatly improved my understanding of a number of complex issues. As a result, for this second edition I felt it necessary to rewrite much of the first half of the book, and significant sections of the second half. The text has grown by at least 20%, with numerous new illustrations, troubleshooting charts, and tables. The result is a volume that I feel is, both in small ways and large, far superior to the first edition.

In the course of writing this new edition, I have corresponded with, and received help from, literally dozens of boat and equipment manufacturers and individuals. Some have devoted considerable amounts of time and resources to reviewing and correcting draft chapters; others have shown me their plant and equipment or helped in other ways. I am especially indebted (in no particular order) to Alan Fitzpatrick of Marine and General Battery, Rick Proctor of the Cruising Equipment Company, David Smead of Ample Technologies, Bob Ajeman of Professional Mariner, Paul Michaelcyck of Ancor, Chuck Hawley at West Marine, Jack Honey of Marine Technology, David Potter of Kemp Spars, Julian Whitlock of Whitlock Marine, Gordan Lyall of Simpson Lawrence, Michael Adler of Adler Barbour, Kevin Alston of Glacier Bay, Jack Durrant of Ampair, Bill Owra of Everfair Enterprises, John Surrette of Rolls Battery Co., Tom Hale and Lsyle Gray at the American Boat and Yacht Council, Dick Troberg of Fluke, Wally Ivison of Norseman Marine, Don Kavenagh, associate editor of *Ocean Navigator* magazine, Bob Loeser, Professors Geoffrey Swain and Harry Lipsitt, experts in corrosion, and Ron Colby.

The following companies have also provided information and support: ABI, AC/Delco, Allcraft Corporation, Allison Marine Transmissions, American Insulated Wire Corp., Ampair, Aquadrive, Arco, Atlantic/Trident Solar Products, Autohelm, Automate, Balmar, Barient, Barlow, Battery Council International, Beckson Marine, Bertram Yacht, Blake and Sons, Blue Seas, Borg Warner Corporation, Brookes and Gatehouse, C. H. Corporation, Camper and Nicholson, Carol Cable Co., Caterpillar Tractor Co., Cetrek/Navstar, Climate Control Inc., CPT Inc., Danforth, Danfoss, Dart Union Co., Delco Remy, Detroit Diesel, Dole Refrigeration Co., Don Allen Co., Edson International, Force 10, Forespar, Four Seasons, Frigoboat, Frigomatic, Furuno, Furlex, Garrett Automotive Products Co., Givens Buoy, Gougeon Brothers, Groco, Grunert Refrigeration, Guest, Halyard Marine Ltd., Hamilton Ferris, Harken, Hart Systems Inc., Heart Interface, Henderson Pumps, Holset Engineering Co., Hood Yacht Systems, Hurth, Hydrovane Yacht Equipment Ltd., Interstate Batteries, ITT/Jabsco, Kenyon Marine, Kohler Corporation, L.Q. Moffit, Lasdrop Shaft Seal, Leeward Rigging, Lewmar Marine, Lirakis Safety Harness Inc., Loos and Co., Lucas Marine, Paul Luke and Sons, Lunaire Marine, Mansfield Sanitary, Marine Power Ltd., Marine Vane Gear Ltd., Marinetics Corporation, Marlec, Mars Electronics, Martec, MaxProp, MDC, Mercantile Manufacturing, Merriman Yacht Specialties, Metalmast Marine, Micrologic, Morse Controls, Munster Simms Engineering Ltd., Navico, Navstar, Navtec, New-Mar, Nicro Fico, NMEA, Norseman/Gibb, Onan, Parker Hannifin Corporation, Parker Industrial, PDC Labs International, Perkins Engines Ltd., Plastimo, ProFurl, PYI, Raritan, Raytheon Marine Co., Rolls Battery Engineering, RVG, S and F Tool Co., Sailomat, Sailtec, Sanden International, Schaefer, Sea Frost, Sea Inc., Sealand Technology, Shaft Lok Inc., Shakespeare, Shipmate Stove Division, Signet Marine, Solar Power Corporation, Southwire Company, SpaCreek Inc., StaLok, Stowe, Stream Stay, Surrette Storage Battery Co., Tartan Marine Co., Taylor's Para-Fin, Tecumseh, Trace Engineering, Tracor Instruments, Universal Enterprises, VDO Marine, Vernay Products, Wagner Marine, Walker and Sons, Wallas Marin, Westerbeke Generators, Whale, Whitlock Marine, Wilcox-Crittenden, Wolter Systems, and York.

My editors at International Marine, in particular Tom McCarthy, have been as helpful as ever. Jim Sollers, illustrator extraordinaire, has done an astounding job interpreting my rough sketches. Molly Mulhern, the International Marine art and production director, has shown great patience with the rest of us and somehow kept the manuscript and illustrations organized and on schedule.

So you see, although it is my name on the cover, this book is really a collective effort. My thanks to everyone.

Nigel Calder
Maine, September 1995

Introduction

In the past two or three decades boat equipment has taken a quantum leap in complexity. It is no longer possible to keep things operating with a monkey wrench, hammer, and grease gun. More and more equipment needs specialized servicing, and the cost of professional help is going through the roof. While the public may think that boatowners are rich, in reality most are middle-income salary earners who strain their budgets to support their boating habit. The boatowner of today with limited funds needs a good working knowledge of all systems aboard, the ability to keep up with maintenance, and the means to troubleshoot and repair a broad range of breakdowns.

This book is intended to make these three objectives a realistic possibility with respect to the basic equipment found on most modern, midsized boats, both power and sail. In developing its contents, the biggest problem I have had is in deciding where to draw the line between what a talented amateur in a jam can reasonably be encouraged to undertake, and leading people into trouble. Since I have a high regard for most people's capabilities, I have gone well beyond the information typically available to the general boating public.

I have taken great pains to ensure the accuracy of this book. All information is given in good faith. Nevertheless, I must caution the reader: If you doubt what you are doing, leave things alone. I cannot accept liability for any damage or injuries arising from the reader's attempts to follow the procedures in this book. If you wreck a piece of equipment, sink the boat, or hurt yourself, the responsibility has to be yours.

Now that I've got that off my chest, a word on how to use this book. There are four distinct levels at which it can be useful:

- Many maintenance problems and equipment failures are the result of inadequate or improper installations. A quick skimming of the book, skipping over the detailed sections on equipment repair, may well highlight a number of potential difficulties on your boat and enable you to take corrective action before something goes wrong. This is especially relevant for anyone buying a new boat. Proper liaison with the boatbuilder can eliminate most built-in problems at a fraction of the cost of a later cure.
- When buying new equipment, a review of the pertinent section(s) will give you an idea of what can go wrong. Although I don't recommend one brand name over another, I can arm you with appropriate questions to ask about any brand. This may save a lot of grief later.
- Routine maintenance is covered in some detail in each chapter with an annual haulout (winterizing) summary in Appendix A.
- When equipment does malfunction or break down, the table of contents and index will point you to the relevant sections on troubleshooting and repair.

After reading this book, boatowners may think that maintenance and repair is a full-time job in itself. Sometimes it does seem like that. But in reality, most routine maintenance procedures take little time. The key is to be methodical and organized. And keep in mind that boat equipment likes to be used frequently. In the marine environment, more things seize up from lack of use than from being used. Your boat will be least troublesome if you get the maintenance done, then go out on the water as often as possible.

Happy Boating!

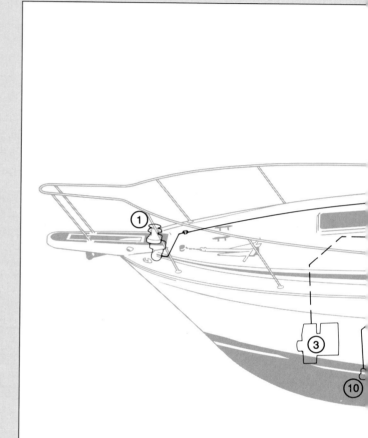

CHAPTER 1

Figure 1-1. These two representative boats illustrate just how complicated the electrical system of an average modern pleasure boat has become. *(Jim Sollers)*

—————————— 12 VDC

— — — — — — 120 VAC

(1) anchor windlass
(2) macerator pump
(3) air conditioner
(4) engine instruments, radios, navigation instruments
(5) engine starter switch
(6) distribution panel
(7) battery isolation switch
(8) 120-VAC shoreside receptacle
(9) bilge pump
(10) sump pump
(11) batteries
(12) air conditioning compressor
(13) blower
(14) starter motor
(15) refrigerator
(16) water heater
(17) head pump
(18) cabin lights
(19) navigation lights
(20) pressure water pump

Establishing a Balanced Battery-Powered Electrical System

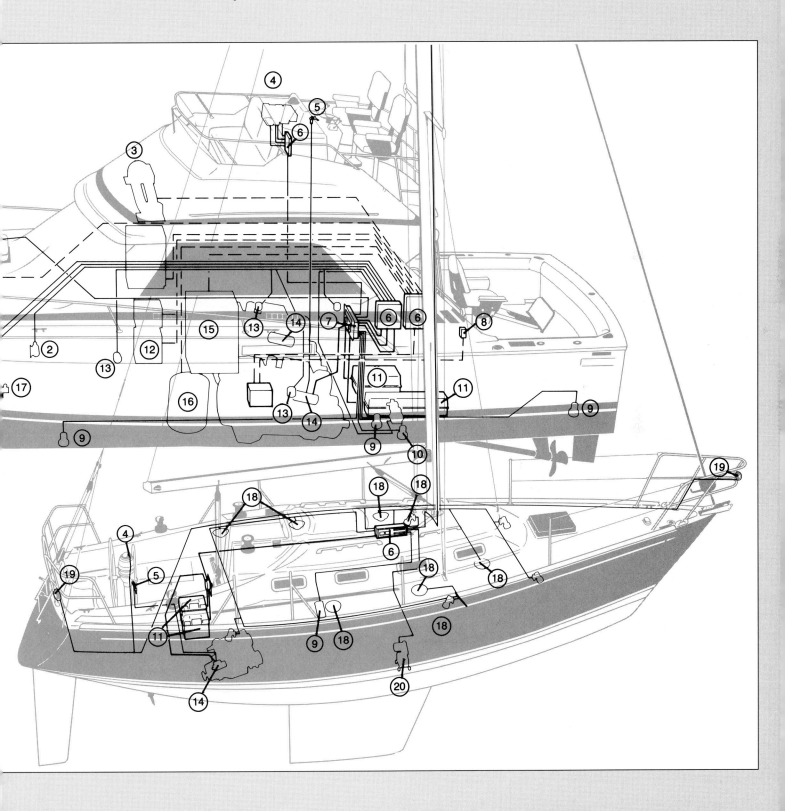

Introduction

Today's pleasure boats have become increasingly dependent on electricity. Most engines can't be started without it; many boatowners can't navigate without it; a growing number of toilets can't even be flushed without it! While the explosive growth of electrical and electronic equipment over the past decade or two has brought about a revolution in comfort and ease of boat handling, electrical equipment malfunctions have become the most common maintenance problem aboard boats, especially those with aging, hodgepodge, or jury-rigged electrical circuits.

The marine environment is a terrible place for electricity. To be troublefree, electrical circuits must be installed with great care and to the highest standards—topics which are dealt with in Chapter 3. But no matter how carefully an electrical installation is carried out, the entire system must be properly balanced in the first place or it will soon become a source of endless problems and a constant drain on the pocketbook.

Because of improperly set up systems, many boatowners repeatedly find themselves with dead batteries, outright battery failures, and lengthy charging times. Fixing immediate problems does nothing to resolve the overall imbalance in the system, guaranteeing that the next difficulty is just around the corner. A large number of boats come straight off the production line with these potential problems built in. Thus the first requirement for electrical problem solving and repair is to understand the peculiar needs of a boat's 12-volt electrical system, and to make sure that the overall system is in balance. This chapter takes a look at these general considerations; Chapter 2 deals with detailed maintenance, troubleshooting, and repair procedures for specific pieces of 12-volt electrical equipment. Although I focus on 12-volt systems, all information is equally applicable to 24 or 32 volts.

The Peculiarities of Boats

Consider first an automobile. A 12-volt battery provides the energy to crank a starter motor, normally for just a second or two, after which the engine fires up and the alternator cuts in. The alternator subsequently supplies all the car's electrical needs, plus an extra margin to replace the juice the starter motor withdrew from the battery. The car's electrical system runs on the energy supplied by the alternator, not that supplied by the battery. Although starter motors use a tremendous amount of energy, they do so for a very brief period of time, and thus pull next to nothing from a battery. For example, a 400-amp starter motor (this is a large starter motor) would consume 400 amp-hours of energy in 1 hour,

but cranking it for 15 seconds (which is far longer than normal) drains the battery by only $400 \div (4 \times 60) = 1.66$ amp-hours, which is not very much! (The distinction between amps and amp-hours is drawn on page 9.) This drain is replenished by the alternator in just a few minutes. In normal usage a car battery is almost always fully charged, and the batteries do very little work. This holds true for all cars, regardless of size, electrical complexity, or use. The only variable from one car to another is the capacity of the alternator—cars with high electrical loads need bigger alternators.

Contrast this with a sailboat. The "average" boat spends most of its time in a slip. Periodically the owner cranks the engine, motors out of the slip, shuts the engine down, and goes sailing. Apart from the time spent motoring, the boat's electrical system runs directly off the battery. The battery will be discharged more deeply than an automobile battery, while the engine will be run far less than an automobile engine, providing minimal charging time.

Now consider the "average" powerboat. The engine will be run for longer periods of time than a sailboat's, with usage patterns often similar to those of an automobile. But even so, most powerboats, especially cruising boats, will have extended periods when the engine is shut down and the boat's electrical system is running off the batteries. Although larger powerboats may have a 24-hour-a-day generating capability, with a battery charger left permanently "on" so that battery service closely resembles that of an automobile, this is not necessarily the case; an increasing number of boatowners with onboard AC generators and substantial power requirements are discovering that with a good-quality DC/AC inverter (see Chapter 5), they can shut down their generators for most of the day, enjoying peace and quiet while on the hook and saving money at the same time! In this case too, battery use closely resembles that of cruising sailboats.

What this adds up to is that in contrast to automotive use, one way or another at some time almost all boats run their DC systems off the battery, deeply discharging it. As a result, the working environment for all the major DC system components—the battery, alternator, and voltage regulator—is very different from that found in the automotive field, and yet, primarily for reasons of cost, it has been customary to use transplanted automotive equipment in marine applications with little or no modification. Not surprisingly, this leads to numerous problems, most of which have their origins in the limitations of existing battery technology. To see why this is so, and how to correct problems, we need to delve into this technology.

Batteries

How They Work

A battery is composed of one or more *cells* (Figure 1-2). Each cell contains alternating negative and positive *plates*, between which are plate *separators* (insulators). All the negative plates are connected together, as are all the positive plates. Each plate has a *grid* configuration, and within the grid is bonded the plate's *active material* (Figure 1-3). The grid provides the physical structure for the plate, and the means for conducting electrons in and out of the plate. The active material is the substance that produces the electrons.

When fully charged, the active material in the negative plates is pure *sponge lead;* in the positive plates, it is *lead dioxide*. The plates are placed in contact with a solution of sulphuric acid (the *electrolyte*). As a battery discharges, the acid from the electrolyte combines with the active material in the battery plates, forming *lead sulphate* and water, the latter diluting the acid solution. When a battery is charged, water is driven from the acid solution, increasing the strength of the electrolyte, while the used portion of the plate material that formed the lead sulphate is reconverted to active material.

The formula describing this process, for those who are interested, is as follows:

$$PbO_2 + Pb + 2H_2SO_4 \leftrightarrows 2PbSO_4 + 2H_2O.$$

Voltage, capacity, and rate of discharge/recharge. Irrespective of plate size, construction, or numbers of plates in an individual cell, any charged lead-acid cell will produce a voltage of around 2.1 volts. This is simply the voltage that results from placing lead dioxide and lead in sulphuric acid (cells using other metals and electrolytes have different voltages—for more on this phenomenon see the section on galvanic corrosion in Chapter 4).

What is not built into the cell chemistry is the *capacity* of a cell (how many electrons the cell can store), how fast the cell can deliver these electrons when connected to a load, and how fast it can be charged.

Crudely speaking, capacity is a function of the amount of lead in a cell. The greater the weight of lead dioxide and lead paste, the greater the storage capacity. A large, thick plate will produce the same voltage as a small, thin plate, but will store many times more electrons.

The ability of a plate to give up its stored energy depends on the ability of the acid in the electrolyte to react with the active material in the plate. The active material is made porous so that the acid can filter (diffuse) through the plate, allowing water to percolate out and fresh acid to

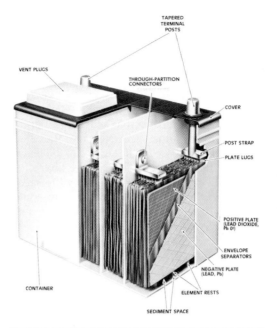

Figure 1-2. Typical automobile-type battery construction. There are six cells; within each is a series of alternating negative and positive plates, each one isolated from its neighbors by intervening insulators, called separators. The plates are immersed in a sulphuric acid solution. The negative plates are connected with each other and with the negative terminal; the positive plates are collectively connected with the positive terminal. *(Battery Council International)*

percolate in during discharges, and the reverse to happen during charges. The thicker a plate, and the denser the active material, the slower this process of percolation and as a result the slower a battery will give up its stored energy, and conversely the slower it can be charged.

When a battery is put under a heavy load, the electrolyte will first react with the accessible (surface) areas of the plates, but once these have given up their stored energy the rate at which electrons can be released from the inner areas of the plates slows down, causing the voltage to fall off. This does not necessarily mean the battery is dead: If it is rested, giving water time to diffuse

Figure 1-3. A collection of battery plates with some of the active material removed to reveal the plate grids. The white areas are sulphated (see page 6).

out of the plates and fresh acid time to filter in, the voltage will recover as fresh areas of active material are brought into service. This is why if a car is cranked until the battery dies and then left for a short period of time, the battery will frequently recover and crank the engine again—the acid has diffused to unused portions of the plates, providing a fresh burst of energy.

When it comes time to charge, the charging current will first reconvert to active material the lead sulphates most accessible to the electrolyte—that is, those on the surface of the plates. This can be done relatively quickly. Thereafter the rate of charge will be limited by the speed with which acid can filter out of the active material, and water filter in, as the charging progresses. It is this diffusion rate that determines the *charge acceptance rate* of a battery, with thick-plate, dense-active-material batteries having a lower charge acceptance rate than thin-plate, low-density-batteries.

Electrolyte Variations

The electrolyte in a battery may take different forms. These in turn will affect the nature of the battery's construction. The principal variations are:

"Wet" or "flooded" electrolyte. The traditional battery has a liquid electrolyte and is known as a *wet*, or *flooded-electrolyte*, battery. During periods of charging, particularly the final stages of charging, some of the charging current breaks down water in the electrolyte into its component parts of hydrogen and oxygen, which then bubble out of the electrolyte—the battery is said to *boil* or *gas*—lowering the level of the electrolyte. This water must periodically be replaced by topping up the battery cells with distilled water, via removable vent caps. (Note that much of this water loss can be prevented by fitting Hydrocaps, available from the Hydrocap Corporation, Miami, FL. These devices contain a catalyst that causes the hydrogen and oxygen to recombine into water. However, Hydrocaps have to be used with caution on the kinds of fast-charging systems I will be discussing later in this chapter.)

The battery plate grids in wet batteries have small amounts of antimony added to the lead during their manufacture. This considerably strengthens the grid and helps to lock the active material in the grids (which reduces shedding—see below), but antimony has the undesirable side effect of promoting internal galvanic currents within a battery, which slowly discharge the battery when it is left idle (a process known as self-discharge). Antimony also intensifies gassing during charging.

Gelled electrolyte. In a *gel-cell*, the electrolyte is formed into a gel with the consistency of soft candle wax. During manufacture this gel is pasted onto the battery plates and separators, which are then packed tightly together. During discharges and charges the active material in the battery reacts with the gel in immediate contact, but there is not the same fluid movement within the electrolyte as in a wet battery. As a result, the battery plates must be kept relatively thin to achieve adequate diffusion of the gel around them.

The gel cannot be replaced during service, so gelled batteries cannot be topped up. They are built as sealed no-maintenance units. Because they cannot be topped up, it is essential to prevent gassing during charging, since this would cause the electrolyte to dry out (it turns to a powder) and the battery to fail. Several methods are used to keep gassing to a minimum:

1. Charge voltage is carefully controlled to prevent overcharging.
2. The antimony used to reinforce conventional battery plates is replaced with calcium. The resulting plate grid is not as strong, but is far less prone to gassing or self-discharge.
3. Some batteries are allowed to build up a certain amount of internal pressure. Under pressure, small amounts of hydrogen and oxygen produced during charges will recombine into water and be absorbed into the electrolyte (as a result, these batteries are sometimes called *recombinant*). Excessive charging, however, will cause excessive amounts of hydrogen and oxygen to be produced, so recombinant batteries always have pressure relief valves to vent excess gases (gel-cell batteries are also sometimes called SVR—sealed valve regulated—batteries). Anytime venting takes place, the electrolyte is drying out and battery life is being reduced.

Note that many so-called maintenance-free batteries are in reality nothing more than wet batteries with excess electrolyte contained in partially sealed cases. During service the excess electrolyte is slowly used up. Because there is no way to top up these batteries, once the plates begin to dry out they are doomed. So it is important to distinguish between these batteries and a true *no-maintenance* battery—i.e., an SVR, recombinant, gelled-electrolyte battery.

Starved, or absorbed, electrolyte. A *starved*

or *absorbed electrolyte* battery is a variation of a gelled-electrolyte, SVR (and therefore recombinant) battery. The difference between it and a gel-cell is that it has even less electrolyte—just enough to soak the separator material. (These are sometimes called *AGM*—absorbed glass mat—batteries.) Consequently, *it is more important than ever to prevent overcharging and drying out of the electrolyte.*

Modes of Failure

With these basic facts in hand we can understand the main reasons why batteries fail. Such an understanding is essential to designing DC systems that will be free from premature failure, and in troubleshooting problem systems. The principal causes of failure are:

Shedding of the active plate material. When a battery is discharged and charged, the chemical processes in the plates, converting sponge lead and lead dioxide to lead sulphate and back again, tend to weaken the bond between the active material and the plate grids (Figure 1-4). Every time a battery is discharged some of the active material is loosened and *shed* from the grid, reducing the overall capacity of the battery. This is a normal process of aging and will eventually result in a complete failure of a battery, either through material building up in the base of the battery until it reaches the

Figure 1-4. Shedding of active material from a battery plate. The material has broken loose from the plate grid and is ready to fall to the bottom of the battery.

level of the plates and shorts them out (Figure 1-5), or through the loss of much of the active material from the plates so that the battery no longer has the capacity to carry out its tasks. (Note that in recent years more and more batteries have been built with *envelope* plate separators, which are sealed on the sides and bottom, so that any shed material remains in the envelope. This reduces the incidence of plate shorting, but not the shedding itself.)

The extent to which a battery will shed its active material in a given situation is almost

Figure 1-5. A severe case of shedding. The positive plate grids in this battery have been entirely eaten away through galvanic corrosion as a result of repeated overcharging. This has allowed the active material to fall to the base of the battery.

Figure 1-6. Close-up of sulphated active material. For photographic purposes the sulphates have been dislodged and turned on end to show that the sulphation is not just a surface phenomenon.

Figure 1-7. Positive plate disintegration as a result of persistent overcharging. The grid structure within the body of the plate is entirely gone.

entirely a matter of its internal construction. Thin-plate, low-density-active-material batteries are far more susceptible to damage than thick-plate, high-density-active-material batteries. The process of shedding is accelerated by deep discharges, very high rates of discharge and charge, and, in the case of liquid-electrolyte batteries, by gassing during periods of overcharge, which will wash active material out of the plates, and possibly also by the sloshing of the electrolyte around the plates when a boat is pounding in a seaway. Gel-cells with their tightly packed plates resist shedding, and when it does occur the shed material tends to be trapped in the gel rather than falling to the base of the battery.

Sulphation. The lead sulphate formed in the

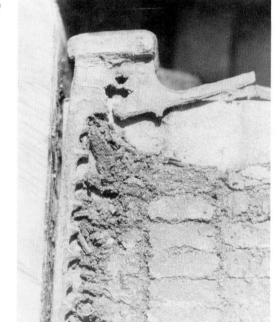

battery plates during discharges is initially soft and relatively easy to reconvert into active material through battery charging. If a battery is left in a discharged state, however, the sulphate hardens into crystals that prove increasingly difficult to reconvert into active material (Figures 1-3 and 1-6). This effectively reduces battery capacity and slowly kills the battery—a process known as *sulphation*. Sulphation can occur in several different ways: from leaving a battery discharged for a prolonged time; from persistent undercharging, so that a percentage of the battery's active material is always left uncharged; and from failing to charge the inner areas of thick plates or plates with dense active material (this is a variant of undercharging). In addition, idle batteries slowly self-discharge and sulphate over time, at a rate largely determined by whether the plates have antimony- or calcium-reinforced grids and by the ambient temperature (the higher the temperature, the faster the rate of discharge). When discharged, gel-cells have a slower rate of sulphation than other batteries. This is due to the recombination of oxygen—the presence of which accelerates sulphation in other batteries—into water, and its reabsorption into the gel.

Overcharging. Overcharging can be just as damaging as undercharging, since it leads to *gassing*. If this results in water loss and the lost water is not replaced, sooner or later the plates dry out. Gel-cells are particularly susceptible to damage: They have less electrolyte than wet-cells to begin with, and there is no way to replace lost electrolyte. Once active material is allowed to dry out, it is permanently lost.

During overcharges, galvanic activity within a battery also attacks the positive plate grids, causing them to deteriorate, reducing their current-carrying capability, and finally disintegrating them completely (Figure 1-7). The grids in thin-plate batteries fail sooner than those in thick-plate batteries.

Buckling of battery plates. A battery has an internal resistance that increases as the battery comes up to charge. As with any resistance, the more current driven through it, the warmer it gets. The normal result of excessively high rates of charge is that the battery heats up internally until the plates distort, shorting out adjoining plates and killing the battery.

Automotive (Cranking) Versus Deep-Cycle Batteries

From the foregoing we can see why automotive batteries are a bad choice in many marine applications. Automotive batteries are designed for engine starting, which requires the rapid release of a tremendous burst of energy. To make this possible, these batteries have many thin plates containing low-density active material. This maximizes the plate surface area and minimizes the diffusion time of acid through the plates. These construction features accelerate the rate at which the charge can be withdrawn from the battery.

But thin plates and low-density active material cannot handle repeated deep discharges and recharges (known as *cycling*). With each cycle—some of the active material literally falls out of the plate grids. This is of little concern in automotive (cranking) use since the batteries are rarely discharged more than a few percent, so very little shedding occurs. But in marine use, where repeated deep discharges are common, automotive batteries can quickly fall apart internally, a process accelerated by any pounding at sea. In fact, poorly constructed automotive batteries fail in as little as a dozen complete discharge/recharge cycles, while even the better-quality ones are unlikely to survive more than 30 to 40 such cycles (which may be just a month's cruising on some boats!). At the other end of the spectrum, the flimsy plate grids in automotive batteries cannot tolerate much overcharging during charging cycles without disintegrating.

A *deep-cycle* battery (in the UK a *traction* battery) is needed for cycling applications (Figures 1-8 and 1-9). Deep-cycle batteries have much thicker plates, stronger grids, denser active material, heavier plate separators, and generally tougher construction than automotive (cranking) batteries. There is still some shedding of active material from the plates with every discharge cycle, but nowhere near as much as from thin-plate batteries. *Deep-cycle batteries tolerate repeated discharges in a way that no automotive (cranking) battery can.* The heavier grids also withstand considerable abuse during charging (Figure 1-10).

Life cycles (cycle life). The differences between automotive and deep-cycle batteries are matters of degree (thicker plates, stronger grids, heavier separators, a tougher case, etc.) rather than fundamental differences in design. Thus, there is no clear dividing line between them. Some high-quality automotive batteries are as well built as some cheap "deep-cycle" batteries. It is not possible simply to rely on a manufacturer's description of a battery as "deep-cycle" when determining its quality (Figure 1-11)! The key in judging one battery against another is *life cycles*: the number of times a battery can be pulled down to a certain level of discharge, and then recharged, before it fails.

Figure 1-8. **Deep-cycle battery anatomy. Compare this battery's sturdy construction with the automotive-type battery in Figure 1-2.** *(Surrette America)*

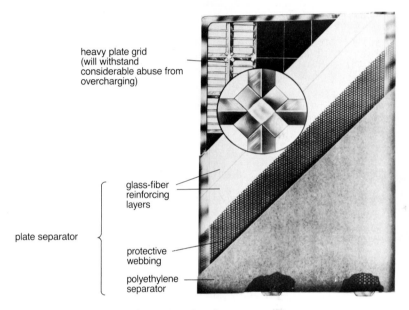

heavy plate grid (will withstand considerable abuse from overcharging)

plate separator

glass-fiber reinforcing layers

protective webbing

polyethylene separator

Figure 1-9. **A cutaway view of a positive plate from a top-of-the-line deep-cycle battery: The lead dioxide has been removed to show the heavy grid. Note the complexity of the multilayered plate separators.** *(Surrette America)*

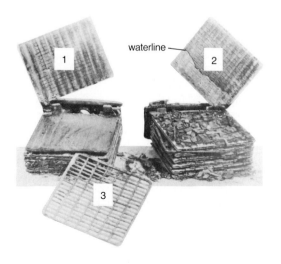

waterline

Figure 1-10. **Effects of overcharging on battery plates. The group of plates marked 1 is from a deep-cycle battery; that marked 2 is from an automotive battery. The topmost negative plate of both groups has been folded up to expose the positive plate below. The deep-cycle plate marked 3 has had all its active material removed to show that the grid is still intact in contrast to the positive plate grid of the automotive battery, which has disintegrated. The automotive battery was shorted out and using a lot of water, hence the low waterline mark on plate 2.** *(Surrette America)*

Figure 1-11. **The effects of cycling on battery plates.** This series of positive plates, each containing a different density of lead dioxide, has been subjected to 136 discharge/recharge cycles. Number 1 is typical of lightweight automotive batteries; number 6 is from a top-of-the-line deep-cycle battery. Note the almost total loss of plate material from the former while the latter is virtually intact. The densities of lead dioxide (grams per cubic inch) in each plate are as follows: #1, 50; #2, 55; #3, 60; #4, 65; #5, 70; #6, 75. *(Surrette America)*

Figure 1-12. **Life cycles as a function of depth of discharge at each cycle.**

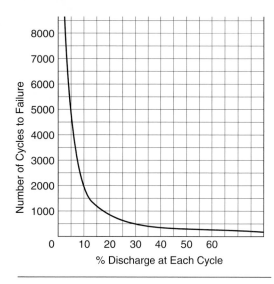

When assessing life cycles, it is important to make sure apples are compared with apples. Some manufacturers may estimate life cycles using a 50% discharge and recharge cycle. Others might use an 80% or even 100% discharge/recharge cycle. In general, the greater the depth of discharge in each cycle, the fewer the life cycles (i.e., the shorter the life expectancy of the battery). So if one battery has the same number of life cycles at an 80% discharge as another has at a 50% level of discharge, the former is superior; it will have far more life cycles at a 50% discharge than the latter (Figure 1-12). For our purposes, *the number of life cycles at the 50% level of discharge is the key criterion in assessing battery suitability for cycling applications.*

The other factor to consider in judging life-cycle data is the manufacturer's definition of battery "death." To some, death comes when the shedding of active plate material reduces the battery's capacity to 80% of its original value; to others, the battery dies only when it has fallen to as little as 60% of original capacity (which will artificially inflate the number of life cycles).

When comparing deep-cycle batteries, ask the battery supplier for this information. If it is not available, the battery is quite likely not suitable for marine deep-cycle applications.

Batteries for marine use. We are now in a position to make appropriate choices. If a battery is to be used *solely* for engine cranking and *immediately recharged by an engine-driven alternator*—in other words, where its usage directly parallels automotive use—an automotive cranking-type battery is perfectly adequate. To avoid premature plate disintegration under the rigorous conditions found at sea, especially the pounding that takes place from time to time, you'd want a good-quality, heavy-duty cranking battery. Its capacity should be at least as great as the cold cranking amps (see the accompanying sidebar, Battery Capacity Ratings) specified in the engine's manual.

For all other applications, you should assume that the batteries will be cycled at some time, especially batteries that are to be used for *house* as opposed to engine-cranking service. These should be good-quality deep-cycle batteries. The really contentious issue revolves around

Battery Capacity Ratings

Battery capacity is defined in three different ways: amp-hours, reserve capacity (or minutes), and cold cranking amps.

Amp-hours: This rating defines capacity in terms of the number of amp-hours that can be pulled from a battery at 80°F (26.7°C), at a relatively slow rate of discharge, before it dies (i.e., its voltage falls below 1.75 volts per cell, which is 10.5 volts for a 12-volt battery). In the USA the discharge period is normally 20 hours; in the UK, 10 hours. This means that a battery rated at 100 Ah is capable of delivering 5 amps for 20 hours in the USA (known as the *C20* rate), or 10 amps for 10 hours in the UK (known as the *C10* rate). Shorter time periods are sometimes used, notably 5 hours on some deep-cycle (traction) batteries (the *C5* rate, in which case a 100 Ah battery would be capable of delivering 20 amps for 5 hours).

Because of limitations in the speed of acid diffusion through its plates, *the faster a battery is discharged, the smaller the portion of its overall capacity it can deliver before its voltage falls to the threshold level.* In other words, a battery has a lower Ah capacity at higher rates of discharge (Figure 1-13). If a USA-rated 100-Ah battery (C20 rate) is discharged at a rate of 10 amps (the C10 rate) it will deliver only 84 Ah before its voltage falls to the threshold level, whereas a UK-rated 100-Ah battery (C10 rate) will deliver the full 100 Ah at this rate. Put another way, a 100-Ah C10-rated battery has a greater capacity than a 100 Ah C20-rated battery. *When comparing battery ratings, make sure the same rating period has been used.*

Reserve capacity (or *minutes*) is an automotive industry rating that is increasingly used with marine batteries. If a car's alternator dies, the whole electrical load (which at night includes lights) will be thrown on the battery. The reserve capacity tells us how long, in minutes, a battery at a temperature of 80°F (26.7°C) will sustain a certain load before its voltage falls below 1.75 volts per cell (10.5 volts for a 12-volt battery). The normal rating load is 25 amps, but sometimes other amperages are used. *For valid battery comparisons the same load must be used.*

Cold cranking amps (CCA) rate engine cranking ability. As temperatures decrease it takes more energy to crank an engine, while at the same time batteries have less available power. (Figures 1-14 and 1-15). The standard USA cold-cranking rating assumes a cold day (0°F; −17.8°C) and a recalcitrant engine that needs to be cranked for 30 seconds. It tells us the maximum discharge rate (in amps) the battery can deliver to the starter motor without falling below 1.2 volts per cell (7.2 volts for a 12-volt battery). Lately we have seen the introduction of *marine* cold cranking amps, in which it is assumed the temperature is 32°F (0°C), which inflates the CCA figure. In Europe different parameters may be used. In the UK, the British Standard Rate is based on a temperature of 0°F (−17.8°C), but with cranking sustained for 180 seconds down to a final terminal voltage of 1.0 volt per cell; the International Electrotechnical Commission rating is at the same temperature, but with cranking sustained for 60 seconds down to a final terminal voltage of 1.4 volts per cell. Once again, *when making battery comparisons, see that the same test methods are used.*

Note: An *amp* (*ampere*) is a measure of the *rate of flow* of electric current. It represents a specified number of electrons passing a given point every second, in the same way that gallons per minute in fluid systems represent a certain volume of fluid passing a given point in 1 minute.

An *amp-hour* (abbreviated to *Ah*) is a measure of the *quantity* of electric current. One Ah is the total number of electrons that will pass a given point if a current of 1 amp is sustained for 1 hour. It says nothing about the rate of flow, since the same number of electrons could be supplied by a 60-amp current for one minute, or a 3,600-amp current for 1 second. In the same way, 100 gallons of water could be supplied by a 1 gallon/minute pump running for 100 minutes, or a 100 gallon/minute pump running for 1 minute.

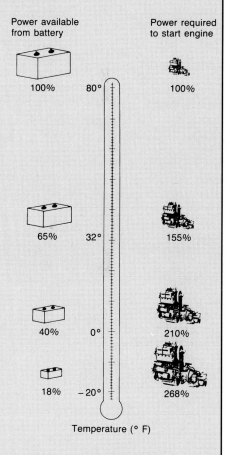

Figure 1-14. As the temperature falls, a battery's starting power (cold cranking amps) declines while the energy required to crank an engine increases. A cranking battery must have a sufficient energy reserve to deal with the worst anticipated situation.

Power available from battery

Power required to start engine

100% 80°	100%
65% 32°	155%
40% 0°	210%
18% −20°	268%

Temperature (° F)

Figure 1-13. Battery capacity as a function of the rate of discharge: 100-Ah battery, USA (20-hour) rating. *(Battery Council International)*

(graph: Amps vs Hours)
44 Ah
54 Ah
70 Ah
84 Ah
100 Ah

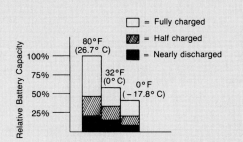

= Fully charged
= Half charged
= Nearly discharged

80°F (26.7°C)
32°F (0°C)
0°F (−17.8°C)

Relative Battery Capacity: 100% 75% 50% 25%

Figure 1-15. The effects of temperature and state-of-charge on battery capacity. *(Battery Council International)*

determining which make the better deep-cycle batteries for marine applications: wet-cells or gel-cells?

Wet-Cells Versus Gel-Cells

In the first edition of this book I recommended top-of-the-line wet-cells (notably Surrettes) over gel-cells for cycling applications. This judgment was based on the then considerably higher cost, amp-hour for amp-hour, of the recently introduced Prevailer gel-cells, and doubts about their ability to stand up to heavy cycling in marine use. Six years later, with the Prevailers manufactured under license in the USA, their cost has fallen into line with top-quality wet-cells, while they have withstood marine service well. Their success has spawned several clones, Dynasty and Lifeline batteries being the most widely advertised. It is time to reevaluate.

The following discussion pertains only to the best deep-cycle batteries, such as the Surrette (Tilton, NH) and Rolls (Salem, MA) wet-cells and the Prevailer gel-cells (East Penn, Lyon Station, PA). (In the UK, Lucas/Yuasa makes excellent traction batteries, while the Prevailers are sold by FWO Bauch under the Sportline DryFit label.) The discussion will prove a useful way to recapitulate much of the preceding material on batteries.

Wet-cells. Wet-cell deep-cycle batteries get their long cycling life from heavy, antimony-reinforced plate grids; thick plates with high-density active material; multiple plate separators; and very rugged cases. If properly cared for these batteries can be cycled *thousands* of times. But this powerful cycling performance is paid for not only in cost—the batteries are several times more expensive than an automotive battery—but also with a loss of performance in other respects.

The thick plates and dense active material slow the rate of acid diffusion through the battery and thus the rate at which a charge can be withdrawn or replaced. Anytime these batteries are placed under a high load (such as when cranking an engine), the battery voltage tends to fall off. Aside from cranking applications, this voltage drop is particularly significant with DC to AC inverter use (see Chapter 5); depending on the inverter, some loads (notably microwaves) will suffer a serious loss of performance as battery voltage declines.

Short-term high loads take the charge off the battery plate surfaces. Long-term lower loads (such as lights) drain a battery steadily over a number of hours, allowing it time to stabilize internally, which drains the charge from less accessible plate areas as well as the surface areas. When it comes time to recharge, these inaccessible inner plate areas must also be recharged, which requires time enough for the electrolyte to diffuse in and out. If charging times are limited the battery will not be fully charged—some of the lead sulphates formed in the inner plate areas when the battery was discharged will remain. These will slowly crystallize until no amount of charging will reconvert them to active plate material—the battery will become sulphated.

In other words, *the very steps taken to reduce damage from cycling—increasing plate thickness and density—increase the chances of damage from sulphation!* There is another problem with wet-cell batteries: The antimony used to reinforce the plate grids causes minute discharge currents within the battery itself. These currents will steadily *self-discharge* an unused battery. If the battery is not regularly recharged, the lead sulphates forming in the plates will harden, causing a permanent loss of capacity. *The search for maximum cycling strength increases the chances of damage from sulphation.*

To minimize damage from sulphation, a wet-cell deep-cycle battery must be periodically (at least once a month) returned to a full charge and then, if it has been heavily discharged during the month, given a *controlled overcharge*—a process known as *equalization* or *conditioning*. The purpose of this overcharge is to soften up hardened sulphates and put them back into active service. It is done by charging the battery at around 3% to 5% of its rated amp-hour capacity (i.e., 3 to 5 amps for a 100-Ah battery) until the battery voltage is driven to between 15.0 and 16.2 volts (for a 12-volt battery). During this period the battery must be isolated from all loads, since these high voltages can damage sensitive electronic equipment. Equalization requires specialized equipment and takes several hours. I discuss it in more detail on page 47.

All wet-cell batteries tend to gas to a certain extent as they approach full charge. A *Surrette or Rolls* subjected to an equalization charge will bubble away steadily like a simmering cook pot! Explosive gases are given off, corrosive vapors are vented from the filler caps, and the battery uses water, necessitating regular refills to replace what is lost. None of these consequences is desirable.

In short, wet-cell deep-cycle batteries have their problems. The gel-cells minimize these problems, but not without introducing drawbacks of their own, which deserve a little investigation.

Gel-cells. There is less electrolyte in a gel-cell. As we have seen (page 4), during construction the separators and plates are saturated with the gelled electrolyte and then tightly packed together. Since there is not the same movement of electrolyte in and out of the plates as in a wet battery, the plates must be thinner. Close spacing of multiple, thinner plates enables gel-cells to be discharged and recharged rapidly but at the expense of longevity. In terms of absolute cycle life, gel-cell deep-cycle batteries fall somewhere between a cranking battery and a top-quality wet-cell deep-cycle battery. Whereas a Surrette or Rolls *theoretically* can be cycled through 50% of its capacity more than two thousand times, a Prevailer yields four hundred cycles at a 50% level of discharge. The other gel-cells are certainly no better.

These figures, however, are theoretical when it comes to the wet-cells. In practice, because of their slow charge acceptance rate (the time it takes for the acid to diffuse through the thick plates), wet-cell batteries are frequently not fully charged and as a result slowly sulphate. *Given equal charging time, the gel-cells, with their higher charge acceptance rate, will be more fully charged. This may well result in a higher cycle life for the gel-cell.*

The gel-cells use plate grids in which the lead has been strengthened by alloying it with calcium rather than antimony. The result is a less rugged grid, but one that has a far lower rate of internal self-discharge—many times below that of a wet-cell battery. These weaker grids are another factor contributing to the theoretically shorter cycle life, but on the other hand, *if a wet-cell is allowed to lose its charge and sulphate, it will never live up to expectations, whereas a gel-cell can sit unattended for months without suffering damage.* Once again, in a given set of circumstances, *this may well result in a higher cycle life for the gel-cell.*

The ability of a gel-cell to give up its charge rapidly means that under heavy loads the battery voltage will hold up better than that of a wet-cell. If the battery is to be used for cranking or with an inverter, a smaller-capacity Prevailer will do as well as a larger-capacity Surrette or Rolls.

I mentioned that wet-cell batteries benefit from periodic controlled overcharges, which require specialized charging equipment. *For the gel-cells, any charging regimen that causes gassing, resulting in loss of electrolyte, spells certain death.* The gels are sealed, maintenance-free batteries that cannot be opened and topped up. Periods of sustained overcharging will cause them to dry out and fail. *Overcharging is probably the number one cause of failure of these batteries* (Figure 1-16).

As a result, the gel-cells need carefully regulated charging devices, but not specialized charging equipment. East Penn insists the voltage be kept between 13.8 and 14.1 volts. Given correct

Figure 1-16. **Dried-out gel-cell as a result of overcharging. The liquid has been driven out of the electrolyte, leaving a dry powder.**

regulation, in contrast to the wet-cells, venting of gases is minimal, there are no corrosive vapors, and no maintenance is required.

Making the right choice. Much more could be said about wet-cells versus gel-cells, but we already have enough information to settle the main questions. The first point to note is that *with proper charging and maintenance, a top-quality wet-cell deep-cycle battery will have a longer service life in a cycling application than any gel-cell.* However, and this is a big however, *these batteries are rarely charged or maintained properly*, with the result that very few live up to their potential. And of course absolute cycle life is not the only issue.

In circumstances where the slower charge acceptance rate of a wet-cell battery prolongs charging times and therefore engine running, a gel-cell may well be the better proposition. If a boat is to be left unattended for months at a time without its batteries being charged, as so many are, the lower self-discharge rate of a gel-cell battery will almost certainly make it the better choice. And if the owner habitually neglects even minimal battery maintenance, as so many do, the maintenance-free gel-cell is once again the best option. Added to which, of course, the gel-cell voltage holds up better under high-load discharges; the gel-cell gives off no explosive gases or corrosive fumes in normal use; and it cannot spill acid into the bilges if the boat is well-heeled or knocked down. In short, the typical sailor who uses his or her boat infrequently and does not have sophisticated charging devices with equalization capability will find the gel-cells hard to beat *so long as charging devices are properly regulated.*

On the other hand, when an owner does take care of batteries, has the devices to adequately charge them, can afford the necessary charging time, does not allow them to self-discharge over long periods, and does not mind the maintenance, wet-cell batteries give a longer cycle life at less cost. But it is the rare owner who pampers batteries in this way.

Golf-cart batteries. Finally, golf-cart batteries should be mentioned. These are constructed similarly to a wet-cell deep-cycle battery, and have similar operating characteristics. They do not have as high a cycle life, but on the other hand they will take a charge a little faster and are far more readily available and considerably cheaper. In terms of amp-hours per dollar in cycling applications, they may well be the best value of *any* battery on the market.

Nicads—The Ultimate Battery

Nickel-cadmium batteries are virtually indestructible, with a life span of up to 25 years. They will accept a fast charge right up to full capacity and maintain a high discharge voltage until almost dead. They can be discharged completely flat, left shorted out indefinitely, and still be recharged without damage! When idle, they have an extremely low rate of self-discharge. But amp-hour for amp-hour they are bulkier and far more costly than any lead-acid battery, and for these reasons are rarely used in boats. They also operate at slightly different voltages than lead-acid batteries, and as a result require different charging voltages. If a boat is kept for the life of the batteries and they can be afforded, nicads will pay for themselves handsomely as long as an appropriate voltage regulator is used. After a number of years the electrolyte will deteriorate and will need replacing; consult the manufacturer.

Getting Down to Specifics

Determining the type of battery to be used in marine applications is just the first step in evaluating a DC system. Earlier I referred to "average" sail- and powerboats, when in reality there is no such thing as an "average" boat. Some have shoreside power and a permanently connected battery charger in their slip, while others cruise and anchor out for months at a time with little or no engine-running time; some have auxiliary generators running 24 hours a day, keeping the boat's batteries constantly topped up, while others have solar panels and wind generators providing intermittent sources of power; and so on. No two boats—even identical production-line boats—end up with the same equipment, experience the same usage, or have the same electrical needs. *When discussing boat electrical systems it is not possible to deal in the same kinds of generalities that can be used with cars. Every boat must be treated as a unique entity with the peculiar requirements of its electrical system evaluated in relation to its usage.*

There are four steps to take in such an evaluation:

1. determine the power requirements of the boat

2. provide the necessary battery storage capacity

3. provide adequate charging capabilities

4. establish correct voltage regulation levels to maintain system harmony

All four interact, but for clarity they are treated separately here. The following sections focus broadly on the needs of a midsized cruising boat—sail or power—that has a moderate electrical load and relies on its batteries to supply power for extended periods of time. The needs of a boat with a different set of parameters can be readily extrapolated.

Determining Power Requirements

Overall power needs are normally calculated on a 24-hour (daily) basis on the assumption that, away from the dock, the batteries will be recharged daily. For some boats, 24 hours may not be a suitable interval, but it is easily adjusted: For example, divide by 24 to find hourly use; multiply by three to find needs for 3 days.

All electrical appliance loads are rated in either *watts* or *amps*—a 100-watt lightbulb, a 3-amp electric motor. The magnitude of the current flowing through an appliance is measured in amps; the work done by that current is measured in watts. The rating will be in the manufacturer's installation bulletin or on a label attached to the equipment. When adding up loads on an electrical system, it does not matter if watts or amps are used, just as long as the choice is consistent (although it is generally easier to use amps). In any case, watts and amps are easily interchangeable, since watts = volts × amps, and amps = watts ÷ volts.

Most boats have 12-volt systems, but some do not. The following examples can readily be converted to 24 or 32 volts by substituting the appropriate voltage.

Let's say we have a 25-watt lightbulb on a 12-volt system, and we want to know our load in amps. How many amps is this?

Amps = 25 watts ÷ 12 volts = 2.08 amps.

Perhaps our DC refrigeration unit has a 7-amp, 12-volt motor. How many watts does it draw?

Watts = 12 volts × 7 amps = 84 watts.

The first step, then, in calculating our daily load is to list all the onboard electrical equipment and convert the power needs into either watts or amps (Table 1-1). The next step is to estimate the normal daily usage, in hours or fractions of an hour, for each piece of equipment. The load for each piece is then multiplied by duration of use and the items are added up to give a *total daily load*, expressed in *watt-hours* or *amp-hours*. (For these calculations it is not necessary to understand the definition of watt-hours and amp-hours; what is important is to grasp the method by which the figures are derived.)

We have answered the first question: How much power does our boat demand each day? The sample system in Table 1-2 has a daily load of 100 Ah. The next question we must resolve is how much battery storage capacity we need to meet this demand.

Table 1-1. Typical Power Consumption of Electrical Loads (12 Volts)

Anchor light	1.0 amp
Anchor windlass	40 – 300 amp
Autopilot	⅓ – 30 amp
Bilge blower	2.5 amp
Bilge pump	5.0 amp
Cabin fan	0.2 – 1.0 amp
Cabin light (incandescent)	1.5 – 3.5 amp
Depth sounder	0.1 – 0.5 amp
Fluorescent light	0.7 – 1.8 amp
Freshwater pump	5.0 amp
GPS	0.5-1.0 amp
Knotmeter	0.1 amp
Loran	1.0 – 1.5 amp
Masthead light	1.0 – 1.7 amp
Radar	4.0 – 8.0 amp
Refrigerator (typical)	5.0 – 7.0 amp
Running lights (port, starboard, and stern)	3.0 amp
SatNav	0.2 – 0.8 amp
Spotlight	10.0 amp
Spreader lights	8.0 amp
SSB (receive)	1.5 – 2.0 amp
(transmit)	25 – 35 amp
Strobe light	0.7 amp
Stereo/tape deck	1.0 amp
VHF (receive)	0.7 – 1.5 amp
(transmit)	5.0 – 6.0 amp
Wind speed indicator	0.1 amp

Providing the Necessary Capacity

The required battery capacity is intimately related to the intervals between charges. A boat such as our sample boat in Table 1-2, which uses an engine-driven alternator as its principal means of battery charging and restricts engine

Table 1-2. Daily Power Requirements (12 Volts) of a Hypothetical Cruising Boat Anchored Off a Bahamian Beach

Equipment	Rating	Hours of Use (in 24 hours)	Total Load (in 24 hours)
6 lights	1.5 amps each	2 hours each = 12	18 amp-hours
1 refrigeration compressor	5 amps	10 hours	50 amp-hours
Masthead navigation lights	1.5 amps	8 hours	12 amp-hours
2 fans	1 amp each	5 hours each = 10	10 amp-hours
VHF radio, tape deck, etc.	2 amps total	5 hours total	10 amp-hours
		TOTAL	100 amp-hours

Notes:
1. Power consumption will vary enormously according to the boat's intended cruising area; refrigeration and fan usage in northern climates will be a fraction of that in the tropics.
2. Large items of occasional and short-term use, such as an electric anchor windlass, can in most instances be ignored, since they have little impact on the overall picture. On the rare occasions when sustained use is required, as when breaking out a deeply embedded anchor, the engine can be run during operation to provide a charging backup.

usage to once a day, must be capable of storing and delivering the desired 100 Ah between charges. This is a typical usage pattern for a cruising boat—sail or power—that spends much of its time at anchor. A boat with onboard power sources equal to demand, however, such as a boat that uses the main engine continuously, or runs a battery charger off a constantly operating auxiliary generator, or has large banks of solar panels or a wind- or water-driven generator, is in a position similar to an automobile: The battery is primarily for engine starting. The main engine, auxiliary generator, solar panels, or wind generator supply the boat's electrical needs and keep the battery topped up.

As solar panels and wind generators become more popular and widespread, most boats fall somewhere between these two extremes. But it must always be remembered that auxiliary generators break down, the sun may not shine for days, and the wind may fade away. At other times these charging sources may not meet all the electrical demands, and the battery will become a power source. When determining battery capacities, in order to ensure an adequate margin for all eventualities it is best to omit such charging methods from the calculations, assuming recharging will take place from the alternator alone, and therefore predicating recharge intervals and consumption between recharges on anticipated engine-running intervals.

So how much battery capacity do we need to deliver our 100 Ah a day? The answer is determined by three variables:

The depth to which the batteries are discharged. This is extremely important. Assuming a 100-Ah daily consumption, if we plan to discharge our batteries 100% at each cycle, a 100 Ah battery will meet our immediate needs (but will leave no emergency reserve for engine starting). However, no battery should ever be fully discharged. This applies to deep-cycle batteries just as much as to automotive batteries. Repeated 100% discharge of any battery, even the best deep-cycle battery, will drastically shorten its life (refer back to Figure 1-12).

But if we do not fully discharge a battery, we cannot utilize its full capacity. If we need 100 Ah, and we intend to discharge the battery only to the 50% level, we will need a 200-Ah battery. Bigger batteries last longer, but they cost more, weigh more, and take up more space. Somewhere we must make a trade-off between battery size and the degree of discharge in daily use (i.e., battery life). With deep-cycle batteries this is normally done at around the 50% level of discharge. We try to set up our total electrical system so that the battery is not discharged beyond 50% of its capacity in normal use. Occasional discharge to 80% or so can then be taken in stride.

The extent to which the batteries are routinely recharged. A discharged battery can be recharged rapidly to around 70% to 80% of its fully charged level. At this time the surface areas of the plates—those areas most accessible to the electrolyte—will have been recharged while the inner plate areas will be lagging behind. The acid and water will require time to diffuse in and out of the plates. Beyond the 70% to 80% level of charge, a battery's charge acceptance rate slows dramatically—the rate of charge must be tapered off sharply or battery damage will result. *It takes hours to bring a battery up the last 20% to a full charge*; the thicker and denser the plate material, the longer it takes. Since charging time is at a premium on most boats, in normal use it makes sense to bring batteries back merely to the 80% level (with the caveat that at least once a month we bring the battery to a full charge, so as to arrest incipient sulphation, and if it is a wet-cell battery we apply an equalization charge—see page 47). As we are discharging only to the 50% level, *our regular, usable storage capacity is now reduced to just 30% of overall battery capacity*.

The age factor. Over time a battery ages, losing capacity and performance. This results primarily from the progressive shedding of active plate material, but also from the gradual erosion of the positive plate grids. In order to take account of this aging process, it is customary to build an allowance—a "fudge factor"—into battery sizing calculations. Twenty percent is a fair ballpark figure.

Where does this leave us? *To support our hypothetical boat's 100-Ah daily consumption, taking a conservative approach utilizing only 30% of battery capacity, we need 333-Ah of battery capacity. Adding in a 20% fudge factor, we need 400 Ah of battery capacity.* This is approximately the capacity of two size 8D batteries wired in parallel (see below), which in point of fact is an excellent combination for most of today's electrically loaded midsize boats. (The designation "8D" refers only to the external dimensions of the battery; it says nothing about its all-important internal construction.) If we are a little less conservative and are using top-of-the-line deep-cycle batteries, we might decide to discharge these batteries to 30% of capacity before recharging, in which case we would need a battery capacity of only 250 Ah to meet a 100 Ah daily demand. However, this would be a *minimum*, leaving almost nothing in reserve, and

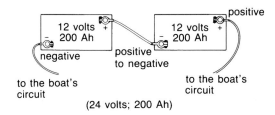

negative to negative · positive to negative · positive

12 volts 200 Ah — 12 volts 200 Ah

to the boat's circuit · to the boat's circuit

(24 volts; 200 Ah)

Figure 1-17A. Series connection. The Ah capacity is unchanged from a single battery's capacity, but output voltage is doubled. Twelve-volt batteries should never be connected in series on a 12-volt electrical system—the resulting high voltage will seriously damage equipment.

Figure 1-17B. Four 8-volt batteries connected in series to produce an output of 32 volts. *(Surrette America)*

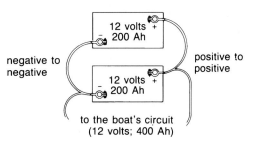

negative to negative · 12 volts 200 Ah · 12 volts 200 Ah · positive to positive

to the boat's circuit
(12 volts; 400 Ah)

Figure 1-18. Parallel connection. Output voltage remains the same as that of the individual batteries, but Ah capacity is doubled.

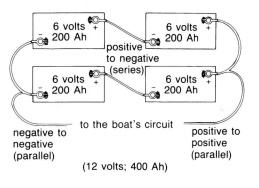

6 volts 200 Ah · 6 volts 200 Ah
positive to negative (series)
6 volts 200 Ah · 6 volts 200 Ah

negative to negative (parallel) · to the boat's circuit · positive to positive (parallel)

(12 volts; 400 Ah)

Figure 1-19. Series/parallel connection. In this example, each pair of 6-volt batteries connected in series delivers 12 volts, while connecting the pairs in parallel doubles system capacity. Thus this array achieves the same effect as two 12-volt batteries in parallel, but permits the use of high-capacity 6-volt batteries, which are individually lighter and easier to handle than high-capacity 12-volt batteries.

would virtually halve anticipated battery life compared with a battery discharged to 50% of capacity (Figure 1-12).

Series and parallel. In the example above, we are using two 8D batteries. When more than one battery is included in an electrical system, each can be hooked into the boat's circuits independently, via a suitable battery isolation switch (see page 28), or all can be connected together to boost output, either in *series* or *parallel*.

A *series* connection is made by tying the positive post of one battery to the negative post of another and then using the remaining positive terminal on one and negative terminal on the other to make the connection to the boat's circuits (Figures 1-17A and 1-17B).

When in series, *the total amp-hour capacity of the two batteries together remains the same as the amp-hour rating of either one, but the output voltage is doubled.* In our example, with two 200-Ah 12-volt batteries, series connection would still give us a 200-Ah capacity, but at 24 volts. *Twelve-volt batteries should never be connected in series on a 12-volt electrical system:The resulting high voltage will seriously damage equipment.*

A *parallel* connection is made by tying together the positive posts on two or more batteries, and also tying together the negative posts. The boat's circuit is connected to these combined positive and negative posts (Figure 1-18).

Paralleling batteries leaves the system voltage unchanged, but doubles its amp-hour capacity. Two 200-Ah 12-volt batteries in parallel will produce only 12 volts, but will have a 400-Ah capacity. *Connecting additional batteries in parallel increases system capacity at a given voltage.* The Ah capacity of all the paralleled batteries is added to find the system's total Ah capacity.

Both series and parallel connections are often made where a large storage capacity is needed but single batteries would be too cumbersome to handle. Typically, in a 12-volt system, two 6-volt batteries are placed in series to give 12 volts, and then another two 6-volt batteries, also in series,

are connected in parallel with the first two to double capacity while maintaining 12 volts (Figure 1-19).

There are those who claim that paralleling batteries is a poor practice, since if a cell fails in one battery it may drag down all the others in both batteries, and that in any case small circulating currents between the two batteries will increase their rate of self-discharge. These people argue that the only way to build up large-capacity 12-volt systems is to use two high-capacity 6-volt batteries in series. If the 6-volt batteries become too heavy to handle, the use of six individual 2-volt cells, connected in series, is advocated.

Then there are those who claim that there is no evidence to support this position, and that there is nothing wrong with paralleling batteries. What is more, they claim that whereas a failed cell in one battery will cripple both batteries if they are connected in series, a failed cell in a parallel situation will simply drag down the voltage on the other battery while leaving it operational.

At times there's a lot of hot air blown on this subject! I'm not sure the boatowner needs to be too concerned—I certainly would not hesitate to parallel a couple of batteries if that was the most convenient way to increase capacity. What *is* important, however, in both series and parallel connections, is *not to connect different types of batteries* (e.g., wet-cells and gel-cells; cranking and deep-cycle) or *batteries of different ages or capacities*—differences between the batteries will accelerate the destruction of both.

Providing Adequate Charging Capabilities

I recently worked on a sailboat, used extensively for cruising, that had seen minimal engine running and therefore minimal battery-charging time. Its frugal electrical system worked well for years; then it changed hands. The new owner installed a small, poorly insulated 12-volt refrigeration unit. The batteries died. The owner concluded that he had insufficient battery capacity and added another battery. This died also. He added two more, and these died! I removed five miscellaneous batteries from the boat, scattered around in different lockers.

Regardless of how much battery capacity a boat has, if the various charging devices are not putting back what is being taken out, the batteries eventually must go dead. The solution to this boat's problem was not more batteries, but a more efficient refrigerator and *more charging capability.* Since the primary source of battery charging for this boat, as for almost all boats, was an engine-driven alternator, the question became: What size alternator did the boat need, and how should it be regulated?

Sizing an alternator. When engine running time is extended, or the depth of discharge of batteries is minimal, a relatively small alternator is all that is needed—the typical 50- to 60-amp model will be more than adequate. The situation is similar to automotive applications, where the function of the alternator is to handle the car's electrical load and top off the battery, which typically is discharged no more than 5%.

But when, as is so often the case on a boat, engine running time must be kept to a minimum, while at the same time the batteries are deeply discharged, the alternator must be large enough to get the charging job done as quickly as possible. In this case, *the determining factor in sizing the alternator is normally the maximum current the batteries can absorb without damage.*

A battery 50% or more discharged will readily accept a rate of charge in excess of 25% of its rated capacity—that is, a 200-Ah battery will accept a charge of 50 amps or more. But as the battery starts to come up to charge, its charge acceptance rate declines; if the alternator continues to pump in a heavy amperage, the battery will begin to heat up and gas. By the time a battery is up to 70% to 80% of full charge, its charge acceptance rate will be down to no more than 10% to 15% of its rated capacity, and thereafter declines rapidly. Thin-plate cranking batteries can be charged faster than thick-plate deep-cycle batteries because the rate of electrolyte diffusion through the plates is greater, but there is still a strict limit to how fast charging can proceed without battery damage.

In order to keep charging times to a minimum, we need to be able to take advantage of the high charge acceptance levels at low states of battery charge. Thus, an alternator should have an amperage output of at least 25% of the total Ah-rating of the batteries it will be charging. To this we must add the boat's DC load while the engine is running (which may be quite high, particularly with some heavy-duty DC refrigeration units).

We need to distinguish *real* alternator output from *rated* output. An alternator is normally given an SAE (Society of Automotive Engineers) rating that describes its maximum output at a given temperature—77°F (25°C)—and speed of rotation. But when operating, the alternator will heat up, which will reduce its magnetism, causing its output to decline by as much as 25%. What is more, in automotive use a typical alternator puts out at full load for just a few minutes (after engine cranking) and then its output

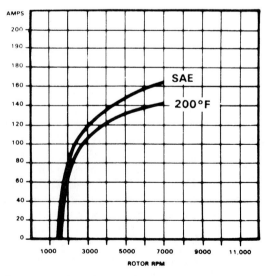

Figure 1-20. Specifications for a large-frame, 160-amp SAE-rated, 130-amp hot-rated, alternator. *(Powerline Division of Hehr International Inc.)*

tapers off. *Many automotive alternators cannot be run continuously at full load in high ambient temperatures* (such as are found in engine rooms on boats in the tropics) *without burning up.* But this is precisely what we want our alternator to do when we try to bring a large-capacity, deeply discharged battery back to full charge in the shortest possible time.

We require an alternator that is capable of continuously producing its full rated output at temperatures up to 200°F (93°C)—what is known in the USA as a *KKK*-rated alternator (Figure 1-20). For long life, even continuously rated marine alternators are best run at less than 100% of full output. To keep an alternator below its full output, an additional fudge factor of 25% should be built in when sizing it.

Where does this leave us? In the case of our two 8Ds, with a total capacity of 400 Ah, we should start with a hot-rated 100-amp alternator (25% of 400), add 25% to keep the alternator below continuous maximum output (bringing us to 125 amps), and then add in the DC load when the engine is running (which may well bring us to more than 150 amps!)

Such a high output alternator will have an important side benefit. Battery charging is frequently done at anchor, with the engine idling and the alternator operating below its rated speed and output. With the correct pulley sizes, a 150-amp alternator will easily reach 100 amps at a little above engine idle speed, but will still not overspeed at full throttle.

High-output alternators come in a *small frame*, which is interchangeable with most automotive alternators, and a *large frame*, which may be hard to mount in some circumstances. As of this writing, small-frame alternators are available with hot-rated outputs up to 130 amps (Table 1-3); there are rumors of breakthroughs in the works with outputs to 200 amps or more. In situations where more amperage is needed than can be supplied by a single small-frame alternator, two can be used, or else a single large-frame alternator. Suppliers in the USA include Ample Technologies, Balmar, Cruising Equipment Company (all of Seattle, WA); and SALT (Marathon, FL); in the UK, Ampair (Poole), Adverc BM (Willenhall), and Energy Control (Cowes). (Note: alternators for use on *gasoline* engines must be *ignition protected* to comply with US Coast Guard and other standards. *A failed ignition-protected alternator should never be replaced with an automotive alternator,* even if the latter is only one-third the price. The alternators mentioned above all have ignition protection.)

Speed of alternator rotation. An oversized alternator does no good if we can't get it up to its

Table 1-3. Typical KKK Alternator Outputs as a Function of Speed of Rotation and Temperature

(A) 140 amps SAE/105 amps hot

Alternator rpm	Alternator amps Cold–Hot
2,000	43–32
3,000	92–70
4,000	113–88
5,000	124–99
6,000	132–105
6,500	139–108

(B) 160 amps SAE/130 amps hot

Alternator rpm	Alternator amps Cold–Hot
2,000	40–30
3,000	100–76
4,000	127–98
5,000	148–112
6,000	157–123
6,500	160–131

(C) 190 amps SAE/165 amps hot

Alternator rpm	Alternator amps Cold–Hot
2,250	87–71
3,000	135–122
4,000	167–150
5,000	180–157
6,000	187–162
6,500	190–165

("Cold" = 77°F; 25°C)
("Hot" = 200°F; 93°C)

rated speed. The pulleys supplied with most alternators are not suitable for marine use because they are geared to automobile engines, which typically cruise at 2,500 to 3,500 rpm, whereas many boat engines spend much of their time refrigerating or battery charging at idle speeds between 700 and 1,000 rpm. *Since boat engines and usage vary considerably, alternator pulley sizes must be geared to individual use.* The following procedure should be used to size alternator pulleys:

1. Determine the alternator speed needed to produce the maximum *required* alternator output as described earlier. Note that this is *not* the maximum *alternator* output, and in general should not exceed 75% of maximum output in order to guard against overloading and overheating. (All alternator manufacturers can supply a graph of output versus speed of rotation;

some high-output and marine alternators are designed to produce their full output at considerably lower speeds than a typical automotive alternator, which makes alternator installation for low engine speeds easier.)

2. Find out the maximum safe operating speed for the alternator (usually 10,000 rpm).

3. Determine the *minimum* engine running speed in normal use (or normal battery charging and refrigerating speed if this is the predominant use, such as on a cruising boat spending much of its time at anchor).

4. Set up the alternator pulley ratio to achieve the maximum *required* output at this *minimum* engine speed, and then check to make sure that the alternator will not overspeed at maximum engine revolutions. If the alternator will overspeed, its pulleys will have to be powered down to the point at which it reaches maximum speed only at maximum engine revolutions.

For example:

• We have a 130-amp alternator and a maximum required output of 100 amps (77% of rated output). The alternator reaches 100 amps at 3,000 rpm.

• The maximum safe operating speed is 10,000 rpm.

• The boat spends much of its time at anchor, running its engine at 1,000 rpm to drive the mechanical refrigeration unit.

We need a pulley ratio of 3:1 to achieve an alternator speed of 3,000 rpm. Maximum engine speed is also 3,000 rpm, giving a maximum alternator speed of 9,000 rpm, which is within safe operating limits.

Tachometers. Many engine tachometers operate by sensing the output frequency of the alternator (in which case the tachometer wire will go from the meter to a terminal on the alternator). If nonstandard pulley ratios are used to drive the alternator, this will throw out the tachometer calibration. In some cases the calibration can be restored by moving the tachometer wire to a different terminal (called a *tap*); in other cases the tachometer itself can be adjusted, using a separate hand-held rpm meter on the end of the engine crankshaft to establish the engine speed. Occasionally, an under- or over-reading tachometer simply has to be lived with.

Horsepower requirements of alternators. An alternator's output is about 14 volts. At 100

amps an alternator is therefore producing: 14 volts × 100 amps = 1,400 watts. There are 746 watts in 1 horsepower; therefore in theory this alternator will require 1400 ÷ 746 = 1.88 horsepower to drive it.

However, alternators are only 50% to 60% efficient in energy conversion, so this figure needs to be doubled to 3.76 horsepower, and then a further factor added for other energy losses such as drive belt and pulley friction! This results in a power requirement of up to 4 to 5 horsepower at 100 amps. Obviously, at reduced loads the alternator will need less power. (Note that large-frame alternators and large pulleys cause less power loss than small-frame alternators and small pulleys.)

A side loading of this magnitude on an engine's crankshaft pulley may damage the crankshaft oil seal or bearing. Before installing a high-output alternator, check with the engine manufacturer to make sure the motor can handle the load. If it can't, side loading can be eliminated by adding a *stub shaft* to the crankshaft, and either directly driving the alternator with the stub shaft (i.e., eliminating the pulleys and belt) or else adding a separate *pillow-block* bearing to the stub shaft to absorb the side load of the alternator.

Another problem that may occur with small engines and large alternators is that the horsepower absorbed by the alternator at times causes unacceptable propulsive power losses. This situation can be alleviated by fitting a sophisticated voltage regulator with a current-limiting capability that is set to keep the alternator's output below a certain level (see the next section).

Establishing Correct Voltage Regulation

So far we have determined the correct type of batteries for a given application (cranking or deep-cycle), sized the batteries to meet the anticipated load, and determined the alternator capability and installation necessary to recharge these batteries. *None of this will be effective in providing a troublefree DC system unless we correctly tailor the alternator's voltage regulator to the needs of our system. Voltage regulation is one of the most neglected aspects of marine DC systems, and as a result improper voltage regulation is one of the single greatest causes of DC problems.*

The water tank analogy. A battery can be compared with a closed tank having a series of baffles inside it, the lower sections of which contain semipermeable membranes. A pump (the alternator) pushes in water (current) on one side (Figure 1-21), and the main section of the tank fills. The rising water is initially contained by

Belts and Pulleys

The horsepower requirements of high-output alternators put considerable loads on the belts. To gear up alternator speeds at engine idle speeds, smaller-than-normal pulleys are often used on the alternator, which further increases belt stresses. To determine what size belt is needed in any given application, all three factors—total hp load, alternator speed, and pulley size—have to be taken into account.

The specifications in the tables below are adapted from information supplied by the Gates Rubber Company for their excellent belts:

Table 1-4. HP Ratings for 3VX Super HC Molded Notch V-Belts (approx. ⅜" belts)

Alternator rpm	Alternator Pulley Diameter										
	2.2"	2.35"	2.5"	2.65"	2.8"	3.0"	3.15"	3.35"	3.65"	4.12"	
1000	0.87	1.02	1.18	1.34	1.49	1.69	1.85	2.05	2.35	2.82	Rated
2000	1.52	1.82	2.11	2.40	2.70	3.08	3 37	3.75	4.32	5.19	hp
3000	2.08	2.50	2.93	3.35	3.76	4.31	4.72	5.26	6.06	7.29	for a
4000	2.56	3.10	3.65	4.18	4.71	5.41	5.92	6.60	7.60	9.11	single
5000	2.96	3.62	4.27	4.91	5.53	6.36	6.96	7.75	8.90	10.6	belt

Table 1-5. HP Ratings for 5VX Super HC Molded Notch V-Belts (between ½" and ⅝")

Alternator rpm	Alternator Pulley Diameter			
	4.40"	4.65"	4.90"	
1000	5.22	5.92	6.62	Rated hp
2000	9.14	10.4	11.7	for a single
3000	12.3	14.1	15.9	belt

Table 1-6. HP Ratings for AX-Section Tri-Power Molded Notch V-Belts (½" belts)

Alternator rpm	Alternator Pulley Diameter										
	2.2"	2.4"	2.6"	2.8"	3.0"	3.2"	3.4"	3.6"	3.8"	4.0"	
1000	1.10	1.32	1.53	1.74	1.95	2.15	2.35	2.56	2.75	2.95	Rated
2000	1.59	1.96	2.33	2.70	3.06	3.41	3.75	4.09	4.43	4.76	hp
3000	1.81	2.32	2.81	3.30	3.77	4.24	4.69	5.13	5.56	5.98	for a
4000	1.83	2.44	3.03	3.61	4.16	4.70	5.21	5.71	6.18	6.63	single
5000	1.65	2.34	3.00	3.63	4.22	4.78	5.31	5.81	6.27	6.70	belt

As can be seen, the company does not size the 5VX belts for use with pulleys below 4.40 inches, although they are commonly used on smaller pulley sizes. What is clear is that a single 5VX belt will handle any alternator load. To see if the smaller 3VX belt will hold up in a given application, the alternator's rated output curve should be used to find the lowest speed at which it reaches full output (generally around 5,000 rpm), and the table entered at this speed to see if the belt can sustain the load for the given pulley size (as determined earlier). In general, once output goes much above 100 amps, a single 3VX belt is not suitable with pulleys under 3 inches in diameter; two belts will be required. The larger the pulleys that can be used, the lower the friction losses and the less likelihood of slippage.

There is one other consideration: The pulley sheaves must be sized so that the belt does not bottom out in the pulley. *The driving force of the belt must be transmitted via the sides of the belt, not the base of the belt.* Often a high-output alternator comes with a ½-inch pulley in which a 3VX belt will just about bottom out. In this case, the 5VX or AX belts should be used.

Regardless of belt and pulley size, belts need tensioning at regular intervals. An accurate way to determine the correct tension is to measure the distance (in inches) from the center of the crankshaft pulley to the center of the alternator pulley, and to tension a 3VX or AX belt such that it takes 3 to 5 pounds of pressure in the center of the longest span of the belt to depress the belt by 1/64 inch for every inch measured above (for example, if the pulleys are 16 inches apart, 3 to 5 pounds of pressure should depress the belt by 16/64, or ¼ inch). For the 5VX belts, 8 to 12 pounds of pressure should achieve the same deflection. New belts should be slightly overtensioned and then checked regularly, since they will stretch in the first day or two of use.

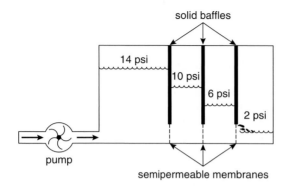

solid baffles

14 psi

10 psi

6 psi

2 psi

pump

semipermeable membranes

Figure 1-21. Battery charge acceptance: the water tank analogy. On charging, the pump first fills the main chamber, compressing the air into the top of the chamber until there is sufficient pressure to drive water through the membrane into the second chamber, and so on. The first chamber will fill rapidly, but thereafter the rate of flow decreases steadily. On discharging, the air pressure in the main chamber will drive much of the water out of this chamber quite rapidly, but thereafter the rate of flow will decrease as the water has to be driven out of the inner chambers through the membranes.

the first membrane, causing the trapped air to raise the pressure (voltage) in this section of the tank until the pressure begins to drive water through the first membrane into the second section of the tank. There will now be a pressure differential between the first and second sections, with the second lagging behind the first. As more water is pumped in, the pressure (voltage) on these two sections will rise until water is driven into the third section, and so on.

In the same way, the surface areas of the plates in a discharged battery are the first to be recharged, but thereafter it takes time for the charge to diffuse into the inner plate areas. The *surface voltage* must build up on the accessible plate areas before the inner areas begin to receive a charge. Surface voltage is what is measured by a voltmeter placed across the battery terminals, and is also what the alternator must contend with when trying to pump more amp-hours into the battery. It is sometimes known as *countervoltage*, since the rising voltage, or pressure, makes it harder for the alternator to drive in the charge.

If the pump in our analogy is stopped, the water will slowly work its way through the membranes until the differing pressure zones inside the tank equalize. In the same way, if charging ceases, the voltage differential inside a battery will slowly equalize until the battery reaches an internal equilibrium, known as an *open circuit* state (this assumes there is no charge being put into the battery and no loads being drawn off it).

If a large pump is put to work on a small tank, it will drive up the pressure in the first section of the tank before much water has time to percolate through the membranes into the other cham-

bers. If the pump has a pressure switch, it will soon reach the set-point and shut down, even though the inner chambers are as yet unfilled. The water will then filter into the inner chambers until the pressures equalize.

In the same way, if a high-output alternator is put to work on a small battery, it will rapidly drive up the surface voltage on the plates without doing much to charge the inner plate areas. If the alternator is set to turn off at a certain pressure (voltage), it will soon reach the set-point, even though much of the battery's capacity remains uncharged. After shutting down, the charge will equalize within the battery, until the voltage stabilizes at the open-circuit voltage.

Raising the pressure set-point on the pump will force water through the inner membranes at a faster pace, but if the setting is raised too high the membranes will rupture. So too, raising the voltage setting on an alternator will charge a battery at a faster pace (it raises the battery's charge acceptance rate), but if the setting is raised too high the battery will be permanently damaged through buckling of the battery plates and other effects of overcharging.

A voltage regulator is akin to a pressure switch on a pump. It switches off its alternator when a certain preset battery voltage (pressure) is reached. When a battery is deeply discharged its voltage (pressure) falls: The voltage regulator drives its alternator to full output in an attempt to bring the voltage back up. Initially the battery will probably be able to accept more charging current than the alternator can produce (its charge acceptance rate exceeds the output of the alternator), so the voltage will remain below the regulator's set-point. Once the accessible plate areas are charged (like the first chamber of the tank filling up), the battery's charge acceptance rate will slow (the water must begin to percolate through the membranes). The alternator will begin to drive up the battery's surface voltage (the pressure in the first chamber of the tank), until this voltage reaches the regulator's set-point. The regulator will then switch off the alternator.

The process of acid diffusion and equalization within the battery will almost immediately lower the battery's surface voltage (the water has filtered from the first part of the tank into inner chambers), causing the regulator to turn the alternator back on. The more fully charged a battery, the slower the rate of diffusion, and the longer the alternator will stay switched off. The process of switching is rapid enough (hundreds of times a second) to produce a relatively even rate of charge, rather than constant changes in alternator output. What an operator will see (if an ammeter is mounted in the circuit) is a

Establishing a Balanced Battery-Powered Electrical System

steadily declining output from the alternator.

A thin-plate cranking battery is comparable to a tank in which the volume of the main chamber is around 60% of the total volume. The many thin plates and low-density active material mean that much of the battery can be recharged rapidly. A thick-plate deep-cycle battery is comparable to a tank in which the volume of the main chamber is as low as 40% of the total volume. The relatively accessible surface areas of the plates form a far smaller percentage of the battery's overall capacity.

Low versus high regulator settings. In typical automotive use we have a thin-plate cranking battery that is rarely discharged by more than a small percentage of its capacity. The act of cranking draws the charge from the surfaces of the plates (the main chamber of the tank), which are then recharged before the battery has time to equalize internally—the inner plate areas retain their charge. In general, the engine and alternator run far longer than is needed to replace this charge. Little charge is needed; it has to be applied only to the surface areas of the plates; and we have excess charging time. In this undemanding environment *voltage regulator settings are kept relatively low in order to avoid damaging the battery through overcharging during extended periods of engine running time.*

In contrast, in many marine applications a thick-plate deep-cycle battery is deeply discharged over a long period of time, allowing the battery to equalize internally and so draining the charge from the inaccessible inner-plate areas. *The engine and alternator are then run for far less time than is needed to restore a full charge.* If a typical automotive voltage regulator setting of around 14.0 volts (for a 12-volt system) is used during charging, the rising surface voltage of the battery will cause the regulator to curtail alternator output soon after the battery is 50% charged (Figure 1-22), which is well before battery safety demands that it be cut back. *This unnecessarily prolongs charging times.*

Since a well-designed deep-cycle battery bank will be cycling primarily in the region of 50% to 80% of full charge, *a typical regulator cripples charging performance in the region of most interest to boatowners!* As a result, many batteries are perennially undercharged and die prematurely from sulphation. In addition, if battery charging is accomplished by running the boat's main engine at anchor, the engine will be run long hours at low loads to little effect, except to increase wear, tear, and maintenance.

In these circumstances the charge rate needs to be accelerated to the limit the batteries can

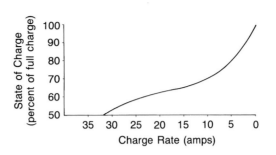

Figure 1-22. Output of an alternator controlled by a conventional voltage regulator when charging a 100-Ah battery. Note that the rising surface voltage causes the charging current to be cut back early in the charging process.

accept, driving the voltage (pressure) as high as can be tolerated, so that the inner plate areas will be charged as rapidly as possible. *But if a regulator's voltage setting is raised to produce the maximum safe charge rate in the 50% to 80% of full charge region, during extended periods of engine running the batteries will be overcharged.* This will result in an excessive loss of electrolyte, destruction of the positive plate grids, and perhaps overheating and buckling of the battery plates.

The dilemma is clear. In many pleasure boat situations, batteries are periodically discharged deeply (to at least the 50% level), but charging times are restricted. Thus, fast charges are required, which call for higher voltage regulator settings than in automotive applications; otherwise the batteries will suffer from undercharging, sulphation, and a permanent loss of capacity. But if voltage regulator settings are raised, extended engine running will likely overcharge the batteries, causing excessive gassing and plate damage.

Voltage regulator solutions. For years, knowledgeable cruisers have resolved this dilemma by bypassing their voltage regulators so that they can manually control the level of alternator output. In this way they can boost charge rates until batteries are almost fully charged, and then cut back to a safe rate of charge during periods of extended engine running time. If irreversible damage is to be avoided, however, this practice requires a thorough understanding of the charging process and close monitoring of the batteries (see page 66 for more on bypass regulators).

In the 1990s these manual devices have been superseded by sophisticated, computer-controlled, *multistep ("smart") regulators* (Figures 1-24 and 1-25; the best-known in the USA are those manufactured by Ample Technologies and the Cruising Equipment Company, and in the UK those by Adverc BM and TWC). These regulators maintain a relatively high voltage setting, boosting charge rates, until a battery is almost fully charged, and then trip to a lower setting to

Charge Rates as a Function of Voltage and Battery State of Charge

To illustrate the relationship between battery state of charge, charge acceptance rates, and alternator output voltage (as determined by the voltage regulator setting), take a look at Figure 1-23. For any given alternator output voltage, find the voltage on the left of the chart, trace across horizontally until a curve is met, and then move vertically down to read the charge acceptance rate at that voltage for a battery in that state of charge. For example, if a regulator is holding 13.6 volts, a fully charged 100-Ah battery will be accepting approximately 1 amp, a three-quarter-charged battery 7½ amps, and a half-charged battery 17 amps. If the regulator is holding 14.4 volts, the figures become 2 amps, 14 amps, and 30 amps respectively. (For a 200-Ah battery these figures can be approximately doubled as long as the alternator has sufficient output to supply the current.) *An increase of only 0.8 volt on the regulator setting almost doubles the charge acceptance rate throughout the critical 50% of charge to full-charge range that we are interested in; this cuts charging times in half.*

Turning these figures around reveals another interesting relationship. If a regulator is holding 13.6 volts, a half-charged battery will be accepting 17 amps; a three-quarter-charged battery, 7½ amps; and a fully charged battery, 1 amp. *The charge is tapering off rapidly.* To go from three-quarter charge to full charge will take a very long time, as the charge rate winds down toward 1 amp. Even if the regulator is holding 14.4 volts the battery's charge acceptance rate from three-quarter charge to full charge winds down from 14 amps to 2 amps. *On a boat where charging is intermittent and engine running time restricted, it will be nearly impossible to bring batteries up to full*

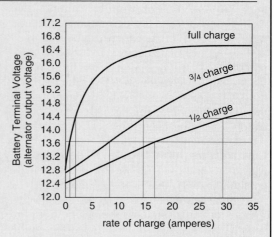

Figure 1-23. Charge acceptance rates of a 100-Ah cranking battery as a function of charging voltage and state of charge. Since it is wise to avoid routine discharges of greater than 50% (failure to do so will shorten battery life), this chart covers the charge states of greatest interest. The implications of the chart are discussed in the text. *(Adapted from a table courtesy the Battery Council International)*

charge, even with an elevated voltage regulator setting.

Now assume a battery is at full charge. A voltage regulator setting of 13.6 volts, producing a charge rate of around 1 amp, will only minimally overcharge a battery. In practice, other losses—both internal and external to the battery—will probably prevent overcharging. But a regulator setting of 14.4 volts, producing a charge rate of 2 amps, will create excessive battery gassing over an extended period, with a consequent loss of electrolyte and potential damage to the battery-plate grids.

avoid overcharging. Most have at least three phases:

1. the *bulk* charge
2. the *absorption* charge
3. the *float* charge

1. The bulk charge. During the bulk charge, maximum alternator output is sustained until the battery comes up to the regulator's absorption voltage (normally in the region of 14.2 to 14.4 volts). Generally (though not always), the bulk charge is more or less a constant-current charge, as opposed to the typical automotive constant-voltage charge. To understand the significance of this differ-

ence, we'll return to our water tank analogy.

The alternator on a constant-voltage system acts like a *centrifugal* pump (see Chapter 12). As the head pressure against which the pump is working increases (the pressure in the first chamber of the tank rises), the flow rate decreases even though the pump is not yet up to its rated maximum pressure. Pump output steadily tapers down well before the pump approaches its high-pressure limit. Finally a pressure is reached at which the pump is still spinning but no water is moving. The pump can continue indefinitely in this state without damage to either the pump or the system.

In contrast, an alternator on a constant-current system acts like a *constant-volume* pump, which moves the same volume of water at each revolution, irrespective of the head pressure on the system, until a pressure switch (the voltage regulator) turns it off. Pump output is constant right up to the high-pressure cutout. If the switch fails, the pump will drive up the head pressure until something breaks.

A constant-current regulator defeats the taper effect inherent in a constant-voltage regulator (Figure 1-26), producing faster rates of recharge. Note this, however: The higher the constant current in relation to a battery's amp-hour capacity, the faster the battery will be driven to the absorption voltage, but the less the battery will be charged, since the alternator will have driven up the surface voltage on the battery plates without allowing time for the inner plate areas to absorb a charge.

It is necessary to avoid extremes. *Charging current with a multistep regulator should be equal to the DC load while the engine is running, plus 10% (minimum) to 40% (maximum) of the battery's rated amp-hour capacity.* In the previous section on sizing an alternator I outlined a good middle point to shoot for, which is the DC load plus 25% of rated battery capacity.

The lower the rate of charge in relation to a battery's Ah capacity, the longer it will take to drive the battery to a given voltage but the more fully charged the battery will be once that voltage is reached (the charge will have had more time to filter into inner plate areas). Conversely, the higher the rate of charge, the faster a battery will be driven to a given voltage, but the less charged the battery will be when the voltage is reached. When fast charging, a higher absorption voltage is needed to drive the battery to the same state of charge as would occur with slower charging to a lower voltage over a longer period of time. So at lower rates of charge, the point at which the bulk charge is terminated can be lower than at high rates of charge (14.2 volts at a 10% rate of charge, rising to 14.4 volts at a 25% rate of charge would be typical). When the cut-off voltage is reached, a battery should be 70% to 80% charged.

2. The absorption (acceptance) charge. If the constant-current charge were to be continued too long it would drive the battery up to potentially damaging voltages. To prevent this, during the *absorption* charge *the alternator output is held to the voltage at which the bulk charge is terminated* (14.2 to 14.4 volts), allowing the charge rate to be determined by what the battery will accept at this voltage setting (the rate at which the charge will percolate into inner plate areas at this pressure). This is therefore a constant-voltage charge. It is continued either for a fixed time or until the battery's charge acceptance rate at this voltage declines to 2% of the battery's amp-hour rating

Figure 1-24. Multistep regulator from Ample Technologies. Note the two potentiometer screws on the right-hand side for adjusting the absorption voltage and absorption time, and the *12-terminal* connector strip at the bottom: wiring these regulators can get quite involved! *(Ample Technologies)*

Figure 1-25. Multistep regulator from Heart Interface/Cruising Equipment Company. Once again, note the potentiometer and timer screws on the right-hand side. *(Heart Interface)*

(the specific mechanism that determines the end of this phase is one of the subtle differences between one regulator and another). The absorption phase gives time for the charge to be "absorbed" by the inner plate areas. At its termination, a battery will be very nearly fully charged.

3. The float charge. At the completion of the absorption phase the regulator trips to a lower constant-voltage float setting (generally between 13.2 and 13.6 volts), which protects the

Figure 1-26. A comparison of the output of a charging device using multistep regulators as opposed to a conventional regulator. Desirable attributes of a marine regulator are: a constant-current output of approximately 25% of the Ah rating of the battery being charged in region A of the graphs, tripping to a constant-voltage setting of around 14.4 volts (on a 12-volt system) at point B, holding this voltage until the charge rate falls to 2% of the Ah rating of the battery, and then tripping to a float voltage of 13.2 to 13.6 volts (point C). As temperatures rise above 80°F (26.7°C) the voltage set-points should be progressively lowered.

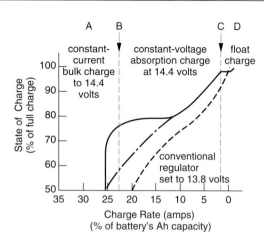

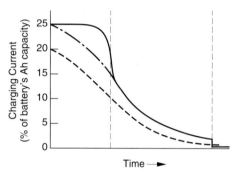

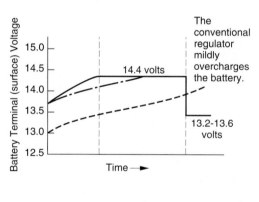

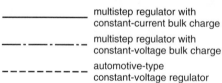

multistep regulator with constant-current bulk charge

multistep regulator with constant-voltage bulk charge

automotive-type constant-voltage regulator

battery from overcharging during periods of extended engine running time.

Additional features. Different regulators have numerous additional features, in particular:

- A fourth *equalization* or *conditioning* phase (Figure 1-27), *which is essential for obtaining the maximum life expectancy from wet-cell deep-cycle batteries* (see page 10 and Chapter 2).

Table 1-7 Gassing Voltages for a 12-Volt Battery as a Function of Electrolyte Temperature

(Absorption voltage on a multistep regulator would want to be adjusted to approximate these voltages at these *battery* temperatures.)

Electrolyte Temperature (°F / °C)	Gassing Voltage of a 12-Volt Battery
122 / 50	13.80
104 / 40	13.98
86 / 30	14.19
77 / 25	**14.34** (this is the standard rating temperature)
68 / 20	14.49
50 / 10	14.82
32 / 0	15.24
14 / −10	15.90
−4 / −20	17.82

- Temperature compensation, which lowers the regulator's voltage set-point if the battery temperature rises (Table 1-7). When coupled to large alternators, the high currents produced by multistep regulators will cause a battery to warm up, which in turn will increase the battery's charge acceptance rate (the warmth accelerates the chemical reactions needed for charging). *Unless the voltage regulator setting is lowered, the battery will steadily absorb more current, further raising its temperature, until damage occurs* (note that the fitting of Hydrocaps to wet-cell batteries exacerbates this problem). In extreme conditions a battery can get into a condition known as *thermal runaway*. This will destroy the battery and can even cause it to blow up! *The maximum safe battery temperature is 125°F (52°C).* Battery charging can be accelerated only until this temperature is reached; the rate of charge must then be tapered off to ensure no further rise in temperature takes place.

Without temperature-sensing equipment, how can you guard against this? Anytime a battery case becomes warm to the touch, it should be suspected that the internal temperature is dangerously high. (Battery temperature can be determined more accurately by using a digital thermometer on the battery post, or withdrawing a sample of electrolyte using a hydrometer with a built-in temperature gauge. See "Testing a Battery" in Chapter 2.)

- A timer on the bulk charge and absorption phases so that, if for some reason the battery does not come up to the trip-to-float voltage, or the charge acceptance rate does not drop to the trip-to-float current, the regulator will still trip to float. This safeguards against overcharging as a result of a shorted cell or some other problem.

- A time-delay function so that the alternator is not switched on until some seconds after an engine cranks. This eliminates cranking difficulties caused by the high loads of a high-output alternator. The alternator output is then sometimes increased gradually *(ramped)* to avoid shock-loading the drive belt.

- A current-limit setting so that the maximum output of a non-hot-rated alternator can be set at a level that will keep the alternator from burning up. The current limit can also be used to hold down the maximum horsepower draw on a small engine.

- A continuous tachometer function. Many tachometers are sensed off the alternator. When a smart regulator trips from the absorption to the float cycle, alternator output temporarily ceases while the battery's surface voltage falls to the float voltage level (the battery equalizes internally), and then the alternator kicks back in. With some multistep regulators the engine tachometer will stop registering during this period; with others it will not.

- Sensing of the battery voltage at the batteries as opposed to the alternator, which is important for accurate monitoring and control.

- Spray-proofing of the units to a greater or lesser extent.

The benefits of multistep regulators. Using a typical automotive voltage regulator, even

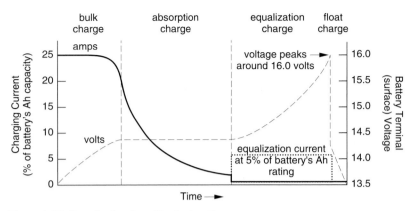

Figure 1-27. Equalization (conditioning) cycle on a multistep regulator. At the end of the absorption phase, instead of tripping to float, the charge rate is raised to a constant-current setting of 3% to 5% of the battery's Ah rating and held at this level for several hours (see Chapter 2 for methods of determining when to end an equalization charge).

with a high-output alternator, *it will take as long as seven hours to fully recharge a heavily discharged battery.* Such lengthy charging times are frequently impractical. As a result, many marine batteries are perennially undercharged, DC systems perform well below par, and the batteries fail prematurely from sulphation (this is probably the number two cause of battery death in the marine environment, with the misapplication of cranking batteries in cycling service being the number one cause).

With a multistep regulator and a high-output alternator the charging period can be cut in half. In fact, if charging to 80% of the fully charged level is acceptable, charging times can be consistently reduced to between 1 and 1½ hours a day (or whatever is the normal interval between charges). *This results in a dramatic improvement in DC system performance and also battery life, which translates into far fewer electrical problems and considerable cost savings—more than enough in many instances to pay for the added cost of the alternator, the regulator, and their installation!*

Putting the Pieces Together

Having selected a decent set of batteries, an adequate alternator, and a suitable voltage regulator for a given application, the next task is installing these components in a way that puts them to work most effectively.

One of the key aspects of the installation is to ensure that there is always a battery in reserve with an adequate capacity to crank the engine. It

is, in any case, a requirement of the American Boat and Yacht Council (ABYC—the industry-wide standards-setting body) that there be a reserved battery for all but hand-cranked engines. This requirement is normally met by either having a dedicated engine-cranking battery, or two house banks that are alternated in use, with the reserve bank kept in a fully charged state (often not the best use of batteries—see below).

In the former case, the reserved battery can be a cranking battery. In the latter case, two banks of deep-cycle batteries will be needed. Many people erroneously believe that deep-cycle batteries are unsuited for cranking applications. They can be used, but because the thicker plates in deep-cycle batteries retard the rate of acid diffusion as compared with thin-plate (cranking) batteries—and therefore retard the rate at which energy can be released—a larger capacity deep-cycle battery is required to produce the same cranking capability as a thin-plate battery.

How much larger? If a deep-cycle battery is to be used for engine cranking it is necessary to make sure that it has a CCA rating at least equal to that specified in the engine manual (or at least equal to the CCA rating of the cranking battery it is replacing).

Is It Better to Have One or Two Battery Banks for House Use?

The popular arrangement of having two house banks alternated in use needs scrutiny before I go any further.

Life cycles. As we have seen, the life expectancy of a battery in cycling service is directly related to the depth to which it is discharged at each cycle—the greater the depth of discharge, the shorter the battery's life (refer back to Figure 1-12).

This relationship between depth of discharge and battery life is not linear. As the depth of discharge increases, a battery's life expectancy is disproportionately shortened. A given battery might cycle through 10% of its capacity 2,000 times, 50% of its capacity something over 300 times, and 100% of its capacity around 100 times.

Let's say, for argument's sake, that a boat has two 200-Ah battery banks, alternated from day to day, with a daily load of 80 Ah. Each bank will be discharged by 40% of capacity before being recharged. The batteries will fail after 380 cycles, which is 760 days (since each is used every other day). If the two banks had been wired in parallel to make a single 400-Ah battery bank, this bank would have been discharged by 20% of capacity every day, with a life-expectancy of 800 days, a 5% increase in life expectancy using exactly the same batteries!

But now let's double the capacity of the batteries so that the boat has either two 400-Ah banks, or a single 800-Ah bank, but with the same 80-amp-hour daily load. The two banks will be cycling through 20% of capacity every

other day, resulting in a total life-expectancy of 1,600 days. Doubling the size of the battery banks in relation to the load has produced a 210% increase in life expectancy. The single 800-Ah battery bank will be cycling through 10% of capacity every day, resulting in a life expectancy of 2,000 days—a 25% increase in life expectancy over the two banks, and a 250% increase in life expectancy over the single 400-Ah battery bank!

There are two immediate conclusions to be drawn from these figures:

1. For a given total battery capacity, wiring the batteries into a single high-capacity bank, rather than having them divided into two alternating banks, will result in a longer overall life expectancy for the batteries; and
2. All other things being equal, any increase in the overall capacity of a battery bank will produce a disproportionate increase in its life expectancy (through reducing the depth of discharge at each cycle).

For battery longevity, a single large bank, the larger the better, is preferable to divided banks.

Battery voltage and other considerations. Besides increased battery life, there are other advantages to the single, large bank.

The efficient functioning of many DC devices is directly related to their input voltage. A small drop in voltage will cause a noticeable reduction in light from an incandescent bulb. Of more significance is the loss of output from electric motors. With declining voltage, a centrifugal bilge pump, for example, will suffer a disproportionate loss of pumping capability, while many other motors tend to overheat, with a distinct risk of burning up—in fact, low voltage is probably one of the primary causes of DC motor failure.

When any battery is discharged, the load on the battery immediately pulls down the voltage, and then causes a steady continuing voltage decline until the voltage suddenly falls off, at which point the battery is effectively dead. The extent to which the voltage initially falls, and then the rate at which it continues to decline, is related to the size of the load *as a percentage of the battery's overall capacity.* The greater the capacity of a battery bank in relation to the load applied to it, the smaller the initial voltage drop and the slower the subsequent rate of voltage decline. Once again, this relationship is not linear. Doubling the size of a battery bank will reduce to less than half the rate at which the battery voltage declines under a given load.

For a given load over a given period of time, a single large battery bank will at all times maintain a higher terminal voltage than a divided bank with each half used alternately.

Aside from electric lights and motors, this has particular significance for many inverter-based AC systems. The majority of inverters found on boats are *line frequency* inverters in which the peak AC output voltage is directly related to the DC input voltage—as the battery voltage falls off under a load, the peak AC voltage also falls (this is covered in some detail in Chapter 5). Much of the time this is of no consequence, but some AC loads, notably many microwaves, are quite sensitive to the peak AC voltage, suffering a considerable loss of efficiency as this voltage declines. The sustained higher DC voltage of a single battery bank, as compared to the voltage of a divided bank, will result in a significantly improved performance from these inverter-powered devices. Not only that, but the voltage on a single bank subjected to a heavy inverter load will take more than twice as long as the voltage on a divided bank to fall to the cut-off threshold of the inverter.

Finally, when it comes to battery installation and management, for a number of reasons a single large bank is easier to manage than two smaller banks. First of all, the bank can be charged directly from an alternator, as opposed to having to use some sort of a switching arrangement (which is always subject to operator error), or using battery isolation diodes (which have problems of their own—see below). Secondly, the voltage regulator can be adjusted for the ideal charging regimen for the single bank, as opposed to the common situation in which, due to batteries of differing sizes, types, or ages in the two banks, none are charged to best advantage. And finally, the single bank is simpler and cheaper to install, requiring less wiring and switches.

A dedicated cranking battery. But none of these advantages would justify a single bank if on just one critical occasion the single bank caused a situation in which the batteries were flat, the engine couldn't be cranked, and as a result the boat and crew were put in peril. To be viable, the single bank must be combined with a pretty-well bulletproof method of ensuring an ability to crank the engine. Since it must be assumed that at some time the house bank will be discharged to the point at which it could not crank the boat's engine, the single house bank must be combined with a separate battery reserved solely for engine cranking, and kept in a state of full charge at all times.

This is achieved by wiring all the house loads to the house bank, and *nothing but the starter motor to the cranking battery* so there is no pos-

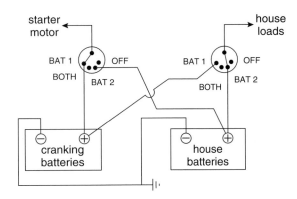

Figure 1-28. An arrangement that allows either battery to be selected for either cranking or house loads while still keeping both batteries isolated from one another.

sibility of accidentally draining the cranking battery in house service. An emergency paralleling switch between the cranking battery and house bank can be added just in case the house bank is needed as a backup for engine cranking, but this function can just as easily be accomplished by keeping a set of jumper cables on board. Alternatively, for maximum flexibility, the batteries can be wired with two "1, 2, BOTH" battery-isolation switches (Figure 1-28). This provides complete flexibility, enabling the engine to be cranked, or the house loads to be supplied, by either battery in isolation from the other. But this comes at the cost of introducing the possibility of paralleling all the batteries in house use and accidentally flattening the lot (through leaving either switch in the "BOTH" position).

The question then is simply how to charge the cranking battery and house bank. By far the best arrangement, particularly if the boat has substantial DC needs, is to leave the existing alternator and voltage regulator wired to the engine-cranking battery, and to add a second high-output alternator, controlled by a multistep regulator, wired to the house bank (Figure 1-29). This way, the cranking battery and house bank can be charged independently, with the voltage regulation parameters on each alternator adjusted to provide the most efficient charging regimen for the individual battery banks. (In practice, the existing regulator will probably not be adjustable, but in any case will provide a regimen suitable for a cranking battery; the multistep regulator can be programmed to achieve the maximum state-of-charge and life-expectancy from the house batteries). If one or other alternator or voltage regulator fails, the emergency battery paralleling switch, or jumper

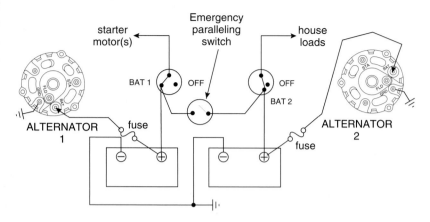

Figure 1-29. Twin alternator installation with independent house and cranking batteries.

cables, can be used to charge both battery banks from the remaining alternator.

Charging More Than One Battery Bank from a Common Alternator

Difficulties arise when two battery banks (either two house banks alternated in use, or independent cranking and house batteries) must be charged from a single alternator. The various batteries must be paralleled while charging, so that both are charged, but then isolated when the engine is shut down, preventing the cranking battery, or reserve bank, from becoming discharged in house service. One of two methods has traditionally been used to accomplish these objectives:

1. A manual battery-selector switch is used to parallel the batteries when the engine is running, and to isolate the cranking battery or reserve bank when the engine is not running; or
2. Battery isolation diodes are used to provide the same service automatically.

Less common methods that deserve consideration are the use of battery paralleling relays, and series voltage regulators. We need to look at all of these.

Battery selector switch. A four-position switch ("OFF"; "1"; "BOTH"; and "2") parallels the various batteries when charging, and is then used to isolate the cranking or reserve house battery when charging is finished. In a conventional two-house-bank installation the switch is generally wired as in Figure 1-30A; with a dedicated cranking battery and a single house bank, the wiring will be as in Figure 1-30B. Note that in

general there should not be any loads wired to the battery side of a battery isolation switch, since this will void the switch's isolation function, but in practice there are almost always a few exceptions to this rule: certain pieces of electronic equipment that need to be hooked directly to a battery to operate properly; automatic bilge pumps, so that the boat can be left with the batteries isolated but the pumps operational; the alternator in certain circumstances (see below and Figure 1-30B); and battery-charging devices that are to operate when the boat is unattended. All of these *must* have over-current protection—fuses or circuit-breakers—as close to the battery as possible (see Chapter 3).

If the alternator is wired to the load side of an isolation switch (Figure 1-30A—a common installation) either battery can be charged independently, or both together, but the alternator needs special protection. Since its output is fed to the batteries via the switch, if the switch is turned to the "OFF" position while the engine is running, the alternator will be *open circuited*, which may destroy its diodes (see Chapter 2). Some battery-selector switches incorporate a *field disconnect* function, which disables the alternator momentarily before the switch circuit is broken, thus preventing damage. If this is not present the switch needs to be clearly labeled: NEVER TURN TO "OFF" WITH THE ENGINE RUNNING.

Alternator damage can also occur when switching *between* battery banks while the engine is running. Since there must be no interruption of the circuit, the switch needs to be of the *make-before-it-breaks* variety—both batteries are first brought on line (the "BOTH" position) and then one disconnected. Even so, dirty or corroded points on the switch can occasionally still lead to alternator damage. A *Zap Stop* or *snubber* (page 51)—a cheap device wired from the alter-

ALTERNATOR

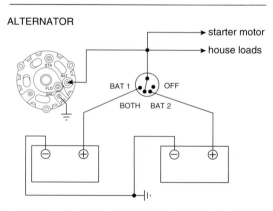

Figure 1-30A. Two battery banks alternated in house use with the unused bank kept in reserve for cranking. The battery isolation/changeover switch is paralleled to charge both batteries from a single alternator. Either battery can also be charged independently of the other by switching to the BAT 1 or BAT 2 positions.

nator output stud to ground, safely shorting-out such spikes—will prevent this damage (available from Ample Technologies, Cruising Equipment Company, SALT, and others).

If the alternator is wired to the house battery (second option in Figure 1-30B), the cranking battery can only be charged in parallel with the house battery (the "BOTH" position on the switch). There is, however, no risk of open-circuiting the alternator.

Charging two battery banks through a battery-selector switch results in a simple and economical installation used by many boatbuilders. However, if two different battery types (for example, a cranking battery and a deep-cycle battery, or a wet-cell and a gel-cell) are charged in parallel, one is likely to be chronically overcharged while the other will be chronically undercharged. In addition, this approach is subject to operator error: If the batteries are not paralleled during charging, one will not be charged; if they are left paralleled after charging, they may both be discharged to the point at which it is not possible to crank the engine.

Finally, in many installations the battery selector switch, which must be accessible to the user, will be in a panel at some distance from the batteries and the alternator, creating some long wiring runs. With larger-capacity DC systems, the battery and alternator wiring is going to consist of heavy cables that can prove both expensive and awkward to handle.

There are many cases in which some other approach to battery selection and charging is needed.

Diodes. Split-charging through battery-isolation diodes is quite common on larger cruising boats, especially when there are more than two battery banks to be charged (for example, a dedicated engine-start battery in addition to two separate house banks). The alternator's output is fed to diodes—semiconductors that allow current to flow in one direction but block it in the reverse direction. A diode is assigned to each battery (or battery bank—Figure 1-31). Any number of batteries can then be charged in parallel, but are isolated from one another when in service, so that the cranking battery cannot be accidentally discharged in house service. All batteries will be charged, while there is no way the operator can open-circuit the alternator.

This seems like the ideal set-up since there is no user interaction required, and the system is therefore "idiotproof," but there is a severe drawback to diodes that is rarely appreciated. Depending on the type of diode, and the current (amperage) flow in relation to its rated current,

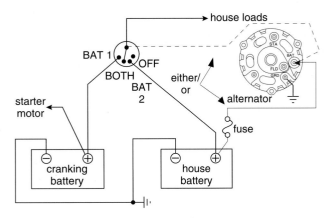

Figure 1-30B. Dedicated cranking battery and single house bank. If the alternator is wired to the load side of the switch, either battery can be charged independently, or both together, but there is a risk of open-circuiting the alternator. If the alternator is wired to the house battery, the cranking battery can only be charged by placing the isolation selector switch in the "BOTH" position, but there is no risk of open-circuiting the alternator.

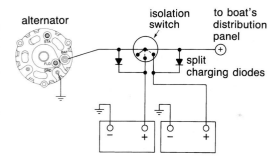

Figure 1-31. Split-charging diodes in combination with a battery isolation/changeover switch. Note that even if the isolation/changeover switch is inadvertently turned off while the engine is running, the alternator is not open-circuited.

a diode will typically produce a voltage drop in a charging circuit of from 0.6 to 1.0 volt. I deal with voltage drop in some detail in Chapter 3. All we need to know here is that the difference between a fully charged battery and a flat battery is only 0.8 to 1.0 volt. As a result, differences on the order of a tenth of a volt in voltage regulator settings will have a major effect on charge rates and charge times, *so the 0.6- to 1.0-volt drop of a diode can play havoc with the charging system.*

This is what happens: A typical automotive voltage regulator is mounted inside its alternator, and senses battery voltage for regulation purposes not at the battery, but at the output terminal on the alternator. With a diode in the charging circuit the regulator may be sensing, for example, 14.2 volts, while the voltage at the battery is only 13.6 volts (Figure 1-32). Unless compensated for, such a 0.6-volt drop through a diode will cause the voltage regulator to curtail the alternator's output long before the batteries are fully charged, prolonging charging times unnecessarily and resulting in chronically undercharged batteries that will die prematurely from sulphation—a major cause of battery death in marine use.

Since few builders and installers compensate for diode-induced voltage drop (see Chapter 2 for methods of doing this), as often as not *fitting an isolator to establish an idiotproof method of ensuring there will always be a charged battery for engine starts unwittingly guarantees that none of the batteries on board will be properly charged!*

Relays. There is a third approach to charging more than one battery bank from a single charging source that I have always liked, and which eliminates both the need for user interaction and also voltage drop in the charging circuit, thus delivering the virtues of isolation diodes (idiotproofing) without the vices (voltage drop).

This approach uses a heavy-duty relay or solenoid (an electrically operated switch) wired between the two battery banks. The circuit energizing this switch is wired either to the engine ignition switch, or to an oil-pressure switch mounted on the engine. Any time the ignition is turned on, or the engine is cranked and builds up sufficient oil pressure to close the oil-pressure switch, the battery banks are paralleled for charging. When the engine is shut down the relay is de-energized, opening the circuit between the battery banks and so isolating them in service. So long as the cables between the batteries and the relay are large enough, battery paralleling while charging will be accomplished without significant voltage drop (Figure 1-33). The paralleling circuit can be quite short (which keeps down the cable sizes and cost), while a relay with a suitable rating for the task (the maximum rated output of the alternator in most cases) will be cheaper than a battery isolation diode.

Note, however, that if the ignition switch is used to power the relay, and the house battery is flat, when the ignition is turned on the cranking battery will discharge into the house battery before cranking takes place. Depending on the relative sizes and states of charge of the batteries, this might result in a high, short-term *inrush* current flow—the paralleling relay and wiring must be rated to handle such a load in order to avoid potentially dangerous overheating. The discharging of the cranking battery that takes place may also hamper cranking attempts. For both these reasons it is preferable to wire the relay to an oil-pressure switch, in which case paralleling will only occur *after* the engine has fired up. This protects the cranking battery from discharge prior to cranking, and also allows the alternator to kick in before the batteries are paralleled, which in turn will begin to drive up the terminal voltage on the house batteries before paralleling occurs, reducing any current surge from the cranking battery to the house batteries.

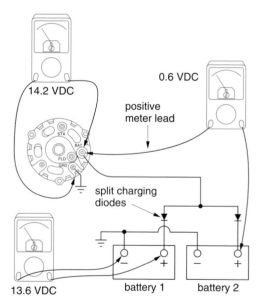

Figure 1-32. Measuring voltage drop between an alternator and batteries with split-charging diodes.

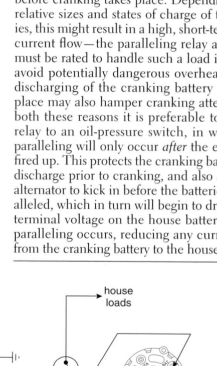

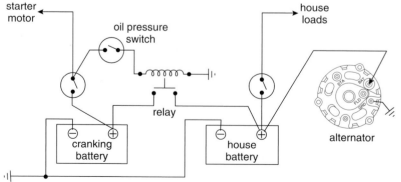

Figure 1-33. Charging through a relay (solenoid). When the engine is cranked the oil pressure switch closes, energizing the relay, which closes the circuit between the two batteries. When the engine is stopped the oil pressure switch opens, de-energizing the relay.

When relay-based battery paralleling is used on a boat with a dedicated cranking battery and a single house bank, the alternator should be wired to the house batteries, since these will need the most charging (this keeps the current flow through the paralleling circuit to a minimum). The engine should be run long enough to bring both sets of batteries to a near-full charge (otherwise repeated short-term operation of the engine on a boat that has a dead house battery will allow the cranking battery to discharge into the house battery each time the engine is cranked until there is insufficient charge to crank the engine).

Electronic relays. Recently a couple of electronically activated relays have been developed that perform the same function as these other relays but without the oil-pressure, or ignition switch, connection. These relays are once again wired between the two battery banks, but instead of an externally activated switch that closes the relay circuit, there is an internal electronic-sensing unit which, in the one case (the *Batt-Link* and *Batt-Maxx* from Wells Marine Technology, Stuart, FL) senses alternator output and in the other case (the *Battery Combiner*, from West Marine, Watsonville, CA), senses battery voltage. Anytime this solid-state controller senses alternator output, or a rising voltage (caused by some charging device coming on line), the relay is activated to parallel the batteries; if the alternator goes off line, or the voltage falls below a pre-set level, the relay is opened, isolating the batteries.

The *Batt-Link* and *Batt-Maxx* are direct replacements for battery-isolation diodes, taking the input from an alternator and feeding it to paralleled battery banks whenever the alternator comes on line, while the *Battery Combiner* is simply wired between the battery banks, leaving the alternator wired to one or other battery bank. Of the two types of device, the *Battery Combiner* is more versatile in that it is triggered into action any time it senses a rising voltage on either battery bank, and as such will respond not only to an alternator, but also to other charging devices such as a battery charger or wind generator. On the other hand, the *Batt-Link* and *Batt-Maxx* are somewhat more ruggedly built (and correspondingly more expensive). The *Battery Combiner* is available in two ratings—70 amps and 130 amps—while the *Batt-Link* and *Batt-Maxx* are available in ratings up to 400 amps. The *Batt-Maxx* has an additional emergency paralleling switch that overrides the internal electronic circuit to enable all batteries to be paralleled for difficult engine starts (this is what differentiates it from the *Batt-Link*).

Installation of a *Batt-Link*, *Batt-Maxx* or *Battery Combiner* is a snap. With the *Battery Combiner*, the engine alternator and other charging devices should once again be wired to the house batteries rather than the cranking battery to avoid a situation in which a fully charged cranking battery is paralleled with heavily discharged house batteries. This would lead to a high current flow through the paralleling circuit (the *Battery Combiner* has an internal circuit breaker that trips if the paralleling circuit is subjected to an overload; the *Batt-Link* and *Batt-Maxx* do not have this feature). When the charging devices are wired to the house batteries, the circuit between the house and cranking batteries will not be closed until the house batteries have a higher voltage, in which case the cranking battery can never be discharged into the house batteries. The one possible drawback to this installation occurs if the house batteries are never charged sufficiently to drive their voltage to the level at which the paralleling circuit closes, in which case the cranking battery will not be charged at all. This, however, is a somewhat speculative and unlikely situation that is easily avoided by ensuring that at least once in a while the engine is run long enough, or some other charging device left on long enough, to drive the house voltage to the level at which the cranking battery also gets charged.

Series regulation. In spite of their benefits, all the means described to date for charging battery banks in parallel suffer from a common disadvantage: once battery banks are paralleled, the batteries in both banks will be charged according to the same charging regimen. But different kinds of batteries are commonly used for house service and cranking service (deep-cycle batteries for the house; a cranking battery on the engine). These batteries accept a charge in different ways. When charged in parallel, one bank will invariably be somewhat overcharged, while the other will be somewhat undercharged, resulting in a reduced life expectancy for all the batteries. Inequalities are likely to be especially pronounced when a single large house bank is paralleled with a relatively small cranking battery.

The only way to get around this problem is to have a voltage regulator for each battery bank, providing a tailor-made charging regimen for each bank. As mentioned previously, with two alternators this is easy. With one alternator it has, until recently, been impossible. But now Ample Technologies has produced what is called a *series regulator* to solve this problem. This is a special kind of voltage regulator that is wired between the house bank and the cranking battery (Figure 1-34). The alternator's output is fed to the house

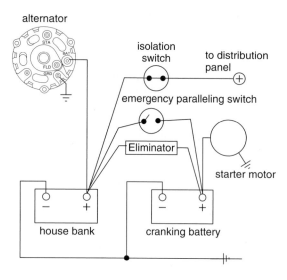

Figure 1-34. Battery charging circuit using an Eliminator.

alternator

isolation switch

to distribution panel

emergency paralleling switch

Eliminator

starter motor

house bank

cranking battery

bank, with the voltage regulator set to charge these batteries to maximum advantage, and then any time the alternator, or some other charging source, comes on line the series regulator (trade-named the *Eliminator*) "siphons off" some of the charge to the cranking battery. The series regulator has its own adjustment points to provide the optimum charging regimen for the cranking battery. Various batteries can be mixed up in house and cranking use without suffering damage, although it should be noted that the *Eliminator* cannot charge the cranking battery at a higher voltage than that being applied to the house batteries, which can, in certain circumstances, limit its usefulness.

Electronics battery. Increasingly, it is necessary to have an electronics battery that is isolated from voltage dips and spikes caused by engine-cranking and the application of other heavy loads. With a dedicated engine-cranking battery, the house battery will normally remain stable enough to carry the electronics load. Otherwise, a third battery bank will be needed, wired into the charging circuit by any of the four methods described above.

Monitoring and Control

To overcome the inherent weaknesses of existing battery technology as applied to many marine applications, we are often forced to drive batteries to their limits, using high rates of charge at elevated voltages to shorten charging times to a minimum.

A variation of just tenths of a volt will make a

considerable difference in the charge acceptance rate of a battery. Referring back to the sidebar on page 22, and Figure 1-23, it can be seen that a 0.2 volt increase in the regulated output of an alternator will increase the charge acceptance rate of a battery by close to 20%. At 14.0 volts a half-charged 100-Ah battery will accept approximately 23 amps of charging current; at 14.2 volts it will accept approximately 27 amps.

If we are to get the most out of a system without pushing the batteries beyond the limits of their tolerance, we must have very precise monitoring and control of the system. Most off-the-shelf distribution panels fitted to boats incorporate *analog* meters (meters with a swinging arm) which measure voltage and current at various points on the panel. These are just about adequate for simple circuits and undemanding situations, but on heavily-loaded boats with complex DC systems (high-output alternators, multistep regulators, wind generators, solar panels, DC/AC inverters, etc.), it is almost mandatory to install one of the new breed of multifunction, highly accurate, *digital* meters (available from Ample Technologies, Cruising Equipment Company, SALT, and others).

We will want to measure the amperage flow into, and out of, the batteries, and the battery voltage *at each battery bank* (*not* the panel, since there may be voltage losses between the battery and panel, resulting in misleading information). In addition, I would recommend a meter that reads the *gross* alternator output (i.e. before any loads are deducted), especially if you are using a multistep regulator or voltage regulator bypass (the gross alternator output is needed to monitor alternator performance, and in some instances to avoid overloading, and burning out, the alternator—see page 17).

Ammeters that read up to around 60 amps are simply wired directly into the relevant circuit, but above this amperage a special *shunt* must be used, with the ammeter wired to the shunt (Figure 1-35). Where battery amperage measurements are concerned, this shunt is normally wired into the negative cable to the batteries, although SALT has a neat device that simply slips around the battery positive cable. With the wired-in shunts, since the entire battery input or output will be flowing through the shunt—including in many installations engine cranking loads and perhaps an electric windlass—a shunt with a *continuous* rating of 200 amps will be required on even quite small boats. Boats with larger loads and heavier equipment will need to go to 400- or even 800-amp shunts.

Even with accurate amperage and voltage measurements it still takes a good grasp of the nature of batteries to gain an understanding of the health of the batteries from the readings. One of the recently introduced *amp-hour* meters will take the guesswork out of these calculations, providing an instant read-out of the state-of-charge of any battery bank (more on this in Chapter 2).

Finally, it is worthwhile considering a meter with programmable alarms for such situations as low- or high-battery voltage, or low state-of-charge. These alarms may well provide warning of a potentially damaging situation long before it would otherwise be noticed.

Putting the pieces together. With the equipment available to boatowners today, it makes sense to wire all the house batteries into a single large bank, with a separate cranking battery reserved solely for engine starts. In the ideal set-up, the original engine alternator will be supplemented, rather than replaced, with a high-output alternator controlled by a multistep regulator. The high-output alternator will charge the house batteries, and the engine alternator the cranking battery, with both alternators regulated to provide the most beneficial charging regime for their respective batteries. Battery state-of-charge will be continuously monitored by an amp-hour meter.

Where only a single alternator is available for charging both the house and cranking batteries, an *Eliminator* can be used if different types of

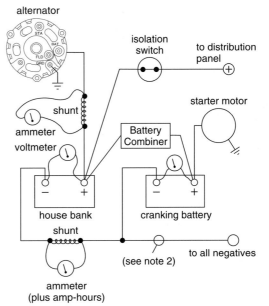

Figure 1-35. Desirable measurement points on a DC system. Notes: 1. One multifunction meter can be used instead of individual meters. 2. With a dedicated cranking battery it is not so important to measure amps in and out, so the ammeter is shown wired to the house batteries. If the batteries are alternated in house use, a second shunt can be placed in the negative cable to the second battery, or else the single shunt can be moved to position 2, where it will measure total current in and out of the batteries. 3. The Battery Combiner could be replaced with an oil-pressure operated relay, a Batt-Maxx, or an Eliminator.

batteries are used for these two functions, or a *Batt-Link, Batt-Maxx,* or *Battery Combiner* (or similar paralleling device) where the same types of batteries are used for both house and cranking service.

Summary: A Balanced System

There is hardly a boat around that does not at some time shut down its engine and run off its batteries, deeply discharging them. Even the best automotive batteries cannot be cycled more than 30 to 40 times before failing. Unless a boat has a permanent charging capability equal to demand, it should be fitted with deep-cycle batteries. The lone exception is a marine cranking battery reserved for engine starting. Then when evaluating a DC system we need to remember the following:

- Auxiliary charging devices such as solar panels, wind generators, and battery chargers powered by onboard generators should be left out of the equation. All may fail to produce at some time or be inadequate to meet total demands, in which case the batteries will be steadily discharged.

- Deep-cycle batteries vary enormously in quality of construction and suitability for marine

use. The key criterion in most boating applications is the number of life cycles at the 50% level of discharge.

- Battery capacity, as a rule of thumb, should be as high as *four times* the anticipated demand between charging periods (although this is often physically impossible to achieve; at any rate, capacity should be a minimum of double the anticipated demand). Charging capability should be up to one third of battery capacity *plus* any additional boat loads during the charging period (once again, not always possible to achieve; 20% to 25% of battery capacity may be a more realistic target).

- A multistep marine voltage regulator is essential to maximize DC system capabilities and minimize problems.

- Charging circuits must be designed to en-sure a proper charging regime for all batteries, with *effective charging voltages at the batteries.*

Table 1-8. Designing Your Boat's 12-Volt Electrical System

Question	Answer
1. Do you regularly or even periodically draw power from your battery or batteries, other than to start the engine, when you aren't charging them (i.e., when the engine isn't running)? Note: Do not consider auxiliary charging devices such as solar panels and wind generators in your answer, since their output is not wholly predictable and your system should be able to function adequately without them.	If your answer is "No," one or more automotive (cranking) batteries will suffice. Go to Question 8, then 10. If your answer is "Yes" (the great majority of cases), you need deep-cycle batteries. Go to Question 2.
2. Does your boat have an engine?	If "No," go to Question 3 through 6, then study Chapter 5 to ascertain how you can provide sufficient charging capability for your battery bank. If "Yes," go to Question 3.
3. How long (in days or in a fraction of a day) between charging intervals? (See page 12. Note that engine running time must be long enough during each charging cycle to bring the battery to a reasonable state of charge. Variables include degree of discharge and voltage regulator setting. See discussion of voltage regulation.)	_____day(s)
4. What is your boat's total 12-volt electrical demand per day? (See Tables 1-1 and 1-2.)	_____amp-hours
5. What is the anticipated battery drain between charges? (Multiply Answer 3 by Answer 4.)	_____amp-hours
6. What is the necessary battery capacity? (Multiply Answer 5 by at least 2 ½, and preferably by 4.)	_____amp-hours
7. Will you carry a separate automotive (cranking) battery for engine starts, or will you have two banks of deep-cycle batteries to be alternated for "house" use and engine starts? Put a checkmark next to your choice. Note: When two deep-cycle battery banks are installed, *each one* should have the capacity computed in Answer 6.	_____Option #1 Cranking battery (go to Question 8, then 10) _____Option #2 Second deep-cycle battery bank (proceed with Question 8)
8. How many cold-cranking amps does your engine need to start in the coldest weather you can imagine? (see page 9)	_____amps
9. If you intend to use your deep-cycle banks for engine starting, does their capacity exceed the foreseen demand in Answer 8? Note: If you plan to install two deep-cycle battery banks, each alone should have the necessary capacity for engine starts. In practice, the capacity computed in Answer 6 is almost certain to suffice. Banks can be paralleled for difficult starts	_____yes _____no
10. What is your maximum required alternator output? Note: Unless your answer to Question 1 was "No," the output should be one-third the capacity of one battery bank *plus* the additional load imposed by the boat's operating systems during charging (see Tables 1-1 and 1-2). This may include refrigeration and other large loads that are turned on only when the engine is running. If your answer to Question 1 was "No," maximum alternator output should equal the boat's load while the engine is running plus a 33-percent margin to prevent alternator overheating.	_____amps
11. What should your alternator pulley ratio be? Note: This is the ratio of the engine output-pulley diameter to the alternator drive-pulley diameter. Adjust the ratio to achieve the output called for in Answer 10 at the minimum projected engine running speed. Make sure the alternator will not exceed its maximum safe operating speed (usually 10,000 r.p.m.) at maximum engine r.p.m. See page 18.	_____ : _____
12. What voltage regulator setting should you maintain? If your answer to Question 1 was "No," an automotive regulator setting of 13.8 to 14.0 volts will be acceptable but automotive regulators are otherwise inappropriate. See the discussion on pages 18-25 in this chapter.	_____volts
13. Through your answers to the preceding questions you have designed a sensible 12-volt system for your boat. You may well be curious about the effects on this equation of power inputs from other sources—DC/AC inverters, wind and water generators, solar panels, and diesel generators. These are the subjects of Chapters 5 and 6.	

- Precise instrumentation is needed for effective monitoring and control.

This simple statement of a balanced electrical system reveals the woeful inadequacy of the electrical systems on most boats. Problems start on the production line. Boatbuilders are constantly pressured to keep costs down: Good-quality deep-cycle batteries, large-capacity alternators with multistep voltage regulators, and accurate monitoring devices are expensive and rarely fitted. In addition, much common electrical equipment is regarded as "extra"; builders frequently install batteries and an alternator barely adequate to handle the factory-installed items; additional equipment rapidly overwhelms the system. The net result is a DC system inherently prone to failure.

Analyzing the DC system, and setting the DC house in order, should be one of the first priorities when taking delivery of any boat, whether it has come straight out of the showroom or is a twenty-year veteran of several circumnavigations!

Postscript

The theme that has run through this chapter is that the limiting factor in many marine DC systems is the nature of existing battery technology. This may change radically in the next decade. Increasing concerns about the environment, which are spawning ever tighter clean air regulations, are speeding the development of electric vehicles. New technologies, such as fuel cells, are being developed, and millions of dollars are being pumped into research to improve the performance of batteries in cycling applications.

Any breakthrough in the automotive field is likely to carry over into the marine field. As a result, what is already a confusing situation will probably become even more so. A thorough understanding of battery technology is going to be more important than ever for well-reasoned choices in the marine world. But at the end of the day we will have ever more powerful and effective DC systems—perhaps, if fuel cells become commercially viable, with undreamed of capabilities.

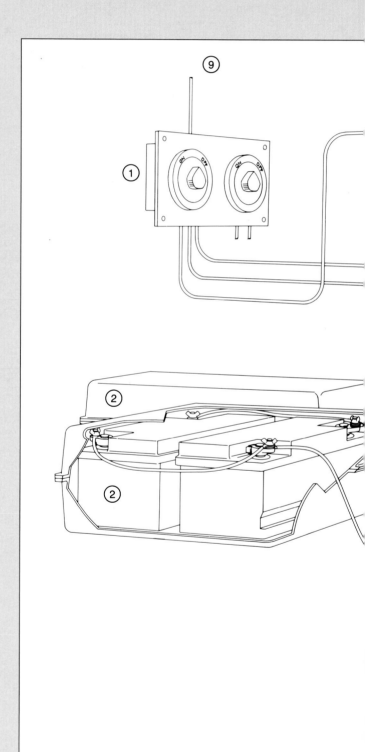

CHAPTER 2

Figure 2-1. Keeping your batteries and charging system trouble free should be the first systems maintenance priority of any boater. *(Jim Sollers)*

(1) battery isolation switch
(2) batteries
(3) starter
(4) to starter
(5) alternator
(6) to positive terminal of battery
(7) common ground point
(8) diode
(9) to distribution panel

Note: This illustration shows a common installation, but it is not the best approach to wiring batteries and alternators—see the text.

Maintaining and Troubleshooting a Battery-Powered Electrical System

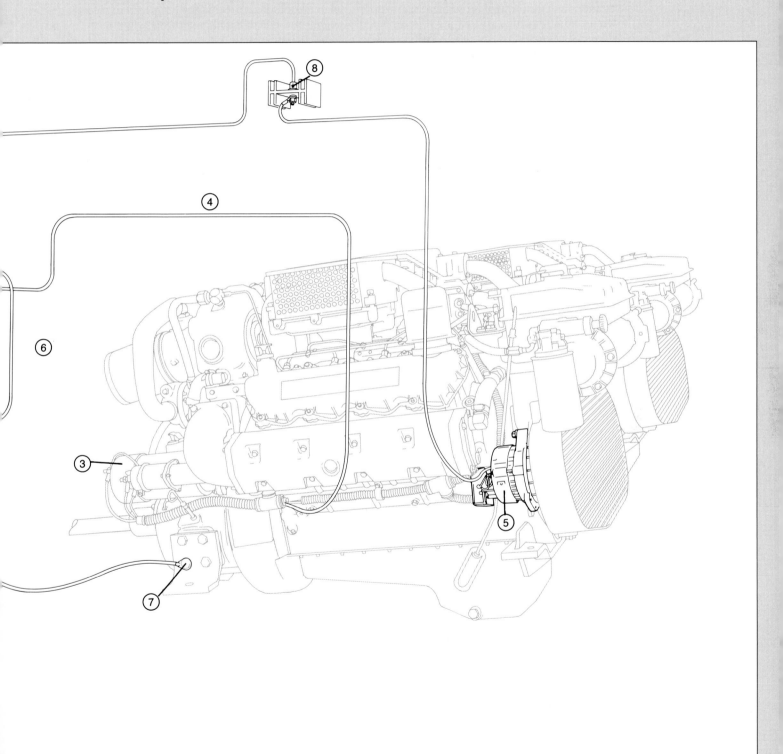

Batteries

Safety

Batteries constitute an underestimated danger aboard boats. A fully charged battery contains a tremendous amount of stored energy—more than enough to melt in half a wrench placed carelessly across its terminals. A battery's electrolyte, a solution of sulphuric acid, will eat through clothing and cause severe burns. Spilled battery acid, when mixed with seawater, will give off deadly chlorine gas.

When working around batteries, always remove jewelry, particularly a wristwatch with a metal band, and be very careful in placing tools. *Take great care with battery acid*; if it gets in the eyes it can cause blindness. Wear some form of eye protection. Immediately douse any splashes with water, then neutralize them with an antacid solution such as baking powder or soda, household ammonia, or antacid medication.

A battery compartment, particularly for a wet-cell battery, needs to be well ventilated. When being charged, batteries emit combustible, lighter-than-air gases: hydrogen and oxygen. Never generate sparks around a charging battery. Batteries can explode, spraying acid in all directions.

Batteries also emit corrosive fumes. Never install electronic equipment near a battery compartment. The equipment will likely suffer irreparable damage.

Batteries should be kept in well-built, acid-proof (plastic, fiberglass, or epoxy-saturated wood) boxes with secure, vented lids (Figure 2-5, page 40). Ventilation is important not just to remove explosive gases but to dissipate heat generated during rapid charging. The degree of ventilation often significantly affects battery life. As long as the batteries don't freeze, the cooler the temperature the longer the life.

Routine Maintenance

Wet-cell batteries must be periodically topped up with distilled water. A battery's internal plates will be permanently damaged by exposure to air. Fluid levels should be maintained at $\frac{1}{4}$ to $\frac{1}{2}$ inch above the plates, but no higher: Overfilling will lead to spewing of electrolyte from the filler caps during charging. *Tap water should not be used*, particularly if it comes from a chlorinated source (most city water) since chlorine will shorten the battery's life. Traces of minerals are also damaging, creating internal galvanic currents. In a pinch, bottled water or clean rainwater is better than nothing at all.

Record keeping is important with wet-cell batteries. Any specific-gravity readings that are taken should be corrected for temperature (see below) and noted, together with the amounts of water that are added. A glance at the record will often give advance warning of problem cells or a general deterioration of the battery (more on this in a moment), enabling you to head off an inopportune failure.

Keep the tops of batteries clean. A small amount of dirt, water, or acid will provide a path for electrical leaks that will drain the battery over time. Wiping with a rag dipped in a solution of baking powder, soda, or household ammonia will neutralize any acid, but never sprinkle baking soda directly on a battery case—if any were to enter a cell through a vent hole, it would cause explosive boiling of the electrolyte and could destroy the cell.

Periodically remove the battery cables (negative first) and clean the terminal posts and clamps. (See Figure 2-2A). When removing the clamps, do not lever them up with a screwdriver. This is likely to damage the battery plates and may tear a terminal post loose, destroying the battery. Loosen the clamp bolt and ease the clamp jaws open; work the clamp gently from side to side and then lift it off. A pair of battery-clamp pullers (Figure 2-2B) is a cheap and excellent investment for the tool box. Why wreck a $400 battery for the lack of a $10 tool? After replacing the cable clamps, coat them and the battery posts liberally with grease or petroleum jelly to inhibit corrosion.

Bring a battery to a full charge any time it is to be left unused for more than a few days. All batteries will discharge slowly when standing idle. The rate of discharge depends to a great extent on temperature and on certain features of internal construction. A wet-cell lead/antimony battery will run down faster than a gel-cell with no antimony in the plate grids. Lead/antimony batteries lose approximately 0.7% of their charge per day at 80°F (27°C), rising to 1.75% per day at 100°F (38°C). The higher the temperature, the greater the rate of discharge (Figures 2-3A and 2-3B). Gel-cells have a rate of discharge at 80°F (27°C) of as low as 0.1% per day.

If a wet-cell battery is left uncharged for more than a month, especially over the summer months, self-discharge will lead to sulphation, the sulphates will harden, and the battery will be

Figure 2-2A. If battery-cable clamps look like this they are long overdue for a clean-up! The corrosion will be causing resistance that will seriously impair DC system performance.

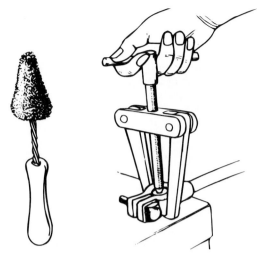

Figure 2-2B. Battery-clamp puller and tapered wire brush for cleaning the inside of the clamp. *(Yachting Monthly)*

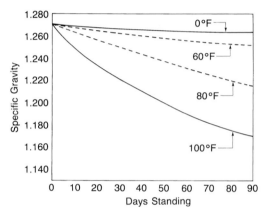

Figure 2-3A. Self-discharge rates for wet-cell batteries. *(Battery Council International)*

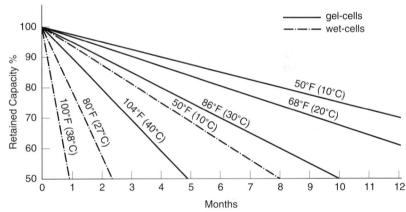

Figure 2-3B. Self-discharge rates for wet-cells and gel-cells as a function of temperature.

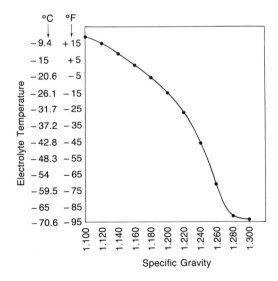

Figure 2-4. Battery freezing points at different states of charge. *(Battery Council International)*

Table 2-1. Electrolyte Freezing Point as a Function of Battery State of Charge

State of Charge (%)	Freezing Point (°F) (°C)
100	−70 (−57)
75	−45 (−43)
50	−10 (−23)
25	5 (−15)
0	15 (−9)

Batteries   39

The battery box illustrated in Figure 2-5A represents the ideal. The vent (which leads outside, and *not* to interior boat spaces) is at the top of the compartment, since the explosive hydrogen gas given off during charging is lighter than air. The removable lid permits ready access for servicing. Batteries are well secured so that even in a capsize they will not break loose. Air is introduced at the base of the compartment to encourage thorough ventilation. The optional fan further increases ventilation, which also increases the efficiency of battery charging. (If a fan is used, it *must* be sparkproof.) The box is constructed of acidproof material such as plastic, fiberglass, or epoxy-saturated wood.

In practice, many boats have no battery box at all, or something that falls far short of this ideal. The owner of any boat venturing offshore would be well advised to fit a decent box if one is not present. Good-quality batteries weigh around three-quarters of a pound per amphour of capacity (at 12 volts); a 200-Ah battery thus weighs about 150 pounds, a 400-Ah battery, 300 pounds. This is a highly concentrated weight, coupled with gallons of highly corrosive sulphuric acid (about 1¾ gallons per 100 Ah of capacity at 12 volts). Batteries that come loose in a seaway constitute a major safety threat. Containing the batteries and battery acid in an acidproof container is a matter of common sense.

Building a simple battery box. Begin with a 4- by 8-foot sheet of ½-inch exterior-grade plywood. Mark it out in panels to form a box ¼ inch longer and wider on its *inside* than the battery or batteries it is to hold, and ½ inch higher than the battery depth (including terminal posts), as in Figure 2-5B. Before cutting out the panels, place a layer of fiberglass cloth (just about any weight will do) over the plywood (Figure 2-5C) and thoroughly wet it out with catalyzed polyester resin or epoxy resin, the latter being preferable for this purpose. Add resin until the weave of the cloth is filled; the cloth will turn transparent, allowing the pencil marks for the panel cuts to show through.

When the resin has cured, cut out the panels and then saturate all the sawn edges with resin.

Glue and nail the box together with the fiberglass on the inside, making sure all the seams are completely filled with glue. Use an epoxy paste (or epoxy resin with appropriate filler) to seal the seams, even if you used polyester resin for the sheathing; polyester resin is brittle and has no gap-filling ability. Radius (round off) the outside corners and bottom edges of the box. Now use masking tape to temporarily affix strips of fiberglass cloth around each corner

and edge, overlapping each side of the seam by 2 inches (Figure 2-5D). Wet out the cloth with resin and, progressing from the corner to the edges, work out the wrinkles and air bubbles to achieve a firm bond.

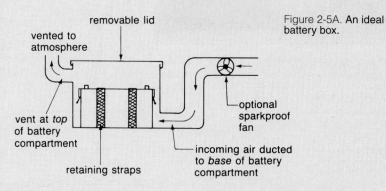

Figure 2-5A. An ideal battery box.

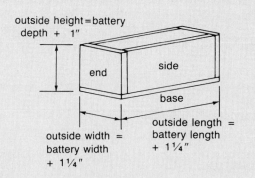

Figure 2-5B. Dimensions for a do-it-yourself box of ½-inch plywood.

Figure 2-5C. The "ingredients": plywood, fiberglass cloth (which will give a smoother, more finished appearance than woven roving), epoxy resin and hardener, a roller and brush, acetone for cleaning tools, and a mason jar for saving used acetone.

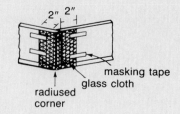

Figure 2-5D. Sealing and reinforcing the outside corners of the box.

continued

Figure 2-5E. The finished box.

Figure 2-5F. Two lengths of ¼-inch line provide a means of lifting the battery out of the box when necessary. Make sure the line is nylon, which is acid-resistant.

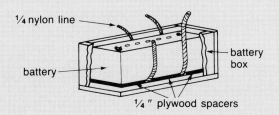

¼ nylon line

battery

battery box

¼ " plywood spacers

Figure 2-5G. Fitting a lid.

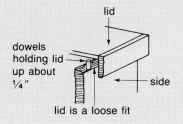

lid

dowels holding lid up about ¼"

side

lid is a loose fit

Lay a second strip of cloth over the first, overlapping its edges by one inch, and repeat. Radius the inside corners with fillets of epoxy paste (Figure 2-5E).

The box will need to be fastened in place, a task that may involve some imagination as well as an appreciation for the forces that could come to bear in a seaway. Any fasteners through the sides or bottom will need liberal bedding, preferably with a polyurethane adhesive such as 3M 5200. If the batteries have no handles, place three spacers of ¼-inch ply in the bottom of the box to separate two lengths of ¼-inch nylon line, the ends of which will emerge above the box sides (Figure 2-5F). With this arrangement the battery can be removed without having to destroy the box!

There remains only the task of fitting a lid. The lid can simply rest on and overlap the box sides, as shown in Figure 2-5G, provided some short dowels or nails are set into the box sides and ends to stick out ¼ inch or so. This holds the lid slightly above the box, permitting adequate ventilation. Alternatively, fit a vent in the lid (a screened hole will suffice).

Strap the lid down with straps sturdy enough to restrain the batteries in the event of a capsize.

The American Boat and Yacht Council *Standards and Recommended Practices for Small Craft* requires that:

1. Batteries must be securely fastened against shifting;
2. Positive terminals must be protected against accidental shorting either with some kind of a boot or else by a battery-box lid;
3. There will be no uninsulated metal fuel line within 12″ of a battery top or sides, and no battery installed directly above or below a fuel tank, fuel filter, or fuel-line fitting;
4. There will be some form of a vent to allow hydrogen to escape;
5. The means of mounting a battery must be impervious to battery electrolyte, while any fasteners must be isolated from areas intended for collecting electrolyte.

(Lloyd's Register of Shipping *Rules and Regulations for the Classification of Yachts and Small Craft* has similar requirements.)

damaged permanently. During any extended layup, *be sure to put wet-cell batteries on charge at least once a month* (a small array solar panel will keep a battery topped up and prevent sulphation—see Chapter 5). A fully charged gel-cell can be left alone for several months.

In cold climates a full charge is also essential to prevent freezing of the electrolyte, which will cause irreparable damage. Table 2-1 and Figure 2-4 show the approximate relationship between a battery's state of charge and the freezing point of its electrolyte.

Keep batteries cool. Some capacity loss will occur at elevated temperatures whether the battery is in use or not. *This loss is irreversible* and is part of a battery's aging process (Figure 2-6). The higher the temperature, the greater the loss. Batteries in storage should be kept as cool as possible without freezing.

Testing a Battery

There are five ways to check the state of charge, and/or health, of a battery:

1. measuring the *specific gravity* of its electrolyte
2. measuring its *open-circuit* voltage
3. using a *load tester*
4. performing a *capacity test*
5. keeping track of the amps going in and out with an *amp-hour meter*

Specific gravity. The electrolyte in a battery is a solution of sulphuric acid, which is denser than water. As a battery discharges, this acid weakens progressively, becoming less dense. Samples of the electrolyte can be withdrawn from each cell in a wet-cell battery using a *hydrometer* (Figure 2-7). A hydrometer contains a floating indicator that comes to rest at a certain level in pure water, this level being calibrated for a *specific gravity* of 1.000. The denser the acid solution, the higher the indicator will float, giving a higher specific gravity reading. As the solution weakens, the indicator will sink. Since specific gravity varies with temperature, better hydrometers incorporate a thermometer that allows any reading to be corrected for nonstandard temperatures. In the USA the standard temperature is 80°F (26.7°C); in the UK it is 60°F (15.6°C). If the electrolyte is at a nonstandard temperature, the conversion charts in Figure 2-8 are used to correct the specific gravity reading. The corrected specific gravity can then, in theory, be corre-

Figure 2-6. Permanent loss of battery capacity for gel-cell batteries as a function of temperature. Note: wet-cell losses will be higher. *(Sonnenschein Battery Co.)*

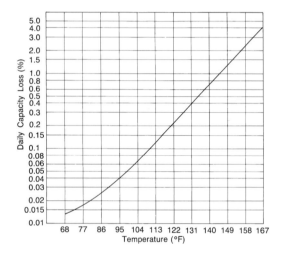

Figure 2-7. A battery-testing hydrometer. The correct method of reading it is shown on the right. The eye should be level with the liquid surface. Readings are made disregarding the curvature of the liquid against the glass parts. *(Battery Council International)*

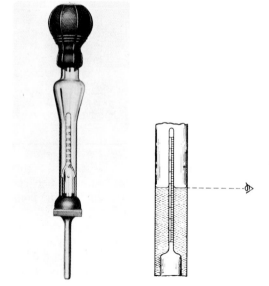

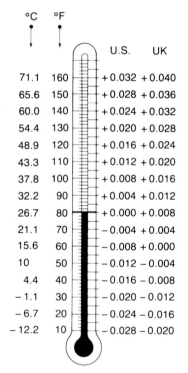

°C	°F		U.S.	UK
71.1	160		+ 0.032	+ 0.040
65.6	150		+ 0.028	+ 0.036
60.0	140		+ 0.024	+ 0.032
54.4	130		+ 0.020	+ 0.028
48.9	120		+ 0.016	+ 0.024
43.3	110		+ 0.012	+ 0.020
37.8	100		+ 0.008	+ 0.016
32.2	90		+ 0.004	+ 0.012
26.7	80		+ 0.000	+ 0.008
21.1	70		– 0.004	+ 0.004
15.6	60		– 0.008	+ 0.000
10	50		– 0.012	– 0.004
4.4	40		– 0.016	– 0.008
– 1.1	30		– 0.020	– 0.012
– 6.7	20		– 0.024	– 0.016
– 12.2	10		– 0.028	– 0.020

Figure 2-8. Temperature corrections for hydrometer readings in the United States and the United Kingdom. Baseline temperature is taken as 80°F (26.7°C) in the USA, and 60°F (15.6°C) in the UK. Given a hydrometer reading of 1.250 and an electrolyte temperature of 20°F, for example, in the USA. 0.024 would be subtracted for a corrected specific gravity of 1.226. Looking in Table 2-2 we see that the battery is about 25% discharged. In the UK, the correction factor for an electrolyte temperature of 20°F (–6.7°C) is –0.016, yielding a corrected specific gravity of 1.234. Turning again to Table 2-2 we see that the battery is once again about 25% discharged.

Maintaining and Troubleshooting a Battery-Powered Electrical System

lated accurately with a battery's state of charge.

It should be noted, however, that if a battery is rapidly discharged or recharged, the chemical reactions will take place between the active material on the surfaces of the battery plates and the immediately accessible electrolyte, but not in the inner plate areas. Following the discharge or charge, if the battery is left alone the acid and water will diffuse in and out of the plates, the battery will equalize internally, and the electrolyte will reach a homogeneous state. *The only time a specific gravity reading will correlate accurately with a battery's state of charge is when the electrolyte is in this homogeneous state.* At all other times, depending on how recently the battery was used and the magnitude of the current in relation to the battery's capacity, specific gravity readings will be off by a certain margin, indicating a more discharged state than is in fact the case during discharges, and a less charged state than is the case during recharges. If the battery has been used vigorously, it can take up to 24 hours for the electrolyte to reach a stable state.

There is another phenomenon that affects specific gravity readings called *stratification*. When recharging, the heavier acid forming in the electrolyte tends to sink to the bottom of the battery, out of reach of the hydrometer. It is not until the battery begins to reach gassing voltages, and the bubbles stir up the electrolyte, that the electrolyte reaches a more homogeneous state. Stratification exaggerates the lag between state of charge and hydrometer readings on recharge (Figure 2-9).

Once the electrolyte is in a homogeneous state, and specific gravity readings have been corrected for temperature, there is a correlation between the specific gravity and the battery's state of charge, which is given in Table 2-2 and Figure 2-10.

The figures in Table 2-2 are for *industry-standard* batteries. In real life the specific gravity of fully charged batteries varies considerably, from 1.230 to 1.300. The lower figure may be found on some deep-cycle batteries sold in the tropics,

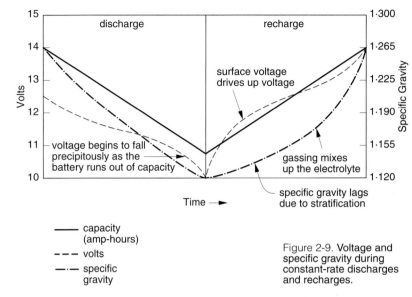

Figure 2-9. Voltage and specific gravity during constant-rate discharges and recharges.

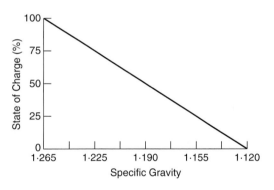

Figure 2-10. State of charge as a function of homogeneous specific gravity.

where the higher prevailing temperatures promote more efficient battery operation, requiring a less concentrated acid solution. The higher figure may be found on cranking batteries sold in cold climates, where more concentrated acid solutions are needed to boost output (Table 2-3).

Table 2-2. Electrolyte Specific Gravity as a Function of Temperature and Battery State of Charge

Specific Gravity:	80°F (26.7°C)	60°F (15°C)	State of Charge (%)
	1.265	1.273	100
	1.225	1.233	75
	1.190	1.198	50
	1.155	1.163	25
	1.120	1.128	0

Table 2-3. Typical Specific Gravity Variations by Region

Region	Fully Charged Specific Gravity
North of Florida and Northern Europe	1.265 –1.280
Florida to San Juan (Puerto Rico)	1.250 –1.265
South of San Juan	1.235 –1.250

After a new battery is installed, it should be fully charged and then tested to establish its actual specific gravity (be sure to compensate for the temperature of the electrolyte); *the figures should be logged for future reference.* (Note that a battery may be assumed to be fully charged when further charging over a 3-hour period fails to produce any increase in the specific gravity of its electrolyte.)

A hydrometer should be found on every maintenance-conscious boat with wet-cell batteries. Be sure to get one designed for battery-testing; some are for antifreeze, others for winemaking! Each is purpose-built to cover an appropriate range of specific gravities.

Open-circuit voltage. A battery is open-circuited when no load is being drawn from it and no charge is being fed to it. The simplest way to open-circuit a battery is to switch off the battery isolation switch. However, this should never be done with the engine running—it can blow out the diodes in the alternator (see previous chapter). There may be some equipment, such as a bilge pump, VHF radio, or solar panel, hooked directly to the battery; such equipment must also be switched off or disconnected to achieve meaningful test results.

Just as with specific gravity readings, battery voltage readings are affected by the initial strength of the battery acid, the rate of previous discharges and recharges, and the amount of time the battery has been *rested*. Following use, a battery will take a while to stabilize internally. If voltage readings are to be a meaningful reflection of the state of charge, the battery must be allowed to sit for at least 10 minutes; an hour or two would be better; overnight would be best (gel-cell batteries may take 48 hours to stabilize). With the battery temperature between 60°F and 100°F (15.5°C and 38°C), the *stabilized* open-circuit voltage can be approximately correlated with state of charge as shown in Table 2-4 and Figure 2-11.

Note that the difference between a fully charged battery and a half-charged battery is only 0.4 volt!

From full charge to full discharge is just 0.8 to 1.0 volt. Most swinging-arm (analog-type) meters are quite useless in these circumstances; a meter with an expanded scale (normally covering the region from 8 to 16 volts) is questionable; *only a good-quality digital meter will give an accurate assessment of the state of charge.* (If an analog meter is used, look for one with an accuracy of ±2% as opposed to the common ±5%; digital meters are typically ±0.2%.)

Since *homogeneous* specific gravity and *stabilized* open-circuit voltage are both measuring states of charge, we would expect some sort of a correlation between the two. The relationship is as follows:
The voltage of a single cell
 = the specific gravity reading (SG) + 0.84.
The voltage of a 12-volt battery
 = $6 \times (SG + 0.84)$.

Load testing. *A battery can show a full or nearly full charge on both an open-circuit voltage test and a specific-gravity test, yet still fail to operate correctly due to a severe loss of capacity resulting from sulphation of the plates or shedding of active material.* The voltage and specific gravity are merely reflecting the fact that the *remaining capacity* is fully charged. To check the capacity itself, some form of a *load test* is needed, normally using a *high-load tester (high-rate discharge tester).* This is a device that is connected either across each cell in turn or across the battery terminals, artificially creating an extremely high load on the battery while measuring voltage. A cell or battery in good condition will maintain a steady voltage for up to 10 seconds, while the voltage on a weak cell or battery will begin to fall off rapidly at some point during the test (the reduced cell or battery capacity is soon exhausted with the result that the rate of discharge cannot be sustained). If a 12-volt battery's voltage falls below 9.5 volts before 15 seconds are up, the battery is in sorry shape.

High-load testers are specialized pieces of equipment found in all automotive parts stores (they can sometimes be borrowed) but rarely

Figure 2-11. State of charge as a function of stabilized open-circuit voltage for a wet-cell battery. (A fully charged gel-cell will have an open-circuit voltage as high as 13.0 volts.)

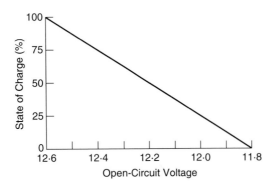

Table 2-4. Open-Circuit Voltage and Battery State of Charge

Open-Circuit Voltage:		Battery State of Charge
Typical Wet-Cell	Gel-Cell	
12.6 or greater	13.0	100%
12.4 –12.6	12.8 –13.0	75% – 100%
12.2 –12.4	12.6 –12.8	50% – 75%
12.0 –12.2	12.4 –12.6	25% – 50%
11.8 –12.0	12.2 –12.4	0% – 25%
Below 11.8	Below 12.2	0%

found on boats. Not to worry. The effect of a high-load tester can be simulated by cranking a diesel engine for 15 seconds. Close the throttle and activate any "stop" lever to keep the engine from starting. If the engine has an automatic starting advance that is difficult to outfox, shut off the fuel supply. Then crank the motor. While it is cranking, monitor the battery voltage constantly. (On a gasoline engine, close off the fuel supply and disable the ignition before cranking.)

As soon as cranking commences, the voltage will drop (on a 12-volt system normally to around 10.5 volts, depending on load, battery capacity, and temperature) but will then more or less stabilize, declining slowly during the rest of the test. If the voltage starts to drop precipitously before 15 seconds are up, the battery is in trouble—it is either seriously discharged or else has lost much of its capacity. The battery should be fully recharged and the test repeated. If the battery fails a second time it should be given a full capacity test (see below).

To avoid overheating the starter motor when simulating a high-load test, *cranking should in no circumstances be continued for more than 30 seconds*. If more than one battery bank is to be tested, the starter motor must be rested for at least 5 minutes between each bank. High-load testing takes very little out of a battery. As I pointed out in Chapter 1, even if the starter motor is pulling 400 amps, at 15 seconds this amounts to a total of only

$$400 \div (4 \times 60) = 1.66 \text{ amp-hours.}$$

Capacity testing. A capacity test is done by simulating a 20-hour capacity test (for a C20-rating; refer back to Chapter 1 for a definition of this rating). The battery is first brought to a full charge. It is then discharged at a rate of *one twentieth of its rated amp-hour capacity* (e.g., at 10 amps on a 200-Ah battery). The load is established by turning on incandescent lights until the required amperage is reached. The time is noted when the test is begun. The test is continued until battery voltage has fallen to 1.75 volts per cell (10.5 volts on a 12-volt battery). The load (e.g., 10 amps) is multiplied by the hours the battery was able to sustain it (say, 15 hours) to give the amp-hour capacity of the battery ($10 \times 15 = 150$ Ah; the battery is down to 75% of its rated capacity). The battery should be immediately recharged to prevent sulphation. (Note that if a battery is rated at the C10 rate it should be discharged at a rate of $1/10$ of its rated capacity. Note also that as the test progresses and the battery voltage declines, the amperage drawn by the lights will also decline, it may be necessary to add another small load to keep the amp draw close to the desired level.)

Any battery below 80% of its rated capacity should be recharged and tested again. If the capacity cannot be brought up to 80% or better, the battery should probably be replaced; once capacity falls much below this level, batteries tend to fail fairly rapidly (note, however, that new gel-cells may test as low as 80% but then gain in capacity over a period of time as the battery is used; see later in this chapter for some techniques that may help restore lost capacity to older batteries, both wet and gel). *Sailors who venture offshore, or for whom the batteries are vital pieces of equipment, should perform a capacity test on all batteries at the beginning of each boating season.*

Amp-hour meters. An amp-hour meter keeps track of the amps going into and out of a battery, maintaining a running total, which is used to indicate the state of charge of the battery (Figure 2-12). This sounds simple, but is in fact incredibly complicated. The meter must first be calibrated to the specific battery it is metering, and then must be able to make appropriate adjustments for the inefficiencies inherent in charging and discharging batteries. Unfortunately, no two batteries have the same efficiency ratings, and even the same battery will be more or less efficient depending on its temperature, state of charge, the rate of charge or discharge, its age, and so on.

Many amp-hour meters are incapable of accurately reflecting this ever-changing efficiency factor and will need some form of periodic recalibration to bring them back into line with the actual state of charge of the battery. Between calibrations the meter will tend to become less and less in sync with the state of charge of the battery. Of the meters on the market, those made by Ample Technologies, the Cruising Equipment Company, and SALT, are excellent. (I have no commercial affiliations with any manufactur-

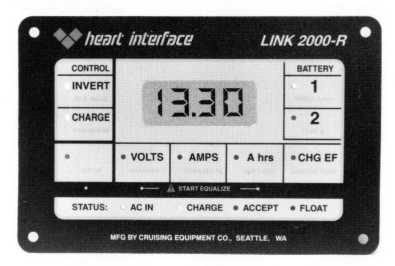

Figure 2-12. Sophisticated metering, including amp-hours, built for Heart Interface by Cruising Equipment Company. *(Heart Interface)*

ers—any references are purely to aid in locating equipment and making choices.)

Problem Batteries

When confronted with batteries that are short on capacity (cannot sustain a load) or going dead prematurely, the normal reaction is to blame the battery, but often it is not at fault. First, check for some hidden drain such as: a piece of equipment left on (especially navigation lights) or the cumulative load of a number of LED's (light-emitting diodes) fitted to distribution panels, switches and meters; leaks to ground in the boat's wiring (see Chapter 3, Ground Faults ["earth" leaks]); or simply dirt and moisture on top of the battery.

Next, consider the possibility that the battery is not receiving a proper charge (see the relevant discussions under Alternators and Voltage Regulators later in this chapter). All too often a boat sets out on a cruise with fully charged batteries. Every day, due to inadequate charging, a little less is put back into the batteries than is taken out (Figure 2-13). Eventually the batteries will not meet the demands placed on them. The owner assumes that the batteries are at fault although it is actually the charging system that is the problem. Batteries repeatedly, and unnecessarily, get replaced—quite a common scenario with cruising boats, particularly those with ferro-resonant battery chargers (Chapter 5) and automotive alternators.

Signs of trouble. Of course, it may be the battery that is defective—all must die sooner or later. Common signs of battery problems are:

A battery that shows nearly full voltage when under no load, but a steadily falling voltage when a load is applied. The battery is short on *usable* capacity. If, on recharging, its voltage comes up rapidly, there is only a limited amount of active material in the plates that is still accepting a charge. This may be due to sulphation or to shedding—in either case the battery will go dead rapidly in use, since only a small fraction of its plate area is still active. In some circumstances, sulphated active material may be brought back to life (see below), but material that has been shed is gone forever.

A wet-cell that never needs topping up with water. The battery is being undercharged. This is certain to lead to sulphation and premature death.

A wet-cell that needs frequent topping up. The battery is being overcharged. Water loss should amount to no more than two ounces of water per cell (12 ounces per battery) in 30 to 50 hours of battery charging time. If just one cell is using excessive water, it is probably shorted.

Uniformly low specific gravity readings on all cells. The battery needs recharging. If it cannot be brought up to full charge (as measured by its specific gravity), it is dying. If the difference between the highest and lowest cell readings is more than 0.030, then the low cell is probably dying. And if, after recharging, the difference remains over 0.030, this cell is almost certainly dying (in all probability shorted).

Figure 2-13. Daily cycling of a battery with inadequate charging. Despite the fact that the battery is properly sized (three to four times the daily load), eventually the battery fails to meet its tasks. Note that long before the problem becomes apparent the battery will have been damaged from sulphation through never being fully charged.

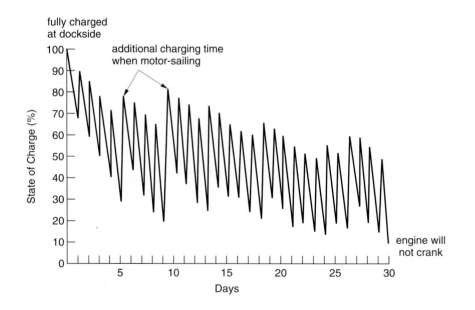

Maintaining and Troubleshooting a Battery-Powered Electrical System

An isolated and unused battery whose voltage shows an appreciable drop (such as from full charge to 75% of charge or less) over two to three weeks. The battery has an internal short—shed material, or what is known as *dendritic growth*, has bridged the gap between negative and positive plates. If the battery is a gel-cell it is not salvageable; in desperate circumstances some wet-cells can be brought back to life. All the electrolyte (acid) must be drained from the battery (be careful!) and stored in a glass or plastic container, such as a plastic milk jug. The battery should be filled repeatedly with water, gently sloshed around and bumped, then drained. (This water will still contain some acid, so take care.) With any luck the water will dislodge the offending debris. The electrolyte should then be strained (pantyhose works well) and put back in the battery. Top up the cells with water as necessary, charge the battery, and test the cells again. If one or more still will not accept a charge, the battery is useless.

A gel-cell with white powder around its vents. The battery has been overcharged to the point that the valves have opened and vented, drying out the electrolyte and wrecking the battery. In desperate circumstances if the valves are forced open and water is added, the battery may be brought back to life temporarily, but it should be noted that *once the valve seals are damaged the battery will soon be history, so do not do this unless it is certain the battery has dried out*. After the valves have been opened, the battery should be treated as a regular wet-cell (i.e., periodically topped up) until it can be replaced.

A gel-cell with a black post. The battery probably has a leaking seal around the post, in which case sooner or later it will dry out and fail. To test the seal, remove the cable clamp, brush a soap solution around the post, and then flex the battery case *for that cell*. If the solution bubbles, the seal is definitely gone.

Finally, a battery may simply be old and dying. It may have an accumulation of problems: sulphating, shorts, shedding of active material, etc. Like everything else, even well-maintained batteries wear out.

Sulphation and equalization: Is there life after death? As we saw in Chapter 1, during repeated charges and discharges lead sulphate builds up throughout battery plates. Initially the sulphate is relatively soft and porous and easily reconverted into active material, but over time it hardens and battery performance declines steadily. Sulphation is a particularly acute problem with deep-cycle batteries that are repeatedly discharged but never brought back up to a 100% charge—precisely the operating conditions of many boat batteries. Thick-plate wet-cells with antimony-reinforced plate grids are more prone to sulphation than gel-cells.

Sulphates need to be dealt with before they harden, so batteries should *never be left in a discharged state* or even a partially discharged state. If sulphates are allowed to harden, they increase the internal resistance of a battery. During charges, the surface voltage of the battery (page 20) rises rapidly, fooling any constant-voltage (automotive-type) regulator into thinking that the battery is fully charged when it is not. The regulator then shuts down the charging output. *Regardless of engine running time, the sulphated areas remain uncharged*.

To bring sulphated areas back to life a battery must be *equalized* (page 10). For equalization, it is necessary to boost charging voltages to a level that will overcome the resistance of the sulphates—sometimes to as high as 16.2 volts. Once the sulphates begin to break down, at these voltages an alternator with a standard automotive-type constant-voltage regulator would pump out too much amperage and cook the battery, with potentially explosive results. Some form of current (amperage) limiting ability is needed to hold the charging amperage to less than 5% of the total amp-hour rating of the battery being equalized (3% to 4% would be better, i.e., 6 to 8 amps for a 200-Ah battery). If the battery voltage rises rapidly, the amperage is too high. The battery temperature will need constant monitoring to make sure it does not go above 125°F (52°C). Quite a bit of gassing will occur, and the battery will need topping up with water when equalization is complete. *This gassing would destroy a gel-cell (or any sealed battery), so equalization is strictly limited to heavy-duty wet-cells*.

Equalization cannot be carried out with a standard automobile voltage regulator. It requires a purpose-built multistep regulator (page 21), a voltage regulator bypass device and a thorough understanding of how to use it (page 66), or a purpose-built battery charger (Chapter 5). A large-array solar panel (3 amps or more for every 100-Ah of battery capacity to be equalized) without voltage regulation and hooked directly to the battery will also work, as will an unregulated wind generator (Chapter 5), so long as careful attention is paid to battery voltage and temperature and the solar panel or wind generator is disconnected when equalization has occurred.

The only sure way to test for proper equalization is with a hydrometer, checking the cells repeatedly until all are up to full charge. Specific gravity will then be around 1.265 for most batteries, but will vary from battery to battery (see Testing a Battery earlier in this chapter). *The battery will accept no more charge when the specific gravity readings remain unchanged for 3 hours.* This testing is a tedious business, especially if the battery is hard to reach. Once it has been done a few times, however, the weakest (slowest to come to a full charge) cell in the battery will become apparent, and then this is the only cell that needs to be monitored. Experience will show at what rate (amperage) the battery can be charged without overheating or excessive gassing.

Important note: Much sensitive electronic equipment has a rated input voltage from around 11 volts DC to 16 volts DC. Equalization voltages of 16 volts may damage such equipment. Whenever equalizing a battery at voltages above 14.5 volts, always isolate the battery in question; at the very least, be absolutely certain all electronic equipment hooked to the battery is turned off, and also *halogen bulbs* (they are particularly sensitive to high voltages).

Dead gel-cell batteries. Gel-cell batteries, particularly if they have been discharged very flat or left in a seriously discharged state for some time, can build up a layer of calcium oxide on the grids, which creates a high resistance and fools most voltage regulators into thinking the battery is charged. The battery will then not accept or hold a charge. The battery can sometimes be brought back into service with one of the following treatments:

1. Place a moderate load on the battery for just a brief period—its voltage will fall. Immediately put the battery on charge for a couple of minutes, then repeat the process (load followed by charge). Do this three times, and then attempt a full charge. If this fails, try the next suggestion.

2. Kill the battery stone dead. Place a load on the battery (10 amps would be fine) and drag it all the way down until it shows a voltage of 1.0 volt or so. Use equipment that will not burn up as the voltage falls, such as incandescent lights.

   When the battery is completely down, finish it off by shorting out its two terminals with a length of heavy-gauge, insulated wire—12 gauge or larger (jumper cables work well). If the wire gets really hot the battery is not down enough; put the load back on. Leave it shorted for several more hours.

   Recharge the battery. It will not recover to full capacity, but after several normal discharge-and-recharge cycles it may come back to nearly full capacity.

3. Use a high-voltage, low-current charge. A charging source well above 12 volts is needed, ideally with a current-limiting function to hold the current down to a few amps, but this is hard to come by (note that one of the multistep regulators with an equalizing function can be used). In a bind it might be possible to use two good 12-volt batteries wired in series to produce 24 volts, but be sure to disconnect all 12-volt loads from the batteries. The defective gel-cell battery is hit repeatedly with the high voltage for short periods (a few seconds at a time if using the two batteries; a few minutes if using the equalizing function on a multistep regulator), and then put back onto a normal charge. The high voltage may be sufficient to get the plates accepting a charge once again. The battery should be run through several charge/discharge cycles to restore as much capacity as possible.

Alternators

How They Work

A magnet (the *rotor*) is spun inside a series of coils (the *stator*), as shown in Figures 2-14 and 2-15. As the north and south poles of the rotor pass the coils in the stator, an electrical pulse is generated—positive for the north pole, negative for the south pole. This is alternating current (AC), so called because the direction of current flow alternates from positive to negative and back. Two alternations make a *cycle*, which can occur from a few times to several million times per second. The number of cycles per second is the *frequency*, expressed as *Hertz* (Hz). Household current (AC) is commonly 60 cycles per second in the USA (50 cycles per second in the UK); in other words, its frequency is 60 Hz. The voltage and amperage generated in the alternator are determined by the strength of the magnetic field in the rotor, the number of *poles* in the rotor, the number of turns of wire in the stator coils, and the speed of rotation.

Instead of having fixed (permanent) magnets in the rotor, an alternator rotor has a soft-iron core

Figure 2-14. Alternator. *(Lucas/CAV)*

Figure 2-15. Alternator operating principles. The rotor contains the field winding. The voltage regulator varies the direct current passing through the field winding and thus the strength of the resultant magnetic field. Three sets of windings (A, B, and C) are built into the stator, each producing AC output.

wrapped in a coil of wire (the *field winding*). When *direct current* (DC), which flows in only one direction, passes through the coil, the iron core is magnetized. The stronger the current, the greater the degree of magnetism. Alternator output is controlled (*regulated*) by varying the current (the *field current*) fed to the field winding.

Current is fed to the field winding via two slip rings—smooth, round, insulated discs mounted on the rotor shaft (Figure 2-16)—each connected to one end of the field winding and each contacted by a spring-loaded carbon brush contained in a brush holder fixed to the alternator housing.

A refinement of the system is attained by compounding the rotor in multiple interlocking fingers. This has the effect of producing multiple north and south magnetic poles when the field winding is energized.

As noted, when these north and south poles spin inside the coils of the stator, alternating current is generated in the coils. Regardless of the number of coils or windings (this varies among alternators), they are hooked up in such a way as to produce just three effective coils—the resulting power output is known as *three phase* (Figure 2-17).

Despite the multiple phases, the current from each phase is still alternating. To be of any use in charging a battery it must be *rectified* to direct current. This is done with *silicon diodes*. A diode is an electronic switch or check valve that allows electricity to flow in only one direction.

Imagine first a single-phase alternator. Each end of the stator winding is connected to two diodes. The first diode is placed so it passes only positive impulses, and is connected to the battery's positive terminal. The second diode is oriented to pass only negative impulses, and provides a return path from the battery's negative terminal to the winding. The complete diode setup is known as a *bridge rectifier* (Figure 2-18A). Despite a constantly reversing current flow in the

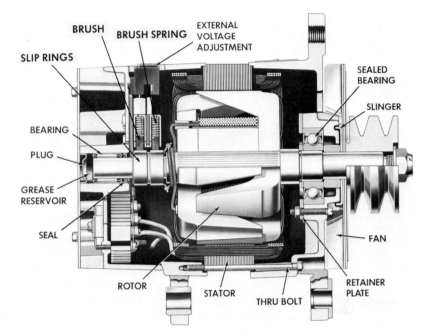

Figure 2-16. Alternator construction. *(AC Delco)*

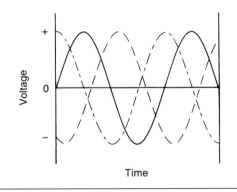

Figure 2-17. Three-phase alternator output.

stator, current flows in only one direction to the battery. In a three-phase alternator the configuration is a bit more elaborate. Three positive diodes are tied together to form the alternator's positive terminal, which is connected to the positive terminal of the battery. Three more diodes are generally grounded to the alternator frame and con-

Alternators   49

Figure 2-18A. Operation of a single-phase bridge rectifier. In the symbol for a diode, the arrow indicates the direction in which the diode will pass current. In the left-hand schematic, current is flowing in one direction from the stator winding through diode D to the battery's positive terminal. Diodes C and B block the flow in the other direction. The return path from the battery's negative terminal to the winding (necessary to complete the circuit) is through diode A. In the schematic on the right, the AC current flow from the stator winding has reversed, passing through diode B to the positive terminal. The return path is through diode C. *The generated current has reversed direction but still flows in the same direction into the battery.*

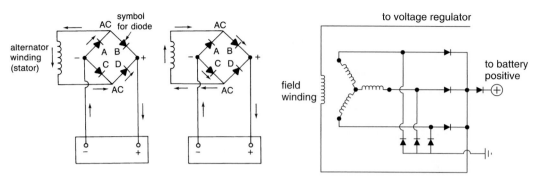

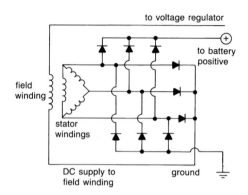

Figure 2-18C. Schematic with a single output diode.

Figure 2-18B. Schematics of two common three-phase bridge rectifiers. The only difference between the two is the manner in which the stator windings are connected. This is not a distinction with which we need to be concerned.

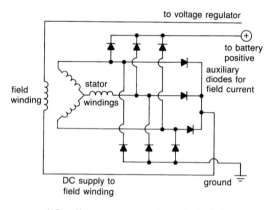

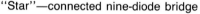

"Star"—connected nine-diode bridge

"Delta"—connected nine-diode bridge

nected to the battery via the engine block and the battery ground strap. Another three auxiliary diodes (for an overall total of nine diodes) frequently are installed on the positive side of the three phases, feeding positive current to the voltage regulator and rotor field winding (via the brushes and slip rings) to energize and control the alternator (Figure 2-18B). Sometimes there is only one auxiliary diode (Figure 2-18C); occasionally none.

Hot-rated, marine, and isolated-ground alternators. As always, there are cheap ways and expensive ways of making alternators. *If an alternator is to be used to recharge heavily discharged, large-capacity battery banks, it is going to be worked many times harder than an automotive alternator, and as a result needs to be more ruggedly built.* Key features are the ability to operate *continuously at full output in high temperatures*, oversized bearings, heavy-duty brushes, and heavy-duty diodes (all features of what, in the USA, are known as *KKK*-rated alternators—Figure 2-19). In addition, to withstand the marine environment the alternator should have noncorrosive brush holders (normally

brass), plated brush springs and other metal parts (the springs are especially important), and impregnated windings to maintain insulation levels in a damp environment. These features are not so common, although Lucas (in the UK) builds a line of *marine* alternators like this.

A marine alternator should be *ignition-protected*, which is to say the slip rings and brushes are enclosed in a vapor-tight housing, or the ventilation openings have screens. This will stop internal arcing within the alternator from igniting explosive vapors (e.g., gasoline, butane, or propane) in the engine room. Ignition protection is essential with gasoline engines.

Finally, it is desirable for a marine alternator to be constructed with an *isolated ground*: Instead of using the normal practice of grounding the negative side to the alternator case, *the negative is brought out to a separate insulated stud, which must then be wired to the battery's negative terminal.* This eliminates the otherwise high currents that flow through the engine block to ground when the alternator is operating, potentially contributing to stray-current corrosion (see Chapter 4). Isolated-ground alternators are uncommon and expensive, but in certain circumstances, notably on metal boats, are important.

Installation and Maintenance

If installed properly, alternators are virtually maintenance and trouble free. Key aspects of installation are using large enough cables to avoid voltage drop (see below and Chapter 3); getting the correct polarity on the cables; making sure the alternator is never open-circuited when running; and supporting the cables against vibration. Maintenance is a matter of keeping the drive belt tensioned and the alternator clean and protected from corrosion.

Open-circuit and reverse polarity. Anytime an alternator is electrically disconnected (such as by turning off the battery isolation switch) *while still running*, the residual energy in the stator and the field windings momentarily produces continued output with no place to go. This voltage can easily peak at several hundred volts or more, blowing out all the diodes and the voltage regulator. This can happen in a fraction of a second! Never disconnect a running alternator! The diodes will be blown out even more certainly by connecting a battery with reverse polarity—connecting the positive lead to the negative terminal and vice versa (Figure 2-20). *When reconnecting batteries be absolutely sure to get the cables the right way around!* Be especially careful when installing new batteries; the position of the terminals may be reversed from one model to another.

It is possible to fit *snubbers* (reverse-avalanche silicon diodes; available from Ample Technologies, Cruising Equipment Company, and SALT)—otherwise known as surge-protection devices—between an alternator output terminal and ground. These special diodes are set to close well above alternator output voltage, but well below the destruction voltage of the alternator diodes. Anytime an alternator is open-circuited, the snubber senses the rising voltage and dumps the alternator output to ground, de-energizing the field winding, stopping any further output, and so saving the diodes. Snubbers have a limited load-carrying capability; larger alternators would need to have two or more fitted in parallel.

It is also possible to fit special *fast fuses* that will protect against accidental reverse polarity. Lucas makes three sizes suitable for alternators up to 120 amps' output.

Vibration. A problem that is becoming more common with the increasing use of high-output alternators is the positive cable's coming adrift

Figure 2-19. Construction details of a hot-rated (KKK) alternator. Note the large diodes and heavy, impregnated stator windings.

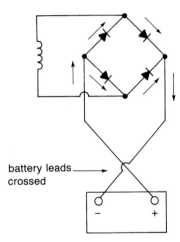

Figure 2-20. The effect of reverse polarity on diodes. The result is a direct electrical path from positive to negative terminal—a dead short. Full battery current will flow, burning out the diodes instantly.

battery leads crossed

from the positive stud. Whenever outputs go above 100 amps, large cables are needed, which tend to be stiff and heavy. Engine-transmitted vibration can cause the cable-securing nut to work loose. The loose cable then arcs between its lug and the mounting stud, until the stud is burned through and the cable drops off the alternator. Depending on the charging circuit, this cable may be connected directly to a battery with no intervening diodes and switches. If such a cable should land on the engine block, or some other grounded surface, *it will cause a highly dangerous short circuit across the battery, which may well start a fire or even cause the battery to blow up. It is essential to ensure that the nut holding the output cable to its stud is locked in some way* (e.g., a *nyloc* nut, or the addition of a locking nut) and that the cable is properly supported so that it places no strain on the stud (the best way to do this is to add a small arm to the alternator, so that the arm is vibrating in sync with the alternator, and to fasten the cable to this arm—Figure 2-21).

Belt tension and bearings. The high loadings of a high-output alternator can be met only by top-quality belts that are regularly tensioned. If twin belts are fitted, when renewing them they must be replaced as a *matched* set. To tension a belt, the alternator mounting bolts are backed off a turn or two, a lever is slipped between the alternator case and the engine, and the alternator levered out, holding the tension while the bolts are tightened. A short broom handle, hammer handle, or something similar is better for this job than a metal tool since it will not cause shorts or damage the alternator case (Figure 2-21). Note: Some modern alternator cases are quite thin, so tensioning must be done with care; special tools are available for belt tightening.

Belts are especially prone to slip immediately after engine start-up, when alternator loads are at their highest. A slipping belt will frequently give off a high-pitched, often cyclical squeal. (Note that the tachometer on many engines works by measuring the frequency of the alternator's AC output—before rectification—which varies directly with engine speed. Any time a tachometer reading is low or erratic, suspect a slipping alternator drive belt.) If a common belt is used for the water pump and alternator, a slipping belt will also result in an overheated engine.

If a belt is allowed to slip for any length of time it can heat up its pulley, which then transmits the heat along the shaft to the rotor, which demagnetizes the rotor, crippling alternator output. Belts must be kept tight!

Bearings are generally longlived. The pulley-end bearing is the one most likely to fail—it will make a distinctive, medium-pitched rumble. If the bearings are suspect, the belt should be removed and the pulley flexed from side to side and in and out. There should be no sideways movement, and only minimal in and out movement. Next, turn the pulley by hand—it should turn freely. Worn bearings can often be felt as a slight roughness as the pulley turns. If the bearings are damaged, when installing the new alternator check the pulley alignment carefully since misalignment may have been the cause of the damage.

Cleanliness and corrosion. Marine alternators are subjected to prolonged periods of high loading in hot engine compartments, which will tend to overheat bearings, diodes, and voltage regulators, and cause any of these to fail. Excess heat will also melt the thin, lacquered insulation on coils. This could result in a short circuit or could burn through the coil wire like a fuse, breaking the circuit. Burned coils have a distinctive smell—once encountered, easily remembered!

Any dirt will tend to trap heat. The cooling fans on alternators located in dirty, greasy, smoky engine rooms pick up the oily mist and blow it through the alternator. In time a greasy buildup of dirt coats and *insulates* coils, diodes, etc., causing the alternator to run hot, making burnout more likely. This kind of gook is hard to clean out; the answer is to keep the engine running cleanly in the first place.

Exposure to salt spray, or just to the marine atmosphere, will lead to corrosion of parts and electrical terminals. Moving parts tend to freeze with intermittent use; brush springs are particularly prone to failure. A periodic shot of WD 40 or electrical cleaner in and around alternator housings goes a long way toward keeping things moving and reducing corrosion on terminals.

Finally, alternators should not be painted, even to slow corrosion. However nice they look, that paint is just one more layer of insulation!

Charging Problems

When faced with charging problems, don't be too hasty about tearing into the equipment! One of the following three situations is likely: *undercharging; overcharging;* or *no output at all.* First determine which category covers the problem. Then work through the relevant pro-

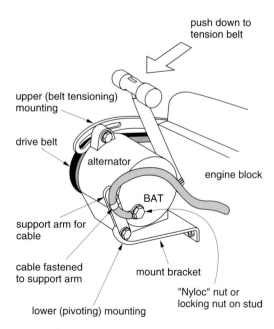

Figure 2-21. Tensioning an alternator. Note the additional cable support bracket to prevent the heavy output cable from vibrating loose from the output stud.

push down to tension belt

upper (belt tensioning) mounting

drive belt

alternator

engine block

BAT

support arm for cable

cable fastened to support arm

mount bracket

"Nyloc" nut or locking nut on stud

lower (pivoting) mounting

cedure below before jumping to any conclusion as to where the problem lies.

Persistent undercharging from an otherwise functioning alternator (Troubleshooting Chart 2-1). The alternator may be just fine. *First check the batteries.* As discussed earlier in this chapter, dead and dying batteries will not accept a charge. If the batteries are not the problem:

- Check the belt tension. It should not be possible to depress the longest stretch of belt with moderate finger pressure more than ⅜ to ½ inch. If the output has been fluctuating wildly—especially on initial start-up—perhaps accompanied by belt squeal, the belt is loose.

- Check that the alternator is adequately sized for the demands being made on it and that its speed of rotation is not too slow (see Chapter 1, Sizing an Alternator)

- *Check for voltage drop between the output terminal on the alternator and the positive battery post.* (Voltage drop is covered in detail in Chapter 3. At this time it is not necessary to understand the concept, simply how to test for it.) With the engine off, turn on some loads (lights, etc.) for a few minutes to discharge the battery. Now start the engine. The alternator will go to full output to replace the current drained from the battery. Immediately after cranking, *while the alternator is still at full output,* test between the *alternator output terminal* (the largest one, with an insulated base and the largest cable coming from it—it will also probably be labeled BAT) and the *battery positive post* with a multimeter set to the DC volts scale (Figure 2-22A). The meter's positive lead goes to the alternator output terminal; the negative to the battery. Stay clear of the alternator drive belt! If the meter has multiple scales (most analog types do) start with the 10-volts DC scale and then if this shows no deflection or only a slight deflection, switch to a lower scale (2.5 volts DC). (Multimeter use is covered in Chapter 3.)

In a system with split-charging diodes the meter should show no more than 1.0 volt at full alternator output; without diodes, no more than 0.5 volt. These figures are the volt drop on the circuit (Figures 2-22A and 2-22B). *Any reading above these indicates excessive voltage drop;* the wiring is inadequate or there is unwanted resistance in the circuit, possibly caused by loose, dirty, or corroded terminals (see Chapter 3, "Troubleshooting With a Voltmeter"). Clean up all connections and try again. If the voltage drop persists, *the wiring is*

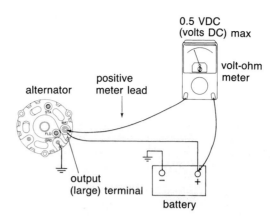

Figure 2-22A. Measuring the voltage drop between an alternator and a battery with no split-charging diodes. First draw down the battery by turning on cabin lights, a freshwater faucet, etc., with the engine off. Then start the engine and immediately hook up the voltmeter as shown, being careful to avoid the alternator drive belt. There should be no more than a 0.5 volt drop. Repeat this test from the alternator case to the battery negative post.

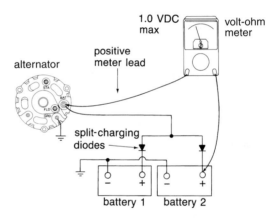

Figure 2-22B. Measuring the voltage drop between an alternator and a battery with split-charging diodes. There should be no more than a 1.0 volt drop on the positive side of the circuit, and no more than a 0.5 volt drop on the negative side (testing from the alternator case to the battery negative post).

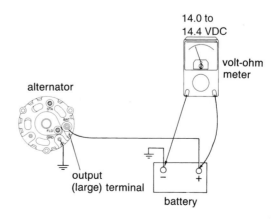

Figure 2-23. Testing for the maximum voltage to which an alternator is driving a battery during charging.

Symptom: Battery never seems to regain full charge.

Is the battery dying or dead? **NO** **TEST:** Check the specific gravity or open-circuit voltage; charge up and run a load test or capacity test.	**YES** **FIX:** Look for equipment inadvertently left on, dirt or moisture on the battery, or a leak to ground in the boat's wiring. Run an equalization charge on wet-cells; try the dead-battery recovery procedure on gel-cells. If battery fails to respond, replace it.
Is belt tension adequate? **NO** **TEST:** Listen for belt squeal; watch for fluctuating tachometer; depress belt—should not move more than ½ inch under moderate finger pressure.	**YES** **FIX:** Increase tension.
Is the alternator too small or its speed of rotation too slow? Is charging time inadequate? **NO** **TEST:** Compare demands on alternator with its size and speed of rotation as outlined in Chapter 1. Try charging the battery for at least 3 hours.	**YES** **FIX:** Match alternator with demands (see Chapter 1). Increase routine charging time.
Is there excessive voltage drop in the circuit between the alternator and the battery? **NO** **TEST:** Use multimeter to test for volt drop at full alternator output, between the alternator positive stud and the battery positive, and the alternator negative and the battery negative.	**YES** **FIX:** Clean and tighten loose, dirty, or corroded terminals; replace faulty or undersized wiring; be sure to check the engine ground-strap connections.
Is the voltage at the battery too low for effective charging? **NO** **TEST:** As the battery comes to charge, monitor the voltage across the battery terminals. Does it stabilize below 14.0 volts?	**YES** **FIX:** Adjust voltage regulator upward; compensate for diode-induced voltage drop (see the text). If this is not possible, replace the voltage regulator with a more appropriate model.
Is the voltage regulator wiring defective? **NO** **TEST:** Check external connections and wiring.	**YES** **FIX:** Repair or replace.
If the above tests fail to reveal a problem, check the brushes, diodes, rotor, and stator windings in the alternator (see pages 59-62).	

almost certainly undersized for this application and needs to be upgraded (see Chapter 3 for determining wire sizes). *Undersized wiring is a common problem on boats, crippling the effectiveness of many a charging system.*

- Repeat the same voltage drop test, with the alternator once again at full output, placing the positive meter lead on the battery's *negative post*, and the negative meter lead on either the *alternator case or a ground terminal on the alternator* (which will probably be labeled GRD; if the alternator has an insulated ground—desirable, but rare—the ground terminal must be used). *If the volt drop is even as high as 0.5 volts on any system, there is serious resistance in the circuit that needs to be cleaned up.* Since most alternators are grounded through the case and then through the mount bracket, engine block, and engine ground strap, clean all the connections in the circuit (mounting brackets and bolts, and engine ground-strap terminals). On all but insulated-ground alternators, it is a good idea to install a short ground strap, at least as heavy-duty as the alternator's output cable, from the alternator case to the boat's *main negative bus* (see Chapter 4).

- Run the engine for a while with all loads off so that the battery has a chance to come to a full charge. While doing this, monitor the battery voltage with a multimeter placed *across the battery terminals*. The battery voltage will rise steadily and then level off. *This level voltage is the actual voltage to which the battery is being driven when the alternator has reached the regulated set-point established by its voltage regulator (Figure 2-23). The voltage should be at least 14.0 volts, and on many marine systems as high as 14.4 volts. If the measured voltage is less than this, the battery is being undercharged.* The reason for undercharging may be an improperly adjusted voltage regulator, but most likely it is as a result of voltage drop in the circuit that may be caused by inadequate wiring and connections (see above) but *is also commonly caused by installing isolation diodes without compensating for the voltage drop of 0.5 to 1.0 volt caused by the diodes* (for an explanation of this, see Chapter 1; for solutions to the problem, see page 69).

- Check all the connections in any external field circuit (see below, page 65) to make sure they are clean and tight.

Only if none of the preceding tests turns up a problem should the alternator be suspected. One or more diodes or stator windings may be open-circuited (page 59), or the brushes may be worn or not making good contact with their slip rings, in which case output is likely to be erratic (page 60). Such problems are uncommon—an alternator is far more likely to fail outright than it is to partially fail (remember, the heading of this section is "Persistent undercharging *from an otherwise functioning alternator*"—for "No output," see below).

Persistent overcharging (Troubleshooting Chart 2-2). There is a problem with the batteries or voltage regulator *but not the alternator*. As batteries, especially wet-cell batteries, reach their last legs, they tend to absorb a higher charging current, gas more than usual, and require frequent topping up. These are also symptoms of overcharging. So before blaming the charging system, check the batteries (high-load and capacity test—see earlier this chapter). If the batteries are OK, the alternator's voltage regulation circuit is the problem (see Troubleshooting Voltage Regulators, Persistent Overcharging, later in this chapter).

No output (Troubleshooting Chart 2-3; see page 58). If an alternator appears not to be charging at all (the ignition warning light stays on, the battery remains discharged, etc.), the first task is to confirm that it is really the alternator that is at fault.

- With *the engine shut down*, all auxiliary charging devices (wind generator, solar panels) turned off, *the battery switched into the starting circuit* (the relevant battery isolation switch "on"), and *the engine ignition switch "on"* (but without the engine running), check the battery voltage *across the battery terminals*. It should be around 12.5 volts (Figure 2-24A).

- Now check the voltage between *the output, or positive, terminal* (the big one) on the alternator and *a good ground*, or negative, such as a clean spot on the engine block (unless the alternator has an insulated return—see page 50—in which case the ground or negative connection must be made at the negative terminal on the alternator or the battery).

    In a battery installation without isolating diodes, *the voltage at the alternator output should be the same as battery voltage* (Figure 2-24A). If isolating diodes are fitted between the alternator and the batteries, *the voltage at the alternator output* (with the engine shut down) *will read 0* (Figure 2-24B). *If the voltage is neither battery voltage nor 0, there is a problem in the circuit between the alternator and the battery.* (Note that in some circumstances leakage current through a diode will

Troubleshooting Chart 2-2. Battery/Alternator/Regulator Problems: Overcharging		
Symptoms: Battery overheats, "boils," requires frequent topping up with water, and gives off an acrid smell.		
Is the battery dying or dead? If so, it may behave as if overcharged, but will not come to or hold a full charge. **NO** **TEST:** Check specific gravity, measure open-circuit voltage, or use load tester or capacity test (page 44).	**YES** **FIX:** Replace.	
Is the battery in a location that is too hot? **NO** **TEST:** Measure temperature of battery compartment. If excessively hot, should be remedied.	**YES** **FIX:** Increase ventilation to compartment, or move battery.	
Is the voltage regulator set slightly high for faster charge rates? **NO** **TEST:** Monitor the battery voltage during charging. As the battery comes up to full charge, its voltage should not go above 14.4 volts for a wet cell, 14.2 volts for a gell cell.	**YES** **FIX:** It may be wise not to "fix" this. Occasional mild overcharging is often the price to be paid for realistically fast charge rates. See text.	
Is a voltage regulator bypass device being used incorrectly? **NO** **TEST:** Monitor battery voltage and battery temperature during charging. Voltage should not go above 14.4 volts on a wet cell (except during equalization, page 47) and 14.2 volts on a gell cell. Battery temperature should not go much above 110°F (43.3°C).	**YES** **FIX:** Adjust manual rheostat on bypass device to reduce alternator output. Switch off manual bypass when battery is fully charged.	
Is an unregulated wind generator or solar panel overcharging the battery? **NO** **TEST:** As above. See Chapter 5 to estimate probable inputs from these sources.	**YES** **FIX:** See Chapter 5.	
Is the voltage regulator's battery-sensing wire disconnected or broken? Has a diode been installed backwards in the sensing wire? Both will lead to violent overcharging, causing vigorous boiling and rapid water loss. **NO** **TEST:** Visual inspection. Corroded sensing-wire terminals will have a similar though less dramatic effect.	**YES** **FIX:** Replace sensing wire. Clean terminals. Put the diode in correctly (see page 70).	
Is the voltage regulator short-circuited? This will lead to violent overcharging. **TEST:** Fit a spare and see whether problem disappears.	**YES** **FIX:** Replace voltage regulator.	

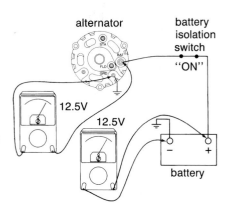

Figure 2-24A. Measuring voltage at the battery and at the alternator output terminal: no split-charging diodes. The battery isolation switch and the ignition switch are on, but the engine is *not* running. There should be about a 12.5-volt reading across the battery terminals (more or less fully charged battery), with the same reading between the alternator output terminal and ground (its case, unless it has an insulated ground).

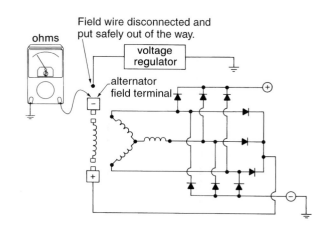

Figure 2-25B. N-type alternator schematic—the voltage regulator is on the negative side of the field winding. See accompanying text for test procedure.

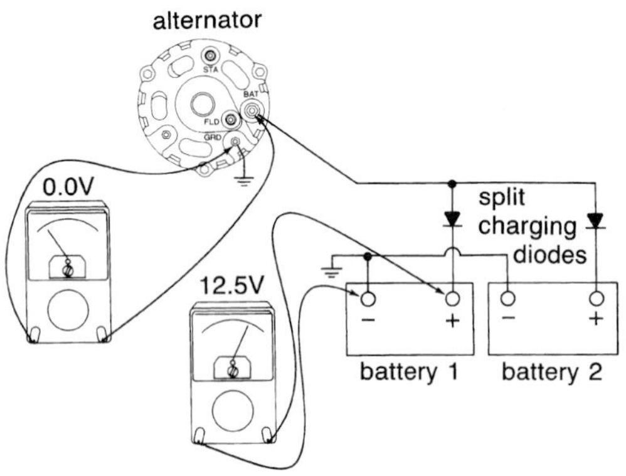

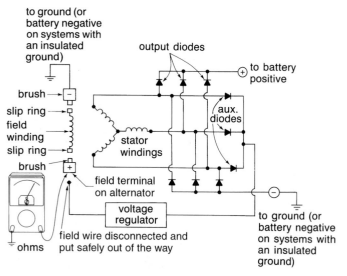

Figure 2-24B. Measuring voltage at the battery and at the alternator output terminal with split-charging diodes. The battery isolation switch and the ignition switch are on, but the engine is *not* running. The voltage reading across the battery terminals should be around 12.5 volts (more or less fully charged battery); the reading between the alternator output terminal and ground should be 0.

be high enough to cause a voltage reading at near battery voltage; before condemning the circuit, check with a test lamp—Figure 2-26A—from the alternator output terminal to ground. The lamp should not light. If it does, the diode has failed. For other methods of testing diodes, see page 58.)

• If the circuit seems okay, start the engine, speed it up, and recheck the voltage at the alternator output. *Whatever the system, it should read a volt or more above the original battery voltage.* If it does, the alternator is functioning. If it does not, there is a problem with the alternator or its voltage regulator; the next task is to decide which.

P- and N-type alternators. Some alternators have internal regulators, and in this case there is little to be done when a problem is traced to the alternator or regulator except fit a new alternator/cum regulator. (The section on voltage regulators later in this chapter has a few more suggestions.) Many alternators, however, have external regulators controlling the current to the alternator field winding via a terminal on the back of the alternator marked F, DF, or FLD. Most external regulators are connected on the positive side of the field winding (these are P-type alternators, Figure 2-25A), but a few are connected between the negative side of the field winding and ground (N-type alternators, Figure 2-25B). More on this in the section on voltage regulators, later in this chapter. For now, the first task is to decide whether the alternator is a P- or N-type.

Shut down the engine, *turn off the ignition and battery isolation switches,* and disconnect the

Figure 2-25A. P-type alternator schematic—the voltage regulator is on the positive side of the field winding. See accompanying text for test procedure.

field wire from the alternator. Using the ohms function of a multimeter (on its lowest—R × 1— scale if it is an analog meter), test between *the field terminal* on the alternator and *ground* (Figures 2-25A and B). A P-type alternator will give a reading near 0 ohms; an N-type will give a high reading.

Voltage regulator or alternator? Once you have established the type of alternator, you need to bypass the voltage regulator so that field current can be supplied *directly to the alternator field winding.* If this causes the alternator to work, *the voltage regulator is bad.* If the alternator still fails to work, *the alternator itself is at fault.* To bypass the voltage regulator, make up a test light as shown (Figure 2-26A), with a minimum 12-watt (1-amp) lightbulb. Disconnect the field wire at the field terminal (F, DF, or FLD) on the alternator and put it safely *out of the way, where it cannot short out.*

If the alternator is a P-type, connect the test light *between the positive terminal on the battery and the field terminal* (Figure 2-26B).

If the alternator is an N-type, connect the test light between *the field terminal and a good ground* (Figure 2-26C).

Start the engine and test the voltage *across the battery terminals.* If the voltage is now normal (a volt or more above the battery voltage when the alternator is not running) *the alternator is okay, but its voltage regulator is defective* (the current flowing through the test light is energizing the field winding and so bypassing the voltage regulator, which is why there is now alternator output). *If the alternator still does not produce output, the alternator itself is defective.*

If a multimeter is not available, or if there is any doubt as to whether the alternator is a P- or N-type, with the engine running try connecting the test light from the field terminal first to the battery positive and then to ground. If there is no output on either test, the alternator is bad.

Excitation tests: the last test. If the test light from the battery to the field terminal produced output from a P-type alternator, *reconnect the field wire from the voltage regulator* and crank the engine. Connect the test light *momentarily* between the battery and the field terminal *with the engine still running.* This is known as *flashing the field* (Figure 2-26D). If the test light restores output and *the alternator continues to work after the light is disconnected,* the problem is nothing more than a failure of the excitation circuit, which is easy to fix (page 68).

N-type excitation is a little more complicated. If an N-type excitation circuit has failed, none of the tests to date will have produced any output.

N-type alternators with external regulators

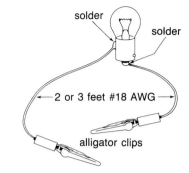

Figure 2-26A. Test light.

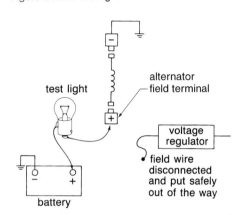

Figure 2-26B. Bypassing a P-type voltage regulator. Connect the test light as shown, start the engine, and measure the alternator output voltage as in Figure 2-23. If it is normal (a volt or more above original battery voltage), the regulator is defective; if it is not, the alternator is defective.

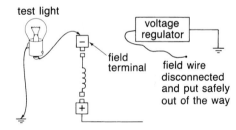

Figure 2-26C. Bypassing an N-type voltage regulator.

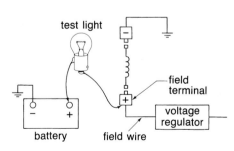

Figure 2-26D. "Flashing the field" on a P-type alternator. If the test in Figure 2-26B showed normal output, shut down the engine and reconnect the field wire from the voltage regulator. Start the engine. With the engine running, connect the test light momentarily between the battery and the field terminal. If alternator output is restored (test as in Figure 2-23), the excitation circuit has failed.

Troubleshooting Chart 2-3.
Battery/Alternator/Regulator Problems: No Alternator Output

Symptoms: Ignition warning light stays on, battery remains discharged.

Is the drive belt loose or broken? **NO** **TEST:** The belt should respond to finger pressure with no more than ½ inch give at its midpoint.	**YES** **FIX:** Tighten or replace.
Is the circuit between the alternator and battery at fault? **NO** **TEST:** Shut down the engine, isolate or shut down auxiliary chargers (solar panels, wind generator, etc.), turn on battery isolation switch, turn on engine ignition switch (but without starting engine), and check voltage (1) across the battery terminals and (2) between alternator output and ground. If voltage at alternator output terminal is neither about the same as battery voltage (no isolating diodes) or 0 (isolating diodes, dual battery installation), the circuit between alternator and battery is faulty. (Note: Diodes may sometimes show voltage—see text.)	**YES** **FIX:** Check all wiring and connections. Clean and replace as necessary.
Does the alternator have an internal voltage regulator? **NO** **TEST:** Look for absence of alternator field terminal, field wire, and external regulator.	**YES** **FIX:** If a lack-of-output problem has been traced this far and the regulator is internal, there is little option but to install a new alternator.
If the voltage regulator is external, is it a P-type or an N-type? **NO** **TEST:** Shut down engine, turn off ignition and battery isolation switches, and disconnect field wire from alternator. Measure resistance between field terminal and ground. P-type = reading near 0 ohms; N-type = high reading.	**YES** **P-type FIX:** Proceed with Steps 1-3 below. **YES** **N-type FIX:** Proceed with Steps 4-6 below.
(1) Does the alternator fail to work when the P-type voltage regulator is bypassed? **NO** **TEST:** Connect a test lamp between alternator field terminal and battery positive terminal. Start engine. Look for alternator output in excess of battery voltage.	**YES** **FIX:** Alternator is broken. Check for shorted or open-circuited rotor, stator or diode. See pages 59-62 for possible repair procedure.
(2) If the alternator worked in Step 1, the voltage regulator is defective. Is it merely a failure of the excitation circuit? **NO** **TEST:** Shut down the engine. Reconnect the alternator field wire. Restart the engine. Connect the test lamp momentarily between the field terminal and the battery positive terminal. If alternator output is restored and continues after the light is disconnected, the excitation circuit is at fault.	**YES** **FIX:** Repair is comparatively simple (page 68).

continued

generally have either an auxiliary output terminal (sometimes marked AUX; in any case it will be a second, insulated, stud on the back of the alternator) or an external excitation wire supplying current to the field winding (sometimes both; see Voltage Regulators, page 65). Connecting the test light *momentarily* between *the battery positive and either the auxiliary or excitation terminal*, while the alternator is running and with all normal wiring in place, will restore lost excitation—if the alternator begins to work and stays working, once again the problem is a failure of the excitation circuit.

Last resort. With a really dead battery many alternators just will not start producing output, and none of the above tests is possible. If the engine has a hand crank and can be started, a 6-volt battery or half a dozen flashlight (torch) batteries can be connected in series to provide enough current to get the alternator going once again. The negative side of the flashlight battery's ground is connected *to the alternator case* or a good ground on the engine, the engine is cranked, and the alternator field is flashed as described in the previous excitation tests i.e., touching the flashlight battery's positive wire to the field terminal on a P-type alternator, and to the auxiliary or excitation terminal on an N-type. In the case of an alternator with an insulated ground, connect the flashlight battery's ground to the boat battery's negative terminal or the alternator's negative terminal.

Miscellaneous diode tests. Finally, I have three quick and easy diode tests that should be performed in the case of unexplained battery failures or loss of charge:

1. Connect a voltmeter in the AC-volts mode across *the alternator output stud and a good ground* (the alternator case, unless it has an insulated ground) *with the alternator running.* The meter will read the AC *ripple* superimposed on the alternator's DC output (Figure 2-26E). To understand this, refer back to Figure 2-17. After rectification, rather than being a straight line, the DC output of an alternator is composed of the tops of the three curves that form the three phases of the AC output of the alternator, and as such the output line forms a continuous sequence of shallow waves. When measuring the AC ripple, a meter will be measuring the depth of these waves. *The AC ripple should be no more than 0.5 volts—if it is greater than this, one or more of the diodes is damaged. Excessive AC ripple is destructive to batteries, especially gel-cells.*

2. *With the engine shut down*, disconnect the alternator positive cable and then insert a DC milliammeter *between the output cable and the output stud on the alternator, that is*, in series with the output cable and stud (Figure 2-26F). The meter will be reading any leakage current through the alternator's diodes. This will generally be on the order of 0.5 milliamps, but in any event *should not be higher than 2.0 milliamps*. If it is, one or more of the diodes has a problem.

3. *With the engine shut down and all cables disconnected from the alternator output stud*, test with an ohmmeter from the alternator output stud to ground, and then reverse the meter leads and test again. The meter should show *infinity* in one direction, and *either infinity or a very high resistance* in the other direction (depending on the voltage developed by the meter in its ohms-testing mode—see Chapter 3). If the meter has a *diode-testing* capability (Chapter 3), using this function will show *no voltage* in one direction and around *0.9 volts* with the meter leads reversed. If the test results are different from these, there is a problem with one or more diodes.

Repairing Alternators

If the above tests have pinpointed the alternator as the source of a charging problem, the most likely failures are in the diodes and the brushes. However, determining what is the problem is generally academic since repair parts are unlikely to be on board! Those adventurous souls wishing to get heavily into alternator repairs should obtain a copy of *The 12-Volt Doctor's Alternator Book*, by Edgar J. Beyn (Plath North America, 1989). The rest of us should always carry a spare alternator and have the deceased rejuvenated by a professional alternator rebuilder; it then becomes the spare.

If you are exploring further, diode testing is covered later in this chapter. An open-circuited diode will simply disable its particular stator winding, leaving the alternator to run at reduced output on the other two windings. A short-circuited diode can be removed, insulating the end of its stator winding if no replacement diode is available and continuing to operate the alternator at reduced output. Brushes, rotors, and stators can be checked as follows:

Brushes. Since an alternator's brushes carry only the small amount of current needed to energize the field winding in the rotor, they are subject to very little load and wear and rarely

Troubleshooting Chart 2-3, *continued*

(3) If Step 2 failed to restore continuous output, the regulator needs to be replaced.

(4) Does the alternator work when the N-type voltage regulator is bypassed?	**YES** **FIX:** Voltage regulator is defective and needs to be replaced.
NO **TEST:** Connect a test lamp between alternator field terminal and a good ground. Start the engine. Look for alternator output in excess of battery voltage.	
(5) Is the voltage regulator's excitation circuit defective?	**YES** **FIX:** Repair is comparatively simple (page 68).
NO **TEST:** Shut down the engine. Reconnect the alternator field wire. Restart the engine. Connect the test lamp momentarily between the battery positive terminal and the alternator auxiliary or excitation terminal. See whether alternator output voltage comes up and stays up.	

(6) If Step 5 failed to restore output, the alternator is defective. Check for shorted or open-circuited rotor, stator, or diode. See pages 59-62 for possible repair procedures.

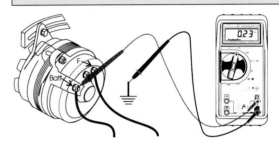

Figure 2-26E. Checking ripple voltage. Ripple voltage (AC voltage) can be measured by switching the multimeter to AC volts and connecting the black lead to a good ground and the red lead to the "BAT" terminal on the back of the alternator (not at the battery). A good alternator should measure less than 0.5 VAC with the engine running. A higher reading indicates damaged alternator diodes. *(Fluke)*

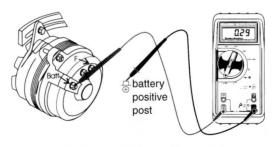

Figure 2-26F. Alternator leakage current. To check alternator diode leakage, connect the multimeter between the alternator output terminal and the battery positive post when the engine is not running. Leakage current should be a couple of milliamps at most; more often, it will be on the order of 0.5 milliamps. Use care when disconnecting the alternator output wire; make sure the battery is disconnected first. A leaking diode can discharge the battery when the engine is off. *(Fluke)*

require maintenance. In time, however, they wear down, spring pressure decreases, and the brushes fail to seat properly on their slip rings. Corrosion of brush springs can also cause a loss of spring tension, resulting in poor brush contact with slip rings. This will lead to arcing and pitting of the slip rings. Such problems in turn will lead to improper energizing (*excitation*) of the field winding and erratic or failed alternator output. Even if no replacement brushes are on board, simply cleaning up the old ones and the slip rings will sometimes temporarily restore output to a problem alternator.

Brush inspection, clean-up, and replacement is generally straightforward. Unfortunately, however, there are not just dozens but hundreds of different alternators so it is difficult to lay down general rules. Some alternators have external brush holders; some have internal brush holders; and some have the brush holders incorporated in an externally attached voltage regulator housing. If the brush holders are not self-evident, but the alternator has an externally attached regulator—often a fairly compact, boxlike unit, normally held on with two screws—unscrew this and the brushes usually will be found inside.

Independently mounted external brush holders generally consist of a small plastic housing held with one or two screws, within which are one or two spade terminals. The housing is withdrawn from the alternator and the spade terminals released by pressing down their retaining tags with a small screwdriver and pushing them inward; this will free the brushes. The housing needs cleaning before new brushes are fitted. When being fitted, some brushes must be held in place in their housings with a small screwdriver or a toothpick inserted through a hole in the body of the alternator.

Internal brushes are trickier. The whole rear end of the alternator—generally held on with four bolts—must be removed. Be careful not to damage or break any wire as the rear end comes loose. Make a note of the position of any wiring that is disconnected. The brush holders will be self-evident, probably the brushes will already have popped out of their holders under their spring pressure. A toothpick will once again likely be needed to trap the brushes in their brush holders during reassembly (Figures 2-27A,

Figure 2-27A. **Brush location and replacement on an alternator with an external voltage regulator but internal brushes.** This is a back view of the alternator.

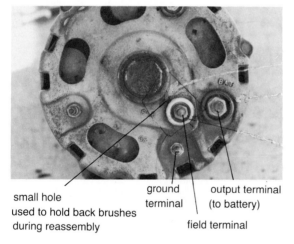

small hole used to hold back brushes during reassembly

ground terminal

output terminal (to battery)

field terminal

field terminal

Figure 2-27B. **A toothpick in the hole holds back the brushes.** (The nut and insulating washer on the field terminal have been removed.)

Figure 2-27C. Internal views of the same alternator.

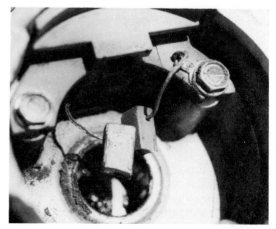

Maintaining and Troubleshooting a Battery-Powered Electrical System

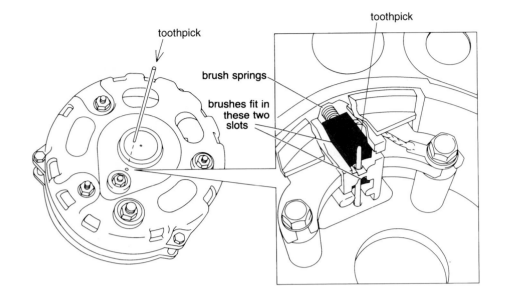

toothpick

toothpick

brush springs

brushes fit in these two slots

Figure 2-27D. Close-up of the brush holder with the brushes in place. The two alternator halves must be separated and the rotor removed in order to gain access to the brushes. In this alternator the brush holder does not have to be unscrewed to change the brushes; the brushes pop out of the holders under their spring pressure when the rotor is removed. The new brushes are pushed in against their springs and held with the toothpick until the rotor is replaced. *(Jim Sollers)*

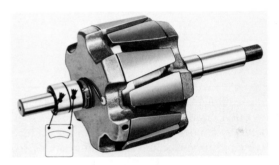

Figure 2-28. Alternator rotor testing with a multimeter set to its ohms function (R × 1 scale on an analog meter). Touching the probes to the two slip rings as shown should yield a low reading. A high reading indicates an open circuit in the rotor. Check also from each slip ring to the rotor shaft (R × 100 scale on an analog meter); there should be no continuity (i.e., the reading should be infinity). *(AC Delco)*

2-27B, 2-27C and 2-27D). While the rotor is out, clean its slip rings, polish them with 400- or 600-grit wet-and-dry sandpaper, and test the rotor for shorts or an open circuit —see below).

Rotors. The following test can be made with the alternator still in place and with minimal disassembly (although for clarity I show the test in Figure 2-28 with the rotor removed from its alternator), but first *isolate the alternator electrically* (switch off the battery isolation and ignition switches). This is essential to avoid damaging the multimeter.

On alternators with external regulators, disconnect the field wire coming from the voltage regulator; disconnect the alternator output lead; set a multimeter to its ohms function (R × 1 scale on an analog meter), and test between *the field terminal* and the *alternator case*. This will test the circuit from the field brush, which in turn is connected to one end of the field winding, to ground.

With P-type alternators, the meter should give a very low reading—close to 0 ohms— since the other end of the field winding should be grounded, through the second brush, to the alternator case (Figure 2-29A, Test 1). A very high reading indicates an open circuit in the field winding (it is burned out) or that the brushes are not in contact with their slip rings. Try turning the alternator while making the test: If the reading flickers up and down, check the brushes and springs before writing off the rotor. With a low reading the field winding may be okay, but then again it may be shorted

to ground; most meters are insufficiently sensitive to tell. To test for a short, connect a line containing a low-amperage fuse (10 to 15 amps—the fuse is *important*) from the positive terminal of the battery to the field terminal of the alternator (Figure 2-29A, Test 2). If the fuse blows, the rotor is shorted.

With N-type alternators, a multimeter (R × 100 scale if it is an analog meter) connected between *the field terminal* and ground (with the field wire disconnected) should show an open circuit (a very high reading—Figure 2-29B). A low reading indicates a short to ground. The high reading may also be due to an open circuit in the rotor itself, but there is no easy way to check this without further disassembly.

Rotors on alternators with internal or attached regulators (i.e., with no external field terminal) can be tested if access can be gained to the brushes or slip rings. The multimeter leads are touched to the two slip rings for the ohms test. Both P- and N-types should give a

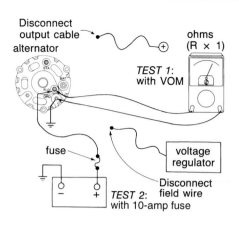

Figure 2-29A. Rotor testing, P-type alternator, external regulator. BAT is the output terminal (leading to the battery positive terminal); FLD is the field terminal.

TEST 1: with VOM

TEST 2: with 10-amp fuse

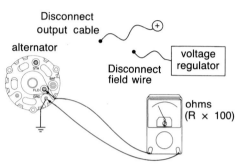

Figure 2-29B. Rotor testing, N-type alternator, external regulator.

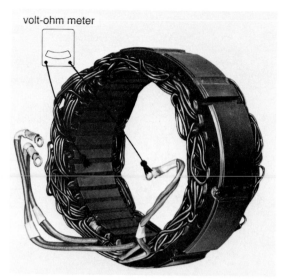

Figure 2-30. Testing a stator. *(AC Delco)*

low reading. A high reading (infinity) indicates an open circuit in the rotor. The fuse test is made by connecting the wire from the battery to the positive brush or slip ring. If in doubt, try both brushes. With P-type alternators, only the negative brush should blow the fuse; with N types *neither* brush should blow the fuse. If both brushes blow the fuse, regardless of alternator type, the rotor is shorted.

Stators. If the two alternator halves are separated and the three stator winding wires are removed from their diodes (the wires will probably have to be unsoldered) the stator windings can be tested with a multimeter set to its ohms function (R × 1 scale on an analog meter). There should be *no continuity* (i.e., an open circuit) when testing from any of the three wires to ground (the steel laminations around which the wires are wound—see Figure 2-30); there should be continuity, showing only a low resistance (difficult to distinguish from a short) when testing across any two wires (since this is testing the resistance in the winding; it will vary according to the alternator's rated output, with the resistance being lower on high-output alternators). Continuity from any wire to ground indicates a shorted winding; no continuity between any two wires indicates an open-circuited winding. Neither is repairable in the field. With the wires off the diodes, now is a good time to test the diodes (page 58).

Voltage Regulators

How They Work

A voltage regulator controls the output of an alternator by varying the current supplied to the field winding (page 48). Although it is called a *voltage* regulator, it is in fact a *current* regulator, both in terms of the field current and also the alternator's output! However, what it does is hold the alternator's output current to whatever level a battery will accept at a given charging voltage (page 20), hence the misnomer "voltage regulator."

A change of only 1 amp in the field current will alter an alternator's output by up to 50 amps—field current is anywhere from 2% to 6% of alternator output. Formerly, voltage regulation was a mechanical affair, but now it is almost always done with solid-state electronics. Whatever the method, the process is essentially the

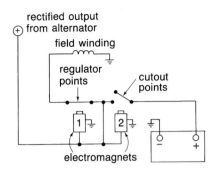

Figure 2-32A. Operating principles of a P-type mechanical voltage regulator. The engine is at rest. The cutout points are open; the regulator points closed. The field winding is isolated from the battery.

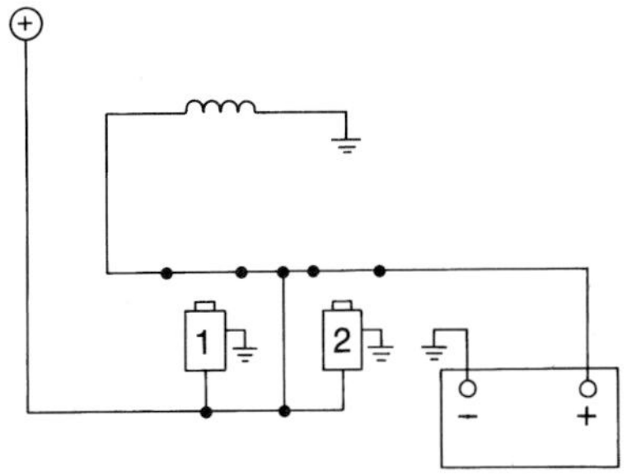

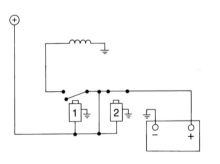

Figure 2-32B. Initial generator output. Electro-magnets are energized. Electromagnet 2 closes the cutout points, allowing charging current to reach the battery. But generator output is insufficient for electromagnet 1 to open the regulator points against the spring pressure. The generator also feeds the field winding.

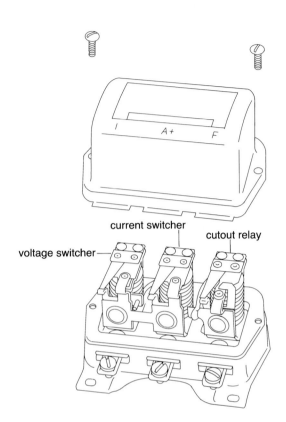

Figure 2-31. **An external voltage regulator.** *(Jim Sollers)*

Figure 2-32C. As generator output increases, the cut-out points are held closed while increasing magnet-ism on electromagnet 1 opens the regulator points against the spring pres-sure. This cuts the field current, causing the gener-ator's output to decline. Electromagnet 1 loses magnetism until the regula-tor points close once again, restoring the field current and causing output to build back up. This cycle is repeated hundreds of times a minute.

same, and is most easily understood by referring to mechanical regulators.

Mechanical regulators. These normally are found with generators (dynamos) and invariably are mounted as a separate unit from the generator (*external* regulators—Figure 2-31). The regulators have spring-loaded switches (*points*). One set of points (the *cutout* points) is held open when the generator is not producing current; the other set (the *regulator* points) is held closed. The open cutout points isolate the generator so that no current drains from the battery into the field winding when the unit is not running (Figure 2-32A).

When the generator is running, it feeds current into an electromagnet on the cutout points, energizing it, which closes the cutout points and completes the circuit back to the battery. When the engine stops, the generator stops generating current, the electromagnet de-energizes, the spring opens the cutout points, and the circuit is broken once again (Figure 2-32B).

Holding charging voltage to a certain level is the function of the regulator points. When the generator starts to generate, current to the field winding passes through the regulator points and through the points' electromagnet, energizing it

and pulling open the points against a spring. This open-circuits the field winding, its magnetism declines, and the output of the generator falls off, in turn reducing the current to the electromagnet holding open the regulator points; the electromagnet loses magnetism, and the spring closes the regulator points once again, restoring current flow to the field winding and restarting the process. Typically the regulator points open and close hundreds of times a minute. By altering the spring pressure on the points, it is possible to regulate the voltage at which they open, and thus regulate the output of the generator (Figure 2-32C).

There may well be a third set of points, operating in much the same fashion, to limit the maximum output (amperage) of the generator and so protect it from overloading and burning up.

These will be connected in series with the regulator points (Figure 2-31).

Solid-state regulators. Alternators are almost all equipped with solid-state regulators (Figure 2-33). The principles of operation are the same as with mechanical regulators, except that the mechanical contact points are replaced with transistors. These are set to open at a certain voltage, cutting the current to the field winding (rotor). When output voltage has fallen to a preset level, the transistors close. This cycle happens *hundreds of times a second* (as opposed to hundreds of times a minute in a mechanical regulator), making for extremely precise voltage regulation, but at the cost of often severe radio interference (Chapter 7).

Since the rectifying diodes in an alternator prevent the flow of current from a battery back into the field winding (rotor) when the unit is at rest (page 49), solid-state regulators require no cutout circuit. However, should a battery be hooked up backwards (negative and positive leads crossed over), reverse current will flow through the diodes, which will overheat and blow out immediately. A new alternator will be needed. I'll risk being redundant: *Hook a battery up correctly — negative to negative, positive to positive.*

Ignition circuits and excitation. The observant reader will have noticed that the generator or alternator output is used to supply current to the field winding. However, when a generator or alternator is first started, there is no output. Without output there is no field current. Without field

current there can be no output. Some initial *excitation* of the field winding is needed to break this vicious circle. Two approaches are used:

1. The field winding in the rotor is designed to retain a certain amount of residual magnetism when the generator or alternator is shut down. This is sufficient to produce a low output when the generator or alternator rotor begins to spin. This output feeds back to the field winding, builds up its magnetism, and restores full output. This approach to excitation is uncommon.

2. A separate feed from the battery to the field winding provides initial excitation (Figure 2-34). Since the field winding would drain the battery through this line when the generator or alternator is shut down, a switch is incorporated in the circuit. This is normally an ignition switch, but sometimes an oil pressure or fuel pressure switch (or both) is used. With a pressure switch the engine must build up pressure to close the switch before the generator or alternator will kick in. (If problems are experienced with excitation, try jumping out the switches.)

An ignition warning light included in an excitation circuit will glow as long as current flows from the battery through the field winding to ground. Once the generator or alternator starts to put out, it supplies current to the winding. There is now the same, or nearly the same, voltage at both ends of the excitation circuit: generator or alternator output at one end, battery voltage at the other. Without a

Figure 2-33. Solid-state regulator inside the back of an alternator. *(AC Delco)*

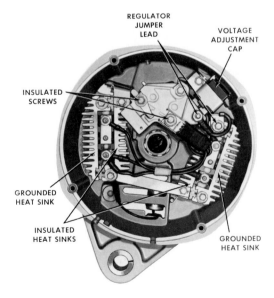

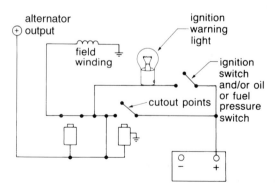

Figure 2-34. Mechanical voltage regulator (P-type) with excitation circuit. Closing the switch provides initial field current. The battery discharges through the ignition light into the field winding, lighting up the lamp. When the generator output builds, the cutout points close. There is now equal voltage on both sides of the ignition warning light, and the light goes out.

voltage differential no current will flow (see Chapter 3) and the warning light goes out.

Different Regulators: Internal, External, P and N

There are hundreds of different regulators in common use. Many are completely internal; others are classified as internal but are attached to the alternator's outside casing, which makes them and their wiring more accessible. Some alternators—especially high-output alternators—have separate, external regulators mounted as an independent unit. These are preferred in boat use as they make troubleshooting and emergency repairs so much easier.

Regulators fall into two broad types: P and N. As we have seen, all regulators function by repeatedly making and breaking the current to the field winding. It is irrelevant whether this is done on the supply side (P, positive) of the winding or the return side (N, negative, or ground): The end result is the same (see Figures 2-25A and 2-25B). Almost all external regulators are P type; most internal regulators, especially on smaller alternators (up to 55 amps), are N type.

Charging Problems, earlier in this chapter, outlined a procedure for testing *external* regulators and determining their type (page 56). Some *attached* regulators can be unscrewed and their wires disconnected without removing the brush holders. These can be tested the same way. If the alternator has a wire to only one brush, it is probably a P type (the other brush is grounded). If wires run to both brushes, it is probably an N type. In any event, to double-check, *turn off the ignition and battery isolation switches, disconnect the voltage regulator leads from the brushes,* and test in turn *between each brush and ground* with a multimeter set to its ohms function (the lowest scale—R × 1—on an analog meter). P types will read near 0 ohms on both brushes; N types will give high readings.

Identifying wiring. Regardless of alternator and regulator type, somewhere all will have a field wire and a battery-sensing wire, and almost all will have an excitation wire.

The field wire. Alternators with external regulators have a terminal on the back to receive the field wire. This terminal will be labeled F, DF, or FLD. Externally attached internal regulators must be unscrewed from the back of the alternator to expose the field wire or wires. Some externally sensed units have two field wires: one connected to the battery excitation line, the other to the volt-

age regulator. The latter is the main field wire. The field wire normally is connected by a spade terminal (marked F or DF) to one of the two brushes. In the absence of internal identification, or in the case of completely internal regulators, determining the field wire becomes rather involved and is beyond the scope of this book.

The excitation wire. If fitted, the battery excitation wire will come from the alternator (internal regulator) or regulator (externally attached and external regulators) to a pressure switch mounted on the engine block and/or to the ignition switch, generally via an ignition warning light.

The battery-sensing (voltage regulation) wire. The battery-sensing wire, which determines voltage regulation, may come from the battery itself (*battery sensed*) but is more likely to be taken from the alternator (*machine sensed*), either from an auxiliary terminal (sometimes labeled AUX) on the back of the alternator (external and attached regulators) or from inside the alternator itself. Where fitted, an auxiliary terminal will have an *insulated* stud and will have *no connections to ground.* Normally it will be smaller than the main output terminal.

Common alternators. The most commonly found alternators in the USA are made by Motorola and Delco Remy. The most popular high-output alternators in the USA are made by Powerline and Lestek (sold by Balmar). In the UK, Lucas/CAV and Bosch are most common, with Powerline alternators sold by Ampair and Lestek by Energy Control. The wiring on those alternators with external regulators should be clear enough.

Many Motorola alternators with attached regulators have the following wiring: A white wire with its own separate spade terminal is the excitation line; the black wire goes to ground; and the red wire goes to an auxiliary terminal post on the back of the alternator. This is the battery-sensing (voltage regulation) line. The field wire(s) is (are) under the regulator.

Delco Remy alternators with internal regulators have two spade lugs on the back. The lug numbered 1 is the excitation connection; number 2 is the battery-sensing (voltage regulation) terminal.

Powerline alternators with external regulators have two spade lugs on the back. The lug marked R is for a tachometer; that marked F is the field connection. These are P-type alternators.

Voltage regulator adjustments. Mechanical regulators are adjusted by altering spring tension; most solid-state regulators are not adjustable, although some Delco Remys do have a four-

Figure 2-35. Voltage regulator adjustments on some Delco-Remy alternators. In this enlarged view the adjustment cap is in the "low" position. *(AC Delco)*

position cap that can be rotated for different settings (Figure 2-35); some Lucas/CAVs have high-, medium-, and low-output wires; and some external regulators—particularly multistep regulators—have one or more *potentiometer* (variable resistor) screws to fine-tune the voltage setpoint(s).

If a regulator is adjustable, any adjustments should be made only while charging into *fully charged batteries in good condition*. Make alterations in regulated voltage *a little at a time* (even a 0.2 volt change can have a major impact on charging rates) and then *give the system plenty of time to stabilize at the new level* before considering further adjustments. After making changes, it is a good idea to lock a potentiometer screw against vibration by putting a dab of silicone or polyurethane sealant over the screw head.

Voltage Regulator Bypass Devices

As we saw in Chapter 1, when a battery comes up to charge, its internal voltage rises. The regulator senses this rising voltage and cuts back the charging current. Because battery voltage rises faster than the state of charge (refer back to Figure 1-22), the charge current starts to taper off around the 50% to 60% charged level, approaching 0 near the fully charged level.

However, most batteries in good condition will accept a relatively high rate of charge all the way up to 70% to 80% of the fully charged level, at which point the battery will start to gas vigorously and heat up internally. The rate of charge must then be reduced to avoid permanent battery damage (in the case of gel-cells, *it must be*

cut back before vigorous gassing occurs). The slower rate of charge then allows the acid to diffuse through the interior areas of the plates, which is necessary to produce a completely charged battery.

Charging at a maximum practical rate all the way to the 80% level will reduce battery-charging times considerably. To this end, a number of devices on the market effectively bypass the voltage regulator altogether, allowing a *constant current* to be pumped into the batteries. Some are manually operated; others have a *trip* point at which they turn themselves off and return the system to its voltage regulator when the battery reaches a preset voltage level. The best known are the Auto-Mac and T-Mac units manufactured by C-Plath (Figure 2-36). These can really shorten charging times, but with the attendant risk of cooking alternators, voltage regulators, and batteries due to equipment malfunction or operator error.

Voltage regulator bypass devices leave all existing wiring and regulators in place. They are connected to the existing alternator field terminal *in parallel* with the voltage regulator. On P-type alternators, the bypass is connected between the field terminal and the battery positive terminal; on N-type alternators, between the field terminal and ground (Figures 2-37A and 2-37B). A manual rheostat controls current to the alternator field winding, thus controlling alternator output. Bypass units *must* incorporate an ammeter and voltmeter in the charging circuit to monitor alternator output and battery voltage (Figure 2-38).

A deeply discharged battery can be charged at a rate of 25% or more of its amp-hour rating; an alternator should be kept to 75% or less of its rating. The rheostat is turned until the ammeter

Figure 2-36. Voltage regulator bypass devices for alternators up to 75 amps (left) and above 75 amps (right). *(C-Plath)*

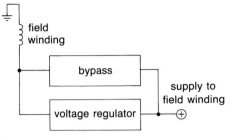

Figure 2-37A. Voltage regulator bypass device for a P-type alternator.

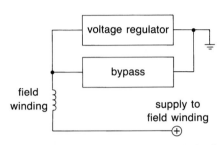

Figure 2-37B. **Voltage regulator bypass device for an N-type alternator.**

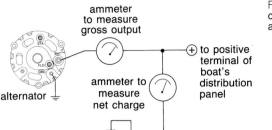

shows a rate of charge equal to the lesser of these two figures. For example, assume a 200-Ah battery with a 60-amp alternator. The battery can take up to 50 amps, but 75% of the alternator rating is 45 amps; therefore output should be increased only to this level. With a 90-amp alternator, 75% of its rating would be 68 amps; in this case the limiting factor would be the battery charge acceptance at 50 amps.

In practice, things are not quite this simple. The boat's own DC load may be 20 amps while the engine is running. In this case the *net* charge (what is actually going into the battery) of the 60-amp alternator operating at 75% of its full rating would be 45 – 20 = 25 amps; and of the 90-amp alternator, would be 68 – 20 = 48 amps—neither figure coming up to the maximum battery charge acceptance rate. The alternators are the limiting factor in this situation.

This brings up another point. The usual practice is to install ammeters in such a way as to measure *net* charge to the batteries. *But we cannot tell from this what the alternator is really doing.* With voltage regulator bypass devices *a second ammeter that measures gross alternator output should be fitted* (Figure 2-38). Otherwise there is a risk of overloading and burning up the alternator, especially on electrically loaded boats.

It is essential to monitor the battery continuously the first few times a bypass device is used. If its temperature starts to rise much above

110°F (43°C), the charge rate is too high. When the battery voltage rises and a wet-cell battery begins to gas noticeably, it is time to reduce the charge rate or to switch back to the voltage regulator. *Because of the sensitivity of gel-cells to overcharging, and the inability to tell if a gel-cell is gassing until permanent damage has been done, voltage regulator bypasses should not be used on these batteries,* and if they are used, care should be taken to see that the voltage does not rise above 14.1 volts.

Some bypass units incorporate a voltage-sensing circuit that turns the unit off when battery voltage rises to a preset level (normally around 14.2 volts) and returns control of the alternator to its voltage regulator. I have had reports of factory cutout settings ranging from 13.8 volts, useless for effective charging, to 14.8 volts, which will fry the batteries. Check the cutout voltage carefully the first time you use a unit, and reset it as necessary with the potentiometer that should be located somewhere in the unit. Note that if the unit's automatic shutdown circuit fails, the batteries will surely fry; automatic or not, it is still important to keep an eye on battery voltage. If used on wet-cell batteries, units with automatic voltage trips should have a manual override to make periodic battery equalization possible (see page 47).

Note that even when the trip point is reached a battery will be only about 80% charged. The bypass regulator will have completed the *bulk-charge* phase (Chapter 1). For full charges an *absorption* (constant voltage) phase is still needed, which an automatic bypass regulator is incapable of providing.

Other units are strictly manual. The battery voltage must be monitored and the unit turned off when the voltage comes up. *Failure to do so just once will result in battery damage—even explosion.* If the voltage rises high enough, electronic equipment hooked to the battery will be damaged. Some manual units incorporate a timer to switch off the unit after a preset period of operation. Once again, the unit will have completed just the bulk charge phase of charging. An absorption charge can be applied to the battery *but only by continuously monitoring the voltage and progressively cutting back the charging current to hold this voltage steady.*

All these devices provide a constant field current to the alternator (determined by the rheostat setting). If engine speed is increased, alternator output also will increase even though the field current is unchanged. The field current must be cut back to compensate for speed increases or alternator and battery damage are likely.

Voltage regulator bypasses must be used with circumspection, with a full understanding of what is being done, and with a recognition of the limits of what is possible without equipment damage or risk of battery damage or explosion. It also should be noted that most are not made with heat-protected components. With a powerful alternator it is quite possible to overload many units, with a consequent fire risk. A boosted alternator output may also overload the capacity of existing circuits. All wiring will need to be checked to ensure it has sufficient current-carrying capability (see Chapter 3).

When you are using a voltage regulator bypass, a lapse of attention on just one occasion can do irreparable harm to batteries and cause a potentially dangerous situation. In recent years voltage regulator bypasses have been superseded by multistep regulators, which do a better job without risk of operator error (see page 21).

Troubleshooting Voltage Regulators

No alternator output at all. Charging Problems (page 55) outlined a procedure for *external* regulators to determine if the alternator or regulator is at fault (Figure 2-26). Some at-tached regulators can be removed without disturbing the brushes and treated in a similar fashion (page 65).

If these tests indicate that the voltage regulator is malfunctioning, we have an open circuit (no current) to the field winding. This may be the result of a defective switch circuit on battery-excited alternators, a broken or shorted wire, blown diodes or transistors on solid-state regulators, or open points on a mechanical regulator.

Battery-excited alternators. Always suspect the switches first. The excitation line may run to an oil-pressure or fuel pressure switch mounted on the engine block, to the ignition switch, or to both (Figure 2-34). *Rig a jumper wire incorporating a minimum 12-watt test light from the battery positive terminal, crank the engine, and touch the jumper for just a second or two to the battery exci-*

tation terminal on the voltage regulator. If the alternator now works we know this circuit is faulty. The alternator may continue to work after the jumper is disconnected, but when the engine is shut down and then restarted the alternator field winding will need re-exciting to get things going again.

Self-exciting alternators. These are designed so that the iron core of the field winding retains sufficient residual magnetism when the unit is shut down to get things moving again when it is put back in operation. Sometimes, however, this residual magnetism will decline to the point at which it will not bring the alternator back to life. Revving up the engine may bring the alternator back into commission. If not, give the field winding its initial excitation with a small positive current to the field or auxiliary terminal on the alternator. The easiest way to do this is to connect a minimum 12-watt test light from the battery positive terminal to the field or auxiliary terminal (Figure 2-26).

Continuity tests. If the excitation tests fail to restore alternator output, with the ignition off *and the battery isolation switch off,* use a multimeter set to its ohms function (placing an analog meter on its lowest—R × 1—scale) to test the regulator wiring for continuity. We should get a reading of 0 ohms (needle all the way to the right) when the meter probes are touched to both ends of an individual wire. Infinite ohms indicate a break in the wiring. It may prove necessary to push the probe tip through the insulation at the voltage regulator end of the wires as the connections are inaccessible on many regulators.

If earlier tests showed the regulator is at fault, but all its wiring and external circuits are okay, the regulator needs replacing. If no spare is on board, an emergency regulator can sometimes be rigged up as detailed on page 71.

Mechanical regulators. These are easier to troubleshoot since all wiring, connections, and points are accessible. If the internal wiring has burned, the ends will be visible—just like a blown fuse. Emergency repairs can be made with copper wire of approximately the same diameter. Contact points should be cleaned with 400- or 600-grit wet-and-dry sandpaper. To make a crude test of the regulator, run up the engine and gently hold the regulator points open and shut. The generator or alternator should not put out at all with the points open (or at a very low level if externally excited), and then put out at full blast with the points closed. Don't keep the points closed for any length of time, or something is likely to burn up!

Persistent undercharging of the battery.

The alternator may just be too small for the demands being placed on the system, its speed of rotation too slow (wrong pulleys, see page 17), its belt slipping, or its charging time inadequate. Given a correctly sized alternator and pulleys and sufficient charging time, however, persistent undercharging must be the result of incorrect voltage regulation for the system in question.

- First, it is necessary to bring the battery(ies) to full charge by one means or another. (This is important; test wet-cells with a hydrometer.) Then set the engine to its normal charging speed and check the battery voltage *across the battery terminals*. This will show the regulated voltage from the alternator that is actually reaching the battery. Depending on the design parameters of the system, this should be anywhere from 13.8 to 14.4 volts. Most boats will want to be somewhere between 14.0 and 14.4 volts for reasonably rapid battery charging without risk of excessive overcharging. An exception to this is a boat fitted with one of the multi-step regulators previously mentioned. In this case, if the battery is *fully charged*, the regulator may have tripped to a float setting between 13.2 and 13.6 volts. If so, turn the regulator off and back on to put it into its absorption phase (see page 23).

- *If voltage levels are down, no amount of engine running time will bring the battery(ies) to full charge.* In this case, check the voltage *at the output terminal on the alternator*. With the engine running, test between the terminal and a good ground (the alternator case). On alternators with an insulated ground, test between the output terminal and the ground terminal. Voltage may well be a volt or more higher than the battery voltage already measured.

- Voltage drop from the alternator to the batteries can be caused by inadequate wiring and poor connections (see Chapter 3) but is more likely to occur as a result of battery isolation diodes fitted to allow charging of two or more batteries from the same alternator (see Chapter 1 and Figures 2-39A and B). *Unless a voltage regulator is compensated for diode-induced voltage drop, the batteries will be permanently undercharged.* If an alternator is undercharging because of diode-induced voltage drops, one of the following procedures will correct the situation:

Adjustable regulators. Raise the voltage setting—see earlier in this chapter. Remember, all adjustments should be made only with a *fully charged* battery and in *small increments,*

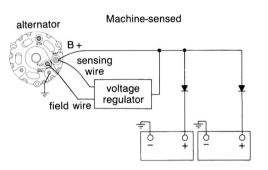

Figure 2-39A. Correct voltages on systems with split-charging diodes when the batteries are fully charged. Voltage drop can be measured directly between the alternator output terminal and the battery's positive post as shown.

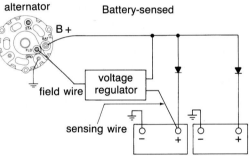

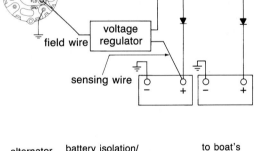

Figure 2-39B. Machine- (opposite) and battery-sensed (below) voltage regulators. B+ is the alternator's output terminal. FLD is the field terminal.

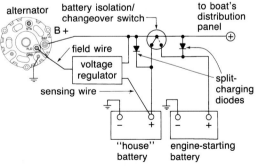

Figure 2-39C. Battery-sensing wire connected to a "house" battery.

allowing the system to stabilize before making further changes.

Nonadjustable regulators. Either (1) take the regulator sensing wire *directly to the battery positive terminal,* thus bypassing any diodes (Figure 2-39C), or (2) *fit a diode with the same* *voltage drop as the battery isolation diodes into the sensing wire* (Figure 2-39D). Either way the regulator is now sensing more or less the same voltage that the battery is receiving.

1. *Battery-sensing wire connected to house battery.* If the sensing wire is moved to the battery, make sure it does not pass through any switches that may be opened while the engine is running. If this happens *the regulator will sense no voltage and will respond by increasing field current to its maximum.* The sensing wire can go to only one battery; otherwise the batteries would be paralleled via the sensing wire, defeating the purpose of the diodes. *If the sensed battery is fully charged and the other battery is low, the alternator output will shut down and the second battery will be inadequately charged.* Normal practice is to connect the sensing wire to the battery on the boat's house circuit (as opposed to engine cranking), as this battery is generally in the lowest state of charge. Should the engine-starting battery be lower, the batteries should, if possible, be paralleled manually during charging (e.g. by turning a battery isolation/changeover switch to the "BOTH" position): Remember to isolate the batteries when charging is complete!

Unfortunately, the sense line on most internal regulators is inaccessible. Some degree of alternator disassembly is needed to find it, and also an understanding of the regulator wiring once the alternator is disassembled. Note that the various multistep regulators have external sensing lines that can be run to the battery terminals, bypassing any diodes.

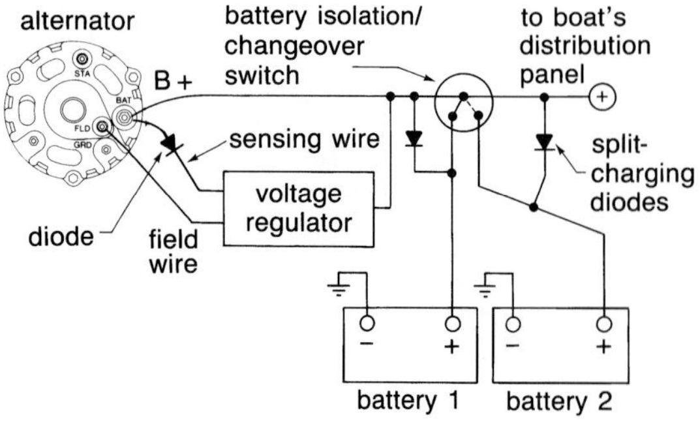

2. *Diode installed in sensing wire* (Figure 2-39D). The diode will impose approximately the same voltage drop on the sensing wire as is imposed on the output cable by the isolation diodes, thus canceling out the negative effect of the output diodes on the regulating circuit. Once again, finding the sensing line may be a problem. Any diode must be installed with its arrow pointing *toward the voltage regulator. If it is fitted in reverse it will block the sensing line altogether; the regulator will respond with maximum field current at all times, and the batteries will be overcharged* (if nothing burns up first).

Persistent overcharging of the battery.
The battery or batteries overheat, boil or gas, use excess water, and give off an acrid, acid smell. Gel batteries dry out and fail.

First, check the batteries. Dead and dying batteries will frequently gas and lose electrolyte as if they were overcharged. Note that *excessively hot batteries will automatically overcharge*; there may be no fault in the system itself. The batteries will need to be moved to a cooler location.

Next, check for improper use of a voltage regulator bypass (page 66), excessively high setpoints on a multistep regulator, or overcharging from an unregulated wind generator or solar panel (Chapter 5). Note that since regulators in marine use frequently are set to achieve faster charge rates through higher voltage settings than in automotive use, extended engine running generally will result in mild overcharging and moderate water loss on wet-cell batteries; this is to be expected. These conditions will spell death for a gel-cell!

Regardless of the size of an alternator, serious overcharging cannot occur with correct voltage regulation. If battery voltage is above 14.4 volts, the battery is gassing vigorously, or a wet-cell is experiencing a substantial water loss on all cells, in all probability the voltage regulator's battery-sensing wire is disconnected or broken, or the regulator itself has shorted. If the sensing circuit is broken, the regulator senses no voltage and responds by increasing field current to its maximum. Pay particular attention to *battery-sensed* regulators that have a long wire running to the batteries rather than a short one to the alternator *(machine-sensed)*. Any voltage drop *in the sensing wire*, such as would result from corroded terminals, will have a similar, though less dramatic, effect.

A short circuit on the voltage regulator will result in permanent maximum output since the regulator supplies maximum field current at all times, a situation similar to the loss of the sensing wire. This, however, is not repairable. Carry a spare.

Figure 2-39D. A diode installed in a sensing wire to compensate for voltage drop caused by split-charging diodes.

Emergency Voltage Regulation

The excitation current for almost all alternators ranges up to a maximum of around 5 amps at full output, although some high-output alternators may go as high as 7 to 8 amps. Any external source can be used to supply this current if the voltage regulator is first removed or disconnected. A test wire connected to a 12- or 15-watt DC lamp (Figure 2-26A) will feed approximately 1 amp to the field winding (12-volt system). The lamp acts as a fixed resistance, preventing excessive amperage from reaching the field winding. The higher the lamp wattage, the more amperage it will pass. Divide the wattage by the system voltage to find out how many amps. For example, a 15-watt bulb on a 12-volt system will pass 1.25 amps; a 40-watt bulb, 3.33 amps.

With P-type alternators, the lamp must be connected between the battery's positive terminal and the alternator's field terminal (Figure 2-26B). With N-type alternators, it is connected between the field terminal and ground (Figure 2-26C).

Alternator output and battery voltage must be monitored closely to guard against overheating and overcharging. If output is too high, the lamp wattage should be decreased, or two lamps should be wired *in series*; if output is lower than desired, lamp wattage can be increased, or two lamps can be wired *in parallel*. When the battery is fully charged this field current must be switched off or disconnected; likewise when the engine is shut down. If it is left hooked up, it will drain the batteries through the field winding.

Diodes

Frequent reference has been made in these first two chapters to diodes. They will crop up over and over again in other contexts. This is as good a place as any to look at them in a little more detail.

Identification and Rating

Identification. Diodes are imprinted with an arrowhead-like symbol with its tip crossed by a perpendicular line (Figure 2-40). The arrow points in the direction of current flow; the perpendicular line symbolizes the resistance to current flow in the opposite direction. Smaller diodes simply have a black band at one end, which corresponds to the perpendicular line (i.e., current flow is from the other end to this end—for those who are interested, I am sticking with the popular conception that current flow is from positive to negative).

Smaller diodes have pigtail leads at each end. Larger diodes have a terminal on one end and a threaded stud on the other—one connection is made to the terminal on the diode's top, the other to the threaded stud on its base. If the arrow points from the terminal to the stud, conduction is from the terminal to the stud. If the arrow points from the stud to the terminal, conduction is from the stud to the terminal.

Rating. Diodes are rated in terms of their *maximum forward current*, their *peak inverse voltage*, and their *forward voltage drop*.

- The *maximum forward current* specifies the maximum current rating of the diode (the maximum number of amps it can conduct without failure).
- The *peak inverse voltage* specifies the maximum voltage the diode will block in the

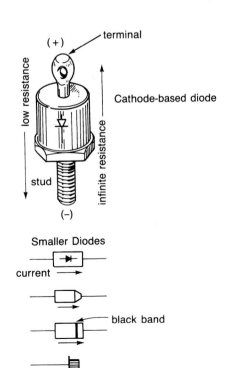

Figure 2-40. Diode identification. Diodes are rated according to: (1) their current-carrying capacity when conducting (e.g., 50 amps) and (2) the voltage they are capable of blocking in the other direction, known as *peak inverse voltage* or PIV (e.g., 50 PIV). The bottommost of the smaller diodes is frequently used in alternators, pressed into a heat sink, in which instance the diode case is electrically in common with the heat sink, and usually grounded (or negative).

reverse direction. Once voltage goes above this level, the diode will break down and conduct in both directions (a shorted diode).

- The *forward voltage drop* specifies the voltage at which the diode begins to conduct in the forward direction, which is also the voltage drop it will impose on the circuit when carrying its full rated current. In other words, if the forward voltage drop is 0.6 volts (a typical silicon diode), the diode will not begin to conduct until the voltage on the circuit is at least 0.6 volts, and once it is conducting the voltage "downstream" of the diode will be 0.6 of a volt less than upstream of it. The "lost" voltage represents energy that is dissipated as heat (which is important—see below). Some diodes have a lower forward voltage drop than others. Conventional silicon diodes run as high as 1.0 to 1.5 volts at full current; Schottky diodes as high as 0.5 to 0.7 volts at full current.

Diodes come in different sizes to fit different needs. *Since the full charging output of an alternator passes through battery isolation diodes, they must be rated to accept this high amperage. If you are upgrading to a high-output alternator, any existing battery isolating diodes will most likely also need upgrading.* This can be done by fitting additional diodes in parallel with the original ones.

Heat Sinks

Current passing through a diode heats it up. More current produces more heat. The quantity of heat at full current rating can be calculated approximately by taking the diode's forward current rating and multiplying this by its forward voltage drop. For example, if we have a Schottky diode as an isolation diode on a 150-amp alternator, it will generate up to (150 amps × 0.7 volts) 105 watts of heat. If this heat is allowed to build up it will destroy the diode, so diodes are generally mounted on some kind of a *heat sink*, frequently a finned, aluminum plate. Note: If a heat sink is installed on a vertical service, the fins should be aligned vertically since this will maximize the cooling effect.

Since one side of a diode is connected electrically to its heat sink via the mounting stud, *heat sinks are live.* If the heat sink is connected to the battery positive terminal, shorting *out the heat sink to ground is much the same as shorting out the battery terminals. If the heat sink is connected to the alternator, it will be hot (live) whenever the engine is running* (Figures 2-41A and 2-41B).

If the heat sink is common with the battery positive terminal, it is not possible to mount two

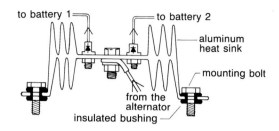

Figure 2-41A. Diodes mounted on a shared heat sink for battery isolation. Note that the heat sink is live during alternator operation.

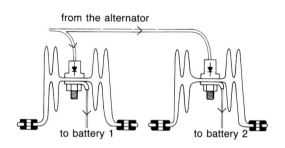

Figure 2-41B. In this setup, the heat sinks are connected to the two battery positive terminals via the diode cases, hence the use of independent, electrically-isolated heat sinks to avoid paralleling the batteries.

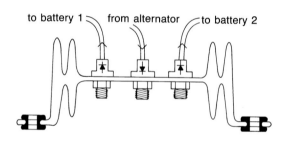

Figure 2-42. Three-diode split-charging setup. Note that the voltage drop is doubled relative to that of a two-diode configuration. The heat sink is still live during alternator operation.

diodes on the same heat sink; this will parallel the batteries through the heat sink and defeat the purpose of the diodes. If the heat sink is common with the alternator output, any number of diodes can be mounted on the same heat sink without affecting the batteries.

Some battery isolation units use three diodes: The alternator feeds one, then another two feed the batteries. Note that *the voltage drop to the batteries is doubled* (Figure 2-42), which will exacerbate any voltage regulation problems. The diodes are sometimes mounted in an insulated block fitted to the heat sink. In this case the heat sink is permanently electrically isolated from its diodes.

Soldering and connections. Excessive heat will damage a diode. Do not solder to the top terminal with the diode mounted on its heat sink; the heat sink will draw the heat down into the diode. Use a large enough soldering iron to get the job done as quickly as possible and so avoid the need to hold the iron to the terminal for prolonged periods. When soldering small diodes with attached wires, clamp a pair of small Vise-Grips or pliers around the wire between the solder joint and the diode. This will act as a heat sink and protect the diode (Figure 2-43). Alternatively, wrap a strip of aluminum cut from a soft drink can around the wire. For more information on soldering, see Chapter 3.

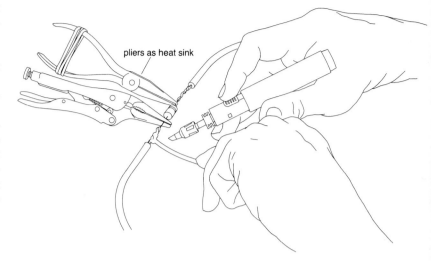

Figure 2-43. **Soldering small diodes.** *(Jim Sollers)*

Testing Battery Isolation Diodes

All diodes create a voltage drop, normally around 0.6 volt, but sometimes over 1.0 volt. To find out how much, check with a DC voltmeter across the two diode terminals *while the alternator is running at full output* (set an analog meter to the 2.5-volt scale). The positive meter lead goes to the alternator side of the circuit (Figure 2-44).

To test an isolation diode's operation, shut down the alternator and turn off the ignition and battery isolation switches. Check with a voltmeter (or test light) from the *battery side* of the diode *to ground*. It will show battery voltage (or light). Now test from the alternator side to a good ground. It should show no or very little voltage (there may be a small leakage current—if a meter shows voltage, try with a test light; it should not light). If there is battery voltage on the alternator side (if the test lamp lights), the diode is shorted, another diode in the charging circuit has been installed backward, or some equipment has been wired incorrectly in such a way as to bypass the diodes. If the diode is shorted, the battery will still receive a charge, but will not be isolated from other batteries (although other batteries may still be isolated from this one via their own isolating diodes). If one of the diodes is in backward the relevant battery will receive no charge when the alternator is running and will soon go dead.

Diodes can also be tested with an ohmmeter, *but only after disconnecting the batteries* (otherwise the ohmmeter will be damaged). An analog meter is set to its lowest ohms scale (R × 1). The probes are touched to the two diode terminals. The probes are then reversed. If the diode is functional it will show continuity in one direction (0 or near 0 ohms) and an open circuit in the other (infinite or very high ohms). Where there is continuity the direction of flow is from the negative probe to the positive probe. A shorted diode will show continuity in both directions. An open-cir-

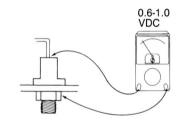

0.6-1.0 VDC

Figure 2-44. **Testing for voltage drop across a diode.** The positive meter lead goes on the alternator side of the circuit.

cuited diode will show infinity in both directions.

(Note that *some meters may not have the necessary forward voltage to show a circuit in either direction*; it is best to use a meter with a specific *diode-testing* function. Rather than testing resistance, these frequently test the voltage drop across the diode: a properly functioning diode will show a voltage, generally around 0.6 volt, in one direction and "infinity" in the other direction; a shorted diode will show 0 volts in both directions; an open-circuited diode will show "infinity" in both directions.)

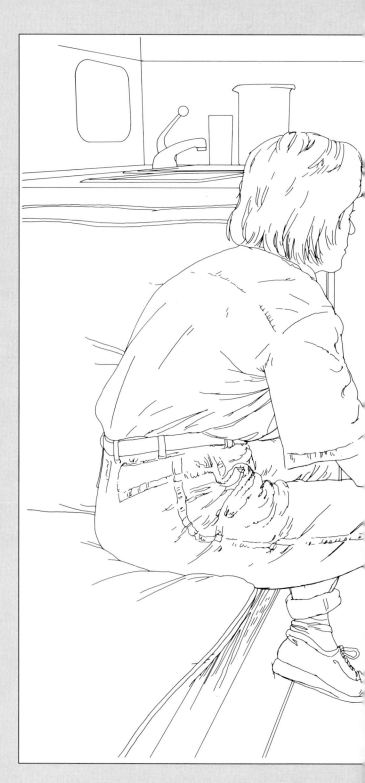

CHAPTER 3

Figure 3-1. Effective troubleshooting of recalcitrant electrical circuits begins and ends with a thorough understanding of the dynamics involved. *(Jim Sollers)*

Understanding and Troubleshooting Electrical Circuits; Proper Installation Practices

Basic Concepts & Measurements

Electrical circulation is analogous to the circulation of water in a pressurized water system. Since most people have little trouble understanding water flow, there should in principle be few obstacles to understanding electrical circuits. But even with such an understanding, because electricity is invisible we still cannot do effective troubleshooting without some kind of a tool that will let us "see" inside a circuit. This tool is the multimeter. With these two things—a grasp of basic concepts and a multimeter—it is the rare electrical problem that cannot be solved.

The Water Analogy

In a pressurized water system the *rate of flow* through any given pipe is governed by the *pressure of the water* and the *size of the pipe*. The higher the pressure, the greater the potential flow; the larger the pipe, the greater the potential flow, up to the capacity of the system's pump.

In an electrical circuit the rate of flow *(amperage)* through any given wire is governed by the pressure in the wire *(voltage)* and the size of the wire. The higher the pressure (voltage), the greater the potential flow (amperage). The larger the wire, the greater the potential flow, up to the capacity of the system's generator or battery.

With a pipe of a given size, the longer the pipe, the more the cumulative resistance and therefore the less the flow. Moreover, pressure will decline steadily along the length of the pipe, but the *flow rate* will be the same at all points. If 4 gallons per minute comes out at the far end, four gallons per minute must go in at the beginning, and 4 gallons per minute will flow through the pipe at all points (Figure 3-2).

With a wire of any given size, the longer the wire the more the cumulative resistance *(ohms)* and therefore the lower the rate of flow (amps). Moreover, pressure (voltage) will decline steadily along the length of the wire (this is called *voltage drop*, and is very significant in boat electrics, as we have already seen), but the rate of flow (amps) will remain constant at all points.

Flow rates and pressure; amps and volts.
Consider an open tank of water with a pump on its outlet feeding a pipe with a valve. The outlet from the valve runs through a second pipe onto the ground. The pump is running but the valve is closed, creating, in effect, infinite resistance to flow. In other words, there is no flow through the pipes. The pump will build system pressure upstream of the valve.

An open *switch* is the electrical equivalent of a closed valve; it offers infinite resistance to electrical flow. In other words, it stops all flow through the system. System pressure (voltage) will build upstream of the switch.

Water is used if the valve is opened and water allowed to flow. If the valve is barely cracked (Figure 3-3A) it offers a very high resistance to flow and allows only a small amount of water to pass. The pump is more than capable of maintaining system pressure upstream of the valve while water flows through the valve out onto the ground at no pressure. In other words, the pressure drop from one side of the valve to the other amounts to the pressure on the system.

Electricity is used when a switch is closed and electricity is allowed to flow. Current flowing through a high resistance, such as a light bulb, is the electrical equivalent of a barely cracked valve; it allows only a small amount of current to flow. Upstream of the resistance there will be full sytem voltage. Downstream from the resistance the circuit runs to ground—either the negative terminal on a battery or *ground potential* on an AC system (see AC Circuits later in this chapter). Voltage falls to 0 volts. *The voltage drop from one side of the resistance to the other will amount to the voltage on the system.*

The more the water valve is opened, the lower the resistance to flow and the more water will pass through the valve. At some point, if the pipe and valve are large enough and the resistance to flow is low enough, the rate of flow will exceed the ability of the pump to maintain system pressure, and pressure will begin to decline upstream of the valve (Figure 3-3B).

The lower the resistance in a circuit, the more current (amperage) will flow. At some point, if the wire is large enough and the resistance is low enough—a starter motor is a good example—the rate of flow will exceed the ability of the generator or battery to maintain system pressure (voltage). This is why battery voltage falls, generally to around 10.5 volts, when cranking an engine.

As long as the pipes leading to and from the valve are large enough to accommodate the flow without resistance, and as long as the rate of flow does not exceed the capability of the pump to maintain system pressure, the water pressure will always be at pump pressure above the valve and at no pressure downstream from the valve (Figure 3-3A again). At very high rates of flow, however, the pipes themselves may begin to offer resistance. There will now be a pressure drop along the length of the pipes, followed by a drop of the remaining system pressure across the valve (Figure 3-3C).

As long as the wires leading to and from a resistance *(load)* are large enough to accommodate the flow (amperage) and free of extra resistance, such as loose or corroded connections, and as long as the rate of flow (amperage) does

Understanding and Troubleshooting Electrical Circuits;
Proper Installation Practices

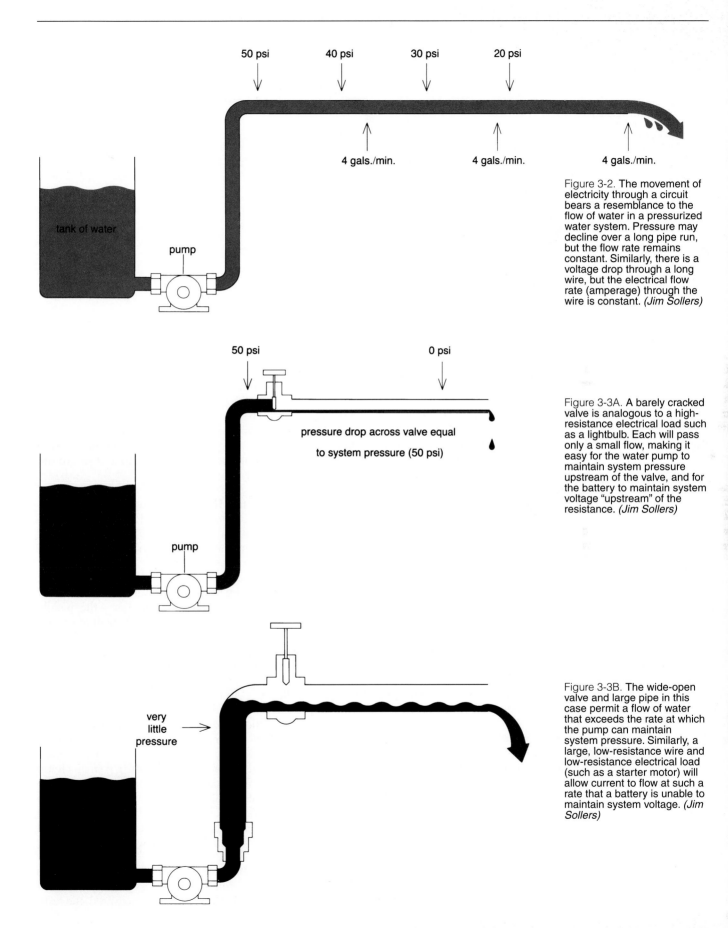

50 psi   40 psi   30 psi   20 psi

4 gals./min.   4 gals./min.   4 gals./min.

tank of water

pump

Figure 3-2. The movement of electricity through a circuit bears a resemblance to the flow of water in a pressurized water system. Pressure may decline over a long pipe run, but the flow rate remains constant. Similarly, there is a voltage drop through a long wire, but the electrical flow rate (amperage) through the wire is constant. *(Jim Sollers)*

50 psi   0 psi

pressure drop across valve equal to system pressure (50 psi)

pump

Figure 3-3A. A barely cracked valve is analogous to a high-resistance electrical load such as a lightbulb. Each will pass only a small flow, making it easy for the water pump to maintain system pressure upstream of the valve, and for the battery to maintain system voltage "upstream" of the resistance. *(Jim Sollers)*

very little pressure →

Figure 3-3B. The wide-open valve and large pipe in this case permit a flow of water that exceeds the rate at which the pump can maintain system pressure. Similarly, a large, low-resistance wire and low-resistance electrical load (such as a starter motor) will allow current to flow at such a rate that a battery is unable to maintain system voltage. *(Jim Sollers)*

Basic Concepts and Measurements

77

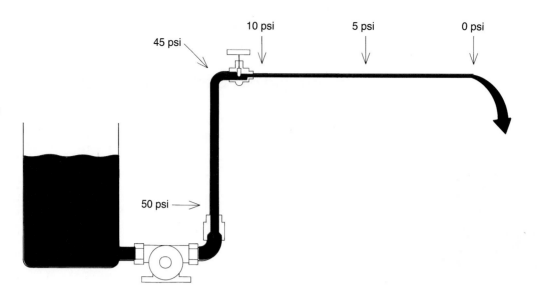

Figure 3-3C. At high flow rates a narrow pipe or undersized wire (or faulty connection) will create its own pressure or voltage drop. The pressure (voltage) drop measured across the valve (or electrical load) will now be something less than the pressure (voltage) at the pump (battery). *(Jim Sollers)*

not exceed the capability of the generator or battery to maintain system pressure (voltage), the pressure (voltage) will always be at system pressure (voltage) above the resistance (load) and drop to 0 volts downstream from the resistance. At very high rates of flow (amperages), the wires and/or their connections may begin to offer their own resistance to flow: They will heat up. There will now be a pressure (voltage) drop along the length of the wires, followed by a drop of the remaining system pressure (voltage) across the resistance (load).

Making Measurements

In a pressurized water system we can insert gauges at any point to measure the pressure and rate of flow. So too with electrical circuits. We can even go one better and measure resistance to flow (ohms) quite easily; this must be deduced in the water system.

Measuring pressure (voltage). Water pressure is measured by teeing in a small line and leading it to a pressure gauge. Voltage is measured the same way, with one difference: Water pressure gauges are calibrated with reference to atmospheric pressure. Since atmospheric pressure is all around us, this reference point can be built into the meter quite simply by leaving one side open to atmosphere; only one connection is needed to the water pipe. What we are measuring is the pressure *differential* between the system pressure and atmospheric pressure.

Voltage is measured with reference to *ground* (or *ground potential*). A *voltmeter cannot measure without being connected to this reference*

point in some way; a hole in the side of the meter will not work! Therefore *two* connections are needed to measure voltage: one to the pressure point in the circuit and one to its ground (Figure 3-4). This ground connection performs the reference function of the open side of the water pressure gauge; we are measuring the pressure *differential* between the system and its ground potential.

Measuring flow (amperage). In a water system, rate of flow is measured by installing a paddle wheel in the pipe and seeing how fast it spins. Amperage is measured in the same way by installing an *ammeter*—the electrical equivalent of a paddle wheel—in the electrical circuit.

With larger volumes of water it is impractical to measure the whole flow rate—the paddle wheel would have to be huge. A small restriction is made in the main pipe to cause a slight pressure drop. A smaller pipe bypasses this restriction. The slight pressure drop in the main pipe causes water to flow through the bypass pipe, and a paddle wheel in this pipe measures the rate of flow. This is multiplied by a suitable factor to determine the rate of flow in the main pipe.

High amperage is measured in a similar fashion. A specially calibrated, low-resistance *shunt* is installed in the main wire *(cable)*. A small circuit containing a voltmeter is connected across the terminals of the shunt. The voltmeter measures the voltage drop across the shunt, which is then multiplied by a suitable factor and reconfigured to give the overall rate of flow (amperage).

Measuring resistance (ohms). If water is pumped through a pipe at a carefully regulated pressure and the rate of flow measured, the resis-

Understanding and Troubleshooting Electrical Circuits;
Proper Installation Practices

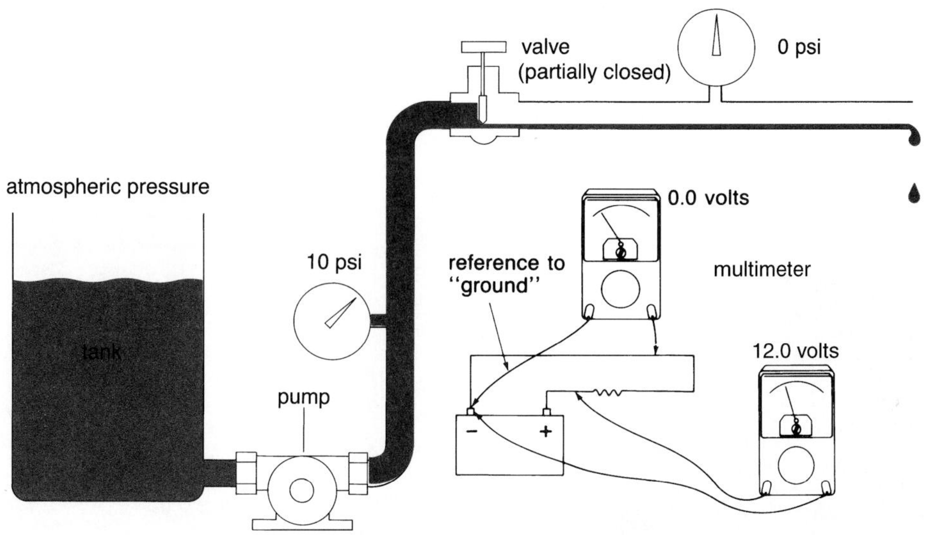

Figure 3-4. Pressure and voltage measurements. *(Jim Sollers)*

tance can be deduced. The greater the flow, the less the resistance.

In electrical work, this is the function of an *ohmmeter*. The meter contains its own power source (a battery), which is the electrical equivalent of a pump and reservoir of water. The meter supplies current (amperage) at a carefully regulated pressure (voltage) to the circuit to be tested—the same as a pump pushing water through a pipe at a carefully regulated pressure. The meter measures the rate of flow (amperage); the less the flow, the greater the resistance (ohms). Instead of displaying this rate of flow (amperage), the meter dial is simply reconfigured to display ohms of resistance.

Ohm's law. As we have seen, pressure (voltage), rate of flow (amperage), and resistance to flow (ohms) are all interrelated. This relationship is summed up in a simple formula known as Ohm's law (named for Georg Simon Ohm [1787–1854], a German physicist):

$I = E \div R$, where I = amperage, E = voltage, and R = resistance (ohms)

The formula can be rearranged to find either voltage or resistance:

$E = I \times R$ or $R = E \div I$

With this formula, if we can measure any two of voltage, amperage, or resistance, we can easily calculate the third. The means to measure them is provided by a multimeter.

The Multimeter: An Essential Tool

A multimeter is an essential electrical troubleshooting tool. In fact, given a knowledge of how to use it, I would go so far as to say that it is possibly *the single most important tool on a boat!*

There are two kinds of meter: analog (swinging arm) and digital (Figures 3-5 and 3-6). In general, the digital meters are easier to use and are more accurate than the analog meters (particularly when dealing with DC systems, where accurate measurements of readings as low as a tenth of a volt are sometimes needed). Since a reasonable digital meter can be bought from West Marine and other discount catalogs (USA) for less than $70, there is really no excuse not to have one on board.

There is, however, a notable quirk to cheaper *(high impedance)* digital meters. Through a process known as *capacitive coupling*, one AC circuit can at times impose a measurable "ghost voltage" on another circuit even though the two are electrically isolated. This typically occurs with cables that are in a common bundle, or around transformers (used principally in battery chargers, inverters, and fluorescent lights). The current generated by this capacitive coupling is minuscule. As a result, as soon as any kind of a load is applied to the circuit the ghost voltage disappears. But it can be very confusing, for example, if a test is made from a battery charger negative terminal to its case and the meter shows 60 volts! Some more expensive digital meters apply a built-in internal load that enables the meter to distinguish ghost voltages from actual voltage on the circuit.

A second problem with cheaper meters is that they are electrically fragile. It is possible, for example, to generate a high enough voltage from static electricity by shuffling across a carpet to blow out a meter! Finally, cheap meters lack protection circuitry, which is needed to guard against injury to the user and damage to the

Basic Concepts and Measurements

Figure 3-5. **An inexpensive analog meter.**
(Professional Mariner)

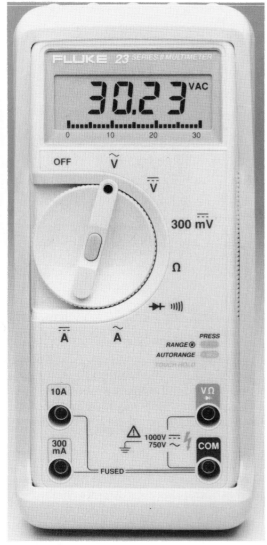

Figure 3-6. **A more expensive, but more useful, digital multimeter.** This meter has numerous functions, including important safety features, not found on cheaper meters. *(Fluke)*

meter if the meter is accidentally used when switched into the wrong mode, or with the meter leads in the wrong sockets (see below).

When buying a meter, boatowners should look for the following refinements:

- A DC-amps capability of 10 amps or more. The more common *milliamp* scales are useful only for troubleshooting ground leaks and electronics, and the latter are best left alone by the average boatowner. (Note that with the addition of a current clamp, a device that plugs into the milliamps scale of most meters, currents up to 1,000 amps can be measured, but the clamp is likely to cost more than the meter!)

- Accuracy at the low end of the ohms scale (many of the cheaper analog meters are particularly inaccurate when measuring low resistances).

- The ability to test diodes. As mentioned on page 72, it takes a certain *forward voltage* to make a diode conduct; some meters will not always develop the necessary internal voltage, making diode testing unreliable. It is preferable to buy a meter with a specific *diode testing* function.

- An *auto-ranging* function, which eliminates the need to switch up and down different voltage, amperage, and ohms scales when using the meter, and thus eliminates one more potential source of error and damage.

- Protection circuitry, to guard against injury and meter damage if the meter is used incorrectly.

As with most things, quality costs money. The industry standard in meters is set by Fluke (Everett, WA), whose top-of-the-line models run

Understanding and Troubleshooting Electrical Circuits;
Proper Installation Practices

as high as $300 but are fully waterproof and virtually indestructible.

Using a multimeter. AC CIRCUITS CAN KILL! IF YOU ARE IN DOUBT ABOUT WHAT YOU ARE DOING, DON'T GO POKING AROUND AC CIRCUITS!

AC and DC circuits frequently share the same distribution panel. Be sure to disconnect the AC power cord and turn off any DC/AC inverters before opening such panels. Merely switching off the incoming breaker will NOT do since it will leave hot wires on the supply side in the panel.

A meter's different functions and scales are accessed by plugging jacks into different holes and/or by turning a multiposition switch (preferable). The meter will have two output leads: one red, one black. Red is hot (+ or POS); black is ground (– or COMMON). Switch-type meters sometimes have a different plug-in point for AC and DC measurements; the meter will be clearly marked. Resistance readings are made using the DC output terminals.

When taking AC voltage readings it is immaterial which way the leads are used, but for reading DC voltages and amperages the red (+) lead must go to the positive side of the circuit and the black (–) to the negative side, or the meter will read backward. On most resistance tests the leads can be either way around unless the circuit contains a diode.

Any voltage (AC or DC) can blow out an unprotected meter (and possibly injure the operator) when the meter is in the resistance or amps mode. When measuring ohms be absolutely certain to electrically isolate the relevant circuit. When measuring amps be careful not to bridge the power leads with the meter probe.

In order to avoid draining its internal battery, turn a meter off when it is not in use, or to the highest AC volts scale if it has no OFF position.

Measuring voltage. You can measure voltage at any point in a circuit by connecting the meter between *a ground* and *an uninsulated terminal or section of wire*—the meter will be *bridging the voltage differential* between the terminal or wire and ground (Figure 3-7). Most meter probes have sharp points; if necessary you can force the probe into contact with a conductor through a wire's insulation, although you should not do this unless it is absolutely necessary. You can seal the hole in the insulation with a dab of non-silicone sealant (silicone is slightly moisture-absorbent and acid-cured, which causes corrosion).

Unless the meter has an auto-ranging function, always begin by selecting the highest potential voltage scale. For example, if the boat has 240- and 120-volt AC circuits, set the meter to

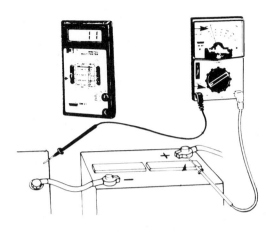

Figure 3-7. Using multimeters.

Check batteries   DC voltage

the 250-VAC scale initially, even when checking 120-volt circuits. If you inadvertently tap a 240-volt line, the meter will not be damaged. Switch down to a more appropriate scale, such as 150 volts, only after the meter probes are positioned properly (the meter will be more accurate and easier to read the closer the measured voltage is to the limit of the scale being used; 120 volts will be displayed more accurately on a 150-volt scale than on a 250-volt scale).

Measuring amperage. Note that in general, amperage is far lower in AC circuits than in DC circuits. This is easy to understand. Since watts = volts × amps, amps = watts ÷ volts. Therefore, a 100-watt appliance will draw only 0.83 amps (100 ÷ 120) on a 120-volt system, whereas the same appliance will draw 8.3 amps (100 ÷ 12) on a 12-volt system.

Amperage (AC and DC) can be measured by connecting a meter (or a shunt and meter) *in series* with the conductor (Figure 3-8A). This method requires the circuit to be broken to insert the meter (or shunt) into it. It also means that *the circuit's full current (amperage) will flow through the meter (or shunt)*. Since many meters cannot handle more than 250 mA (thousandths of an amp) and very few appliances draw less than half an amp, the amperage scales are frequently of little use except for troubleshooting electronics and ground faults (*earth leaks*; see below).

DC stereos, fans, and pumps generally draw from 0.5 amp to a maximum of 6 or 7 amps. For these, a meter with a capability of 10 amps DC is very useful. Electric winches, windlasses, sail-furling systems, and starter motors have power-hungry motors, well beyond this range; measuring their amps requires a *current clamp*.

Basic Concepts and Measurements   **81**

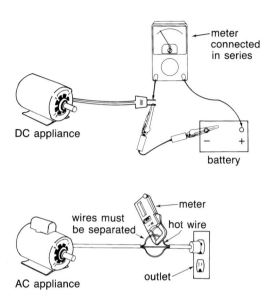

Figure 3-8A. Measuring current draw (amps) of a DC appliance.

Figure 3-8B. Measuring current draw (amps) of an AC appliance. This purpose-built meter (Amprobe is one brand) clips around individual hot wires to measure their induced magnetism, which is directly related to the current they carry. A simple device known as a line splitter can be inserted between the plug and outlet to obviate the need for separating the wires in the cable as shown here.

A current clamp is simply clipped around the hot wire(s) in a circuit. The circuit need not be broken, but the clamp must be clipped around individual hot wire(s); if there is more than one hot wire, the clamp must be clipped around each in turn (Figure 3-8B). In an AC circuit, each hot wire must be separated from the neutral and ground wires and from any other hot wire. Special "line splitters" can be bought to separate leads in a common housing without having to cut into the insulating sheath.

Measuring resistance. An ohmmeter is a delicate instrument. If it is hooked into a circuit under pressure, such as a circuit connected to a *power source*, the existing pressure may blow out the meter (analog meters are particularly vulnerable to damage; most digital ohmmeters have a greater degree of circuit protection built in). *An ohmmeter can be used only on disconnected circuits—that is, those that have been isolated from voltage input.* When isolating DC circuits, solar panels are frequently overlooked, but even the limited output of a small solar panel will blow an ohmmeter fuse.

On an analog meter, ohms scales range from small values on the right to large values on the left, in contrast to voltage and amperage scales. That is, 0 ohms reads all the way to the right; infinite ohms reads all the to the left. Most analog meters have three ohms scales: R × 1, R × 10, and R × 100. On R × 10 and R × 100, the displayed meter reading must be multiplied by 10 and 100 respectively.

Since the internal power source, and therefore the reference point, for an ohmmeter comes from a battery whose state of charge declines over time, a meter must be recalibrated

to the existing state of charge of the battery before every use. With an analog meter, this must be done by the user; most digital meters are self-calibrating. Calibration is done by touching the meter probes *firmly* together and turning a knob until the meter reads 0 ohms. *Every time an analog meter is reused or the ohms scale changed (e.g., from R × 1 to R × 100), the meter needs recalibrating.* If the needle does not move when the probes are touched together— i.e., it stays all the way to the left on infinity— the probe wires are broken, the fuse is blown, the battery is dead or missing (or its terminals corroded and not making electrical contact), or the meter is defective.

When the meter probes are touched to two points in a circuit, the resistance is measured between these points (e.g., on either side of a switch). However, if the circuit has not been properly isolated, the meter may be measuring the resistance around the rest of the circuit rather than that between the two probes! *In order to avoid confusion, always disconnect the specific pieces of equipment—wires, switches, and so on— that are being tested* (Figure 3-9). Don't touch the meter probes when measuring high resistances since the meter will record the resistance through your body, which may confuse you!

Testing diodes. A specific diode-testing function is normally required to get meaningful test results from diodes. A meter with such a capability will show the test results in one of two ways: either by displaying the voltage drop mea-

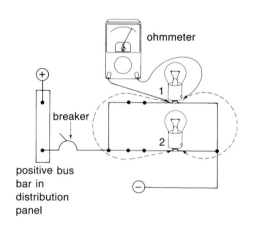

Figure 3-9. Testing a circuit using an ohmmeter. In this example two lights are installed with common supply and ground wires. Because the breaker is open, it might be thought that lightbulb 1 is being tested, whereas it is just as possible that the circuit all the way around through lightbulb 2 is being tested (the dotted lines). To avoid ambiguity, the circuit or piece of equipment being tested should always be isolated.

Understanding and Troubleshooting Electrical Circuits; Proper Installation Practices

sured through the diode (which should be on the order of 0.6 volts with the meter leads applied one way around, and 0.0 volts with the meter leads applied the other way around) or else as a resistance (which should be moderately low with the meter leads applied one way around, and very high with the meter leads applied the other way around). To test a diode, it must always be isolated from its circuit (which generally requires unsoldering a lead).

DC Circuits

Direct current circuits are easy to understand. The flow of electrons—the fundamental unit of electricity—is all in one direction, making a DC system directly analogous to the flow of water in a pressurized water system. Unfortunately, the flow is from *negative to positive* (a fact that was not appreciated until after these terminals were named!), but to avoid confusion I am going to stick to the popular conception of a circuit running from *positive to negative.*

Ground Versus Insulated Return

Ground return. The type of DC circuit that people are most familiar with is the *ground-return* circuit found on automobiles (Figure 3-10A). This utilizes the car's frame as the ground (negative) side of the system. *Hot* (positive) wires carry current through switches to all lights, instruments, etc.; these are then *grounded* (earthed) to the car frame. The negative terminal on the battery is connected by a heavy cable to the engine block, which in turn is connected to the car's frame via its mounts to complete the circuit. The big advantage of such a system is that only one (hot) wire needs to be run to electrical equipment.

Almost all marine engine installations use a ground-return circuit. That is to say, electrical equipment on the engine, such as the starter motor or alternator, is grounded to the engine block, which in turn is connected to the battery's negative terminal with a heavy cable.

Although it is commonly used, this is not the best practice for boats. Imagine a poor (resistive) connection between the battery ground strap and the engine block. The battery's negative post will usually be tied into the boat's *common ground point* (Chapter 4), which in turn will likely have the bonding strap connected to it (more on this later). Various through-hull fittings will be connected to the bonding strap. *Rather than take the electrical return path through the resistive battery ground strap, equipment grounded to the engine block may find a path back to the battery via the pro-*

peller shaft and propeller, through the water, into a through hull, up the bonding strap, through the common ground point, and so back to the battery. Stray current corrosion will follow (more on this later).

Insulated return. Engine-mounted electrical equipment should ideally be of the *insulated-return* type (Figure 3-10B). This requires purpose-built alternators and starter motors, or mounting of the equipment in such a way as to electrically isolate it from the engine block. A second ground conductor is then installed to form an insulated return path to the battery. The engine block is never part of the circuit.

Some purpose-built marine alternators and starter motors have insulated grounds, but they

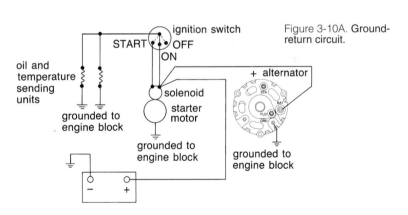

Figure 3-10A. Ground-return circuit.

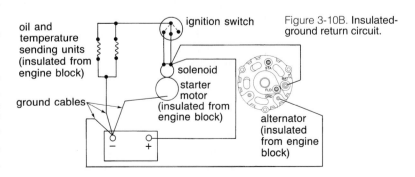

Figure 3-10B. Insulated-ground return circuit.

are uncommon. Existing ground-return alternators can be converted to insulated-ground types by drilling out all the mounting holes and installing nylon bushings and washers so as to completely insulate the alternator from the engine block. Then a separate ground wire must be run from the alternator case to the battery's negative post (or, preferably, the boat's common ground point). *This wire must be at least as heavy as the main output wire from the alternator, since it will be a full current-carrying conductor.*

However, it is not easy to electrically isolate a noninsulated alternator and still ensure a sufficiently rigid installation. A compromise approach is to connect a *heavy* ground wire *from the alternator case to the boat's common ground point.* This will provide a direct electrical path to the battery that bypasses the engine block, discouraging leakage currents. For additional insurance against corrosion, check the engine ground strap periodically to ensure that its connections are electrically perfect.

Uninsulated starter motors are even harder to insulate than alternators, but since they operate for only a second or two, the duration of any leakage currents will be strictly limited.

The electronic sending units that are mounted on most modern engines to monitor oil pressure and water temperature are generally grounded through the block, as is other electrically operated equipment such as solenoid-type fuel shutdown valves. *Anytime the ignition is on, potentially damaging small currents flow to ground through these units.* The only way to eliminate these currents is to replace the sending units (and other devices) with purpose-built insulated-ground units. These will have a separate ground wire, carried back to the battery's negative terminal. VDO (VDO-Yazaki, Winchester, VA), among others, makes insulated-ground sending devices (see page 287).

The boat's wiring. Whether or not engine installations use a ground-return circuit or have an insulated ground, *the rest of the DC system should never use a ground-return circuit, even if possible* (such as on a steel boat, or a fiberglass boat with a copper bonding strap running the length of the boat). Using the hull in a metal boat as a ground circuit, or the bonding strap in a fiberglass boat, will result in different parts of the hull and underwater fittings having slightly different voltages. *Corrosion will be rampant.*

All non-engine-mounted DC equipment on boats must have a separate insulated-ground cable that runs back to the ground (negative) side of the distribution panel. The panel ground will, in turn, be connected to the battery's negative terminal. *At no point can the hull or any fittings or fixtures be used as an electrical path. To do so is to invite corrosion.*

Troubleshooting with a Voltmeter

The following tests all refer to a voltmeter and assume a 12-volt circuit. A test lamp (Figure 3-11) could be used to duplicate the tests. Where the meter shows 12 volts, a test lamp would light; no volts, no light; low volts, dim light (or the test lamp barely glows). Remember: To get a voltage reading, or to make the test lamp light up, *a voltage differential must be bridged.*

Basic circuit test. The most basic circuit test is simply to connect the meter between the positive and negative terminals on a 12-volt battery to read battery voltage directly from *hot* to *ground.*

Load on circuit. Now let us make a circuit from the positive terminal to the negative terminal and put a piece of electronic gear in it (i.e., a resistance). We are placing a load on the circuit (Figure 3-12).

The line all the way to the resistance is *hot* and all the way back from it is at battery *ground potential.* A meter connected anywhere from the hot side to the ground side, right up to the two terminals on the equipment, will show 12 volts, *but a meter with both probes on one side of the equipment or the other will give no reading* (the meter is not bridging any voltage differential).

Circuit with switch. Now let's put in a battery isolation switch (Figure 3-13). When the switch is closed we have exactly the same situation as in the test above and the same procedures apply. A meter placed across the switch will not read anything since it is not bridging any voltage differential. However, when the switch is open ("off"), *only the cable from the battery positive terminal to the switch is hot*; the rest of the circuit will be "bled down" to ground. *A meter placed across the switch will read system voltage, but if placed across the resistance (the piece of equipment) will read nothing.*

Consider the analogy with a pressurized water system. If a valve is placed in the line before a restriction (resistance), as long as the valve is open, the pressure (i.e., voltage) will be constant all the way to the restriction (resistance) and will then drop on the other side of the restriction (resistance). But if the valve is closed, the pressure will bleed off the whole system downstream of the valve and the only pressure differential will be across the valve.

Understanding and Troubleshooting Electrical Circuits;
Proper Installation Practices

Test Lights

In the absence of a multimeter, many useful tests can be made with a test light. On occasion a test light may give even better results than a multimeter.

For example: The points on a switch are badly corroded. The switch is closed, but there is no load (i.e., amperage flow) on the circuit. Because of its high sensitivity and low current draw, the voltmeter may show 12 volts downstream of the switch, whereas the test light will impose a small load on the circuit, which will reveal the resistance in the switch (the light will glow dimly).

To understand this, think of a pressurized water pipe with a severe restriction in it and a closed valve farther down the line. (The closed valve is the equivalent of no load, therefore no flow, on the the electrical circuit.) Pressure will equalize on both sides of the restriction all the way to the closed valve, and a pressure gauge will not reveal the restriction. However, if we open the valve a little and let some water flow, pressure will drop downstream of the restriction and thus reveal its presence. The drain caused by a test light is the equivalent of opening the valve a little.

We can draw a useful conclusion from this analogy. When possible, circuits should be tested under normal load rather than in a no-load situation. This will reveal weaknesses that otherwise may be hard to find.

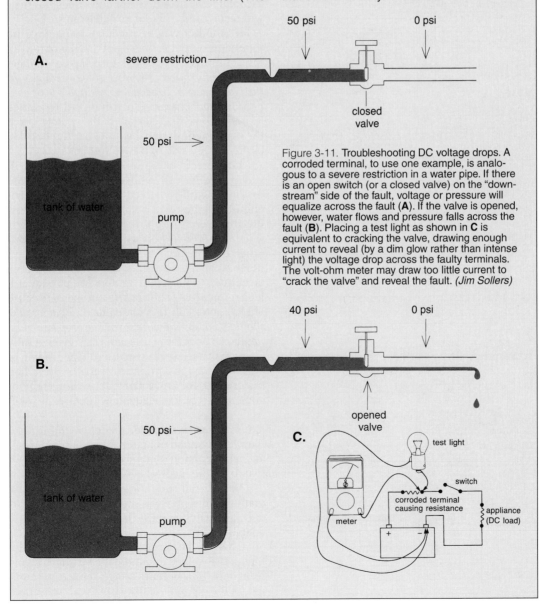

Figure 3-11. Troubleshooting DC voltage drops. A corroded terminal, to use one example, is analogous to a severe restriction in a water pipe. If there is an open switch (or a closed valve) on the "downstream" side of the fault, voltage or pressure will equalize across the fault (**A**). If the valve is opened, however, water flows and pressure falls across the fault (**B**). Placing a test light as shown in **C** is equivalent to cracking the valve, drawing enough current to reveal (by a dim glow rather than intense light) the voltage drop across the faulty terminals. The volt-ohm meter may draw too little current to "crack the valve" and reveal the fault. (*Jim Sollers*)

Unwanted resistance. Now let's put some wear and tear on our switch so that the points are dirty and pitted and the switch causes a resistance. When the switch is open ("off"), the situation is the same as when it is open in the test above. When the switch is closed, it is electrically the same as placing a second load (resistance) in the circuit in series with the equipment load. In effect we have the situation shown in Figure 3-14.

There will be a voltage drop across both resistances. What is more, *the voltage drop across each resistance will be proportional to the amount of its resistance as a percentage of the total resistance in the circuit.* What does this mean in practice?

On a *closed* circuit, if a voltage test across the input and output terminals of any switch, terminal block, or length of wiring reveals *any* voltage, *there is unwanted resistance in the switch, terminal block, or wire.*

The unwanted resistance is proportional to the voltage shown. For example, a reading of 6 volts on a 12-volt circuit indicates that the resistance is half the total resistance in the circuit. In other words, it is equal to the resistance of the equipment in the circuit, and the equipment will receive only half of its rated amperage. A reading of 3 volts indicates a resistance of 25% of the total resistance in the circuit; the equipment will receive only 75% of its rated amps.

Put another way, if a voltage test across the input and output terminals of a piece of *operating* equipment reveals less than battery voltage, *we have unwanted resistance somewhere else in the circuit due to inadequate wiring or poor connections and switches.* The unwanted resistance is proportional to the extent of the voltage loss at the equipment. It may be on either the hot side or the ground side of the equipment.

Many pieces of equipment (e.g., lights) will run perfectly well with a 10% voltage drop: Assuming a fully charged battery with an open-circuit voltage of 12.6 volts, the voltage across the input and output leads to the equipment *when it is switched on* will read 11.3 volts. But other equipment is sensitive to voltage drop, notably voltage regulators (see Chapter 1), some electronics, and electric motors (which may suffer a serious loss of power; the number one cause of DC motor failure is low voltage). *Boat circuits should be designed to limit voltage drop to a maximum of 3% at the equipment* (e.g., given a fully charged battery at 12.6 volts, a voltage reading of 12.2 volts *at the equipment when in use*). The major causes of unwanted voltage drop are poor connections and inadequate wiring (see below).

Circuit with multiple switches and a fuse. Now let us extend our circuit one more time and add a distribution panel with a breaker, another switch for the piece of equipment, and a fuse.

There is really nothing new here, just an elaboration of the previous situation. To make a circuit, all switches must be closed and the fuse operative. Any voltage drop across a *closed* switch or a fuse indicates unwanted resistance; the higher the voltage, the more the resistance. Anything less than system voltage across the terminals of the equipment likewise reveals unwanted

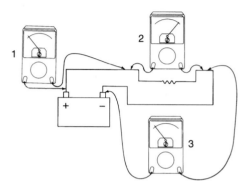

Figure 3-12. **Voltage readings.** In a healthy circuit meter 1 will show no voltage reading, meter 2 will read the system voltage, and meter 3 will again show no voltage.

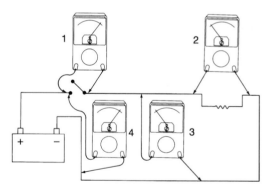

Figure 3-13. **Voltage readings.** Meters 1 and 4 should both show the full system voltage. Meters 2 and 3 should read 0 volts.

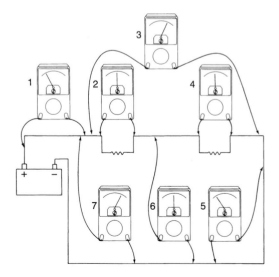

Figure 3-14. **Voltage readings.** There are two resistances in series, each of which (meters 2 and 4) will show a voltage drop of less than the total system voltage. Meter 3 will show the system voltage, as should meter 7. Meter 6 should give the same reading as meter 4, and meters 1 and 5 should read 0 volts. One of the two resistances is unwanted (a faulty switch, for example), and these tests will find it.

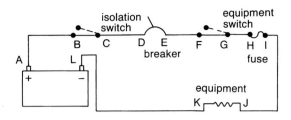

Test sequence (left to right)

Readings	A to L	A to B	B to C	C to L	C to D	D to E	E to L	E to F	F to G	G to L	G to H	H to I	I to L	I to J	J to K	K to L
Battery check; should read about 12.6 volts	•															
Should be no reading. To be certain, switch down progressively to the lowest voltage scale on the meter. Low reading indicates unwanted resistance; 12.6 volts, a break in the line.		•			•			•			•			•		•
Should be no reading. To check, switch down to the meter's lowest scale again. Low reading indicates dirty or corroded switch terminals or points, or too small a switch; 12.6 volts, an open switch or, in H to I, a blown fuse.			•			•			•			•				
Should be 12.6 volts. No reading indicates an open switch; or in I to L, a blown fuse. Less than 12.6 volts in C to L, a voltage drop between A and C. Less than 12.6 volts in J to K indicates unwanted voltage drop somewhere in the circuit.				•			•			•			•		•	

resistance in the circuit, on either the hot or the ground side.

If there is no voltage or reduced voltage at the equipment, a comprehensive and logical procedure to test every part of the circuit would be to close all switches, check the fuse, and then test for voltage following the 16 tests in Figure 3-15. Naturally no one wants to run through such an involved procedure, so what we need are a few simple steps to narrow down the location of a problem.

Simplified troubleshooting procedure with a voltmeter. If a piece of electrical equipment fails to operate, or operates at below par, *it should be turned on* (if this is not safe or possible, see Troubleshooting with an Ohmmeter below) and the voltage checked *across the power leads*. This will yield one of three results (Troubleshooting Chart 3-1):

- The meter shows system voltage. In this case, the equipment itself is at fault—most likely a blown fuse, poor connection, or burnout (for further diagnosis see Troubleshooting with an Ohmmeter).

- The meter shows less than system voltage. There are three possibilities: The battery is flat; there is a *short circuit* (see below) or partial short in the load, which is dragging down the voltage on the battery; or else there is a voltage drop in the circuit. In all cases the equipment may be working, but at below par (motors run slowly, lights are dim, and electronic equipment is subject to random errors). To distinguish the three situations, *the load should be left "on," while the voltage is tested across the battery posts.*

If the voltage is the *same* at the battery as at the load, the entire system is being dragged

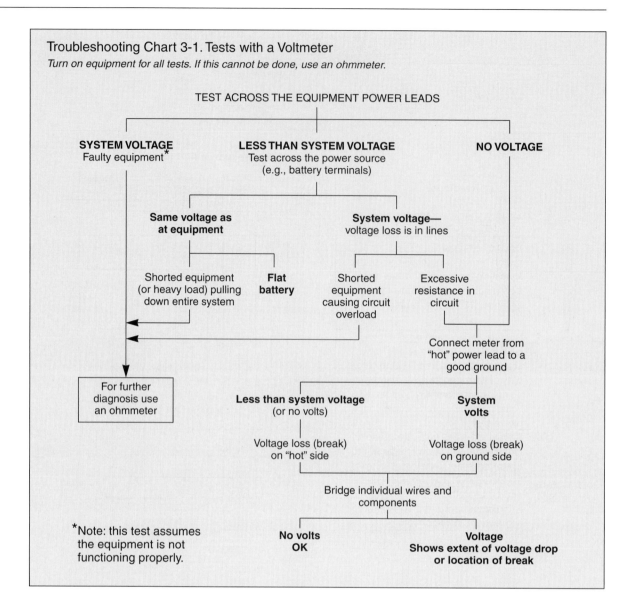

Troubleshooting Chart 3-1. Tests with a Voltmeter

Turn on equipment for all tests. If this cannot be done, use an ohmmeter.

TEST ACROSS THE EQUIPMENT POWER LEADS

SYSTEM VOLTAGE
Faulty equipment*

LESS THAN SYSTEM VOLTAGE
Test across the power source
(e.g., battery terminals)

NO VOLTAGE

**Same voltage as
at equipment**

System voltage—
voltage loss is in lines

Shorted equipment
(or heavy load) pulling
down entire system

**Flat
battery**

Shorted
equipment
causing circuit
overload

Excessive
resistance in
circuit

For further
diagnosis use
an ohmmeter

Connect meter from
"hot" power lead to a
good ground

Less than system voltage
(or no volts)

**System
volts**

Voltage loss (break)
on "hot" side

Voltage loss (break)
on ground side

*Note: this test assumes
the equipment is not
functioning properly.

Bridge individual wires and
components

**No volts
OK**

**Voltage
Shows extent of voltage drop
or location of break**

down, but without voltage drop—the battery is probably flat, but if not, the equipment has a short (the exception being very-heavy-draw DC items, such as a starter motor or electric windlass, which can be expected to pull even a healthy 12-volt DC system down to as low as 10.5 volts, at which point the voltage should stabilize for at least 15 seconds before falling any lower). If, on the other hand, the voltage at the power source remains at or near system voltage while it *falls* at the load, there is a voltage drop on the circuit.

The source of the voltage drop can once again be narrowed down by connecting the meter from the equipment positive lead to a known good ground (J to L in Figure 3-15). *With the load "on,"* if the meter shows *less than system voltage,* there is a voltage loss on the *positive* side. If the meter shows *system*

voltage, the loss is on the *negative* side. *There may be losses on both sides!* The voltage loss can be further isolated by using the meter leads to bridge every length of wire and individual component (switches, fuses, and terminal blocks) in the faulty side of the circuit. If at any time the meter gives a reading, this indicates the extent of the voltage drop in this part of the circuit.

Resistive wires need renewing with properly sized marine-rated cable (see later in this chapter). Resistive connections need to be undone, cleaned, refastened and coated with a corrosion inhibitor. You can sometimes make resistive switches and breakers serviceable by switching them on and off repeatedly, or if this fails, by cleaning the points with a fine file or wet-and-dry sandpaper (400 to 600 grit); otherwise they will have to be replaced.

Understanding and Troubleshooting Electrical Circuits;
Proper Installation Practices

- The meter shows no voltage. There is a break in the circuit, most likely a switch or breaker is "off", or a fuse is blown, but if not there is some other discontinuity such as a broken wire. To determine on which side of the load (hot side or ground side) the break lies, *with all switches "on,"* connect the meter from *the equipment positive lead to a good ground* (such as the negative battery post if this can be reached—i.e., J to L in Figure 3-15). If the meter now shows *system voltage*, the break is on the *negative* side; if it still shows *no voltage,* the break is on the *positive* side. To further narrow down the break, use the meter leads to bridge every individual length of wire and component (switches, fuses, and terminal blocks) in the offending side of the circuit. As noted earlier, this should produce readings of 0 volts; when the meter reads system voltage, the break in the circuit is being bridged.

Limitations of a voltmeter. To be effective many voltage tests, particularly voltage-drop tests, must be made with a circuit *under load,* but sometimes it is just not possible to turn on the relevant equipment to make the tests (for example, if a *short circuit* keeps tripping a breaker or there has been an electrical fire). In this case an ohmmeter is the appropriate troubleshooting tool. In addition it has, as we will see, a specific application in troubleshooting electrical equipment itself.

Troubleshooting with an Ohmmeter

An ohmmeter can be used to duplicate many of the procedures described for a voltmeter. But, first, remember that *when using an ohmmeter the circuit or equipment being tested must ALWAYS be electrically isolated from the battery or other power source.*

If a piece of equipment fails to run, placing the meter probes at either end of the positive supply circuit and then the negative circuit will reveal any problem in the circuit (Troubleshooting Chart 3-2). A *break* in the circuit will produce a reading of *infinite* ohms; *excessive resistance,* causing voltage drop, will show up as a *specific ohms* reading; and a *good resistance-free circuit* will give a reading of 0 ohms (or very near 0 ohms—sensitive meters will produce a low ohms reading, particularly on circuits rated for a low load and therefore using small-gauge wires).

Breaks and high resistance in a circuit can also be isolated in much the same way as with a voltmeter by bridging individual lengths of wire and components (switches, fuses, and terminal blocks) in turn. *Any break will show up as a reading of infinite ohms; excessive resistance will show as a significant ohms reading.*

Checking equipment. Beyond these uses, an ohmmeter has other useful functions all its own (Troubleshooting Chart 3-3). For example, if preliminary testing indicates a problem with a specific piece of equipment, the internal resistance of the equipment can be checked by testing across its input leads (with any internal fuses in place, and any *equipment-mounted* switch—*not* the power switch—turned "on"). Some resistance is to be expected; how much depends on the nature of the equipment, with low-power items showing a higher resistance than heavy-duty equipment.

In theory, if the amp draw of the equipment is known the precise resistance to be expected can be calculated by using Ohm's Law (resistance = voltage ÷ amperage—see page 79). In practice, however, many resistances are not

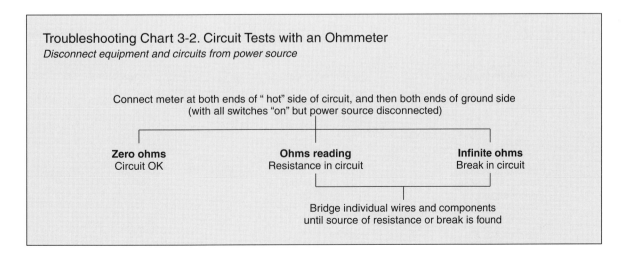

Troubleshooting Chart 3-2. Circuit Tests with an Ohmmeter
Disconnect equipment and circuits from power source

Connect meter at both ends of " hot" side of circuit, and then both ends of ground side
(with all switches "on" but power source disconnected)

| **Zero ohms** | **Ohms reading** | **Infinite ohms** |
| Circuit OK | Resistance in circuit | Break in circuit |

Bridge individual wires and components
until source of resistance or break is found

Troubleshooting Chart 3-3. Equipment Tests with an Ohmmeter

Disconnect equipment and test across its input leads

Zero ohms	**Ohms reading**	**Infinite ohms**
Internal short (except for heavy-draw DC equipment—see text)	Check against known resistance of equipment*	Open circuit: check fuses, switches, brushes and internal wiring (for breaks)

*Note: Many resistances are not what you would expect from a strict application of Ohm's law (R = E ÷ I). Incandescent lightbulbs, for example, measure much lower than their operating resistance, which rises as the filament heats up.

---

what might be expected, particularly incandescent lightbulbs and electric motors, which for different reasons tend to measure low (lightbulbs several times lower than expected; when they warm up, their resistance increases dramatically). In any case, most times precise resistance readings are not needed.

A reading of *infinite* ohms indicates an *open circuit* inside the equipment: a lightbulb or heating element is burned out; an electric motor may simply have a blown fuse, have a problem with its brushes, or a dirty commutator (Chapter 6), but otherwise it is also burned out. A reading of *0* ohms indicates a *dead short* (except on certain very-heavy-draw DC motors, such as a starter motor, which have such low internal resistances that only a good-quality meter will differentiate between a normal resistance and a short).

Short circuits. This matter of shorts deserves more attention. A *short circuit is a direct connec-* tion from the hot side of a circuit to the ground side, bypassing the load itself. It can be a minor current leak or a *dead* short, in which case very high currents will flow. In the latter case, *if the circuit is not properly protected with a fuse or circuit breaker, it is likely to catch fire. Note that the fire may well NOT be at the source of the short, but instead will occur at the most resistive part of the new (short) circuit*—generally the smallest-gauge wire in the circuit—since this is where the excessive current flow will generate the most heat. *Replacing the burned wire will not resolve the problem.*

An ohmmeter is the perfect tool for tracing shorts (Troubleshooting Chart 3-4). It will show a circuit *(continuity)* where none should exist. Given a short or a suspected current leak (for example, if the batteries die slowly when no equipment is turned on), the circuit to be tested is *disconnected from its power source*, and the load is disconnected from the circuit. The equipment is tested as above. If this fails to reveal a

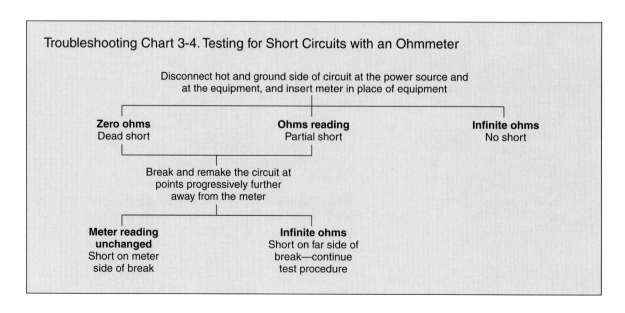

Troubleshooting Chart 3-4. Testing for Short Circuits with an Ohmmeter

Disconnect hot and ground side of circuit at the power source and at the equipment, and insert meter in place of equipment

Zero ohms	**Ohms reading**	**Infinite ohms**
Dead short	Partial short	No short

Break and remake the circuit at points progressively further away from the meter

Meter reading unchanged	**Infinite ohms**
Short on meter side of break	Short on far side of break—continue test procedure

problem, *with the circuit still disconnected from the power source, and the equipment still disconnected from the circuit*, put all switches and circuit breakers in the "on" position and test from any part of the hot side of the circuit to any part of the ground side—the terminals where the equipment was disconnected are generally the most accessible place (Figure 3-16A). The meter should show *infinite ohms. Any other reading indicates a short; the lower the reading the more serious the short.*

The source of a short can be further narrowed down by leaving the meter connected across the wires to the equipment and progressively breaking the circuit (turning off switches, pulling fuses, or undoing terminals) further and further back from the meter (Figures 3-16B and 3-16C). If, after a break is made, the meter reading is *unchanged, the short is on the meter side of the break*; if the meter jumps to *infinity*, the short is on the *other* side. In the latter case the break should be closed and another break made further from the meter. If the meter reading now remains unchanged, the short is between the two break points; if it jumps to infinity once again, the short is still further back and the test procedure needs to be continued.

Ground Faults ("Earth" Leaks)

One of the more insidious problems on board is leakage of very small amounts of current through poor wiring, switches, connections, and equipment insulation to ground. Such leaks slowly drain batteries and can also contribute to devastating stray-current corrosion (more on this later). Leaks to ground are an ever present possibility in the damp marine environment, especially from bilge pumps and other equipment or wiring located in damp areas of the boat or actually in water.

To locate ground faults, look for current flow to ground that bypasses normal circuits but is not normally great enough to show up as a short circuit. Depending on where in a circuit the leak is, it may occur either only when equipment is switched on or all the time.

Preliminary test. Switch off absolutely all equipment and *disconnect any solar panels*, but leave the battery isolation switch "on." Disconnect the positive cable from the battery and connect a multimeter on an appropriate scale for 12 volts DC between the battery post and the cable (Troubleshooting Chart 3-5). *The voltmeter should give no reading.* If it reads 12 volts, one of two things is happening:

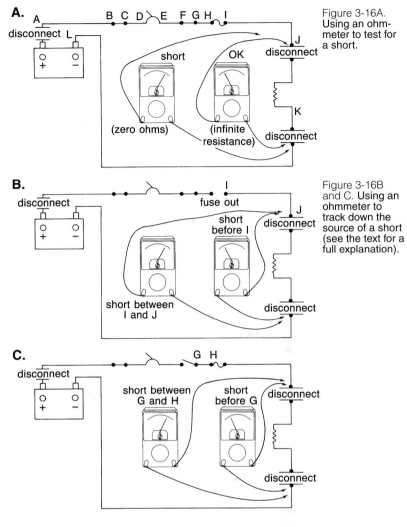

Figure 3-16A. Using an ohmmeter to test for a short.

Figure 3-16B and C. Using an ohmmeter to track down the source of a short (see the text for a full explanation).

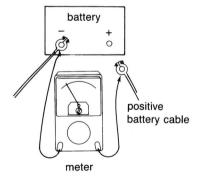

Figure 3-17. Pinpointing a ground leak with an ohmmeter. Disconnect the cable clamp from the positive terminal, and connect the meter between the disconnected positive cable clamp and the negative terminal. Readings may be interpreted as follows: less than 10 ohms = equipment left on; 10 to 1,000 ohms = serious ground leak; 1,000 to 10,000 ohms = minor ground leak; greater than 10,000 ohms = little or no leak.

1. One or more circuits are still on, providing a path to ground. Double-check all circuits.
2. There is a ground leak between the battery and the various switches and breakers that are turned "off" (depending on the type of meter, this leak may be anywhere from a fraction of a milliamp on up).

Using an Ohmmeter to Test a Masthead Light Circuit

There are some circuits, such as masthead lights, that are inaccessible for much of their length. Isolating faults can be difficult. The ohmmeter will make things much easier. First, disconnect the circuit at the base of the mast and test across the two mast leads. A very low (close to 0 ohms) reading (unusual) indicates a short inside the mast or at the masthead; a low ohms reading (typically 10 to 20 ohms) indicates that both the in-mast wiring and the bulb are good—the problem lies elsewhere; an infinite ohms reading indicates a break in the circuit inside the mast or at the masthead.

If the ohmmeter gives an infinite reading, twist the two wires together, go to the masthead, and remove the bulb. Test the bulb across its two terminals—an infinite reading shows a blown bulb, a low reading tells us that the bulb is working, in which case a test is made across the two wire terminals at the masthead. Since these wires have been shorted together at the base of the mast, this last test should show a low ohms reading—if it is infinite, there is a break in the mast circuit (check for dirty or broken terminals at the light fixture before condemning the in-mast wiring).

Many navigation lights on new boats now use quartz halogen lights since they provide more light for less amp draw. These bulbs are extremely delicate and must be handled with care (especially at $10 to $15 a lamp!). *Do not touch the bulb*; always grip it in a piece of paper. The bulbs are simply pulled out of their sockets or pushed in—no twisting is needed. Each quartz halogen bulb has two wires that stick straight out; be sure the wires are straight before fitting a new bulb. At the base of the bulb is a small indentation that will mate up with a spring clip in the fixture to hold the bulb in place.

Note that quartz halogen bulbs are sensitive to high voltages, even the elevated voltages common with multistep regulators. *Given a charging device regulated to anything over 14.2 volts, it might be better to stick with incandescent bulbs* (these will also suffer a decline in their life expectancy, but since they are so much cheaper this is less significant).

Note: With an aluminum mast, when testing the wiring at the base of the mast make an additional test from each wire to the mast itself. Anything other than infinite resistance indicates some sort of a short to the mast. This could cause serious corrosion.

The meter shows a leak. If the meter gives a reading, it should be connected between *the disconnected cable clamp* (NOT the battery post) and the negative battery post (Figure 3-17), and then switched to its most sensitive ohms (resistance) function (R × 1 scale on an analog meter). The meter is now registering any circuit to ground within the boat's wiring.

A reading of less than 10 ohms indicates a piece of equipment left on; 10 to 1,000 ohms, a low-drain piece of equipment left on or a serious leak; 1,000 to 10,000 ohms (the meter may need to be switched to the R × 100 scale), a minor leak; and anything over 10,000 ohms, an insignificant leak.

The magnitude of any leakage current can be found with a meter capable of measuring DC amps. However, many multimeters are limited to a maximum of 250 milliamps, in which case the meter should not be used in this mode if the resistance reading was less than 50 ohms. A meter with a 10 amps capability can be used with resistance readings as low as 1.5 ohms.

Place the meter, set to read DC amps, back in line between the positive battery post and the

disconnected cable clamp. If an analog meter shows no measurable deflection of its needle, progressively switch it down to lower milliamps scales until the leakage current can be measured. Less than 1mA is insignificant; 1 to 10mA, a minor leak; 10mA to 1 amp, a major leak or some equipment left on; over 1 amp, equipment left on.

Isolating leaks. To track down a leak, first trip the battery isolation switch. If the leak persists, it is on *the battery side* of the switch, most likely in some piece of equipment wired directly to the battery. In this case, disconnect the individual wires to the battery clamp one at a time until the leak disappears, indicating which is the offending circuit (Figure 3-18, Test 1).

If, on the other hand, the leak disappears when the battery isolation switch is tripped, the leak is "downstream" of the switch. Isolating it becomes rather more involved. First, the isolation switch is turned back "on." From the switch there is likely to be a positive feed to a distribution panel, at which point most circuits will have either a fuse or a circuit breaker. If any

Understanding and Troubleshooting Electrical Circuits;
Proper Installation Practices

equipment has been turned off at the equipment, but its circuit breaker is still "on," now is the time to trip the breaker or, in a fused circuit, to pull the fuse. If at any time the leak disappears, the offending circuit has been found.

If the leak persists, the next step is to disconnect the hot wires to any circuits not on a circuit breaker or fuse (for example, the starter motor and starting circuit—Figure 3-18, Test 2). If disconnecting a cable makes no difference to the meter reading, this cable should be reconnected before moving to the next. If disconnecting a circuit causes a partial drop in the meter reading, this indicates some leakage current in this circuit, but also that there is more than one leak.

If a leak still persists after all circuit breakers have been tripped, fuses pulled, and unbreakered or unfused circuits disconnected, one of the panel breakers must be leaking, or the panel itself is leaking. Breakers and panel wiring can be checked with an ohmmeter (set to the R × 1 scale on an analog meter). A breaker that is "off" should produce a reading of infinite ohms across its two terminals, as should any test between the hot side of the panel's wiring and a good ground (for example, the negative bus bar).

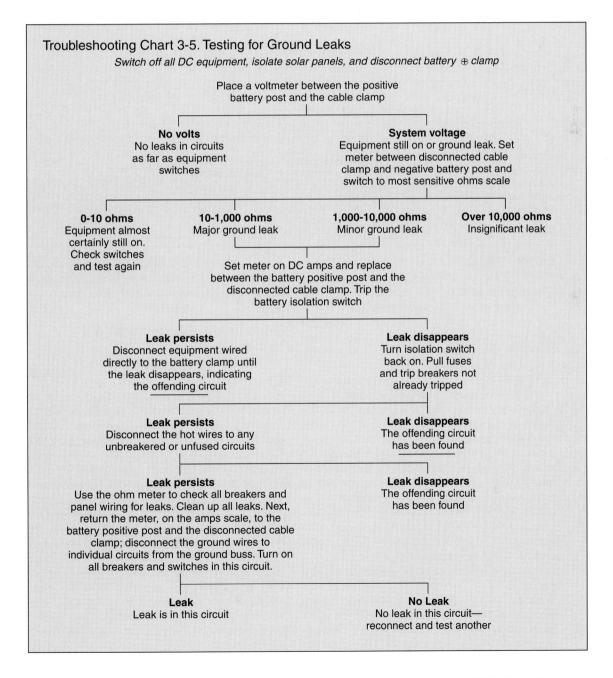

Troubleshooting Chart 3-5. Testing for Ground Leaks

Switch off all DC equipment, isolate solar panels, and disconnect battery ⊕ clamp

Place a voltmeter between the positive battery post and the cable clamp

No volts
No leaks in circuits as far as equipment switches

System voltage
Equipment still on or ground leak. Set meter between disconnected cable clamp and negative battery post and switch to most sensitive ohms scale

0-10 ohms
Equipment almost certainly still on. Check switches and test again

10-1,000 ohms
Major ground leak

1,000-10,000 ohms
Minor ground leak

Over 10,000 ohms
Insignificant leak

Set meter on DC amps and replace between the battery positive post and the disconnected cable clamp. Trip the battery isolation switch

Leak persists
Disconnect equipment wired directly to the battery clamp until the leak disappears, indicating the offending circuit

Leak disappears
Turn isolation switch back on. Pull fuses and trip breakers not already tripped

Leak persists
Disconnect the hot wires to any unbreakered or unfused circuits

Leak disappears
The offending circuit has been found

Leak persists
Use the ohm meter to check all breakers and panel wiring for leaks. Clean up all leaks. Next, return the meter, on the amps scale, to the battery positive post and the disconnected cable clamp; disconnect the ground wires to individual circuits from the ground buss. Turn on all breakers and switches in this circuit.

Leak disappears
The offending circuit has been found

Leak
Leak is in this circuit

No Leak
No leak in this circuit— reconnect and test another

Figure 3-18. Testing for ground leaks. At the start of each test, set the meter to the highest amps scale and then progressively switch it down to see if there is a leak.
Test 1: Battery isolation switch "off"; all circuits connected to the battery clamp (and therefore bypassing the distribution panel) turned "off." If there is a leak, disconnect the individual wires from the battery clamp to find the offending circuit.
Test 2: Battery isolation switch "on"; all other switches "off." If there is a leak, disconnect unfused or unbreakered cables (e.g., the engine cranking cable) at the isolation switch or panel. If the leak disappears, it is in the circuit just disconnected.
Test 3: Battery isolation switch "on"; individual ground cable for a given circuit disconnected at the negative bus bar; all switches and breakers *for the disconnected circuit only* turned "on." Any leak represents a leak to ground in this circuit.

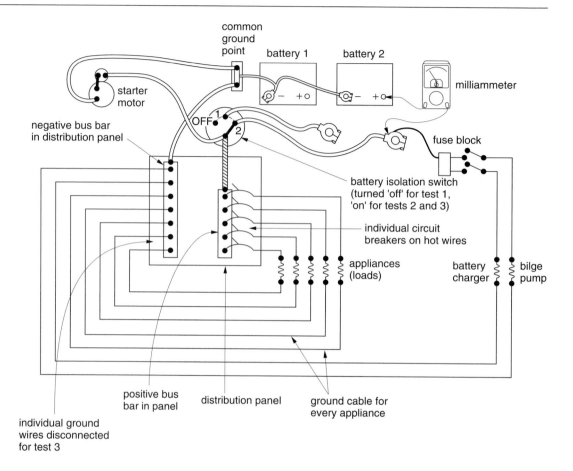

common ground point
battery 1
battery 2
milliammeter
starter motor
negative bus bar in distribution panel
OFF
battery isolation switch (turned 'off' for test 1, 'on' for tests 2 and 3)
fuse block
individual circuit breakers on hot wires
appliances (loads)
battery charger
bilge pump
positive bus bar in panel
distribution panel
ground cable for every appliance
individual ground wires disconnected for test 3

Further tests. The tests to date will reveal ground leaks in unbreakered circuits and in other circuits *up to the various equipment switches, breakers, or fuses, but not beyond this point.* If the equipment is switched at the distribution panel (much of it is on modern boats) *this may leave the greater part of the boat's circuits untested.*

To test for ground leaks in the rest of the circuits, you will have to disconnect the ground lead to each circuit in turn at the bus bar in the distribution panel (Figure 3-18, Test 3). If more than one circuit shares the same switch or breaker, the grounds to all the relevant circuits will need disconnecting from the negative bus bar. Replace any fuses that were previously removed from the circuit being tested, and turn on all switches and circuit breakers in this circuit. Set the meter to the amps scale and once again insert it between the battery positive post and the disconnected cable clamp.

Any current flow indicates a leak to ground in the disconnected circuits(s), finding its way back to the battery through other (still connected) circuits. If the path to ground includes underwater hardware (for example, through bilge water to an engine block, the propeller shaft, the propeller, and then a grounded radio ground plate), corrosion is likely. The leak needs to be tracked down and cleared up.

Don't Leave Port Without a Multimeter

There is nothing in these procedures that is terribly complicated. Rather, it is a matter of being logical and methodical. With more complex circuits and difficult-to-isolate problems, it often pays to begin by sketching on a piece of paper the circuit and all its components, jotting down on this sketch the tests you make. It then becomes a relatively simple matter to draw the correct conclusions from the test results.

It is a rare electrical problem that cannot be cracked in this fashion, using either a voltmeter or an ohmmeter. The more you use a multimeter, the more adept you become in its handling, and the more versatile a tool it turns out to be. This is particularly true of the ohms function, which is frequently poorly understood and therefore rarely used. The multimeter is one of the key components of my toolbox—I would never leave port without one!

Understanding and Troubleshooting Electrical Circuits;
Proper Installation Practices

AC Circuits

Alternating current circuits in their simplest form also have a *hot* and a *ground* side as do DC circuits, although the ground wire is known as the *neutral*. Instead of a battery, as a power source there is a generator, either ashore or on board, or sometimes a DC to AC inverter (see Chapter 5). The hot wire can be considered the electrical supply side of a load; the neutral wire is the return path to the generator or inverter. But then we have a refinement. *At every shoreside generator a connection is made from the neutral terminal to a buried metal plate or rod (Figure 3-19). What this does is hold the neutral side of the circuit at the earth's potential.* When we measure voltage on an AC system *we are measuring the differential between the hot side of the system and the earth's potential (ground potential, sometimes simply referred to as earth)*. The hot side of the circuit is known as the *ungrounded* side; the neutral side as the *grounded* side.

The principal differences between this basic AC circuit and a DC circuit are:

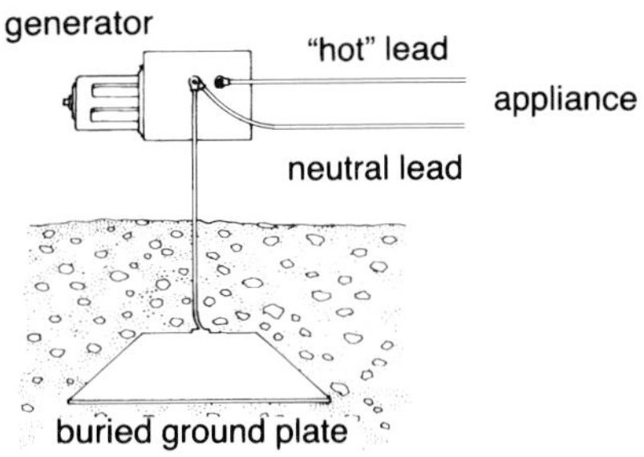

1. The voltage on the AC circuit continuously alternates between positive and negative in relation to ground potential. To all intents and purposes, we can ignore this fact as far as this chap-

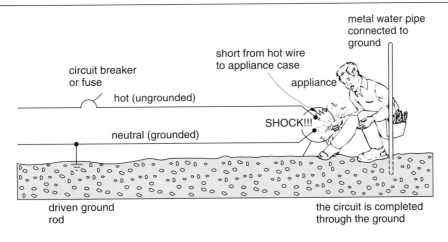

Figure 3-19. Basic AC generator setup.

ter is concerned (more on this in Chapter 5).

2. The voltage on the AC system is typically many times higher than that on a DC system—in the USA a nominal 120 or 240 volts; in the UK 240 volts. *THESE VOLTAGES ARE POTENTIALLY LETHAL, SO SAFETY ISSUES ARE A PRIMARY CONCERN WHEN DEALING WITH AC CIRCUITS.*

The Importance of Grounding

When a house is wired, the two wires—hot (ungrounded) and neutral (grounded)—are run to all fixtures and appliances. The incoming electrical box is considered to be the *generating source* for the house, and as such the neutral cir-

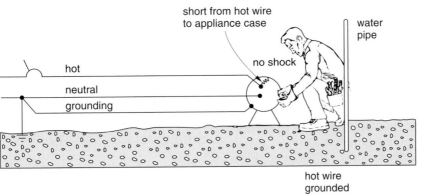

Figure 3-20A. **Two-wire AC circuit.** An appliance has an internal short which has made its case 'live'. Because there is no direct path to ground the circuit breaker has not tripped. A person coming into contact with the appliance completes the path to ground and receives a shock.

Figure 3-20B. **Three-wire AC circuit.** The short-circuit current is being safely conducted to ground by the grounding cable. If the short is severe enough, the high current flow will trip the circuit breaker. The person, who forms a less conductive path to ground, is protected.

Figure 3-21A. Household electrical circuits (USA color code shown). The neutral and ground circuits are tied together at the main panelboard.

Figure 3-21B. Shipboard AC circuits. The neutral and ground circuits are not tied together on the boat—only on shore. The grounding circuit should be connected to the boat's ground as shown.

Figure 3-21C. An onboard generator has its neutral and grounding wires tied together *at the generator case and nowhere else.*

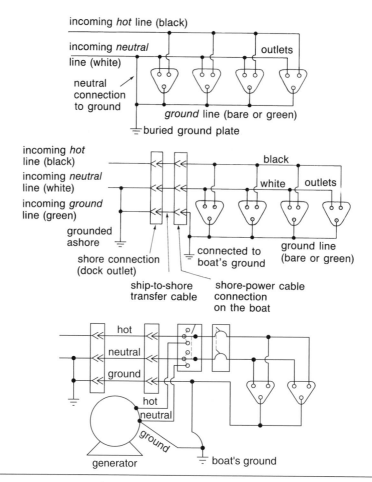

cuits are once again connected to a buried pipe—a *driven ground rod*—at this point, just as at the power station.

In the old days that was it. But if a fault developed such that a piece of equipment became "hot" to touch, anyone coming into contact with this equipment completed the circuit to ground and received a severe shock (Figure 3-20A). What made the situation particularly dangerous was that in many instances the *fault current* could not run to ground *until human or other contact completed the circuit.* In such circumstances fuses and breakers provide no protection: Without a path to ground, the kind of currents necessary to blow the fuse or trip the breaker simply do not flow—the fault remains undetected until the damage is done.

To improve system safety, a third *grounding* wire has now been added to AC circuits (note the term *grounding* is used to distinguish this wire from the neutral or *grounded* wire). The grounding wire is connected to the external cases of appliances and is in turn connected at the power source (incoming panelboard) to the neutral wire, and thus to the driven ground rod (Figure 3-21A). In normal circumstances this grounding wire carries no current, but *should some sort of a*

fault develop that makes an appliance "hot" to touch, this wire will immediately conduct the fault current safely to ground (Figure 3-20B). What is more, *if the leak is a serious one, such as in a short circuit, as soon as it occurs the grounding wire will allow high levels of current to flow, which will immediately blow any fuse or trip a breaker.*

This grounding circuit is thus *a normally redundant path to ground, paralleling the neutral circuit.* It provides an essential degree of protection against many common electrical faults. Rather like a seat belt or an air bag in a car, it doesn't do any good until a problem develops, but then it might save a life. Any break in the grounding circuit, such as would be caused by cutting the ground pin off an extension cord (a common sight around boatyards!) or by a badly corroded ground connection on a shore-power cord, potentially leaves us with the old-style two-wire circuit that provides fault current with no safe path to ground.

Safety Versus Corrosion

For a boat connected to shore-side power the dockside receptacle is, in effect, the power

Understanding and Troubleshooting Electrical Circuits; Proper Installation Practices

As stated in the text, the neutral and grounding wires of an AC circuit are connected to a driven ground rod *at the power source*. In the case of shore-side power this is considered to be *the dockside* (Figure 3-21A); with onboard generators and inverters it is *the generator or inverter* (Figure 3-21C); with an isolation transformer it is *the secondary winding of the transformer* (see page 103). *There is never any connection between the neutral and grounding wires at any other point.* This is important for a couple of reasons:

The neutral is a full current-carrying conductor. Were it to be grounded in more than one place, small differences in ground potential, or perhaps undue resistance in the neutral circuit itself, might induce some of the return current to find a path to ground through the grounding circuit, creating a potential shock hazard (Figure 3-22).

In the case of a shore-power circuit, if the neutral is grounded on board and the boat is then connected with reverse polarity (either through improper wiring ashore or on board, or through inserting a two-pronged shore-power cord the wrong way around), *any neutral-to-ground connection on board the boat will cause the grounding circuit to become hot (Figure 3-22). If this circuit is connected to the*

DC negative (as it should be—see the text), the entire DC negative circuit will become hot, creating a hazardous environment both on board and in the surrounding water. Fuses and circuit breakers will likely provide no protection against potential shocks since in most cases the resistance of the surrounding water will not allow the passage of sufficient current to blow a fuse or trip a circuit breaker. (If the total resistance of the path through the water is above 10 ohms, for example, this will limit the current flow from a 120-volt circuit to 12 amps, which is not enough to trip a typical 15-amp breaker but is more than enough to kill someone.)

Note that if a boat has two shore-power connections (as many powerboats and large yachts do) the two neutral circuits on board must also be isolated from each other. Should the neutrals be connected and one of the shore-power cords be plugged in with reverse polarity, all wires on the other circuit would be live!

It is worth repeating that shore-power-based AC circuits never have the neutral grounded on board. Finally, it should be noted that for historical reasons some domestic electric clothes dryers and electric stoves do have a neutral-to-ground connection on the appliance frame. If such an appliance is used on board, this connection must be cut.

Figure 3-22. The neutral and grounding circuits have been improperly wired together on this boat. There is a resistive connection in the neutral circuit. As a result, the return current from the appliances will now find an alternative (lower resistance) path to ground through the grounding circuit. Since this is (correctly) tied to the DC ground, it can create a shock hazard both on board and for swimmers. If the boat is connected to shore-power with reverse polarity, the entire grounding system will be "hot."

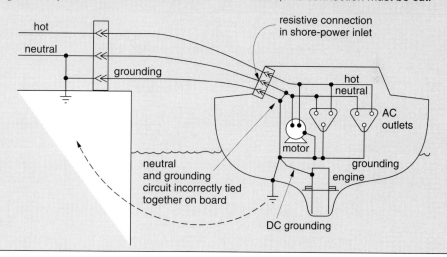

source. The neutral and grounding cables will be grounded to a driven metal rod somewhere near the dockside panel that contains the main overcurrent protection device (main circuit breaker). When the boat is plugged into shore-power, the neutral circuit on the boat and the grounding circuit are connected to their respective cables, and consequently both are grounded ashore at the point where the cables connect to the driven rod.

Just as in a house, if the case of an appliance becomes hot, the fault current will be conducted safely ashore via the grounding wire. Even in the damp marine environment we still have excellent protection against shock hazards. There is, however, a snag: The same green, or uninsulated, grounding wire that is providing such essential people protection may be contributing to galvanic corrosion. *This corrosion can take place even if the AC circuits are perfectly installed*

Swimmers Beware

Recently evidence has been mounting that some deaths around marinas that were classified as drownings were, in fact, caused by electric shocks. When improper or faulty grounding of either onboard or dockside wiring is combined with AC leaks to ground, enough current can be fed into the water to paralyze the muscles of a swimmer, resulting in a drowning that leaves no physical evidence of the causative shock.

When a person is in the water, it takes very little current to cause muscle spasms or seizure: Currents on the order of 50 milliamps (0.05 amps) sustained for 2 seconds, or 500 milliamps sustained for just 0.2 seconds, can, in certain circumstances, cause ventricular fibrillation; currents as low as 5 milliamps can cause muscle seizure. But for any current to be lethal it has always been assumed that there must be a significant voltage present: I am told there has never been a documented case of electrocution *on shore* with a voltage much below 50 volts.

However, it seems a different criterion is needed to determine dangerous voltage levels when the current is flowing through the water. For the purposes of an illustration let us assume a boat that is connected to shore-side power using an extension cord from which the grounding pin has been cut off. A piece of onboard AC equipment, which is in some way or another grounded to the DC negative (as it should be if the boat is properly wired—see the text) develops a short. The fault current, denied a path to ground through the normal ground wire, runs to ground through a bonded underwater fitting.

The fault current will develop a *field* around the boat. At the fitting that is discharging the current into the water the voltage will be at the full fault voltage (as high as 240 volts). Resistance within the water will cause the voltage to decrease the further the distance from the boat until ground potential—i.e., 0 volts—is reached. Depending on the water's resistance and other factors, there will be a voltage *gradient,* creating a declining voltage the farther one moves from the boat. This gradient can be measured in *volts per foot (or meter).*

A swimmer entering this electrical field will have one part of his or her body at one voltage potential, and other parts at another potential. If the voltage differential that is bridged is great enough, current will pass through the body. As a general rule of thumb it appears that *if the voltage gradient is above 2 volts per foot (6 volts per meter) the situation is potentially lethal.* When this figure is looked at in combination with those given above for potentially dangerous current levels, it becomes immediately apparent that *quite small leakage currents and voltages can be deadly.*

AC leaks into fresh or brackish water are considered to be more dangerous than the less resistive salt water. Leaks into salt water tend to follow the shortest path to ground, directly to the bottom or to adjacent vessels with well-grounded systems, whereas leaks in fresh water radiate out into the surrounding water from the fitting that is feeding the current into the water. (Note that in salt water there could still be a severe shock hazard for someone cleaning a boat bottom or checking the propeller or other hardware.)

---

and functioning faultlessly. It has, in fact, nothing to do with the AC system itself but is simply a parasitic problem that comes aboard with a proper AC installation.

What happens is this. Let's say two boats are lying alongside one another. Both are connected to shore-power, and are properly wired with the AC grounding circuit connected both ashore and also to the onboard DC negative and bonding system (more on this in Chapter 4). The underwater hardware on one boat is protected by zincs, but on the other it is not. In effect what we have is a giant battery: The zincs on one boat form the negative plate; bronze underwater fittings on the other boat form the positive plate; and the water in which the boats are floating is the electrolyte. As soon as both boats plug into shore-power the AC grounding wire completes the circuit between the two "battery terminals" (i.e., underwater hardware on the boats), *causing galvanically generated DC current to flow along the AC grounding wire* (Figure 3-23). The least noble (galvanically most active) metal will corrode (in this case the zincs—see Chapter 4). When the zincs are depleted, the next least noble metal (i.e., some underwater fitting) will start to go.

As long as a shore-power-based AC system is properly grounded, *if an unmodified AC system is plugged into shore-power, it will always invite corrosion. The problem is caused by precisely those steps deemed necessary to safeguard the people on board and swimmers in the water. We end up with an apparent conflict between people safety and boat protection.* The challenge is to find an acceptable response to this situation that sacrifices neither.

Understanding and Troubleshooting Electrical Circuits;
Proper Installation Practices

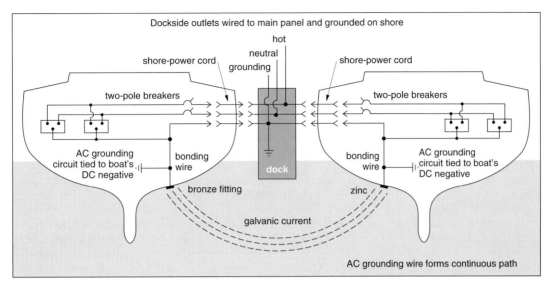

Dockside outlets wired to main panel and grounded on shore

hot
neutral
grounding

shore-power cord

shore-power cord

two-pole breakers

two-pole breakers

AC grounding circuit tied to boat's DC negative

bonding wire

dock

bonding wire

AC grounding circuit tied to boat's DC negative

bronze fitting

zinc

galvanic current

AC grounding wire forms continuous path

Figure 3-23. Two vessels connected to shore-power both have their grounding circuits properly grounded to the boat's ground. But now the AC grounding wire provides a direct electrical connection between the underwater hardware on both boats. The seawater surrounding the hardware is an electrolyte (an electrically conductive liquid). We have, in effect, a giant battery with two dissimilar metals immersed in an electrolyte and interconnected! Galvanic activity will cause a current to flow along the AC grounding wire; the most easily corroded metal will be steadily eaten away (see Chapter 4). *(Ocean Navigator)*

Breaking the galvanic circuit. From time to time an ill-conceived recommendation is made to cut the connection between the AC and DC grounding circuits. In theory, this isolates the AC grounding circuit from underwater hardware, breaking the path from shore to water for DC galvanic currents, while still maintaining the shore-side AC grounding connection for people protection. On the surface of things, this is a simple, cost-effective solution to the corrosion problem that does not compromise safety, but in reality *it can result in a highly dangerous situation that has almost certainly caused some deaths.*

There are at least three reasons why this is an unacceptable practice:

1. There are times when there may be a serious AC leak into the DC negative circuit, the most likely cause being a defective battery charger or a short between adjacent AC and DC wiring. *Without the AC grounding to DC negative connection, this fault current has no safe path back ashore.*

2. *Proper lightning protection demands that the AC grounding circuit and the DC negative circuit be held to the same voltage potential* in order to minimize the build-up of dangerous voltages in either circuit (Chapter 4). To do this effectively the two must be electrically interconnected.

3. Quite often, even if the AC grounding to DC negative connection were cut, *there would still be some other, unforeseen, path to the DC negative.* This might be through a piece of AC equipment that is itself in some way grounded to the DC system (many generators; air conditioners; nonmarine battery chargers; some water heaters—Figure 3-21C) or through onboard leaks between the two cir-

cuits. *The potential for corrosion would still exist but without the boatowner being aware of it,* with the result that proper preventive measures would not be taken.

The AC grounding to DC negative connection should never be cut. The only correct ways to galvanically isolate an AC circuit are with a *galvanic isolator* or an *isolation transformer.*

Galvanic isolators. These consist of little more than two sets of two diodes wired in parallel to conduct in opposite directions (Figure 3-24). It takes a certain voltage (typically around 1.0 volt) to make the diodes conductive. If a galvanic isolator is installed in the AC grounding wire, unless there is a leakage current or a stray DC current driven by a voltage in excess of 1.0 volt, the diodes simply will not conduct. In normal circumstances the isolator effectively breaks the grounding circuit. But in the event of a leakage current with a voltage above 1.0 volt, the diodes become conductive, ensuring the continuity of the grounding circuit.

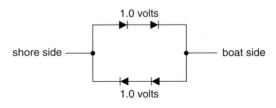

1.0 volts

shore side —————————————— boat side

1.0 volts

Figure 3-24. Basic galvanic isolator schematic. It takes a forward voltage around 0.5 volts to make each diode conduct, and therefore around 1.0 volt to make a pair of diodes in series conduct. As a result, these diodes will block voltages of up to 1.0 volt, whether they originate ashore or on the boat. Faced with voltages above 1.0 volt, the diodes start to conduct, providing a path for current in either direction.

It might seem that the best place to put a galvanic isolator is between the AC grounding and DC negative circuits (see position 1 in Figure 3-25A). In this position an isolator failure would not in any way compromise the integrity of the ship-to-shore grounding connection. However, as noted above, in reality it is often next to impossible to prevent some circuit or other from bypassing the isolator, rendering it completely ineffective (Figure 3-25B). The potential for corrosion will once again exist while the boatowner is under the illusion that the problem has been solved. Added to which, if an isolator installed in this position becomes open-circuited, and a short develops from an AC circuit into the DC circuits, the fault current will have no safe path back ashore (we have, in effect, condition 1 above). As a result the American Boat and Yacht Council standards require a galvanic isolator to be placed *in the incoming AC grounding wire* immediately downstream of the shore-power inlet (see position 2 in Figure 3-25A). It is then a simple matter to ensure that nothing bypasses the isolator (as long as *absolutely no wires, except the shore-power grounding wire, are connected to the shore-power side of the isolator*). If a boat has two shore-power inlets (as many powerboats and

larger yachts do) to be effective *there must be a separate isolator on each inlet.*

Should a galvanic isolator installed in the incoming AC grounding wire fail in the open-circuited position, the grounding circuit will be broken, voiding the protective function of the grounding wire. Alternatively, should the diodes fail in the conductive (shorted) position, there will be no protection against galvanic currents.

Given that diode failure in most instances is not externally visible, *it is essential to have a high-quality isolator with both a continuous-current rating and a short-circuit rating at least as high as that of the main breaker on the circuit in which it is installed* (in practice higher, since breakers typically trip at around 1.3 times their nominal current rating; it will soon be an ABYC standard to have isolators rated for at least the amperage rating of the shore-power outlet feeding the boat). On a USA 30-amp dockside outlet this means a continuous-current rating of at least 40 amps and a short-circuit rating of 3,000 amps; on a 50-amp outlet the relevant figures are 70 amps and 5,000 amps (the short-circuit current has to be sustained only for the time it takes to trip a circuit breaker). There are galvanic isolators that do not have this current-car-

Figure 3-25A. **Two possible locations for a galvanic isolator. Location 1 might seem best, but may end up with the isolator being bypassed (Figure 3-25B). It can also create a hazardous situation (see the text). Location 2 is required by the ABYC standards. However, should the isolator fail in the open-circuited mode, the boat will lose AC grounding protection; should it fail in the close-circuited mode, it will lose galvanic protection.** *(Ocean Navigator)*

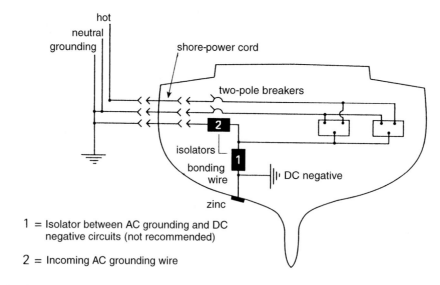

1 = Isolator between AC grounding and DC negative circuits (not recommended)

2 = Incoming AC grounding wire

Figure 3-25B. **A bonding circuit bypassing, and therefore negating, a galvanic isolator placed between the AC grounding circuit and the boat's ground.**

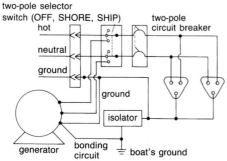

Understanding and Troubleshooting Electrical Circuits;
Proper Installation Practices

rying capability and as a result are potentially lethal—it is a case of buyer beware! The other factor to be considered is the temperature of the isolator when asked to carry these kinds of currents. Most isolators now on the market become dangerously hot—hot enough, at times, to set fire to surrounding hardware and laminates. By the time this is published the ABYC should have established standards governing isolator construction; only those that meet these standards should be used.

Beyond this, isolator design gets controversial.

The problem is that in the damp marine environment there is often a low-level AC leakage into the grounding circuit. This may be high enough to make the diodes conductive (above 1.0 volt) but low enough to remain undetected. In such cases the isolator is doing nothing to block galvanic currents.

One school of thought holds that a capacitor—a device that conducts AC but not DC—should be wired around the diodes. The capacitor will allow alternating currents of several amps and volts to be shorted to ground without the diodes

Simple Test Procedures for Grounding Circuits on Boats
without an isolation transformer

For people protection *it is essential to maintain an effective grounding connection between the boat and the dock.* To test, plug the shore-power cord into the boat but *not the dock,* turn off any onboard generator or AC/DC inverter, set a multimeter to its lowest (R × 1 on an analog meter) ohms function, and then touch the two probes to the grounding socket of any AC outlet on board and the grounding blade of the shore end of the cord (Test 1). There should be a low ohms reading. If not, the grounding circuit is faulty and must be fixed. (If a galvanic isolator is installed, the meter will give a higher ohms reading—see "Testing a Galvanic Isolator." The probes should be reversed and the test repeated. It should produce the same results in both directions.)

If the circuit passed this first test, keep the one meter probe on the grounding stud of the shore-power cord and touch the other to the

engine block (Test 2). There should be a low ohms reading (except with a galvanic isolator, when the results should be as above). If not, *the AC grounding to DC negative connection is faulty and should be fixed.*

With the shore-power cord still *unplugged,* any generator or inverter turned off and *switched out of the AC circuit* (this is important), and *all AC breakers turned on,* put one probe in any grounding socket of an onboard AC outlet and the other in any *neutral* socket (Test 3). There should be an infinite ohms reading (an open circuit; boats with an isolation transformer will show a dead short, i.e., 0 ohms.) If there is a low reading, the neutral and grounding circuits are incorrectly tied together on board and need to be separated (note that some polarity indicators will give a high ohms reading—above 25,000 ohms—rather than show an open circuit).

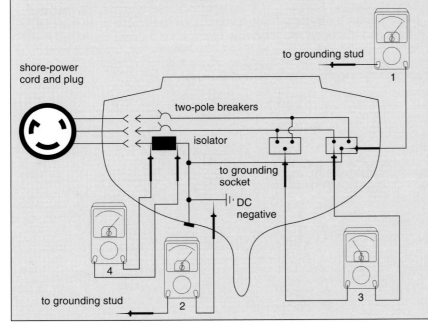

Figure 3-26. Test procedures for grounding circuits. *Unplug the shore end* of the shore-power cord, leaving the *boat end* plugged in and turn off any onboard generator or DC to AC inverter. Bring the cord aboard for easy access to the grounding lug. See the text for the test procedures. *(Ocean Navigator)*

to grounding stud

shore-power cord and plug

two-pole breakers

isolator

to grounding socket

DC negative

to grounding stud

conducting. In other words, the capacitor will maintain galvanic isolation up to higher AC leakage levels than the diodes alone, without compromising grounding safety. Once the carrying capacity of the capacitor is exceeded, the diodes will become conductive as with any other isolator.

The alternative viewpoint is that the boatowner needs to be aware of, and take steps to cure, any leakage current, either AC or DC, driven by a voltage in excess of 1.0 volt. According to this view, the correct method of isolator installation is not to include a capacitor, but to combine the isolator with a meter or warning device that will alert the boatowner to any leakage voltage high

enough to make the diodes conductive. Such devices are readily available but rarely used.

There is little doubt that the galvanic isolators with capacitors provide better protection than those without; the drawback is cost (they are typically two to three times more expensive, but this is insignificant when set against the potential costs of corrosion). Whichever view is adopted, the reality is that the majority of galvanic isolators presently in service neither contain a capacitor nor are fitted with a warning device. *There are many that, because of improper installation or voltage leaks in excess of 1.0 volt, are not providing galvanic isolation.*

Testing a Galvanic Isolator

With the shore-power cord disconnected use a length of wire to short the two isolator terminals (this will discharge any capacitor in the isolator) and then place an ohmmeter across these two terminals (Figure 3-26, Test 4). If the terminals are not accessible, test from the grounding pin of the shore-power inlet to the AC grounding bus in the distribution panel, or to any grounding socket on an AC outlet (any capacitor can also be discharged by shorting these two points). Wait for the meter reading to stabilize (if the isolator contains a capacitor, this can take anywhere from a minute or two up to ten minutes, depending on the type of meter being used and the rating of the capacitor). Note the reading. Short any capacitor once again, and then reverse the meter leads: The meter should show the same ohms reading within 10% to 12% in both directions. A high reading in either direction indicates open-circuited diodes; a 0 ohms reading means shorted diodes. If the meter has a diode testing capability, the same test procedure can be repeated with the meter in this mode—it should produce a voltage drop

reading of around 0.9 volts in both directions.

With the shore-power cord *connected on board* but dis*connected ashore,* place the leads of a DC ammeter on the *grounding* blade of the shore-power cord and on *any grounded metal ashore (the metal rim of the dockside receptacle should be grounded; Figure 3-27). There may be voltage and current present at the grounding connections,* coming from leaks ashore or on other boats, *so don't touch the meter probes when making the connections.* Set the meter to its highest DC amps scale and then progressively switch down to lower scales. *The meter should give no reading* (if the meter's fuse blows, there is a current flow on the grounding wire that exceeds the meter's amperage rating!). If any current flow is present, the isolator is conducting and therefore not blocking galvanic currents. (Sometimes small leakage currents of 10 to 15 milliamps may be present. On a properly bonded boat with well-maintained zincs, the zincs will corrode so slowly that this current will not be a concern.)

Figure 3-27. Testing a galvanic isolator.

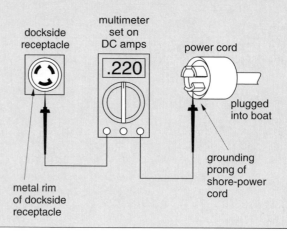

Understanding and Troubleshooting Electrical Circuits; Proper Installation Practices

Isolation transformers. Galvanic isolators are a low-cost but only partially effective response to the people-versus-boat-protection conundrum. Ultimately the only way to provide full people protection without courting the risk of galvanic corrosion is to install an *isolation transformer* on the incoming shore-power line.

The concept of an isolation transformer is straightforward. Shore-power is fed into one winding (the *primary*) and transferred *magnetically* to another (the *secondary*). The primary winding has a *shield*, which is grounded ashore. The secondary winding may or may not be grounded on board. *Either way, there is no direct electrical connection whatsoever between the shoreside supply and the onboard AC circuit.* We get two desirable consequences:

1. Since the boat's power source is now the secondary side of the transformer, *the only path for onboard leakage currents is back to the transformer, not the dockside supply*—leaks will not find a path to ground through the water.

2. Since the shore-side grounding wire is not connected to the boat's grounding circuit, there is no ship-to-shore path for galvanic currents.

Although the onboard circuit is sometimes ungrounded (in which case it is said to be *floating*), the ABYC standards require *one side of the secondary winding to be grounded on the secondary side of the transformer, with a boat's grounding circuit tied in at this point, and the two then connected to the boat's DC negative* (Figures 3-28 and 3-29). This has the effect of producing a *polarized* circuit on board in which the grounded side of the transformer is the neutral. In the event of either a short in a piece of AC equipment or a leak into the DC circuits, the fault current has a direct path back to the transformer through the grounding circuit.

At first sight the connection to the DC negative appears to bring the earth's ground back into the picture, creating the potential for shock hazards to swimmers. But on reflection it can be seen that regardless of this connection, *the only path for fault current is back to its source, which is the transformer.* Earth ground has no part to play in this circuit. The *fault-current circuit* is completely contained within the boat and its wiring—swimmers will be safe.

It is important to distinguish an isolation transformer from a *polarization transformer*. The primary and secondary windings in the latter function as in an isolation transformer, creating a *floating* AC circuit on board, one side of which is once again made the neutral by tying it to the boat's grounding circuit. This establishes a con-

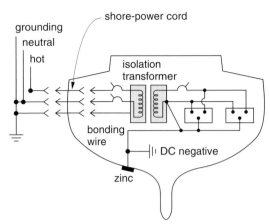

Figure 3-28. ABYC-recommended isolation transformer circuit with the neutral grounded on board. *(Ocean Navigator)*

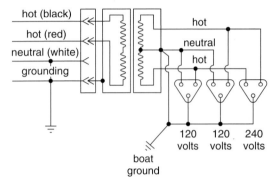

Figure 3-29. Isolation transformer circuit for 120/240 volts AC (USA). The neutral is not brought on board. The 240-volt appliances are wired to the two "hot" wires and the safety grounding wire. 120-volt appliances are wired to one or the other hot wire, the onboard neutral wire, and the safety grounding wire.

stant polarity on board, regardless of the polarity at the shore-side receptacle. But on the polarization transformer *the shoreside grounding connection is fastened to both sides of the transformer, and ultimately to the boat's DC negative: The transformer does nothing to provide galvanic isolation.* To get galvanic isolation with such a transformer, it is necessary to once again fit a galvanic isolator in the grounding circuit. It is worth repeating that as long *as the grounding wire is carried on board and connected to the boat's AC grounding and DC negative circuits there will be no galvanic isolation.*

Typical AC Circuits Afloat

Note: In what follows I deal only with what are known as *single-phase* circuits—the kind that are found in every household. Some large yachts with heavy equipment will have industrial-type *three-phase* circuits, but these will never be found on smaller boats.

Color codes. The basic 120-volt AC circuit in the USA consists of a *black* hot wire, a *white* neutral, and a *green or bare* ground. The same three-wire circuit in the UK will carry 240 volts. The old UK color code had a *red* hot, a *black* neutral, and a *green or bare* ground (earth). The new European standard code uses *brown* for hot (positive), *light blue* for neutral, and *green and yellow* for ground (earth).

The USA also has a 240-volt circuit, but this is established by supplying a second 120-volt (hot) circuit and wiring 240-volt appliances (typically electric stoves, clothes dryers, and larger air-conditioning units) to both hot circuits (Figure 3-30). This second hot circuit is color-coded *red*. The incoming breaker box will have two hot *bus bars*, one connected to the black wire and one connected to the red; it will also have the neutral bus bar and ground connection. One-hundred-twenty-volt appliances will be connected to either the black or the red bus bar, together with the normal neutral and ground connections. Usually an attempt is made to spread the load of 120-volt appliances equally between both hot bus bars. The 240-volt appliances will be connected to *both* the black and the red bus bars, and the green (or bare) safety wire to ground.

In the following text all colors refer to USA color codes:

    Red — hot (ungrounded)
    Black — hot (ungrounded)
    White — neutral (grounded)
    Green or bare — ground (grounding)

Ship-to-shore cables. The connection from shore-power to a boat is made with a shore-power cord. These cables are often subjected to unfair strain, and may be exposed to saltwater and fresh-water spray — they clearly need to be assembled from high-quality components to high-quality standards. The cables themselves must be flexible yet designed for hard service, with oil- and water-resistant insulation. In the USA applicable cable types are labeled SO, ST and STO (see Table 3-1 on page 113). The terminals at both

ends of the cable should have some form of a spray-proof locking cap, although too often all that is available on the shore-power end is a standard household-type outlet, which therefore does not meet ABYC standards. It is particularly important to have the boat end of the cable well secured; if it should come loose and fall in the water it will be potentially lethal. It is best to buy a commercially made shore-power cord with preassembled terminals.

The shore-power *outlet* on a dock must have a *female* receptacle; the *inlet* on the boat must have a *male* receptacle. On boats with isolation transformers or galvanic isolators, the shore-power inlet must be isolated from the hull (it will be anyway in a fiberglass hull, but metal hulls require either a nonmetallic inlet or some form of insulation from the hull). The ABYC standards call for a warning sign on the boat's shore-power inlet (Figure 3-31). Different styles of outlets and plugs are mandated for different voltage and current ratings (Figure 3-32). None is interchangeable. This is fine until you pull up at a dock with the legally correct shore-power cord and find it won't fit the available outlets! Once again, shore-power cord manufacturers can supply preassembled adapters, which are preferable to attempting to jury-rig a connection that may well be unsafe.

Mixing and matching outlets and plugs. In some USA situations dockside power is available at a USA 50-amp, 250-volt receptacle, but the boat has two 30-amp, 125-volt inlets. It is common to use a Y-adapter (Figure 3-33) to split the supply to the two inlets. This is an acceptable practice as long as the total amperage drawn from the two legs does not exceed the rating of the components in the single leg.

There is another situation that is the reverse of the above, in which the dockside has two 30-amp, 125-volt outlets, but the boat has a 50-amp, 250-volt inlet. A standard Y-adapter is often installed in reverse. This is dangerous for two reasons:

1. After one 30-amp plug is connected at the dockside, if any 240-volt load is turned on aboard, *the protruding terminals on the second plug will be live.*
2. If either of the dockside outlets has reverse polarity, when both are plugged in it will short-circuit the power supply, creating a fire hazard.

If two dockside receptacles must be used to feed a common inlet on the boat, a special kind of Y-adapter (Figure 3-34) is needed with internal circuitry that checks the polarity and does not complete the circuit until both plugs are in place.

Figure 3-30. A 240-volt AC circuit (USA). As in Figure 3-21B, the neutral line is not grounded on board. The 120-volt appliances are spread equally between the two "hot" bus bars in order to balance the electrical load. The 240-volt appliances have two hot terminals.

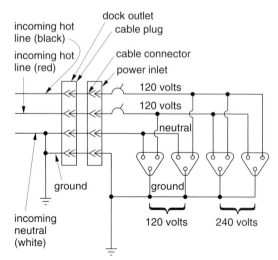

Understanding and Troubleshooting Electrical Circuits;
Proper Installation Practices

Figure 3-31. ABYC-recommended notice for a shore-power inlet.

WARNING

To minimize shock and fire hazards:

(1) Turn off the boat's shore connection switch before connecting or disconnecting shore cable.

(2) **Connect** shore-power cable at the boat first.

(3) If polarity warning indicator is activated, immediately disconnect cable.

(4) **Disconnect** shore-power cable at shore-outlet first.

(5) Close shore-power inlet cover tightly.

DO NOT ALTER SHORE-POWER CABLE CONNECTORS.

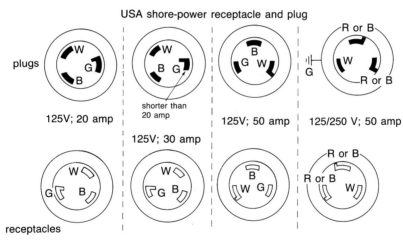

USA household receptacle and plug rated for 125 volts and 15 amps

plug

receptacle

USA shore-power receptacle and plug

plugs

125V; 20 amp

shorter than 20 amp

125V; 30 amp

125V; 50 amp

125/250 V; 50 amp

receptacles

Figure 3-32. USA-style receptacles and plugs. W = neutral (white); R or B = hot (red or black); G = ground (green or bare).

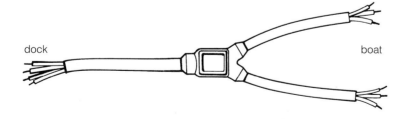

dock

boat

Figure 3-33. Blank Y-adapter assembly which can be used with different end fittings. *(Marinco)*

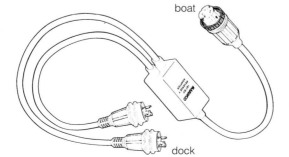

boat

dock

Figure 3-34. Reverse Y-adapter with built-in safety device. *(Marinco)*

Note also that a proper 50-amp, 250-volt USA dockside supply consists of two 125-volt legs that are supposed to be *out of phase*. As I said earlier, I am not going to discuss the subject of phases. It is enough to know that with two out-of-phase legs, *the maximum current that will flow down the neutral wire is the highest current on a single phase*, but if the two 125-volt legs are from the same phase, wired in parallel, *the current flowing through the neutral wire will be the sum of the current flowing through both hot wires*, which at full load will be *double the rating of the cable, meaning that the neutral may melt down*. To check for proper wiring, test with a voltmeter between the two incoming hot lines—if they are out of phase, the voltmeter will read around 240 volts; if in phase, around 0 volts. A purpose-built Y-adapter (mentioned above) will sense if the two hot lines are in phase, in which case it will not complete the connection to the boat.

Loose neutrals. Even if the two incoming 125-volt legs on a USA 240- or 250-volt supply are correctly out of phase, there is still a problem that sometimes develops which is known as a *loose neutral*. Let us assume that there is a heavy draw 120-volt appliance on one leg (for example, an air-conditioner) which is wired from one of the incoming hot legs to the onboard neutral. There is a low-draw 120-volt appliance (for example, a TV) wired from the other leg to the neutral (refer back to Figure 3-30). The air-conditioner and TV are both "on."

There is a poor connection between the neutral pin on the shorepower cord and the neutral socket in the dockside outlet (this is the *loose neutral*) which is creating a high resistance at this point. The air-conditioner has a low internal resistance. The net result is that instead of the neutral line from the air-conditioner being at ground potential (0 volts), it is at something close to line voltage (120-volts) all the way to the resistance (the dockside receptacle) and only at ground potential on the ground side of this resistance (refer back to Figure 3-14, resistances in series). The TV, which is wired across the other hot leg and the same neutral will now effectively be wired across two hot legs, which is to say it will be wired into something approaching 240 volts—it is likely to burn up (perhaps setting fire to the boat in the process—this example is taken from a real-life situation which resulted in the loss of a large motor yacht).

Boats with USA-style 240-volt systems, in which 120-volt appliances are spread between the two hot legs, must ensure that the neutral connections in the shorepower cord are in good condition. Better yet is to use a polarization or isolation transformer since the shoreside neutral is

not brought on board (refer back to Figure 3-29) and the onboard neutral is *bolted* at the transformer (just as it is bolted at the panelboard in a house) so there is no possibility of a loose neutral developing.

Onboard AC power: specific components.
The potentially hazardous marine environment, and the peculiarities of boat AC installations require one or two components not generally found ashore. These are:

Two-pole circuit breakers. Household circuits use single-pole circuit breakers in the hot lines to appliances, as opposed to two-pole breakers which cut both the hot and neutral lines simultaneously (Figure 3-35). It is an ABYC requirement that in order to protect against hazardous reverse polarity situations *the main incoming AC breaker on a boat should be of the two-pole type*. Better yet, two-pole breakers should also be used on all branch circuits; but if the onboard circuits are polarized, the ABYC allows use of single-pole breakers in the hot side of branch circuits, as in a house. (Note: The ABYC requires the main breaker to be within 10 feet of the boat's shorepower inlet. If not, additional fuses or breakers are required within 10 feet of the inlet.)

No breaker, switch, or fuse is ever placed in the green (or bare) ground (earth) line. This would defeat its purpose—to provide a permanent, redundant path to ground to protect against electrical system failures.

Polarity testers. A polarized system is one in which the grounded (neutral) and ungrounded (hot) conductors are connected in the same relation to all terminals. It is important to ensure safety on board. The polarity of a household circuit is established by tying the neutral to ground (earth). The polarity of a boat circuit is established in the same way through the shore-side grounding and grounded connections, tied together at a buried rod, or else through tying the neutral and grounding circuits together at an onboard generator frame, an inverter frame, or the secondary side of an isolation transformer (see above).

The wiring for an inverter or generator is all contained within the boat—if it is done correctly, proper polarization will be assured. But even if the boat's AC circuits are properly wired, with a shore-power cord there is always the possibility of plugging into a shore-side receptacle with reverse polarity. If the shore-power cord is feeding into an isolation or polarization transformer on board, the transformer will still ensure the correct polarity, but *without such a transformer the neutral side of the boat's circuits will*

Understanding and Troubleshooting Electrical Circuits;
Proper Installation Practices

now be hot. As long as the neutral is not grounded aboard (which it should not be—see page 97), the AC circuits will still function just fine. If all branch circuits have two-pole breakers (see above), these will provide adequate protection for those on board, but if (as is more common) all the branch circuits have single-pole breakers, *even with the breakers turned off, the entire AC circuit from the shore-power inlet through the appliances back to the breakers in the AC panel will still be live,* creating a potentially hazardous situation.

To provide a warning of such a situation, the ABYC requires onboard circuits with single-pole breakers and no isolation or polarization transformer to have a *reverse-polarity* indicating device. This must be wired in such a way as to be permanently lit or audible in the event of reverse polarity. The normal way is to wire a light or buzzer from the incoming neutral wire to the grounding wire; in the event of reverse polarity, the neutral becomes hot, causing the alarm to activate. In order to keep leakage currents into the grounding circuit to a minimum, the reverse polarity device is required to have a very high resistance (25,000 ohms or more). (Older panels with polarity lights may be wired from the hot to ground. If these glow green, polarity is correct, if the lamp fails to light, polarity is reversed.)

In the absence of a polarity indicator, polarity is checked easily. Connect a voltmeter or test light (120-volt in the USA, 240-volt in the UK) between the *incoming* AC hot wire(s) and a good ground, such as a *grounding* socket on an AC outlet or a through-hull fitting that is below the waterline (Figure 3-36). *REMEMBER, THIS CIRCUIT IS LIVE. IF YOU ARE AT ALL UNSURE OF WHAT YOU ARE DOING, DO NOT DO THIS TEST!* The meter should show system voltage or the light should glow. Next connect the meter or light between the incoming neutral line and ground. The meter should read no volts or the light should remain unlit. If there is voltage or the lamp lights between neutral and ground, but nothing happens between the hot side and ground, polarity is reversed. If there is nothing on either side, the shore power is not hooked up or switched on, or the test light is grounded improperly.

Three-prong outlets. The third prong on 120-volt and 240-volt (both USA and UK) plugs is the grounding plug (Figure 3-37). Two-prong outlets and plugs (commonly seen on lamps, small appliances, and electric hand tools) have no grounding connection and so lack this important safety feature. *Two-prong outlets should never be used on a boat—they are not suitable for the damp marine environment.* In the USA, 120-

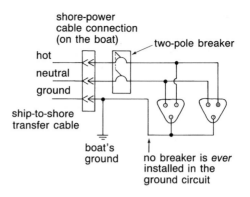

Figure 3-35. Two-pole circuit breaker. When a two-pole breaker trips, it stops the current flow to the entire circuit regardless of whether polarity is normal or reversed.

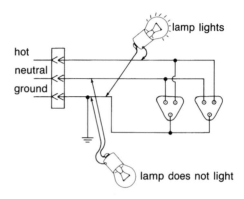

Figure 3-36. Polarity testing. A test lamp should light when placed between the "hot" wire and ground; if it does not light, either the polarity is reversed or the circuit is dead. The lamp should not light when placed between the neutral and ground. If it lights, polarity is reversed. A permanently installed polarity light should have a resistance of at least 25,000 ohms to keep current flow to a minimum.

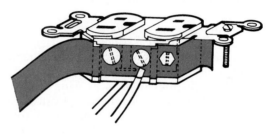

Figure 3-37. A three-prong outlet with a grounding socket (USA).

volt outlets are wired with the black (hot) lead to the black or brass screw and the white (neutral) lead to the silver screw. Switching these will lead to reverse polarity. (Wiring tip: When wiring an outlet, give the grounding—green or bare wire—an extra length of wire. If for some reason the outlet gets ripped out, the grounding wire will be the last to come undone.)

For obvious reasons, the ABYC requires that receptacles and matching plugs for AC use *must not be interchangeable* with those for DC use.

Ship-to-shore transfer switch. Boats with a shore-side hookup and an onboard AC generating capability and/or a DC/AC inverter use the same AC circuits on board, regardless of the power source. *If ever two AC power sources are switched into an AC circuit at the same time, one or the other power source is likely to suffer extensive damage.* Therefore a proper two-pole, ship-to-shore-type transfer switch is needed that breaks both current-carrying conductors from

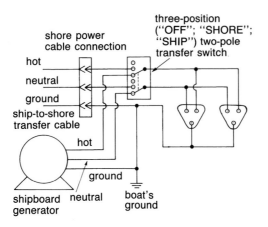

shore power cable connection

Ground-fault circuit interrupters (GFCI's). A *ground-fault circuit interrupter* (GFCI), also known as a *residual current circuit breaker* (RCCB), is a device that senses the current flow through both a hot and a neutral wire in a circuit. Any short to ground, such as someone receiving a shock, creates an imbalance (less current flows through the neutral wire than the hot), and the GFCI trips the circuit. GFCI's are incredibly sensitive and fast acting, and provide a large measure of safety from shock.

The very effectiveness of GFCI's is sometimes a drawback. In the marine environment, there are invariably minute current leakages in AC systems. The accumulation of these over half a dozen individual branch circuits on a boat often will be enough to trip a central GFCI even when no real (or curable) problem exists (in the USA the trip limit is set at a very low 5 milliamps; in Europe higher and therefore less sensitive limits are used). To avoid nuisance tripping, it is preferable to install an individual GFCI on each branch circuit rather than have one central unit. Note: *GFCI's provide no protection against touching both hot and neutral wires at the same time,* since the current flow through both is affected equally and the GFCI senses no imbalance.

one power source before making the connection to another power source (Figure 3-38). *It must never be possible to switch two AC power sources into the same circuit at the same time.* This ship-to-shore transfer switch must at the same time *isolate the shore-power inlet any time the AC supply is coming from an onboard generator or inverter.* Without this isolation, an onboard AC supply would cause the male prongs in the shore-power inlet to be live, creating a potentially dangerous situation.

Volt and frequency meters. Boats venturing abroad will find a variety of different voltages and frequencies. Even "at-home" voltages in many marinas may be low because of voltage drop in inadequate wiring. Appliances with resistive loads, such as lightbulbs, heaters, toasters, or ovens, will tolerate fairly wide variations in voltage and frequency. Most appliances that use induction motors, such as refrigerators, freezers, washing machines, tape decks, and sewing machines, will not. Because we need to know the voltage and frequency of AC power, all AC circuits should have a voltmeter and frequency meter connected at the main breaker.

The most commonly encountered problem is stepping up from 120 to 240 volts (USA to UK), or down from 240 to 120 volts (UK to USA) with a concomitant change in frequency from 60 Hz to 50 Hz (USA to UK) or 50 Hz to 60 Hz (UK to USA). The voltage change is easy enough: It merely requires an appropriate transformer. A frequency change is a little trickier.

A 120-volt motor designed to operate on 60 cycles will overheat and ultimately fail if fed 120 volts at 50 cycles. Changes in frequency also will affect the speed at which motors turn. This is immaterial with most appliances but obviously critical for tape decks and record players. The only effective way to compensate for speed changes is by altering internal pulley ratios—an involved procedure.

Testing AC Circuits

REMEMBER, AC VOLTAGE CAN KILL. IF YOU ARE IN ANY DOUBT ABOUT WHAT YOU ARE DOING, DON'T DO IT! Before working on AC circuits always disconnect the shore-side cable, and turn off any generator or DC/AC inverter. *Pay particular attention to inverters*—many have a "sleep" mode that drops the AC output to a low voltage, not measurable with many voltmeters, when there is no load on the circuit, thus reducing the standby drain on the DC system to a minimum. The AC circuit may appear to be dead, but *if a load is accidentally applied the inverter will almost instantaneously switch to full voltage.*

Dockside. AC troubleshooting generally starts at the dockside. Things to look for are correct voltage, correct polarity, and ground faults.

1. Correct voltage: Test with a multimeter on the 250 volts AC scale. There will be three sockets in a dockside receptacle. A 120-volt system (USA) should give the following results:

Hot to ground   120 volts
Hot to neutral   120 volts
Neutral to ground   less than 5 volts
                                 (see note below)

A 240-volt system (USA) should give the following results:

Hot 1 to neutral	120 volts
Hot 2 to neutral	120 volts
Hot 1 to hot 2	240 volts
Hot 1 to ground	120 volts
Hot 2 to ground	120 volt
Neutral to ground	less than 5 volts (see note below)

A 240-volt system (UK) should give 240 volts for hot-to-ground and hot-to-neutral tests and less than 5 volts for the neutral-to-ground test.

Note: In theory, the neutral-to-ground voltage will be 0 because the two conductors are tied together at the dockside power source. In practice, the voltage will not be 0 if the circuit being tested is feeding a load. This is because the neutral is a current-carrying conductor, and therefore subject to voltage drop from one end of the conductor to the other. Since the ground carries no current, the voltage between neutral and ground at the load end of the neutral conductor will equal the voltage drop in this conductor. In marina wiring, if a shore-side outlet is feeding more than one boat, even if there is no load on the receptacle being tested, a load on another circuit wired to that same outlet will cause a small voltage drop to be registered. If at any time this exceeds 5 volts, the wiring is undersized for the load, or there is some other fault in the circuit (such as a loose neutral—see page 106).

2. Correct polarity: The hot and neutral sockets are as shown in Figure 3-32. If the meter shows them to be reversed, the receptacle is wired with reverse polarity. *Unless the boat has an isolation or polarization transformer, do not plug in. To do so will be hazardous to people on board and in the water.*

3. Ground faults: *The grounding (green or bare wire) side of an AC circuit is never a current-carrying conductor in normal use.* To test 120-volt receptacles (240 volts in the UK) put one probe of a voltmeter in the *grounding* (green or bare wire) socket of the receptacle (*BE ABSOLUTELY SURE TO GET THE RIGHT SOCKET; DO NOT TOUCH THE METER PROBES; DO NOT DO THIS TEST IF YOU ARE AT ALL UNSURE WHICH IS THE GROUNDING SOCKET!*) and dangle the other probe in the water (Figure 3-39). On 240-volt receptacles (USA), touch the first probe to the metal shell of the receptacle. Progressively switch down to the lowest AC volts scale. If there is any indication of voltage, there is a serious ground leak. This can be measured by switching to the amps and milliamps scales. If the meter shows any leaks to ground whatsoever, the shore-power cord

should not be plugged in (except when the boat has an isolation transformer).

Note that it is possible to buy portable ground-fault and reverse-polarity indicators (Figure 3-40). In the USA Radio Shack sells a couple of models at very cheap prices. One of these is an excellent investment—use it always before making a hookup.

Onboard circuit testing. As we have seen, a 120-volt circuit (240 volts in the UK) is essentially the same as a 12-volt circuit with one hot (black in the USA; red or brown in the UK) wire to the equipment, and one wire, the neutral (white in the USA; black or blue in the UK), back. The third wire (green or bare in both the

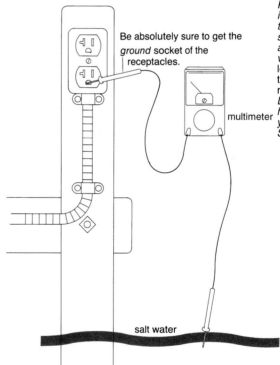

Switch down to the lowest voltage scale: *any reading indicates a serious leak.*

Be absolutely sure to get the *ground* socket of the receptacles.

multimeter

salt water

Figure 3-39. Using a multimeter to test a shore-power receptacle for leaks. *Remember the receptacle is live—be sure to place the probe in the ground socket of the receptacle and start with a high AC voltage scale,* switching to lower scales as necessary to increase sensitivity. Any reading indicates a leak. *Do not do this test if you have any doubt about what you are doing. (Jim Sollers)*

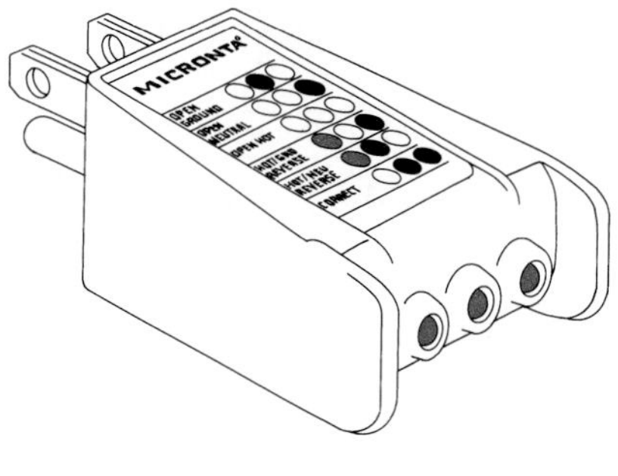

Figure 3-40. Multifunction ground-fault tester. *(Jim Sollers)*

USA and UK, with green and yellow in newer UK installations), although called a grounding wire, is not part of the circuit in normal circumstances. If you are in any doubt about this, read the section on page 95 once again. The same voltage tests can be made between the hot and neutral sides of the circuit (using an appropriate AC scale) as between the hot and ground sides of a DC circuit, KEEPING IN MIND THE LETHAL NATURE OF AC VOLTAGE. SEVERAL OF THE FOLLOWING TESTS ARE DONE ON "LIVE" CIRCUITS. DO NOT TOUCH THE METER PROBES. DO NOT DO THESE TESTS IF YOU ARE AT ALL UNSURE OF WHAT YOU ARE DOING.

With shore power connected any test from a hot wire to the safety grounding wire should yield 120 volts (240 volts in the UK), and from the neutral wire to the grounding wire, 0 volts. If the hot and neutral are reversed, so is polarity. *If the dockside receptacle did not show reverse polarity, the wires are crossed on board and need sorting out.*

A 240-volt circuit (USA) is a little different since it has two hot wires and no neutral wire. Again, the third (green or bare) wire is not part of the circuit in normal circumstances. Any test across the two hot wires should yield 240 volts; any test from either wire to the green or bare grounding wire should yield 120 volts.

Open-circuit and short-circuit testing is done on all circuits using an ohmmeter, just as with DC circuits, but only after *disconnecting the shore-power cable, shutting down any generator,*

and switching off any DC/AC inverter. The following additional tests can be made for ground leaks and short circuits.

With the AC selector switch turned to SHORE, and all equipment unplugged or switched off, but *with the various AC circuit breakers turned "on,"* with an ohmeter (R × 1 scale on an analog meter) test first between the hot wire(s) and the ground wire (green or bare), and then between the neutral wire and the ground wire (Figure 3-41). This is most easily done by poking the ohmmeter probes into an AC receptacle socket. *There should be no continuity at any time*—i.e., the meter reading should stay on infinity (a polarity indicating device may produce a very high resistance reading, above 25,000 ohms). The sole exception is when a polarized isolation transformer (one leg grounded on the boat) is fitted. In this case, break this leg loose from the ground and proceed with the rest of the tests.

Any continuity indicates a leak to ground in the wiring circuits. If the neutral wire is at fault, it may have been incorrectly wired into the boat's ground point. If so, disconnect it. Now, *with the shoreside power still disconnected,* plug in and switch on all appliances, one piece at a time. Any continuity from either a hot or neutral wire to the green or bare wire shows a short or leak to ground in that piece of equipment. *The equipment is dangerous and needs repairing*

The ohmmeter can be used for another test. Once again, *with the shoreside cable disconnected,* the AC selector switch turned to SHORE, and all

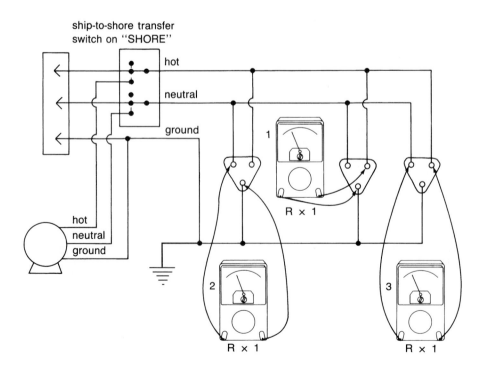

Figure 3-41. Testing AC circuits without an isolation transformer. *These resistance tests are carried out with the shore-power cord disconnected, any inverter or generator shut down,* and all appliances unplugged or switched "off," but with the boat's main breaker turned on. Meters 1 and 2 should show no continuity; a reading of less than infinity indicates a leak to ground (except for some polarity-indicating devices and frequency meters that will give a reading above 25,000 ohms). Meter 3 should also show no continuity.

ship-to-shore transfer switch on "SHORE"

hot

neutral

ground

1

R × 1

hot

neutral

ground

2

R × 1

3

R × 1

equipment unplugged or switched off, but with the AC breakers turned "on," test between the hot and neutral wires (USA, 120 volts; UK, 240 volts), or the two hot wires (USA, 240 volts). Boats without isolation transformers should show infinite ohms—anything less indicates a leak between the wires, or some equipment plugged in and left on. (Note: A frequency meter in the circuit will give a high ohms reading.) Boats with isolation transformers will show a low reading (near 0 ohms), since the meter now in effect is connected across the secondary coil in the transformer. With such circuits, the next step is to trip the main breaker—the meter should jump to infinity, since the transformer has been taken out of the circuit. Any reading other than infinity now indicates a leak, assuming the meter is connected on the downstream side of the breaker.

Proper Electrical Installations

A while back we were having a problem with our VHF radio. It would receive, but then cut out the minute we keyed the mike to transmit. Since we were in the West Indies far from help, we simply stopped using the radio.

Months later, back at the dock, I prepared to remove the unit and send it in for repairs. When I opened up the fuse holder I noticed a trace of corrosion on the tip of the fuse. I cleaned the fuse, replaced it, and the radio was back in commission! The corrosion was such that it would allow the passage of the small amounts of current required to receive, but created excessive voltage drop whenever an attempt was made to pass the higher currents needed to transmit. If I had spent five minutes performing a voltage drop test I would have found the problem immediately!

With my curiosity aroused I now peeled back a section of insulation on the coaxial cable to the antenna. The copper braid was severely tarnished and corroded (Figure 3-42). I continued peeling back the insulation, working up the cable. After seven feet there was still no sign of a reduction in the corrosion. I replaced the entire cable.

Our boat is exceptionally dry down below. We have never taken on any appreciable quantities of salt water, and the radio and its associated wiring have not even been subjected to any spray. And yet we had a corrosion problem. This example just goes to show that in the marine environment the electrical circuits on even the driest of boats are still liable to deteriorate simply from salt and moisture in the atmosphere. When wiring electrical circuits, the only sure way to postpone problems for as long as possible is to use the best available materials and to install them to the highest possible standards.

Cables

Cables need: strength to resist the vibration and pounding experienced in boats, adequate insula-

---

Checking Fluorescent Lights

Fluorescent lights are a little more complex than incandescent lights. Most incorporate a transformer (also known as a *ballast*) and a starter, a cylinder that plugs into a fixture inside the lamp base (12-volt fluorescents do not have starters). If a fluorescent lamp flickers on and off or will not come on:

• Check the power supply and voltage drop at the appliance as always.
• Switch off the unit, remove the tubes, clean all contacts and pins (with a clean rag or 400- to 600-grit wet-or-dry sandpaper) on the light fixture and tubes, replace the tubes, and try again. Remove the tubes by twisting through 90 degrees and pulling down gently.

• Still no light? Try a new tube. If the unit has more than one tube, replace all tubes.
• Still no light? Try a new starter if the unit incorporates one.
• Still no light? Replace the ballast. The new one will have a wiring diagram with it, or one will be glued to the lamp base.

Fluorescent lights wear out: The more frequently they are turned on and off, the more quickly they wear out. This is more of a determining factor than the amount of time they remain on. Single-tube fluorescents are likely to cause more radio interference than double-tube units, but all can cause problems (Chapter 7, Radio Interference).

Figure 3-42. **Severe corrosion of a coaxial cable caused simply by salt-laden moisture wicking up the wire strands. This section of the cable was 7 feet from the cable termination! The cable had never been subjected to immersion or spray of any kind. Tinned cable would have prevented this corrosion.**

tion to prevent ground leaks, and sufficient size to minimize voltage drop.

Cable construction. Nothing but copper cable is suitable for use in the marine environment. Sometimes aluminum cable is found in household wiring, but this has a lower conductivity than copper and builds up a layer of aluminum oxide on the surface of the cable which creates resistance in connections and terminals—it is not suited to marine use (similarly, because of the corrosion problem, aluminum and unplated steel are not to be used for studs, nuts, washers, and cable terminations). An added measure of protection against corrosion can be gained by drawing the individual strands of a copper cable through a tin "bath" before assembling the cable, to form what is known as *tinned* cable. Tinned cable is more expensive than regular cable, but will provide troublefree service for much longer and is, in the long run, an excellent investment.

Cables in boat use are subjected to vibration and, at times, considerable shocks. Solid-cored cable of the kind used in household wiring is liable to fracture. Stranded cable must be used in boats. The ABYC lists three types, based upon the number of strands (column 6 of Table 3-6 on page 116). Recently the use of Type 1 cable (solid) has been discontinued for marine use; the more flexible Type 2 (19 strands) is recommended for use in general-purpose boat wiring, with Type 3 (many strands—the number varies with cable size) used if frequent flexing occurs.

Insulation is the other critical factor in cable construction. It must be able to withstand the ever present salt-laden atmosphere; contamination by various chemicals, particularly oil, diesel, and dirty bilge water; and exposure to ultraviolet rays from sunlight.

The most commonly available wire in the USA that may be suitable for general-purpose marine wiring is classified as THWN (Thermoplastic, Heat resistant, for Wet locations, and with a Nylon jacket—Table 3-1), or XHHW (cross-linked polyethylene, High-Heat resistant, for Wet locations). Other grades are MTW (Machine Tool Wire), which is rated for wet locations and is oil-, gasoline-, and diesel-resistant, and AWM (Appliance Wiring Material), which is similar to MTW but with a Higher Heat rating (up to 221°F; 105°C), making it suitable for engine rooms.

Wire insulation will frequently carry more than one designation, for example: THHN/THWN. In this instance the insulation has a higher heat (HH) rating in dry locations (up to 194°F/90°C) than it does in wet locations (up to 167°F/75°C).

The problem with Table 3-1 is that the requirements that have to be met for these designations are not rigorous enough to determine whether the cable is really suitable for marine use. A good-quality marine-rated cable will exceed all existing UL, Coast Guard, and ABYC standards. Consequently it is not possible simply to recommend buying a cable that meets a particular standard or has a certain designation, although in the USA it should at the least be labeled as meeting "BC5W2" or "UL1426." To be on the safe side, *tinned, multi-stranded* cable should always be bought from a recognized marine outlet. The cable will be more expensive than that bought from a local electrical wholesaler or retailer, but the added cost is insignificant when compared to the cost of troubleshooting and rectifying faulty circuits in the future.

No normal insulation is suitable for prolonged immersion in water. Sooner or later current leaks will develop. Even good-quality boat cable

Understanding and Troubleshooting Electrical Circuits; Proper Installation Practices

Table 3-1 Common Electric Cables Acceptable to the ABYC and Their Designations (USA)

TW: *T*hermoplastic insulation (usually PVC), suitable for *W*et locations (60°C/140°F heat- resistance rating).

THW: *T*hermoplastic insulation (usually PVC), *H*eat resistant (75°C/167°F rating) suitable for *W*et locations.

HWN: *H*eat-resistant (75°C/167°F rating) suitable for *W*et locations, with a *N*ylon jacket for abrasion resistance.

THWN: Same as for HWN, but with *T*hermoplastic insulation.

XHHW: Cross-linked synthetic polymer insulation, *H*igh *H*eat resistant (90°C/194°F rating) suitable for *W*et locations (but in this case de-rated to a 75°C/167°F rating).

MTW: *M*achine *T*ool *W*ire. Usually thermoplastic insulation (PVC) or thermoplastic with a nylon jacket. Moisture-, heat-, and oil-resistant. Most MTW is rated 60°C/140°F. *The ABYC requires it to be rated 90°C/194°F.*

AWM: *A*ppliance *W*iring *M*aterial. Usually thermoplastic insulation (PVC) or thermoplastic with nylon jacket. Thermosetting. 105°C/221°F rating.

BC5W2 and UL 1426 "Boat Cable": Any cable with this designation is good for general- purpose boat wiring. 5 = the heat rating in a dry environment (there are 5 ratings: 1 = 60°C; 2 = 75°C; 3 = 85°C; 4 = 95°C; and 5 = 105°C); 2 = the heat rating in a wet environment (there are two ratings: 1 = 60°C and 2 = 75°C). The insulation on UL 1426 cable is self-extinguishing, which is to say in a fire it will simply char down and drip rather than melt.

For shore-power cords:

SO: Hard *S*ervice cord, *O*il resistant compound.

ST: Hard *S*ervice cord, *T*hermoplastic.

STO: Hard *S*ervice cord, *T*hermoplastic with *O*il- resistant rating.

All are available with several temperature ratings (e.g., 60°C/140°F and 75°C/167°F)

Key: T = *T*hermoplastic, a plastic that can be softened by heating, as opposed to *T*hermosetting, a plastic that is heat-cured into an insoluble and infusible end product

W = *M*oisture-resistant

H = *H*eat-resistant (75°C/167°F rating)

HH = *H*igher-*h*eat-resistant (90°C/194°F rating)

N = *N*ylon jacket

X = Cross-linked synthetic polymer, a plastic in which polymers are linked chemically by polymerization

BC = *B*oat *C*able

should not be run through perpetually damp or wet areas of a boat. For this, special waterproof, oil-resistant insulation is required, and naturally this is more expensive.

Welding cable. Welding cable is sometimes used on boats for high-current DC circuits (notably for high-output alternator and DC/AC inverter installations), and in fact I recommended it for these purposes in the first edition of this book. The reason for using welding cable is its extreme flexibility, which is particularly useful when running heavy cables in tight quarters, and its tolerance of vibration (for example, when attached to the back of an alternator). The problem with welding cable is that its flexibility comes from its large number of very small strands and its soft insulation. These strands tend to wick up moisture, encouraging corrosion, and the insulation is not as moisture-resistant as other insulation and is easily damaged. For these reasons I am persuaded that welding cable should not be used on boats: It does not, in any case, meet the applicable ABYC standards.

Color coding. A standardized system of DC color coding has been adopted by the ABYC (Tables 3-2 and 3-3). However, in many instances it is not feasible to follow this entirely. The primary consideration (USA) is to use red leads on DC positive circuits, and black or yellow on DC negative. AC color coding is explained on page 103. (Note that black is also used for the "hot" leads on AC circuits in the USA, creating the possibility of dangerous confusion. When rewiring a boat I would strongly recommend the use of yellow for the DC negative).

Cable sizes. Selecting the proper wire size for a given application is critical, especially when electric motors are concerned. Undersized cables introduce unwanted resistance, resulting in voltage drop at appliances, reduced performance, and premature failure.

In the USA, two tables developed by the ABYC are commonly used to determine wire sizes in the marine field. The first assumes that a 10% voltage drop at the appliance is acceptable; the second is based on a 3% voltage drop (Tables 3-4 and 3-5). The tables are entered on

Table 3-2. ABYC DC Color Coding

Color	Use
Red	DC positive conductors
Black or Yellow	DC negative conductors
Green or Green with Yellow stripe(s)	DC grounding (bonding) conductors (see Chapter 4)

Table 3-3. ABYC Color Code for Engines and Accessory Wiring

Color	Item	Use
Yellow w/Red Stripe (YR)	Starting Circuit	Starting Switch to Solenoid
Brown/Yellow Stripe (BY) or Yellow (Y)—see note	Bilge Blowers	Fuse or Switch to Blowers
Dark Gray (Gy)	Navigation Lights	Fuse or Switch to Lights
	Tachometer	Tachometer Sender to Gauge
Brown (Br)	Generator Armature	Generator Armature to Regulator
	Alternator Charge Light	Generator Terminal/Alternator
		Auxiliary Terminal to Light and Regulator
	Pumps	Fuse or Switch to Pumps
Orange (O)	Accessory Feed	Ammeter to Alternator or Generator Output and Accessory Fuses or Switches
	Accessory Feeds	Distribution Panel to Accessory Switch
Purple (Pu)	Ignition	Ignition Switch to Coil and Electrical Instruments
	Instrument Feed	Distribution Panel to Electrical Instruments
Dark Blue	Cabin and Instrument Lights	Fuse or Switch to Lights
Light Blue (Lt Bl)	Oil Pressure	Oil Pressure Sender to Gauge
Tan	Water Temperature	Water Temperature Sender to Gauge
Pink (Pk)	Fuel Gauge	Fuel Gauge Sender to Gauge
Green/Stripe (G/x) (Except G/Y)	Tilt down and/or Trim in	Tilt and/or Trim Circuits
Blue/Stripe (Bl/x)	Tilt up and/or Trim out	Tilt and/or Trim Circuits

NOTE: *If yellow is used for DC negative, blower must be brown with a yellow stripe.* (ABYC)

one side by the total length of the wiring in a circuit (which includes both the hot and the ground wire) and on the other side by the maximum current draw (amps) of the appliance on the circuit. The required wire size, in American Wire Gauge (AWG), for the given voltage drop is then read in the body of the table. Note that the larger the AWG number, the smaller the wire size.

If more than one appliance is to be operated from common cables, *the cables must be rated for the total load of all the appliances. The ground cables to all fixtures must be sized the same as the hot cables, since they carry an equal load.*

Many appliances, particularly lights, will work with a 10% voltage drop, but nevertheless I recommend that you use the 3% voltage drop tables at all times. Given the harshness of the marine environment, it just does not pay to start out by trying to cut calculations as fine as possible.

Cable ampacity. All wire has some internal resistance, and so the passage of any current will generate heat. If this heat builds up faster than it dissipates, the cable will eventually pose a fire hazard. The extent to which this is so depends on the nature of the cable insulation and, in AC circuits, on how many cables are bundled together.

Table 3-8 has been developed by the ABYC to indicate the maximum allowable current (ampacity) of different types of cable, both inside and outside engine spaces. *The correction factors at the bottom are to be applied when bundling current-carrying AC cables.* (Note that in a 120-volt circuit [240-volt UK circuit] the hot and neutral conductors are both current-carrying; in a 240-volt circuit [USA] the two hot conductors are current-carrying. In other words, regardless of the system voltage, there are normally two current-carrying conductors in each circuit.)

Understanding and Troubleshooting Electrical Circuits; Proper Installation Practices

Table 3-4. Conductor Sizes for 10% Drop in Voltage

(Total current on circuit in amps) — (Length of conductor from source of current to device and back to source—feet)

Amps	10	15	20	25	30	40	50	60	70	80	90	100	110	120	130	140	150	160	170
12 volts																			
5	18	18	18	18	18	16	16	14	14	14	12	12	12	12	12	10	10	10	10
10	18	18	16	16	14	14	12	12	10	10	10	10	8	8	8	8	8	8	6
15	18	16	14	14	12	12	10	10	8	8	8	8	8	6	6	6	6	6	6
20	16	14	14	12	12	10	10	8	8	8	6	6	6	6	6	6	4	4	4
25	16	14	12	12	10	10	8	8	6	6	6	6	6	4	4	4	4	4	2
30	14	12	12	10	10	8	8	6	6	6	6	4	4	4	2	2	2	2	2
40	14	12	10	10	8	8	6	6	6	4	4	4	2	2	2	2	2	2	2
50	12	10	10	8	8	6	6	4	4	4	2	2	2	2	2	1	1	1	1
60	12	10	8	8	6	6	4	4	2	2	2	2	2	1	1	0	0	0	0
70	10	8	8	6	6	4	4	2	2	2	2	1	1	0	0	0	0	2/0	2/0
80	10	8	8	6	6	4	4	2	2	2	1	1	0	0	0	2/0	2/0	2/0	2/0
90	10	8	6	6	6	4	2	2	2	1	1	0	0	0	2/0	2/0	2/0	3/0	3/0
100	10	8	6	6	4	4	2	2	1	1	0	0	0	2/0	2/0	2/0	3/0	3/0	3/0
24 volts																			
5	18	18	18	18	18	18	18	18	16	16	16	16	14	14	14	14	14	14	12
10	18	18	18	18	18	16	16	14	14	14	12	12	12	12	12	10	10	10	10
15	18	18	18	16	16	14	14	12	12	12	10	10	10	10	10	8	8	8	8
20	18	18	16	16	14	14	12	12	10	10	10	10	8	8	8	8	8	8	6
25	18	16	16	14	14	12	12	10	10	10	8	8	8	8	6	6	6	6	6
30	18	16	14	14	12	12	10	10	8	8	8	8	8	6	6	6	6	6	6
40	16	14	14	12	12	10	10	8	8	8	6	6	6	6	6	6	4	4	4
50	16	14	12	12	10	10	8	8	6	6	6	6	6	4	4	4	4	4	2
60	14	12	12	10	10	8	8	6	6	6	6	4	4	4	2	2	2	2	2
70	14	12	10	10	8	8	6	6	6	6	4	4	4	2	2	2	2	2	2
80	14	12	10	10	8	8	6	6	6	4	4	4	2	2	2	2	2	2	2
90	12	10	10	8	8	6	6	6	4	4	4	2	2	2	2	2	2	1	1
100	12	10	10	8	8	6	6	4	4	4	2	2	2	2	2	1	1	1	1

Table 3-5. Conductor Sizes for 3% Drop in Voltage

(Total current on circuit in amps) — (Length of conductor from source of current to device and back to source—feet)

Amps	10	15	20	25	30	40	50	60	70	80	90	100	110	120	130	140	150	160	170
12 volts																			
5	18	16	14	12	12	10	10	10	8	8	8	6	6	6	6	6	6	6	6
10	14	12	10	10	10	8	6	6	6	6	4	4	4	4	2	2	2	2	2
15	12	10	10	8	8	6	6	6	4	4	2	2	2	2	1	1	1	1	1
20	10	10	8	6	6	6	4	4	2	2	2	2	1	1	1	0	0	0	2/0
25	10	8	6	6	6	4	4	2	2	2	1	1	0	0	0	2/0	2/0	2/0	3/0
30	10	8	6	6	4	4	2	2	1	1	0	0	0	2/0	2/0	3/0	3/0	3/0	3/0
40	8	6	6	4	4	2	2	1	0	0	2/0	2/0	3/0	3/0	3/0	4/0	4/0	4/0	4/0
50	6	6	4	4	2	2	1	0	2/0	2/0	3/0	3/0	4/0	4/0	4/0				
60	6	4	4	2	2	1	0	2/0	3/0	3/0	4/0	4/0	4/0						
70	6	4	2	2	1	0	2/0	3/0	3/0	4/0	4/0								
80	6	4	2	2	1	0	3/0	3/0	4/0	4/0									
90	4	2	2	1	0	2/0	3/0	4/0	4/0										
100	4	2	2	1	0	2/0	3/0	4/0											
24 volts																			
5	18	18	18	16	16	14	12	12	12	10	10	10	10	10	8	8	8	8	8
10	18	16	14	12	12	10	10	10	8	8	8	6	6	6	6	6	6	6	6
15	16	14	12	12	10	10	8	8	6	6	6	6	4	4	4	4	4	2	2
20	14	12	10	10	10	8	6	6	6	6	4	4	4	4	2	2	2	2	2
25	12	12	10	10	8	6	6	6	4	4	4	4	2	2	2	2	2	2	1
30	12	10	10	8	8	6	6	4	4	4	2	2	2	2	2	1	1	1	1
40	10	10	8	6	6	6	4	4	2	2	2	2	1	1	1	0	0	0	2/0
50	10	8	6	6	6	4	4	2	2	2	1	1	0	0	0	2/0	2/0	2/0	3/0
60	10	8	6	6	4	4	2	2	1	1	0	0	0	2/0	2/0	3/0	3/0	3/0	3/0
70	8	6	6	4	4	2	2	1	1	0	0	2/0	2/0	3/0	3/0	3/0	3/0	4/0	4/0
80	8	6	6	4	4	2	2	1	0	0	2/0	2/0	3/0	3/0	3/0	4/0	4/0	4/0	4/0
90	8	6	4	4	2	2	1	0	0	2/0	2/0	3/0	3/0	4/0	4/0	4/0	4/0		
100	6	6	4	4	2	2	1	0	2/0	2/0	3/0	3/0	4/0	4/0	4/0				

Notes: These tables are based on SAE wiring sizes. SAE-rated cables are typically 10% to 12% smaller than AWG-rated cables of the same nominal size (see Table 3-6, columns 2 and 3). Consequently, if a cable is sized by reference to these tables, and then AWG-rated wire of the same nominal size is substituted for SAE, the cable will be somewhat oversized for the application, which is all to the good. Although SAE-rated wiring can be used in DC circuits, *AWG-rated wiring must be used in AC circuits* (If you find this confusing, blame the ABYC and not me!).

Table 3-6. Conversion of American Wire Sizes to European Standards

1	2	3	4	5	6		
Conductor Size	Minimum Acceptable Circular Mil[1] (CM) Area (SAE specs and ABYC for DC Wiring)	Minimum Acceptable Circular Mil[1] (CM) Area (UL specs [AWG] and ABYC for AC Wiring)	Conductor Diameter (mm)	Conductor Cross-sectional Area (mm²)	Minimum Number of Strands		
					Type 1	Type 2	Type 3
25			0.455	0.163			
24			0.511	0.205			
23			0.573	0.259			
22			0.644	0.325			
21			0.723	0.412			
20			0.812	0.519			
19			0.992	0.653			
18	1537	1620	1.024	0.823	7	16	
17			1.15	1.04			
16	2336	2580	1.29	1.31	7	19	26
15			1.45	1.65			
14	3702	4110	1.63	2.08	7	19	41
13			1.83	2.63			
12	5833	6530	2.05	3.31	7	19	65
11			2.30	4.15			
10	9343	10380	2.59	5.27	7	19	105
9			2.91	6.62			
8	14810	16510	3.26	8.35	7	19	168
7			3.67	10.6			
6	25910	26240	4.11	13.3		37	266
5			4.62	16.8			
4	37360	41740	5.19	21.2		49	420
3			5.83	26.7			
2	62450	66360	6.54	33.6		127	665
1	77790	83690	7.35	42.4		127	836
0 (1/0)	98980	105600	8.25	53.4		127	1064
00 (2/0)	125100	133100	9.27	67.5		127	1323
000 (3/0)	158600	167800	10.40	85.0		259	1666
0000 (4/0)	205500	211600	11.68	107.2		418	2107
00000 (5/0)	250000		13.12	135.1			
000000 (6/0)	300000		14.73	170.3			

1. 1 circular mil (CM) = 0.0005067 mm², and 1 MCM = 1,000 CM = 0.5067 mm²

NOTES:
Type 1 no longer accepted in boat wiring by ABYC.
The lesser ABYC requirements for DC circuits reflects the fact that much of the industry is using SAE-rated cable. Using the UL specs for both DC and AC is preferable.

USA Cable-Sizing Formula

The ABYC tables have been developed by the application of the following formula:

$$CM = (K \times I \times L) \div E \text{ where:}$$

CM = Circular Mil area of the conductor (a measure of its cross-sectional area)

K = 10.75 (a constant representing the mil-foot resistance of copper)

I = the maximum current (amps) on the circuit

L = the length in feet of the conductors in the circuit

E = the maximum allowable voltage drop (in volts) at full load

Use the formula to calculate wire sizes for loads and voltage drops not covered by the tables. For example, if voltage drop is to be limited to 3%, what size cables would be required for a 12-volt electric windlass that pulls 200 amps at full load and which will be situated 25 feet from its battery?

3% of 12 volts is 0.36 volts.

$$CM = (10.75 \times 200 \times 50) \div 0.36 = 298611$$
Circular mils.

Table 3-6 converts Circular Mils to AWG. In our example a humongous, and totally impractical, 6/0 cable is required. Two 3/0 cables could be run in parallel, but in all probability we would settle for a 10% voltage drop at full load, which can be met with a 2/0 cable (still big!).

Column 2 of Table 3-6 gives minimum SAE (Society of Automotive Engineers) cable specifications, which the ABYC considers adequate for DC wiring, and column 3 gives minimum UL (Underwriters Laboratories) cable specifications (AWG), which the ABYC considers necessary for AC wiring. For a given cable size, UL cables (AWG) are larger than SAE (wiring is one of those confusing areas where there are several different standards). Using the UL standards (AWG) for both DC and AC wiring will ensure the best results.

Understanding and Troubleshooting Electrical Circuits;
Proper Installation Practices

UK Cable-Sizing Procedures

In the UK a slightly more involved procedure is used to determine cable sizes. The allowable volt-drop-per-amp-per-meter must be calculated. Taking the windlass example, a 3% volt drop on a 12-volt circuit is 0.36 volts. At a maximum current of 200 amps, this gives an allowable volt-drop-per-amp of:

0.36 ÷ 200 = 0.0018 volts (1.8 millivolts [mV, thousandths of a volt]).

Now we have a hitch. Some UK volt-drop tables are based on the *total length of the circuit* (as in the ABYC tables), but other tables are constructed on the basis of the *meter run* of the circuit, which means it is necessary to measure only the distance *in one direction* in order to enter the table. Table 3-7 is a *meter-run* table. The circuit is 7.5 meters (25 feet) in one direction, so the allowable volt-drop-per-amp-per-*meter run* is:

0.0018 ÷ 7.5 = 0.00024 volts (0.24 mVolts).

Table 3-7 is entered in the DC millivolt (mV)

column. Reading down we find 0.25mV, which is very close to the 0.24 mV we are looking for. Reading across to the left-hand side, we find we need a cable with a cross-sectional area of 185 mm² (which is pretty close to AWG 6/0—see Table 3-6). If we decide to accept a 10% volt drop on the circuit, the allowable volt-drop-per-amp-per-meter run is now:

1.2 ÷ (200 × 7.5) = 0.0008 volts (0.8 mV).

Entering Table 3-7, we find the nearest mV readings are 0.67 and 0.96. When we cannot find an exact correlation, we always use the *larger* cable which in this case is 70 mm². This is pretty close to AWG 2/0—the formula worked again! (Unless precise electrical engineering is needed, UK readers can use the ABYC tables to determine an American Wire Gauge size for a cable, and then use Table 3-6 to convert this to mm², but remember that the American tables require measurements in *feet*, both *to and from* the load.)

Table 3-7. Continuous Current Ratings for Cables

Conductor nominal cross-sectional area	Current rating DC or single-phase AC or 3-phase AC	Volt-drop-per-ampere-per-meter		
		DC	Single-phase AC	3-phase AC
1	2	3	4	5
mm²	A	mV	mV	mV
1.0	17	53	53	46
1.5	21	34	34	29
2.5	30	18	18	16
4	40	12	12	10
6	51	7.6	7.6	6.6
10	71	4.5	4.5	3.9
16	95	2.7	2.7	2.3
25	125	1.7	1.7	1.5
35	155	1.2	1.2	1.2
50	190	0.96	0.98	0.87
70	240	0.67	0.69	0.63
95	290	0.48	0.52	0.49
120	340	0.38	0.42	0.43
150	385	0.31	0.36	0.38
185	440	0.25	0.32	0.34
240	520	0.19	0.27	0.31
300	590	0.15	0.24	0.29
	DC	AC			
400	690	670	0.12	0.23	0.28
500	780	720	0.093	0.22	0.27
630	890	780	0.071	0.21	0.26

NOTES:

1. There are different tables for different types of cable in different ambient temperatures. This is a conservative table based on insulation rated for 60°C (140°F). A cable with insulation rated for higher temperatures will be able to carry higher currents. Since any good-quality boat cable should exceed the 60°C (140°F) temperature rating, this table can be safely used to size just about any cable.

2. This table is based upon distances measured in *meter-runs*—i.e., it is necessary to measure only the circuit *in one direction*. See the text for an explanation of how to use it.

Table 3-8. Allowable Ampacity of Conductors

CONDUCTOR SIZE AWG	Temperature Rating of Conductor Insulation												
	60°C (140°F)		75°C (167°F)		80°C (176°F)		90°C (194°F)		105°C (221°F)		125°C (257°F)		200°C (392°F)
	OUTSIDE ENGINE SPACES	INSIDE ENGINE SPACES	OUTSIDE ENGINE SPACES	INSIDE ENGINE SPACES	OUTSIDE ENGINE SPACES	INSIDE ENGINE SPACES	OUTSIDE ENGINE SPACES	INSIDE ENGINE SPACES	OUTSIDE ENGINE SPACES	INSIDE ENGINE SPACES	OUTSIDE ENGINE SPACES	INSIDE ENGINE SPACES	OUTSIDE OR INSIDE ENGINE SPACES
18 (0.8)	10	5.8	10	7.5	15	11.7	20	16.4	20	17.0	25	22.3	25
16 (1)	15	8.7	15	11.3	20	15.6	25	20.5	25	21.3	30	26.7	35
14 (2)	20	11.6	20	15.0	25	19.5	30	24.6	35	29.8	40	35.6	45
12 (3)	25	14.5	25	18.8	35	27.3	40	32.8	45	38.3	50	44.5	55
10 (5)	40	23.2	40	30.0	50	39.0	55	45.1	60	51.0	70	62.3	70
8 (8)	55	31.9	65	48.8	70	54.6	70	57.4	80	68.0	90	80.1	100
6 (13)	80	46.4	95	71.3	100	78.0	100	82.0	120	102.0	125	111.3	135
4 (19)	105	60.9	125	93.8	130	101.4	135	110.7	160	136.0	170	151.3	180
2 (32)	140	81.2	170	127.5	175	136.5	180	147.6	210	178.5	225	200.3	240
1 (40)	165	95.7	195	146.3	210	163.8	210	172.2	245	208.3	265	235.9	280
0 (50)	195	113.1	230	172.5	245	191.1	245	200.9	285	242.3	305	271.5	325
00 (62)	225	130.5	265	198.8	285	222.3	285	233.7	330	280.5	355	316.0	370
000 (81)	260	150.8	310	232.5	330	257.4	330	270.6	385	327.3	410	364.9	430
0000 (103)	300	174.0	360	270.0	385	300.3	385	315.7	445	378.3	475	422.8	510

Maximum Allowable Amperage

Correction Factors for Bundling of AC Cables

No. of current-carrying conductors	Correction factor
3	0.70
4-6	0.60
7-24	0.50
25+	0.40

(ABYC)

This table, and these correction factors, are used to double-check the adequacy of cables selected by using the voltage-drop tables. For example, a 2/0 cable on a 200-amp circuit: If this is to be run through an engine space, Table 3-8 tells us the cable insulation must be rated for 167°F/75°C; if the only cable available has a 140°F/60°C rating, the 2/0 cable cannot be used to carry 200 amps in the engine room, but would be adequate outside it.

Table 3-9 converts American wire gauge sizes to European specifications.

Connections and Terminals

Poor connections are the bane of many an otherwise excellent electrical installation. The keys to success are using the proper terminals, installing them with the proper tools, and keeping moisture out of the terminal.

Proper terminals. Crimp-on connectors and terminals have gained almost universal acceptance in marine wiring. However, it should be noted that every one is a potential source of trouble: The exposed end of the cable core, protruding from the terminal, provides an entry path for moisture to wick up into the wiring, causing corrosion and resistance; the terminal forms a hard spot in the wiring so that any vibration will tend to cause the wire to fracture where it enters the terminal; and the terminal itself will be fastened to a terminal block or piece of equipment that may use a screw of a dissimilar metal, opening up the possibility of galvanic corrosion.

It makes sense to use the very best terminals available, and as usual there is more to this than meets the eye. A quality terminal will include the following features (none of which are likely to be found on the cheap terminals available at auto parts stores!):

- an *annealed, tin-plated,* copper terminal end. The annealing softens the copper so that the retaining screw will bite into it for maximum conductivity. The tin plating enhances conductivity and corrosion resistance.

- a *seamless* tin-plated brass or bronze sleeve to crimp onto the cable, preferably with a serrated inside surface to enhance its mechanical grip. A seamless sleeve can be crimped from any angle and will hold the wire better than a seamed sleeve.

Understanding and Troubleshooting Electrical Circuits;
Proper Installation Practices

Table 3-9. Comparison of Conductor Cross-Sections

AWG Ga.	AWG mm²	ISO mm²	Ampacity AWG	Ampacity ISO
18	0.82	0.75	20	12
		1.0		18
16	1.31		25	
		1.5		21
14	2.08		35	
		2.5		30
12	3.31		45	
		4.0		40
10	5.26		60	
		6.0		50
8	8.39		80	
		10.0		70
6	13.3		120	
		16.0		100
4	21.2		160	
3	26.6	25.0	180	140
2	33.6	35.0	210	185
1	42.4		245	
0	53.5	50.0	285	230
2/0	67.7	70.0	330	285
3/0	85.2		385	
		95.0		330
4/0	107		445	
250 kcm	127	120	500	400
300 kcm	152	150	550	430

ISO = International Standards Organization, the governing body for European standards.
(ABYC)

- *a long, nylon insulating sleeve,* extending up over the wire insulation. Nylon will not crack or punch through when crimping, and is UV-, diesel-, and oil-resistant (unlike the PVC found on cheap terminals). If the long sleeve contains an extra brass sleeve, a double crimp can be made—once on the terminal barrel, and once on the sleeve around the wire insulation—to provide maximum strain relief.

On wire sizes larger than 4 AWG, uninsulated *lugs* are used to terminate cables. Key features to look for in such lugs are once again an annealed terminal end, tin plating, and a seamless construction. In addition, *the lower end of the barrel should be closed to prevent water entry.* A long barrel will enable a double crimp to be made.

A terminal must be matched to both its cable and its retaining screw or stud. Terminals are given a simple color code: red for 22-18 gauge wire (0.5 to 1.0mm²); blue for 16-14 gauge (1.5 to 2.5mm²); and yellow for 12-10 gauge (3.0 to 6.0mm²).

Ring-type terminals are preferred to spade, since they cannot pull off a loose screw. Locking spades are preferred to straight spades (Figure 3-43).

Wire nuts are frequently used to make connections in household circuits in the USA, though not in the UK. They are not suitable for marine use since the threaded metal insert is made of steel and will rust; what is more, the lower end of the nut is open to the atmosphere. If used, wire nuts should always be installed with the open end down so that the nut does not become a water trap. It is a good practice then to seal the nut with polyurethane sealant (it is a better practice to "just say no").

Proper tools. *It is simply not possible to turn out successful crimps without the right tools.* This means a *properly sized* insulation stripper (not a pocket knife, see Figure 3-44), and a *properly sized* crimper.

There are two types of crimp: an indented crimp, in which a deep slot is made in the terminal, and an elliptical crimp, in which the terminal is compressed around its circumference.

Proper Electrical Installations   119

Figure 3-43. Wiring installation tips. Several acceptable connections are shown. Wire nuts are *not* recommended for marine use. Drip loops should be incorporated into all connections to keep water from the wire ends and terminals. *(Jim Sollers)*

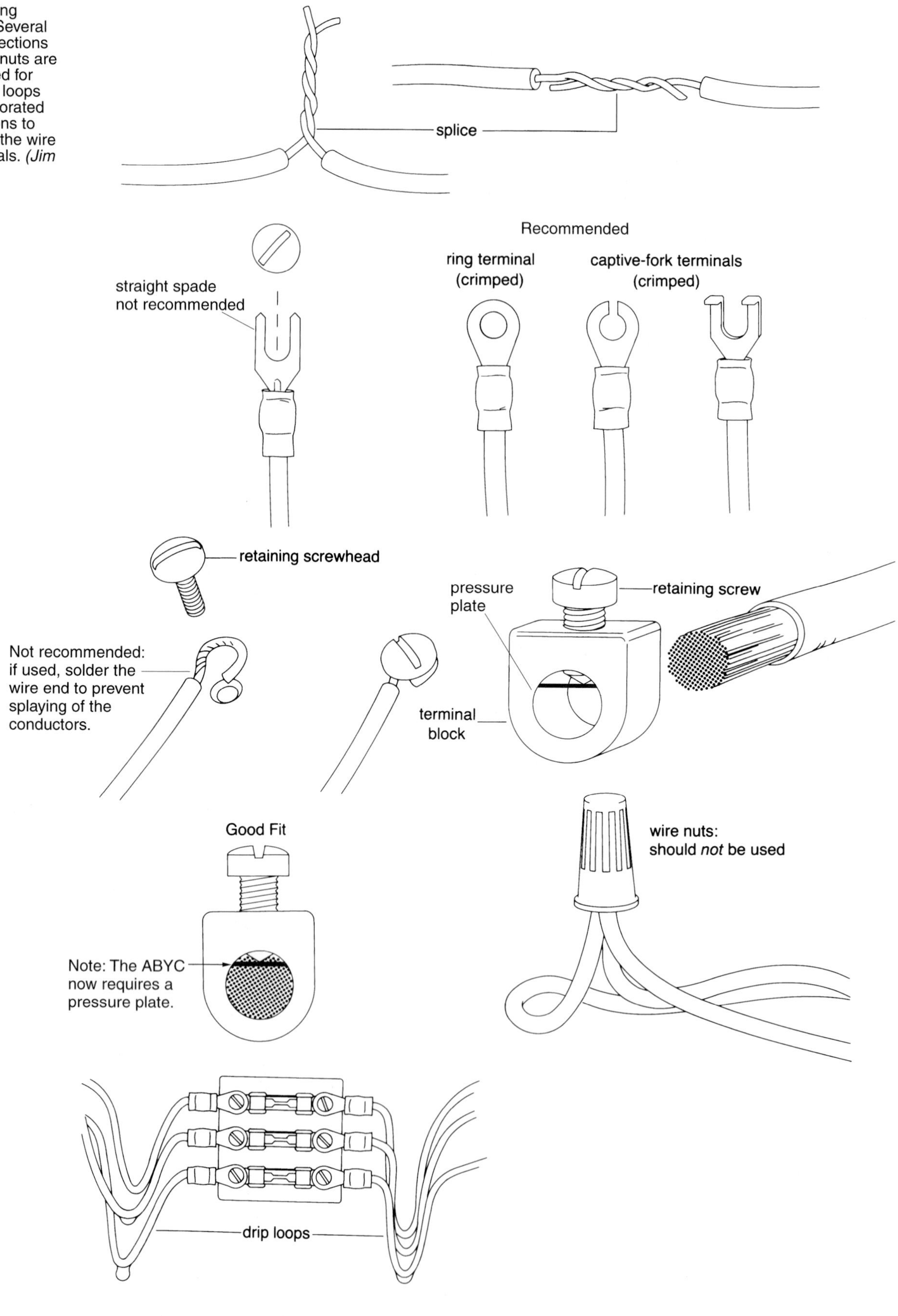

splice

straight spade
not recommended

Recommended

ring terminal
(crimped)

captive-fork terminals
(crimped)

retaining screwhead

Not recommended:
if used, solder the
wire end to prevent
splaying of the
conductors.

pressure
plate

retaining screw

terminal
block

Good Fit

Note: The ABYC
now requires a
pressure plate.

wire nuts:
should *not* be used

drip loops

Understanding and Troubleshooting Electrical Circuits;
Proper Installation Practices

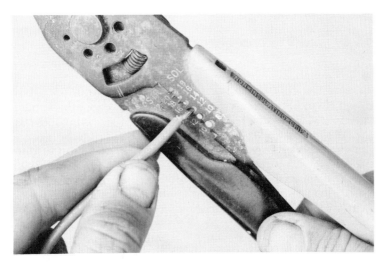

Figure 3-44. Wire stripper in use on a cheap multi-purpose crimping and stripping tool. Note that the stripping holes are numbered with their AWG sizes—the numbers on the left-hand side are for stranded cable; those on the right-hand side for solid cable. The threaded holes in the tool (top left) are for cutting terminal retaining screws to length. The screws are threaded in from the numbered side, cut to length, and backed out. This tool has both indent and elliptical crimping slots (not shown).

Figure 3-45. A ratcheting-type crimper that does a perfect job every time. This one makes a double crimp (see Figure 3-46).

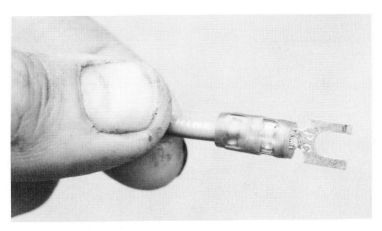

Figure 3-46. Double crimp, once on the terminal barrel and once on the insulated sleeve. Note that these are elliptical crimps, not indent crimps, because this is an insulated terminal (although in point of fact, an indent crimp could have been used in this case since this is a nylon sleeve).

To avoid the risk of cutting through any insulation, *an indent crimp is normally made only on an uninsulated terminal* (although it is permissible to use it on *nylon-sleeved* terminals, since the nylon resists cracking); for insulated terminals it is important to use an *elliptical* crimp (most cheap crimping tools will do both—its simply a matter of choosing the right slot).

But rather than use a cheap crimping tool, every maintenance-conscious boatowner should have a ratcheting-type crimper in the toolbox (Figures 3-45 and 3-46). These will assure a perfect crimp every time.

Special crimping tools are needed for larger cable sizes, but these need not be expensive (the Ancor catalog is an excellent source for marine-grade wiring products and installation tools: Ancor, Cotati, CA). These large cables will be carrying heavy loads, which require perfect electrical connections if problems are to be avoided. (Ohm's law tells us that voltage = amperage × resistance. On a 100-amp circuit a resistance of just one-hundredth of an ohm (0.01 ohm) will cause a 1-volt drop, which is close to 10% on a 12-volt circuit. Since watts = volts × amps, this will generate 100 watts of heat.)

While on the subject of tools, let me also mention *split-shank* screwdrivers. These have a blade divided into two sections that can be squeezed apart in the slot of a screw, gripping the screw. This is an invaluable tool when trying to do up terminal screws in cramped quarters.

Soldering. Soldering is a controversial subject. A properly soldered connection creates the best electrical connection, but all too often the soldering is not done properly. In any case, ABYC regulations require that every joint have a *mechanical* means of connection other than solder. The reason for this is that if the joint gets hot (through excessive resistance or a high current flow) the solder may melt and the joint fall apart. So soldering frequently becomes just an adjunct to a crimped connection, but in this case the solder wicking up the cable creates a hard spot, which is then liable to fail from vibration. *The consensus among professionals is that a properly made crimp, done with the proper tools, is frequently a more reliable termination than soldering.*

Recently low-temperature solder connections with a heat-shrink sleeve have been introduced to the US market. The terminals come lined with solder and enclosed in the heat shrink. The wire is simply slipped into the terminal and a heat-gun applied (Figure 3-47). The solder melts into the wire at the same time as the sleeve shrinks down. It seems like a neat idea, but unless the wire is spotlessly clean the solder may not tin properly; the solder penetration is frequently poor; and the solder melting point is so low that if the joint heats up it may well fail. Additionally, as mentioned, the ABYC does not allow solder to be the sole means of mechanical support in a connection. Although the heat shrink provides a degree of mechanical connection, this is not the same as a crimp. For these reasons, these terminals are not recommended.

Sealing terminals. In recent years heat-shrink tubing has become widely available. Heat shrink consists of a plastic tube that is slipped over a terminal and then heated, preferably with a proper heat gun, but a small propane torch or even a cigarette lighter will do. The tubing contracts to form a tight fit around the terminal barrel and wire (Figures 3-49A, 3-49B and 3-49C).

There are three types of heat shrink: *thin wall*; *dual wall* (which is thin wall lined with an adhesive); and *heavy wall with sealant*. The thin wall (which is commonly found at Radio Shack in the USA) provides insulation, but *not weatherproofing*; the adhesive in the dual wall and heavy wall is squeezed out of both ends of the tubing as it contracts, *forming an extremely effective barrier to moisture penetration*. The heavy wall provides an added margin of abrasion resistance over the dual wall. One or two companies now have a line of "waterproof" terminals that have a length of heat shrink tubing already built onto the terminal sleeve.

Some joints that need insulating are an awkward shape with protruding corners and screws. In these instances, electricians' putty comes in handy. It is a pliable substance, similar to plasticene, which is molded around the connection to fair it so that it can be wrapped smoothly with heat shrink tape (this can be bought in rolls; it is known as *self-amalgamating tape* in the UK). The putty itself has a high insulating value but is too soft to be left uncovered.

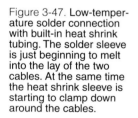

Figure 3-47. Low-temperature solder connection with built-in heat shrink tubing. The solder sleeve is just beginning to melt into the lay of the two cables. At the same time the heat shrink sleeve is starting to clamp down around the cables.

Understanding and Troubleshooting Electrical Circuits;
Proper Installation Practices

Soldering on Board

Most soldering aboard can be done with a 50- to 100-watt soldering iron; a few large jobs are best done with a propane torch. Soldering irons can be bought for use with 12-volt systems but are electrically greedy (a 50-watt iron will draw close to 5 amps). Since the iron is used intermittently and for short periods, this is not a great problem. Also available now are small, pocket-sized temperature-controllable butane soldering torches.

Solder is always used with a *flux,* an agent that helps to keep the metal surfaces clean while being soldered. Fluxes are either acid based or rosin based. Only rosin-based fluxes can be used in electrical work, acid fluxes will corrode copper wire.

There are numerous grades of solder, rated by their percentage of tin, lead, or silver. The best all-around solder for electrical work is 60/40 (60% tin; 40% lead). Avoid cheap solders with higher percentages of lead. Solder comes in rolls of either solid or rosin-cored wire, the latter having a hollow center with flux already in it whereas solid solder requires an external application of flux. The rosin-cored solder is suitable for most marine uses and is much more convenient.

The keys to successful soldering are having a well-tinned soldering iron and tinning the individual pieces to be bonded *before* the joint is made. To tin the iron, clean its tip down to bare metal with a file, heat it up, and then touch rosin-cored solder to it. The solder should flow over the whole tip to form a clean, shiny surface. If it will not adhere to areas of the tip, there are impurities. Sometimes scratching around with a knife and the solder (to lay on more rosin) will clean these areas, but it may be necessary to go back and start again with the file. During soldering, the tip of the hot iron should be wiped periodically with a damp rag to remove burnt flux and old solder.

To tin wire ends and terminals, clean them down to bare, shiny metal and then hold the iron to the part to heat it. Touch the solder *to the part,* not to the iron. When the part is hot enough, the solder will flow over and into it, at which point the iron can be withdrawn—the tinning is complete. Once again, if the solder will not adhere to certain areas, they are not clean enough. To speed the heating of the part, place a drop of solder on the iron itself where it is in contact with the part; the actual tinning should always be done by applying the solder as described above.

Figure 3-48. Soldering practices. Note that an alligator clip or a strip of aluminum used as a heat sink will protect the insulation from melting. When tinning (applying solder to the wire—not necessary on tinned wire), touch the solder to the wire, not to the iron. As a preparatory step, sandpaper or file the tip of the iron to a pyramid-shaped point of bright metal, then heat the iron, file it bright again, and, working fast, run on a little solder. Try to achieve a good coating of solder over the entire point and 1/2 inch or so down the tip. Before making a joint, scrape the wire clean and bright. Place the parts to be soldered in firm contact. Use enough heat, but don't overheat. Keep the joint and wire immobile while the solder cools. *(Jim Sollers)*

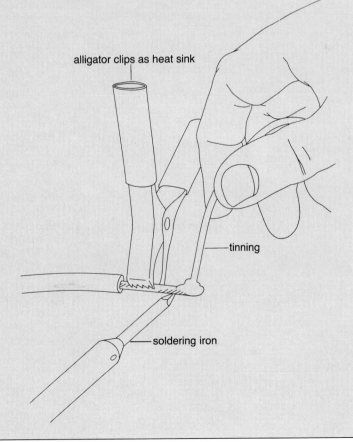

alligator clips as heat sink

tinning

soldering iron

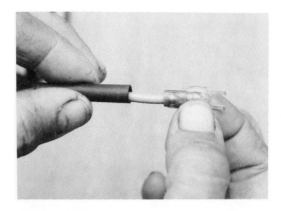

Figure 3-49A. Sliding a length of heat shrink tubing over a terminal.

Figure 3-49B. Heating the heat shrink with a heat gun.

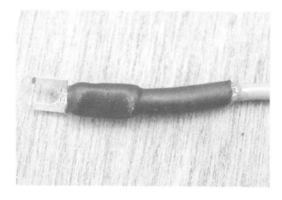

Figure 3-49C. The completed terminal. Note the glue squeezed out of the heat shrink tubing. The heat-shrink sleeve will not only provide waterproofing, but also a fair measure of strain relief at the hard spot where the cable exits the terminal.

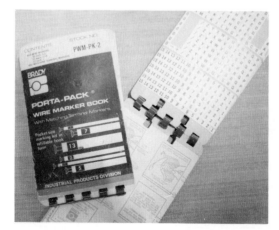

Figure 3-50. Book of wire markers.

Installing Cables

Under ABYC regulations, no individual cable, unless housed in a common sheath with other cables, should be smaller than 16 AWG. This is to provide a minimum physical strength. Also *AC and DC cables cannot be run in a common bundle or sheath*, although they can be run side-by-side in separate bundles or sheaths.

Where cable runs come close to sensitive electronic equipment and compasses, twisted conductors should be used, preferably within a mylar or braided shield—this helps to reduce magnetic influences and interference. Long wire runs can be twisted rapidly by securing one end of the cables and then clamping the other end in an electric drill chuck and running the drill slowly (keep the wires taut to avoid a terrible tangle!).

Making and supporting cable runs. As each cable is run both ends should be labeled. This is most easily done using self-adhesive wire markers, which come in a book or dispenser containing all the letters of the alphabet, a collection of numbers, and + and − symbols (Figure 3-50). Wire markers can be obtained from any electrical wholesaler. Alternatively, a handwritten note can be used and covered with clear heat shrink tubing (the heat shrink is also a good idea over wire markers since they tend to come unglued over time).

When renewing cables inside masts and other inaccessible locations, attach the new wires to the ends of the old and pull the new into place as you withdraw the old. It is a good idea to pull a piece of string through along with the new wires and to leave this in place in case of future additions. Anytime a cable is run through an area where it may chafe (e.g., passing through a bulkhead) or suffer other damage (e.g., from loose objects rattling around in a locker), it must be fully protected. Holes through bulkheads should be lined with rubber grommets or grommet material (which can be bought in rolls), except in the case of watertight bulkheads in metal hulls. In the latter case, a pipe stub is usually welded through the bulkhead, with the cable passing through it. The end of the stub is threaded, and an appropriate watertight cable seal is screwed on.

Inside lockers, and anywhere else cables need protection, PVC pipe can be used as a conduit. The pipe is cheap, widely available (any hardware store), and easy to work with (all that is needed is a hacksaw and PVC cement). Any conduit must have a good-sized drain hole (at least ¼ inch) drilled at all low spots to prevent water entrapment.

Understanding and Troubleshooting Electrical Circuits;
Proper Installation Practices

Cables not run in conduit will need to be bundled together and supported against vibration at least every 18 inches. A broad variety of plastic cable ties and clips with which to do this are readily available. A very neat job of bundling can be done with plastic spiral wrap, which comes in diameters from ¼ inch up. Note that black plastic has a greater resistance to UV degradation than colorless. It should be used on all external wiring, and also preferably on internal wiring unless aesthetic reasons dictate otherwise.

No cable should be run closer than 2 inches to a wet exhaust, and 9 inches to a dry exhaust.

For AC circuits, the ABYC requires that all current-carrying connections (i.e., hot and neutral lines) be made inside some form of an enclosure (so that the connections cannot be touched accidentally).

Wires should, if possible, always enter junction boxes from the base. In order to avoid trapping moisture form a "drip loop" in the wire before making a terminal fast. Note that under the ABYC standards no more than four terminals can be stacked up on a single stud.

Distribution Panels

A distribution panel, as its name implies, takes battery or AC current and distributes it to all the individual circuits on the boat. A number of (sometimes contradictory) factors need to be taken into account when choosing a location for a distribution panel. The back of the panel must be readily accessible to simplify wiring and troubleshooting tasks. The best situation is a permanent mount in a bulkhead with a clear approach to the other side. Failing this, the panel must be set in a hinged frame.

Although the panel must clearly be kept dry, it is normally located most usefully in the navigation area, which is generally close to the companionway hatch. If spray is ever likely to be a problem, protect the front of the panel with a clear plastic screen. If at all possible, the panel should also be close to the boat's batteries to keep the heavy cable runs to a minimum.

Panel size and layout. For obvious reasons, it is an ABYC requirement to keep AC and DC panels and wiring separate. This is often hard to do in practice, particularly on smaller boats (Figure 3-51). Nevertheless, where AC and DC circuits are in close proximity there should still be a clear separation. It is also an ABYC requirement that it should not be possible to access the back of an AC panel without having to undo a fastener of some sort (a screw or bolt—this will stop children getting in the panel).

Panel size is a function of available space,

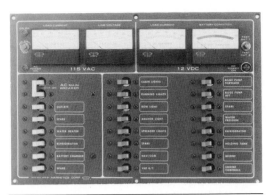

Figure 3-51. Combined AC and DC panel. Note, however, the clear separation of AC and DC breakers, with different colors used for the two sets of breakers. *(Marinetics)*

budget, and the number of circuits in a boat. The ideal, seldom realized, is to have an individual breaker for every circuit on the boat, but this can result in enormous panels (both in terms of size and expense—the largest I ever saw was 6 feet by 3 feet with upwards of 200 breakers, each with its own LED light!).

There is almost always a need to develop some logical groupings to cut down on the overall number of breakers. When doing this, it is only natural to think of placing similar fixtures (e.g., lights) on a common breaker, but this is not necessarily the best approach. Should the light circuit fail, all the lights will go out at once. So it is best to break things up a little and build in some redundancy if possible, for example having the port-side lights on one breaker and the starboard-side lights on another, the SatNav on one breaker and the GPS or Loran on another, and so on. If there is more than one bilge pump, they should be on separate breakers (unless they bypass the distribution panel altogether—see below).

Finally, there should be a logical sequence for the breakers in the panel, especially if it is a large one, for example placing all the navigation-related breakers in one block, the pumps in another, and so on.

Panel wiring. The positive side of the batteries is fed from an isolation switch through a main breaker (note that on AC panels the main breaker *must* be a *two-pole* breaker—see page 106) to a copper or brass bar, known as a *bus* bar, to which are connected a series of individual circuit breakers (which are normally single pole; this is acceptable on AC circuits only if the circuits are *polarized*—see page 106). These breakers feed the individual circuits on the boat. The ground side of the circuits (neutral on AC circuits) returns to a second bus bar. A connection is made from the DC negative bus (but not the AC neutral bus) to the boat's "common ground point," and then back to the negative side of the batteries. (The green or bare AC grounding wires are run to another bus which *is* connected to the boat's "common ground point.")

Older panels with single-pole breakers tend to have the negative (and neutral on AC circuits) bus bar built in alongside the positive bus, leading to a multiplicity of cables in a small space. Since there is no reason to have the ground and neutral wires even enter the panel (except where double-pole breakers are used), it will greatly simplify the wiring if a separate negative or neutral bus is established at a convenient but close-by, out-of-the-way location. This bus can be a terminal block with all the terminals interconnected with metal "bridging" plates to form an electrically continuous strip, or else a solid copper or brass bar drilled and tapped to take a series of brass screws (Figure 3-52). An AC neutral bus will need a cover to comply with the ABYC requirement that all exposed current-carrying connections be made within some sort of an enclosure.

If possible, the negative or neutral bus should be made long enough so that each individual ground or neutral wire in the boat's circuits can be given its own terminal. In any event, no more than four wires should be connected to each terminal. A single heavy cable, which must be sized to handle the boat's entire load, is led from the negative bus (DC system) to the main negative bus bar or common ground point, and from here back to the batteries' negative terminal posts (the connection from the AC grounding bus to the common ground point can be much lighter). The AC neutral bus is wired to the neutral half of the incoming two-pole main breaker.

On the positive side, once again it is desirable to have just one cable attached to each breaker (Figure 3-53). If the breaker serves more than one circuit, this single cable can be taken to a bridged terminal block, and the individual circuits taken off this block (Figure 3-54).

The final step in a panel installation is to form all the cables into neat bundles and to fasten them properly against vibration. It is essential to make sure that any battery cables are under no strain since, with their weight, they can occasionally vibrate loose. If a hot cable makes contact with a grounded terminal there will be an uncontrolled arc welder at work in the back of the panel!

If a panel is hinged, all the cables are led to the hinged side and then given a small excess loop so that they will be flexed minimally, and not be put under any strain, when the panel is opened and closed.

Breakers. Any kind of a short in a DC or AC circuit allows electrical current to by-pass the designed load on that circuit. If the path of the short circuit has a lower resistance than the load, currents in excess of the designed limit on the circuit will flow. If the current is high enough, the circuit will heat up to the point at which it starts fires. Given a short, even quite small batteries have more than enough stored energy to start fires or to do other serious damage; the potential energy that can flow around AC circuits is far higher.

Sizing breakers. The purpose of a circuit breaker is to detect overcurrent situations and break a circuit before it becomes dangerously hot. Since the most heat in any circuit will be developed by the section of wiring with the highest resistance (the smallest wire), for any given circuit, a circuit breaker is sized to protect the smallest gauge wire in the circuit. The current-carrying capability (*ampacity*) of cables is given in Table 3-8. Under ABYC regulations if there is not an exact match between cable ampacity and available breaker ratings, the next highest rated breaker can be used so long as its rating does not exceed 150% of the ampacity of the cable it is protecting (for example, if a cable is rated at 17

Figure 3-52. A collection of neatly installed bus bars and terminal strips. Note that everything is labeled, which will help in future troubleshooting. The four terminals stacked on one stud at the top left are acceptable under ABYC recommendations but would have been better spread out over a couple of studs. In the lower left the cable sheath clearly reads "Boat Cable"—this is, in fact, tinned, multi-stranded UL 1426 cable. A spare bus bar (middle right) has been fitted for future needs.

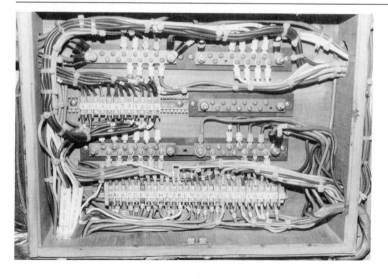

Understanding and Troubleshooting Electrical Circuits;
Proper Installation Practices

amps in a given environment, but the only breakers available are rated at 15 and 20 amps, the 20 amp breaker, at 117% of the cable rating, is acceptable).

Note that a circuit breaker is intended for circuit protection, not for equipment protection. If a GPS, which draws minimal current, is hooked into a circuit wired with AWG 12 wire, *the circuit breaker should be rated to protect the wire from meltdown, not the GPS*. Separate protection (generally a fuse—see below) should be provided for the individual pieces of equipment.

However, if a breaker serves a circuit to a single load, and the protection required by the load is less than that required by the circuit, the breaker can always be sized to protect the load, down to about 5 amps, which is typically the smallest breaker available. Since breakers generally don't trip until the load exceeds their rating by 15% to 30%, any breaker sized for the load will still have a margin to handle minor overloads.

If a breaker serves several circuits, its sizing is a little more complex. There are two factors to be considered: the total load of all the electrical equipment to be served by the breaker, and the current-carrying capability of the *smallest* wire being protected by the breaker. The breaker must be sized according to the *lower* of the total load or ampacity of the smallest conductor.

If a breaker feeds another subsidiary panel or fuse block, and if all the conductors from the panel or fuse block to individual appliances are protected by their own breakers or fuses, *the only conductor that the breaker has to protect is the feeder cable to the subsidiary panel*. The breaker will be rated according to the lower of the total load on the subsidiary panel or the ampacity of the conductor to the panel.

Breaker types. There are two broad categories of breakers: thermal and magnetic. The thermal breakers heat up as current passes through them; once a certain temperature is exceeded, the breaker trips. In high ambient temperatures they may be subject to nuisance tripping (for every 10°F/5°C rise in temperature above 80°F/27°C they are de-rated by approximately 10%). For this reason, magnetic breakers are preferred (these sense the magnitude of the current magnetically and are unaffected by temperature).

Some breakers can be overridden manually. These are not acceptable in marine use. What is needed are *trip-free* breakers, which cannot be overridden or reset until the overcurrent condition has been eliminated. Handles may be the toggle or rocker type. The marine industry seems to have standardized on the toggle type, which can be easily knocked "off "or "on" by

Figure 3-53. A block of breakers. Note the "hot" bus bar on the left of the breakers with the individual circuits to the loads on the right. The bus bar shows some signs of corrosion. It is not a good idea to make multiple connections to a breaker as at the upper right (see the text).

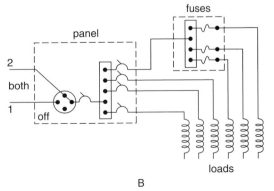

Figure 3-54. If a breaker serves more than one circuit it is preferable to run a single cable to a bridged terminal block (A) and take the individual circuits off this block, or to run the cable from the breaker to a "common hot feed" fuse block and run the individual circuits from the various fuses (B).

accident, even though the rocker type is far less prone to such accidents.

Breakers are given a specified current rating. However, two breakers with the same rating may not perform the same way. Some are designed to trip rapidly once a threshold current is exceeded, and some to respond more slowly—the latter are needed primarily on electric-motor circuits where the *inrush* current to the motor may be several times its operating current.

Fuses and motor protection. Circuit breakers are generally used to protect wiring from overcurrent situations; fuses are generally used to protect the equipment at the end of the wiring.

The *inrush*, or *start-up*, current of some loads (notably electric motors, but also incandescent lights) can momentarily be up to seven times the operating current. To protect such equipment a fuse is needed that is rated somewhere close to the operating load but can handle this inrush current. Such a fuse is a *slow-blow* fuse. But then there are other pieces of equipment, notably electronics, that pull a steady current and will be damaged by just about *any* overload. These need a *fast-blow* fuse with no tolerance for even momentary overcurrents. The manufacturer's data sheet for a piece of equipment should specify both the *rating* and the *type* of any recommended fuse.

Fuses actually blow at around 130% of their rating, but this is temperature dependent. The hotter the fuse, the lower the current it will carry. At 125°F (52°C) a fuse will blow at well below its rated current. Corrosion on fuse terminals will create resistance, which in turn creates heat. If a fuse begins to blow regularly with no apparent explanation, the ambient temperature should be checked and the fuse and fuse holder inspected for corrosion.

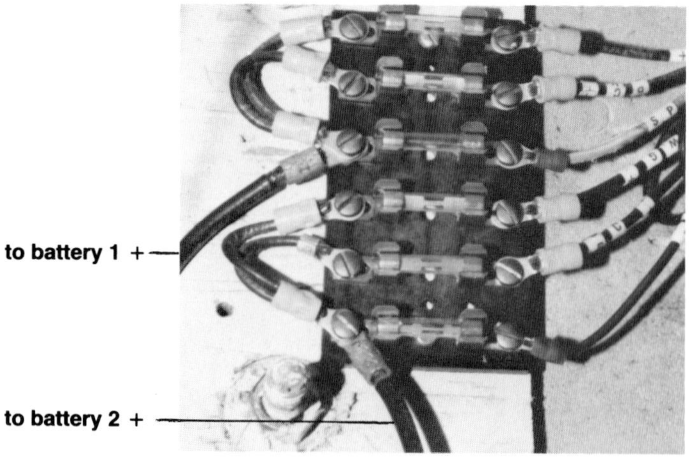

One situation needs particular attention. If a motor gets into what is known as a *locked-rotor* state (which means the motor is jammed—for example, a bilge pump with a piece of trash in the impeller), its current draw rises sharply, potentially overloading the circuit and/or melting down the pump housing. If the rise in current is high enough, and the circuit or motor is properly breakered or fused, the breaker or fuse will trip or blow.

But sometimes, particularly with bilge pumps, there is a long run of marginally sized wiring to the motor. If a locked-rotor condition develops, the *total resistance in the circuit may be sufficient to limit the current flow to a level that will not trip the breaker or blow the fuse but which nevertheless is high enough over time to start a fire*. Using a lower-rated fuse or breaker is not the answer since it may lead to nuisance tripping with normal inrush currents. *The wire size needs to be increased so that the voltage drop on the circuit is lowered to a level at which sufficient current to trip the breaker or blow the fuse can flow*. In any event, the ABYC requires that *all motors and motor circuits be designed and protected in such a way that they can withstand a locked-rotor condition for seven hours without creating a fire hazard*.

Circuits that bypass a panel. There are certain circuits that may need to bypass the battery isolation switch and distribution panel. These include charging devices and bilge pumps that are to be left on when the boat is unattended, and some sensitive electronic equipment that will suffer from interference problems if connected directly to a battery.

A short in any circuit wired directly to a battery will create a dead short across the batteries. I know of one boat that was burned to the waterline by a simple fault in the unfused wiring to a small solar panel. *All such circuits must be properly fused as close to the batteries as possible* (Figures 3-55A and 3-55B).

The ABYC does, however, allow any conductor wired directly to the battery positive post to be unprotected for a length of up to 72 inches, and cables to starter motors require no overcurrent protection at all (although, on boats over 26 feet in length, the ABYC standards do require a battery isolation switch in the cranking circuit). Other cables tied into this cranking circuit may be unprotected for up to 40 inches so long as the cables are in a sheath or conduit (Figure 3-56—typically these include the alternator output cable, the positive feed to the engine panel, and sometimes the positive feed to the distribution

to battery 1 +

to battery 2 +

Figure 3-55A. The correct way to install any equipment connected directly to a battery (bypassing the distribution panel and battery isolation switch). This particular setup is for a two-battery system. The six incoming cables on the right are (top to bottom) wind generator, battery charger, and solar panel for battery 1, and the same three for battery 2.

Understanding and Troubleshooting Electrical Circuits; Proper Installation Practices

panel, all of which are commonly connected to the positive terminal on the starter solenoid, which in turn is wired to the battery positive.)

These exceptions originate in the automotive field where starter motor and alternator output cables are short and well secured. In the marine field where cranking and alternator circuits may be long, and alternator outputs may be at welding amperages, a hazard may be created. High-capacity fuses (up to 800 amps) are now readily and cheaply available (Ample Technologies, Cruising Equipment Company, Blue Sea Systems [Bellingham, WA], and others—Figure 3-57).

If a car catches fire the occupants can pull over and jump out; if a boat catches fire it is not so simple. *It makes no sense to have any unprotected circuits on a boat* (with the possible exception of cranking circuits on larger engines since the inrush currents are high enough to make it very difficult to provide over-current protection).

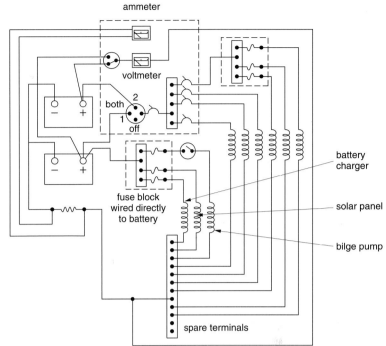

Figure 3-55B. Circuits connected to a battery post fed by a common-hot-feed fuse block.

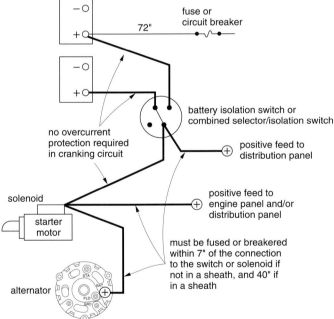

Figure 3-56. Maximum unfused or unbreakered cable lengths under ABYC standards. Note that although the ABYC accepts unprotected cables up to the lengths shown, it is preferable to provide full overcurrent protection *at the batteries for all cables* (see the text).

Figure 3-57. A collection of high-current fuses on a 70-foot schooner with a very powerful DC system.

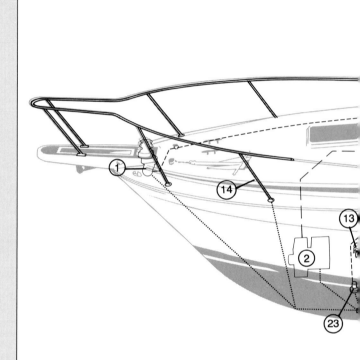

CHAPTER 4

Figure 4-1. Effective bonding and grounding techniques will head off problems with corrosion and electrical interference, not to mention minimize damage from lightning strikes. *(Jim Sollers)*

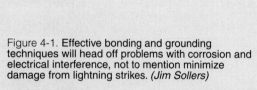

― ― ― ― ― ―	12 V ground (return)
― ― ― ― ― ―	120 VAC grounding
....	bonding strap jumper
▨▨▨▨	engine ground
▨▨▨▨	immersed ground

(1) windlass
(2) air conditioner
(3) bonding strap
(4) freezer
(5) air conditioner compressor
(6) refrigerator
(7) water heater
(8) radio and instruments
(9) steering and engine controls
(10) batteries
(11) battery isolation switch
(12) fuel tanks
(13) through hull
(14) stanchions
(15) metal keel
(16) chainplates
(17) deck fills
(18) stem fitting
(19) metal rudder
(20) distribution panel
(21) generator
(22) struts
(23) pump
(24) blower
(25) lights
(26) lightning rod

Corrosion, Bonding, Lightning Protection, and Grounding

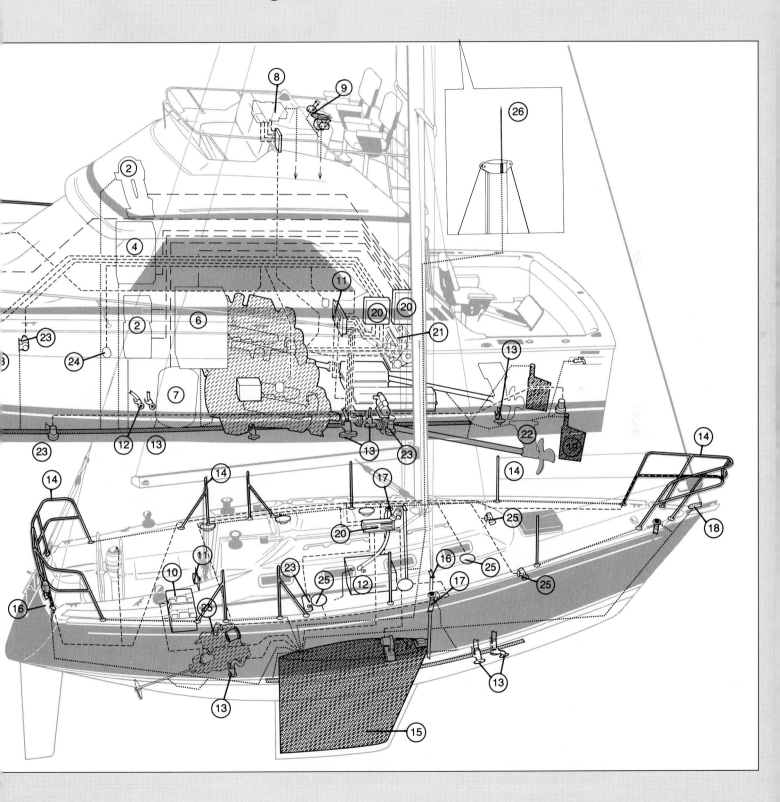

Corrosion

Corrosion is an ever present fact of life with boats. The mixing of salt water and different metals is, in itself, enough to cause *galvanic corrosion*; the addition of electricity can be a potent catalyst leading to highly destructive *stray-current* corrosion.

Galvanic Corrosion

It is a "fact of nature" that all metals when immersed in an electrically conductive fluid (an *electrolyte*) have a specific *electrical potential* which is measurable as a voltage. It is another "fact of nature" that no two metals have the same electrical potential. As a result, if two different metals are placed in the same electrolyte, their differing electrical potentials will produce a voltage difference, measurable simply by placing the probes of a sensitive voltmeter on the two pieces of metal.

If we take one piece of metal and put it in an electrolyte and then one at a time place a whole series of different metals in the same electrolyte, measuring the voltage difference between the first metal and each of the others, we will be able to construct a table, ranking all the metals in terms of the extent of their voltage difference with the first *(reference)* metal (Figures 4-2, 4-3, and 4-4). It

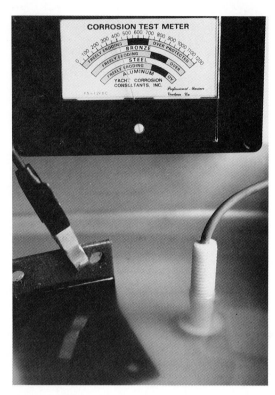

Figure 4-3. When the same meter is connected to a piece of steel, the voltage reading jumps to 410 millivolts.

Figure 4-2. The "natural voltage" of a bronze water pump with respect to a reference metal (in this case a silver/silver chloride half cell) is here around 120 millivolts.

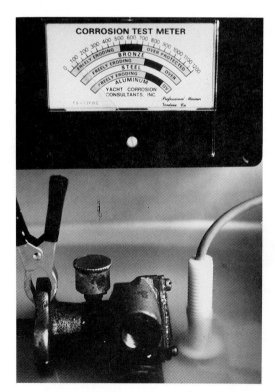

Figure 4-4. Connected to an old zinc anode, the reading jumps to 850 millivolts.

Table 4-1. Galvanic Series of Metals in Seawater[1]

Metals and Alloys	Corrosion-Potential Range in Volts[2]	
Magnesium and Magnesium Alloys	−1.60	to −1.63
Zinc	−0.98	to −1.03
Galvanized Steel or Galvanized Wrought Iron	NA	
Aluminum Alloys	−0.76	to −1.00
Cadmium	−0.70	to −0.73
Mild Steel	−0.60	to −0.71
Wrought Iron	−0.60	to −0.71
Cast Iron	−0.60	to −0.71
13% Chromium Stainless Steel, Type 410 (active in still water)	−0.46	to −0.58
18/8 Stainless Steel, Type 304 (active in still water)	−0.46	to −0.58
Ni-Resist	−0.46	to −0.58
18.8, 3% Mo Stainless Steel, Type 316 (active in still water)	−0.43	to −0.54
Inconel (78% Ni, 14.5% Cr, 6% Fe) (active in still water)	−0.35	to −0.46
Aluminum Bronze (92% Cu, 8% Al)	−0.31	to −0.42
Naval Brass (60% Cu, 39% Zn)	−0.30	to −0.40
Yellow Brass (65% Cu, 35% Zn)	−0.30	to −0.40
Red Brass (85% Cu, 15% Zn)	−0.30	to −0.40
Muntz Metal (60% Cu, 40% Zn)	−0.30	to −0.40
Tin	−0.31	to −0.33
Copper	−0.30	to −0.57
50-50 Lead − Tin Solder	−0.28	to −0.37
Admiralty Brass (71% Cu, 28% Zn, 1% Sn)	−0.28	to −0.36
Aluminum Brass (76% Cu, 22% Zn, 2% Al)	−0.28	to −0.36
Manganese Bronze (58.5% Cu, 39% Zn, 1% Sn, 1% Fe, 0.3% MN)	−0.27	to −0.34
Silicone Bronze (96% Cu max, 0.80% Fe, 1.50% Zn, 2.00% Si, 0.75% MN, 1.60% Sn)	−0.26	to −0.29
Bronze, Composition G (88% Cu, 2% Zn, 10% Sn)	−0.24	to −0.31
Bronze, Comp. M (88% Cu, 3% Zn, 6.5% Sn, 1.5% Pb)	−0.24	to −0.31
13% Chromium Stainless Steel, Type 401 (passive)	−0.26	to −0.35
90% Cu − 10% Ni	−0.21	to −0.28
75% Cu − 20% Ni − 5% Zn	−0.19	to −0.25
Lead	−0.19	to −0.25
70% Cu − 30% Ni	−0.18	to −0.23
Inconel (78% Ni, 13.5% Cr, 6% Fe) (passive)	−0.14	to −0.17
Nickel 200	−0.10	to −0.20
18/8 Stainless Steel, Type 304 (passive)	−0.05	to −0.10
70% Ni − 30% Cu Monel 400, K-500	−0.04	to −0.14
18.8, 3% Mo Stainless Steel, Type 316 (passive)	−0.0	to −0.10
Titanium	−0.05	to +0.06
Hastelloy C	−0.03	to +0.08
Platinum	+0.19	to +0.25
Graphite	+0.20	to +0.30

anodic → least noble → ← most noble ← cathodic

1. Each metal has a unique voltage potential.
2. Half-cell reference electrode, silver/silver chloride.

(ABYC)

doesn't matter what metal is used as the reference metal—the order of the metals in the table will come out pretty much the same (there may be some minor variations), although the voltages measured at each test will vary according to which metal is used as the reference.

In the marine world the most commonly used *reference electrode* is what is known as a *silver/silver chloride half cell*, and the situation of most interest to boatbuilders is generally that of metals immersed in *moving seawater* (the movement resulting from a boat's being underway, or from tidal flow at a mooring or anchorage). Taking these as the benchmarks, and further defining moving seawater as being between 50°F (10° C) and 80°F (26.7° C) and flowing at a rate of 8 to 13 feet per second (5 to 8 knots approximately), we end up with Table 4-1, which is known as the *Galvanic Series* table.

Voltage is akin to pressure in a water system. If we have two tanks of water at differing pressures and we make a connection between the two tanks, water will flow from the higher-pressure tank to the lower-pressure tank until an equilibrium is reached. In much the same way, if we have two different metals immersed in an electrolyte, resulting in a voltage difference between them, anytime a connection is made between these two metals, an electrical current, measurable with a sensitive ammeter, will flow through the connection (Figure 4-5A).

There is a difference, however, between the metals and the water tanks, for no matter how much current flows, the natural potential of the two metals will never equalize (remember, this voltage difference is a "fact of nature"). It is rather as if the lower-pressure water tank has a hole in it, and so the flow of water will not cease until the higher-pressure tank runs out of water. The problem, when it comes to metals, is that

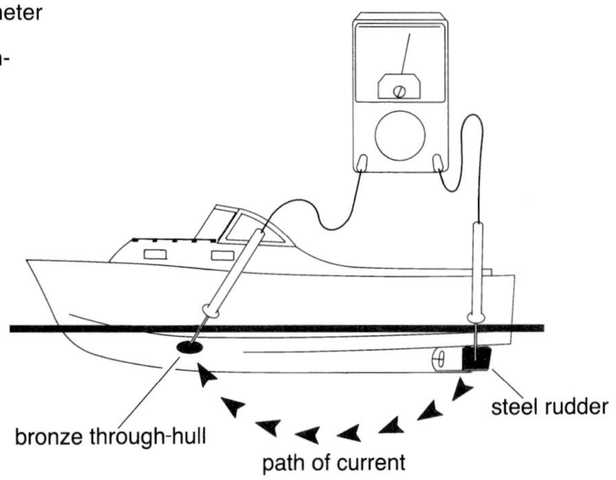

Figure 4-5A. **If an ammeter is placed between the rudder and the through-hull it will read a small current.** *(Jim Sollers)*

bronze through-hull

path of current

steel rudder

Figure 4-5B. **A simple galvanic cell.** *(Professional Boatbuilder)*

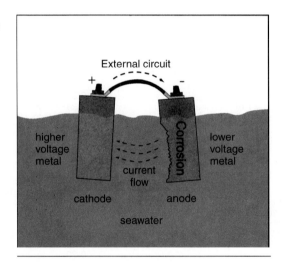

External circuit

+

−

higher voltage metal

Corrosion

lower voltage metal

current flow

cathode

anode

seawater

this "running out of water" is arrived at *through the dissolution of one of the metals involved in the flow of current.*

What happens can crudely be described as follows: Given any two metals immersed in an electrolyte, when an electrical connection is made between them the current flows from the higher-voltage metal to the lower-voltage metal. The effect of this is to raise the voltage of the lower-voltage metal above its natural potential. In an effort to reestablish equilibrium, the lower-voltage metal discharges a current into the electrolyte. This current flows through the electrolyte to the higher-voltage metal, completing the electrical circuit between the two pieces of metal. Unfortunately, *the current flowing through the electrolyte is generated by an electrochemical reaction that steadily consumes the lower-voltage metal*—a process known as *galvanic corrosion* (Figure 4-5B).

As long as the external circuit remains in place between the two metals, the current being electrochemically generated at the lower-voltage metal flows back around the circuit through the

external connection, preventing the lower-voltage metal from reestablishing equilibrium at its natural potential, and so causing the reaction to continue. We have what is known as a *galvanic cell* or *couple.* Eventually the lower-voltage metal will be entirely consumed, while the higher-voltage metal will remain intact. The metal that is feeding the current into the electrolyte is known as the *anode;* the metal that is receiving the current from the electrolyte, and discharging it into the external circuit, is known as the *cathode.*

The most commonly known galvanic cell is the lowly flashlight battery, which contains two dissimilar metals and an electrolyte, with the cathode forming the positive terminal and the anode forming the negative terminal. When an external circuit is made (for example, through a flashlight bulb), the anode is steadily consumed until it is destroyed, at which point the battery is dead.

Since the cathode in a galvanic cell does not dissolve, it is also referred to as the *most noble,* or *passive,* metal in this relationship, while the anode is referred to as the *least noble,* or *active,* metal. It should be noted that this relationship is entirely relative: Depending on its position in the galvanic series table, a metal will be cathodic with respect to metals that have a lower electrical potential, but anodic with respect to those with a higher potential.

Galvanic corrosion via the green wire. For a galvanic cell to be formed, it is necessary only to have two different metals immersed in the same electrolyte (body of water) and electrically connected in some way. Corrosion will occur, even if the metals are on different boats. This fact has become abundantly clear in recent decades, with the rapid expansion of shorepower-based electrical systems. Many of these pass galvanic currents from one boat to another, or to the dockside, down the grounding (green or bare) wire of the AC shorepower cord (refer back to Chapter 3).

As we saw in Chapter 3, this kind of galvanic couple is easily broken with a galvanic isolator or an isolation transformer, although all too often one of these devices is not fitted and corrosion proceeds, sometimes at a devastating rate. *All boats, particularly metal boats, should break the galvanic connection between the boat and the AC grounding wire with either a galvanic isolator or an isolation transformer, with the latter being by far the preferable option.*

Dezincification and crevice corrosion. So far I have considered galvanic cells containing two dissimilar metal objects. But most metallic materials in marine use are *alloys*—mixtures of more than one metal. Even "pure" metals contain impurities. Add a little salt water and many can generate internal galvanic corrosion—a notorious example being screws made of brass, an alloy of copper and zinc. In the presence of an electrolyte these two metals, being widely separated on the galvanic scale, become highly interactive, eating up the zinc in the alloy and leaving a soft, porous, and worthless fastener (identifiable by a change in color from the yellow brass to red copper).

To a certain extent, the prerequisites for the establishment of these internal galvanic cells vary from alloy to alloy. Steel, for example, requires not only an electrolyte but also oxygen. However, since oxygen is readily available both in the atmosphere and in dissolved form in seawater, galvanic corrosion (evidenced by rust) is an ever present possibility. The waterline area on a steel boat is especially vulnerable, for here the hull is constantly wetted in a highly oxygenated atmosphere.

Untreated steel is particularly susceptible to corrosion. It often comes from the foundry with a coating of *mill scale*. Mill scale has a potential about 0.3 volts above that of regular steel. In the presence of an electrolyte and oxygen a galvanic cell is established between the underlying plate and the scale, with the plate as the anode, pitting the plate until the scale becomes loosened and falls off. Once the mill scale is gone, impurities in the steel itself will ensure that the process of galvanic interaction (rusting) continues.

The manner in which aluminum and stainless steel establish internal galvanic cells is somewhat different. First of all, whereas there is very little difference in the rate of rusting of one grade of steel as compared to another, there are marked differences in the susceptibility to corrosion of different grades of both aluminum and stainless steel—*it is absolutely essential to use marine-grade alloys in boat construction, and also for fasteners and hardware.* Second, in contrast to steel, the presence of oxygen *slows* the corrosion process, with both aluminum and stainless steel developing an inert oxide film. When oxygen is removed, this oxide skin breaks down. If an electrolyte is then added, corrosion is likely to be rampant.

Oxidized stainless steel is called *passivated*, and is one of the more corrosion-resistant alloys available for marine use (Table 4-1), whereas without the oxide layer stainless steel becomes *active*, making it vulnerable to localized attack. Active areas of stainless steel frequently evidence themselves by rust stains. Since oxygen is readily available in the atmosphere and in seawater, there is little risk of corrosion in most circumstances, but *if stainless steel is used in an area where stagnant water can collect, sooner or later its passivity will break down and it will become active* (normally in isolated pinholes and crevices) and will begin to "feed" on itself, just as the copper in a brass screw feeds on the zinc (Figure 4-6). The active area is the anode; the passive area the cathode. In such localized instances of corrosion, the surrounding passive stainless steel forms a large cathodic area in relation to the small anodic pinhole or crevice, resulting in rapid corrosion of up to ¼ inch per year (see the accompanying sidebar)!

Preventing galvanic corrosion. What we have seen so far is that for galvanic corrosion to occur, three preconditions must be met:

1. There must be two dissimilar metals, or dissimilarities within one piece of metal.
2. The dissimilar metals must be in contact with an *electrolyte* (an electrically conductive fluid).
3. There must be an electrical connection between the metals (other than the path provided by the electrolyte).

If these three preconditions are met, a galvanic cell will form in which one metal (the anode) will corrode while the other (the cathode) will be unharmed.

Figure 4-6. **Crevice corrosion on a stainless steel propeller shaft caused by stagnant water of low oxygen content in the stern tube.**

Is Stainless Steel Really Stainless?

When first discovered in 1913, stainless steel was heralded as a wonder metal, and in many ways it is. However, eight decades and many millions of dollars of research later, it is clear that it has very definite limitations, particularly in a marine environment, that boatowners would do well to recognize.

There are more than 500 different "grades" of stainless steel, all of which get their stainless quality by alloying chromium with iron (steel). In the presence of oxygen, the chromium forms a relatively inert skin that is highly resistant to corrosion: Stainless with this oxidized "skin" is known as *passivated*. The minimum percentage of chromium in the alloy required to create this condition is around 12%, with higher levels providing greater corrosion resistance. Typically, up to 20% chromium is used for "better" grades of stainless steel.

In addition to chromium, nickel is sometimes added to the mix, which further enhances corrosion resistance. Stainless steels without nickel, or with very low levels of nickel, fall into two broad categories known as *ferritic* and *martensitic;* those with higher levels of nickel fall into a category known as *austenitic*. Ferritic and martensitic stainless steels are not suitable for marine use. Rather conveniently, they are easily identifiable since they are magnetic (Figure 4-7), whereas austenitic stainless steels are nonmagnetic or have very low levels of magnetism. (All too often ferritic or martensitic fasteners are found on boats, steadily rusting away, notably the screws on many "all stainless" hose clamps. If the screw is undone a turn or two, the band will be found to be seriously corroded where it has been in contact with the screw—Figure 4-8. Hose clamps for marine use should be stamped "all *300* stainless steel"—see below—or come from a manufacturer, such as *AWAB* [Parker Merrick Company, Ft. Lauderdale, FL], who uses nothing but austenitic stainless steel—Figure 4-9.)

Different alloys of stainless steel are given an identification number. The ferritic and martensitic steels fall in the 400 series (with individual numbers between 400 and 450); the austenitic steels are mostly 300 series, although a few are 200 series. Of the austenitic stainless steels, 304 is widely used in the marine field for fasteners, stainless steel fittings, propeller shafts, rigging, and so on. It is sometimes also known as 18-8 since it has 18% chromium and 8% nickel in its mix.

Despite its widespread use, 304 is not the best of the austenitic stainless steels. 316,

Figure 4-7. "All-stainless" hose clamp with a screw of an inferior (magnetic) corrosion-prone grade of stainless.

Figure 4-8. A perfectly good-looking "all-stainless" hose clamp which, when the screw was backed off a turn or two, revealed considerable corrosion inside the screw housing, caused by using an inferior grade of stainless steel for the screw.

Figure 4-9. Good-quality all-stainless hose clamp using a 300-grade corrosion-resistant screw.

continued

which has a slightly higher nickel content, and 2% added molybdenum (which further enhances its corrosion resistance), or other more specialized alloys (such as Nitronic 50 and Aquamet 22) are preferable, especially in any areas where corrosion is particularly likely. And there are many such areas.

As noted in the text, the corrosion resistance of stainless steels is dependent upon the integrity of the oxide layer formed by the chromium. There are several ways in which the integrity of this layer can be breached. One is if there are microscopic water-retaining cracks or scratches on the surface of the metal—these will lead to crevice corrosion. Another is if there are microscopic impurities on the surface of the metal—in the presence of an electrolyte, these are likely to result in the formation of a galvanic cell causing pitting. More generally, anytime an oxygen deficiency at the surface of the metal leads to the oxide layer's breaking down in the presence of an electrolyte, corrosion is pretty well certain. Locations in which this commonly occurs are:

- Between a propeller shaft and a propeller, in the threads under the propeller nut, around the keyway, where the rubber sleeve of a Cutless bearing is in contact with the shaft, under barnacles, and under monofilament fishing line if it gets wrapped around a propeller shaft. In all instances, problems are reduced by frequent boat use since this provides a regular supply of freshly oxygenated water.

- Any damp areas where stainless steel fasteners are deprived of oxygen, such as below-the-waterline wooden-boat plank fastenings (bronze, or galvanized steel, screws should always be used). (Note that if a boat is moored in a protected harbor, or in a canal where there is little or no current, it is a good idea to move the boat at least once a week to ensure that there is a fresh supply of oxygen-laden water in contact with any underwater stainless steel hardware.)

Sailboats are vulnerable in a number of additional locations:

- Inside the lower terminals of swaged-on rigging fittings, which tend to collect water, and inside barrel-type turnbuckles. In both instances corrosion is invisible and the first sign of trouble is likely to be a rigging failure.

- Inside centerboard trunks—particularly around hinge pins—where the water is stagnant and oxygen levels are depleted.

- Wherever stainless steel fasteners pass through the hull, deck, or spreaders—if any moisture becomes trapped in the hole the moisture will eventually become deoxygenated, causing the stainless to turn active, often with no external evidence (through-deck chainplates are particularly vulnerable since the flexing of the rig almost always eventually breaks down any caulking seal, allowing moisture to penetrate).

Besides using 316 stainless steel or some other specialized alloy, you can enhance corrosion resistance by polishing the surface of the metal (either electrochemically or mechanically) and by ensuring that if a fastener must be used in an area where moisture may penetrate, the fastener is properly bedded in a completely waterproof sealant (5200, for example, but not silicon, which is minutely porous). Despite these measures, stainless steel, despite its popularity, is not the best choice in many instances for applications in which it is commonly used. (Note that even where pitting and crevice corrosion are not a problem, austenitic stainless steels in certain environments are subject to *stress corrosion cracking* and *corrosion fatigue,* both of which occur at the microscopic level, making problems almost impossible to detect until a sudden failure occurs).

Finally, it should be noted that when many stainless steels are welded, the differential heating of the metal in the area of the weld causes the chromium to combine with carbon in the steel, removing the chromium from its passivating film-forming role. These areas become anodic with respect to the rest of the stainless steel, leading to galvanic corrosion that goes under the name of *weld decay,* or *intergranular corrosion* (particularly noticeable around the welds on many stainless steel fuel and water tanks, which soon develop leaks). On small welded pieces intergranular corrosion can be avoided by heating the entire piece, after welding, to around 2,000°F (600°C), and then rapidly cooling it. For larger structures where this is not practicable *a low-carbon-content stainless steel should be used* (identified by the letter "L" after its number, e.g., 304L or preferably 316L) *for all welded structures.*

The rate of current flow in a galvanic cell, and therefore the rate at which the anodic metal dissolves, depends on a number of factors, the most important of which are:

1. The voltage difference between the two metals (the greater the difference, the more the potential for corrosion). Anytime the voltage difference, as shown in Table 4-1, exceeds 0.25 volts, corrosion is pretty well certain.

2. The relative exposed surface areas of the two metals: the *area effect*. A large cathodic area (a bronze rudder, for example) connected to a small anodic area (a steel heel bearing) will soon destroy the anode, whereas a large anode (a steel rudder) in relation to a small cathode (a bronze heel bearing) will corrode only slowly.

3. A process known as *polarization*. When two metals form a galvanic cell they are initially quite reactive, but soon some of the by-products of that reaction (various salts and oxides of the metals) insulate the surface of one or the other metal, reducing the rate of reaction and thus of corrosion. The effect of polarization varies markedly from one metal to another, and according to such factors as whether the water is moving or not (moving water tends to flush the salts and oxides away, keeping the reaction going) and how much oxygen it contains.

4. The conductivity of the electrolyte. Salt water is relatively conductive, whereas fresh water sometimes is not—it depends on the level of dissolved salts and minerals, which is highly variable from one lake or river to another.

Knowing these facts, many times it is possible to build a boat and install equipment in such a way that *one or more of the three preconditions for galvanic corrosion is not present, in which case such corrosion simply will not occur.* If prevention is not entirely possible, a grasp of the factors determining the rate of corrosion can be used to implement measures that slow corrosion to "acceptable" levels. Either way, key considerations are:

Use the right metals. Use *marine-grade* alloys, and ensure that they are used in appropriate applications. For example, use only austenitic stainless steels, and if *stress corrosion cracking* or *corrosion fatigue* are possible, substitute monel or titanium.

Don't mix underwater metals. This minimizes differences between the voltages of the various metals in the boat, minimizing the potential for corrosion.

In metal-boat building, whatever grade of steel or aluminum is used for the hull plating should be used also in the hull reinforcement, and for deck stringers, pipe stubs, and any other metal fixtures in physical contact with the hull. On all other boats, anytime two pieces of metal are likely to be in contact with the same body of water (even if this is nothing more than a few drops of salt water caught in the head or threads of a fastener), the same metals should be used.

If mixing of metals is necessary, Table 4-1 can be used to ensure that the metals are galvanically close to one another. However, this table is not in itself an infallible guide, since it does not take account of polarization effects. If we need to fasten an aluminum cleat, for example, with something stronger than an aluminum fastener, looking at the table we see that all the bronzes and brasses are galvanically closer to aluminum than passivated stainless steel, and so we might be tempted to select a bronze fastener. However, both aluminum and stainless steel develop inert oxide films which, in the absence of other disturbing influences, reduce galvanic interaction to a minimum, whereas in the presence of moisture any copper-based fastener (bronze and brass) will continually break down the protective film on the aluminum, causing extensive corrosion. *Copper alloys should never be used in combination with aluminum*; passivated stainless steel or monel is normally the appropriate choice for fasteners.

Minimize any area effects. Do this by ensuring that all fasteners, and metals used for welding, are *at least as noble as, and perhaps a little more noble than, the metals they are fastening.* This will create a small cathodic area in relation to a large anodic mass, protecting the fastener or weld from corrosion while generating very little corrosion in the anode.

Keep electrolytes away from metal surfaces. Do this by avoiding structural elements that will form pockets of trapped dirt and moisture and by using proper coatings and sealants. Without an electrolyte in contact with metal, there can be no galvanic corrosion.

In order to keep moisture away from metal surfaces, attention has to be paid to the placement of frames, stringers, and floors in metal boats, and the provision of limber holes for drainage. Discontinuous welding, particularly on box-section frames, is an invitation to trouble. Ventilation, to eliminate condensation, is especially important. Beyond this, there are numerous modern coatings that create a surface that is impervious to moisture. In all cases such coatings have to be planned for *at the design stage,* both to ensure adequate surface preparation of the underlying metal, particularly in inaccessible areas on the interior of the hull, and also to eliminate sharp or rough edges which will result in thin coats of paint that are easily breached.

Steel can be given a substantial amount of extra protection with a coating of zinc—*galvanizing*—prior to painting. Since zinc is more anodic than steel, any time the paint layer is damaged, allowing moisture access to the metal and so establishing a localized galvanic cell, the zinc will corrode, protecting the steel and in fact plating out on the steel to "heal" the scratch. Proper coatings are not so important with aluminum (which will develop its own relatively inert oxide skin) or many bronze fittings (which are naturally resistant to corrosion; however, note that *manganese bronze*, unlike other bronzes, has a high percentage of zinc and as a result is susceptible to *dezincification*—it should more properly be called a *brass*). Stainless steel should *not* be painted since the exclusion of oxygen from the surface of the metal may cause its protective oxide film to break down.

A word of caution must be be sounded at this point. Painting a *cathodic* metal to isolate it from galvanic activity will *always* help to slow, or stop, corrosion at an interconnected anodic metal, since the paint reduces the exposed cathodic area which in turn reduces the level of galvanic current generated at the anode. But when an *anodic* metal is painted, if there is a galvanic connection to any unprotected cathodic surface, the galvanic current will be concentrated at any flaws in the paint job on the anode (scratches or pinholes, for example). We now have a very unfavorable area effect—a relatively large cathodic area drawing current from a very small anodic area—which may well cause *severe localized pitting* of the anode. The resulting damage is frequently more harmful than would have been the case with modest corrosion over the entire surface of the anode. It is sometimes better to leave an anodic surface unpainted, allowing it to suffer mild generalized corrosion, rather than to risk this concentrated corrosion.

Electrically isolate individual pieces of metal. This will break any potential galvanic circuits between them.

As well as isolation from an electrolyte, in many cases a surface coating will also provide a fair measure of electrical insulation (depending on the type of paint). However, when two metal objects are fastened together minor projections on one or the other surface are likely to cut through the paint job to make a connection. Additional insulating materials are best used. These may range from some form of grease,

thread compound, or caulking around a fastener (zinc pastes, proprietary products such as Lubriplate, TefGel, and Duralac, or compounds such as 5200) to a gasket of neoprene or PVC with an insulating sleeve around any bolt and an insulating washer under its nut, or a rugged, nonconductive insert fitted to the hull of a metal boat to which a through-hull is mounted (Figure 4-10A and B—it is an ABYC requirement that *any galvanically incompatible below-the-water-line fitting be insulated from a metal hull*).

Beyond these measures, further corrosion protection can be provided *cathodically*, either via a *bonding system* or with an *impressed current system* (see Bonding and Cathodic Protection below).

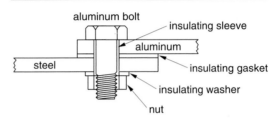

Figure 4-10A. The use of insulating washers and sleeves to electrically isolate dissimilar metals that are fastened together.

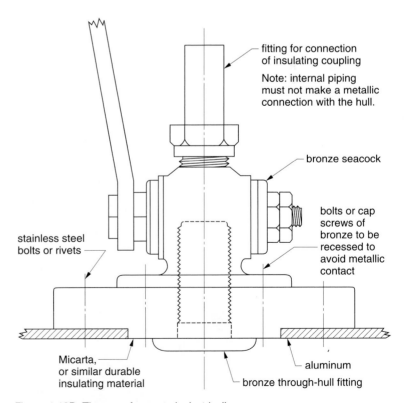

Figure 4-10B. The use of a rugged, electrically non-conductive, insert to isolate a bronze seacock from a metal hull. *(ABYC)*

Stray-Current Corrosion

Galvanic corrosion can set up currents between fittings measured in milliamps and millivolts—a *thousandth* of an amp or volt. Faulty electrical circuits can establish currents *hundreds* and even *thousands* of times stronger. Such *stray currents* can originate from within a boat, from shoreside fittings and ship-to-shore cables, or from neighboring boats. In all cases a leak from a "hot" wire allows current to find a path to ground through bilge water, damp areas of the boat, or the seawater rather than through proper channels.

Any metal fitting that feeds a current into water may be corroded. Galvanic corrosion is by its nature a relatively slow process (the metals themselves have to generate the current), but stray-current corrosion, with its potential for far higher levels of current flow, can be devastating. In worst-case scenarios, *stray currents can wipe out hardware in a matter of hours (Figure 4-11A and B)*.

DC stray currents are particularly destructive, whereas there is some debate as to whether AC leaks lead to any corrosion at all. However, in many instances this is academic. DC leaks are frequently superimposed on AC circuits, so careful attention needs to be paid to eliminating sources of stray currents from both.

In normal circumstances, electric currents are confined to the cables and the equipment in their circuits. For a stray current to develop there must first of all be a mechanism for the current to "escape" from a circuit—a short circuit, or some other fault, which feeds the current to hardware in contact with water—and second there must be some reason for the current to "run to ground" through water rather than through other cables. Anytime these two preconditions are met, corrosion is pretty well certain. The following are some real-life examples:

1. A bilge-pump float switch had a leaking seal that allowed salt water to penetrate the float until the water reached the level of the two switch terminals. Current then tracked through the water from one switch terminal to the other. The terminal feeding the current into the water was corroded until its cable fell off, at which point the switch was no longer operative and the boat began to fill with water (Figure 4-12).

2. A 12-volt bilge pump was wired with undersized wiring which created a 10% voltage drop (1.2 volts) on the ground side of the circuit (not at all unusual). Either through a fault or a deliberate connection between the pump motor and its case, the motor was grounded to its case. In normal circumstances this would not create a problem. But because of the voltage drop on the circuit, when the pump was running the ground side of the pump was 1.2 volts positive with respect to the battery negative. That was enough to cause some of the current passing through the circuit to find a path to the battery negative via the pump housing, bilge water, an unbonded through-hull, the surrounding seawater, the propeller and propeller shaft, the engine block, and

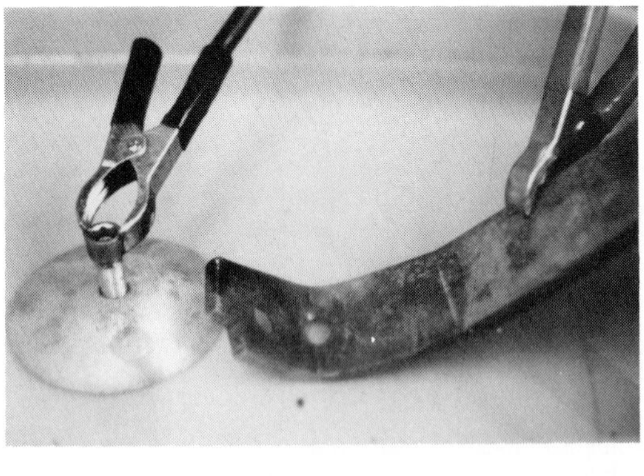

Figure 4-11A. **Test rig to simulate stray-current corrosion. 5-amps of DC current is being passed from the stainless steel flat bar to the zinc anode via the electrolyte (salt water).**

Figure 4-11B. **After less than three hours the stainless steel is severely corroded whereas the zinc is unharmed.**

Figure 4-12. **Bilge pump switch with a leaking seal. Salt water penetrated and rose to the level of the switch terminals, at which point the power supply cable began feeding current directly into the water to the other terminal. The supply cable was eaten through until it fell off its terminal.**

finally the engine ground strap back to the battery negative. The pump housing and through-hull, which were both feeding the current into water, were corroded.

3. This time the bilge pump was wired with cables that were not properly color-coded. In the course of making the connections, the positive and negative cables got crossed over. The pump didn't care, but now the entire circuit through the pump back to its float switch was "hot" at all times, while the switch created an infinite resistance in the ground circuit whenever the pump was not running. Regardless of the quality of the wiring and connections on the ground circuit, if there had been any kind of an electrical leak from the pump it would have had no path back to ground except through the water and various fittings in contact with it—corrosion would have been rampant.

4. A situation similar to the preceding example occurred when a compass light was wired with the switch in the negative side of the circuit. A connection from what should have been the ground side of the light (but which was now the hot side) to the binnacle allowed current to find a path to ground through the compass housing, the binnacle, the steering cable, and an unbonded rudderpost to the propeller, and so back to the engine and the battery negative. The rudderpost, being the part that fed the current into the water, corroded until the rudder dropped off!

Sources of stray currents. Given the fact that all electrical currents, whether AC or DC, seek the path of least resistance back to their source, as we have just seen, stray currents almost always arise as a result of (1) some defect in wiring or a piece of equipment that allows an electrical leak into damp areas of the boat, bilge water, or the surrounding water, combined with (2) *a resistance in the proper path to ground so that the path through the boat and the water now has less resistance than the path through the ground circuit*. Some of the more common sources of stray currents are (Figure 4-13):

- Faulty insulation and poor connections in damp areas of the boat, or leaks within equipment from the hot side to the equipment case and thence through bilge water or damp areas of the boat to ground.
- Salt "bridges" between one terminal and another on terminal strips and junction blocks.

- Screws, staples, or other fasteners through wiring.
- Inadequate wiring or corroded terminals, leading to voltage drop, particularly on the ground side, so that different parts of the ground circuits are at different voltages, encouraging current to find other paths to ground.
- Any grounding system that haphazardly grounds different circuits and pieces of equipment to through-hulls, bonding conductors, and lightning conductors (see Lightning Protection below), resulting in voltage differences from one part of the ground circuit to another. *All equipment should have an insulated ground that leads back to a central ground bus bar in the main distribution panel*, which in turn leads to a *common ground point* or bus (see The Common Ground Point below), and from there back to the battery negative terminal.
- Voltage drop in radios with external (immersed) ground plates. The voltage on the plate will differ from the negative battery terminal voltage, generating currents between the plate and any underwater metal grounded to the battery, such as the engine and the propeller shaft.
- Shore-power circuits that do not have an isolation transformer or a functioning galvanic isolator (Chapter 3).
- Any AC circuit that causes a galvanic isolator to be bypassed. Examples are:

  1. A nonmarine battery charger (without an isolation transformer). The shoreside neutral will be connected to the boat's DC ground (Chapter 5). This provides a path for galvanic or stray currents along the neutral wire, bypassing any galvanic isolator.
  2. Tying the neutral side of a shore-power AC system into the boat's grounding system, once again bypassing any galvanic isolator. The neutral side of a shore-power-based AC system is grounded only ashore, never on board (Chapter 3).
  3. Some reverse polarity lamps, which function by making a low-resistance connection between the hot or neutral wire and the grounding circuit, providing a path for galvanic or stray currents to bypass any galvanic isolator. To prevent this, many older reverse polarity lamps have a spring-loaded (normally off) switch that is held on momentarily to check polarity, and remains off the rest of the time, isolating the polarity indicator; more recent ABYC regulations require a permanent light or alarm in a situation of reverse polarity, but with a resis-

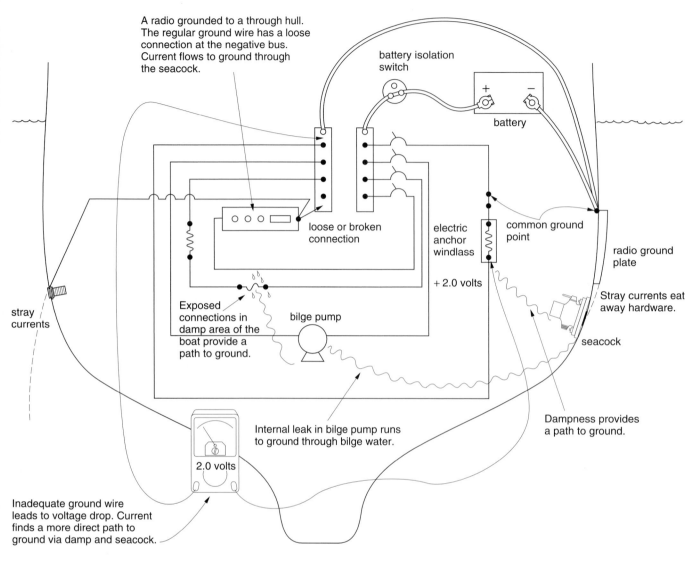

A radio grounded to a through hull. The regular ground wire has a loose connection at the negative bus. Current flows to ground through the seacock.

battery isolation switch

battery

loose or broken connection

electric anchor windlass

+ 2.0 volts

common ground point

radio ground plate

Stray currents eat away hardware.

seacock

Exposed connections in damp area of the boat provide a path to ground.

bilge pump

stray currents

Internal leak in bilge pump runs to ground through bilge water.

Dampness provides a path to ground.

2.0 volts

Inadequate ground wire leads to voltage drop. Current finds a more direct path to ground via damp and seacock.

Figure 4-13. Stray-current sources.

tance of at least 25,000 ohms, which will eliminate stray currents.

4. Cable TV, since the TV will likely be grounded on board, while the grounded sheath of the incoming cable will bypass any isolator or isolation transformer.

5. Any conductive connection from a metal hull to the shore, such as an aluminum ladder from the deck to a dock, since this will once again bypass any galvanic isolator or isolation transformer.

Preventing stray-current corrosion. As noted, stray-currents can arise only when faulty electrical equipment or wiring not only allows a current to "escape" from a piece of equipment or its circuit, but also creates a situation in

which *a lower-resistance path back to the energy source is found outside of the boat's wiring.* Once this point is grasped, a number of key measures for preventing stray-current corrosion become clear:

• Electrical equipment used on boats must be rated for marine use. There are frequently subtle differences in design and materials that reduce the chances of "leaks" from the equipment. Battery chargers are a notable case: Many automotive chargers have a direct connection between the incoming AC side and the DC side, whereas all "marine" chargers have the two sides of the transformer isolated from each other.

• All electrical cabling needs to be kept out of damp areas of a boat. If this is not possible, at the very least *no connections should be made in damp locations.*

- Marine electrical systems should always use a *grounded negative*, with *no switches, fuses, or breakers in the ground side.* In the event a leak develops from a piece of DC equipment, as long as the equipment is grounded and as long as the ground circuit is unbroken, the leak will be conducted back to the battery without causing corrosion.

- Marine wiring must be of the *insulated-return* type, which is to say a separate ground wire is run back from every piece of equipment to the ground bus, as opposed to using the hull in a metal boat, or the bonding system or some other circuit in a nonconductive boat. This is to once again ensure an unbroken, low-resistance path back to the battery.

- Ground cables must be sized *at least as large as* positive cables to avoid voltage drop on the ground side of the circuit (any voltage drop will encourage current to seek a lower-resistance path back to the battery). In gen-

eral, although a 10% voltage drop is often considered acceptable in marine wiring, 3% is a far better figure to shoot for.

- The use of a single ground cable to ground more than one appliance should be avoided for a couple of reasons. First of all, this requires added connections in the grounding circuit, every one of which is a potential source of corrosion, resistance, and voltage drop. Second, unless the cable is carefully sized, if more than one load is turned on at the same time, excessive voltage drop is likely.

- *Multistranded, tinned wire with marine-quality terminals* should be used for all wiring. This is the only way to ensure corrosion-free, and therefore resistance-free, circuits in the long run.

- A bonding circuit (see below) should be connected to all major metal fixtures that may be in contact with water. In the event an electrical leak makes any of these fixtures "hot," the bonding circuit will provide a *low-resistance path straight back to the battery negative*, discouraging the leakage current from

Figure 4-14. Bonding and ground leaks.

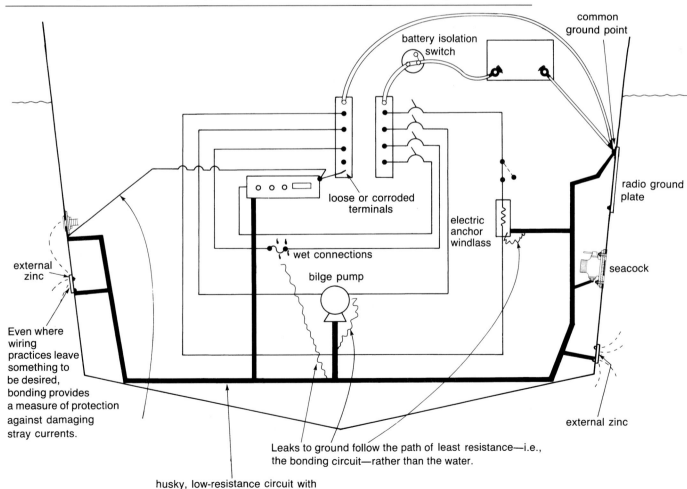

common ground point

battery isolation switch

loose or corroded terminals

electric anchor windlass

wet connections

bilge pump

radio ground plate

seacock

external zinc

external zinc

Even where wiring practices leave something to be desired, bonding provides a measure of protection against damaging stray currents.

Leaks to ground follow the path of least resistance—i.e., the bonding circuit—rather than the water.

husky, low-resistance circuit with electrically tight connections

finding any other potentially corrosive path.

- The engine on a metal boat should have insulated ground sending units and a heavy ground strap from the alternator ground to the boat's common ground point (or, even better, an insulated ground alternator and starter motor—see page 83).

- All DC ground circuits, AC grounding circuits, bonding, and lightning-protection circuits should terminate at a *single* common ground point or bus (see The Common Ground Point below) which will then hold

these circuits to a common voltage, discouraging stray currents from circulating around the different circuits.

The key thing to remember is that even if a stray current should develop, *as long as it has a low-resistance path back to the battery* (or to the AC source in the case of AC circuits), and *as long as this path does not include discharging the current into an electrolyte*, it will not cause stray-current corrosion (see Figure 4-14, preceding page).

Bonding and Cathodic Protection

Bonding is the practice of electrically tying together, and connecting to the boat's ground, major metal objects on a boat: rigging and chainplates, engine and propeller shaft, stove, metal fuel and water tanks, fuel deck-fill fittings, metal cases on electrical equipment, etc.

The purpose of a bonding system is to provide a low-resistance electrical path between otherwise isolated metal objects, *preventing the buildup of voltage differences between these objects* (Figure 4-15). This circuit is then connected to the boat's ground, which in turn is connected, through underwater hardware, to the earth's ground. A bonding circuit provides another redundant path to ground for potentially dangerous AC leaks (Chapter 3), provides a path to ground for the high voltages and currents associated with a lightning strike (see Lightning Protection below), minimizes radio frequency interference (RFI—see Chapter 7), and can prevent damage to underwater hardware from stray currents originating within the boat by providing these currents with a direct path to ground to preclude their passing through any underwater hardware.

(Note that if a bonding system is installed solely for corrosion control, it needs to only include hardware in contact with water, either external or internal. Other items are included for safety and RFI-suppression reasons, with the comprehensiveness of the bonding circuit varying markedly from boat to boat. Metal fuel tanks and fuel-fill fittings are *required* to be bonded when gasoline engines are installed, but this is optional with diesel engines.)

To be effective a bonding circuit needs electrically perfect connections with conductors that ensure no voltage differences between bonded fittings. Given the small currents that a bonding system is normally expected to handle, it would

seem that quite small cables could be used. However, with bonded electrical equipment if the DC negative cable or the AC neutral cable fails, the bonding cable may become a full current-carrying conductor, so the general rule of thumb is to size the bonding cable the same as the DC negative or AC neutral (which means, in the case of any connections to or between engines, that *the bonding cable must be rated to handle the full engine-cranking load*).

When it comes to nonelectrical fittings (such as chainplates) the bonding cable generally doubles as a lightning ground cable (see Lightning Protection below), and since the latter are required to be at least #6 AWG, this becomes the size of the bonding cable. So far as zincs are concerned (see Cathodic Protection below), to ensure minimal voltage drop between a zinc and the bonding system, any connection should be at least #8 AWG.

Putting a stainless steel bolt through a zinc and connecting a bonding wire to the bolt *will not do* when connecting remotely placed zincs to wood and fiberglass hulls. The zinc will soon corrode where it contacts the stainless steel, and the connection will deteriorate. Zincs should have *cast-in plates and fasteners* to maintain a good electrical contact throughout the life of the zinc. On wooden hulls, the zinc and its fastenings should be insulated from the hull to reduce the possibility of alkali attack (see page 148).

Zincs must never be painted, and need replacing *before* they wear out (see sidebar "Sizing Zincs").

Finally, propeller shafts need special attention. The connection between the propeller shaft coupling and the engine is not adequate for bonding purposes (especially with flexible couplings). A jumper wire should be connected across the coupling and a spring-loaded bronze brush set up against the shaft and tied into the bonding strap (Figure 4-16). Rudderstocks should be bonded with a similar brush arrangement, or else a flexible strap can be attached to the stock.

Cathodic Protection

So far so good. But when two dissimilar pieces of metal with different voltages, such as a stainless steel propeller shaft and a copper radio ground plate, are immersed in seawater, *bonding the two will make precisely the circuit needed to promote galvanic corrosion!* Bonding may be a case of jumping from the frying pan into the fire. However, *if the bonding system is in turn connected to a piece of zinc immersed in seawater, the zinc, being less noble than any boatbuilding metal, will be the object to corrode, providing protection to all the more noble metals on the galvanic table.* When the zinc is gone, the next least noble metal that is connected into the bonding circuit will start to corrode (the hull on a steel or aluminum boat!).

This explains the logic behind sacrificial zinc anodes. All the boat's underwater metal fittings are bonded, and the bonding system is connected to one or more well-placed zincs in reasonable proximity to the metal fittings they are protecting (or attached to them in the case of metal hulls and rudders). The zincs are eaten up, and thus protect the hardware. In technical parlance, the zincs drive the rest of the hardware cathodic. As long as the zincs supply enough current, corrosion will be held at bay. Clearly it is vital to renew the zincs from time to time to provide fresh sacrificial material.

To protect most metals against corrosion, their voltage must be reduced approximately 200 millivolts (0.20 volts) below the voltage given in Table 4-1, page 133. A steel hull, for example, which Table 4-1 shows as being −0.60 to −0.70 volts relative to a silver/silver chloride half cell, should be reduced to −0.80 to −0.90 volts (the ABYC currently recommends −0.84 volts). Aluminum is something of a special case. According to Table 4-1, an aluminum hull should be reduced to somewhere between −0.96 and −1.20 volts (depending on the alloy), but because aluminum is sensitive to overprotection (see below) it should, in fact, not be reduced much below −1.00 volt. Since the voltage of a zinc with respect to a silver/silver chloride half cell is around −1.00 volt (Table 4-1), if enough zincs are provided, the potential of any steel or aluminum hull can be reduced to −1.00 volt, providing more than enough protection for steel hulls and just about enough for aluminum.

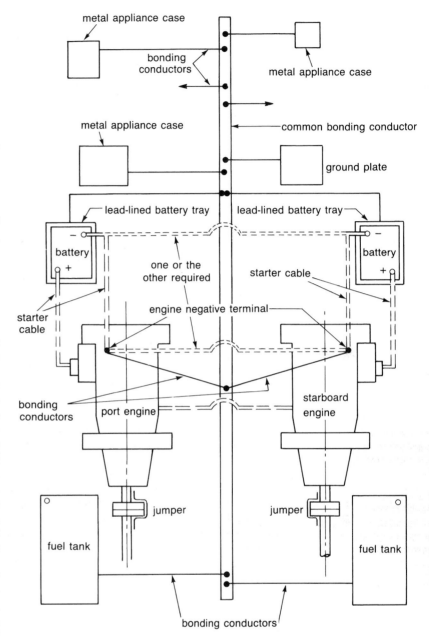

Figure 4-15. **Bonding system.** *(ABYC)*

The amount of current required to achieve the 200-millivolt negative shift needed for cathodic protection will depend primarily on the area of metal to be protected and the insulating effect of any paint layer (or oxide film in the case of bare aluminum); the greater the exposed area, the higher the current needed for protection. The hardware on a fiberglass hull will require very little current, whereas a steel hull with a defective paint job will require quite a bit. Current requirements also rise in moving water.

The current that a zinc produces depends on its exposed surface area; its overall capacity (its ability to maintain this current over time) depends on its weight. Zinc surface area and

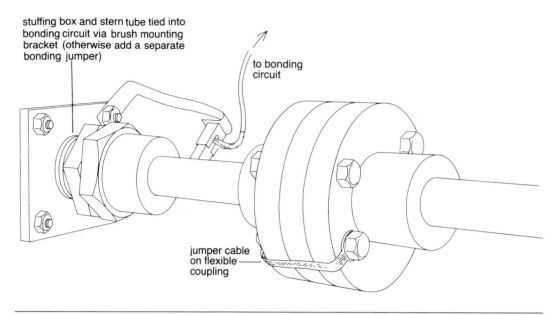

Figure 4-16. Bonding of propeller shaft and flexible coupling. *(Jim Sollers)*

stuffing box and stern tube tied into bonding circuit via brush mounting bracket (otherwise add a separate bonding jumper)

to bonding circuit

jumper cable on flexible coupling

weight, therefore, have to be matched to the amount of metal to be protected, the rate at which the zinc(s) customarily corrode, and the frequency of haulouts. A certain amount of trial and error may be needed to get the balance right (see sidebar Sizing Zincs).

Direct fastening—for example, to a metal hull or rudder—makes an excellent electrical connection, but in general the best *current distribution*—that is, the most effective distribution of the galvanic current generated by zincs—will be obtained by remotely mounting the zincs more-or-less equidistant from the metals to be protected. Depending on the amount of metal to be protected and its distribution, more than one zinc may be required—the use of several anodes rather than one large one will provide better current distribution.

Finally, it should be noted that a zinc will protect only those metals that are both *wired to it and immersed in the same body of electrolyte.* From the standpoint of galvanic corrosion, the bodies of raw water inside a heat exchanger, refrigeration condenser, engine block, or bilge all constitute independent electrolytes. For cathodic protection, any metal components in contact with these bodies of water require *their own zincs* (particularly important for heat exchangers and condensers since here we find high temperatures and high water velocities, both of which tend to accelerate corrosion).

Impressed currents. Zinc anodes work by generating a small galvanic current that makes the boat's underwater fixtures cathodic with respect to the zinc. The same effect can be produced by feeding controlled amounts of DC current through the water to fittings (and the hull, if metallic). This is the basis for *impressed-current* cathodic protection systems.

A *reference electrode* senses the voltage of the metal to be protected. A control unit then uses the boat's batteries to send an appropriate current to one or more anodes projecting through the hull. This current flows to the underwater metals, driving them cathodic (just as does the current generated by a zinc anode).

The amount of power required to operate such a system varies enormously. Looking at a steel hull as an example, we find that depending on the quality of the paint job, to provide cathodic protection, anywhere from 0.1 milliamps to 10 milliamps of protective current will be required for every square foot of submerged hull area. On a 30-foot boat this translates to between 4.5 and 450 amp-hours per week, with a "fair average" probably being around 100 amp-hours a week. With a poor paint job, or a hull bottom scraped clean of paint in a grounding, this figure could easily climb to more than 250 amp-hours—a substantial energy requirement. As a result, impressed-current systems tend to be confined to larger vessels with a 24-hour-a-day generating capability (the notable exception being the impressed-current systems widely available for MerCruiser inboard/outboard installations, in which the battery drain is kept down by meticulous attention during manufacture to the paint job on the outboard unit, the addition of separate zincs on the lower unit, and a current limit of 200 milliamps on the controller).

Some impressed-current systems adjust the protective current automatically, but others have to be set manually (the MerCruiser system is automatic). Either way, it is important to avoid overprotection. A side effect of any cathodic pro-

Sizing Zincs

The ABYC outlines the following general procedure for determining zinc area, using a millivolt meter with a *silver/silver chloride half cell:*

1. Isolate the *underwater* (it has to be in contact with the seawater) metal to be protected (disconnect any bonding wire), suspend the half cell in the nearby water, and then measure with the millivolt meter between the metal and the half cell. The meter should give a reading that corresponds to those given in Table 4-1 (for example, −50 to −100 millivolts for *passivated* 304 stainless steel; −460 to −580 millivolts if *active*—Figure 4-17).

2. Now place the zinc anode in the water, connect it to the bonding circuit, reconnect the bonding wire to the metal, and measure the voltage again. The sacrificial zinc is working and has a large enough surface area if there is at least a 200-millivolt shift in the reading (e.g., to between −250 and −350 millivolts for passivated 304 stainless steel, or −660 to −780 millivolts for active 304 stainless steel (Figure 4-18); note that many "corrosion" meters have the dial arranged to read these millivolt figures as positives rather than negatives, but the numbers will be the same). If the metal in the bonding circuit has been without protection for some time, it will take a while to polarize, and for the voltage reading to stabilize; the time to stabilize will vary according to the time since protection was removed, the area of the zinc, the area of the metal, the motion of the water, and other factors.

Over time a zinc is consumed. As surface area diminishes and corrosive residues build up, protection declines. *A zinc needs upgrading or replacing anytime the voltage produced by it drops below the level required for the protection of the type of metal in the circuit.* If this occurs sooner than the next planned haulout, the weight of the zinc (not its surface area) should be increased (Table 4-2).

Figure 4-17. Millivolt reading from a keel bolt wired to a lightning grounding system but not connected to a zinc. Note that the reading of −300 millivolts is close to that given for lead in Table 4-1.

Figure 4-18. The millivolt reading from the same piece of metal after wiring to a bonding system which in turn is connected to a zinc. The 400-millivolt shift in the voltage reading indicates that the zinc is providing more than enough cathodic protection.

Table 4-2: Weight of Zinc (in Pounds) for Cathodic Protection of Boats

Hull Material	Boat Length				
	22' Cruiser	30' Cruiser	32' Sailboat	40' Cruiser	48' Cruiser
Wood or fiberglass	1.5	16	3.6	35	44
Steel	31	81	53	128	185
Aluminum	23	38	44	64	100

Source unknown. These are conservative figures designed to provide protection for at least a year, and with a substantial allowance for faster-than-anticipated zinc consumption.

The following formula can also be used for determining zinc weight: $W = kL(B + 2d)/15.6$ where: W = weight of zinc in pounds; L = waterline length in feet; d = draft in feet; B = breadth in feet; k = 0.165 for fiberglass hulls, 1.000 for steel boats and 0.625 for aluminum hulls. (*Courtesy Wood Marine Ltd.*)

tection system is that it makes the electrolyte alkaline in the vicinity of the cathode. Anytime steel or aluminum is reduced much below –1.00 volt, this alkalinity will reach levels that are corrosive to aluminum (the threshold for damage is around –1.20 volts; because of the risk of severe hull damage the ABYC does not recommend the use of impressed-current systems on aluminum hulls), and at the same time hydrogen bubbles will begin to evolve at the cathode, and these are liable to lift off paint (known as *cathodic disbondment*—blistering paint with clean metal beneath it is a pretty good indication of overprotection). Since the greatest current density at a cathode will be found closest to its anode (therefore the most likely area for damage), the anodes on impressed-current systems must be mounted in metal hulls with an insulating shield that extends over the surrounding area of the hull (the width of the shield is determined by the maximum current output of the anode).

Overprotection and wooden boats. Wood hulls, and the wooden backing blocks often found with bronze through-hulls fitted to fiberglass boats, are even more sensitive to overprotection than steel or aluminum. Once protection voltages go below –0.500 volts or less, the wood surrounding a cathode will come under increasingly severe alkali attack: In some cases the wood can be, to all intents and purposes, destroyed in just a year or two (Figure 4-19). Since these kinds of voltages are just as easily

achieved with zincs as with impressed currents, *cathodic protection on wooden boats has to be applied with a great deal of care.* Isolated bronze through-hulls should probably not be protected at all (the ABYC states: "Protection… for metal appendages on nonmetallic boats may not be justified if the metals are galvanically compatible."); other fixtures should be given the minimum necessary protection current, well below the capability of a zinc. To make this possible a "corrosion controller"—a variable resistance coupled to a millivolt meter—is sometimes installed between the zinc and the hardware, and the resistance adjusted to produce the desired voltage at the hardware. Otherwise the zinc surface area must be kept low enough to keep the protection voltage in the desired range.

Unbond and Isolate

The opposite approach to bonding and cathodic protection, which is more prevalent in Europe than the USA, is to unbond all underwater fittings, isolate them electrically, and allow them to reach equilibrium at their own voltage. For this to work it is necessary to have *all top-quality underwater fittings (e.g., bronze), of a similar metal, and insulated from all electrical circuits.* In practice, since most through-hulls on fiberglass boats are connected to rubber or plastic hoses, the through-hulls are already electrically isolated unless connected by a bonding circuit. On metal boats, through-hulls should in any case be mounted on insulated blocks to reduce galvanic interaction between the hull and fittings. (Note that *manganese bronze*, which is frequently used for propellers and has been used for propeller shafts and through-hulls, contains a high percentage of zinc; *it will dezincify if used without cathodic protection.*)

An unbonded hull will need electrical systems of the insulated-return type (which should be mandatory in boats in any case, with the possible exception of engine circuits). In addition, *the AC system should have an isolation transformer.* Failing that, the AC grounding circuit will need a galvanic isolator (Chapter 3).

We had an unbonded boat in warm tropical and semitropical waters for twelve years with no signs of corrosion except for minor pitting around the bronze housing to the knotmeter impeller and a trace of corrosion between the bronze propeller and its stainless steel shaft. Part of our success with an unbonded hull was undoubtedly due to the fact that our internal circuits were wired to high standards throughout with very heavy wire, and we had no external radio grounds or other potential sources of stray current.

Figure 4-19. Destruction of wood due to over-protection of underwater metal fittings. Because of alkali attack the entire bow area of this wooden boat has had to be heavily patched with epoxy filler.

The integrity of a bonding circuit is critical to both cathodic protection and the elimination of stray-current corrosion. It should be checked from time to time. With a boat on dry land, testing is simple. The two probes of a good-quality digital ohmmeter are placed on any two pieces of hardware tied into the bonding system. There should not be a reading in excess of 1 ohm (Figure 4-20—the reading should be as low as 0.01 ohm, indicating a near-perfect circuit). Similarly, there should be no reading in excess of 1 ohm from a zinc anode to any hardware it is protecting.

Once a boat is in the water the current produced by the zinc and other underwater metal makes such readings impossible. The easiest way to test the bonding system under these circumstances is to obtain a *millivolt* meter and a *silver/silver chloride half cell* (obtainable from Professional Mariner and others). Unplug the shore-power cord and disconnect the battery from the DC circuits. Lower the half cell over the side into the water on the end of a long extension cable, which is plugged into one socket of the meter, while you touch the other meter probe to the various pieces of underwater hardware.

Take a voltage reading from each piece of metal and note it. *The voltage on all underwater hardware connected into the bonding system should be the same—if it is not, there are problems in the wiring or connections.* If the bonding system is working, and the zincs are in good condition, the voltage will be at least 200 millivolts below the voltage given in Table 4-1 for the most negative metal protected by the bonding system. If the voltage shift produced by the zinc is less than this, the bonding circuit is not properly protecting the lower-voltage fittings; the fittings are likely to corrode.

Next, reconnect the battery to the DC system and turn on one circuit after another, checking the millivolt reading at any fitting each time. *If at any time the voltage reading changes, there is a leak into the bonding circuit from the DC circuit that has just been turned on.* This may simply be the result of poor connections or wiring, or may be the result of a partial short somewhere. To check the wiring, run a jumper wire from the battery to the piece of equipment on the circuit and check the millivolt reading; repeat this from the ground side of the equipment to the battery; if either test corrects the millivolt reading, the problem lies in the wiring on the side of

Figure 4-20. The resistance between a bronze propeller and the shaft zinc protecting it and its stainless steel propeller shaft is 0.1 ohms, indicating a good connection.

the circuit being jumped out; if neither test corrects the problem, the equipment is at fault.

Finally, plug in the shore-power cord. This may result in a change in the millivolt reading. What this indicates is that the bonding system is tied into the AC grounding system (as it should be) and that the AC grounding system has no galvanic isolation transformer, in which case galvanic corrosion through the shore-power cord is likely (a galvanic isolator or isolation transformer should be installed). Now turn on the AC circuits one at a time, checking once again for any *permanent* change in the voltage readings as each circuit is turned on. *Any leaks, either AC or DC, must be tracked down and cleaned up.*

Unbonded boats will still need sacrificial zinc anodes at specific spots, such as a zinc collar where a stainless steel propeller shaft interacts with a bronze propeller (we have a variable-pitch propeller on which it is not possible to mount a shaft collar, hence our corrosion) and zincs in the raw-water engine-cooling circuit and any refrigeration condensers. Steel hulls and rudders will need their own zincs.

Unbonded boats are likely to have problems providing adequate lightning protection (see below) and adequate grounding systems for SSB radio and lorans (see Chapter 7).

Lightning Protection

In some parts of the world lightning is a rarity, but in others it can be quite common—in any given minute, worldwide there are 2,000 thunderstorms in progress, for a total of more than 16 million a year! Parts of the eastern seaboard of the United States are notorious for electrical storms. Since lightning tends to strike the highest object in its vicinity, boats out on the water are peculiarly vulnerable—a sailboat, with its tall mast, is an obvious target! The traditional response to this situation has been to put the mast to use as a lightning rod, conducting a strike "safely" to ground, and so providing a degree of protection for the boat and its occupants; more recently there have been claims that it is possible to prevent strikes altogether. Let's look first at lightning rods.

The Importance of Grounding

The concept underlying a lightning rod has been understood for some time. When the conditions are right for a thunderstorm—a lot of heat and moisture in the air—the turbulent air strips electrically negative electrons from the moisture molecules, leaving the clouds with a positive electrical charge. The surface of the earth or the ocean beneath the clouds becomes loaded with an abundance of negative electrons. The voltage difference between the cloud and the surface of the earth or water becomes huge, and the pressure to regain an equilibrium enormous. However, air is normally a pretty good insulator, so a charge has to build up to a tremendous intensity before it becomes sufficient to jump the gap from the earth or sea to the cloud above. But once the energy reaches this level the resultant giant spark (actually, a series of increasingly long sparks, known as *stepped leaders*) *ionizes* the path through the air. Ionized air happens to be a good conductor, so now the whole system balances out in a fraction of a microsecond with an enormous current flow (the main lightning strike).

The purpose of a lightning rod is twofold: (1) to bleed off electrons from the surface of the earth to the surrounding air in hopes of dissipating the electrons and so preventing a lightning strike, and (2) if this is not successful, to limit the damage done by a strike by providing a low-resistance path between the two oppositely-charged bodies, thus preventing the lightning from following more hazardous paths. To carry out these tasks, a pointed conductor is raised as high as practicable and connected electrically to the earth or the ocean (Figure 4-21A). Negatively charged electrons from the surface of the ocean are attracted to the positive cloud above, accumulating on the point of the lightning rod. Here the physical constraints caused by the geometry of the point greatly increase the electron density. Since the electrons are all of the same negative charge, and like charges repel one another, there is a pressure to push electrons off into the surrounding atmosphere where they neutralize the positive charge above.

There is a school of thought that holds that this process of attracting charged particles to the lightning rod actually increases the possibility of a strike and that therefore a lightning rod should *not* be fitted to a boat. This position is not supported by the evidence. When the charge density begins to approach the level needed for a lightning strike, electrons will accumulate on the surface of any object in the vicinity, including a mast, and will not care if the mast is grounded or not, or even if it is a poor conductor. Any lightning bolt will then follow the path of least resistance to equalize the points of maximum charge density. *The top of the mast, with or without a lightning conductor, is likely to be one of these points.* At this stage in the cycle, the poorly grounded mast merely offers a greater probability that the strike will be a powerful one since the electrons will not have been bled off by a functioning lightning rod. Damage will be greater than with a lightning rod because of the higher current levels and *the lack of a low-resistance path for the current.*

Failure to provide an adequate path to ground will cause a lightning strike to find its own route.

If this is through people (for example, crewmembers standing close to, or holding, a stay or shroud) it may kill them. If tracking down a wet wooden mast, the resistive path will generate a tremendous amount of heat, explosively boiling moisture in the mast and perhaps blowing its seams wide open. If running to ground through an internal chainplate and then jumping to the ocean outside the boat, it may blow a hole in the boat. If running to a through-hull with an inadequate surface area to dissipate the heat caused by the strike, it will likely blow the through-hull out of the boat, or melt the surrounding resin. And so on—the examples are many. A well-grounded lightning rod will not stop a lightning strike, but it may reduce the chances of a strike, and will tend to lessen the extent of the damage should a strike occur.

The zone of protection. There is a concept that a well-grounded lightning rod provides a *zone of protection* for an area around its base with a radius equal to the height of the rod (Figure 4-21B and C). Given the height of a sailboat mast, if it is used as a lightning conductor the whole boat will fall within this zone of protection, whereas powerboats need some form of elevated lightning rod to establish such a zone (see below) and even then the whole boat may still not be within the zone of protection (particularly the bow)—the occupants will need to stay clear of these areas during lightning storms.

It should be noted, however, that this zone of protection is by no means absolute. The main conductor from a mast-mounted lightning rod to ground inevitably has some internal resistance. Given a lightning strike, this resistance will encourage part of the strike to follow other paths to ground—what are known as *parallel paths*. In the case of a sailboat, the rigging is one likely parallel path. The extent to which the lightning strike will follow these parallel paths is proportional to the resistance of these paths as compared to the resistance offered by the main lightning conductor. Even if the resistance of the parallel paths is relatively high, given the enormity of the voltages and amperages involved in a lightning strike the parallel paths will still be highly charged—perhaps to tens of thousands of volts. If these parallel paths do not themselves have a low resistance path to ground, the behavior of the strike will become quite unpredictable, passing, for example, through any people bridging the gap between a charged piece of rigging and a grounded fitting on the boat (such as the steering wheel), or generating dangerous *side flashes*.

As a result, the best *people protection* will be had by keeping out of the water and remaining

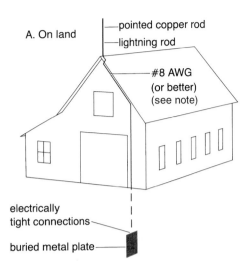

Figure 4-21A. Conventional lightning protection on shore. *(Jim Sollers)*

A. On land
— pointed copper rod
— lightning rod
#8 AWG (or better) (see note)
electrically tight connections
buried metal plate

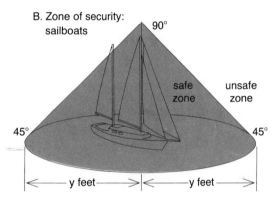

B. Zone of security: sailboats
90°
safe zone
unsafe zone
45°
45°
←— y feet —→ ←— y feet —→

Figure 4-21B and C. Lightning protection. Note that on power boats it may prove impossible to include all deck areas in the theoretical *zone of protection* (and that in any case, this may not be completely effective—see the text). A grounded metal spike higher than any mast-mounted antenna will provide additional protection on both power and sailboats. *(Jim Sollers)*

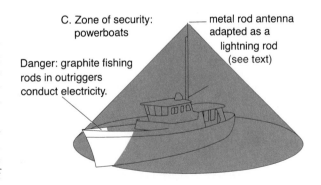

C. Zone of security: powerboats
— metal rod antenna adapted as a lightning rod (see text)
Danger: graphite fishing rods in outriggers conduct electricity.

inside a closed boat, so far as this is possible, during thunderstorms. If forced to remain on deck, do not dangle arms or legs overboard, and unless necessary for safe boat handling, avoid contact with any metal objects. *It is especially important not to bridge two such metal items, since in the event of a strike they may be at very different voltage potentials, encouraging the current to run to ground through the bridging body.*

The Path to Ground

Whatever is used as a lightning rod, it should terminate in a sharp point, and its tip should be at least 6 inches (150 mm) above anything else on the boat. So even an aluminum sailboat mast should be capped by some form of a masthead rod (Figure 4-22). This must then be connected as directly as possible to a good ground. The key to success is to keep the lightning moving in a straight line, and to conduct it to as large an immersed ground plate as possible.

Previous ABYC and other standards required that any lightning conductor must be #8 AWG copper wire or larger, but these standards are being revised to require the main down conductor from the lightning rod to the external ground plate (see next paragraph) to be #4 AWG cable, and all other conductors in the lightning grounding system to be at least #6 AWG. An aluminum mast is adequately conductive as the main down conductor; a wooden mast needs a #4 AWG cable run down the mast.

The direct path to ground should be maintained from the base of a mast or other lightning conductor all the way to an external ground plate. On a metal-hulled boat, the ground plate can be the hull itself. On wood and fiberglass boats an external keel or metal centerboard plate will do well. Otherwise a ground plate will need

to be fitted—it should be of corrosion-resistant materials (e.g., copper, monel, or bronze) with a *minimum* area of 1 square foot (930 cm²; the current International Standards Organization requirement, which is applicable in Europe, is for 0.25 of a square meter [approximately 2.5 square feet]), and so placed that it remains immersed at all times. Interestingly, recent research has shown that a lightning strike is dissipated primarily from the edges of a ground plate, so that a long metal strip (say, 1 inch by 12 feet [25 cm by 3.6 meters]) will be up to *six times* as effective in dissipating a strike as a square metal plate with the same surface area. The edges of the strip must be kept clean and clearly defined, rather than faired into the hull. Fresh water is less conductive than salt—as much as ten times the contact area may be needed to safely dissipate a strike. All electrical connections must be made with heavy-duty connectors to first-class standards, and properly protected against corrosion (heat-shrink tubing and various anticorrosion sprays or greases).

(Note that although the sintered ground plates frequently used for radio grounds have an effective surface area many times that of their actual surface area, the area of the water just micro-inches away from the plate is no more than that of the outside dimensions of the plate. This seems to be the limiting factor in dealing with the incredibly high current flows of a lightning strike, in which case the effective grounding area is no more than the plate's actual surface area. What is more, there are numerous reports of sintered ground plates disintegrating when confronted with a lightning strike—presumably the water in the pores of the plate boils explosively.)

In addition to the main down conductor, any potential parallel paths for lighting must be effectively grounded. To do this, connect a minimum #6 AWG cable from the base of the rigging (the chainplates), and any other parallel paths, to the ground plate. Lightning does not like to turn corners, so to the extent possible in making these connections, run a cable directly from the base of each chainplate and fixture down to the ground plate (as opposed to running a grounding cable horizontally around the boat, with a single connection down to the ground plate). Grounding the parallel paths in this fashion has the added advantage that most of the grounding cables will be running more or less vertically, whereas most of the boat's electrical wiring will be more or less horizontal. The two sets of cables will intersect more or less at right angles, which in the event of a lightning strike will minimize the extent to which the boat's wiring becomes electrically charged (see Protecting Electrical Circuits and Electronics

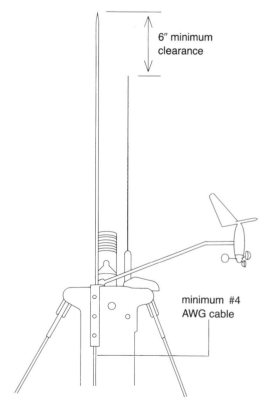

Figure 4-22. Lightning rod installation. The current draft of the NFPA standards recommends that the main down conductor from such a lightning rod be #4 AWG cable (as opposed to the previously required #8 AWG cable). *(Jim Sollers)*

6" minimum clearance

minimum #4 AWG cable

below), which in turn will minimize electrical and electronic damage.

If an external grounding strip is used in place of a grounding plate, and if this strip is run above the bilge-water level (but below the waterline at all angles of heel), a parallel grounding strip (a grounding *bus*) can be run on the inside of the hull, with the two through-fastened. The various grounding cables can then be connected to this grounding bus. This is a particularly attractive arrangement for many fiberglass sailboats since the stemhead fitting can be tied into the bus at the forward end, the backstay and the engine at the aft end, and the various chainplate and other grounding cables along the length of the bus.

To minimize the chances of side flashes, if a bend is needed in a grounding cable, the bend must not form an arc of more than 90 degrees, and the minimum radius of the bend must be 8 inches (203 mm) or more. For added security from side flashes, any substantial metal object within 6 feet (1.8 meters) of any of the paths to ground needs to be tied into the grounding system with #6 AWG cables (as with bonding, good-quality metal through-hulls are probably better excluded).

Protecting engines. Engines, being such large hunks of metal, should be tied into the grounding system regardless of whether they are within 6 feet (1.8 meters) of a grounding conductor or not. Most already have a connection to ground via the propeller shaft and propeller, but oil coating the various bearings can make this resistive. If high currents pass this way, the resistance can create enough heat to damage the bearings. So although a propeller in most instances has enough surface area to dissipate a lightning strike in salt water, and has occasionally been recommended as a candidate for a ground plate, current should be *discouraged* from following this path to ground, and this is best done by directly connecting the engine to the ground plate, grounding strip, or grounding bus. On metal boats a #6 AWG connection also must be made from the engine block to the hull (a stringer or frame in a dry area) to reduce the chances of side flashes.

Lightning rods for powerboats. As noted, a powerboat may have a problem in establishing a high-enough lightning rod. An outrigger with conductivity better than or equal to #4 AWG copper cable can sometimes be raised up sufficiently to provide the necessary zone of protection, but otherwise a lightning rod will have to be mounted on a short mast. In all cases, as on a sailboat, a minimum #4 AWG cable with excellent electrical connections must lead as directly

as possible to an adequate ground plate.

The use of an antenna is sometimes recommended as a lightning rod, but many have various *impedance-matching circuits* that will reduce their effectiveness. If an antenna is used, to be effective it will have to be a *metal* one (most are fiberglass), it will need to be properly grounded via a *lightning arrestor*, and if it has a loading coil (a cylinder at the base of the antenna) this will need a *lightning bypass* (Figure 4-23).

A *lightning arrestor* is a device that is inserted in the line between the coax cable and the antenna at the base of the antenna. It has another connection (minimum #6 AWG copper wire) to the boat's lightning ground plate. In normal circumstances the lightning arrestor is nonconductive to ground, but when hit by very high voltages it shorts to ground, in theory causing a lightning strike to bypass the coax (although the effectiveness of such devices is a matter of some dispute). Lightning arrestors are available through various marine catalogues, or from Radio Shack (USA).

A *lightning bypass* is a simple device that is fitted in parallel with a loading coil. It contains a small gap that will not conduct in normal circumstances, but which lightning can easily bridge, bypassing the loading coil and providing a direct path to ground (once again, with debatable effectiveness).

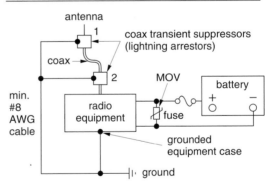

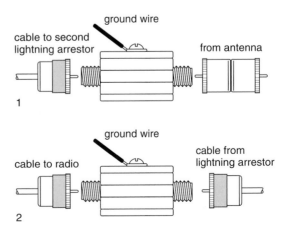

Figure 4-23. The use of lightning arrestors and MOV's to protect electronics and other equipment from the effects of a lightning strike. The various devices create a path to ground for the high voltages and currents associated with a strike. However, the efficacy of the lightning arrestors is disputed by some authorities. (Ocean Navigator)

Protecting Electrical Circuits and Electronics

So far the emphasis has been on protecting people and the boat. Electrical systems and electronics are another matter. A lightning strike may have a potential of up to 100 million volts, resulting in multiple current surges of up to 175,000 amps, with temperatures running as high as 60,000°F. The near instantaneous buildup and then cessation of these massive currents creates an intense magnetic field. Any conductor within the expanding and contracting magnetic field will have a current induced along its length (this is the same principle—passing a wire through a magnetic field or vice versa—employed to generate electricity in alternators and generators). The effects can be felt hundreds of feet away. So aside from the massive voltages and currents produced by the strike, there may be substantial voltages and currents induced in any part of the boat's wiring.

Electronic equipment. While there is nothing that can provide sure protection from a direct hit, or from these induced voltages and currents, certain measures can improve the chances that the electrical gear on board will come through in one piece. When installing such equipment, keep all leads (power, ground, and antenna) as short as possible, without any loops, and as far as practicable, run them at right angles to lightning grounding cables (certainly not in the same bundle!). During electrical storms disconnect these leads (with the exception of grounding cables to metal equipment cases or chassis).

In practice such measures are rarely taken. The relevant leads are frequently inaccessible, and in any case the equipment may be needed during the storm. So the next best option is to build the protection into the equipment leads. *A circuit breaker does not constitute adequate protection*—the response time to current surges is too slow, and even if a breaker is already tripped, lightning can bridge the breaker terminals.

Power lines can be protected with a *metal oxide varistor* (MOV), which is a variation on the lightning arrestor already discussed. Called *despikers, line surge protectors*, etc., these cheap devices, which are available from Radio Shack (USA) or other electronics parts stores, have two leads that are connected across the power leads to both AC and DC equipment at the point at which the leads enter the equipment. MOV's are normally open-circuited, but when the voltage exceeds a predetermined point (normally between 400 and 1,000 volts) they instantly become conductive, producing a direct short across the power leads that cuts off any voltage spike before it affects the rest of the circuit (i.e., the equipment).

Antennas. There are many stories of vaporized antennas. Antennas are almost impossible to protect in the event of a direct strike, even with the use of lightning arrestors and bypass devices. The best form of lightning protection for all antennas, and the equipment to which they are attached, is to disconnect them completely from associated equipment and to ground the antenna cable—both the inner conductor and the outer braided shield—by clipping on a heavy jumper cable and running this to a good ground.

On a ketch, placing antennas on the mizzen rather than the mainmast will increase their chances of not being hit directly. On vessels with single masts it might be worth considering some place other than the masthead, particularly when the transmission and reception range of the equipment is unrelated to the height of the antenna (for example, a satnav or GPS).

At the end of the day it must be recognized that there is no such thing as a lightning-proof boat, only a lightning-protected boat. In a major strike the forces involved are so colossal that no practical measures can be guaranteed to protect sensitive electronic equipment (especially microprocessors). However, the structural integrity of the boat and the safety of its occupants can be assured, and in the process the boat's electrical circuits and electronics may also be saved. The measures needed to attain this degree of protection are neither complex nor particularly expensive—it makes sense to carry them out.

Note: After a strike, or nearby strike, of any size the compass (even a fluxgate) should be swung to check for deviation.

Lightning Prevention

All the foregoing has been predicated upon the impossibility of preventing a lightning strike, and has therefore focused on means to dissipate the strike with as little damage as possible. However, in recent years there has been a certain amount of evidence to show that it may actually be possible to prevent a strike in the first place. The theory once again rests upon the concept that negatively charged electrons from the surface of the earth can be made to congregate on a metal point, where the physical constraints caused by the geometry of the point will result in electrons being pushed off into the surrounding atmosphere.

What is done is to build a *lightning dissipator* that has not just one point, but very many points (Figure 4-24—in the case of the No-Strike device

[Island Technology, Cherry Hill, NJ] more than two thousand—the unit looks like an old-fash-ioned bottle brush and is, in fact, built just the same way!). The claim is that *with proper connection to the earth's surface*, the static electrical charge can be bled off as fast as it builds up, with the result that the voltage differential between the earth and any charged clouds in the vicinity of the boat is kept down to a level at which the boat is "invisible" to lightning and so will not get struck.

Once again, the key to success lies in proper grounding, which is necessary to bleed off the earth's surface charge. All the steps outlined above should be followed, in which case should the device not work as predicted the boat will still be as well protected as possible from the effects of any lightning strike. Only time will tell if the lightning dissipators are as effective as their proponents claim; if they are, every boat should have one.

Figure 4-24. Bottle-brush type lightning dissipator. (This mast is horizontal since it is off the boat.)

The Common Ground Point

Proper *grounding* practices have formed a major part of both Chapter 3 and this chapter, specifically in relation to AC grounding, bonding for corrosion prevention (both galvanic and stray current), and lightning protection. When you also include the two *grounded* circuits found on most boats (the AC neutral and the DC negative) it can all get a little confusing. What I need to do is to tie the pieces together.

The first thing to keep in mind is that the *grounded* circuits (AC neutral and DC negative) are full current-carrying circuits, whereas the *grounding* circuits are not current-carrying in normal circumstances (with the exception of the small currents generated by a cathodic protection system). The second thing to remember is that *the AC neutral is never grounded on board* (except with isolation transformers, inverters, and onboard generators—see Chapter 3) and can be ignored for the purposes of this discussion.

Next, although the DC negative (current-carrying) cables and the various grounding (non-current-carrying) cables may be run in a common bundle, the two sets of circuits are kept *electrically separate* with the exception of a *single common connection* to the boat's *common ground point* or bus bar (see below). This separation is maintained because the DC negative conductors are subject to a certain amount of voltage drop when conducting, so different parts of the DC negative circuit will at different times be at different voltages (not quite at ground potential). If the DC negative circuits were to be tied to the grounding circuits at more than one spot, this would encourage small circulating currents within these circuits which could cause stray-current corrosion.

The purpose of the various normally non-current-carrying grounding systems is to provide a path to ground *within the boat's wiring* for AC fault currents, stray currents, and lightning. In order to do this it is *not* necessary to have separate AC grounding, bonding, and lightning conductors fastened to all major metal objects—in theory the same cable can serve all three purposes, *as long as it is rated for the job*.

However, in practice the AC grounding cable is always run as a separate circuit to all AC appliances and outlets, terminating at the AC grounding bus, from where a connection is made to the common ground point or bus bar. In most circumstances, the #6 AWG cable required for lightning grounding is then more than adequate for combined lightning and bonding purposes, the exception being heavy-draw DC equipment, notably starter motors, on which any bonding cable must be at least as large as the DC negative cable (see page 144). When a heavier cable is required for bonding purposes than is needed for lightning protection, the bonding cable serves also for lightning protection.

The cables on those items that require bonding (for cathodic protection) but do not need to be tied into the lightning grounding system (for example, some bilge pumps) are sized as described on page 144.

The various *current-carrying DC negative cables* are brought to one or more *DC negative buses*. There is normally an *(accessory)* bus close to the DC distribution panel, which in turn is connected to a heavy-duty *(main negative)* bus to which are fastened the battery negative, the engine ground strap, and any other heavy-duty DC negative cables (for example, a direct connection to an alternator case, or the negative

Figure 4-25. **Common ground point.**

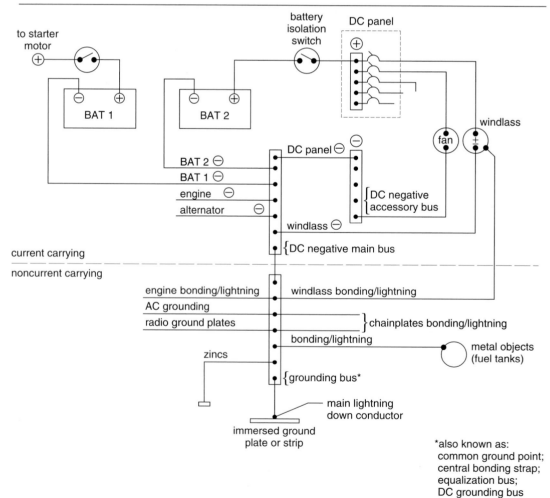

from an anchor windlass—Figure 4-25). Note that although it is a common practice to select a substantial bolt on the engine block to serve the function of the DC main negative bus, this is not the best choice and should not be done on boats with a fully insulated ground system (see page 83); it is preferable to set up a separate bus bar as described above.

Another grounding point or bus should be established as the boat's *common ground point*. All the *non-current-carrying grounding conductors* are fastened to this bus, including:

- a connection to the DC negative bus (this will not be current-carrying since it is not part of the circuit to the batteries)
- the grounding wire (green or bare) from the AC distribution panel (but never the neutral wire)
- the lightning/bonding circuits
- ground connections to radio ground plates
- the external ground plate or strip (for lightning dissipation)
- any zincs for cathodic protection

The function of this common ground point is to hold the DC negative circuit and the various grounding circuits to a common (earth) potential.

This common ground bus is what used to be referred to as a boat's *central bonding strap*, and is now sometimes called an *equalization bus* or *DC grounding bus*. It is the same thing as any internal *grounding strip* for lightning grounding purposes (page 152). As with the DC negative, it need not be more than a single substantial bolt (bearing in mind that the ABYC limits to four the number of connections to a single terminal), which is normally connected directly to the immersed ground plate, but it is best made of a substantial bronze or copper bus bar (the ABYC requires a minimum width of ½ inch and a minimum thickness of 1/32 inch). If possible, a grounding bus bar should be mounted directly over the external ground plate or strip (to maintain a straight path to ground for lightning). If this is not possible, *the main down conductor from the lightning rod or dissipator should go directly to the ground plate*, with the grounding bus tied in via a separate conductor.

(Note that in practice one large bus can serve as both the main DC negative bus and the common ground point. Conceptually, however, it helps to separate them, and it is also not a bad idea in practice since it is often advantageous to have the main DC negative bus and the common ground point in separate physical locations. If they are physically separated, it is important to maintain the current-carrying and non-current-carrying distinction between the two buses.)

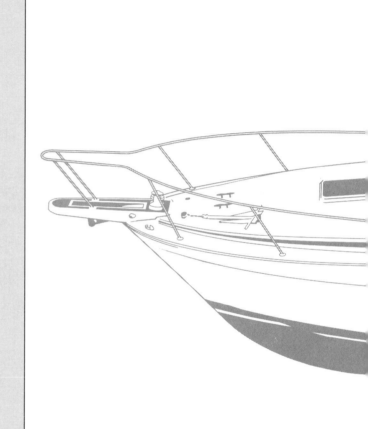

CHAPTER 5

Figure 5-1. Alternative sources of electrical power can go a long way toward easing life aboard. Become your own power company. *(Jim Sollers)*

—————————— 12 VDC

— — — — — — 120 VAC

(1) wind generator
(2) batteries
(3) 110-VAC shoreside receptacle
(4) shunt regulator
(5) 110-VAC load center
(6) to AC appliances
(7) generator set
(8) distribution panel
(9) DC/AC inverter
(10) battery charger
(11) solar panel
(12) isolation transformer

Battery Chargers, Inverters, Wind and Water Generators, and Solar Panels

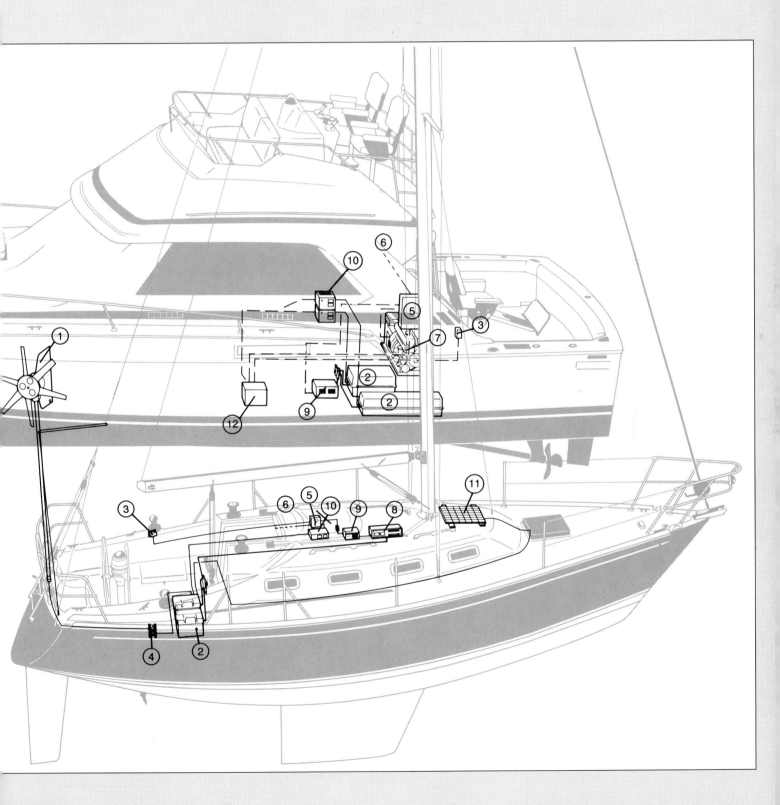

This chapter deals with various auxiliary power sources, both AC and DC. Battery chargers and DC/AC inverters are opposite sides of the same coin, one converting AC power into DC power for battery charging, the other transforming a battery's DC into AC power. Wind and water generators and solar panels produce direct current for battery charging.

Battery Chargers

How They Work

To understand both battery chargers and inverters, some understanding of the nature of alternating current (AC) is needed. Alternating current is generated by spinning a magnet inside a set of coils (an alternator—see Chapter 2) or by spinning a set of coils inside a magnet. As the positive and negative poles of the magnet pass a coil, positive and negative pulses are generated in the coil, causing the electrical output to oscillate continuously from positive to negative and back again, rather than flowing in one direction as in a DC circuit. From a positive voltage peak to a negative voltage peak and back to a positive voltage peak is one cycle. A graph of voltage against time forms a series of sine-waves (Figure 5-2). The number of cycles in 1 second is the *frequency* (*Hertz*, or *Hz*) of the current. In the USA, AC generators are held to a speed of rotation that produces 60 cycles a second (60 Hz). In the UK and Europe frequency is held to 50 Hz.

In a battery charger, AC power is fed into a transformer—a device for changing voltages. The incoming AC voltage (generally 120 volts in the USA and 240 volts in the UK) is stepped down to near-battery voltage: 12, 24, or 32 volts, depending on the system. But this is still alternating current. To use it for battery charging, it must be *rectified* to direct current using electronic check valves or switches of one kind or another.

Types of charger. The two basic components of a battery charger—a transformer and rectifiers—can be put together in numerous different ways. The most common in the marine field is the *ferro-resonant* charger, which has a transformer wound such that given the rated input voltage and frequency (for example, 120 VAC at 60 cycles a second), the desired output (*finishing*) voltage (for example, 13.8 VAC) results. All that remains to be done is to rectify the output to DC, something that can be readily accomplished with diodes (Figure 5-3).

Other types of charger use a *linear* transformer. The transformer is wound to produce a higher finishing voltage than that of a ferro-resonant transformer. The output is then *regulated* by some electronic circuitry (Figure 5-4A and B) using *SCR's* (silicon-controlled rectifiers), *triacs*, or *MOSFET's* (*metal oxide semiconductor field effect transistors*)—all devices for switching circuits on and off in response to a control signal.

SCR's and triacs are found in conventional battery chargers, with SCR's operating on the secondary (battery) side of the transformer and triacs operating on the primary (incoming or *line voltage*) side of the transformer. MOSFET's are used

Figure 5-2. Characteristics of AC power. The current cycles back and forth from positive to negative polarity. The number of cycles in 1 second is its frequency (Hertz or Hz).

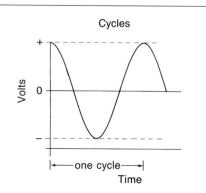

Cycles

one cycle

Time

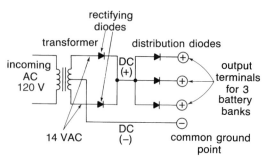

Figure 5-3. Basic battery charger circuit. The transformer steps down the incoming 120- or 240-volt AC power to around 14.0 volts (12-volt charger). The rectifying diodes convert this to DC, which is then fed to the battery. If more than one battery is to be charged, the output is channeled through distribution diodes.

in the latest wave of chargers—*high-frequency switchers (switch mode)*—which are an outgrowth of power supplies in the computer market. In a switcher, before entering the transformer sophisticated electronics are used to pump up the incoming AC line frequency from 50 or 60 cycles a second to 50,000 or even 100,000. *The higher the frequency, the greater the efficiency of the transformer.* The high-frequency output of the transformer is rectified with MOSFET's, which also regulate the charger's output by using more or less of the available *pulse (pulse width modulation).* The end result is a charger that is smaller, lighter, more sophisticated, and more powerful than anything else on the market, but also considerably more complex.

Ferro-Resonant as a Yardstick

Given the market dominance of ferro-resonant chargers over the past few decades, a good way to open up a discussion on the subject of battery chargers is to look at the pros and cons of this type.

The most obvious advantage is the extreme simplicity of the design. It is relatively economical to produce and has proved incredibly reliable over the years. But price and reliability are one thing; performance is another. The simplicity of design that produces this excellent track record is also the ferro-resonant's chief stumbling block. Since there are no regulating circuits, the only way to avoid overcharging a battery with a ferro-resonant charger is to wind the transformer in such a way as to keep its finishing voltage below 14.0 volts (for a nominal 12-volt system—in practice most manufacturers set a target of between 13.6 and 13.8 volts). Once a battery's voltage has been driven up to this level, the transformer's construction must ensure that its output is down to 0 amps (or at least, no more than milliamps).

The nature of the transformer is such that the current tapers off as the finishing voltage is approached (Figure 5-5). As a result, once a battery is just 50% charged many ferro-resonant chargers are already below 50% of rated output. *By the time the battery is 75% charged, the output of even a large charger will be down to a trickle of amps.* To bring a deeply discharged battery back to a state of full charge is likely to take the better part of 24 hours.

If a boat is used only for weekends and then left in a slip with shore power for the following week, the necessary extended charging times will not be a problem. But in any kind of a situation where there is pressure on charging times, the batteries will not be properly charged and sooner or later will succumb

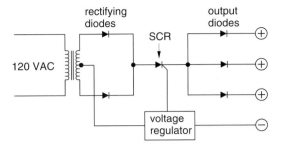

Figure 5-4A. **Simple SCR-controlled battery charger schematic.**

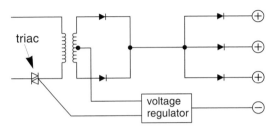

Figure 5-4B. **Simple triac-controlled battery charger schematic.**

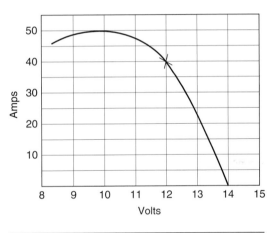

Figure 5-5. **Charging curve for a nominal 40-amp ferro-resonant charger. Note how rapidly the charging current declines as the battery voltage rises.**

to progressive sulphation (Chapter 1).

Despite this weak charging performance, *once batteries are fully charged the continuing trickle charge from many a ferro-resonant charger is high enough to slowly boil away the water or dry out the gel in any unused battery that is left permanently connected* (which is precisely the operating condition of many boat batteries when a boat is left in its slip connected to shore power). Numerous boatyards, marinas, and battery dealers have horror stories relating to ferro-resonant chargers.

There is another problem. Since the output voltage and current are determined by the input voltage and frequency, fluctuations in the line voltage or frequency (which are quite common with inadequate dockside wiring and onboard generators) will cause uncontrolled fluctuations in the output, resulting in under- or overcharging. The frequency, in particular, must be accurate to within 2 cycles.

Overall, this is not a very rosy picture. The bottom line is that *if high performance is wanted, a different design is needed.*

Performance Implies Regulation

To achieve fast charge rates *a transformer must be wound to give a finishing voltage well above the voltage on the DC system.* The charger will then have the ability to maintain a high voltage differential over the batteries it is charging. The higher the differential, the more current that can potentially be pumped in, depending on the overall capability of the charger and the battery's ability to absorb the charging current.

However, the other side to this picture is that *any charger that has the capability to pump in high amperages at high battery voltages also has the capability to destroy the battery.* Some kind of a regulation circuit is essential to control the output of the charger as the battery comes up to full charge.

A basic SCR or triac charger is likely to have a *constant-voltage* regulation circuit similar to that found on an automotive alternator (Chapter 1). The charging curve (Figure 5-6) is not too dissimilar to that of a ferro-resonant charger, with the significant exception that *the rate of charge is considerably higher during the important latter stages of charging.* Once the battery reaches the regulator's voltage set-point, the charger either switches off or trips to a lower *float* setting to avoid overcharging. In addition to a better output curve, the higher potential finishing voltage on the transformer, which is then regulated down, provides some leeway to compensate for changes in line voltage and frequency. The net result is a significant gain in performance but with an increase in complexity.

This has pretty much been the state of the art until the recent introduction of *smart (multistep)* chargers. These have a transformer that is wound with the capability of giving *continuous full output at high charging voltages.* The regulator,

which may be of the SCR, triac, or MOSFET type, is then controlled by a microprocessor or microcomputer. *The sophistication of the charging regimen is now limited solely by the ingenuity of the programmer.* In theory, a customized program can be tailor-made for any battery in any application. In practice, most smart chargers have a similar program consisting of a *bulk* charge, perhaps an *absorption* charge, a *float* charge, and maybe an *equalization* cycle (Figure 5-7). A few have *sulphation recovery* programs.

Bulk, absorption, and float charges are described in detail in Chapter 1. Note that *effective battery charging requires the absorption charge.* So-called *two-step* chargers do not have this function; they simply trip to float once a battery has been driven to the bulk-charge termination voltage. *The batteries are likely to be persistently undercharged.*

A *sulphation recovery* program can, in certain circumstances, bring completely flat and badly sulphated batteries back to life. Resurrection is achieved by hitting the battery with very high voltages (20 volts or more on a 12-volt system) at very low amperages until the battery begins to accept a current and then backing off the voltage levels as the battery state of charge comes up.

While some multistep charger programs are almost entirely factory preset, others allow the user to determine the various voltage trip points, current- and time-limiting parameters, and the equalization program. A charger may have a single output, but most have at least dual outputs.

Line frequency versus high frequency. Such multistep programs can be used with both standard-frequency *(line-frequency)* transformers, whose output is regulated by SCR's and triacs, and also with high-frequency transformers regulated with MOSFET's. There is an ongoing debate about the merits of the two approaches. On the one hand we have the "conservatives" who see high-frequency switchers as notoriously unreliable—the electronics are very complex and difficult to regulate. On the other hand are those who point out that in the computer world everybody went away from ferro-resonant to high-frequency switchers about five or six years ago, and that problems have long since been solved.

There is no question that the high-frequency switchers have significant advantages over conventional battery chargers, and not just in terms of size and weight. The very nature of the high-frequency process makes these chargers both *insensitive to input frequency,* whether it be the fluctuating frequency of a poorly governed AC generator or the difference between European and American frequencies, and also *tolerant of high variations in input voltage*—many nominal 120-volt chargers will still produce full output with input voltages as

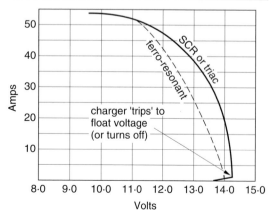

Figure 5-6. Basic SCR or triac charger output as compared to a ferro-resonant. Although the two curves look similar, at 13.0 volts the SCR or triac is producing 34 amps as compared to 25; at 13.5 volts the SCR or triac is producing 25 amps as compared to 13; and at 13.8 volts the SCR is producing 15 amps while the ferro-resonant is below 1 amp.

low as 80 volts or as high as 150 volts. The output of a high-frequency charger is also *pure* DC, in contrast to many conventional chargers that have a superimposed AC *ripple*, which can be destructive to batteries, particularly gel-cells.

On the other side of the coin there is the question of complexity (Figure 5-8) and its potential impact on reliability, and the fact that high-frequency technology, in its "raw" state, is very dirty electrically—the rapid "on" and "off" switching of high currents has a tendency to generate large amounts of radio frequency interference (RFI, see Chapter 7). Manufacturers of high-frequency switchers have invested and are continuing to invest, with varying levels of success, considerable sums of money to overcome (*filter out*) RFI.

The wave of the future? The new generation of microprocessor-controlled chargers represents not simply a linear development of ferro-resonant chargers but a radical advance. The computer age has caught up with this segment of the marine marketplace.

The charger is no longer seen simply as a crude device for pushing current into a battery, but is regarded as an essential element in ensuring a battery's good health. Not only will batteries be kept more fully charged in less time than was previously possible, but their life expectancy will also be extended, sometimes by several times over. The larger and more expensive the batteries, the greater the potential benefit—a good-sized bank of deep-cycle batteries may well repay the cost of a high-tech charger out of extended battery life alone.

But as always there are drawbacks, the principal one being that the likelihood of charger failure increases with its complexity. For this reason ferro-resonant chargers will remain attractive to the sailor whose boat spends much of its time in a slip with shore power and who is concerned primarily with cost and reliability rather than performance. While the hare can win the race sometimes, the turtle will always finish!

In contrast there are many, from the professional bass-fishing guide to the bluewater cruiser, who will benefit from a powerful, fast-return, sophisticated high-tech charger, and will find the new breed of chargers to be an invaluable tool. That is, so long as these chargers can prove themselves reliable in marine use, and only time can show this to be the case.

Troubleshooting

Safety. Before attempting to open any battery charger, unplug it from its power source and disconnect all its batteries. AC POWER CAN

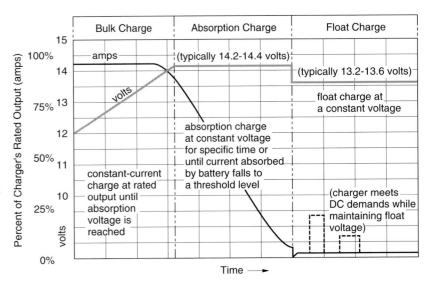

Figure 5-7. Output curves of a multistep charger. One line represents amps; the other, volts. The transformer is wound so that the charger is capable of producing continuous full output to high charging voltages. The output is regulated to provide a bulk charge at a constant current to a relatively high-voltage, an absorption charge at this voltage, and then a float charge at a much lower voltage.

Figure 5-8. Ferro-resonant construction versus high-frequency. On the left-hand side are all the components from *two* ferro-resonant chargers—two transformers, two capacitors, and two sets of diodes—while on the right is the complex circuitry of a single high-frequency charger. Despite their size and weight, these two ferro-resonants taken together provide less performance than the single compact and lightweight high-frequency charger! (*Professional Mariner*)

KILL. Accidentally shorted DC circuits can blow out diodes and expensive electronics.

Warning. Most chargers now incorporate at least some solid-state circuitry. Shorting out the battery leads to test for output (to see if the leads will spark) or connecting batteries in reverse may blow out expensive electronic circuits. Some chargers may be damaged by turning them "on" when they are not connected to a battery. Good chargers, however, are protected against all these eventualities—this kind of protection is well worth paying for.

Comparing Battery Charger Outputs

There are no industry standards for rating battery chargers, which makes comparisons a difficult process. Some chargers will produce, or even exceed, their rated output at all states of battery charge; others are far below their rated output at any likely state of battery charge, making their nameplate rating borderline fraudulent.

Take ferro-resonants, for example. The general practice is to rate these chargers at 2.0 volts per cell (i.e., 12.0 volts if intended for a 12-volt system). That is to say, a charger rated at 80 amps can be expected to produce this level of output at 12.0 volts. At higher voltages, due to the nature of ferro-resonant design, the output falls dramatically.

The only time a charger will be charging into a battery at 12.0 volts is when the battery is stone dead! In a properly designed DC system the batteries will not fall below 50% of charge, giving an open-circuit voltage of around 12.2 to 12.4 volts on a 12-volt system. To put a charge in the battery, the charger must drive the voltage to 13.0 volts or higher. At these voltages *the output of a ferro-resonant charger will already be less than half its rated output, and as the batteries more nearly approach a full charge the output will continue to fall off rapidly* (Figure 5-9). It follows that a 12.0-volt yardstick for rating output is meaningless for judging real-life charging performance!

For a comparison of the effective charging capabilities of different battery chargers, the output at a higher charging voltage must be used. The problem is in determining how much higher. Fast-charging a battery requires a higher voltage than trickle-charging. Fast chargers need to be compared on the basis of their output at 14.0 volts or more, but at these voltages the output of a ferro-resonant charger will be, *by design,* down to milliamps.

Comparison, as a result, becomes a relatively complicated process. The required charger output (amperage) will be a function of the available charging time, the total number of amp-hours to be put back into the batteries, and the DC load to be sustained while charging (see the sidebar on the next page). *The voltage level at which this output must be sustained* will be a function of the rate of charge needed, as a percentage of battery amp-hour capacity (for example, a 25-amp charge into a 400-amp-hour battery bank is a 6.25% rate of return, which can be accomplished at a lower charging voltage than if into a 200-amp-hour battery bank, a 12.5% rate of return; in the latter case a higher charging voltage is needed to drive up the batteries' charge acceptance rate—refer back to Chapter 1).

The choice of a voltage at which to compare charger outputs thus becomes a somewhat arbitrary affair. The important points to remember are: (1) to choose a voltage related to the desired rate of charge—say 13.6 volts for float charging with continuously available AC power; 14.0 volts when there is not a great deal of pressure on charging times; and 14.4 volts for a fast charger—and (2) to then use charger output *at this voltage* as a basis for comparison of performance (all charger manufacturers have output curves containing this information, though some are reluctant to give them up). It is also worth noting how rapidly the charger output rises or falls (if at all) on either side of the chosen voltage—this will give some idea of performance in early and late stages of charging.

Figure 5-9. The output curves of a nominal 80-amp ferro-resonant charger on a well-discharged 200-Ah battery. Note that within a few minutes battery voltage is above 13.0 volts, and charger output is below 26 amps, although in practice the battery is still almost completely discharged. It takes 14 hours to bring the battery to anything near a full charge. *(Adapted from a graph, courtesy Ample Technologies)*

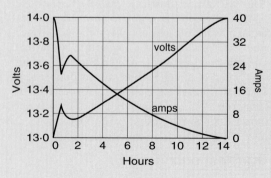

What Size Battery Charger?

There are several factors to consider when sizing a battery charger for a given application, the most important being: (1) whether the charger is intended for continuous use or intermittent use (the time available for recharging); (2) the amp-hours that must be put back into the battery; and (3) the typical DC load (if any) on the battery while charging is taking place.

To determine a minimum battery charger capability, or in a situation where a continuous source of AC power is available (for example, at the dockside or with a 24-hour-a-day AC generator), the charger should be sized to keep up with the average DC load, with sufficient extra output to maintain the batteries on a float charge. To do this, *at a float voltage of somewhere between 13.2 and 13.6 volts*, the charger needs to have a rated output equal to the continuous DC load, *plus 5% to 10% of the amp-hour capacity of the batteries it is charging*. (When a multistep charger is being used, some industry sources feel 10% should be the lower limit—if output is much less than this the charger may have trouble driving the batteries to the bulk-charge termination voltage, creating the potential for damage through overcharging. All smart chargers should have some sort of a *time-limiting* circuit to terminate the bulk-charge phase in case of these kinds of problems.)

When AC power is only intermittently available, the charger must be able not only to keep up with the DC load but also to recharge the batteries in the available time. The *average* charge rate needed can be established by taking the total charge that must be put into the batteries (in amp-hours), dividing this by the number of charging hours available, and adding in the DC load while charging. Regardless of charger type, such a charging current will still not fully recharge the batteries due to the tapering charge acceptance rate as a battery comes to charge: An initial charge rate of up to double the figure arrived at will be needed to compensate for this!

It sometimes seems that it is impossible to have too much charger capability, but this is not necessarily the case. In a well-designed DC system, boat batteries are rarely discharged by more than 50%. Due to internal resistance in a battery, at a 50% level of discharge, and at a charger output regulated to 14.2 volts, a liquid electrolyte battery will not accept a rate of charge much above 25% of its overall amp-hour capacity. As its state of charge rises, this charge acceptance rate declines below 25%.

Gel-cells will accept a higher rate of charge, but even so *there is generally little practical advantage to having a charger capability, at charging voltages, much in excess of 25% of the battery's overall amp-hour capacity*. To this must be added the boat's DC load while the charger is in operation. This will determine the maximum practical battery-charger capability in most situations. If the calculations of charger requirements produce a figure higher than this, the chances are that *no amount of charging capability will bring the batteries to a full charge in the available time*.

For any given charger (or alternator) output, even with a multistep regulator, David Smead of Ample Technologies points out that the length of time required for a full charge can more or less be found by taking the current available for battery charging (i.e., first subtracting any DC loads coming off the charger), multiplying this figure by 0.8 (to take account of inefficiencies in the charging process), dividing the result into the number of amp-hours that must be put back into the battery, and then adding 30 to 45 minutes for a gell-cell or 60 to 90 minutes for a wet-cell (to allow for the battery's declining charge acceptance rate as it comes to charge). If this figure exceeds the available charging time, once again the chances are the battery will not be fully charged.

No output. Before blaming the charger:

- Check the incoming AC shore-power connection or onboard generator.

- Check all relevant circuit breakers.

- Check the charger's incoming AC fuses—often there are two. If the fuses blow repeatedly, see below.

- Check the charger's AC switch.

- Double-check the hot and neutral AC terminals *at the charger* with a voltmeter or test light to make sure the charger really is receiving power (Chapter 3, Testing AC Circuits).

Where present, a remote control for a charger is wired in series with the AC "ON/OFF" switch, but will be in the circuit *after* the "on" light (if fitted). If the remote control is "off," the "on" light will glow, *but the charger will be off*. Check that the remote switch is "on" and double-check

Transformers

A battery charger intended for marine use must have an *isolation transformer* in which the incoming AC power flows through one coil and transfers power magnetically to a *totally separate* coil. This second coil, which is electrically isolated from the incoming AC side, supplies power to the DC side. All marine battery chargers use isolation transformers, but some automotive chargers do not: *The neutral AC wire may be common to both sides of the transformer* (Figure 5-10). Should the incoming neutral and hot leads get crossed, the common line will be hot! This can happen quite easily with improper wiring, or by inserting a two-prong plug the wrong way around. In this case there will be a reverse polarity situation in which *the entire negative side of the boat's DC system may be charged at full AC voltage, creating a severe shock hazard aboard and for swimmers* (see Chapter 3). Even without reverse polarity, *an automotive-type common neutral connection will bypass any galvanic isolator and encourage stray-current corrosion.*

Testing for an isolation transformer. With the battery charger completely disconnected, test with an ohmmeter *that has a diode-testing capability* between all output terminals and all incoming AC leads, *reversing the meter leads at each test.* An isolation transformer should read an open circuit (infinite ohms) between any input wire and any output terminal.

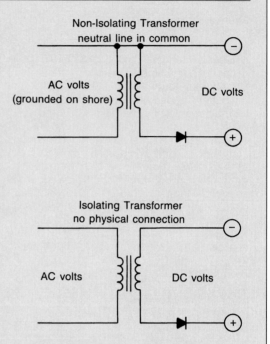

Figure 5-10. Marine battery chargers use an isolation transformer to eliminate any direct electrical connection between the incoming shore power and the boat's AC system.

---

for AC power across its two terminals on the charger. If in doubt, fit a jumper wire across its terminals (*unplug the charger to do this!*).

AC side OK but no output to the batteries (ammeter does not register).

1. Check that the battery selector switch is in the correct position.
2. Check the leads from the charger to the batteries, and any fuses or switches in the line; make sure the battery leads are connected with the correct polarity.
3. Turn the charger "off" and test the battery voltage. It should be around 12.0 to 12.5 volts. Turn on the charger and test across its positive and negative terminals: *If the voltage is now higher than the previously measured battery voltage, the charger is putting out.* (If the battery is already fully charged, an automatic charger may simply have turned itself off. If it has a manual switch, turn it to manual. If not, put a load on the battery for a few minutes to drop its

charge below the regulator kick-in voltage. Note that a *completely dead* battery will sometimes not accept any charge—in this case, try another battery.)

4. If the charger is hot, let it cool down. It may simply be tripping on its *thermal-overload* protection. In this case it will cycle on and off almost inaudibly at intervals of several minutes (most likely with simple SCR chargers).
5. If the charger has an ignition-protection circuit disconnect the wires leading to it and test again. When the engine is shut down these wires should be sensing no voltage; if they are sensing voltage, the charger will not come on line. If the charger works with the circuit disconnected, it can be used in this fashion but *must be switched off before cranking the engine or it may be damaged.*
6. An overloaded charger with a DC overload circuit breaker will cycle on and off with an audible click (once again, this is most likely with simple SCR chargers). Reduce the load and check for shorts in the boat's wiring or DC equipment. If the circuit breaker trips *with the*

thermistor and/or varistor protects
against voltage spikes and temperature-
compensates output

capacitor on
incoming AC
line
protects against
voltage spikes

voltage regulator,
ignition protection,
automatic circuit
control, thermal
overload, noise
suppression
filters

Figure 5-11. Basic battery charger schematic with
voltage regulator.

AC *power off*, the charger has a shorted
distribution (output) diode.

7. Still no output? If the charger has an
internal DC circuit breaker and/or an
ammeter, bridge across it/them with
jumper wires.

**AC fuses blow immediately upon
plugging in.** The high-frequency and
multistep chargers contain a fair amount
of sophisticated electronics, which are
well beyond the scope of this book. Low-
tech chargers, particularly ferro-resonants,
have very simple circuitry (Figure 5-11)
which will include a transformer and
diodes and perhaps:

1. A circuit to compensate for variations
in incoming AC voltage. This is
known as *line compensation*.

2. A *thermistor* and/or a *varistor* con-

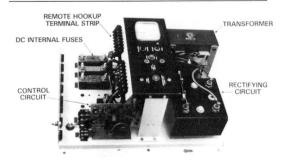

Figure 5-12. Component layout of a simple charger
(this is a ferro-resonant charger, but with an automatic
shutdown circuit to avoid overcharging batteries).
(Marine Development Corporation)

Troubleshooting Chart 5-1.
Battery Charger Problems: No Output.
Checking the AC Side
Warning: AC power can kill. Before opening any battery charger, unplug it
from the power source and disconnect all its batteries. Accidentally shorted
DC circuits can blow out diodes and expensive circuits.

Is AC voltage reaching the charger? (Use a voltmeter or test light on the incoming AC terminals to check for incoming voltage.) **YES** ⬇	**NO** ➡ Check the AC supply: the incoming shore power or onboard generator; fuses, breakers, and switches (including remote control switch if present); and wiring.
Are the charger's AC fuses blowing every time it's plugged in? **YES** ⬇	**NO** ➡ Go to "Checking the DC Side" below.
If a capacitor is fitted across the incoming AC lines, remove it and try again. Do the fuses still blow? **YES** ⬇	**NO** ➡ Fit a new capacitor.
Repeat the test above with any thermistor or varistor, and the rectifying diodes. Do the fuses still blow? **YES** ⬇	**NO** ➡ Fit new thermistor, varistor, or rectifying diodes.
Replace the transformer.	

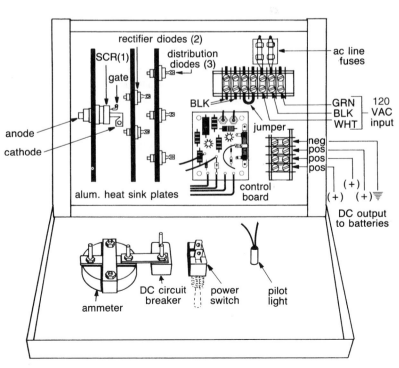

Checking the DC Side

With the charger connected to a charged battery check the output voltage at the charger first with it off and then with it on. Is there a voltage increase? **NO**	**YES** The charger is OK. Perform the same test at the battery. If there is no voltage rise, the circuit between the charger and battery is defective—check all terminals, breakers, switches and wiring. If there is a voltage increase, the charger is working but may be suffering from voltage drop (page 86).
Does the charger have an automatic shutdown circuit? **NO**	**YES** Override it with a manual switch (if fitted) or discharge the battery for a few minutes and try again.
Does the charger have an ignition-protection circuit? **NO**	**YES** Disconnect it and try again. If the charger now works it can be used without this circuit, taking care to switch the charger off before firing up the engine.
Is the charger hot? **NO**	**YES** It may have tripped on its thermal overload protection. Reduce the DC load, allow it to cool, and try again.
Did the charger show maximum amperage before tripping off (probably with an audible click)? **NO**	**YES** It is tripping on overload. Disconnect all DC loads from the battery and try again. Check for shorts in the boat's DC equipment and wiring, or overloading of the charger. Maybe the battery itself is shorted.
Open the charger (see the warning above) and put a jumper wire across the two terminals to any internal breaker and the ammeter. Does the charger now work? **NO**	**YES** Replace the breaker or ammeter.

If all tests to this point fail to isolate the problem, call a specialist.

nected across the low-voltage side of the AC transformer to adjust output for changes in temperature and to protect against voltage *spikes*.

3. A capacitor connected across the high-voltage (incoming AC) side of the transformer.

4. Current-limiting and voltage-regulating circuits.

5. Automatic "off" and "on" circuits.

6. An *ignition-protection* circuit, which shuts down the charger during engine cranking and running. This prevents overload from the starter motor, and conflict between alternator and battery charger voltage regulators.

7. Various *filters* to reduce radio interference.

If the components can be identified, the following tests may isolate a problem.

Look for a shorted transformer, capacitor (if fitted), rectifying diode, or thermistor or a varistor (if fitted). The transformer is a bulky unit with two AC supply wires running into it and two or more wires running out to the rectifying diodes (Figure 5-12). A capacitor (if fitted) is a cylindrical object wired *across* the incoming AC wires; a thermistor or varistor is a much smaller electronic component, which will be wired across the output wires to the rectifier diodes.

1. Disconnect any capacitor and try the charger again. Note that *long after a battery charger is shut down, a capacitor can hold a lethal charge—before handling a capacitor use a length of INSULATED wire to short out its two terminals*, which will discharge any residual charge. If the charger works without the capacitor, install a new one with the same rating (see the symbols on its side—for capacitor testing, see page 204).

2. Disconnect the thermistor or varistor and try again; if the charger works, install a new thermistor or varistor.

3. Disconnect the two wires to each rectifying diode (they may need to be unsoldered); if the fuses still blow, the transformer is shorted. If not, the diodes are shorted.

4. After unsoldering the diode connecting wires, test the diodes with an ohmmeter that has a diode-testing capability; they should show continuity in only one direction (see Chapter 2, Diodes).

Battery will not come to charge:

1. Check for some load that may inadvertently have been left on the battery, or a leak to ground (Chapter 3).

2. Many battery chargers with multiple-battery-charging capabilities have only one battery-voltage sensing line. If this line senses a fully charged battery, *no matter how dead the other batteries are, the charger will stay "off" until the voltage on the sensed battery falls below the charger's kick-in point*. In this case, the *most-used* battery should be connected to the charger output terminal that has the battery-sensing capability. Alternatively, during battery charging, connect all batteries in parallel via the battery selector switch.

3. If problems with undercharging persist, load up the batteries, then turn on the charger so that it is putting out at its full rate. Check the

output voltage on the charger and at the batteries. If there is a significant difference (more than 0.3 volt), there is an unacceptable voltage drop in the wiring and switches (Figure 5-13). The battery charger will sense a higher voltage than the battery actually receives and will shut down too soon. Measure voltage both at the battery posts and the battery terminal clamps; any difference here indicates a poor connection that needs cleaning.

Voltage drop caused by inadequate wiring is a major cause of undercharging. Situate a charger as close to its batteries as possible, no more than 10 feet away. However, do not place a battery charger in or over a battery compartment with wet-cell batteries. Gases emitted during charging will corrode sensitive electronic parts. Use Table 3-5 to determine wire size based on maximum charger output and maximum 3% voltage drop—the larger the wire, the better.

4. Now bring the batteries to a full charge by one means or another then check the charger's output voltage. If it equals the rated output voltage (probably around 13.8 volts), the charger is Okay. In this case, if the previous test showed no voltage drop to the batteries, the charger may have too low a charging voltage to effectively charge the batteries, it may be undersized for its job, or the batteries may be failing.

5. If the charger output voltage is low, before trying to adjust it (if it is adjustable), be certain the batteries are fully charged and check the incoming AC power *at the charger*. Low input voltage will produce low output voltage if the charger does not have *line compensation*.

Persistent overcharging. The batteries boil and lose water; gel-cells dry out and fail. Many ferro-resonants left permanently connected to shore-power will produce a low-level overcharge—the charger should be switched off once the batteries are charged, or else a small DC load (for example, a cabin light) can be left on to absorb the excess output. On other chargers, overcharging may be the result of improper regula-

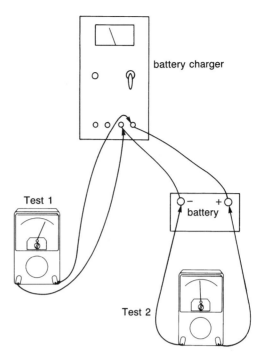

Figure 5-13. Checking battery charger output. Load up the battery so that the charger goes to full output, then test the voltage between the charger's output terminals (Test 1), and between the battery's terminals (Test 2). There should be no difference between Test 1 and 2. If 2 is lower, there is a voltage drop in the wiring and/or connections between the charger and the battery. This should not exceed 3% of system voltage (i.e., 0.36 volts on a 12.0-volt system).

tion, or once again the batteries may be at fault, most likely from one or more shorted cells. Batteries will often overcharge when housed in hot locations, unless the charger has temperature compensation based on temperature-sensing *at the batteries* (rare) or else an external adjustable switch that the user can set for different ambient temperature conditions.

If the output voltage on constant-potential chargers is higher than rated, check the incoming AC voltage; high input will produce high output unless the charger has line compensation. Continuously high output to good, cool batteries will be the result of an internal short in the voltage regulation circuit (where fitted, i.e., non-ferro-resonant battery chargers); this requires a specialist's attention.

Inverters

Inverters, which convert battery power to AC power, hold out the enticing prospect of being able to use all kinds of useful household gadgets on board without the noise, weight, space requirements, exhaust fumes, and expense of a generator. Blenders, toasters, coffeemakers, even microwaves—seemingly no problem! Few recent innovations have such far-reaching potential to improve shipboard living standards. But is there a down side? That depends on whether the right choice is made between competing inverters, and on whether the boat's DC system is properly set up to handle the chosen inverter.

How They Work

To understand inverters it is necessary to delve a little deeper into the nature of AC power. As noted above, AC voltage cycles continuously from positive to negative and back. A graph of voltage against time forms a series of sine-waves (Figure 5-2).

The nominal system voltage—120 volts, 240 volts, etc.—is in fact more or less an average known as *root mean square*, or RMS voltage. The voltage at the peak of the sine-waves—both positive and negative—is actually considerably higher than the nominal (RMS) voltage of the system (Figure 5-14). Peak voltage is found by multiplying the RMS voltage by 1.414, or dividing by 0.707. A 120-volt (RMS) circuit has an actual peak voltage of 169.7 volts; and a 240-volt (RMS) circuit has a peak voltage of 339.36 volts.

Why use such an odd divisor as 0.707? Because from any given peak voltage *this gives us an RMS voltage that will do the equivalent amount of work as the same DC voltage*: 169.7 peak volts of AC will do the same work as 120 volts of DC

$(120 \div 0.707 = 169.7)$.

The earth—meaning the planet, globe, world—is the common reference point for AC electrical circuits. The earth has its own ground potential or voltage, which is given a value of 0 (just as the negative side of a DC circuit is given a value of 0). Alternating current of 120 volts surges first to 169.7 volts positive and then to 169.7 volts negative, for an RMS value of 120 volts with respect to this common reference point.

Types of inverter. A DC/AC inverter essentially reverses the mechanism of a battery charger, producing line voltage, (i.e., 120- or 240-volt AC) from DC battery voltage. In essence, two steps are required: the first to convert DC to AC, and the second to step the AC up to the required voltage.

Inverters fall into two broad categories: those that produce a true *sine-wave* output equivalent to that produced by a generator or an electricity company, and those that produce a *stepped-square-wave* (generally referred to as a *modified-sine-wave*) output. There are two technologies for producing either waveform, one based on *line-frequency* switching, the other on *high-frequency* switching. This gives us four possible combinations: line-frequency stepped-square-wave; line-frequency sine-wave; high-frequency stepped-square-wave; and high-frequency sine-wave.

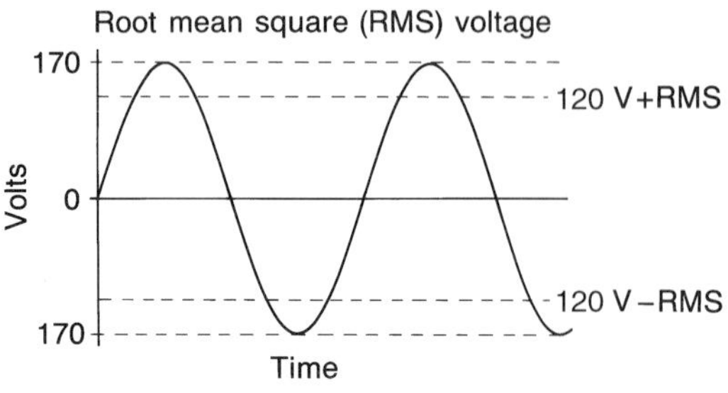

Line frequency inverters. Inside a *line-frequency stepped-square-wave* inverter there is a transformer with a primary (low-voltage) winding and a secondary (high-voltage) winding. The negative side of a battery is fed through two banks of high-current switches (*FET's—field effect transistors*) to each end of the primary winding. The positive side of the battery is connected to the center of the winding (Figure 5-15). The switches are turned on and off alternately at a rate determined by a high-frequency *crystal oscillator* (a device that holds a very stable frequency).

When the switches at one end of the winding are turned on, current flows through the coil in one direction; when the switches at the other end are turned on, current flows in the opposite direction—we have alternating current, with its frequency regulated by the oscillator. This alternating current is stepped up by the transformer to produce alternating current in the secondary winding at the desired output voltage.

The rate at which the FET's switch on and off determines the frequency of the AC output and is set to produce 60 cycles a second in the USA, 50 cycles a second in Europe—the same as the power companies, hence the designation *line-frequency* for these inverters. Since the FET's are either "on" or "off," the waveform produced by such an inverter is a stepped-square-wave as opposed to a true sine-wave (Figure 5-16).

The transformers are wound in such a way that with normal battery voltages the peak of the

Figure 5-14. Peak voltage and RMS voltage in AC circuits (nominal 120-volt AC).

Root mean square (RMS) voltage

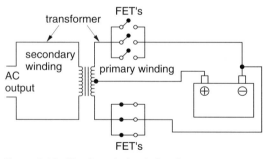

Figure 5-15. Circuitry of a basic line-frequency stepped-square-wave inverter. Current from the negative side of the battery is fed through banks of field effect transistors (FET's) to the primary winding in the transformer. The "on" and "off" cycling of the switches produces alternating current which is stepped up by the transformer to the appropriate voltage.

Battery Chargers, Inverters, Wind and Water Generators, and Solar Panels

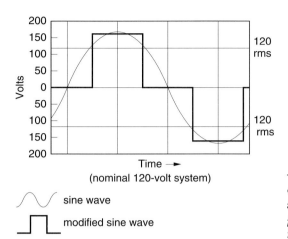

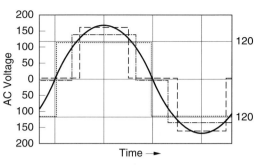

Figure 5-16. **Stepped square wave ("modified sine-wave").** The peak voltage is lower than with a true sine-wave, but the RMS voltage is the same.

Figure 5-17. Pulse width modulation on a modified-sine-wave inverter maintains a constant RMS voltage at differing battery input voltages.

stepped-square-wave is lower than that of a true sine-wave. The length of the wave is then regulated to maintain an RMS voltage of 120 volts. As the load on such an inverter increases, so too does the load on the battery that is powering it. The heavier the load, the lower the battery's voltage will be. Since this type of inverter's output voltage is *directly proportional* to its input voltage, the output voltage will also fall. To compensate for the falling voltage the wave length has to be increased so that the inverter maintains its RMS voltage, but with a resultant loss of the *resemblance to a sine-wave* (Figure 5-17). This process of changing the length of the stepped-square-wave to maintain a constant RMS voltage is known as *pulse width modulation*.

A line-frequency *sine-wave* inverter uses much the same technology as a line-frequency stepped-square-wave inverter, but with some proprietary circuitry that produces *a peak output voltage and a true sine-wave that remain constant over a broad range of battery input voltages*. The process is clearly more complex, and as a result these inverters are more expensive.

High-frequency inverters. These once again have a center-tapped transformer with FET's at either end of the primary winding, but these FET's switch on and off *thousands* of times a second (anywhere from 16,000 on up) to produce high-frequency AC voltage at battery voltages. This low-voltage, high-frequency AC is stepped up by a transformer to some voltage above 140 volts in the secondary side of the transformer (for a 120-volt system). The high-voltage, high-frequency AC is then rectified to DC to produce high-voltage DC. This high-voltage DC is fed through another bank of FET's switching at line frequency to produce AC at the correct fre-

quency. *The higher the frequency of the initial switching operation, the smaller and lighter it is possible to build the transformers, and thus the inverter.*

A *stepped-square-wave* high-frequency inverter produces the same single positive and negative pulse in each AC cycle as a stepped-square-wave line-frequency inverter. On some the voltage and pulse width also vary with battery input voltage, just as with the line-frequency pulse-width-modulated inverters, but on others an additional regulation circuit produces a constant voltage and pulse width.

A *sine-wave* high-frequency inverter uses carefully regulated multiple steps (many thousands in each cycle) to create a sinusoidal output waveform that is indistinguishable, so far as AC equipment is concerned, from a true sine-wave. What is more, the peak voltage and waveform are unaffected by changes in battery voltage—in fact, the output is frequently "cleaner" than that from a power company!

Pros and cons of different technologies. What are the pros and cons of the different technologies? The first point that is immediately apparent is the physical difference between line-frequency and high-frequency inverters. A 2,000-watt line-frequency model (either stepped-square-wave or sine-wave) will weigh in at around 50 pounds and occupy approximately a cubic foot of space; its high-frequency counterpart (once again, either stepped-square-wave or sine-wave) may weigh in at as little as 8 pounds and occupy one-third the space (Figure 5-18).

However, the high-frequency inverter is more likely to generate radio frequency interference (Chapter 7); and it has a much higher component count, which historically has translated into a higher failure rate. In addition, the high-frequency process is not easily "reversible," whereas a number of the line-frequency inverters can be run "backward" to charge batteries when another source of AC power comes on line.

Within the general class of high-frequency inverters, the sine-wave inverters have additional handicaps. They are frequently less efficient than

Figure 5-18. Line-frequency versus high-frequency inverter construction. The line-frequency inverter (occupying most of the picture) is rated at 1,000 watts, while the high-frequency inverter (the small unit in the foreground) is rated at 1,500 watts! Each of the three small transformers in the center of the high-frequency inverter (the square units) is capable of producing 500 watts of output, as compared to the 1,000 watts from the heavy and bulky transformer that dominates the line-frequency inverter.

other inverters in converting DC to AC (typically 80% efficient as opposed to 90% for a stepped-square-wave inverter), and have a higher *standby* drain (the amount of current consumed when the inverter is "on" but not powering a load—*this is particularly important for cruising sailors: Where DC resources are limited, but an inverter is to be left on for long hours, the standby drain can become a significant part of the boat's overall DC load*). Finally, all sine-wave inverters (both line-frequency and high-frequency) are more expensive than other inverters in terms of dollars per watt of output. Is there any reason to pay this extra money for a sine-wave?

How important is the waveform? Many AC loads, such as incandescent lights, toasters, hair dryers, and coffeemakers, are *resistive*. These are not in the least bit sensitive to waveform. In fact, they will run as well on DC as on AC as long as the voltage is correct. At the other end of the spectrum are certain loads, mostly high-tech electronics (such as laser printers and SCR- or triac-based electronic controllers), that not only will not function on a stepped-square-wave, but may also self-destruct. In between we have a gray area.

With a stepped-square-wave there is likely to be some picture degradation on the TV and hum on the stereo, and there will probably be some loss of efficiency on some induction motors. Microwaves, a popular appliance to run off an inverter, are an interesting case. They appear to be sensitive to both peak voltage and waveform. When powered by a modified-pulse-width stepped-square-wave inverter, many become increasingly inefficient the lower the battery input voltage—and therefore the lower the output voltage and the wider the output pulse (more on this in a moment).

In the final analysis, unless there are specific pieces of equipment that demand a true sine-wave, the point at which a loss of performance in

other equipment tips the balance in favor of the extra cost of a sine-wave inverter is very much a matter of individual choice.

Batteries: The Limiting Factor

Regardless of inverter choice, keeping up the battery voltage is, as often as not, the single biggest problem faced by any inverter user. It is not hard to see why.

Take a 1,200-watt, 120-volt microwave. Since watts = volts × amps, amps = watts ÷ volts. When in use, the current absorbed by the microwave will be

$1,200 \div 120 = 10.0$ amps.

But if we take that same microwave and power it with an inverter connected to a 12-volt battery, the current drain on the battery will nominally be $1200 \div 12 = 100$ amps. In reality an inverter is not 100% efficient in converting battery power to AC power. The current drain will be 5% to 15% higher than this—i.e., between 105 and 115 amps—more than ten times as much as on the 120-volt system. This will impose a tremendous strain on any battery bank.

There are two factors at work here:

1. the high rate of discharge that some AC loads impose on the battery
2. the overall drain on the battery if AC loads are sustained for any length of time

High-rate discharges. Battery Ah ratings are based on a slow rate of discharge (over a period of 20 hours in the USA; 10 in the UK). As the rate of discharge increases, the battery's Ah capacity declines sharply (Chapter 1, Figure 1-13). Even a small 300-watt DC/AC inverter will impose a load of up to 27.5 amps on a 12-volt system ($300 \div 12 = 25 + 10\%$ for inefficiency = 27.5 amps). A 1,500-watt inverter can impose a staggering load as high as 137.5 amps—close to that of a small starter motor. Imagine what cranking an engine continuously for half an hour would do to the batteries!

At these kinds of loads, battery capacity will be only a fraction of its rated capacity. Output voltage will fall off sharply after only a short period of time and the inverter will trip off due to low battery voltage (Figure 5-19). The battery will recover and tolerate another short burst of energy, but not as long as the first. Repeated high-load discharging of batteries for prolonged periods will cause internal damage sooner or later.

It should be noted that in terms of deep-cycle batteries, gel-cells can deliver their stored current faster than the wet-cells. Given equal-capacity batteries, subjected to equal loads, the terminal voltage will hold up better on a gel-cell than a wet-cell. This has particular significance when using a line-frequency stepped-square-wave inverter on loads that are sensitive to peak AC voltage, notably many microwaves. As the battery terminal voltage declines, the peak AC voltage will decline, and microwave efficiency will decline (Figure 5-20)—the gel-cell will, because of its higher terminal voltage, do a better job than the wet-cell in maintaining microwave efficiency. Both types of battery will do even better if the battery voltage is boosted by the output from an engine-driven alternator.

Overall drain on the batteries. The intensity of a load is just one aspect of the impact of inverters on batteries; the duration of the load is the other. A microwave used for 15 minutes a day will pull fewer amp-hours (around 30 Ah) out of a battery than a typical DC lighting load. But sustained use of just about any AC item will put a heavy drain on the batteries. *A single 100-watt lightbulb run off an inverter powered by a 12-volt battery for 24-hours will drain the battery by 220 amp-hours!*

To avoid excessive discharges, *battery capacity should total at least 2.5 and preferably 4 times the anticipated need between charges* (Chapter 1). An inverter load is obviously a cyclic load—the batteries are discharged and then recharged. *Only good-quality deep-cycle batteries will withstand this kind of treatment for any length of time* (Chapter 1). So although it is a relatively easy matter to find an inverter that meets typical AC needs (see sidebar, "Calculating AC loads"), it is nowhere near as easy to supply the batteries and battery-recharging capabilities needed to support the inverter. Unless a boat has enormous battery banks, large-capacity inverters should be used at their full rated output only on rare occasions and for brief periods of time. Where inverters really shine is on light (300 watts or less), moderate-duration AC loads, or short-term heavier loads.

Battery protection. Repeated discharging below 50% of full charge will eventually kill even the best deep-cycle batteries. Because inverters can discharge batteries rapidly, they invariably incorporate a low-battery-voltage shutdown circuit. Under a heavy load, however, battery voltage falls rapidly while overall capacity is not necessarily affected greatly, especially if the load is of short duration. Most inverters therefore have a low-voltage trip point of 10 to 11 volts to prevent the inverter from kicking off under heavy, short-duration loads. But under a light load, any battery that is pulled down to 10 volts will be *stone dead*. In other words, *the low-volt-*

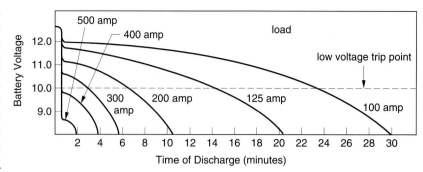

Figure 5-19. Battery voltage as a function of load. The greater the load put on a battery, the steeper and more rapid the drop in battery voltage. The graph assumes a fully charged 100-Ah battery. Simultaneous use of three typical "morning appliances," such as a hair dryer, coffeemaker, and toaster, will pull the battery below 10 volts in less than 4 minutes!

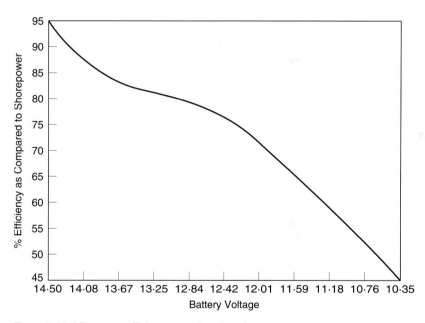

Figure 5-20. Microwave efficiency, as a function of battery voltage, when powered by a modified-sine-wave inverter. *(Adapted from a graph, courtesy Ample Technologies)*

age trip protects the inverter, not the battery. It is useless to rely on an inverter's low-voltage cutout to protect batteries; some other means of monitoring them is needed (Chapter 1).

Recharging the batteries. Whatever is pulled out of the batteries must be replaced (plus up to 20% to allow for inefficiencies in the charging process). Given the ability of even a moderate-size inverter to deplete a battery bank rapidly, unless inverter use is sandwiched between extended periods of battery charging, some form of high-capacity fast charging is essential for the survival of the DC system. For example, on a boat with an anticipated daily demand of around 120 Ah, a battery bank of up to 480 Ah will be needed, while the boat will need a recharging capability of around 145Ah per day (120×1.2).

Many line-frequency stepped-square-wave inverters can be used "backwards" to charge a battery. Two-thousand-watt inverters have 100+ amp charging capabilities at 12 volts, controlled by sophisticated multi-stage regulation programs designed to recharge batteries at the fastest safe rate (Figure 5-21). Without such a battery-charging option a high-capacity (and relatively expensive) battery charger may well be required to support the inverter.

This is all very well if there is a regular independent source of AC power with which to charge the batteries, but what happens when this is not the case? At such times the principal means of recharging batteries will be the boat's main engine and alternator. However, there is little point in transferring the AC load to the DC system if the engine then has to be run long hours to recharge the batteries! If battery-charging hours are to be kept to a minimum, the engine-driven alternator must be upgraded to a high-output model with a multistep regulator. In the above instance, *to support the inverter alone* an alternator output of up to 120 amps can be used (25% of the Ah rating of the batteries). To keep the alternator below its full-rated output, a 160-amp alternator would be advisable.

Matching the Demand to the System

Light AC demands. If AC demands are occa-

sional and light and if, as is so often the case, a boat is used on weekends only and then kept in a slip with shore power throughout the week, an inverter can readily be wired into existing circuits. It will be important to fit deep-cycle batteries appropriately sized for the weekend load, but beyond this, little need be done.

Inverter size can be calculated as described in the sidebar. The type will depend on whether there is to be any waveform-sensitive equipment on board, and on questions of size, weight, radio frequency interference, historical reliability, standby drain, and cost. If a "reversible" inverter is used, the inverter's battery-charging capability will recharge the batteries during the nonuse period. With all other inverters, if the boat does not currently have a battery charger, it will almost certainly need one.

Moderate AC demands. The picture becomes a little more complex with heavier AC demands. A more substantial battery bank is required. The inverter's battery charger, or an independent battery charger, may well need to be backed up by a high-output engine-driven alternator coupled to a multistep regulator. Many sailboats, which typically use their engines less than powerboats, will still find themselves with limited battery-replenishment capabilities, but may be able to make up the deficit with solar panels and/or a wind generator. One way or another, most owners of powerboats up to 30 feet in length and cruising sailboats up to around 40 feet would find that an inverter offers considerable improvement in creature comforts with very few drawbacks.

Heavier AC demands. As the anticipated AC load increases, there comes a point at which the DC system will be overwhelmed even if the inverter is not. In such circumstances it is time to think of a dual inverter/generator setup. *The key to a successful inverter/generator system is to concentrate all the high-load AC items into 1 or 2 hours a day, during which time the generator is run, and to then power the light AC loads from the inverter alone throughout the rest of the 24 hours* (Figure 5-22). During the generating hours the generator will not only meet the AC need, but also provide the power either for a battery charger or for the inverter to switch into its battery-charging mode. The battery-charging amps can be supplemented by attaching a high-output alternator with a multistep regulator to the generator engine. The inverter or battery charger, together with the alternator, will provide a formidable overall battery-charging capability that is able to compensate for the demands on the DC system during the rest of the day.

Since the strengths and weaknesses of genera-

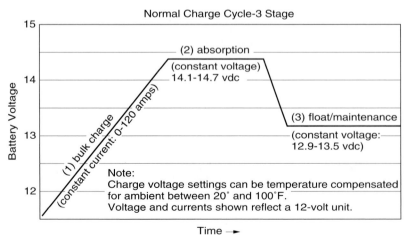

Figure 5-21. Battery charger program for a modified-sine-wave inverter. *(Trace Engineering)*

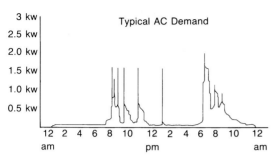

Typical AC Demand

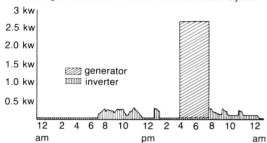

Usage Pattern with Inverter and Generator System

▨▨▨ generator
▥▥▥ inverter

Figure 5-22. Combined inverter/generator use: Patterns of AC use on board. Top: Uncontrolled use, requiring the generator to be operated (and underutilized) 24 hours a day. Note the heavier usage at meal times and when AC-powered entertainment equipment is used. Bottom: Controlled use, concentrating the use of high-load AC equipment into a limited period of generator operation and running the AC system from a DC/AC inverter for the rest of the day. *(Heart Interface)*

tors and inverters tend to be mirror images, this can be an ideal arrangement. For example, generators like to be run at close to full load, but without an inverter it is not unusual to have a boatowner run the generator just to watch the TV or VCR. This is wasteful of fuel and hard on the generator, whereas inverters are efficient at this kind of light load. Or there might be a heavy load, but of short duration, such as when warming something in the microwave for three minutes. With an inverter there is no need to crank the generator and then shut it down again. Finally, when the main engine is running, the inverter can be used for AC power rather than the generator, with no drain on the batteries (the alternator will be supplying the current).

Eventually, of course, the AC load becomes so great that only a 24-hour-a-day AC generator can meet it. Air-conditioning, in particular, is such a power hog that there is just no way around the generator. But the level of AC consumption at which a 24-hour-a-day generator becomes necessary is far higher than many people realize.

The comforts of home. So the enticing prospect of constantly available AC power on board without the need for a generator is a real

one, but only in a limited sense, and even then not one that can be met by simply wiring an inverter to the ship's batteries. First, you must choose an appropriate inverter for the task at hand and then, as with any additional DC load, particularly such a potentially heavy load, you must look at the boat's overall power equation and take whatever steps are necessary to keep this in balance.

Without such a holistic approach the inverter is likely to become a cancer that destroys key components of the DC system; with such an approach one truly can enjoy many of the comforts of home, although the cost of upgrading the DC system to handle the inverter may be more than the cost of the inverter itself!

Inverter Installation

Inverter installation is generally straightforward, bearing in mind the following points:

Location. An inverter is a complex electronic device, incorporating different metals. With the addition of moisture, all the ingredients for galvanic and stray-current corrosion—water, electricity, and dissimilar metals—are present. An inverter must be kept dry and be protected from spray or condensation. Additionally, performance is related to temperature. Particularly at high levels of output, an unrestricted flow of cool air is needed to carry off the heat of operation (some inverters that don't already include a fan have a temperature-activated fan as an option—this is highly recommended in boat use). The inverter should be as close to its batteries as possible without actually being in the battery compartment, since batteries give off corrosive and explosive fumes.

The DC side. It is critical to avoid voltage drop in the supply cables from the battery. Very heavy cables are needed—larger inverters on 12-volt systems have peak currents up to 1,000 amps, requiring 4/0 cables on even 5 to 10 foot cable runs.

These large cables are awkward and hard to handle. As likely as not there will be others, connecting to the starter motor, the boat's distribution panel, a high-output alternator, and perhaps an electric windlass. *Do not attempt to attach all these cables at the battery posts.* Instead, establish substantial negative and positive distribution posts or bus bars at a suitable location (Figure 5-24) with a single very heavy cable leading back to each battery terminal.

Any short circuit in the supply cables will create a very dangerous dead short across the bat-

Calculating Loads

Calculating AC loads. An inverter must be sized to handle the peak anticipated AC load. This is simply done. A list is made of all the AC appliances to be run from the inverter, together with the power draw (in watts) of each item (Table 5-1). A determination is made of which appliances are likely to be used simultaneously. The wattages are added to find the maximum likely demand at any given point in time, and an inverter is chosen with a continuous rating equal to this demand. But note:

• Induction-type AC motors (AC refrigerators and air-conditioning systems, pumps, washing machines) can pull three to six times their rated power on initial start-up (Table 5-2). A 400-watt refrigeration compressor motor may draw up to 2,400 watts momentarily. When making load calculations, a separate accounting must be made of these *surge* loads. No individual surge load may be greater than the inverter's surge capacity, and two or more appliances with high surge ratings must never be switched on simultaneously if their combined rating exceeds the inverter's surge rating. In practice, if the inverter is sized for the continuous load, it will almost always have the capability to handle the surge load.

• Resistive loads (incandescent lights, heaters, toasters, electric stoves) can pull several times their rated load while heating up. A 100-watt lightbulb can momentarily draw 700 watts when it is first switched on!

• Power factors. In DC circuits, watts = volts × amps. Not so with many AC appliances. Here watts = volts × amps × power factor (PF). Resistive loads have a power factor of 1.0, so watts *really do* equal volts × amps. But induction motors and fluorescent lights, to name two common items, have a PF of less than 1.0, sometimes as low as 0.5. What this means in practice is that the rated wattage of an appliance gives a false idea of its power consumption. Consider a 60-watt fluorescent light with a PF of 0.5. At first sight it would seem to draw

$60 \div 115 = 0.52$ amp.

But, watts = volts × amps × PF. Therefore, amps = watts ÷ (volts × PF). So amps = $60 \div (115 \times 0.5) = 1.04$ amps. *The amp draw is doubled.* When calculating wattage for induction motors and fluores-

Table 5-1. Typical AC Appliance Loads

Appliance/Tool	Watts	Start Up Watts
13″ Television	80	NA
19″ Television	100	NA
VCR deck	50	NA
Stereo	50	NA
Curling Iron	50	NA
Lamp	100	NA
Blender	300	NA
⅜″ power drill	500	NA
Small hand sander	500	NA
Ice maker	200	1000
Small coffee maker	1000	NA
3 cu. ft. refrigerator	150	750
Compact microwave	750	NA
20 cu. ft. refrigerator	750	3750
Medium-size microwave	1200	NA
Hand vacuum cleaner	800	NA
Hair dryer	1250	NA
Toaster	1200	NA

NA = not applicable (resistive load)

Table 5-2. Typical Loads for Induction Motors

Motor Requirements	¼ h.p.	⅓ h.p.	½ h.p.	¾ h.p.	1 h.p.	2 h.p.	3 h.p.
Starting watts (in-rush)	750+	1,000+	1,500+	2,000+	3,300+	4,000+	5,000+
Running watts	350	400	600	750	1,100	2,000	3,000

Table 5-3. Sample Load Calculations

Appliance	Watts	Hours of Use	Watt-Hours
TV	100	2	200
VCR	50	2	100
Stereo	50	2	100
Coffeemaker	1,000	0.2 (12 mins)	200
Toaster	1,200	0.1 (6 mins)	120
Microwave	1,200	0.3 (18 mins)	360
Blender	300	0.2 (12 mins)	60
Vacuum cleaner	800	0.1 (6 mins)	80
Hair dryer	1,250	0.1 (6 mins)	125

Total Watt-Hours = 1,345

Total Amp-Hours = 1,345 ÷ 12 = 112 (12-volt system)

Adding a 10% conversion inefficiency = 112 × 1.1 = 123 amp-hours

(continued)

Calculating Loads, *continued*

cent lights, in the absence of specific information on power factors it is best to take the rated watts and allow half again as much. In other words, count a 60-watt fluorescent light as a 90-watt load.

The greatest likely AC load is combined use of the microwave and the coffeemaker. An inverter with a *continuous* rating of 2,500 watts will be more than large enough (in fact, given the short time a coffee maker is at full power, a 2,000-watt inverter would likely be more than adequate. With separate use of the microwave and the coffeemaker, a 1,500-watt inverter will suffice).

Finally, note that there are no standards for rating inverters. The *continuous* rating on one may really be a continuous rating, whereas on another it may be a 30-minute rating; the surge rating may be for several minutes or for a few seconds. The temperature at which the inverter is rated may be 70°F (21°C) or 80°F (27°C). *The only reasonably accurate way to compare outputs and surge capabilities*

is to compare graphs of output (in watts) versus time, at a given temperature (all manufacturers have these, though some may be reluctant to give them up—Figure 5-23).

Calculating DC loads. List the wattage of all the AC appliances to be run off the inverter, making allowances for power factors. Estimate each item's hours of daily use. Multiply the wattage by the hours to get a total daily load for each appliance. Add the loads and then divide by the DC system voltage (12 on a 12-volt system) to find the total daily amp-hour draw. Multiply this by 1.1 to allow for inefficiencies in the inverter (Table 5-3). If the inverter is to be run off the house batteries, add in the load of any DC appliances that will be run concurrently (Chapter 1) to give the total load on the batteries between battery charges.

Figure 5-23. Typical output curve at 70°F (21°C) of a continuously rated 1,000-watt inverter. But note that 70°F (21°C) is in many circumstances an unrealistically low rating temperature—real-life performance may be down by 10% or more.

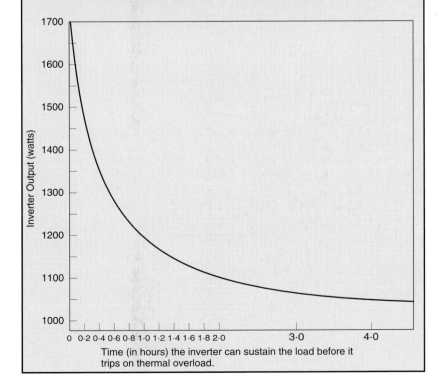

Time (in hours) the inverter can sustain the load before it trips on thermal overload.

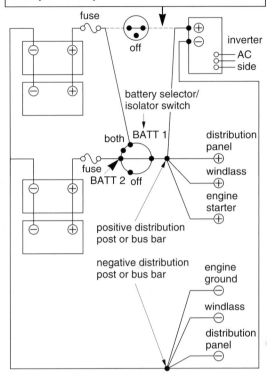

Alternative installation with independent battery isolation switch if:
1. Inverter load exceeds battery selector switch rating
2. Panel mounted battery selector switch involves excessively long cable runs
3. Only one battery bank is to be used with the inverter

Figure 5-24. Wiring diagrams for an inverter: DC side, 1 or 2 battery banks.

teries. Install a high-capacity circuit breaker (very expensive) or slow-blow fuse (up to 250-amp capacity on a 2,000-watt 12-volt inverter) as close to the batteries as possible.

Note that in order to minimize the standby power drain, *most inverters are not protected against reverse polarity* (protection would require power-consuming diodes). *If the battery cables are connected in reverse, instant and catastrophic damage will occur.*

The AC side. *AC power can be lethal. When in the standby mode, many inverters will not give a voltage reading with a typical multimeter but the instant a load is applied (such as a person touching the output cable!), the inverter will go to full output. Whenever wiring or troubleshooting an inverter or working on the AC circuits on an inverter-equipped boat, make sure the inverter is isolated from its batteries.*

If another AC source is connected to an inverter's AC output, instant and catastrophic damage is likely. This is so even if the inverter

Table 5-4. Sizing DC/AC Inverters

STEP	ANSWER
1) Do you know the AC load in watts for each appliance on your boat? Note: Where a power factor is appropriate, such as with induction motors or fluorescent lights, multiply the load rating by the power factor to obtain a true rating. See Table 5-1 for typical loads for AC appliances. If you have no specific power factor add half again as many watts to the rating (e.g. a 60-watt fluorescent light counts as a 90-watt load).	If your answer is no, list all onboard AC appliances and find out their rating in watts. If the surge or start-up load rating is greater than the operating load rating, list it in a separate column. Then go to Step 2. If your answer is yes, go directly to step 2.
2) How many hours a day is appliance drawing power?	List hours of use in a column by each appliance's load rating.
3) Multiply the (true) rating by the daily use of each appliance (Answers to Question 1 times Answers to Question 2). Add all appliance sums together to get the total 24-hour AC load in watts-hours.	_____ total watt-hours/day
4) How often do you fully charge your battery? Give answer in days—2 times a day, 1 time every 2 days, etc.	_____ day(s)
5) If charging more than once a day, divide Answer 3 by Answer 4 to find the maximum AC demand between charges (e.g. divide by 2 if charging two times a day). If charging less than once a day, multiply Answer 3 by Answer 4 (e.g. multiply by 2 if charging once every two days). Answer 5 is your total AC load between battery changes	_____ watt-hours
6) Divide Answer 5 by 12 on a 12-volt system (24 or 32 on 24- or 32-volt systems) to get an approximate amp-hour demand on your DC system. Note: Multiply by 1.1 to account for inverter inefficiencies and add in the standby drain of the inverter between battery charges (e.g. a 200 milliamp drain [0.2 amps] for 24 hours = 0.2 x 24 = 4.8 amp-hours).	$\dfrac{\text{watt-hours demand of AC appliances}}{\text{system voltage}}$ x 1.1 = _____ amp-hours demand
7) Add to Answer 6 the amp-hour demand placed directly on the battery by DC appliances, as calculated from Chapter 1, to get total amp-hour demand.	_____ total amp-hour demand
8) Multiply Answer 7 by a minimum of 2½, and preferably 4, to get the Ah capacity of the battery bank that will be needed to power the inverter. Note: Use only top-quality deep-cycle batteries. Answer 8 is your needed battery capacity.	_____ Ah capacity
9) Is Answer 8 totally impractical for your boat or budget?	If your answer is no, go to Step 11. If your answer is yes, go to Step 10.
10) You will have to limit your AC load based on your boat's battery bank. Determine your maximum battery bank Ah size; divide this by a minimum of 2½, preferably 4; subtract the amp-hour demand you anticipate from those DC appliances you wish to use; divide the quotient by 1.1 to determine a maximum amp-hour draw; and multiply the resulting figure by 12 for 12-volt systems (24 for 24-volt systems, 32 for 32-volt systems) to give a maximum AC demand in watt-hours. Go back to Steps 1, 2, and 3 to find ways of bringing the total AC load down to the maximum allowable level. Take high-demand AC items and arrange to use them when other sources of AC power are available so that their load is not thrown onto the DC system.	_____ watts based on _____ Ah capacity of the battery bank
11) Calculate the maximum foreseeable continuous AC load—or peak load—by adding the true ratings of all the AC appliances listed in Step 1 that might be used at the same time.	_____ watts peak load
12) Now calculate the maximum foreseeable AC surge rating by adding the surge ratings of all AC appliances that might come on line simultaneously. The inverter must be large enough to handle the larger of Answers 11 and 12.	_____ watts surge load
13) Take Answer 7 and multiply it by 1.1 to find the amp-hours that must be put back in the battery bank.	_____ amp-hours
14) Take Answer 8 and divide it by 4 to get a desired rate of charge from a battery charger or alternator. Add any residual DC loads when charging. Multiply the sum by 1.3 to find the continuous rating of an alternator.	_____ rate of charge (amps) + _____ residual DC load (amps) _____ sum (amps) x 1.3 = _____ min. rating (amps)

has an AC-sensing and transfer function (see below). In this case, there will be provision for a separate AC input to the inverter. *Under no circumstances should it be possible to bring the inverter and another AC source on line on the same circuit.* Figures 5-25A, B, and C illustrate several different wiring options that will prevent such an occurrence.

Many newer inverters have an *automatic transfer switch.* Other sources of AC power (shore power or a generator) are routed through the inverter (Figure 5-25B). Anytime the inverter senses another AC source on line, it automatically switches to the battery-charging mode (if fitted) or to "off." If the other source of AC power drops out, the inverter switches back to the AC mode. It is important to ensure that loads beyond the capability of the inverter, and any independent battery charger, are not included in this circuit (see below).

If the inverter does not have the capability to handle some onboard loads (notably air-conditioning), these loads must be supplied from an AC panel that is independent of the inverter (Figure 5-25C). Note also that *if an independent battery charger is fitted, it must be on this independent AC panel to avoid a situation in which the inverter is trying to run the charger which is charging the inverter's battery. This kind of loop will be wasteful of battery energy at best, and may damage the inverter and charger.*

All inverters in marine use must connect the inverter's neutral to its grounding circuit when in inverter use (this complies with the need to ground the neutral at the power source—see Chapter 3), but break this connection when another AC source is on line (so as not to ground the neutral at any other place other than the power source).

Troubleshooting

No output. If the unit has just been installed, double-check the installation for correct polarity. Reverse polarity will likely have caused irreparable damage. Check all wiring and switches; check for DC input and AC output *at the inverter.* Feel the inverter to see if it is hot, and see if any of the protection devices have tripped.

Note that unless the inverter produces a pure sine-wave, *most voltmeters will read 10 to 20 volts low when measuring the AC output.* Only true RMS voltmeters will be accurate. When the inverter is in the standby mode, with no load on line, there may be only a very low voltage reading. Depending on the nature of the load-sensing circuit, small AC loads may not trigger

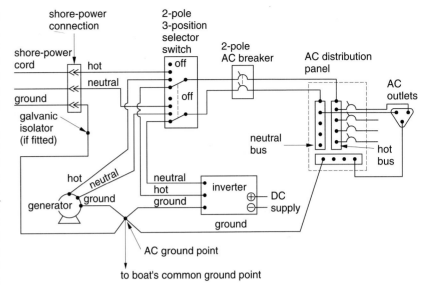

Notes:
1. This is for a typical AC installation *without an automatic transfer switch.*
2. If there is no onboard generator, a 2-pole, 3-position selector switch is needed ('off', 'shore-power', 'inverter').
3. If a separate battery charger is fitted, see Figure 5-25c.

Figure 5-25A. **AC wiring diagram for an inverter** *without* an automatic transfer function.

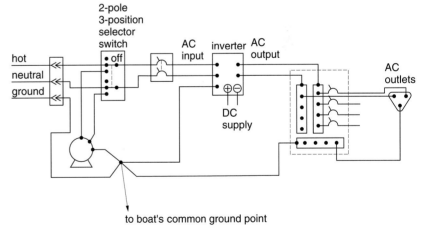

Note: If any loads exceed the capacity of the inverter, or a separate battery charger is fitted, see Figure 5-25c

Figure 5-25B. **AC wiring diagram for an inverter** *with* an automatic transfer switch.

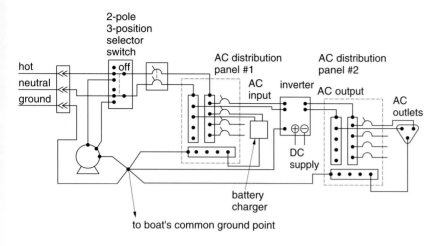

hot
neutral
ground

2-pole
3-position
selector
switch

• off

AC distribution
panel #1

AC distribution
panel #2

AC
input

inverter

AC output

AC
outlets

DC
supply

battery
charger

to boat's common ground point

Figure 5-25C. **AC wiring diagram for an inverter with an automatic transfer function, and two AC panels wired to isolate the inverter both from heavy loads that it cannot handle and also from an independent battery charger. AC distribution panel #1 handles loads that are not to be supplied by the inverter, such as a water heater, an electric stove, and the battery charger. These appliances can be used only when shore power is available or the generator is on line.**

the inverter into action; before concluding there is a problem, try a heavier load.

Inverter is hot. Most likely the high-temperature cutoff has tripped. Allow the unit to cool and try again. If the inverter has an internal fan, check its operation. The unit may be in an area without adequate ventilation, such as an engine room.

Overload tripped. Switch off all appliances

and reset (if manual trip). Bring appliances back on line one at a time and see if any trip the inverter. The overload may be a result of excessive starting surge loads or a short in an individual piece of equipment or its wiring. Also check for undersized DC cables (they will be warm) or voltage drop across loose or corroded connections (Chapter 3).

Low voltage tripped. Most likely the battery capacity or charging capability is inadequate for the loads being placed on the system. Check battery state of charge and condition. Check also for undersized cables and loose or corroded terminals.

Note that some trips reset automatically; others must be set manually. There may also be manual circuit breakers inside some units. Check the instruction book.

Erratic operation. The inverter trips continually on low voltage when appliances are turned on. Check for a starting overload (high surge), undersized cables, and loose or corroded connections. Check the voltage drop from one end of the DC cable to the other *when under full load*. Feel the cables to see if they are warm. Check the condition of the battery.

Equipment problems. Appliance motors run slow and hot, transformers "hum," microwave is slow, TV has lines on it, etc. The inverter output is probably closer to a square wave than a modified sine-wave! Moreover, the greater the load and the lower the battery voltage, the squarer it will get (check the batteries). To reduce problems, it may be necessary to use sensitive equipment only at the batteries' peak state of charge and with no other AC equipment on line, or with an engine-driven alternator running to keep the battery voltage up. If this doesn't work, a pure-sine-wave inverter is needed.

Wind and Water Generators

Wind generators and water generators are essentially the same units fitted with different propellers (impellers, turbines, vanes). Wind generators in particular are making a tremendous impact on the cruising scene. The rest of this section focuses on them, although almost all the information is equally applicable to towed water generators.

How They Work

A wind generator is a simple device that uses a propeller, or turbine, to convert wind energy to a rotating force that is used to spin a generating device. There are a couple of interesting relationships that hold in this conversion process: All other things being equal, (1) *a doubling of the propeller diameter produces a theoretical fourfold increase in generator output*, and (2) *a doubling of the wind speed produces a theoretical eightfold increase in output*.

In practical terms, at wind speeds of less than 5 knots *the wind has insufficient energy to produce output from any wind generator*. At 5 knots the more efficient generators will begin to trickle-charge a battery, whereas less efficient designs may not "kick-in" until the wind speed has picked up to as high as 7 knots. This "kick-in" speed is of some importance for sailors, particularly in areas of generally light winds. Once the kick-in speed is reached, the output of the various devices on the market picks up slowly at first, and then rises with ever increasing rapidity as the wind speed rises. Above 10 knots or so, for any given wind speed *output is broadly determined by blade diameter*. The wind itself, *in conjunction with an appropriately sized propeller*, contains sufficient energy to meet the electrical needs of just about any cruising sailor.

Two basic types. The propeller may be used to spin either a custom-built alternator or a DC electric motor. The differences need not concern us here except to note that although both types produce alternating current (AC) in the output windings, in the alternator-type this output is *rectified* to DC with *diodes* (see Chapter 2, Alternators), while in the DC-motor type the output is rectified to DC using a *commutator* and *brushes* (see Chapter 6).

Until recently the alternator types all had small propellers (turbines), a relatively low output, and were made in Europe (e.g., the Ampair 100, the LVM, and the Rutland Windcharger), while the DC-motor types had large propellers, higher outputs, and were made in the USA (e.g., the Neptune Supreme, Fourwinds, WindBugger, and RedWing). This neat classification is breaking down. There are at least two DC-motor manufacturers (Fourwinds and Windstream) with downsized propellers, and a correspondingly reduced output, and there are now available alternator type with outputs exceeding the larger DC-motor types (the Wind Baron Neo Plus and several models from Southwest Windpower).

A few models will double up as water generators (the Ampair, Neptune Supreme, RedWing, and Fourwinds II and III). In this configuration the propeller is removed so that a towed impeller can be used to spin the generator. Typically a boat moving at near hull speed will generate more than enough electricity to keep up with the entire DC demand—a very useful capability, especially on transoceanic downwind runs when apparent wind speeds tend to be light and wind generators, as a result, are ineffective.

Pros and Cons

The alternator types need no brushes to generate electricity, and so in this sense are "maintenance-free," whereas the DC-motor types need brushes to pick up the current from the commutator. The commutator and brushes require periodic maintenance. In addition, a poor contact between the brushes and commutator can create annoying radio frequency interference (RFI—see below).

The lower-output wind generators are almost silent. Of more significance is the fact that they can be used in any wind speed without damage, which means that they can be left operating when a boat is unattended. Their biggest drawback is that, except in sustained strong winds, they simply do not have the capacity to keep up with the demands of an electrically-loaded boat, particularly one with DC refrigeration.

In the past some of the higher-output wind generators, which do have this capacity, have been quite noisy. In addition, in strong winds the centrifugal forces developed by the large propellers (from 54 to 60 inches in diameter) have also caused some units to self-destruct! Improving blade design, materials, and manufacturing tolerances, combined with methods to regulate the top speed of these generators, have eliminated these problems with some, but not all, generators. But even where there are no limits on the wind speed that can be tolerated, the high output can, in itself, be a problem: when a boat is left unattended with little or no load to absorb the generator output, the batteries can be seriously overcharged (particularly gel-cells) unless some means is found to regulate the generator. These two issues of speed control (*governing*) and voltage regulation need a closer look.

Speed control. Five different approaches are used to keep the speed of large wind generators under control. The first is simply to tie off the blades when the wind pipes up (the RedWing)—in strong winds and rough seas this can be a nerve-wracking operation! The second, adopted by the WindBugger, is to have a centrifugally activated friction brake inside the generator housing. This brake, however, is not powerful enough to handle sustained wind speeds much above 35 knots. In these conditions the generator once again has to be tied off.

The third, in use on the Fourwinds II and on the Neptune Supreme, is an optional centrifugally-operated air brake that is effective in sustained heavy winds. It is possible, from a mechanical point of view (though perhaps not from an electrical one—see below), to leave a generator with an air brake in operation on an unattended boat for extended periods.

The fourth, used on the Wind Baron Neo Plus, the larger LVM's and Southwest Windpower models, and the Windstream, is a *furling* or *tilt-back* mechanism that progressively turns the machine out of the wind as the wind speed picks up (Figure 5-26).

The fifth is to design the blades in such a way that they flutter and stall out at higher wind speeds (Southwest Windpower). It is very effective but can also be exceedingly noisy.

Voltage regulation. With an effective governor, any wind generator can be kept going in just about any wind condition. However, the boat's DC system may not be able to handle the output! To take an extreme example, one of the high-output generators in a sustained wind of 25 knots or more will produce up to 400 amp-hours a day at 12 volts. Without a heavy load on the DC system, this will eventually cook even the largest battery bank. There are times when some form of regulation is needed.

A conventional alternator is regulated by varying the field current to the field coil, altering its magnetism (Chapter 2). *All* wind generators, however, have *permanent magnets with a fixed level of magnetism*, so this option is not available for controlling output.

Three methods are used to regulate a wind generator's output:

1. Monitor the battery voltage and shut the generator down *manually* when the battery is charged (WindBugger, RedWing). This approach is entirely dependent on the operator, and *cannot be used if a wind generator is to be left unattended* for even a few hours—our WindBugger was caught in a 50-knot squall while we were ashore; the resulting high output melted down the brush holders.

2. Use a device that senses battery voltage and open-circuits the generator (i.e., disconnects it from the battery) when the battery voltage reaches a certain level. But unless the generator has a governor, *releasing the load can allow the generator to speed up uncontrollably and dangerously.* The Windstream uses this method with a blade design and furling tail that keep the maximum speed below damaging levels; the Neptune Supreme also uses it but in this case the manufacturer recommends the optional air brake to control blade speed.

3. Dissipate the wind generator's unwanted output as heat, which can be done through transistors mounted on a heat sink (a *shunt* regulator—Ampair, LVM, Windcharger, and Fourwinds II and III), or by diverting the generator's output to another load (a *dummy* load) as the battery comes up to charge (a *charge-divert* regulator; the output is normally fed to a fixed resistor, but it could be switched into a hot water tank and put to useful work—Wind Baron Neo Plus).

Shunt regulation. Shunt regulation is generally of the constant-voltage type: The wind generator output is cut back progressively as battery voltage rises, rather than simply being chopped off when a set voltage is reached. Normally regulators are set to around 14.4 volts, which means generator output starts to taper off around 13 volts—too low for effective fast charging, or equalizing, of deep-cycle batteries. Shunt regulators therefore should have a disabling switch (Figure 5-27) so that at times the full generator output can be maintained until the batteries come up to 14.0 volts or higher. Note, however, that anytime a wind generator is used with the regulator disabled, the battery voltage must be monitored since it is quite possible to do some serious, and permanent, damage through overcharging.

When a shunt regulator dissipates excess

Figure 5-26. Tilt-back mechanism for controlling (governing) maximum speed on a wind generator. Note that as the unit tips back, the blades will be spinning in a more horizontal plane. There must be adequate clearance from all rigging. (*Wind Baron*)

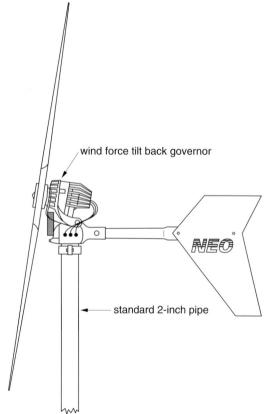

wind force tilt back governor

NEO

standard 2-inch pipe

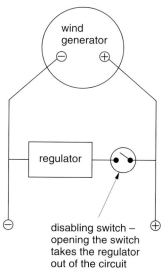

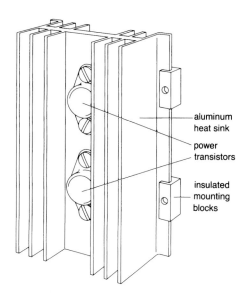

Figure 5-28. Shunt regulator. The regulator is a solid-state device sensitive to battery voltage. As the voltage approaches a preset limit (for example, 14.0 volts for a 12-volt battery), the regulator allows current to be diverted increasingly from the battery to be dissipated as heat through the heat sink. *(Jim Sollers)*

aluminum heat sink

power transistors

insulated mounting blocks

disabling switch — opening the switch takes the regulator out of the circuit

Figure 5-27. **Shunt regulation circuit.**

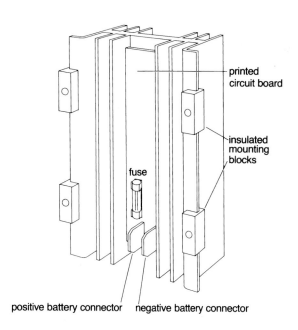

printed circuit board

insulated mounting blocks

fuse

positive battery connector   negative battery connector

charging current it creates heat—sometimes quite a bit of heat. A regulator must be in a cool place with good airflow (Figure 5-28). Shunt regulators generally have a fairly low amperage rating, sufficient only to handle the loads of the wind generator in question. If the wind generator output is teed into the ship's battery-charging circuits, the engine-driven alternator can feed back through the shunt regulator, burning it up and causing a severe fire risk. A protective diode sized to handle the wind generator's full output must therefore be installed between the shunt regulator and the ship's battery-charging circuit (Figure 5-29).

This diode may be built into the regulator, in which case the regulator's set-point will be compensated for the diode-induced voltage drop on the charging circuit (Chapters 1 and 2), but if a diode has to be added it will cause a voltage drop of around 0.6 volt. Now the regulator will start to cut in when the battery voltage is around 12.4 volts and limit output at the battery to 13.8 volts. If the regular charging circuit also incorporates diodes for split charging, there will be an *additional* 0.6-volt drop (Figure 5-30A), producing a cut-in voltage at the battery of 11.8 and a final voltage of 13.2—much too low to be of any use. In other words, the wind generator must be hooked in *downstream* from any alternator split-charging diodes, and if the wind generator regulator is adjustable its setting must be raised to compensate for the total voltage drop on the charging circuit. To charge two batteries independently, a wind generator will need its own pair of split-charging diodes to avoid paralleling the batteries through its charging line (Figure 5-30B).

Note that the Fourwinds shunt regulator is

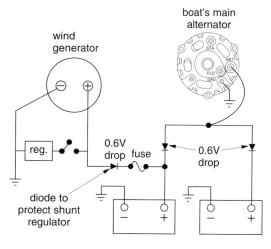

wind generator

boat's main alternator

reg.

0.6V drop   fuse

0.6V drop

diode to protect shunt regulator

Figure 5-29. Wiring schematic for a wind generator charging a single battery, using a shunt regulator.

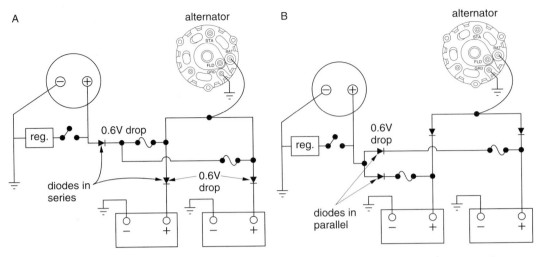

Figure 5-30B. Charging two batteries—correct installation.

currently the most sophisticated available with a two-step charging program, allowing settings either for bulk charging and float charging or else for bulk charging and equalization of liquid-electrolyte batteries.

Charge divert regulation. The principle is the same as that for shunt regulation. Excess wind generator output is fed to a resistor and dissipated as heat. With a larger wind generator a lot of heat can be created! The resistor must be placed in a location with good airflow, particularly if the generator is to be left in operation when the boat is unattended.

The Wind Baron Neo Plus regulator is mounted on the negative side of the batteries, where it can interact adversely with any other regulator set to a higher voltage. If, for example, the wind generator regulator is set to hold the wind generator output to 14.0 volts, but an alternator has a bulk-charge voltage setting of 14.4 volts, once the battery voltage is above 14.0 volts, the wind generator regulator will divert the alternator's output to its resistive load instead of charging the batteries! *The solution to this conflict is to disable the wind generator regulator when the alternator is on line* (and also when equalizing wet-type deep-cycle batteries). Wind Baron provide a couple of leads to do this. These can be wired either to a manually operated switch (mounted next to the engine ignition switch) or to an oil pressure switch on the engine (in which case the wind generator regulator will be disabled automatically whenever the engine is running).

Making choices. Making sense of these many factors to effect an informed choice between wind generators is not easy. First one must assess the boat's power needs, the type of cruising that will be engaged in, and the available winds in the cruising grounds. For example, someone intending to do transoceanic passages would probably benefit from a water generation option, while another person intending to cruise the Gulf of Maine in the summertime, where winds are characteristically below 10 knots much of the time, might consider solar panels a better investment!

In making a choice the tendency is to go for the higher-output wind generators on the assumption that more must be better. Although this is often so, it is not necessarily the case. If a boat is used on weekends and for an annual vacation but is kept on a mooring for the rest of the year, the primary function of a wind generator is likely to be to keep up with the loads on the mooring—the bilge pump, perhaps a 12-volt refrigeration unit (although this may be more than a small generator can handle), and a float charge on the batteries—rather than the load when cruising. A lower-output wind generator that will safely run continuously—the Ampair, LVM, Rutland Windcharger, Windstream, or Fourwinds III—may prove a better investment than one of the high-output units. The low-output unit will be essentially maintenance-free, quiet, and unobtrusive. It will continue to produce electricity in storm conditions on ocean passages after many of the higher-output types have been shut down. To be sure, over a weekend's cruising it will not keep up with the load and the batteries will slowly be discharged, but then they can be replenished during the week. On longer vacations the engine-driven alternator will be needed to supplement the wind generator.

At the other end of the scale from a boat used only infrequently is a boat used for extended cruising in, for example, the Caribbean. Fan and refrigeration loads will be high and one of the

Comparing Wind Generators

There are no industry-wide standards for comparing wind generator outputs. Some specifications are borderline fraudulent, others just hopelessly optimistic.

Certain of the alternator types have stator coils that will overheat at higher levels of output. To protect the coils from burning up, a temperature-sensitive switch is added (a *winding protection thermostat*). As the wind pipes up, or in a particularly hot environment, the switch may be off more than it is on, crippling output. Beware a product description in which the small print reads "typical performance, cold windings," or "voltage limiter inoperative" or something similar—Figure 5-31!

As with battery chargers *it is essential to know at what voltage the rated amperage is attained*. Most companies use the output at 12.0 volts for rating purposes, although this is too low for battery charging! For any given wind speed, a much better basis for comparison would be the output (amps) at 14.0 volts (for a 12-volt system). In any event, when making comparisons, use the same voltage.

What is less obvious is that *the kick-in speed is also affected by battery voltage*—the higher the voltage, the higher the kick-in speed. When making comparisons between generators, *be sure the kick-in speed is at 12.0 volts*. At this voltage some wind generators will get going in 5 knots of wind, while others will need 7 or 8, *severely affecting their utility in most popular*

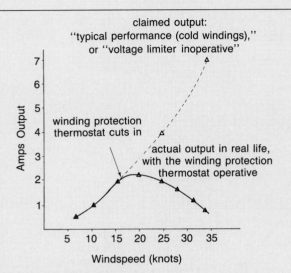

Figure 5-31. Performance curve of a wind generator with a "winding protection thermostat."

cruising grounds. It is also important to remember that even in the trade wind belt (e.g., the Caribbean) most boats spend most of the time anchored in relatively protected anchorages where wind speeds much above 10 knots are uncommon. As a result, *so far as output is concerned the two key indices are the kick-in speed at 12.0 volts and the output at 14.0 volts given a wind speed of 10 knots*.

Table 5-5. Wind Generator Comparisons

Machine	Type diam.	Prop. (inches)	Weight (pounds)	Governor option	Regulator option	Water option	Output (amps) at 10 knots	Warranty period (years)
Fourwinds II	DC-M	60	22	yes	yes	yes	5.6	3
Fourwinds III	DC-M	40	20	NA	yes	yes	4.0	3
Neptune Supreme	DC-M	60	25	yes	yes	yes	4.5	1
WindBugger	DC-M	54	38	no	no	no	4.0	1
RedWing	DC-M	60	35	no	no	yes	2.0	1
Windstream	DC-M	42	20	yes	yes	no	1.0	1
Ampair	Alt	36	20	NA	yes	yes	1.2	3
LVM 3	Alt	33	15	NA	yes	no	1.0	1
LVM 5	Alt	60	30	yes	yes	no	3.0	1
Rutland Windcharger	Alt	36	28	NA	yes	no	1.3	1
Wind Baron Neo Plus	Alt	60	20	NA	yes	no	5.0	2
Southwest Windpower "Air Marine"	Alt	45	11	NA	Incl.	no	2.0	3

Notes:
All figures are based on manufacturers' specifications. When it comes to output ratings some are more optimistic than others!
DC-M = DC-motor
Alt = alternator
NA = Not Applicable (does not need overspeed control)
Inc. = included
Output (amps) = the *manufacturer's* given output at 10 knots windspeed. (Rating methods vary widely—there are no industry standards. This column can be taken only as a *very rough* guide, it *is inherently unfair to those manufacturers who rate their products conservatively*.)
At the time of writing (1994) the Wind Baron Neo Plus is a new model, untested in the marine field.

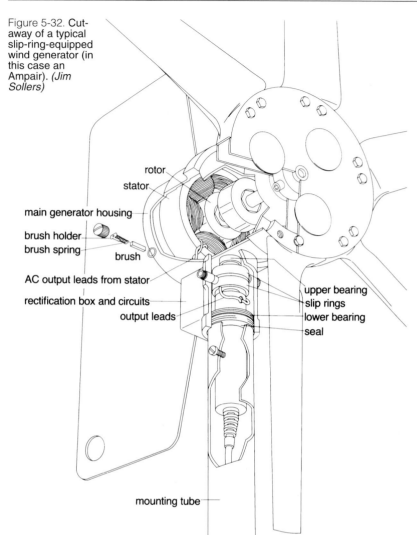

Figure 5-32. Cut-away of a typical slip-ring-equipped wind generator (in this case an Ampair). *(Jim Sollers)*

rotor
stator
main generator housing
brush holder
brush spring
brush
AC output leads from stator
rectification box and circuits
output leads
upper bearing
slip rings
lower bearing
seal
mounting tube

higher-output wind generators will be a far more valuable investment than a small generator. Factors determining which generator is chosen will likely include the reputation of the manufacturer, the ability to leave the generator operating in any wind speed, the availability of a voltage regulator if the unit is to be left operating unattended, and, of course, price.

Either way, on any boat that does not have an AC generator running 24 hours a day, a wind generator can transform a cruising lifestyle. There is no other device on the market that can come close to generating as much power without having to run an engine. In many instances a wind generator can almost completely free a sailboat from any need to run its engine, with major savings on fuel and maintenance bills, not to mention the reduction in noise and elimination of exhaust fumes.

Installation and Maintenance

Although some wind generators are mounted in a fixed alignment, this severely limits their effectiveness. Much to be preferred is a wind-seeking capability, produced by hanging the generator in the rigging, or by placing it on a pole-mounted bearing assembly into which are built *brushes* and *slip rings* (Figure 5-32). The brushes, rotating with the generator, receive its output, feeding this output to the fixed slip rings (or vice versa), which transmit the output to the batteries. (Note, however, that sometimes a generator is mounted on a bearing assembly *with-*

Figure 5-33. Wind generator schematic with shunt regulation, extended to include electric braking, a "bump-start," and volt and amp meters. Notes:
1. The electric brake functions by shorting out the generator output. This must be done using a *momentary-type* switch, that cannot accidentally be left "on" (see the text).
2. The "bump-start" switch can be used only with DC-motor-type wind generators. It allows battery current to be used to get the generator spinning in marginal wind conditions. It too must be a momentary-type switch. 3. *It must never be possible to operate an electric brake and a bump-start device at the same time, since this would put a dead short across the battery!*

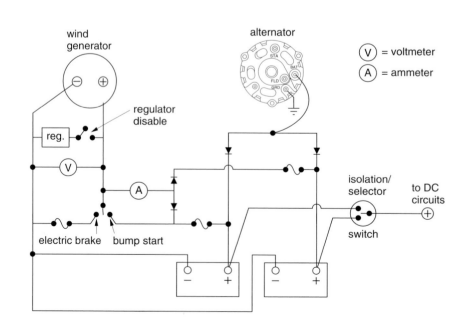

wind generator
alternator
reg.
regulator disable
electric brake
bump start
isolation/selector switch
to DC circuits
Ⓥ = voltmeter
Ⓐ = ammeter

out slip rings. In this case, when the generator turns, it twists its output cable. Statistically speaking, the cable should unwind itself, but in some instances it will need to be unwound manually from time to time.)

Clearly any generator must be mounted high enough, or in a sufficiently out-of-the-way location, to avoid being a hazard to people moving around on deck. But on the other hand, unless it has a remotely operated brake (as do some models of the Fourwinds II and the Air Marine), it has to be accessible enough for the operator to be able to shut it down (by turning it out of the wind) and tie off the blades, sometimes in rough conditions when the unit will be swinging wildly from side to side. These contradictory requirements are not easy to balance. Inevitably there are times, particularly with the larger generators, when shutting a machine down can be quite hazardous. (Wind generators can be braked electrically by shorting the output leads, locking the generator magnetically—Figure 5-33. The problem with electric braking is that when it is done at high speeds and levels of output, it tends to burn up the generator, and in any case still may not stop it.)

Wiring a generator is simplicity itself. Almost all are attached directly to a battery so that when the boat is unattended, and the battery isolation switch is turned "off," the generator can still be left "on line." In any event, the wiring must be such that *whenever the battery is isolated from the ship's circuits, the wind generator is also isolated* (Figure 5-33). If a wind generator is left connected to the DC circuits without a battery to absorb its output, *it can drive up the voltage to a level that will destroy most of the electrical equipment on board!* Wire should be sized for a maximum 3% voltage drop at full rated output (Chapter 3).

The DC-motor types require a diode in the positive cable to prevent a reverse drain from the batteries when the generator is not running (this diode may already be present with some regulators); the alternator types already have this diode in the rectification circuit. All models must be fused in the positive cable close to the batteries. *This fuse is an essential safety device: It prevents a short in the generator circuit from putting a dead short across the battery and so melting down the wind generator wiring.*

The problem with such a fuse is that if it blows, it will open-circuit the generator, which may, in high winds, then self-destruct. To avoid this situation the fuse rating must be at least as high as the *maximum possible output from the generator*, which, in the case of the larger generators, may be 25 amps or more. A 40-amp fuse will, in most instances, serve the purpose of ulti-mate wiring protection without threatening the generator.

It is desirable, but by no means necessary, to install an ammeter to monitor performance. Battery voltage can be measured with existing meters.

Maintenance. Given the wide variety of wind generators available, it is possible to make only a few general points on maintenance. Brushes and brush springs are the most obvious point of failure (Figure 5-34). Alternator types will have brushes only on the slip rings, and none at all if no slip rings are present. DC-motor-type generators will have brushes to collect the output from the commutator, as well as slip ring brushes if they are fitted. Some larger generators have four brushes on the commutator.

Check brushes and brush springs periodically for wear, corrosion, and loss of tension. If brushes or springs are defective, inspect the commutator or slip rings for burning or pitting (see page 216).

Check the shaft bearing occasionally by gripping the blades and attempting to move the shaft up and down and side to side. Any play indicates the need for bearing replacement, which will require generator disassembly. See below for one or two precautions to observe when taking the unit apart.

Check all external fasteners periodically. Most wind generators are subject to a certain amount of vibration, and fasteners will sometimes work loose. Add a drop of Loctite thread-sealing compound when replacing them.

To cure excessive vibration, if the turbine blades can be detached individually take them off in *opposite pairs*, weigh them on a postal scale, and correct any differences. Be sure to mark them so that they can be replaced as matched pairs. After reinstallation, check the alignment as shown in Figure 5-35.

Fiber-reinforced plastic blades are UV-degradable in sunlight. If the surface becomes crazed and powdery, sand them lightly and paint with a two-part polyurethane paint.

The leading edge of unprotected spruce blades will wear down just from the impact of bugs, rain, etc. The blades must be kept smooth for maximum efficiency and noise reduction; recoat the blades with epoxy or two-part polyurethane.

Many generators have aluminum housings with stainless steel fasteners, shafts, and bearings. Add salt spray and this is a recipe for corrosion. Rinse the housings from time to time with fresh water. Watch closely for any signs of galvanic interaction. If present, remove the relevant fastener or part, apply a corrosion inhibitor (such as Tefgel, Duralac or a teflon-based grease), and

Figure 5-34. Wind generator components—alternator type. **(Top)** This rotor has two permanent magnets; each has a set of stator coils. One set of coils can be seen on the right in the generator housing; the other set is in the other half of the housing, which has been removed. **(Below left)** Looking into the base of the same generator. The output shaft and slip rings (see above) have been removed to expose the brushes. **(Below right)** A complete wind generator kit.

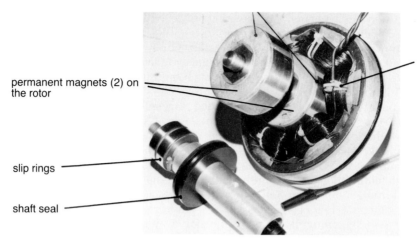

permanent magnets (2) on the rotor

slip rings

shaft seal

one set of stator coils (another set in the other half of the generator housing goes with the second permanent magnet)

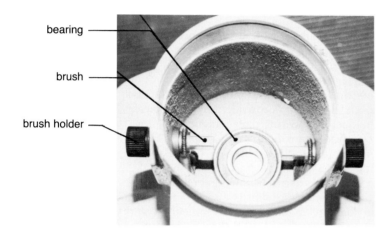

bearing

brush

brush holder

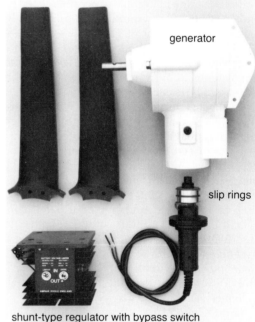

blades (6 to a set)

generator

slip rings

shunt-type regulator with bypass switch

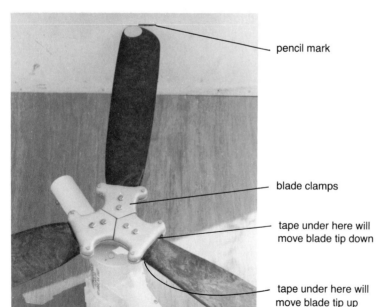

pencil mark

blade clamps

tape under here will move blade tip down

tape under here will move blade tip up

Figure 5-35. **(Left)** To check wind generator blade alignment, place the generator, blades up, on a flat surface with one blade tip just touching a wall. Draw a pencil mark on the wall at the blade tip and slowly rotate the blades, checking the alignment of each as it passes the mark. If blades are out of alignment, adjust them by putting pieces of tape, or some other shim material, under the blade clamp.

replace. Pay particular attention to the pivot points on any air-brake, furling, or tilt-back mechanism, making sure that these are free and lubricated.

Troubleshooting and Repair

Radio frequency interference. A poor contact between a brush and a slip ring or commutator can create arcing that generates *radio frequency interference* (RFI). The frequency will vary with the wind generator speed, but is most likely to interfere with ham radio operations, sometimes on boats a good distance away. The DC-motor type of wind generator is the worst offender. Solutions are to keep brushes in good condition and commutators and slip rings clean. If problems persist, capacitors should be wired across the output leads of the wind generator as close to the brush holders as possible. Bill Owra, manufacturer of the Fourwinds, suggests three in parallel, rated at 7.5 microfarads, 0.01 microfarads, and 0.001 microfarads (available from electronics stores; some are polarity sensitive, and must be installed the right way around, while others are not).

Erratic output. If the generator has brushes (DC-motor type, or any wind-seeking generator with slip rings), check the brushes for adequate spring tension and the slip rings and/or commutator for a clean mating surface. Otherwise look for loose or corroded connections (see the various voltage and resistance tests in the next paragraph).

No output from the generator:

1. Check all fuses and switches (there may be a fuse inside any voltage regulator).

2. With the generator spinning in a wind usually high enough to produce output, check the voltage across the output leads *as close to the generator as possible.* It should be a little above battery voltage (normally around 0.5 volts higher—a good digital multimeter is needed), in which case the wind generator is working. If it is high (it may run to 40 volts or more), the charging circuit is open at some point; check the fuses and switches once again. Open-circuited wind generators can give quite a shock at high speeds; *be careful.*

3. Check the continuity of all wiring with an ohmmeter (see Chapter 3). Be sure to disconnect the generator from the batteries first and immobilize its blades; any output is likely to damage the ohmmeter.

4. With the generator still disconnected from the battery, let the blades spin and check the open-circuit voltage. It should be well above battery voltage.

5. If there is no output, disconnect any voltage regulator and try again.

6. Still no output: Check all brushes and brush springs for possible sticking.

7. Still no output: If a rectifier is fitted (alternator types), test the diodes as outlined on page 73. On DC-motor types inspect the commutator (see page 216).

8. Finally, as a crude test disconnect the output leads from the batteries, short them together, and try spinning the propeller blades by hand. If everything is working, they should be noticeably more difficult to turn than normal. If not, there is likely some internal fault in the generator; check the stator (alternator types) or armature (DC-motor types).

Generator hard to turn. The output leads may be shorted (see above), but otherwise there is a mechanical problem. Most likely are (1) corroded bearings from the failure of a shaft seal—both bearings and seals need replacing; (2) friction from a bent shaft—it may be possible to remove it and straighten it; or (3) magnets coming loose and binding (the generator will probably be "squeaking"). Many magnets are simply glued in place; moisture in the marine environment can cause corrosion under the glue bond, causing the bond to give way. If no other damage has been done, after you've cleaned the seating surfaces you can glue the magnets back in place with an epoxy glue (MarineTex, often found on boats, will do), *making sure that each magnet goes back in the same place from which it came, and the same way around* (don't let them get mixed up or turned around!). Handle magnets with care (they will shatter if dropped), and clamp them gently while the glue sets (they are brittle and easily cracked).

If there is evidence of moisture inside a wind generator, it is a good idea to flush the various coils with mineral spirits, blow them dry (with an air compressor if available, but otherwise with the exhaust from a vacuum cleaner or even a bicycle pump) and then bake the unit in an oven at no more than 200°F (93°C) for several hours.

Disassembly. It is impossible to be specific, but these are a few points to watch for:

1. It is frequently crucial to align housing halves to within plus or minus 1 degree. Before separating any housings, mark the two halves for an exact realignment. A line scribed across the joint works best.

Troubleshooting Chart 5-2.
Wind Generator Output Problems.
Symptom: Generator provides no battery charging when battery voltage is below the preset cutoff level of the voltage regulator (if one is fitted).

Note: Many of the following tests involve checking the voltage on an open-circuited generator. An open-circuited (i.e., disconnected from its battery) wind generator can produce up to 100 volts and give a severe shock. Be careful.

Disconnect the generator leads at the battery and check for voltage with the generator spinning. Is voltage present?	**YES** Generator is OK.
Disconnect the output leads at the generator and check for voltage at the generator output terminals with the generator spinning. Is voltage present?	**YES** Generator is OK. The fault is in its circuit. Check all fuses, switches, breakers and terminals. Bypass any diode or voltage regulator to see if this is the problem.
Inspect all brushes and brush springs for wear, corrosion, loss of tension, or sticking. Replace as necessary and spin again. Is voltage present?	**YES** Generator is OK.
DC-motor-type generators: Inspect the commutator for burning and pitting (page 216); *Alternator-type generators:* Test the rectifying diodes (page 73); repair as necessary and spin again. Is voltage present?	**YES** Generator is OK.
Short together the output leads from the generator and turn the generator by hand. Is there more resistance to turning than normal?	**YES** The generator is probably OK. Go back to the beginning.

The generator is probably defective: Check its stator or armature (see Chapters 2 and 6).

2. The permanent magnets used in wind generators are powerful and hold housings together with a strong magnetic force. Some housings have threads for the addition of jacking screws to aid in separation; others must be levered apart carefully with screwdrivers. When replacing them, keep fingers well out of the way: The magnets may grab the housings and pull them together uncontrollably.

3. The magnets will attract any metal particles or flakes lying around. *Work in a scrupulously clean environment and check the magnets before reassembling.* It is particularly important to keep the air gap between the magnets and the stator (armature) clean.

4. Whenever a unit is opened, pay special attention to any shaft seals where the drive shaft exits the housing. Some units rely solely on "sealed" bearings and have no additional shaft seals. These bearings do not always keep out salt water for long and may need replacing.

5. Various armature and stator tests can be carried out as outlined in the sections on universal motors (Chapter 6) and alternators (Chapter 2).

6. Any glued-in-place magnets should be given a tug to make sure they are still firmly bonded.

Solar Panels

Solar panels can be an expensive minefield for the unwary. The promise is great—"free energy from the sun"—but the reality can be extremely disappointing if an installation is not sized and mounted correctly, and if the panels themselves cannot withstand the marine environment—and many can't. This is not to say that solar panels do not have a place on boats, particularly for maintaining batteries at full charge when a boat is left unattended. It is just a matter of getting things in perspective.

Basic Terminology

Solar panels are silicon-based semiconductors that convert sunlight directly into electrical energy. There are three types:

1. *single crystal* units, in which each cell is cut from a single silicon crystal

2. *polycrystalline* units, in which the individual cells are composed of multiple smaller crystals

3. *amorphous* silicon units, in which vaporized silicon is deposited on some substrate

Where single cells are visible in a panel, each cell has an *open-circuit* voltage in direct sunlight of around 0.5 volts *regardless of its size*; the open-circuit voltage of the panel can be roughly determined by adding the number of cells (30 cells = 15.0 volts). The output (amperage) of a cell, on the other hand, is *directly proportional to its surface area*. Since amorphous silicon panels are only about half as efficient as the others, twice the surface area is required for a given level of output (the amorphous silicon panels also suffer an additional loss of output of up to 10% in the first year or two after manufacture, but then stabilize).

Open-circuit (oc) voltage is measured by disconnecting a panel from its battery and placing a voltmeter across its leads. Specification sheets also include *short-circuit (sc) current*, which is the maximum current a panel can produce with its output terminals shorted, at which point its voltage will drop to 0. *Neither describes real-life performance*. For this we need to measure the output (amperage) at *battery-charging voltages*. In the specifications these figures are generally given as the *load current (Imp, or current at peak power)* and the *load voltage (Vmp, or voltage at peak power)*. These two multiplied together give a panel's *rated wattage (peak power—Figure 5-36)*. Sometimes only the wattage (peak power) and the voltage (load voltage, Vmp, or voltage at peak power) are given, in which case the current (load current, Imp, or current at peak power) can be found by dividing the voltage into the wattage.

The current will vary with the voltage—the lower the voltage, the higher the current. *There is no industry standard voltage at which current is rated*—each panel will be rated at a different voltage. When making comparisons of output, *it is essential to take the rating voltage into account*: If two panels have the same load current rating, but one has a higher load voltage, *the latter is more powerful* (more on voltage in a moment).

Key Factors in System Design

How many amps? Solar panels are rated in a certain set of standard test conditions, the two most important of which (from a boatowner's point of view) are the assumption of *direct overhead sunlight* and *a panel temperature of 25°C (77°F)*.

On land, solar panels are set up on angled mounts that are designed to intercept as many of the sun's rays as possible. But if this is done on a boat, every time the boat turns, the panel will lose the sun! As a result, a solar panel on a boat is almost always mounted more or less horizontally in a fixed location.

Even in the tropics the sun is directly overhead (known as *solar noon*) for only a brief period each day. For the rest of the day the sun's rays intersect the panel at ever shallower angles and with decreasing intensity. Figure 5-37 indicates the decline in panel output on either side

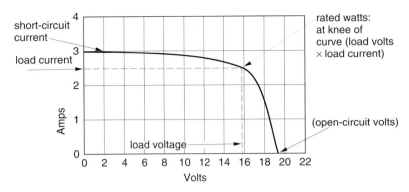

Rated Power	40 Watts
Current (typical at load)	2.55 Amps
Voltage (typical at load)	15.7 Volts
Short-Circuit Current (typical)	3.0 Amps
Open-Circuit Voltage (typical)	19.5 Volts

Figure 5-36. Typical solar panel specification sheet.

of solar noon. Should a cloud obscure the sun or a shadow be cast over the panel (e.g., from rigging, sails, or a boom), there will be a further, dramatic, fall in panel output.

The net result is that even in sunny climates daily panel output will rarely exceed more than the equivalent of the panel's rated output sustained for 4 to 5 hours a day, perhaps 6 hours in some locations in the summer; it is best to base calculations on the assumption of 4 hours a day. A 6-watt panel in a 12-volt system can be expected to produce only 24 watt-hours = 2 amp-hours a day; a 30-watt panel, 120 watt-hours = 10 amp-hours a day (i.e., amp-hours per day at 12.0 volts = rated wattage ÷ 3). In many instances a panel will not do even this well. Given a desired daily output (for example, 60 amp-hours), the necessary panel wattage (for a 12-volt system) can be determined by multiplying by 3:

$$(60 \times 3) = 180 \text{ watts}$$

At what voltage? When charging a battery, if a solar panel is to deliver its rated output, the panel must be able to maintain a healthy voltage differential over the battery's rising voltage. The panel must be able to produce its rated current while maintaining a voltage of from 14.0 to 14.4 volts *at the battery*.

A 12-volt solar panel will have anywhere from 30 to 36 cells in series, giving a nominal *open-circuit voltage* of from 15.0 to 18.0 volts. This would seem to be more than adequate for battery charging, but in fact this is not always the case.

As solar noon approaches, the black silicon in a solar panel heats up. In the tropics the panel temperature is certain to exceed the 25°C (77°F) temperature used for rating purposes, producing a decline in the panel voltage of approximately 1.0 volt for every 15°C (27°F) temperature rise (Figure 5-38). At 50°C (122°F—not uncommon in

Figure 5-37. Output voltage and amperage in relation to solar noon. Note the drop in voltage as the temperature rises at solar noon and on into the early afternoon, and the relatively narrow band of time during which a panel puts out at anywhere near its rated output. Panel output can be considerably increased by adjusting the angle of the panel during the course of the day to maintain as near to a right angle to the sun as possible.

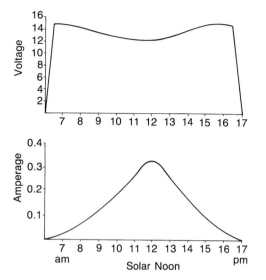

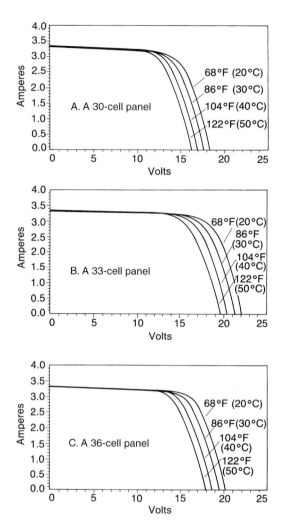

Figure 5-38. The relationship between temperature and output for three popular panels. These curves represent maximum output in bright sunlight, rather than realistic output in normal operating conditions. At 50°C (122°F), output on a 36-cell panel begins to taper off at 15 volts; on the 30-cell panel, at 11 volts—the latter is much too low for effective battery charging in hot climates. *(Siemens Solar)*

the tropics) the nominal voltage of a 30-cell panel will be reduced to 13.3 volts; that of a 33-cell panel to 14.8 volts; and that of a 36-cell panel to 16.3 volts. The 30-cell panel is below effective battery-charging levels and will suffer a steady decline in its output as a battery comes up to charge.

At the time of installation a blocking diode is also frequently added to the wiring to the battery (see below—such diodes are in addition to the bypass diodes found in some panel junction boxes and are not to be confused with them). Diodes cause an additional voltage drop of around 0.6 volts. *A 30-cell panel with a blocking diode, particularly in a hot climate, will be almost completely ineffective for battery charging;* even a 33-cell panel will start to suffer a decline in its output as a battery comes up to charge.

In the tropics, any 30-cell panel is likely to prove a marginal battery-charging source. A 33-cell panel will develop effective battery-charging voltages, but with little margin for other losses (e.g., voltage drop through diodes and in transmission lines; resistive connections; poor sunlight). A 36-cell panel will develop effective battery-charging voltages in just about any application. In *temperate climates* a 33-cell panel will develop adequate battery-charging voltages on all but the hottest days.

In general terms, for effective battery charging in hot climates a panel needs a *load voltage* (at standard test conditions), *after deducting the voltage drop of any diode,* of 16.0 to 17.0 volts; in temperate climates a load voltage after a diode of 15.0 to 16.0 volts is adequate.

Blocking diodes. The reason for installing blocking diodes is that while a solar panel puts

out in sunlight, it takes back after dark (although the reverse current flow is much less). But *the voltage drop through a diode will often reduce the output of a panel by more than the nighttime drain back into the panel!* So although such diodes are fitted routinely, *they would often be better left out.* The key factor here, once again, is the number of cells in series in a panel. A 36-cell panel generally has a high enough voltage to be able to handle a diode in all circumstances with no appreciable loss in performance; a 33-cell panel will suffer some loss of performance, especially in high-temperature applications; and a 30-cell panel will suffer a serious loss of performance in almost all applications.

The one time a blocking diode is more or less

mandatory is when it is intended to cover the panel for any length of time (e.g., when you are not using the boat) while leaving the panel connected to the battery—it will steadily drain the battery (unless it has one of the new type of voltage regulators with a *nighttime dropout*—see below). However, panels are rarely covered (unless a boat has a covered slip), and such a situation would in any case best be handled by putting a switch in the circuit, rather than a diode, so that the panel can simply be disconnected from the battery.

Voltage regulation. Figure 5-38A typifies the output of a so-called *self-regulated* solar panel. Actually, this panel is constructed with just 30 silicon cells, keeping down the output voltage. As battery voltage rises and more nearly equalizes with panel voltage, panel output declines. As we have seen, if we add temperature projections for warmer climates (especially the tropics), a diode, and perhaps minimal voltage drop in a circuit, *a self-regulating solar panel will frequently fail to charge a battery adequately*, regardless of the claimed output. For effective charging, more cells are needed.

But a panel that will maintain an effective battery-charging voltage may have enough capacity to overcharge a battery slowly when a boat is not in use. The critical point comes if *the panel's rated output at 14.0 volts is above 0.5% of the amp-hour rating of the battery to which it is connected* (i.e., above 1 amp when connected to a 200 amp-hour battery bank). If the panel's capacity exceeds this level it should be turned "off" when leaving the boat, or else a voltage regulator should be fitted (Figure 5-39).

Solar panel voltage regulators have come a long way in the last few years with some now having sophisticated multistep charging programs. Other desirable features are a *nighttime dropout* function, which disconnects the panel from the battery anytime the regulator senses a negative current flow and thus eliminates the need for a blocking diode. Also desirable is some form of an *equalizing* or disabling switch, so that at times the regulator can be taken out of the circuit, concentrating the panel's full output on the battery.

Float charging. To combat sulphation many boatowners leave their batteries hooked to a battery charger when in the slip, but this can cause overcharging, and in any case the shore-power cord may bring with it the risk of galvanic corrosion and stray currents (Chapter 4) that will consume zincs and then attack underwater hardware.

An alternative is to unplug the shore-power cord and hook in a small solar panel to each battery bank on the boat (Figure 5-40). All that is needed is a rated panel capacity at 14.0 volts of around 0.3% of the amp-hour capacity of the battery bank to be floated (e.g., a 1.2-amp—15 watt—panel on a 400-amp-hour battery bank). *As long as there is no drain on the battery bank*, and the batteries are in good condition, this will indefinitely maintain the batteries in a state of full charge with only minimal water consumption (but note, even an LED on a bilge pump circuit will eventually run down the batteries). With good-quality deep-cycle batteries the panels will pay for themselves in extended battery life alone.

Installation

Given the fact that solar panel output is so sensitive to even small voltage drops, marine-quality wiring and terminals must be used when making an installation. The terminals at the panel are particularly vulnerable to corrosion and need to be completely sealed. *There should be no other*

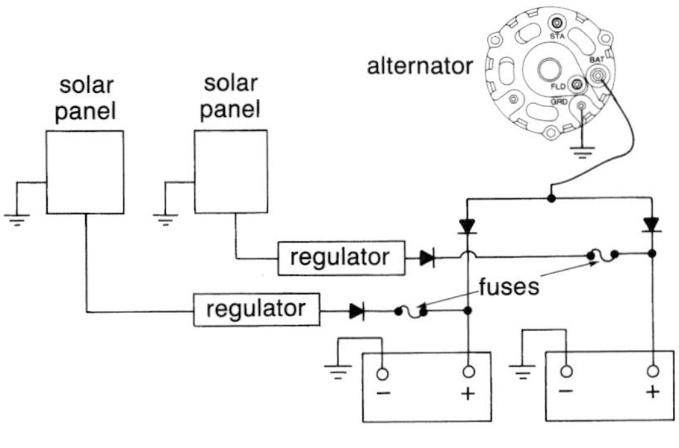

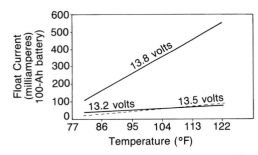

Figure 5-39. Regulated solar panels with diodes in the regulators. Note that some regulators with a *nighttime dropout* function do not require a diode.

Figure 5-40. Float current versus temperature and battery float voltage. Using 13.2 to 13.5 volts as a desirable float voltage, a constant float current of 50 milliamps would be sufficient for a 100-Ah battery at 86°F (30°C). 50 milliamps x 24 hours = 1.2 amp-hours. 1.2 × 3 (the factor for converting amp-hours to watts at 12-volts—see page 191) = 3.6. A panel output of 3.6 watts is needed for every 100-Ah of battery capacity to be floated.

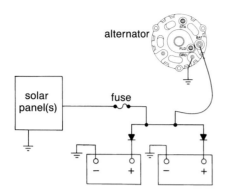

Figure 5-41A. Unregulated solar panel. If the panel is installed upstream of the main blocking diodes, it will not need its own diode.

alternator

solar panel(s)

fuse

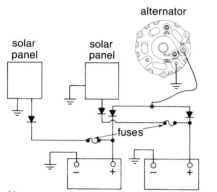

Figure 5-41B. Unregulated solar panels with diodes. The diodes may be better omitted (see the text).

solar panel   solar panel   alternator

fuses

Note: separate panels for each battery bank

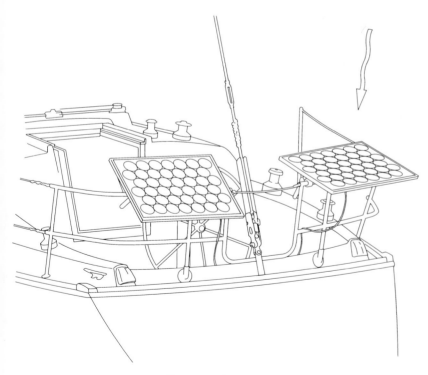

Figure 5-42A and B. (**Above** and **top right**, following page) Typical solar panel placements. *(Jim Sollers)*

connections in this circuit above deck—a continuous length of cable should be run directly to a deck seal. Any connections, if necessary, should be made *inside* the boat.

A good rule of thumb for determining a cable size is to take the maximum *short-circuit current* (see the panel specifications sheet) of all the panels in a particular circuit, multiply this figure by 1.25, and treat this result as the required current-carrying capacity of the panel wiring. Then refer to the 3% voltage drop table in Chapter 3 to select an appropriate cable size.

If the panel is to be hooked directly to a battery (which it will have to be for float charging—see the preceding circuit diagrams), *there must be a fuse in the wiring as close to the battery as possible. Without such a fuse, any short in the wiring will cause a dead short across the battery and likely start a fire.*

Multibattery systems. Many split-charging systems use isolation diodes (Chapters 1 and 2). These introduce a voltage drop of around 0.6 volts. If a solar panel is to be used in a split-charging system with isolation diodes, *it will not need its own blocking diode*, which would only introduce an extra unwanted voltage drop. The panel should be installed upstream from existing diodes (Figure 5-41A).

If, on the other hand, a panel has a *built-in* diode, the wiring to the battery should be connected *downstream* of any split-charging diodes. But in this case the panel's output can be fed to only one battery—if fed to two it would parallel the batteries via its wiring. Where two batteries need to be charged independently, two separate panels should be used as in Figure 5-41B.

If a panel uses a voltage regulator, the regulator will quite likely include a diode of its own. In this case additional diodes are not needed and the installation should be as in Figure 5-39.

Location. Published specifications apply only to solar panels in direct sunlight, angled to intercept the sun's rays at approximately 90 degrees. This is virtually impossible to achieve on a boat! If the panels are set up on angled mounts, as is normally the case on land, they will lose the sun every time the boat turns (Figure 5-42A). As a result, panels are almost always flat-mounted (Figure 5-42B), which is generally the best compromise. (In this case *they should be mounted on blocks to keep them off the deck and maintain an air space that will help cool them.*) In the tropics, with the sun nearly overhead, the panels will perform quite well; the farther north one goes the poorer the angle becomes.

Although a solar panel does not require direct sunlight to reach its maximum output voltage, anything that restricts the impact of the sun (including poor angles) has a marked effect on the amperage produced. Even small shadows that partially shade the panels can cause a significant drop (the loss of output varies markedly from one make and type of panel to another, which is of some significance when making choices in many applications). On sailboats, mast, boom, sail cover, and even rigging shadows can ruin output completely. An outboard mount aft is probably the best location for output, but may be vulnerable to pooping waves or docking damage. Another good spot is on top of a bimini or pilothouse.

Troubleshooting

Panel construction is the principal factor limiting solar panel life in marine use, with water ingress through delamination, poorly sealed cable boxes, and cracking of cases and covers being the main problem. If a solar panel has a warranty in marine use of less than 10 years, I would consider its construction suspect and would look for another product.

If a panel is physically sound but appears not to be working, disconnect it and check its open-circuit voltage in sunlight (Troubleshooting Chart 5-3). If it is between 16 and 20 volts, the panel itself is functioning, although it may have a reduced output due to internal shorts from moisture ingress. The output can be checked by placing an ammeter in series with the output cable. The blocking diode (if fitted), wiring, and connections should be checked for undue resistance (Chapters 2 and 3), but before using an ohmmeter, be sure to disconnect the solar panel. Its output is capable of damaging the meter.

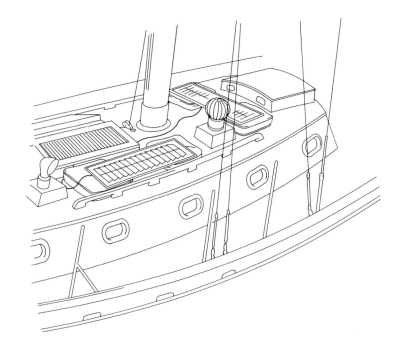

Troubleshooting Chart 5-3. Solar Panel Problem: No Apparent Output.	
Disconnect the panel's leads *at the battery* and check for voltage *in bright sunlight*. Is there voltage? **NO**	**YES** ▶ If the voltage is 16 volts to 20 volts, the panel is probably OK. If the voltage is less than 16 volts, check fuses, connections, wiring and any blocking diodes for discontinuities and voltage drop (see Chapter 3). Note: Before making any tests with an ohmmeter, *block out the panel* to avoid damaging the meter.
Disconnect the panel's leads *at the panel* and check for voltage across the panel's output terminals *in bright sunlight*. Is there voltage? **NO**	**YES** ▶ If the voltage is 16 volts to 20 volts the panel is probably OK but its wiring is defective. Check as above. If the voltage is less than 16 volts there are problems with the panel and its internal wiring.
The panel is defective: If it has a built-in diode, jump it out and test again.	

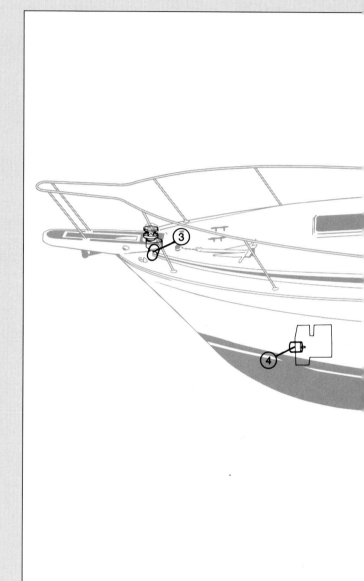

CHAPTER 6

Figure 6-1. Electric motors and generators are found throughout modern pleasure boats. Although initially mysterious, they are readily maintained and repaired. *(Jim Sollers)*

(1) starter motor
(2) pump
(3) anchor windlass
(4) air conditioner fan motor
(5) freezer compressor
(6) air conditioner compressor
(7) blower
(8) refrigerator compressor
(9) bilge pump
(10) freshwater pump
(11) macerator pump

AC Generators and Electric Motors (DC and AC)

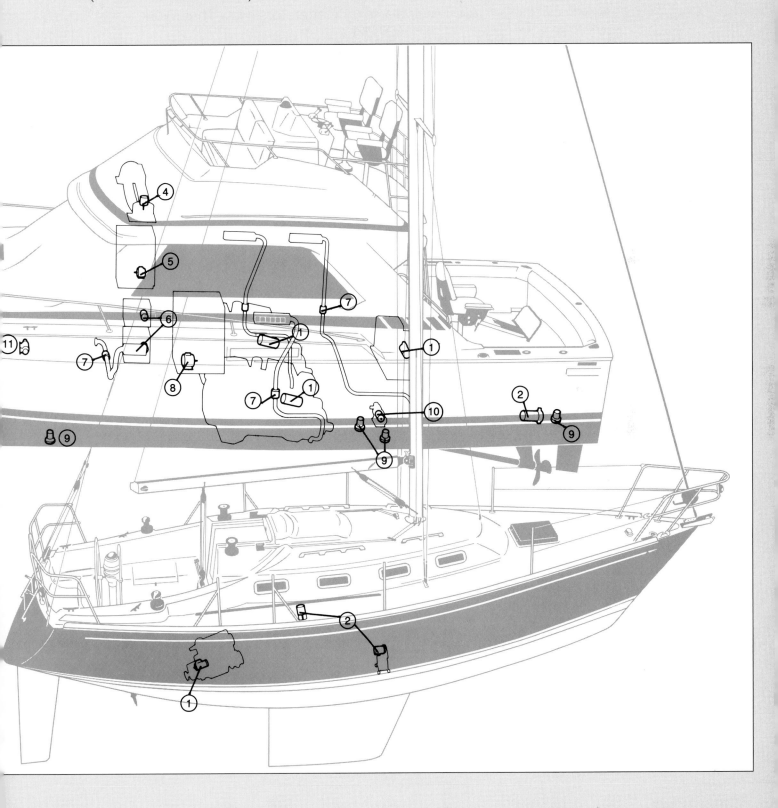

AC Generators

AC power requires a stable frequency of 60 Hz (USA) or 50 Hz (UK). Traditionally, the frequency has been established by running an electric generator at a virtually constant speed regardless of the load placed on it. However, with the advent of modern solid-state electronics it is now possible to produce a stable output frequency from a fluctuating generator frequency, allowing stable AC power to be produced from a variable-speed power source. This results in a number of different approaches to powering generators:

1. An entirely separate engine, regulated (*governed*) to a constant speed and coupled directly to a generator—the traditional stand-alone generator set (*genset*).

2. A variable-speed clutch, belt-driven off the boat's main engine, that *mechanically* compensates for changes in engine speed, imparting a constant speed of rotation to a generator (e.g., Mercantile Manufacturing Company's AutoGen).

3. A hydraulic pump, belt-driven off the main engine, that powers a constant-speed hydraulic motor coupled to a generator (e.g., Onan's Hydra-Gen).

4. Solid-state variable-speed technology (VST), which takes the fluctuating output of an engine-driven alternator and feeds it through a modified inverter to produce stable AC power (Balmar's VST generators; SeaPower AC alternators [USA] and Sterling AC alternators [UK]). Regardless of the power source, all are similar at the generator end of things.

Generators: How They Work

Onboard AC generators can be separated into two broad categories: *alternator* types, which produce AC by spinning a magnet (*rotor*) inside a set of coils (a stator—see Chapter 2, Alternators, How They Work); and *armature* types, which spin the coils inside magnets (Figure 6-2).

Alternator types. Just as with an automotive alternator, a DC current is passed through a set of *field windings* on the rotor, creating a magnetic field that induces output in the stator windings. But unlike an alternator, when a generator is shut down, the rotor retains a degree of *residual magnetism*. This is sufficient to induce a low-level output in the stator when the generator is restarted. This stator output is then used to supply the field current necessary to produce full generator output. The generator is said to be *self-exciting*.

In operation, some alternator-type generators tap one of the stator windings for the field current, using a *bridge rectifier* (Chapter 2) to convert part of the AC output of the stator to the DC current required by the field windings. This current is then fed to the rotor via brushes and slip rings. Just as with an alternator, a voltage regula-

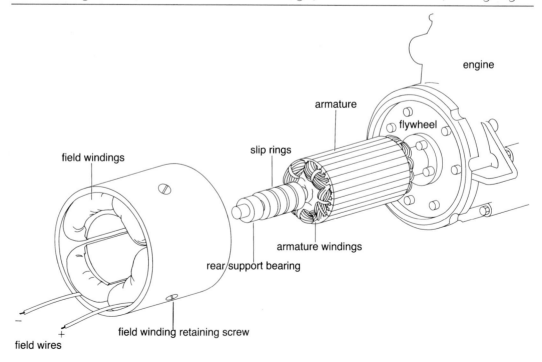

Figure 6-2. Armature-type AC generator, with frame and field windings removed. *(Jim Sollers)*

field windings

slip rings

armature

engine

flywheel

armature windings

rear support bearing

field winding retaining screw

field wires

tor is used to control the field current, and thus the generator's output voltage.

Most alternator-type generators, however, are *brushless*. On start-up the residual magnetism in the rotor stimulates a separate *exciter winding* in the stator which in turn induces AC output in a winding on the rotor. Diodes built into the rotor rectify this output to DC, which is used to power the field windings. No brushes or slip rings are neeeded to supply the field current to the rotor. (Figure 6-3A—a few expensive automotive alternators are built the same way, but these rarely turn up in the marine field.)

In addition to the exciter windings and the main stator windings, many brushless generators include another auxiliary winding in the stator. The output from this winding is rectified to DC and controlled by a voltage regulator. On larger generators (8.0 kW and up) this output is normally used to power and control the exciter windings (Figure 6-3B). On smaller generators it will charge the generator engine's starting battery (Figure 6-3A). In the former case, failure of the auxiliary winding, its rectifier, or the regulation circuit will disable the output of the generator. In the latter case, a failure of the auxiliary winding circuit will have no effect on the main AC output: It can safely be ignored when troubleshooting the generator's AC output.

Armature types. Multiple coils are wound around the rotor or *armature*, and two or more electromagnets are mounted in a fixed position inside the generator case. The armature is spun inside these magnets, producing alternating current in the armature coils. This AC output is fed to slip rings on the end of the armature shaft, where it is picked up by spring-loaded brushes and conveyed to the boat's AC distribution panel.

The generator field windings are once again designed to retain a degree of magnetism when the generator is at rest. This is sufficient to produce a low level of output in the armature when the armature is first spun. This output is tapped for *field current*. Since generator output is AC, and field windings require DC, the field current must first be rectified via a *bridge rectifier*. (A few generators, notably AutoGen, supply current to the field windings by a direct feed from the boat's batteries, thus eliminating the need for a rectifier.)

This type of generator may have two, three, or four slip rings and brushes, depending on internal configuration and power output. The simplest (small, 120-volt AC generators in the USA; 240 volts in the UK) have two slip rings and brushes: one hot, the other neutral (which is grounded to the generator frame, thus preserving the requirement to ground the neutral at the power source, as discussed in Chapter 3—Figure

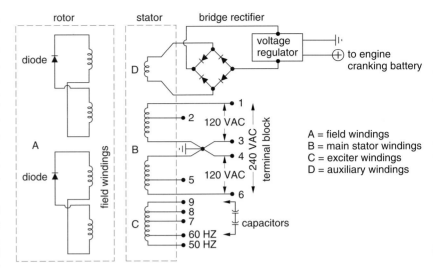

Figure 6-3A. Simplified wiring schematic for a brushless AC generator—in which the auxiliary windings are used for battery charging. Note that: (1) The windings for the main stator (B), exciter (C), and battery-charging circuits (D) are all built into the stator. (2) The battery-charging circuit (D) is independent of the generator's AC output. (3) The rotating field, or rotor (A), has no slip rings or brushes and its diodes are built-in. (4) This generator is self-regulating—there is no voltage regulation circuit. Output voltage is determined principally by the speed of rotation, but is also affected by generator load. No-load voltage can be altered by plugging a different numbered lead (7, 8, or 9) into the capacitors in the exciter circuit (C). (5) Frequency can be changed from 60 Hz to 50 Hz by changing the engine rpm. Because this will alter voltage as well, it will be necessary to tap different capacitor and output terminals (on the terminal block) to get the desired voltage (e.g., in the UK, 240 volts at 50 Hz).

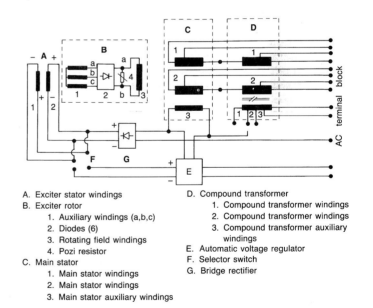

A. Exciter stator windings
B. Exciter rotor
  1. Auxiliary windings (a,b,c)
  2. Diodes (6)
  3. Rotating field windings
  4. Pozi resistor
C. Main stator
  1. Main stator windings
  2. Main stator windings
  3. Main stator auxiliary windings

D. Compound transformer
  1. Compound transformer windings
  2. Compound transformer windings
  3. Compound transformer auxiliary windings
E. Automatic voltage regulator
F. Selector switch
G. Bridge rectifier

Figure 6-3B. Simplified wiring schematic for a brushless AC generator—in which the auxiliary windings are used to power the generator voltage regulation circuit. Voltage regulation is found only on larger generators. Most smaller generators will be of the type illustrated in Figure 6-3A. *(Westerbeke)*

6-4A). Small 120/240-volt AC generators (USA) have three slip rings and brushes: two hot (120 volts each) and the third neutral (which once again is grounded to the generator frame—Figure 6-4B).

Figure 6-4. Wiring
schematics for armature-
type AC generators.
(Westerbeke)

Figure 6-4A. (**Top left**) Two
brush, 120 volts.

Figure 6-4B. (**Top right**)
Three brush, 120/240
volts.

Figure 6-4C. (**Bottom**)
Four brush, 120/240 volts.

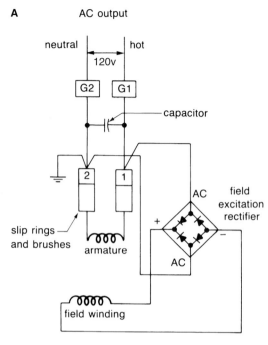

A

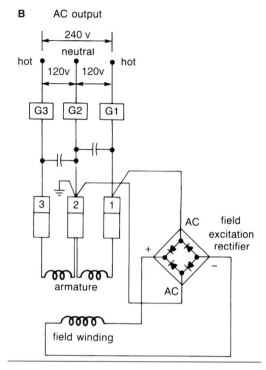

B

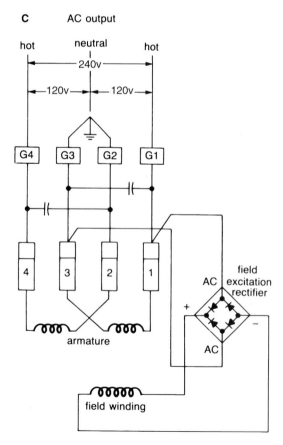

C

Larger generators (both 120-volt and 120/240-volt) have four slip rings and brushes (Figure 6-4C): two hot and two neutral, the latter being tied together and grounded to the generator frame at some point.

The field windings are bolted to the inside of the generator case. The simplest generators have two field windings (a two-pole generator) to produce one magnetic field (north and south), but most have two sets of windings (a four-pole generator).

General Maintenance

Most generators have bearings that are sealed for life. A few have grease fittings, which need one shot once or twice a year, but *no more*. The only other thing that needs attention are any brushes. Those on armature-type generators carry the full output current of the generator. If they are allowed to wear down or stick in their brush holders so that they make an imperfect contact with their slip rings, arcing will occur and expensive damage will be done to the slip rings.

These brushes need to be checked regularly (Westerbeke recommends every 200 hours) and replaced once they are worn to half their original length. They must move freely in their brush holders and have reasonable spring tension. If in doubt, replace. *Brushes must always be put back in the same holders and the same way around.* To avoid confusion, remove and replace them one at a time. New brushes are bedded in as described on page 217.

Any brushes on alternator-type generators carry the low-level rotor excitation current, not generator output current, and so are far less subject to wear. They need checking only every 500 hours.

Occasionally, vibration will cause a field winding to work loose on armature-type generators. The windings are mounted with bolts through the outside of the generator case. These bolts will be evenly spaced on either side of the case with two-pole generators, or spaced every 90 degrees with four-pole generators. Check them for tightness from time to time.

Troubleshooting Operating Problems

WARNING: THE OUTPUT FROM A GENERATOR CAN KILL! Some of the following tests involve working around an operating generator. At all times keep hands, clothing, and hair away from moving parts, and IF YOU ARE IN ANY DOUBT ABOUT WHAT YOU ARE DOING, DON'T DO IT!

If a generator has a circuit for remote starting, make sure it is disabled before working on the unit.

Frequency wrong. A frequency meter is a necessity, not a luxury, for effective control, adjustment, and troubleshooting of any onboard generator. In the absence of a meter, frequency can be checked using an electric clock with a second hand, and another *accurate* timepiece, such as the time beeps from station WWV on the 2.5-, 5-, 10-, 15-, and 20-MHz single-sideband frequency. If the electric clock runs slowly, frequency is low. If it runs fast, frequency is high.

Given a correctly functioning generator, frequency is directly related to speed of rotation (ignoring, for the time being, VST generators). Depending on internal construction, a generator will come to its designed frequency at several different speeds (e.g., 1,200, 1,800, and 3,600 rpm), but *only one is correct for the designed voltage output.* If a generator comes up to its designed speed slowly, the frequency meter may well come up to the correct frequency, go past it and off the scale, and then come up again. It may do this as many as three times, which is quite normal.

Once the generator speed has stabilized, frequency should be as designed (60 Hz in the USA, 50 Hz in the UK). However, most boat generator governors (speed-regulating devices) are not sensitive enough to hold a constant speed from no load to full load. The governors are set to permit mild overspeeding (maximum 63.5 Hz in the USA) on no load, to be about right at half load, and to permit mild underspeeding on full load. As a result frequencies will normally vary

Table 6-1. Typical Generator Speeds, Frequencies, and Voltages[1]

Load	Speed	Hz	Voltage (120)	Voltage (240)
No load	1,830	61	129	258
Half load	1,800	60	120	240
Full load	1,755	58.5	115	230

1. Generator governed to a nominal 1,800 rpm. Variations outside this range indicate improper governing or, when frequency drops off and an engine *bogs down,* an overloaded generator or a malfunctioning engine. If the load is not reduced rapidly, expensive electrical damage is possible.

(usually plus or minus 5%) from a couple of cycles over to a couple of cycles under (Table 6-1). Belt-driven variable-speed-clutch generators (AutoGen) are likely to show a wider variation with changes in engine speed.

Frequency low: Switch off the load and check again. If the frequency returns to normal, the generator is probably overloaded (or its propulsion unit is losing power through mechanical problems). Beware the starting loads of many electric motors, which can be *several times* the motor rating and can bog a generator down. If frequency is still low after shutting down the loads, check the speed of the propulsion unit before blaming the generator. Most engines have mechanical governors that are adjusted by loosening a locknut and turning a screw—check the engine manual. With belt-driven generators, check belt tension and constant-speed clutches; on hydraulic units, check the oil level.

Frequency too high: The propulsion unit is overspeeding. Adjust the governor accordingly.

Frequency varies erratically: Check the AC circuit for high, varying loads, such as the cycling on and off of a refrigeration compressor, or a microwave on anything less than full power. (Microwaves on defrost cycle or lower cook-power settings are *not* actually operating on less than full power. The microwave simply cycles on and off at timed intervals, sometimes only a second or two apart. A full-size, 1,500-watt microwave will give a small 3-kW generator's governor a very hard time.)

If the frequency continues to wander with all AC loads off, the governor on the propulsion unit is defective. Governors sometimes will *hunt,* a condition in which they constantly and rhythmically cycle the engine speed up and down. Refer to the engine manual.

Voltage wrong. Voltage is generally a function

of generator speed and load: The faster the generator spins and the less the load, the higher the voltage. Unless the generator reaches its designed minimum speed, it cannot reach its designed output voltage. This is particularly true of belt-driven variable-clutch units. If the driving pulleys are sized wrongly, or the boat's engine turns over too slowly, the generator cannot reach its designed voltage.

A generator is rated at a certain maximum output (in kilowatts or amps) at a particular voltage (e.g., 5 kW or 42 amps at 120 volts). At anything less than full output, as the load is decreased the voltage will rise. Externally excited generators prevent voltage from going too high by using a voltage regulator to reduce the current to the field windings, just as with an alternator. Internally excited generators tend to be less tightly controlled.

Since voltage is related to speed, if voltage is off, first check the speed by checking the frequency. As previously noted, in extreme cases frequency may be correct but at a completely wrong speed, but this is not a problem likely to arise in normal use. Since generator speed is likely to vary somewhat with load, some variations in voltage are to be expected (Table 6-1). Typical ranges from no load to full load may be as much as 130 volts down to 108 volts (on a 120-volt genset) or 260 volts down to 225 (on a 240-volt genset). Voltages above and below these levels may damage onboard equipment and must be corrected. Some external voltage regulators incorporate a *potentiometer* (a variable resistor) with a small screwdriver slot in the end for fine-tuning generator voltage.

Low voltage: Always check the voltage *at the generator:* Low voltage may simply be the result of voltage drop through inadequate wiring. Before making any adjustments (where they are possible), perform all the tests outlined for low frequency. Next, feel the voltage regulator (if external) or generator to see if it is hot (hot is too hot to touch). Overheating will play havoc with some of the solid-state components and can lead to erratic regulation or a slow tapering off of output voltage—to as low as half voltage. If it is hot, allow the unit to cool down and hope that no damage has been done.

Check the condition of any brushes and brush springs and ensure that they are making good contact with their slip rings (see below).

With *external regulation*, if the voltage is still low adjust the potentiometer. If voltage cannot be brought up enough, *do not force the potentiometer.* Check generator speed yet again. Perhaps it really is in the wrong speed range. Otherwise, the voltage regulator is probably defective.

With *internally excited* generators, check the diodes and the field windings as detailed below.

High voltage: Check engine speed and frequency. If correct, adjust the voltage regulator potentiometer on units with external regulation. If the voltage cannot be brought down, the voltage regulator probably has an internal short.

Erratic output. This may be due to a fault in the voltage regulator, or it may be the result of worn, badly seated, and arcing brushes on those generators that have brushes. If the slip rings have also been burned, pitted, or worn out of round, the armature will have to be sent to a machine shop to be *turned down.* A step in a slip ring is acceptable. For more on this, see the section on Commutator Cleaning on page 215.

No Output: Armature Type

WARNING: THE OUTPUT FROM A GENERATOR CAN KILL! Some of the following tests involve working around an operating generator. At all times keep hands, clothing, and hair away from moving parts, and IF IN ANY DOUBT ABOUT WHAT YOU ARE DOING, DON'T DO IT!

Preliminary test. First remove all the loads from the generator. With the unit running, check for voltage at the generator's AC terminals. The generator may be working, but there may be an open switch or broken wire to the boat's circuits. Next check the engine tachometer to see that the generator is spinning at or close to its rated speed. Still no output?

If the generator is externally excited by the boat's 12-volt battery, there will be an external field (F or FLD) terminal on the back of the generator. With the generator circuit switched "on" (but not necessarily running), test between this and a good ground. It should read at least several volts DC. If not, there is a fault in the external excitation wiring or voltage regulator. If voltage is present, there is a fault in the field windings, armature, brushes, or capacitors (see relevant sections below).

If the generator is internally excited, remove whatever covers are necessary to expose the bridge rectifier and disconnect the field leads from the positive (+ or red) and negative (− or black) terminals. Label the leads so that they can be reconnected correctly, and then place them safely out of the way. (If the negative terminal is not marked, it is the one *opposite* the positive terminal.) Operate the generator with no load and measure for voltage between the hot and neutral output leads. There should be a low voltage generated by the residual magnetism in the field windings. (Figure 6-5—on Westerbeke two-brush units it is around 5 volts AC; three-and four-brush units, 2.5 volts AC.) If residual voltage is present, the armature, brushes, and capacitors (if fitted, they will bridge the output leads) are almost certainly OK and the problem lies in the rectifier, field windings, or regulation circuit (see next section). If residual voltage is *not* present, the unit may simply have lost its residual magnetism. Otherwise the problem is in the armature, brushes, or capacitors (see below).

Residual voltage present. Connect a 12-volt battery to the field leads that were disconnected from the bridge rectifier—positive to positive, negative to negative. Run the generator without a load and measure the voltage at the output leads. If voltage is now present (50 to 70 volts on Westerbekes), the generator itself is OK, but there is a fault in the bridge rectifier. If voltage does not rise, the field windings (or their wiring) are defective.

To test a bridge rectifier: First make sure the generator is fully isolated. Leave the positive and negative leads disconnected and disconnect the two AC leads (the other two leads, sometimes color-coded yellow). Using an ohmmeter with a diode-testing capability (R × 1 scale on an analog meter), connect the positive meter lead to the positive terminal and touch the negative meter lead to the other terminals in turn (Figure 6-6). All should show infinite resistance (no needle deflection). Reverse the leads and repeat. All should show a circuit with a small resistance (between 5 and 50 ohms on Westerbekes). Check across the two AC terminals, then reverse the leads and recheck. Both tests should show infinite resistance. If the rectifier fails *any* of these tests, one or more diodes are defective.

To test field windings: First make a close visual inspection of the wires running into and out of each field winding, looking for broken, burned, or chafed spots. If the wiring seems intact, connect an ohmmeter (R × 1 scale on an analog meter) between the positive and negative field wires (previously disconnected from the bridge rectifier), or in the case of externally excited generators, between the field terminal and a good ground, such as the generator case (scratch a spot bare to make a good contact). A 0 reading indicates a shorted winding; most field windings will show a resistance varying between 12 and 40 ohms—the lower the output of the generator, the higher the resistance. A very high

Troubleshooting Chart 6-1. Armature-Type AC Generators: No Output.	
Is there output voltage at the generator's AC terminals? **NO** **TEST:** Check for AC volts at the terminals after disconnecting all electrical loads from the generator.	**YES** Generator is OK. The problem is in the boat's circuits. Look for a broken wire or an open switch.
If the generator is *externally* excited, is there DC voltage at the field terminal? **NO** **TEST:** Locate the field terminal on the back of the generator. With the generator switched on but not necessarily running, attach a DC voltmeter between the terminal and a good ground. It should register several volts.	**YES** **FIX:** Check the capacitors, brushes, and armature. Check the field windings. Replace any defective parts.
Check the excitation circuit and voltage regulator.	
If the generator is internally excited, there residual voltage? **NO** **TEST:** Expose the bridge rectifier and label and disconnect the positive and negative field wires, placing them out of the way. Operate the generator with no load and measure the voltage between the hot and neutral output leads. Presence of a low voltage indicates that there is residual magnetism in the field windings.	**YES** **FIX:** Connect 12 volts to the disconnected field wires, run the generator and test for AC voltage at the output terminals. If there is voltage check the rectifier. It likely needs repair or replacement. If there is no voltage, check the field windings and replace as necessary.
Is there voltage when you flash the field? **NO** **TEST:** Reconnect all leads. With generator shut down, connect a battery across the field winding terminals and hold for 10 seconds. Try the generator again.	**YES** The generator is OK.
Check the capacitors, brushes, and armature (see text).	

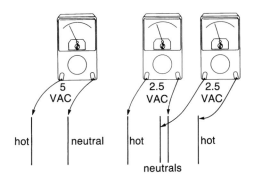

hot   neutral   hot   hot
neutrals

Figure 6-5. Checking for residual voltage.

reading (R × 100 scale on an analog meter) indicates an open circuit in the field windings or their attendant wiring. Finally, on internally excited generators test between each of the field

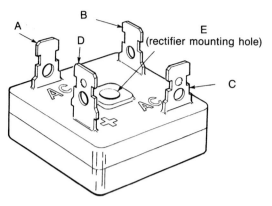

Figure 6-7. Capacitors store electricity. Their capacity to do so is measured in microfarads (abbreviated MFD, or μF). Because there often is sufficient electricity stored to administer a shock, discharge capacitors with a lightbulb (see text) or a screwdriver as shown before working with them.

wires going to the bridge rectifier (the ones previously disconnected) and the generator case (R × 1 scale on an analog meter). Any continuity (zero or low reading) shows a short to ground.

Residual voltage not present. The unit has lost its residual magnetism or there is a fault in the armature, brushes, or capacitors (if fitted). Residual magnetism is easily restored by *flashing the field*. Reconnect any leads to the rectifier. *With the generator shut down*, simply connect a 12-volt battery (or even a 6-volt flashlight battery) across the positive and negative field winding terminals—positive to positive, negative to negative—and hold for 10 seconds.

Be sure to connect the leads from the battery to the rectifier the correct way around. Reverse polarity will blow out the diodes. Make the connections at the rectifier before making those at the battery to avoid waving around hot leads that might accidentally blow something out. After flashing the field, disconnect the battery and operate the generator. If output is not restored, it is time to check the armature, brushes, and capacitors (if fitted).

To **test a capacitor***:* Capacitors (round or nearly round cylinders with one or two spade terminals) must be discharged before testing (Figure 6-7), as they store electricity and can pack a *POTENTIALLY LETHAL PUNCH, EVEN WHEN DISCONNECTED FROM A POWER SOURCE.* Discharging is often done by bridging the capacitor terminals with a screwdriver, but this can be hard on the capacitor (and the screwdriver!). Better to rig a 120-volt lightbulb (240 volts in the UK and Europe) with two test leads and touch the leads to the capacitor terminals. Now connect an ohmmeter (R × 100 scale on an analog meter) to the capacitor terminals. The meter should go to zero ohms and slowly return to high (Figure 6-16, page 217). Reverse the meter leads and repeat—the same results should be obtained. If the meter fails to go down,

the capacitor is open-circuited; if the meter goes down and stays down (zero ohms), the capacitor is shorted. Check between each capacitor terminal and its case. There should be an open circuit. If not, there is a short. Capacitors are rated in *microfarads*, and additionally are rated for continuous and intermittent duty. Replace with the same size and type.

To test an armature and brushes: Armature winding resistances are very low (typically around 1 ohm) and so can only be measured by a very accurate meter. With most meters it will be difficult to distinguish between a low resistance and a short. Nevertheless, I have included the test procedure for those with sufficiently sensitive meters.

Isolate the generator. Discharge and disconnect any capacitors (see above). Connect an ohmmeter between each brush in turn and the generator case (a good ground). The neutral (grounded) brushes should show a short (i.e., zero ohms) and, in fact, should be wired to the generator case at some point. If they do not show a short, the wiring to the brush is defective.

On a two-brush generator, one brush is hot and one neutral. On a three-brush generator, the two end brushes are hot and the middle one is neutral. On a four-brush generator, the two end brushes are hot and the middle two are neutral.

The hot brushes will show a low resistance (around 1 ohm). If they show no resistance (R × 1 scale on an analog meter), the armature is shorted. If they show high resistance (R × 100 scale on an analog meter), the armature is open-circuited. In either case it needs rewinding. Note: An open circuit may also be the result of a brush that fails to make electrical contact with its slip ring, and *not necessarily the brush being tested* since the circuit from a hot brush to the generator case is completed through a neutral brush. Be sure the brushes are seating properly.

Before condemning an armature, remove and inspect all the brushes and their springs. Connect the ohmmeter between the slip rings. With two slip rings, there should be a low reading (around 1 ohm). With three slip rings, there are three possible measurements: between 1 and 2, 1 and 3, and 2 and 3. 1-and-2 and 2-and-3 should give a low reading (R × 1 scale on an analog meter), and 1-and-3 a higher reading—approximately double.

With four slip rings, there are six possible combinations! Between 1 and 2, 3, or 4; 2 and 3 or 4; and 3 and 4. 1-and-3 and 2-and-4 should give approximately the same low reading (R × 1 scale on an analog meter); all the others, no reading (open circuit). If any continuity is found between 1-and-2, 2-and-3, 3-and-4, and 1-and-4, there is a short in the armature.

Finally, test between each slip ring and the armature shaft (R × 100 scale on an analog meter). There should be no continuity between any slip ring and the shaft. A 0 reading at any time indicates a short in the armature.

No Output:
Alternator Type with Brushes

WARNING: THE OUTPUT FROM A GENERATOR CAN KILL! Some of the following tests involve working around an operating generator. At all times keep hands, clothing, and hair away from moving parts, and IF YOU ARE IN ANY DOUBT ABOUT WHAT YOU ARE DOING, DON'T DO IT!

With the unit running, check for AC voltage *at the generator.* If this is OK, the boat's AC circuit is at fault. If there is no voltage at the generator, *shut it down,* locate the voltage regulator, and check its fuse (if fitted). If OK, check the brushes and brush springs to ensure they are making contact with the slip rings. If OK, disconnect the positive and negative field leads from the voltage regulator to the brushes, first labeling them so that they can be replaced properly. Connect a 12-volt battery to the field leads—positive to positive, negative to negative—and run up the generator (Figure 6-8A). It is now being externally excited by the battery. Check for AC output. If present (it may range anywhere from 20 to 100 volts), the voltage regulator or its stator winding is probably defective. If there is no AC output, the rotor or the stator is probably defective.

Testing the rotor. Make a visual inspection for damaged insulation, windings, or slip rings. Pitted or burned slip rings will have to be turned down in a lathe. Spin the rotor by hand and flex its shaft to check the bearings. Check between

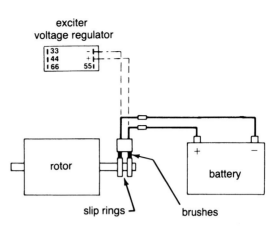

exciter
voltage regulator

33	–
44	+
66	55

rotor

slip rings

brushes

battery

+   –

Figure 6-8A. Externally exciting a brush-type AC alternator. *(Kohler)*

the slip rings with an ohmmeter (R × 1 scale on an analog meter): Resistances are typically from 3 to 5 ohms. Check for continuity between each slip ring and the rotor shaft (R × 100 scale on an analog meter). Any continuity indicates a short.

Testing the stator. Label and disconnect all leads from the terminal block. Test between the leads on each set of stator windings (R × 1 scale on an analog meter). Resistances are very low (typically from 0.06 to 0.34 ohm—Figure 6-8B) and indistinguishable from a dead short on most meters. The windings that supply the voltage regulator will have a slightly higher resistance (typically from 1 to 4 ohms). Test between each lead of a winding and the leads on *other* windings (R × 100 scale on an analog meter). There should be no continuity.

No Output:
Brushless Alternator Type

WARNING: THE OUTPUT FROM A GENERATOR CAN KILL! Some of the following tests involve working around an operating generator. At all times keep hands, clothing, and hair away from moving parts, and IF YOU ARE IN ANY DOUBT ABOUT WHAT YOU ARE DOING, DON'T DO IT!

Check for AC voltage *at the generator.* If this is OK, then the problem is in the boat's AC circuit.

Winding and diode tests. If no voltage is present at the generator, shut it down and remove its covers. Test all the windings as explained below: stator, rotor, exciter, and, for larger generators only, the auxiliary winding if it powers the exciter windings.

Stator windings. These terminate in the main output terminal block. Disconnect all leads,

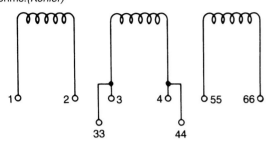

Figure 6-8B. **(Right)** Stator leads on Kohler generators. **(Below)** Stator winding resistance readings, when cold, in ohms. *(Kohler)*

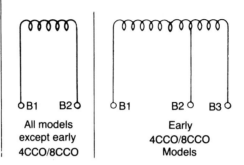

Note: New stators have the center-tapped B2 lead removed and re-identify B3 as B2.

All models except early 4CCO/8CCO

Early 4CCO/8CCO Models

Leads	4CCO	4CCFO	7CCFO	8CCO	10.5CCFO	12.5CCO	12.5CCFO	16CCO	16.5CCFO	20CCO
1-2, 3-4, 33-44	.25	.34	.18	.14	.07	.07	.07	.07	.07	.07
55-66	2.8	4.2	1.26	1.1	1.1	1.1	1.1	1.4	1.4	1.4
B1-B2 (w/o center-tapped winding)	.15	.20	.10	.08	.06	.06	.06	.06	.06	.06
B1-B2 (with center-tapped winding)	.10	—	—	.06	—	—	—	—	—	—
B1-B3 (with center-tapped winding)	.15	—	—	.08	—	—	—	—	—	—

grounds, and interconnections from the terminal block, first labeling everything and noting positions so that it can all be put back correctly.

Each set of stator windings will have at least two leads—three if the generator can be used on both 50 Hz and 60 Hz. (On these units, the outermost leads on a winding are for 50 Hz; the lead tapped closer to the center of the winding is for 60 Hz.) Test the resistance between the two outermost leads on each winding (R × 1 scale on an analog meter). These readings will be very low—on the order of 0.2 to 0.6 ohm (smaller generators will show higher resistance). All but the most sensitive meters will show a dead short. Infinity indicates an open-circuited coil.

Now test from every stator lead to ground (R × 100 scale on an analog meter), and from the leads on one stator coil to another. Any continuity indicates a short to ground or between windings.

Rotor windings. The rotor may have up to three sets of windings, and as many as six diodes, located on or around the rotor. Turn the rotor over to identify the diode(s).

1. *Diodes screwed into the end of the rotor* (smaller generators; Figure 6-9A). To test the winding(s), quickly check (R × 1 scale on an analog meter) between the top connection and the base of the diode. It should read about 1 to 4 ohms (the smaller the generator, the

lower the reading). Again, less-sensitive meters will show this as a short. If resistances are out of line, to test the windings more thoroughly, unsolder the wires from the top(s) of the diode(s), using the lowest heat possible and making sure no solder splashes onto the windings since it will melt the thin, lacquered insulation. Remove the diode(s), and test between the unsoldered wire(s) and the wires that were attached to the base of the diode(s). A 1- to 4-ohm resistance should be present. Check for continuity between each lead and the rotor shaft (R × 100 scale on an analog meter). Any continuity indicates a short in a winding.

2. *Diodes spread around the rotor* (larger generators). The individual winding resistances can be measured with the diodes in place by measuring between each diode on each side of a winding. Do not include the diode (see Figure 6-9B).

3. *Diode testing.* Diodes cannot be checked in place with an ohmmeter. However, a test can be made using a 12-volt battery and a lamp with attached jumper leads (Figure 6-9C). The lamp should light brightly one way and glow faintly with the leads reversed. If the lamp lights in both directions, the diode is shorted; if it doesn't light at all, the diode is open-circuited.

Should diodes be removed for any reason, they can be tested using an ohmmeter with a diode-testing capability (Chapter 3). If the meter measures the resistance, with the leads applied in one direction the meter will show infinity (open circuit); in the other, a circuit. Typical resistances may range from below 10 up to several hundred ohms (Figure 6-9D). If the meter measures voltage drop, with the leads applied in one direction the meter will show a low voltage (typically around 0.6 volts); in the other, an open circuit. Readings other than this indicate a failed diode.

Exciter windings. This will be the only set of connections left untested, excluding any battery-charging circuit. If the terminals are bridged by one or more capacitors (Figure 6-10), then the excitation windings are not powered by an auxiliary circuit (smaller generators). On the other hand, if there are no capacitors, we have an auxiliary circuit to deal with (larger generators).

Capacitor-type circuit. Discharge the capacitor or capacitors as described earlier in this chapter, label all connections, and unplug.

As with the stator windings, the exciter windings will probably be tapped for both 60 Hz and 50 Hz. Measure resistance (R × 1 scale on an analog meter) between the two leads farthest apart. It should be anywhere from 0.5 to 3 ohms (a short on most meters). The smaller the generator, the higher the resistance. Measure from each lead to ground (R × 100 scale on an analog meter) and to all stator leads. Any continuity indicates a short.

Test capacitors as before. Note that where a brushless generator with capacitor-type excitation windings (small generators) suffers from low voltage, *the capacitor may be at fault even if it checks out OK with the tests outlined.* Try changing the capacitor.

Auxiliary winding-type circuits. Small brushless generators do not use the auxiliary winding in the stator to feed the exciter windings. Thus the auxiliary winding and its bridge rectifier and regulation circuit can be ignored when troubleshooting generator output. In larger generators that use the auxiliary winding (no capacitors on the excitation windings), the resistance of the excitation windings can be read from the positive and negative terminals of the bridge rectifier. Resistances may be considerably higher than in capacitor circuits. Measurements from either of these points to ground (R × 100 scale on an analog meter) should read infinity. If not, a winding is shorted.

The bridge rectifier can be disconnected and tested as outlined earlier in the chapter.

After disconnecting its leads, the auxiliary winding in the stator can be tested across its two output leads, at least one of which will run to

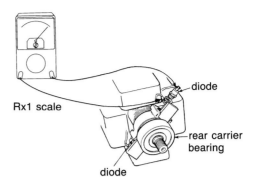

Figure 6-9. Diode placement on brushless generators.

Figure 6-9A. Small generators (one or two diodes). Test field winding resistance at leads shown. *(Westerbeke)*

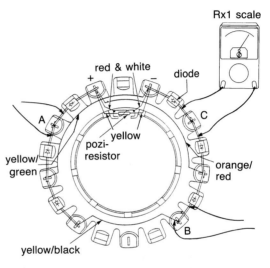

Figure 6-9B. Larger generators (six diodes). Check resistance of field windings A, B, and C at the points shown.

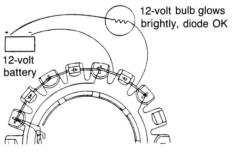

Figure 6-9C. Testing a diode in place, using a 12-volt battery and a lamp equipped with jumper leads.

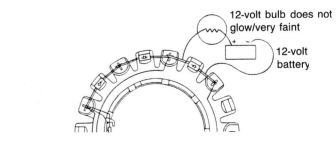

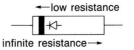

Figure 6-9D. Testing a diode removed from the rotor. Use an ohmmeter (R × 1 scale on an analog meter).

Figure 6-10. Exciter winding capacitor connections on brushless generators. The frequency of the generator is changed from 60 Hz to 50 Hz by changing the engine speed. Voltage is then adjusted by connecting the relevant lead to the capacitor and leaving the other one loose. The no-load voltage of the generator can be raised or lowered by switching leads 7, 8, and 9. The higher the number on the lead connected, the higher the no-load voltage. *(Westerbeke)*

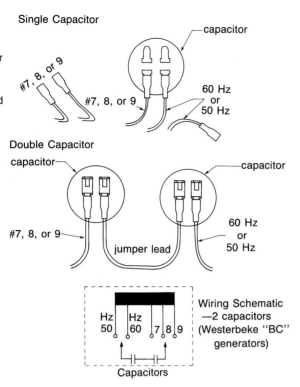

one of the AC terminals on the bridge rectifier. Once again resistances are low (1 to 2 ohms). No continuity (R × 100 scale on an analog meter) should be found between either auxiliary winding lead and ground or any other winding lead (stator windings and excitation windings). If continuity is present, there is a short.

If at this stage no problem has been found, the voltage regulation circuit needs testing. That, unfortunately, is getting too complex for this book.

Flashing the field. On rare occasions exciter windings may lose their residual magnetism. This can be restored by flashing the field with a 12-volt battery. *With the engine running and all wiring in place,* momentarily touch the leads from the battery to the two capacitor terminals (small generators) or the positive and negative terminals (be sure to get the correct polarity!) on the bridge rectifier (large generators). If two capacitors are fitted, touch the two capacitor terminals that have the leads, not the two terminals that are bridged.

No output on battery-charging circuit (if fitted). Identify the bridge rectifier. The auxiliary stator winding will have two leads running to the two AC terminals on the bridge rectifier. Disconnect these terminals and measure the winding resistance across the two leads (R × 1 scale on an analog meter). It should be very low (0.5 to 0.2 ohms) and indistinguishable from a dead short on most meters. Check from each

lead to ground (R × 100 scale on an analog meter). Any continuity indicates a short. Check to all other stator leads. Once again, any continuity indicates a short.

Remove the DC connections from the bridge rectifier (label as necessary) and test it as described earlier in the chapter.

The output from the rectifier will be regulated by a solid-state voltage regulator. About all that can be done with this is to check all wiring and terminals. It will be subject to all the same problems regarding voltage drop, undercharging, etc., outlined in Chapter 2, Troubleshooting Voltage Regulators.

Disassembly and Bearing Replacement

Worn bearings make a distinctive rumble and should be replaced as soon as detected. If these are left unattended, armature or rotor vibration will lead to accelerated wear and ultimately to damage to any brushes and slip rings, while various wires are likely to work loose or chafe through. The field windings on armature-type generators may come loose and start rubbing on the armature.

Generators have few parts, and disassembly is straightforward. If the generator is belt driven, begin by removing the pulley. Remove any brushes, taking care to note the position of all wires, which way around the brushes go, and in which brush holders. Unbolt and remove the end bearing retaining plate; the bearing will be a press fit in the plate or will be held with a small retaining plate. To get at the bearing in the other end, you must withdraw the armature/rotor taking care not to drag it against the field windings/stator coils.

This procedure leaves the field windings/stator coils and any rectification and voltage regulation circuits still attached to the generator case. To reassemble the unit, reverse the process.

Variable-Speed Technology (VST)

There are two principal limitations with a traditional genset:

1. To achieve the desired output frequency a generator must be run at 1,800 or 3,600 rpm (USA; 1,500 or 3,000 rpm in the UK). Unfortunately, these speeds do not coincide with the peak power ratings of most engines! As a result, engines normally have to be oversized and even at full generator load are run at less than 100% of their rated output.

2. Regardless of the load on the generator the engine must be run at this required generating speed. Even on standby, a 12-kW generator will still be running at full speed! Aside from being inefficient and unnecessarily noisy, low-load operation, particularly with diesels, is damaging to the engine and will run up maintenance bills while shortening engine life.

Variable-Speed Technology (VST) solves both these problems. An engine is used to drive a specially wound alternator that, even at low engine speeds, produces three-phase AC (as with an automotive alternator—Chapter 2), but in excess of the desired AC voltage (120 or 240 volts) and at some frequency that will vary with engine speed. This variable output is rectified to high-voltage DC, and then fed through an inverter to produce AC at the desired frequency and voltage (Chapter 5). As with other inverters, this output may be in the form of a modified sine wave (a stepped square wave) or a true sine wave. For a given output, VST generators are smaller and lighter than traditional generators. What is more, the output voltage and frequency are very tightly regulated, as opposed to the fluctuating voltage and frequency on many traditional generators.

VST generators consist of two principal components—the engine-driven alternator and the electronics box (inverter)—plus, in most instances, a remotely mounted monitoring and control panel. These generators can be belt-driven off an existing propulsion engine (usually the boat's main engine) or directly coupled to a separate engine to form a stand-alone genset.

Belt-driven VST generators. At the time of writing, belt-driven VST generators are available in the USA with outputs of 2.5 kW and 5.0 kW, with the ability to mount two 5.0-kW units on one engine to produce 10.0 kW. UK ratings tend to be lower. Early models had a stepped-square-wave output, which suffers from the same limitations as a stepped-square wave inverter, but newer models are shifting to true-sine-wave output.

Pros and cons. Unless a boat has some partcularly high-load AC appliance that exceeds the capability of a DC/AC inverter, and which is to be used only intermittently, it is difficult to see the benefits of a belt-driven VST generator over those of an inverter. (The one clear exception is a powerboat that spends a good bit of time under way with the air-conditioner running. A belt-driven VST generator attached to the main engine will enable the air-conditioner to be used without having to run the auxiliary generator.)

In most circumstances a VST generator will be more expensive than an inverter, is more complicated to install (requiring special mounting brackets and perhaps idler pulleys), requires more maintenance (belt loadings are high; the belts require regular attention), and will produce AC power only when the engine is running; whereas the inverter is available 24 hours a day. A stepped-square-wave inverter will have the added advantage that it can be used as a battery charger when connected to shore power. (This capability may soon be added to the inverter part of some VST generators. It should be noted that the present generation of stepped-square-wave VST inverters will not run many stand-alone battery chargers, and may in fact actually damage some.)

Belt-driven VST generators are less efficient than most other generators because of the horsepower absorbed by the drive belt, and the small losses in the inverter. Overall, it takes close to 2 horsepower to produce 1 kW of output (as opposed to 1.3 to 1.5 horsepower with a traditional generator). The power absorbed by the generator can also be a problem if the unit is mounted to a relatively small auxiliary sailboat engine. A 2.5-kW unit requires 4.25 horsepower at full load, and a 5.0-kW unit needs 8.5 horsepower—there may be times when a belt-driven VST generator simply can't be used. For a given level of output they are, however, considerably cheaper than a traditional genset (because there is no need to pay for the engine!).

Stand-alone VST generators. Currently the only stand-alone VST generators of which I am aware are produced by Balmar (Seattle, WA). A specially wound stator is bolted up to the rear end of an engine, with a brushless, superconducting permanent magnet (the rotor) coupled directly to the end of the crankshaft. There are no belts, pulleys, brushes, adjustments, or maintenance requirements of any kind. Outputs of up to 10 kW are currently available, with higher capabilities planned.

The alternator is incredibly compact—the 6-kW generator is typically half the size and weight of a traditional generator—and more efficient than a traditional generator. The inverter box produces a true-sine-wave output that is not only cleaner and more stable than that of any traditional generator, but also cleaner and more stable than that produced by most electricity companies! These generators clearly have a great future in those applications where AC demands exceed the capabilities of a DC/AC inverter installation. The only drawbacks are the complexity of the electronics (it remains to be seen how they will stand up in the marine environment) and the price (which is currently about 30% above that of a comparably-rated traditional genset, but should fall as production runs increase).

Troubleshooting VST generators. The inverter end of things is liable to have various overtemperature and overload protection devices—see Chapter 5 (Inverters).

Low voltage (generator bogs down). The engine speed on belt-driven VST generators is set manually; that on stand-alone generators may be either manually or electronically controlled. If a generator is unable to handle a load, there are two options: to reduce the load or to increase the engine speed.

Sometimes the *surge* or *start-up* load of a large AC motor may overwhelm a generator. The solution is to turn off the load, increase the engine speed, and try again. If the engine bogs down from full speed, the load is simply too great for the generator. Where more than one high-surge-load motor may come on line simultaneously (e.g., a dive compressor and an air-conditioner), a *load sequencing* device can be installed that will automatically delay the start-up of one motor until the other is up to speed.

The newer Balmar generators have electronic governing in which a device senses the instantaneous current draw of the AC loads and automatically adjusts the engine speed to meet the load. If a heavy load suddenly hits a lightly loaded (and therefore idling) generator, the engine may take a moment to respond but will then pick up (this is no different from a conventional genset).

Belt-driven generators: Just as with a regular alternator, belt alignment and tension are critical to long life—if output is erratic, accompanied by belt squeal when a heavy load is applied, the belt is loose. If output is erratic but the belt is okay, the brushes are probably not making proper contact with the slip rings (see page 60). In the case of no output, the various tests outlined on pages 55-58 can be carried out to determine if it is the alternator's voltage regulator circuit that is at fault or the alternator itself, remembering that *any output from the alternator is potentially lethal high-voltage AC and must be treated with the appropriate respect. IF YOU ARE IN DOUBT ABOUT ANY TEST, DON'T DO IT!*

Electric Motors

How They Work

All electric motors, regardless of type, operate on the same general principles. A magnetic field is established inside the motor case, either with fixed permanent magnets, or by using electromagnets—coils of wire (field windings) wrapped around iron shoes that become magnetized when a current is passed through the windings.

An armature or rotor is mounted on bearings inside this magnetic field. An armature contains another series of windings on an iron frame that also becomes magnetized when a current is passed through the windings. A rotor contains a set of fixed metal bars. In either case, like or opposing magnetic fields between the motor case and the armature or rotor drive the armature or rotor around in its bearings—we have an electric motor. Depending on methods of construction and details of operation, electric motors fall into three broad categories: universal motors, permanent-magnet motors, and induction motors.

Universal motors. The magnetic field inside the motor case is created by a couple of field windings. This type of motor uses a wound armature with anywhere from four windings on up (depending on motor construction). Each armature winding terminates in a copper bar. These bars are separated by insulation and arranged in a circle on the end of the armature shaft to become a *commutator*. Electricity is conducted to both the field windings and the armature windings (via spring-loaded brushes—Figure 6-11). The individual armature winding connected to the commutator bars in contact with the brushes is magnetized, and this magnetic attraction or repulsion (depending on the direction of rotation) interacts with the magnetic field produced by the field windings causing the armature to turn.

As the armature turns, the brushes connect with another segment of the commutator, de-energizing the first winding on the armature and energizing the next. It in turn is attracted or repelled by the field windings and keeps the armature turning.

The brushes are offset slightly from the field windings so that when the energized armature winding is attracted or repelled by the field mag-

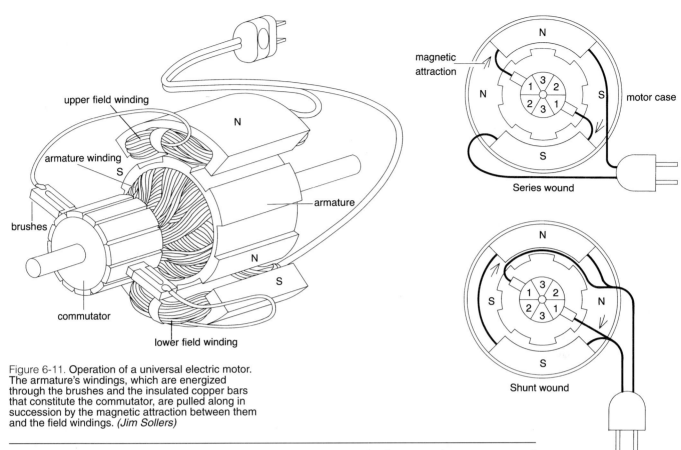

Figure 6-11. Operation of a universal electric motor. The armature's windings, which are energized through the brushes and the insulated copper bars that constitute the commutator, are pulled along in succession by the magnetic attraction between them and the field windings. *(Jim Sollers)*

net, the armature is pulled (or pushed) around. Without this offset, the motor would remain locked in one position.

Some motors (*series-wound* motors) have the field and armature windings connected in series: The current flows first through a field winding, into a brush, through an armature winding, out the other brush through the second field winding, and then back to the power source. Others (*shunt-wound* motors) have the field and armature windings in parallel. The current flows from a common terminal through both the field and armature windings, then back to another common terminal.

The speed of a series-wound DC motor is governed by its load. If this type of motor is run without a load, it will run faster and faster until it ultimately self-destructs. This is why these motors are used inside a sealed, composite unit with the load permanently attached to the shaft.

Permanent-magnet motors. Permanent-magnet motors replace the field windings with permanent magnets. These motors resemble universal motors in all other respects (brushes, commutators, wound armatures).

Induction motors. Induction motors work on AC power only. They contain field windings but they have no windings on the armature and therefore have no brushes or commutator. This type of armature is generally referred to as a rotor, and comprises a number of copper bars. These motors rely on the pulsating nature of AC power. The current through the field windings, alternating from positive to negative and back, sets up a pulsating magnetic force that alternately attracts and repels the copper bars in the rotor. Once an induction motor starts spinning, it will keep spinning as long as current flows. The problem is to get it moving in the first place. Two different methods are used to start induction motors:

Split-phase (resistance) starting. A separate set of *phase* or *start* windings is added to the field windings, offset from the *run* windings and designed to generate an offset magnetic force and get the motor moving (Figure 6-12A). As the motor comes up to speed, a centrifugal switch or a current-sensing switch generally cuts off the start windings, often with an audible click (Figure 6-12B).

Capacitor-start motors further refine the starting process by the addition of one or two capacitors—round or oval cylinders with two spade terminals on one end, usually fitted under a cover on top of the motor, that store an electric charge.

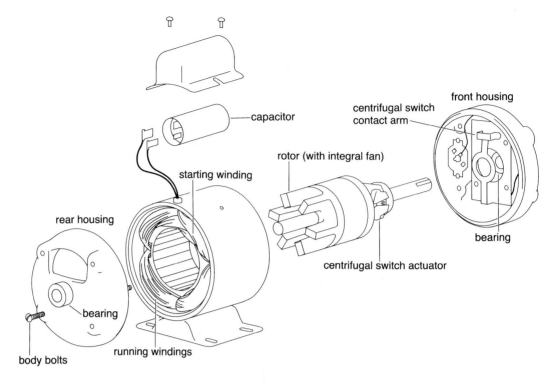

Figure 6-12A. Split-phase capacitor-start induction motor. *(Jim Sollers)*

capacitor

front housing

centrifugal switch contact arm

rotor (with integral fan)

starting winding

rear housing

bearing

centrifugal switch actuator

bearing

body bolts

running windings

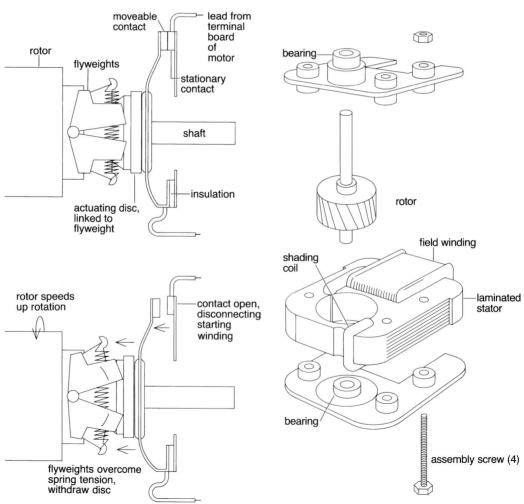

Figure 6-12B. (**Left**) Operation of the centrifugal switch on a split-phase motor.

Figure 6-12C. (**Right**) Shaded-pole induction motor.

rotor

flyweights

moveable contact

lead from terminal board of motor

stationary contact

shaft

actuating disc, linked to flyweight

insulation

bearing

rotor

field winding

shading coil

laminated stator

rotor speeds up rotation

contact open, disconnecting starting winding

flyweights overcome spring tension, withdraw disc

bearing

assembly screw (4)

Some capacitor-start motors have no switch on the start windings, which remain energized at all times; others have a switch. Where two capacitors are fitted, the second maintains partial current to the start windings even after the main start circuit is switched off. This makes for smoother running and reduces *hum*.

Shaded-pole starting: Shaded-pole motors have a copper strap around a section of the field magnet that creates a magnetic asymmetry and gets the motor moving (Figure 6-12C). Shaded-pole motors are simple, inexpensive, and reliable, but since the magnetic asymmetry is a permanent feature, even when they are running at full speed, they are also inefficient.

Speed Regulation

Universal motors. Universal motors are commonly controlled by varying the current to the field windings. This is done either by a multiposition switch or with a rheostat and knob, which permits continuous adjustment of the field current. Newer devices may have solid-state regulators similar to the voltage regulators found on alternators, but with an added manual controller to adjust output. On such devices a short circuit will result in maximum speed at all times; an open circuit will disable the motor. Motors designed to run at a single, constant speed are likely to have a governor.

Tapped-field speed control. The field winding has three to six connections at different points along its length. The closer a connection is to the end of the winding, the shorter the length of winding energized when current is applied, and therefore the less the resistance (since resistance is a function of wire length). The less the resistance, the greater the current flow. The greater the current flow, the more the magnetism. The more the magnetism, the faster the motor will spin! So, by connecting (tapping into) the field winding at different points, we vary motor speed. The different points are accessed by a multiposition selector switch (Figure 6-13A).

Rheostats. A rheostat generally consists of a circular coil with a spring-loaded contact that can be rotated to any point on the coil. Current is fed into the coil at one end and flows along it until reaching the contactor, which then becomes the exit path for the current. As more coil is included in the circuit the resistance increases, causing less current to flow. The rheostat is placed into the supply line to the field windings, controlling the current fed to the wind-

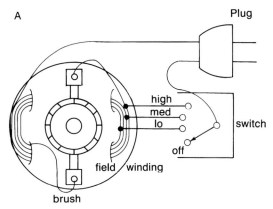
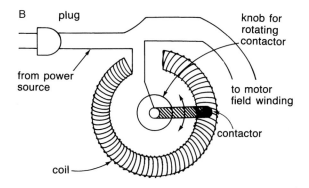
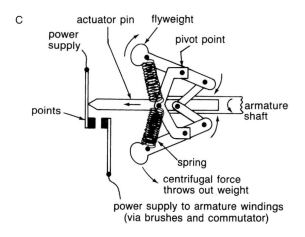

Figure 6-13. Regulating the speed of universal motors. (A) Multiposition switch. (B) Rheostat (variable resistor). (C) Mechanical governor.

ings and therefore motor speed (Figure 6-13B).

Governors. A governor is mounted on the end of an armature shaft (Figure 6-13C). As the armature spins, the governor's flyweights are thrown outward by centrifugal force against spring pressure. As a result the various levers move the actuator pin out, and this in turn opens the points, cutting off the current to the armature windings. The motor slows, centrifugal force declines, the weights are pulled back in by the springs, the points close, power is restored to the armature windings, and the motor speeds up once again. Motor speed is set by adjusting the

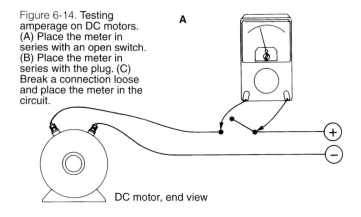

Figure 6-14. Testing amperage on DC motors. (A) Place the meter in series with an open switch. (B) Place the meter in series with the plug. (C) Break a connection loose and place the meter in the circuit.

DC motor, end view

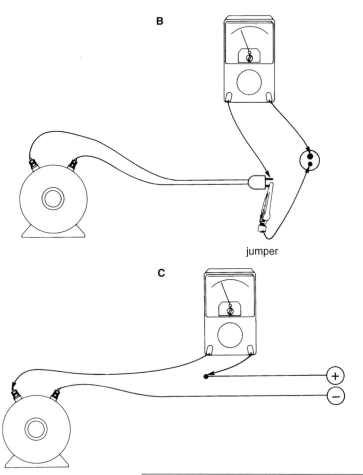

jumper

power, their speed is tied directly to the frequency in the AC system (e.g., 60 Hz in the USA, 50 Hz in the UK). As such, speed is not variable. The motors may have anywhere from two to six or more field windings (*poles*). Speed is broadly governed by the number of poles. At 60 Hz, two poles will yield approximately 3,500 rpm., four poles 1,750 r.p.m., and six poles 1,160 r.p.m. Speed regulation of induction motors is generally available only by switching poles into or out of the circuit.

Troubleshooting

Preliminary testing: all motors

Voltage test: Check the voltage at the motor, preferably across its input and output terminals. If these are inaccessible, check at the nearest power outlet or terminal block. Switch the motor on and off. Severe voltage drop results from a dead battery, defective wiring and switches, or a shorted motor.

Amperage test, DC motors below 10 amps: If an ammeter with a 10-amp DC rating is available, connect the meter *in series* with the hot lead (Figure 6-14). This can be done either by turning off the switch and jumping it out with the meter leads, or by unsoldering or otherwise breaking loose a connection. If the motor is pulling more amps than rated, it has a short; if pulling no amps, it is open-circuited. This could result from a blown fuse, tripped breaker, turned-off switch, broken or disconnected wire, brushes not contacting the commutator, or a burned winding in the motor itself.

Amperage test, DC motors above 10 amps: Fluke and other companies make clip-on DC ammeters, which are simply plugged into a regular multimeter and clamped around the DC cable. These are capable of measuring up to 1,000 amps DC, or 750 amps AC.

Amperage test, AC motors: Use a clip-on ammeter (Chapter 3) to compare the amp draw with the rated load (Table 6-2). On 240-volt AC motors (USA), test both power leads one at a time—they should be pulling approximately the same number of amps. Induction motors are notoriously inefficient—the smaller the motor, the greater the inefficiency. If the motor is rated in watts, its *rated* amperage can be found by dividing the watts by system voltage. *Actual amperage may be more than twice this*, and on initial start-up as much as six times higher! This makes it difficult to distinguish partial shorts.

spring pressure on the flyweights; the more pressure, the greater the centrifugal force needed to open the points, and therefore the faster the motor will spin before the points are opened (Figure 6-13C). Things to look for when troubleshooting governors are burned or corroded points, a dirty or rusty shaft (interfering with the movement of the actuator pin), and any dirt or corrosion on the rest of the linkage or the springs.

Induction motors. Since induction motors work by utilizing the pulsating nature of AC

Dead shorts will draw heavy amperage continuously; open circuits, no amps.

Resistance tests: Disconnect the motor from its power source and connect an ohmmeter (R × 1 scale on an analog meter) between the hot and ground leads (12-volt motors), the hot and neutral leads (120-volt, USA, or 240-volt, UK), or the two hot leads (240-volt, USA). The meter should show a small resistance, depending on the type and size of the motor. In general, the more powerful the motor, the lower the resistance. Note, however, that the resistance is likely to be less than that calculated by an application of Ohm's law to the motor's rated voltage and amperage (or wattage). This is because an operating motor develops a higher resistance than a static motor, and motors are rated at their operating characteristics.

If the meter shows 0 ohms, the motor has an internal short. However, DC motors that have a heavy current draw, such as starter motors, may show so little resistance that only the most sensitive meters can distinguish between normal internal resistance and a short. If the meter shows infinite resistance (R × 100 scale on an analog meter), the motor is open-circuited at some point. Likely causes are an open switch, a broken wire, burned brushes or brush springs, or a burned winding.

Leave the meter connected (R × 1 scale on an analog meter) and turn the motor by hand. On motors with brushes the reading may flicker up and down uniformly, but any sudden or erratic differences probably indicate problems with the brushes or the commutator.

If the motor has variable speeds, such as a food processor, switch through the range (or turn the speed-adjusting knob) and observe the ohms reading. It should increase or decrease gradually. Any sudden deviations indicate a problem. An exception is when the switch is turned off: The reading should jump to infinity. If it does not, the switch is defective.

If the preceding tests indicate a problem in the motor, it needs to be dismantled. Generally this is a simple and obvious procedure. Take care not to break any wires when removing end covers and housings, especially on universal motors, where brush and field winding wires may be attached to two different parts of the casing. Motor casings and covers often must be reassembled exactly as they came apart. It is always a good idea to make a couple of punch marks or scratches in the paint across a joint so that they can be realigned exactly. Universal and permanent-magnet motors with spring-loaded brushes are likely to launch them during incautious disassembly. Extra care is needed.

Table 6-2. Typical Running Amperages for 120-Volt Induction Motors[1]

Horsepower	120-Volt Motor	240-Volt Motor
⅙	4.4 amps	2.2 amps
¼	5.8	2.9
⅓	7.2	3.6
½	9.8	4.9
¾	13.8	6.9
1	16	8
1½	20	10
2	24	12

1. Starting currents for split phase motors are 5 to 7 times higher, for capacitor-start motors 2 to 4 times higher.

Electrical problems.

Universal motors. The most likely problem areas are the brushes and the commutator. The brushes must be free-moving in their holders, have sufficient spring tension to contact the commutator firmly, and as a general rule, should be at least as long as they are wide. When worn beyond this point they need replacing. The commutator must be clean, relatively shiny (a light film or surface mottling is OK), and smooth (a step worn by the brushes is okay). Any pitted or darkened segments indicate a short or open circuit in one of the armature windings (Figure 6-15A); the armature needs replacing or rewinding.

Commutator testing: The armature and commutator can be tested with an ohmmeter. Touch one probe to one commutator segment and the other probe to the adjacent segment. The ohms reading should be low, but not 0. Test adjacent segments all around the commutator; all should read about the same. No ohms (needle all the way to the right on an analog meter) indicates a short between windings (except with some cheap meters insufficiently sensitive to distinguish normal readings from a short). High ohms (needle all the way to the left on an analog meter) indicates an open circuit (a burned winding). Finally, test between the armature shaft and each commutator segment (R × 100 scale on an analog meter). A 0 reading at any time indicates a short to ground (Figure 6-15B).

Commutator cleaning: A dirty commutator that checks out okay and is in reasonable shape (not pitted, out of round, or excessively worn) can be cleaned by pulling a strip of fine sandpaper (600- or 400-grit wet-or-dry) lightly back and forth until all the segments are uniformly shiny

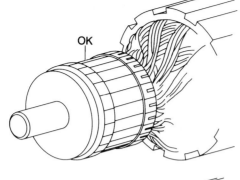

Figure 6-15A. Maintenance procedures for universal motors. A worn and grooved commutator is OK as long as the ring is shiny. A pitted or dark bar results from an open or short circuit in the armature winding. *(Jim Sollers)*

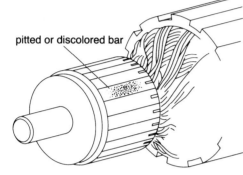

Figure 6-15B. Testing an armature. Testing between adjacent bars on the commutator should give a low ohms reading; all readings about the same. Testing from each commutator bar to the shaft should show infinity, indicating an open circuit. *(Jim Sollers)*

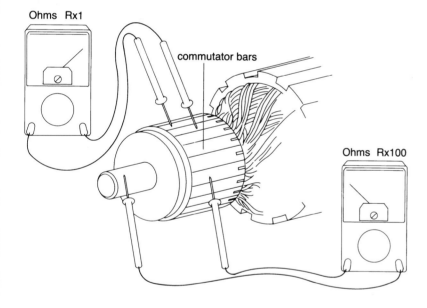

(Figure 6-15C). Cut back the insulation between each segment of the commutator to just below the level of the copper segments by drawing a knife or sharp screwdriver across each strip of insulation. Take care not to scratch the copper or burr its edges (Figures 6-15D and E). Use a triangular file to bevel the edges of the copper bars. Always renew the brushes at this time.

Brush renewal: Pull out the old brushes and thoroughly clean away all traces of carbon from the commutator and motor housing with a pro-

prietary cleaner, such as Electroclean or WD-40. Dry thoroughly afterward. Slip in the new brushes, *which must slide in and out of their holders without binding.* The *commutator* ends of the new brushes will need *bedding in:* Wrap some fine sandpaper (600- or 400-grit wet-or-dry; *not emery cloth*) around the commutator under the brushes (Figure 6-15F), with the sanding surface facing out. Spin the armature, or work the sandpaper backward and forward, until the brushes are bedded to the commutator; they should be almost shiny over their whole surface. Remove the sandpaper and blow out the carbon dust.

Field winding testing: The field windings will have a wire running into one winding, around to the other(s), and out. One end may or may not be grounded to the motor case. Test with an ohmmeter (R × 1 scale on an analog meter), between the ungrounded end of the field winding wire and the other wire or the motor case (scratch around to get a good ground). If the meter reads 0, the field windings or wires are shorted to ground (except on large motors being tested with a cheap meter not sensitive enough to read field-winding resistances). A high reading (analog meter on R × 100 scale) indicates the field windings or their wiring are open-circuited (burned through like a fuse, or a broken wire).

On those motors with governor-type speed controls, check the governor for free movement, the springs for reasonable tension, and the points for any signs of pitting and corrosion.

Permanent-magnet motors. These are tested and repaired in exactly the same way as universal motors, with the exception that there are no field windings to worry about.

Induction motors. Induction motors have no brushes, commutator, or armature windings to concern us. Field windings are tested as for universal motors. Shaded-pole motors have little else to go wrong electrically. Split-phase motors have one or two special problem areas.

Thermal overload trip: If the motor is very hot (too hot to touch), let it cool down. Some thermal overload trips reset themselves; others have to be reset by pushing a button on the motor housing.

Motor hums but does not start: Probably the start windings are not energizing. Spin the motor by hand (switch turned on). If it goes, the start circuit is bad. Check for a centrifugal switch in the open position or one that has dirty or corroded points. If present, the switch will be on the end of the rotor shaft. Clean it and ensure free movement. If the motor has capacitors, test these (Figure 6-16).

Motor starts and kicks off: The start windings are not switching off when the motor comes up

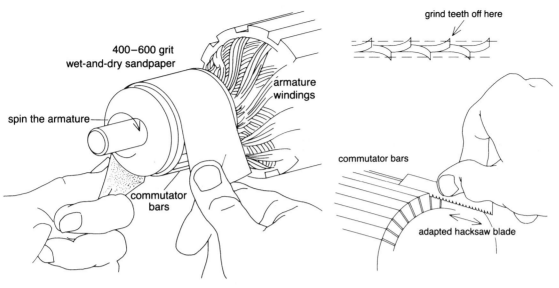

400-600 grit
wet-and-dry sandpaper

spin the armature

armature
windings

commutator
bars

grind teeth off here

commutator bars

adapted hacksaw blade

Figure 6-15C. (**Top Left**) Polishing a commutator. *(Jim Sollers)*

Figure 6-15D. (**Top Right**) Cutting back the insulation on a commutator. Modify a hacksaw blade as shown. *(Jim Sollers)*

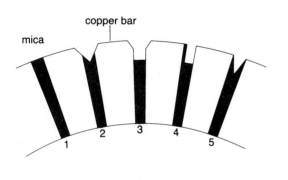

mica

copper bar

1 2 3 4 5

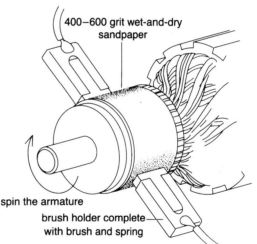

400-600 grit wet-and-dry sandpaper

spin the armature

brush holder complete with brush and spring

Figure 6-15E. (**Bottom Left**) Cutting back the insulation on a commutator. At 1, the mica insulation is flush with the commutator bars. Cut back as in 2 (good) or 3 (better). Avoid cutting back as in 4 or 5. *(Jim Sollers)*

Figure 6-15F. (**Bottom Right**) Bedding in new brushes. *(Jim Sollers)*

to speed. Check the centrifugal switch, if fitted.

Mechanical problems. Motors are mechanically very simple. A bearing supports the armature (rotor) at both ends. Sometimes a fan is added to the shaft.

Small motors have bushings for bearings (brass or bronze sleeves), which require a very little light machine oil periodically. Do not overdo it: Excess oil will carry dirt into the motor windings.

Larger motors have ball bearings. Most are sealed for life, but a few older ones have external grease nipples (one shot of grease occasionally). Worn bearings produce distinctive rattles and rumbles. With the power off, armatures (rotors) should turn freely by hand with no catches or rough spots. There should be no up-and-down or sideways movement, and almost no in-and-out movement (end play).

The clearance between an armature (rotor) and its field winding shoes (or magnets) is quite small. Any misalignment or serious bearing wear will cause the armature to rub on the shoes (magnets). This will produce a shiny spot on both the armature and shoe and must be fixed. If the armature and its bearings appear to be in

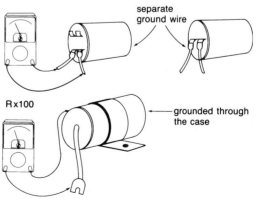

separate ground wire

R x 100

grounded through the case

Figure 6-16. Testing capacitors. Discharge first (see Figure 6-7). Test across the capacitor terminals with an ohmmeter (R × 100 scale on an analog meter). The meter should jump to 0 ohms and slowly return to high. If it fails to go down, the capacitor is open-circuited. If it goes down and stays down (0 ohms), the capacitor is shorted. Testing from any terminal (or lead) to the case (R × 100 scale on an analog meter) must show infinity. If not, the capacitor is shorted.

good shape, check any fastenings to the field windings. On some motors the windings are bolted through the motor case and can work loose with vibration.

Starter Motors

Starter motors are universal motors, but with one or two special quirks that merit attention.

Starter-motor circuits. The heavy amperage draw of a starter motor requires heavy supply cables. Ignition switches are frequently located some distance from the battery and starter motor. To keep cable runs to a minimum, a remotely operated switch—a *solenoid*—that is operated by the ignition switch turns the starter motor on and off (Figures 6-17A, 6-17B, and 6-17C).

A solenoid contains a plunger and an electro-magnet. When the ignition switch is turned on it energizes the magnet, which pulls down the plunger, which closes a couple of heavy-duty contacts, thus making the circuit to the starter motor (Figures 6-17D and 6-17E).

Some starting circuits utilize a *neutral start* switch, or solenoid, which prevents the engine from being cranked when it is in gear. Some heavy-duty circuits fit a second solenoid, which, when energized by the ignition switch, closes a set of points to energize the first solenoid, which then closes the starter-motor points. (This is done because the main solenoid itself draws a moderately heavy current, requiring fairly heavy cables.

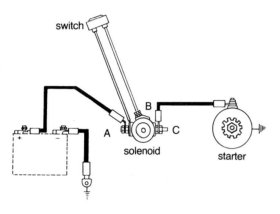

Figure 6-17A. Starting circuit with an inertia starter. To bypass the switch, connect a jumper from A to B. To bypass the switch and the solenoid, connect a heavy-duty jumper (for example, a screwdriver) from A to C.

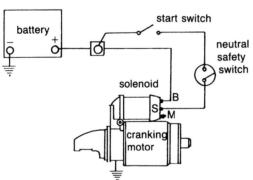

Figure 6-17B. Starting circuit with a preengaged starter. To bypass the switch, connect a jumper from terminal B to terminal S on the solenoid. To bypass the solenoid and switch, connect a heavy-duty jumper (for example, a screwdriver) from terminal B to terminal M. See also Figure 6-19A. (PCM)

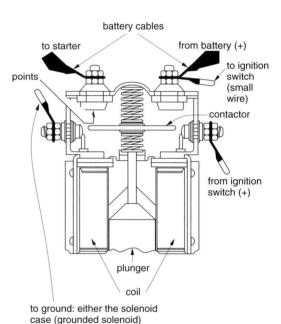

Figure 6-17D. Solenoid operation. Upon closing the ignition switch, a small current passing through the solenoid's electromagnet pushes the contactor up against spring tension, completing the circuit from the battery to the starter motor.

Figure 6-17C. Starting circuit with main and auxiliary solenoids. To bypass the switch circuit, connect a jumper from B to S on the main solenoid; to bypass the solenoid and switch, connect a heavy-duty jumper from B to M.

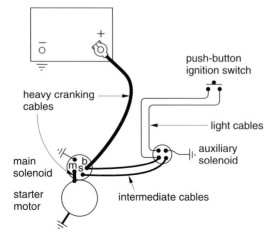

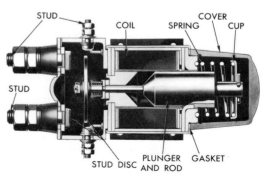

Figure 6-17E. Cut-away of a typical solenoid. (Detroit Diesel)

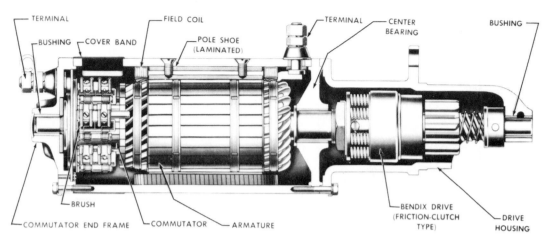

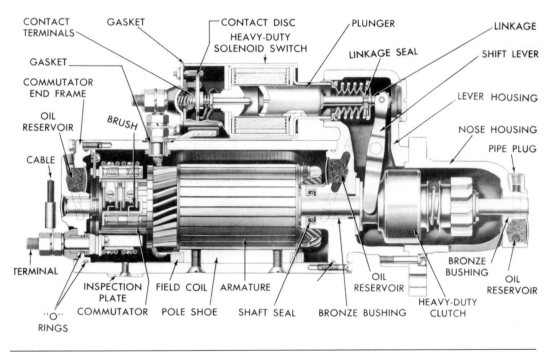

Adding a second light-duty solenoid enables lighter wires to be run to the ignition switch.)

The ground side of a starter-motor circuit almost always runs through the starter-motor case and engine block to a ground strap, which is connected directly to the battery's negative terminal post. However, sometimes an insulated ground is used, in which case the starter motor is isolated electrically from the engine block; a separate cable grounds it to the battery.

Inertia and preengaged starters. Starter motors are of two basic kinds: inertia and preengaged. The solenoid for an inertia motor is mounted independently, at a convenient location. The starter-motor drive gear that turns the engine over—the *pinion*—is keyed into a helical groove on the motor shaft. When the solenoid is energized, the motor spins. Inertia in the gear causes it to spin out along the helical groove and into contact with the engine flywheel, which is then turned over (Figure 6-18A).

Sometimes an inertia starter's pinion will stick to its shaft and not be thrown into engagement with the flywheel. In this case the motor will *whir* loudly without turning the engine over. A smart tap on its case while it is spinning may free it up (don't do this too often, it's hard on the gear teeth). At other times the pinion may jam in the flywheel and not disengage. In this case access can often be gained to the end of the armature shaft via a cover, normally located in the center of the rear housing of the starter motor. *With the engine shut down* turning the squared-off end of the shaft back and forth with a wrench should free the pinion.

Troubleshooting Chart 6-2.

Starting Circuit Problems: Engine Fails to Crank.

Note: Before jumping out solenoid terminals, completely vent the engine compartment, especially with gasoline engines, since sparks will be created.

Turn on some lights and try to crank the engine. Do the lights *go out*? **NO** ↓	**YES** ➡ If the solenoid makes a rapid "clicking" the battery is probably dead—replace it. If the solenoid makes one loud click the starter motor is probably jammed or shorted—free it up or replace it as necessary. While the starter is out, try turning the engine over by placing a wrench on the crankshaft pulley nut. If the engine won't turn this is the problem—there may be water in the cylinders (page 257) or it may be seized up.
When cranking, do the lights *dim*? **NO** ↓	**YES** ➡ Check for voltage drop from poor connections or undersized cables. Try cranking for a few seconds, then feel all connections and cables in the circuit—battery and solenoid terminals, and battery ground attachment on engine block. If any are warm to the touch, they need cleaning. If this fails to show a problem use a voltmeter as shown in Figure 6-20, then try to crank the engine. If there is no evidence of voltage drop, check for a jammed or shorted starter.
Is the ignition switch circuit faulty? **NO** ↓ **TEST:** With a jumper wire or screwdriver blade, bridge the battery and ignition switch terminals on the solenoid. If the starter motor now cranks, the ignition circuit is defective.	**YES** ➡ Replace ignition switch or its wiring as needed.
Is the solenoid defective? **NO** ↓ **TEST:** Use a screwdriver blade to jump out the two heavy-duty terminals on the solenoid. (This procedure is tricky: Observe all precautions outlined in accompanying text.) If the starter now spins, the solenoid is defective.	**YES** ➡ Replace the solenoid.
Is there full battery voltage at starter motor when cranking? **NO** ↓ **TEST:** Check with VOM between the starter positive terminal and the engine block when cranking.	**YES** ➡ The starter is open-circuited and needs replacing. First check its brushes for excessive wear or sticking in their brush holders.
The battery isolation switch is probably turned "OFF"!	

The solenoid of a preengaged starter is *always* mounted on the starter itself (a surefire indicator!). When the solenoid is energized, the electromagnet pulls a lever, which pushes the starter-motor pinion into engagement with the engine flywheel; the main solenoid points now close, allowing current to flow to the motor, which spins at full speed, and (we hope) starts the engine. Preengaged starters mesh the drive gear with the flywheel *before* the motor spins, greatly reducing overall wear (Figure 6-18B).

Circuit testing. Never crank a starter motor for more than 15 seconds continuously when performing any of the following tests. Because starter motors are designed for only brief and infrequent use, they generally have no fans or cooling devices. *Continuous cranking will burn them up.* Note: *Some of these tests will create sparks. Be sure to vent the engine room properly, especially with gasoline engines.*

Remember: A battery that is in reality almost dead may show nearly full voltage on an open-circuit voltage test. If a starter motor fails to work, turn on a couple of lights (wired to the cranking battery) and try to crank the engine. The lights should dim but still stay lit. If the lights remain unchanged, no current is flowing to the starter; if the lights go out, the battery is dead or the starter is shorted. Check the battery first (Chapter 2, Testing a Battery).

Preliminary tests. A couple of quick steps will isolate problems in the starting circuit. The solenoid will have two heavy-duty terminals: one attached to the battery's positive cable, the other with a second cable (or short strap in the case of preengaged starters) running to the starter itself. There will also be one or two small terminals. If only one of the small terminals has a wire attached, this is the one we need. If both small terminals have wires attached, one is a ground wire; we need *the other one* (it goes to the ignition switch). If in doubt, turn "off" the ignition and battery switches and test from both solenoid terminals to ground with an ohmmeter (R × 1 scale on an analog meter). The ignition switch wire should give a small reading; the ground wire will read 0 ohms.

Switch the battery isolation switch back "on." Bypass the ignition switch circuit (and neutral start switch if fitted) by connecting a jumper wire or screwdriver blade from the *battery terminal* on the solenoid to the *ignition switch* terminal (Figures 6-19A and B). If the motor cranks, the ignition switch or its circuit is faulty. If the solenoid clicks but nothing else happens the battery may really be dead (check it again) or the starter is probably bad (but note that the solenoid on a preengaged starter will sometimes throw the pinion into engagement with the flywheel but then fail to energize the motor due to faulty main points, so *always check the solenoid before condemning the motor*). If nothing at all happens there is either no juice to the solenoid (check the battery isolation switch) or the solenoid is defective.

If the starter failed to work use a screwdriver to jump out the *two heavy-duty terminals* on the solenoid (Figures 6-19A and C). Be warned: *The full battery current may be flowing through the screwdriver blade.* Considerable arcing is likely. A big chunk may be melted out of the screwdriver blade. Do not touch the solenoid or starter case with the screwdriver: This will create a dead short. Hold the screwdriver *firmly* to the terminals. If the starter now spins, the solenoid is defective. If the motor does not spin, *it* is probably faulty. If no arcing occurred, there is no juice to the solenoid.

A motor with an inertia starter can be cranked by jumping a defective solenoid as described. A preengaged starter, however, will merely spin without engaging the engine flywheel since the solenoid is needed to push the starter pinion into engagement with the flywheel. In this case, have someone hold the start switch "on" while you jump the main solenoid terminals. If the cranking problem is a failure of the solenoid *points* (most likely), this will crank the engine; but if the problem is a failure of the solenoid *coil, the* pinion will still fail to engage the flywheel. In the latter case, you can remove the solenoid to access the pinion fork, allowing you to manually engage

Figure 6-19A. Typical preengaged starter motor and solenoid. Jumping across 1 and 2 bypasses the ignition switch; 1 and 3 bypasses both the ignition switch and the solenoid. The starter should spin but will not engage the engine's flywheel.

Figure 6-19B. **Bypassing the ignition switch by** jumping out the two smaller wires.

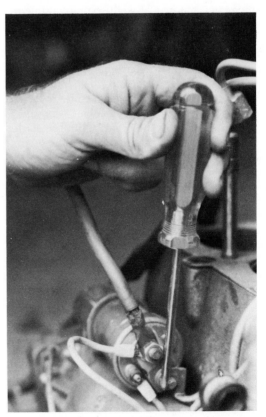

Figure 6-19C. **Bypassing the solenoid altogether by** jumping out the two main cable terminals.

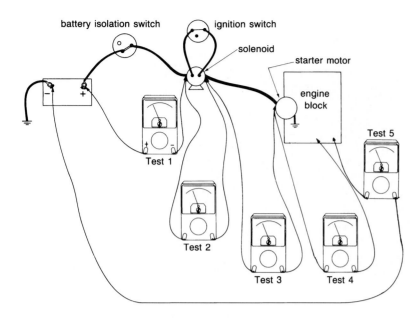

Figure 6-20. Testing for voltage drop in starter motor circuits. Test while the engine is being cranked (see the text).

the gear while you jump out the main solenoid points. This should get the engine going in an emergency, but may leave the pinion rattling up against the flywheel when the engine is running.

Voltage-drop tests. The above tests will quickly and crudely determine whether there is juice to the starter motor and whether or not it is functional. More insidious is the effect of poor connections and undersized cables—these create voltage drop in the circuits, rob the starter motor of power, and result in sluggish cranking or failure to crank at all, especially when the engine is cold. A potential result is a burnt-out starter motor.

A quick test for voltage drop can be made by cranking (or trying to crank) for a few seconds and then feeling all the connections and cables in the circuit: both battery terminals, both isolation switch terminals, solenoid terminals, and the battery ground attachment point on the engine block. If any of these are warm, there is resistance and voltage drop; the connection needs cleaning.

More accurate tests can be made with a voltmeter. Run the positive meter probe to the battery positive post (not the cable clamp), and the other to the solenoid positive terminal, and crank the engine (Figure 6-20, Test 1). Switch down the voltage scales on an analog meter. *Any voltage reading shows voltage drop in this part of the circuit.* Clean all connections and repeat the test.

Switch back up the voltage scales and perform the same test (cranking the engine) across the two main solenoid terminals (Test 2). Switch down the scales. Any voltage indicates resistance in the solenoid (see below for cleaning dirty and pitted points).

Repeat the same tests from the solenoid outlet terminal to the starter motor hot terminal (Test 3); from the starter motor case to the engine block (Test 4); and from the engine block back to the battery negative post (not the cable clamp—Test 5). The latter test frequently reveals poor ground connections.

Motor disassembly, inspection, and repair. Before removing a starter motor from an engine, isolate its hot lead, or better still, disconnect it from the battery. The starter will be held to the engine by two or three nuts or bolts. If it sticks in the flywheel housing, a smart tap will jar it loose (but check first to see that you didn't miss any of the mounting bolts!).

Inertia starters. Remove the metal band from the rear of the motor case. Undo the locknut from the terminal stud in the rear housing. Do not let the stud turn; if necessary, grip it carefully with Vise-Grips (Mole wrenches). Note the order of all washers. These insulate the stud, and it is essential that they go back the same way.

Undo the two (or four) retaining screws in the rear housing. If tight, grip with a pair of Vise-Grips from the side to break them loose. Lift off the rear housing with care; it will be attached to the motor case by two brush wires. Lift the springs off the relevant brushes and slide the brushes out of their holders to free the housing.

Preengaged starters. To check the solenoid points on a preengaged starter, remove the battery cable, the screw or nut retaining the hot strap to the motor, and all other nuts on the stud(s) for the ignition circuit wiring. Undo the two retaining screws at the very back of the solenoid. The end housing (plastic) will pull off to expose the *contacter* and the *points*. (Note: The spring in here that will probably fall out goes on the center of the contactor.) Check the points and contactor for pitting and burning and clean or replace as necessary. A badly damaged contactor can sometimes be reversed to provide a fresh contact surface. In a similar way, the main points can sometimes be reversed in the solenoid end housing, but take care when removing them because the Bakelite housing is brittle.

To remove the solenoid *coil* (electromagnet), undo the two screws at the flywheel end of the solenoid and turn the coil housing through 90 degrees. The coil will now pull straight off the piston. The piston and fork assembly generally can be removed only by separating the starter motor case from its front housing (see below).

If it is necessary to undo the pivot pin bolt on the solenoid fork, mark its head so that it can be put back in the same position. Sometimes, turning this pin adjusts how far the pinion is *thrown* when it engages the flywheel.

Remove the two starter-motor retaining screws from the rear housing and lift off the rear cover; it comes straight off and contains no brushes. This will expose the brushes and commutator.

All starters. The motor case, complete with field windings, can now be pulled off to expose the armature. If the end cover was held with four short screws as opposed to two long ones, there will be four more screws holding the motor case at the other end. Note that both end housings will probably have small lugs so that they can be refitted to the motor case in only one position.

Inspect the commutator and brushes for wear as previously detailed in the section on universal motors. Without a very sensitive ohmmeter, it will be impossible to distinguish between normal resistances and a short when doing the various winding and resistance tests. Any high resistances indicate an open circuit.

There will be four brushes instead of two, to handle the high loads. Some brush leads are soldered in place; other brushes are retained with screws. If replacing soldered brushes, cut the old leads, *leaving a tail long enough to solder to.* Tin this tail and the end of the new brush wire and solder them together (see Chapter 3 for more on soldering).

The brushes attached to the field windings are insulated; those to the end housing or motor case are uninsulated. When replacing the end housing of an inertia starter, hold the brushes back in their holders and jam them in this position by lodging the brush springs against the *side* of the brushes. Once the plate is on, slip the springs into position with a small screwdriver, and then put the metal band back on the motor case.

The pinion. Given the intermittent use of boat engines and the hostile marine environment, the pinion (or drive gear, often known as a *bendix*) can be especially troublesome. Pinions are particularly prone to rusting, especially where salt water in the bilges has contacted the flywheel and been thrown all around the flywheel housing.

Inertia starters are more prone to trouble than preengaged starters. Dirt or rust in the helical grooves on the armature shaft will prevent the pinion from moving freely in and out of engagement with the flywheel.

Figure 6-21.
Disassembling a preengaged starter.

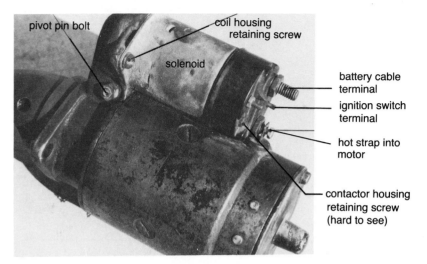

Figure 6-21A. **Identifying the main components.**

Figure 6-21B. **Removing stubborn end-plate bolts.**

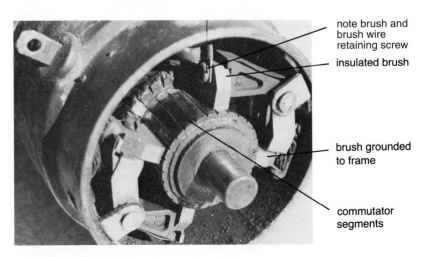

Figure 6-21C. **End housing removed.**

Figure 6-21D. Solenoid disassembly.

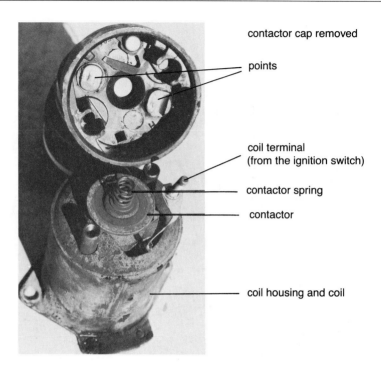

contactor cap removed

points

coil terminal
(from the ignition switch)

contactor spring

contactor

coil housing and coil

Figure 6-21E. Coil unit removed.

plunger

pivot pin bolt

contactor

coil

Figure 6-21F. Starter motor armature and commutator.

commutator

armature

AC Generators and Electric Motors (DC and AC)

Figure 6-21G. Preengaged starter motor disassembled.

case with field coils and brushes

end housing with bushing

solenoid coil with contactor and spring

solenoid contactor housing

solenoid plunger

pinion

clutch

solenoid plunger forks

armature and commutator

A small resistance spring in the unit keeps the pinion away from the flywheel when the engine is running. If this spring rusts and breaks, the gear will keep vibrating up against the flywheel with a distinctive rattle.

In automotive use, the shaft and helical grooves are not oiled or greased since the lubricant picks up dust from any clutch plates and causes the pinion to stick. In marine use, however, there are no clutch plates in the flywheel housing and the shaft should be greased lightly to prevent rusting.

The pinion assembly is usually retained by a spring clip (a snap ring or circlip) on the end of the armature shaft, occasionally by a *reverse-threaded* nut and cotter pin (split pin). An inertia starter has a powerful *buffer* spring that must be compressed before the clip can be removed. Special tools are available for this, but a couple of small C-clamps or two pairs of adroitly handled Vise-Grips usually will do the trick.

Figure 6-21H. Testing between bars on a commutator (R × 1 scale on an analog meter). Very low resistance (indistinguishable from a short with this meter).

Figure 6-21I. Testing from commutator bars to the armature shaft (R × 100 scale on an analog meter). Very high resistance—no continuity.

Electric Motors   225

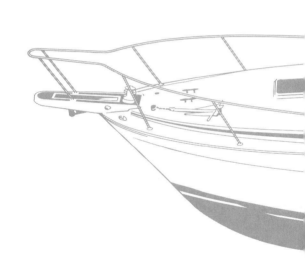

CHAPTER 7

——————— 12 VDC

- - - - - - - - 12 V ground
(return)

— — — — 120VAC

.... bonding
strap jumper

▨ ground

Figure 7-1. Trouble-free marine electronics depend to a large extent on proper installation. *(Jim Sollers)*

(1) satnav antenna
(2) loran antenna
(3) insulated backstay SSB antenna
(4) copper mesh ground plane
(5) radar
(6) VHF antenna
(7) wind indicator
(8) weatherfax
(9) radios
(10) antenna tuner
(11) copper foil ground plane
(12) depth sounder/speed/log transducers
(13) instruments
(14) battery isolation switch
(15) batteries

Marine Electronics

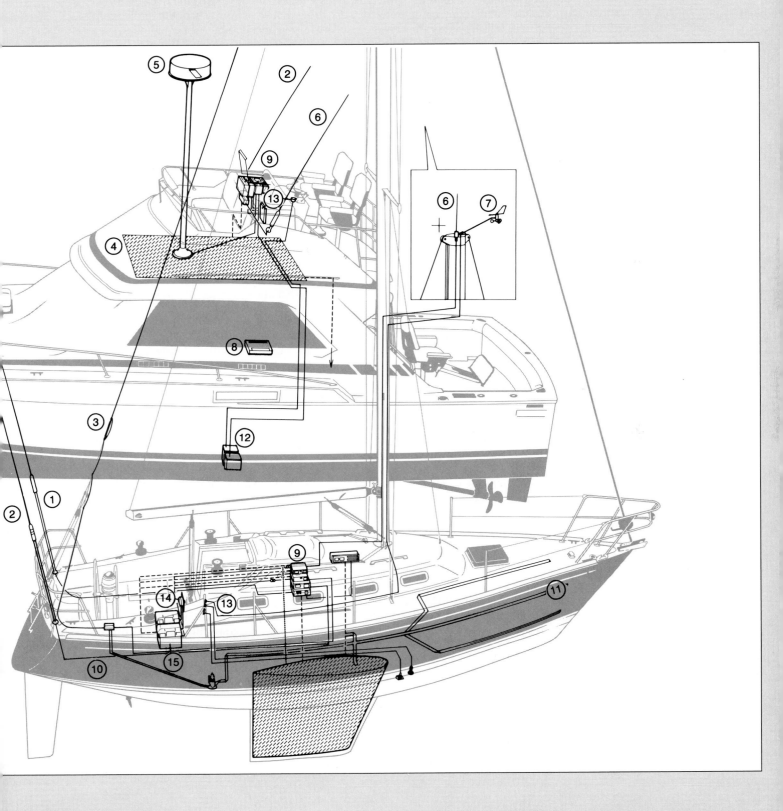

Troubleshooting Electronic Equipment

Troubleshooting printed circuit boards (pc-boards) and solid-state electronics is a highly skilled and specialized field far beyond the experience of the average layperson (myself included). As more and more computerized technology worms its way into every aspect of our lives, we find ourselves increasingly at the mercy of electronics manufacturers and repair technicians. Fortunately, however, most electronic equipment is highly reliable *as long as it is kept cool and dry*. Equipment that is placed in well-protected and ventilated areas, with unobstructed cooling vents, should give years of troublefree use. Difficulties that do arise are more often than not a result of problems that are *external* to the equipment. These we can often do something about, and this is the focus of this chapter.

Preliminary Troubleshooting

Unit will not come on line. As with all other electrical equipment, the primary suspect is always the power supply. Check all switches, breakers, and fuses. Check the manual to see if there are any internal fuses that might have blown. Some units—most notably radar—may have more than one fuse.

Check the voltage across the power leads as close to the equipment as possible. Check for voltage-drop *with the unit switched on*. Check radios in the *transmit* mode, since this draws the most current.

If voltage drop is present, check the voltage across the battery, once again with the equipment in its maximum-current-draw mode. If the voltage falls at the battery, the battery is the problem (Chapter 2). If the battery voltage holds up, the problem is in the circuit—check all connections, terminal blocks, fuse holders, and switches for voltage drop (Chapter 3).

An example: After seven years of flawless operation, our VHF radio started to act up. The problem turned out to be no more than a buildup of a thin layer of corrosive residue on the tip of one of the contacts in the in-line fuse holder. A voltage-drop test would have immediately revealed the problem.

Unit comes on line but gives no data (or obviously incorrect data). The device has power, and a voltage drop test has shown no unacceptable losses in the line. The problem lies elsewhere.

Operator error. The number one suspect is the *operator*, especially with more sophisticated devices such as lorans, satnavs, and GPSs. Failure to study owner's manuals, and memory lapses from infrequent use, contribute to such problems. But perhaps the most difficult errors to spot are those that arise from a firm but faulty memory of how to operate a piece of equipment, since we are convinced we are doing things right!

Difficulties also arise from entering incorrect data. For example, common errors include confusion between local time, daylight saving time, and GMT; entering latitudes as south instead of north; entering longitudes as east instead of west; and punching in the wrong coordinates on waypoints.

Voltage problems. A number of problems are associated with low- or high-voltage conditions. Engine cranking will frequently pull system voltage levels below a critical minimum needed to maintain internal memories, which become corrupted and must be reset and reprogrammed. Some large electric winches may affect memory-based equipment the same way. *The solution is to connect electronic equipment to a separate battery* (which can be the house battery), *which is not subjected to these loads*, or to turn off the electronics during periods of high battery demand.

Voltage spikes and surges can have a similar, or more damaging, effect. When a heavy electric motor, such as a starter motor or an anchor windlass, is turned off, the collapsing magnetic field in the motor windings causes a sudden voltage rise. In normal circumstances the boat's batteries act as a giant filter to absorb such transient voltages, but not always. The solution is once again to connect electronic equipment to a separate battery.

Whatever the battery, it should be noted that while most 12-volt electronic equipment will digest a wide range of input voltages—from 10 to as much as 40 volts—some equipment (notably depth sounders) cannot tolerate voltages even as high as 16 volts. To be on the safe side, *whenever equalizing batteries at high voltage levels be sure to isolate electronic circuits*. (Halogen lightbulbs are also particularly sensitive to overvoltage, while the operating life of any incandescent lightbulb will be dramatically reduced by elevated voltages.)

Much electronic gear depends on internal memories powered by small Nicad (nickel cadmium) batteries that maintain the equipment in a user-ready state when shut off. These batteries have a life expectancy of from 2 to 3 years on up (we have one still functioning after 7 years). As they begin to die memory lapses occur, especially when units are switched off for longer periods of time. Normally the equipment will still be

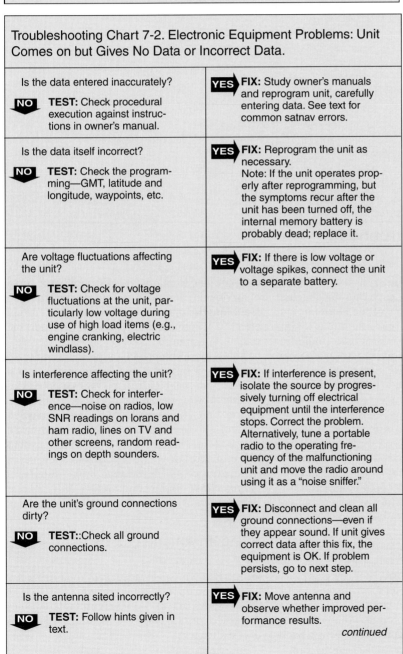

Troubleshooting Chart 7-1
Electronic Equipment Problems: Unit Will Not Come on Line.
Symptom: No lights, no beeps, etc.

Is there a problem with the voltage supply? **NO** **TEST:** Check the voltage at the equipment when it is turned on.	**YES** **FIX:** If no volts or low volts, check the battery, switches, fuses, connections, etc., for voltage drop as outlined in Chapter 3.
Are there blown fuses or tripped circuit breakers within the unit? **NO**	**YES** **FIX:** Replace or reset as necessary.

If unit still will not come on line, call a specialist.

Troubleshooting Chart 7-2. Electronic Equipment Problems: Unit Comes on but Gives No Data or Incorrect Data.

Is the data entered inaccurately? **NO** **TEST:** Check procedural execution against instructions in owner's manual.	**YES** **FIX:** Study owner's manuals and reprogram unit, carefully entering data. See text for common satnav errors.
Is the data itself incorrect? **NO** **TEST:** Check the programming—GMT, latitude and longitude, waypoints, etc.	**YES** **FIX:** Reprogram the unit as necessary. Note: If the unit operates properly after reprogramming, but the symptoms recur after the unit has been turned off, the internal memory battery is probably dead; replace it.
Are voltage fluctuations affecting the unit? **NO** **TEST:** Check for voltage fluctuations at the unit, particularly low voltage during use of high load items (e.g., engine cranking, electric windlass).	**YES** **FIX:** If there is low voltage or voltage spikes, connect the unit to a separate battery.
Is interference affecting the unit? **NO** **TEST:** Check for interference—noise on radios, low SNR readings on lorans and ham radio, lines on TV and other screens, random readings on depth sounders.	**YES** **FIX:** If interference is present, isolate the source by progressively turning off electrical equipment until the interference stops. Correct the problem. Alternatively, tune a portable radio to the operating frequency of the malfunctioning unit and move the radio around using it as a "noise sniffer."
Are the unit's ground connections dirty? **NO** **TEST::**Check all ground connections.	**YES** **FIX:** Disconnect and clean all ground connections—even if they appear sound. If unit gives correct data after this fix, the equipment is OK. If problem persists, go to next step.
Is the antenna sited incorrectly? **NO** **TEST:** Follow hints given in text.	**YES** **FIX:** Move antenna and observe whether improved performance results. *continued*

Troubleshooting Chart 7-2, *continued*

Is the coaxial cable or its connectors faulty?	
TEST: Remove the coax connection from the back of the equipment and inspect closely for corrosion; repeat for any other in-line connectors. Just behind the coax connection to the equipment (or any other in-line connectors) carefully peel back a small piece of the outer coax insulation and inspect the braid for tarnishing and corrosion. If both ends of the coaxial cable can be disconnected, test with an ohmmeter (R x 100 scale) from the center pin of one connector to its case. Any reading less than infinity indicates an internal short (probably in one of the connectors). Now short the center pin on the connector to its case and test between the pin and the case on the other connector (R x 1 scale). Any reading of more than 2 or 3 ohms indicates excessive resistance.	**FIX:** Clean connections. Replace shorted or defective cable and connectors. If the braid is corroded, replace the coax and its connection. If the braid is clean and shiny, replace the insulation and seal with 3M 5200 or some other sealant.

usable, but only by reprogramming at every use. If dead batteries are left in place, they may begin to weep and corrode expensive circuit boards. They may do this even before giving signs of failure. To be on the safe side memory batteries should be checked every couple of years for any signs of external corrosion and replaced immediately if such signs are present.

Then there are a host of problems associated with *antennas, ground planes,* and *electrical interference (noise)*—the subjects of the next three sections.

Antennas and Grounds

Antennas come in a bewildering array of shapes and sizes. To be effective, each must be matched to the operating frequency of the equipment to which it is attached. This is a simple matter where the equipment operates on a single frequency (loran, satnav, and GPS) or on a narrow band of frequencies (VHF radio) but becomes quite complex where a wide band of frequencies is covered (high-frequency radio, specifically ham bands and SSB).

Knowledgeable radio operators frequently make their own antennas, tuning the antenna length to the specific frequency being used. Dipole antennas (in which a *transmission line* from the radio feeds two equal-length antenna arms) are particularly useful since there are not the same grounding problems (see below) as with the typical *vertical* antenna (either an *untuned whip* antenna or an *insulated backstay*). There are plenty of books that discuss antenna construction in great detail. For the rest of us, except in special circumstances, it is best to follow the equipment manufacturer's recommendations concerning an antenna, which normally results in buying a whip antenna or using a backstay. For high-frequency transmissions this is then coupled to an *antenna tuner* (either manual or automatic) that electronically manipulates the fixed-length antenna to produce the correct effective length for the frequency on which the radio is transmitting.

Since most antennas look pretty much alike externally, it is hard to judge one brand against another. Internal construction varies markedly in quality, however. Such features as all-soldered connections, high-quality brass sleeves, rugged mounting brackets, etc., serve to differentiate antennas for the long haul from antennas that will probably have to be replaced in a few years. *Always buy a quality antenna from a reputable manufacturer.* Radio equipment is only as good as the antenna to which it is fitted (Figure 7-2).

Siting an Antenna

Gain. The principal yardstick for measuring relative antenna performance is *gain,* expressed in decibels, or "dB." A 3-dB-gain antenna doubles the power of outgoing and incoming signals, 6 dB quadruples it, 9 dB magnifies it eight times.

Increased performance (decibel rating) is

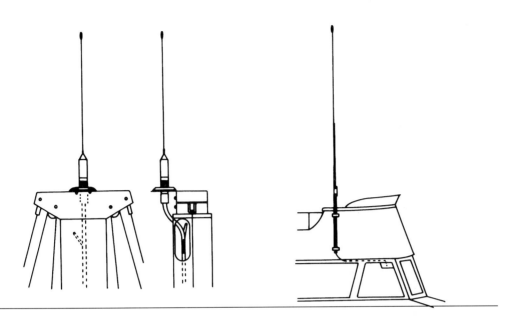

Figure 7-2. Correct antenna mount and placement. *(Ocean Navigator)*

achieved by concentrating the signal into a narrower beam width. A 0-dB antenna radiates uniformly in all directions, including straight up. A 3-dB antenna concentrates horizontal radiation at the expense of the vertical, but still radiates in a 360-degree arc around the antenna. This horizontal concentration is carried even further in 6-dB and 9-dB antennas (Figure 7-3A).

Signal concentration can be taken only so far. If a boat is rolling heavily, a highly concentrated signal may well undershoot or overshoot another station: The signal will tend to fade in and out. The higher the gain of an antenna, the more sensitive it is to heeling—at a 40-degree angle of heel the useful signal strength of a 9-dB antenna will be no more than that of a 0-dB antenna. For this reason, and to avoid overly long antennas, sailboats rarely use antennas with a higher gain than 6 dB, and 3 dB is the norm (Figure 7-3B).

With VHF radios, radio transmission is *line of sight*, making antenna height a more important factor than gain in determining antenna performance. Since high-gain antennas are generally longer and more expensive than low-gain antennas, a small, 3-dB masthead antenna often will

outperform a deck-level, 14-foot, 6-dB-gain antenna—and at considerable savings (Table 7-1). Of course if the mast ever goes over the side, the antenna goes with it.

High-frequency radio. The height of an antenna has a different effect with SSB and ham radios. If an untuned vertical antenna is used, which is then coupled to an antenna tuner, the antenna tuner must be grounded (see below). When transmitting, the cables from the antenna tuner to the antenna and to the ground become parts of the radiating system, and in doing so dissipate part of the signal strength into the boat, the water, and any wiring that is close by. To reduce these losses, these conductors should be as short and direct as possible.

Elevating an antenna simply produces a longer ground connection with greater losses. It is preferable to mount the antenna as close as possible to the ground, even if this puts it low on the boat (for example, on the transom of a powerboat, with the antenna tuner in a locker immediately below, and the ground plates on the outside of the hull immediately below this). For *fiberglass*

Table 7-1. VHF Antenna Range in Nautical Miles

Receiver Antenna Height (feet)	Transmitter Antenna Height (feet)							
	8	12	24	40	60	120	200	400
8	8	9	11	13	15	19	23	32
12	9	10	12	14	16	20	24	33
24	11	12	14	16	18	22	26	35
40	13	14	16	18	20	24	28	37
60	15	16	18	20	22	26	30	39

Antennas and Grounds   231

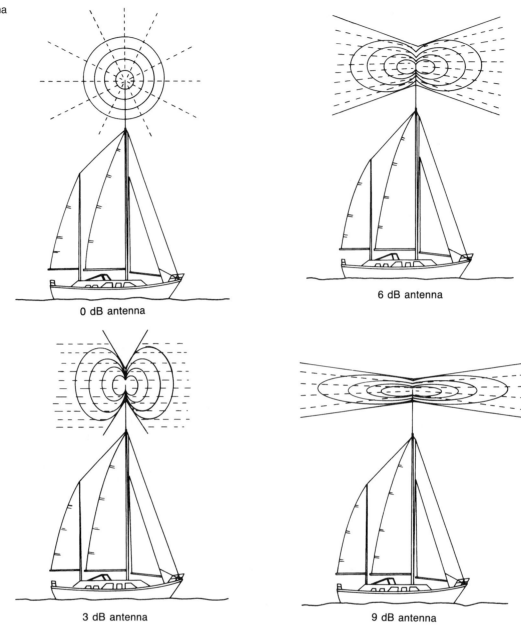

Figure 7-3A. VHF antenna gain and signal radiation patterns—the higher the antenna gain, the more concentrated and far-reaching the signal.

0 dB antenna

6 dB antenna

3 dB antenna

9 dB antenna

Figure 7-3B. Antenna gain versus boat stability. A very-high-gain antenna is not suited for a small boat; the narrow signal pattern can overshoot or undershoot distant stations when the boat rolls. (*NMEA*)

antenna

sailboats with insulated backstays, the lower backstay insulator can be omitted (the fiberglass hull provides sufficient insulation at high frequencies), and the antenna tuner can be wired directly to one of the chainplate bolts, with a short connection from the tuner to ground. A jumper cable will be needed from the stay to the chainplate to bypass any resistive connections between the wire terminal and the chainplate.

Antenna Installation

The signals collected by antennas are measured in *millionths* of a volt. Only antennas sited correctly, with perfect electrical connections, will work properly. Poor performance on newly installed equipment is nearly always a result of inadequate antenna or ground installations, particularly with SSB, ham radios, and lorans. Deteriorating performance on older units is likely to result from corrosion in coax cables and connectors.

Coax cable. Coaxial cable consists of an inner core of copper wire surrounded by a substantial insulating sleeve (the *dielectric*), which is further enclosed in metal braid and topped with another insulating sheath (Figure 7-4). The signal received by an antenna is trapped between the wire core and the braid and conducted to the receiver. The braid also excludes unwanted signals radiating from other sources, such as rigging, wiring circuits in the boat, etc.

Coax cable comes in different resistance ratings, sizes, and qualities.

Resistance. Almost all marine antennas require 50-ohm coax, but TV antennas use 75-ohm coax. *TV antenna cable, regardless of its quality, is not suitable for marine antennas.*

Size. The most commonly found coax cables in marine use, ranging in size from the smallest to the largest, are called *RG-58, RG-8X (RG-8*

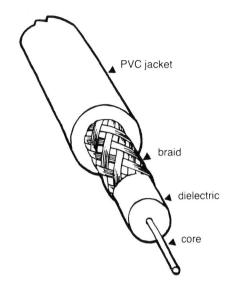

Figure 7-4. Coaxial cable construction. Coaxial cable consists of an inner core of copper wire surrounded by a substantial insulating sleeve (the dielectric), which is enclosed in a metal braid, and topped with another insulating sheath.

mini, or *RG-8M*), and *RG-8* (Table 7-2; the RG stands for *Registered Government* specifications; the number is sometimes followed by a U, meaning *Universal Specification*, and this in turn may be followed by a letter, which refers to the set of specifications to which the cable conforms, with more recent specifications having a designation further into the alphabet). The larger the cable, the lower the losses in transmitting and receiving a signal, but since these losses are also related to the frequency of the signal, it is not possible to give absolute figures (losses are specified as so many *decibels per 100 feet* at a particular *frequency*—the higher the frequency, the higher the aggregate loss).

The large RG-8 costs more than other cables, is more obtrusive, and is stiff and awkward to run. As a result, RG-8X (RG8-mini or RG8-M) cable is used for most marine applications. When used with equipment that operates at lower frequencies (up to 100 MHz) such cable is good for runs up to 100 feet; for higher-frequency equipment, the maximum allowable run should be reduced, and if it needs to be exceeded, the lower-loss RG-8

Table 7-2. Typical Coaxial Cable Specifications

Wire Type	Insulation	Braid Coverage	Impedance (Ohms)	Attenuation Per 100 Ft.		
				at 50 mHZ	100 mHZ	1000 mHZ
RG-58	PVC*	96%	50	3.3 dB	4.9 dB	21.5 dB
RG-8X	PVC	96%	50	2.5 dB	3.7 dB	13.5 dB
RG-8	PVC	96%	52	1.3 dB	2.2 dB	8.9 dB

(These will vary somewhat from manufacturer to manufacturer. These are for Ancor cable—high-quality, fully-tuned, cable.)

* noncontaminating insulation

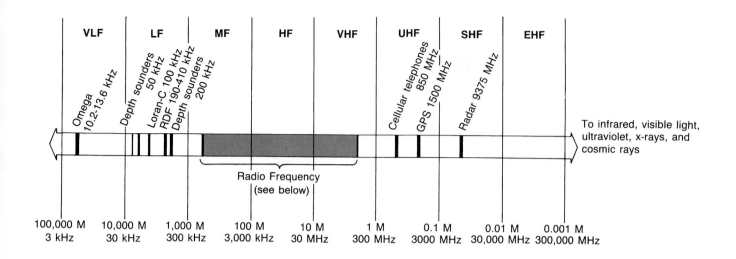

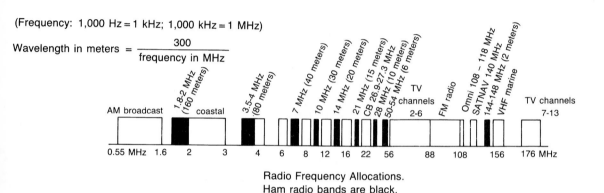

Radio Frequency Allocations.
Ham radio bands are black.

Figure 7-5. The frequency spectrum, including the radio frequencies commonly used by boats.

cable should be substituted (for example, if a VHF radio—which operates at around 160 MHz [Figure 7-5]—is to be installed, coupled to a masthead antenna that requires a cable run of much more than 50 feet, to maximize signal strength RG-8 cable should be used).

Quality. Insulation is important. Many coax cables have a *foam-core* dielectric, which reduces power losses in the line compared to a solid polyethylene dialectic. However, some foam is open cell and acts as a wick, allowing any moisture that finds its way through improperly sealed connections to corrode the core conductor and the braid, whereas other foam is closed cell and does not suffer from a wicking problem. In marine applications, use only cable with a *closed-cell* foam or *solid polyethylene* dielectric.

The external insulation on cables varies tremendously in its thickness, quality, and resistance to ultraviolet (UV). Better-quality cables are *noncontaminating*, a designation meaning that when it is subjected to UV, the outer insulation does not shrink to the point at which the braid below *prints through*. Given a choice, non-contaminating cable is the best buy, although some other cables (such as those manufactured by Ancor) do have UV-resistant insulation even though it does not meet the specific provisions of the noncontaminating standard.

The braid is equally important. Some coax uses aluminum braid—out of the question for marine use. *It must be copper*, preferably *tinned* copper (with the inner core also tinned). There are further differences in the *tightness of the weave*. Cheap coax has loosely woven braid, which is electrically "leaky," leading to signal loss, distortion, and interference. Braid is described by a percentage figure: 98% is the best.

To summarize: Coax for marine use should be tinned (both the braid and the core), with at least a 96% braid and if possible a noncontaminating jacket. RG-8X will serve for most purposes, except where long cable runs are needed for VHF's and equipment with higher operating frequencies, in which case RG-8 should be used. At the top of the line is RG-213, the same size as RG-8 but with a completely waterproof and ultraviolet-resistant insulation. Twice the quality but twice the price and a little hard to work with—even professionals have to struggle with connectors on RG-213—and not worth fooling with except on some special radar systems.

(Note: The cable supplied with some antennas and many depth sounders *cannot be cut or shortened*, read the instructions carefully before modifying prewired equipment.)

Coax connections. Faulty antenna connections rank right up there with power supply deficiencies and operator error as a principal cause of electronic malfunctions. Anytime equipment performance is unsatisfactory, check all connections, particularly those exposed to the weather.

Although noncontaminating cable is waterproof, it can still wick up considerable amounts of water through its ends, just from humidity in the air—never mind rainwater and salt spray. The water is sucked along the copper braid by capillary action, corroding the braid and ruining line efficiency (this is where tinned wire once again more than pays for itself in the long run). Coax connections must be made with proper connectors and then sealed to keep out all moisture. The connectors themselves must be high quality—the regular connectors found in Radio Shack (USA) do not stand up to the marine environment; better choices would be their "Premium" fittings, or those manufactured by Amphenol (available through one or two marine catalogs and various marine electronics suppliers).

Regardless of the terminal, all connections should be made bearing the following points in mind (Figures 7-6A and 6B):

- The connector must match the cable. The standard terminal is a PL-259, which fits RG-8 and RG-213U cable. This mates with an SO-239 socket. RG-8X (RG-8M) uses a UG-176U adapter to neck the PL-259 down to cable size, while RG-58 uses a UG-175U adapter. Two cables are connected by screwing their respective PL-259s into a *barrel connector*, sometimes numbered PL-258. More esoteric types of connectors are available, such as BNC connectors, but these rarely find an application on board. Any good electronics store should have all these connectors.
- *Coax connectors should always be soldered.* Because of installation errors with soldered connections, many manufacturers now include pressure-crimped terminals with their equipment. These are not recommended for marine use. Sooner or later (generally sooner) corrosion will develop in the terminal, creating resistance and interfering with the signal. What is more, to install them properly special tools are required.

- Installation procedures are illustrated in Figure 7-6. If a waterproof jacket is to be fitted (available quite cheaply from Radio Shack and other electronics stores), slide this up the cable before doing anything else. Before fitting a connector, tin the core cable and the braid (if not already tinned), and make absolutely certain that no stray wires from the braid can short the core cable. (This would make the antenna inoperative and might do expensive damage to the equipment.) The braid must make a clean fit inside the connector, all the way around. When soldering the braid, avoid excessive heat, which may melt the dielectric. If you are inexperienced in soldering, get help.
- Unless a custom-made waterproof boot has been fitted, coat the connector with a waterproof sealant or with an electrician's putty, such as Coax Seal; then seal the whole joint with heat-shrink or self-amalgamating tape. (Allow the sealant, if used, to partially set before adding the tape.) Install drip loops (Figure 7-6C) even on well-insulated connections. When checking a connector, look for corrosion around the center pin and tarnish on the braid.

Testing coax and connections. *Never short the center pin and connector housing on a cable connected to an antenna or electronic equipment. Expensive damage may result.*

If the coax can be disconnected at both ends, test with an ohmmeter ($R \times 100$ scale on an analog meter) from the case of one of the connectors to its center pin. Anything less than infinite resistance shows a short (probably in the connector installation, or at a sharp bend). Now clip a jumper wire between the pin and the case on one connector and test at the other end ($R \times 1$ scale on an analog meter). Resistance should be close to 0 (depending on the length of the cable). Higher readings show unwanted resistance, such as corroded wire or poor connections.

Emergency VHF antenna. A serviceable temporary antenna can be made from any 19-inch (480-mm) length of wire (a coat hanger, for example) stuck in the antenna socket in the back of a radio. The range will be limited because of the antenna's minimal height above sea level. Care must be taken not to short this antenna to the outside of the terminal socket, as this might damage the radio. The radio should be used only on low power and as little as possible since lengthy transmissions could eventually do damage.

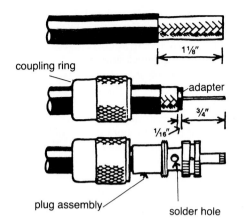

Figure 7-6A. Method of installing coax connectors without adapters (RG-8, RG-213U). (**1**) Cut the end of the cable even. Remove the vinyl jacket 1 ⅛ inches—do not nick the braid. Make sure the braid is evenly distributed. (**2**) Bare ¾ inch of center conductor—do not nick the conductor. Trim the braided shield ¹⁄₁₆ inch back from the end of the dielectric and tin the braid. Slide the coupling ring onto the cable. (**3**) Screw the plug assembly onto the cable. Solder the plug assembly to the braid through the solder holes. Solder the conductor to the contact sleeve. Make sure no loose strands of braid can short out the core.

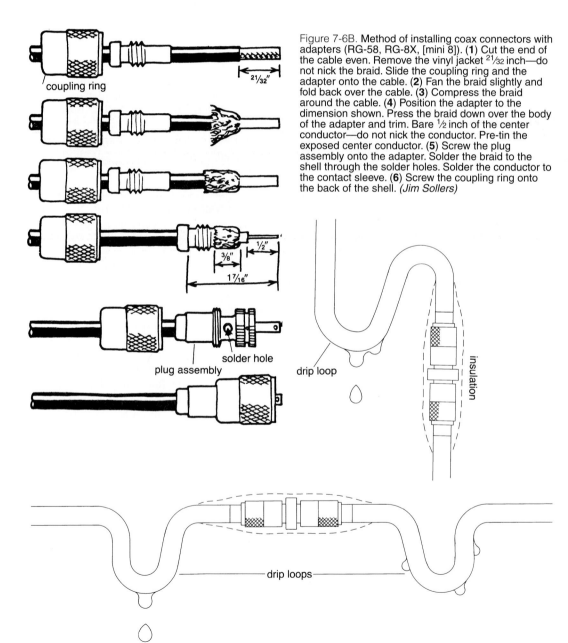

Figure 7-6B. Method of installing coax connectors with adapters (RG-58, RG-8X, [mini 8]). (**1**) Cut the end of the cable even. Remove the vinyl jacket ²¹⁄₃₂ inch—do not nick the braid. Slide the coupling ring and the adapter onto the cable. (**2**) Fan the braid slightly and fold back over the cable. (**3**) Compress the braid around the cable. (**4**) Position the adapter to the dimension shown. Press the braid down over the body of the adapter and trim. Bare ½ inch of the center conductor—do not nick the conductor. Pre-tin the exposed center conductor. (**5**) Screw the plug assembly onto the adapter. Solder the braid to the shell through the solder holes. Solder the conductor to the contact sleeve. (**6**) Screw the coupling ring onto the back of the shell. *(Jim Sollers)*

Figure 7-6C. Install drip loops—even on well-insulated connections. *(Jim Sollers)*

236　　Marine Electronics

Grounds

Although not critical with VHFs and satnavs, a good ground is essential for effective ham and SSB transmissions (particularly when using a vertical antenna), and for loran performance. On these types of equipment, the ground system complements the antenna, and one will not function with full efficiency without the other. This relationship, known as a *counterpoise*, is somewhat analogous to a diver (the radio signal) on a springboard (the ground). A better spring makes for a better dive; a better ground makes for a better signal.

Metal boats have a wonderful ground in the hull, but what constitutes a good ground in wood and fiberglass boats is debatable. Experts call for anywhere from 9 to 100 square feet of flat metal surface (copper mesh, metal foil tape, aluminum plate, etc.). For high-frequency radio transmission, the Coast Guard requires an underwater ground that is at least the equivalent of 12 square feet of copper. Anything made of metal that is flat and *fractions of an inch* (this is important—the farther the distance, the less the effect) from the water has proven effective.

A tremendous ground can be bonded directly into the hull or placed under internal ballast of boats under construction. Any boat with a solid ballast casting—internal or external—can use this as a ground either by tapping directly into the casting or by connecting to a keel bolt. On bonded boats a ground is sometimes established by running copper foil tape—available in 3- and 6-inch (8- and 15-cm) rolls from good marine electronics stores—in parallel with the bonding wires and connecting this to all through-hulls, the engine, etc.

On unbonded boats, where a common ground strip may invite the risk of galvanic corrosion, isolating capacitors can be placed in the ground system between the ground strap and underwater hardware. The capacitors will block stray DC currents but allow radio frequency ground currents to flow. Consult a knowledgeable electronics technician about details of the installation.

Ground areas can be distributed throughout the boat, and need not be in actual contact with the seawater. Grounds that are spread out in different locations should be tied together with copper foil tape, with joints that are mechanically sound and *soldered*.

Always choose flat tape over round cables in a ground system. The tape itself should be folded rather than rolled around corners (Figure 7-7). Make all equipment connections to ground with the same tape. To connect to a single terminal on the back of a piece of equipment, fold the tape into an arrowhead and drill it to fit over the terminal. Ground *all* pieces of radio equipment in this fashion: receivers, transmitters, antenna tuners, radar, etc.

For boats with an inadequate ground plane,

Figure 7-7. Radio grounds. Any boat with a solid ballast casting—internal or external—can use this as a ground by connecting to a keel bolt as shown here, or by tapping directly into the casting. Boats with an inadequate ground plane can use a sintered bronze ground plate—always get the largest practical size. You can't have too much ground plane.

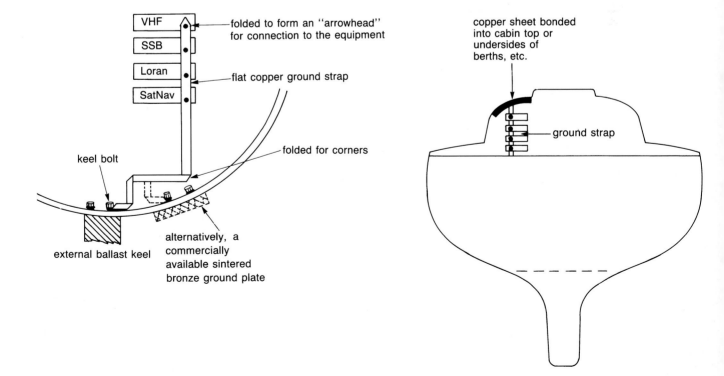

sintered bronze ground plates are available. These are made of a porous bronze that allows seawater to permeate the whole plate, increasing its actual surface area many times over its external dimensions. A relatively small plate (12 by 3 inches, or 300 by 75 mm) theoretically has a total surface area of several square feet. There is some debate as to the efficacy of these plates in real use, and some question as to their ability to dissipate a lightning strike (Chapter 4), so it is always best to get the largest practical size. It is not possible to have too much ground plane.

Radio Interference

The abundance of radio-based equipment on modern pleasure boats and the plethora of circuits in close proximity to one another (antenna cables, power cables, engine-charging circuits, AC circuits, etc.) make interference problems (electrical *noise*) increasingly commonplace.

Interference is caused by unwanted radio frequency energy, much of it generated on board, although a small proportion can be traced to external origins. This energy is picked up by antenna systems and wiring circuits and fed to receivers, which may not be able to distinguish between noise and signal if they share similar frequencies. Hissing, buzzing, crackling, popping, and other undesirable noises on radios will compete with the true signal, perhaps making it unintelligible. Depth sounders and radio direction finders (RDF) may give false readings, and lines and ripples are likely on TV screens. The SNR (signal-to-noise ratio) meter on a loran will show a loss of signal when equipment generates interference on its wavelength.

Interference is transmitted principally by conduction and radiation. Conducted interference flows from its source through circuits directly to receivers; radiated interference is picked up by wiring circuits acting as antennas and then conducted to receivers. Wires conducting interference can themselves act as antennas, reradiating the signal and creating a complex of radiated and conducted signals (Figure 7-8).

Sources of Interference

The principal sources of onboard interference are anything that abruptly varies or switches a current, including:

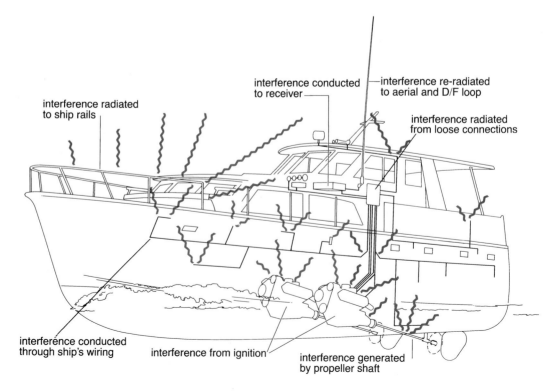

Figure 7-8. **Interference is caused by unwanted radio frequencies; receivers cannot distinguish between noise and signal if they share a similar frequency.** *(Jim Sollers)*

interference radiated to ship rails

interference conducted to receiver

interference re-radiated to aerial and D/F loop

interference radiated from loose connections

interference conducted through ship's wiring

interference from ignition

interference generated by propeller shaft

- Alternators
- Voltage regulators
- Ignition systems on gasoline engines
- Electric tachometers
- Static electricity from rotating propeller shafts
- Electric motors, especially those with commutators and brushes (DC motors used in pumps, electric winches, etc.)
- Sparks at switch contacts
- AC voltage peaks superimposed on DC circuits (mostly through alternators, battery chargers, and fluorescent lights)
- Televisions, microcomputers, radar inverters, and modulators

Anything that generates sparks or voltage pulses—even loose rigging—can create interference. The more power generated or consumed by any device, the more likely it will be to create noise.

Tracking Down Interference

To track down interference in a radio or some other electronic gear, leave it switched on (or tune a hand-held RDF to the interference frequency) and shut off all the boat's circuits one at a time: fluorescent lights, the engine, AC circuits, etc. If the interference ceases at any point, the offending circuit has been pinpointed. If it continues when all circuits are shut down, the interference is probably coming from adjacent boats or the shoreside. But note: Radio interference, particularly as it affects low-, medium-, and high-frequency units such as loran, SSB, and ham radio, may be generated by sources about which we can do nothing, including sunspots, solar flares, the aurora borealis, and distant thunderstorms.

A cheap transistor radio tuned to the AM band can become an effective noise sniffer. Tune it between stations, so that it picks up only interference, and move around the boat close to suspect items. The radio will crackle and hiss louder where interference is generated.

Engines have a number of potential noise-makers (especially gasoline engines). When tracking down a culprit, start with the alternator. If it has an external field lead, disconnect this to disable the alternator; otherwise remove its belt. Crank the engine. If the interference has ceased, it is in the charging circuit. If it persists, it is either in the ignition circuit (gasoline engines) or the result of static electricity generated by the rotating propeller shaft. The latter generally produces intermittent *crackles* as the static dis-

charges, rather than the rhythmic interference keyed to engine rpm associated with alternators and ignition circuits.

Propeller-shaft interference can be eliminated by fitting a bronze brush to the propeller shaft and wiring it to ground or to the boat's bonding system (these brushes are available in the USA from Professional Mariner, Ventura, CA). This is a good practice in any case to reduce the risk of galvanic corrosion. Flexible couplings should be bridged with a jumper wire (refer back to Figure 4-16).

Charging circuits. If disabling the alternator indicated that the problem is in the charging circuit, and if the alternator has an external regulator, to determine whether it is the alternator or its voltage regulator that is at fault disconnect the field wire *from the regulator* and run the field wire *temporarily* to the battery *positive* (P-type alternator—see Chapter 2) or to a good *ground* (N-type alternator) and restart the engine. This will drive the alternator to full output. If the noise reoccurs, the alternator is at fault; if it does not, the regulator is the problem (in either case, see below for fixes).

Preventing (Suppressing) Interference

Since receivers cannot distinguish between a useful signal and noise at the same frequency, interference needs to be suppressed at its source rather than in the receiver. Suppression measures fall into three broad categories: shielding, filtering, and bonding.

Shielding. Any wire carrying a fluctuating current (AC or DC) will radiate interference. If the wire forms a loop, the signal will be magnified. But if the wire is encased in metal braid (*shielded*), the unwanted signals will be trapped inside (just as with coax cable, which in fact makes excellent shielded cable in certain applications). Shorting the braid to ground should eliminate the interference (Figure 7-9), but the braid itself may become an antenna, receiving and radiating signals. Thus it must be grounded to a boat's bonding system *at regular points along its length*. Where shielded cables leave and enter equipment, the braid must make a good electrical contact with the equipment case at both ends to avoid leaks. If individual wires need shielding, it is sometimes possible to slide a piece of soft copper tubing over the wire. The copper tube is then grounded. (Don Kavenagh of *Ocean Navigator* magazine points out that "shielding a wire is like taking aspirin for a brain

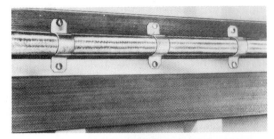

Figure 7-9. Shielded cable—note the cable retaining clamps are grounded to a copper strap, which is itself connected to the boat's ground. *(Lucas Marine)*

Figure 7-10A. Shielded alternator.

Figures 7-10B and 7-10C. Screening or shielding techniques. Since voltage regulators are a major contributor to interference, some are shielded with a metal box. The large threaded fitting (**A**) is where a screened cable screws onto the box. This cable carries all the wiring to the alternator. Any wiring coming into the box acts as an antenna both inside and outside the box, unless effectively filtered where it enters the box. The round protrusions (**B**) are built-in filters for all unscreened incoming wires, such as the battery positive wire. The nut (**C**) is the grounding connection for the screening box itself.

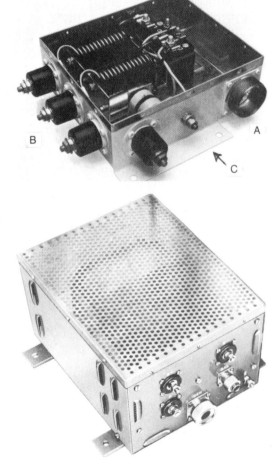

tumor." The answer is to treat the problem at its source, rather than deal with the symptoms.)

Since alternators and voltage regulators are major contributors to interference, a few expensive alternator installations are shielded (Figures 7-10A, B, and C). The alternator's metal case grounds out radiated noise produced within; the various leads to and from the regulator are run through a shielded cable; and the regulator itself is placed in a metal box. A special ferrule ensures adequate grounding where the braided cable enters the alternator and regulator housings. The cable run is kept as short as possible (no loops!) and grounded at points along its length if necessary. The engine, alternator, regulator box, and screened wiring harness are all grounded. These measures should, however, rarely be needed—most alternator noise can be dealt with as outlined below.

Filtering. Shielding will take care of radiated noise, but conducted noise is another matter. For this, special *filters* are needed, which are a combination of coils *(inductors)* and capacitors.

Radio frequency energy is alternating current; it forms waves of different lengths. An inductor provides a high-resistance path to alternating current (the higher the frequency, the more the resistance) but offers very little resistance to direct current, depending on the size and length of the wire used to wind the coil. An inductor installed in series in a DC line will tend to block radio frequency energy while passing direct current.

A capacitor, on the other hand, conducts alternating current but blocks direct current. The higher the frequency, the lower the resistance of the capacitor to AC currents. So if we combine an inductor with a capacitor we can "hold up" radio frequencies with the inductor and then short them safely to ground with the capacitor without causing a short in the DC circuit. This is the principle behind filters. Since the wiring of the inductor will be carrying the full current of the circuit that is being filtered, it must clearly be rated to carry the load (which may be more than 100 amps in some alternator installations).

Filters are fitted in hot (positive) leads as close to offending equipment as possible to reduce the potential area for conducting and radiating unwanted frequencies (Figures 7-11A and B). The filters are then connected to a ground. (In severe cases of interference, filters are sometimes added to both hot and ground cables.)

Bonding. Note that both shielding and filtering take unwanted frequencies and *short them to ground.* Bonding all equipment cases and metal objects to a common ground helps reduce interference by holding everything at the same

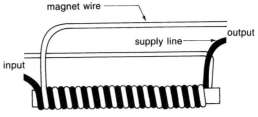

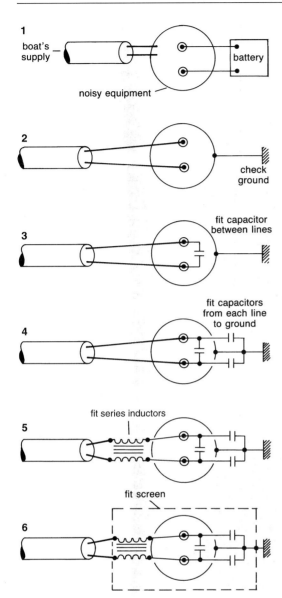

Figure 7-11B. Making an inductor. (1) Use insulated magnet wire (copper) obtainable at radio supply stores. The size depends on the current drawn by the appliance as indicated on the table below. (2) Take a length of $^3/_8$-inch ferrite rod (used for portable radio antennas, also obtainable at radio supply stores) as indicated below. The rod can be cut to length by filing a groove in it and breaking it over a sharp edge. (3) Make 20 turns around the rod with the equipment supply line and magnet wire as shown in the illustration. (4) Slip a piece of PVC tubing over the inductor and dip it in varnish to seal it. (5) Connect both ends of the magnet wire to ground.

Equipment current rating (amps)	Wire size (AWG)	Ferrite rod length (inches)	(mm)
1	23	1.5	40
2	20	2	50
5	17	3	75
10	14	4	100
15	12	5	130
20	11	6	150
25	10	6	150

Specific measures for noise suppression.

Effective RFI suppression involves good design and good discipline in the manufacture and installation of equipment, especially charging equipment. A fully screened, isolated-ground marine alternator properly fitted as original equipment will be far more effective in reducing electrical noise than any number of filters and other devices tacked onto the system at a later date. Even without such screening, using properly sized cables, including a ground cable from the alternator to the common ground point (regardless of whether or not the alternator is grounded through its mount bracket), with sound connections, will go a long way toward eliminating problems. Motto: Do it right in the first place. It may seem to cost more, but in the long run it will not only be cheaper, but will perform better than patched up electrical circuits. This will become even more true in the future, given the explosive growth in onboard electronic equipment and microprocessors.

If you are experiencing problems with interference, one of the following measures may help to bring them under control. (Note: Frequent use is made of pigtail capacitors, which have one hot lead and a mounting plate that serves as a ground connection, or coaxial capacitors, which have two leads, one of which goes to ground.

Figure 7-11A. Specific ways to reduce interference. (1) If possible, disconnect the piece of equipment suffering from interference from its power supply and provide power via a separate battery with short leads. If this reduces interference, supply-line filters will be effective. (2) Next, if the equipment has a metal case, make sure it is effectively grounded. (3) Try a 1-μF capacitor between the supply leads (positive and negative). (4) Connect a 1-μF capacitor from each terminal to ground. (5) Make up inductors as outlined in Figure 7-11B and fit these in the supply lines. (6) Place the equipment in a screening box and use feed-through filters on all lines. (7) If all else fails, try moving the equipment and/or its leads. *(John French, Electrics and Electronics for Small Craft, Beekman Publishers)*

potential (voltage). If there are no voltage differences and a good ground with seawater, there will be no arcing or buildup of static electricity (hence the brush on propeller shafts). Proper bonding is an important part of any electrical installation.

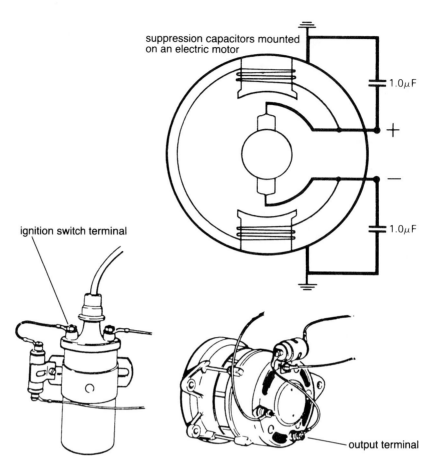

suppression capacitors mounted on an electric motor

1.0μF

+

−

1.0μF

ignition switch terminal

output terminal

Figure 7-11C. Noise suppression on electric motors, alternators, and coils. Note that radio interference from ignition systems produces a distinct popping that is synchronized with the engine speed. Alternator interference produces whining, whistling, and howling noises that are tied to the alternator output rather than the engine speed.

Connections are made as indicated in the text; the mounting plate is fastened firmly to ground. Leads must be kept as short as possible. *Cut them down if possible*; it will improve the operating characteristics of the capacitor.)

Gasoline engines. Ignition systems produce a distinct popping synchronized with engine speed. Specific measures to reduce interference are:

- Fit resistor-type spark plugs (auto parts store).
- If copper-cored (wire-cored) high-tension (HT) leads are used between the distributor and spark plugs, fit *suppressed* plug caps and distributor cap, or else change to suppression/resistance HT leads.
- If suppression/resistance (resistive) HT leads are used, fit *screened* plug caps and distributor

cap (auto parts store). In a marine environment the HT leads should be replaced every two years.

- Install a suppressor resistor (auto parts store) in the HT cable from the coil to the distributor cap. Mount the coil on the engine to keep the lead to the distributor as short as possible. Keep the low-tension (LT) and high-tension (HT) leads as far apart as possible.
- Put a 1.0-μF (microfarad), 200-volt capacitor (electronics store) between the ignition coil's hot terminal (the one from the ignition switch, *not* the one going to the distributor) and ground (the engine block), or
- Fit a filter at the coil *in series* with the wire from the ignition switch. A suitable filter is a low-pass PI-type LC filter rated at 5 amps (auto parts store). Mount it to the engine or coil bracket as close as possible to the coil and ground it well.
- Make sure the coil case is well grounded to the engine block.
- If the engine has a tachometer that takes its pulses from the alternator, make sure the

tachometer wire is shielded properly and the shield grounded at both ends.

Alternators and voltage regulators. These produce whining, whistling, and howling noises, the intensity varying with alternator output rather than engine speed. Radiated noise decreases by the square of the distance from the source to the receiver, so its impact can be greatly reduced by keeping sensitive electronics away from charging devices. Conducted noise in the regulation circuit can be minimized by keeping a voltage regulator close to its alternator. Beyond this, try the following (Figure 7-11C):

- If the alternator is grounded through its mount to the engine block (most are), fit a separate ground strap from the alternator to the engine block, or better yet, to the boat's common ground point (see Chapter 4).
- Connect a 1.0-μF, 200-volt capacitor between the output terminal on the alternator and ground, or
- Fit a filter rated at the full alternator output in series with the output line.
- Connect a 1.0-μF, 200-volt capacitor from the voltage regulator's battery connection to ground.
- Alternator *ripple* (a superimposed AC waveform carried over from the alternator's AC side to the DC side) requires heavy medicine: A 10,000- to 20,000-μF capacitor (readily available for computers) can be wired in parallel with the previous capacitor to eliminate interference at the loran frequency.

Electric motors (brush type):

- Clean the commutator and brushes.
- Connect a 1.0-μF, 200-volt capacitor across the input and output leads as close to the motor as possible (inside the case if it can be done).
- If this fails, connect a 1.0-μF, 200-volt capacitor from each brush lead to the motor case (Figure 7-11C).

TV's and fluorescent lights. Turn off the offending equipment. Newer fluorescent lights have built-in noise-suppression circuits; notwithstanding any claims made for them, however, fluorescent lights are still a major source of interference, especially where lorans are concerned. With 12-volt-powered fluorescent lights, interference tends to increase with higher battery voltages, and so may be more pronounced when the battery is charging. Two fluorescent lights mounted within 10 feet of each other can set up *harmonics*, which magnify problems. Power line filters are available (Marine Technology Inc., Long Beach, CA); these are fitted on the power supply to the light. A screening material can be put inside the light cover to block interference radiated from the tubes (see below under Video Displays).

Battery chargers. Some chargers (particularly half-wave-rectified ferro-resonant chargers, and some high-frequency switchers; see Chapter 5) can be quite noisy. While experimenting with various chokes and filters will sometimes help, a better approach is to check the battery charger installation itself; in particular, make sure the charger is close to the batteries—no more than 10 feet away—and wired to the batteries with adequately sized cables for minimal voltage drop. Check all terminals, switches, and connections to see that they are clean and tight. If the noise problem persists, return the charger to the manufacturer!

Video displays. CRT display tubes (video depth sounders, raster-scan radars) radiate interference *through the face of the tube*. This affects loran reception in particular. If you suspect this as a source of trouble, cover the display tube temporarily with aluminum foil. If the tube is at fault, the interference will cease. CRT-produced interference can be eliminated by installing a transparent conductive shield in front of the tube. Made from plastic coated with a very thin metal film, this will reduce light transmissions from the tube by around 5%—hardly noticeable—and impart a slight tint.

Radio installations. Antennas, antenna cables, and power leads to equipment should be routed as far as possible from likely sources of interference, especially engine-charging circuits, fluorescent lights, and TV's. The power leads themselves are a potential source of interference. Those supplying electric motors in particular should maintain a 3-foot separation from antenna cables. Ideally, power leads should run at right angles to antenna leads. This may not be feasible, but they at least should not be bundled up with antenna leads. Power leads should be short and large enough to prevent significant voltage drop. Equipment cases should be thoroughly grounded to the bonding system. Finally, an antenna matched correctly to its equipment and tuned efficiently will give the best possible signal-to-noise ratio (SNR) and enable the equipment itself to filter out much unwanted noise.

Loose rigging. Tighten turnbuckles. If necessary, connect jumper cables across turnbuckles (rigging screws) and shackles, and connect the chainplates to the bonding system (if installed—in any case rigging should be grounded for lightning protection).

Saving Soaked Equipment

Anytime electronic equipment takes a bath, if it was not already "off," turn it "off" immediately to prevent internal shorts from damaging sensitive circuits. Salt is then the big problem. Salt is hygroscopic, which is to say it attracts moisture. Salt dissolved in moisture forms an electrolyte that promotes galvanic reactions between dissimilar metals, such as a piece of wire and its soldered terminal.

In the humid marine environment, any electrical equipment into which salt has insinuated itself is more or less doomed—sooner rather than later. For instance, after a particularly wet and wild beat from Venezuela to Grenada, our autopilot went haywire, making all kinds of random responses. A day later it seemed to be working fine, but then developed a random tendency to go nuts. Although I'm generally reluctant to tear into electronic units, circumstances forced me to take it apart. Eventually I found one tiny grain of salt, no bigger than a small pinhead, which had been left behind by an evaporating drop of water. Every time the humidity rose, this speck of salt absorbed moisture and shorted out a sensitive circuit board. I was able to rinse it out with a cotton swab dipped in fresh water, and we and the autopilot have been in business ever since.

Electrical equipment that has suffered saltwater intrusion will need to be opened and flushed thoroughly with clean fresh water (first remove any internal battery). If the equipment can't be worked on immediately, it is better to store it in fresh water than to let the salt go to work. *As long as the unit is dried completely before being reconnected to a power source,* the fresh water may do no harm—certainly less harm than the salt! Mineral spirits and stove alcohol can also be used for flushing—alcohol, in particular, is itself hygroscopic, and so will tend to draw water out of components. WD-40 or some other penetrant/dispersant will have much the same effect.

When flushing, pay particular attention to terminal blocks: Remove the wires, rinse the cable ends, and use a syringe to flush the block. Remove fuses from their holders and wash both the fuse and holder. A coaxial cable connector, unless fully waterproofed, will hold salt and moisture, which will likely short the terminal—it will need to be opened, throroughly flushed, and dried; if there is sufficient cable, it should be cut off and replaced.

After flushing, the real difficulty lies in drying out some of the labyrinthine passages in electronic equipment, and in drawing water from encased components, such as capacitors. A good airflow will drive water from many inaccessible areas. An air compressor is best; failing that, use a fan or a vacuum cleaner's exhaust. A prolonged period of low heat—bright sunshine, or perhaps an oven, no higher than 150°F (66°C)—may be needed to draw out all the water from individual components. The part *must be dry* before reentering service. Any moisture is likely to create internal shorts and cause rapid and irreparable damage. Before placing the unit on line, test for normal resistances if known (R × 1 scale on an analog meter); then test between the power leads and equipment case for any signs of shorts.

Even if a rescue attempt is succesful, the equipment should thereafter be treated as suspect: At the first opportunity return it to the manufacturer or an authorized dealer for thorough testing and servicing.

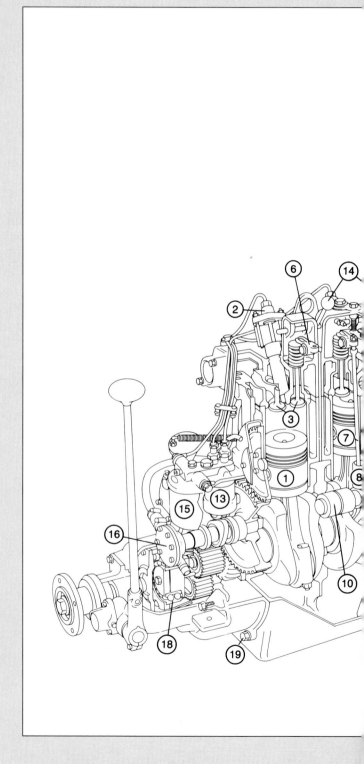

CHAPTER 8

Figure 8-1. Diesel engines can deliver years of trouble-free service—given proper preventative maintenance procedures. *(Jim Sollers)*

(1) piston
(2) injector
(3) valve
(4) turbocharger
(5) oil filter
(6) valve rocker
(7) pushrod
(8) cam follower
(9) air intake
(10) camshaft
(11) starter
(12) lube oil pump
(13) fuel injection pump
(14) compression release
(15) fuel filter
(16) water pump
(17) crankshaft
(18) cone clutch
(19) oil drain

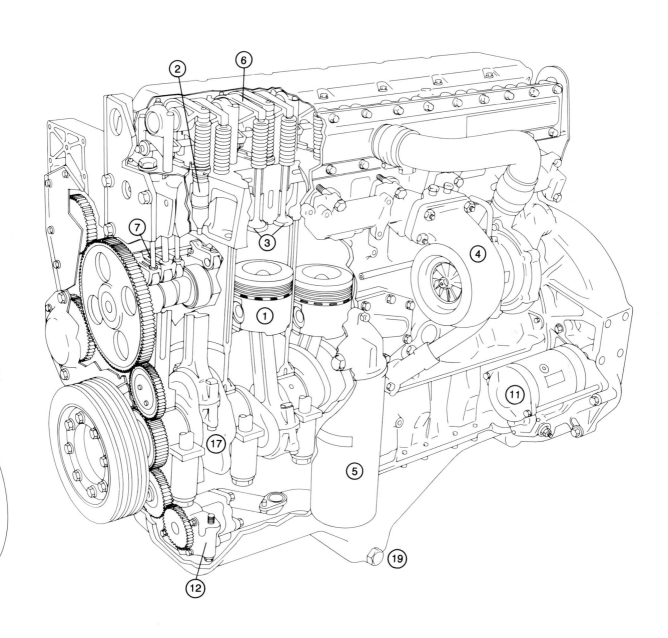

Operation and Maintenance

Diesel engines are remarkably simple in principle, and require little in the way of routine maintenance, although what little is required is essential to a long life.

How They Work

A piston compresses air in a cylinder. Compression is measured in terms of the *compression ratio*, the cylinder volume with the piston at the bottom of the cylinder compared with the volume when the piston is at the top of its stroke. The more air is compressed, the hotter it becomes. At compression ratios between 16:1 and 23:1, air temperature rises to over 1,000°F (580°C), well above diesel fuel's ignition temperature of 750°F (400°C).

When the piston is near the top of its stroke, diesel is sprayed (injected) into the cylinder of compressed, superheated air and ignites immediately, raising temperatures and pressures even higher, which drives the piston forcefully back down the cylinder—a *power stroke*. (Diesels are frequently called compression-ignition [CI] engines since they do not have a true ignition system. *The diesel fuel is ignited solely by the high temperatures attained by compressing air.*)

Four-cycle engines have two more piston strokes in the cycle (Figure 8-2). On its next upward stroke the piston expels the burned gases through an *exhaust valve*; on its next downward stroke it sucks clean air into the cylinder via an *inlet valve*. The cylinder is now filled with clean air, and the piston is at the bottom of its stroke, ready to start over.

Some diesel engines operate on *two cycles*, reducing the four cycles described into two strokes of the piston, once up and once down the cylinder. The best known are the Detroit Diesels, widely used in powerboats.

Detroit Diesels have a mechanically driven supercharger mounted in the air inlet; this compresses the incoming air (Figures 8-3A and B). As the piston nears the bottom of its power stroke, exhaust valves are opened and most of the exhaust gases exit the cylinder. A moment later the descending piston uncovers a series of *ports* in the cylinder wall, and the pressurized inlet air rushes in, driving the remaining exhaust gases out the exhaust valves and refilling the cylinder with fresh air. The piston now has reached the bottom of its stroke and is on its way back up the cylinder. The exhaust valves close and then the ascending piston blocks off the inlet ports in the cylinder wall. The cylinder is full of clean air and a new compression stroke is underway.

Preventive Maintenance

Most diesels will run troublefree for thousands of hours with little more than regular air-, fuel-, and oil-filter changes. The procedures are detailed below. One or two grease points may also need periodic attention (the engine manual will indicate where), and belts to auxiliary equipment must be kept tight (no more than ½ inch or 13 mm of deflection under moderate finger pressure in the center of the longest belt run). *Any*

Figure 8-2. The four cycles of a four-stroke diesel engine. **(1)** Inlet stroke: Air is drawn into the cylinder. **(2)** Compression: The air is compressed and becomes hot. **(3)** Injection: Fuel is sprayed into the hot air, ignites, and burns. **(4)** Exhaust: the burned gases are expelled from the engine. *(CAV/Lucas)*

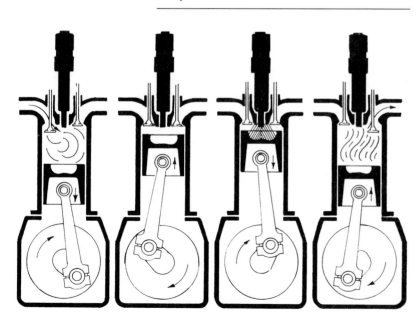

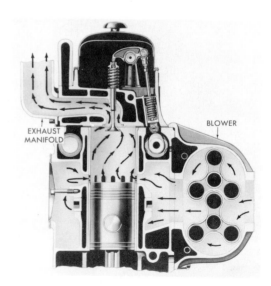

Figure 8-3A. Operation of a two-cycle Detroit Diesel—the principal components. *(Detroit Diesel)*

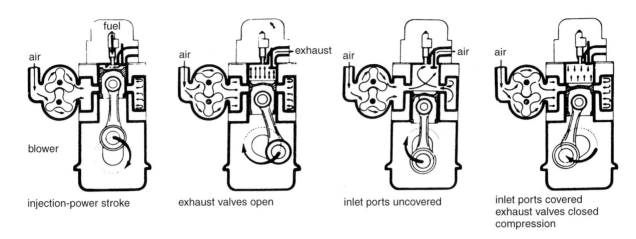

injection-power stroke — exhaust valves open — inlet ports uncovered — inlet ports covered exhaust valves closed compression

Figure 8-3B. Operation of a two-cycle Detroit Diesel—refer to the text for an explanation. (Detroit Diesel)

zinc anodes in the cooling system (the raw-water side) need replacing well before they are consumed (Figure 8-4A). If this turns out to be more than once a season, you must solve a corrosion problem before a heat exchanger is eaten through or some other expensive damage is done (zincs are frequently neglected at great cost).

Typically, exhausts are water cooled. The cooling water is injected at an elbow coming out of the exhaust manifold. Sooner or later the elbow itself will corrode through, and so it should be inspected periodically. Carry a spare. A temporary repair can be made by wrapping a strip of rubber cut from an inner tube tightly around the elbow and clamping with two hose clamps or Jubilee clips (Figures 8-4B and C).

Engine manufacturers lay down specific schedules for overhaul procedures; Table 8-1 shows typical maintenance intervals and can serve as a general guide. The marine environment and engine use are so varied, however, that one engine may need work much sooner than another. For this reason I tend to subscribe to the philosophy "If it ain't broke, don't fix it!" At the first sign of trouble, however—whether it be difficult starting, changes in oil pressure or water temperature, a smoky exhaust, vibration, or a new noise—the problem must be resolved right away; delay may cause expensive repair bills (see the sections on Troubleshooting).

The air system. The efficient running of a diesel depends on its maintaining compression. *Even small amounts of fine dust passing through a ruptured air filter or a leaking air-inlet manifold can lead to rapid piston-ring wear and scoring of cylinders,* which pave the way to expensive repairs. What is more, *once dirt gets into an engine, cleaning it out properly is impossible.* Small particles become embedded in the relatively soft surfaces of pistons and bearings, and no amount of oil changing and flushing will

Figure 8-4A. A zinc anode in the cooling system of a Yamaha diesel engine.

Figure 8-4B. A corroded galvanized exhaust elbow. The hot gases and water from the engine exhaust have eaten right through it.

Figure 8-4C. The same corroded exhaust elbow patched with rubber inner tube and hose clamps. This repair held for 200 hours of engine-running time.

Table 8-1. Basic Preventive Maintenance for Marine Diesel Engines

Immediately after start-up	Daily (when in regular use)	Weekly (when in regular use)	Semi-annually (or more often)	Annually (or more often)
· Check oil pressure. · Check raw water flow from the exhaust (unless engine has dry exhaust).	· Check engine oil level. · Check freshwater coolant level in the header tank. (Do not open when hot!)	· Check transmission oil level. · Check pulley belt tensions. · Check any grease points. · Clean raw water strainer, if necessary. · When in dusty environments, check air filter and replace if necessary. · **Change the engine oil and filters** every 100 to 150 operating hours (including any turbocharger oil filter).	· Take a sample of fuel from the base of the fuel tank. Check for water and/or sediment. · Check cooling system zinc anodes and replace as needed. · When in clean environments, check air filter and replace as necessary. · **Change the fuel filters** every 300 operating hours or more frequently as needed.	· Check all coolant hoses for softening, cracking, and bulging. · Check all hose clamps for tightness. · Check the raw water injection elbow on the exhaust for signs of corrosion. Replace as needed.

break them loose. This dirt accelerates wear.

Even if a filter is not ruptured, as it filters the air it becomes plugged, progressively restricting airflow to the engine. This limits the amount of oxygen reaching the cylinders, and combustion, especially at higher loads, suffers. The engine begins to lose power, and the exhaust shows black smoke from improperly burned fuel. Pistons, valves, turbochargers, and exhaust passages carbon up, further reducing efficiency and leading to other problems. The engine is likely to overheat, and in extreme cases, to seize.

Air filters must be kept clean! The interval for changing filters depends on the operating conditions. In general, the marine environment is relatively free of airborne pollutants, making filter changes an infrequent occurrence (except when pets are kept on board—it is surprising how fast hairs can clog a filter). Long filter change intervals, however, can lead to complacency and a forgotten air filter; *changing the filter at a set interval, even if it appears to be clean, is far better than forgetting it.*

Air filters. Most small diesels have replaceable paper-element-type filters (Figure 8-5A). Less common is the oil-bath type (Figure 8-5B). The latter forces the air to make a rapid change of direction over a reservoir of oil. Particles of dirt are thrown out by centrifugal force and trapped in the oil. The air then passes through a fine screen, which depends on an oil mist drawn up from the reservoir to keep it lubricated and effective.

In time, although the oil may still look clean, the reservoir fills with dirt, the oil becomes more viscous, less oil mist is drawn up, and the filter's efficiency slowly declines. Periodically the oil must be emptied from the reservoir and the pan thoroughly cleaned with diesel or kerosene. At this time, the screen should also be flushed with diesel or kerosene and blown dry. When refilling the reservoir with oil, *be careful not to overfill it*—excess oil can be sucked into an engine causing damaging *runaway* (page 280).

The fuel system. A fuel-injection pump is an incredibly precise piece of equipment that can be disabled by even *microscopic* pieces of dirt or traces of water. It is also *the single most expensive component of an engine*, and about the only one that is strictly off-limits to the amateur mechanic. Attempts to solve problems invariably make matters worse. It is therefore of vital importance to be *absolutely fanatical about keeping the fuel clean.* Yet so many boatowners treat their fuel systems with indifference. According to CAV, one of the world's largest manufacturers of fuel-injection equipment, the result is that *90% of diesel engine problems result from contaminated fuel.*

Fuel is contaminated by dirt, water, and bacteria. Even minute particles of dirt can lead to the seizure of injection-pump plungers, or to scoring of cylinders and plungers. If the dirt finds its way to the injectors themselves, it can cause a variety of equally damaging problems, such as plugged or worn injector nozzles.

Water in the fuel opens another can of worms. It leads to a loss of lubrication of injection equipment, resulting in seizures. In the combustion chamber it causes misfiring and generally lowers performance. In addition, water droplets in an injector can turn to steam in the high temperatures of a cylinder under compression. *This happens with explosive force, which can blow the tip clean off an injector!* Raw fuel is then dumped into the cylinder, washing out the film of lubricating oil while the injector tip rattles around, beating up the piston and valves. During extended periods of shutdown, which are quite common with most boat engines, water in the fuel system will also cause rust to form on many of the critical parts.

Bacteria can grow in even apparently clean diesel fuel, creating a slimy, smelly film that plugs filters, pumps, and injectors. The microbes live in the fuel/water interface, requiring both liquids to survive. They find excellent growth conditions in the dark, quiet, nonturbulent environment found in many fuel tanks. Two types of biocide are available to kill these bacteria. The first is water soluble, the second diesel soluble—the latter is preferred. Follow the instructions on the can if adding these chemicals to a tank. Various other diesel-fuel treatments on the market are not generally recommended by fuel injection specialists. Some, for example, contain alcohol (to absorb water), but this attacks O-rings and other nonmetallic parts in some fuel system equipment.

Clean fuel. Biocides will help to ameliorate some problems after they develop, but by far the best preventive measures are those that avoid taking on contaminated fuel in the first place and detect and remove any contaminants that are taken on board rather than neutralize them. To do this:

- Ensure that all cans used for carrying fuel are spotlessly clean.

- If taking on fuel from a barrel, first insert a length of clear plastic tubing to the bottom of the barrel, plug off the outer end with a finger, and then withdraw the tube. It will bring up a sample of fuel from all levels of the barrel, enabling you to see serious contamination.

- *Filter all fuel*, using a funnel with a fine mesh or, preferably, one of the multistage filter funnels now available through various marine catalogs and at some marine chandlers. If

Figure 8-5A. **A replaceable paper element for an air filter.** *(Caterpillar Tractor Company)*

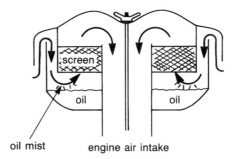

Figure 8-5B. **An oil-bath air cleaner.**

there are *any* signs of contamination, *stop refueling at once*.

- *Take regular samples from the bottom of the fuel tank to check for contamination.* If there is no accessible drain valve, find some means of pumping out a sample of fuel. *At the first sign of contamination, drain the tank or pump out the fuel until no trace of contamination remains.* Any especially dirty batch of fuel should be *completely discarded*—it's not worth risking the engine for the sake of a tankful of fuel. After refueling, we *always* allow the tank to settle for a few minutes *and then pump a sample from the base of our fuel tank before restarting our engine*—twice we have found serious contamination which we have been able to remove before it did any damage.

- When leaving the boat unused for long periods (e.g., when it is laid up over the winter), fill the fuel tank to the top. This eliminates the air space and cuts down on condensation in the tank. Add a biocide.

- *Periodically flush the fuel tanks to remove accumulated sediment.*

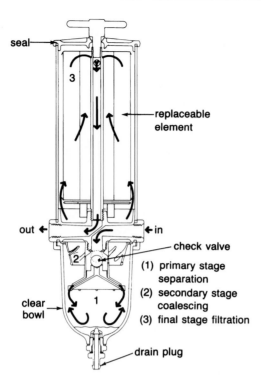

seal

3

replaceable element

out ←   ← in

check valve

(1) primary stage separation

(2) secondary stage coalescing

(3) final stage filtration

2

clear bowl

1

drain plug

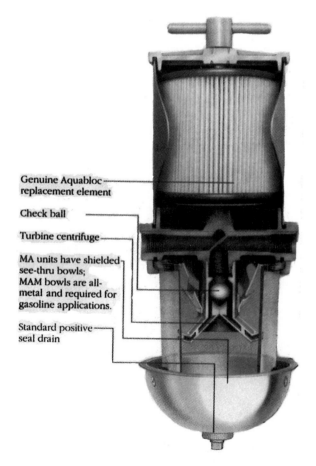

Genuine Aquabloc replacement element

Check ball

Turbine centrifuge

MA units have shielded see-thru bowls; MAM bowls are all-metal and required for gasoline applications.

Standard positive seal drain

Figure 8-6B. Cutaway of a good-quality primary filter. (Racor)

Fuel filters. Most people regard fuel filters as the first line of defense against contaminated fuel. As should be clear by now, I regard them as *the last line of defense* whose function is to deal with any *minor* contamination that escapes the measures designed to keep the fuel tank clean.

Without exception, every marine diesel engine should have both a primary and a secondary fuel filter. All engines come from the manufacturer with an engine-mounted secondary filter located somewhere just before the fuel injection pump. *If this is the only filter, a primary filter MUST be installed* (Figures 8-6A and B). This needs to be mounted *between* the fuel tank and the lift pump, not *after* the lift pump because any water in the fuel supply that passes through a lift pump gets broken up into small droplets that are hard to filter out.

Primary and secondary filters do not have the same function. A primary filter is the main defense against water and larger particles in the fuel supply, but it does not guard against microscopic particles of dirt and water. These are filtered out by the secondary filter.

A *primary filter* needs to be of the *sedimenter* type specifically designed to separate water from fuel. Sedimenters are extremely simple, generally consisting of little more than a bowl and deflector plate. The incoming fuel hits the deflector plate, then flows around and under it to the filter outlet. Water droplets and large particles of dirt settle out. The better-quality filters then pass the fuel through a relatively coarse filter element (10 to 30 microns—a micron is one-millionth of a meter, or approximately 0.00004 inch).

A primary filter should have a see-through bowl with a drain *plug* so that water can be rapidly detected and removed (note: The ABYC does not permit drain *valves*). Beyond this, the filter may have an electronic sensing device that sounds an alarm if water reaches a certain level, a float device that shuts off the flow of fuel to the engine if the water reaches a certain level, or both.

Powerboats should have two or more primary filters mounted on a valved manifold that allows either filter to be closed off and changed without shutting down the engine (Figure 8-7). This way, if there is a problem with dirty fuel, the filters can be changed with the engine running. Such an arrangement would also be a good idea on many motorsailers. A *vacuum gauge mounted between the primary filters and the lift pump is an excellent troubleshooting investment.* A rising vacuum indicates that the filters are starting to plug (procedures for changing filters are covered below).

A *secondary filter* is designed to remove very

Figure 8-7. A set of valved primary filters, which allows any one to be changed while the engine is running. *(Racor)*

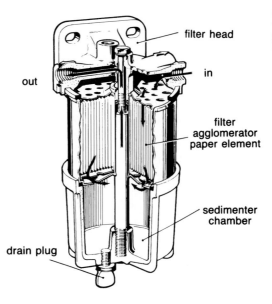

Figure 8-8. Secondary filter. This one has a separate water-collecting bowl; many don't. *(Lucas/CAV)*

small particles of dirt and water droplets (Figure 8-8). It cannot handle major contamination because its fine mesh will soon plug up. Secondary filters are normally of the spin-on type and contain a specially impregnated paper element that catches dirt. Water droplets are also too large to pass through the paper and therefore adhere to it. As more water is caught, the droplets increase in size (*coalesce* or *agglomerate*) until they are large enough to settle to the bottom of the filter, from where they can be periodically drained. The filter mesh should be in the range of 7 to 12 microns. In certain special applications it may be as small as 2 microns.

The lubrication system. Lubricating oil in a diesel engine works much harder than in a gasoline engine, owing to the higher temperatures and greater loads encountered. This is especially the case with today's lightweight, high-speed, turbocharged diesels. Diesel engine oil also has other problems to contend with, notably acid and soot formation.

Diesel fuels contain traces of sulphur. *Although it is a thoroughly destructive practice, which should be avoided in every way possible,* many cruising boat engines, particularly those in auxiliary sailboats, are operated for long hours at light loads when charging batteries and running the refrigeration unit at anchor. The engines run cool, which causes moisture to condense in the engine. These condensates combine with the sulphur to make sulphuric acid, which attacks sensitive engine surfaces. Low-load and cool running also generate far more carbon (soot) than normal. This soot gums up piston rings, and coats valves and valve stems, leading to a loss of compression and numerous other problems.

Diesel engine oils are specially formulated to hold soot in suspension and deal with acids and other harmful by-products of the combustion process. Using the correct oil in a diesel engine is vitally important. Many perfectly good oils designed for gasoline engines are not suitable for use in a diesel engine. The American Petroleum Institute (API) uses the letter C (for Compression ignition) to designate oils rated for use in diesel engines, and the letter S (for Spark ignition) to designate oils rated for use in gasoline engines. The C or S is then followed by another letter to indicate the complexity of the additive package in the oil, with the better packages having letters further into the alphabet. Thus any oil rated CC, CD, CE, or CF-4 is suitable for use in diesel engines, with the CF-4 oil being the best at the time of writing (Detroit Diesels use CD-II). Cruisers going to Third World countries should carry a good stock of the best-grade oil money can buy.

As the oil does its work, the additives and detergents are steadily used up. The oil wears out. It must be replaced at frequent intervals—far more frequently than in gasoline engines. In particular, if high-sulphur-content fuels, such as are likely to be found in many Third World countries and much of the Caribbean, are taken on, or extended periods of low-load running are increasing the soot content, oil-change intervals should be shortened to as little as every 50 hours. Every time the oil is changed, a new filter must be installed to rid the engine of its contaminants.

If regular oil changes are not carried out, sooner or later the acids formed will start to attack sensitive engine surfaces, and the carbon will overwhelm the detergents in the oil, forming a thick black sludge in the crankcase and in the oil cooler (if fitted). The sludge will begin to plug narrow oil passages and areas through which the oil moves slowly, eventually causing a loss of supply to some part of the engine. A major mechanical breakdown is under way, and all for the sake of a gallon or so of oil, a filter, and less than an hour's work. One major bearing manufacturer estimates that 58% of all bearing failures are the result of dirty oil or a lack of oil.

Centrifuges and bypass filters. A typical *full-flow* engine oil filter has a mesh size of around 30 microns, which is relatively large (a finer mesh would plug up faster and need changing more often). Particles of dirt smaller than 30 microns pass through the filter and circulate continuously with the oil. Various studies have shown that of the microscopic particles that pass through the filter, *the most destructive in terms of engine wear are those in the 10- to 20-micron range.* Two methods have been developed to catch these particles: centrifuges and bypass filters, both of which are tapped into the pressurized oil gallery that leads to the engine bearings

and bleed off a certain percentage of this oil (normally around 10%) and drain it back to the crankcase (Figure 8-9; the amount of oil bled off must be kept low so as not to cause a damaging drop in engine oil pressure).

In the case of a *centrifuge,* this oil is fed through a bowl mounted on bearings and then out a couple of small nozzles on the base of the bowl. The oil is driven out of these nozzles under pressure from the engine oil pump, causing the assembly to spin at a high speed (the size of the nozzles, coupled to the engine oil pressure and the oil's viscosity, is what determines the rate of flow through the filter). The centrifugal force generated by the spinning bowl causes entrained particles of dirt to be thrown out of the oil onto the centrifuge's outer housing (Figure 8-10). Here the dirt accumulates as a dense, rubbery mat. Periodically the outer housing is removed and the dirt cake dug out.

Centrifuges will remove particles down to 1 or 2 microns in size. Their principal drawback is that to date none has been manufactured to operate on the relatively low oil-flow rates of an auxiliary engine. Centrifuges are big-engine devices (100 to 200 hp on up).

A *bypass filter,* on the other hand, can be bought for any size engine. These contain a fine mesh filter element which, depending on the manufacturer and the element, can filter particles down to 1 micron in size. A restriction built into the filter at some point keeps the flow rate down to a level that will not cause a drop in the engine oil pressure. One brand of bypass filter (manufactured by TF Purifiner, Boynton Beach, FL) also includes a heating element that vaporizes any water or fuel in the oil.

The net result of either a centrifuge or a bypass filter will be far cleaner oil with a considerable reduction in engine wear. Engine life in many applications is doubled! The cost, relative to the return, is minimal. Many larger engines come fitted with one or the other as standard equipment, but few smaller engines have either—they are definitely worth considering as add-on equipment.

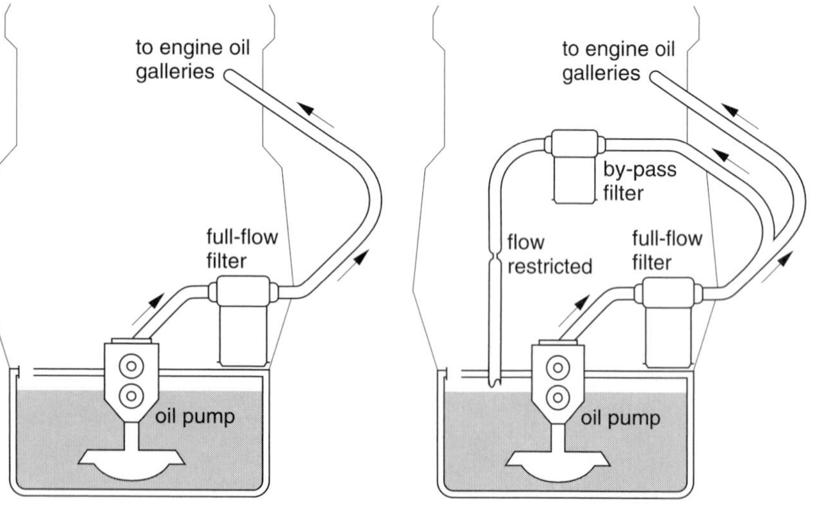

Oil analysis. The other tool that can greatly help to extend engine life is regular oil analysis. If an oil sample is taken at each oil change, or at least once a year, and sent to a laboratory for analysis, all kinds of trouble in the making can be detected at an early stage and headed off before serious damage is done (Figure 8-11). The cost of analysis is between $10 and $15; the time and trouble involved in taking a sample is minimal.

To be of maximum benefit, oil samples must be taken on a regular basis so that a typical wear

Figure 8-9. A bypass filter removes smaller particles from the oil than does a full-flow filter. The bypass loop has a restriction that limits the oil flow through the circuit to around 10% of the total oil flow through the engine. After 10 to 20 minutes of operation all of the oil in the engine will have passed through the bypass filter. *(Ocean Navigator)*

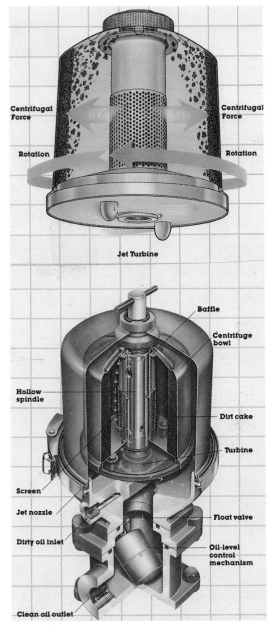

Figure 8-10. The innards of the Spinner II oil centrifuge. Oil entering through the central axis is driven by the engine's oil pump out of the jets at the bottom, causing the drum to spin. Since dirt is heavier than oil, it is thrown outward to accumulate on the outer walls of the unit. *(TF Hudgins)*

pattern can be established for an engine, enabling detection of abnormalities when they occur. Oil samples have to be taken when the oil is hot, from approximately the mid-sump level, so that the sample is representative of the oil in the engine. Clearly *the sampling pump and bottle have to be spotlessly clean* to avoid misleading contamination. The laboratory will need to know what type and grade of oil is in the engine, *how many hours it has on it,* and how much oil has been added since the last oil change. The more information that is provided, the more useful the results of the analysis are likely to be.

Many marinas, marine surveyors, boatyards, or mechanics can provide the address of a local laboratory. The lab will be able to provide sample bottles, labels, and sampling pumps. Better labs will also provide some literature to help in understanding the results of the analysis.

Changing filters. Changing fuel and oil filters is straightforward enough, but note that most diesel fuel systems need *bleeding* after a filter change (page 265). Note also that some turbochargers have their own oil filter. *This must be replaced whenever the engine oil filter is changed.* To change a filter:

1. Scrupulously clean off any dirt from around the old filter or filter housing (Figure 8-12).
2. Provide some means to catch any spilled fuel or oil—I find disposable diapers (especially the ones with elasticized sides since they can be formed into a bowl shape) to be ideal!
3. Most primary fuel filters have a central bolt or wing nut that is loosened to drop the filter bowl. Screw-on filters (both fuel and oil) are undone with the appropriate filter wrench. This should be a part of the boat's tool kit (note that more than one size of filter wrench may be needed for fuel and oil filters). In the absence of a filter wrench, wrap a V-belt around the filter, grip it tightly, and unscrew the filter. Failing this, a large screwdriver can be hammered through the filter—it may be messy, but at least it will enable removal of the filter.
4. If a fuel filter has a replaceable element, take a close look at the old one. If it isn't spotless—as it should be in a well-maintained fuel system—find out where the contamination is coming from and stop it before it stops the engine!
5. Fuel filters are often filled with clean diesel before installation. This reduces the amount of priming and bleeding that has to be done, but this practice carries with it the possibility of introducing contaminants directly into the injection system. For this reason, *never fill the secondary filter before installing it.* Normally the priming can be done by operating the lift pump manually (page 267) or with a built-in electric lift pump, but sometimes on larger installations it pays to install an additional electrically operated lift pump on a separate bypass manifold. This pump is placed before any filters and is used to push fuel through the filters, priming the system.
6. If the new filter has its own sealing ring, *ensure that the old one doesn't remain stuck to the fil-*

Figure 8-11. An oil analysis reporting the results of a series of tests performed on the oil of the Ocean Navigator's *Ocean Star*. The earliest analysis is at the bottom; the latest at the top. The second analysis revealed problems with the freshwater cooling system (glycol in the oil); the third, problems with saltwater intrusion into the engine from a faulty exhaust installation (indicated by the high sodium levels). *(Ocean Navigator)*

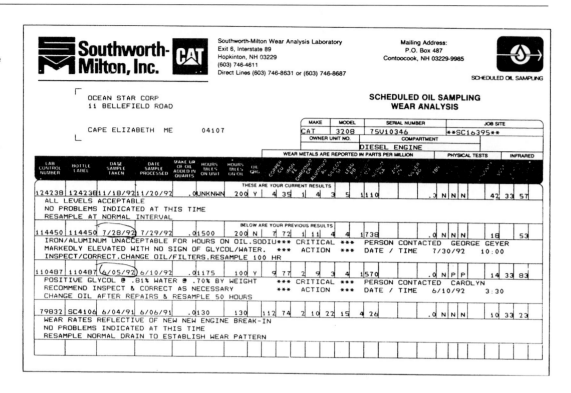

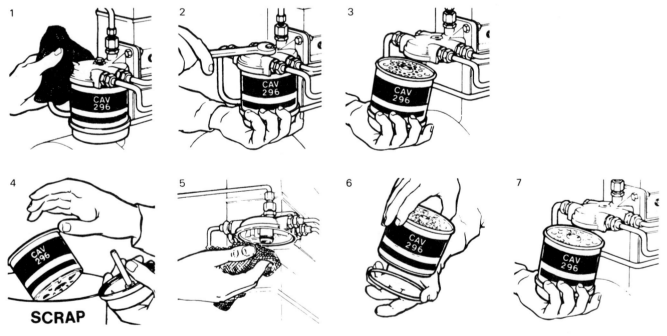

Figure 8-12. Changing a filter element with a replaceable element. (1) Clean off all external dirt from the unit before attempting to service. Unscrew the thumbscrew in the base and drain the accumulated water and sludge. (2) Unscrew the center bolt and at the same time hold the base of the unit to prevent it from rotating. (3) Release the filter element complete with base, by pulling the element downward and at the same time turning it slightly so that it come free from the internal O-ring. (4) Detach and discard the element. Detach and inspect the lower sealing ring for damage. Renew the ring if defective. (5) Clean out the sedimenter base. Complete cleaning by rinsing with clean fuel oil. Clean the unit head and inspect both the upper sealing ring and the O-ring for damage. Renew any imperfect sealing ring. (6) Replacement sealing rings may be obtained from the supplier of the filter element. (7) Check that the upper sealing ring and O-ring are positioned correctly in the head and fit a new filter element to the head. Rotate the element slightly when fitting it to slide easily over the O-ring. Ensure that the lower sealing ring is positioned correctly in the base and offer up the base to the assembled head and element. Guide the center stud through the center tube of the element and engage it with the center bolt. Make sure that the rims of the element and base are seating correctly before tightening the center bolt. Do not overtighten. *(Lucas/CAV)*

ter housing. If the new filter has no sealing ring, the old one will have to be reused. In order to prevent this, buy a stock of rings and fit one at each filter change. Note that some sealing rings have a square cross section—they *must* go in without twisting.

7. The sealing rings of screw-on filters should be lightly lubricated before installation. These filters are done up hand tight, and then given an additional three-quarters of a turn with the filter wrench. If a fuel filter is done up with a wing nut, check closely for leaks around the nut when finished. This is a likely source of air in a fuel system and one of the first places to look if an operating problem develops immediately after a filter change.

Please don't dump old oil overboard or down the nearest drain! Save it in some oil or milk jugs and take it to a proper disposal facility.

Routine oil and filter changes take little time and are relatively inexpensive but are too often neglected. *Nothing will do more to prolong the life of an engine than this routine maintenance.*

Troubleshooting Part 1: Failure to Start

It is necessary to distinguish two differing situations when dealing with an engine that will not start. The first is a failure to crank—the engine will not turn over at all. The second is a failure to fire—the engine turns over but does not run (see below).

Failure to Crank

When an engine will not crank at all, the problem is almost always electrical (Chapter 6, Starter Motor Circuits), but occasionally it is the result of water in the cylinders or a complete seizure of the engine or transmission. Before checking the electrical system, see if the engine can be turned over by hand with the hand crank (if fitted) or by placing a suitably sized wrench on the crankshaft-pulley nut (turn the engine in its normal direction of rotation to prevent accidentally undoing the nut). If the engine has a manual transmission, it can be put in gear and turned with a pipe wrench on the propeller shaft, but only after wrapping a rag around the shaft to avoid scarring it.

If the engine is locked up solidly, it has probably seized and will need professional attention. If it turns over a little and then locks up, or turns with extreme difficulty, water may have siphoned into the cylinders through a water-cooled exhaust (see sidebar, Siphon Breaks). The other way it may have got in is from excessive cranking, since anytime an engine is cranked the raw-water pump will push water into the exhaust, but until the engine fires there will not be the necessary exhaust gases to lift the water out. Eventually enough water can accumulate to flood the engine. If an engine requires extensive cranking, any water-lift silencer will need periodic draining.

Water in the engine. Water, especially salt water, that remains for any length of time will do expensive damage to bearing and cylinder surfaces, requiring a complete engine overhaul. If the water is discovered in time, it can be eased out of the exhaust and the engine will continue to operate.

To remove water, *close the throttle so that the engine will not start.* If the engine has decompression levers and a hand crank, simply turn it over several times. Otherwise, flick the starter motor on and off, or use a wrench on the crankshaft-pulley nut to turn the engine over bit by bit, turning in the normal direction of rotation and pausing between each movement. Take it slowly—if you rush the process, you may damage piston rings and connecting rods.

Once an engine has turned through two complete revolutions, it should be free of water. Spin it a couple of times *without starting it.* Now check the crankcase for water in the oil. If any is present, change the oil and filter. Start the engine and run it for a few minutes to warm it, shut it down, and *change the oil and filter again.* Now give the engine a good run to drive out any remaining moisture. After 25 hours of normal operation, or at the first sign of any more water in the oil, *change the oil and filter for a third time.*

Put appropriate siphon breaks in the cooling and exhaust system (see the sidebar).

Engine Cranks but Won't Fire

If an engine will not start as usual, it is important to stop cranking and start thinking! Those extra couple of cranks in the hope that some miracle will happen very often flatten the battery to the point at which the engine cannot be started at all. Most starting problems are simple ones that

On any engine that is below the waterline, both the water-injection line and the exhaust pipe create the potential for water to siphon back into the exhaust, fill it, and flow into the engine via open exhaust valves. The injection line must have an effective siphon break (Figure 8-13). The exhaust pipe can be looped up above the waterline and discharged well up in the hull. In sailboats, it should have an *accessible* positive shutoff valve to close it, in case following seas threaten to drive up the back of the boat.

Siphon breaks tend to plug up with salt crystals (the newer spring-loaded siphon breaks are far less prone to plugging than the traditional rubber-flap type). Once plugged, they are inoperative. They can also spray salt water all over the running engine and its electrical sys-

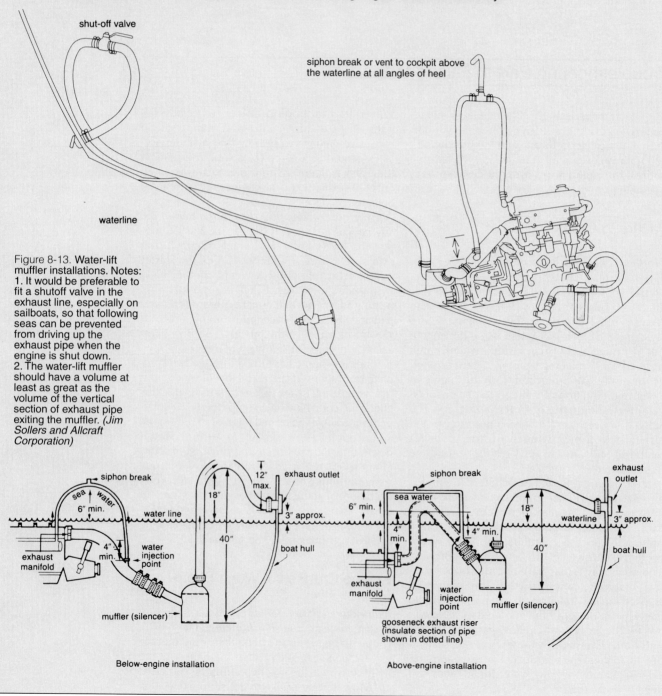

Figure 8-13. Water-lift muffler installations. Notes: 1. It would be preferable to fit a shutoff valve in the exhaust line, especially on sailboats, so that following seas can be prevented from driving up the exhaust pipe when the engine is shut down. 2. The water-lift muffler should have a volume at least as great as the volume of the vertical section of exhaust pipe exiting the muffler. (*Jim Sollers and Allcraft Corporation*)

Siphon Breaks, *continued*

tems, adding insult to injury. It is better to remove the valve element, add a hose to the top, and vent this well above the waterline (into the cockpit works well—Figures 8-14A and B).

The higher an exhaust is looped above the waterline, the greater the security from siphonic action, but the greater the back pressure (see page 280) since the cooling water has to be lifted farther. (Note also that when the engine is shut down, the water in the vertical section of the exhaust pipe will run back into the water lift silencer—the silencer must have a volume at least as great as that of this vertical section of pipe.) To keep back pressure within acceptable limits, the vertical lift of the cooling water should not exceed 40 inches (1 meter) on naturally aspirated engines (i.e., without turbochargers). This corresponds to a back pressure at full load of somewhere around 1.5 psi. On turbocharged engines the water lift should be kept down to 20 inches (½ meter) to give a full-load back pressure of around 0.75 psi.

In situations where a standard water-lift exhaust will create excessive back pressure, a *standpipe* exhaust can be used in which the silencer is raised as in Figure 8-15. In general, the less the back pressure, the less the silencing effect, so an additional in-line silencer (muffler) may be required. The dry section of exhaust from the exhaust manifold to the standpipe needs effective insulation.

Figure 8-14B. A siphon break on an engine cooling circuit that has been adapted removing the valve and adding a length of hose, which is vented into the cockpit.

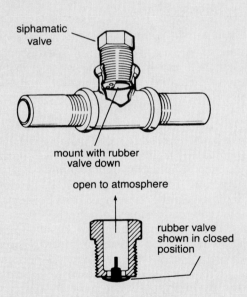

Figure 8-14A. A Kohler siphon break. *(Kohler)*

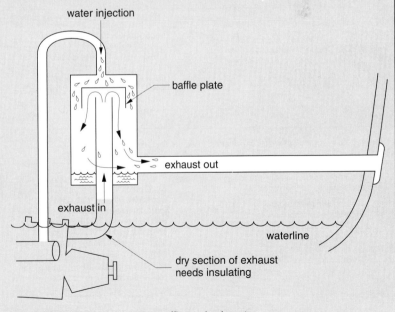

Figure 8-15. A standpipe-type muffler and exhaust installation.

Troubleshooting Chart 8-1.
Diesel Engine Problems: Engine Cranks but Won't Fire.
Note: See Chart 6-2 if engine won't crank.

Is the engine cranking slowly? Note: Stop cranking and save the battery! **NO**	**YES** Try the methods for boosting speed listed in the text under Cranking Speed. If slow cranking is due to cold, see below. If these fail, recharge the batteries.
Is the engine too cold? **NO** Check cold-start devices. If glow plugs and manifold heaters are working, the cylinder head will be noticeably warmer. Plugs can be tested by using a multimeter, or unscrewing the plug and holding it against a good ground. See text under "Achieving Ignition Temperatures" for details.	**YES** Replace faulty glow plugs or manifold heaters; warm the engine, inlet manifold, fuel lines, and battery using a hair dryer, light bulb or kerosene lantern. Raise temperature slowly and evenly—concentrated heat can crack the engine castings.
Is the air supply obstructed? Check any air flaps, air filter, and exhaust seacock for blockage or closure. **NO**	**YES** Open air flap; replace air filter element; open exhaust seacock.
Is the fuel level too low? Check the fuel level in the tank. **NO**	**YES** Add fuel. It will probably also be necessary to bleed the fuel system (see page 265).
Is the fuel delivery to the engine obstructed? **NO** Check to see that no kill devices are in operation; all fuel valves are open; no fuel filters are plugged; the remote throttle is actually advancing the throttle lever on the engine; and any fuel solenoid valve is functioning.	**YES** If stop or kill control has been pulled out, push it in. Check power supply to and operation of fuel shutdown solenoid valve by connecting it directly to the battery with a jumper wire. If see-through fuel filters are plugged, change filters. Open the throttle wide.
Is the fuel delivery to the injectors obstructed? **NO** **TEST:** Open throttle wide, loosen an injector nut and crank the engine.	**YES** If no fuel spurts out, check primary, secondary, and lift pump filters and bleed the system. Check fuel lift pump for diaphragm failure. If fuel still does not flow, go back and check system for fuel level, blockages, and air leaks. Only after all else has been eliminated, suspect injection pump failure.
Note: If fluid spurts out when conducting previous test, make sure it is fuel, not water.	
Is the compression inadequate to achieve ignition temperature? **NO** (a) Suspect inadequate cylinder lubrication or piston blow-by. . . . (b) Suspect valve blow-by. . . .	**YES** **FIX:** On engines with custom-fitted oil cups on the inlet manifold, fill cups with oil and then crank engine. On others remove air filter and squirt oil into the inlet manifold as close to the cylinders as possible *while* cranking. See Compression in text. **FIX:** If valves are poorly seated, a top-end overhaul is needed.
If you have exhausted these tests, you can suspect incorrect timing, a worn fuel-injection pump, worn or damaged injectors.	**YES** **FIX:** Replace pump or injectors. Timing problems indicate a serious mechanical failure; correction requires a specialist.

can be solved with a little thought—and frequently in a whole lot less time than it will take to recharge a dead battery!

A diesel engine is a thoroughly logical piece of equipment. If the airflow is unobstructed, the air is being compressed to ignition temperatures, and the fuel injection is correctly metered and timed, it more or less has to fire. Troubleshooting an engine that won't start boils down to finding the simplest possible procedure to establish which of these three preconditions for ignition is missing.

Checking the airflow. A failure to reach ignition temperatures or problems with the fuel supply are the most likely causes for starting failures. The airflow is the easiest to check, however, so it should be investigated first.

Does the engine have air? This may seem to be a stupid question, but certain engines (notably Detroit Diesels) have an emergency shutdown device, a flap that completely closes off the air inlet to the engine and guarantees that no ignition will take place. Once the flap is activated, even if the remote operating lever is returned to its normal position the flap will remain closed until manually reset *at the engine*. (*Note that stopping an engine by closing the air flap will soon damage the supercharger's air seals and should be done only in an emergency, such as engine runaway—more on this later.*)

If the engine doesn't have an air flap, what about the air filter? It may be plugged, especially if the engine has been operated in a dusty environment. It may have a plastic bag stuck in it, or even a dead bird (which I found on one occasion). If the boat has been laid up all winter, a bird's nest may be in there.

Does the engine have a turbocharger? Poor oil-change procedures or operating behavior (particularly racing the engine on start-up and just before shutdown—more on this later) may have caused the shaft to seize in its bearings. Remove the inlet ducting and use a finger to see if the compressor wheel turns freely.

The other side of the airflow equation is the ability to vent the exhaust overboard. Starting problems, particularly on Detroit Diesels, may sometimes be the result of excessive back pressure in the exhaust. The most obvious cause would be a closed seacock. Other possibilities are excessive carbon buildup in the exhaust piping or in the turbocharger. In cold weather, there could be frozen water in a water-lift-type muffler, which has the same effect as a closed seacock.

Achieving ignition temperatures. If there is no obstruction in the airflow, perhaps the air charge is not being adequately compressed to achieve ignition temperatures. Although numerous variables may be at work here, an attempt must be made to isolate them in order to identify problems.

Cold-start devices. The colder the ambient air, the lower its temperature when compressed, and the harder it is to get it up to ignition temperatures. As if this were not problem enough, cold thickens engine oil, which makes the engine crank sluggishly. Slower cranking gives the air in the cylinders more time to dissipate heat to cold engine surfaces and more time to escape past poorly seated valves and piston rings. In addition, a battery that puts out 100% of its rated capacity at 80°F (27°C) will put out 65% at 32°F (0°C), and only 40% at 0°F (–18°C).

Cold is a major obstacle to reliable engine starting (refer back to Figure 1-14). As a result, most engines incorporate some form of a cold-start device to boost the temperature of the air charge during initial cranking. The most common device is a glow plug—a small heater installed in a pre-combustion chamber. Glow plugs are run off the engine-cranking battery, becoming red hot when activated.

Other devices include a heater in the air inlet manifold—perhaps a heating element, or a *flame primer* (a device that ignites a diesel spray in the inlet manifold, thus warming the entering air—Figure 8-16), or a carefully metered shot of starting fluid to trigger the initial combustion process (some Detroit Diesels—but note that starting fluid *should not be used in most instances*—see accompanying sidebar, Starting Fluid and WD-40).

If glow plugs and manifold heaters are working, the cylinder head or manifold will be noticeably warmer near the individual heating devices. If they are not working, first check the wiring in the circuit. There is frequently a solenoid activated by the ignition switch or a preheat switch, in the same way that a starter motor solenoid is activated by the ignition switch. The same kinds of circuit tests can be made to this circuit as to a starting circuit (see Chapter 6, Starter Motor Circuits, but substitute "glow-plugs" for "starter motor").

Glow plugs can be checked further by unscrewing them, holding them against a good ground (the engine block), and turning them on. They should glow red hot (Figure 8-17). An ammeter can be used to test the power drain (5 to 6 amps per plug), or an ohmmeter to test the resistance (around 1.5 ohms per plug).

To test the amp draw, place a suitable DC ammeter in the power supply line between the main hot wire and each glow plug *in turn* (not in the main harness itself since this may carry up to

Figure 8-16. **A flame primer (*Thermostart*).** *(Lucas/CAV)*

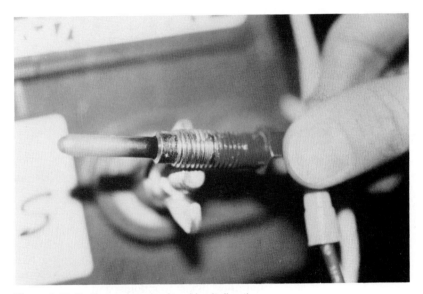

Figure 8-17. Testing a glow plug by wiring it directly across a battery. The plug can be held at the top, but the probe should not be touched!

40 amps on a six-cylinder engine). Test resistances by disconnecting the hot wire from each glow plug and checking from the hot terminal on the plug to a ground, using the most sensitive ohms scale on the meter (Figure 8-18). Only a good ohmmeter will be accurate enough to distinguish between a functioning glow plug and a shorted plug.

If a flame primer is not working, check its electrical connections and its fuel supply. If the unit is removed, the heating coil can be tested by jumping it from the battery, and the fuel discharge and atomization can be checked, but *not at the same time since this may result in an uncontrolled flare up.*

Troubleshooting Part I: Failure to Start   261

Figure 8-18. Using a
multimeter to test a glow
plug. *(Jim Sollers)*

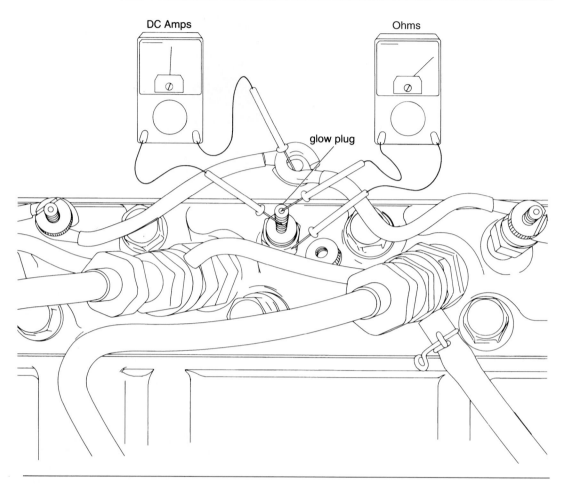

DC Amps

Ohms

glow plug

Any safe means used to boost the temperature of the engine, battery, and inlet air will help with difficult starting. This includes using a hair dryer, lightbulb, or kerosene lantern to warm fuel lines, filters, manifolds, and the incoming air; removing oil and water, warming them on the galley stove, and returning them; heating battery compartments with a lightbulb; or removing the battery, putting it in a heated crew compartment, and returning it once it is warm.

A propane torch flame can also be used to boost temperatures. Gently play the flame over the inlet manifold and fuel lines, and across the air inlet when the engine is cranked so that it heats the incoming air. *A torch cannot be used in the presence of gasoline or propane vapors.* Do not play the torch flame over electrical harnesses, plastic fuel lines and fittings, or other combustibles!

Raise temperatures slowly and evenly, playing the heat source over a broad area. Concentrated heat may crack an engine's castings. Boiling water or very hot oil may do the same.

Compression. When an engine is operating, the lubrication system maintains a fine film of oil on the cylinder walls and the sides of the pistons. This oil plays an important part in main-

taining the seal of the piston rings on the cylinder walls. After an engine is shut down, the oil slowly drains back to the crankcase. An engine that has been shut down for a long period of time may suffer a considerable amount of *blowby* when an attempt is made to restart it because the lack of oil on the cylinder walls and piston rings reduces the seal, therefore compression.

An engine that grows harder to start over time is probably also losing compression, but this time because of poorly seated valves and piston-ring wear. *(Note that a Detroit Diesel exhibits the same symptoms if the blower is defective.)* The air in the cylinders is not compressed enough to produce ignition temperatures.

Short of a *top end* overhaul, there is not a lot that can be done about valve blowby. Piston blowby and a loss of cylinder lubrication, however, can be cured temporarily by adding a little oil to the cylinders. The oil dribbles down and settles on the piston rings, sealing them against the cylinder walls.

If there is plenty of battery reserve, set the throttle wide open and crank for a few seconds. Then let the engine rest for a minute. Three things will be happening: The injected diesel will be dribbling down onto the piston rings; the initial

Starting Fluid and WD-40

Unless specific provision for the use of starting fluid is made on an engine (e.g., some Detroit Diesels and Caterpillars), do not use it at all. It is sucked in with the air charge and, being extremely volatile, will often ignite before the piston is at the top of its compression stroke. This can result in serious damage to pistons and connecting rods. For some reason, Detroit Diesels seem to tolerate starting fluid better than four-cycle diesels.

If starting fluid must be used, do not spray it directly into the air inlet manifold. Rather, spray it onto a rag and hold this to the air intake. This will control the amount being drawn in. Adding a little diesel to the inlet manifold will also help the engine to pick up once the starting fluid fires.

Diesels will run on WD-40 (don't ask me why) at far less risk of premature detonation than that imposed by starting fluid. In fact, if the battery is low but it is necessary to do some extended cranking—such as when you are having problems purging a fuel system—you can open the throttle wide and spray a continuous stream of WD-40 into the air inlet while cranking. The engine will fire and continue to run as long as the spray is maintained. The engine speed can be controlled by varying the rate of spray until the fuel system is bled and the engine takes over. This is also an effective way to get a drowned engine running again, after the water has been driven out of the cylinders and the oil and filter changed. Note, however, that *WD-40 should not be used in conjunction with manifold heating devices since it may ignite in the manifold and blow back, causing a fire.*

---

heat of compression will be taking the chill off the cylinders; and the battery will be catching its breath. Try cranking again.

If the engine still won't start, or if little battery reserve remains, introduce a small amount of oil directly into the engine cylinders.

On engines with custom-fitted oil cups on the inlet manifold (for example, many older Sabbs—Figure 8-19), fill the cups with oil, then crank the engine. On others, remove the air filter and squirt oil into the inlet manifold as close to the cylinders as possible, while cranking the engine. The oil will be sucked in when the engine cranks. Let the engine sit for a minute or two to allow the oil to settle on the piston rings. After starting, the engine will smoke abominably for a few seconds as it burns off the oil—this is OK. Put the air filter back in place as soon as the engine fires.

When applying oil to the cylinders, use only a couple of squirts in each cylinder. Oil is incompressible; too much will cause damage to piston rings and connecting rods. Also, keep the oil can clear of turbocharger blades—a touch of the can will result in expensive damage.

Oil used in this fashion is often a magic—albeit a temporary—cure for poor starting, but the engine needs attention to *solve* the compression problem.

Cranking speed. No diesel will start without a brisk cranking speed (at least 60 to 80 rpm; most small diesels will crank at 200 to 300 rpm). The engine, especially when it is cold, just will not

oil cup on an inlet manifold of a Sabb 2JZ

air filter on cylinder #2

air inlet to cylinder #1

Figure 8-19. Adding oil to inlet manifolds to increase combustion chamber pressure.

attain sufficient compression temperature to ignite the injected diesel. If a motor turns over sluggishly, stop cranking and save the battery.

Check the battery's state of charge. If it is fully charged, check for voltage drop (which may be robbing the starter motor of power) between the battery and the starter motor (Chapter 6). Assuming a good battery and a properly functioning starting circuit, the techniques in the sections on Cold-Start Devices and Compression will help generate that first vital power stroke. Sometimes the following tricks will also boost cranking speeds:

- If fitted with decompression levers and a hand crank, turn the engine over a few times by hand to break the grip of the cold oil on the bearings. Assist the starter motor by hand cranking until the engine gains momentum, then knock down the decompression levers.

- Disconnect all belt-driven auxiliary equipment (refrigeration compressor, pumps, etc.) to reduce the starting load.

- Place a hand over the air inlet while cranking. Restricting the airflow will reduce compression and help the engine build up speed. Once the engine is cranking smartly, remove your hand—the motor should fire. *Never block the air inlet on an operating engine—the high suction pressures generated may damage the engine and cause injury.*

- An additional trick for *sailboats with a manual transmission* is to sail the boat hard in neutral with the propeller freewheeling, then start cranking and throw the transmission into forward. The additional momentum of the propeller may bump-start the engine.

Solving fuel problems. If an engine is cranking smartly, with sufficient compression to produce ignition temperatures, but still won't start, the culprit is almost certainly the fuel system. Unfortunately, the fuel system has the potential for causing a considerable number of problems! Some are easy to check but others can only be guessed at.

Check the obvious. Diesel engines are shut down by closing off the fuel supply. On some engines this occurs when the throttle is closed; others continue to idle at minimum throttle settings and have a separate *stop* control to shut off the remaining fuel supply. Has the stop control inadvertently been left pulled out? Has an emergency shutdown device, such as the air flap on a Detroit Diesel, been inadvertently tripped? Is the throttle open to the position specified for starting by the engine manufacturer? *A diesel will never*

start with the throttle closed. Trace the throttle cable from the throttle lever in the cockpit to the engine and make sure that it is actually advancing the throttle lever on the engine.

Is there plenty of fuel in the tank? The fuel suction line is probably set an inch or two off the bottom of the tank; if the boat is heeling, air can be sucked in even when the fuel level appears to be adequate. Is the fuel valve (if fitted) open? If there is fuel and the valve is open, but no fuel is reaching the engine, there may be a small filter screen, which has become plugged, inside the tank on the suction line. If such a screen is fitted, *throw it away*—this is not the proper place to be filtering fuel.

Most engines have mechanical lift pumps, but a few have electrical pumps. With the latter there should be a quiet clicking when the ignition is first turned on. If you are in doubt about an electric pump's operation, loosen the discharge line and see if fuel flows.

Solenoid valve. Many newer engines have a solenoid-operated fuel shutdown valve which is held in the closed position by a spring when the ignition is turned off. When the ignition is turned on, it energizes a magnet, which opens the valve. Any time the electrical supply to the solenoid is interrupted, the magnet is de-energized and the spring closes the valve. Any failure in the electrical circuit to the valve will automatically shut off the fuel supply to the engine.

Some solenoid fuel valves are built into the back of the fuel-injection pump—these are identified by a couple of wires coming off the pump close to the fuel inlet line. Others are mounted separately but close to the pump (Figure 8-20).

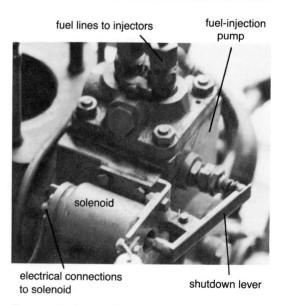

Figure 8-20. A solenoid-operated fuel shutdown valve.

A rod coming from the back of the valve actuates a lever on the pump. The operation of a solenoid valve can be checked by connecting it directly to a battery with a jumper wire. Take care to get the positive and negative leads the right way around. If the valve has only one wire, this is the positive lead; if two, one will run to ground and we want the other one.

Fuel filters. The primary fuel-filter should have a see-through bowl, which should be checked for water and sediment (Figure 8-21). If it is opaque, open the drain on its base and take a sample. On many fuel systems, this will let air into the system, which will then need *bleeding* (see below). It is not uncommon for a primary fuel-filter element to be completely plugged up. If this is the case, don't take chances—replace it along with the secondary filter element and drain the tank or pump it down until all traces of contamination are removed. If filters clog repeatedly, it is likely that sediment has built up inside the tank to the level of the fuel pickup. The tank needs opening and flushing.

If there is no primary filter, or if there is any sign of contamination making its way past the primary filter, *check the filter screen in the lift pump*, which can normally be found by undoing the center bolt and removing the cover (Figures 8-22A and B).

Assuming the tank has fuel and the filters are clean, the next step is to find out if the fuel lines have air in them.

Bleeding (purging) a fuel system. Air trapped in the fuel system can bring many diesels to a halt, although the extent to which this is true varies markedly from one engine type to another. Detroit Diesels can be purged simply by opening the throttle and cranking, whereas many older diesels can be completely disabled with even tiny amounts of air. When air has to be purged from a fuel system, the process is known as *bleeding*.

With the exception of Detroit Diesels, typical fuel systems are shown in Figures 8-23A and B. Fuel is drawn from the tank by a lift pump (sometimes called a feed pump) and passes through the primary filter. The lift pump pushes the fuel on at low pressure through the secondary filter to the injection pump. (On some engines, the lift pump is incorporated into the back of the fuel-injection pump rather than being a separate item.) The injection pump meters the fuel and pumps exact amounts at precise times and at very high pressures, down the injection (*delivery*) lines to the injectors, then into the cylinders. Any surplus fuel at the injectors returns to the secondary filter or tank via *leak-off*, or return, pipes.

The more cylinders an engine has, the greater

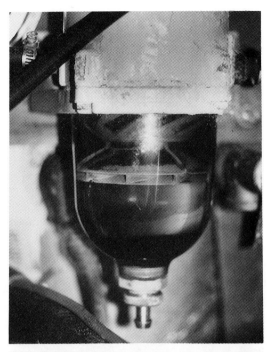

Figure 8-21. **A primary fuel filter with a see-through bowl. The sediment is a sure sign that the tank needs flushing. (This filter does not meet current Coast Guard regulations because it has no protective metal deflector plate around its base.)**

Figure 8-22A. **The fuel filter inside the top of a lift pump.**

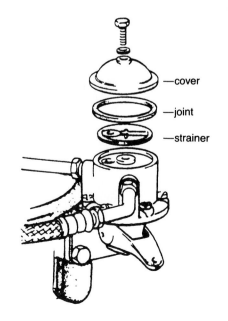

—cover

—joint

—strainer

Figure 8-22B. **To clean a lift-pump filter, undo the central retaining bolt, lift off the cover, remove the filter screen, flush it in clean diesel, and then replace it. Make sure that the cover gasket is undamaged, and that a good seal is made when the cover is replaced—any leakage here will let air into the fuel system.** *(Perkins Engines Ltd.)*

Figure 8-23A and 8-23B. Fuel system schematics. Note the two different types of fuel-injection pumps in common use on four-cycle engines—distributor type and jerk type. They are easily distinguished since the fuel lines are arranged in a circle on the former and in a straight line on the latter. *(Lucas/CAV)*

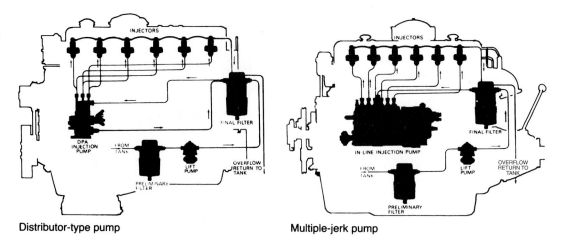

Distributor-type pump

Multiple-jerk pump

Figure 8-24. Internal fuel lines. Shown here are the fuel lines inside a valve cover and their point of entry into the engine. *(Caterpillar Tractor Company)*

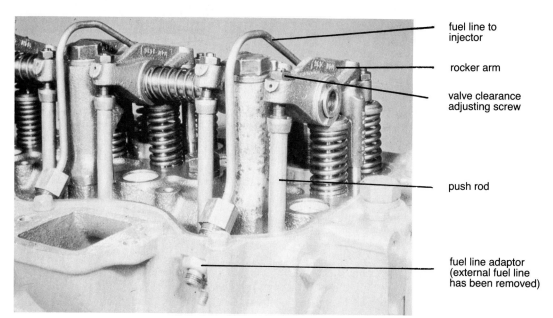

fuel line to injector

rocker arm

valve clearance adjusting screw

push rod

fuel line adaptor (external fuel line has been removed)

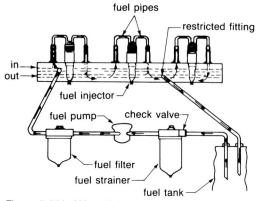

fuel pipes

restricted fitting

in
out

fuel injector

fuel pump   check valve

fuel filter

fuel strainer

fuel tank

Figure 8-25A. **(Above)** A typical two-cycle diesel engine fuel system. *(Detroit Diesel)*

Figure 8-25B. **(Right)** A Detroit Diesel (common rail) fuel system. *(Detroit Diesel)*

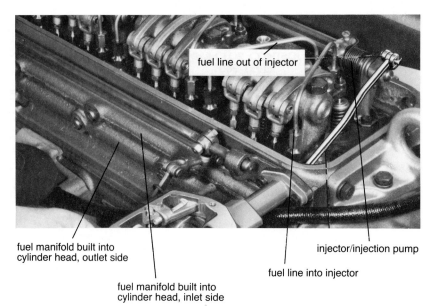

fuel line out of injector

fuel manifold built into cylinder head, outlet side

fuel manifold built into cylinder head, inlet side

injector/injection pump

fuel line into injector

the number of fuel lines. The various filters and lines can sometimes become a little confusing. Just remember that the secondary fuel filter is generally mounted on the engine close to the fuel-injection pump, whereas the primary filter is generally mounted off the engine, or on the engine bed, closer to the fuel tank. The filters should have an arrow on them to indicate the direction of fuel flow; sometimes the ports will be marked IN and OUT.

There will be an injection line (delivery pipe) from the injection pump to every injector, but the leak-off pipes go from one injector to the next, then down a common pipe to the secondary filter or fuel tank. This makes it easy to distinguish delivery pipes and leak-off pipes on most engines. A few engines, however (notably many Caterpillars), have *internal* fuel lines and injectors that are hidden by the valve cover. In this case, each delivery pipe runs from the fuel-injection pump to a fitting on the side of the cylinder head, and from there all is hidden (Figure 8-24). Detroit Diesels are as shown in Figures 8-25A and B.

At various points in the system there will be bleed nipples—normally on the filters and the injection pump (Figure 8-26). There should be one on the top of the secondary filter. On the base of a mechanical lift pump is usually a small handle, enabling it to be operated manually (Figure 8-27). Pump this handle up and down. If it has little or no stroke, spin the engine a half turn or so to free the manual action. (See the section on lift pumps below for an explanation of this.) Electric pumps are activated by turning on the ignition.

Engines that have neither an external lift pump nor an electric pump generally have a manual pump attached to the injection pump or one of the filters or at some other convenient point in the system (Figure 8-28). Bleeding follows the same procedure as that used on a mechanical lift pump.

Open the bleed nipple on the secondary filter and operate the lift pump (Figure 8-29A). If the filter has no bleed nipple, loosen the connection on the fuel line coming out of the filter. Fuel should flow out of the bleed nipple or loosened connection *free of air bubbles*. If bubbles are present, operate the lift pump until they clear, then close the nipple or tighten the connection. This should have purged the air from the suction lines all the way back to the tank, including both filters. If any of the fuel lines have a high spot, however, a bubble of air may remain at this point and be extremely hard to dislodge.

Take the trouble to catch or mop up all vented fuel. Diesel will soften, and eventually destroy, most wire insulation and also the

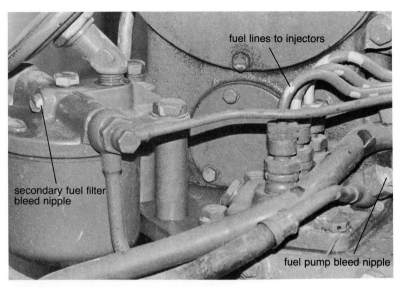

Figure 8-26. **The bleed points on a Volvo MD 17C.**

Figure 8-27. **Operating a manual fuel lift (feed) pump.** *(Perkins Engines Ltd.)*

rubber feet on flexibly mounted engines.

The next step is to bleed the fuel-injection pump. Somewhere on the pump body there will be one or perhaps two bleed nipples. (Some of the modern pumps are self-bleeding and have no nipples.) If the pump has more than one nipple, open the low one first and operate the lift pump until fuel that's free of air bubbles flows out (Figures 8-29B, C, and D). Close the nipple and repeat the procedure with

Figure 8-28. A manual fuel pump mounted on a fuel filter.

electronic water-sensing device

manual pump

filter drain

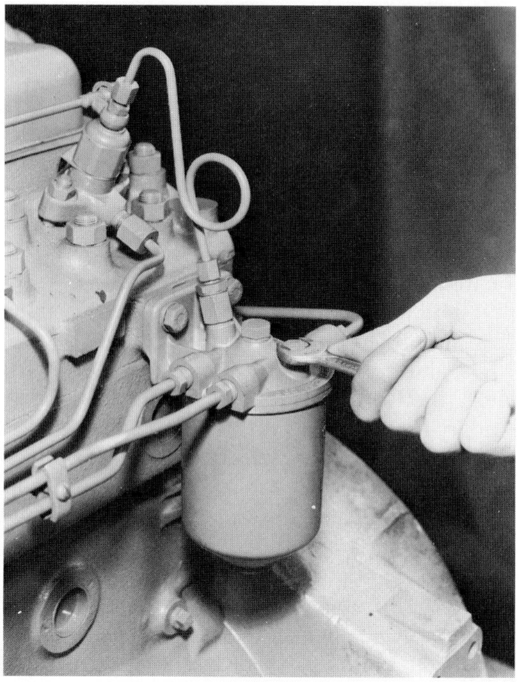

Figure 8-29A. **Bleeding a secondary fuel filter.** *(Perkins Engines Ltd.)*

Figure 8-29B. (**Left**) Bleeding the fuel inlet pipe to a distributor-type fuel-injection pump. *(Perkins Engines Ltd.)*

Figure 8-29C. (**Right**) Bleeding the lower nipple on a CAV DPA distributor-type fuel-injection pump. *(Perkins Engines Ltd.)*

Figure 8-29D. (**Left**) Bleeding the upper nipple on a CAV DPA distributor-type fuel-injection pump. *(Perkins Engines Ltd.)*

Figure 8-30A. (**Right**) The location of the injector nut.

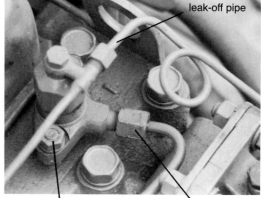

leak-off pipe

injector hold-down bolts

injector nut

Valve cover

Injector hold-down nut

Injector leak-off pipe

Decompression lever (in decompressed position)

Injector nut

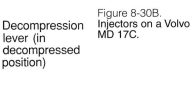

Figure 8-30B. Injectors on a Volvo MD 17C.

the higher one. The injection pump is now bled.

Bleeding the fuel lines from the injection pump to the injectors is the final step. To do this, set the governor control (throttle) *wide open* (this is essential) and crank the engine so that the injection pump can move the fuel up to the injectors. This should take no more than 30 seconds. In any event, a starter motor should not be cranked for longer than this at any one time because serious damage can result from internal overheating. If the engine has decompression levers and a hand crank, turn it over by hand to avoid running down the battery.

If the engine has no hand crank, the injection pump must be properly bled before attempting this last step. Frequently the battery is already low because of earlier cranking attempts; therefore, pumping up the injectors one time, let alone having to come back to try again if rebleeding is necessary, will be touch and go.

When the fuel eventually reaches the injectors, provided the engine is not running, a distinct *creak* will be heard at the moment of injection. It's a useful noise with which to be familiar. If it is present when any attempt is made to crank an engine, there is no need to bleed the fuel system (unless water is being injected!).

If the engine will still not fire, loosen one of the injector nuts (these hold the delivery lines to the injectors—Figures 8-30A and B) and crank again. A tiny dribble of fuel, free of air, should spurt out of this connection at every injection stroke for this cylinder (every second engine revolution on a four-cycle engine). If there is no fuel, or there is air in the fuel, the bleeding process has not been done adequately and needs repeating. On engines with internal fuel lines, loosen the nuts on the delivery pipes where they enter the cylinder head, *not the nuts on the injectors*, so that none of the vented diesel gets into the engine oil.

Do not overtighten injector nuts because this may collapse the fitting that seals the delivery pipe to the injector (tighten the nuts to 15 pounds-feet if you don't know the manufacturer's recommended setting). *Anytime an injector nut is loosened, it must be checked for leaks once the engine is running. Fuel leaks on engines with internal fuel lines will drain into the crankcase, diluting the engine oil and possibly leading to engine seizure.*

Detroit Diesel (common rail) fuel systems are self-purging. As long as the tank has fuel in it, the suction line is free of breaks, and the fuel pump works, the diesel flowing through the system will drive out any air. To check the fuel flow, undo the return line from the cylinder head to the tank, then crank the engine—a steady flow should come out (not the little dribbles that come from other injection pumps).

Persistent air in the fuel supply. One of the more aggravating problems on many four-cycle diesels can be persistent air in the fuel system. Air can come from poor connections, improperly seated filter housings (especially if the problem occurs after a filter change), and pinholes in fuel lines caused by corrosion and vibration against bulkheads or the engine block. Since the only part of the fuel system under a suction pressure is that from the tank to the lift pump, this is the most likely problem area. Sometimes fuel tanks are deeper than the lifting capability of the pump; the pump may fail to raise the fuel when the tank is almost empty, or fail to raise enough fuel (*fuel starvation*) at higher engine loadings. If the tank vent is plugged, over time the tank will develop a vacuum and once again starve the engine of fuel.

If the primary filter has a see-through bowl, loosen the bleed nipple on the secondary filter, operate the hand pump on the lift pump, and

Figure 8-31A. The diaphragm on a fuel lift (feed) pump.

diaphragm cover screw

diaphragm

manual operation lever

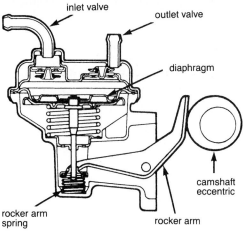

Figure 8-31B. A typical mechanical fuel pump. *(AC Spark Plug Division, General Motors Corp.)*

inlet valve

outlet valve

diaphragm

camshaft eccentric

rocker arm spring

rocker arm

watch the bowl. Air bubbles indicate a leak between the fuel tank and the primary filter, or in the filter gasket itself. No air: The leak is probably between the filter and the pump.

In the absence of a see-through bowl, locate the fuel line that runs from the lift pump to the secondary filter. Disconnect it *at the filter*. Place it in a jar of clean diesel and pump. If there is a leak on the suction side, bubbles will appear in the jar.

Any air source on the lift pump's discharge side should reveal itself as a fuel leak when the engine is running. When the engine is shut down, the fuel may suck in air as it siphons back to the tank. Next time the engine is cranked, it will probably start and then die. A similar problem can arise when the leak-off pipe from the injectors is teed into a fitting on the secondary fuel filter with another (overflow) line running from here back to the tank (this is a common arrangement). When the engine is shut down, fuel will sometimes siphon down the overflow line and cause air to be sucked into the system. In this situation, there is no external evidence of the air source, making for frustrating detective

work! To cure the problem, either move the leak-off pipe so that it runs directly to the fuel tank (in which case, if there is more than one fuel tank, the fuel must be directed to the one in use) or add a length of flexible fuel line between the injectors and the secondary filter. Loop this above the level of the filter and injectors and drill a small (1/16 inch) hole in it at its highest point. This will act as a siphon break.

Lift pump (feed pump) failure. Many small four-cycle diesels found in boats use a diaphragm-type lift pump (Figures 8-31A and B). Newer engines tend to use electric pumps. Larger engines and Detroit Diesels use a gear-driven pump (Figures 8-32A and B).

A diaphragm pump has a housing that contains a suction and a discharge valve, plus the diaphragm. A lever, which is moved up and down by a cam on the engine's camshaft or crankshaft, pushes the diaphragm in and out. This lever can also be operated manually, but if the engine is stopped in a position that leaves the diaphragm lever fully depressed, the manual lever will be ineffective until the engine is turned over far enough to move the cam out of contact with the lever.

Diaphragm pumps are nearly foolproof, but eventually the diaphragm will fail. When this happens, little or no fuel will be pumped out of the fuel system's bleed nipples when the lift pump is operated manually. Older pumps often have a drain hole in the base from which fuel will drip if the diaphragm has failed, but recent Coast Guard regulations have banned this for newer pumps.

A spare diaphragm, or better yet a complete pump unit, should be part of the spares kit on boats that cruise offshore. Diaphragms are accessible by undoing a number of screws (generally

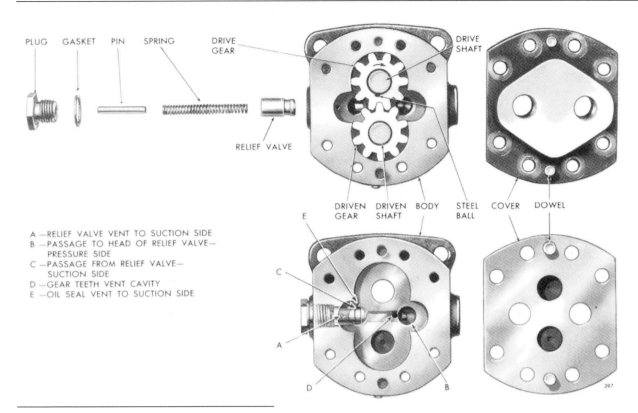

A — RELIEF VALVE VENT TO SUCTION SIDE
B — PASSAGE TO HEAD OF RELIEF VALVE—
     PRESSURE SIDE
C — PASSAGE FROM RELIEF VALVE—
     SUCTION SIDE
D — GEAR TEETH VENT CAVITY
E — OIL SEAL VENT TO SUCTION SIDE

six) around the body of the pump and lifting off the top half. The method of attaching the diaphragm to its operating lever varies—it may be necessary to remove the whole pump from the engine (two nuts or bolts) and play with, or remove, the operating lever (Figure 8-33).

If the air inlet and exhaust are unobstructed, compression is good, the tank has fuel, and the system is properly bled, it is time to feel nervous, check the bank balance, and call a mechanic!

Addendum: fuel tanks and fittings. After about ten years of use, many metal fuel tanks begin to develop pinholes. Depending on how hard it is to get at a tank to repair it or replace it, this may create major difficulties and expenses. Since tanks are not addressed anywhere else in this book, this is as good a place as any to slip in a few comments on tank construction and installation.

Tanks for both gasoline and diesel fuel can be made from copper (tin-plated on the inside), steel, galvanized steel, aluminized steel, aluminum, stainless steel, fiberglass and cross-linked polyethylene ("plastic").

Tin-plated copper was once quite common but is less so today. Over time the tin-plating can react with gasoline to form a gum that fouls carburetors, and the sulphur content in diesel fuels can be corrosive to the tank.

Steel, despite its tendency to corrode, particu-

Figure 8-32A. **A breakdown of a gear-type lift pump showing how the various parts fit together.** *(Detroit Diesel)*

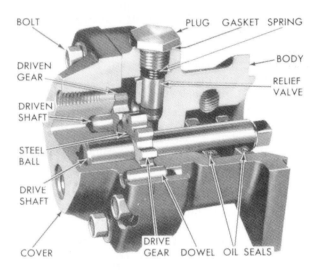

Figure 8-32B. **Cutaway of a gear-type lift pump.** *(Caterpillar Tractor Company)*

larly when exposed to salt water, is not a bad tank material. It is cheap and can be made thick enough to substitute mass for corrosion resistance. In gasoline applications it should be hot-dip-galvanized both internally and externally, but in diesel applications galvanizing should never be used on the inside of a tank since the

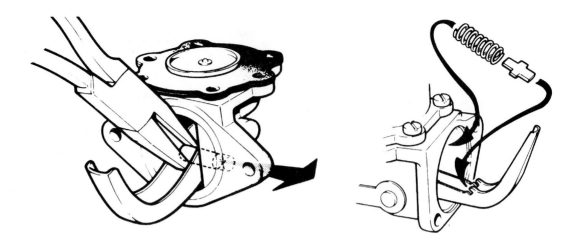

Figure 8-33. Diaphragm replacement on a lift pump.
(*Volvo Penta*)

sulphur in the fuel will dissolve the galvanizing, causing a sludge that is damaging to the fuel system. A steel tank that is properly primed and painted with a two-part epoxy will be as resistant to corrosion as most aluminum and stainless-steel tanks, but at far less cost.

Aluminum corrodes when exposed to salt water, and is also particularly susceptible to galvanic corrosion in damp areas and in contact with other metals. Corrosion will be slowed by using magnesium-bearing alloys ("marine" grades of aluminum) as opposed to copper-bearing alloys. *Any copper-based fittings* (common in fuel systems) *must be isolated from the aluminum*, while any fasteners used to attach fittings such as a fuel-tank level sensor, must be at least as corrosion resistant as "300" series stainless steel (refer to Table 4-1). Any copper bonding wire should be attached by means of a stainless steel bolt or stud, with the bonding-cable terminal clamped between two nuts so that the copper does not come into contact with the aluminum.

Stainless steel is considered by many to be the ultimate fuel tank material, but in fact it can be worse than the other metals! First, a good grade of *low carbon content* (see page 137) stainless is needed (high in nickel—preferably 316L, although 304L is far more common), which must be properly welded using the correct welding wire (stainless welds are far more prone to stress failure than either steel or aluminum welds). Secondly, to avoid crevice corrosion the tank must be installed in such a way as to keep it dry and ensure a good airflow over it (the points at which a tank rests on its bearers are notorious for developing pinholes).

Regardless of the material used, to slow corrosion all metal tanks should be:

1. Designed so that there are no external dips or hollows that can accumulate water;
2. Installed away from bilge water, with non-metallic, non-moisture-absorbent, nonabrasive strips separating the tank from its supports, retaining straps, or tie-downs
3. So placed that there is an air space around the entire tank (unless the tank is welded into the hull of a steel or aluminum boat—*integral* tanks are acceptable with diesel but not with gasoline)

Many aluminum tanks are foamed in place, using closed-cell foam. The problem here is that if any cracks or fissures develop in the foam, or the aluminum is not properly prepared to ensure a 100% bond between the foam and the tank, sooner or later corrosion will set in. When the tank needs replacing it will literally have to be chiseled out of the boat!

With metal tanks corrosion is inevitable in time. Corrosion can be eliminated altogether, however, by using fiberglass or plastic tanks. Although they are not often used, fiberglass tanks on a diesel-fueled boat have the advantage that they can be built directly into a fiberglass hull (integral tanks are, once again, not acceptable with gasoline).

The inside of a fiberglass tank should be laid up with several layers of resin-rich mat to ensure that the tank is well sealed. Nonintegral

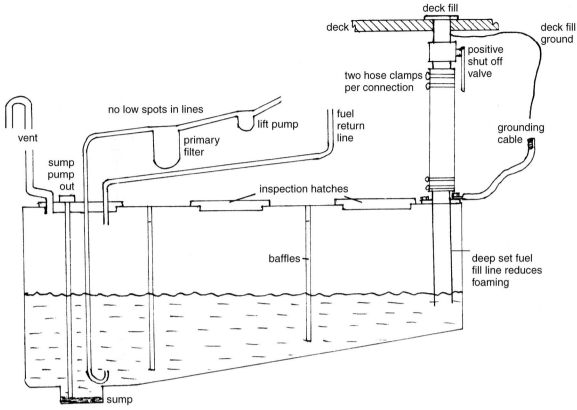

Figure 8-34. A "proper" fuel tank.

tanks are best made over a male mold so that the inside of the tank is smooth, and also because the exclusion of air from the surface against the mold promotes a better curing of the inner laminate. A one-off tank can be built around a suitably faired block of Styrofoam: When complete, an access hole is cut in the tank and the Styrofoam broken up and pulled out (if no access hole is wanted, gasoline poured through the fill-fitting hole will dissolve the Styrofoam).

Cross-linked polyethylene is arguably the best available fuel tank material. Any size and shape tank can be produced with a seamless construction that is noncorrosive and impervious to just about any damage other than severe impacts. The drawbacks are (1) tooling up for tank production is expensive, so an off-the-shelf tank, which might not be the most desirable shape or size, will have to be bought for most applications; and (2) installing baffles is difficult, which limits the size of tanks. When polyethylene tanks get hot, the tops tend to sag, so design and installation need to be geared to the prevention of water accumulation. Polyethylene tanks also absorb fuel, "growing" by approximately 2% when first put in service. This growth must be

allowed for in the installation.

Larger tanks need to be baffled at least every 30 inches (Figure 8-34). All tanks should be designed and installed with a distinct low spot that will act as a sump from which contaminants can periodically be removed (it is not permissible to have any drains on gasoline tanks—these have to be pumped out from above—but it is permissible on a diesel tank). All other tank openings should be in the top of a tank. The standard fill hose has a 1½-inch internal diameter (ID)—see Chapter 11 for more on hoses), and the minimum vent hose a 9/16-inch ID. Fill hoses should run to within an inch or so of the bottom of the tank (this reduces foaming, and also effectively seals any vapor in the fill line until the tank is almost empty).

Fuel lines are sized according to the application. The suction line should be run to within an inch or so of the bottom of the tank, but no closer, in order to allow sediment and water to settle out beneath it. Diesel engines have a fuel return line: If a boat has more than one tank, it is essential to design and label the suction and return valves such that the fuel cannot be drawn from one tank and returned to another (which might cause the second tank to overflow). If

Troubleshooting Part I: Failure to Start   273

there are crossover lines between tanks, these should either be fully protected from damage or else be built strong enough to be stood on. If sight gauges are fitted (permitted on diesel tanks, but not gasoline), there should be a valve at both the top and the bottom of the sight glass, with the valves opened only to read the level and then closed again, to avoid the risk of rupturing a glass and draining the tank.

Troubleshooting Part 2: Operating Problems

Overheating

Engines are either *air cooled* (rare in marine use); *raw-water* cooled (Figure 8-35A: the seawater is circulated directly through the engine—also rare); or *heat-exchanger* cooled. Engines with heat exchangers have an enclosed (*freshwater*) cooling circuit with a header tank. The cooling water passes through a heat exchanger, which has seawater on its other side, carrying off the engine heat.

Heat exchangers are either inside the boat (Figures 8-35B and C), complete with their own raw-water circuit and pump, or fitted to the outside of the boat in direct contact with the seawater (a *keel cooler*) and so requiring no raw-water pump.

Almost all engines with a raw-water pump and circuit pass the raw water through any oil coolers (for the engine and hydraulic transmission) and then discharge it into the exhaust. (Detroit Diesels include the engine oil cooler and transmission oil cooler in the freshwater circuit.) Even some keel-

Figure 8-35A. **Raw-water cooling.**

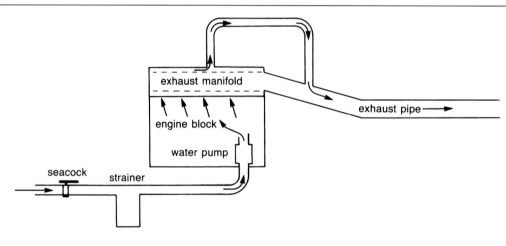

Figure 8-35B. **Heat-exchanger schematic.**

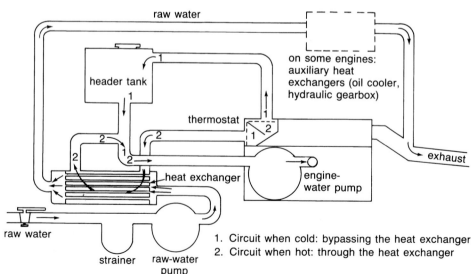

1. Circuit when cold: bypassing the heat exchanger
2. Circuit when hot: through the heat exchanger

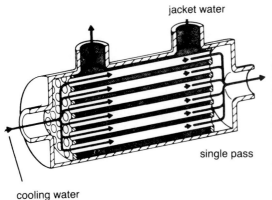

jacket water

single pass

cooling water

jacket water

two-pass

Figure 8-35C. **Single-pass and double-pass heat exchangers.** *(Caterpillar Tractor Company)*

Figure 8-36. **A raw-water filter.**

Figure 8-37. **A raw-water pump on a Volvo MD 17C.**

Figure 8-38A. **A raw-water pump with its cover removed. Three out of six vanes on the impeller are missing!**

cooled engines have an extra raw-water circuit specifically to cool the engine oil and exhaust.

Overheating can be the result of a number of things, but the primary suspect is always a loss of flow in the raw-water circuit. For this reason, as well as to prevent following waves from driving up the exhaust pipe, a water-cooled exhaust should ideally exit fairly high in the stern. It will then be possible to see at a glance whether the raw-water side of a cooling system is functioning. *It should be an iron habit to check the exhaust for proper water flow every time the engine is started.*

Overheating on start-up. The seacock on the raw-water circuit is probably closed! If not, check the raw-water filter (Figure 8-36) and then the pump. Almost all raw-water pumps are the rubber impeller type (Figure 8-37). If the pump runs dry, the impeller will tear up.

Check the pump drive belt. If this is OK, remove the pump cover (usually six screws) and check the impeller (Figures 8-38A and B). Make sure that when the pump turns, the impeller is not slipping on its shaft. If the impeller is damaged, pull it out with needle-nosed pliers or pry it out with two screwdrivers; a few have a locking screw or a retaining circlip (Atomic 3 diesel; if the shaft comes out with the impeller, the pump will

Troubleshooting Chart 8-2
Overheating on Start-up.

Is water coming from the raw-water discharge? **NO**	**YES**	Check the coolant level in the fresh-water circuit (if fitted). Caution: do not remove header-tank pressure-cap when hot. If the level is low, refill and find the leak.
Is the raw-water seacock closed? **NO**	**YES**	Open and then check the raw-water overboard discharge. The raw-water pump may have failed from running dry.
Is the raw-water strainer plugged? **NO**	**YES**	Clean and then check raw-water discharge as above.
Has the raw-water pump failed? Inspect the drive belt and tension or replace as necessary. Make sure any clutch is operative. If the belt and clutch (if fitted) are OK, remove the pump cover and inspect the impeller vanes. Make sure the impeller turns when the engine turns. **NO**	**YES**	Tighten or replace the drive belt as necessary. Replace a damaged impeller. Track down any missing vanes. See also troubleshooting chart 5-2 on page 71.

Check for collapsed or kinked raw-water hoses, an obstruction over the raw-water inlet on the outside of the hull (break a below-the-waterline hose loose as close to the raw-water seacock as possible and see if there is a good flow into the boat), or a plugged raw-water injection nozzle into the exhaust. Is the water-lift silencer frozen?

Troubleshooting Chart 8-3
Overheating in Operation.

Check the raw-water overboard discharge. Is the flow less than normal? **NO**	**YES**	Check for obstructions in the raw-water circuit. (see Troubleshooing Chart 8-2). In addition, check the raw-water circuit for siting, scale and other partial obstructions (see the text).
Check the oil level. Is it low? **NO**	**YES**	Refill with the correct grade and viscosity of oil.
Is the boat overloaded? (Check for a rope around the propeller; a heavily fouled bottom; adverse conditions; excessive auxiliary equipment; an oversized propeller.) **NO**	**YES**	Reduce the loading.
Check the coolant level in the fresh-water circuit (if fitted). Caution: do not remove the header-tank pressure-cap when hot. Is the level low? **NO**	**YES**	Refill and find the leak.
Is the freshwater circuit air-locked? (With the header-tank pressure-cap off, check for signs of flow when the engine is running—you may have to wait for the engine to cool down and the thermostat to close.) **NO**	**YES**	Break the hoses loose at the freshwater pump and water heater (if fitted) and bleed off any air.
Is the thermostat operating incorrectly? (Remove and test as outlined in the text.) **NO**	**YES**	Replace.

There is probably a mechanical problem (e.g. faulty fuel injection; a partial seizure)—see the text.

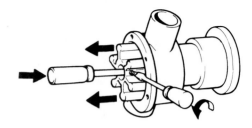

Figure 8-38B. Most flexible water pump impellers can be pried or pulled out . . . but some are secured to the shaft with a circlip (not shown) or setscrew (illustrated). The latter can be removed by prying out the shaft far enough to access the setscrew. *(Volvo Penta)*

have to be unbolted from the engine in order to replace an adapter in the back of the pump). Any missing vanes need tracking down—they will most likely be found in the heat exchanger (if fitted—Figures 8-39A and B). For rebuilding, see Chapter 12.

If the raw-water circuit is functioning as normal and the engine is freshwater cooled, check the level in the coolant recovery bottle (if fitted) or expansion tank. *Warning: Never remove the cap when it's hot. Serious burns may result.* If the level is low, find out where the water is going (adding red food dye may help in tracing leaks). Possibilities are leaking hose connections, heat exchanger or oil cooler cooling tubes that have corroded through (see Water in the Crankcase later in this chapter), or a blown head gasket. A blown head gasket will likely cause air bubbles in the cooling system when the engine is running, and these will be visible in the header tank; the header tank may also smell of exhaust fumes. Finally, note that a pressure cap on the header tank with too low a pressure rating, or a failure of the pressure cap, will allow the coolant to boil away over time (the pressure rating will be stamped on the cap; the required pressure is given in the engine specifications).

Overheating during normal operations. *Check the oil level.* If a low oil level is causing the engine to overheat, expensive damage may be in the making.

The raw-water inlet screen (if fitted) on the outside of the hull may be blocked with a piece of plastic. Throttle down, put the boat in reverse, throttle up, and then shut the engine down once the boat has reverse way on it. With a little luck, the reverse propeller thrust and water flow will wash the plastic clear. To confirm this, loosen a hose below the waterline and see if water flows into the boat. If the flow is restricted, check also for barnacles on the inlet screen or in the water intake.

Check the raw-water filter. If it contains a lot of silt, the heat exchanger (or the engine itself on raw-water cooled boats) may be silted up. Feel the freshwater inlet and outlet pipes to the heat exchanger—if it is doing its job, there should be a noticeable fall in the temperature of the water leaving the heat exchanger. Many heat exchangers have removable end caps and can be rodded out with a suitable wooden dowel. Note that if a refrigeration condenser is fitted in line with the engine cooling circuit, any obstruction in the condenser will reduce the raw-water flow to the engine.

Check for collapsed cooling hoses, a loose raw-water pump drive belt, or poor pump performance. This is another reason that a high-set overboard discharge is useful—the pump flow can be gauged at a glance.

Where the raw water is injected into the exhaust (on both raw-water-and heat-exchanger-cooled engines) a relatively small nozzle is sometimes used to direct the water down the exhaust pipe and away from the exhaust manifold. If scale forms in the raw-water circuit, this nozzle is likely to plug, restricting the water flow (Figure 8-40).

If the raw-water flow is normal, check any header tank as above, but *only after allowing the engine to cool.*

Perhaps the engine is overloaded (a rope around the propeller, an oversized propeller, a badly fouled bottom, or too much auxiliary equipment). Maybe the ambient water temperature is higher than normal. A boat moving into the tropics may experience a 40°F (22°C) rise in water temperature, and engine temperatures may rise a little.

An overheated engine can generate hot spots that cause pockets of steam to build up in the cylinder or head. These can sometimes air-lock cooling passages, the cooling pump, the heat exchanger, or the expansion tank, especially if the piping runs have high spots where steam or air can gather. (*Note that where a domestic water heater is plumbed into the engine cooling circuit, as most are, there is frequently a high spot in the tubing, which can cause an air lock.*) In certain instances, if the raw-water intake is not set low enough in the hull, a well-heeled sailboat can suck in air and air-lock the raw-water pump.

The thermostat may be malfunctioning (some raw-water engines don't have thermostats). It will be found under a bell housing near the top and front of the engine (Figures 8-41A and B). Take it out and try operating without it. This will make most engines run cool, but will cause a few—for

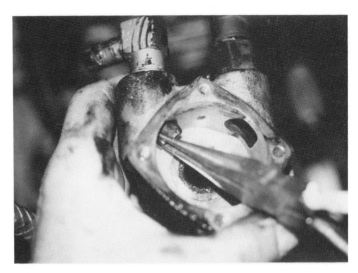

Figure 8-39A. Tracking down the missing vanes from the impeller shown in Figure 8-38A. The first one was found in the pump discharge elbow; the second in the tubing; and the third . . .

Figure 8-39B . . . . in the heat exchanger (the most likely place to find missing vanes). Note the smaller pieces of rubber lodged in two of the heat exchanger tubes.

Figure 8-40. Checking a raw-water injection nozzle for obstructions—this is a likely spot for debris to build up.

Figure 8-41A. The
thermostat housing on a
Volvo MD 17C.

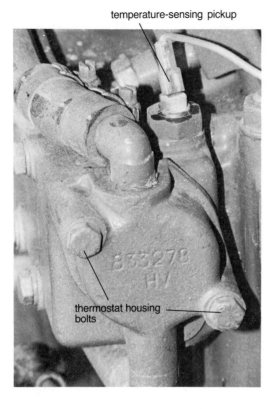

temperature-sensing pickup

thermostat housing
bolts

thermostat

Figure 8-41B. The thermostat removed from a Volvo
MD 17C.

Figure 8-42. **Checking the
operation of a thermostat.**
(Volvo Penta)

example, some Caterpillars—to run hot, and in
that case should not be done. To test the thermostat, put it into a pan of water and heat it (Figure
8-42). It should open between 165°F and 185°F
(74°C to 82°C), except on some Caterpillars,
which open as high as 192°F (89°C), and some
raw-water engines, which open between 140°F
and 160°F (60°C and 71°C).

Raw-water-cooled engines are likely to develop
scale around the cylinders over time (Figure
8-43), especially if run above 160°F (71°C).
Descaling requires professional advice.

Finally, problems with temperature gauges are
rare. If suspected, consult the section on Problems with Engine Instrumentation (page 285).

Figure 8-43. Corrosion in a raw-water-cooled cylinder
head. Note the scale partially plugging the water
passage on the right-hand side of the photograph.

Smoke

The exhaust of a diesel should normally be perfectly clear. The presence of smoke can often point to a problem in the making, and the color of the smoke can be an even more useful guide.

Black smoke. When unburned particles of carbon from the fuel blow-out of the exhaust, black smoke results. On many older engines, any attempt to accelerate suddenly will generate a cloud of black smoke as the fuel rack opens and the engine slowly responds. Once the engine reaches the new speed setting, the governor eases off the fuel rack and the smoke ceases immediately. This smoke is indicative of a general engine deterioration—the compression is most likely falling, the injectors need cleaning, and the air filter should be changed. If the engine is otherwise performing well, there is no immediate cause for concern, but the engine is serving notice that a thorough service is overdue.

If smoking persists when the load is eased off, the engine is crying out for immediate attention. The following are likely causes for the smoke:

- Obstruction of the airflow through the engine. Likely causes are a dirty air filter, or restrictions in the air inlet ducting, or a high exhaust back pressure (see below). Turbocharged engines in particular are sensitive to high back pressure. Many engines on auxiliary sailboats are tucked away in little boxes. As often as not these boxes are fairly well sealed to cut down on noise levels. Unless they are adequately vented, *this can strangle the engine*, particularly at higher engine loadings and in hot climates, where the air is less dense.
- Overloading of the engine, for example, by wrapping a rope around the propeller. The governor reacts by opening the fuel control lever until more fuel is being injected than can be burned with the oxygen that's available. This improperly burned fuel is emitted as black smoke. Black smoke on new boats should raise the suspicion of an overloaded engine caused by the wrong propeller or too much auxiliary equipment.
- Defective fuel-injection. If an engine is not overloaded, and the airflow is unobstructed, poor injection is the number one suspect for black smoke.
- Excessively high ambient air temperatures (e.g., in a hot engine room on a boat operating in the tropics). The density, thus the weight, of the air entering the engine will be reduced, leading to an insufficient air supply, especially at high engine loadings.

Blue smoke. Blue smoke comes from burning oil. Oil can find its way into the combustion chambers only by making it up past piston rings; down valve guides and stems; or in through the air inlet from leaking supercharger or turbocharger seals, from an overfilled oil-bath air filter, or perhaps from a crankcase breather.

Engines that idle or run at low loads for long periods do not become hot enough to expand the pistons and piston rings fully. These then fail to seat properly, and oil from the crankcase finds its way into the combustion chamber. In time, the cylinders become *glazed* (very smooth), while the piston rings get gummed into their grooves, allowing more oil past. Oil consumption rises and compression declines. Blowby down the sides of the pistons raises the pressure in the crankcase and blows an oil mist out of the crankcase breather. Carbon builds up on the valves and valve stems and plugs the exhaust system. Valves may jam in their guides and hit pistons. *Prolonged idling and low-load running will substantially increase maintenance costs, including major overhauls, and shorten engine life.*

White smoke. White smoke is caused by water vapor in the exhaust or by totally unburned, but atomized, fuel. The former is symptomatic of

Troubleshooting Chart 8-4.	
Smoke	
Black	**Blue**

Obstruction in the airflow:
   Dirty air filter
   Defective turbo/supercharger
   High exhaust back pressure
	Worn or stuck piston rings
	
	Worn valve guides

Excessively high ambient air
   temperature
	Turbo/supercharger problems:
	   worn oil seals
	   plugged oil drain

Overload:
   Rope around the propeller
   Oversized propeller
   Heavily fouled bottom
   Excessive auxiliary equipment
	Overfilled oil-bath-type air
	   filter
	
	High crankcase oil level/
	   pressure

Defective fuel injection	
White Lack of compression Water in the fuel Air in the fuel Defective injector Cracked cylinder head/leaking head gasket	

Note: when an exhaust is water cooled, it is difficult to distinguish white smoke from the normal exhaust.

dirty fuel, or possibly a leaking head gasket, cracked head, or cracked cylinder allowing water into the combustion chamber. The latter generally indicates that one or more cylinders are failing to fire. Air in the fuel supply will, on occasion, cause misfiring with little puffs of white smoke. Unfortunately, it is generally not possible to distinguish any of these conditions on a boat because of the water normally present in the exhaust that is injected from the cooling system!

Loss of Performance

High back pressure. The exhaust is an integral part of the airflow through an engine. Any restriction will generate *back pressure* (see accompanying sidebar, Measuring Exhaust Back Pressure). This will cause an engine to lose power, overheat, and probably smoke (black). The most likely causes of high exhaust back pressure are:

- A closed, or partially closed, sea valve on the exhaust exit pipe
- Too small an exhaust pipe, too many bends and elbows, too great a lift from a water-lift muffler to the exhaust exit (refer back to Figure 8-13), or a kink in an exhaust hose
- Excessive carbon formation in the exhaust system caused by long hours of operation at light loads (such as when battery-charging or refrigerating at anchor)
- In wintertime, frozen water in a water-lift-type muffler at initial start-up. This may produce a hissing immediately after cranking, or bubbles in the raw-water strainer, as the trapped exhaust looks for a path to escape.

An exhaust should be broken loose and inspected annually. A heavily sooted exhaust will need cleaning—so will the exhaust passages on the engine, and the turbocharger if fitted.

Knocks. Diesel engines make a variety of interesting noises. Each of the principal components creates its own sound, and a good mechanic can often isolate a problem simply by detecting a specific *knock* coming out of the engine.

The symphony, however, is frequently garbled by a variety of fuel and ignition knocks. Differences in the rate of combustion can cause noises that are almost indistinguishable from mechanical knocks, especially on two-cycle diesels. But if the engine is run at full speed and then the governor control lever (the throttle) is shut down, a fuel knock will cease at once, whereas a mechanical knock will probably still be audible, albeit not as loudly as before because the engine is now merely coasting to a stop. Knocks that gradually get louder over the life of an engine (especially if accompanied by slowly declining oil pressure when the engine is hot) are almost certainly mechanical knocks.

Some fuel knocks are quite normal, especially on initial start-up—diesels are much noisier than gasoline engines and have a characteristic *clatter* at idle, especially when cold. The owner of a diesel will have to become accustomed to these noises in order to detect and differentiate out-of-the-ordinary fuel knocks. These can have several causes, such as poor-quality fuel (low cetane rating, dirt or water in the fuel), faulty fuel-injection, injection timing too early, and oil in the inlet manifold from leaking turbocharger or supercharger seals. (The oil is then sucked into the cylinders causing premature ignition. In extreme cases, enough oil can be drawn in to cause engine *runaway*—the engine speeds up out of control and will not shut down when the fuel rack is closed. Runaway is more prevalent on two-cycle diesels than four-cycles, and that's why Detroit Diesels have the emergency air flap that cuts off all air to the engine and strangles it. In the absence of an emergency air flap, the only way to stop runaway is to cut off the oxygen supply to the engine with a CO_2 [carbon dioxide] fire extinguisher or by jamming a boat cushion in the air inlet.)

The more common mechanical knocks arise from worn piston pin or connecting rod bearings, worn pistons, and worn main bearings. Aside from checking the fuel quality, *all these mechanical problems require professional help. Do not ignore new noises!*

Misfiring. Diesels idle unevenly due to the difficulty of accurately metering the minute quantities of fuel required at slow speeds. This is not to be mistaken for misfiring, which will be felt and heard as rough running at all speeds.

Misfiring may be rhythmical or erratic. The former indicates that the same cylinder(s) are misfiring all the time; the latter means that cylinders misfire randomly. Rhythmical misfiring is caused by a specific problem with one or more cylinders, such as low compression or faulty fuel-injection. If it occurs on start-up and then clears up once the engine warms, it is almost certainly due to low compression. The air in the cylinder is not initially reaching ignition temperature, but as the engine warms the air gets hotter until the cylinder fires.

The guilty cylinder(s) of a rhythmical misfire can be tracked down by loosening the injector nut on each injector in turn (with the engine

Measuring Exhaust Back Pressure

Exhaust back pressure can be checked with a very sensitive pressure gauge designed to measure in *inches of mercury* or *inches of water* rather than in pounds per square inch (psi). (See Table 8-2 for conversion of one to the other). It can also be checked with a homemade *manometer*. This need be nothing more than a piece of clear plastic tubing of any diameter greater than ¼ inch, fixed in a U-shaped loop to a board about 4 feet long. The board is marked off in inches (Figure 8-44).

Set up the board on end and half fill the tubing with water. Connect one side of the tubing to a fitting on the exhaust as close to the exhaust manifold as possible (but 6 to 12 inches *after* a turbocharger). Leave the other end of the tubing open. If the manifold has no suitable outlet to make the connection, drill an ¹¹⁄₃₂-inch hole, tap this for a ⅛-inch pipe fitting (standard pipe thread), and screw in an appropriate fitting. When finished, remove the fitting and fit a ⅛-inch pipe plug.

Note the level of the water in the tube with the engine at rest. Then crank the engine and *fully load* it. *This is important—if necessary, tie the boat off securely to a dock, put it in gear, and open the throttle.* The exhaust back pressure will push the water down one side of the tubing and up the other. The difference between the two levels, measured in inches, is the back pressure in *inches of water column*. On naturally aspirated engines and Detroit Diesels, it should not exceed 40 inches of water (3 inches Hg); on turbocharged engines, including turbocharged Detroit Diesels, 20 inches of water (1.5 inches Hg). However, it is frequently hard to keep an exhaust with a water-lift-type muffler within these tolerances.

Figure 8-44. A simple homemade manometer to check exhaust back pressure.

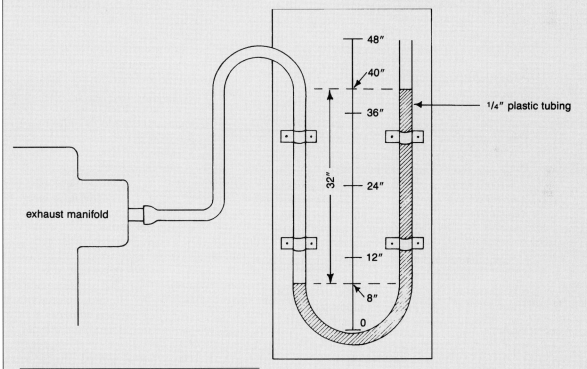

Table 8-2. Pressure Conversion Factors

To convert	Into	Multiply by
Psi	Hg″	2.036
Hg″	Psi	0.4912
Psi	H₂O″	27.6776
H₂O″	Psi	0.03613
H₂O″	Hg″	0.07355
Hg″	H₂O″	13.5962

running) until fuel spurts out (don't do this with a Detroit Diesel—fuel will flood out!). If the engine changes its note or slows down, the cylinder was firing as it should; the nut can be retightened. If no change occurs, the cylinder is misfiring, and needs to be investigated further (of course, if no fuel spurts out, we know why it's not firing!). If the engine has internal fuel lines, loosen the delivery pipes *at the external fittings on the cylinder head* so that fuel doesn't run down into the crankcase. On a Detroit Diesel, individual injectors can be checked by removing the valve cover and then, while the engine is running, holding down the rocker arm on individual injectors, which has the same effect as loosening the injector nut on other engines (this is a messy business since oil tends to splatter everywhere).

Erratic misfiring on all cylinders is the result of a general engine problem, frequently contaminated fuel. If the misfiring is more pronounced at higher speeds and loads, in all probability the fuel filter is plugged. If it is accompanied by black smoke, the air filter is probably plugged, or there is some other problem with the airflow (carbon in the exhaust, defective turbocharger, etc.).

Poor pickup. Poor pickup, or a failure to come to speed, is most likely a result of one or more of the following:

- Insufficient fuel caused by a plugged filter or a nearly empty tank
- A clogged air filter, in which case the engine is likely to be emitting black smoke. *This is about the fifth time that plugged filters have been mentioned in connection with various problems! This is no accident. Routine attention to filters is neglected time and time again.*
- Supercharger or turbocharger malfunction—black smoke is likely
- Overloading due to an improperly matched propeller, a heavily fouled bottom, too much auxiliary equipment, or perhaps a rope around the propeller
- Excessive back pressure in the exhaust
- Low compression, perhaps resulting in misfiring
- Improper fuel-injection
- Too much friction—a partial seizure is under way

Seizure. Seizure of the pistons in their cylinders is an ever present possibility anytime serious overheating occurs or the lubrication breaks down. Overheated pistons expand excessively and jam in their cylinders. An engine experiencing a seizure *bogs down*—that is to say, fails to carry the load, slows down progressively, probably emits black smoke, and becomes extremely hot. If immediate steps are not taken to deal with the situation, total seizure—when the engine grinds to a halt and locks up solidly—is not far off.

If the beginning of a partial engine seizure is detected, the correct response is not necessarily to shut the engine down immediately—as it cools, the cylinders are likely to lock up on the pistons. The load should be instantly thrown off and the engine idled down as far as possible for a minute or so to give it a chance to cool off. This action assumes that the seizure is not due to the loss of the lubricating oil or cooling water. In either of those situations, there is no choice but to shut down as soon as possible.

Water in the Crankcase

A certain amount of water can find its way into the crankcase from condensation of steam formed during combustion, but appreciable quantities can come only from the cooling system. The sources are strictly limited: water siphoning in through exhaust valves from a faulty water-cooled exhaust installation (see page 258), leaks around injector sleeves (where fitted), a leaking cylinder head gasket, a cracked cylinder liner (or one with a pinhole caused by corrosion from the water-jacket side), a leaking O-ring seal at the base of a wet liner, or corrosion in an oil cooler.

The cooling tubes on oil coolers with raw water circulating on the water side (as opposed to water from an enclosed engine cooling circuit) are especially prone to damage. The combination of heat, salt water, and dissimilar metals is a potent one for galvanic corrosion. All too many oil coolers are made of materials unsuited to the marine environment (e.g., brass). Oil coolers are expensive and often hard to find. Before starting on a long cruise, make sure a cooler is marine grade (bronze and cupronickel) and *adequately protected with sacrificial zinc pencil anodes (Figure 8-45). These zincs should be checked every month or so and replaced when only partially eaten away* (no more than 50%). Some engines in the tropics will consume their zincs in as little as 30 days—be sure to bring a good supply of spares.

When an oil cooler tube fails during engine operation, oil is likely to be pumped into the cooling system. On a raw-water cooled oil cooler, the oil will show itself as an overboard slick. On a freshwater cooled oil cooler, the oil will appear in the header tank. When the engine is at rest, water from the cooling system may find

Figure 8-45. A heat exchanger that has been patched with Bondo. Note that the zinc, which should be screwed into the pipe plug that is set on top of the heat exchanger, has been completely eaten away. It would have been a whole lot less trouble and expense to replace the zinc than it was to patch up the heat exchanger!

Figure 8-46. Emulsified oil inside a valve cover (the cover has been removed from the engine). In this instance the problem was caused by a blown head gasket.

its way into the oil side of the cooler and siphon into the crankcase.

If fittings can be found to bypass the oil and water sides of a failed oil cooler, the engine can still be run until a replacement cooler is found, but only at low loadings and only after changing the engine oil and filter. Keep a close eye on the oil-pressure and engine-temperature gauges.

One condition may be encountered that is sometimes mistaken for a water leak into the engine but in fact is not. This is condensation in the valve cover, leading to emulsification of the oil in the valve cover (it goes gooey and turns a creamy color—Figure 8-46) and rusting of the valve springs and other parts in the valve train. This happens from time to time when the owner periodically runs the engine for relatively short periods of time to charge a battery, or just to make sure it is still working. The engine never warms up properly, but it generates enough heat to create condensation in the valve cover.

If an engine is started, it should be run long enough and hard enough to thoroughly warm up. If possible, tie the boat off firmly, put the engine in gear, and open the throttle a little.

Low Oil Pressure

Low oil pressure is a serious problem, but occurs infrequently. Many people, confronted with low oil pressure, assume that the gauge or warning light is malfunctioning and ignore the warning. Given the massive amount of damage that can be caused by running an engine with inadequate oil pressure, this is the height of foolishness. *Anytime low oil pressure is indicated, immediately*

shut down the engine, find the cause, and fix it.

The problem is likely to be one of the following:

- Lack of oil, *the most common cause of low oil pressure and the least forgivable.*
- The wrong grade of oil in the engine—with a viscosity that is too low.
- Lowering of the oil viscosity by overheating, even though the correct grade is in the engine.
- Diesel dilution of the oil from leaking internal fuel lines. (Once enough diesel has found its way into the oil to lower the pressure to a noticeable extent, it will be possible to smell the fuel in the oil if a sample is taken from the dipstick.)
- Worn bearings (these do not, as a rule, develop overnight—a very gradual decline in oil pressure occurs, especially at low engine speeds when the engine is hot). *Any rapid loss of oil pressure accompanied by a new engine knock indicates a specific bearing failure that needs immediate attention.*
- Oil pressure relief valves sometimes malfunction, venting oil directly back to the sump, with a consequent loss in pressure. Problems with pressure relief valves are rare but are simple to check. Almost invariably, the pressure relief valve is screwed into the side of the block somewhere and can easily be removed, disassembled, cleaned, and put back. The spring is liable to be under some tension, so take care when taking the valve apart. After cleaning, reset the spring's tension to maintain the manufacturer's specified oil pressure. Run the engine until it is warm and check the oil pressure. If it is low, shut down the engine and tighten the relief valve spring a little (if it is adjustable). If no amount of screwing down on the spring brings the oil pressure up to the manufacturer's specifications, the problem lies elsewhere.

- A well-heeled sailboat will sometimes cause the oil pump suction line to come clear of the oil in the pan (sump), allowing the pump to suck in a slug of air. The oil pressure will drop momentarily, generally with a sudden, alarming *clatter* from the engine. This is especially likely to happen if the oil level is a little low. Check the level, top up as necessary, and put the boat on a more even keel.
- The failure of an external oil line or gasket (e.g., to an oil cooler) will cause a sudden, potentially catastrophic loss of oil and pressure. The engine is likely to suddenly *clatter* loudly. It must be shut down immediately. There will be oil all over the engine room! Less easy to spot is the loss of oil that accompanies a corroded cooling tube in an oil cooler. The oil will be pumped out of the exhaust (or into the header tank), and sometimes water will enter the crankcase (see above).
- Oil pumps rarely, if ever, give out as long as the oil is kept topped up and clean and the filter is changed regularly. Over a long period of time, wear in an oil pump may produce a decline in pressure, but not before wear in the rest of the engine creates the need for a major rebuild. At this time, the oil pump should always be checked.
- The oil pressure gauge is unlikely to malfunction (see below for troubleshooting engine instruments).

Inadequate Turbocharger Performance

Poor turbocharger performance will cause symptoms similar to those caused by a plugged air filter: reduced power, overheating, and black smoke. Be sure to check the airflow through the engine (including looking for: obstructions in the exhaust; any air leaks between the turbocharger and the inlet manifold, or exhaust leaks between the exhaust manifold and the turbocharger; and dirt plugging the fins on any intercooler or aftercooler) before turning attention to the turbocharger.

Turbochargers spin at up to 120,000 rpm; the speed of the blade tips can exceed the speed of sound; temperatures are as high as 1,200°F (650°C)—hot enough to melt glass. The degree of precision needed to make all this possible means that *repairing turbochargers is strictly for specialists.*

A turbocharged engine should *never be raced on initial start-up*—the oil needs time to be pumped up to the bearings. Similarly, *never race the engine before shutting it down*; the turbine and compressor wheel will continue to spin for some time but without any oil supply to the bearings, and the residual heat will turn any oil in the bearings into abrasive carbon.

Clean oil is critical to turbocharger life—the bearings will be one of the first things to suffer from poor oil-change procedures. Many engines have a bypass valve fitted to the oil filter so that if the filter becomes plugged, *unfiltered* oil will circulate through the engine—if the filter is neglected for long, the turbocharger will soon be damaged. Note that some turbochargers also have their own oil filter, which must be changed at the same time as the engine oil filter.

Any loss of engine oil pressure, such as from a low oil level or the use of the wrong grade of oil in the engine, will also threaten the turbocharger. When a turbocharger is under load, insufficient oil for as little as 5 seconds can cause damage. Damage to bearings will allow motion in the shaft, permitting the turbines to rub against their housings.

A dirty or damaged air filter or leaks in the air inlet ducting will allow dirt particles into the turbocharger which will erode the compressor wheel and turbine. The resulting imbalance and loss of performance will lead to other problems.

Before condemning a turbocharger, make the following tests:

1. Start the engine and listen to it. If a turbocharger is cycling up and down in pitch, there is probably a restriction in the air inlet (most likely a plugged filter). A whistling sound is quite likely produced by a leak in the inlet or exhaust piping.
2. Stop the engine, *let the turbocharger cool,* and remove the inlet and exhaust pipes from the turbine and compressor housings (these are the pipes going into the *center* of the housings—Figures 8-47 and 8-48). This will give a view of the turbine and compressor wheels. With a flashlight, check for bent or chipped blades, erosion of the blades, rub marks on the wheels or housings, excessive dirt on the wheels, or oil in the housings. The latter may indicate oil seal failure, but first check for other possible sources, such as oil coming up a crankcase breather into the air inlet, oil from an overfilled oil-bath-type air cleaner, or a plugged oil drain in the turbocharger, causing oil to leak into the turbine or compressor housings.
3. Push in the wheels and turn them to feel for any rubbing or binding. Do this from both sides.

If these tests reveal no problems, the turbocharger is probably OK. If it failed on any count

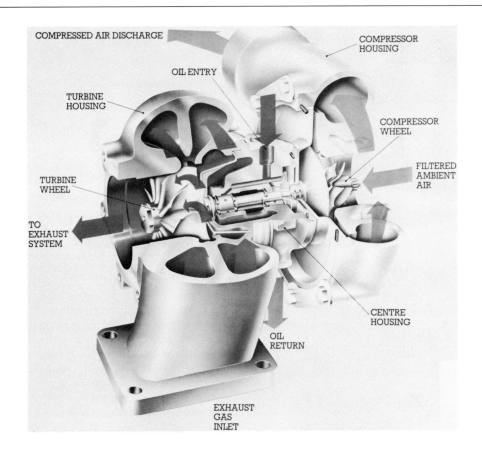

Figure 8-47. Cutaway view of a turbocharger. *(Garrett Automotive Products Co.)*

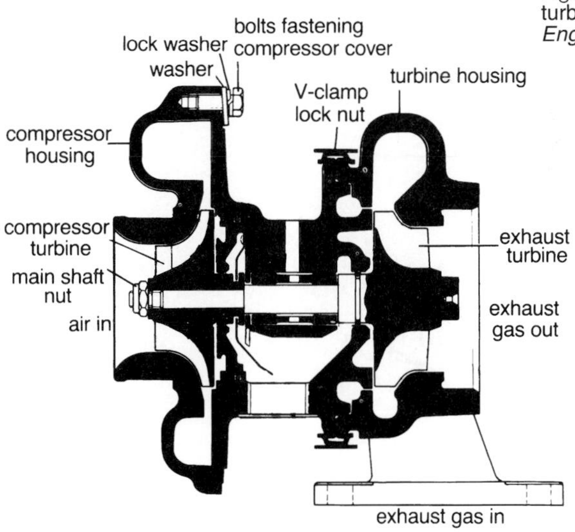

COMPRESSED AIR DISCHARGE

COMPRESSOR HOUSING

OIL ENTRY

TURBINE HOUSING

COMPRESSOR WHEEL

FILTERED AMBIENT AIR

TURBINE WHEEL

TO EXHAUST SYSTEM

CENTRE HOUSING

OIL RETURN

EXHAUST GAS INLET

Figure 8-48. A typical turbocharger. *(Holset Engineering Co. Ltd.)*

bolts fastening compressor cover

lock washer
washer

V-clamp lock nut

turbine housing

compressor housing

compressor turbine

main shaft nut

air in

exhaust turbine

exhaust gas out

exhaust gas in

(except dirty turbine or compressor wheels), it should be removed as a unit and sent in for repair.

Cleaning turbocharger wheels. Mark both housings and the center unit with scribed lines so that they can be put back together in the same relationship to each other. Allow the unit to cool before removing any fasteners or the housings may warp. If the housings are held on with large snap rings (circlips), leave them alone—they will come apart easily enough but will require a hydraulic press to put back together! Those held with bolts and large clamps can be taken apart (Figure 8-49).

If the housings are difficult to break loose, tap them with a soft hammer or mallet. Pull them off squarely to avoid bending any turbine blades. Turbines can be cleaned only with noncaustic solutions (degreasers work well—I am told that various carburetor cleaners also do a good job) using soft-bristle brushes and plastic scrapers. Do not use abrasives; resultant damage to the blades will upset the critical balance of the turbines. Make no attempt to straighten bent blades—the turbocharger demands a specialist's help.

After reassembly, spin the turbines by hand to make sure they are turning freely. Before starting the engine, crank it for a while to get oil up to the turbocharger bearings.

Problems with Engine Instrumentation

Some engines are still found with thermometer-type temperature gauges and mechanical pressure gauges and tachometers. All will have some kind of a metal tube from the engine block to the back

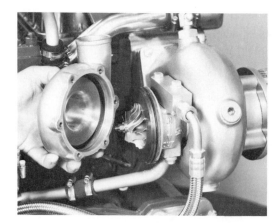

Figure 8-49. Removing a turbocharger housing. *(Perkins Engines Ltd.)*

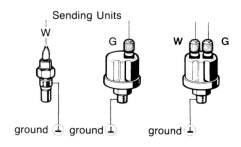

W = warning light or alarm wire
G = gauge wire

Sending Units

W   G   W   G

ground ⏚ ground ⏚   ground ⏚

Figure 8-51. Sending units for alarms and gauges. (**Left**) Simple sensor with a warning contact "W," as used, for example, with an oil pressure warning light. (**Middle**) Sensor for use with a gauge. (**Right**) Sensor with contacts for both a gauge and a warning device. *(VDO)*

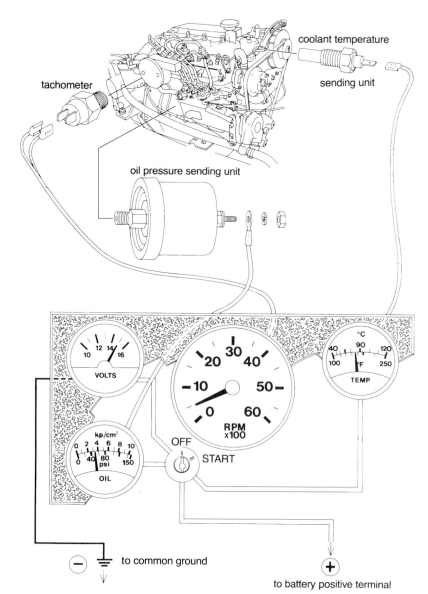

Figure 8-50. Sending units and gauges on a typical engine. *(Jim Sollers)*

of the gauge. Gauge failure is normally self-evident—the gauge sticks in one position. Temperature gauges and their sensing bulbs have to be replaced as a complete unit; oil pressure gauges may just have a kinked sensing line; tachometers perhaps a broken inner cable.

Most engines today use electronic instruments comprising a sending unit on the engine block connected to a gauge, warning light, or alarm (Figure 8-50). Detecting problems is not quite so straightforward.

Ignition warning lights. Most alternators require an external DC power source to *excite* the alternator before it will start generating power (Chapter 2). An ignition warning light is installed in the *excitation line* to the alternator. When the ignition is turned on, current runs from the battery down this line to the alternator, causing the light to glow. When the engine fires up, and the alternator begins to put out, the light is extinguished. If the light fails to come on when the ignition is switched on, check the bulb first. If it is OK, the most likely problem is a break in the wire to the lightbulb, or in the excitation line running to the alternator, or an electrically poor connection. If the light comes on and stays on after the engine is running, the alternator is almost certainly not putting out (Chapter 2).

All other warning lights and alarms. These use a simple switch. Positive current from the battery is fed via the ignition switch to the alarm or warning light and from there down to a switch on the engine block. If the engine reaches a preset temperature, or oil pressure drops below a preset level, the switch closes and completes the circuit.

Most switches (sending units) are the earth-

Figure 8-52. Warning light, alarm, and gauge circuits.

Warning light or alarm

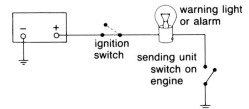

Gauge

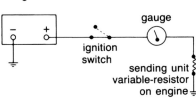

Combined alarm and gauge

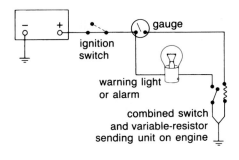

Combined alarm and gauge (another approach)

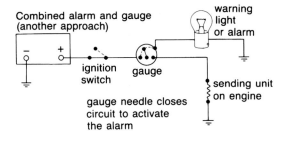

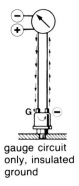

gauge circuit
only, insulated
ground

Figure 8-53. An insulated-return sending unit and gauge circuit, similar to the circuit in Figure 8-52, but with a separate ground wire (as opposed to using the engine block). This reduces the potential for stray-current corrosion. *(VDO)*

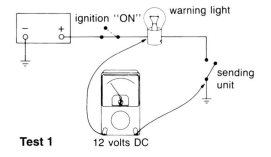

Test 1   12 volts DC

Figure 8-54. Testing a warning light, or alarm, circuit.

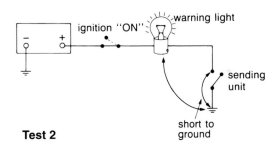

Test 2

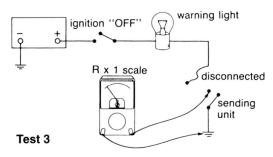

Test 3

return type—that is, grounded through the engine block (Figures 8-51 and 8-52). However, some are for use in insulated circuits, in which case they have a separate ground wire. Many sending units incorporate both an alarm and a variable resistor, which connects to a gauge. In this case there will be two wires on an earth-return unit, and three on an insulated unit (Figure 8-53).

If you suspect problems with an *alarm* or *warning light* (for *gauges*, see below), turn on the ignition switch and:

1. Test for 12 volts between the alarm or light positive terminal and a good ground—Figure 8-54, Test 1). No volts: The ignition cir-

cuit is faulty. 12 volts: Proceed to the next step.

2. To test the alarm or light itself, disconnect the wire from the sending unit and short it to a good ground (Figure 8-54, Test 2). The alarm or light should come on. If not, make the same test from the second terminal on the back of the alarm or light (the one with the wire going to the sending unit) to a good ground. No response: The alarm or light is faulty. Response: The wire to the sending unit is faulty.

3. If the alarm or light and its wiring are in order, the sending unit itself may be shorted (the alarm or light stays on all the time) or open-circuited (it never comes on, even when it should). Switch off the ignition, disconnect all wires from the sending unit, and test with an ohmmeter (R × 1 scale on an analog meter) from the sending unit terminal to a good ground (Figure 8-54, Test 3). A temperature warning unit should read infinite ohms, unless the engine is overheated, in which case it reads 0. An oil warning unit reads 0 with the engine shut down and infinite ohms at normal operating pressures.

Temperature and pressure gauges. Positive current is fed from the battery via the ignition switch to the gauge and from there down to a variable resistor on the engine block and then to ground (Figure 8-55).

To test a gauge:

1. Test for 12 volts from the gauge positive terminal to a good ground (Figure 8-55, Test 1). No volts: The ignition switch circuit is faulty. 12 volts: Proceed to the next step.

2. Disconnect the sensing line (which goes to the sending unit) *from the back of the gauge* (Figure 8-55, Test 2). A temperature gauge should go to its lowest reading; an oil pressure gauge to its highest reading, although just to confuse things a few behave the same as a temperature gauge!

3. Connect a jumper (a screwdriver will do) from the sensing line terminal on the gauge to the negative terminal on the gauge (or a good ground on the engine block if there is no negative terminal—Figure 8-55, Test 3). A temperature gauge should go to its highest reading; an oil pressure gauge to its lowest reading (except as noted above).

4. If the gauge passed these tests it is OK. Reconnect the sensing line and disconnect it at the sending unit on the engine (Figure 8-55, Test 4). A temperature gauge should go to its lowest reading; an oil pressure gauge to its highest reading (except as noted above). Short the sensing line to the engine block. A temperature gauge should go to its highest reading; an oil pressure gauge to its lowest reading (except as noted above). If not, the sensing line is faulty (shorted or open-circuited).

5. To test a sending unit, switch off the ignition, disconnect all wires, and test with an ohmmeter (R × 1 scale on an analog meter) from the sending unit to a good ground (Figure 8-56). Most temperature senders vary from around 700 ohms at low temperatures through 200 to 300 ohms at around 100°F (40°C), down to almost 0 ohms at 250°F (120°C), while most oil pressure senders vary from around 0 ohms at no pressure to around 200 ohms at high pressure. However, there are differences from one manufacturer to another, and some gauges

Figure 8-55. Testing a gauge circuit.

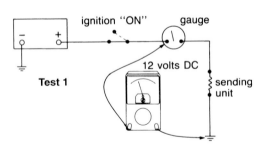

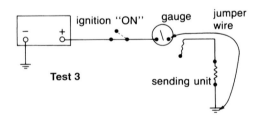

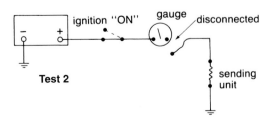

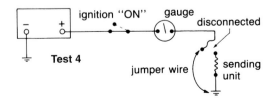

may work in the opposite direction—the important thing is to get a clear change in resistance with a change in temperature or pressure.

Tank-level gauges. Old-style tank-level gauges have been electronic, but in recent years pneumatic gauges have become increasingly popular.

Electronic gauges. A float is put in the tank either in a tube or on a hinged arm. As the level comes up, the float or arm rises, moving a contact arm on a variable resistance (a kind of rheostat). Positive current is fed from the battery via the ignition switch to the gauge, down to the resistor, and from there to ground (Figure 8-57). The gauge registers the changing resistance.

The same tests apply to the gauge, the sensing line, and the sending unit as for an oil pressure gauge. Sending-unit resistances are similar—near 0 ohms on an empty tank, up to around 200 ohms on a full tank.

Should everything check out OK, but the unit always reads "empty," the float on the sending unit is probably saturated or there is a mechanical failure—for instance, a broken or jammed arm. A saturated swinging-arm-type float can be made temporarily serviceable by strapping a piece of closed-cell foam to it.

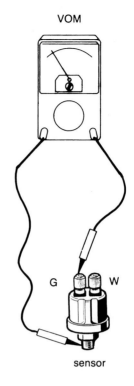

Figure 8-56. **Testing a sending unit.** *(VDO)*

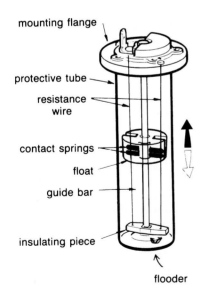

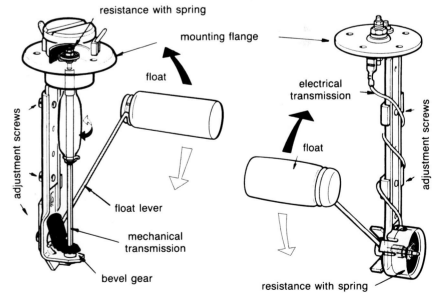

Figure 8-57. **(Left)** Electronic fuel tank sensor. Because of its construction, the immersion pipe sensor is suitable only for use with fuel tanks. The float unit is mounted on the guide bar, making contact with the two resistance wires via the contact springs. Resistance varies according to the height of the float, varying the gauge reading. The protective tube and the flooder provide excellent damping. **(Middle and Right)** Typical differences between a swinging-arm-type water tank sensor (middle) and a fuel tank sensor (right). For electrically conductive media, the electrical resistance element must be positioned in the assembly flange, with the level of the liquid transmitted mechanically up to the element. *(VDO)*

Figure 8-58. Pneumatic tank-level gauge. The gauge has been calibrated to the various tanks in the boat, with the relationship between the gauge reading and the tank volumes codified in the tables beneath the meter.

Pneumatic sensors. These are becoming increasingly popular due to their versatility and simplicity. A tube is inserted to the bottom of the tank and connected to a small hand pump mounted on the tank gauge panel. The gauge itself is teed into the tube just below the pump (Figure 8-58).

When the pump is operated, air is forced down the tube and bubbles out into the tank. Depending on the level in the tank (and hence in the tube) more or less pressure is needed to drive all the fluid out of the tube. The gauge registers this pressure in *inches of water* (in the tank) or *inches of diesel*. The owner draws up a table converting the gauge readings to gallons—the conversion will vary from tank to tank depending on the tank size and shape. The gauges come with instructions on how to draw up this table. If the instructions are missing, or your tank is an odd shape, the best bet is simply to empty the tank, then keep adding known quantities of fluid (e.g., 5 gallons at a time), stroking the hand pump and noting the gauge reading after each addition.

Pneumatic level gauges are more accurate than electronic gauges. What is more, apart from leaking connections or kinked tubes, there is nothing to go wrong. As many as ten tanks can be measured with one gauge simply by switching the gauge and pump into the individual tank tubes. Since there is no fluid in the tubes beyond the level of the tanks themselves, there is no possibility of cross-contamination from one tank to another. This means diesel and water tanks can both be measured with the same unit.

Winter Layup

1. Change the oil at the *beginning* of the winter, not the end. The used oil will contain harmful acids and contaminants that should not be allowed to go to work on the engine all winter long! The transmission oil should be changed at the same time.

2. Change the antifreeze on freshwater-cooled engines. The antifreeze itself does not wear out, but it has various additives to fight corrosion that do. Always mix the water and antifreeze *before* putting it in the engine.

3. (a) Either: Drain the raw-water system, taking particular care to empty all low spots. Clean the strainer. Remove rubber pump impellers, grease lightly with petroleum jelly, and replace. Leave the pump cover screws loose; otherwise the impellers have a tendency to stick in the pump housings. Leave a prominent note as a reminder of what has been done! Run the engine for a *few seconds* to drive any remaining water out of the exhaust. Drain the base of a water-lift muffler.

(b) Or: Close the raw-water seacock, make a routine inspection (as above) of the strainer and raw-water pump impeller, and then disconnect the engine suction hose from the seacock, dip it in a 50/50 solution of antifreeze and water, and run the engine until the solution emerges from the exhaust. (Note: *ethylene* glycol—commonly found in antifreeze—is harmful to the environment, so use *propylene* glycol instead, which is commonly used for winterizing drinking water systems.)

4. Wash the valves on any vented loops in warm water to clean out salt crystals.

5. Break the exhaust loose from the exhaust manifold (not visible in illustration) and check for carbon build-up; inspect the raw-water injection elbow for corrosion. Remove the raw-water hose from the injection nipple and check for any obstruction (this is a likely spot for scale and debris to get trapped).

6. Check the fuel filters and fuel tank for water and sediment, and clean as necessary. If the tank is kept full, it will cut down on condensation.

7. Squirt some oil into the inlet manifold and turn the engine over a few times (without starting) to spread the oil around the cylinder walls.

8. Grease all grease points.

9. Seal all openings into the engine (air inlet, breathers, exhaust) and the fuel tank vent. Put a conspicuous notice somewhere as a reminder to unseal everything at the start of the next season.

10. Remove the inner wires of all engine control cables from their outer sheaths. Clean, inspect, grease, and replace them. Check the sheathing as outlined on page 303.

11. Inspect all flexible feet and couplings for signs of softening (generally from oil and diesel leaks) and replace as necessary.

12. Inspect all hoses for signs of softening, cracking, or bulging, especially those on the hot side of the cooling and exhaust systems. Check hose clamps for tightness and corrosion, especially where the band goes inside the worm gear. (Undo the clamps a turn or two to inspect the band. When undoing clamps, push in relatively hard on the screwdriver so that the screw does not come out of its housing, leaving the band stuck to the hose!)

13. Remove the inlet and exhaust ducting (not visible in illustration) from any turbocharger and inspect the compressor wheel and turbine for excessive deposits or damage. Clean as necessary.

14. *Make sure that batteries* (not visible in illustration) *are fully charged* and, in the case of wet-cells, that they are topped up and recharged monthly.

15. Lightly spray the alternator and starter motor with WD-40 or some other moisture dispersant/lubricant; loosen belts.

Recommissioning

1. Unseal engine openings and tighten the raw-water pump cover if loose. If the paper gasket is rubbed with grease or petroleum jelly it will not stick to the cover or pump body next time the cover is removed.

2. Replace all zincs.

3. Capacity-test the batteries.

4. Tighten alternator and other belts.

5. Prime the cooling system.

6. Crank the engine without starting it until oil pressure is established.

7. Once running, check the oil pressure, the raw-water discharge, and the engine for oil and water leaks.

8. After the boat has been in the water for a few days, check the engine alignment.

For more on diesel engines, see my *Marine Diesel Engines, Second Edition*, published by International Marine.

Seizure	Excessive oil consumption	Rising oil level	Low oil pressure	High exhaust back pressure	Loss of power	Overheating	Poor idle	Hunting	Misfiring	White smoke	Blue smoke	Black smoke	Knocks	Low cranking speed	Lack of fuel	Low compression	Poor starting	Cause
															●		●	Throttle closed/fuel shut-off solenoid faulty/tank empty
					●										●		●	Lift pump diaphragm holed
					●		●		●						●		●	Plugged fuel filters
					●		●		●	●			●		●		●	Air in fuel lines
					●		●		●	●		●	●				●	Dirty fuel
					●		●		●			●	●				●	Defective injectors/poor quality fuel
					●		●		●						●		●	Injection pump leaking by
					●	●	●		●			●	●				●	Injection timing advanced or delayed
						●						●						Too much fuel injected
	●				●		●		●	●	●					●	●	Piston blow-by
					●		●		●	●						●	●	Dry cylinder walls
					●	●	●		●	●						●	●	Valve blow-by
											●							Worn valve stems
					●		●		●	●						●	●	Decompressor levers on/valve clearances wrong/valves sticking
									●	●							●	Pre-heat device inoperative
					●				●			●					●	Plugged air filter
				●	●												●	Plugged exhaust/turbocharger/kink in exhaust hose
●			●			●												Oil level low
●	●		●											●				Wrong viscosity oil
●		●	●															Diesel dilution of oil
			●															Dirt in oil pressure relief valve/defective pressure gauge
							●	●										Governor sticking/loose linkage
								●										Governor idle spring too slack
●						●												Defective water pump/defective pump valves/air bound water lines
●						●												Closed sea cock/plugged raw-water filter or screen/plugged cooling system
●						●				●	●					●	●	Blown head gasket/cracked head/water in cylinders
●						●												Uneven load on cylinders
			●													●	●	Worn bearings
						●											●	Seized piston
					●									●			●	Auxiliary equipment engaged
														●			●	Battery low/loose connections
●					●		●					●						Engine overload/rope in propeller

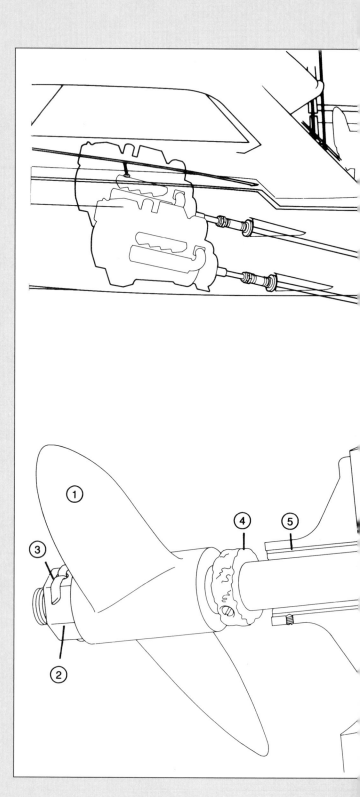

Figure 9-1. The mysterious space between engine and propeller is easily maintained, yet is all too often neglected. *(Jim Sollers)*

(1) propeller
(2) retaining nut
(3) cotter pin
(4) zinc
(5) cutless bearing
(6) bearing
(7) stern tube
(8) propeller shaft
(9) flexible stuffing box
(10) packing rings
(11) locking nut
(12) compression spacer
(13) adjusting nut
(14) shaft coupling
(15) output shaft
(16) transmission
(17) input shaft
(18) clutch discs

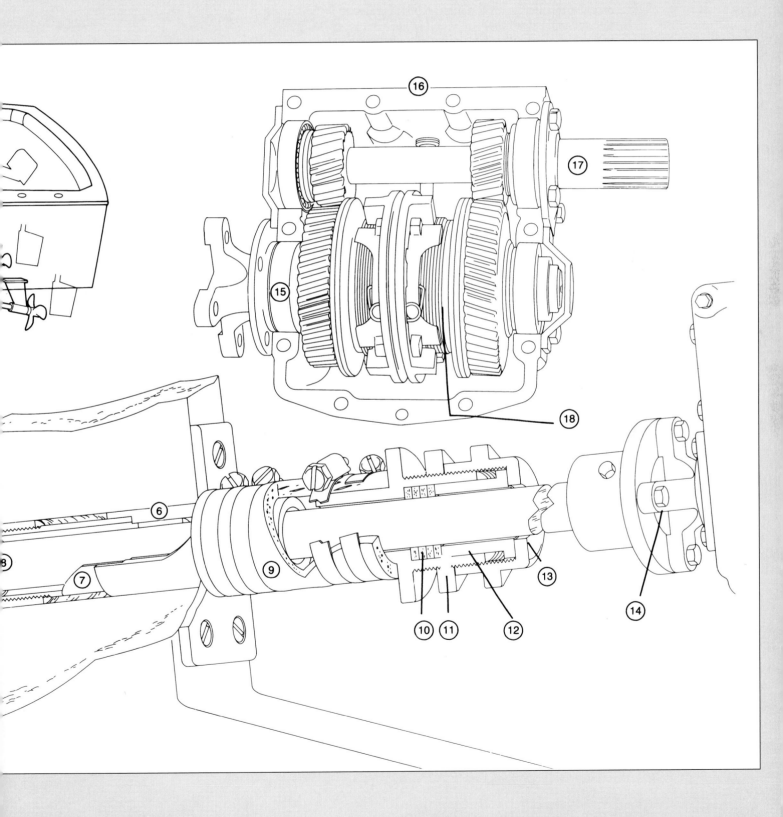

An inboard engine almost always has an attached transmission, or gearbox, coupled directly to the propeller shaft. The propeller shaft is sealed in the boat with a *stuffing box (packing gland)* or one of the newer mechanical or lip-type seals, and then supported just in front of the propeller with a Cutless-type bearing inserted in the deadwood, or in an I (P) or V (A) bracket (strut). (Cutless is a registered trademark of L. Q. Moffitt.)

Transmissions and Shaft Brakes

Transmissions: How They Work

Manual transmissions (gearboxes) are still found in some boats, and they are generally of the planetary, or epicyclic, type, but far more common are hydraulic planetary transmissions (Figure 9-2) and two-shaft transmissions.

Planetary transmissions. The engine turns a drive shaft which rotates constantly in the same direction as the engine (Figure 9-3). Deployed around and meshed with a gear on this shaft are two or three gears (the *first intermediate* gears) on a carrier assembly. These mesh with more gears (the *second intermediate* gears), also mounted on the carrier assembly. The second intermediate gears engage a large geared outer hub. The carrier assembly, with its collection of first and second intermediate gears, is keyed to the output shaft of the transmission.

On one end of the drive shaft is the forward clutch. Engaging forward locks the entire drive shaft and carrier assembly together—the whole unit rotates as one, imparting engine rotation to the output shaft of the transmission via the carrier assembly (Figure 9-4A).

Reverse is a little more complicated. The forward clutch is released and a second clutch engaged. This locks the outer geared hub in a stationary position. Meanwhile the drive gear is still rotating the intermediate gears. Unable to spin the outer hub, the intermediate gears rotate around the inside of the hub in the *opposite* direction to the drive gear. The carrier assembly imparts this reverse motion to the output shaft (Figure 9-4B).

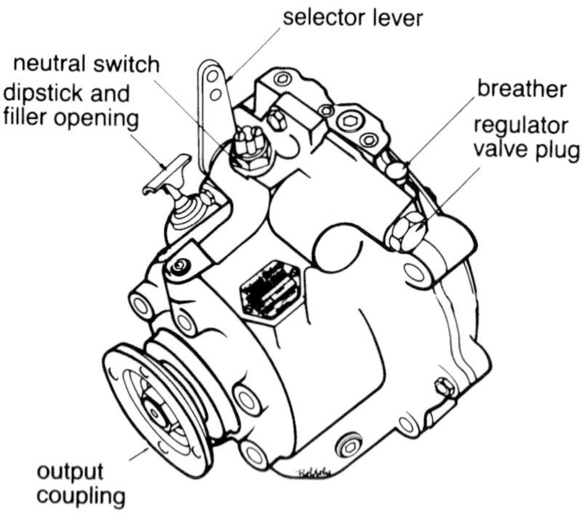

Figure 9-2. Typical hydraulic transmission. (Borg Warner)

selector lever

neutral switch
dipstick and
filler opening

breather

regulator
valve plug

output
coupling

Figure 9-3. An internal view of a planetary-type hydraulic transmission. In reality, the gears have teeth all the way around; to simplify things the artist has drawn the teeth only where one gear contacts another. (Borg Warner)

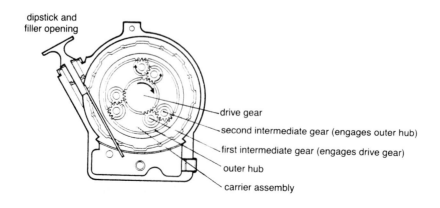

dipstick and
filler opening

drive gear

second intermediate gear (engages outer hub)

first intermediate gear (engages drive gear)

outer hub

carrier assembly

From Transmission to Propeller

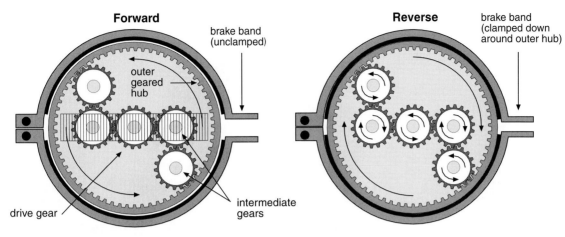

Forward

brake band
(unclamped)

outer
geared
hub

drive gear

intermediate
gears

Reverse

brake band
(clamped down
around outer hub)

Figure 9-4. Forward and reverse in a manual planetary (epicyclic) transmission. *(Michael D. Ryus)*

Figure 9-4A. In forward gear, the brake band is unclamped while the forward clutch locks the drive gear, carrier assembly and geared hub together so that they rotate as one (schematically represented by the band across the center of the drawing, locking all the gears). Engine rotation is imparted to the output shaft.

Figure 9-4B. When in reverse the forward clutch is released, leaving the carrier assembly free to rotate around the drive gear, while the brake band is clamped down, locking the geared hub. The carrier assembly is driven around the hub in the opposite direction to the drive gear, imparting reverse rotation to the output shaft.

Manual and hydraulic versions of a planetary box are very similar. The principal difference is that the reverse clutch of a manual box consists of a brake band that is clamped around the hub, whereas in a hydraulic box a second clutch, similar to the forward clutch, is used.

A manual box uses pressure from the gear shift lever to engage and disengage the clutches. A hydraulic box incorporates an oil pump. The gearshift lever merely directs oil flow to one or the other clutch; the oil pressure does the actual work. While quite a bit of pressure on the gear lever is needed to operate a manual transmission, gear shifting with a hydraulic transmission is a fingertip affair.

Two-shaft transmissions. The engine is coupled to the input shaft, to which two gears are keyed, one at either end. A second shaft, the output shaft, has two more gears riding on it; one of these engages one of the input gears directly, and the other engages the second input gear via an intermediate gear (Figure 9-5A). These two output gears are mounted on bearings and rotate freely around the output shaft.

The drive gears impart continuous forward and reverse rotation to the output gears. Each output gear has its own clutch, and between the two clutches is an engaging mechanism. Moving the engaging mechanism one way locks one gear to the output shaft, giving forward rotation; moving the mechanism the other way locks the other gear to the shaft, giving reverse rotation (Figure 9-5B).

In a *manual* two-shaft transmission, when the clutch-engaging mechanism is first moved to either forward or reverse, it gently presses on the relevant clutch. This initial friction spins a *disc carrier*, which holds some steel balls in tapered grooves. The rotation drives the balls up the grooves. Because of the taper in the grooves, the balls exert an increasing pressure on the clutch, completing the engagement (Figure 9-6). Only minimal pressure is needed to set things in motion, and thereafter a clever design supplies the requisite pressure to make the clutch work, but without the necessity for oil pumps or oil circuits. Gear shifting is once again a fingertip affair. In a *hydraulic* two-shaft transmission an oil pump provides the pressure for operating the clutches, just as in a hydraulic planetary transmission.

V-drives and inboard/outboards. A *V-drive*

Transmissions and Shaft Brakes   297

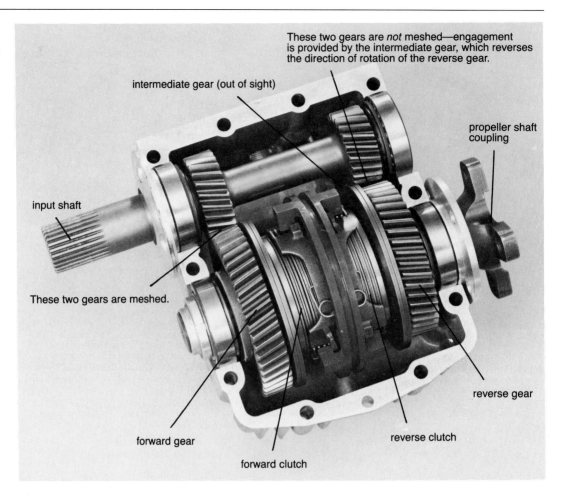

Figure 9-5A. A two-shaft Hurth transmission with the cover removed. *(Hurth)*

intermediate gear (out of sight)

These two gears are *not* meshed—engagement is provided by the intermediate gear, which reverses the direction of rotation of the reverse gear.

propeller shaft coupling

input shaft

These two gears are meshed.

reverse gear

forward gear

forward clutch

reverse clutch

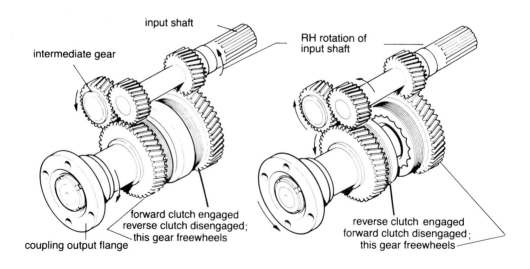

Figure 9-5B. Forward and reverse in a two-shaft transmission. When the forward clutch is engaged (left), the output shaft rotates in the opposite direction to the input shaft; when the reverse clutch is engaged (right), the output shaft is rotated in the same direction as the input shaft, via the intermediate gear. *(Hurth)*

input shaft

RH rotation of input shaft

intermediate gear

forward clutch engaged reverse clutch disengaged; this gear freewheels

coupling output flange

reverse clutch engaged forward clutch disengaged; this gear freewheels

298   From Transmission to Propeller

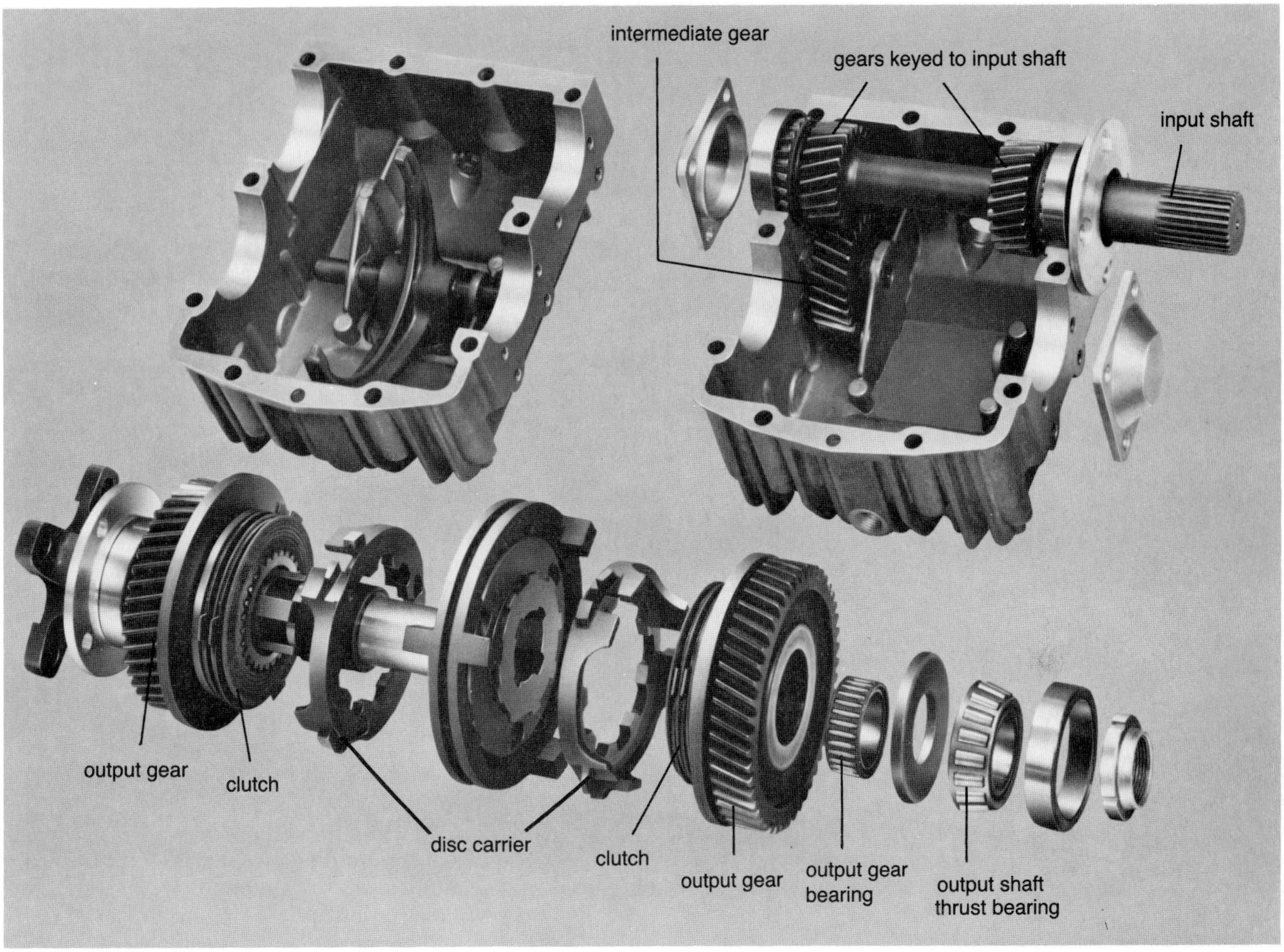

Figure 9-6. **A Hurth two-shaft transmission disassembled.** *(Hurth)*

is simply an arrangement of gears that allows the engine to be installed *backward*, placing it directly over the output shaft (Figure 9-7). This enables far more compact engine installations to be made, and in particular enables sportfishing boats and other planing-type hulls to have the engine installed right in the stern of the boat, which is the best spot from the point of view of weight distribution.

Inboard/outboards are exactly what their name implies—an inboard engine coupled to an outboard-motor-type drive assembly and propeller arrangement (Figure 9-8). These units have definite advantages in planing craft, notably:

- Inboard/outboards allow an engine to be mounted in the stern of the boat, which is the best place in terms of weight distribution on many planing hulls.

- The outboard unit can be pivoted up and down hydraulically. This enables these boats to take full advantage of their shallow draft to run up onto beaches. It also permits infinite propeller-drive-angle to hull-attitude adjustments for changes in boat trim, and makes trailering easy.

- The whole outboard unit turns for steering, greatly increasing maneuverability and removing the need for a separate rudder.

- There is no propeller shaft, stern tube, or stuffing box to leak into the boat.Naturally, there are drawbacks. The extra gearing and sharp changes in drive angle absorb a little more power than a conventional transmission; the U-drives in the transmission tend to have a relatively high failure rate if driven hard; and above all, most outboard units are built of relatively corrosion-susceptible materials. If the

Transmissions and Shaft Brakes   299

Figure 9-7. V-drive transmission. (Borg Warner)

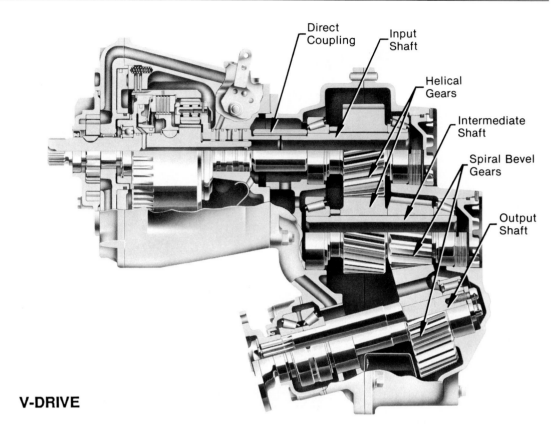

Direct Coupling

Input Shaft

Helical Gears

Intermediate Shaft

Spiral Bevel Gears

Output Shaft

V-DRIVE

Figure 9-8. An inboard/outboard. (Volvo Penta)

boat is kept dry-docked between use or the outboard unit is raised out of the water, this latter point is not a great problem, but if the unit is left in the water it can be.

Observing all maintenance schedules is important, particularly oil changes, greasing of U-joints, and replacing those all-important zincs.

Maintenance

Transmission maintenance is minimal (Figure 9-9). It generally boils down to keeping the exterior clean (important for detecting oil leaks); periodically checking the oil level (Figure 9-10—unless there is a leak, it should never need topping up); checking for signs of water contamination (water emulsified in engine oil gives it a creamy texture and color; in automatic transmission fluid it looks more like strawberry frappe!); and changing the oil annually. If there is an oil screen, a magnetic plug, or both in the base of the transmission, inspect them for any signs of metal particles or other internal damage when changing the oil. If the transmission has an oil cooler, especially a raw-water-cooled oil cooler, *the sacrificial zinc anodes must be checked regularly and changed when only partly eaten away.*

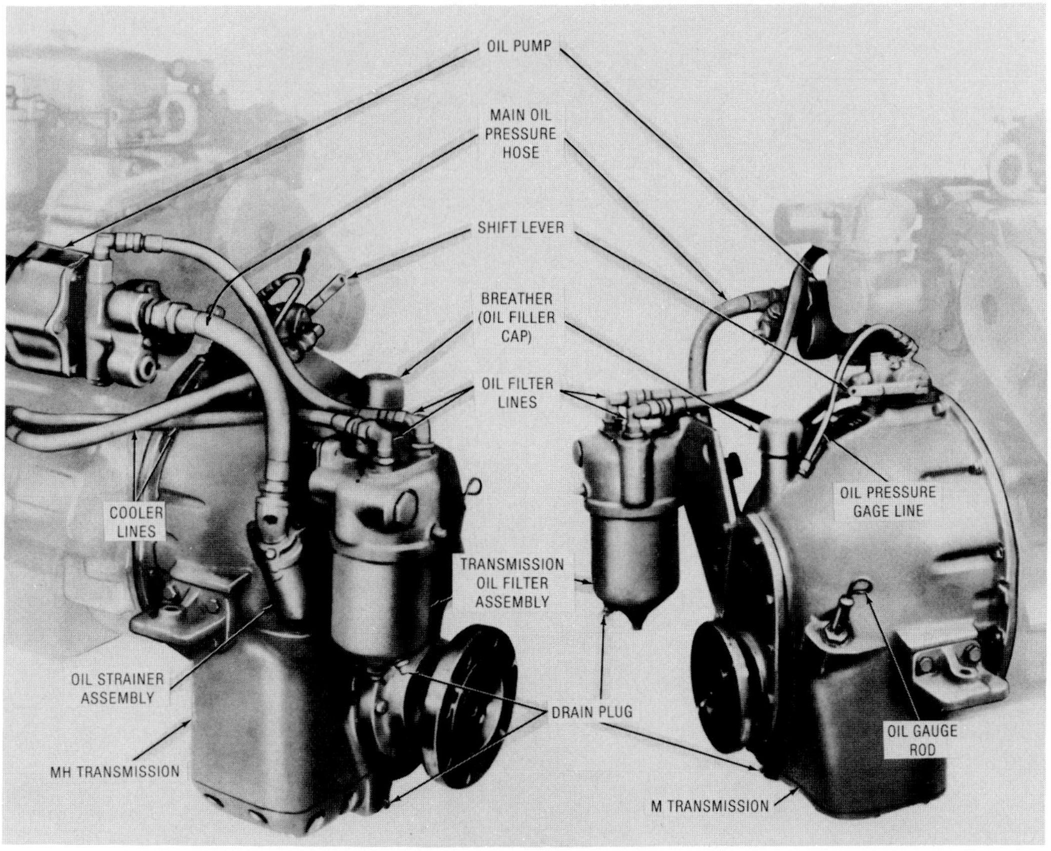

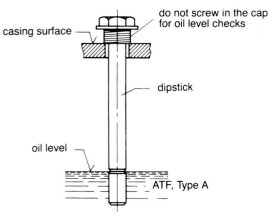

Figure 9-9. Principal external components on a relatively large hydraulic transmission. (Detroit Diesel)

OIL PUMP

MAIN OIL PRESSURE HOSE

SHIFT LEVER

BREATHER (OIL FILLER CAP)

OIL FILTER LINES

OIL PRESSURE GAGE LINE

COOLER LINES

TRANSMISSION OIL FILTER ASSEMBLY

OIL STRAINER ASSEMBLY

DRAIN PLUG

OIL GAUGE ROD

MH TRANSMISSION

M TRANSMISSION

Most transmissions operate on 30-weight engine oil or F-type transmission fluid. The latter is preferred by many manufacturers (see the manual). When checking the oil level, run a hydraulic transmission for a couple of minutes, and then shut it down to make the check.

Troubleshooting

The majority of transmission difficulties arise as a result of improper clutch adjustments (manual transmissions) or problems with the control cables (hydraulic transmissions), rather than from problems with the transmission itself (see below— Hurth clutches, in particular, are very sensitive to improper cable adjustments). However, before discussing these, there are a couple of problems peculiar to hydraulic boxes that must be noted.

A buzzing sound indicates air in the hydraulic circuit, generally as a result of a low oil level. This will lead to a loss of pressure and slipping clutches. Most hydraulic transmissions also have an oil pressure regulating valve that passes oil back to the suction side of the oil pump if excess pressure develops. If the valve sticks in the open

do not screw in the cap for oil level checks

casing surface

dipstick

oil level

ATF, Type A

Figure 9-10. Checking the oil level on a Hurth transmission. (Hurth)

position, the clutches may slip or not engage at all. If, on the other hand, the valve sticks closed, the clutches will engage roughly (as they also will do if gear shifting is done at too high an engine speed). The valve is generally a spring-loaded ball or piston screwed into the side of the transmission—removing it for inspection and cleaning is easy (Figure 9-11).

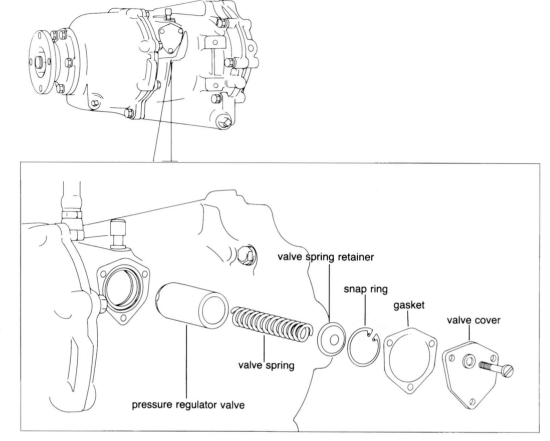

Figure 9-12. **(Below)** Operating principles of a Paragon transmission—a common manual planetary gearbox. For forward, the lever (1) is pushed toward the engine; the shift yoke (2) moves back the other way (toward the coupling), sliding the shift cone (3) along the output shaft (3a), thus moving the cam levers (4) out. The cam levers bear on the pressure plate (5), compressing the friction discs (6) in the clutch. The friction discs press against the gear carrier (7), causing the motion of the input shaft (8) to be transmitted to the output shaft (3a). The pressure plate is adjusted by backing out the lock bolt (5a), screwing up the castellated nut (10), and retightening the lock bolt. For reverse, the gear lever (1) is moved the other way, compressing the reverse band (9), which locks around the gear carrier like a huge hose clamp. *(Jim Sollers)*

valve spring retainer

snap ring

gasket

valve cover

valve spring

pressure regulator valve

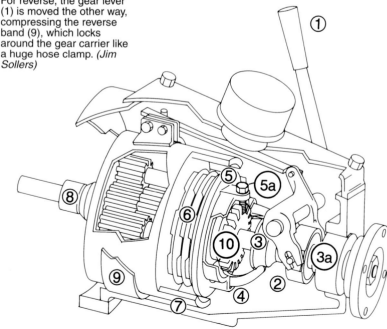

Clutch adjustments. The top of most manual transmissions unbolts and lifts off. Inside are adjustments for forward and reverse gears. Reverse is easier.

Move the gear lever into and out of reverse— the brake band will be clearly visible as it clamps down on the hub and unclamps (Figure 9-12). On one side of the band will be an adjusting bolt. If the transmission is slipping in reverse, tighten the bolt a little at a time, engaging reverse between each adjustment. When the gear lever requires firm pressure to go into gear, and clicks in with a nice, clean feel, adjustment is correct.

It is important not to overdo things. Put the box in neutral and spin the propeller shaft by hand. *If the brake band is dragging on the hub, it is too tight; the box is going to heat up and wear will be seriously accelerated.* If no amount of adjustment produces a clean, crisp engagement, the brake band is worn out and needs replacing—or at least relining.

To adjust the forward clutch, first put the transmission into and out of gear a few times to see what is going on. The main plate on the back of the clutch unit (it pushes everything together) will have either one central adjusting nut or between three and six adjusting nuts spaced around it. Tighten the central nut by one flat. For multiple adjusting nuts, put the box into neutral and turn it over by hand, tightening each adjustment nut as it becomes accessible by one-sixth of a turn. After going all the way around, try engaging the gear again. Repeat until the gear lever goes in firmly and cleanly. Lock the adjusting nuts. Do not tighten to the point at which the clutch drags in neutral (the propeller shaft will turn slowly when the engine is running); if over-tightening seems necessary, the friction pads on the clutch plates are probably worn out and need replacing.

Control cables. With the exception of manual boxes, which have a gear shift handle, most transmissions today use a push-pull cable to move the shift lever on the box (Figure 9-13). A push-pull cable is one that pushes the lever in one direction and pulls it in the other. *More transmission problems are caused by cable malfunctions than anything else. Faced with difficulties, always suspect the cable before blaming the box.*

If the transmission operates stiffly, fails to go into either or both gears, stays in one gear, or slowly turns the propeller when in neutral (*clutch drag*), make the following checks (Troubleshooting Chart 9-1):

- See that the transmission actuating lever (on the side of the transmission) is in the neutral position when the remote control lever (in the cockpit or wheelhouse) is in neutral.

- Ensure that the actuating lever is moving fully forward and backward when the remote control is put into forward and reverse. This is particularly important on Hurth boxes.

- Disconnect the cable at the transmission and double-check that the actuating lever on the box is *clicking* into forward, neutral, and reverse. Note: Hurth boxes do not have a distinct *click* when a clutch is engaged. However, the lever must move through a minimum arc of 30 degrees in either direction. Less movement will cause the clutches to slip. More is OK. *As the clutches wear, the lever must be free to travel farther.* If the transmission actuating lever is stiff, or not traveling far enough in either direction, make sure that it is not rubbing on the transmission housing or snagging any bolt heads.

- While the cable is loose, operate the remote control to see if the cable is stiff. If so, replace the cable. Note that forcing cables through too tight a radius when routing

them from the control console to the engine is a frequent cause of problems.

- Inspect the whole cable annually, checking for the following (Figure 9-14): seizure of the swivel at the transmission end of the cable conduit; bending of actuating rods; corrosion of the end fittings at either end; cracks or cuts in the conduit jacket; burned or melted spots; excessively tight curves or kinks (the minimum radius of any bend should be 8 inches); separation of the conduit jacket from its end fit-

Troubleshooting Chart 9-1. Transmission Problems. Symptoms: Failure to engage forward or reverse; clutch drag in neutral; or tendency to stick in one gear.	
Move the remote control lever through its full range a couple of times. Does it move the operating lever on the transmission itself through its full range? **YES**	**NO** Check for a broken, disconnected, slipping, or kinked cable.
Is the remote control lever free-moving? **YES**	**NO** Break the cable loose at the transmission and try again. If still stiff, remove the cable from its conduit, clean, grease, and replace. If the cable moves freely when disconnected from the transmission, move the transmission lever itself through its full range. If binding, the transmission needs professional attention.
When the remote control is placed in neutral, is the transmission lever in neutral? **YES**	**NO** Adjust the cable length.
Is the transmission oil level correct? (Most transmissions have a dipstick; hydraulic transmissions frequently make a buzzing noise when low on oil). **YES**	**NO** Add oil and run the engine in neutral to clear out any air.
Does the transmission output coupling turn when the transmission is placed in gear? **YES**	**NO** The transmission needs professional attention.
Does the propeller shaft turn when the transmission coupling turns? **YES**	**NO** The coupling bolts are sheared or the coupling is slipping on the propeller shaft. Tighten or replace set screws, keys, pins and coupling bolts as necessary.
There must be a fault with the propeller: 1. It may be missing or damaged; 2. A folding propeller may be jammed shut; 3. A variable-pitch propeller may be in the "no pitch" position; 4. If this is the first trial of a propeller, it may simply be too small and/or have insufficient pitch.	

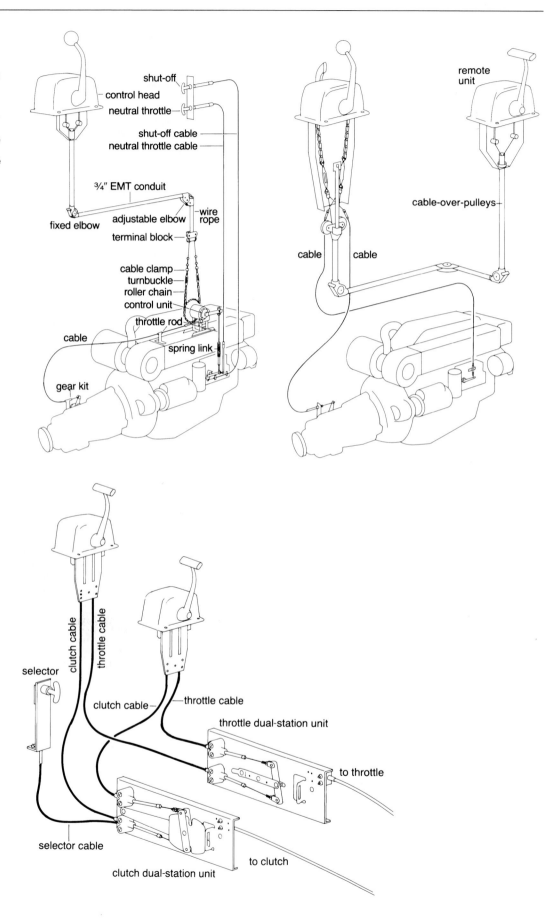

Figure 9-13. Typical remote engine and transmission controls. These comprise three sections: (1) the pilothouse control; (2) the cable system; and (3) the engine control unit. (**Left**) an enclosed cable-over-pulley system. (**Right**) a dual-station installation, with the main station using push-pull cables, and the remote station using a cable-over-pulley system. (**Below**) a dual-station installation using remote bellcrank units and single-lever controls. *(Morse Controls, adapted by Jim Sollers)*

shut-off

control head

neutral throttle

shut-off cable

neutral throttle cable

¾″ EMT conduit

fixed elbow

adjustable elbow

wire rope

terminal block

cable clamp

turnbuckle

roller chain

control unit

throttle rod

cable

spring link

gear kit

remote unit

cable-over-pulleys

cable   cable

selector

clutch cable

throttle cable

clutch cable

throttle cable

throttle dual-station unit

to throttle

selector cable

to clutch

clutch dual-station unit

tings; or corrosion under the jacket (it will swell up). If at all possible, remove the inner cable and grease it with a Teflon-based waterproof grease before replacing. Replace cables at least every 5 years and keep an old one as a spare.

Miscellaneous operating problems. If the oil is kept clean and topped up and the clutch or cables are properly adjusted, problems tend to be few and far between.

Overheating. Heavily loaded transmissions, especially hydraulic transmissions, tend to get hot (too hot to touch). In fact, many that do not have an oil cooler would benefit from the addition of one. Excessively high temperatures, however, are likely to arise only if the oil level is low (a smaller quantity of oil has to dissipate the heat generated), if the clutches are slipping (creating excessive friction), or if an oil cooler is not operating properly.

A slipping clutch should be evident from a loss of performance. The intense heat generated will soon warp clutch plates and burn out clutch discs. The oil in the transmission will take on a characteristic black look and may well smell burned.

Oil cooler problems may arise on the water and oil sides. Transmission oil generally remains pretty clean, but a slipping clutch and other problems occasionally create a sludge that can plug up the oil side of a cooler. More likely is silt, corrosion, and scale interfering with the heat transference on the water side, especially if the cooler is raw-water cooled.

Water in the transmission. If the transmission has an oil cooler, this is the most likely source of water, especially if the cooler is the raw-water type. Pinholes form in cooler tubes just as in engine-oil coolers. *Regular inspection and changing of sacrificial zinc anodes is essential.* The only other likely source of water ingress is

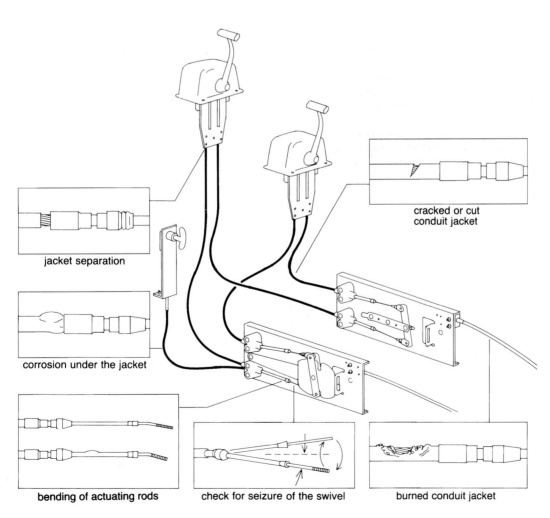

Figure 9-14. Checking transmission control cables. *(Morse Controls, adapted by Jim Sollers)*

jacket separation

corrosion under the jacket

bending of actuating rods

check for seizure of the swivel

cracked or cut conduit jacket

burned conduit jacket

through the transmission output seal. For this to happen, the seal must be seriously defective and the bilges must have large amounts of water slopping around, both of which were far more common years ago, when leather seals and wooden boats were the norm.

Loss of the transmission oil. The rupture of an external oil line will produce a sudden, major, and catastrophic loss of oil, which will immediately be obvious. Less obvious will be the loss of oil through a corroded oil cooler. If it is raw-water cooled, the oil will go overboard to form a slick; if freshwater cooled, it will rise to the top of the header tank.

Although the seal around the clutch actuating lever or the seal on a hydraulically operated shaft brake (see below) occasionally leak small quantities of oil, the most likely candidate for this kind of leak is the output-shaft oil seal. This is true particularly if the engine and propeller shaft are poorly aligned (which leads to excessive vibration), or if the propeller shaft has been allowed to freewheel when the boat is under sail. Alignment checks and seal replacement are dealt with below. On rare occasions, since the oil pressure in hydraulic transmissions tends to be higher than that in engines, the oil gets pumped through some ruptured seal into the flywheel housing or the engine crankcase.

Replacing an output-shaft seal.

1. Unbolt and separate the two halves of the propeller coupling (Figure 9-15). Mark both halves so that they can be bolted back together in the same relationship to each other.

Figure 9-15. Transmission oil seal and output coupling arrangement. The recesses machined into the faces of the two coupling halves assist in shaft alignment. *(Jim Sollers)*

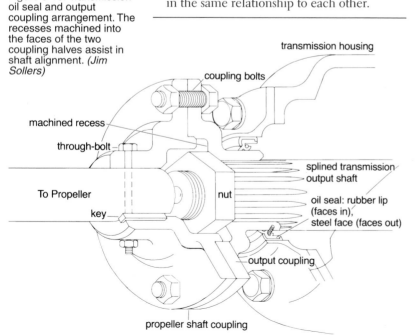

transmission housing

coupling bolts

machined recess

through-bolt

To Propeller

key

nut

splined transmission output shaft

oil seal: rubber lip (faces in), steel face (faces out)

output coupling

propeller shaft coupling

On some boats with vertical rudderposts, the propeller shaft cannot be pushed far enough aft to provide the necessary room to slide the transmission coupling off its shaft! The propeller hits the rudderstock and will go no farther. In this case, the rudder has to be removed or the engine lifted off its mounts to provide the necessary space—an awful lot of work to change an oil seal.

2. The coupling half attached to the transmission output shaft must be removed. This coupling is held in place with a central nut, which is done up tightly on most modern boxes but on some older boxes is just pinched up and then locked in place with a cotter pin (split pin).

The coupling rides on either a splined shaft (one with lengthwise ridges all the way around) or a keyed shaft. In the latter case, do not lose the key down in the bilges when removing the coupling. The key will most likely stick in the shaft. If there is no risk of its falling out and getting lost, leave it there; otherwise hold a screwdriver against one end and tap gently until the end can be pried up and the key removed.

Some couplings are a friction fit on their shafts and should be removed with a proper puller (Figure 9-16). This is nothing more than a flat metal bar bolted to the coupling and tapped to take a bolt in its center. The bolt screws down against the transmission output shaft, forcing off the coupling.

3. Transmission oil seals are a press fit into either a separate housing or the rear transmission housing. Most seals consist of a rubber-coated steel case with a flat face on the rear end and a rubber lip on the front end (the end inside the transmission). A spring inside the seal holds this lip against the coupling face to be sealed.

Removing a seal from its housing is not always easy. If at all possible, the housing should be unbolted from the transmission and taken to a convenient workbench. This is often fairly simple on older boxes and boxes with reduction gears, but may not be feasible on many modern hydraulic boxes. The seal may be dug out with chisels, screwdrivers, steel hooks, or any other implement that comes to hand; it doesn't matter if the seal gets chewed up, *as long as the housing and shaft (if still in place) are unscratched.*

4. New seals go into the housing with the rubber lip facing into the gearbox, and the flat face outside. Place the seal squarely in its housing and then tap it in evenly using a block of wood and a hammer. *If a seal is forced in cockeyed it will be damaged.* The block of wood is

necessary to maintain an even pressure over the whole seal face—*hitting a seal directly will distort it*. Push in the seal until its rear end is flush with the face of the transmission housing. Once in place, some seals require greasing (there will be a grease fitting on the back of the gearbox), but most need no further attention.

5. Reassembly of a coupling and propeller shaft is the reversal of disassembly. Check the alignment of the propeller shaft (see below) any time the coupling halves are broken loose and reassembled.

Many transmissions have what are called *preloaded* thrust bearings. The transmission output shaft, on which the coupling is mounted, turns in two sets of tapered roller bearings—one facing in each direction (Figure 9-17). Between the two is a steel sleeve. When the coupling nut is pulled up, this sleeve is compressed, maintaining tension on the bearings and eliminating any play. Anytime the coupling nut is undone, use a torque wrench and note the pressure that is needed to break loose the nut. When reinstalling the nut, tighten it to the same torque *plus 2 to 5 pounds*. In any event, the torque should be at least 160 foot-pounds on most Borg-Warner boxes, but the couplings should still turn freely by hand in neutral with only minimal drag. If the transmission needs a new spacer between the thrust bearings, a special jig and procedure are called for, and the whole transmission reduction gear will have to go to a professional.

On an older transmission in which the coupling nut is done up less tightly and restrained with a cotter pin, it is essential that the nut be replaced properly. The best approach is to moderately tighten the nut, make sure everything is properly seated, then back it off an eighth of a turn or so before inserting the cotter pin. The transmission should be put in neutral and the coupling turned by hand to make sure there is no binding. This type of coupling sometimes leaks oil between the shaft and the coupling, in which case a little gasket sealer should be smeared around the inside of the coupling before fitting it to the shaft.

Shaft Brakes

When a boat is being towed or is under sail with the motor shut down, the flow of water over a fixed-blade propeller will spin the propeller unless the propeller shaft is locked in some way. This is of little concern with manual and two-shaft transmissions, except that it creates unnec-

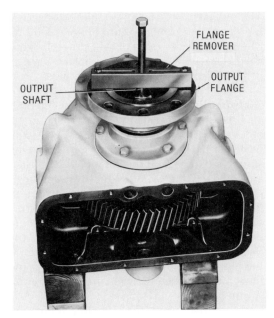

Figure 9-16. **Removing an output shaft coupling with a simple coupling puller.** *(Allison Transmission)*

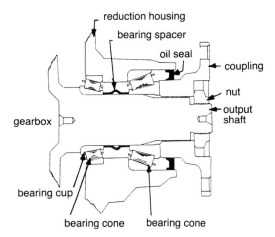

Figure 9-17. **Preloaded thrust bearings.** *(Borg Warner)*

essary wear on bearings, oil seals, and the stuffing box (or alternative seal). But *on some hydraulic transmissions (e.g., some Detroit Diesels), it will lead to a complete failure of the transmission* since no oil is pumped to the bearings when the engine isn't running. Some output-shaft oil seals (particularly rawhide seals) will also fail. Freewheeling propellers can also make quite a racket.

If an engine has a manual transmission the shaft can be locked simply by putting it in gear.

This will not work with a hydraulic box because there will be no oil pressure for gear shifting when the engine is shut down. A shaft brake is needed (except with folding and feathering propellers). There are essentially two choices.

Hydraulic units. Hydraulically operated units all have a spring-loaded piston. The spring is opposed by oil pressure, and the oil line is connected to the hydraulic transmission. When the engine is at rest the spring forces out the piston and operates the brake. When the engine is started, oil pressure from the transmission oil pump forces the piston back against the spring pressure, releasing the brake. These units are thus automatic in operation, overcoming the main objection to older manual units, which is the probability of leaving the brake on at some time, putting the transmission in gear, and burning up the brake.

Four variations on the hydraulic theme are widely available:

1. *Caliper disc brakes*, operating as on a car. A disc is bolted between the two propeller-shaft coupling halves. A hydraulically operated caliper grips the disc to stop rotation.

2. *Cam disc*. Similar to the above except that the disc has several cams. A hydraulically operated arm locks into the cams.

3. *Brake band*. A hydraulically operated brake band clamps around the propeller-shaft coupling.

4. *Plunger type*. A slotted sleeve is clamped around the shaft, and a hydraulically operated plunger locks into one of the slots.

Manual units. In the older manual units, a brake pad simply clamps around a block on the shaft or coupling. There is the obvious inherent risk that the owner will forget the brake when the engine is next started and, as a result, burn up the brake. Newer manual units, however, have a notched disc clamped to the propeller shaft, with a plunger engaging the notch. If the brake is left engaged while the engine is started and put in gear, the plunger is simply forced out of the notch and held back by another spring-loaded pin until it is set manually once again (Figures 9-18A and B).

Problem areas:

- Hydraulic oil leaks through faulty piston seals, connections, or hoses on the automatic units will cause the loss of the transmission oil and ultimately transmission failure. Adding a hydraulic shaft lock may, in fact, void a transmission warranty.

- The manual plunger types have a tendency to jump out during hard sailing. Spring tension on the latching pin can be increased to hold the plunger in place, but then it becomes more difficult to disengage the plunger.

- The cam disc, the hydraulic plunger, and the manual notched-disc plunger-style units can be set only at low propeller speeds. Ignoring this rule is likely to result in damage to the former unit; in the latter two cases the plunger will jump out. It may be necessary to slow the boat and reduce propeller freewheeling before engaging the device; in other words, these devices are shaft locks rather than shaft brakes.

Maintenance:

Hydraulic units. Pay close attention to the hydraulic lines and inspect them regularly for any signs of leaks around the piston seals. Check the brake linings on caliper and brake band units for wear. *Don't allow them to slip*—a lot of heat will be generated. Check any sleeve mounting bolts from time to time.

Manual units. The control cable is a Morse

Figure 9-18A. **A manual propeller-shaft lock.** *(Shaft Lok)*

type. Figure 9-14 shows a number of points to watch for with Morse cables. The plunger unit is mounted on a bearing within which the propeller shaft rotates. The bearing is sealed for life. Check for undue play once in a while, and while at it check the setscrews that lock the central sleeve to the propeller shaft.

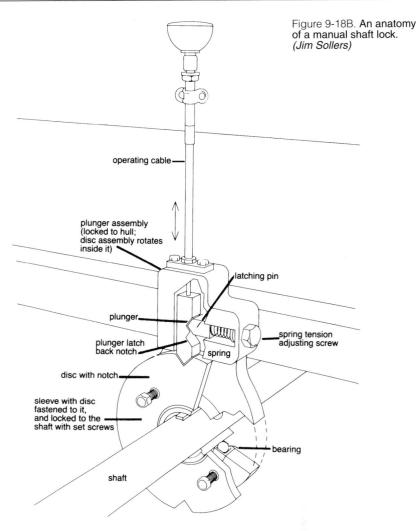

Figure 9-18B. **An anatomy of a manual shaft lock.** *(Jim Sollers)*

operating cable

plunger assembly (locked to hull; disc assembly rotates inside it)

latching pin

plunger

plunger latch back notch

spring tension adjusting screw

spring

disc with notch

sleeve with disc fastened to it, and locked to the shaft with set screws

bearing

shaft

Connecting a Transmission to a Propeller Shaft

Couplings

Couplings should always be keyed to their shafts and then pinned or through-bolted so that they cannot slip off (Figure 9-19). The practice of locking a coupling with setscrews is not very seaworthy. If a coupling is held this way, be sure the setscrews seat in good-sized dimples in the shaft, and preferably are tapped into the shaft a thread or two so that there is no risk of slipping. *Should they slip, the propeller and shaft are liable to pull straight out of the boat in reverse, leaving the ocean pouring in through the open shaft hole!* Just for insurance it is a good idea to place a stainless steel hose clamp (Jubilee clip) around the shaft in front of the stuffing box; if the coupling should ever work loose, the hose clamp will stop the shaft from leaving the boat (with high-speed shafts, use two hose clamps with the screws on opposite sides of the shaft in order to provide some sort of balance or else use a specially made collar bolted around the shaft).

Of course, anytime it becomes necessary to remove a coupling (e.g., for shaft removal), it is generally found to be frozen immovably in place! A stubborn coupling can be jacked off by making up a coupling puller as in Figure 9-16 or by separating the coupling halves, inserting a length of pipe on the end of the shaft (it must have a diameter less than the size of the hole in the coupling), and then pulling the coupling halves together again with elongated bolts (Figure 9-20). Be sure to pull the bolts up evenly to avoid distorting the coupling halves. If the coupling won't come, the propeller shaft will have to be cut, and both shaft and coupling replaced.

keyway

pin

set screws

pin

Figure 9-19. Shaft couplings may be keyed and pinned in place (**left** and **center**), or restrained by set screws seated in dimples in the propeller shaft (**right**).

Figure 9-20. Using a short length of pipe to jack a coupling off its propeller shaft.

propeller shaft coupling

length of pipe

transmission coupling

elongated bolts

Figure 9-21. Using a spring scale to eliminate shaft droop during engine alignment. The scale is tensioned until it reads one-half the free-hanging weight of the shaft plus the weight of the coupling. *(Jim Sollers)*

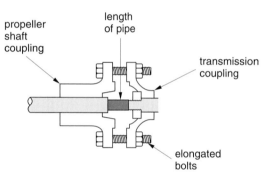

spring scale

line around shaft

Engine Alignment

Most engines use conventional couplings, either solid or flexible, between the transmission and the propeller shaft. Accurate alignment is critical to smooth, vibration-free running and a long life for the transmission bearings, transmission oil seal, and the Cutless bearing. Engine alignment should be checked once a year, always in the water (the hull may well have a different shape there than on land—it is preferable to wait a few days to a week after launching a boat to give the hull time to settle, especially a wooden hull). However, alignment cannot be checked unless the propeller shaft is straight and the two coupling halves are exactly centered on and square to their shafts, so *a coupling should be fitted to its shaft and machined to a true fit in a lathe before putting the shaft in the boat.*

Checking and adjusting engine alignment. To check alignment, undo the coupling bolts and separate the coupling halves. In cases where a long run of propeller shaft is unsupported by a bearing, the shaft will sag down under its own weight and the weight of its coupling half. In this case, the correct procedure is to calculate half the weight of the protruding shaft, add to it the weight of the coupling, and then pull up on the shaft by this amount with a spring scale of the type used for weighing fish (Figure 9-21). In practice, smaller shafts can generally be flexed up and down by hand to get a pretty good idea of the centerpoint, and then supported with an appropriately sized block of wood. A notch in the wood will hold the shaft and allow it to be rotated.

There should be a machined step on one coupling that fits closely into a recess on the other. Bring the two halves back together—the step should slip into the recess cleanly and without snagging at any point. If it does not, the shafts are seriously misaligned and the engine must be jacked around until the two halves come together.

Assuming they do come together cleanly, bring them almost into contact and then measure the gap at the top with a feeler, or thickness, gauge. Repeat at the bottom and on both sides. The difference from any one point to another should not exceed 0.001 inch per inch of coupling diameter (for example, 0.003 inch on a 3-inch-diameter coupling, or 0.06 mm on a 6-cm-diameter coupling).

If the difference exceeds tolerable limits, turn the propeller shaft coupling through 180 degrees while holding the transmission coupling stationary, and then measure the clearances again. If the widest gap is still in the same place, the engine alignment needs correcting. If the widest gap has also rotated 180 degrees, either the propeller shaft is bent, or its coupling is not squarely on the shaft, or both. The shaft and the coupling should be removed from the boat and *trued up (faced)* by a machine shop (Figure 9-22).

To adjust alignment, the engine must be jacked around and moved from side to side until the clearances all around the coupling are in tolerance. Some engines have adjustable feet, which greatly simplifies things; others need thin strips of metal (shims) placed under the feet until acceptable measurements are reached. Make sure that all feet take an equal load, otherwise when the mounting bolts are tightened there is a risk of distorting the engine block and causing serious damage. Engine alignment can be a time-consuming and frustrating business. When everything looks fine, tightening down the engine bolts may throw the alignment out again. Patience is the order of the day.

Flexible feet and couplings. Most engines today are mounted with flexible feet and couplings. *These are not substitutes for accurate engine alignment.* Modern, lightweight hulls tend to *work* in a seaway, whereas engines are necessarily extremely rigid. The principal reason for flexible feet is to absorb hull movements and lessen hull-transmitted engine vibrations, not to compensate for inadequate alignment. Flexible feet slowly compress over time while the rubber is subject to softening, especially if it becomes oil or diesel soaked. The feet should be inspected annually and replaced if deteriorated. (Yanmar recommends every two years!)

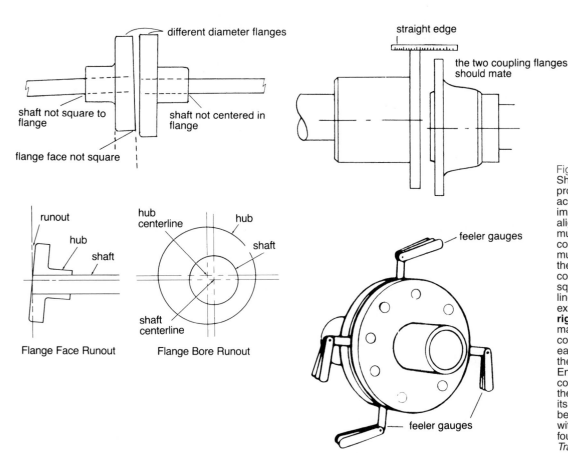

different diameter flanges

shaft not square to flange

flange face not square

shaft not centered in flange

straight edge

the two coupling flanges should mate

runout

hub

shaft

Flange Face Runout

hub centerline

hub

shaft

shaft centerline

Flange Bore Runout

feeler gauges

feeler gauges

Figure 9-22. (**Far left**) Shaft and coupling problems that will make accurate engine alignment impossible. For effective alignment: (1) Both shafts must be square to their couplings; (2) the shafts must be centered exactly in their couplings; (3) the coupling faces must be square; and (4) the coupling diameters must be exactly the same. (**Upper right**) Bore alignment. the machined step on one coupling half must slip easily into the recess on the other. (**Lower right**) Engine alignment. Once the coupling flanges match and the machined step fits into its recess, check the gap between the two flanges with a feeler gauge on all four sides. *(Caterpillar Tractor Company)*

Connecting a Transmission to a Propeller Shaft   311

Figure 9-23. (**Right**) Constant-velocity joints, such as this Aquadrive unit, compensate for shaft misalignment. (**Below**) How constant-velocity joints handle different types of misalignment. *(Aquadrive)*

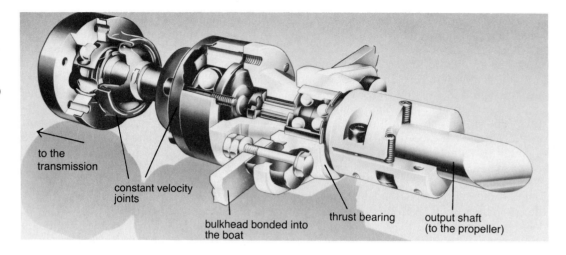

to the transmission

constant velocity joints

bulkhead bonded into the boat

thrust bearing

output shaft (to the propeller)

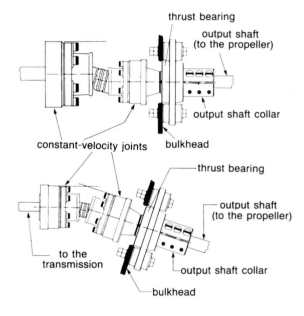

thrust bearing

output shaft (to the propeller)

output shaft collar

bulkhead

constant-velocity joints

thrust bearing

output shaft (to the propeller)

to the transmission

output shaft collar

bulkhead

Constant-Velocity Joints

Back in the 1950s, constant-velocity joints (CVJ's) were developed for front-wheel-drive cars. These are a special refinement of a universal joint, allowing a limited amount of shaft play in all directions. CVJ's have since been adapted for marine installations, notably by Aquadrive, a Swedish company (Figure 9-23).

CVJ's are used in pairs, one joint having a short, splined shaft that slides into a splined collar on the other. The entire unit is bolted between the transmission and propeller shaft, and, according to the makers, will permit misalignment of up to ½ inch or 13 mm! Since reverse thrust of the propeller would pull the two sliding shafts apart, the unit has to be combined with a *thrust bearing*. The propeller shaft is locked into this bearing, which in turn is fastened to a *hull-bonded bulkhead*, absorbing all forward and reverse thrust from the propeller and leaving the CVJ's to cope solely with misalignment.

CVJ's require no maintenance; the various bearings are packed in grease and sealed in rubber boots. Since all the main components are steel, however, a careful eye will have to be kept out for corrosion, especially on boats with wet bilges. Should the rubber bearing boots ever get damaged, they will need immediate replacement. Despite the tolerance of CVJ's for extreme misalignment, their life expectancy will be increased if alignment is kept fairly accurate.

Shaft Seals

The few pages on shaft seals in the first edition of this book provoked more reader response than any other topic. This is clearly a subject of concern to many boatowners, so in this edition I will take a more detailed look at the options. Most boats still have a traditional stuffing box, or packing gland, but increasingly, innovative new approaches are found. Notable among these are *mechanical* seals and *lip-type* seals (Figure 9-24).

Stuffing Boxes (Packing Glands)

In all forms of stuffing box a chamber is formed around a shaft, rings of greased flax are pushed in, and some form of a cap is tightened down to compress the flax around the shaft, creating a close fit which excludes almost all water from the shaft/flax interface (Figures 9-25A and B). Some stuffing boxes have grease fittings, and in this case a bronze spacer ring is generally incorporated between the second and third rings of packing and directly below the grease fitting, allowing the grease to be distributed around the stuffing box (Figure 9-25B). A shot of grease (or one turn on the grease cup) should be put in about every 8 hours of engine running time.

At one time most stuffing boxes were bolted up to the deadwood on a boat *(rigidly mounted, often incorporating a stern bearing—Figure 9-26A)*, but today the majority are flexibly mounted in a length of hose that in turn is fastened to the inner end of the shaft log *(sterntube—Figure 9-26A and 9-26B)*. *If this hose fails, water will pour into the boat at an alarming rate.* The hose must have two *all-stainless-steel* hose clamps at each end, with *300-grade* stainless steel screws (many "all-stainless" clamps have inferior screws that soon rust; quality clamps have 300 SS or AWAB stamped on them; the screws will be *nonmagnetic*—see Chapter 4). Annually, inspect the hose for any signs of cracking or bulging, and undo the clamps a turn or two *to make sure that galvanic corrosion is not eating away the band where it contacts the worm screw.* Should it be necessary to replace the hose, the propeller shaft coupling will have to be broken loose and the coupling removed from the shaft (see above).

Stuffing box blues. The concept of a stuffing box is simple enough. Done right, *on a properly installed and aligned engine*, the packing will not leak when a shaft is at rest, but when the shaft is in motion it will allow the occasional drip. Done wrong, the stuffing box will leak continuously, or else the shaft will be permanently damaged.

Note the emphasis on *the engine installation and alignment*. It is an unfortunate fact of life that many engines are not properly aligned, or else suffer from other installation problems such as a misaligned strut or Cutless bearing. In these cases the shaft whips around inside the stuffing box, beating the flax back against the sides of the

Figure 9-24. **A collection of mechanical and lip-type seals.**

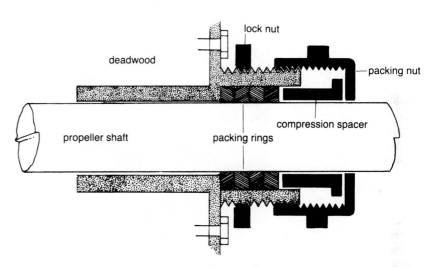

Figure 9-25A. **Cross section of a rigid stuffing box.** *(Ocean Navigator)*

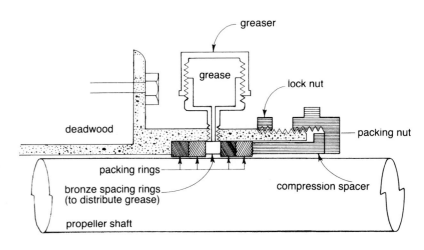

Figure 9-25B. **Cross section of a stuffing box equipped with a greaser.** The screw-down cap-style cup greaser could be replaced with a standard grease nipple or a remote greaser. *(Ocean Navigator)*

Shaft Seals   313

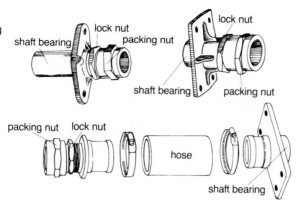

Figure 9-26A. Rigid stuffing boxes (**top**) and a flexible stuffing box (**bottom**). (Wilcox Crittenden, adapted by Jim Sollers)

shaft bearing — lock nut — packing nut — shaft bearing — lock nut — packing nut — packing nut — lock nut — hose — shaft bearing

Figure 9-26B. Flexible stuffing box. The hose is attached to the shaft log on the left; the transmission is to the right.

Figure 9-27. There is not enough room in this installation to back off the packing nut; as a result the packing has not been changed in 10 years! The stuffing box has been leaking profusely, corroding the coupling and everything else in range of the saltwater spray that is produced when the shaft is turning. The transmission controls were close to failing, and an electric water heater almost corroded through. The leak was such that a dead battery, or a failed bilge pump, could have resulted in the loss of the boat in just a few days.

box, allowing more and more water into the boat both with the shaft turning and with it at rest. Regardless of the skill of the mechanic who fitted the packing, the stuffing box will need constant attention and will still never give satisfactory service.

Even on a properly installed engine, a stuffing box needs some maintenance, including adjustment and greasing and periodic replacement of the packing, which otherwise hardens over time and may then damage the shaft. Access to many a stuffing box is, to say the least, poor, making such maintenance an onerous chore—it is not uncommon to have to hang upside down in a cockpit locker with insufficient room to swing the necessary wrenches. In extreme cases, notably some V-drives and boats with very short propeller shafts, the packing cannot be reached or replaced without removing either the propeller-shaft coupling or the engine (Figure 9-27—this is in clear violation of ABYC standards, which call for sufficient clearance "along the shaft line to permit replacement of the packing without uncoupling the shaft or moving the engine").

Poor access and difficulties in packing adjust-

ment and replacement often lead to neglect. Add a little engine misalignment and vibration and the stuffing box is soon dripping when the engine is at rest as well as when the shaft is turning. In time this drip becomes a trickle. When the engine is running, salt water is sprayed all over the back of the engine room; when the boat is left unattended, the automatic bilge pump and its battery become the sole line of defense against a sinking—the loss of the pump can result in the loss of the vessel. Small wonder then that many owners regard their stuffing box with hostility, little realizing that in most instances the engine installation is the source of their problems rather than the stuffing box. It's the old story of shooting the messenger rather than heeding the message!

Packing adjustment and replacement. A stuffing box is meant to leak. When the shaft is turning, two or three drops a minute are needed to keep the shaft lubricated. If the leak is worse than this, tighten down the nut or clamp plate to compress the packing a little more. If a greaser is fitted, pump in a little grease first. Tighten down the nuts no more than a quarter turn at a time. With a clamp plate, tighten the two nuts evenly.

Start the engine and put the transmission in gear for a minute or so. *Shut down the engine.* Feel the stuffing box and adjacent shaft: *If they are hot, the packing is too tight.* A little warmth is acceptable for a short while as the packing beds in, but any real heat is unacceptable—it is quite possible (and common) to score grooves in shafts by overtightening the packing, in which case the shaft will never seal and will have to be replaced. (Sometimes it can be turned end for end to place a different section in the stuffing box.)

If the shaft cannot be sealed without heating,

the packing needs to be replaced. It should, in any case, be renewed every year or so, since old packing hardens and will score a shaft when tightened up. The hardest part of the job generally is getting the old packing out. *It is essential to remove all traces of the old packing or the new wraps will never seat properly.* With a deep, awkwardly placed stuffing box, it is next to impossible to pick out the inner wraps of packing with screwdrivers and ice picks; a special tool is needed, consisting of a corkscrew on a flexible shaft (Figure 9-28—available from Drip-Free Packing—see below). Unless this tool is on hand it is not advisable to start digging into the packing, especially if the boat is in the water. Appreciable quantities of seawater may start to come into the boat as the packing is removed, in which case speed is of the essence.

Packing itself comes as a square-sided rope in different sizes: ³⁄₁₆ inch (4 mm), ¼ inch (6 mm), ³⁄₈ inch (8 mm), etc. It is important to match the packing to the gap between the shaft and cylinder wall. Packing can be bought as preformed rings to match the stuffing box (the best option for most people), or by the roll. When cutting rings off a roll, make about five tight wraps around the propeller shaft at some convenient point and then cut diagonally across the wraps with a very sharp knife.

To fit new rings of packing, grease each with a Teflon-based waterproof grease before installation, and tamp each ring down before putting in the next. I use some short pieces of pipe slit lengthwise, slipped around the shaft, and pulled down with the packing nut or clamp plate to *gently* pinch up the inner wraps (not too tight, or the shaft will burn). Stagger the joints from one wrap to another by about 120 degrees. Don't forget the greasing spacer (if one is fitted) between the second and third wraps.

"Drip-Free" packing. Although many of the problems with traditional stuffing boxes result from poor engine installations, there are some that can be attributed to the nature of the packing itself. Greased flax has done sterling service over the years, but it is an ancient product. It is not unreasonable to expect that late-20th-century technology might produce more effective packing compounds and this is, in fact, the case. In the first edition of this book I mentioned graphite packing tape, which we have used for 10 years now, but also mentioned potential problems with galvanic corrosion (graphite is high on the noble scale). Since I wrote the first edition, the ABYC has specifically prohibited the use of graphite packing tape, but this is of no concern because there is now something even better—a mixture of shredded Teflon in a heavy hydrocarbon base known as *Drip-Free* packing (available from Drip-Free Packing, Ft. Lauderdale, FL).

Drip-Free, which has a texture akin to somewhat dry bread dough, is installed in a conventional stuffing box, sandwiched between an inner and an outer ring of flax (Figure 9-29—the flax keeps the material from working its way out of the stuffing box). After the first ring of flax is installed, the Drip-Free is formed into a ring if possible, or else crumbled, and pushed into the stuffing box until the box is almost full. The sec-

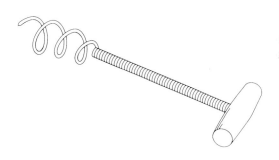

Figure 9-28. (**Left**) Packing removal tool. *(Jim Sollers)*

Figure 9-29. (**Bottom**) Teflon-impregnated grease ("Drip-Free" packing) installed between inner and outer rings of flax. *(Ocean Navigator)*

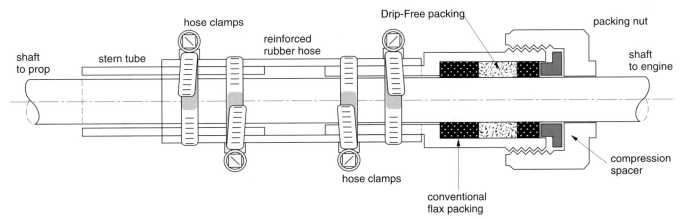

Shaft Seals

ond ring of flax is then added and the packing nut tightened until any leaks stop. And that's it! There should be no leak with the shaft at rest *or in motion.*

Being moldable, Drip-Free will conform to even corroded and grooved shafts. It will not eliminate drips in cases of severe engine misalignment or shaft vibration, but it does work exceptionally well in most situations. Once installed, it never needs renewing, and very rarely needs adjustment. Typically, problems arise from improper installation (not reading the instructions!) and from overtightening the packing nut. The packing begins to run hot. In this case, because the Drip-Free does not reexpand when the nut is loosened, it has to be picked out, recrumbled, and put back in. (In normal use, because Drip-Free shuts off the water in the seal altogether, there is often a little heat in the stuffing box, but as long as the box is not hot enough to blister a hand it will probably do no harm. In the worst case the Drip-Free will simply melt and run out, leaving the inner and outer flax rings. The stuffing box will leak, but not catastrophically.)

Mechanical Seals

Mechanical seals are not an adaptation of the traditional stuffing box, but instead are a complete replacement. A mechanical seal has two components: a boot or bellows, which is attached to the inner end of a shaft log, and a sealing ring *(rotor)*, which is attached to the shaft and rotates with it (Figure 9-30A and B). The face of the boot has a hard machined surface (a *stationary flange*); the sealing ring sometimes consists of a stainless steel unit, but at other times consists of a second machined surface embedded in another boot. One or the other of the two components either contains a spring or is constructed in such a way as to resist compression. On installation the two components are pushed together against the spring or boot resistance, and then the sealing ring is clamped to the shaft so that pressure is maintained. As the shaft rotates, the machined faces of the stationary flange and the sealing ring form a close enough fit to keep water out of the boat.

On a properly installed and aligned engine, such a seal will eliminate all leaks. Once installed there is no adjustment or maintenance beyond a routine inspection of the hoses, clamps, and sealing faces. Since no part of the seal is bearing on the propeller shaft, there is no risk of overheating or scoring the shaft. What is more, the seal will be effective regardless of the state of the shaft. This is an impressive list of attributes.

Many a face seal works perfectly. After five or ten years the owner hasn't seen a drip and is ecstatic. But then there are the ones with problems…The problems that have arisen have not generally stemmed from an outright failure of the seal itself, but have resulted from unforeseen operating conditions or improper engine installation and alignment. For example: A one-cylinder diesel engine placed on flexible mounts jiggles all over the place. When the throttle is pushed forward, the force of the prop can push the engine ahead as much as $\frac{3}{8}$ inch, which allows the seal faces to move away from each other and spray water everywhere. In addition, there is the movement that occurs when the boat is under sail. As the boat comes about, the heavy mass of the engine sways, causing the seal face to move sideways, potentially resulting in a severe leak until the boat rights itself.

As a result, some installations require a greater initial compression than others. So far as sideways movement is concerned, some seals have a broad seating surface, which allows the seal to oscillate without loss of contact, while others have either a lip or a chamfer built into the face of the stationary seal and sealing ring so that the two are held in a positive mechanical alignment.

The nature of the boots or bellows has come under close scrutiny over the years. Some early bellows were susceptible to diesel, oil, and gas that softened them and reduced their operating life. These were weak in compressive force and got weaker over time. Some seals containing a spring had one or two failures when the spring came through the bellows. Any kind of a bellows failure is, of course, potentially catastrophic. Nowadays, newer, more chemical resistant and resilient materials, and expensive high-tech construction methods, are mostly used.

Regardless of the engineering that has gone into a mechanical seal, its success and life expectancy in any given application will be dependent to a considerable extent upon the conscientiousness of the seal installer. Shafts must be deburred before installation, and sealing rings properly secured to the propeller shaft, with the fasteners locked against vibration. If a bellows is attached to a shaft log cockeyed, or the seal is inserted crookedly into the other end of the bellows, the seal faces will be subjected to uneven pressure: Even if the seal does not leak, it will wear rapidly. And finally, if provision is not made to lubricate a seal, it will eventually burn up.

Two situations can typically cause a loss of lubrication. The first is high boat speed, which creates a vacuum that sucks the water out of the sterntube; the second is a haulout, which allows the water to drain out of the shaft log. To combat

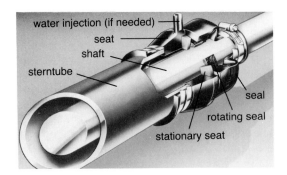

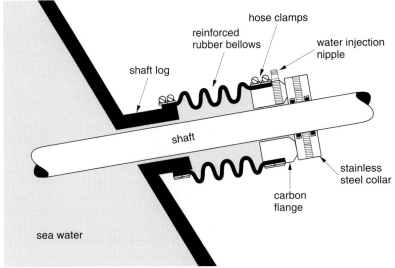

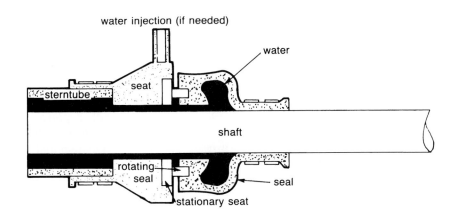

Figure 9-30A and B. Two types of mechanical seal. Mechanical seals all work on the same principle: Two sealing surfaces are held in contact by some sort of "spring" pressure. (**Top**) A PSS shaft seal. (**Left**) A Crane shaft seal. (*Ocean Navigator and Halyard Marine*)

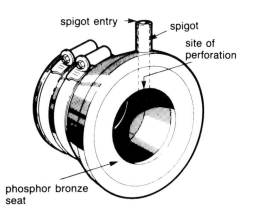

both situations most rotating seals include an option for water injection using water from the engine's raw-water circuit. If water injection is not used, there may be an air-vent valve which will release trapped air after a haulout, allowing the sterntube to refill with water. If not, *it is essential*, once a boat is back in the water, *to pull*

back and hold the boot until water spurts out of the seal face.

With a decade of engineering and experience behind them, properly installed mechanical seals will perform as advertised, even under adverse conditions. But it must still be recognized that mechanical seals are *two-part* seals (the boot and

Shaft Seals   317

sealing ring) in which the two parts are not, and cannot be, fastened together. If the two halves become separated, or the seal between them is damaged, the seal is likely to leak far more rapidly than a traditional stuffing box.

Lip-Type Seals

It is this nagging fear of a major leak as much as any other factor that causes many boatowners to remain wary of mechanical seals. The various lip-type seals on the market attempt to address these concerns by seeking to eliminate the leaks of a stuffing box without in any way increasing the risk of a catastrophic failure. This is done, essentially, by replacing the packing in a conventional stuffing box with a nitrile lip seal of the type universally used to seal crankshafts and output shafts in engines and transmissions.

Just as with mechanical seals, while the concept is straightforward, the engineering can get quite complex. The simplest units are *water lubricated* and closely resemble a flexible stuffing box. One end of the seal body is fastened to the shaft log with a length of hose; the other end has a recess into which is slipped the seal. In order to keep the seal lubricated, provision is made to maintain a water supply from the engine's raw-water circuit. Experience has shown that unless corrected for, shaft vibration will cause such a seal to leak, so a Cutless-type bearing is built into the inside of the seal body, forming a close fit around the propeller shaft. This keeps the seal in a constant alignment with the shaft, regardless of engine misalignment and other problems (Figure 9-31).

Other seals are *oil lubricated*. These are physically similar in appearance, but instead of a single seal at the inboard end they have seals at both ends (Figure 9-32). Lubrication is provided by a gravity feed tank of oil set above the seal. There seems little doubt that the oil-lubricated seals will last longer, but on the other hand the oil reservoir must be checked regularly, and should it be allowed to run dry, the seal will heat up and fail—unlike the water-lubricated seals, these shaft seals require a minimal level of operator attention and maintenance.

In practice, operator error has been a nuisance but not a big issue. As with mechanical seals, *the number one reason for lip seal failures is improper installation*. The seals are generally installed over the inboard end of the propeller shaft and then slid into place toward the outboard end. The lip on the seal is facing aft. *If the end of the shaft is not adequately chamfered during installation there is a good possibility that the lip will be rolled under (Figure 9-33). If the seal is put in at all cockeyed it will probably leak*. Neither of these situations is easily detected until the boat is in the water, at which point it must be hauled back out and the propeller-shaft coupling removed in order to repair the seal—an expensive and time-consuming business.

Even if properly installed, *a lip-type shaft seal will leak unless the shaft upon which it is seating is in an unblemished condition and polished*. A recently patented British design (the SealMaster from Ambassador Marine) may eradicate these potential problems. The seal has an inner sleeve, which is fastened to the propeller shaft, and an oil-filled outer sleeve, containing a bearing surface and lip seals, which is fastened with a bel-

Figure 9-31. Water-lubricated lip seal.

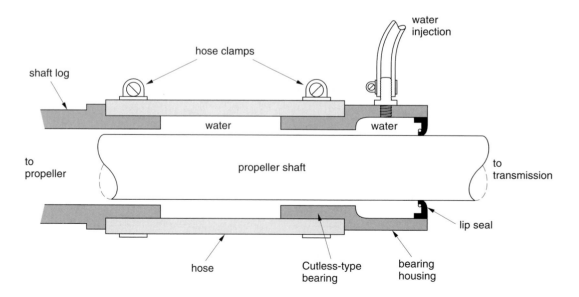

From Transmission to Propeller

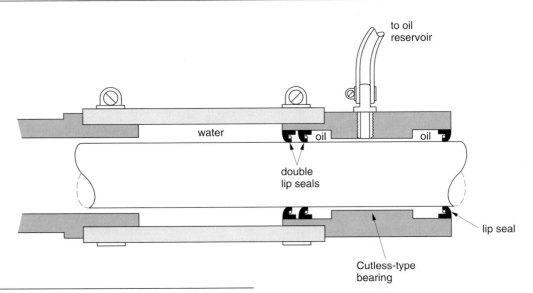

Figure 9-32. Oil-lubricated lip seal.

to oil reservoir

water

oil

oil

double lip seals

lip seal

Cutless-type bearing

lows to the stern tube. The unit comes preassembled, so *there is no risk of damaging the lip seals during assembly, and since the inner sleeve is now the seal-seating surface, the condition of the propeller shaft is not critical.* What is more, the inner and outer sleeves can be machined at the factory to fine tolerances, guaranteeing an effective bearing surface, and so reducing problems caused by misalignment.

It is too early to draw conclusions about the suitability of these lip seals for different applications, the extent to which they can handle misalignment and other common engine-installation problems, and whether they offer any improvement in performance over the mechanical seals. Such judgments can be made only after years of experience in the field. In the meantime it is fair to say that they clearly work well in some situations, but that whereas the mechanical seals are maintenance-free, the *oil-filled* lip seals (not the water-lubricated ones) do require a minimal level of maintenance. Which seals will hold up the longest remains to be seen. With a lip seal, should neglect, or some other failure, cause a complete seal failure the rate of leakage is not likely to exceed that of a badly leaking stuffing box—the potential for a major failure is less than that of a mechanical seal.

A Dripless Future?

So where does this leave us? Properly installed, with a proper engine installation, just about any shaft seal will work well. Even a traditional stuffing box can be almost drip-free; with Drip-Free packing it can be completely dripless.

Unfortunately many engines are not properly installed, or subsequently develop alignment or shaft problems. In such instances the traditional

stuffing box begins to leak, and requires more and more attention, and Drip-Free packing will be unable to do more than perhaps reduce the rate of leakage. In contrast, the mechanical and lip seals will clearly tolerate a wider range of deficiencies while still maintaining a dripless seal. Which is the better seal in a given application is to some extent a question of the type of deficiency being dealt with (e.g., a mechanical seal will handle a damaged shaft that would destroy most lip seals), and to some extent a subjective judgment based upon one's perception of the potential for a major leak, and also upon incomplete evidence as to the long-term effectiveness of lip seals.

Eventually, installation deficiencies are such that NO seal will work properly. The failure to recognize this is at the root of many of the complaints concerning stuffing box replacements. The owner sees a mechanical seal or a lip-type seal as the solution to a *stuffing-box* problem instead of recognizing that the boat has an *engine-alignment* or *propeller-shaft* problem. When the stern-tube continues to leak, the disgruntled owner blames the seal and the seal installer.

Bearings and Propellers

Cutless Bearings and Struts

Most Cutless bearings consist of a metal or fiberglass pipe with a ribbed rubber insert in which the shaft rides (Figure 9-34). Water circulates up the grooves to lubricate the bearing. Externally mounted bearings (in a strut, Figure 9-35) need no added lubrication, but some bearings installed in hull bottoms and deadwoods (Figure 9-36) have an additional lubrication channel into the sterntube. In place of the ribbed rubber, various plastics are sometimes used.

With a properly aligned engine most Cutless bearings will last for years (unless operated in silty water, which accelerates the wear), as long as they are lubricated adequately. They require no maintenance. At the annual haulout, flex the propeller shaft at the propeller; if there is more than minimal movement ($\frac{1}{16}$ inch of clearance between the shaft and bearing per inch of shaft diameter), the bearing needs replacing. If not renewed, a worn Cutless bearing will allow excessive shaft vibration, which will rapidly wear stuffing box and transmission bearings and seals. A Cutless bearing worn on only one side is a sure sign of engine misalignment.

Most bearings are a simple sliding fit; some are locked in place with setscrews but others are not (the ABYC says they should be, with at least two setscrews). Once any setscrews are loosened, a strut-mounted bearing can sometimes be replaced with the propeller shaft still in place. The problem is that there generally is not enough room between the hull and strut to maneuver the tools needed to knock the bearing aft. However, if a piece of pipe with an outside diameter of a little less than the bearing is slid up the propeller shaft, the bearing can be knocked up the shaft into the space between the strut and hull (Figure 9-37). Its outer case can then be filed or ground down until it will slide back easily through the strut and off the shaft.

In almost all other cases the shaft must come out to renew a Cutless bearing. A strut-mounted bearing can generally be knocked out from the inner side of the strut, but care must be taken not to damage the strut or its mounting. To do the same on a hull-mounted bearing, the stuffing box has to be removed from the inner end of the sterntube.

Figure 9-34. **Cutless bearings.** *(BF Goodrich)*

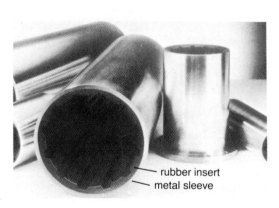

— rubber insert
— metal sleeve

Figure 9-35. **A propeller shaft supported by an external strut.** *(Jim Sollers)*

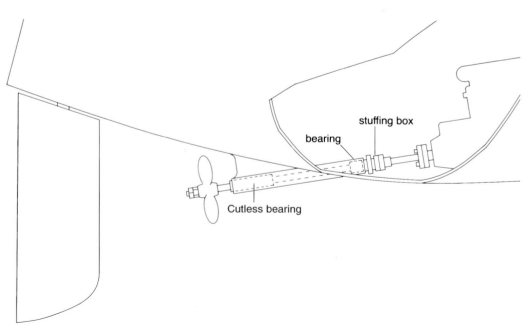

stuffing box

bearing

Cutless bearing

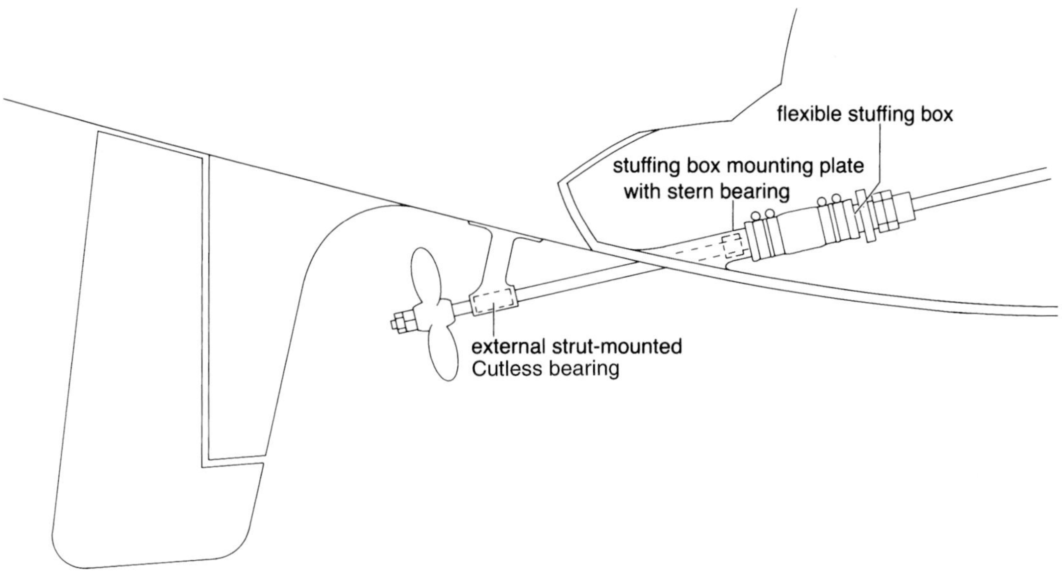

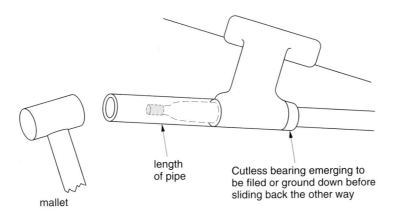

Figure 9-36. A propeller shaft supported in a sterntube. *(Jim Sollers)*

flexible stuffing box

stuffing box mounting plate
with stern bearing

external strut-mounted
Cutless bearing

Figure 9-37. Cutless bearing removal from a strut, with the propeller shaft still in place.

length
of pipe

Cutless bearing emerging to
be filed or ground down before
sliding back the other way

mallet

Figure 9-38. Homemade tool for Cutless bearing removal. The Cutless bearing is drawn out by tightening the nuts.

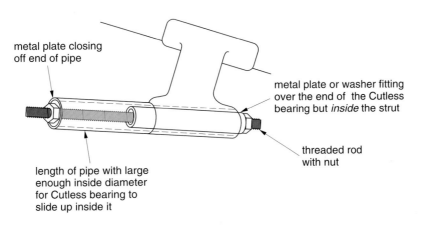

metal plate closing
off end of pipe

metal plate or washer fitting
over the end of the Cutless
bearing but *inside* the strut

threaded rod
with nut

length of pipe with large
enough inside diameter
for Cutless bearing to
slide up inside it

Bearings and Propellers

Not infrequently the Cutless bearing refuses to dislodge. In this case, given a strut, a simple puller can be made as shown in Figure 9-38, on previous page. In the case of a hull-mounted bearing, or in the absence of a puller, two longitudinal slits will have to be made in the bearing with a hacksaw blade so that a section can be pried out, allowing the rest to be flexed inward. Take care not to cut through the bearing into the surrounding strut or sterntube. A new bearing is then lightly greased and pushed in, using a block of wood and *gentle* hammer taps. The bearing should not be a tight (interference) fit, since it may distort. If a bearing is packed in ice before installation it will shrink a few thousandths of an inch—enough to ease the installation.

Any retaining setscrews *must tighten into dimples in the bearing case*, and should be locked in place with Loctite or something similar. Set screws must not press on the bearing case, since this could distort it, causing friction between the rubber bearing and the propeller shaft. The shaft itself should *not* be a tight fit in the bearing sleeve.

Most bearing cases are made of naval brass or stainless steel. Fiberglass/epoxy (FE) cases are becoming more common, however. This material works just as well as the metals and is especially recommended for steel and aluminum hulls, where it will eliminate the risk of galvanic corrosion. Its only disadvantage is that if the bearing is a tight fit, there is a greater risk of damaging the bearing when knocking it in or out.

All too often struts are mounted inadequately. The stresses from a fouled propeller or bent shaft

will work them loose, especially I (P) brackets. Check the fasteners annually, and tighten as necessary. If the bolts are a loose fit in the hull due to elongated holes, a good dollop of bedding compound combined with a good-sized, well-bedded backing block will tighten things up.

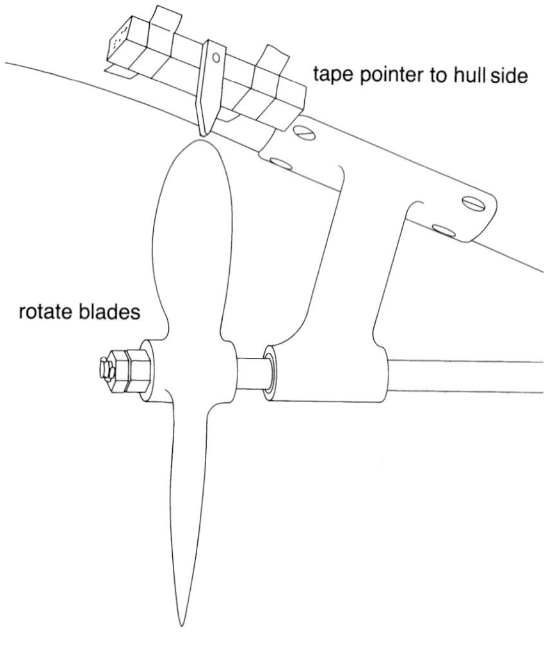

Propellers

The number one problem with propellers is fouled lines, generally one's own! These can be a devil of a job to clear. Before resorting to snorkeling gear and a hacksaw, shut down the engine, put the transmission in neutral and have someone pull on the fouled line while a second person rotates the propeller shaft by hand in the opposite direction from which it was turning when the line was caught. Often the line will simply unwind. Very effective line cutters can be installed on a propeller shaft that will cut right through trailing lines, but I must say I have mixed feelings about these: First of all because I would rather salvage than destroy our lines, but second, and more importantly, because if we foul a fishing or lobster-pot line I feel we have some moral obligation to protect it rather than destroy someone else's livelihood.

Bent propeller blades can cause quite a bit of vibration. It is advisable to check them at the annual haulout. Set up a pointer (a piece of wood or a pencil) on the hull side or strut so that it nearly touches the tip of one propeller blade (Figure 9-39). Rotate the propeller by hand. Any differences in the blade clearances will become apparent immediately.

Many propellers are made of little more than high-tensile brass (for example, manganese bronze is approximately 60% copper, 40% zinc). Without adequate cathodic protection such propellers will suffer from dezincification (Chapter 4) and will crumble in time (dezincified manganese bronze takes on a pinkish hue). There will also be galvanic interaction between many propellers and their propeller shaft. The normal means of providing galvanic protection is to fit a zinc collar to the propeller shaft, but many of these come loose after they have been partially eaten away. The better ones have an internal nonzinc band that remains firmly clamped to the shaft at all times.

Standard propellers. Propellers are mounted on keyed and tapered shafts, retained by a propeller nut with either a second locking nut or else a cotter pin (split pin). There may or may not be a *fairing piece* over the top of the nut to smooth out the water flow (Figure 9-40).

To remove a propeller, back off the retaining

Figure 9-39. **Using a pointer to check for propeller-blade misalignment.** *(Jim Sollers)*

tape pointer to hull side

rotate blades

From Transmission to Propeller

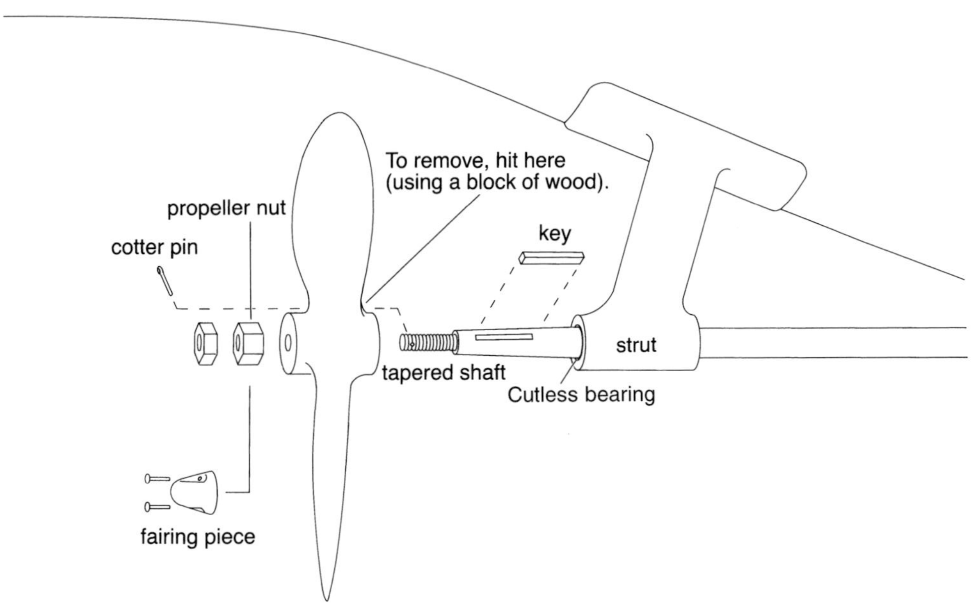

Figure 9-40. **Propeller installation.** The half nut, which would be between the blades and the locking nut, can be dispensed with when a fairing nut is used. *(Jim Sollers)*

nut *(but not all the way)*. If a propeller puller is not available use a piece of hardwood and a hammer to hit the propeller smartly behind its boss and jar it loose from the taper on the shaft. If it won't come, concentrate on the spot with the keyway—this is the most likely point of binding. If it still won't move, it will be necessary to heat the propeller hub with a propane torch. Move the torch around the hub in a circular fashion to avoid excessive localized heating.

When refitting a propeller, fit it first without its keyway and place a *nongraphite* (i.e., nonpencil) mark on the shaft at the inboard end of the propeller hub. Then remove the propeller, grease the shaft to help in future removal, and refit the propeller with its key, checking to see that the hub comes back up to the mark. This will ensure that the key is not oversized or improperly seated. Lock the retaining nut securely.

Feathering propellers. By their very nature, feathering propellers are sailboat specific.

The old style has two hinged blades. When sailing, the blades are held in the closed position by the flow of water over the propeller. When the engine is cranked and put in forward, the centrifugal force opens the blades partway, and then the developed thrust drives them all the way open, sometimes with considerable force. In reverse, any thrust developed tends to close the blades. This tendency is counteracted by centrifugal force, but efficiency is minimal.

The most common problem with this type of propeller is a failure to open at all because of weeds or barnacles in the hinge. Partial opening of one or other blade will result in severe vibration. These propellers must be kept clean.

The new style has a gear on the base of each propeller blade that engages a central gear mounted on the propeller shaft. The whole unit is enclosed in a case (Figures 9-41 and 9-42).

When the engine is cranked and put in gear, the propeller shaft, and the gear mounted on it, turn while the case and blades tend to lag due to inertia. The blades will be in a feathered position. The rotating gear on the propeller shaft turns the propeller blades inside the case. The blades have a preset "stop" such that they cannot rotate beyond a certain point. Once this stop is reached, the propeller shaft spins the whole unit, including the case.

When the engine is shut down, water pressure on the blades forces them back to the feathered position.

When put in reverse, the propeller shaft once again drives the blades to their full pitch before spinning the whole unit, thus ensuring maximum efficiency in reverse. (Note that the blade pitch can be adjusted by altering the stops, but this can be done only by disassembling the case and, in the case of the Luke propeller, machining the stops. In other words, although the

Bearings and Propellers   323

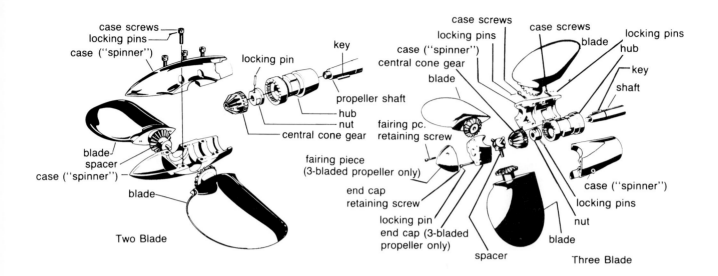

Two Blade

case screws
locking pins
case ("spinner")

locking pin

key

propeller shaft

hub
nut
central cone gear

blade
spacer
case ("spinner")

blade

case screws
locking pins
case ("spinner")
central cone gear
blade

fairing pc.
retaining screw

fairing piece
(3-bladed propeller only)

end cap
retaining screw

locking pin
end cap (3-bladed
propeller only)

spacer

case screws

blade

locking pins
hub

key

shaft

case ("spinner")

locking pins

nut

blade

Three Blade

Figure 9-41. (**Top**) One of the new style of fully feathering propellers. (**Right**) The operation of Max-Prop propellers. Under sail, the Max-Prop feathers to a low drag shape. In forward, the torque of the prop shaft acts on the differential-type blade design to force the blades open to a preset pitch at any throttle setting. In reverse, as in forward, the torque of the shaft will rotate the blades 180 degrees, presenting the same leading edge and pitch in reverse. (*Max-Prop*)

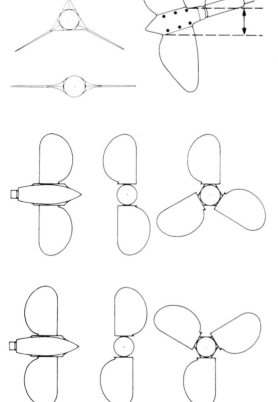

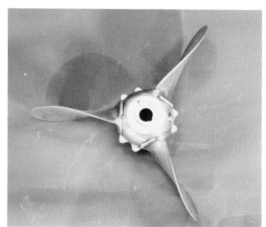

Figure 9-42. The Luke fully feathering propeller—a very rugged design that is particularly easy to maintain. (*Paul E. Luke Inc.*)

mechanism looks broadly similar to a variable-pitch propeller, this is in fact a fixed-pitch blade with a fully feathering characteristic.)

Maintenance is simply a matter of checking sacrificial zinc anodes regularly and renewing the grease every 1 or 2 years. To renew the grease some units must be taken apart (e.g., Max-Prop) whereas on others a grease fitting is simply screwed into the case (e.g., Luke). In the former case, make a careful note of where everything goes and put it all back the same way. A waterproof bearing grease such as Lubriplate Marine A works well. Lighter Teflon greases will be washed away.

If the propeller blades are stiff to rotate by hand, or have *hard* spots, it may simply be the result of too much grease—take a little out. If not, check for small burrs on the gears or minor damage on any of the bearing surfaces (the propeller blade bases; bearing surfaces in the case; and the hub). Remove the cone gear and reassemble the unit. Now check each blade for stiffness individually, and test the rotation of the case around the hub; you should be able to isolate problem areas. *Dressing up* with emery cloth or a fine file will solve most problems.

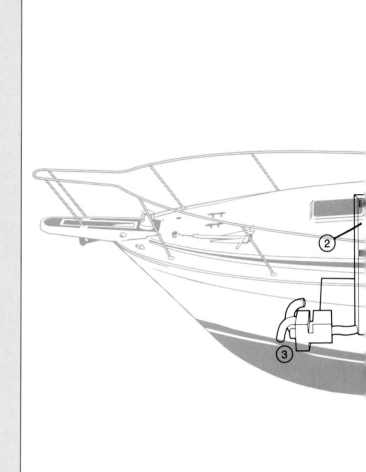

CHAPTER 10

Figure 10-1. Problems aboard can crop up almost anywhere, but most can be ignored as long as the beverages and the mahi-mahi are kept cold. *(Jim Sollers)*

- (1) compressor
- (2) plenum
- (3) air-conditioner
- (4) freezer
- (5) refrigerator
- (6) pump
- (7) strainer
- (8) air-conditioner raw-water intake
- (9) holding plate in icebox
- (10) belt-driven compressor
- (11) condenser (in engine raw-water intake line)

Refrigeration and Air-Conditioning

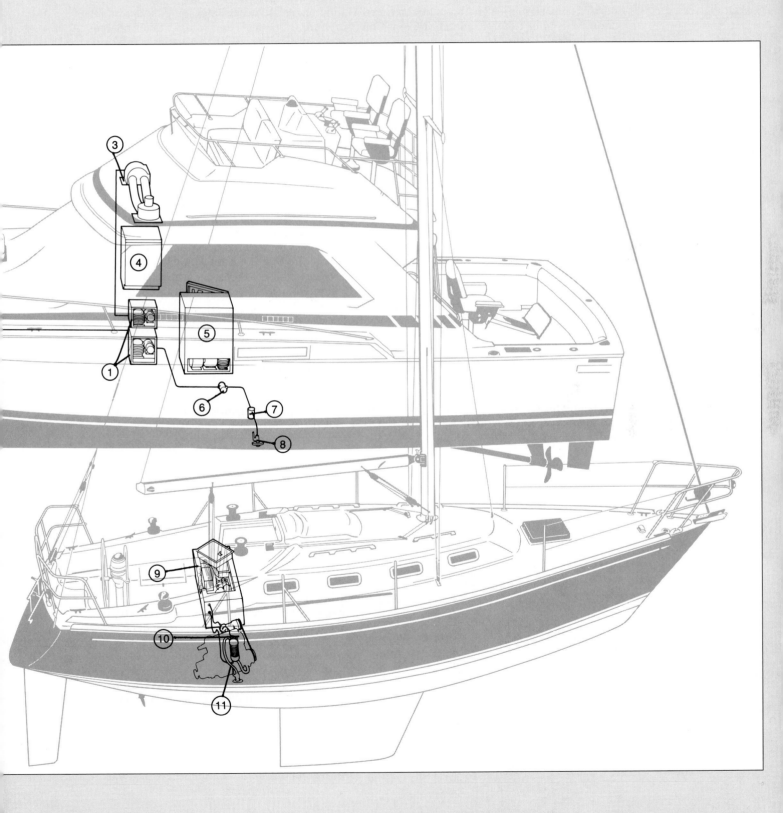

CFCs and the Ozone Hole

In the few years since the first edition of this book was published the refrigeration world has been turned upside down. CFCs, which include *R-12 (Freon-12)*, the substance used as the refrigerant in all marine and household refrigeration units prior to 1991, and HCFCs, which include *R-22 (Freon-22)*, the substance used in almost all air-conditioning, have been fingered as two of the main culprits in the destruction of the earth's ozone layer. Worldwide, governments have moved with unaccustomed alacrity to deal with the problem. The Montreal Protocol of 1987 laid down a schedule to phase out the production of CFCs by the year 2000 and HCFCs by the year 2030. Subsequently this schedule has been accelerated on several occasions (Figure 10-2). Soon after this edition is published, a complete ban on the production of CFCs will be in place (December 31, 1995); HCFCs will be scheduled for phase-out by the year 2020, and perhaps sooner. In the space of a few short years every existing marine refrigeration unit has been made obsolete!

When these production bans were first mooted it was commonly assumed that the major chemical companies would find a *drop-in* replacement for R-12—that is to say, a non-ozone-depleting substance which could simply be exchanged for R-12 within the confines of an existing system. Such a substance has yet to be produced.

The automotive-air-conditioning and household-appliance refrigeration industries, with mixed levels of enthusiasm, have been driven to adopt a substance known as *HFC 134a* as the substitute for R-12. HFC 134a causes zero ozone depletion, and performs in a similar fashion to R-12, but unfortunately it requires special oils and is *incompatible with the mineral oils that have always been used to lubricate R-12 systems*. In addition, its use necessitates some modifications of compressor seals and other rubber components (primarily hoses) and a minor tweaking of system-operating parameters.

Marine Refrigeration

The move to HFC 134a left much of the marine refrigeration industry out on a limb for several reasons:

1. Many pleasure-boat refrigeration systems have been, and still are, built around a 12-volt hermetic compressor from Danfoss (the BD 2.5). Early trials of this compressor with HFC 134a resulted in repeated failures; it was not until recently that teething problems were overcome. The first units of the new HFC 134a-compatible compressor were shipped in late 1993.

2. Even those systems built around automotive compressors had some problems with HFC 134a. Initially HFC 134a was used with what are known as *polyalkylene (PAG)* oils, but these are incredibly hygroscopic (moisture attracting), which is an obvious liability in the humid marine environment. There is now a trend toward what are known as *polyolester* oils (*esters*), which are still many times more hygroscopic than mineral oil, but not nearly as bad as PAG oils.

3. At the low temperatures commonly found in marine refrigeration, HFC 134a is, on paper, not as efficient as R-12.

4. There are very real difficulties in educating the diffuse marine service sector in the use and handling of HFC 134a.

In a search for environmentally clean products that would resolve these issues, marine refrigeration manufacturers have taken different tacks:

1. Those producing systems built around automotive air-conditioning compressors have concentrated on making HFC 134a work, primarily through the use of the latest generation of ester-based oils and some system reengineering that improves the efficiency of HFC 134a at low temperatures.

2. In 1993 and 1994 several manufacturers who rely on the Danfoss compressor turned to cer-

Figure 10-2. **This graph demonstrates the accelerating phaseout of CFCs over the past few years.**

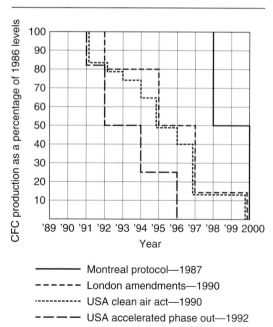

Montreal protocol—1987

- - - - London amendments—1990

········· USA clean air act—1990

– – – USA accelerated phase out—1992

tain *blends* (which include HCFCs) as an environmentally acceptable interim solution while problems with HFC 134a were resolved (by late 1994 most of these companies were switching to HFC 134a). Two DuPont blends in particular have been found to work with the Danfoss compressor at least as well as R-12 with almost no system modifications. "MP 39" is used in refrigeration units, "MP 66" in freezer units. The great thing about these blends is that although the recommendation is to use another, recently developed, synthetic oil *(alkybenzene)*, they will work with mineral oil, with mixtures of different oils, and with partial charges of R-12. In other words, they are very forgiving. In addition, no system reengineering is needed. The one major drawback is that, since they contain HCFCs, they are still, in the long term, slated for abolition.

The blends may also solve the nagging problem of what to do with all those existing units charged with R-12 and mineral oil, which may be quite expensive to retrofit with HFC 134a (although the perspective on this question is changing at the time of writing). For the time being, as long as R-12 is available, these units can be serviced with R-12. As the supply of R-12 dries up and the economics of the situation change, one of the blends could be substituted along with alkybenzene oil. For this to be successful, no more than a routine evacuation of the system, with the recommended replacement of the filter/dryer (which would in any case ordinarily be replaced at any service) is needed.

The legal framework. Concurrent with the phaseout of CFCs has been a remarkable rise in the price of these substances. In five years R-12 went from around $1 a pound to $10 a pound; the price is still rising. Not only have traditional refrigerants become expensive, but their use, and that of the replacement refrigerants, has also been regulated by stringent new laws. For example, in the USA:

- Since July 1, 1992, *it has been illegal to vent controlled refrigerants* (CFCs and HCFCs, including the blends) *to the atmosphere.* "De minimus" releases are permitted, which basically covers the unavoidable venting that occurs when connecting and disconnecting refrigeration gauge sets to perform service work.
- Since November 15, 1992, *it has been illegal to sell cans of controlled refrigerants* of less than 20 pounds *to the general public* (this measure removed the popular 14-ounce cans from auto parts stores and hardware stores).

This ban on refrigerant sales to the general public was extended, on November 15, 1994, to include *all* cans—only technicians certified by the Environmental Protection Agency (EPA) can now buy refrigerant.

- Since July 13, 1993, anyone servicing or opening CFC- or HCFC-based refrigeration or air-conditioning equipment (including that using blends) has had to posses at least one EPA-certified piece of recovery and recycling equipment, capable of removing and saving just about all the refrigerant from the system that is to be worked on.
- Since August 12, 1993, *it has been illegal for all but EPA-certified technicians to service refrigeration and air-conditioning equipment containing CFCs and HCFCs* (including the blends).
- As of November 15, 1995, these regulations will be extended to *all* refrigerants (including HFC 134a).

The cruising sailor. The situation of an *uncertified* cruising sailor who has been accustomed to carrying a can of refrigerant on board, and topping off a refrigeration system from time to time, is an interesting one. It is not illegal to carry such cans on board. But when it comes to connecting the can to the system we enter a gray area.

The primary concern of the EPA is to prevent unnecessary releases of refrigerant. As long as care is taken to minimize releases when purging the hoses, simply connecting a can to top off a unit *probably* does not constitute an offense. Although one part of the regulations implies that since August 12, 1993, such topping off can be done only by a certified technician with access to recovery and recycling equipment, the wording is ambiguous. *The EPA has told me quite explicitly that the relevant section was not intended to cover topping off and that "you can go ahead and charge your own systems. You don't need, and will not need, to be certified or to have recovery equipment."* However, if hose connections and disconnections cause "unnecessary" releases, such as would occur, for example, if a high-pressure hose were to be disconnected while filled with liquid, this would violate the "de minimus" rule on releases.

On one thing there is no discussion. *Since August 12, 1993, the only people allowed to open a refrigeration system have been certified technicians. Any procedure beyond a simple topping off clearly constitutes "servicing" or "opening" an appliance and as such falls under the provisions of the regulations.*

When it comes to enforcement, a staff attorney at the Coast Guard's Division of Maritime and

International Law stated that *the Coast Guard has the legal authority to enforce all applicable US laws on US-registered vessels (whether Coast Guard–documented or simply State-registered) in all international waters, and also within the waters of other nations if granted permission to do so by that nation*. In other words, it is no good thinking these regulations can be avoided when overseas. Whether or not the Coast Guard will actually play a role in enforcement is another question. It has been suggested to me that their policy may be that violations detected in the process of a routine vessel inspection would be reported to the EPA for further action.

Penalties for lawbreakers are severe: fines up to $25,000, with rewards up to $10,000 for those turning in violators.

Steering a prudent course. So where does this leave us? R-12 is history. The best advice (for both environmental and economic reasons) for the tens of thousands of boatowners who have an existing R-12 system is to give it a thorough check as soon as possible and to fix any leaks or problems right away. A well-built system, particularly a hermetic system (one that does not have an external drive belt), should run for many years without the need for further attention. If problems do arise and R-12 is found to be unavailable, for a relatively modest cost the unit can probably be converted to one of the blends and kept in service for the rest of its "natural" life.

For anyone in the market for a new refrigeration unit to buy an R-12 system is simply to buy potential trouble down the road. If, for some reason, you still decide to buy such a system, at least make an effort to see that it is lubricated with a *synthetic* oil, preferably an *ester* oil, and that *not a drop of mineral oil enters the system*—this will ease the conversion to HFC 134a in the future. If you buy a unit that is charged with HFC 134a or one of the blends, *it is essential to ensure that the installing technician is familiar with the system*. The best approach is to use the manufacturer's recommended dealer so that if the technician screws up it will be possible to get any problems resolved under warranty. If the unit is to be owner-installed, *the instructions must be followed to the letter, particularly when using HFC 134a*.

The greatest danger to these systems is going to be if they need servicing overseas or during the next year or two while the service sector is still unfamiliar with the new refrigerants. For such work the best advice is once again to go through an *established dealer network*. But in any event, it will do no harm to check that the technician is using *the correct oil and refrigerant* (both should be clearly identified with labels on the unit and in the literature that came with it), and is familiar with the system in question, and that in the case of an HFC 134a system, *any gauge set and equipment being used is dedicated to HFC 134a and nothing else* (this is to prevent the possibility of cross-contamination from another system). Cruisers going overseas with a system charged with HFC 134a or a blend would be well advised to carry both oil and refrigerant if only to have it available for use by a local technician.

Balancing Refrigeration Needs with Boat Use

So much for the general picture. Let's get into specifics. The keys to successful refrigeration are, first, matching the unit to the boat's energy resources and patterns of use, and, second, ensuring a proper installation. If these two things are got right, the unit will gives years of satisfactory use. If either is wrong, it is likely to become a millstone around the boatowner's neck. Our present system, with which I am finally satisfied, is our third. I have wasted thousands of dollars in tailoring it to our specific needs, which is not uncommon for tropical cruisers. In fact, we have met numerous cruisers who have invested thousands and still don't have a satisfactory system.

Problems are especially likely with boats coming from temperate climates (such as northern Europe or the northern United States) to hotter climates such as the Mediterranean, the Caribbean or Baja California. The higher ambient air and water temperatures increase the power demands of the refrigerator or freezer while at the same time decreasing the efficiency of the refrigeration unit—all the variables are moving in the wrong direction. It is not unusual to find boats that have perfectly adequate refrigeration at home having to run engines 3 or 4 hours a day to keep up with refrigeration demands in the tropics, or to keep up with battery charging necessitated by the refrigeration unit, sometimes still with poor results. As often as not, if the refrigeration unit is DC powered they will also suffer repeated battery failures.

Iceboxes: The Key to Sizing

At the heart of many refrigeration failures is the icebox. The function of a refrigeration unit is to combat heat gain by an icebox, thus keeping the contents cold. The icebox is therefore the key component in determining the necessary size of a refrigeration unit. In terms of heat gain, there are two factors at work: the overall dimensions of the icebox (since the larger it is the greater will be its surface area and therefore its heat absorption) and the quality of its construction.

Unfortunately, many iceboxes installed in even expensive boats are unnecessarily large and then poorly built. The following is a summary of the key construction features to look for (Figure 10-3): Insulation should be only of the closed-cell (urethane) foam type (polystyrene should never be used since its granular structure allows moisture to penetrate, which cuts its insulation properties in half). Iceboxes to be used for a refrigerator should have 4 inches of foam on the sides and bottom, 2 inches on the top; those to be used for a freezer, 6 inches of foam on the sides and bottom, 3 inches on the top. All access hatches should be in the tops of the boxes, and should have double seals. Drains, where fitted, must have a U-trap, or valve, to stop cold air from sinking out the bottom of the icebox.

Table 10-1 indicates approximately the kind of heat losses to be expected in tropical climates from a well-constructed icebox of a given size. The accompanying sidebar outlines a procedure to determine the heat losses from an icebox of unknown construction.

Refrigeration Choices

Once the overall energy demand of an icebox has been determined, a choice needs to be made as to what kind of refrigeration unit to use to meet this demand.

Refrigeration is not something that can just be tacked onto a boat. It is a major power consumer, particularly in the tropics where DC refrigeration (the most common) frequently accounts for between 50% and 75% of a boat's total DC demand. *A refrigeration unit has to be carefully integrated into a boat's available power supplies,* which in turn are going to be a function of the use to which the boat is put (Figure 10-4). A boat used for weekend cruising, for example, will have shore power available in its slip all week, whereas one used for long-term offshore cruising will not. It may well be the case that two identical production-line boats with similar-capacity refrigeration demands are best served by radically different types of refrigeration units. In practice, for most boatowners there are three common choices, and one less common:

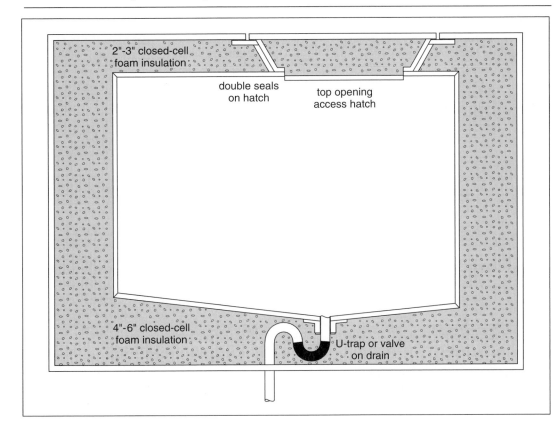

Figure 10-3. A "proper" icebox. The better insulated the box, the less the refrigeration unit will have to run to keep it cold. *(Ocean Navigator)*

2"-3" closed-cell foam insulation

double seals on hatch

top opening access hatch

4"-6" closed-cell foam insulation

U-trap or valve on drain

Constant-cycling DC refrigeration. The refrigeration unit is permanently hooked to the ship's batteries and controlled by a thermostat in the icebox (Figure 10-5). Every time the temperature rises beyond a set-point, the unit kicks on until the icebox is cooled down, and then the unit switches off—it constantly cycles on and off (just as a household refrigerator does).

Constant-cycling DC refrigeration is the cheapest *initial* option. Almost all units currently available use the Danfoss BD 2.5 compressor (or its new HFC 134a version), which has a limited output, especially in a freezer application. From a conservative viewpoint, I would consider the upper limits of such a system to be 1,500 Btus per day in a refrigerator, and would not use such a system on a freezer.

When running, most constant-cycling DC units produce a battery drain of around 5 to 7 amps on a 12-volt system. 1,500 Btus of refrigeration will require around 8 hours total running time (that is, 20 minutes an hour), resulting in a total daily battery drain of around 50 amp-hours. In practice, since these units are often asked to handle greater loads than this, or the system is operating at well below peak efficiency, running times in the tropics often exceed 30 minutes in the hour, and daily power consumption is generally from 70 amp-hours on up.

Unless there is some kind of a continuous battery charging device that keeps up with the demands of the refrigeration unit, this kind of a load will *cycle* the ship's batteries on a daily basis. *To be effective and reliable, any kind of DC refrigeration on a distance cruising boat must be sup-ported by a high-capacity DC system* including deep-cycle batteries, a high-output alternator, a multistep regulator, and preferably a large-capacity wind generator (7 to 15 amp maximum output) with backup solar panels. If not already installed, such a DC system will cost several times more than the constant-cycling DC refrigeration unit!

Constant-cycling DC refrigeration is therefore an appropriate choice only on a boat with limited refrigeration needs, and one that is to be used for weekend cruising, or, if going offshore, already has a high-capacity DC system. One essential modification will still be needed for the tropics.

Table 10-1. Heat Loss as a Function of Icebox Size, Insulation, and Use

Heat loss, 24 hours (BTUs)	Insulation thickness					
	Refrigerator use			Freezer use		Icebox volume in cubic feet
	3"	4"	6"	4"	6"	
1,000	1	1.5	2			
1,500	2	3	4		1	
2,000	4	5	8	1.5	2	
2,500	6	8	12	2.5	3	
3,000	8	13	18	3.5	5	
3,500	11	18	24	5	7	
4,000	15	24		6.5	9	
4,500	19			8	11	
5,000	24			10	13	

Courtesy Grunert

Testing an Existing Icebox for Its Heat Loss

To approximate tropical conditions, close up the boat and heat its interior to at least 90°F (32°C), preferably 100°F (38°C), making sure that the boat is uniformly hot all around the icebox area. Stock the box with a typical sampling of food and drink and then suspend a large block of ice of known weight (10 to 20 pounds) as high in the box as possible. Simulate normal use by opening and closing the box, removing items, and adding fresh produce, etc. After a measured period of time (I would recommend at least 6 hours), remove the remains of the block of ice and reweigh it.

The heat gain of the box during this period, in British Thermal Units (Btus), is found by multiplying the reduction in the weight of the block of ice (in pounds) by 144. The 24-hour (daily) heat gain will be this figure, divided by the number of hours of the test (e.g., 6), and multiplied by 24. This will approximate the daily heat gain of this box in refrigerator use in the tropics. For freezer use this figure should be doubled. If the figures are much above those shown in Table 10-1, there is a problem with the icebox.

Depending on how far short of the recommended standards an icebox falls, it may be possible to improve its performance by modifying hatches and drains and by adding insulation. (In particular, there are frequently large voids between existing insulation and adjacent bulkheads and cabinetry. These voids can be filled by drilling holes in surrounding countertops and pouring in a two-part urethane foam mixture.) However, *if an icebox is seriously delinquent, for effective tropical refrigeration it may prove necessary to bite the bullet, rip the icebox out, and start from scratch.*

Figure 10-4. Refrigeration Choices

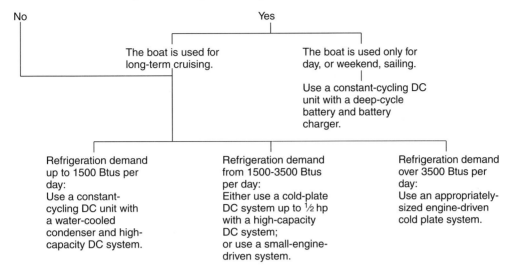

Does the boat have shorepower in its regular mooring?

No   Yes

The boat is used for long-term cruising.

The boat is used only for day, or weekend, sailing.

Use a constant-cycling DC unit with a deep-cycle battery and battery charger.

Refrigeration demand up to 1500 Btus per day:
Use a constant-cycling DC unit with a water-cooled condenser and high-capacity DC system.

Refrigeration demand from 1500-3500 Btus per day:
Either use a cold-plate DC system up to ½ hp with a high-capacity DC system;
or use a small-engine-driven system.

Refrigeration demand over 3500 Btus per day:
Use an appropriately-sized engine-driven cold plate system.

Note: For boats with an AC generator, see the text.

Most units come with an air-cooled condenser—the vital component that dissipates the heat taken out of an icebox. In the tropics the air temperature in a closed-up boat will rapidly climb to 100°F (38°C) or more, rendering an air-cooled condenser increasingly ineffective just when the refrigeration demands of the icebox are at their highest. The unit will start to run almost continuously, draining the batteries, probably still not refrigerating properly, and with a distinct risk of burning up.

It is absolutely essential to fit a water-cooled condenser to any refrigeration unit to be used in the tropics. Water is a far more efficient cooling medium than air, and the water temperature in the tropics rarely exceeds 85°F (30°C). *The absence of a water-cooled condenser is the number one cause of refrigeration problems in the tropics.*

The critical ambient temperature at which water cooling becomes more energy efficient than air cooling (in spite of the added energy consumption of the water pump attached to the water-cooled condenser) is around 95°F (35°C). This temperature is the temperature *in the space occupied by the air-cooled condenser*, not the temperature in the boat (which may be considerably cooler). Below 95°F (35°C), a water-cooled condenser may be *less efficient in terms of overall power consumption* than an air-cooled condenser, because of the added power drain of the water pump (this only applies to small, constant-cycling refrigeriation units; all large-capacity units, such as those below, require the added heat-removal capabilities of water cooling).

Cold-plate DC refrigeration. Cold-plate re-

frigeration employs one or more tanks filled with a solution that has a freezing point below that of water (Figure 10-6). The tanks are fitted in the icebox. When the refrigeration unit is running, it freezes the solution in the tanks, and then the unit shuts down (Figure 10-7). The tanks slowly thaw out, keeping the icebox cold. When the

Figure 10-5. Constant-cycling DC refrigeration. Note the substantial air duct to the air-cooled condenser. If this becomes obstructed, or there is not an equal-size duct to disperse the hot air from the other side of the condenser, performance will suffer drastically. *(Adler Barbour)*

Figure 10-6. **Cold-plate** construction. *(Dole Refrigeration Company)*

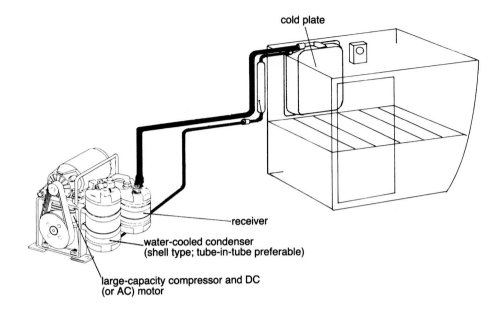

cold plate

receiver

water-cooled condenser (shell type; tube-in-tube preferable)

large-capacity compressor and DC (or AC) motor

tanks have almost defrosted, the unit is turned back on to refreeze them. In a well-designed system, even in the tropics the tanks will hold down the temperature in the icebox for 24 hours, and will then require no more than 1 to 2 hours refrigeration running time to be refrozen.

The ability of a typical cruising boat's batteries to drive a refrigeration compressor is strictly limited. There are thus two options: to install a large DC system, but keep the engine running whenever it is in use so that an engine-driven alternator supplies the power, or to limit the size of the compressor to whatever the batteries can handle. The first approach, though sometimes used, has no rationale—since the engine must be run whenever refrigerating, a directly engine-driven unit (see below) will be a far better choice: The engine-driven unit will be both cheaper and more powerful, resulting in more refrigeration at less cost for less engine running time. This leaves the second option (Figure 10-8).

A suitable bank (250 Ah or more) of good-quality deep-cycle batteries can sustain a refrigeration load of up to $\frac{1}{2}$ hp for extended periods (1 to 2 hours at a time). The current draw of a $\frac{1}{2}$-hp unit will be around 40 amps at 12 volts. Coupled to cold plates, this will comfortably provide a refrigeration capability of 3,500 Btus a day in refrigerator use, or around 2,000 Btus a day in freezer use. However, such a system will function only if backed with a high-capacity DC system as outlined above.

A DC cold-plate system is expensive, even ignoring the cost of upgrading the DC system should that be necessary. But it is more efficient than a constant-cycling system, which means that although it consumes far more power *when running*, it will provide an equivalent refrigera-

tion capability for less *overall* power consumption, or a greater capability for the same overall power consumption. What is more, if the DC system includes a large wind generator and/or a large-enough array of solar panels, quite considerable refrigeration needs can be met when cruising without having to crank the engine.

Engine-driven refrigeration. Cold plates are used once again, but this time the refrigeration compressor, the central component in a refrigeration unit, is directly belt driven from an engine instead of being driven by an electric motor (Figure 10-9). The system capacity is limited only by the ability of the cold plates to absorb the compressor's output, or the ability of the engine to drive the compressor. In practice, automotive air-conditioning compressors are invariably used, providing a refrigerating capability of up to 8,000 Btus per hour, and a freezer capability of up to 5,000 Btus per hour (although these outputs are rarely achieved).

Engine-driven systems are powerful. They are generally the only choice for those with substantial refrigeration needs. Although expensive, if a cruising boat does not already have an adequate DC system to support DC refrigeration, an engine-driven unit will also compare very favorably in terms of *total* cost.

The big drawback is the need to run the engine when refrigerating. At sea, if the engine has to be run anyway, as is so often the case (e.g., to charge batteries), this is not a problem. The difficulties arise at dockside. To get around these an auxiliary DC or AC (see below) unit is often built into the system. But this of course escalates the cost, particularly if the DC system is to be used with anything other than a battery charger run from shore

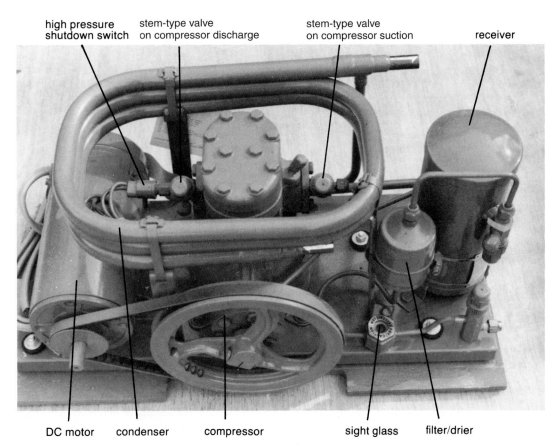

high pressure shutdown switch   stem-type valve on compressor discharge   stem-type valve on compressor suction   receiver

DC motor   condenser   compressor   sight glass   filter/drier

Figure 10-8. The "condensing unit" (compressor, condenser, and associated vessels) for an intermediate-sized DC unit designed for use with cold plates.

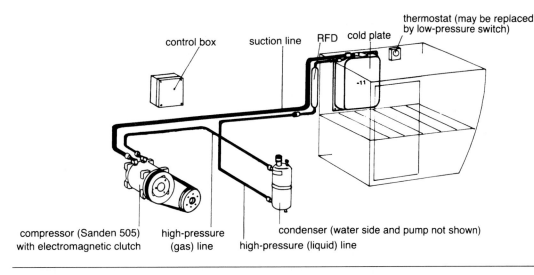

control box   suction line   RFD   cold plate   thermostat (may be replaced by low-pressure switch)

compressor (Sanden 505) with electromagnetic clutch   high-pressure (gas) line   high-pressure (liquid) line   condenser (water side and pump not shown)

Figure 10-9. Engine-driven refrigeration with cold plates. *(Frigoboat)*

power, since the boat's DC system will need to be upgraded to handle the cycling loads.

AC refrigeration. Large boats with 24-hour-a-day AC generation can obviously use large household-style AC refrigeration units. On smaller boats constant-cycling AC refrigeration is sometimes used as a shoreside supplement to an engine-driven unit, or else a stand-alone AC

unit is installed in a cold-plate configuration, with the compressor run off an intermittently operated generator.

Unlike a DC unit installed as a dockside assist to an engine-driven system, a constant-cycling AC unit can serve as an emergency backup at sea only if a constant source of AC power is available. In the past this has not often been the case, but the increasing popularity of DC/AC invert-

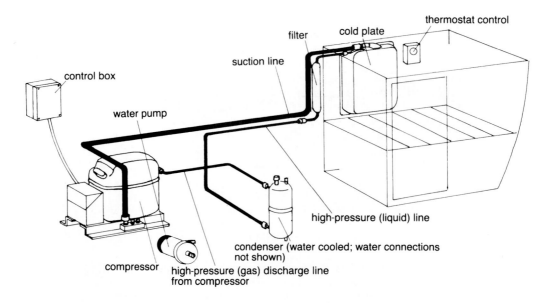

ers is now making it more and more commonplace. (However, running a refrigeration unit from an inverter creates greater energy losses than in most other systems—it would be better to get a DC system in the first place.)

Cold-plate AC refrigeration (Figure 10-10) requires intermittent operation of a generator. Running a generator engine in order to turn a generator that is used to power an electric motor that spins a refrigeration compressor that could have been driven directly off the engine in the first place involves an awful lot of energy losses! What is more, the directly engine-driven compressor will, in most instances, have a higher output than the AC unit, and therefore a reduced refrigeration *pull-down* time! In other words, *it is rarely worthwhile to run a generator simply for refrigeration purposes, but if the generator is to be used for other loads (e.g. water making, water heating, or cooking) it will likely have surplus capacity which can usefully be diverted to an AC refrigeration system.* The AC unit will, of course, be operable with shore power. In addition, it will use a hermetic compressor, enabling a sealed system to be built that will not suffer from the small leaks of a belt-driven system. However, *careful design and control of hermetic compressor systems are needed in the low-temperature and low-pressure environment of cold-plate refrigeration if risk of compressor damage is to be avoided.*

Postscript. The June 1995 issue of *Cruising World* includes detailed performance comparisons for most of the major marine refrigeration systems on the US market. This article is well worth reading if you are in the market for a refrigeration system. In terms of manufacturers, the clear winner on just about all counts was Glacier Bay (San Mateo, CA).

Operation, Troubleshooting, and Repair

Given a properly chosen and installed refrigeration unit, the key to being able to troubleshoot any problems that might arise is an understanding of how the unit works and what its normal operating parameters are.

How Refrigeration Works

Water boils at 212°F (100°C). Or does it? In a pressure cooker, water boils at more than 240°F (116°C), which is why food cooks so much faster (Figure 10-11A). The reason for this is that anytime pressure is increased, the boiling temperature goes up, and conversely, when pressure is decreased, the boiling temperature goes down. Water boils at 212°F *only at sea level atmospheric pressure.* At any other pressure the boiling temperature is higher or lower.

There is a corollary to this. If the temperature of a vessel of steam, which is at atmospheric pressure, falls below 212°F (100°C), the steam will

Refrigeration and Air-Conditioning

condense into water. *At higher pressures this condensation will take place at higher temperatures.*

When water turns into steam at atmospheric pressure the water is at 212°F (100°C) and so too is the steam. But *quite a bit of energy is needed to bring about this change of state from water to steam, even though no change of temperature occurs* (Figure 10-11B). This is seen easily. Put a thermometer in a pot of water, bring the water to a boil, and then boil it all away. The water will start to boil quite quickly but will take some time to boil away even though there will be no further rise in temperature. The converse also applies: In the process of condensing, steam *gives up* a large amount of heat even though the steam and water are both at 212°F (100°C).

Because heat absorbed and lost during changes of state does not result in a change in temperature (and cannot be measured with a thermometer), it is called *latent heat*. For a vapor (or gas) to condense into a liquid it must give up *latent heat of condensation;* for a liquid to boil into a vapor or gas it must absorb *latent heat of vaporization*.

These two concepts—the changing of boiling or condensation temperatures with changes in pressure, and the latent heat of vaporization and condensation—are at the heart of almost all refrigeration and air-conditioning systems. Let's see how it works, using R-12 (Freon-12) as a refrigerant. (Although it is being phased out, R-12 is still the refrigerant in the overwhelming majority of units, and in any case the new refrigerants operate in a very similar fashion.)

The refrigeration cycle. At atmospheric pressure, liquid R-12 vaporizes, or boils, into a gas at –21.6°F (–29.7°C), just as water boils at 212°F (100°C). When R-12 is pressurized, its boiling temperature rises (Figure 10-12). At 100 psi (pounds per square inch), R-12 boils at 90°F (32.2°C), or, put another way, if it is already in gaseous (vapor) form at 100 psi and if its temperature falls below 90°F (32.2°C), it will condense into a liquid. At 170 psi its boiling/condensation temperature is 125°F (51.7°C). At 220 psi the boiling/condensation temperature is 145°F (62.9°C). (Note: Air-conditioners, both past and present, generally use R-22 as a refrigerant; R-22 operates the same way as R-12, but with different boiling/condensation temperatures.)

In a refrigeration system R-12 gas is pulled into a compressor and compressed (Figures 10-13A and B), generally to between 125 and 175 psi. At 125 psi the gas will condense if its temperature falls below 104°F (40°C); at 175 psi, below 127°F (52.8°C). The hot gas is cooled in a *condenser;* its temperature falls below its con-

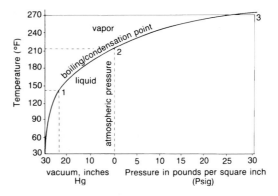

Figure 10-11A. The relationship between pressure and the boiling point of water. At position 1 (24 inches Hg vacuum) water boils at 142°F (61°C). At position 2 (atmospheric pressure) water boils at 212°F (100°C). At position (3) (30 psi) water boils at 272°F (133°C).

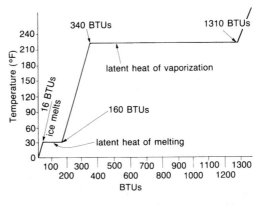

Figure 10-11B. Latent heat graph for water. This graph shows the amount of heat required to turn 1 pound of ice at 0°F (−17.8°C) into steam at 212°F (100°C).

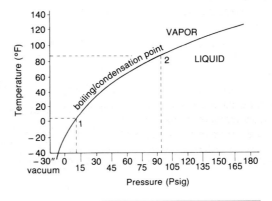

Figure 10-12. Temperature/pressure curve for R-12 refrigerant. At position 1 (11.79 psi) the vaporization/condensation temperature is 5°F (−15°C). At position 2 (93.34 psi) the vaporization/condensation temperature is 86°F(30°C).

densation point at this pressure and it turns into a liquid. In liquefying, it gives up a large amount of latent heat of condensation to the condenser.

The pressurized liquid enters a receiver/filter/drier (RFD for short; the receiver and the filter/drier are often two separate units). An RFD is nothing more than a tank with a fine screen and some desiccant (water-absorbing substance). The RFD filters out trash, absorbs moisture, and acts as a reservoir of liquid R-12. It is worth noting that most RFD's have a sight glass on top (more on this later), or one located nearby.

From the RFD the pressurized liquid R-12 goes to the refrigerator or freezer. There it is sprayed through a very small orifice into a length of finned tubing known as an *evaporator*, much like the radiator of a car. The orifice may consist

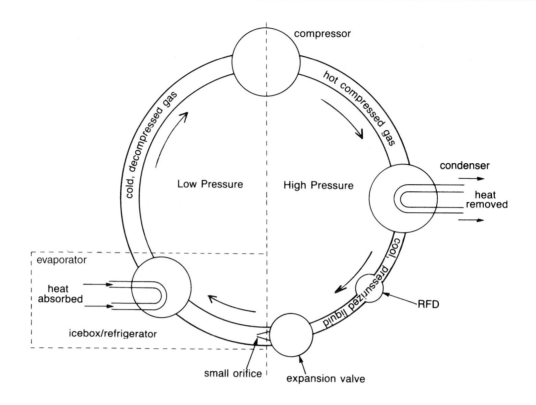

Figure 10-13A. The refrigeration cycle.

compressor

hot compressed gas

cold, decompressed gas

Low Pressure   High Pressure

condenser

heat removed

cool pressurized liquid

evaporator

heat absorbed

RFD

icebox/refrigerator

small orifice

expansion valve

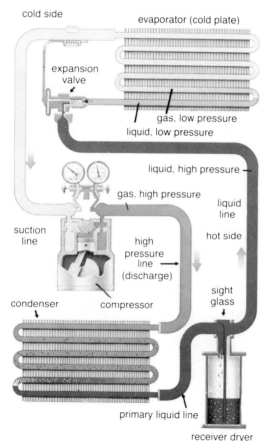

Figure 10-13B. Typical refrigeration system. Follow the arrows from the compressor through the condenser to the receiver/dryer, expansion valve, and evaporator, and then back to the compressor. (This is an air-cooled condenser—fan not shown.) *(Four Seasons)*

cold side

evaporator (cold plate)

expansion valve

gas, low pressure
liquid, low pressure

liquid, high pressure

gas, high pressure

liquid line

suction line

high pressure line (discharge)

hot side

condenser   compressor

sight glass

primary liquid line

receiver dryer

of nothing more than a very small piece of *capillary* tubing, or it may be incorporated in a special valve that regulates the size of the orifice according to the needs of the system—a *thermostatic expansion valve* (TXV for short).

The evaporator tubing is connected directly to the suction side of the compressor so that its pressure is held well down—typically anything from 30 psi down to a substantial vacuum, maybe as low as –10 inches of mercury. At 30 psi, liquid R-12 evaporates (vaporizes) at any temperature above 32°F (0°C); at –10 inches of mercury it evaporates (vaporizes) at any temperature above –40°F (–40°C).

When the pressurized liquid R-12 sprays into the low pressure zone of the evaporator, the sudden drop in pressure causes it to vaporize—it boils off into a gas. In doing so it absorbs large amounts of latent heat, pulling this heat out of the refrigerator or freezer and thereby cooling it down. The gas returns to the compressor, is recompressed, and goes back to the condenser where it is converted back into a liquid. The latent heat of condensation given up in the condenser is the same latent heat of vaporization that was absorbed in the evaporator; the heat has been taken from the food compartment of the refrigerator or freezer and transferred to the condenser.

The condenser dissipates the heat it has gained in one of two ways: Either a fan blows air over a radiator and the air carries the heat off (just as with a car radiator), or seawater is pumped through the condenser, carrying the heat overboard (just as with a heat exchanger on an engine's cooling circuit). Water-cooled condensers are up to 25 times more effective than air-cooled. Only small constant-cycling refrigeration units will have air-cooled condensers, and many of these would be better off with water cooling. All other systems are water cooled.

An air-conditioner works in exactly the same fashion, except that it uses R-22. All refrigeration and air-conditioning units are lubricated by oil, which circulates with the refrigerant. Refrigerant oils are specially blended for extremely low temperatures, and for specific refrigerants, and no other type can be used. As noted, the new refrigerants require new oils, and in many instances different oils and refrigerants are *totally incompatible*—it is essential to get the correct oil and refrigerant for a system!

Routine Maintenance

Properly installed, refrigeration units require little maintenance. If the condenser is water cooled, it should have sacrificial zinc anodes, which will need inspecting on a regular basis and replacing well before they are corroded away. If corrosion is rapid (the zinc needs replacing more than once a season), *there is a galvanic or stray-current problem that needs resolving before the condenser fails*, an event that can result in the total destruction of a refrigeration system.

During a winter layup be sure to drain the condenser, or it is likely to freeze and burst. The drain must be at the lowest point and effectively remove all water. Alternatively, mix up a 50% antifreeze solution, break the pump suction loose, and pump this through the water circuit.

Belts on belt-driven compressors must be correctly aligned (Figure 10-14A). With the belt off, a length of ½-inch (13-mm) doweling should drop cleanly into the grooves on the two pulleys. The belts should be set up moderately tightly—tighter than alternator belts (Figure 10-14B). Compressors must be extremely rigidly mounted. Without a solid mount, correct alignment, and adequate tension the compressor will chew up belts at regular intervals. If the belts vibrate excessively, particularly when long belt runs are involved, an idler pulley is needed to bear against the center stretch of the belt.

At certain speeds compressors will sometimes set up harmonic vibrations, which are amplified through the compressor mounts, bulkheads, etc.

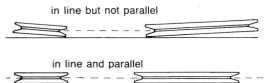

in line but not parallel

in line and parallel

Figure 10-14A. Pulley alignment.

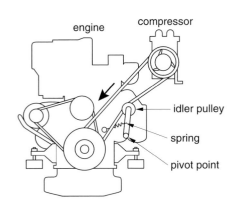

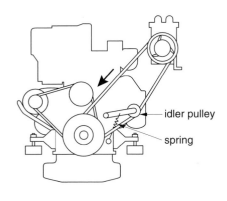

engine   compressor

idler pulley

spring

pivot point

idler pulley

spring

Figure 10-14B. Idler pulley arrangements. An idler pulley goes on the slack side of a belt.

The belt may well dance or jump. There is nothing wrong with the compressor. Try tightening the drive belt a little; perhaps add an idler pulley on the slack side of the belt. Check the alignment of the pulleys, and stiffen the compressor mount.

The brushes and commutator in DC motors need inspecting every year or two, depending on the amount of use (Chapter 6).

Belt-driven compressors tend to leak minute amounts of refrigerant from around the shaft seal. Just as with an automotive air-conditioner, the system should be topped off every year or so.

Troubleshooting and Repair

Troubleshooting starts long before a problem develops. Identify all the components and get a feel for normal operating temperatures at different points (feel the lines from time to time, particularly those going into and out of the compressor, the condenser [both refrigerant and water lines], the expansion valve, and the evapo-

Troubleshooting Chart 10-1.
Refrigeration and Air-Conditioning Problems: Brief Overview.

Unit fails to run: Is there a fault in the AC or DC circuit to the compressor or compressor clutch? **TEST:** Check the voltage *at the compressor or clutch.*	**FIX:** Check all fuses and shutdown devices. Reset or bypass any over-temperature or over-current shutdown device mounted on the compressor itself. Jump out the compressor or clutch directly to check its operation. If OK, jump out individual shutdowns to find the problem in the circuit.

Unit still fails to run: The compressor or clutch is faulty. Test motors as outlined in Chapter 6, or replace the clutch unit (pages 343–347). Hermetically sealed compressor will need replacing.

Unit cycles on and off: Is the condenser hot? **TEST:** Feel the condenser (water cooled) or inspect the fan and fins (air cooled). Check water flow or air ducting.	Check the flow of cooling water and its temperature. If the condenser is air-cooled, check its fans and fins. If the boat has recently moved into warmer ambient conditions the condenser may be undersized.
Unit cycles on and off: Is it undercharged? **TEST:** Check the sight glass—a mass of bubbles indicates a low refrigerant charge. If the sight glass is clear, switch off the unit, wait 15 minutes, and turn it back on. Watch closely: If the sight glass remains clear, the unit is out of refrigerant.	Recharge as necessary.
The unit runs but fails to cool the icebox or boat properly: Is the condenser hot? **TEST:** See above.	See above.
The unit runs but fails to cool the icebox or boat properly: Is it undercharged? **TEST:** See above.	See above.
The unit runs but fails to cool the icebox or boat properly: Is the compressor vibrating or excessively noisy? **TEST:** Listen to the compressor.	Run the compressor tests outlined in the text (page 348).
The unit runs but fails to cool the icebox or boat properly: Is there a temperature differential across the RFD or at any point in the lines? **TEST:** Feel with your hand.	The RFD or line is blocked. It will need replacing.

The expansion valve may be plugged or frozen, or its superheat setting too high (see the text). The unit may simply be undersized for the demands being placed on it.

rator). Find the sight glass and observe it during a number of starts—from a warm unit and from an already cold unit. See how quickly the stream of bubbles appears and then disappears as the condenser produces liquid. Check the sight glass at least monthly: If the bubbles begin to take longer to clear, or refuse to clear at all, the unit is losing refrigerant and the compressor may be in danger of burning up.

If a water-cooled condenser has its own overboard discharge (which I would recommend for troubleshooting reasons), measure the cooling water flow. Get a thermometer and measure the temperature of the seawater and then the temperature of the overboard discharge. Do this at different points of the cycle for a cold-plate refrigeration unit to gain some idea of typical in-and-out cooling water differentials. These figures can be used to crudely calculate the efficiency of the system as follows:

1. Take the cooling water flow rate in gallons per minute and multiply this by 7.5 (US gallons) or 8.3 (imperial gallons) to convert it into pounds.
2. Find the temperature differential between the cooling water coming out of the condenser and going into it in *degrees Fahrenheit*.
3. Multiply (1) by (2), and then multiply the result by 60. This will give the approximate rate of heat removal in Btus per hour. The figure will overstate performance; to improve accuracy multiply by 0.9 if the cooling water is salt water, and then by 0.75 to take account of various extraneous heat sources. This will give a fairly conservative approximation of system performance. The unit will probably be well short of its advertised capabilities—this is quite normal!

Pressures. Before problems develop, the adventurous may want to hook up a set of gauges (see below) and get an idea of normal operating pressures in different conditions.

Suction and discharge (head) pressures are affected by a dozen different factors. Nevertheless, a few broad generalizations can be made. Let's look first at refrigerators and freezers, using R-12. If an icebox and evaporator are warm to start with, initial suction pressures will probably run around 30 psi, discharge pressures around 175 psi. The pressures in a small, constant-cycling water-cooled unit will come down gradually, perhaps to about 10 psi and 140 psi (air-cooled units in hot climates may have discharge pressures as high as 180 psi). Large-capacity units with holding plates will keep coming down steadily. Suction pressures at the cold part of the cycle may range anywhere from 10 psi down to minus 10 inches of mercury (a considerable vacuum); discharge pressures range from 125 psi to as low as 100 psi. MP 39 and 66 units will be much the same; HFC 134a units will tend to run slightly higher on the high side, and slightly lower on the low side.

Air-conditioners with R-22 run at higher pressures and temperatures. They should stabilize fairly rapidly (after a few minutes) with suction pressures of 60 to 80 psi and discharge (head) pressures anywhere from 150 to 250 psi (the warmer the ambient air temperature and the cooling water, the higher the pressures). In extremely hot conditions pressures may go as high as 90 psi and 300 psi. If the unit is started on a freezing day, the ranges will be lower.

Leak detection. Refrigerant leaks are the number one problem in boat refrigeration and air-conditioning. There are three ways of detecting leaks:

Electronic leak detectors. These are ultrasensitive, in fact too much so around belt-driven compressor seals, where a small leak is both normal and permissible. Note that a special detector is needed with HFC 134a.

Halide leak detectors (will not work with HFC 134a). A fitting screws onto a standard propane torch. The flame heats a catalyst, and a hose is used to *sniff* around the refrigeration unit. If refrigerant is present the flame will change color: no leak, pale blue; slight leak, pale green; medium leak, brilliant green; serious leak, brilliant peacock blue. Halide leak detectors are ideal for boats and reasonably cheap (around $25). If *any* leak is detected, it needs fixing.

Soap solutions (50% dishwashing liquid). Sponge or brush the solution onto the part in question. If the solution bubbles, there is a bad leak.

Note that leaks often leave a telltale trace of refrigeration oil.

If a unit slowly loses efficiency over a month or two and no leak can be found, suspect the hoses. Neoprene and hydraulic hoses are sometimes used in place of proper refrigeration hose and these have been found to leak several ounces per foot per year through pores in the hose itself, but since the leak is not concentrated at any one point, leak detection equipment very often will not pick it up (note that HFC 134a requires special nylon-lined hoses).

Failure to run. On AC and DC units check the voltage at the compressor as described in Chapter 3. Remember, *AC VOLTAGES CAN KILL*. Many electrically powered compressors have overload (high-temperature) and low-voltage cutouts. If tripped, these may require manual resetting, or the unit may have to cool down before it will reset automatically. If the unit can be made to run, *check for voltage drop at the compressor during operation.*

Larger AC compressors have starting capacitors. If the motor hums but won't start, the capacitor may be faulty. Test as outlined in Chapter 6 or replace with a good one.

Hermetically sealed compressors that will not work despite adequate voltage will have to be replaced as a unit, but first turn it off and give it a smart *knock* with a soft-faced mallet—it may simply be stuck! On engine-driven compressors check the operation of the magnetic clutch and replace as necessary (see below).

If there does prove to be an electrical problem, trace it back through the circuit. Primary suspects, as always, are fuses, circuit breakers, and connections (Figures 10-15A, B, and C). Additionally, there are likely to be one or more high- and low-pressure or temperature cutout switches or solenoids on the system itself (as

Figure 10-15A. Schematic of a simple engine-driven refrigeration system. To operate, all switches and breakers must be closed and any fuses intact. To troubleshoot the clutch or water pump, first check the ground connection, then connect a jumper wire from the positive terminal, as shown. If the unit now works there is a problem in the circuit. Jump out individual switches to isolate the problem as shown, starting from the positive supply end of the circuit.

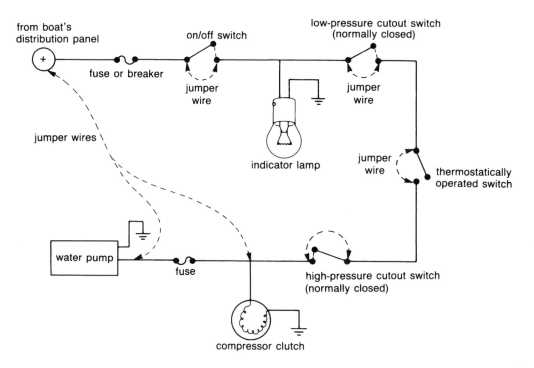

Figure 10-15B. Schematic for a unit with dual cold plates and thermostats. The thermostats supply power to close a solenoid, which then supplies power to the clutch and water pump circuit. With either thermostatic switch closed, power is supplied to close the solenoid; when both are open the curcuit is broken.

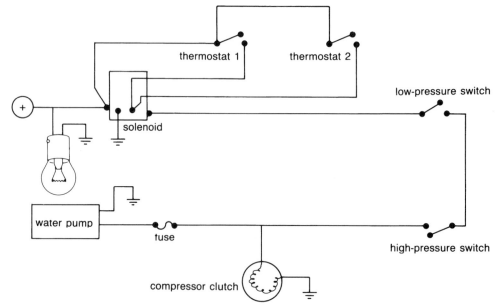

Refrigeration and Air-Conditioning

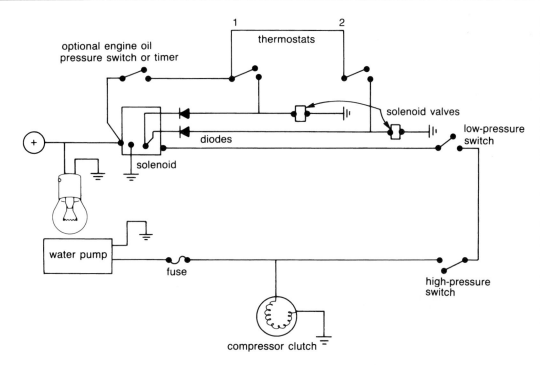

optional engine oil
pressure switch or timer

thermostats

1   2

solenoid valves

low-pressure
switch

diodes

solenoid

+

water pump

fuse

high-pressure
switch

compressor clutch

Figure 10-15C. Schematic of a more complex system, with dual cold plates and thermostats, and individual shutdown solenoids on each cold plate to close off the flow of refrigerant to that plate. The thermostats supply power to close the main solenoid, and also open individual solenoid valves on the liquid lines to each expansion valve. When a thermostat opens (i.e., breaks the circuit) its liquid line solenoid closes and shuts down its cold plate. The diodes prevent power from one thermostat feeding back via the common connection on the main solenoid to the other thermostat's liquid line solenoid valve, which would keep the solenoid valve open when it should be closed. When both thermostatic switches open the circuit is broken and the unit shuts down.

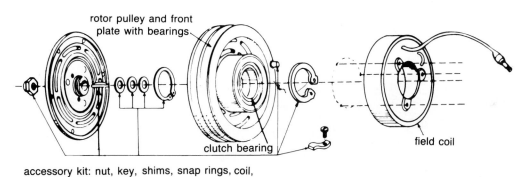

rotor pulley and front
plate with bearings

clutch bearing

field coil

accessory kit: nut, key, shims, snap rings, coil,
lead wire clamp with screw, retainer screws

Figure 10-16. An exploded view of a Sanden clutch. (Sanden International)

opposed to the compressor) and maybe a relay or two. Bypass each in turn to see if it is causing a problem. If it is, before condemning it make sure it is not performing its proper function (for example, cutting out because of genuinely low pressure due to a loss of refrigerant).

Magnetic clutches. Engine-driven compressors employ an electromagnetic clutch using 12 volts from the boat's battery. The drive pulley freewheels around the clutch unit, which is keyed to the drive shaft. Energizing the clutch locks the unit and drives the compressor. When the engine is running with the clutch disengaged, the pulley turns but its center hub remains stationary. When the clutch is energized the center hub turns with the pulley (Figure 10-16).

If the compressor fails to operate, energize the clutch and *make sure the center hub is turning*. If

it is not, check the voltage at the clutch and check its ground wire. If there is no voltage, or a severe voltage drop, test the clutch by jumping it out directly from the positive terminal on the battery. If the clutch still fails to work, it needs replacing. This is reasonably easy with Tecumseh (Blissfield) and York compressors, but Sankyo/ Sanden compressors require two special tools, which cruising sailors are well advised to buy: a clutch front-plate wrench (spanner) and a front-plate puller (Figures 10-17 and 10-18). A couple of other tools—a rotor puller and installer set, and a clutch plate installer—are useful but not necessary. (Tecumseh/Blissfield, York, and Sanden compressors account for the vast majority in engine-driven applications.)

To remove a York or Tecumseh (Blissfield) clutch assembly, a special tool is normally used to lock the pulley hub so that the pulley retaining nut can be undone. Some means of holding

Figure 10-17. Special tools used in servicing Sanden compressors. *(Sanden International)*

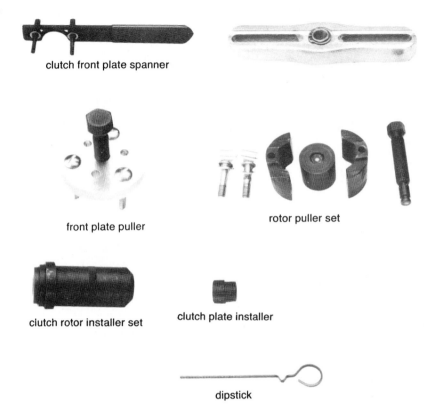

clutch front plate spanner

front plate puller

rotor puller set

clutch rotor installer set

clutch plate installer

dipstick

Figure 10-18. Replacing a clutch on a Sanden compressor. *(Sanden International)*

Figure 10-18A.**(Left)** 1. Insert the two pins of the front plate spanner into any two threaded holes of the clutch front plate. Hold clutch plate stationary. Remove hex nut with ³⁄₄-inch (19mm) socket.

Figure 10-18B.**(Right)** 2. Remove clutch front plate using puller. Align puller center bolt to compressor shaft. Thumb tighten the three puller bolts into the threaded holes. Turn center bolt clockwise with ³⁄₄-inch (19 mm) socket until front plate is loosened.
NOTE: Steps **1** and **2** must be performed before servicing either the shaft seal or clutch assembly.

Figure 10-18C.**(Left)** For HD-series compressors, remove bearing dust cover as shown.

Figure 10-18D.**(Right)** 3. Remove shaft key by lightly tapping it loose with a screwdriver and hammer.

Refrigeration and Air-Conditioning

Figure 10-18E.(**Left**)
4. Remove the internal bearing snap ring by using snap ring pliers (pinch type).

Figure 10-18F.(**Right**)
Note: On some later model clutches, the snap ring is below the bearing, and step 4 will not be necessary.

Figure 10-18G.(**Left**)
5. Remove the external front housing snap ring by using snap ring pliers (spread type).

Figure 10-18H.(**Right**)
6. Remove rotor pulley assembly. First insert the lip of the jaws into the snap ring groove (snap ring removed in step 4). Then place rotor puller shaft protector (puller set) over the exposed shaft.

Figure 10-18I. Align thumb-head bolts with puller jaws and finger tighten.

Figure 10-18J, K. Turn puller center bolt clockwise using ¾-inch socket until rotor pulley is free.

Figure 10-18L. (**Left**) **7**. Remove field winding; loosen winding lead wire from its clip on top of compressor front housing. (Early models do not use this clip; 1979 and later models use a snap-ring retainer for the field coil; 1978 and prior model 508s are held with screws.)

Figure 10-18M. (**Right**) Use spread-type snap ring pliers to remove snap ring and field coil.

Figure 10-18N. (**Left**) Clutch installation: (**1**) Install field coil. Reverse the procedure outlined in step 7, "Remove field winding." Coil flange protrusion must match hole in front housing to prevent coil movement and correctly locate lead wire. (**2**) Replace rotor pulley: Support the compressor on the four mounting ears at the compressor rear. If using a vise, clamp only on the mounting ears—never on the compressor body. Then align rotor assembly squarely on the front housing hub.

Figure 10-18O. (**Right**) Using rotor installer set, place the ring part of the set into the bearing cavity. Make certain the outer edge rests firmly on the outer race of the rotor bearing. Now place the tool set driver into the ring as shown.

Figure 10-18P. (**Left**)Tap the end of the driver with a hammer while guiding the rotor to prevent binding. Tap until the rotor bottoms against the compressor's front housing hub (there will be a distinct change of sound during the tapping process). (**3**) Reinstall internal bearing snap ring with pinch-type pliers. (**4**) Reinstall external front housing snap ring with spread-type pliers. (**5**) Replace front plate assembly. Check that the original clutch shims are in place on the compressor shaft. Next replace compressor shaft key. Then align front plate keyway with compressor shaft key.

Figure 10-18Q. (**Above, Right**) Using shaft protector, tap front plate onto shaft until it bottoms on the clutch shims (there will be a distinct sound change). (**6**) Replace shaft hex nut. Torque to 25 to 30 foot pounds. Note: SD-505 torque is 156 ± 26 in./lbs.; 180 ± 30 kg./cm.

Figure 10-18R. (**Right**) (**7**) Check air gap with feeler gauge to 0.016 to 0.031 inch. If air gap is not consistent around the circumference, lightly pry up at the minimum variations; lightly tap down at points of maximum variation. Note: The air gap is determined by the spacer shims. When reinstalling or installing a new clutch assembly, try the original shims first. When installing a new clutch onto a compressor that previously did not have a clutch, use 0.040, 0.020, and 0.005 shims from the clutch accessory kit. If the air gap does not meet the specification in step 7, add or subtract shims by repeating steps 5 and 6.

Refrigeration and Air-Conditioning

the hub will have to be devised. A universal deck plate key works well (Figure 10-19). Place a wrench on the bolt and hit it smartly to jar it loose. Take out the bolt.

Do not hit the pulley rim to break it loose from its tapered shaft. Find a ⅝-inch NC (coarse thread) bolt to fit the threads in the center of the pulley and wind in the bolt to back the pulley off. Unbolt the clutch retaining plate from the compressor block (four bolts). Replace the whole clutch and pulley assembly as one.

Unit cuts on and off. One of the temperature or pressure switches is cutting in and out. The switch is probably working correctly, indicating a fault in the system. If the unit is cutting out on high pressures, check the condenser (see below). If it is cutting out on low pressures, check the refrigerant charge (see below).

If high pressures are combined with heavy frosting on the suction line back to the compressor and a clear sight glass, and refrigerant has just been added, the unit is probably dangerously overcharged, and the compressor is at risk of serious damage.

Unit fails to cool down or cools too slowly. Likely causes are a loss of refrigerant, condenser

Figure 10-19. Clutch replacement on a York compressor (Tecumseh/Blissfield are the same).

Figure 10-19A. Use a universal deck plate key to hold the pulley stationary while undoing its retaining bolt.

Figure 10-19B. Screw off the pulley with a ⅝-inch NC (coarse-thread) bolt.

clutch coil retaining bolt

Figure 10-19C. The pulley has been removed to reveal the clutch coil. Undo the four bolts—one in each corner of the base plate.

Figure 10-19D. The clutch has been removed to reveal the shaft seal assembly.

problems, or compressor problems; less likely are capillary tube or expansion valve problems.

Loss of refrigerant. Check the sight glass. A steady stream of fast-moving bubbles indicates the unit is low on refrigerant. If the sight glass is completely clear, it is filled either with air (completely out of refrigerant) or with liquid (functioning OK). Faced with a clear sight glass, shut the unit down and give it 15 minutes to allow pressures to equalize internally. Restart it while watching the sight glass. If no bubbles appear, there is no refrigerant. Watch closely: The bubbles may appear for just a few seconds, and then only as a large, slow-moving bubble hovering in the top of the sight glass; if this happens the refrigerant charge is OK.

Hook up the gauge set (see below). When not running, a *warm* unit low on refrigerant will show pressures of 50 psi or less on both gauges. (Note: A fully charged cold unit will also show low pressures, so make sure the unit is warm.) When running, a unit low on refrigerant will have generally low pressures on both the suction and discharge sides, and the compressor discharge temperature will be lower than normal.

Condenser problems. If the condenser is operating inefficiently, the compressor discharge and suction temperatures and pressures will be abnormally high.

Air-cooled condensers are totally dependent on a good flow of cool air over the condenser fins. If the condenser is in an enclosed space or an engine room, ambient air temperatures will climb, and condenser efficiency will fall dramatically. Likewise, if the cooling fins are plugged with dust, efficiency will fall. Make sure any air-cooled condenser has an adequate flow of cool air. If necessary, duct air into the bottom of the condenser compartment (minimum 4-inch or 100-mm duct) and vent the top of the compartment (minimum 4-inch-diameter vent). Never obstruct the ducts. Fan motors require no maintenance except an occasional light oiling of shafts and bearings. Note that DC fans, if connected with reverse polarity, will run in reverse, greatly reducing efficiency. If the motor fails to operate, make all the usual voltage tests at the motor before condemning it.

The efficiency of a *water-cooled* condenser is directly related to the rate of water flow through it, and to the temperature of the cooling water. Any decrease in flow or rise in water temperature will have a marked effect on performance. Many condensers that work just fine in cooler climates prove inadequate in the tropics. If the condenser has a separate overboard discharge, measure the flow rate and compare this against the previously measured rate. If it has fallen, inspect the intake strainer for plugging and all hoses for kinking or collapsing. Next check the pump impeller (Chapter 12). Finally, some condensers have a removable cover, which allows the water tubes to be *rodded out* (use a wooden dowel with care), but most do not.

If a condenser is proving inadequate due to higher ambient water temperatures, before condemning it try increasing the water flow. If it is using the engine's water pump, the flow rate may be only 1 to 2 gallons a minute, especially at engine idle. Installing a separate pump could easily increase this to 4 to 6 gallons a minute.

Compressor problems. If noise levels are above normal, check discharge temperatures (this is when it is handy to have a sense of normal operating temperatures). If these are high, check the condenser.

If the compressor's valves are leaking, or the head gasket is blown between the high and low sides, the compressor will once again run hot. A failed valve will often make a *clacking* noise at idle speeds. If the compressor has stem-type service valves (as opposed to Schrader valves—see Charging and Topping-Up Procedures below), hook up a gauge set and make the following tests:

- Run the compressor, closing the suction-side service valve *to the system* (all the way in, clockwise). The compressor should rapidly pull a complete vacuum (–28 to –30 inches of mercury). Shut down the compressor.
- If a vacuum of –28 inches of mercury cannot be pulled, the suction valve or head gasket is bad (or the stem valve is not properly closed).
- If a vacuum of –28 inches of mercury can be pulled, but it rises fairly rapidly to atmospheric pressure (0 psi) after the compressor is shut down, the shaft seal is leaking.
- If a vacuum of –28 inches of mercury can be pulled, but it rises fairly rapidly to a positive pressure after the compressor is shut down, the discharge valve or head gasket is leaking.

If the compressor has Schrader-type service valves, run it normally for 5 minutes and then shut it down. If the suction and discharge pressures equalize in less than 2 minutes, the head gasket or valves are almost certainly bad.

Capillary tube or expansion valve problems. Capillary tubes either work or they don't. There is no adjustment. The tube should be warm where the liquid refrigerant goes in, and cold where it sprays out.

Expansion valves have a remote sensing bulb,

which is strapped to the exit pipe from the evaporator or cold plate and connected to the top of the expansion valve with a length of capillary tubing: The bulb controls expansion valve operation. *If the capillary tube is broken or kinked, the whole valve needs replacing.*

An expansion valve should be warm where the liquid refrigerant enters it and cold where the evaporator tubing exits. There will generally be a filter screen on the inlet side. If the valve is frosted all the way up the body and close to the inlet, the filter is probably plugged. Gauges will show an abnormally low suction pressure and the unit will not cool down properly—the filter will need cleaning (call a technician).

Any moisture in the system will freeze in the expansion valve orifice and plug it up. Gauges will show an abnormally low suction pressure, and the unit will not cool down. The compressor discharge line will run cooler than normal, and the evaporator side of the expansion valve will be warmer than normal. These symptoms are similar to those accompanying a plugged filter. To distinguish the two, allow the whole system to warm up and then restart it. With a plugged filter, the suction gauge will immediately show abnormally low pressures; if moisture is the problem, it will take a minute or two to produce abnormally low pressures. To combat frozen moisture, repeatedly shut down the unit and allow the expansion valve to warm up. Start the unit again. With any luck the ice will thaw out and be picked up by the drier. If the expansion valve still freezes, the unit will have to be bled down and the drier replaced—a certified technician with recovery equipment will once again be needed.

To test the operation of an expansion valve, hook up a set of gauges, run the unit until it is cold, then, with the unit still running, warm the remote sensing bulb (wrap a hand around it). After a few seconds the suction pressure gauge should show a slight rise (a pound or two) as the expansion valve opens and admits more refrigerant. The suction line to the compressor will probably start frosting up. *Let the bulb cool back down* or else excess liquid refrigerant may pass through the evaporator and cause *liquid slugging* at the compressor (which may damage the compressor's valves). The suction pressure should drop again. If the valve appears to be working, its *superheat* may simply need adjusting (see below).

Air-conditioners. Check the filter on the air inlet to the evaporator at regular intervals. A plugged filter will result in rising pressures and temperatures, with a general loss of performance. Check the fan, making all the usual voltage tests. *Remember, this is AC voltage. IT CAN KILL!*

Superheat. *Superheat* is not an easy concept to grasp. When the liquid refrigerant boils off in an evaporator, it absorbs latent heat of vaporization, thus cooling the evaporator. At any given compressor suction pressure, there is a specific temperature above which the liquid refrigerant will boil. Once the evaporator cools down to this temperature, no more refrigerant will boil off. If the expansion valve continues to let in liquid refrigerant, it will pass straight through the evaporator in liquid form with a risk of liquid slugging at the compressor.

The purpose of an expansion valve is to limit the flow of refrigerant, at any given compressor suction pressure, to an amount that will not quite cool the evaporator to the temperature at which liquid slugging will occur (Figures 10-20A and B). The difference between the theoretical minimum boiling temperature of the refrigerant at the given suction pressure and the actual temperature of the evaporator is known as superheat. In a well-set-up system it is generally maintained at 6°F to 10°F (3.3°C to 5.5°C).

To check superheat settings, use a gauge set to determine the compressor's suction pressure and then read across the gauge needle to the various temperature scales in the center of the gauge. Select the appropriate scale for the refrigerant in use (R-12, R-22, etc.) and then read off the temperature given. *This is the minimum boiling temperature of this refrigerant at this pressure.* Next, *precisely measure the temperature of the compressor suction line where it exits the evaporator* (this is generally where the sensing bulb is strapped on). This temperature measurement requires a sensitive electronic thermometer. *The amount by which this temperature exceeds the temperature read off the suction pressure gauge is, in theory, the degree of superheat in the system.*

A problem arises at this point. Frequently the compressor may have a long suction line containing bends and restrictions. The pressure measured at the compressor will be lower than that at the evaporator outlet, and *it is this latter pressure that is needed to determine the superheat.*

Some idea of the pressure drop in the suction line can be gained by watching the suction gauge while the unit runs and then cutting off the compressor. The pressure will jump and then slowly climb until it equalizes with the high side. This initial jump is fairly indicative of the pressure drop to the evaporator (if this jump is more than a pound or two, the suction lines are undersized—a relatively common problem). The pressure registered immediately after the jump is the pressure to be used when reading off the minimum boiling temperature of the refrigerant.

All this is rather academic, since equipment

Figure 10-20A. **(Top)** Expansion valve operation. The compressor is holding the pressure in the evaporator coil to 10 psi. At this pressure, the liquid R-12 emerging from the expansion valve will boil at any temperature above 2°F (−16.7°C). Since the cold plate is at 20°F (−6.7°C) the refrigerant rapidly boils off, pulling heat from the cold-plate. Once the refrigerant has boiled off, the vapor continues down the evaporator slowly equalizing (more or less) with the cold-plate temperature of 20°F (−6.7°C). The difference between the refrigerant's boiling temperature at this pressure (2°F [−16.7°C]) and the temperature at which the refrigerant emerges from the evaporator (20°F [−6.7°C]) is its superheat (18°F [10°C]), which in this case is excessively high. The expansion valve bulb contains a sealed charge of R-12. This too will equalize at the temperature of the evaporator coil at the outlet to the cold-plate (20°F [−6.7°C]). At this temperature, R-12 in a sealed chamber has a pressure of 21 psi. There is thus an 11 psi (21 − 10 = 11) pressure difference between the evaporator coil and the pressure transmitted by the bulb to the diaphragm in the expansion valve. This pressure differential is counteracted by the spring in the expansion valve. Adjusting the spring determines the extent to which the valve will open, and thus regulates the refrigerant flow and the superheat.

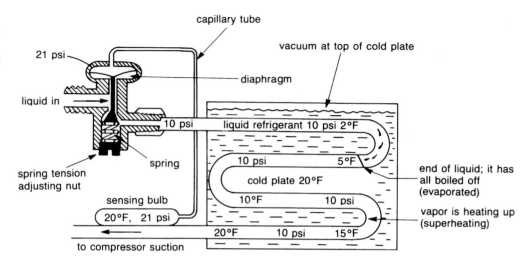

Figure 10-20B. **(Bottom)** Cutaway view of an expansion valve. *(ALCO Controls)*

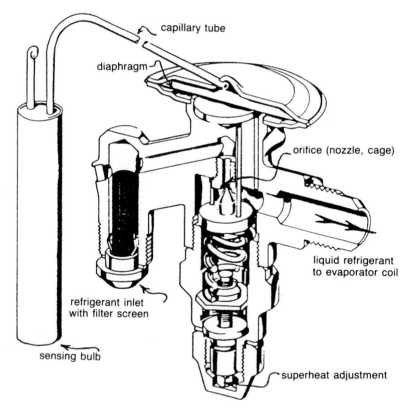

sensitive enough to measure evaporator temperatures accurately is unlikely to be available. In practice, cruder methods for setting up the superheat generally have to be used.

Superheat adjustments. Most expansion valves have a screw or squared-off stem in the body of the valve, covered with a ¾-inch cap nut. Remove the nut. Moving the screw beneath it in and out alters the amount of fluid passing through the expansion valve. (If there is no external superheat adjusting screw, the screw will be inside the discharge port of the expansion valve, and the valve must be taken out of the system to get at it! These valves should be avoided like the plague.)

A system must be properly charged before making superheat adjustments.

Superheat adjustments are made while the unit is running, but only on a cold unit. To do otherwise is to invite liquid slugging at the compressor when the unit cools.

When making superheat adjustments, *never move the screw more than a half turn at a time, and wait several minutes for the system to stabilize* (up to 20 minutes on a large-capacity holding-plate unit).

If the flow of refrigerant is increased, the suction pressure will rise slightly and the suction line at the evaporator outlet will cool. If the flow of refrigerant is decreased, the opposite happens. If at any time the suction line frosts heavily all the way back to the compressor and down the compressor side, excessive refrigerant is passing through the system and the compressor is in danger of liquid slugging. (This situation also arises with overcharging of refrigerant.) Restrict the flow or shut down the unit before damage occurs.

When a refrigeration or freezer system is cold, superheat can be adjusted to permit frosting of the suction line where it exits the evaporator. No damage to the compressor will occur as long as this frosting does not reach the compressor. (Even if it does, there is generally a degree of safety built in.)

Cold-plate units with multiple plates *in series* (one after the other) should be adjusted to permit frosting of the suction line where it exits *the last plate*. If the plates are *in parallel*, each will have its own expansion valve, which should be adjusted to permit mild frosting of the suction line where it exits the cold plate.

Air-conditioning units operate at higher pressures and temperatures, and the suction line should be cool at the compressor. If it is not, the expansion valve should be opened farther. *The suction line should never frost*; if it does there is danger of liquid slugging at the compressor.

Cold plates fail to hold over. If this has always been the case, the icebox may have inadequate insulation or the unit and cold plate may just be too small. If the failure is a new problem, check the items covered on page 347 under Unit Fails to Cool Down or Cools Too Slowly. In addition:

1. Consider whether a recent change in operating conditions (such as a move to warmer waters) is showing up a basic weakness for the first time.

2. Check the seal on the icebox lid or door (see page 331).

3. Has the icebox usage changed? For example, are some recently arrived heavy beer drinkers continually putting fresh cans of warm beer into the fridge? This is the WB (warm beer) factor!

4. Are the cold plates heavily iced? This will insulate them and reduce the rate of heat removal from the icebox.

Charging and Topping-Up Procedures

In what follows it is essential to remember that in the USA at least, and on US-registered vessels, *it is illegal for the uncertified boatowner to do more than top off a system, and even when topping off, there must be no more than minimal releases of refrigerant to the atmosphere.*

Handling Refrigerant

Refrigerants are reasonably safe and inert gases, but a few precautions must be observed:

1. The gases are heavier than air and in large quantities will displace the oxygen needed to breathe. In the small enclosed space of a boat, leaks will sink into the bilges and gradually displace the air in the cabin. Any serious leaks need to be dispersed with a good airflow through the cabin.

2. It is not safe to solder or braze on a system with refrigerant in it. At high temperatures R-12

will produce a gas similar to phosgene, which was used in the trenches in World War I.

3. No refrigerant should ever be added to the high-pressure side of a unit when it is running. The high pressures may blow up the can of refrigerant.

4. Refrigerant containers should not be left in direct sunlight or allowed to heat up beyond 125°F (52°C).

5. Cans of refrigerant contain liquid in the bottom, gas in the top. If the can is inverted when charging a system, liquid will come out. This is sometimes done by professionals, but amateurs should always play it safe: Charge with gas; never invert the can (the exception being the blends, which need to be charged as a liquid—consult a technician).

6. Evaporating refrigerant is extremely cold. It can cause frostbite, and permanent damage to eyes. Wear safety glasses.

7. Different refrigerants and oils are incompatible—*be absolutely sure to use the correct one for a given unit.*

Gauge Sets

A refrigeration gauge set is not expensive ($20 to $50—shop around) and is an *essential* troubleshooting tool. Newer gauge sets have what are called *low-loss* fittings; these minimize refrigerant releases and are recommended. If using more than one refrigerant (in different systems), *use a dedicated gauge set for each system to avoid the possibility of cross-contamination.*

A gauge set includes one red and one blue gauge screwed into a *manifold*, and below each gauge is a hose (Figure 10-21). On either side of the manifold is a valve. A third hose, the service hose, is located between the two gauge hoses. When the gauge valves are closed, the gauges will register the pressure in their respective hoses. When either valve is opened, its hose is connected with the service hose. When both valves are opened at the same time, all three hoses equalize with one another. The blue side of a gauge set always connects to the suction (low-pressure) side of a compressor, the red side to the discharge (high-pressure) side. Suction and discharge connections will be found on the

suction and discharge fittings on the compressor. Belt-driven compressors generally have the cylinder head stamped SUCT and DISCH; hermetically sealed compressors may not be labeled, but it doesn't matter. *The suction line is always larger than the discharge line* (Figure 10-22). There may also be other hose connections around the system, but the two closest to the compressor are the ones to use.

Making connections. *It is vitally important that no dirt enter a system. Before making any connections make sure that everything is spotlessly clean. Tighten the hose fittings by hand only.*

The hose connections on the compressor will be fitted with service valves. There are two kinds: *Schrader* valves and *stem-type (Rotolock)* valves (Figure 10-23). Schrader valves are the same as valves on bicycle and car tires, with a spring-loaded pin. One end of each hose on the gauge set has a metal piece for depressing the pin in a Schrader valve—this end must always go on the valve.

Stem-type valves have a squared-off shaft, which is screwed in and out to open and close the valve (Figure 10-24). There are three possible positions: all the way out (counterclockwise or anticlockwise) closes off the gauge hose to the system but leaves the compressor hooked in; the middle position (a turn or so clockwise) opens the gauge hose to the system while still leaving

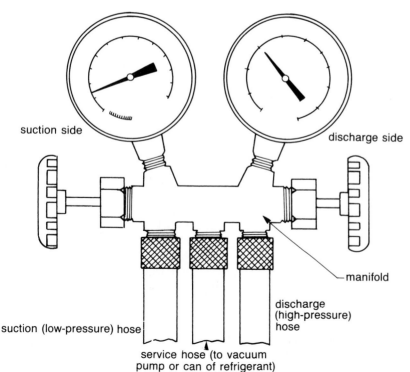

suction side

discharge side

manifold

suction (low-pressure) hose

discharge (high-pressure) hose

service hose (to vacuum pump or can of refrigerant)

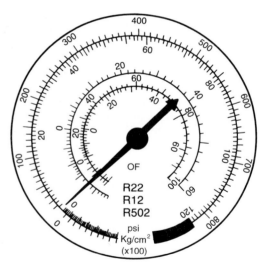

400
300
500
200
600
100
700
800
OF
R22
R12
R502
psi
Kg/cm² (x100)

Figure 10-21. (**Left**) A refrigerant gauge set: an essential tool for self-sufficient, refrigeration-equipped boats. (**Right**) Suction-side gauge. The outer band indicates pressure; the inner bands the evaporation/condensation temperature (°F) of R-22, R-12, and R-502 refrigerants at any given pressure.

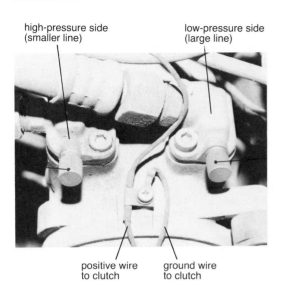

high-pressure side (smaller line)

low-pressure side (large line)

positive wire to clutch

ground wire to clutch

Figure 10-22. Engine-driven compressor gauge connections.

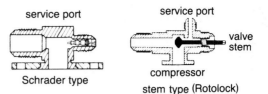

service port

Schrader type

service port

valve stem

compressor

stem type (Rotolock)

Figure 10-23. Schrader valve and stem-type (Rotolock) valve—the two most commonly found types of service valve.

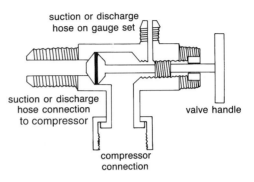

suction or discharge hose on gauge set

suction or discharge hose connection to compressor

valve handle

compressor connection

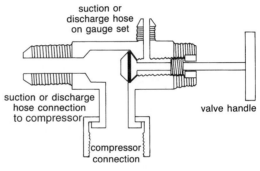

suction or discharge hose on gauge set

suction or discharge hose connection to compressor

valve handle

compressor connection

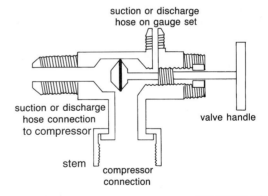

suction or discharge hose on gauge set

suction or discharge hose connection to compressor

valve handle

stem

compressor connection

Figure 10-24. Stem-type (Rotolock) valve operation. (**Top**) Valve is closed to system but open to gauge set (for compressor removal, etc.). (**Middle**) Valve is closed to gauge set but open to system (for normal operation). (**Bottom**) Valve is open to both system and gauge set (for monitoring performance, etc.).

the compressor hooked in; and all the way in (clockwise) closes off the compressor to the system but leaves the gauge hose connected to the compressor. A proper ¼-inch square ratchet wrench—obtainable from refrigeration supply houses—is highly recommended for stem-type valves. The use of adjustable wrenches or pliers soon messes up valve stems.

Purging a gauge set. Once a refrigeration or air-conditioning unit is charged *it is essential that no air be allowed to enter the system.* What this means in practice is that anytime a gauge set is hooked up for charging, air must be purged from the gauge set hoses and replaced with refrigerant before making the final connections. When doing this, *refrigerant releases must be kept to an absolute minimum.* To purge a gauge set, first shut down the unit (if it is running). There are then two methods (Figures 10-25A and B):

Using refrigerant already in the system (presupposing it has at least a partial charge). Close *both gauge valves,* loosen the hoses below the gauges, and prepare to screw the hoses onto their compressor connections.

If the compressor has Schrader valves: as each hose is done up it will open the Schrader valve and refrigerant gas will blow out of the loosened connection at the gauge manifold. Snug up the connection. This hose is purged.

If the compressor has stem-type valves: turn the valves fully counterclockwise before making any connections. Attach the hoses at the compressor

and snug up, but leave the hoses loose at the gauge manifold. Turn the stem valves clockwise one-half to one turn. Refrigerant will blow out of the loosened connections at the gauge manifold. Snug up these connections. The hoses are purged.

For all types of valve: connect a can of refrigerant to the service hose, leaving the hose loose at the can. Crack open either one of the gauge valves—refrigerant will blow out of the loose connection at the can. Snug up the connection. Purging is complete. (Note that if the can has a Schrader valve, the pin on the service hose must go on the can.)

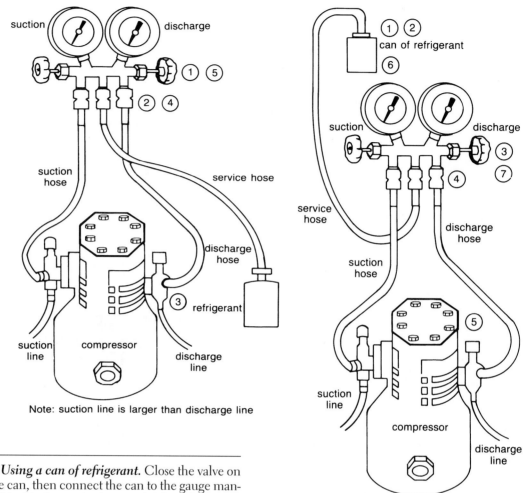

Figure 10-25A. **(Left)** Purging a gauge set using refrigerant already in the system. Preliminary step: If the system has stem-type valves, fully backseat the valves. **(1)** Close both gauge valves. **(2)** Loosen the suction and discharge hose connections at the gauge set; tighten the service hose connection. **(3)** Tighten the suction and discharge hose connections at the compressor one at a time. **(4)** Schrader valves: Allow refrigerant to blow out of the loosened connections at the gauge set and then snug up. Stem-type valves: Turn the valves clockwise one-half to one turn, allowing refrigerant to blow out of the loosened connections at the gauge set, and then snug up. **(5)** Connect the service hose loosely to a can of refrigerant, crack open either gauge valve, allow refrigerant to blow out of the loosened connection at the can of refrigerant, and then snug up. Purging is complete.

Figure 10-25B. **(Right)** Purging a gauge set using a can of refrigerant. Preliminary step: If the system has stem-type valves, fully backseat the valves. **(1)** Close the valve on the can of refrigerant. **(2)** Tighten the service hose at the can of refrigerant. **(3)** Close the gauge valves. **(4)** Tighten all three hose connections at the gauge manifold. **(5)** Fit the hoses loosely at the compressor. **(6)** Open the valve on the can of refrigerant. **(7)** Crack each gauge valve in turn, allowing refrigerant to blow out of the loosened connection at the compressor, then snug up. Now close the gauge valve if the compressor has Schrader valves (to avoid adding refrigerant to the system). Purging is complete.

Note: suction line is larger than discharge line

Using a can of refrigerant. Close the valve on the can, then connect the can to the gauge manifold with the service hose and tighten both connections. Tighten the other two hoses at the manifold and connect them *loosely* at the compressor (we do not want to open a Schrader valve at this stage). Close both gauge valves and open the valve on the can of refrigerant. Crack each gauge valve in turn, blowing refrigerant out of the loose hose connection at the compressor before tightening the connection. If the compressor has Schrader valves, close the gauge valves to avoid adding refrigerant to the system. Purging is complete. On a unit with Schrader valves, once the hoses are tightened the gauges are always open to the system, but where stem-type valves are fitted the valves must be opened one-half to one turn clockwise.

Charging a system. Purge the hoses. Check to see that *both gauge valves are closed* and the stem-type valves on the compressor (if fitted) are open one turn. *Make sure the can of refrigerant is upright.* Open the valve on the can of refrigerant. Open the suction-side gauge valve. Refrigerant will enter the unit. Wait until the pressure in the system has settled down (probably at around 60 to 70 psi, but this depends on ambient temperatures). Then close the suction valve on the gauge set.

Locate the sight glass on the system. It will probably be on top of or next to the RFD. (Some air-conditioning units do not have a sight glass— see below.) Take a look in it; it will be clear. Now start the unit and watch the sight glass. Fairly soon foamy, fast-moving bubbles will appear as the first liquid refrigerant comes out of the condenser mixed with gas bubbles. The bubbles should steadily decrease. In a fully charged, fully cold system they will disappear altogether, leaving a sight glass that is once again completely clear, but this time filled with liquid.

If a unit is very low on refrigerant, this initial charge of refrigerant is not going to be enough to clear the sight glass. The problem is to determine how much more to put in—too much will damage the compressor. The final charge can be determined only with the unit cold. In the case of air-conditioners and refrigeration units with-

Refrigeration and Air-Conditioning

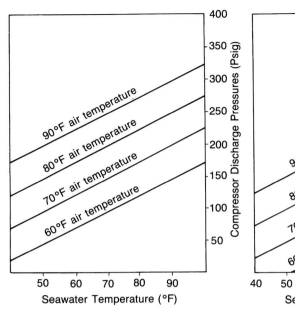

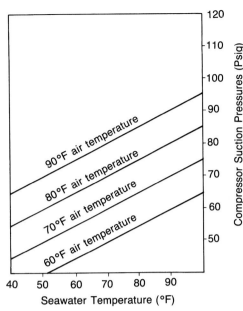

Figure 10-26. Typical operating pressures for an air-conditioning unit using R-22 with a water-cooled condenser. For a given seawater temperature and ambient air temperature, read off the anticipated compressor suction and discharge pressures. For example, with a 70°F (21°C) seawater temperature and an 80°F (27°C) ambient (in the cabin) air temperature, on this unit expect a suction pressure of 70 psi and a discharge pressure of 200 psi. Add refrigerant a little at a time until these pressures are approximated. If at any time the suction begins to frost, the unit is overcharged. *(Lunaire Marine)*

out cold plates this will take only 5 minutes or so, but where cold plates are fitted, if the plates are warm, it may take 20 minutes to a half hour, perhaps even longer.

Monitor the sight glass continually. If the stream of bubbles is still pretty steady once the unit has cooled down a bit, with the unit running open the suction-side gauge valve to let in more refrigerant. The bubbles will start to decrease. After a while there may be just one big bubble hovering in the top of the sight glass. Close the gauge valve and let the unit stabilize. If more bubbles appear, add more refrigerant. Let the unit get really cold—don't rush things—before doing the final topping off. Eventually the sight glass should be completely clear (all liquid). Don't add any more refrigerant. If compressor discharge pressures become excessively high (much over 200 psi on a refrigeration unit or 250 psi on an air-conditioner), and/or the suction line on a refrigeration unit starts to frost heavily all the way back to the compressor, the system is almost certainly overcharged. There should be no frosting of the suction line in an air-conditioner.

Charging a unit without a sight glass. Many air-conditioning manuals specify a set of operating pressures at certain ambient air and cooling water temperatures (Figure 10-26). Measure the air and water temperatures, enter the graphs provided, and read off the suction and discharge pressures. Continue adding refrigerant until these pressures, or something close to them, are reached. When charged and in operation, the compressor suction line will be cool and proba-

bly sweating. If it is warm, the charge is inadequate; if it is frosting, the charge is excessive. (This applies to air-conditioners only; many refrigeration and freezer units run colder, and some frosting of the suction line is acceptable.)

Removing a gauge set. *Shut down the unit.* Close off any can of refrigerant, but leave its hose connections tight. Open both gauge valves until the system equalizes, with both gauges reading the same pressure. Close both gauge valves. Loosen the hose connection at the can of refrigerant, allow the hose pressure to bleed off, and remove the hose from the can of refrigerant.

Schrader valves. Remove each hose in turn at the compressor as fast as possible. Refrigerant will vent as long as the valve stem is depressed, which is why the hoses must be undone quickly.

Stem-type valves. Backseat the valves counterclockwise. Crack one of the gauge valves and bleed off its hose through the service hose. Close the gauge valve and observe the pressure—if it climbs back up, the stem valve is not properly seated (the high-pressure side may show a slight pressure rise initially but then should stabilize). When the stem valve is holding, bleed off the hose and remove it. Repeat this process for the other hose.

Cap all valves and hose ends to make sure that no dirt can enter the system.

For an in-depth look at marine refrigeration, see my *Refrigeration for Pleasureboats*, published by International Marine.

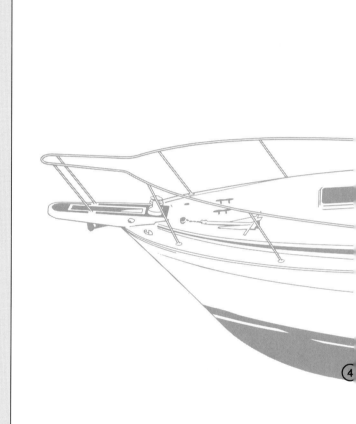

CHAPTER 11

Figure 11-1. Problems with onboard plumbing can ruin a cruise faster than anything else. A familiarity with the system—and where everything is located—is highly recommended. *(Jim Sollers)*

———————— cold water

------------------ hot water

(1) Y-valve
(2) macerator pump
(3) toilet pump
(4) shower sump
(5) lavatory basin
(6) vented loop
(7) galley sink
(8) icemaker
(9) shower
(10) freshwater fill
(11) head overboard discharge
(12) head raw-water intake
(13) holding tank
(14) lavatory basin drain
(15) galley sink drain
(16) water heater
(17) air conditioner raw-water intake
(18) engine cooling water intake
(19) auxiliary raw-water intake
(20) freshwater tank
(21) freshwater pump
(22) washdown system
(23) holding tank pump-out
(24) bilge pump
(25) bilge pump strainer
(26) collection box
(27) foot pump

Plumbing, Toilets, and Through-Hull Fittings

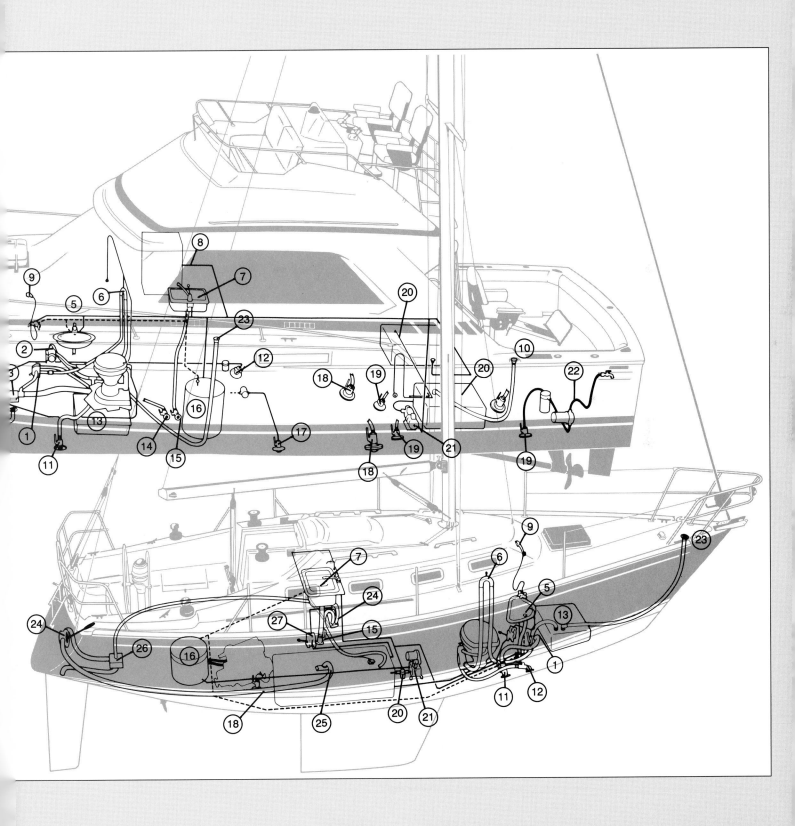

Plumbing

Plumbing can be a bit of a nightmare aboard a boat. To avoid mismatches between equipment and pipes or hoses, and untoward plumbing failures, it is necessary to understand how pipes and hoses are specified, the suitability of different pipes and hoses for different applications, and proper installation practices.

The *nominal* sizes of most pipes, hoses, and fittings do not correspond to their *actual* sizes, either the *outside diameter* (OD) or the *inside diameter* (ID). In addition, there is no universal standard governing sizes. Given two items that are nominally the same size (e.g., ¾ inch or 20 mm) it is quite likely that neither will actually be this size, and, what is more, that they will not be the same size as each other!

Pipes and fittings are commonly copper, metal (*black* or *galvanized*), or plastic (*PVC* or *CPVC*). Copper pipe in the USA is subdivided into *water* pipe or tubing and *refrigeration* pipe or tubing (pipe comes in straight lengths; tubing in coils).

Copper Pipe or Tubing

Water pipe (USA) has a purely nominal size (Table 11-1). In other words, *its nominal size does not correspond to either its ID or its OD. Refrigeration* pipe or tubing, on the other hand, *is measured by its outside diameter* (OD)—½-inch (13-mm) refrigeration tubing really has a ½-inch (13-mm) outside diameter. Copper fittings (connectors, elbows, tees, etc.) *are made mostly to water pipe sizes.* Since water pipe of any given nominal size is actually one size larger than refrigeration pipe of the same nominal size, when buying fittings for use with refrigeration pipe or tubing, *generally you must buy the next smaller size of fitting down* (e.g., ⅜-inch fittings for ½-inch refrigeration pipe or tubing—see Table 11-2).

Copper pipe and tubing is further defined by its wall thickness. In the USA it is given a K, L, or M rating, with the K having the thickest wall. Type L is generally used for household and refrigeration plumbing. In the UK copper pipe and fittings (I believe!) are all standardized according to the outside diameter of the pipe or tubing (8-, 10-, 15-, 22-, 28-mm, etc.).

Specific *refrigeration* tubing or pipe should always be bought *for refrigeration purposes*—it is specially cleaned, dehydrated, and capped to keep out moisture. For water systems, either refrigeration or water tubing or pipe can be bought from any hardware store. Tubing has the advantage that it can be worked around the awkward shapes of a boat with very few joints. It generally comes in 50-foot rolls. When making tubing runs, the copper should be bent *as little as possible*; with constant flexing it *work-hardens* and then is prone to kink or crack. If tubing does become hard, it can be resoftened by heating to a cherry red color with a propane torch and then dousing with cold water (*annealing*—for some reason copper is annealed the opposite way to other metals, which are heated and then cooled *slowly*).

Table 11-1. Table of Pipe Sizes[1]

| Nominal Inside Diameter (inches) | Actual Outside Diameter (inches) | | | | | Wall Thickness (copper tubing, in inches) | | | | |
| | Schedule 40 Pipe | | | Copper Tubing | | Water Tubing | | | Refrigeration | |
	Metal[2]	PVC	CPVC	Water	Refrigeration	K	L	M	K	L
⅛ (0.125)	0.405	-	-	¼	N.A.	0.032	0.025	0.025	N.A.	N.A.
¼ (0.250)	0.540	-	-	⅜	N.A.	0.035	0.030	0.025	N.A.	N.A.
⅜ (0.375)	0.675	-	-	½	⅜	0.049	0.035	0.025	0.032	0.032
½ (0.500)	0.840	0.840	⅝	⅝	½	0.049	0.040	0.028	0.049	0.032
⅝ (0.625)	N.A.	-	-	¾	⅝	0.049	0.042	0.030	0.049	0.035
¾ (0.750)	1.050	1.050	⅞	⅞	¾	0.065	0.045	0.032	0.049	0.035
⅞ (0.875)	N.A.	-	-	N.A.	⅞	N.A.	N.A.	N.A.	0.065	0.045
1 (1.0)	1.315	1.315	-	1⅛	N.A.	0.065	0.050	0.035	N.A.	N.A.
1⅛ (1.125)	N.A.	-	-	N.A.	1⅛	N.A.	N.A.	N.A.	0.065	0.050
1¼ (1.250)	1.660	1.660	-	1⅜	N.A.	0.065	0.055	0.042	N.A.	N.A.
1⅜ (1.375)	N.A.	-	-	N.A.	1⅜	N.A.	N.A.	N.A.	0.065	0.060
1½ (1.500)	1.900	1.900	-	-	-	-	-	-	-	-
2 (2.0)	2.375	2.375	-	-	-	-	-	-	-	-
2½ (2.500)	2.875	2.875	-	-	-	-	-	-	-	-

1. N.A. = Not Applicable.
2. Metal pipe includes brass, bronze, black, and galvanized

Table 11-2. Size Relationships

Nominal Copper Fitting Size (inches)	Fits Refrigeration Tubing with OD of (inches)
1/8	1/4
1/4	3/8
3/8	1/2
1/2	5/8
3/4	7/8
1	1 1/8

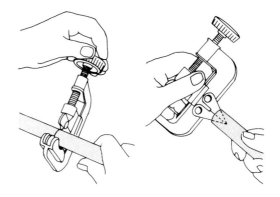

Figure 11-2. Using tubing cutters.

Tight bends are liable to flatten out, kink, or both, unless made with proper bending tools or springs. Bending springs, which simply slip over the outside of the tubing and are then removed when the bend is complete, are quite cheap, and available from plumbing suppliers.

If possible, tubing and pipe should always be cut with tubing cutters since this is the only way to ensure a smooth and square cut (especially important for making flare connections—see below). To make a cut, clamp the cutters *lightly* around the tube or pipe and make a full turn (Figure 11-2). Tighten the handle a half turn after each turn until the cut is complete. On the back of the cutters will be a hinged arrowhead fitting—use this to clean any burr on the inside of the cut.

In both the USA and the UK copper pipe and tubing can be joined with compression fittings, flare fittings, and solder fittings.

Compression fittings. Compression fittings are in many ways the easiest to make but the least reliable in service.

1. Slide a nut up the tube or pipe and then slip on a compression ring, or *olive* (Figure 11-3).
2. The tube or pipe fits into a recess in the compression fitting. The fit must be perfectly square.
3. The nut slides up onto the fitting and is tightened, *keeping the tube or pipe pressed into the recess at all times.*
4. The compression ring is squeezed against the fitting and into the soft metal of the tube or pipe, forming an effective seal.

Flare fittings. Flares are made with a special tool. There are a number of relatively inexpensive flaring kits on the market, and one or two real Cadillacs for around $80. The cheaper kits consist of a clamp that fits around the tube or pipe and has a machined bevel in its face. A

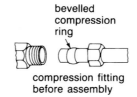

bevelled compression ring

compression fitting before assembly

Figure 11-3. A compression fitting.

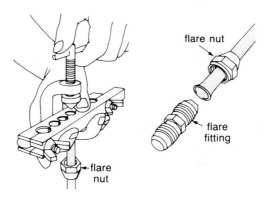

flare nut

flare fitting

flare nut

Figure 11-4. Making a flare connection.

horseshoe-shaped bracket with a threaded bolt in its center fits over the clamp. On the base of this bolt is a spinner—a block of metal cut to the same taper as the bevel in the clamp. The spinner is screwed into the mouth of the tube or pipe and forces its sides out against the bevel (Figure 11-4). The flare is complete.

Here are some tips:

1. The nut must be put on the line before making the flare! If possible use long-nosed flare nuts (as opposed to the more common short ones), since they provide more support to the joint and reduce the chances of cracking due to vibration.

2. The end of the tube or pipe must be *cut square and cleaned of all burrs inside and out.*

Any dirt, trash, or metal filings will especially come back to haunt refrigeration and gas systems.

3. Warming the tube or pipe before screwing down the spinner will help prevent cracking (ideally, the tube should be *annealed*).

4. Depending on clamp configuration, the tube or pipe may need to protrude above the face of the clamp by one-third to one-half the depth of the bevel to permit an adequate flare. If it is set flush with the face of the clamp, the resulting flare will be skimpy and prone to leak. When made, the flare should just fit into, but not hang up on, the sides of the flare nut.

5. The spinner should be oiled when making the flare.

6. *The spinner should not be screwed down too tightly*—it will weaken the flare. When the joint is done up, the flare nut will pull the flare snugly onto the flared fitting.

7. If the flare looks uneven or in any other way unsatisfactory, it must be cut off and remade. Doing so right away will be a lot easier than doing so later.

Soldering. Solder fittings (sweat fittings) can be used on both copper tubing and pipe. A wide range of fittings is readily available. Some fittings are presoldered (omit steps 4 and 5 below), but most are not.

1. Clean both surfaces to be soldered with fine (400- to 600-grit) wet-or-dry sandpaper *until the entire surface to be soldered is shiny* (Figure 11-5). *Do not use emery cloth*—oils in the cloth backing will spoil the soldering.

2. Apply soldering flux immediately but sparingly to both surfaces. Push the fitting onto the tube or pipe and twist to spread the flux evenly. The flux is there to keep out oxygen and contaminants *once the joint is clean*. Flux is no substitute for cleaning.

3. Heat the joint evenly with a propane torch.

4. Touch solid solder to the joint periodically until the tube or pipe and fittings are hot enough to melt the solder. *The solder itself is not heated by the torch*—if the metal in the joint is not hot enough to melt the solder, it will not flow properly.

5. Let solder flow into the joint. Apply only enough heat to keep the solder melting; more will overheat the joint. Generally the flame can be held at some distance or turned away from the joint and passed over it quickly a couple of times.

6. When solder shows all around the fitting, the joint is complete. Remove the heat. Any more solder added to the joint will merely flow out the other side and into the tube or pipe, causing a partial blockage.

7. When the joint is cool, thoroughly clean away the excess flux.

Figure 11-5. **Soldering:** refer to the text for a step-by-step description of the process.

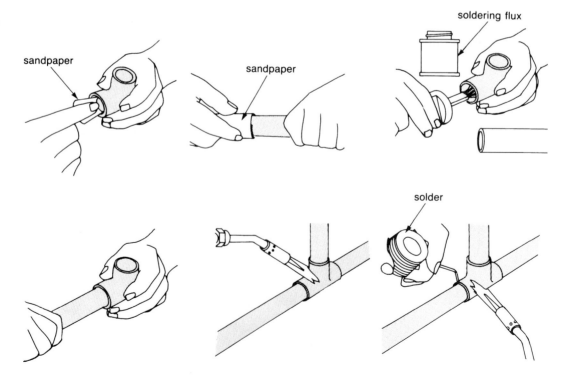

sandpaper

sandpaper

soldering flux

solder

Plumbing, Toilets, and Through-Hull Fittings

If you experience problems in getting leak-proof joints, the most likely culprit is contamination of the soldering surface on the pipe or in the fitting. To be certain of making successful joints, the surfaces to be soldered can be tinned (i.e., given a thin film of solder) prior to being mated. If the solder will not spread out evenly, the copper is not clean enough. Once tinned, the pipe may not push into the fitting, in which case you need a little heat to melt the solder while seating the pipe.

Metal Pipe

Black pipe is plain steel (technically, *black* metal is *wrought* iron, but today the term is used to describe plain rolled steel); it is used in some commercial boat applications but not on pleasure boats. *Galvanized* pipe is steel pipe coated with zinc to resist corrosion, but even so has only limited applications. It is sometimes found in fuel systems but *should never be used with diesel fuel* since the diesel will dissolve the zinc, which will then clog the fuel system.

Pipe sizes are standardized, but as can be seen from Table 11-1, the actual outside diameter of metal pipe is considerably more than its nominal diameter. The thickness of a pipe is given as its *schedule*. Schedule 20 is thin-wall pipe, unsuitable for boat applications; schedule 40 is standard pipe, and suitable for most applications; schedule 80 is thick-wall pipe, and once again rarely used. The additional thickness is gained by narrowing the inside diameter, so regardless of a pipe's schedule, *a given fitting will fit any pipe of the same nominal size.*

Pipe fittings. Metal pipe is almost invariably joined with threaded fittings; threads are, once again, standardized. Pipe fittings are labeled according to the nominal size of pipe they will accommodate. A 1½-inch (38-mm) fitting, for example, fits a 1½-inch (38-mm) pipe. Since the 1½-inch (38-mm) pipe is actually around 1⅞-inch (48-mm) in diameter, and the fitting must go around the pipe, a 1½-inch (38-mm) fitting will be more than 2 inches (52 mm) in diameter.

Pipe threads are tapered. As a pipe or fitting is screwed up, it becomes progressively harder to turn. A certain amount of experience is required to gauge how tightly to do up differently sized fittings. A threaded pipe joint is rarely water- or gas-tight without the addition of some kind of a sealant to the joint. Various pastes can be bought for this purpose, but by far the most useful thing to carry on board is several rolls of *Teflon (PTFE)* tape, which is available at any hardware store.

The most useful general-purpose size is ½ inch (12 or 13 mm). Wind the tape around the male fitting *in the opposite direction to which it will be screwed into the female fitting*. Three or four wraps is more than enough. Then stretch the tape until it breaks, and smooth the loose end down.

Although it is commonly done, it is not a good idea to screw metal pipes into plastic *adapters* (see below) — hardening of the plastic with age, combined with expansion and contraction of the metal, is liable to crack the plastic fitting. Plastic adapters screwed into metal fittings, on the other hand, rarely fail.

Plastic Pipe

PVC pipe is commonly used for cold-water applications, while CPVC pipe is used for hot-water applications. The two are not interchangeable! Nominal and actual dimensions are given in Table 11-1 (standard UK sizes are 10, 15, 22, 28, 35 and 42 mm).

Both types of pipe are joined with glued fittings. It is important to match the type of glue to the type of pipe (best of all is to buy a quality glue suitable for both types of pipe). Adapters are available with a glue-type terminal on one end and a threaded fitting on the other so that it is possible to go from metal pipe and metal-pipe fittings to glued pipe and fittings (but note the caveat above). Once again, Teflon tape will be needed on the threads. Various compression-type fittings are also now available for use with plastic pipe.

Plastic pipe, which is available from any hardware store, is excellent for many plumbing jobs on board, and as conduit for electrical wires. It is readily cut with a hacksaw, comes with a tremendous range of fittings, and can be glued together in seconds. It is easily cut up and glued back together for later modifications. Prior to gluing, lightly sand the end of the pipe and the inside of the fitting with 400-grit wet-and-dry paper, then clean with a solvent cleaner (available from any hardware store), and finally coat with the cement. *Immediately* press the pipe home, twisting a half turn or so to spread the glue evenly. Hold for about 30 seconds to give the glue a chance to grip, and do not subject the joint to pressure for at least half an hour. Once installed, plastic piping is maintenance-free.

Note: Solvent cleaners and plastic-pipe glues are highly flammable and evaporate rapidly, giving off toxic fumes. They should be used only in well-ventilated, nonsmoking environments. Read the labels carefully and observe all cautions.

Hoses

Hoses are almost always specified by their *inside diameter* (ID); a 1-inch (25-mm) hose will have a 1-inch (25-mm) inside diameter. Sizes in the USA are almost all multiples of ⅛ inch or ¼ inch (Europe is comparable in metric sizes); since the outside diameter of metal pipe and PVC pipe are very rarely multiples of ⅛ inch or ¼ inch, *hoses rarely make a clean fit on pipes*: adapters are needed (the exception is CPVC pipe, which normally has an outside diameter of ⅝ inch or ⅞ inch). Adapters are readily available as either threaded fittings with *hose barbs* or glued fittings with hose barbs, but sometimes the necessary combination (i.e., the specific pipe size and hose size) cannot be found in a single fitting, in which case the threaded or glued end has to be sized up or down using *bushings*.

Hoses play a critical role aboard any boat, but given the bewildering array on the market it is not always easy to pick the right one for a particular job. The first thing to note is a tremendous variation in quality. Quality hoses will generally be labeled as meeting some standard—in the USA typically UL (Underwriters Laboratories), SAE (Society of Automotive Engineers), or CG (Coast Guard) standards; in the UK typically ISO (International Standards Organization) standards. However, it is not unknown for foreign-made hoses to be falsely labeled. When buying hoses, particularly below-the-waterline hoses, it is best to buy only those manufactured by a reputable domestic producer.

Fuel fill, vent, and supply hoses. In the USA these must meet SAE J1527. The Coast Guard has a classification based upon the permeability of a hose and its fire resistance. Type A passes the fire test; class 1 passes the most stringent permeability tests. *Those hoses continuously filled with fuel (all fuel lines) must be CG Type A1*. Fuel-tank *fill* hoses and *vent* hoses can be CG Type A2 or B2. It is required that the hoses be labeled. It is worth checking existing hoses to see that they meet the standards; if they don't, replace them. The minimum inside diameter of a fuel-tank fill hose is 1½ inch (38 mm); that of a vent hose ⁹⁄₁₆ inch (14 mm).

Exhaust hose. Hose is by far the best material to use in a wet exhaust system. It is easy to run, helps to dampen exhaust noise, and lasts for years if properly installed. Surprisingly, there are currently no standards *required* of exhaust hose manufacturers, although there is a tough UL standard (UL 1129), which few hoses pass (it includes a requirement to be able to withstand 2 minutes of dry running). The subject of standards is actively under discussion by the SAE and the ISO. For the present, any hose that meets UL 1129 will be excellent but hard to find; more common is hose stamped "Type Certified" or "Wet Exhaust," which, if domestically manufactured, should be good quality; in the future we should expect to see hose that meets SAE J2006 and whatever standard the ISO produces.

As a general rule of thumb, any run of exhaust hose that is longer than four times the inside diameter of the hose (this covers all but the shortest of runs) should be *wire reinforced* (called *hardwall*, as opposed to nonreinforced *softwall*).

Notwithstanding the lack of standards, it is essential to buy a quality exhaust hose. It is going to have to withstand heat, oil, acids, salt, some pressure, a certain amount of weight (when filled with water), vibration, and constant pulsation when the engine is running. A leak can be anything from a minor inconvenience to fatal (particularly if it allows carbon monoxide into accommodation spaces).

Water hose. Some, such as that on engine cooling circuits and domestic hot-water systems, has to be able to withstand quite high temperatures; other hose must tolerate quite high pressures (pressurized water systems) or considerable vacuums (an engine cooling pump or bilge pump sucking against a plugged filter). There are no standards, with the exception of hose for drinking water applications which, in the USA, should be made of FDA-approved materials (this will generally *not* be stamped on the hose—it is necessary to check with the supplier). For any application where a vacuum might be encountered, some sort of reinforcement is necessary.

Fresh water hose has traditionally been clear PVC or nylon-reinforced clear PVC. I have never understood the rationale for this—it lets light into the water system, which promotes the growth of algae and other undesirable organisms. Hard pipe (copper or plastic) or opaque tubing (now available in FDA-approved materials) will keep the drinking water cleaner.

For all below-the-waterline applications, although there are no standards, only a top-quality hose should be used. I well remember the occasion when some spilled acetone ate through our plastic cockpit drain hoses *in seconds*—we immediately (the same day!) replaced all hoses attached to through-hulls with heavy-duty, fabric-reinforced, oil- and acid-resistant water hose.

Sanitation hose. Even when watertight, many hoses are not *odor-tight*. Specific *sanitation* hose is needed for toilet discharge lines and holding-tank connections (including the vent line). This hose should have a *smooth interior* to inhibit clogging and scaling (see below).

Federal regulations in the USA, and ISO standards in Europe, require pump-out fittings to be a nominal 1½ inch (38 mm) pipe size (which is, of course, nearer 1 ⅞ inch in actuality—Figure 11-6). Many pump-out fittings in marine catalogs and chandleries are marked 1½ inch, but this refers to their *actual* size; in terms of pipe sizes they are only 1¼ inch, *which is not legal*. Both properly sized fittings, and the undersized fittings are generally designed to take a 1½ inch (38 mm) ID hose—this is pretty much the international standard for pleasure boats.

When it comes to holding-tank *vent fittings*, the ISO standard requires a 1½ inch (38 mm) ID hose, whereas US boatbuilders have traditionally used something far smaller (typically ¾ inch).

Connecting hoses. Various hoses (water, bilge, sanitation) can be bought with a spiral (*threaded*) outer casing. On some, the inside is also ribbed, but on others it is smooth (for sanitation use, it should definitely be smooth). Some hose has a *right-handed* thread, and some a *left-handed* thread. End fittings (*cuffs*—Figures 11-7A and B) and couplings screw right onto the hose either to make a connection to a hose barb or else to join two lengths of hose. Clearly a right-handed hose needs a right-handed fitting and a left-handed hose a left-handed fitting. The end of the hose is liberally coated with plastic pipe cement (for PVC or CPVC pipe) and then immediately screwed into the cuff until it bottoms out. This makes a clean and watertight connection. If the cuff is properly matched to the hose barb or pipe on which it will go, this too will make a clean and watertight connection.

Many times, however, a hose or cuff is not quite the right size for the pipe or barb it is to go on. In certain circumstances (notably exhaust systems and fuel systems) *the ABYC flatly requires that it BE the right size*, but in other instances it is possible to fudge a little. *If the hose is a loose fit* a little caulking (3M 5200 works well) smeared over the surface of the pipe or hose barb (Figure 11-8) will spread out on the inside of the hose and make a good joint (as long as it is given time to set up). *The caulking should not be applied to the inside of the hose* since the pipe or barb will simply push it up the hose to form a blockage. Clearly the hose must be clamped down tightly enough to also produce a mechanical connection—the caulking is simply there to make a seal.

If a hose is a tight fit, a little dishwashing liquid will do wonders as a lubricant. If this is not

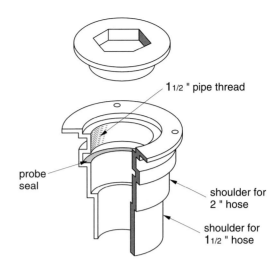

Figure 11-6. Internationally agreed upon standardized pump-out deck fitting. The 1½-inch pipe thread is purely nominal—the outside diameter is closer to 1⅞ inch. The 1½-inch hose diameter is the actual inside diameter of the hose.

1½ " pipe thread

probe seal

shoulder for 2 " hose

shoulder for 1½ " hose

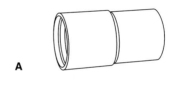

Figure 11-7A. **Hose cuff.**

A

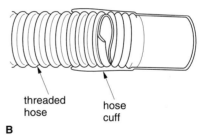

Figure 11-7B. **Hose cuff screwed onto a hose.**

threaded hose

hose cuff

B

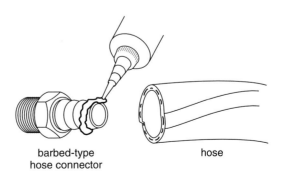

Figure 11-8. **Adding sealant to a poorly fitting hose connection.**

barbed-type hose connector

hose

enough, soften the hose by holding it in a pot of boiling water for a few seconds and then try the dishwashing liquid.

Most people, myself included, still recommend two *all-stainless-steel* hose clamps on below-the-waterline hoses. But there are others who argue that this is overkill and that in fact at times there is not enough room to space two clamps properly, with the result that one is too close to the end of the hose (it should be in ¼ inch) and the other is half off the pipe or hose barb. Regardless of opinion, on wet exhausts the ABYC requires two clamps, each with a minimum ½-inch (13-mm) band width.

Many *all-stainless* hose clamps utilize an inferior grade of stainless for the screw (*400 series*) which soon rusts and then corrodes the band inside the screw housing (see Chapter 4). *These screws can be detected with a magnet.* Better-quality screws are made of *300-series* stainless (which is nonmagnetic, or almost nonmagnetic—the clamp will be marked 300); the best clamps have *316-series* screws (notably all hose clamps manufactured by AWAB).

Hydraulic hoses. Hydraulic systems, particularly winches and windlasses, may experience pressures of thousands of pounds per square inch. It is essential to use only the specified tubing, hoses, and fittings, and to assemble them with great care. In addition, most hydraulic systems are supersensitive to dirt—absolute cleanliness and careful clean-up of all shavings and particles if a hose has to be cut are critical when assembling systems. Always cap hoses when they are not connected, especially if passing them through bulkheads or lockers where they might pick up dirt, and always flush new hoses with hydraulic oil before connecting them to a system.

As a general rule, hydraulic hose should meet one of the following standards: Aeroquip 2651,

SAE 100R7, or ISO DIS 3949. Any of these hoses have adequate burst pressures for most pleasure boat systems (2,000 psi or more in smaller sizes); they all have a rubber outer cover which protects the inner braid (if metal) against corrosion; and perhaps most importantly they are designed for use with *reusable* (as opposed to *crimp*) fittings, which facilitates repairs in the field (note that not all SAE 100R7 hose is suitable for reusable fittings). Other commonly available rubber-coated hoses suitable for reusable fittings are Aeroquip 2781 and SAE 100R2A, but these hoses have higher burst pressures (5,000 psi in smaller sizes) and will be overkill in most situations. In the kind of low-volume hydraulic systems found aboard pleasure boats, unless otherwise specified, hose runs of up to 50 feet (16 meters) can be ½-inch (13-mm) ID, while those more than 50 feet should be ⅝-inch (15- or 17-mm) ID. Hoses should never have tight bends (Figure 11-9), and should be fastened at regular intervals (sudden pressure changes can make them move around).

Specialized equipment is needed to install crimp-type fittings, whereas reusable fittings require just a vice and a couple of adjustable wrenches (Figure 11-10). Note that of the reusable fittings, some require a *mandrel* for assembly while others do not. The mandrel type can be fitted without the mandrel, but only at the risk of the fitting cutting into the hose wall—check carefully when done to see that the hose is not damaged.

Various fittings are available with different threads and angles on the seating surfaces. Since there is no international standardization, matching replacement fittings to existing equipment can be a minefield for the unwary cruiser: In the USA 37-degree *flares* are the most common, with some 45-degree flares; in Germany and many parts of the world a 24-degree *cone* is common; in the UK a 60-degree cone is the most common; but besides these there are at least a *dozen* other flares and cones with varying thread patterns! Before leaving port, *be sure to lay in a stock of correctly matched reusable end fittings for any critical hydraulic systems.* End fittings can be male or female, swiveling or non-swiveling, threaded or quick-connect. (The latter have a spring-loaded knurled ring that is pulled back while pushing the connector onto its fitting and then locks the connector in place. *A quick-connect should always be checked for dirt before making a connection, and kept capped when not in use.*)

Since hydraulic service technicians are few and far between outside Western cities, the voyaging cruiser should carry whatever fittings are needed to splice the hoses in the system, and preferably sufficient hose to replace the longest run of hydraulic hose or pipe on board.

Figure 11-9. Right and wrong ways to make a bend in a hydraulic hose.

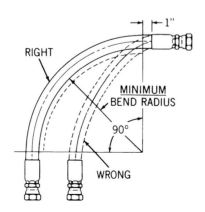

Plumbing, Toilets, and Through-Hull Fittings

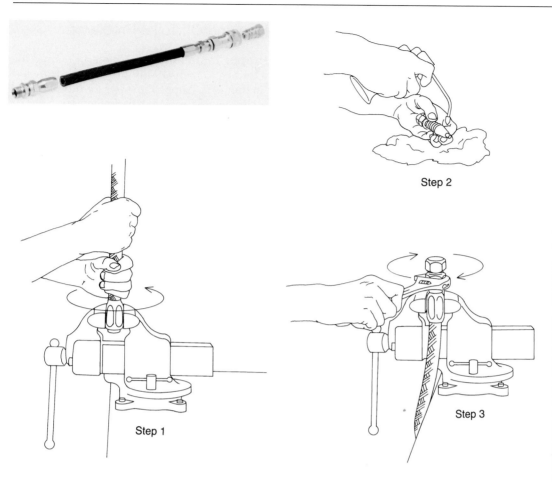

Figure 11-10. Adding end fittings to hydraulic hoses. A special assembly tool—a *mandrel*—is sometimes required for assembly, but is not absolutely necessary. **Step 1**: Cut the hose square with a fine-toothed hacksaw or cutoff wheel. Clean the hose bore. Put the end fitting socket in a vise and screw the hose in counterclockwise until it bottoms out. Back off one-quarter turn. **Step 2**: Liberally oil the end fitting nipple, the assembly tool (mandrel) if used, and the inside of the hose, using a heavy oil such as STP or Aeroquip Lube Oil. **Step 3**: Push the assembly tool (if used) into the nipple. Add a few drops of oil and then screw the nipple clockwise into the socket and hose. Tighten the nipple, leaving a clearance of 0.030 to 0.060-inch (0.8 to 1.6 mm) between the nipple hex and the socket. Clean the assembly by blowing out with dry air or washing with warm water. Inspect the hose internally for a cut or bulged tube and general cleanliness. Check for the proper gap between the nut and socket or hex and socket—nuts should swivel freely. Cap the ends to keep the hose clean. *(Jim Sollers)*

Step 1

Step 2

Step 3

Marine Toilets (Heads)

Discharge Regulations

Discharge of untreated raw sewage is illegal anywhere within the United States' three-mile limit and in many areas in Europe. In the USA, any installed toilet *(marine sanitation device or MSD)* in a vessel *shorter than 65 feet* must conform to one of three types.

Type I MSDs. These break up the sewage so that no visible floating solids remain. The sewage is treated chemically to kill bacteria and then discharged overboard.

Type II MSDs. These are similar but treat the sewage to more exacting standards.

Type III MSDs. These include portable toilets, eliminating overboard discharge in prohibited areas. The usual method is to store the sewage in a holding tank and then to discharge it either through a dockside pump-out facility or overboard beyond the three-mile limit (Figures 11-11A and B).

Vessels longer than 65 feet can use only type II or III systems. Type I and II devices must be properly certified and have a certification label. Holding tanks require no certification provided they store sewage only at ambient temperatures and pressures (usually provided by venting the tank to atmosphere via a through-hull fitting). Currently it is perfectly legal to have a toilet and holding tank with a Y-valve such that the toilet can be pumped directly overboard (beyond the three-mile limit) or into the holding tank. The valve must be secured in the holding tank position when in territorial waters. Padlocking, removal of the valve handle, or use of a plastic wire tie are all considered adequate methods of securing the valve.

There is increasing concern that the chemicals used to treat the effluent in many Type I and II systems are themselves damaging to the environment. We can expect moves to restrict the use of these devices. In the meantime both in the USA and Europe considerable resources are being put into developing the network of pump-out stations (in 1992 the USA appropriated $40 million for this purpose). Type III devices are the way to go.

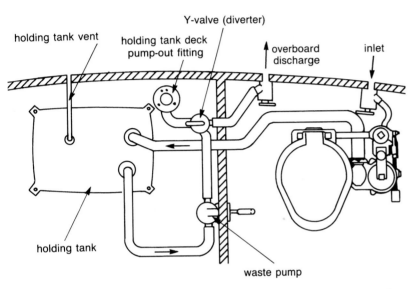

Figure 11-11A. Typical arrangement of an onboard waste disposal system with a holding tank and overboard discharge. In this configuration, all effluent first passes through the holding tank before being pumped overboard. The inlet and discharge lines should be looped above the waterline and fitted with vented loops. *(Simpson Lawrence)*

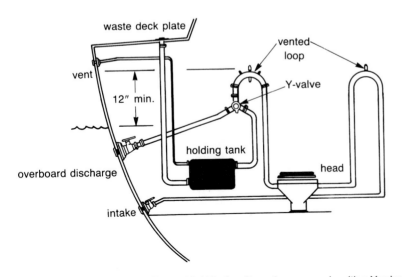

Figure 11-11B. An alternative approach, with a Y-valve (diverter) before the holding tank.

Heading Off Toilet Problems

Proper installations. Almost all marine toilets use a ¾-inch (19-mm) ID (inside diameter) suction hose (supplying water for flushing) and a 1½ inch (38 mm) ID discharge hose. Suction hoses must be noncollapsible—any good-quality, reasonably firm water hose will do. Discharge hoses must be proper *sanitation hose*.

Vented loops. Almost all sailboat toilets, and many powerboat toilets, are installed below the waterline. The toilets have valves on both the suction and discharge sides, but even so, any leakage past either a suction or discharge valve can siphon water into the toilet, eventually sinking the boat if not discovered in time. Many boats have sunk this way. *It is absolutely essential to fit some form of a siphon break on both suction and discharge lines (Figures 11-12A and B).*

A siphon break is formed by looping the line above the water level and installing at the high point of the loop a valve that allows air to be drawn into the line. This valve must be above the water level *at all angles of heel.*

The usual configuration consists of a U-bend with a small tee containing a rubber flap. Several problems may arise:

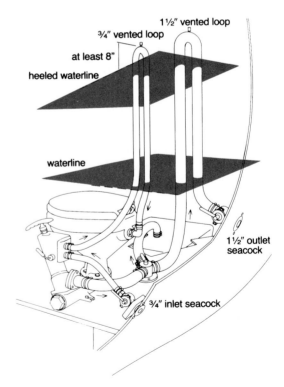

Figure 11-12A. A "proper" toilet installation. *(ITT/Jabsco)*

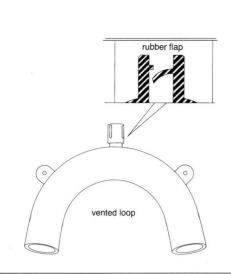

rubber flap

vented loop

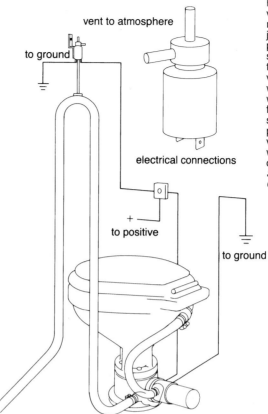

vent to atmosphere

to ground

electrical connections

to positive

to ground

Figure 11-12B. (**Far left**) a vented loop with a simple rubber flap valve, or even just a very small hole, to prevent water from being siphoned into the boat through a leaking inlet valve. (**Left**) a vented loop with a solenoid valve, which prevents excess air from being sucked into the system by the head's pump. (**Bottom**) a recent variation on a vented loop, which provides access for clearing blockages. *(Jim Sollers/Wagaman Graphics)*

1. The vent will sometimes plug up, notably with salt crystals in the suction line, rendering the loop inoperative. Periodically the vent valve should be unscrewed and washed in warm fresh water.

2 Air can be drawn into a suction pump through a vented loop. This will reduce the water flow to the toilet and in extreme cases can lead to a loss of prime and subsequent air locking of the suction pump. A U-trap in the suction line, close to the toilet, will retain some water and keep the pump wetted. This simple measure may not suffice for some electric pumps, however, in which case a solenoid valve should be installed on the vent in such a way that the solenoid closes when the toilet is flushed, and opens when flushing is completed (a normally open solenoid valve).

3. A vented loop in the discharge line will allow foul odors into the boat. It is best to attach a small hose to the vent and run this overboard. Its exit must be above the waterline at all times or it will siphon into the boat and negate the purpose of the vented loop.

Some vented loops for discharge lines incorporate a cleanout fixture—a useful addition to any system.

General maintenance. Marine toilets require little maintenance. Periodically it is worthwhile to half-fill the bowl with warm water, add some biodegradable laundry detergent, and flush this through the system. Follow with another half bowl of warm water containing a little mineral or baby oil—the oil will help keep all rubber parts (valves, impellers, and seals) supple and in good condition. A little Teflon-based waterproof

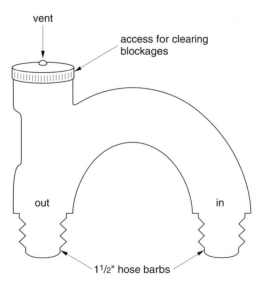

vent

access for clearing blockages

out

in

1½" hose barbs

grease smeared on the pump piston rod pro-longs the life of the piston rod seal on a manual toilet.

Never use toilet bowl cleaners, drain cleaners, bleaches, or deodorants unless they are made specifically for marine toilets. Most will attack and swell up rubber parts.

All wire terminals on electric toilets should be checked periodically for corrosion and cleaned when necessary. Keep a sharp eye out for external signs of leaking pump seals, since these are a major cause of pump failures.

Winterizing. Improper winterization is a significant cause of toilet failure. It is not enough just to pump the toilet dry and leave it. Water remains trapped in low spots in both the suction and discharge lines as well as in the pump housing.

1. Close the suction seacock, disconnect the hose, and dip it in a can of antifreeze. Use propylene glycol (available from hardware stores and chandleries for winterizing fresh-water systems; ethylene glycol, the usual antifreeze, is harmful to the environment and so should not be flushed overboard, and alcohol, which is sometimes used as an antifreeze, will swell up rubber parts). Pump the toilet until the antifreeze washes down the bowl sides and flows out the discharge.
2. Close the discharge seacock, disconnect the hose, and drain it.
3. The toilet can either be pumped dry or be left with the antifreeze in it. Holding tanks and treatment systems (if present) must be drained and winterized separately. Some specialized types (such as Raritan's LectraSan) should be disconnected *before* antifreeze is put in the system, since the antifreeze will cause problems.

Troubleshooting and Repair

Problems common to all marine toilets. Regardless of type, all toilets will at some time smell, get clogged, and slowly plug up with calcium (if saltwater flushed)—normally at sea in rough conditions!

Odors. The obvious source of odors is a leak. Less obvious are the following:

1. Permeable hose. Rub a cloth on the hose and then sniff it. If the cloth smells, the hose is permeable and should be replaced with proper sanitation hose.
2. Marine life, especially eel grass, in the flushing water. This gets caught on the underside

of the toilet bowl rim and gives off a rotten-egg smell. Where this is a constant problem, a strainer may be needed on the suction line seacock (Figure 11-13).

3. The discharge line vented loop. A piece of hose should be attached to the vent and led outside cabin areas, but *be sure the hose is never under water at any angle of heel.*
4. Clogged vent on the holding tank. This generally results from overfilling the tank and driving solid waste up the vent. ISO standards require a 1½ inch (38 mm) vent, but US boat-builders typically use something far smaller.

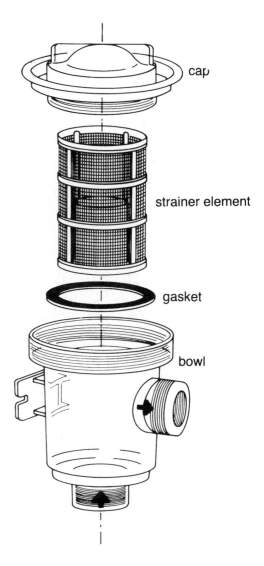

cap

strainer element

gasket

bowl

Figure 11-13. **A raw-water strainer such as this may be needed in the inlet line to exclude marine life—such as eel grass or mussels—which may want to colonize the waste disposal system. Such filters need frequent checking as the strainers themselves often become colonized and plugged.** *(Raritan Engineering)*

5. Low spots in the holding tank vent lines. These may fill with liquid and act as a U-trap, effectively plugging the vent.

6. Defective discharge valve. The result can be that raw sewage backs into the toilet bowl, a problem that may not be obvious since the water in the bowl may appear clean. However, the bacteria present will cause the bowl to stain rapidly—overnight in warm climates.

7. A worn O-ring or piston rings on a manual toilet with a double-acting piston (see below). This will allow raw sewage to work up past the piston into the flushing side of the pump. The pump must be dismantled and rebuilt.

Clogging. Marine toilets use little water (commonly as little as 1 quart per flush) and contain pumps, impellers, and valves that cannot handle solid objects. Clogging is an ever present problem, so much so that many experienced cruising sailors keep a separate receptacle for waste toilet paper and put *only* human waste down the toilet (this, however, is not necessary with a proper installation).

There are special short-fiber toilet papers on the market for use on boats. These break down quickly, reducing the risk of clogging. But the key is to keep paper usage to a minimum. No fibrous substances (rags, sanitary napkins) should ever be put down a marine toilet. In fact, aside from toilet paper, nothing that hasn't been eaten first should be put down the head!

Never combat a blockage with drain cleaners; these will attack sensitive parts in the toilet. The best bet is to add water to the toilet bowl and leave it overnight. Usually the waste will break down enough to pump out the following morning.

Sooner or later, however, we all have to face a clogged toilet that won't clear (such as when our daughter threw a piece of coconut down the toilet!). There is nothing to be done but to take it apart.

Calcium build-up. Calcium deposits, similar to the deposits in tea kettles, build up in time, primarily on discharge valves, lines, and seacocks. In extreme cases the calcium can pretty well plug a toilet. If a toilet has become progressively harder to flush over a period of time, with an ever increasing tendency to clog, or if its discharge line is constantly leaking back into the bowl, calcium is a likely culprit.

A good dose of vinegar (acetic acid) on a regular basis—say once a month—will go a long way toward keeping things free, but if the lines begin to clog, stronger treatment is needed. Muriatic (hydrochloric) acid, obtainable from many boat chandleries and hardware stores, dis-solves the calcium but also will attack metal parts in the toilet, albeit at a much slower rate. Place a 10% solution in the bowl, observing all the warnings on the bottle. The solution will *fizz* as it works, until the bowl and its immediate drain are free of calcium.

When the bubbling has ceased, pump the bowl almost dry. This will move the acid solution into the pump and the first part of the discharge line. Wait awhile and then flush the toilet a few strokes more to move the solution farther through the line. Continue in this manner until the entire discharge line has been covered. Thoroughly flush the system to remove all traces of acid.

The acid is used up as it bubbles. In severe cases of calcification it may be necessary to treat the system several times. Once it is clear, a small dosage at irregular intervals should keep it clear. If the acid treatment fails, the only recourse is to break down the toilet and discharge lines and chip out the calcium. Hoses can be beaten on the dockside to break loose the deposits but replacing them would be preferable.

Manual and electrified manual toilets. The central component in these toilets is a double-acting piston pump, either operated by hand or, in the electrified manual toilets, driven by an electric motor. The suction water is led to the top of the pump cylinder and from there to the toilet bowl rim. The discharge line leads to the bottom of the pump cylinder and from there to a holding tank or overboard discharge (Figures 11-14A and B). There are "in" and "out" valves on the suction and discharge sides. (A few toilets—notably Baby Blakes—have separate suction and discharge pumps and pump cylinders [Figure 11-14C], but the majority are as described.)

On its downward stroke, the pump piston pulls flushing water into the top of the cylinder while driving sewage out the bottom end. On its upward stroke, the piston forces the flushing water into the toilet while sucking effluent into the base of the cylinder.

Since the piston rod is attached to the top of the piston and therefore passes through the flush-water end of the pump cylinder, the flushing-side volume is less than the waste-discharge-side volume by the amount of space occupied by the piston rod. In theory the pump will always pump out more than it sucks in, thus keeping the bowl dry. To make sure, a manual valve is invariably fitted on the suction side enabling the flushing water to be turned off while the bowl is evacuated.

Internal suction and discharge valves may be one of three types: spring-loaded ball valves; flapper valves; and joker (*duckbill*) valves.

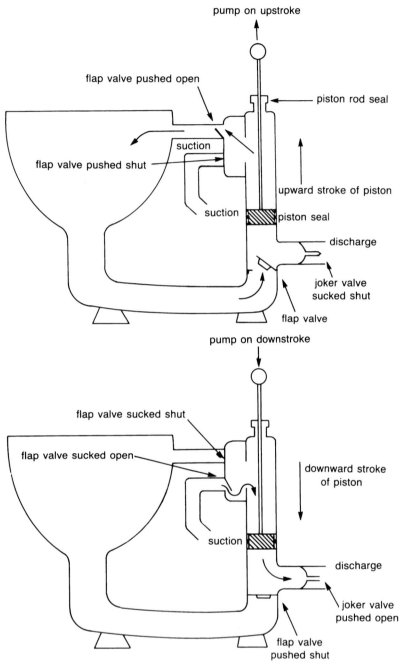

pump on upstroke

flap valve pushed open

piston rod seal

suction

flap valve pushed shut

upward stroke of piston

suction

piston seal

discharge

joker valve
sucked shut

flap valve

pump on downstroke

flap valve sucked shut

flap valve sucked open

downward stroke
of piston

suction

discharge

joker valve
pushed open

flap valve
pushed shut

Figure 11-14A and B. The
operation of a double-
acting piston toilet.

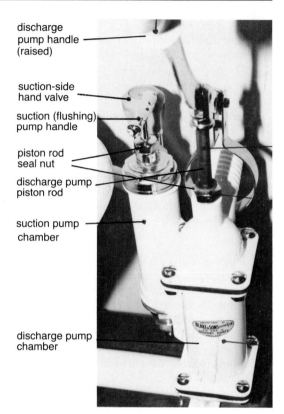

discharge
pump handle
(raised)

suction-side
hand valve

suction (flushing)
pump handle

piston rod
seal nut

discharge pump
piston rod

suction pump
chamber

discharge pump
chamber

Figure 11-14C. Blake toilet, with independent flushing
and discharge pumps.

hemisphere, to the convex surface of which is attached a rubber sleeve (the *duck's bill*). Fluid pushing through the base of the hemisphere opens the slit and sleeve; fluid approaching the hemisphere from the other side collapses and closes it (the discharge valve in Figure 11-15B).

Leaking seals. Where the piston rod exits the top of its cylinder on a manual toilet there is a seal—the familiar grease-type seal consisting of a metal case and a rubber lip to grip the rod. Sooner or later these seals always seem to start leaking and have to be replaced. Note that what is leaking is clean water, not effluent; a minor leak is annoying but can safely be left until a repair is convenient.

Most seals are accessible from the outside, but some can be reached only by dismantling the pump, which is a very poor design and extremely aggravating. When buying, avoid these toilets.

External seals. Close the seacocks. Lift the pump handle, wrap the piston rod with tape, and grip gently with Vise-Grips (Mole wrench). Unscrew the handle, knob, or yoke (depending

Ball valves are held against a seat by a weak spring. Pressure from the opposite side of the seat lifts the ball off the seat, allowing water to flow past; pressure from the other direction combines with the spring pressure to push the ball against the seat and hold the valve closed. A flapper valve is nothing more than a weighted flap resting on a baseplate (Figure 11-15A). Fluid can flow one way, lifting it off its seat, but flow in the other direction forces the flap down onto its seat. A joker valve is a slitted rubber

Plumbing, Toilets, and Through-Hull Fittings

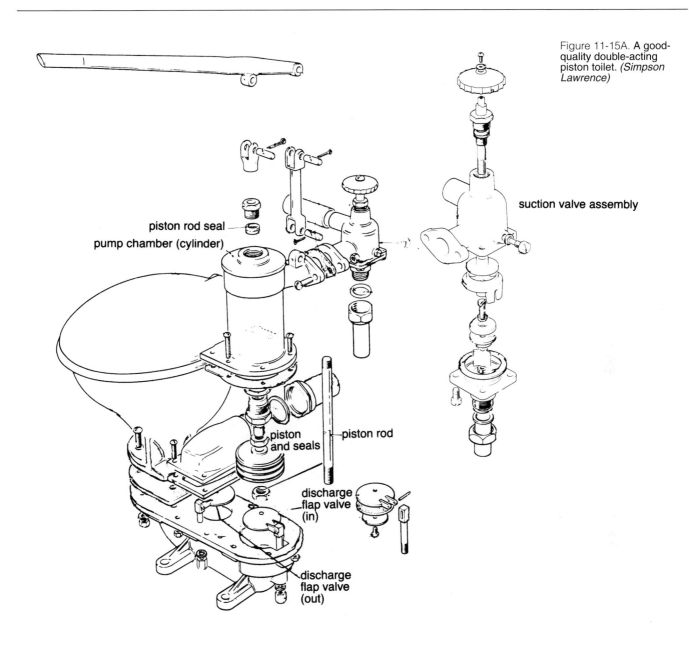

Figure 11-15A. A good-quality double-acting piston toilet. *(Simpson Lawrence)*

piston rod seal

pump chamber (cylinder)

suction valve assembly

piston
and seals

piston rod

discharge
flap valve
(in)

discharge
flap valve
(out)

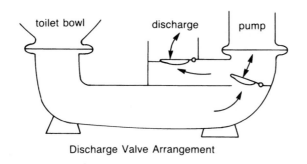

toilet bowl

discharge

pump

Discharge Valve Arrangement

Marine Toilets (Heads)   371

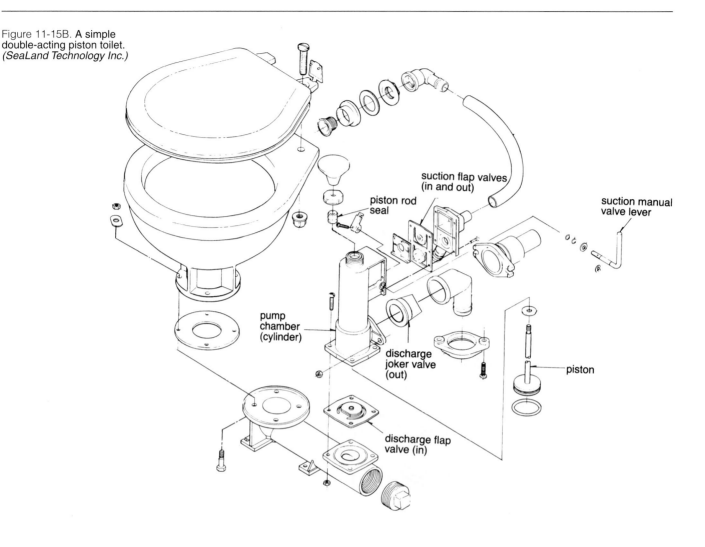

Figure 11-15B. **A simple double-acting piston toilet.** *(SeaLand Technology Inc.)*

suction flap valves (in and out)

piston rod seal

suction manual valve lever

pump chamber (cylinder)

discharge joker valve (out)

piston

discharge flap valve (in)

on make and type of pump action—Figure 11-16), *taking great care not to let go of the rod, since it may drop down inside the pump*! Unscrew the seal assembly (or remove the retaining snap ring or circlip) and slide the assembly off the piston rod, temporarily removing the Vise-Grips to let the assembly past. Before installing a new seal, lightly tape the threads on the top of the piston rod to avoid damaging the seal when it slides over. The lip of the seal, if present, faces toward the pump cylinder (i.e., down).

Internal seals. Remove the pump body from the toilet by unscrewing it from its base and disconnecting the suction and discharge hoses (Figure 11-17). Wrap a piece of tape around the piston rod, gently grip the rod with Vise-Grips, and unscrew the handle or knob. The piston and rod can then be knocked out of the bottom of the pump (after removing any calcium deposits as described above).

The seal fits into a recess at the top of the pump housing and must be pried out, which is

frequently a time-consuming and frustrating business. Straighten a piece of stiff wire (such as a coat hanger), file a point in its end, and bend the last ¼ inch (6 mm) in at 90 degrees. Poke this through the top of the piston housing and try to force it between the seal and its seat. Once the seal starts to work loose, it is important to work it from side to side or it will get cockeyed and jam.

Tape the threads at the top of the piston rod and slide on a new seal with its lip facing down (toward the piston). Put the piston rod back in the pump housing and use the piston to push the new seal gently into place.

In time, the plastic bore around the piston rod (at the top of the cylinder) wears, and the rod action becomes sloppy. Once this happens, the seal fails more quickly. One solution is to add a small length of hose to the top of the pump housing and clamp a second seal into this to form a flexible stuffing box (packing gland). It may be necessary to file down the top of the housing to get the hose to fit. The pump stroke

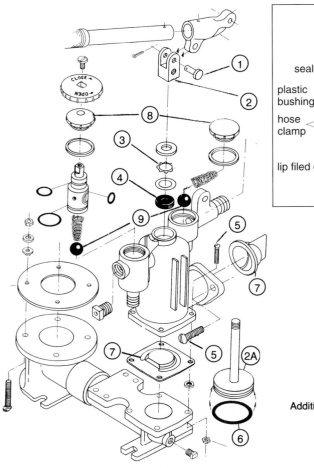

Figure 11-16. To replace an external piston-rod seal, remove the pump handle (**1**); remove the yoke (**2**) from the piston rod (**2A**); remove the star washer or packing nut (**3**); and replace the seal (**4**). To access the discharge valve and the piston seal (**6**), remove the cylinder retaining screws (**5**) and the hoses; check the piston O-ring (**6**) and the discharge valve (**7**). To check the suction valves, remove the two covers (**8**) to provide access to the springs and ball valves (**9**). *(Raritan Engineering)*

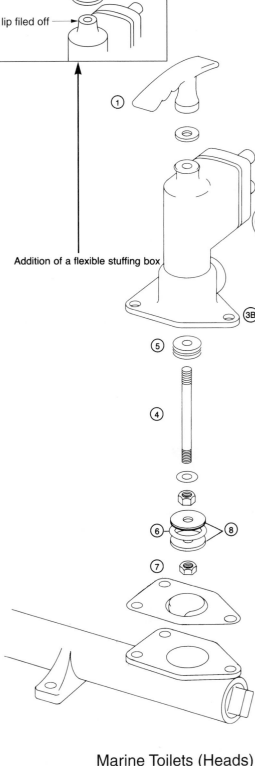

Addition of a flexible stuffing box

(and therefore capacity) will be reduced by the length of the hose, and the toilet therefore will require a little more pumping. The life of this second seal will be extended if a spacer is fabricated out of a piece of plastic and inserted as shown in Figure 11-17—it should be drilled to make a reasonably close fit around the pump shaft, and will then act as a kind of Cutless bearing, maintaining the alignment between the shaft and the seal.

Bowl fills faster than it drains. As noted, pumps are designed to empty the bowl faster than it fills. If the reverse happens, it is almost always because a discharge flapper or joker valve is stuck partially open. Vigorous pumping will

Figure 11-17. To replace an internal piston-rod seal, remove the pump handle or knob (**1**), remove the suction hoses (**2**), remove the pump cylinder retaining screws, knock the piston rod (**4**) out of the base of the cylinder, and then pick out the old seal (**5**) and put in a new one. If necessary, replace the piston seal O-ring (**6**) by taking off the piston retaining nut (**7**) and separating the two halves of the piston (**8**). Inset: Alleviate leakage due to wear-induced slop in the piston rod by adding a flexible stuffing box. *(Jim Sollers)*

generally clear it unless the problem is a result of scale buildup or valve failure. Try the muriatic acid treatment. If all else fails, dismantle the toilet and replace the valves (see below).

Bowl fills when not in use. Either the suction or the discharge valve or valves are leaking. Close first one seacock and then the other, observing the bowl level, to find out on which side the problem lies. The toilet will have to be dismantled to check the valves. In addition to the internal suction valve, many toilets have a hand-wheel-type manual valve on the suction line (e.g., Blakes). These often seem to leak after a few years. They are not repairable and must be replaced.

Handle is pumped but nothing happens. If strong resistance is felt, check that the seacocks are open and that the inlet valve is in the correct position. Check also that the holding tank is not full. If little or no resistance is felt, the piston nut has probably fallen off, allowing the piston to drop off its shaft. The pump needs dismantling.

Electric pump operates slowly or not at all. First check the voltage *at the motor, while it is running.* If there is no voltage (it will not be running!) check all fuses, breakers, connections, etc. If the voltage is low, check the ship's battery and recharge as necessary. If the battery is OK, there must be excessive voltage drop between the battery and the motor (no more than 10% is permissible). Refer to Chapter 3.

Because of the heavy electrical loads and long wiring runs, some pumps use a solenoid *(relay)* to close the motor circuit, with a remotely operated switch at the toilet. The principle is the same as that of an engine-starting circuit. Check the solenoid for voltage drop (see pages 218–222 for troubleshooting this type of circuit).

If the voltage is adequate, disconnect the electric drive (normally one bolt—Figures 11-18A and B) and operate the toilet manually. If it works normally, check the electric drive gears (normally a worm-gear arrangement) and linkage for binding.

Repairing valves and pistons. Disassembly and reassembly are simple. Two to four screws remove the pump from its base; two or more screws undo the discharge manifold; suction hoses are generally held with hose clamps.

Inspect flapper valves for damage, swelling, or dirt and calcium buildup, any of which could prevent them from seating properly. Inspect joker valves for obstructions in the sleeve (duckbill). Calcium deposits can be broken up by flexing the rubber or by putting the valves in a 10% muriatic acid solution (observe all cautions on the acid bottle). Check ball-valve springs for corrosion and adequate tension, and the balls and their seats for trash and pitting.

Flapper valves are replaced with the weight uppermost. Make sure the side of the valve that

Figure 11-18A and B. Electrified toilet and drive mechanism. To disconnect the drive, remove the drive bolt (**4**) and operate the toilet manually. Check the connecting rod (**3**) and worm gears (**2A** and **2B**) for binding. Test the motor (**1**) for voltage drop and shorts. *(Raritan Engineering)*

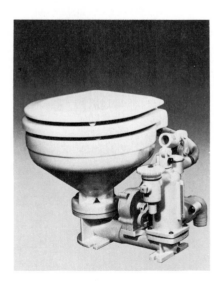

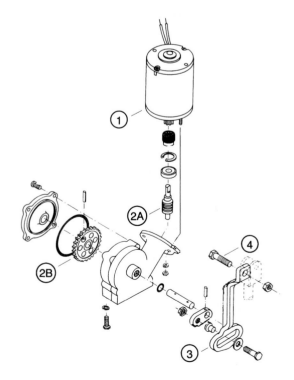

hinges is matched to the belled outside of its housing; otherwise the valve will fail to open or will hang up in operation.

Joker valves are fitted with the sleeve or duck-bill facing *away* from the toilet, *toward* the holding tank and seacock.

Pistons generally consist of two dished washers trapping an O-ring, and held to the end of the piston rod with a nut. If the O-ring needs replacing, simply undo the nut and separate the washers. Make sure the new O-ring is mounted squarely, and be sure the piston retaining nut is adequately locked to its shaft with a lock washer, liquid adhesive (such as Loctite), or by peening (hammering) the shaft threads over once the nut is on. Grease the cylinder wall with Vaseline before replacing the piston.

Scrupulously clean all mating surfaces before reassembly; otherwise leaks are almost certain. Do not overtighten screws, especially on plastic toilets. A little silicone gasket cement or sealing compound smeared on mating surfaces before reassembly will prevent most minor leaks.

Lavac toilets. Lavacs (made by Blake) are beautifully simple. The toilet lid is designed to make a seal with the bowl. When the waste is pumped out (with the lid down), a vacuum is created in the bowl, which sucks in the flushing water (Figure 11-19A). No inlet pump or valves

are needed. There is almost nothing to go wrong. Lavacs use diaphragm pumps on the discharge (Chapter 12). These are far less troublesome than piston pumps. Where an electric diaphragm pump is fitted, it is advisable to install a manual diaphragm pump *in series* with it as a backup (Figure 11-19B). This is the same pump minus the motor drive, so only one set of spare pump valves and diaphragm is needed. The suction line has no valves—merely a vented loop. Should it start siphoning into the bowl, the vented loop must be plugged. The bowl can always be pumped dry with the lid open.

The most likely problem is a loss of vacuum in the bowl, leading to a reduction or complete loss of the flushing water. Older Lavacs have plastic-coated aluminum bowls. Once they start to corrode and the seal fails between the bowl and the lid, the bowl will need replacing with one of the newer (post–1981) porcelain bowls.

If the bowl is OK, check the sealing face on the underside of the lid. If this is sound, check all the suction hose connections for an air leak.

Electric toilets. At the base of these toilets is a multipurpose pump (Figure 11-20A), usually comprising the following components mounted on a common shaft: a small rubber impeller pump, supplying flushing water to the toilet bowl; a macerator pump (a device that breaks

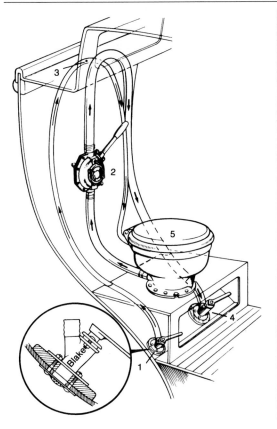

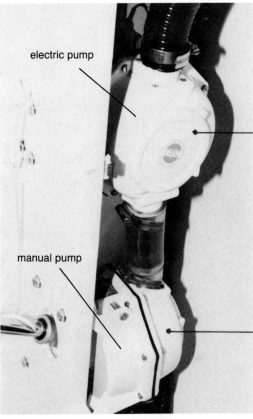

Figure 11-19A. (**Left**) Blake's Lavac toilet. As the waste is pumped overboard (or to the holding tank, not shown) the resulting vacuum draws in flushing water through the inlet. (**1**) Inlet seacock; (**2**) diaphragm discharge pump; (**3**) air bleed valve—a simple plastic plug with a hole drilled in it (the size of the hole controls the level of water remaining in the bowl: the larger the hole, the less the water); (**4**) discharge seacock; (**5**) bowl. *(Blake and Sons)*

Figure 11-19B. (**Right**) Lavac toilet with electric and manual diaphragm pumps in series.

Marine Toilets (Heads)   375

up the sewage into tiny particles); and a good-sized rubber impeller or centrifugal pump to discharge the waste (Figure 11-20B).

Bowl fills faster than it drains. Waste is probably caught in the discharge valves. Close the inlet, pump down, and then open the inlet and flush through to clear the discharge lines. If the problem persists, check the discharge pump impeller, valves, and lines for wear, obstructions, or calcification.

Inadequate flushing. The pump may be running slowly because of a variety of electrical problems that usually involve low voltage; the suction pump impeller may be worn; or the pump may be sucking air through a loose connection or through the vented loop (see above, page 367). The suction seacock may even be coming out of the water when the boat is heeled.

Motor runs but either suction or discharge fails to operate. The pump impeller, particularly if it is the rubber-impeller type, is probably stripped. *Most pumps cannot tolerate being run dry for more than a few seconds without damage.* But before pulling the pump apart, check that all valves and seacocks are open and the pump is primed. Note that when a pump is run dry not only the impeller(s) but also the seal(s) are likely to be damaged.

Motor repeatedly blows fuses. This is especially likely at the start of a new season. During the winter, rubber impellers frequently get stuck to their pump housings; they then overload the motor and fuse on startup. Try lubricating the pump (pour some water in the bowl and suction lines), and if possible turn it by hand. The other common problem is the swelling of pump impellers caused by inappropriate chemicals (toilet bowl cleaners, deodorants, drain openers) put down the toilet. In this case the pump will need to be dismantled and the impeller replaced.

Figure 11-20A. **Typical electric toilet.** *(Raritan Engineering)*

Figure 11-20B. **An exploded view of an electric toilet.** *(ITT/Jabsco)*

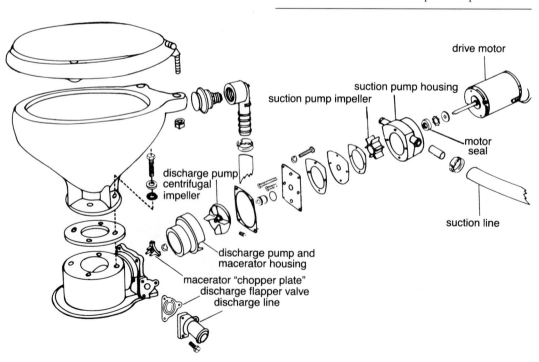

Plumbing, Toilets, and Through-Hull Fittings

Loud noises from the pump. There may be a solid object jammed in the macerator, or the motor bearings may be worn out. The latter is generally because leaking seals allow water into the bearings. In either case the pump needs disassembling (see below).

Water leaks around pump housings. One of the pump seals is leaking (some pumps have one seal; others have a central motor with pumps on both ends of the shaft, in which case there is a seal at both ends). *Any defective seal needs immediate corrective action. Seal leaks are one of the principal causes of bearing and motor failures*

Motor operates sluggishly or erratically. Check for low voltage at the motor. If the voltage is OK, the pumps may be partially plugged, or the motor brushes may be worn or hanging up in their holders. The brushes should be accessible after a couple of covers are removed. Check the brush springs and the free movement of the brushes in their holders. While the brushes are out, check the commutator for excessive carbon and signs of arcing and burning (Chapter 6).

Motor burnout. The principal causes of burned-out motors are:

1. Seal leaks into the motor causing a short circuit.
2. Overheating as a result of low voltage, pump clogging, or *extended running.* Motors are rated for intermittent use—some as little as 2 minutes at a time; some as long as 15 minutes. Motors should have momentary-type switches— switches that must be held "on" against a spring pressure—to guard against their accidentally being left "on".

Overhauling pump and motor. Disassembly is usually reasonably obvious and straightforward. There will be one or more flap and/or joker valves on the discharge side. The first unit encountered is generally the macerator, with the discharge pump behind it (the latter may be either a centrifugal pump or a rubber-impeller pump). PAR toilets have the suction pump mounted behind this, followed by a seal and the motor. Raritan toilets have a double-ended motor shaft, with the suction pump on one end and the macerator and discharge pump on the opposite end. In this case both ends of the motor shaft have a seal.

Nearly all suction pumps are the rubber-impeller type. Inspect the vanes for wear on their outer edges (they should be rounded and not flat) and for adequate flexibility with no signs of distortion or cracking.

Seal replacement. Old seals can be pried and pushed out with bent coat hangers, screwdrivers, etc., taking great care not to score the seal housing. The housing must then be scrupulously cleaned. New seals must be pressed into position with equal care; this is the most important part of any rebuilding job. If the seal is at all cockeyed, bent, or distorted, it will leak and the motor will fail in a short time.

New seals are placed in their housings with the lip that encloses the motor shaft facing *toward* the pump chamber that is being sealed. A piece of dowel or a socket of the same diameter as the seal should be used to push the seal home; use the minimum pressure and keep the seal square to the housing at all times.

Testing the motor. Motors are the universal type (Chapter 6). Older motors usually have field windings; newer motors are the permanent-magnet type. The various tests outlined in Chapter 6 can be applied to armatures, commutators, field windings, and brushes. The armature should be flexed and spun to check the bearings and to make sure it is not rubbing on the field winding shoes or magnets.

If there is any problem with the armature, field windings, or bearings, it is better to replace the entire motor than to disassemble it. Motors are constructed to very close tolerances in order to eliminate vibration and shaft seal leaks. It is impossible to meet these standards without specialized bench equipment.

When refitting pumps, be sure to get the positive and negative wires the right way around. Polarity is not necessarily critical on motors with field windings, but it is absolutely critical on the more common permanent-magnet types. The usual color coding on DC motors comprises a red or orange wire for the positive, and a black wire for the negative. On AC motors a black wire is normally hot (ungrounded), a white wire neutral, and a green wire ground (USA color codes; see Chapter 3 for UK and European equivalents).

Macerator pumps. These are used to break up and pump out the waste from many holding tanks, and are almost the same as the pumps on electric toilets, with the exception that there is no flushing pump built into the unit (Figure 11-21). Pumps may be inside or on top of the holding tank or may be mounted separately. In the event of a problem, make all the usual voltage tests. If a pump mounted above the holding tank spins but fails to pump, before pulling it apart, disconnect the discharge hose and pour in some water to make sure it is primed. It may just be airbound.

Never run a macerator pump dry; the seal and impeller will burn up. Never run it continuously; the motor will burn up. Motors are rated for intermittent use only—2 to 15 minutes, depending on the make of the pump. It is best to fit only momentary-type switches—i.e., spring-loaded buttons or switches that must be held in the "on" position.

LectraSan holding tanks. LectraSan is a sewage treatment system manufactured by Raritan that qualifies as a Type I MSD, and as such overboard discharge of its end product is becoming increasingly restricted. Waste is pumped into a small holding tank that has approximately a four-flush capacity. In the holding tank the waste is chopped up by a macerator pump in one chamber and stirred by a mixer in another chamber. In between, through an electrolytic process, two electrodes immersed in the suspension manufacture hypochlorous acid from the seawater used for flushing (Figure 11-22). This is done without the addition of chemicals. The acid kills bacteria, and further toilet flushes push the treated waste out of the tank and overboard.

The LectraSan system must be used *every time the toilet is flushed.* Failure to do so will overload the macerator and clog the system. The unit goes through a pretreat cycle of approximately 30 seconds and then a treatment cycle of 2 minutes. The unit must be turned on *before flushing,* it must be flushed *during the pretreat cycle,* and it must *not* be flushed, or flushed again, during the treatment cycle. In other words, once the toilet is flushed the unit must be allowed to complete the cycle before reflushing.

LectraSans have a high current draw (45 amps on 12 volts) but for only 2 minutes—on a 12-volt system this comes to 1.5 amp-hours per flush. Clearly, with a boatload of guests this could add up! Between flushes there is no current drain. In the event of a problem, make all the usual voltage drop tests *at the unit while in operation.*

Check above for macerator pump and electric motor tests.

The control unit has a meter indicating low, normal, and high treatment levels. Treatment levels are related to battery voltage, water salinity, and temperature—the higher the voltage, salinity, and temperature the higher the meter reading. In fresh or brackish water, salt must be added to maintain salinity, either manually when flushing or via a special tank. If meter readings are low, check first for voltage drop during operation. If the voltage is OK, try adding salt. If meter readings are too high, quite likely excessive salt is being added.

The holding tank and electrodes may become calcium-encrusted in time. Flush muriatic acid through the unit as described previously. Rinse well before reusing. If more extensive inspection and cleaning is needed, lift off the whole top and lift out the electrode pack.

Never allow toilet bowl cleaners, drain openers, or deodorants into LectraSan units. If any of these chemicals should enter a unit, flush the toilet repeatedly before turning the LectraSan on again. Otherwise, damaging chemical reactions with the hypochlorous acid formed during operation are likely.

Thermopure waste treatment system. This is a newcomer to the market, manufactured by Groco (Hanover, MD). Heat, either from AC power (run off shore power, an AC generator, or an inverter) or from a heat exchanger plumbed into the engine's cooling circuit (used when the engine is running) is used to kill bacteria. The unit comes with a 10- or 20-gallon holding tank. When the tank is 10% filled, the unit turns on, which is to say that if AC power or engine heat is available it will use either (or both) to heat the tank. When the temperature reaches 167°F (75°C) the contents of the tank are discharged

Figure 11-21. A macerator pump. (ITT/Jabsco)

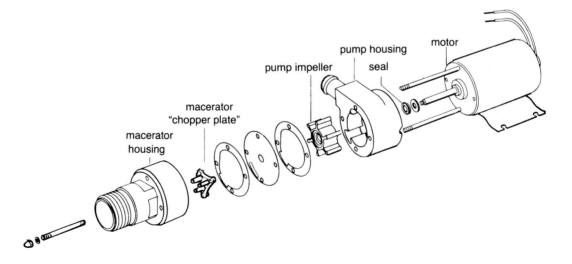

maceerator housing

maceerator "chopper plate"

pump impeller

pump housing

seal

motor

Plumbing, Toilets, and Through-Hull Fittings

main unit

salt feed tank

control panel

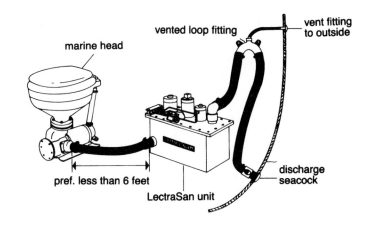

marine head

vented loop fitting

vent fitting to outside

pref. less than 6 feet

LectraSan unit

discharge seacock

Figure 11-22. The LectraSan, an alternative to a holding tank, acts much like a municipal sewage plant, macerating and chlorinating waste and then discharging it directly overboard. Installation options: **top right**, basic electric toilet; **second from top**, basic manual toilet; **next**, electric toilet with salt feed tank; **bottom left**, manual toilet with salt feed tank; **bottom right**, the LectraSan unit itself. *(Raritan Engineering)*

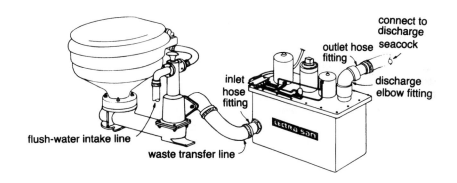

connect to discharge seacock

outlet hose fitting

inlet hose fitting

discharge elbow fitting

flush-water intake line

waste transfer line

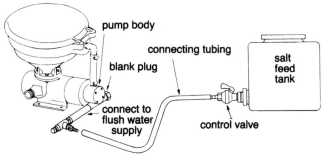

pump body

blank plug

connecting tubing

salt feed tank

connect to flush water supply

control valve

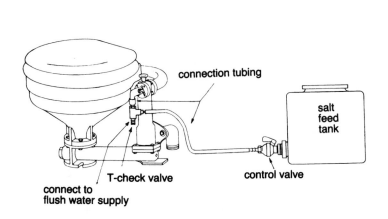

connection tubing

salt feed tank

T-check valve

control valve

connect to flush water supply

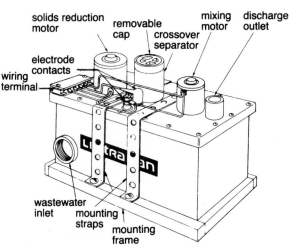

solids reduction motor

removable cap

mixing motor

discharge outlet

crossover separator

electrode contacts

wiring terminal

wastewater inlet

mounting straps

mounting frame

Marine Toilets (Heads)   379

overboard. If no heat source is available, the tank continues to fill. At the 75% full level, an alarm is activated, telling the operator it is time to provide a heat source, or to quit flushing the toilet until the system has had time to reach the discharge temperature.

It is too early to assess reliability. It is worth noting that this is a Type I MSD, and such devices are becoming increasingly restricted in their use, and that it has *significant power demands*. Below 10% full, the unit draws just milliamps, but at 10% various relays close, pulling 1.5 amps at 12 volts. This draw is continued until the unit has been pumped down. In the case of a cruising boat on which the engine or generator is only run once a day, this could result in a drain of up to 36 Ahs a day just for the control circuits. The AC heating element is 1,100 watts (9 to 10 amps at 110 volts); the discharge pump 17 amps at 12 volts. A 75% full tank in typical water and ambient temperatures will take around an hour to heat to the discharge temperature (if run off an inverter, this will amount to around 100 Ahs at 12 volts). This is not a device for a power-starved cruising boat, but may be excellent in many powerboat applications and aboard larger sailboats with extended generator running hours.

VacuFlush toilets. VacuFlush toilets are manufactured by SeaLand Technology Inc. These toilets utilize a vacuum pump and a vacuum chamber (Figure 11-23). Depressing a foot pedal in the base of the toilet opens a ball valve. The waste is sucked out and passed to a holding tank or overboard. The vacuum pump then kicks in and pulls down the vacuum chamber (to −10 inches Hg), ready for the next flush. Water for rinsing the bowl is normally taken from the boat's *pressurized freshwater* supply (a pint to a quart per flush) although seawater can be used (but this would considerably increase maintenance and would require an additional pump to pressurize the water supply). The rinsing valve is connected to the foot pedal, opening just before the main ball valve and closing just after it.

It takes 60 to 90 seconds for the vacuum pump to pull down the vacuum chamber ready for use. The pump will then kick in after every flush (15 to 45 seconds). Because of a slow loss of vacuum,

the pump can be expected to come on as often as once every 2 hours even if the toilet is not flushed. At 12 volts, the pump pulls 4 to 6 amps, which comes to around 0.03 to 0.1 Ah per flush, with an additional drain of around 1 Ah a day to maintain the vacuum.

If the pump runs longer than 90 seconds or more frequently than once every 2 hours between flushes, a more serious vacuum leak is present. Likely sources include faulty hose connections, poor seals on the main ball valve, and leaking check valves. (There are several joker-type valves in the system.) Tighten all hose clamps. Pour a little water in the bowl; if it is sucked away, the seals are leaking. In this case, try tightening the main clamp ring, but beware of overtightening, which will jam the valve or prevent it from closing properly. If check valves are suspected, try repeated flushings. If this fails, add muriatic acid to dissolve calcium deposits (page 369). If all else fails, take the valves apart and inspect.

A lack of flushing water will arise from low pressure on the freshwater system, a plugged freshwater valve (there is a filter screen on the inlet), or a defective water valve. If the water will not turn off, the valve may be stuck open due to a bent operating lever or dirt on the valve seat, or the valve itself may be defective.

The various rubber parts need replacing every 3 to 4 years with freshwater use; perhaps as often as annually with seawater use. The pump is a bellows or diaphragm type. These are covered in Chapter 12.

Jet Head toilets and the Royal Flush. Jet Head toilets, built by Raritan, and the Royal Flush, built by Headhunter (Ft. Lauderdale, FL) are for seagoing vessels only. A high-capacity centrifugal pump directs a powerful jet of water into the toilet bowl, breaking up waste and flushing it away. These toilets use far more water than conventional marine toilets (1.0 to 1.5 gallons per flush) and as such are not suitable for use with typical holding tanks. Power consumption is high, but for a very short time, resulting in a relatively small overall drain (on a 12-volt system the Royal Flush pulls 57 amps, but for just 10 to 20 seconds, resulting in a drain of 0.15 to 0.3 Ah per flush).

Through-Hulls and Seacocks

Consider this. In one survey, boatyard personnel and marine surveyors estimated that 40% to 50% of the seacocks they inspect are seized (mostly in the open position), and 15% are subsequently found to be corroded to the point of being non-repairable. Of the through-hulls and seacocks

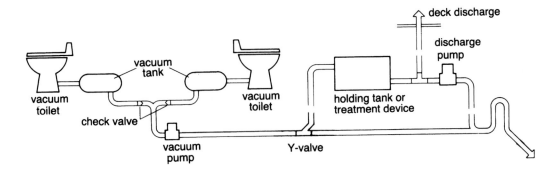

deck discharge

discharge pump

vacuum tank

vacuum toilet

vacuum toilet

holding tank or treatment device

check valve

vacuum pump

Y-valve

Figure 11-23. VacuFlush toilet from SeaLand Technology. (**Top**) A central vacuum pump is used to transfer waste to the holding tank or treatment device. (**Middle**) The main foot-operated valve and freshwater rinsing valve. (**Bottom**) In-line check valves. (*SeaLand Technology Inc.*)

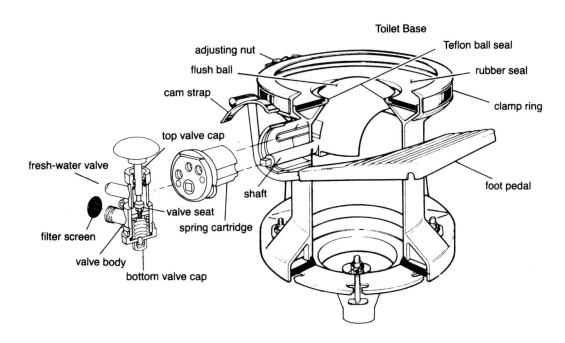

Toilet Base

adjusting nut

Teflon ball seal

flush ball

rubber seal

cam strap

clamp ring

top valve cap

fresh-water valve

shaft

foot pedal

filter screen

valve seat

spring cartridge

valve body

bottom valve cap

In-Line Check Valve

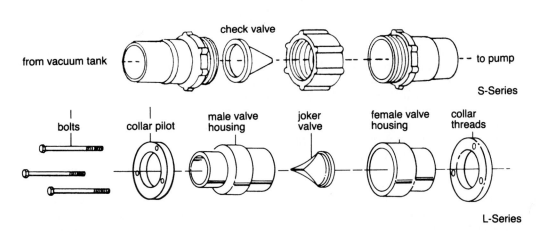

check valve

from vacuum tank

to pump

S-Series

bolts

collar pilot

male valve housing

joker valve

female valve housing

collar threads

L-Series

that are repaired or replaced, 25% can be reached only with difficulty, and 5% to 10% are totally inaccessible. Given the huge amounts of water that a failed through-hull or seacock can allow into a boat, these are pretty scary statistics. The boatowner is well advised to *track down all the through-hulls and seacocks on board* to ensure that all are *marine-grade fittings installed to marine standards* and that they are both *accessible and operative*.

Types of Seacock

Traditionally, all seacocks and through-hulls (skin fittings) were bronze, the seacocks having a tapered plug generally held in place with a ring and two bolts or screws. Now there is a much greater diversity of types and materials. Common alternatives include gate valves and ball valves, and materials such as plastics, stainless steel, brass, and rubber.

Traditional seacocks. It takes but a quarter turn on the handle to open or close a seacock, and it is instantly obvious whether it is open or shut. When it is open, the handle lines up with the tailpiece; when shut, the handle is at a right angle to the tailpiece. Construction is simple, rugged, and more or less chemical-proof (Figure 11-24A).

The tapered plug and seat have a high surface area with the potential for considerable friction. A traditional seacock needs regreasing annually and the keeper nuts or plug-retaining nut should be tightened only enough to stop the seacock from leaking. Overtightening will squeeze out the grease, and the resulting metal-to-metal contact will lead to accelerated wear and seizure.

A seized plug can generally be freed by tapping on the handle with a hammer. Many plugs are installed across the barrel of the seacock and can be tapped from the base after loosening the plug retaining nut.

In time, the plug tends to become wasp-waisted, and water leaks around the plug sides. The seacock fails to hold. Overtightening keeper nuts or the plug-retaining nut will not solve this problem, but merely create others. The plug should be removed, smeared with grinding paste (available from automotive parts stores), and then worked around and around in its seat until a smooth metal-to-metal contact is reestablished on all surfaces. Clean away all traces of the grinding paste, then regrease the plug.

If the plug and its seat are worn beyond restoration, a new seacock is called for. Dezincification as a result of galvanic corrosion (Chapter 4) will also sometimes occur with manganese bronze fittings, in which case the fitting will take on a pinkish blush; it will once again need replacing. Plugs and seats come in matched pairs, and it is generally not possible to replace one without the other.

Rubber-plug seacocks. This popular variation is sold by Groco, among others. Replacing the tapered plug of a conventional seacock is a solid rubber bung, through which is a metal-lined hole. The bung seats on a metal plate, or disk. A threaded locking handle (wing nut) is set into the body of the seacock. When the handle is tightened it forces the metal plate against the bung, compressing the rubber, squeezing it against the sides of the seacock, and sealing it (Figure 11-24B).

To operate the seacock, loosen the locking handle until the seacock can be turned, and then tighten it just until the seacock stops dripping from around its plug-retaining (*keeper*) ring, also called simply a *cover*. Overtightening will deform the rubber, especially when the seacock is closed, forcing the sides of the bung up into the seacock inlet and discharge ports.

These seacocks are not suitable for applications where chemicals may be present (e.g., toilets and sinks). The rubber swells, jamming the bung and making it next to impossible to turn. Maintenance involves annual regreasing. A bung that has swelled into the ports can be salvaged by filing down the excess rubber with a coarse wood file (or belt sander).

Gate and globe valves. Gate valves have a metal disc (the *gate*) that moves in a slot in the body of the valve. The gate rides on a threaded rod; turning the rod via a handle raises and lowers the gate (Figure 11-24C). Globe valves are similar but instead have on the end of the threaded rod a disc which screws down against a seat.

Gate and globe valves have no place on boats. Most are made of brass and will dezincify in time (see page 134), falling apart. Even when the body is made of bronze they suffer from several drawbacks: the interior parts may not be bronze; it is not possible to tell by looking at the handle whether the valve is open or shut; trash is easily trapped under the gate or disc, keeping the valve from sealing; the threaded rod on which the gate or disc rides is relatively thin and easily sheared if the valve jams; and, lacking a mounting flange, the valve cannot be independently fastened to the hull (see installation below).

When opening a gate or globe valve, open it fully and then turn the handle back a half turn so that it is free. There is then likely to be less confusion as to whether the valve is open or shut (when closed, the handle will be tight; when

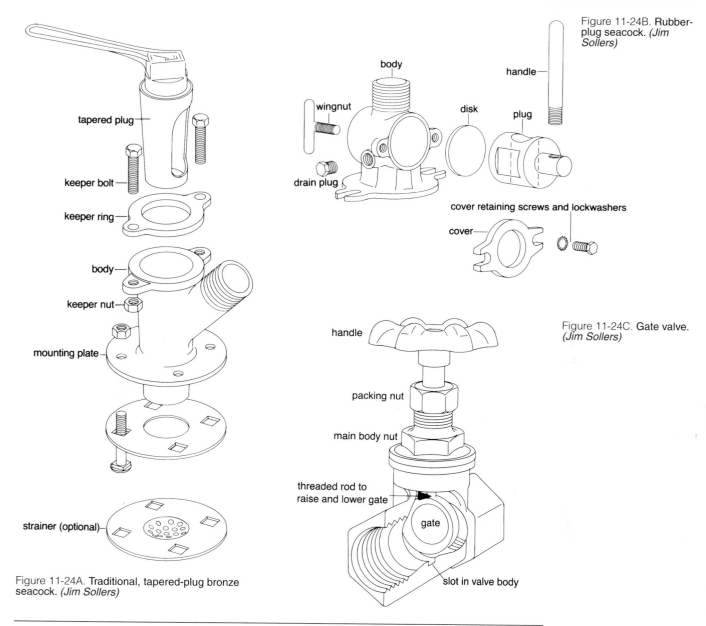

Figure 11-24B. Rubber-plug seacock. (Jim Sollers)

body

handle

wingnut

disk

plug

drain plug

cover retaining screws and lockwashers

cover

Figure 11-24C. Gate valve. (Jim Sollers)

tapered plug

keeper bolt

keeper ring

body

keeper nut

mounting plate

strainer (optional)

handle

packing nut

main body nut

threaded rod to raise and lower gate

gate

slot in valve body

Figure 11-24A. Traditional, tapered-plug bronze seacock. (Jim Sollers)

open, loose) and less likelihood of forcing the handle the wrong way and shearing the stem.

It is advisable to disassemble gate and globe valves annually, inspect them closely for corrosion, and regrease stems and threads. To do this, unscrew the main housing nut on the valve body. When reassembling the valve, screw the gate partially up before tightening the main housing nut, otherwise the gate or disc may bottom out in its slot and suffer damage. The small nut around the stem is a packing nut; tighten it gently if the stem leaks, and repack if necessary.

Ball valves. A ball with a hole through it fits into a spherical seat with inlet and discharge ports. Turned one way the hole in the ball lines up with the ports and allows flow; turned the

other way it closes the ports (Figures 11-24D, E).

Ball valves are efficient and foolproof. The metal versions generally have bronze bodies with chrome-plated bronze balls riding in Teflon seals. Plastic ones have reinforced-plastic bodies and balls again riding in Teflon seals.

To disassemble a ball valve, undo the main body nut. The balls, whether plastic or bronze, should be greased annually. In my experience the plastic stems on many plastic valves are the weak spot, tending to harden and become brittle with age. *Do not force them or they will break.* Plastic seacocks have one other major disadvantage: In a fire they will melt. On the other hand, they will not succumb to galvanic or stray current corrosion, which is probably the greater threat to most underwater hardware.

Through-Hulls and Seacocks 383

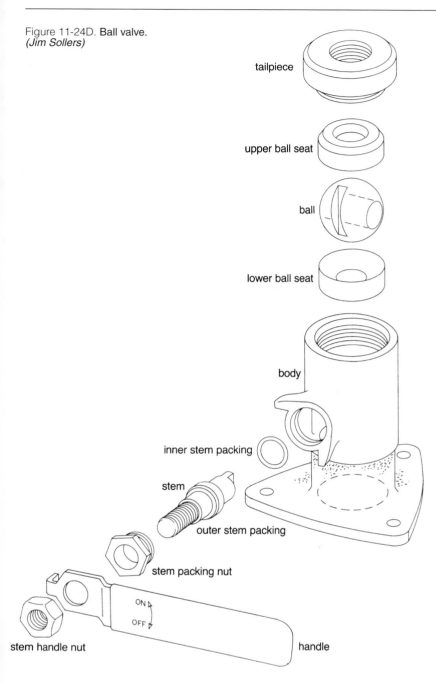

Figure 11-24D. Ball valve.
(Jim Sollers)

tailpiece

upper ball seat

ball

lower ball seat

body

inner stem packing

stem

outer stem packing

stem packing nut

stem handle nut

ON

OFF

handle

Figure 11-24E. An interesting new ball valve from Groco (Hanover, MD). This incorporates a quick-release plug. If the seacock is used on the raw-water intake to an engine cooling circuit, removal of the plug and its replacement with a special adapter allows the seacock to be rapidly converted to an emergency bilge pump (using the engine's raw-water pump). The quick-release fitting can also be used to simplify engine winterizing procedures. (Groco)

Installation

The ABYC requires that any through-hull below the waterline (both static and heeled) be fitted with a seacock (except self-draining cockpits that discharge above the static waterline), that the seacock be manufactured from corrosion-resistant materials (which excludes brass gate and-globe valves), that it be able to withstand a 500-pound weight applied at its inboard end in any direction, for 30 seconds, and that its handle be easy to operate. These *minimal* rules are clearly violated by many installations!

Wood and fiberglass hulls. Through-hulls are fitted as shown in Figure 11-25A. Note the substantial backing block. The through-hull is retained by an external mushroom or flush-mount fitting.

Seacocks (Figure 11-25B) are installed similarly, with the exception that ideally *all seacocks should be flanged and independently fastened* (although many are not). That is, they should not merely rely on the external mushroom or flush-mounted skin fitting for support. Be sure the drain plug in the housing faces down.

Metal hulls. Properly constructed reinforced-plastic through-hulls and seacocks can be installed as above. *Metal through-hulls and seacocks must be insulated from the hull to prevent galvanic interaction.* The seacock must then be electrically isolated from the piping attached to

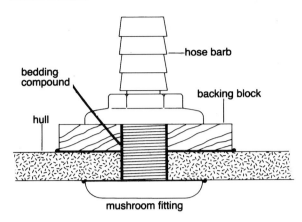

Figure 11-25A. Proper through-hull installation in a wood or fiberglass hull. *(Jim Sollers)*

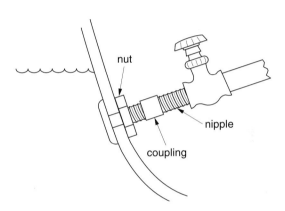

Figure 11-25C. How *not* to install a through-hull or seacock! There is no backing block; the valve should be connected directly to the through-hull fitting to reduce potential stresses (for example, someone stepping on the valve); this is a gate or globe valve, which is not suitable for marine use; and the valve has no independent mounting flange.

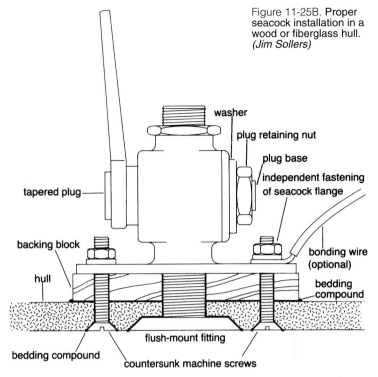

Figure 11-25B. Proper seacock installation in a wood or fiberglass hull. *(Jim Sollers)*

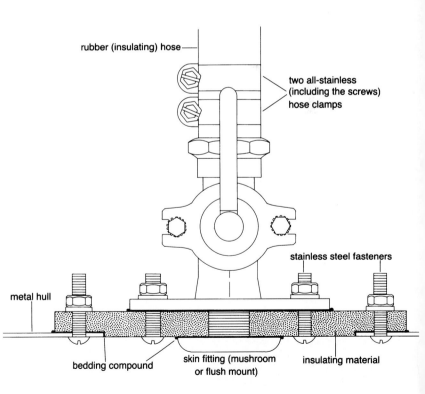

Figure 11-25D. Seacock installation on a metal hull. *(Jim Sollers)*

it by means of an intervening length of rubber hose (Figure 11-25D).

Hose attachments. These should be made with properly matched adapters, hose barbs, or tailpieces. Use two *all 300-series stainless steel* hose clamps. (Make sure the screws are 300-series stainless and not 400-series—see Chapter 4.) The ABYC requires two hose clamps on below the waterline fittings. Check all hoses and clamps at least once a year. The clamps should be undone for inspection, since they frequently rust and fail inside the worm screw unit, where the rust is not visible.

Fids. Keep on board one or two fids (tapered softwood plugs) of a suitable size to (1) ram into seacocks and (2) ram into hull openings occupied by seacocks. In the event of a catastrophic failure of the hose or seacock, or the complete loss of a seacock, you can rapidly plug the hole.

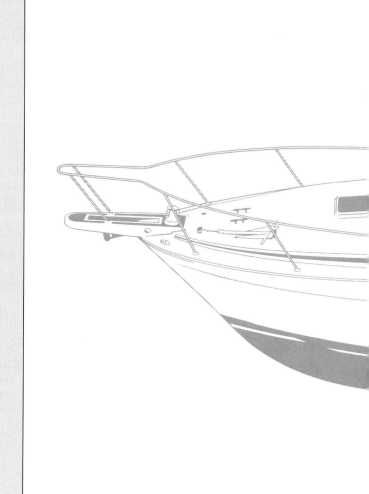

CHAPTER 12

Figure 12-1. A thorough understanding of pumps and their repair could someday keep your vessel afloat in an emergency. *(Jim Sollers)*

(1) toilet pump
(2) bilge pump
(3) macerator pump
(4) collection box
(5) foot pump
(6) engine cooling pump
(7) freshwater pump

Pumps and Pump Switches

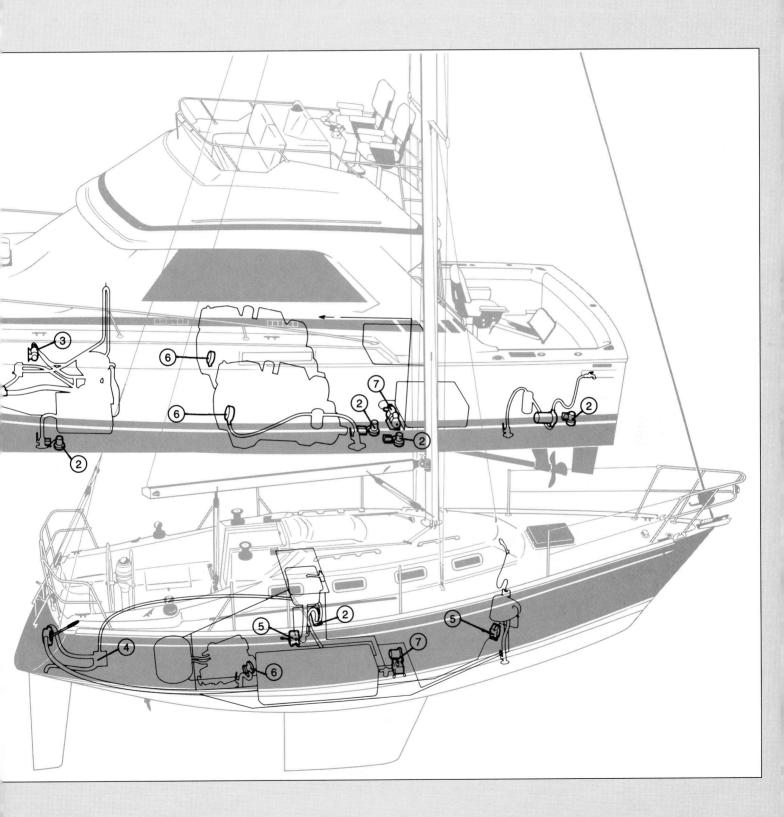

Pumps

This chapter deals with the mechanical (pumping) end of pumps. If problems are experienced with electric motors, refer to Chapter 6, bearing in mind that most old motors are *wound-field-coil universal motors*, while most new ones are *permanent-magnet universal motors*.

How They Work

Pumps on boats fall into three broad categories: *variable-volume impeller* pumps; *centrifugal* pumps; and *positive-displacement* pumps (these are my categories).

Variable-volume impeller pumps. These work on the principle of a change in the displaced volume of the impeller from one side of a pump chamber to another. The most common variety has a flexible impeller turning in a pump body that has one side flattened by screwing a blanking piece (a *cam*) into the body. As the vanes on the impeller reach the cam, they are squeezed down, expelling any fluid trapped between them. As the vanes pass the cam, they spring back up, drawing in more fluid (Figure 12-2).

Less common variations on the same theme are vane and rotary pumps. On vane pumps, the drive shaft is permanently offset in the pump housing such that the impeller (*rotor*) is always closer to the pump body at some points than at others. Set in slots in the rotor are hard vanes, which are held against the pump body. As the rotor spins, the vanes move in and out of their slots, thus maintaining contact with the pump body. The changing volume between the vanes alternately draws in and expels fluid in much the same manner as the vane action in a flexible impeller pump (Figure 12-3).

In rotary pumps the impeller does not actually rotate! Instead it is mounted on, but not keyed to, an *eccentric* shaft. The shaft is centered in the pump housing but with an offset section where it passes through the impeller bearing. The impeller is kept from spinning by an impeller guide (Figure 12-4) held in the pump body and fitting in a slot in the impeller. As the shaft turns, the impeller oscillates in a circular pattern but without actually turning, pulling in and expelling fluid as it goes.

Finally we have gear pumps in which fluid is trapped between the teeth of two gear wheels and then driven out at the point where the gear teeth mesh. Gear pumps are used primarily as oil pumps on engines and hydraulic systems; they are capable of pumping to very high pressures.

Centrifugal pumps. These have an impeller with vanes designed in such a way that fluid drawn into the center of the impeller is thrown out by centrifugal force (Figure 12-5). The momentum generated in the fluid keeps it moving and is what makes the pump work. A less

Figure 12-2. Operation of a variable volume, flexible impeller pump. (**A**) Upon leaving the offset cam, the flexible impeller blades expand, creating a vacuum that draws liquid into the pump body. (**B**) As the impeller rotates, each successive blade draws in liquid and carries it to the outlet port. (**C**) The liquid is expelled when the flexible impeller blades are again compressed by the offset cam, creating a continuous, uniform flow. *(ITT/Jabsco)*

  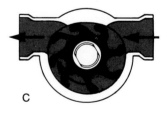

Figure 12-3. Operation of a variable-volume vane pump. (**A**) Upon leaving the eccentric portion of the pump body's liner, the vanes create a partial vacuum, which draws in fluid. (**B**) As the rotor rotates, each successive vane draws in liquid and carries it to the discharge port. (**C**) When the vanes again contact the eccentric portion of the liner, they force liquid out the discharge port. *(Jim Sollers)*

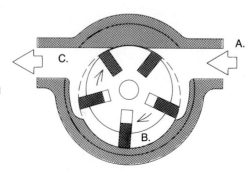

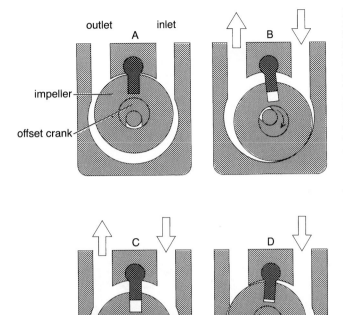

outlet   inlet

impeller

offset crank

Figure 12-4. Operation of a rotary pump. (**A**) The pump at rest. (**B**) The impeller oscillates over and down, opening a space between the impeller and impeller guide, which draws in fluid through the inlet port. (**C**) Suction-side volume increases steadily, drawing in more fluid. At the same time, the dishcarge-side volume decreases, expelling fluid. (**D**) Discharge-side volume near minimum; most fluid is expelled. Suction-side volume is still increasing, drawing in more fluid. *(Jim Sollers)*

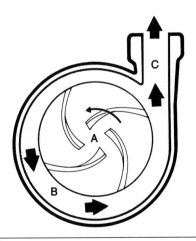

Figure 12-5. Operation of a centrifugal pump. (**A**) Liquid enters the inlet port in the center of the pump. The level of liquid must be high enough above the pump for gravity to push it into the pump, or the pump must receive initial priming. (**B**) Centrifugal force generated by the rotating and curved impeller forces the fluid to the periphery of the pump casing, thence toward the discharge port. (**C**) The velocity of fluid discharge translates into hydraulic pressure in the system downstream from the pump. The flow rate is dependent upon restrictions in the inlet and outlet piping, and the height that the liquid must be lifted. *(ITT/Jabsco)*

common variation on the same principle is a *turbine* pump, which has a somewhat different arrangement of the vanes on the impeller but is otherwise the same.

Positive-displacement pumps. This type moves a *diaphragm, bellows,* or *piston* in and out of a pump chamber, alternately increasing and decreasing its volume (Figures 12-6A, 12-6B, and 12-7). These pumps, unlike the others, can work only with a set of valves—one valve lets the fluid into the chamber and traps it; another lets it out and stops it from being sucked

back in. Since there is no impeller, there is no shaft entering the pump chamber and therefore no shaft seal and associated leaks (except on some piston pumps; see the section Piston Pumps later in this chapter).

Pros and Cons

The most important factors in terms of choosing a pump for a given application are its ability to *self-prime,* the effect of *head pressure* on its performance, and its tolerance for *solids, chemicals,*

Figure 12-6A. A manual diaphragm pump. *(Munster Simms)*

Figure 12-6B. Operation of a manual diaphragm pump. (**A**) As the handle is pulled back, the flexible diaphragm expands, creating a vacuum that pulls back the inlet check valve and draws fluid into the pump chamber. (**B**) When the handle is pushed down, hydraulic pressure forces the inlet check valve to close, at the same time opening the outlet check valve and expelling the fluid.

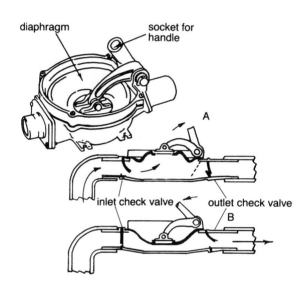

Figure 12-7. Operation of a piston pump. (**A**) The handle is depressed. Fluid is trapped between the base of the piston and the foot valve and forced up into the pump body through the check valve in the base of the piston. (**B**) As the handle is lifted, the check valve closes, and fluid is lifted to the outlet. At the same time, a vacuum is formed below the check valve, which draws more fluid into the pump chamber through the foot valve.

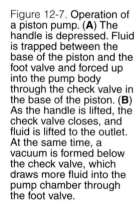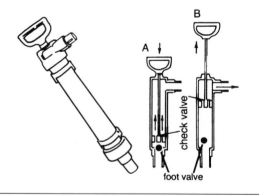

and *running dry*. The *duty rating* of electric pumps must also be taken into consideration.

Self-priming or not. All pumps, excluding the centrifugal ones, are self-priming—in other words, they have the capability to draw fluid up to themselves. *Centrifugal pumps have no self-priming capability whatsoever* and must always be installed below the liquid level they are to pump, *at all angles of heel*. (Note: The addition of a check valve in the suction piping to a centrifugal pump will retain fluid in the pump when it is shut down, thus maintaining its prime. Installed like this, a pump can be placed above the liquid it is pumping, but should the check valve leak back when the pump is shut down, the pump will lose its prime and will have to be hand-primed in some manner—generally by disconnecting the discharge line at some point above the pump and pouring water into the line.)

The effect of head pressure. Head pressure refers to the resistance to flow that a pump must overcome. It includes (1) the vertical height the

Pumps and Pump Switches

fluid must be lifted (from the suction intake to the discharge point) and (2) *the effect of resistance within the piping or tubing runs*. This latter aspect is frequently ignored, but can in fact cause more resistance than the vertical lift itself.

Vertical lift. Vertical lift is easy to measure: It is simply the difference in height of the suction and discharge points. However, it is important to remember the effects of heeling on vertical lift. Let's say we have a submersible bilge pump mounted on the centerline of a boat; the boat has a 14-foot beam. The discharge fitting is 5 feet above the pump, in the side of the boat. If the boat is heeled 30 degrees this vertical lift will decrease to 1.5 feet on one tack, *but will increase to 8.5 feet on the other tack*. (Note that if the discharge line is looped up under the deck, the vertical lift will be the height to the *top of the loop* rather than to the discharge point in the side of the hull.)

The resistance effect of piping and tubing runs. The resistance effect of piping and tubing runs is harder to measure. I have made some gross simplifications in Tables 12-1 and 12-2 to arrive at approximate figures. The tables are based on the resistance of schedule 40 pipe, the internal diameter of which, rather conveniently, is only marginally larger than its nominal size (Chapter 11), so *these tables can also be used for hose of the same size with reasonable accuracy*.

To calculate the resistance of a piping run we must first determine its nominal size (for pipe) or internal diameter (for hose), and then note all the bends and elbows, and any seacock or other valves. Table 12-1 is used to determine what length of pipe or hose would generate the same amount of resistance as the bends, elbows, and fittings. For example, consider a submersible bilge pump that has a 1½-inch discharge hose containing three long bends, culminating in a 180-degree bend (or vented loop) under the deck. Table 12-1 tells us that each of the three 1½-inch bends has the same resistance as 2.2 feet of 1½-inch pipe (giving a total of 6.6 feet of pipe) and the 180-degree bend has the resistance of 6.0 feet of pipe. The bends have a total resistance equal to that of 12.6 feet of pipe. Next we measure the actual length of the discharge hose and find it to be 12 feet, so we have a combined resistance equal to that of 24.6 feet of pipe (12.0 + 12.6 = 24.6).

The second step in determining the resistance effect of piping and tubing is to relate the size of pipe or tube to the rate of flow through it. Our bilge pump is rated at 3,000 gallons per hour (gph), which is 50 gallons a minute. From Table 12-2, reading across the 50-gallon-a-minute column (these are American gallons; to convert imperial gallons to American gallons, multiply by 1.2) to the 1½-inch-pipe column we find that the resistance of every foot of pipe at these rates of flow is equal to 0.284 feet of vertical head. Multiplying our 24.6 feet of pipe by 0.284 we discover our 12-foot tubing run with its bends has the same resistance as 7.0 feet of vertical head!

Adding the vertical lift and the effect of resistance in the tubing run, we find that on the tack which already has 8.5 feet of vertical lift, the total head pressure is 15.5 feet (8.5 + 7.0) while

Table 12-1. Resistance of Various Common Fittings Expressed as *Feet of Pipe*

Fitting	Pipe size (nominal schedule 40 pipe)				
	¾"	1"	1¼"	1½"	2"
In-line seacock (fully open)	0.4	0.5	0.7	0.9	1.2
90° seacock (fully open)	5.0	7.0	10.0	12.0	15.0
45° elbow (bend)	0.8	1.0	1.4	1.7	2.4
90° elbow (bend)	1.4	1.8	2.5	3.0	4.2
Long elbow or bend (90°)	1.0	1.3	1.8	2.2	3.0
180° bend or vented loop	2.5	3.5	5.0	6.0	8.0

For any fitting of a given pipe or hose size read off its approximate resistance in "feet of pipe" of the same size. For example, 3 long bends and a vented loop in the 1½" discharge hose from a bilge pump have the same resistance as: [(3 x 2.2) + 6.0] = 12.6 feet of 1½" hose.

Note: Intuitively this table seems wrong, since in reality the larger a pipe size the less the resistance for a given rate of flow, but yet this table shows the larger the fitting the *greater* the equivalent length of pipe. However, when the length of pipe is multiplied by the factors in the next table it all works out!

Table 12-2. Resistance Per Foot of Pipe, Expressed as *Feet of Head*, as a function of pipe size and water flow rate.

GPM	Pipe size (nominal schedule 40 pipe)				
(US)	¾"	1"	1¼"	1½"	2"
5	0.105	0.033	0.008	0.004	0.002
10	0.380	0.117	0.030	0.014	0.005
15	0.800	0.250	0.065	0.030	0.010
20	1.360	0.420	0.111	0.052	0.018
25		0.640	0.166	0.078	0.027
30		0.890	0.230	0.110	0.038
35		1.190	0.312	0.147	0.051
40		1.520	0.400	0.188	0.066
50			0.600	0.284	0.099
60			0.850	0.396	0.139
70			1.130	0.530	0.184

For any given flow rate and pipe or hose size, read from the body of the table the resistance in feet of head per foot of pipe length. Multiply this by the length of the pipe or hose to find total resistance in feet of head. For example, 24.6 feet of 1½" hose at 3,000 gph = 50 gpm. The factor is 0.284. Total resistance is 24.6 × 0.284 = 6.986 feet of head.

even with an even keel, at 3,000 gph rate of flow the total head pressure is 12.0 feet (5.0 + 7.0). We now have to see what effect this has on different types of pump.

Centrifugal pumps. To find out bilge pump performance we have to go a step further. The above calculations were based on the *rated* flow of the bilge pump (3,000 gallons an hour). Almost all submersible bilge pumps are centrifugal pumps. These are rated under what are known as *open-bucket* or *open-flow* conditions,

which means the pump has no discharge piping connected and is not lifting the water at all. *These are totally unrealistic conditions.* As soon as a discharge line is added to the pump and some lift is factored in, *output drops dramatically.* Some smaller centrifugal pumps stall out entirely with just 4 or 5 feet of head pressure!

All pump manufacturers have graphs that show pump output as a function of head pressure (Figure 12-8). We need to superimpose on such a graph *the total head pressure of our system at different rates of flow.* Referring back to Table 12-2, we find that at 10 gallons a minute (600 gph) resistance to flow *per foot of 1½-inch hose* is equal to 0.014 feet of head. With the equivalent of a 24.6-foot tubing run, this gives us a total of 0.344 feet of head (24.6 × 0.014 = 0.344); at 20 gpm (1,200 gph) the resistance factor is 0.052, for a total of 1.3 feet of head (24.6 × 0.052 = 1.3); at 30 gpm (1,800 gph) the resistance factor is 0.110, for a total of 2.7 feet of head (24.6 × 0.110 = 2.7); and at 40 gpm (2,400 gph) the resistance factor is 0.188, for a total of 4.6 feet of head. If we add these figures to the even keel head of 5 feet and the maximum heeled head of 8.5 feet, we get the results in Table 12-3.

If we plot these results on the graph (the dashed lines on Figure 12-8), *the point at which the dashed line crosses the performance curves will give us the pump capability when the boat is at rest and also heeled 30 degrees.* As can be seen, *output is related to voltage:* If the engine is running, so the alternator has the battery voltage well up, this 3,000 gph pump *in this installation* will have an output of 1,750 gph on an even keel and 1,250 gph when heeled; if the engine is shut down, but the batteries are fully charged, and

Figure 12-8. **Typical centrifugal pump performance curves.**

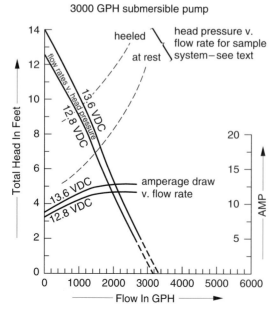

Pump Performance
3000 GPH submersible pump

Pumps and Pump Switches

Table 12-3. Total Head Pressure

Flow rate (US gph)	Even-keel head (feet)	Maximum heel head (feet)	Effect of tubing (feet)	Total head (feet): Even-keel	Heeled
600	5.0	8.5	0.3	5.3	8.8
1,200	5.0	8.5	1.3	6.3	9.8
1,800	5.0	8.5	2.7	7.7	11.2
2,400	5.0	8.5	4.6	9.6	12.9
3,000	5.0	8.5	7.0	12.0	15.5

there is no voltage drop in the pump circuit (impossible to attain), output will fall to 1,450 gph on an even keel and 980 gph when heeled. Interpolating a little, we can see that if the voltage at the pump is down around 12.0 volts (very typical on a sailboat with some voltage drop in the wiring even with a fully charged battery), the pump output will be down to little more than 1,250 gph on an even keel and 700 gph when heeled. Note: Electric bilge pumps are invariably rated at an unrealistic 13.6 volts (for a 12-volt system); there is a 10% to 12% reduction in rated output if this voltage is lowered to a more realistic 12.0 volts.

These figures are for a high-capacity bilge pump with a reasonably well-charged battery in a rather typical installation; imagine what a pitiful stream of water a small pump with a half-dead battery would be moving! Figure 12-9 gives the published specifications for a popular pump rated at 630 gph. Its maximum flow rate at 12.0 volts and 3 feet of head is 345 gph, while at 12.0 volts its maximum lift is just 6.0 feet (at which point flow rate is down to 0 gph). *These specifications are derived from a new pump in ideal test*

conditions. Add a bit of wear, and a couple of hairs wrapped around the impeller, and the pump will be virtually useless in many applications. Its a little shocking, isn't it? (Table 12-4 gives the flooding rate in gallons *per minute* of different-size holes, at different depths, in a hull. It gives some sense of how large a pump is needed to deal with even small holes.)

The single greatest improvement in the performance of centrifugal pumps will come from reducing the total effective head pressure. Given that the vertical lift component is more or less fixed by the physical dimensions of the boat, the only component of head pressure that can be readily

```
Rated flow: 630 gph
Open flow (13.6 volts) 630 gph
Open flow (12.0 volts) 570 gph
3' head at 13.6 volts 450 gph
3' head at 12.0 volts 345 gph
Maximum head at 13.6 volts 7'8"
Maximum head at 12.0 volts 6'0"
```

Figure 12-9. Published pump data for a popular submersible bilge pump.

Table 12-4. Flooding Rate of Various Size Openings at Various Depths (gpm)

Depth of Hole in Feet	Diameter Opening in Hull (Inches)							
	1	1.5	2	2.5	3	3.5	4	6
1	20	44	79	123	177	241	314	707
2	28	62	111	174	250	340	444	1000
3	34	77	136	213	306	417	544	1224
4	39	88	157	245	353	481	628	1414
5	44	99	176	274	395	538	702	1581
6	48	108	192	301	433	589	770	1731
7	52	117	208	325	468	636	831	1870
8	56	125	222	347	500	680	889	1999
9	59	133	236	368	530	722	942	2121
10	62	140	248	388	559	761	993	2235

(Based on formula in U.S. Navy Salvors Handbook)

reduced is that created by the hose run: *There is a clear need to use the largest possible size of hose, to keep the hose run as short and direct as possible, and to avoid any additional resistance such as is imposed by check valves or dirty suction filters.*

The second greatest improvement in performance will come from wiring the pump with adequately sized wire so as to minimize voltage drop. Many pump manufacturers specify wiring based upon the 10%-voltage-drop table; *the 3%-voltage-drop tables should always be used* (Chapter 3). (Note that if an external switch is used to turn the pump on and off—e.g., a float switch—this switch will be wired *in series* with the pump, which is to say *the full pump current will be flowing through the switch and its wiring.* Many of the cheaper switches have a current rating that is barely adequate for normal pump operation and will not handle continuous overloads such as those that occur when an impeller is partially obstructed. The switch points or wiring are likely to burn out. *On such a critical piece of equipment as a bilge pump, there is no substitute for a properly sized—preferably oversized—switch.*)

Finally, *the bilge pump must be properly fused in accordance with the manufacturer's recommendation.* Aside from the usual kinds of problems against which protection is needed (accidental shorts, etc.), there is always the possibility that a bilge pump will become jammed with debris, which in the case of a centrifugal pump will produce a *locked rotor* state in the electric motor. In such circumstances the current draw of the motor increases sharply. Without a fuse the pump may burn up or, more seriously, the pump housing or wiring (maybe the switch wiring) may melt down.

Variable-volume impeller pumps. These are far less sensitive than centrifugal pumps to head pressure. They suffer little loss of performance until the head pressure begins to exceed 10 to 20 feet, and then the loss is gradual rather than sudden (most are, in any case, rated at 10 feet of head as opposed to the open flow of a centrifugal pump). As head pressure rises, the flexible-impeller pumps will suffer a loss of capacity a little faster than the vane or rotary type. With rising head pressure the motor will steadily draw more current. Beyond a certain point something will burn out or break (see below).

Positive-displacement pumps. These suffer almost no loss of pumping ability as head pressure rises. With rising head pressure the motor will once again steadily draw more current. Beyond a certain point something will burn out or break (see below).

Blockage of the discharge. The more restricted the discharge, the higher the head pressure. As we have seen, a centrifugal pump simply responds by moving less fluid until it simply spins to no effect; the less the flow, the less work the pump is doing and the less its power requirements (less amp draw if electrically driven). All other types of pump operate in a completely opposite fashion—the higher the head pressure, the harder the pump works, and the more energy it draws, until eventually something fails (fuses blow, motors burn up, or hoses burst).

Any variable-volume impeller pump or positive-displacement pump used in a system where the flow gets cut off while the pump is running (e.g., a freshwater system or a saltwater wash-down system with a garden-hose-type shutoff nozzle) *must have some form of a built-in pressure switch to protect the system.*

Passing solids. Centrifugal pumps have a moderate tolerance for solids, depending largely on the size of the pump—the particles simply get flushed along in the fluid stream. Variable-volume impeller pumps (all types), on the other hand, have little tolerance for solids—anything stuck between a vane and a pump body will cause a loss of performance and likely damage the impeller or the body. Positive-displacement pumps have a very variable tolerance for solids—the valves on the smaller diaphragm and piston pumps are easily put out of action, whereas the flap valves on many a larger pump have the greatest tolerance for solids of all the pump types.

Running dry. *Diaphragm pumps can run dry indefinitely without damage.* Piston pumps are less tolerant, generally depending on the nature of the piston seals. On all other pumps there are two considerations: the impeller and the pump shaft seals.

No flexible-impeller or vane pump can run dry for more than a few seconds without damage—the fluid pumped is critical for lubrication. (The Globe Rubber Co., Rockland, MA, has developed a flexible impeller that will run dry for up to 15 minutes—considerably more expensive, but well worth the price.) All centrifugal pump impellers can run dry indefinitely. Most rotary pumps fall somewhere between these two extremes.

However, even when an impeller can tolerate running dry, the shaft seal probably cannot. No lip-type seal can run dry for very long without heating up its shaft and damaging the seal. Carbon/ceramic seals are more tolerant, but again there are very definite limits (see below for more information on seals).

If a pump is likely to run dry, a diaphragm or bellows pump must be used, or a centrifugal pump that is rated for dry running.

Chemicals tolerance. This is an important consideration in many applications even if it is not obvious at first. Galley sinks and shower drains handle many kinds of soap, detergents, and bleach; bilges contain traces of oil and diesel; effluent systems have to handle urine, which is acidic, and are frequently subjected to powerful toilet bowl cleaners, drain openers, deodorants, and bleaches (though they most definitely should *not* be—see Chapter 11); even freshwater systems handle traces of chlorine and other chemicals.

Flexible impellers are the most susceptible to chemical damage—they swell up and bind in their pump housings. Fuses blow and/or vanes strip off. The standard impeller is normally made of neoprene (which is generally the worst choice!), but nitrile, polyurethane, and Viton are all available for special applications (Table 12-5). Positive-displacement pumps also have diaphragms and valves that are susceptible to chemical damage. Centrifugal pumps and many vane and rotary pumps have relatively inert bronze and plastic (phenolic or epoxy) impellers and vanes; however, they may still have chemical tolerance problems with lip-type shaft seals. (Note: Carbon/ceramic seals are far more chemicals tolerant, but generally are sealed in pump housings and on shafts with rubber *boots* and O-rings that may not be tolerant.)

Continuous duty. Most pump motors are designed for *intermittent* use only—sometimes as little as 2 minutes at a time. The motor must then be allowed to cool down or it may burn up. Other motors can run indefinitely without damage. Check the manuals that come with a pump to ascertain its limitations.

Note that to pass ABYC requirements, *a bilge pump must be able to withstand a locked rotor condition (jammed impeller) for 7 hours without creating a fire hazard* (Chapter 3).

Choosing a pump. The five most common uses for a pump aboard a boat are for engine cooling, refrigeration cooling, freshwater systems, bilge pumping, and deck wash-down (Table 12-6).

Engine cooling pumps will be specified by the manufacturer—the user rarely has to make a choice. Refrigeration cooling pumps are about evenly split between centrifugal pumps and flexible-impeller pumps. A centrifugal pump has the edge in terms of being less prone to breakdown and requiring less maintenance. However, it *must be installed below the waterline at all angles of heel*—if this is not possible, a flexible-impeller pump is needed.

A freshwater system almost always uses an electrically driven diaphragm pump, which is ideal. The pumps are reliable, relatively quiet, and can tolerate dry running if the tank should run out but the pump fails to turn off. The most likely source of trouble is the pressure switch; fortunately these tend to fail in the open ("off") position rather than the closed ("on") position, since the latter situation results in something else breaking (a pipe bursts or the motor burns out).

The same electric diaphragm pumps are frequently used for gray water (i.e., shower and sink drains) and bilge pumping applications, *for which they are not so well suited*. On the one hand they are self-priming, can be mounted in a dry area—which protects the electrical side of things—and can be run dry, but on the other hand *quite small solids, or hairs and other detritus, can disable the valves*. As a result, these pumps must be protected with a relatively fine mesh strainer. These strainers, however, plug easily, and are especially prone to plug when the pump is most needed (on a wild night when the boat is shipping water and the motion has shaken all kinds of debris into the bilge).

Submersible centrifugal pumps offer the best overall bilge-pumping capability, *as long as the pump is powerful enough to compensate for the losses generated by the head pressure on the system*. A centrifugal pump can be used with a relatively coarse and easily cleaned strainer (strum box), is reliable, requires little maintenance, and can be run dry. When it comes to *manual* bilge pumps, *a high-capacity diaphragm pump* (preferably a *double-diaphragm* pump) *is unbeatable*.

Just about any pump will do for deck washdowns as long as it can generate a flow of 3 or 4 gallons a minute at a reasonable pressure (say, 30 psi—this will exclude most centrifugal pumps). Diaphragm-type pumps in general are more troublefree than variable-volume impeller pumps. With all but centrifugal pumps, the system will need a pressure cutoff switch to protect the pump and its plumbing.

Maintenance, Troubleshooting, and Repair

Flexible-impeller pumps (Figure 12-10). The principal causes of failure are impeller damage from solids, running dry, and chemicals.

Flexible-impeller pumps like to be used often. If left for long periods without running (e.g., over the winter) the impeller vanes have a tendency

Table 12-5. Chemical Compatibility for Impellers[1]

Chemical or Compound		Impeller Material						
	Bronze	316 Stainless	Phenolic	Epoxy	Poly-propylene	Neoprene	Nitrile	Viton
Acetone	1	1	1	3	1	3	3	3
Alcohol, ethyl	1	1	1	1	1	1	2	2
Alcohol, isopropyl	1	1	1	1	1	1	2	1
Alcohol, methyl	1	1	1	1	1	2	3	3
Ammonia	3	1	1	1	1	1	2	3
Antifreeze,								
Most brands	1	1	1	1	1	1	1	1
Prestone	1	1	1	1	1	3	1	2
Pyro Super	1	1	1	1	1	3	1	—
Valvoline	1	1	1	1	1	2	2	—
Beer	1	1	1	1	3	1	—	—
Butter	3	1	3	1	1	2	1	1
Carbolic acid	1	1	3	1	1	2	—	—
Chlorox (bleach)	1	1	3	1	1	1	2	2
Citric acid (lemon juice, etc.)	2	1	1	1	1	1	2	—
Corn oil	2	1	1	1	—	2	1	1
Cottonseed oil	1	1	1	1	1	2	1	1
Deodorants, some	1	1	1	1	1	3	3	—
Detergents	1	1	—	1	1	1	1	—
Diesel fuel	1	1	—	1	2	3	2	1
Disinfectant deodorant	1	1	1	1	—	2	1	1
Gasoline	1	1	1	1	2	3	3	1
Grease	1	1	2	1	—	3	3	1
Horseradish	—	—	—	1	—	1	3	—
Hydraulic oil	1	1	3	1	3	3	2	1
Hydrogen peroxide	3	2	3	1	1	3	1	—
Kerosene, paraffin	1	1	1	1	1	3	2	1
Ketchup	2	1	3	1	—	2	1	1
Lard	1	1	3	1	1	2	1	—
Lemon oil	—	1	1	1	—	2	—	1
Linseed oil	1	1	3	1	—	3	1	—
Mayonnaise	3	1	—	1	—	1	2	1
Mineral oil	1	1	1	1	1	2	1	1
Muriatic acid	2	3	1	1	2	1	2	1
Phosphoric acid	2	1	3	1	2	1	1	1
Pine oil	3	1	2	1	—	3	3	1
Propylene glycol	1	1	1	1	1	2	1	—
Rapeseed oil	1	1	—	1	—	2	—	1
Refrigeration gases, R-12	1	3	—	1	1	2	2	2
R-22	1	2	—	1	1	2	2	3
Sesame seed oil	1	1	—	1	1	2	1	1
Soap solutions	2	1	1	1	1	2	1	1
Soybean oil	1	1	3	1	1	3	1	1
Starch	1	1	1	1	1	1	2	1
Toothpaste	1	1	3	1	—	2	1	1
Turpentine	2	1	—	1	2	3	1	1
Urine	2	1	1	1	1	3	1	—
Varnish	1	1	1	1	1	3	2	—
Vegetable juice	2	2	1	1	1	2	2	—
Vegetable oil	1	1	2	1	1	2	1	1
Vinegar	2	1	—	1	1	2	2	3

1. Note how poorly neoprene performs and yet this is the standard flexible pump impeller!
Key: 1 = OK; 2 = Proceed with caution; flush after use; 3 = Rapid deterioration; — = no information.

Pumps and Pump Switches

Table 12-6. Pump Types and Common Applications

Common Application	Flexible Impeller	Vane	Rotary	Centri-fugal[1]	Electric Diaphragm	Manual Diaphragm	Piston
Engine cooling:							
Raw water	X	-	-	X	-	-	-
Fresh water	-	-	-	X	-	-	-
Refrigeration condensers	X	-	-	X	-	-	-
Deck wash down	X	-	-	X	-	-	-
Bilge:							
Electric	-	-	-	X	X	-	X
Manual	-	-	-	-	-	X	X
Sink discharge	-	-	-	-	X	X	-
Toilets:							
Electric	X	-	-	X	-	-	-
Manual	-	-	-	-	-	X	X
Showers	-	-	-	-	X	-	-
Fresh water:							
Pressurized	X	-	-	-	X	-	-
Manual	-	-	-	-	-	X	X
Fuel transfer[2]	-	X	X	-	-	-	-

1. Must be installed below the waterline.
2. Must be compatible with diesel.

Bilge Pump Plumbing

A bilge pump is, by definition, installed below the waterline. If its discharge line should also be submerged at any time, there is the potential for water to siphon into a boat. *The discharge side of a bilge pump must exit the hull above the waterline at all angles of heel.* If this is not possible (for example, on low-freeboard, tender vessels), the discharge line from the pump must be looped high enough to put it above the waterline at all angles of heel and fitted with a vented loop (siphon break) at the high point.

The discharge hose from a centrifugal pump must maintain *a steady rise, at all angles of heel,* up to its through-hull or vented loop. Otherwise, when the pump stops running after pumping the bilge, although most of the line to the pump will drain down, the low spots will trap water. When the pump restarts, the trapped water can act as a plug, *air-locking* the pump, effectively stalling it.

Regardless of how clean a bilge is kept, it is advantageous to mount a bilge pump or its strum box (suction filter) on a small pedestal. Heavier sediments will settle out below the level of the pump or filter, from where they can periodically be cleaned out manually. In addition, whenever a centrifugal pump is shut down, the water column in the discharge hose returns to the bilge, back-flushing the system. With the pedestal, contaminants will be washed clear of the pump. (Note that in situations with a long discharge hose, and small-volume bilges, the residual water in the hose may raise the bilge level enough to activate a level switch, causing the pump to cycle "on" and "off" repeatedly. In this case some form of a check valve will be needed in the line, but this is not particularly desirable since these valves are prone on the one hand to sticking in the open position and on the other to getting plugged—any such valve will need to be accessible for maintenance.)

Beyond this, it is important to understand the potential weaknesses of a given installation and to stress fundamental aspects of housekeeping and seamanship. The bilge must be kept clean, objects must be properly stowed, and above all *it should be a part of the ship's routine to check the bilge on every watch.*

Figure 12-10. **Typical flexible-impeller pump.** *(ITT/Jabsco)*

to stick to the pump housing. When the pump is restarted, it may blow fuses or strip off its vanes. If this is a constant problem, try fitting an over-thick gasket (see below—this technique results in a small loss of pump efficiency). Otherwise the pump cover must be loosened until the pump starts spinning.

Other common problems are leaking seals (again quite likely as a result of running dry) and worn or corroded bearings. Apart from normal wear, bearings will be damaged by water (from leaking seals), improper belt tension (too tight), and misalignment of drive pulleys or couplings. Optimum belt tension permits the longest stretch of a belt to be depressed ⅓ inch to ½ inch with moderate finger pressure. Pulley alignment can be checked by removing the belt and placing a rod in the groove of the two pulleys; any misalignment will be clearly visible.

Winterizing. Loosen the end cover to drain the pump. It is best to leave the cover loose in case any more fluid finds its way in. The impeller should be withdrawn, lightly greased (petroleum jelly or Teflon-based waterproof grease), and put back. This will keep the impeller from sticking to the pump body and aid in priming the pump the next time it is run.

Troubleshooting Chart 12-1.

Flexible Impeller, Vane, and Rotary Pump Problems: No Flow.

If the pump is belt-driven, is the pump pulley turning? **YES** ⬇	**NO** ➡ Tighten or replace the drive belt.
If a clutch is fitted, is it working? (The center of the pulley will be turning with the pulley itself.) **YES** ⬇	**NO** ➡ Adjust or replace the clutch.
For gear-driven pumps and for belt-driven pumps on which the pulley is turning, proceed as follows:	
Remove the pump cover: Are the impeller vanes intact? **YES** ⬇	**NO** ➡ Replace the impeller and track down any missing vanes. The pump probably ran dry; find out why. Check for a closed seacock, plugged filter, collapsed suction hose, or excessive heeling that causes the suction line on a raw-water pump to come out of the water. Less likely is a blockage on the discharge side causing the pump to overload.
Are the vanes making good contact with the pump body? **YES** ⬇	**NO** ➡ The impeller is badly worn and needs replacing. On vane and rotary pumps the vanes may be jammed in the impeller and just need cleaning.
Does the impeller turn when the pump drive gear or pulley turns? **YES** ⬇	**NO** ➡ The impeller, drive gear, or pulley is slipping on its shaft, or the clutch (if fitted) is inoperative. Repair as necessary.
If the impeller turns, the pump may just need priming. Otherwise the suction or discharge line must be blocked. Check for a closed seacock, plugged filter, collapsed suction hose, or excessive heeling that causes the suction line on a raw-water pump to come out of the water.	

Impeller removal and inspection. Despite the thousands of different flexible-impeller pumps, most share many construction similarities (Figure 12-11). Removal of the end cover (four to six screws) will expose the impeller. Almost all impellers are a sliding fit on the drive shaft (either with splines, square keys, Woodruff keys, one or two flats on the shaft, or a slotted shaft). Using a pair of needle-nose pliers, grip the impeller and pull it out. Note that some impellers are sealed to their shafts with O-rings; most are not. If the impeller will not come, it may be one of the few locked in place with a set, or Allen, screw (some Volvo, Atomic Four, and Universal engines in particular). If the screw is inaccessible, the drive side of the impeller will have to be disassembled and the impeller knocked out on its shaft.

The vanes should have rounded tips (not worn flat), with no signs of swelling, distortion, or cracking of the vanes, or any kind of a *set* (i.e., bend). If in doubt, replace the impeller. If an O-ring is fitted to the shaft, check it for damage. If the impeller has a tapered metal sleeve on its inner end (*extended insert* impellers), inspect the sleeve and discard the impeller if there is any sign of a step where the sleeve slides into the shaft seal.

Wear plate and seal removal. If it is necessary to remove the cam (e.g., to replace a *wear plate*—see next paragraph), loosen the cam retaining screw, tap the screw until the cam breaks loose, and then remove the screw and cam. Clean all surfaces of sealing compound.

Some impellers have a wear plate at the back of the pump chamber. If fitted, the plate can be

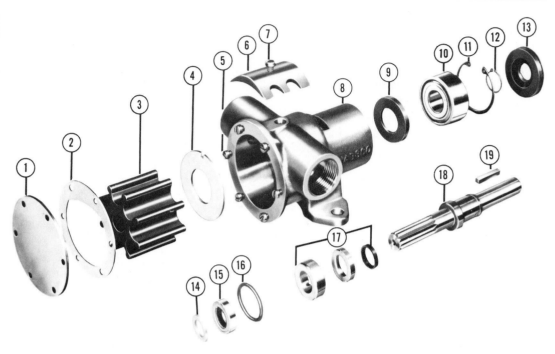

Figure 12-11. **An exploded view of the pump shown in Figure 12-10. 1.** Pump cover. **2.** Gasket. **3.** Impeller (splined type). **4.** Wear plate. **5.** Pump cover retaining screws. **6.** Cam (mounted inside pump body). **7.** Cam retaining screw. **8.** Pump body. **9.** Slinger (to deflect any leaks away from the bearing). **10.** Bearing. **11.** Bearing-retaining circlip. **12.** Shaft-retaining circlip. **13.** Outer seal. **14, 15, 16.** Inner seal assembly, lip type, or **17.** Inner seal assembly, carbon-ceramic type. **18.** Pump shaft. **19.** Drive key. (*ITT/Jabsco*)

hooked out with a piece of bent wire. Note the notch in its top; this aligns with a dowel in the pump body. If the wear plate is grooved or scored, replace it.

Shaft seals are of three types:

1. Lip-type seals, which press into the pump housing and have a rubber lip that grips the shaft.
2. Carbon/ceramic seals, in which a ceramic disc with a smooth face seats in a rubber *boot* in the pump housing and a spring-loaded carbon disc, also with a smooth face, is sealed to the pump shaft with a rubber sleeve or O-ring. The spring holds the carbon disc against the ceramic disc and the extremely smooth faces of the two provide a seal.
3. An external stuffing box (packing gland), which is the same as a propeller-shaft stuffing box. These are not very common. For care and maintenance see page 313.

Although it is possible to hook out and replace some carbon/ceramic seals with the shaft still in place (this cannot be done with lip-type seals), in most cases the shaft must be taken out to replace a seal. To do this, take apart the drive end of the shaft. First unbolt the pump from its engine or remove the drive pulley if belt driven; then proceed as follows:

If the pump has a seal at the drive end of the shaft (part number 13 in Figure 12-11), hook it out. When removing any seals, *be extremely careful not to scratch the seal seat.* A bearing-retain-

ing circlip will usually be found behind the seal in the body of the pump (pumps bolted directly to an engine housing may not have one). Remove the circlip, flexing it the minimum amount necessary to get it out. If it gets bent, it should be replaced rather than straightened.

Support the pump body on a couple of blocks of wood and tap out the shaft, hitting it on its *impeller* end. (Figure 12-12—Exception: those pumps with impellers fastened to the shaft; these must be driven out the other way.) Do not hit the shaft hard; be especially careful not to burr or flatten the end of the shaft. It is best to use a block of wood between the hammer and the shaft, rather than to hit the shaft directly.

If the shaft won't move, take another look for a bearing-retaining circlip. If there truly is none, try hitting a little harder. If the shaft remains fast, try heating the pump body in the area of the bearings with hot water or gentle use of a propane torch. The shaft will come out complete with bearings.

The main shaft seal can now be picked out from the impeller side of the body with a piece of bent wire. There may well be another bearing seal on the drive side and quite probably a *slinger* washer between the two. If the washer drops down inside the body, retrieve it through the drain slot.

Bearing removal and replacement. To remove the bearings from the shaft take the small bearing-retaining circlip off the shaft, support the assembly with a couple of blocks of wood placed *under the inner bearing race*, and tap out the

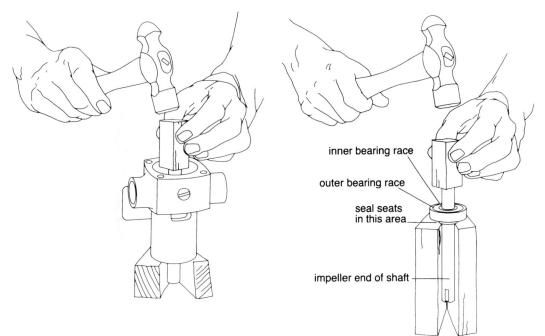

Figure 12-12. **(Left)** Removing a pump shaft. Remove the end cover and impeller. Support the pump body with a couple of blocks of wood, impeller end up. Protect the end of the impeller shaft with a block of wood, and lightly tap the shaft free. *(Jim Sollers)*

Figure 12-13. **(Right)** Removing a bearing from the pump shaft. Remove the bearing-retaining circlip from the shaft; support the bearing with a couple of blocks of wood placed under the inner bearing race; protect the shaft end with a block of wood; and lightly tap the shaft free from the bearing. *(Jim Sollers)*

inner bearing race

outer bearing race

seal seats in this area

impeller end of shaft

shaft, hitting it on its drive end (Figure 12-13).

Inspect the shaft for any signs of wear, especially in the area of the shaft seal. Spin the bearings and discard if they are rough, uneven, or if the outer race is loose. Scrupulously clean the pump body, paying special attention to all seals and bearing seats. Do not scratch any bearing, seal, or seating surfaces.

To fit new bearings to a shaft, support the inner race of the bearing and tap the shaft home. To make the job easy first heat the bearing (e.g., in an oven to around 200°F [93°C] but no more) and cool the shaft (in the icebox). The shaft should just about drop into place. Replace the bearing-retaining circlip, flat side toward the bearing.

Seal and shaft replacement. Now is the time to put the new shaft seal in the pump body—also the inner bearing seal (if fitted). Lip-type seals have the lip *toward the impeller.* Carbon/ceramic seals have the ceramic part in the pump body, set in its rubber boot with the shiny surface facing the impeller.

Lip-type seals are lightly greased (petroleum jelly or a Teflon-based, waterproof grease), but *carbon/ceramic seals must not be greased.* The seal faces must be wiped spotlessly clean—even finger grease must be kept off them—and the seals lubricated with water.

All seals must be centered squarely and pushed in evenly. If the seal is bent, distorted, or cockeyed in any way, it is sure to leak. A piece of hardwood doweling the same diameter as, or a little bigger than, the seal makes a good drift

(Figures 12-14A and B). The seal is pushed down until it is flush with the pump chamber.

If the pump has a slinger washer, slide it up through the body drain and maneuver the shaft in from the drive side of the body (Figure 12-15), easing it through the slinger and into the shaft seal. Pass the shaft through any seals very carefully.

Seat the bearings squarely in the pump housing, support the pump body, and drive the bearings home evenly, applying pressure to the *outer* race (Figure 12-16: A socket with a diameter just a little smaller than the bearing works well). Once again, heating the pump body and cooling bearings will help tremendously. Refit the bearing-retaining ring (circlip) with the flat side to the bearing and press home the outer bearing seal (if fitted), lip side toward the pump impeller.

Turn now to the pump end (refer to Figure 12-11). If the pump has a carbon/ceramic seal, clean the seal face, lubricate it with water, and slide the carbon part up the pump shaft, with the smooth face toward the ceramic seat. Some seals use *wave* washers to maintain tension between the carbon seal and seat; most use springs. (Figure 12-17: If the seal has both, discard the wave washer.)

Wear plate, cam, and impeller replacement. Replace the wear plate, locating its notch on the dowel pin. Lightly apply some sealing compound (e.g., Permatex) to the back of the cam and to its retaining screw. *Loosely* fit the cam. Lightly grease the impeller with petroleum jelly, a Teflon-based grease, or dishwashing liquid and

Figure 12-14A. (Left)
Replacing a pump seal.
Seat the seal squarely in
its housing. Using very soft
hammer taps and a piece
of hardwood doweling the
same or larger diameter as
the seal, push the seal
down until flush with the
pump chamber. *(Jim
Sollers)*

Figure 12-14B. (Right)
When replacing a pump
seal, make sure the
hardwood doweling seats
on the seal's metal rim and
not the rubber lip. The seal
goes in with the rubber lip
toward the pump chamber.
(Jim Sollers)

Figure 12-15. (Left)
Replacing a slinger
washer. Push the washer
up through its slot in the
pump body, threading the
shaft through it and into
the shaft seal. *(Jim
Sollers)*

Figure 12-16. (Right)
Driving home a bearing.
Use a ratchet-drive-type
socket with a diameter
slightly smaller than the
outer bearing race. *(Jim
Sollers)*

Figure 12-17. Carbon-
ceramic pump shaft seals
are of two basic types:
wave-washer seals
(uncommon), and coil-
spring seals. In either
case, the ceramic seal and
rubber boot are pressed
into place in the pump
body, and the carbon-ring
seal and retainer are fitted
to the pump shaft.
(ITT/Jabsco)

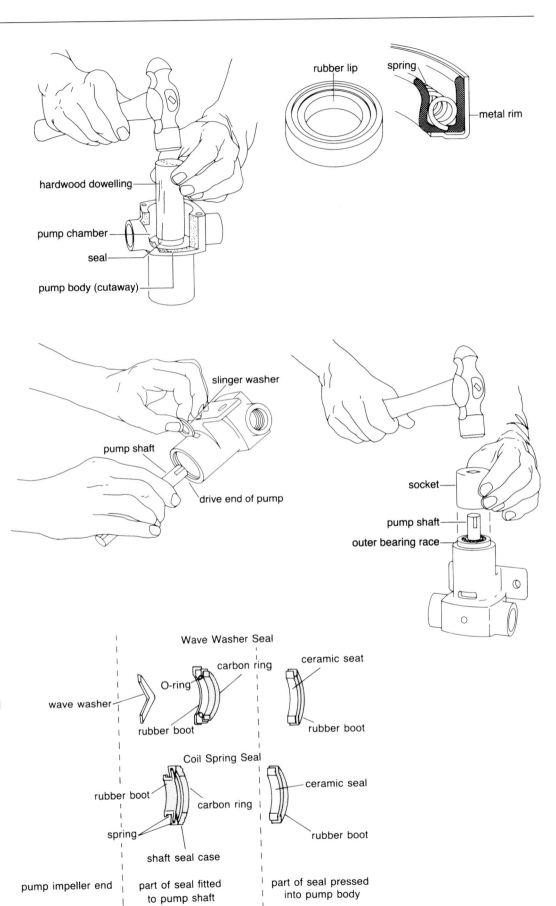

rubber lip
spring
metal rim

hardwood dowelling
pump chamber
seal
pump body (cutaway)

slinger washer
pump shaft
drive end of pump

socket
pump shaft
outer bearing race

Wave Washer Seal
wave washer
O-ring
carbon ring
rubber boot
ceramic seat
rubber boot

Coil Spring Seal
rubber boot
carbon ring
spring
shaft seal case
ceramic seal
rubber boot

pump impeller end
part of seal fitted
to pump shaft
part of seal pressed
into pump body

push it home, bending down the vanes in the opposite direction to pump rotation. Replace the gasket and pump cover. Tighten the cam screw.

The correct gasket is important—too thin, and the impeller will bind; too thick, and pumping efficiency is lost. Most pump gaskets are 0.010 inch (ten-thousandths of an inch) thick, but on larger pumps this may be 0.015 inch. As noted previously, some impellers on pumps used only intermittently have a tendency to stick in their housings and, if electrically driven, blow fuses when the pump is started. To stop this, loosen the pump cover on initial startup, and then tighten it back down (the same result can be achieved with a small loss in pumping efficiency without loosening the cover screws by fitting an overthick gasket).

When refitting a flanged pump to an engine, be sure the slot in the pump shaft, or the drive gear, correctly engages the tang or gear on the engine, and make sure the pump flange seats squarely *without pressure*. Some pumps have spacers or adapters that go between the end of the pump shaft and the engine drive shaft. Pulley-driven pumps must be properly aligned with their drive pulleys, and the belt correctly tensioned.

Manual clutches. Some pump pulleys are turned on and off via manually operated clutches (Figure 12-18). The pulley spins on a bearing mounted on an *adapter ring*. The adapter ring in turn fits on an assembly known as a *body plug and engaging sleeve*. The engaging sleeve is threaded (screwed) onto the body plug. On the back of the pulley, a tapered fric-tion surface fits loosely inside a tapered housing, the *clutch cone*, which is locked to the pump shaft. The pulley freewheels and the pump remains stationary until the clutch lever is operated. Then the operating lever turns the adapter ring, which in turn *backs out* the engaging sleeve on the threaded body plug, forcing the pulley's tapered friction surface into contact with the clutch cone; this locks up the whole assembly and the pump turns.

In time the clutch wears and begins to slip. It can be adjusted by unscrewing the engaging sleeve a little more from the body plug, but this solution is limited by the number of threads between plug and sleeve. The engaging sleeve (and therefore the pulley) will start to wobble, accelerating wear, if it is unscrewed too much.

This adjustment is made by engaging the clutch and then loosening the clutch-operating ring (also called the *lever ring* and the *engaging clamp ring*) where it fits around the adapter ring. Jam the adapter ring in place with a screwdriver and rotate the operating ring backward around the adapter ring (it may be necessary to wedge open the slit in the operating ring with a second screwdriver). Move the operating ring 20 degrees or so, retighten its securing bolt, and try the clutch. Repeat if necessary, but if the ring has to be moved more than a total of 45 degrees, the clutch is badly worn and needs replacing.

Clutch kits contain the body plug and engaging sleeve assembly, pulley, bearing, adapter ring, and instructions for fitting. Note that the body plug and engaging sleeve are a matched set and should always be replaced together.

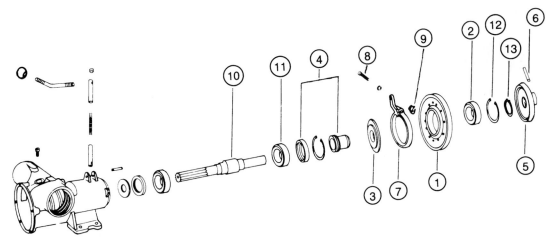

Figure 12-18. An exploded view of a manual clutch for a pump. **1.** Pulley. **2.** Pulley bearing. **3.** Adaptor ring. **4.** Body plug and engaging sleeve. **5.** Clutch cone. **6.** Clutch-cone locking pin. **7.** Clutch-operating ring. **8.** Clutch-operating-ring securing bolt. **9.** Clutch-operating-ring securing nut. **10.** Pump shaft. **11.** Bearing. **12.** Pulley-to-bearing retaining ring. **13.** Engaging-sleeve-to-bearing retaining ring. To adjust this type of clutch: (**A**) Engage the clutch. (**B**) Loosen nut (**9**) and the clutch-operating-ring securing bolt (**8**). (**C**) Open up the slot in the operating ring by prying with a screwdriver. (**D**) Hold the adaptor ring (**3**) stationary and rotate the clutch-operating ring backward 20 degrees. (**E**) Retighten the operating ring nut and bolt. *(ITT/Jabsco)*

Electric clutches. The device here that locks a pulley to its shaft is a *field coil* (Figure 12-19), which is energized electrically and locks a free-wheeling pulley to its hub by electromagnetic force. An electric clutch cannot be adjusted—it either works or it doesn't. If it fails, first check that there is full voltage at the coil and that it is grounded properly.

To replace either a pulley and bearing assembly, or the field coil, remove the pulley. Undo its center retaining bolt (it will probably be necessary to remove the pump cover and hold the impeller to stop the shaft from turning). If the bolt proves tough to break loose, place a correctly sized wrench (spanner) on it and hit the wrench smartly with a hammer—the shock should do the trick.

The end of the pump shaft, where the pulley fits on, is tapered. Between the shaft and the pulley is a key. Tap the pulley loose with a soft-faced mallet or a hammer and a block of wood. Watch out for the key; don't let it fall into the bilges. The field coil is unbolted from either an adapter or the pump body. To reassemble the clutch, reverse these steps—be sure to put the key back.

Rotary and vane pumps. In most cases removing an end cover provides access to the impeller, which will slide off its shaft (Figures 12-20 and 12-21). The vanes on vane pumps tend to fall out of the rotor. Since it is best to put them back in the same slots and the same way around,

slip a rubber band around the rotor when it is half out. This holds the vanes in place.

Besides the usual seal, shaft, and bearing inspections, check old vanes against a new vane (spares should always be carried on board) for signs of wear. If any are worn down more than one-third of their original length, replace the whole set. If the new vanes have a radiused edge, this faces out (toward the pump wall). Some vane pumps have removable liners; replace the liner if the one in place is excessively scored.

Seal and bearing replacement for vane and rotary pumps is similar to this procedure for flexible-impeller pumps.

Centrifugal pumps. The most common problem is loss of prime, which can generally be restored by removing the discharge hose, and pouring in a cup of water.

Gradual wear of the impeller blades increases clearances between the impeller and its housing, resulting in a slow loss of pumping efficiency. If the pump is installed in a pressurized system it will run for longer periods until finally its output pressure cannot reach the cutout point of the pressure switch; the pump then stays on all the time. Wear will cause centrifugal bilge pumps with a considerable lift to pump at a slower and slower rate.

Removal of the end housing gives access to the pump impeller (Figures 12-22A and B). Some impellers are held on with setscrews

Figure 12-19. An exploded view of a pump with an electromagnetic clutch. *(ITT/Jabsco)*

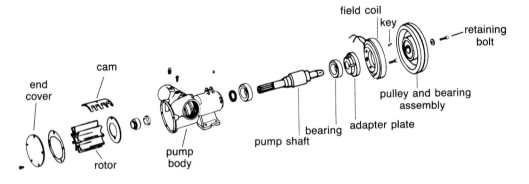

Figure 12-20. An exploded view of a vane pump. *(ITT/Jabsco)*

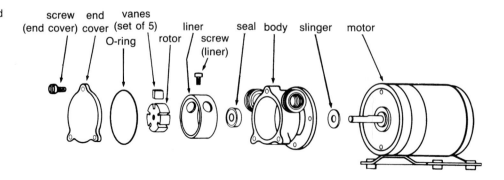

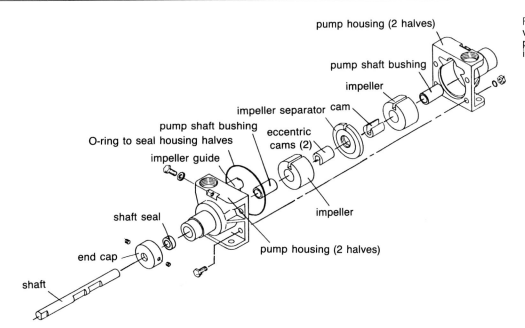

pump housing (2 halves)

pump shaft bushing

impeller

impeller separator cam

cam

pump shaft bushing

O-ring to seal housing halves

eccentric cams (2)

impeller guide

shaft seal

impeller

end cap

pump housing (2 halves)

shaft

Figure 12-21. An exploded view of a rotary pump. This particular one has twin impellers. (Groco)

Troubleshooting Chart 12-2.
Centrifugal Pump Problems: No Flow or Reduced Flow.

Is the pump refusing to spin? **NO** **TEST:** Check the voltage at electric motors while switched on, or the drive mechanism on other pumps (gears, belt, pulley, clutch); check for trash jammed in the impeller on a bilge pump.	**YES** Remove trash. Repair or replace belt, or refer to Chapter 6 for problems with electric motors. (Note: Most old motors are wound, field-coil universal motors; newer ones are permanent-magnet universal motors.)
Has the pump lost its prime? **NO** **TEST:** Prime the pump by disconnecting a discharge line and pouring in fluid to fill the pump chamber. Run the unit again. If there is flow, the pump is OK.	**YES** 1. Check that the pump is below the waterline (including when the boat is heeled) or, if above the waterline, that it has a check valve in the suction line. If the valve is fitted, check that it is not leaking back. 2. Check that the suction line is not kinked or blocked (by a closed seacock or plugged filter, for example). 3. Check that the suction line makes a continuous run up to the pump with no U-bends that can trap air. 4. Check that all suction line connections are tight and not sucking air.
Are there obstructions in the discharge line? **NO** **TEST:** Check for common obstructions in the discharge line, such as a kinked hose or closed seacock.	**YES** **FIX:** Straighten hose or open seacock and try running the unit again. If there is flow, the pump is OK.
Is the head pressure too high? **NO** **TEST:** Disconnect the discharge line at its overboard discharge, lower it in relation to the pump, and try running the unit again.	**YES** Reduce the head or get a more powerful pump. If the pump has worked previously as installed, the loss of pumping ability is likely due to a worn impeller. Replace the impeller.

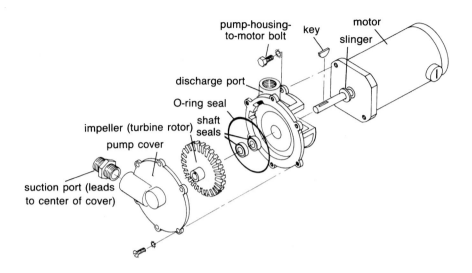

Figure 12-22A. An exploded view of a centrifugal pump with a turbine impeller. *(Groco)*

pump-housing-to-motor bolt

key

motor

slinger

discharge port

O-ring seal

shaft seals

impeller (turbine rotor)

pump cover

suction port (leads to center of cover)

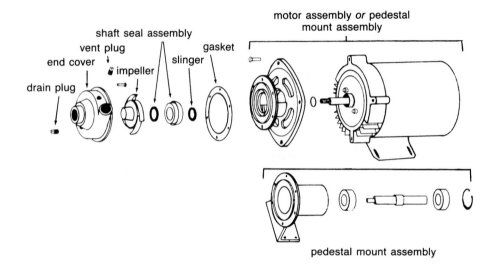

Figure 12-22B. A spiral-vane centrifugal pump. *(ITT/Jabsco)*

shaft seal assembly

vent plug

end cover

impeller

slinger

gasket

drain plug

motor assembly *or* pedestal mount assembly

pedestal mount assembly

(Allen screws); others are screwed onto their shafts. To undo the latter, tape the drive shaft and grip it with Vise-Grips; unscrew the impeller (generally counterclockwise when viewed from the impeller end).

The procedure for seal and bearing replacement for centrifugal pumps is similar to that for flexible-impeller pumps.

Piston pumps. A piston fits in a cylinder, with a valve on the base of the piston and one in the cylinder (or else "in" and "out" valves in the cylinder). When the piston is pulled up, it draws fluid into the cylinder. When it is pushed down, the valve in the cylinder (the inlet valve) closes and the trapped fluid pushes past the valve in the piston, or out of a second valve in the cylinder (the discharge valve). If the fluid has moved past the piston into the upper side of the cylinder, the next upward stroke of the piston drives

it out of the discharge port. On this type of pump, the piston rod must be sealed where it enters the cylinder in order to prevent leaks (Figures 12-23A and B).

Many different valve types are used on both pistons and cylinders. Older pistons may have a dished leather washer screwed to the lower end. As the piston descends its cylinder, trapped fluid in the cylinder pushes in the sides of the washer and forces its way up past the piston. When the piston is withdrawn, the fluid pressure pushes the sides of the washer out against the cylinder wall to form a seal. Modern pistons of this type are sealed with a neoprene cup washer. Another approach is to use an O-ring to seal the piston in its cylinder and fit a ball or flapper valve into the piston's base.

Cylinder valves may be simple rubber or metal flaps, balls, or a rubber disc with a central retaining valve stem. As fluid is sucked in, the

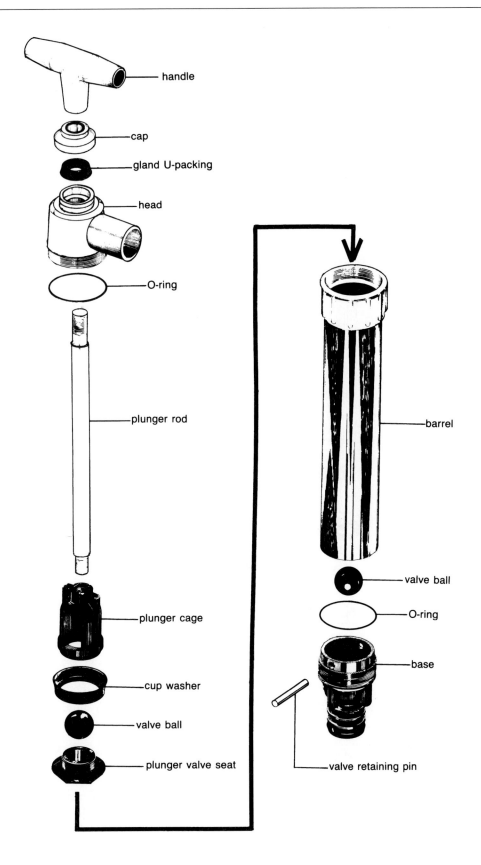

Figure 12-23A. A piston pump with ball valves. *(Munster Simms)*

handle

cap

gland U-packing

head

O-ring

plunger rod

plunger cage

cup washer

valve ball

plunger valve seat

barrel

valve ball

O-ring

base

valve retaining pin

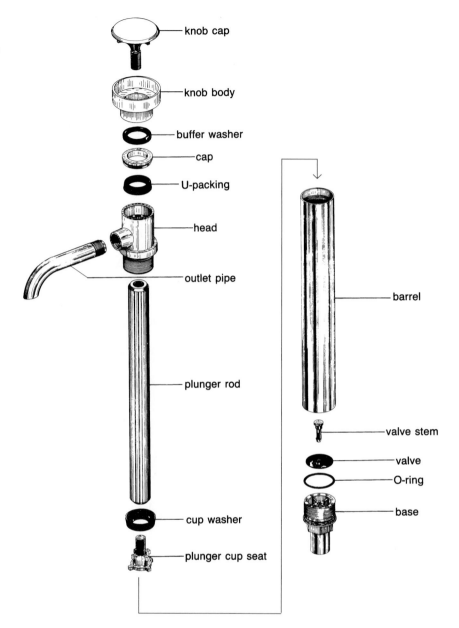

Figure 12-23B. A piston pump with a cup washer on the piston, and a modified flap valve (rubber disc with center stem) on the cylinder. *(Munster Simms)*

knob cap

knob body

buffer washer

cap

U-packing

head

outlet pipe

plunger rod

cup washer

plunger cup seat

barrel

valve stem

valve

O-ring

base

valves, regardless of type, are lifted off their seats. When fluid is discharged, the valves are forced down against their seats.

Foot-operated piston-type galley pumps have spring-loaded pistons. Foot pressure pushes the piston in; the spring brings it back out.

Problems. The most common piston-pump problem is trash in valve seats; this causes a loss of prime and ability to pump. A failure of a piston's dished washer or O-ring will have the same result. Before blaming the pump, check for air leaks in the suction line. Vigorous pumping will sometimes restore prime and clear valves.

The piston-rod seals will leak eventually, especially after a winter shutdown. Most have a cap, which can be tightened to improve the seal.

Overhaul and repair. Most pistons are withdrawn by unscrewing the piston-rod seal from the top of the cylinder. Damaged dish washers can be replaced with a piece of thin leather (e.g., from an old wallet) if no spares are available. Cut the washer a little larger in diameter than the cylinder bore, screw it to the piston, and then lubricate with water. Form the edges up around the base of the piston until the washer fits the cylinder.

Cylinder valves generally unscrew from the base of the cylinder—although on cheaper pumps they are housed in a rubber boot that simply pushes on and pulls off. If the valve consists of a rubber disc, inspect it closely for small tears and nicks, which might not be immediately apparent. Look for and remove pieces of trash between all valves and seats.

Manual diaphragm pumps. A handle moves a lever (rocker arm or *fork*) which arcs backward and forward around a pivot point or fulcrum. Attached to the lever is a diaphragm. As the diaphragm moves out, it draws fluid into a pump chamber; as it moves in, it expels the fluid (Figures 12-24A and B). Simple flap or joker valves (Chapter 11) on the inlet and outlet allow the fluid in and out.

A *double-diaphragm* pump has a diaphragm and pump chamber on both sides of the lever—as one diaphragm moves in, the other moves out, and vice versa (Figure 12-25). Each pump chamber has its own inlet and outlet valves; the two suction and discharge ports feed into common suction and discharge manifolds. Some double-diaphragm pumps have a spring in one chamber to return the operating handle unfailingly to the same position. Foot-operated diaphragm pumps have a spring-loaded plunger instead of an operating handle and lever (Figure 12-26). Standing on the plunger moves the diaphragm in; the spring brings it back out.

Problems. There is almost nothing to go wrong with a diaphragm pump. If the pump fails to prime, suspect an air leak in the suction hose or improperly seated valves. A less likely possibility is a ruptured diaphragm.

Valve problems generally arise as a result of pieces of trash lodging in the valves and holding them open. Chemicals also swell up the rubber flaps, which either fail to seat properly or hang up in the open position on the side of the valve housing. In some applications, calcium builds

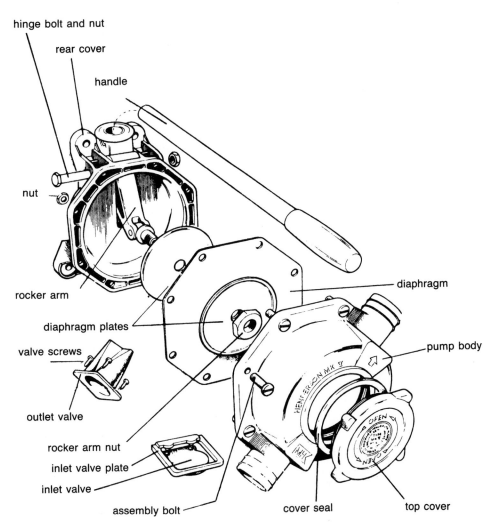

Figure 12-24A. A manual diaphragm pump with an internally mounted handle. *(Munster Simms)*

hinge bolt and nut
rear cover
handle
nut
rocker arm
diaphragm plates
valve screws
outlet valve
rocker arm nut
inlet valve plate
inlet valve
assembly bolt
diaphragm
pump body
cover seal
top cover

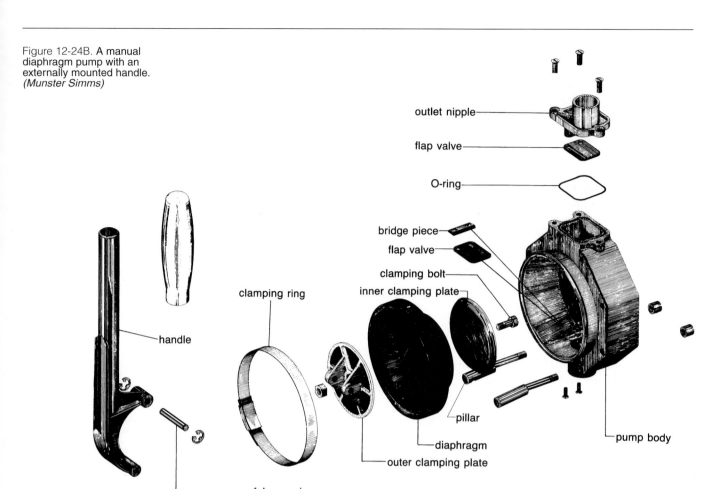

Figure 12-24B. A manual diaphragm pump with an externally mounted handle. *(Munster Simms)*

outlet nipple

flap valve

O-ring

bridge piece

flap valve

clamping bolt

inner clamping plate

handle

clamping ring

pillar

pump body

diaphragm

outer clamping plate

fulcrum pin

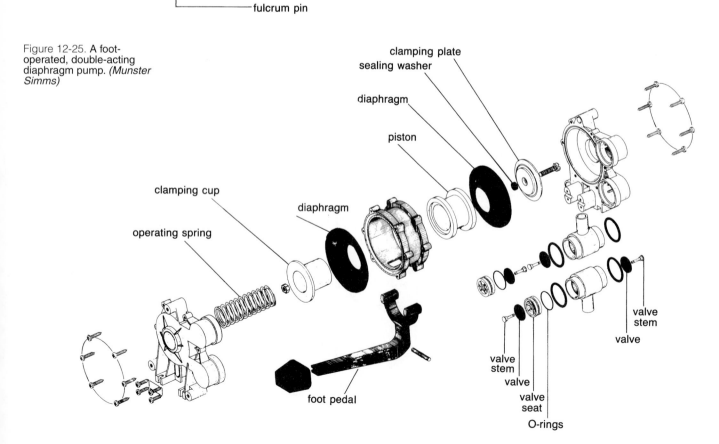

Figure 12-25. A foot-operated, double-acting diaphragm pump. *(Munster Simms)*

clamping plate

sealing washer

diaphragm

piston

clamping cup

operating spring

diaphragm

valve stem

valve

valve stem

valve

valve seat

O-rings

foot pedal

up on valve seats (Chapter 11). Eventually fatigue will cause the flaps to tear and come loose.

Diaphragms are constructed of several layers of fabric. Before a complete failure occurs, the layers may delaminate, trapping fluid in between. Complete failure is close. Rarely, one of the diaphragm plates (on each side of the diaphragm) will fracture, and the broken pieces will punch a hole in the diaphragm.

Many pump housings and levers are cast aluminum while hinge pins are stainless steel. Galvanic corrosion and seizure may occur, especially if the pump is rarely used. On some models, pump handles have a nasty habit of collapsing and breaking where they slot into, or over, the rocker arm (lever arm). Always carry a spare handle.

Overhaul and repair. Almost all diaphragm pumps are very simple to dismantle and reassemble. The greatest problems arise with stainless steel fasteners frozen in aluminum housings; they often shear off when you try to undo them (see Freeing Frozen Fasteners, Appendix B).

Diaphragms are variously retained by screwed-in retaining plates, slotted clamping rings, and large hose clamps (Jubilee clips). On either side of a diaphragm is a plate, held together with one central bolt or with several screws. Two things are important when fitting a new diaphragm: (1) make sure that all seating surfaces are spotlessly clean; and (2) properly line up the lever (fork) pivot point on the outer plate with the lever (fork) before tightening down the diaphragm-retaining device. Where a diaphragm is held with a retaining ring and a number of screws, tighten the screws evenly, alternating from side to side.

Some valves are changed by unscrewing the valve ports from the outside of the pump body (the hoses must first come off); access to others is from inside the pump body (the diaphragm normally must be removed). Valves are variously retained by valve plates, *bridge pieces*, and clips. Remember, the key points are: (1) scrupulously clean all mating surfaces; (2) make sure the valves are inserted the *right way up* (inlet valves flapping inward; outlet valves outward; joker valves on the discharge side with the *duck's bill* facing *away* from the pump); and (3) make sure the valves are in the *right way around* (some valve housings are asymmetrical; if the valves are inserted improperly, they either will not open or will hang up on the valve housing).

Electric diaphragm pumps. These pumps are widely used in pressurized freshwater systems (Figures 12-28A, B, and C) and sometimes

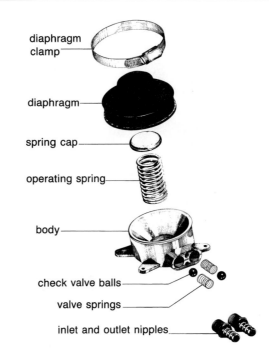

Figure 12-26. **A foot-operated, single-diaphragm pump.** *(Munster Simms)*

diaphragm clamp

diaphragm

spring cap

operating spring

body

check valve balls

valve springs

inlet and outlet nipples

as bilge, shower, and effluent pumps. In a pressurized water system, the pumps are likely to be fitted with a check valve on the discharge side, a pressure switch, an accumulator tank, and possibly a low-tank-level switch. None of these is likely in other applications. The following troubleshooting sections refer specifically to pressurized freshwater systems, but cover most other situations.

Pump fails to operate. Check the voltage at the motor (Chapter 3). If there is no voltage, bypass the pressure switch (see below, High Pressure Switches). If the pump now runs, the switch is defective. Since these are mostly sealed units, the switch will need replacing (if not sealed, check the points for pitting, burning, or corrosion). If the pressure switch is OK, maybe there is a low-tank-level switch that has cut out. If the voltage at the motor is OK, check the motor itself (Chapter 6). Some motors have a high-temperature switch that may have tripped—if so, push the reset button, which will be somewhere on the motor housing.

Pump operates but no water flows. First check to see if the motor, if externally mounted, is turning the pump—the drive belt or coupling may be broken, the connecting rod loose, etc. If the pump itself is operating, open all faucets to reduce any back pressure on the pump. Check the water tank level, especially if the boat is heeled. If the pump has a suction strainer, inspect it. In some situations, the suction line may have an in-line check valve or foot valve—

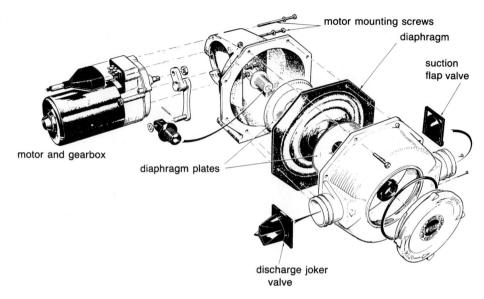

Figure 12-27. An electrified manual diaphragm pump. This is the same pump as shown in Figure 12-24A, with the exception of a modified rocker arm and a rear housing adapted to take a motor. *(Blake and Sons)*

motor mounting screws

diaphragm

suction flap valve

motor and gearbox

diaphragm plates

discharge joker valve

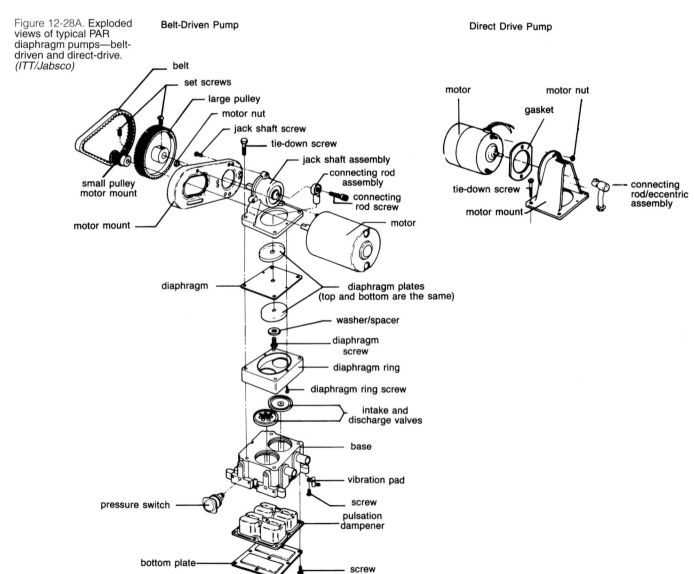

Figure 12-28A. Exploded views of typical PAR diaphragm pumps—belt-driven and direct-drive. *(ITT/Jabsco)*

Belt-Driven Pump

Direct Drive Pump

belt

set screws

large pulley

motor nut

jack shaft screw

tie-down screw

jack shaft assembly

connecting rod assembly

connecting rod screw

small pulley
motor mount

motor mount

motor

diaphragm

diaphragm plates
(top and bottom are the same)

washer/spacer

diaphragm screw

diaphragm ring

diaphragm ring screw

intake and discharge valves

base

vibration pad

screw

pulsation dampener

pressure switch

bottom plate

screw

motor

motor nut

gasket

tie-down screw

motor mount

connecting rod/eccentric assembly

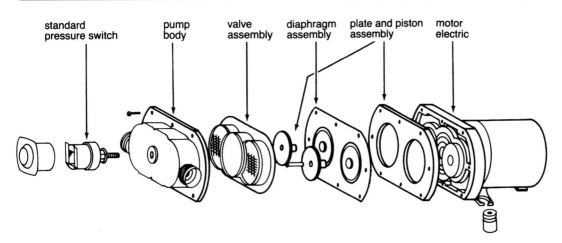

standard pressure switch

pump body

valve assembly

diaphragm assembly

plate and piston assembly

motor electric

Figure 12-28B. In-line electric double-diaphragm pump. *(ITT/Jabsco)*

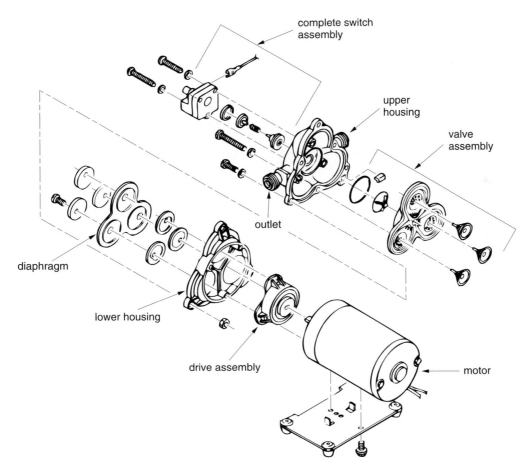

complete switch assembly

upper housing

valve assembly

diaphragm

lower housing

drive assembly

outlet

motor

Figure 12-28C. Triple-diaphragm pump. Inside the lower housing is a *wobble plate*, which oscillates when the motor is running. The oscillating plate drives three separate sections of the diaphragm backward and forward, pulling water in and out of three separate chambers in the upper housing, each with its own valves. The chambers are supplied by a common inlet, and discharge into a common outlet. The same principles can be used with any number of cylinders (four-cylinder pumps are quite common). *(Shurflo)*

make sure it is not plugged or stuck shut. The suction hose may be kinked or plugged. Any air leaks (loose connections) will stop the pump from priming. Finally, there may be problems with the pump itself—most probably trash stuck under the valves, but perhaps a hole in the diaphragm (see the section Dismantling and Repairing). Break loose the discharge line and try blowing back through the pump. If this can be done there is definitely a problem with the valves or diaphragm.

Pump operates roughly, noisily, and vibrates. The suction line may be kinked, plugged, or too small, thus restricting flow, but more likely the pump itself is the problem. The pump must be securely mounted with vibration-absorbing pads. Loose drive pulleys and/or excessive play in the connecting rod and various bearings on those pumps with external motors could be causing the noisy vibration; check them and tighten them if necessary. Some pumps have a rubber *pulsation dampener* or a *surge chamber*, designed to smooth out flow through the pump; as a last resort, take the bottom plate off the pump and check this dampener to see if it is deformed or ruptured (see Pulsation Dampener Replacement).

Pump fails to cut off when faucets (taps) are closed. Check the water tank; it is probably empty! If not, the pump may be air-bound; open a faucet, allow enough water to flow through so that the pump is primed, and then close the faucet. The pressure switch may be stuck "on"—make sure its points are open (if accessible). Last, check the voltage at the motor—a low voltage will cause the pump to operate slowly and perhaps not come to pressure. The motor will be in danger of burning up.

Pump cycles on and off when faucets are closed. Water may be leaking from a loose connection, an open faucet, or perhaps a toilet if fresh water is used for flushing (e.g., VacuFlush). Otherwise pressure is bleeding off the system *back through the pump*—the discharge check valve (if fitted) or valves are leaking (see below).

Pump cycles rapidly on and off in use; water knocks in the piping. Most pressurized water systems use an *accumulator* tank (Figures 12-29A and B). This is an air-filled tank that tees into the discharge side of the pump. As the pump operates it fills the tank with water, compressing the air within it, until pressure reaches the cutout setting on the pump pressure switch. When a faucet is opened, the compressed air forces water back out of the tank and through the faucet until pressure has fallen to the cut-in

point on the pump pressure switch. The pump then kicks in and recharges the accumulator tank. The net effect is to reduce the amount of cycling on and off that the pump does, which reduces wear on both the pump and the pressure switch points.

Two types of accumulator tank are in use. The first is just a simple tank. The second has a built-in rubber diaphragm with a tire valve on the outside of the tank. Air is pumped in through the valve to pressurize the tank (generally to around 20 psi; the pressure should be approximately the same as the *cut-in pressure setting* on the pressure switch). Water enters the tank on the other side of the diaphragm, forcing the diaphragm in against the air cushion.

Both tanks can become *waterlogged*. The simple tank becomes so when the initial tankful of air is slowly dissolved and carried away by the water entering and leaving the tank; the diaphragm tank is affected if the pressure bleeds off the air side of the diaphragm or the diaphragm ruptures. In either case, the pump will cycle on and off at shorter and shorter intervals. This causes sudden pressure changes in the plumbing, which, in turn, not only damages pumps but can produce some surprisingly loud knocks (sometimes called *water hammer*).

Turn off the pump and *open a faucet to bleed all pressure off the system*. The simple tank must be completely drained to renew the air charge; if it has no drain plug, it may be necessary to break the connection loose at its base. The diaphragm type is pumped back up again, generally with a bicycle pump.

Excessive pressure. Some shoreside hookups have pressures that will damage valves and diaphragms. Most pumps are protected with a built-in check valve in the discharge fitting. Even so, a pressure regulator (to around 35 psi) should always be fitted on the shoreside connection.

Dismantling and repairing. Turn off the power and bleed down the system through the faucets.

Pumps with external motors: Removing four screws allows the complete drive and diaphragm assembly to be lifted off, providing access to the valves. Inspect new valves carefully—if one has a small hole in it, this is the intake valve. Be sure to put the valves in the same way up as the old ones.

The diaphragm is disconnected by undoing the screws in the diaphragm-retaining ring and pulling off the ring, which provides access to the central bolt or screw holding the diaphragm and its plates together. If fitting anything other than a circular diaphragm, take care to align it properly

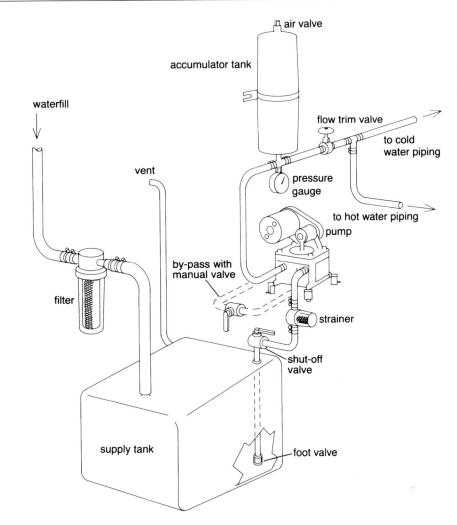

air valve

accumulator tank

waterfill

vent

flow trim valve

to cold
water piping

pressure
gauge

to hot water piping

pump

by-pass with
manual valve

filter

strainer

shut-off
valve

supply tank

foot valve

Figure 12-29A. Accumulator tanks (pressure tanks), like the one shown in this scematic of a typical onboard pressurized water system, serve as a water reservoir, providing pressurized water between pump cycles, and reducing the frequency with which the pump must run. These tanks are susceptible to waterlogging—a reduction in tank air volume as the initial charge of air dissolves into the water. This increases pump cycling, and can lead to system damage. (Jim Sollers)

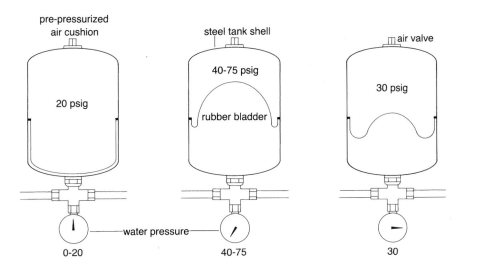

pre-pressurized
air cushion

steel tank shell

air valve

20 psig

40-75 psig

rubber bladder

30 psig

water pressure

0-20

40-75

30

Figure 12-29B. A captive-air, or pre-pressurized, accumulator tank. When the pump starts, water enters the reservoir. At maximum preset pressure, the sytem is filled and the pump shuts off. When water is used, pressure in the chamber forces water into the system. The pump stays off until the minimum pressure setting is reached; then the pump turns on. By isolating the water within a rubber bladder, water-logging is largely eliminated. The air charge is readily renewed with a bicycle pump. (ITT/Jabsco)

so that it does not get twisted. When replacing the diaphragm assembly, make sure the surfaces are clean, and tighten the screws evenly.

The discharge fitting in some pumps has a check valve, which generally cannot be repaired. In the event of failure the whole fitting must be replaced. Remove the old fitting, carefully noting its orientation so that you will put the new one in the right way around!

Pumps with internal motors: The motor is generally held to the pump head with three or four screws, while another three or four screws hold the cover on the pump. Removing either is easy. The cover is taken off for valve and diaphragm access and replacement.

Pulsation dampener replacement (pumps with external motors). Mark the baseplate(s) and pump body so that they can be put back properly.

Remove all the screws from the baseplate(s). Pull out the rubber pulsation dampener(s) and check for deformation, ruptures, or cuts. When doing the baseplate screws back up, first tighten the center screws on each side and then work out toward the corners. Do not overtighten.

Winterizing. Pumps with pulsation dampeners generally can freeze without damage, but the rest of the water system cannot, so winterize the whole system. Either drain the pump and all its piping, or disconnect the suction line from the tank and pump *propylene glycol* antifreeze through it.

Note: Automotive antifreeze is made from ethylene glycol and is poisonous—*do not use it in freshwater systems.* Propylene glycol has almost identical antifreeze properties and is safe to use. Flush the system at the start of the new season.

Pump Switches

Pressure Switches

High pressure switches. Used in freshwater systems and on wash-down pumps. The switch opens the electrical circuit to a pump at a preset pressure, and then closes it once the pressure falls by a certain amount. These switches are increasingly sealed units either screwed into or built into the body of a pump. They are not user serviceable or repairable—a failed switch is simply replaced.

To determine if a switch has failed, its wiring must be accessed and bypassed so that the pump is connected directly to the electrical supply. WARNING: If the pump is AC powered, turn off the power before accessing the switch terminals. REMEMBER, AC POWER CAN KILL. If at all unsure about what you are doing, don't do it! A pump can be run with its switch bypassed, but a failure to turn it "off" just one time after use will result in a blown-out system or a burned-out pump motor.

Older and larger pumps tend to have adjustable switches. A central retaining screw allows the cover to be lifted off, exposing the points and two adjusting screws. Dirty, pitted, and/or corroded points are a frequent source of trouble; inspect them and all wire terminals closely. The points can be cleaned with a fine grade of wet-or-dry sandpaper (400-grit). The operation of the points can be checked by prying

them apart and pushing them together with a screwdriver. There may be a small spark; a large spark indicates a problem with the points or with the pump motor (it may be shorted). If the points close but the pump fails to come on, bridge the wire terminals with a jumper wire to see if it is the switch that is defective (observe all necessary safety precautions with AC-powered pumps).

The two adjusting screws control the pump cut-in and cutout pressures. Generally, turning down one screw increases both pressures; turning down the other raises the cutout pressure without altering the cut-in pressure. Adjustment procedure, therefore, is to set the cut-in pressure with the first screw, and then to fine-tune the cutout pressure with the second screw.

Low-pressure switches. Low-pressure-switches are mechanically similar to high-pressure switches, although their function is different. They are mounted on the discharge side of a pump. They break the circuit when pressures are abnormally low, as would happen if a tank ran dry (e.g., 6 psi on a system set to maintain 20 to 40 psi). A low-pressure shutdown switch may well be built into the same unit as a pressure-regulating switch. Adjustment and points maintenance follow pressure switch procedures. Once tripped, or on initial start-up of a system (before pressure has built up), most have to be reset manually.

Level Switches

Float switches. The concept of a float switch is simple. A rising water level lifts a hinged float that is used to turn on a switch (Figures 12-30A and B). A falling level drops the float, which turns off the switch. Many of these switches have a sealed vial in the float that contains a drop of mercury (a highly conductive liquid metal). When the float rises, the mercury runs to one end of the vial, closing a circuit between two terminals to turn on the pump. When the float drops, the mercury runs the other way, opening the circuit.

Mercury switches can develop problems if the drop of mercury breaks up, reducing its current-carrying capability. The switch heats up, melting the insulation on nearby wiring, which may cause shorts through the bilge water, and in any case will cause the insulation to go hard, reducing its flexibility. So instead of mercury, some switches use a rolling ball that mechanically triggers the switch (the ball itself is not part of the electrical circuit).

There are two problems with any switch in which the wires are carried into the float. The first is that the wires constantly flex or twist as the float moves up and down, with an obvious risk of eventual failure, especially if the insulation has become hard. A way around this is to mount the switch in the fixed part of the unit with a sealed diaphragm over the switch. As the hinged float moves up and down with changing fluid levels, a lever on its base operates the switch. The wires themselves remain static but now there is the problem of sealing the switch itself.

The second problem is that the switch and its wires are necessarily immersed. If the switch seals fail there will almost certainly be current leaks from the positive cable into the water leading to stray-current corrosion (Chapter 4). There is not much that can be done to prevent this, other than buying a high-quality switch.

Location of a float switch in relation to its pump is important. Should a switch be mounted in a position where it is offset from its pump, when the boat is heeled on one tack the switch will not respond until considerably more water is in the bilge than is needed for a level-state response; on the other tack there is a very real danger that the switch will stay energized after the pump has sucked itself dry, causing the pump to run continuously, creating a heavy drain on the batteries and a risk of pump failure. A *float switch should always be mounted as close to its pump as possible, and in the same fore-and-aft plane.* In practice, many are simply clipped into the base of the pump, but in this case *it is essential to ensure that the switch is aligned fore and aft:* If it is set to one side of the pump, the pump will definitely run dry on one or other tack.

The very nature of a float switch is such that the change in water level between switching on and turning off is only an inch or two. Even with a switch mounted on the same fore-and-aft line as its pump, when a boat pounds into a head sea or rolls from side to side, the action of a small amount of water surging backward and forward in the bilge can flick the switch "on" and "off" until eventually something fails (the wiring, the switch points or motor, or the hinge on the switch). This situation also creates an unnecessary drain on the batteries.

From a mechanical point of view, the hinge on these switches is vulnerable. As we and many

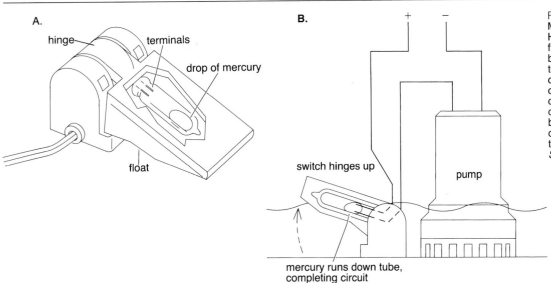

Figures 12-30A and B. Mercury float switches: How they work. A rise in fluid level causes the buoyant end of the switch to rise. The electrically conductive mercury contained in the switch cavity flows to the bottom of the switch, where it bridges two terminals, completing the circuit, and turning on the pump. *(Jim Sollers)*

others have found, a relatively small piece of trash caught in the hinge can jam the switch in either the "off" or "on" position. Some switches include a cover to keep debris away from the switch, but since the cover must have holes to allow the free flow of water, this can be only a partial solution to the problem.

The Ultimate switch. The Ultimate switch (Ultra Safety Systems, Riviera Beach, FL) is the most foolproof float switch on the market. It consists of a perforated cylinder with a magnetized float riding loosely on a central column. Rising fluid level lifts the float until its magnet triggers a sealed switch in the top of the unit. These switches are very rugged and reliable and have no immersed electrical components, but are also bulky and expensive.

Air switches. An air switch has a bell housing that is installed with the open end facing down (Figures 12-31A and B). A length of tubing connects the top of the housing to a diaphragm within a separate switch housing. Rising water in the bilge first closes off the bottom of the bell housing, trapping the air within it, and then raises the air pressure within the housing. This in turn moves the diaphragm to operate the switch (this is the same mechanism that is used for setting the level switch on a washing machine).

The clear advantages of such a system are that there is no electrical wiring in the bilge and that there are no moving parts in the bilge to jam or break. But there are drawbacks. Once again, the range between "on" and "off" is quite narrow (less than 2 inches) and the unit must be installed on the same fore-and-aft axis as the pump. In turbulent conditions water sloshing around the bilge can displace the air in the bell housing with the result that the switch is not activated until the water level is higher than normal; if the tubing from the bell housing to the switch has *any dips at any angle of heel* water can gather at the low spot, effectively blocking the action of the switch; if the tubing gets kinked or crushed or holed, the switch will fail to operate; and if there is a long run of tubing, changes in the ambient temperature will affect the response of the switch (higher bilge level in cold weather; lower in hot).

Electronic switches. An electronic switch avoids many of the problems with float and air switches but introduces new ones of its own!

Conductivity sensors. The traditional type has two stainless steel sensors mounted a small distance apart. If the water level rises to the level of the sensors it forms a circuit between them that activates the bilge pump switch. When the water level falls below the sensors, the circuit is broken, opening the switch. This seems straightforward enough, but in real life the conductivity of the liquids the sensors are likely to encounter varies widely, which causes difficulties. Fresh water, particularly clean rainwater, has a very low conductivity, whereas salt water, especially dirty salt water, is highly conductive; oil is nonconductive whereas some bilge cleaners are not only quite conductive but will also form a slimy film across the sensors.

Figure 12-31A and B. Pneumatic level switches: how they work. When the fluid level rises, air trapped in the bell housing is pressurized and pushes in the diaphragm. This closes the switch points and completes the circuit, turning on the pump. *(Jim Sollers)*

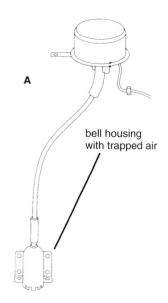

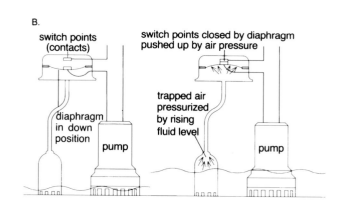

If the sensor circuitry is set to react to fresh water, the switch may well end up staying permanently "on" when coated with bilge cleaner. On the other hand, if the sensitivity is reduced, a coating of oil may add enough resistance to cause the switch to stay permanently "off." A Teflon coating on some sensors helps to reduce the extent to which various contaminants can adhere to the sensors, improving reliability, but even so, a balance still has to be struck in terms of sensitivity settings. If the sensors are not kept reasonably clean, the switch may malfunction.

Light-activated switches. Instead of measuring conductivity, some newer electronic sensors use a beam of light to detect the presence of fluids (Index Marine, Blandford, Dorset, England). In a typical unit the sensor emits a short pulse of light at timed intervals (e.g., every 30 seconds). In the absence of fluid the light is reflected back by a special lens and the system remains quiescent. When the lens is covered by fluid the light is refracted through the fluid, which triggers the control unit into activating the pump. These sensors will work in just about any fluid, including heavily contaminated oil. Depending on the complexity of a system, multiple sensors can be used to operate more than one pump, or to sound a high-bilge-level alarm, and so on.

Time delays. Assuming functioning electronic sensors, it is no good having the pump come on the second the sensors detect fluid. For one thing, the level would immediately drop, turning the pump back off, causing the pump to cycle frequently at short intervals, and for another, any surging of the water in the bilge would cause the switch to repeatedly flick "on" and "off." Some sort of a built-in delay is needed. This can be achieved with sensors at different heights, with the higher one activating the circuit and the lower one breaking it. The other way is to program the unit such that a single sensor must be *continuously* immersed for a certain length of time (e.g., 12 seconds) before the switch is activated, with the switch remaining activated for a certain length of time (e.g., 12 seconds once again) after the sensor is no longer immersed.

Current sensors. Recently we have seen the introduction of another kind of electronic switch which tracks fluid levels through the current draw of the bilge pump motor. The sensing unit and the switch are built into the pump itself. There is a timer which turns the pump on at preset intervals (every 2½ minutes in the case of one popular unit). If there is water in the bilge the pump will have to work harder than if there is no water, in which case its current draw will be higher than in the no-load situation. The sensing unit measures the current draw to determine whether to keep the pump running or not. Once it senses a no-load draw, it shuts the pump down.

These *automatic* bilge pumps have certain obvious advantages. Since the sensing unit and switch are built into the pump itself, there is no need for any external switching device, which makes installation simpler and immediately solves all problems with offset switches and fluctuating (surging) water levels. The principal disadvantage is that *the pump is cycling on and off repeatedly whether there is a leak into the bilge or not* (every 2½ minutes is 24 times an hour, 576 times a day, 4,032 times a week, 17,472 times a month, and 209,664 times a year!). This is bound to accelerate pump and switch wear, and will impose an unnecessary drain on the batteries (albeit a small one—for a 12-volt pump rated at 1,100 gph the manufacturer claims a 0.25 amp-hour drain per day). A less obvious problem, but perhaps more serious, is that *if the pump impeller develops an increased resistance to movement (such as might happen with pet hairs wrapped around the impeller or some other obstruction), the sensor will interpret this as water in the bilge and keep the pump running constantly. It won't take long to flatten a battery.*

Choosing a switch. The plethora of switches on the market is testimony to the fact that no one type has been found to be universally satisfactory for bilge-pumping applications. However, one general point is clear: *To put an expensive boat in the hands of a cheap float switch is foolhardy.*

The better-quality float switches are pretty reliable, especially if the bilges are kept clean, and the Ultimate is just about foolproof. Properly installed, the air switches work well, but tubing runs should be kept *short, vertical, and protected.* The conductivity sensors should be used in a bilge that is kept clean *without the use of bilge cleaners.* The light-activated switches may turn out to be the most reliable and versatile of all, but it is early days to render an opinion. The current-sensing switches seem to me to be a misconceived idea, but that's just an opinion!

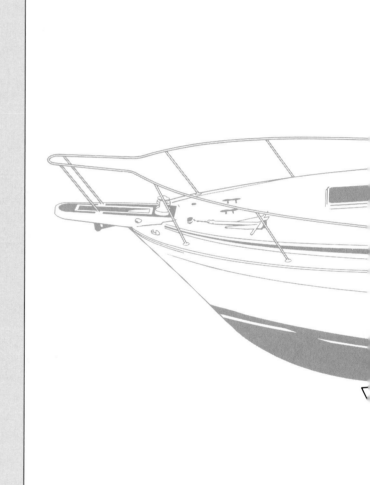

CHAPTER 13

Figure 13-1. Types of steering and self-steering systems are as diverse as types of boats, but all follow logical installation and maintenance procedures. *(Jim Sollers)*

(1) wind vane self-steering
(2) rudder
(3) pedestal
(4) wheel
(5) autopilot
(6) hydraulic steering station with integral pump
(7) check valve
(8) hydraulic reservoir
(9) steering cylinder

Steering Systems, Autopilots, and Wind Vanes

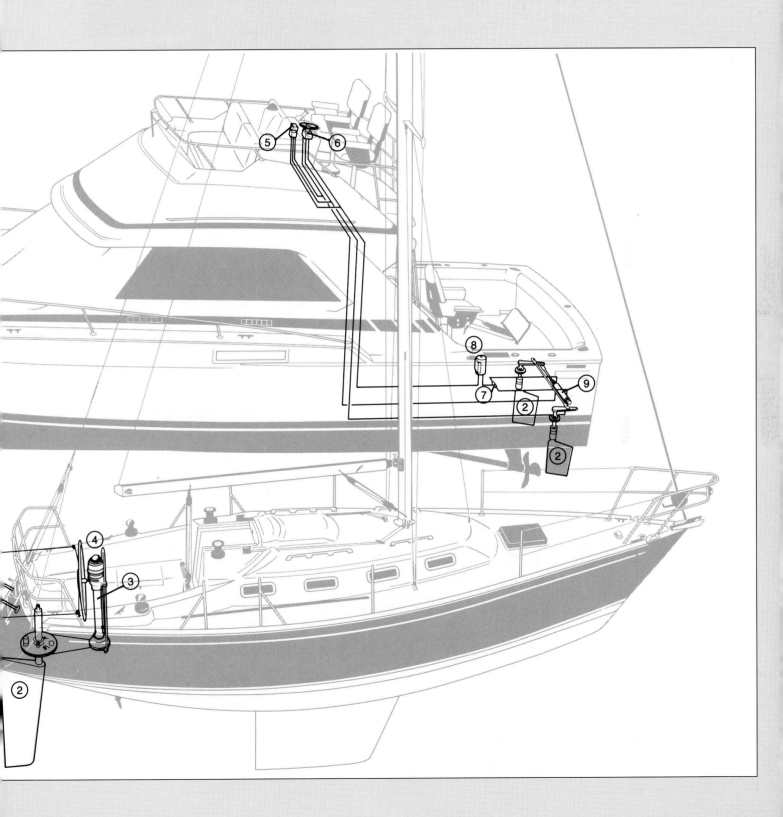

Steering Systems

Types of Steering

It used to be that most rudders were hinged either to the stern of the boat and a full-length keel (aft-hung rudders—Figures 13-2A and B) or else underneath the boat to the trailing edge of a shorter keel or separate skeg (or half skeg—Figure 13-2C). The hinge used is known as a *gudgeon* (the strap part or socket) and *pintle* (the hinge pin—Figure 13-2D). At the base of the rudder is a *heel* bearing to support the weight of the rudder (Figure 13-2E).

A rudder hinged by its forward edge is *unbalanced*. When it is turned, the force of the water acting on it is all in one direction. Pivoting a rudder at a point set back from its forward face counterbalances the forces and makes the rudder much easier to turn. Such *balanced* rudders are popular. On sailboats a balanced rudder commonly appears with a fin keel that is set well forward; the skeg is dispensed with, and the rudder—a *spade* rudder—is simply suspended beneath the boat (Figure 13-2F). This is also the typical way of mounting a powerboat rudder.

Most aft-hung rudders are extended above deck level with a reinforcing pad on either side (*cheek blocks*) and a tiller slotted between the pads. Most other rudders have a hollow or solid pipe (the *rudderstock* or *post*) with a framework

Figure 13-2A. **A transom-mounted (outboard) rudder.**

Figure 13-2B. **A full-skeg rudder.**

Figure 13-2C. **A half-skeg rudder.**

welded or bonded to it (the *web*), around which the rudder is built.

Where a rudderstock enters a boat there is a bearing, and at the top of the stock another bearing. In order to prevent the entry of seawater around the stock, either a seal is placed on top of the lower bearing or the bearing and stock are contained inside a pipe (the *bearing tube*), which is sealed into the bottom of the boat. This bearing tube generally rises above water level to the second bearing. There may or may not be a seal on top of the second bearing, depending on its relationship to the boat's waterline.

There are a number of different methods used to turn rudders, some of the most popular being:

Tiller steering. A piece of wood simply slots in between the cheek blocks on aft-hung rudders or between two metal straps attached to the head of the rudderstock (Figure 13-3A). For maximum strength, it is important that the tiller be constructed of straight-grained wood, or better still, laminated of several thin layers of wood.

All other steering configurations use a wheel.

Rack-and-pinion steering. The steering wheel is keyed to a shaft (drive shaft) on the other end of which is a beveled gear (the *pinion*). This gear engages a circular bevel-geared *quadrant* (the *rack*), which is fastened to the rudderstock and turns the rudder (Figure 13-3B). There is generally a universal joint between the wheel and the quadrant.

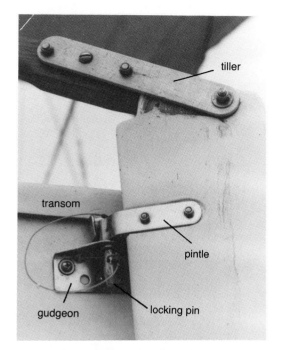

Figure 13-2D. **Gudgeon and pintle.**

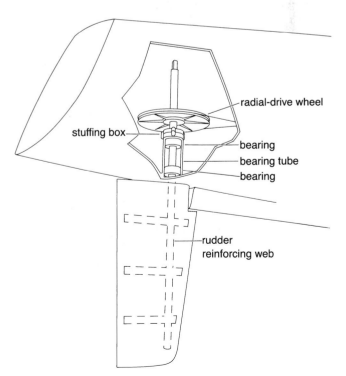

Figure 13-2F. **A typical spade rudder.** *(Jim Sollers)*

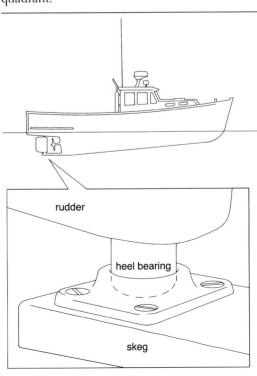

Figure 13-2E. **Heel bearing arrangement.** *(Jim Sollers)*

Figure 13-3A. There are even more ways to control rudders than there are types of rudders. This tiller installation shows a support ring to accept the weight of the rudder.

support ring

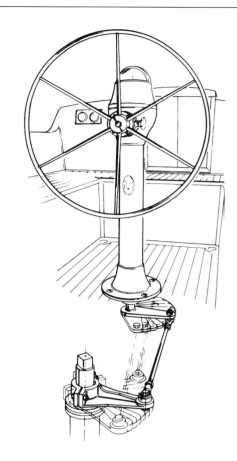

Figure 13-3B. (**Right and below**) Mechanical-linkage wheel steerers, although not inexpensive, are easily maintained and provide positive steering action. Shown here is rack-and-pinion steering.

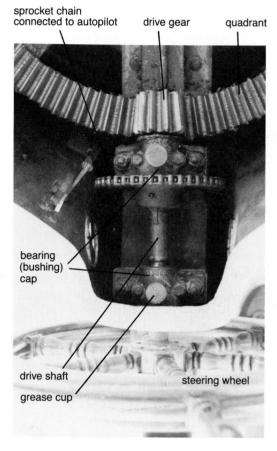

sprocket chain connected to autopilot   drive gear   quadrant

bearing (bushing) cap

drive shaft

grease cup

steering wheel

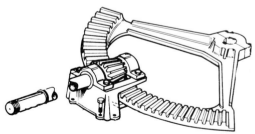

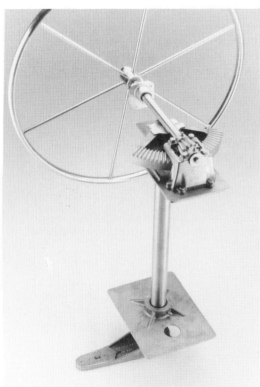

Figure 13-3C. (**Top**) Rack-and-pinion, pedestal-drive steering. (*Whitlock Marine*); photo shows a similar pedestal arrangement. (*Tim Sylvia, Edson International*)

Steering Systems, Autopilots, and Wind Vanes

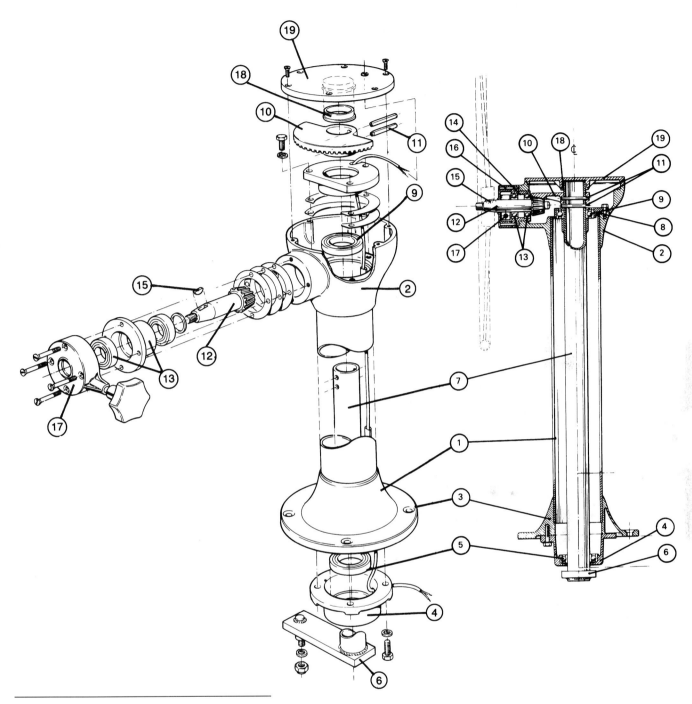

Rack and pinion: pedestal options. Traditional rack-and-pinion steering has to be set up close to, and at roughly the same height as, the rudderhead. In order to make the use of a pedestal possible, another *dummy* ruddershaft is set up in the pedestal. The steering wheel, drive shaft, and rack-and-pinion gear are mounted to the top of this dummy shaft just as in a traditional rack-and-pinion setup. An output lever keyed to the bottom of the dummy shaft is connected by a solid rod to a second lever on the ruddershaft (Figures 13-3C, D, and E).

Figure 13-3D. An exploded view of the steering pedestal from a rack-and-pinion steering system. 1. Pedestal tube. 2. Pedestal bowl. 3. Pedestal base. 4. Lower bearing housing. 5. Sealed ball bearing. 6. Output lever. 7. Down-tube assembly. 8. Output socket. 9. Sealed ball bearing. 10. Gear quadrant. 11. Pin. 12. Input pinion. 13. Sealed ball bearing. 14. Input socket. 15. Woodruff key. 16. Brake cover. 17. Brake clamp assembly. 18. Top cover bearing. 19. Top cover. *(Whitlock Marine)*

Figure 13-3E. For large boats and boats with power-assisted steering, a bevel box such as this often replaces the rack-and-pinion pedestal shown in Figure 13-3D. *(Whitlock Marine)*

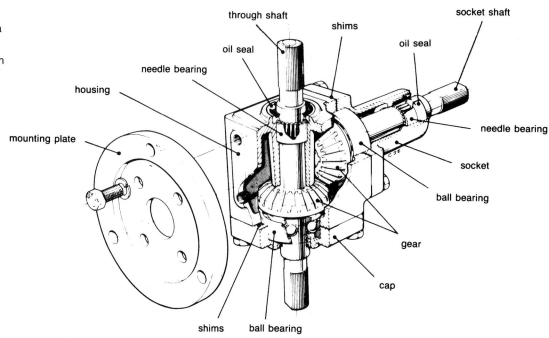

through shaft

shims

socket shaft

oil seal

oil seal

needle bearing

housing

needle bearing

mounting plate

socket

ball bearing

gear

cap

shims   ball bearing

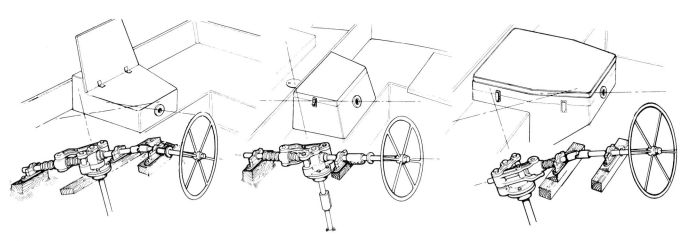

Figure 13-3F. Three different configurations of a worm-drive pedestal steering mechanism. The unit can be adapted to a variety of boats by the use of U-joints. Should the worm seize in operation, the steerer can be unbolted from the rudderhead and the emergency tiller substituted. *(Edson International)*

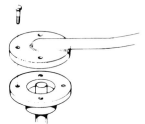

emergency steering tiller

Another type of rack-and-pinion pedestal assembly is sometimes used, with a nonbeveled pinion and a straight, rather than circular, rack. The wheel turns a sprocket. An *endless* roller chain (joined at both ends like a bicycle chain) turns a second sprocket in the base of the unit. This sprocket drives the pinion gear, moving the rack. The rack turns the rudder via a solid link and lever arm.

Worm-drive steering. The drive shaft has a *worm gear* fastened along it. A *traversing nut* rides up and down the worm gear, connected to the rudderhead by various linkages (Figure 13-3F). Moving the traversing nut turns the rudder.

Cable steering. The wheel turns a sprocket, driving a length of roller chain, to which wire cables are attached at each end (Figure 13-4A). There are two methods of running these cables to the rudderhead: open-cable steering uses a series of sheaves (pulley blocks—Figures 13-4B and C); *pull-pull* steering uses enclosed cable conduits (Figures 13-4D and E). Some systems combine both. Open-cable steering is best where there is a

clear cable run from the pedestal to the rudderhead (e.g., aft-cockpit boats); pull-pull works better where there are complex routing problems (e.g., center-cockpit boats). On smaller boats the two cables of a pull-pull system are sometimes replaced with a single *push-pull* cable.

At the rudderhead the cables are attached either to a circular fitting (*radial* or *disc-drive steering*—Figure 13-4B) or to a quadrant (Figures 13-4C, D, and E). The determination of which to use is largely a matter of space and accessibility.

Note that radial steering on an aft-cockpit boat

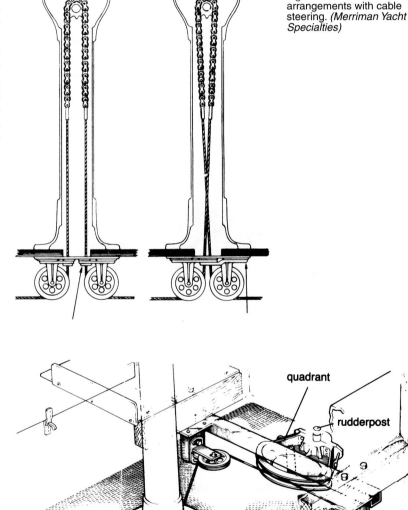

Figure 13-4A. Pedestal arrangements with cable steering. *(Merriman Yacht Specialties)*

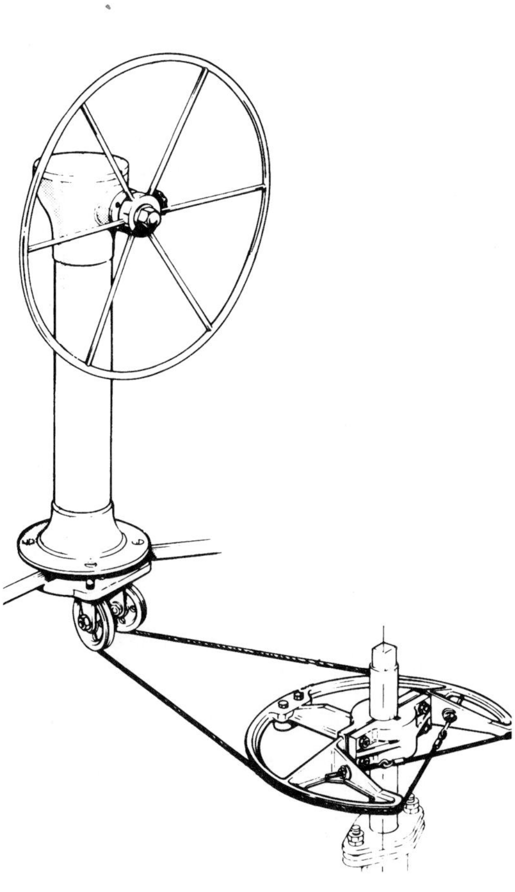

Figure 13-4B. Cable steering using a radial (disc) drive at the rudderhead. *(Whitlock Marine)*

Figure 13-4C. Cable steering using a quadrant at the rudderhead. *(Edson International)*

quadrant

rudderpost

sheave

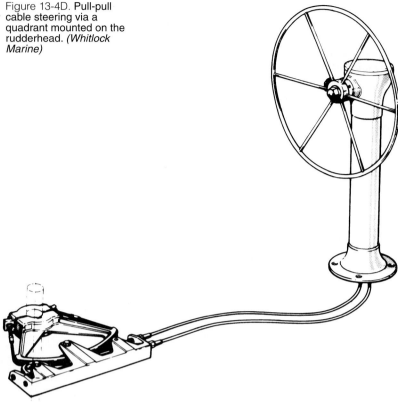

Figure 13-4D. Pull-pull cable steering via a quadrant mounted on the rudderhead. *(Whitlock Marine)*

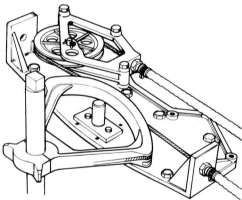

Figure 13-4E. Detail of a quadrant similar to that in Figure 13-4D. *(Edson International)*

eliminates the outboard sheaves that are necessary with the more traditional quadrant steering. This greatly simplifies installation and removes a couple of potential problem areas.

Hydraulic steering. The wheel turns a hydraulic pump, which sends oil under pressure to a hydraulic piston at the rudderhead. This piston turns the rudder via an operating lever on the rudderstock (Figures 13-5A and B). Sometimes the drive shaft on the pump is coupled directly to the steering wheel. At other times the steering wheel turns a sprocket, and an endless (circular) roller chain connects this sprocket to another one on the pump drive shaft.

Maintenance and Troubleshooting

Gudgeons and pintles. At every annual haul-out flex the rudder up and down and from side to side, to check for wear and loose fasteners. If the rudder is fastened with stainless steel gudgeons, *remove it and inspect the pintles closely for any signs of crevice corrosion* (Chapter 4). Many gudgeons ride on Delrin washers—these too need checking and replacing if worn.

Loose fasteners can be a problem with both wood and fiberglass rudders. In wood, if the surrounding area is damaged or rotted, it is best to remove the gudgeon or pintle; drill an oversized hole out to undamaged wood; plug this with epoxy; and then refit the gudgeon or pintle, drilling a new hole for the fastener through the epoxy plug. See Figure 15-5 on page 480 for details.

Most fiberglass rudders have a foam, balsa, or wood core. Entry of water into this core through loose or improperly bedded fasteners, or around loose shafts, can lead to various problems, including delamination, cracking along mold lines, and corrosion of the internal web. If the rudder has become waterlogged it will be necessary to drill a hole in its base and leave it to drain until there is no sign of moisture around the drain hole (this may take weeks) before sealing up the hole and rebedding the fasteners properly with polyurethane caulking (e.g., 3M 5200).

When refitting a rudder be sure to secure it properly. Some have a cotter pin (split pin) through a pintle; others have a threaded pintle with a retaining nut; on a few, one pintle is reversed and must be unbolted to remove and replace the rudder. Be especially careful to lock off nuts. This can be done by tightening two nuts against each other or by using a Nyloc nut, but it is preferable to drill through the pintle and insert a cotter pin.

Rudderstocks, tubes, bearings, and seals. A number of poorly constructed rudders have either inadequate or improperly fastened internal webs. Under a severe load the rudderstock will break loose from the web, causing a complete failure of the rudder. Before this happens the stock may start to twist inside the rudder; failure is imminent. Whenever the boat is hauled, tie off the wheel or tiller and flex the rudder as hard as possible. *If there is any movement between the rudder and rudderstock the rudder must be replaced immediately.* (Note that if water has penetrated a rudder with a stainless steel web, in the de-oxygenated atmosphere inside the rudder corrosion is likely to occur—see Chapter 4; sooner or later the web will fail.)

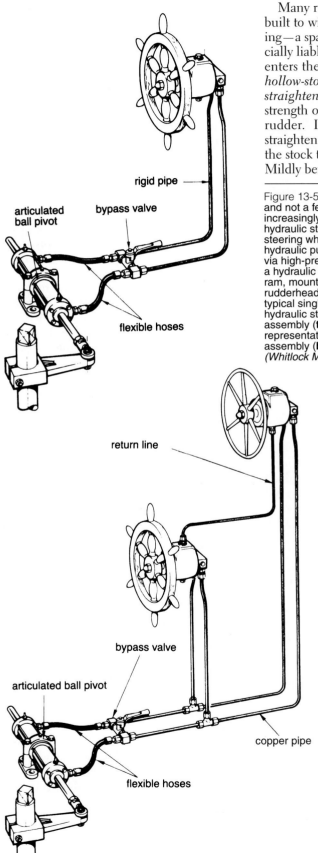

Many rudderstocks are hollow. These are not built to withstand any kind of a serious grounding—a spade rudder with a hollow stock is especially liable to bend at the point where the stock enters the base of the hull (Figure 13-6). *Bent hollow-stock rudders should be replaced, not straightened.* Any straightening reduces the strength of the most highly stressed point of the rudder. If the rudder cannot be replaced, straighten it and insert a second tube down into the stock to reinforce it at the point of the bend. Mildly bent solid stocks can be straightened.

Figure 13-5A. Powerboats, and not a few sailboats, increasingly rely on hydraulic steering. The steering wheel powers a hydraulic pump connected via high-pressure tubing to a hydraulic cylinder, or ram, mounted at the rudderhead. This is a typical single-station hydraulic steering assembly (**top**); and a representative dual-station assembly (**bottom**). *(Whitlock Marine)*

Figure 13-5B. A hydraulic steering system designed for use with pedestal steering. *(Merriman Yacht Specialties)*

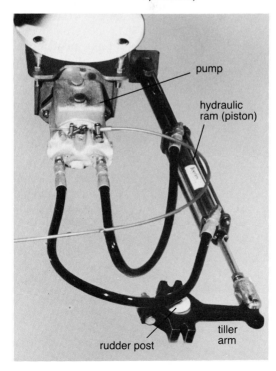

Figure 13-6. Bent (**left**) and broken spade rudders. Their unsupported heels and unprotected leading edges make this type of rudder particularly susceptible to damage.

Bearings. The bearings on smaller boats generally consist of a plastic bushing (Delrin, etc.). On larger boats various roller bearings are used. More recently, self-aligning bearings have become quite common (Tides Marine, Deerfield Beach, FL, and others). These have a plastic bushing riding in an outer case in such a way as to permit considerable rudder stock misalignment or flexing—a highly desirable feature. During a haulout, if the rudder flexing described above reveals more than minimal play, *the bearings need replacing.* (Should they be left and fail in a seaway the rudder will start banging around quite violently and do a considerable amount of damage. If this cracks or breaks the bearing tube, it could even sink the boat.)

Some plastics swell in salt water (Delrin, and especially nylon, suffer from this problem). Dimensional changes of up to 6% have been responsible for a number of seized or tight systems. If the steering on a new boat becomes stiff, *break the cables loose at the rudderhead and turn the rudder. If it is binding, the bearings probably need reaming.*

Two materials that have zero water absorption are PTFE (Teflon) and UHMWPE (ultrahigh molecular-weight polyethylene). PTFE is far too soft for bearing use and has a very low compressive strength in its natural state; therefore it is normally combined with copper or fiberglass. UHMWPE is now readily available from plastics distributors, has zero water absorption, a very low coefficient of friction, and a high compressive strength, making it one of the best materials for bearing use (it is used in all the Tides Marine bearings).

Bearing tubes. Most bearing tubes are fiber-

glass pipes bonded into the base of the hull. The lower bearing (bushing) is pushed up from below and held with either a couple of setscrews or a bead of sealing compound *around its base* (3M 5200 caulk or similar). Do not put caulking up *inside* the bearing tube as it will make later bearing removal very difficult. The bearing tube may terminate in a seal (Figure 13-7A) or be carried up and bonded to the underside of the deck (Figure 13-7B).

The upper bearing (bushing) not only absorbs sideways loading but also holds the weight of the rudder in spade rudder installations (Figure 13-7B again). Either a collar or the rudderhead fitting (quadrant, radial-drive wheel or disc, or tiller strap fitting) rests on the bearing and keeps the rudder in the boat. *Note that loosening this fitting may allow the rudder to fall out of the bottom of the boat, so be warned!*

The bearing-tube-to-hull joint is critical. If it should fail, the boat is in danger of sinking. Bearing tubes in fiberglass hulls are bonded fiberglass; in steel and aluminum hulls they are welded pipes. Inspect the joint annually for any signs of cracking.

Repairing a fiberglass tube:

1. Clean and abrade the hull for 4 to 6 inches (100 to 150 mm) around the bearing tube and up its sides. Be sure to remove all traces of paint, gelcoat, and dirt. Abrade the surface of the fiberglass with a coarse sander. Liberally swab the area with acetone. (Note: Acetone fumes are powerful; if working in confined spaces, ensure adequate ventilation.)

2. If the tube-to-hull joint has a tight radius, this is probably why it is cracking. Fair it out with a paste made from catalyzed polyester resin and a filler such as microballoons or talc. (Prefilled putties are available from chandleries.) In a pinch, use talcum powder for a filler. Cut a piece of stiff cardboard to the desired curvature (in profile) and use this to shave off the excess putty and impart a smooth finish. Practice on a scrap piece before applying the putty to the boat.

3. Fiberglass *cloth* is easier to work into compound curves than either mat or woven rovings, and pound for pound is also stronger. However, it is best laid up over a layer of mat, which holds more resin. This helps to fill in any air spaces in the cloth and provides a better bond with the existing laminate. Cut the mat and cloth into manageable strips (say 3 inches wide by 8 inches long, or 75 mm by 200 mm). When laying up the strips, use a disposable brush to apply the resin, *saturating*

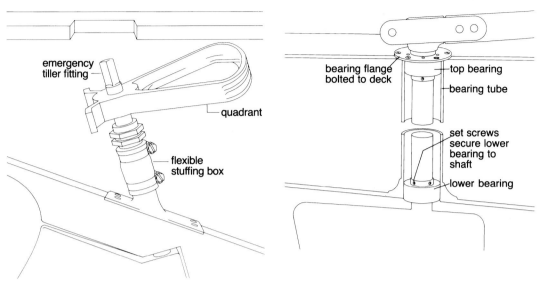

Figure 13-7A. (**Left**) Typical arrangement for wheel steering without a top bearing on the rudderstock. *(Jim Sollers)*

Figure 13-7B. (**Right**) Typical support bearings for a rudderstock with a top bearing. *(Jim Sollers)*

emergency
tiller fitting

quadrant

flexible
stuffing box

bearing flange
bolted to deck — top bearing

— bearing tube

set screws
secure lower
bearing to
shaft

— lower bearing

the mat or cloth and mopping up excess later. The fiberglass becomes completely transparent when fully saturated.

4. Try to lay up successive layers of fiberglass before earlier layers have completely gelled. Stagger all joints to avoid any *hard* edges, which will concentrate stresses. If you lay up more than one layer, use alternate layers of mat and cloth and cut the successive layers longer so that the top layer of cloth makes a smooth transition to the hull and tube sides.

Note that polyester resin is normally used on fiberglass because it does the job and is relatively cheap. Various epoxies, however, will provide a better bond to old fiberglass, and make a stronger and more flexible repair.

Seals. See the section on Shaft Seals in Chapter 9.

Rudderhead fittings. The rudderhead fitting is subjected to tremendous loads from time to time, notably when the rudder is slammed around in heavy seas. Should any play develop between the rudderhead fitting and rudderstock, the movement of the rudder will ceaselessly work away at this weakness until something fails. At the annual haulout, when flexing the rudder with the tiller or wheel tied off, check closely for any play. *Any play at all is unacceptable.*

Rudderhead fittings are clamped to rudderstocks and locked with keys, setscrews, or through-bolts. A key is a length of square metal that fits in matching slots machined in the rudderstock and rudderhead clamp (Figure 13-8). Keys both here and elsewhere in the steering system *must be stainless steel and not brass*, since

brass will not only dezincify and fail, but also cause galvanic corrosion on aluminum quadrants and discs (radial-drive wheels), causing them to fail. (Note that aluminum rudderhead fittings should be used only on aluminum and stainless steel ruddershafts, and never on bronze.) Set screws are frequently threaded into the rudderhead clamp and seated in dimples in the shaft. This is not adequate. It is far better to drill out and tap (thread) the seat in the shaft so that the set screw will positively screw into the shaft. This way the screws cannot slip. Be sure to use some locking compound on the screws so that they cannot work their way out (e.g., Loctite).

Many rudderhead fittings on hollow stocks are through-bolted. If the bolt holes become stretched (elongated), allowing some movement of the bolt, drill out the holes and fit a larger-diameter bolt. Do not take this too far since the loss of metal will weaken the clamp and shaft.

A loose rudderhead clamp can be tightened up either by wrapping a thin piece of galvanically compatible metal around the shaft beneath the clamp or by filing a small amount off the clamp faces so that the clamp pulls up tighter.

Once again, remember that the rudderhead clamp may be the only thing holding a spade rudder in the boat. Before loosening it, *secure the rudder!* (If there is room to fit a hose clamp around the shaft somewhere else, do so as a security measure in case the rudderhead fitting ever slips.)

Rack and pinion (mounted on rudderstock). Rack-and-pinion steering is just about foolproof. The critical factors are to keep the drive shaft at 90 degrees to the quadrant and to keep the quadrant and pinion gears closed up so that the teeth cannot jump. Where the wheel is not mounted

Troubleshooting Chart 13-1.
Wheel Steering Failures: Rack-and-Pinion.

Does the drive shaft turn when the wheel is turned? **YES** ⬇	**NO** ➡ Check for a disengaged clutch or slipping wheel (loose and/or sheared off key).
Does the rack-and-pinion gear turn when the shaft turns? **YES** ⬇	**NO** ➡ Check for a sheared pin locking the rack-and-pinion gear to its shaft, or a slipping universal joint (if fitted). Repair as necessary.
Does the quadrant turn when the gear turns? **YES** ⬇	**NO** ➡ Check for a jumping or stripped gear. Close up the clearance between the gear and quadrant.
Does the rudderstock turn when the quadrant turns? **YES** ⬇	**NO** ➡ The quadrant clamp is slipping on the rudderstock. Tighten or replace bolts and set screws or shim as necessary.
The internal webs in the rudder itself have sheared. Rig a jury rudder. On sailboats, balance the rig.	

bracket has a *contact arm* on which the quadrant rests, worn pinion and quadrant gears can be temporarily closed up by *shimming* the contact arm (sliding a piece of thin metal between it and the quadrant).

The mounting bracket for the pinion gear takes *all* the steering loads—check its fasteners carefully at the annual inspection. Lubricate any universal joint and check for play in the joint, its keyways, or the pins locking it to its shafts. Note that many universal joints are steel and not stainless steel. These should be covered with a grease-filled rubber boot (obtainable from large tool supply houses). In the absence of a boot, grease the universal joint and wrap a length of inner tubing around it, securing the tubing with two stainless steel hose clamps.

Rack and pinion (pedestal type). The top plate and input socket screws (Figure 13-3D) tend to freeze if not removed annually, cleaned, and refitted, preferably with an antiseize compound (Tefgel and Duralac are two good brands).

The fit of the rack-and-pinion gears is adjusted at the factory by placing shims (thin metal spacers) under the face of the pedestal input and output sockets. Any wear that takes place can be removed by taking away a shim *from the input socket only*. This will close up the gears, eliminating play.

Some (older) pedestals use needle bearings (Figure 13-3E) on the output shaft. These will need greasing annually and even when properly maintained have been found to lead to premature wear of the shaft and bearing. Other (newer) pedestals use sealed carbon steel ball bearings, which are essentially maintenance-free. These are liberally coated with a water-repellent grease on assembly to prevent corrosion, but should still be inspected annually for any signs of rust,

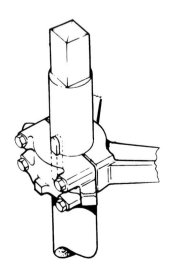

Figure 13-8. Variations on a rudderhead fitting theme. (**Left**) Keyway machined into rudderstock and quadrant. (**Center**) Through-bolted, using a high-tensile bolt. (**Right**) Drilled and pinned, using a high-tensile peg. Because of the potential for extreme point loading at the end of the peg, this method is not recommended. *(Whitlock Marine)*

at a right angle to the quadrant, a universal joint will be fitted to the shaft.

The pinion gear is generally supported in a couple of bronze bushings, which will need lubricating two or three times a season. Some have grease cups or fittings for this purpose (use Teflon-based waterproof grease); if not, engine oil will do. The gears and rack need greasing. The pinion-gear-to-quadrant clearance can often be adjusted by loosening the quadrant clamps on the rudderstock and moving the quadrant slightly up and down its keyway (this *cannot* be done with setscrews or through-bolts on hollow shafts). If the pinion gear mounting

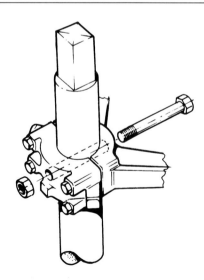

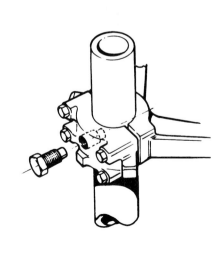

which, if present, should occasion cleaning and recoating.

A lack of rudderstops (see Rudderstops on page 440) and/or incorrect installation of the output lever, operating linkage, and tiller arm will sometimes allow the linkage to come close to, or actually *cam over* center; in the latter event steering reverses! This results in excessive loads on pedestal and rudder bearings and on the linkage. Check to see that *with the rudder straight ahead, the pinion is centered on the rack, and the output lever and tiller arm are both at right angles to the rudder.*

Worm steering. Most of the same considerations apply as above. The wheel must be at 90 degrees to the rudderhead, or else a universal joint is needed. The worm gear and traversing nut need greasing two or three times a year. Worm gears are frequently steel (not bronze). Without adequate and regular greasing they will freeze solid when not in use and prove very hard to free. There are also a number of links, hinge pins, and clevis pins, all of which need lubricating (with engine oil), and probably a central grease fitting on the top of the shaft assembly.

In time, wear between the worm gear and traversing nut and in the various hinges will allow the rudder to rock ceaselessly from side to side, especially at anchor, accelerating the rate of wear. The traversing nut normally has relatively soft threads of babbitt (the white metal found in many bearings), and is designed to wear, thus protecting the worm gear. The threads are renewable at the factory. The various links and clevis pins will need rebushing and renewing as necessary.

Correct alignment on a worm steerer is critical to smooth operation and long life. Once a year separate the two coupling halves at the rudderhead and check the alignment just as for a propeller shaft (Chapter 9).

Troubleshooting Chart 13-2.
Wheel Steering Failures: Cable and Pull-Pull.

Do the cables at the base of the pedestal move when the wheel is turned? **YES** ↓	**NO** ▶ Check for a disengaged clutch, slipping wheel or sprocket, stripped sprocket teeth, or a jumped chain. Repair as necessary.
Does the quadrant (or wheel) turn at the rudderhead when the steering wheel is turned? **YES** ↓	**NO** ▶ **FIX:** Check for broken or jumped cables between the pedestal and rudderhead.
Does the rudderstock turn when the quadrant (or wheel) turns? **YES** ↓	**NO** ▶ The quadrant clamp is slipping on the rudderstock. Tighten or replace bolts and set screws or shim as necessary.

The internal webs in the rudder itself have sheared. Rig a jury rudder. On sailboats, balance the rig.

Cable steering. Galvanized, brass, bronze, aluminum, and plastic sheaves are all in use on cable steering systems. The metal sheaves generally have bronze bushings running on stainless steel or brass shafts, though some have stainless steel needle bearings. There is an obvious potential for galvanic interaction; thus it is important to keep the sheaves clean and lubricated. Use engine oil two to three times a season and at the winter haulout.

Plastic sheaves have plastic bearings; the better ones also incorporate extra ball races to absorb side loading. These bearings do not corrode and need no lubrication, although they will attract dirt and thus need flushing with fresh water periodically.

Once a year slack off the cables and check all sheaves to make sure they are free-spinning without excessive play. Replace sheaves and shafts as necessary.

Table 13-1. Wire Rope and Roller Chain Breaking Strengths[1]

Size		Stainless Steel Wire Rope			Stainless Steel Roller Chain	
Inches	MM	Pounds	Kilograms	#	Pounds	Kilograms
3/16	4.76	2,827	1,285	—	—	—
7/32	5.56	3,857	1,753	—	—	—
1/4	6.35	5,031	2,287	—	—	—
5/16	8.00	7,986	3,630	—	—	—
3/8	9.53	11,330	5,150	—	—	—
7/16	11.00	—	—	—	—	—
1/2	12.70	—	—	40	3,000	—
5/8	16.00	—	—	50	4,700	—
3/4	19.00	—	—	60	6,750	—
1	26.00	—	—	80	—	—

1. Wire strengths are those given in Norseman tables. Other companies differ somewhat.

Mounting and aligning sheaves. Sheaves are sometimes subjected to tremendous loads. All sheaves must be rigidly mounted so that no movement that causes loss of cable tension or alignment can occur. *Screws are not acceptable;* the sheave mounting plate should always be through-bolted. Annually, or before a trip, check all fasteners to make sure they are tight and that the bolt holes are not elongating.

The two final sheaves leading the cables onto a steering quadrant take the highest loads of all. These are normally incorporated into one solid fixture, but if they are mounted independently on either side of the quadrant a rigid brace should be placed between the two bulkheads to which they are fastened (Figure 13-9A).

Accurate alignment of sheaves, rudderhead fittings, and the final lead-in of push-pull and pull-pull cables to a rudderhead fitting is essential to minimize binding, cable wear, and the risk that a cable will jump off a sheave. Most sheaves have adjustable bases (Figures 13-9A and B); some are self-aligning. As an alignment check, a length of doweling placed in one sheave groove should drop cleanly into the next. When the system is all set up put the wheel hard over from port to starboard, observing all sheaves, etc. Sometimes with angled rudderstocks and sheaves, some surprising and unexpected changes in alignment can occur. Take the boat out under full engine power and have someone observe all the sheaves and other system components while the rudder is thrown hard over and back a few times. This should reveal any weaknesses.

Cables. Stainless steel 7 × 19 cables are used universally; 1 × 19 cable is not flexible enough to withstand the constant bending around sheaves, discs, quadrants, etc. The cable needs lubricating: When oiling the sheaves (two or three times a season) soak a rag in the same oil (engine oil) and rub it along the whole length of the cables. If this reveals even one *fish hook* (broken strand of wire), *the cables need replacing.* They should, in any case, be replaced routinely every few years, and a spare set—perhaps an old set taken out of service—should be kept on board.

Wear on cables is greatly accelerated if they are forced through too tight a radius. For example, $^3/_{16}$-inch (approximately 4-mm) cable should have sheaves with a *minimum* diameter of 4 inches; $^1/_4$-inch (6-mm) cable, 6 inches. This gives a ratio of cable diameter to sheave diameter of a little over *1 to 20.* Push-pull and pull-pull cable conduit should never be turned through a radius of less than *8 inches. The fewest possible number of bends and sheaves should be used in routing cables.* If a sheave ever freezes up, inspect the cable closely where it has been dragging over the sheave.

Tension. Cable tension needs to be checked regularly. How frequently depends on the type of steering (open-cable or pull-pull), the length of the steering run, and the amount of boat usage. Six to twelve times a season would not be unreasonable on heavily used open-cable systems. If tension is loose, the steering will be sloppy, with a risk of cables jumping off sheaves and rudder-

Figure 13-9A. To provide troublefree service, open-cable steering must be designed carefully. The sheaves must be mounted rigidly and aligned accurately with one another. Alignment can be checked by laying a thin steel rod in the grooves of two connecting sheaves; the rod should lie absolutely fair. A solid brace should be used between the last pair of sheaves before the rudderhead. The tremendous forces generated can easily collapse sheave-bearing bulkheads in heavy-weather conditions. *(Jim Sollers)*

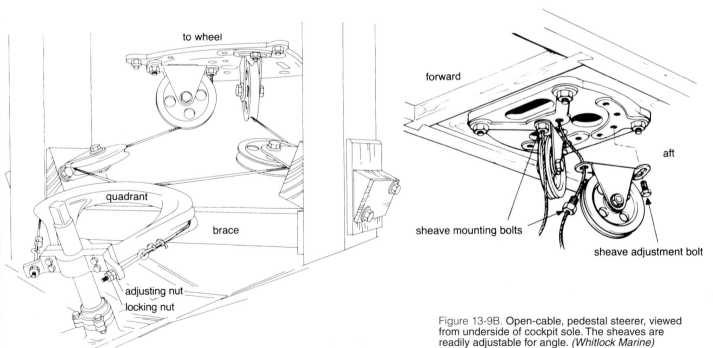

Figure 13-9B. Open-cable, pedestal steerer, viewed from underside of cockpit sole. The sheaves are readily adjustable for angle. *(Whitlock Marine)*

head fittings; too tight and the steering will be stiff, with greatly accelerated wear.

With the wheel tied off, it should not be possible to turn the rudderhead fitting by grasping it and applying torque. As a general rule of thumb for an open-cable system, with moderate finger pressure it should be possible to depress the cable between sheaves 1 inch per foot of cable run, but no more. Because of the inherent friction between cable and conduit in pull-pull systems, cables are kept looser than in open-cable systems; cable tensioners should be only hand tight. A certain amount of slack in the feel of the steering is unavoidable.

Cable adjustments are made at the rudderhead by tightening a tensioning nut on each cable (Figure 13-9A), but first the chain in the pedestal must be centered on its sprocket with the rudder pointing dead ahead. This is hard to check without taking the compass off the top of the binnacle, which should be done in any event once a year to lubricate the pedestal bearings, so this may be a good time to do both.

Before removing a compass make some kind of a mark on the compass and pedestal so that the two can be exactly realigned. Two or three pieces of masking tape stuck across the joint and then slit works well. The compass should be *swung* by a compass adjuster after it is put back, since its characteristics may have changed. (This too should be done annually.)

Some chains have a removable link in the center. If not present, the central link should be determined and identified with a piece of string. Line this up on the center of the sprocket and tie off the wheel. Now adjust the cable tensioners in such a way as to make sure the rudderhead fitting is also centered in the boat. Be sure to lock off the cable adjusting nuts when finished.

Cables in conduits. Pay particular attention to the point where the cables exit the conduits; any misalignment will result in cable and conduit wear. Inspect the conduits closely for any signs of cracking in the jacket, cuts, burned or melted spots, kinks, corrosion under the jacket, or separation of the end fittings from the jacket (Chapter 9). Cables and conduits are not repairable; if any problems exist, replace them both.

Turn the wheel hard over from port to starboard. If any binding, jerking, or stickiness is felt, break the cables loose at the rudderhead and try again. If operation is still rough, the cables probably need replacing (unless there are problems in the pedestal or bulkhead steering; see Wheels, Pedestals and Bulkhead Stations, below).

Once a year remove the cables from their con-

duits and inspect them closely (Figure 13-10A). Refit with a liberal smearing of Teflon-based grease.

Cable-end fittings. Almost all cables terminate in a thimble and two clamps at the rudderhead. Points to check are: the area of the thimble that bears on the cable tensioner; that the cable is snugged up tight around the thimble; that the *saddle* of the cable clamp is over the *standing* part of the cable, and the "U" is over the bitter end (Figure 13-10B); and that the cable clamps are tight.

A variety of fittings can be used at the wheel end for joining cables and chains (Nicopress or Talurit sleeves around thimbles; swaged terminals; etc.—Figure 13-10C). The section on Standing Rigging, Chapter 15 gives points to look for. Remove clevis pins and check for wear; be sure to refit the cotter pins (split pins).

Figure 13-10. Various methods of terminating steering cables.

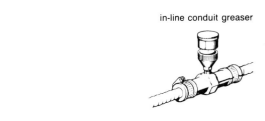

in-line conduit greaser

Figure 13-10A. End fitting used with cables in conduit, commonly used in pull-pull or push-pull steering systems. Less common are in-line conduit greasers, which greatly extend cable life. *(Edson International)*

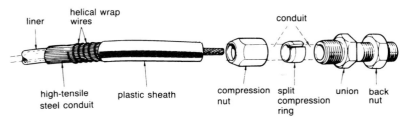

liner helical wrap wires conduit compression nut split compression ring union back nut

high-tensile steel conduit plastic sheath

Conduit-end Compression Fitting

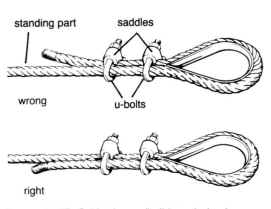

standing part saddles wrong u-bolts right

Figure 13-10B. Cable clamps (bulldog grips): a less elegant, but strong and easily adjusted and repaired end fitting. Make sure the clamp's saddle rests on the standing part of the cable. *(Whitlock Marine)*

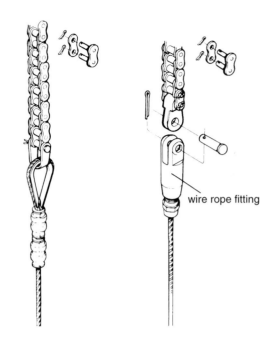

Figure 13-10C. Chain-to-cable connections. On the left, a thimble retained by two compression sleeves (Nicopress, Talurit); on the right, a mechanical end fitting (Norseman, Stalok). *(Edson International)*

wire rope fitting

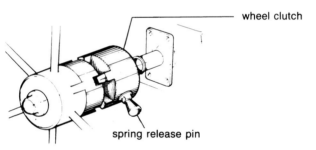

wheel clutch

spring release pin

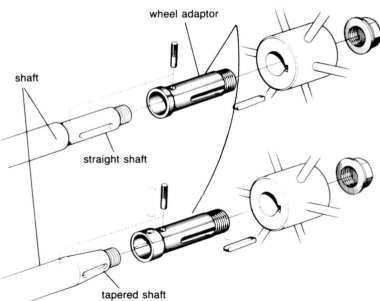

wheel adaptor

shaft

straight shaft

tapered shaft

Figure 13-11. A wheel clutch disengages a wheel from the shaft when an autopilot or another wheel (two-station steering) is in use. Adapters make it possible to install wheels on otherwise incompatible shafts. *(Edson International)*

Wheels, pedestals, and bulkhead stations.

Wheels are keyed to drive shafts and retained with a wheel nut. In some instances, where wheel and shaft do not match, a brass adapter will be fitted between the two. The wheel may or may not have both a clutch and a brake (Figure 13-11).

Clutch units employ a sliding coupling keyed to the drive shaft that can be pushed in and out of engagement with the wheel hub and locked in place with a spring-loaded pin. The wheel is disengaged when certain types of autopilots or a second steering station are in use. Brakes are simply a friction band that clamps around the drive shaft.

Drive shafts run in bronze bushings or needle bearings (Figure 13-12A). The latter are either stainless steel or plastic. A brass or bronze (much preferred) sprocket is keyed to the drive shaft turning a stainless steel chain, except on rack-and-pinion pedestal steering (see previous section).

Clutch hubs, pedestal bearings, and chains all need lubricating at least annually, preferably two or three times a season. The compass will need to be removed from the binnacle (see Tension, above). Engine oil is fine for the clutch where it slides on the drive shaft, and for bronze bushings and chain. Grease should *not* be used on chain since it merely sits on the surface of the links collecting dirt. It *is* used, however, on *stainless steel* needle bearings (Teflon-based waterproof grease, such as Lubriplate A). *Plastic* roller bearings need no lubrication but will benefit from a shot of Teflon spray.

Pedestals are made from various grades of aluminum with different kinds of surface treatment (anodizing, painting, etc.). They merely need washing, and waxing with a good-quality boat or car polish. Pedestals should be tied into the boat's bonding and lightning-protection systems to reduce corrosion and lightning strike hazards (Figure 13-12B).

Trouble spots. Apart from routine wear of all components, galvanic interaction sometimes occurs between stainless steel bearings and aluminum pedestals, causing corrosion and blistering of painted surfaces.

If a bulkhead steerer starts to stiffen up, check the shaft where it passes through the bulkhead; the problem may be nothing more than damp wood swelling and binding on the shaft. In this case, the hole will just need enlarging.

If a rudder is not fitted with rudderstops (see Rudderstops below), or if the rudderstops fail, there is a danger of the chain-to-wire adapters running up onto the sprocket, breaking teeth, damaging adapters, and possibly throwing the

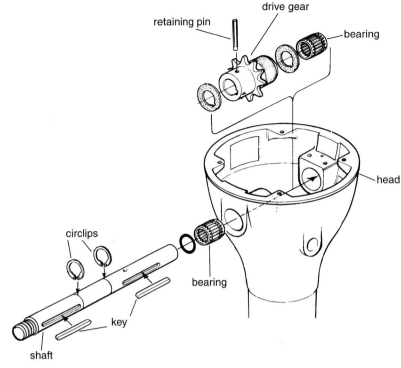

Figure 13-12A. **(Above)** Pedestal with top removed. **(Right)** An exploded view of an open-cable pedestal steerer. *(Merriman Yacht Specialties)*

cable-drive mechanism

chain off the sprocket. Units that have an endless chain driving a second sprocket must be kept tensioned and aligned to stop the chain from jumping off the sprockets; the lower unit will be adjustable.

Pedestal overhaul. Remove the compass, wheel nut, wheel, and clutch (if fitted). Slack off the cables at the rudderhead, lift the chain off the sprocket, and tie it off out of the way. Place some rags in the pedestal to catch any dropped fittings. In most instances the drive shaft is retained in the pedestal solely by the locking pin through the sprocket. Drive this pin out with a hammer and punch (carefully, it may come out only one way). Place a nut back on the shaft and use a block of wood behind the nut to drive the shaft assembly out of the pedestal. Replace worn or broken parts at this time. Reassembly is the reversal of disassembly.

Hydraulic steering. A simple hydraulic system has a single helm station pumping hydraulic fluid to a single steering cylinder. The piston in the cylinder moves a tiller arm fastened to the rudderstock. Sometimes a single helm pump is installed without check valves. In this case, if the rudder is turned (e.g., by a wave hitting it), the wheel will turn. Most pumps, however, incorporate check valves, which prevent the rudder from turning the wheel. Where two or more helm stations or an autopilot are teed into the same hydraulic circuit, check valves are essential to prevent one helm station from *motoring* another, rather than turning the rudder.

A typical check valve assembly's operation is illustrated in Figure 13-13. *All hydraulic steering systems with built-in check valves should have either a manually operated or a solenoid-operated*

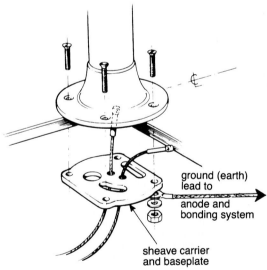

Figure 13-12B. **A** pedestal should be tied into the boat's bonding and lightning-protection system to reduce corrosion and lightning-strike hazards. *(Whitlock Marine)*

bypass valve, as shown in Figure 13-14. In the event of a steering failure the bypass valve is opened, allowing oil to pass freely from one side of the steering cylinder to the other. An emergency tiller can then be installed on the rudderpost and used to steer the boat. (In reality, many systems do not have this bypass valve; in this case, at the very least *the pin that connects the hydraulic cylinder to the rudder arm should be*

Steering Systems 437

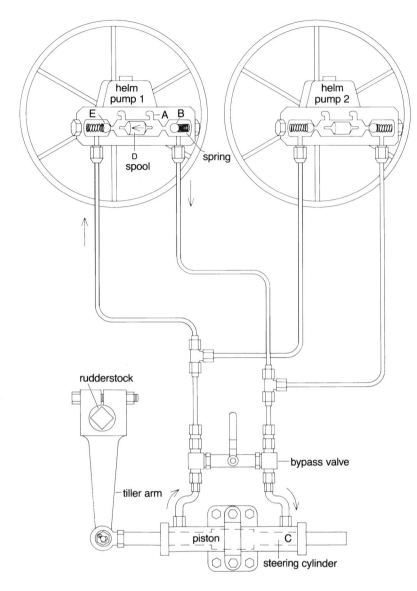

Table 13-2. Hydraulic Oil Recommendations[1]

Manufacturer	ISO 32 Centistokes Grade Mineral-Based Hydraulic Oil
BP	Energol HLP22
Castrol	Hyspin AWS32
Chevron	EP Hydraulic 32, MV, AW Machine 32
Exxon	Nuto H32
Fina	Hydron 32
Gulf	Mechanism LP32, Harmony AW32, Harmony HVI36
Mobil	DTE24, DTE13
Shell	Tellus Oil T32, Tellus Oil 32, Tellus Oil T37, Tellus Oil 37
Texaco	Rondo 32, HD 32, Rondo HDAZ

1. Do not use brake fluid.

both accessible and of a type that can be released quickly, freeing up the rudder.)

Routine maintenance. If the pump is chain driven, check the alignment and tension on the chain every three or four months. Raise or lower the pump on its mount to adjust tension. Pumps are best installed with chain sprockets in a vertical plane; if they are not, loose chains tend to work their way off.

The oil level in pump reservoirs should also be checked every three or four months, and topped up as necessary. *Hydraulic systems are extremely sensitive to dirt; before removing any filler plugs, scrupulously clean the external surfaces of the pump.* If any oil has been lost, check all connections, seals, hoses, and lines. Make sure there is no chafing where hoses and lines pass through bulkheads.

Where two or more helm stations (or an autopilot) are teed into the same hydraulic circuit, the normal practice is to tie all the pump reservoirs together. A line is run from the fill plug on the lowest pump to the drain plug on the next highest, etc. The whole system is topped up via *the fill plug on the highest pump.*

When topping up, use only the specified hydraulic oil; *never use engine oil or brake fluid.* Table 13-2 gives a list of hydraulic oils obtainable worldwide and suitable for most systems. Once a year drain a sample of oil *from the lowest pump* and check for any signs of contamination such as water or dirt. (Moisture can form from condensation in reservoirs—it will cause rust on sensitive valves and spools, leading to failure.) If any moisture or dirt is present, drain the system until only clean oil comes out, and then refill and bleed as necessary (see the following section).

Figure 13-13. (**Above**) The operation of hydraulic steering systems. Imagine the wheel on helm pump 1 is turned clockwise. Oil is pushed down line A; the oil pressure lifts ball valve B off its seat against its spring pressure, and sends oil to piston C. At the same time, the oil pressure moves piston D—the spool—to the left, and the pin on the end of this spool pushes the second ball valve, E, off its seat. This allows return oil from the other side of the steering cylinder back into the helm pump reservoir. The oil pressure pushes both ball valves in the check valve at helm pump 2 against their seats so that no oil flows through the auxiliary steering station. *(Jim Sollers)*

Figure 13-14. (**Below**) Detail of hydraulic steering bypass valve assembly, essential to enable an emergency tiller to be fitted (see page 440). *(Wagner Marine)*

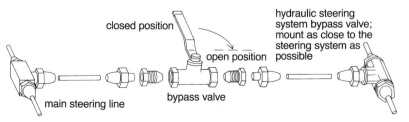

Bleeding a hydraulic system. Oil leaks are the main cause of problems on hydraulic systems. Small leaks can be handled by regular topping up of the reservoir until repairs can be made. However, if any air gets into the system it will cause the steering to feel spongy or even to fail altogether. To test for air, put the wheel hard over in both directions: If it bounces back when released, this is a pretty good indication of trapped air. To remove the air, or after draining and refilling a system, use the following procedure:

1. Fill all pump reservoirs, starting at the lowest (if there is more than one pump) and working to the highest. Replace the fill plugs on the lower reservoirs but leave the upper (or only) one open. Find a length of tubing that will screw into the upper reservoir fill fitting, and a clean funnel that will jam in the tubing. *Maintain a good oil level in the funnel at all times.*

2. Fit two lengths of clear plastic tubing to the bleed nipples on the steering cylinder(s) (Figure 13-15) and place the free ends in a container with a little oil in it. Keep the tubing immersed in the oil to prevent air from being sucked up the lines. (Note that pistons must be installed with the bleed nipples facing up.)

3. Close any cylinder bypass lines. Determine which side of a cylinder will be pressurized when the wheel is turned clockwise, and open the bleed screw on that side.

4. Turn the wheel (the highest wheel, if there is more than one) clockwise slowly. Air and oil will be vented from the cylinder bleed screw. *Keep the funnel topped up.* When no more air is vented, tighten the bleed screw, open the bleed screw on the other end of the cylinder, and turn the wheel counterclockwise slowly until all air is expelled.

5. If the system has more than one wheel, repeat the procedure at each helm station while keeping the funnel on the highest reservoir filled with oil. If the system has twin steering cylinders, open the bleed screws on the same side of both cylinders at the same time, and close each when all the air is vented.

6. The steering may still be spongy due to residual air. This should work its way up into the top reservoir over time. Check its level periodically. If the sponginess persists, the bleeding procedure will have to be repeated.

Tests at the annual haulout. In time—especially if dirt has entered and scored pumps and cylinders—wear on pumps, check valves, and steering cylinders will lead to hydraulic *creep* or *slip*; the rudder will slowly turn independently of the wheel, or it will be possible to keep turning the wheel slowly when the rudder is hard over. This poses no immediate problem, but the unit will need rebuilding at the next haulout.

To determine where the problem lies, close any bypass valves (but not any valves on lines to helm stations), fit the emergency tiller (this will be good practice!) or grasp the rudderhead by hand if there is no emergency tiller, and push the rudder hard in both directions.

1. If the rudder moves but the wheel(s) remains stationary, fluid is seeping down the sides of the piston in the steering cylinder, and it needs rebuilding.

2. If the rudder and steering wheel(s) both move, the check valves in the helm pump are leaking and need rebuilding. (In a single-pump installation with no check valves the wheel will turn; this is OK.)

Amateurs should not attempt pump and piston disassembly; pumps, check valves, and steering cylinders are built to very close tolerances. Seek professional help.

Troubleshooting. So long as the oil is kept clean and the system is properly installed, hydraulic steering is very reliable. The following are the most common problems:

Wheel is stiff. Disconnect the steering cylinder from the tiller arm at the rudderpost and try again. If this eliminates the stiffness, the problem is in the rudder installation (see previous sections) and not the steering system. If the stiffness persists, check the wheel itself for binding (maybe the brake is on!). Other potential sources of trouble are the wrong oil in the system (too viscous) or undersized piping.

Wheel turns but rudder does not respond. Check first to see that a cylinder bypass valve is not open. Check for a mechanical failure (tiller arm slipping on rudderpost, etc.), or a loss of hydraulic oil. If the system has more than one helm station, check to see whether the other wheel (or autopilot motor) is turning. If so, its check valves are defective.

If none of these checks reveals a problem, break the steering cylinder loose at the tiller arm and try moving the cylinder rod in and out by hand. If it can be moved, the internal piston seals have gone and the cylinder needs rebuilding. If the cylinder checks out OK, then the helm pump itself may have failed, though this is uncommon. In any event, ship an emergency tiller (see Emergency Steering below) and seek professional help.

Hydraulic plumbing. Refer to Chapter 11.

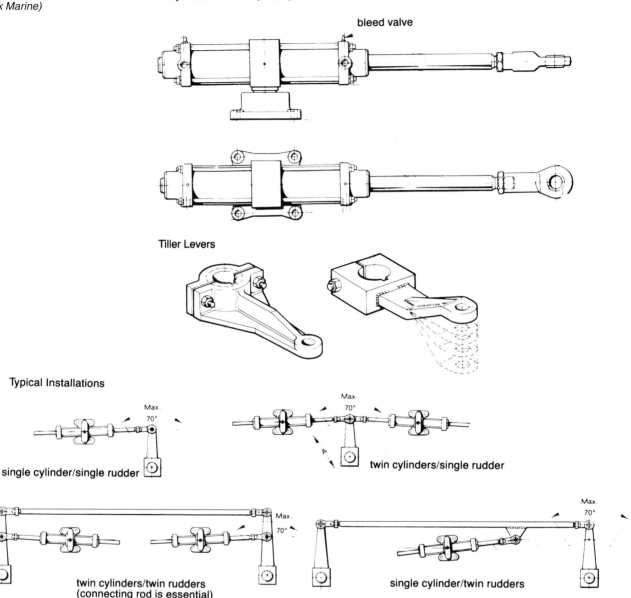

Figure 13-15. Hydraulic piston installations. *(Whitlock Marine)*

Hydraulic Pistons (Rams)

bleed valve

Tiller Levers

Typical Installations

Max. 70°

single cylinder/single rudder

Max. 70°

A

twin cylinders/single rudder

Max. 70°

twin cylinders/twin rudders
(connecting rod is essential)

Max. 70°

single cylinder/twin rudders

Ruderstops. Good, strong rudderstops capable of absorbing sudden heavy shock loads (such as when a rudder is slammed over by a following wave) are essential to protect both the rudder and the steering system. Insofar as possible, mount rudderstops *independently* of the rest of the steering system, rather than building them into quadrants and radial-drive wheels and discs (Figure 13-16).

At a marina or at anchor always tie off the steering so that there is no risk of waves slamming the rudder against the rudderstops.

Annually, check that the rudderstops are secure and that they engage the relevant fitting on the rudderstock cleanly and fully.

Emergency steering. All wheel-steered boats *must* have some form of emergency tiller that can be installed readily if the steering fails (Figure 13-17). What is almost as important is that the skipper and crew practice fitting it *before* an emergency; there may be some surprises.

A solid rudderstock is usually squared off to accept the emergency tiller. Hollow shafts with through-bolted rudderhead fittings take a slotted tiller fitting over the bolt. Since the wheel pedestal is frequently in the way of the tiller, three approaches can be taken to get around it:

1. A very short tiller: This will be of little use in large seas.

Steering Systems, Autopilots, and Wind Vanes

2. A very tall tiller coming over the top of the pedestal. This too will be hard to control, with a serious tendency to bend sideways.

3. A curved tiller bending around the pedestal. This is the preferred solution.

It is extremely hard to fit a long tiller to a rudderstock when the seas are causing the rudder to weave around. Far better to have a tiller in two sections: a short stub to be fitted to the rudder to bring it under control, and the main tiller slotting onto the stub to provide leverage for effective steering. Note that any tiller passing close to a compass should be nonmagnetic.

If hydraulic steering has internal check valves and no bypass valve, the drive cylinder actuating arm will have to be disconnected from the tiller arm before an emergency tiller can be used (unless the hydraulic circuit has failed). Where worm steering is used, the whole steering assembly will have to be unbolted from the rudderstock flange, and a separate, flanged tiller bolted on.

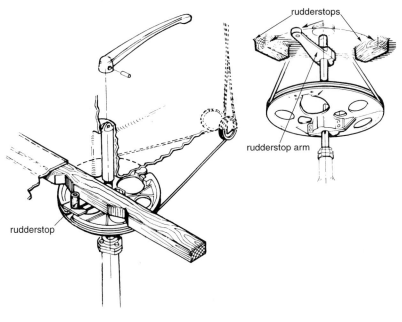

Troubleshooting Chart 13-3.
Wheel Steering Failures: Hydraulic.

Does the hydraulic pump drive shaft turn when the wheel is turned?	**NO** ➤ **FIX:** Check for disengaged clutch; slipping wheel or sprockets; or broken or jumped chain, if fitted.
Does the pump have oil? (Check the reservoir.)	**NO** If the oil is low, fill and bleed (page 439). Check all connections, hoses, and seals for leaks.
Does the piston at the rudderhead move when the wheel is turned?	**NO** Make sure no bypass valve or solenoid is open. Double-check the oil level and bleed again. If this fails to restore steering, the piston and/or pump need rebuilding, or the check valves (if fitted).
Does the rudderstock turn when the piston moves the tiller arm?	**NO** The tiller arm clamp is slipping on the rudderstock. Tighten or replace bolts and set screws or shim as necessary (page 432).

The internal webs in the rudder itself have sheared. Rig a jury rudder. On sailboats, balance the rig.

Figure 13-16. (**Right**) For rudderstops to protect both the rudder and steering system most effectively, it is best that they be mounted independently of the rest of the steering system. In the illustration on the far right, the rudderstop is mounted independently; in the close illustration the rudderstop is mounted on a radial drive wheel. (*Edson International*)

Figure 13-17. (**Below**) Fitting emergency tillers. Use a nonferrous pipe to clear the pedestal. (*Jim Sollers*)

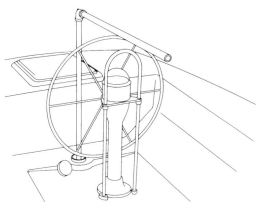

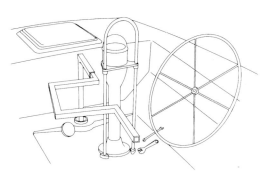

Autopilots

Autopilots are becoming increasingly popular. On long journeys, once that freedom from the wheel has been experienced, there's no going back to hand steering!

How They Work

The boat's course is set on a compass. Two types are used: *fluxgate* compasses, which operate electronically, and *photo-optic* compasses, which utilize a light beam to read the compass.

Any deviation from the preset course is trans-mitted to a central processing unit (CPU)—a minicomputer. This unit then switches power to an electric motor that drives an actuator in order to effect a course correction. The control unit's sophisticated circuitry smooths out rhythmical fluctuations in the course, such as arise from following seas. There may also be a rudder control, which alters the degree of response to any change in the boat's heading: A low rudder control setting will result in small rudder movements; a high setting causes large rudder movements. Some units have a *sea-state* or *deadband* control. This simply determines how far off course the boat may wander before the autopilot responds with a course correction.

All autopilots use an electric motor to move the rudder and make course corrections. Some motors drive a belt or chain (rotary autopilots, Figure 13-18A); others move an arm in and out

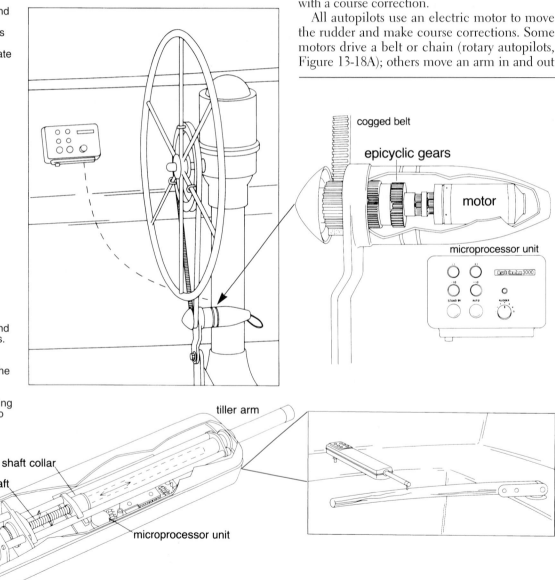

Figure 13-18A. (**Right** and **far right**) This wheel-mounted autopilot utilizes an epicyclic (planetary) reduction gearbox to rotate the wheel via a cogged belt. *(Jim Sollers)*

Figure 13-18B. (**Below** and **right**) Worm gear and planetary gear autopilots. This tiller-mounted unit has a gear running on a worm-geared shaft. As the shaft turns, the gear moves backward and forward. The tiller actuating arm, which is attached to the gear, moves in and out. *(Jim Sollers)*

cogged belt

epicyclic gears

motor

microprocessor unit

tiller arm

shaft collar

worm gear shaft

microprocessor unit

motor

Steering Systems, Autopilots, and Wind Vanes

(linear). This may be done mechanically (via a set of gears) or hydraulically (via a pump and hydraulic piston or *ram*). Almost all motors are geared down: the reduction box may be a *worm* type or a *planetary* type (Figure 13-18B). Mechanical linear drive units must also convert rotary motion to an in-and-out motion; this is generally done via a gear mounted on a worm shaft similar to the worm steering already covered in this chapter, though obviously on a much more compact scale.

Cockpit-mounted units are either rotary, using a belt to turn the boat's steering wheel, or mechanical linear, using an arm to move the tiller backward and forward (Figures 13-18A and B). Below-deck units may be rotary, mechanical linear, or hydraulic linear. Below-deck rotary units use a chain to drive another sprocket and chain linked into existing cable steering, or else operate a completely independent cable system with its own quadrant on the rudder shaft. Mechanical linear and hydraulic units either turn the existing quadrant via an operating arm or else are connected to an independent lever mounted on the rudder shaft (Figures 13-19A, B, and C).

Below-decks hookups. All autopilots using existing steering systems suffer from a major drawback: Any failure of the system will put both the wheel *and* the autopilot out of action (Figure 13-20A).

A preferred approach to a below-decks autopilot installation is to connect the autopilot *directly*

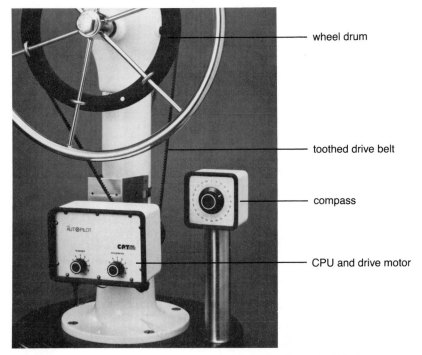

wheel drum

toothed drive belt

compass

CPU and drive motor

Figure 13-19A. Rotary-drive, cockpit-mounted autopilot. *(CPT)*

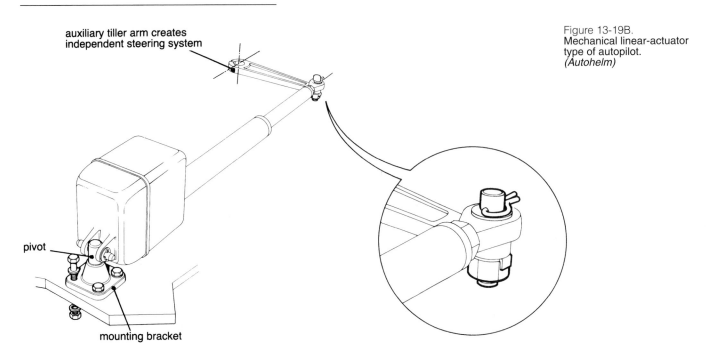

auxiliary tiller arm creates independent steering system

pivot

mounting bracket

Figure 13-19B. Mechanical linear-actuator type of autopilot. *(Autohelm)*

Figure 13-19C. Hydraulic autopilot teed into an existing hydraulic steering system. *(Autohelm)*

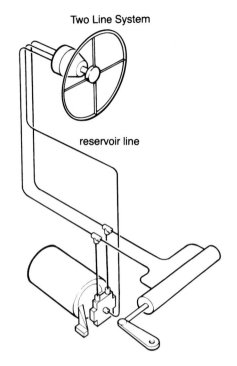

Two Line System

reservoir line

to the rudderhead fitting or even provide it with its own fitting, making it completely independent (Figures 13-20B and C). This creates a separate steering system that can be used if the main system fails. With rack-and-pinion and worm steering the autopilot sprocket is fitted to the steering wheel drive shaft. With hydraulic steering, the main circuit will need a bypass valve, and the autopilot itself will need a bypass valve for when it is not in use (Figure 13-23 below).

Problems with Autopilots

Problems common to all autopilots. There are certain recurrent themes with all autopilots.

The boat slowly veers off to one side. There is insufficient rudder reaction to course changes. Increase the rudder setting.

The boat oversteers and follows an S course. There is too much rudder reaction to course changes. Decrease the rudder setting.

Course corrections are delayed. The boat continually wanders off course before the autopilot reacts. The *deadband (sea-state)* setting is

Figure 13-20A. **(Left)** Typical below-decks autopilot installation. A broken cable or component malfunction anywhere in the system will render the entire steering system inoperative. *(Whitlock Marine)*

Figure 13-20B. **(Top right)** Below-decks autopilot installation using a separate rudder quadrant with its own cables and sheaves. Should either system malfunction, the other can take its place until repairs can be made. *(Merriman Yacht Specialties)*

Figure 13-20C. **(Bottom right)** Independently mounted autopilot unit using a rack-and-pinion arrangement (the regular steering system is radial drive). *(Edson International)*

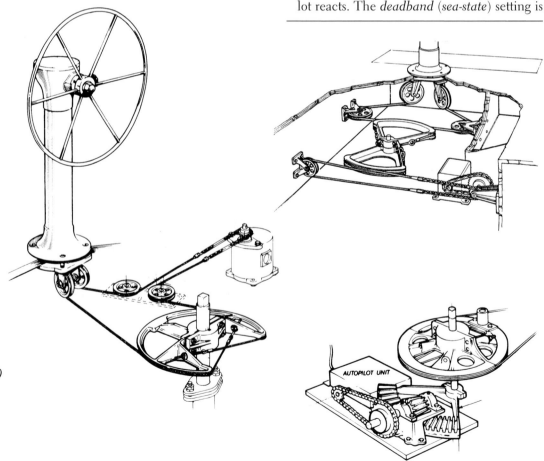

AUTOPILOT UNIT

too high (this may not be adjustable). There may be too much slack in the steering cables, loose linkages, or air in a hydraulic unit (the rudder is weaving independently of the steering system). This will be more pronounced in calm conditions. Tighten cables as necessary. Check the oil level on hydraulic circuits and bleed the circuits of all air. Find out where the oil is going. In particular, check the shaft seals on rams.

The boat heads onto a different course or turns in circles. This is almost certainly the result of *electrical interference*, probably from a *noisy* alternator or SSB (especially when transmitting—see Chapter 7). If it happens only when the engine is running, it is almost certainly the alternator or its regulator. It could also be the result of interaction between the autopilot compass and the boat's compass. They should be at least 39 inches (1 meter) apart; try moving one. Perhaps someone has just placed a radio or other source of magnetic interference close to the autopilot's compass.

The autopilot trips off. This is likely to be the result of either voltage spikes (high-voltage transients) or low voltage. In either case the CPU trips. Does it happen only when a large load kicks in, such as when cranking the engine or using an electric winch? Check for voltage drop at the CPU when the rudder actuator is in operation (Chapter 3). Check all wiring connections, especially terminals and plugs on cockpit-mounted units.

Voltage spikes can be generated by alternators, especially if batteries are in poor shape, or can occur when large loads kick off. It may be necessary to move the CPU power leads to their own battery and/or increase the size of the leads to combat voltage drop.

The autopilot fails to work at all. Check for voltage *at the CPU*. If present, check the polarity (Chapter 3); reverse polarity may have done irreparable damage. If the unit has power and correct polarity, disconnect the leads to the drive motor, set a course, turn the boat, and check to see if there is any output voltage from the CPU. If not, it has an internal problem.

If the CPU is producing output voltage, connect a 12-volt battery (or 24 volts on a 24-volt system) directly to the motor and see if it spins. Reverse the leads; the motor should reverse. Larger motors have a solenoid-operated clutch; if the motor fails to work, identify the solenoid and jump it out to see which item is defective (Chapter 6, Starter-Motor Circuits). If the motor still fails to work, *disconnect it from any actuating mechanism* (since this may be seized) and try

again. If the motor is bad, various motor tests can be performed as outlined in Chapter 6, under Permanent-Magnet Motors.

The autopilot operates sluggishly. Check for low voltage at the drive motor *when it is operating*. Check for binding in the parts of the steering system driven by the motor, such as a wheel brake accidentally left engaged. If necessary, disconnect the motor to check its no-load operation; while doing this, check the free movement of all relevant linkages in the steering system.

The unit operates backward. The power leads from the CPU to the motor are crossed; reverse them. Some units have an internal changeover switch that effectively reverses the leads.

The autopilot exhibits a lack of power. A perennial problem on sailboats. The only answer is to *balance* the sails, even at the expense of performance. For tiller autopilots, see below.

Cockpit-mounted units. Salt water, in one way or another, is the big problem with all cockpit-mounted equipment:

Water in the CPU. All cockpit-mounted units are susceptible to water in the electronics. So far as I know, only one (the Autopilot II) is genuinely waterproof. The rest are merely spray-proof. A good dunking in green water—such as when pooped—may penetrate the seals. CPUs should not be mounted in wet locations, and when stored must be kept in a dry place.

Water in the drive motor. The most likely point of ingress is through the cable gland. If the unit is likely to be subjected to a lot of spray or solid water, check this seal before use, and improve it as necessary—with 3M 5200 caulking, for example.

Corrosion in the power supply socket. Another likely source of trouble! Keep the pins and plugs liberally coated with petroleum jelly. I have found that even when clean, some plugs make a poor contact with the pins; knocking or twisting the plug slightly will break the power supply and cause the CPU to trip off. A bit of judicious bending of pins or plug sockets generally solves the problem.

Cockpit wheel steerers.
Wheel drum centering and motor alignment. Wheel drums are bolted to the center of steering wheels. If the drum is not centered exactly, it will alternately tighten and loosen belt tension as the wheel turns. If not bolted squarely to the wheel, or if the motor is not mounted *directly in line with and square to* the wheel drum, alignment will be out, stressing belts and tending to throw them off. Motor mounting

must be solid and inflexible (Figure 13-21).

Slipping belts. Most belts are toothed (i.e., have ridges across them); the teeth mate with a spline on the end of the motor drive shaft. While some, such as the Autopilot II, have good-sized teeth, others (e.g., Autohelm and Navico) do not; the latter are especially prone to slip when wet and when under a load, or whenever the drum is not properly centered or aligned. Beware of overtightening belts to stop slipping; this will lead to premature bearing failures in the motor. Tension of small-toothed belts should be sufficient to prevent slipping when the steering wheel is turned by hand with the clutch engaged; when the clutch is disengaged, however, the steering wheel should spin freely with no belt drag. If an old belt is glued around the drum with its splines facing out, it will greatly increase traction, but this in turn may lead to the destruction of the gears instead of the slipping of the belt!

Broken belts. Like paper, belts are strong in tension but tear easily if nicked or damaged. Rough spots on wheel drums and poor alignment will shorten belt life.

Stripped drive gears. Most units incorporate a planetary-type reduction gearbox. These will allow the motor to be turned over by the wheel and so absorb some shock loads from the rudder. Nevertheless, a good number of gears are plastic and will strip off under heavy loads.

Some units, however, incorporate larger motors and worm gearing. The motors *cannot* be turned over by the steering wheel (the worm gears exert too much braking action). In this case, the drive pulley will be installed with shear pins, and if overloaded, the pins will give. If the motor shaft turns but the pulley does not, check the shear pins.

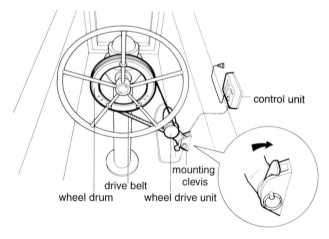

Figure 13-21. Autopilot drive arrangement on a cockpit-mounted wheel steerer. To work properly, the wheel drum must be centered exactly in relation to the wheel's axis, and the drum must be in line with and square to the wheel drive unit. *(Autohelm)*

It seems that most small autopilots are made for the weekend market and not designed for continuous cruising. Manufacturers accept a small percentage of failures from heavy use in order to hold down the cost for the majority of the market. It is my opinion that in most cases one should not take too seriously the manufacturer's claims as to what boat sizes their autopilots can handle!

Tiller steerers.

Seizure of the operating arm. All units use a gear traveling up and down a worm-geared shaft to move the actuating arm in and out through a seal. Many units, such as older Autohelms, use a *steel* gear, which is likely to rust if not properly lubricated and kept dry. Newer Autohelms are stainless steel.

When the actuating arm moves in and out, minor pressure changes occur inside the unit that can draw in humid, salt-laden air. (Some units have a pressure compensation chamber to reduce this effect; newer Autohelms have improved seals.) If salt-laden air does penetrate and the unit is then left unused for an extended period it may seize up solid. If this happens, remove the motor and check motor operation and actuator movement independently of each other to confirm that the actuator is at fault.

It may be possible to free a frozen actuator with liberal doses of WD-40, perhaps some heat from a propane torch, and a judicious application of force! Clean all threads and bearings, grease with a high-quality marine grease, such as Lubriplate A, and *regrease every time the unit is put away for more than a day or two*. Better get a spare; this actuator won't last long.

Autopilot is overpowered by the waves. If the actuating unit is continually overpowered, with the arm being driven in and out against its end stops, sooner or later something will give. The unit had better be unshipped.

We have a heavy-displacement (30,000 pounds), 39-foot ketch, steered by a tiller. Our Autohelm 2000 was repeatedly overwhelmed, and the mounting units at both ends broke at different times. We solved the problem by installing a trim tab on the trailing edge of the rudder with an operating arm at the rudderhead (Figure 13-22). Two cables come forward to a *dummy* operating arm on the tiller. The autopilot actuating unit is mounted on a stainless steel pipe and hooked onto the dummy operating arm. The pipe slots into a hole drilled through the tiller and is locked into place at a right angle to the tiller by a pin pushed down through the tiller and the pipe. The autopilot steers the boat *via the trim tab*, which takes minimal effort—never more than a pound or two of thrust—and uses minimal power.

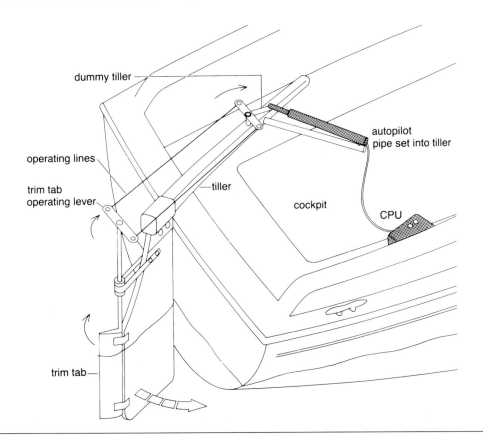

Figure 13-22. Autopilot performance on a tiller-steered boat can be improved by the use of a trim tab. The autopilot is tiller-mounted, and controls the trim tab through a dummy tiller and bell crank assembly. *(Jim Sollers)*

dummy tiller

operating lines

trim tab
operating lever

tiller

trim tab

autopilot
pipe set into tiller

cockpit

CPU

Every time a wave hits the rudder, the whole unit is free to swing and go with the flow; the autopilot is *never* stressed. It has done thousands of miles in all kinds of conditions. It even holds a pretty fair course in sizable quartering and following seas. Given the right size trim tab, this setup can be used to control tiller-steered boats *of any size*. Note that such a setup can be used *only where the CPU is mounted independently of the actuating unit*. Where the CPU is built into the actuator, every time the tiller moves it confuses the CPU!

Below-decks linear actuators (mechanical and hydraulic).

Quadrant failures. Many times a linear actuator is attached to an existing quadrant by simply drilling a hole in the quadrant and through-bolting. Most quadrants, especially lightweight ones, are not designed for this kind of *point* loading. If the actuator must be attached to the quadrant, *a plate of the same material as the quadrant* should be bolted firmly to the quadrant and the actuator bolted to the plate to spread the stresses. The preferred system incorporates an independent operating lever; this provides a completely independent steering system if the main system fails.

Reduction gear failure (mechanical actua-

tors). In all instances a rudder installation must be so designed that the rudder hits its stops before the autopilot actuator is driven into its stops. Otherwise, powerful following seas can slam the rudder over and destroy the actuator.

Actuator jams. Check all mounting bolts. Full steering loads taken by the actuator require it to be mounted as solidly as any other part of the steering system. Note that unless the quadrant or lever arm on the rudderpost and the actuator are in the same plane (mounted at the same angle), their angle to one another will change as the rudder turns. *The actuator installation must accommodate this changing angle.* If it does not, the unit will jam and/or the actuator will be bent or torn from its mounting.

Hydraulic creep. Hydraulic steering may have a pump teed into an existing hydraulic circuit, or it may have a separate pump, reservoir, and actuator operating an independent lever arm at the rudderpost (the latter being highly preferred; see Below-decks Hookups on page 443).

When an autopilot (teed into an existing circuit) is in use, check valves on the steering-wheel-mounted pump prevent flow through that pump (Figure 13-23); when the steering wheel is in use, check valves on the autopilot pump close off the autopilot circuit. If any of the check

Autopilots   447

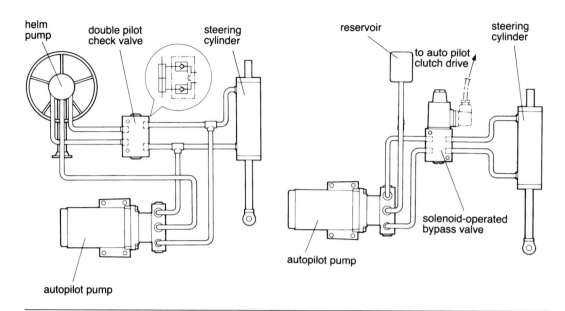

Figure 13-23. Typical hydraulic autopilot circuits. Autopilot teed into existing steering system (**left**). Most helm pumps have built-in check valves, but if these are not fitted, the double-check-valve unit shown will have to be installed to enable the wheel to override the autopilot pump. Independent hydraulic autopilot (**right**). The solenoid bypass valve allows the wheel to override the autopilot, either on command by the helmsman, or if power fails. (*Wagner Marine*)

Diagram labels (left): helm pump; double pilot check valve; steering cylinder; autopilot pump

Diagram labels (right): reservoir; steering cylinder; to auto pilot clutch drive; solenoid-operated bypass valve; autopilot pump

valves fail to seat properly, the steering will creep (i.e., the rudder will move slowly even when the wheel is locked).

Creep may also result from fluid that bleeds down the sides of the piston that drives the actuating arm. This can happen in both teed units and independently mounted units.

Hydraulic emergency override. When an *independently mounted* hydraulic unit is in operation, *it is almost impossible to override it.* Such units should have an emergency bypass solenoid remotely controlled from the steering station so that at the push of a button the hydraulic pump can be bypassed, restoring full control to the steering wheel (Figure 13-23 again). The solenoid should be the *normally open* type so that any power failure (and therefore autopilot failure) will *automatically* open the circuit.

Below-decks rotary autopilots.

Alignment, tension, and mounting. As in other installations, full steering loads are taken by the motor. It must be rigidly bolted down with its chain sprocket correctly aligned and chain tension maintained. Any flex in the motor mounts will accelerate chain wear and run the risk of driving the chain off a sprocket.

Centering of chains and rudderstops. In cases where the autopilot drives a length of chain fitted into a cable system, it is obviously essential that the chain be centered over the motor sprocket when the rudder is centered, and that the rudder hit its stops before the sprocket runs onto the chain-to-wire-rope adapters.

Wind Vane Self-Steering

Wind vane self-steering holds a boat on a certain course *in relation to the wind.* If the wind changes, the course will change to maintain the same relationship.

How It Works

A small *wind vane* is aligned with the wind. When the boat veers off course, the wind continues to hold the vane in alignment—in other words, the boat turns in relation to the vane; this

movement is used to correct the steering. The main problem is the extremely limited amount of force generated by a vane, especially if the boat has changed its relationship to the wind by only a few degrees. This force needs amplifying. Two approaches are used: *trim tabs* and *servopendulum* units. Both utilize water pressure and the boat's speed through the water to produce considerable steering forces.

Trim tabs. Generally an auxiliary rudder is fitted to the stern of the boat with a small rudder

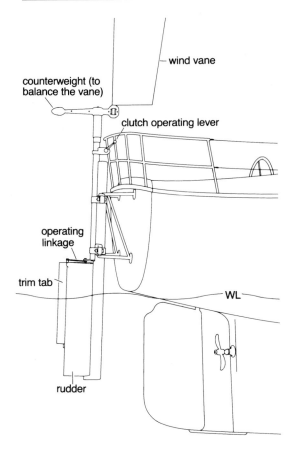

- counterweight (to balance the vane)
- wind vane
- clutch operating lever
- operating linkage
- trim tab
- rudder
- WL

(the trim tab) hinged to its trailing edge; this trim tab is occasionally tacked onto the boat's main rudder, in which case the auxiliary rudder is not needed. The main rudder is tied off (except when the trim tab is attached to it). The boat is put on its chosen course and the wind vane allowed to align with the wind. Then a clutch is engaged to connect the vane to the trim tab (Figure 13-24). Any movement of the vane (such as happens when the boat veers off course) turns the trim tab. This requires little force because of the small size of the trim tab. For various reasons beyond the scope of this book, this small trim tab can develop sufficient hydrodynamic force to turn the auxiliary rudder and correct the boat's course (or turn the main rudder if the trim tab is mounted to it).

Servopendulum units. The wind vane on a servopendulum unit pivots around a *horizontal* axis (Figure 13-25). The vane itself is generally a piece of thin plywood (as opposed to a small sail), weighted at its lower end so that it remains just vertical.

The boat is put on its chosen course and the thin, leading edge of the vane is aligned with the wind. A clutch is engaged, connecting the vane with a *servo-rudder* in the water, which has *its* leading edge lined up with the flow of water past the boat (i.e., more or less fore and aft). If the boat veers off course, the wind vane is brought increasingly broadside to the wind, and the wind blows it down around its pivot point. The base of the vane is connected via a linkage to the shaft holding the servo-rudder. As the wind vane is knocked down, this linkage *pivots* the servo-

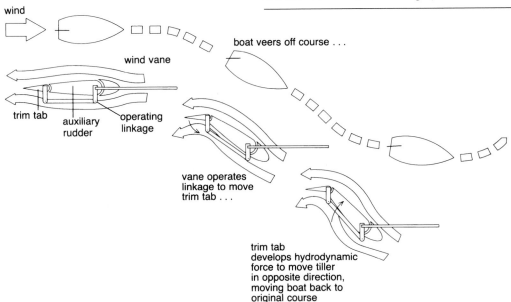

wind

boat veers off course . . .

wind vane

trim tab auxiliary rudder operating linkage

vane operates linkage to move trim tab . . .

trim tab develops hydrodynamic force to move tiller in opposite direction, moving boat back to original course

Figure 13-24. **The operation of trim-tab-type wind vane self-steering.** *(Jim Sollers)*

Wind Vane Self-Steering   449

Figure 13-25.
Servopendulum wind vane self-steering. With the yacht on course, the vane is feathered into the wind. When the yacht goes off course, wind pressure on one face of the vane forces it down around a horizontal axis. This motion is transmitted through a linkage that twists the servo-rudder around its vertical axis, away from its normal position in line with the boat's keel. Pressure from the passing water forces the servo-rudder to swing sideways on its top bearings, and this in turn pulls the steering lines that operate the tiller. *(Marine Vane Gears Ltd.)*

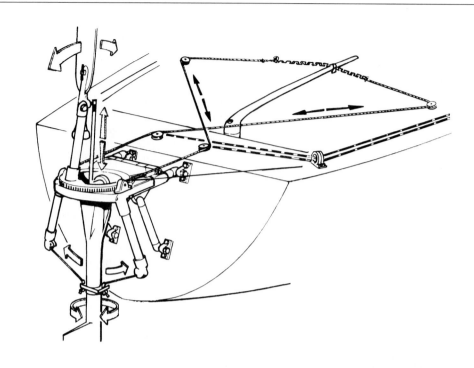

Figure 13-26A and 13-26B. Controlling and adjusting wind vanes: Gear-type clutch. The course adjusting line disengages the ratchet, allowing the vane to align with the wind. Fine-tuning the system is done where the control lines attach to the tiller or wheel drum. *(Marine Vane Gears Ltd.)*

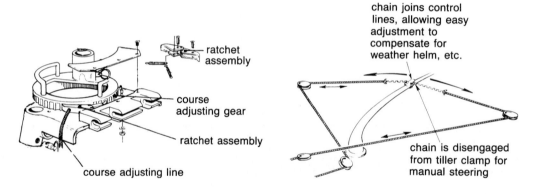

ratchet assembly

course adjusting gear

ratchet assembly

course adjusting line

chain joins control lines, allowing easy adjustment to compensate for weather helm, etc.

chain is disengaged from tiller clamp for manual steering

rudder, which in turn creates hydrodynamic forces that cause the servo-rudder to swing sideways with considerable force. Lines attached to the servo-rudder are fastened either to the tiller or to a special drum on the steering wheel. When the servo-rudder swings, these lines turn the boat's own rudder and correct the course.

Control and adjustment. On many self-steerers the wind vane shaft pivots on a bearing with a toothed gear keyed to the shaft (Figure 13-26A). When the clutch is disengaged, the vane turns to align with the wind. When the clutch is engaged, a ratchet engages the gear and locks the vane to the trim tab or servo-rudder. The principal disadvantage of such a system is that course corrections cannot be made in less than 5- to 10-degree increments, since this is the effect of moving from one gear tooth to the next. Finer adjustment is generally made where the control lines attach to the tiller or wheel drum (Figure 13-26B).

More accurate course adjustments can be made when a *worm gear* is used on the wind vane (Figure 13-27). The gear is disengaged to allow the vane to line up with the wind, and then fine-tuned by rotating the gears; infinite corrections are possible.

A somewhat different approach, which also allows infinite adjustment of the vane's *angle of attack* (its alignment with the wind), is to use a *cone clutch*. The vane shaft has a tapered seat attached to it. A tapered friction pad is keyed to the output shaft. The vane is allowed to free-wheel around the output shaft until it aligns with the wind. The tapered friction pad then is pushed into the tapered seat on the vane shaft, locking the vane to its trim tab or servo-rudder.

Regardless of clutch type, the mechanism needs to be kept clean and lubricated. *It is a matter of basic safety to be able to disengage the wind vane quickly and without difficulty in emergency situations.* Although the forces generated by a

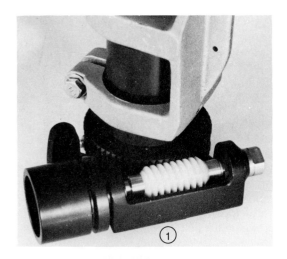

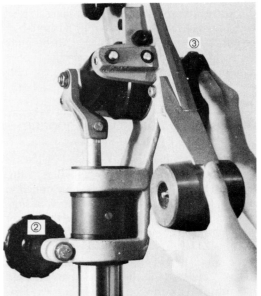

Figure 13-27. Course is adjusted via the line from the worm gear (**1**) to the helm, or by pointing the vane into the wind using a simple friction clamp (**2**). Both provide infinite adjustment. The vane axis is adjusted via the knob (**3**), which enables the vane to be tilted from the vertical for less sensitivity in strong winds. The rudder ratio is adjusted at (**4**) by varying the amount of rudder movement that will occur as a result of any given vane movement, and in so doing varying the degree of steering correction that will occur. (Hydrovane)

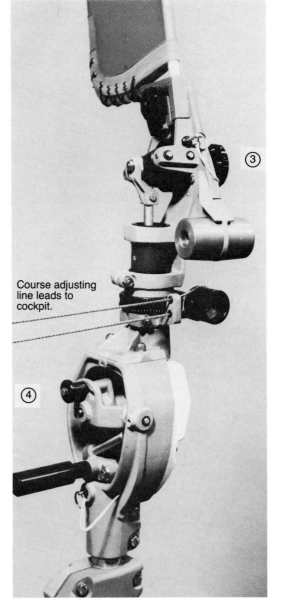

Course adjusting line leads to cockpit.

vane are quite small, on a boat traveling at speed the forces that can be developed by a trim tab or servo-rudder (especially the latter) can be quite astounding (far exceeding the strength of a helmsperson). (Note that any wind vane assembly must be *extremely rigidly* mounted to its transom.)

Maintenance and Troubleshooting

Friction. The initial force developed by a wind vane on any system is quite small. Before this force can be amplified, it must be transmitted to the trim tab or servo-rudder. *Any friction or sloppiness in the linkage between vane and trim tab or servo-rudder will dramatically lessen the unit's performance.* The gear's exposed location ensures the accumulation of salt crystals in bearings and linkages, and if poorly chosen materials are used in construction, corrosion is inevitable. *The linkage needs regular cleaning of dirt or corrosion and should be checked often for free movement* (Figure 13-28). Sloppy movement will allow the boat to wander around the course line before any correction is made. Where adjustment is possible, any sloppiness needs to be taken out, but adjustment must be stopped just short of the point at which friction and binding set in.

Damage control. A self-steerer's exposed location renders it vulnerable to damage from both large waves and collision, such as when docking. Fishing lines can snarl the auxiliary rudder or servo-rudder. Most vanes rely on a combination of brute strength and designed-in weak links to deal with these situations (Figure 13-29).

Wind vanes are mostly thin plywood and easily replaced. *Always carry spares.* Auxiliary rudders are permanent installations and take all the steering loads: *They must be built as strongly as the boat's main rudder.* Servo-rudders will sometimes be thrown sideways violently. Some—such as the Sailomat—can pivot 90 degrees from the vertical without damage, but most can't. Whatever happens, the shock loads must not be thrown on the delicate control linkage. The unit may have break away tubes to relieve stress. If so, carry spares. In any event, think about these things before leaving the dock. Be prepared.

In the past there have been problems with fiberglass auxiliary rudders and trim tabs delaminating (they are generally built in two halves, and the halves will sometimes separate). Watch for telltale cracks in the gelcoat. Many newer rudders—Hydrovane, for example—are built of nylon and are virtually indestructible.

Finally, perhaps the greatest problem comes from installing too small a unit for a given boat in order to cut costs. Not only will performance be unsatisfactory, but the unit will be overstressed and likely to fail. It is far better to err on the conservative side, especially if contemplating ocean crossings.

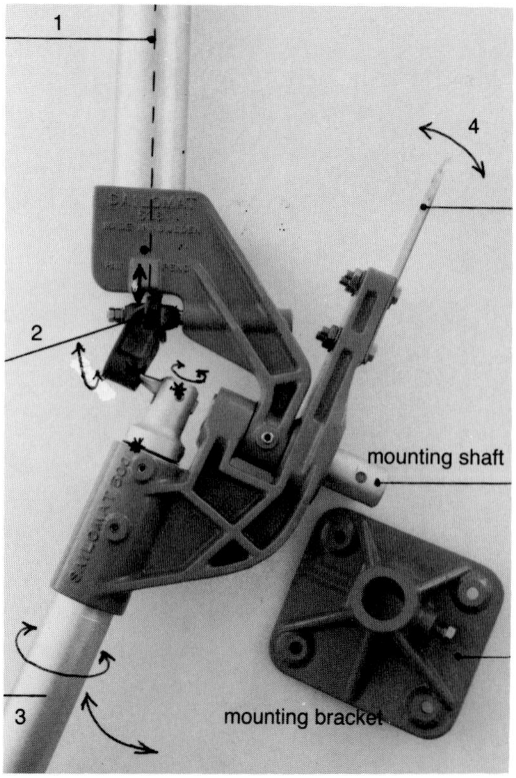

Figure 13-28. Critical maintenance points on wind vane self-steerers. Friction at any of these points will greatly reduce system performance. (1) Linkage inside this shaft connects to the base of the wind vane. When the vane is blown over around its axis, this linkage moves up or down. (2) The linkage is connected here to an offset cam, causing this lever to push from side to side around its axis. (3) This in turn rotates the servo-rudder shaft as shown, causing the rudder to swing sideways. (4) Control lines attached here, and through blocks to the rudder or wheel, translate the sideways swing of the servo rudder into a pull on the helm.

Balancing a boat. Despite the dramatic force amplification achieved hydrodynamically in some conditions, in other conditions the end forces generated by self-steerers are not that powerful, especially in light winds and at slow boat speeds. *No self-steering apparatus will operate effectively unless the boat is balanced first.* This is largely a matter of sail trim, although where an auxiliary rudder and trim tab are used, the main rudder can be tied off in such a way as to correct for helm imbalance (e.g., weather helm).

Most boats will self-steer hard on the wind without a self-steerer. But as the boat comes off the wind, balance is harder and harder to achieve. Few boats can be balanced on a beam reach, and it may be necessary to sacrifice optimum sail trim (e.g., by letting the mainsail luff somewhat or dropping it altogether) in order not to overpower the self-steerer.

When a boat is broad-reaching and running, the more the center of effort can be concentrated in the headsails the easier the boat will be to control. The ideal situation on a downwind run is to drop the main (and mizzen) altogether and set two poled-out jibs. Since *apparent* wind speed is much reduced when a boat is running, the wind vane exerts less force than on any other point of sail. Combine this with the fact that sea conditions are generally at their most difficult to handle when the boat is headed downwind and it is easy to see that the self-steerer will need all the help it can get. Downwind sailing in ocean swells is the acid test of any self-steerer.

Yawing. A self-steerer *reacts* to a change in course and can never *anticipate* wind shifts or wave action. It has, therefore, a built-in tendency to cause the boat to yaw from side to side around the course line. The further the boat is off the wind, the greater the tendency to yaw. Better steerers have a degree of yaw-damping capability; the unit is designed in such a way that as the auxiliary rudder (or boat's rudder) turns in response to instructions from the trim tab or servo-rudder, the force exerted by the trim tab or servo-rudder is lessened (*dampened*). This helps to reduce violent rudder movements and sharp course changes. But even so, no self-steerer will hold a downwind course in following or quartering seas without a fair degree of yawing—just as no helmsperson can. The best that can be hoped for with self-steering is to approximate the performance of a helmsperson.

To deal with yaw and poor downwind performance, hybrid self-steerers have been developed. These operate as straight self-steerers when *on the wind*; on a reach or run, however, the trim tab or servo-rudder is turned directly by an autopilot.

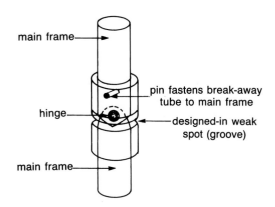

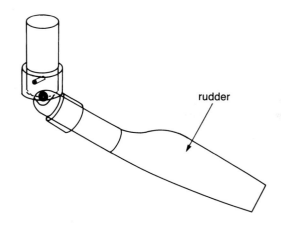

Figure 13-29. Breakaway tubes and other designed-in weak links protect vulnerable and expensive wind vanes from collision damage. Shock loading shears the breakaway tube and allows the main frame to pivot safely out of the way of flotsam.

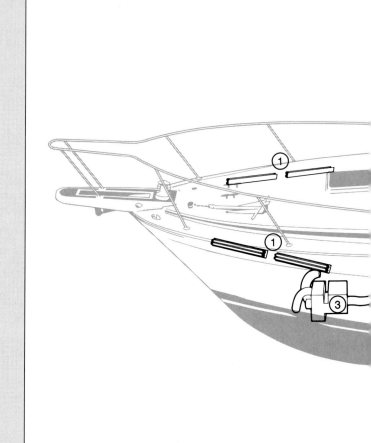

CHAPTER 14

Figure 14-1. Properly maintained, appliances such as these make life aboard a pleasure; poorly maintained they can have quite the opposite effect. *(Jim Sollers)*

 (1) fluorescent lights
 (2) incandescent lights
 (3) air conditioner
 (4) range
 (5) water heater
 (6) propane tank
 (7) propane stove
 (8) propane cabin heater
 (9) navigation lights
(10) kerosene lantern

Stoves, Cabin Heaters, Water Heaters, and Lanterns

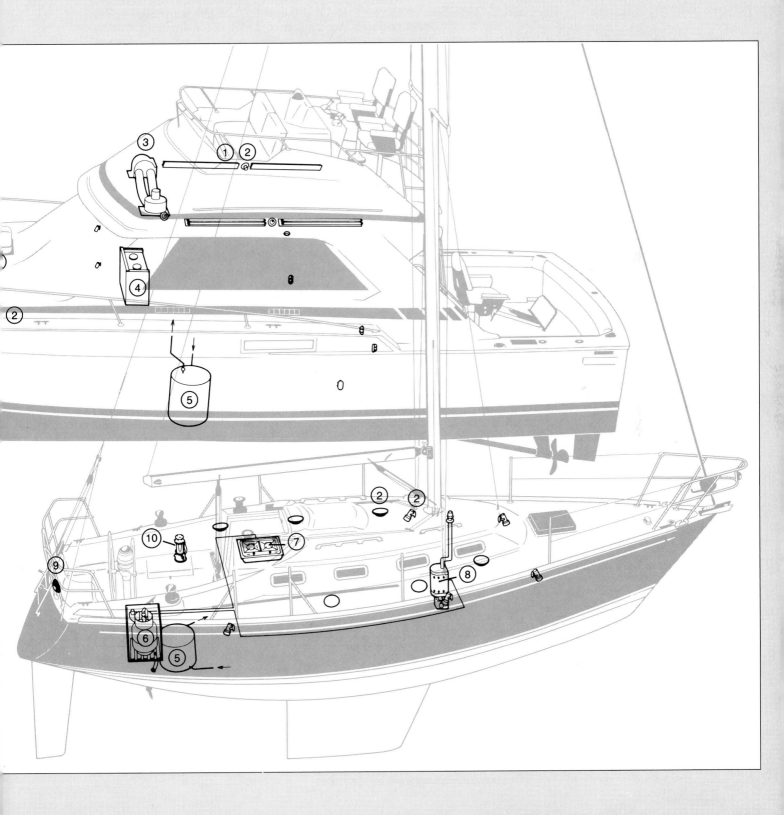

Basic Safety

The method of burning any given fuel—whether it be LPG, kerosene/paraffin, or some other—is more or less the same regardless of the appliance to which a burner is fitted. A kerosene stove operates similarly to a kerosene water heater. It therefore makes sense to focus on fuel types and the methods of burning them, rather than on specific appliances (with the exception of some comments on water heaters at the end of the chapter).

Any fuel that produces a flame consumes oxygen when burning and gives off carbon dioxide (CO_2) and water vapor. Boat interiors have little volume, and cabin spaces are well sealed (they must be to be watertight). The oxygen available in a closed cabin can be consumed quite rapidly. Insufficient oxygen makes the fuel burn improperly, and instead of producing carbon dioxide, it begins to form deadly carbon monoxide (CO).

The combination of oxygen loss and carbon monoxide buildup can be fatal—it has caused a number of deaths over the years. *Always ensure adequate ventilation when burning any fuels* (this includes running diesel engines, which sometimes obtain their air via living spaces despite the fact that they should be independently vented). Any appliance designed for unattended operation (e.g., cabin heaters and water heaters) should have a sealed combustion chamber that has its own air inlet and is externally vented through a flue, thus ensuring a complete separation of the combustion chamber from the air in the boat. This, however, is rare. At the very least *it must have an externally vented flue* (stove ovens are considered an exception to this rule, but these must have a flame-failure safety device that cuts off the gas supply if the oven goes out).

Do not use an appliance for heating unless it is so designed. Never leave a heater on overnight unless it is vented outside the cabin area and adequate air supplies are assured.

Gas

Liquefied Petroleum Gas and Compressed Natural Gas

The three types of gas in widespread use are propane, butane, and compressed natural gas (CNG). The first two are broadly interchangeable and generally lumped together as liquefied petroleum gas (LPG).

Butane and propane both liquefy at low pressures and temperatures—at 100°F (38°C) propane liquefies at 177 psi; butane at 37.5 psi (Table 14-1). When gas is pumped into a cylinder at ambient temper- atures, these pressures are reached quickly. Then, as more gas is pumped in, it liquefies— with the temperature and pressure remaining relatively stable. When a full cylinder is rocked from side to side, the liquid can be heard sloshing around inside. In higher ambient temperatures, pressure in an LPG cylinder will increase somewhat, but never beyond 250 psi for propane and 60 psi for butane; in lower temperatures, it will decrease (for a fuller explanation of these

Table 14-1. LPG Cylinder Pressures[1]

| Gas Composition | Ambient Temperature (°F/°C) | | | | | | | | | | | | | | |
	−30°F −34.4°C	−20°F −28.9°C	−10°F −23.3°C	0°F −17.8°C	10°F −12.2°C	20°F −6.7°C	30°F −1.1°C	40°F 4.4°C	50°F 10°C	60°F 15.6°C	70°F 21.1°C	80°F 26.7°C	90°F 32.2°C	100°F 37.8°C	110°F 43.3°C
100% propane	6.8	11.5	17.5	24.5	34	42	53	65	78	93	110	128	150	177	204
70% propane 30% butane	—	4.7	9	15	20.5	28	36.5	46	56	68	82	96	114	134	158
50% propane 50% butane	—	—	3.5	7.6	12.3	17.8	24.5	32.4	41	50	61	74	88	104	122
30% propane 70% butane	—	—	—	2.3	5.9	10.2	15.4	21.5	28.5	36.5	45	54	66	79	93
100% butane	—	—	—	—	—	—	—	3.1	6.9	11.5	17	23	30	38	47

1. Cylinder pressure in psi as a function of ambient temperature and gas composition.

phenomena, see Chapter 10, Refrigeration and Air-Conditioning).

As long as an LPG cylinder is kept upright, there will always be gas at the top, liquid at the bottom, and *stable pressures*—until the cylinder is almost empty. At this point, the pressure begins to fall as the last of the liquid evaporates.

The principal difference between butane and propane is that the former liquefies at higher temperatures and lower pressures than the latter. In extremely cold weather, liquid butane's rate of evaporation from a cylinder can slow to the point at which appliances fail to work properly. In these conditions propane should be substituted.

Compressed natural gas liquefies only at very high pressures, not found in boat applications. CNG is just that—compressed gas. Consequently, as gas is pumped into a cylinder, pressures rise continuously: A full cylinder at 100°F (38°C) has a pressure of 2,400 psi. As gas is used, the pressure declines steadily.

LPG and CNG are not interchangeable without modification of appliance burners. LPG has a much higher heat output (approximately 21,000 Btus/pound as opposed to approximately 9,000 Btus). Its burners therefore have much smaller orifices than those used with CNG. CNG used in LPG burners will produce less than half the designed output; LPG used in CNG burners will cause high flames and dangerous overheating.

Safety precautions. LPG and CNG both form dangerously explosive mixtures when combined with oxygen in the air. LPG is considerably heavier than air—gas leaks sink to the bilges. CNG is lighter—leaks rise to the cabin-top. A popular fallacy holds that since CNG rises, leaks will dissipate safely through hatches and ventilators. I am living proof that this is not so: I still bear the scars from second-degree burns to my face and hands incurred when I was engulfed by a natural gas explosion on an oil platform. Nevertheless, CNG has an excellent safety record.

LPG leaks are particularly dangerous on boats: Small leaks can remain undetected in deep bilges. A tiny spark (which can be generated by static electricity on any boat) can blow the boat apart.

Boatowners with gas on board would be well advised to invest in a good-quality *sniffer*—a device that will detect small concentrations of gas (well below the explosion point) and sound an alarm. Be sure that the sniffer is totally enclosed, and that it and all associated wiring and switches are sparkproof. I know of one boat that blew up when the sniffer was switched on for a safety check!

Both LPG and CNG are odorless in their nat-ural state but have smelly gases added for resale. When you are refilling cylinders in foreign countries, *if the gas does not smell, it is not safe to have on board*. Regardless of safety devices, gas sniffers, and so on, the boatowner with gas on board should regularly place his or her nose into all potential gas-trapping spaces.

The problem of refills. CNG is virtually unobtainable outside the USA, and is hard to find in some parts of the USA. *For this reason if no other it is not suitable as a fuel on a cruising boat* (in addition to which, it is considerably more expensive per Btu of output than LPG).

So far as LPG is concerned, there is no worldwide standardization of gas usage, gas cylinders, or gas valves and fittings, which also causes problems for cruising sailors, but these are not insurmountable. Propane is the predominant LPG in the US, the Caribbean islands, Australia, New Zealand, and Scandinavia; butane in the UK, the Mediterranean, and many tropical countries (including Brazil, Venezuela, and many South Pacific islands).

Although LPG devices will work on both propane and butane, *propane cannot be stored in a butane cylinder*: Propane has much higher cylinder pressures, which will blow the safety valve on a butane cylinder. Butane, however, *can be stored in a propane cylinder, so for worldwide cruising start out with propane cylinders.*

There are numerous different threads and fittings (both male and female) on LPG cylinders. There are two ways to deal with this when overseas:

1. Connect the boat's gas regulator (see below) to its gas cylinder using fittings that will take *LPG-approved high-pressure hose (ordinary hose will NOT do since LPG attacks rubber and similar materials)*. Then if the gas cylinder cannot be refilled, a local cylinder can be bought with a discharge fitting that accepts a hose, and the hose can simply be connected to this fitting.

2. Keep a cylinder-to-hose adapter, with a length of high pressure hose, on board. When in a foreign country find a suitable local adapter that can be fitted to the other end of this hose so that your cylinder can be refilled from the available supplies.

A cautious sailor would follow both approaches.

Note that in some countries (particularly Europe) it will not be possible to get anything other than *locally approved* cylinders refilled, in which case new cylinders must be bought or rented. A US propane fitting will fit a UK propane cylinder, although in point of fact the threads are marginally smaller, so *this is not recommended*; a UK propane fitting *will not fit a US cylinder*.

When refilling cylinders *it is essential that they are not refilled beyond 80% of their capacity* (70% in hot climates). If a cylinder is completely filled with liquid and the ambient temperature then rises, *the expanding liquid can generate enough pressure to rupture the cylinder*. Another problem is that overfilling cylinders increases the possibility of *liquid carryover into the regulator and the low-pressure lines* to the appliances, which can result in a dangerous *seventyfold increase in pressure* on this side of the system (and can also, even if it does no other damage, destroy the thermostat on a thermostatically controlled oven).

Many cylinders (in the USA and Europe) are so designed that once they are 80% full they begin to vent, but others do not have this important safety device. Every cylinder should be stamped with both its *tare* weight (empty weight) and the weight of refrigerant it is designed to hold (*net fill* weight). A full cylinder can be weighed; if its weight exceeds the tare weight plus the net fill weight, it is overcharged; some of the contents should be vented carefully.

Refilling from another cylinder. One LPG cylinder can be refilled from another as long as the relevant cylinder fittings are available. The procedure is as follows (Figure 14-2):

1. The cylinder to be filled is placed upright, with its valve closed, below the refilling cylinder.
2. The connecting hose is screwed to the refilling cylinder, which is then inverted (with its valve closed) above the cylinder to be refilled.
3. The connecting hose is attached loosely to the cylinder to be refilled, and the valve on the full cylinder is *cracked* just enough to blow off a little gas at the loose connection, which is then snugged up (this purges the hose of air).
4. Both cylinder valves are opened wide. Since the liquid in the full cylinder will be at the valve end, this liquid will flow down to the lower cylinder. The rate of flow will be slow (depending on the size of the fill hose among other things)—it will probably take several hours to get even a moderately full cylinder. The process can be speeded up if the full cylinder is warmer than the cylinder being refilled (this will raise the pressure in the full cylinder); one way to do this is to place the full cylinder in the sun and the cylinder being refilled in the shade. In addition, I have wrapped both in towels, dribbling hot water over one and cold water over the other.
5. To disconnect, close the valve on the upper cylinder first, allow a few minutes for the hose to drain down, and then close the lower valve. *Crack* the fitting at either cylinder, allowing the hose to bleed off, and then remove.

USA LPG cylinders are normally painted white (or else are bare aluminum). *No cylinder should ever be painted a dark color: In direct sunlight a cylinder could absorb enough heat to burst.* In some states it is illegal to paint a cylinder anything other than its original color. A final note: In the USA tanks are required by law to be recertified every twelve years by a qualified testing facility.

Installation

Compartment requirements. Gas bottles, both in use and in storage, must be kept well secured in compartments that are sealed from all machinery and living spaces and are vented

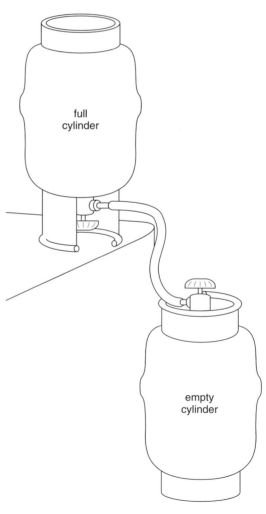

Figure 14-2. **Filling one LPG cylinder from another** (see the text for an explanation).

overboard (Figure 14-3). LPG compartments need to be vented *from the base*, with a minimum ½-inch (13-mm) interior-diameter (ID) vent (preferably 1-inch [25 mm]), *that slopes continuously downward so that no water can form a U-trap, and that exits the hull above the waterline* at all angles of heel. All gas vents must exit well clear of engine exhausts, ventilators, and air intakes. Gas cylinders must be secured in an upright position: If LPG bottles tip over, *liquid*, instead of gas, will come out, with potentially dangerous results.

Pressure gauge. The ABYC requires a pressure gauge immediately *downstream* of the main cylinder valve and *before* the gas regulator (the valve that reduces cylinder pressure to operating pressure). The gauge will then be measuring *cylinder* pressure—a 300-psi (20-bar) gauge is needed on LPG, a 3,000-psi (200-bar) gauge on CNG. The gauge is an essential leak-testing tool (see Periodic Testing below).

Step-down regulator. Regulators should be installed with the vent port *facing down* so that water cannot collect in the vent and enter the system. Different gases are regulated to different pressures. Measurements are made on the low (downstream) side of the regulator in *inches of water column* using a manometer (barometric pressure is used in Europe—multiply inches of water by 2.49 to find *millibars*, which is abbreviated to *m bar*).

The boatowner can construct a manometer

Figure 14-3. Typical LPG installation. Two-tank installations are connected by a selector/shut-off valve, but are otherwise similar. Note: If the regulator is mounted on the bulkhead and connected to the cylinder with a length of hose, it will make it easier to connect to different cylinders when overseas (see the text). *(Jim Sollers)*

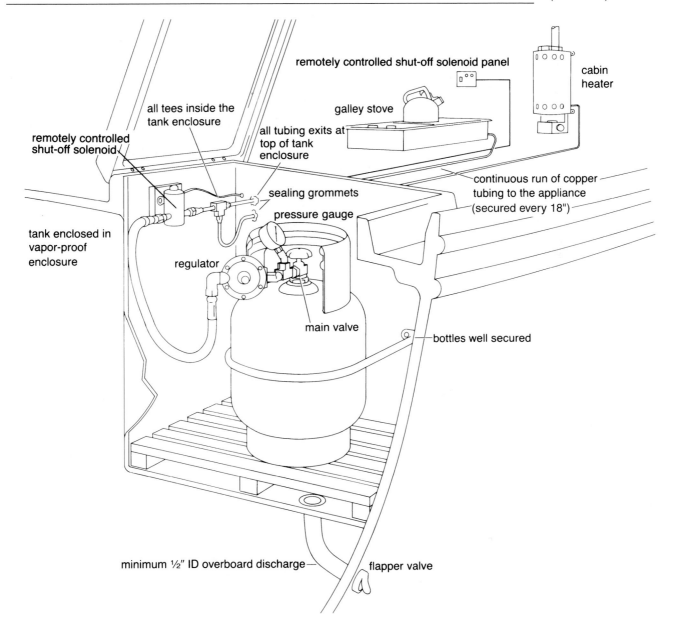

remotely controlled shut-off solenoid panel

cabin heater

all tees inside the tank enclosure

galley stove

remotely controlled shut-off solenoid

all tubing exits at top of tank enclosure

sealing grommets

continuous run of copper tubing to the appliance (secured every 18")

tank enclosed in vapor-proof enclosure

regulator

pressure gauge

main valve

bottles well secured

minimum ½" ID overboard discharge

flapper valve

quite simply (Figure 14-4). Take a board 2 feet long and a few inches wide. Mark it off in inches. Attach a U-shaped piece of ¼-inch (6-mm) or larger (the size is irrelevant) clear plastic tubing. This is a manometer. To use it, set it on end, fill it half full of water, and then connect one end to the gas line being tested, leaving the other end open to atmosphere. Open the gas valve.

The gas pressure will push the water up the other side of the manometer. The difference, in inches, between the two columns of water is the pressure of the gas, given in inches of water.

Most LPG appliances are designed to run with a pressure of around 11 inches water gauge (WG, also called water column; this equals 27 m bar). Propane can be run a little higher than butane, sometimes up to 15 inches WG (37 m bar). *Pressures should never exceed 18 inches* WG (45 m bar; ABYC specifications limit LPG systems to 12 inches = 0.433 psi = 30 m bar). CNG *operates at much lower pressures*—6.5 inches WG is normal (16 m bar). Note that most regulators are made of die-cast aluminum, which can deteriorate rapidly in the marine environment, particularly if left exposed on deck (corrosion is evidenced by a heavy whitish coating), while cylinder valves are made of brass, which can de-zincify (see Chapter 4). Corroded valves will sometimes fail without warning. *Regulators and valves should be replaced at the first signs of significant corrosion.*

Master shutoff valve. After the regulator should come a normally closed, solenoid-operated, master-shutoff valve wired to a remote switch close to the appliance using the gas. The remote switch makes it possible to close off the cylinder (without having to get at it) anytime the appliance is not in use. The ABYC requires that this switch have a light to indicate when the solenoid is open. The cylinder valve should still be closed manually when leaving the boat. However, tripping the battery isolation switch will close the master shutoff valve and provide a pretty fair measure of safety for those who forget to close the cylinder valve manually. Although some stove manufacturers suggest that the master solenoid valve be installed upstream in the line from the regulator, many solenoids (such as the popular Marinetics device) are designed to be installed *downstream* of the regulator as described here. If the valve is to be installed upstream, first make sure it is suitable. The Marinetics valve is too small for larger stoves (three or more burners with an oven). If used in such an installation, two valves will need to be plumbed and wired in parallel (Figure 14-5). This has a side benefit inasmuch as if one solenoid fails the other will still supply gas to the appliances.

Tee fittings. If more than one appliance is to be run from one gas cylinder, the necessary tees should be fitted after the solenoid but *still inside the gas bottle compartment.* For LPG systems unbroken (without fittings), soft copper tubing is run to each appliance. Clean refrigeration or water tubing is used (Type K or L to ASTM standards B-88 or B-280). Tubing sizes are given in Table 14-2. In general, ¼-inch (6-mm) *refrigeration size* tubing (i.e., with an outside diameter the same as its nominal diameter) is adequate for

Figure 14-4. A simple, homemade manometer for measuring gas pressure in an LPG system.

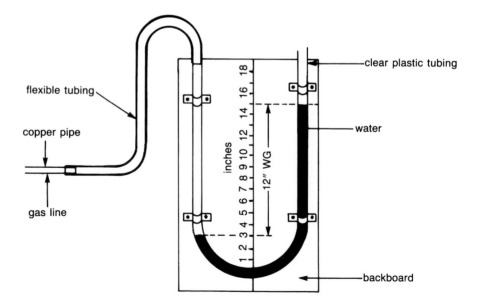

flexible tubing

copper pipe

gas line

clear plastic tubing

water

backboard

inches

12" WG

Stoves, Cabin Heaters, Water Heaters, and Lanterns

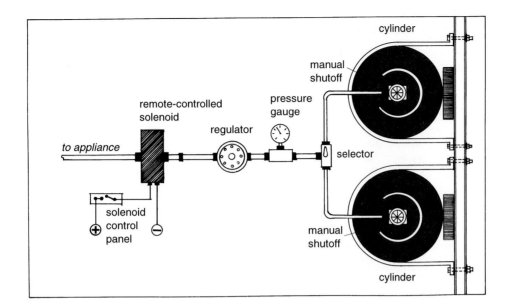

Figure 14-5. Solenoid installations. Top diagram shows a single solenoid; the bottom shows two solenoids plumbed and wired in parallel to increase system capacity. In both cases, a manually operated selector valve upstream of the regulator determines which cylinder is "on line." (Ocean Navigator)

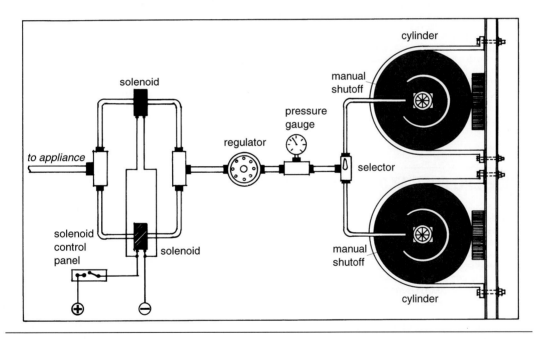

two-burner stoves and small cabin heaters, but ⅜-inch (10-mm) will be needed on larger stoves (three or more burners with an oven). Connections at the regulator end and the appliance should be made with flare fittings (the ABYC does not accept compression fittings—refer to Chapter 11, Plumbing, for more information on these fittings). Flexible connections to gimballed stoves should be made with LPG-approved hose, rated for a minimum of 350 psi and no more than 36 inches in length.

Securing tubing runs. Any tubing run must be securely fastened at least every 18 inches (50 cm). It needs to be protected from abrasion, flex-ing, pinching, or knocks where equipment may bounce around in lockers. Where tubing passes through bulkheads or decks, the hole needs to be sealed.

Periodic testing. The system should be tested at least every two weeks as follows (Figure 14-6):

1. Close all appliance valves.

2. Open the cylinder valve and master solenoid valve.

3. Observe the pressure on the cylinder gauge and let it stabilize. Make a note of the pres-sure.

Table 14-2. Propane Flow[1] as a Function of Tubing Diameter and Length

Tubing Length (feet)	Tubing Outside Diameter, Type L (refrigeration tubing; inches)			
	3/8	1/2	5/8	3/4
10	39	92	199	329
20	26	62	131	216
30	21	50	107	181
40	19	41	90	145
50	18	37	79	131
60	16	35	72	121

1. Output in thousands of Btus; maximum output at 11 inches W.C., based on a 1/2-inch W.C. pressure drop in the tubing.
To determine the tubing size needed, measure the distance from the tank to the appliance farthest from it. Add up the total Btu requirements of all the appliances hooked into the system. (With galley stoves, add all the burners and oven together.) For example, if the tubing run is 30 feet and the appliances use 25,000 Btus, use 1/2-inch outside-diameter tubing.
Note that some safety shut-off solenoids have only 1/4-inch ports. When fitted downstream from the regulator, regardless of tubing size, the entire system essentially has been downgraded to 1/4-inch —about one-third the figures given for 3/8-inch tubing.
Two solenoids plumbed in parallel will double the capacity (see the text). Copper tubing is not acceptable with CNG unless it is tinned on the inside. Special hose is generally used, with permanently attached end fittings (no flares).

Figure 14-6. ABYC-recommended warning label for LPG systems. (0.433 psi = 12 inches WG = 30 m bar). *(Shipmate Store Division)*

USE LPG FUEL AT 0.433 PSI ONLY

1. PLEASE READ INSTRUCTION BOOKLET PROVIDED BEFORE USING THIS GAS SYSTEM.
2. THIS SYSTEM IS DESIGNED FOR USE WITH LPG, LIQUEFIED PETROLEUM GAS (PROPANE OR BUTANE) AT 0.433 PSI (7 OUNCES PER SQUARE INCH OR 12 INCHES WATER COLUMN) PRESSURE ONLY.
3. KEEP CYLINDER VALVES CLOSED WHEN BOAT IS UNATTENDED. CLOSE THEM IMMEDIATELY IN ANY EMERGENCY. IT IS RECOMMENDED THAT CYLINDER VALVES BE CLOSED WHEN APPLIANCE IS NOT IN USE.
4. BE SURE APPLIANCE VALVES ARE CLOSED BEFORE OPENING CYLINDER VALVES.
5. TEST SYSTEM FOR LEAKS AT LEAST EVERY TWO WEEKS AND AFTER ANY EMERGENCY. THE METHOD OF TESTING IS AS FOLLOWS:
   CLOSE ALL APPLIANCE VALVES
   OPEN CYLINDER VALVE AND CLOSE IT IMMEDIATELY
   WATCH THE GAUGE PRESSURE AND SEE THAT IT REMAINS CONSTANT FOR AT LEAST THREE MINUTES
   IF ANY LEAKAGE IS EVIDENCED BY A PRESSURE DROP, CHECK THE SYSTEM WITH LEAK DETECTION FLUID OR A DETERGENT SOLUTION THAT DOES NOT CONTAIN AMMONIA
   REPAIR BEFORE OPERATING THE SYSTEM

NEVER USE FLAME TO CHECK FOR LEAKS

(TO BE POSTED NEAR CYLINDERS)

---

4. Close the cylinder valve, but not the solenoid valve, and wait 3 minutes.
5. Check the cylinder gauge. *If the pressure has fallen at all there is a leak somewhere.*

Never use a flame for leak testing! Mix a 50-50 solution of dishwashing liquid and water; brush this liberally onto all connections between the cylinder valve and the appliance. Any leak will cause the solution to form a mass of tiny bubbles. However, *never use detergents that contain ammonia for leak testing (check the detergent label)—ammonia could cause brass fittings to develop cracks and leaks in a matter of months.*

Troubleshooting Gas Appliances

Gas odors.

- Immediately extinguish all open flames and smoking materials.
- Close the manual and solenoid cylinder valves, and shut down any engines.
- Check to see that all appliance valves are closed.
- Thoroughly ventilate all interior compartments, especially the bilges if LPG is used; do not use any blowers that are not sparkproof (ignition-protected). LPG can be *bailed* with a bucket or pumped out with a manual bilge pump if the pump is sucking air.
- When the boat is free of gas odors, perform a leak test as outlined above and fix any leaks.

No gas at an appliance. Make sure the cylinder valve is wide open (turn counterclockwise) and check the pressure on the cylinder gauge. If a new cylinder has just been put on, air may have entered the line and you will have to purge it by leaving an appliance valve open. Keep a match or light on the burner so that when the gas starts to come through it will burn and not collect in the boat. *Many burners have a safety device that must be overridden when you light the burner* (the most common requirement being to hold in a stove knob against a spring until the burner is lit and hot). Perhaps the safety device is not being overridden: This is one of the most common reasons for not being able to get a burner to light!

Check the voltage at the master solenoid valve. If the voltage is OK, close the solenoid, loosen its downstream connection, reopen the solenoid, and check for gas coming out of the loosened connection. If there is no gas, the solenoid is defective and needs replacing. After tightening, test the connection for leaks.

The line may be kinked or crushed. Inspect its entire length.

The burner may be plugged, especially if something has boiled over on the stove. Remove the burner cap (Figures 14-7A and B) and unscrew the nipple in the center of the burner (use a deep socket). It may be necessary to remove the burner from the appliance to get at the nipple. Clean out the nipple orifice with a sewing needle or a fine piece of wire.

On stovetops with multiple burners but only one central pilot light, if the thermocouple fails (see Thermocouples below), none of the burners will light.

Some of the newer gas appliances have sophisticated electronic controls that may operate another solenoid valve at the appliance. For example, on-demand water heaters operate when a faucet (tap) is turned on. On older models with a constantly burning pilot light, a flow switch on the water line opens a solenoid on the gas line; on newer models with no pilot light, the flow switch initiates an electronic cycle—first an igniter of some sort is activated, and then the gas solenoid valve is opened. Consult any available manuals. Things to look for are: power to the solenoid-valve/electronic panel, and correct polarity. With an on-demand water heater, check the water flow by opening a faucet; the flow switch may be plugged up. Even if the flow is adequate, try jumping out the switch—it may be defective. If the heater has just been installed and has never worked, make sure the hot and cold water lines are hooked up properly.

Igniter fails to work. Light the burner with a match to make sure there is gas flow. If the flame is low, inadequate flow may be the problem (see Unit Ignites Improperly below).

Three types of igniter are in common use: constantly burning pilot lights, spark *(Piezo)* igniters, and filament (glow wire) igniters. Pilot lights themselves may be lit with spark (Piezo) igniters or filaments.

Pilot lights. These are generally lit by holding in a button and then operating a spark (Piezo) igniter. If the pilot fails to light, try a match. If it still fails, check the gas supply. The pilot light orifice may be plugged and need cleaning.

If the pilot lights, but fails to ignite the main burner when it is turned on, check for obstructions between the pilot light and burner. If the pilot light is some distance away, there is often a small tube along which the flame must travel, or a hole in the burner surround through which it must pass (Figure 14-8). This may be incorrectly aligned. A low flame height also may be the cause of this problem. To increase the pilot flame height, trace the pilot line to the main valve. There will probably be a screw underneath a cap on this valve; adjust the screw and check flame height. Both procedures (alignment and adjustment) may be necessary.

(Note: *The latest ABYC regulations ban this type of continuously lit pilot light* except for an oven pilot that operates only when the oven is lit, or a pilot light in a sealed combustion chamber. In spite of this, there are many, many pilot lights still in service that are not covered by these exceptions.)

Spark (Piezo) igniters. Pressing a button moves a magnet rapidly between coils, generating a spark. Some units have a battery; others do not. If fitted, check the battery voltage and connections. The unit may have a remote spark plug with an ignition lead from the sparker. If there is no spark, inspect the lead and its connection. At the pilot light or burner end, there may be a rigid

Figure 14-7A. Gas stove burner, showing thermocouple and spark igniter.

Figure 14-7B. The same burner with the burner cap removed to show the spark igniter, which works (and looks) just like a spark plug. The burner nipple is at the bottom of the center hole.

Figure 14-8. Constantly burning pilot light. When the burner is turned on, gas is directed into the flame tube and ignites.

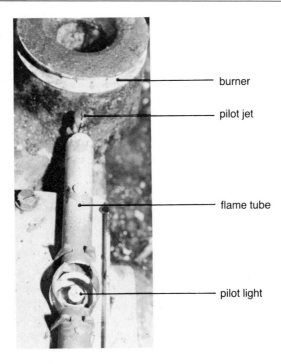

- burner
- pilot jet
- flame tube
- pilot light

Figure 14-9. Piezo spark plug and thermocouple. *(Jim Sollers)*

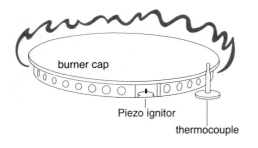

burner cap

Piezo ignitor

thermocouple

spark plug (Figure 14-9) or flexible terminals. If there is a spark plug, the plug head should be approximately $\frac{1}{16}$ inch to $\frac{1}{8}$ inch from the burner rim to which the spark jumps; it may be necessary to adjust its position. If the terminals are flexible, bending the sparker more directly into the gas path may provide more consistent ignition. Note that grease buildup in the area of a sparker will stop it from working.

Filament igniters. A short length of high-resistance wire, the filament, glows red hot, igniting the burner. An external power source is needed, sometimes provided by a flashlight (torch) battery and sometimes by the ship's battery (where the unit is electronically controlled). If the igniter fails to work, check the battery voltage and connections (Chapter 3, Troubleshooting Electrical Circuits). To check the filament, *turn off the gas,* remove any covers to provide a view of the igniter, and activate it—it must glow brightly. If the filament is heating up but still

fails to ignite the burner, check its position in relation to the gas flow and bend it gently into a better position if necessary. Filaments wear out and should be replaced every one or two seasons.

Unit ignites improperly. Ignition is delayed, and then accompanied by a *pop* and a flare-up. What is happening is that excess gas is collecting, due to the delayed ignition, and then exploding.

Gas flow over the igniter may be inadequate (see Inadequate Heat or Flame). Alternatively, the pilot light flame, igniter spark, or filament heat may be weak or improperly placed (see Igniter Fails to Work).

Once lit, unit fails to stay on. All units for marine use should have some kind of safety device that closes the gas valve if the flame goes out. By far the most common cutout is a thermocouple (Figure 14-10), but some electronically controlled units use an optical sensor instead.

Thermocouples. A thermocouple is a device incorporating two dissimilar metals that when heated generate a very small amount of electricity (on the order of $1\frac{1}{2}$ millivolts). This power is used to open a solenoid valve. If the burner goes out, the thermocouple cools and stops generating electricity; the solenoid valve closes.

A thermocouple must get hot before it works, hence the need to hold the gas valve open manually for up to 30 seconds after a unit lights, giving the thermocouple time to heat up and take over. If, after this, the unit goes out when the manual override is released, the thermocouple is defective.

Check first that the tip of the thermocouple (a small bulblike protrusion) is in the center of the pilot light or burner flame. Two wires from the thermocouple terminate in a fitting screwed into the solenoid valve; check that this fitting is not loose. However, do not overtighten it; this will short-circuit the wires and necessitate a new thermocouple. If the valve still fails to open, unscrew the wire fitting and clean the terminals with very fine sandpaper (400- to 600-grit wet-or-dry). If the unit still will not stay on line, replace the thermocouple.

Optical sensors. An optical sensor picks up the burner or pilot-light flame. Loss of the light from the flame causes the sensor to close a solenoid valve. If the unit will not stay on line, make sure that the optical sensor is clean. Some manufacturers that formerly used optical sensors have found them to be unreliable and no longer use them. Before buying an appliance with this

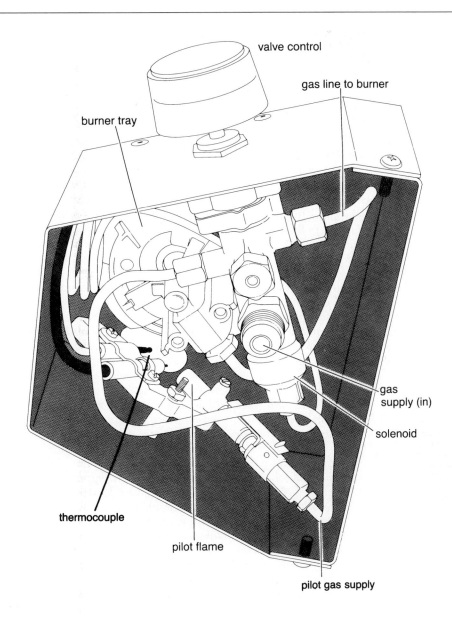

valve control

gas line to burner

burner tray

thermocouple

pilot flame

gas supply (in)

solenoid

pilot gas supply

Figure 14-10. A mouse's-eye view of the burner assembly on a cabin heater. (Jim Sollers)

type of cutout, *check its reliability record in actual boat use.*

Inadequate heat or flame. Make sure the cylinder valve is wide open and check the cylinder pressure. Inspect the gas lines for kinking or crushing. If the problem occurs on initial startup of new equipment, the gas lines are probably undersized. Check the burners for blockages. On stoves, remove the burner caps and check for rust or corrosion that may be plugging either the gas orifice or the air ducts—clean the caps with a wire brush. Make sure any air vents or

chimneys are not obstructed. In extremely cold weather, switch from butane to propane. Make sure CNG has not inadvertently been connected to an LPG system. Use a manometer to check the regulator pressure.

Additional safety devices. Various appliances have safety devices in addition to those already mentioned—an oven-temperature cutout or an oxygen-depletion cutout, for example. Almost all are self-resetting when a problem is resolved (i.e., the unit cools down or oxygen levels recover). Consult the manuals.

Alcohol, Kerosene, and Diesel Appliances

Fuel Quality

The vast majority of problems with alcohol, kerosene (paraffin), and diesel-fueled appliances can be traced to improper or dirty fuel. The orifices in the burners are very small and easily plugged. There are thus two requirements of a fuel:

- It must be spotlessly clean.
- It must contain no contaminants that can form carbon or other deposits in the burner.

We ran a kerosene stove for seven years *without a single blockage* until we ran out of kerosene in Venezuela. We were forced to buy inferior fuel. Within weeks all our burners were plugged. I was cleaning them once a week, then once a day, and finally once every 10 minutes! Then they failed completely and left us without a stove.

Alcohol. There are a number of different types of alcohol on the market, notably butyl alcohol (butanol), methyl alcohol (methanol or wood alcohol), ethyl alcohol (grain alcohol), and isopropyl alcohol (a synthetic alcohol from petroleum gases, not a fermentation product). *Alcohol stoves are designed to run on ethyl alcohol. Both butanol and methanol have low heat production and impurities that clog burners.*

Unfortunately for boat users, the taxation of alcohol in drinks is a major source of revenue for all governments. Ethyl alcohol is what is being taxed. In order to free ethyl alcohol, which is available for sale in other applications, of excise duties, it must be rendered unfit for human consumption—a process known as *denaturing*. In the USA, there are currently about 600 recognized ways of doing this, many of which introduce impurities that will plug up stove burners! (Note: Alcohol in liquor also contains impurities and cannot substitute for fuel.)

Straight ethyl alcohol is best as stove fuel, but it is illegal almost everywhere! The common way to denature ethyl alcohol is to add 5% methyl alcohol (which forms *methylated spirits*), but then other trace elements are put in. Alcohol stove fuel available at marine stores is 95% ethyl alcohol that has been denatured using a process to make it compatible with alcohol burners. Various shellac thinners commonly available in hardware stores are made from denatured alcohol; many of these thinners will also work well in alcohol stoves.

A simple test of alcohol purity can be made by pouring some in an open dish and lighting it. If there is *any* residue after the fuel has burned away, it is not suitable for use as a fuel.

Isopropyl alcohol—the solvent, not the rubbing alcohol—is not readily available but also works well as a stove fuel. It burns hotter than ethyl alcohol, and is slightly smokier. Rubbing alcohol (surgical spirits) cannot be used as fuel because it contains various oils, which will clog burners, and frequently quite a bit of water. Isopropyl alcohol must be a minimum 91% concentration to work properly.

For preheating kerosene (paraffin) burners, any 95% denatured ethyl alcohol or 91% isopropyl alcohol will work fine. In the absence of alcohol a small propane torch played over the burner for 30 to 40 seconds works well.

Kerosene (paraffin) and diesel. The *yellower* the kerosene, the higher its carbon content, and the worse it will be as a stove fuel. Ideally, kerosene should be colorless (except where artificial colors have been added, as in Esso Blue). (Note that in a number of Spanish-speaking countries *kerosena* is diesel, while kerosene is *gasolina blanca*, which translates to *white gas*).

In the USA, any good-quality, colorless kerosene is OK. In the UK, both *pink* and *blue* paraffin are suitable; in Europe and Scandinavia, Esso Blue and Esso Exsol D 60.

Buy the clearest diesel possible. Number 1 diesel is a cold-weather formulation; it is better for stove use year-round.

Cleanliness. Old fuel will collect a certain amount of water. Periodically empty all tanks and start again. Isopropyl alcohol (3 to 5% of the total fuel) added to kerosene tanks will take care of any residual moisture.

At low temperatures (below 5°F [–15°C]) kerosene or diesel may separate out, producing a wax that will plug lines, filters, and burners. The addition of 3% to 5% isopropyl alcohol will help to prevent this. Should blockage occur, run neat alcohol through the circuit—without lighting it—to flush out the wax.

Some cruising people add various carburetor cleaning solutions (such as Carb Out) to their kerosene, believing that it prevents carbon formation. Whether it does or not I cannot say, but I certainly know from bitter experience that no amount of additives will handle truly low-grade fuel. *The only way to have a troublefree kerosene stove is to use clean fuel.*

All fuel taken on board needs to be scrupulously filtered through a very fine mesh. In the absence of a suitable filter, use a pair of pantyhose.

Troubleshooting

The vast majority of alcohol, kerosene, and diesel burners have a tank in which fuel is pressurized. Pressurization is achieved by pumping manually with a bicycle pump or small hand pump built into the tank. The pressurized fuel is led to channels set in the burner head. When the burner is primed, the fuel in the burner is heated and vaporizes. The burner is then lit and the fuel *vapor* is burned.

Fuel tanks. Kerosene tanks are pressurized up to 15 psi, alcohol tanks to 6 or 7 psi, by pumping air (15 to 25 strokes on most tanks and pumps). Tanks that use bicycle pumps just have a check valve built into the tank to which the pump attaches. Tanks with integral pumps have a bicycle-type pump built in, with a check valve at its base (Figure 14-11).

There are a few notable exceptions to these pressurized systems:

1. Wallas Marin has a kerosene stove line in which a small pump supplies fuel to the burner and maintains fuel pressure, while a glow wire on the burner generates enough heat to produce initial vaporization. These stoves need a 12-volt hook-up to work: The glow wire will draw about 6 amps for 2 minutes. In the event of a failure to light, check for voltage drop at the stove during the ignition cycle (Chapter 3).

2. Kenyon has an alcohol stove that also does away with the pressure pump and priming. The small tank (enough fuel to burn for 1 hour) is built into the stove pan. A wick in the center of the burner is lit and heats alcohol in the burner. When this boils, the pressure generated forces vaporized alcohol into the burner where it is ignited by the burning wick. Heat produced by the burner keeps the process going.

3. Diesel drip-pot stoves and heaters rely on a gravity feed (see below) or a small pump.

Pressure tanks. If a pump handle bounces back when pumped, or if the pump handle is pushed all the way back out after a stroke, *the check valve is not holding.*

The check valve is usually a spring-loaded ball. On tanks with external (bicycle) pumps, it is simply unscrewed from the tank. On tanks with integral pumps, the check valve is at the base of the pump cylinder—the piston must be taken out to gain access, and a special long-handled wrench is needed to unscrew the valve (Figure 14-12). *This is an essential tool.*

Examine the valve for dirt on its seat. Clean with a lint-free rag and/or replace as necessary.

Pump cup washer. If the pump requires an excessive amount of stroking to build up pressure, but the tank then holds this pressure, the pump cup washer needs lubricating or replacing.

To get at the pump cup washer, unscrew the top of the pump and pull the piston straight out. On the bottom, held with a nut and washer, is a dish-shaped leather or neoprene washer, the cup washer. When the pump handle is raised, air is pulled down the sides of this washer. When the pump is stroked, the washer's sides push out and seal on the cylinder wall. The cup washer needs

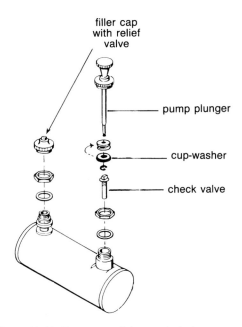

filler cap with relief valve

pump plunger

cup-washer

check valve

Figure 14-11. **Pressure tank for an alcohol or kerosene stove.** *(Kenyon Marine)*

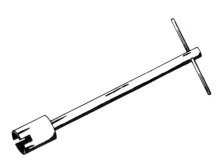

Figure 14-12. **An essential tool for boatowners with pressurized fuel systems equipped with integral pumps: a wrench for removing the check valve located at the pump's base.** *(Force 10)*

Alcohol, Kerosene, and Diesel Appliances   467

periodic lubrication with a little silicone spray or something similar (cooking oil does fine!). Keep a spare on board.

Install the new washer with the sides facing down into the cylinder. In a pinch, a new one can be made from a piece of thin leather cut a little larger than the cylinder bore, screwed to the end of the pump rod, lubricated, and worked down over the lower washer until it can be slid into the cylinder.

Tank filler cap. If the tank loses pressure and needs continual pumping, but the pump handle stays in, the seals around the filler cap or the pump unit are leaking. Some filler caps incorporate a pressure relief valve (safety valve)—this too may be leaking. If the valve can be disassembled, check any seals and make sure the valve seat is clean. If the leak continues, replace the valve.

Burners. Alcohol, kerosene, and diesel burners all behave in much the same fashion and exhibit the same sorts of problems.

No fuel at the burner. Check for fuel in the tank, for tank pressure, and that any valve fitted in the fuel line is open. Alcohol burners have filters in the burner, which may plug up; kerosene and diesel burners have no filters but some may have a restrictor fitting and others an in-line fuel filter, both of which can plug up.

Yellow smoky flame on start-up. Inadequate preheating is one cause. Shut off the burner, let it cool down, and start again. If the burner is difficult to preheat because of drafts, remove both ends of a 3- to 4-inch-diameter can and place this can around the burner to contain the heat while preheating.

Extremely fierce flames when lit, which then die. The unit has a tank valve that was closed while the tank and fuel line were under pressure. The tank valve has not been reopened. The priming process vaporized fuel in the burner and generated high pressures which could not bleed off back into the tank. This pressure caused the initial fierce flame, but then the fuel in the line ran out.

Priming a pressurized burner with a closed tank valve can build up enough force to blow up the burner. For this reason some manufacturers will not fit a tank valve (although the ABYC requires one on all *remotely mounted* tanks, but not integral tanks). If a valve is fitted, it is still better to bleed pressure off the tank after use before closing the valve.

Some yellow flames occur during operation.

This is a result of improper combustion, either from a lack of oxygen (air) or an excess of fuel.

On alcohol burners, hold the burner flange with a pair of pliers and rotate it slightly to adjust the air-to-fuel ratio (Figure 14-13). On all burners check for obstructions to the air supply (or exhaust on vented burners) and if found, remove them.

Let the burners cool down and then check the outer and inner caps for proper seating—misalignment will impede the airflow. While doing this, inspect the caps for any carbon deposits and clean as necessary.

A lack of pressure, blockage in the fuel lines, or excessive restriction of flow with the control knob makes a burner run cool, which can cause improper vaporization of the incoming fuel. Then slugs of unvaporized fuel cause spurts of yellow flame. Problems are exacerbated by colder, draftier conditions.

If the orifice in the nipple is enlarged by improper cleaning, too much fuel comes through and combustion is incomplete. Replace the nipple.

The flame burns correctly but dances away from the burner. This signifies too much oxygen (air). Check the outer and inner caps for proper seating. If they are OK, file three or four notches around the bottom edge of the outer cap. The notches allow some air to bypass the combustion process.

Flame gets progressively smaller. Check the pressure; if it is adequate, carbon is plugging the fuel passages, the needle valve, and/or the nipple orifice. Use a screwdriver or a wrench to tap the body of the burner while it is lit, turning the control knob backward and forward. This may well

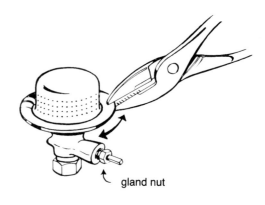

Figure 14-13. Adjusting the air-to-fuel ratio of an alcohol stove by turning the burner flange. *(Kenyon Marine)*

dislodge the carbon, generating a shower of sparks. If the burner has a built-in cleaning needle (or pricker), push it *gently* into the orifice a couple of times. Do not force it—cleaning needles tend to expand, jam up, and break off in hot burners. In general, use the cleaning needle only on a cold burner. (Note that carbon builds up more quickly when burners are run on a low light—run the burners as hot as possible.)

At the first opportunity, dump the fuel and refill the tank with a clean, clear replacement.

Eventually carbon in the fuel passages will plug a burner completely and no amount of normal stripping down and cleaning will clear it out. Generally, the burners must be junked (but see Salvaging a Carboned-Up Burner, Figure 14-14, below).

The flame surges. The burner is too far from the tank and pressure surges are occurring in the fuel line. Fit a surge restrictor in the base of the burner. Note: Some stoves, such as Shipmates, have a built-in pulsation dampener. This is nothing more than a cushion of air trapped in the stove's fuel manifold. It acts like an accumulator tank on a water system (Chapter 12) and, just like an accumulator tank, the manifold can lose its air cushion. To replace it: If the fuel tank is above the stove, maintain tank pressure and use the oven until the tank runs out of fuel; if the fuel tank is below the stove, shut off all burners, release the pressure on the tank, and open the oven burner. The fuel will siphon back to the tank and restore the air cushion.

A small flame burns around the control knob. The packing on the handle stem is leaking. Tighten the packing nut. If this fails, replace the packing (see Overhaul below).

Burner leaks fuel when not in use. If the knob turns 180 degrees or more, the cleaning needle is incorrectly installed (see Burner Reassembly below). Otherwise the knob is in the clean position (needle up) rather than closed, or the needle valve is not seated properly and needs replacing (see Overhaul section). Never attempt to stop a leak by forcing the control knob—this will simply damage the valve or its seat (which may be why it is leaking in the first place).

Overhaul

Kerosene and diesel burners are basically the same (Figure 14-15B); alcohol ones are very similar (Figure 14-15A). Before working on any burner, release all tank pressure. If the burner is above the tank, open the burner control knob and allow the fuel line to bleed back into the tank. If the burner is below the fuel tank, close the tank outlet valve (if fitted) or drain the tank,

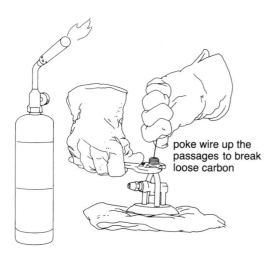

Figure 14-14. Salvaging a carboned-up burner. Remove the old burner and heat it to a *dull red* on a working burner or with a propane torch. Don't overdo it; burners are silver soldered and brazed together—excessive heat will melt the welds. Let the burner cool slowly, and then poke a piece of wire up all the passages. The carbon should break loose and then can be shaken out. *(Jim Sollers)*

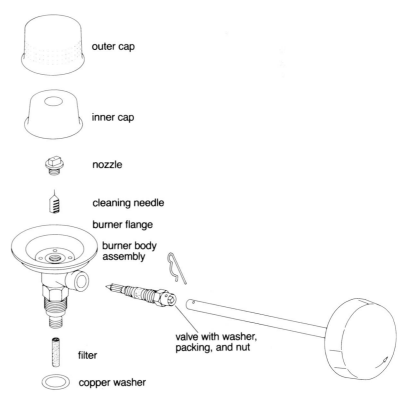

Figure 14-15A. An exploded view of an alcohol burner. *(Kenyon Marine and Jim Sollers)*

Figure 14-15B. An exploded view of a kerosene burner. (Jim Sollers)

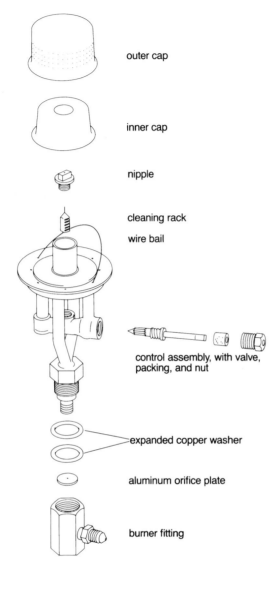

- outer cap
- inner cap
- nipple
- cleaning rack
- wire bail
- control assembly, with valve, packing, and nut
- expanded copper washer
- aluminum orifice plate
- burner fitting

and then break the fuel line loose at the burner and drain it.

Burner removal and replacement. Most burners are factory installed with a high-temperature thread-sealing compound—the burners can prove quite difficult to undo and even harder to seal up again when put back. Since very few problems require burner removal to solve, *remove a burner only when absolutely necessary*. If a burner must be removed, place a wrench on the flat at the burner base; never apply force to the burner top.

When refitting burners it helps to have a supply of soft—or *annealed*—copper washers, or asbestos washers (copper is better). These can be obtained from Force 10 in Richmond, British

Columbia, Canada, to name just one source. Most diesel engine fuel-injection shops will also have a selection of soft copper washers, since they are used for many sealing applications on fuel-injection systems. Finally, you can anneal existing copper washers that have hardened by heating them to a cherry red (with a propane torch or another burner) and dropping them into cold water (although annealing is generally done by heating and cooling *slowly*, copper has unique properties and requires rapid cooling).

If the burner has a priming cup, fit a washer on it and then one on the adapter for the incoming fuel line.

Burner disassembly. Remove the burner's outer and inner steel caps—they pull off (the outer cap may have a retaining wire). The cap may need to be twisted around until two small retaining tags on the burner body line up with flat spots on the rim of the cap before it can be removed.

Unscrew the nipple. This requires a special wrench (Figure 14-12). A piece of masking tape stuck in the end of the wrench will grip the nipple and make it easier to lift out.

Open the control knob. This raises the cleaning needle into the nipple opening. Using a pencil with an eraser on its end, push the eraser down onto the cleaning needle. Continue to open the control knob, lifting gently on the pencil, until the cleaning needle comes free.

Take out the spring clip that holds the control knob stem and remove the control knob. Undo the packing nut from the valve stem. Replace the control knob and continue undoing the valve until the valve threads disengage from the burner body. Pull the valve out (if the packing is tight, it may need a pretty good pull). The packing will come with the valve.

Clean all parts and inspect the tapered end of the valve for any *step*. This is where it seats in the burner body. If the burner has been leaking when turned off, damage to the valve face or seat is a likely cause. Valve faces and seats are not repairable; when these are damaged, the entire burner must be replaced.

A heavily carboned filter may be salvaged as shown in Figure 14-14. Another suggestion from a reader: Make up a strong solution of caustic soda by mixing drain cleaner with water in a glass jar with a plastic lid. Store the burner in this solution for an extended period (weeks if necessary). I am told it will loosen the carbon. In any event, *be sure to observe all cautions on the drain-opener container, and place the jar in a safe place!* Finally, yet another reader tells me that some carburetor cleaners (the OMC brand was mentioned) will also soften carbon.

Filter. Kerosene and diesel burners do not incorporate filters, but most alcohol burners do. The filter is likely to be at the base of the burner on the incoming fuel line. Quite possibly another filter is up inside the body of the burner.

Some filters can be pulled out with tweezers or needle-nose pliers. Others are composed of a sintered bronze material that is jammed in the burner. These may prove impossible to pull out. The filter will have to be drilled out with great care—it will be soft. The drill bit is liable to pass straight through the filter and damage the burner. It is best to drill a little and have another go at tugging and pulling out the rest of the filter. Select a drill bit slightly smaller than the filter so as not to damage any threads in the burner.

Burner reassembly. All stove manufacturers use burners made by Optimus (Sweden) or Hippolyter (Portugal). Quality is about the same, and burners are broadly interchangeable. However, the gearing on the valve spindles and cleaning needle (pricker) units is different, and the nipples (nozzles) and cleaning needles may be different. So, when mixing parts, keep the valve spindles, cleaning needle units, and nozzles as matched sets. When replacing these parts, stay with the same manufacturer.

Thoroughly clean all passages, using compressed air if available. Install any filters; sintered bronze filters are wrapped in braid to make a tight fit. Screw the valve assembly in until it bottoms out in the burner. Push in the valve stem packing, washers, and packing gland nut. Put the control knob back on the valve stem and replace the spring clip. Tighten the packing nut while rotating the control knob backward and forward until the packing begins to bind on the valve stem. Screw the control knob back in until it is closed.

Look through the hole in the top of the burner and locate the valve gear on one side. Skewer a cleaning needle with the eraser on a pencil and lower it into the burner, its teeth facing the valve gear teeth, until the cleaning needle bottoms out on the gear. Press lightly down on the pencil while slowly undoing the control knob. The valve gear teeth will be felt to bounce on the cleaning needle gear teeth: count four distinct *clicks*. (Kenyon stoves have five clicks.)

Slowly screw the control knob back in. It will draw the cleaning needle down into the burner. If it jams, start again. Close the valve all the way and screw the nipple back on with the special wrench.

Open the valve all the way, noting how much the control knob rotates from fully closed to fully open. If it rotates only 90 degrees, the cleaning needle is not down far enough into the burner—

start again. If the knob rotates more than 135 degrees (180 degrees on Kenyon stoves), the cleaning needle is in too far and liable to bottom out before the valve closes, causing the burner to leak when turned off—start again.

Diesel Drip-Pot Stoves

A valve allows a metered amount of fuel into an open combustion chamber, where it is ignited. Air is provided by natural draft or a fan. The burning fuel heats the combustion chamber until incoming fuel is vaporized. At this point the stove functions similarly to a kerosene or alcohol stove, but without the pressurized tank.

The heart of this kind of burner is the fuel-metering valve—a simple device set up in line with, and level with the combustion chamber. The fuel level in the valve determines the (unlit) fuel level in the burner (Figure 14-16).

Because incoming fuel vaporizes on entry into the combustion chamber, the fuel level in the burner is lower than that in the valve. A knob regulates the valve level, and therefore the rate of flow (and heat output of the burner). Raising the valve level increases the differential with the combustion chamber and speeds up the rate of flow.

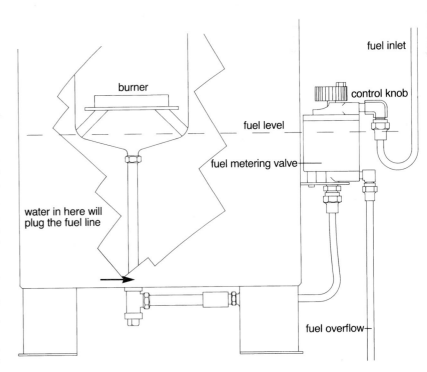

Figure 14-16. **The components of a diesel "drip-pot" burner.** *(Jim Sollers)*

In a boat *the combustion chamber and the valve must be in line fore and aft*; if not, every time the boat heels the valve will either be higher than the combustion chamber, causing flooding, or lower, causing fuel starvation.

Valves are designed to operate with a simple gravity feed from a tank. A fuel pump can be used instead, but its output pressure must be low (less than 3.5 psi on Dickinson stoves and heaters) or it will overwhelm the valve and cause flooding.

Given sufficient draft, drip-pot stoves burn cleanly (no black smoke or soot). The stack (flue or chimney) must be large enough, long enough, and straight up—any bends can cause problems.

One problem I have experienced is that water finds its way down a chimney into the combustion chamber. Since water is heavier than diesel, even a few drops sitting in the fuel inlet will act as a plug and prevent diesel from entering the chamber—the stove will not light. The water can be soaked up with pieces of tissue paper or sucked out with a vacuum cleaner.

Electric Water Heaters and Stoves

Electric stoves commonly have their neutral (grounded) and earth (grounding) wires connected together at the stove frame. *The neutral connection to the frame should be removed* (Chapter 3), leaving just the earth (grounding) cable connected to the frame.

If a stove or heater or water heater fails to work, first check the fuses, breakers, terminals, and the voltage at the outlet supplying the appliance (Chapter 3). If these are OK, *and only if it can be done safely* (the procedure exposes live terminals; *REMEMBER, AC VOLTAGE CAN KILL*), turn on the appliance and check for voltage at the heating element terminals. If voltage is present, the element is almost certainly burned up; if voltage is not present, the switches, thermostats, and/or wiring are faulty. The following tests also can be made.

1. Turn off the power and disconnect the appliance. With an ohmmeter (R × 100 scale on an analog meter) check the resistance from each heating element terminal to the equipment case. *Any continuity shows a dangerous short in the element or its wiring.*

2. Now disconnect the heating element: Stove burners simply unplug; water heater elements have two wires; other elements, such as electric toasters, can be broken loose at one end. Test with an ohmmeter (R × 1 scale on an analog meter) across both element terminals. Resistances are typically low (around 12 ohms per kW on 120-volt systems; 50 ohms per kW on 240-volt systems). *An open circuit indicates a burned-out element.*

The number one cause of a burned-out water heater element is turning on the heater when the water tank is empty. The element will burn out in minutes. *Anytime the heater has been drained, it must be refilled completely before it can be turned on.* To replace an element, drain the tank and unscrew the burned-out one. Put in a new gasket and then screw in the new element. Check for leaks before replacing covers.

Water Heater Problems

Thermostat. Check for voltage across the power leads coming into the thermostat (generally at the top—Figure 14-17). WARNING: these terminals are live. AC VOLTAGE CAN KILL. If in doubt about what you are doing, don't do it! If voltage is present, turn the thermostat on HIGH, press any reset button, and check for voltage at the heating element. If there is none, replace the thermostat. (These tests should be done when the unit is cold.)

The safety valve (relief valve) vents water. Check the thermostat setting—it may be too high. Try reducing it. If the valve still vents, turn off the heater and let it cool. Still venting when cooled? The valve is defective. If the venting stops after the unit has cooled, the thermostat is probably not cutting off.

If the water heater has a heat exchanger and the relief valve (safety valve) vents only when the engine is running, the operating temperature of the engine may be too high for the water heater.

Constantly dripping relief valve. Trash is probably in the valve seat. Take the valve off and clean it.

On-demand water heater cycles on and off with the water pump. The water system accumulator tank has become waterlogged (Chapter 12). Restore its air charge.

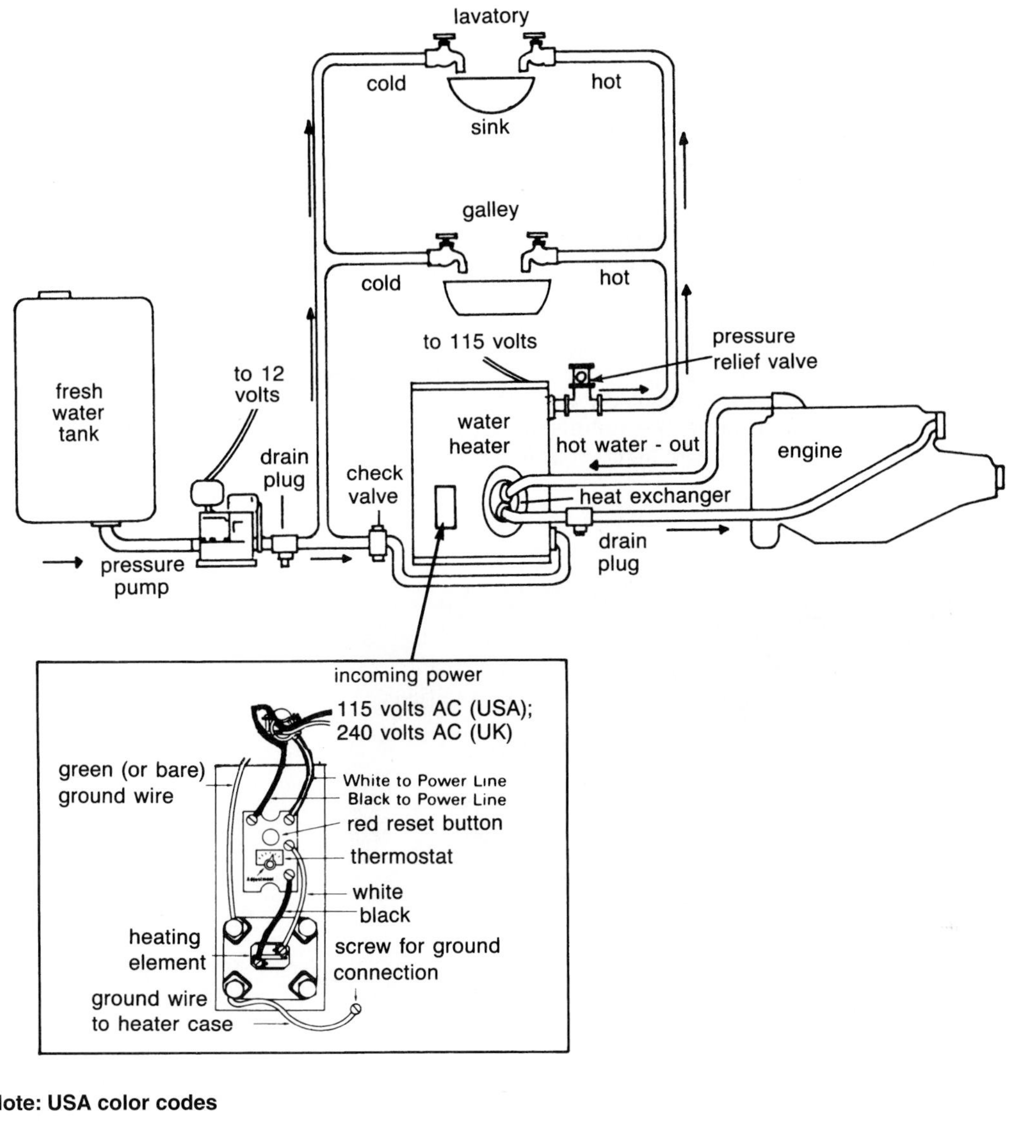

Figure 14-17. Typical onboard water heater installation. Water is heated both by the electric water heater and by engine-cooling water via a heat exchanger. (Allcraft Corporation)

Note: USA color codes

On-demand heater won't kick on. The flow rate is probably inadequate, or the flow valve on the water heater is clogged. Check for kinked lines and pump problems to correct the flow rate. If the valve is clogged, clean it.

Rusty water. "Glass-lined" water heaters are, in fact, made of porcelain-coated steel. All-stainless heaters are preferred in marine use since in time the porcelain cracks and then the steel rusts. When this happens it is time to replace the heater. Before condemning an old water heater, however, make sure that it is really the source of the rust. Break loose a connection on the supply side of the heater; if the water here is rusty, the heater is not

the culprit. Also consider whether the boat has been through any unusual turbulence lately—the "rust" may be nothing more than sediment stirred up from the bottom of the heater's tank.

Freezing. Freezing destroys any water heater; the tank bursts. Be sure to drain the tank when winterizing. Alternately, add *propylene* glycol antifreeze (which is nontoxic), not ethylene glycol (automotive antifreeze, which is toxic).

Kerosene and "White Gas" Lanterns

Principles of lantern burners are the same as for other pressurized burners. The vapor is burned inside a knit sock or bag called a mantle, which becomes white hot, giving off light. Mantles are extremely delicate—the slightest touch will cause them to fall apart.

Mantle replacement is straightforward. Remove all traces of the old mantle, including the asbestos string that was used to tie it on. The new mantle can be handled until first lit. Slide the open end over the ceramic tube in the lantern and tie it on with its asbestos string. Arrange the mantle uniformly around the tube and make sure it is hanging evenly with no major creases (A).

Set the mantle on fire (B). It will smolder slowly, shrinking and giving off unpleasant fumes as a coating on it burns off (C). When all the coating is burned off, the mantle will assume its finished size and shape, and the lantern is ready to use.

After lighting (D), a mantle is extremely fragile. Any sudden knocks—even the slightest touch—will cause it to disintegrate (E). Although a mantle with just a hole in its side will still give off light, it should not be lit. A hot jet of flame will shoot out of the hole, quite likely cracking the lantern glass.

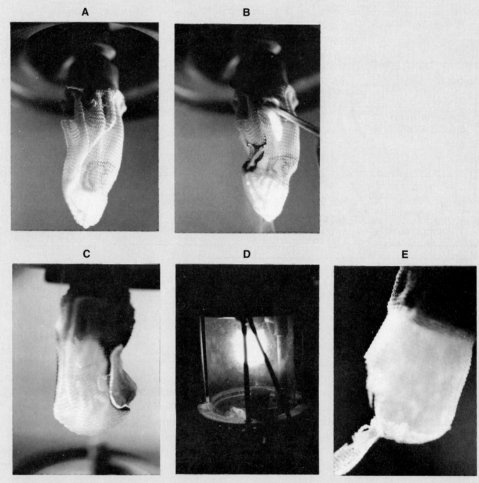

Figure 14-18. Replacing a mantle on kerosene and white gas lanterns.

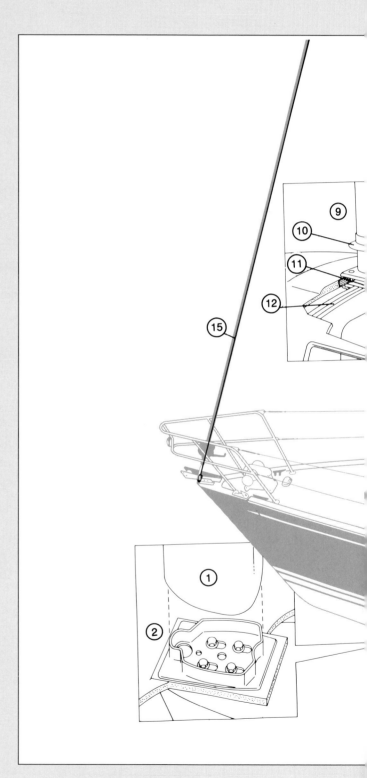

CHAPTER 15

Figure 15-1. Keeping masts aloft is a product of proper design, installation, maintenance, and tuning. *(Jim Sollers)*

(1) keel-stepped mast
(2) mast step
(3) chainplate
(4) backstay
(5) boom
(6) spreader
(7) upper shroud
(8) lower shroud
(9) deck-stepped mast
(10) boot
(11) backing plate
(12) bulkhead
(13) baby stay
(14) turnbuckle
(15) forestay

Spars and Standing Rigging

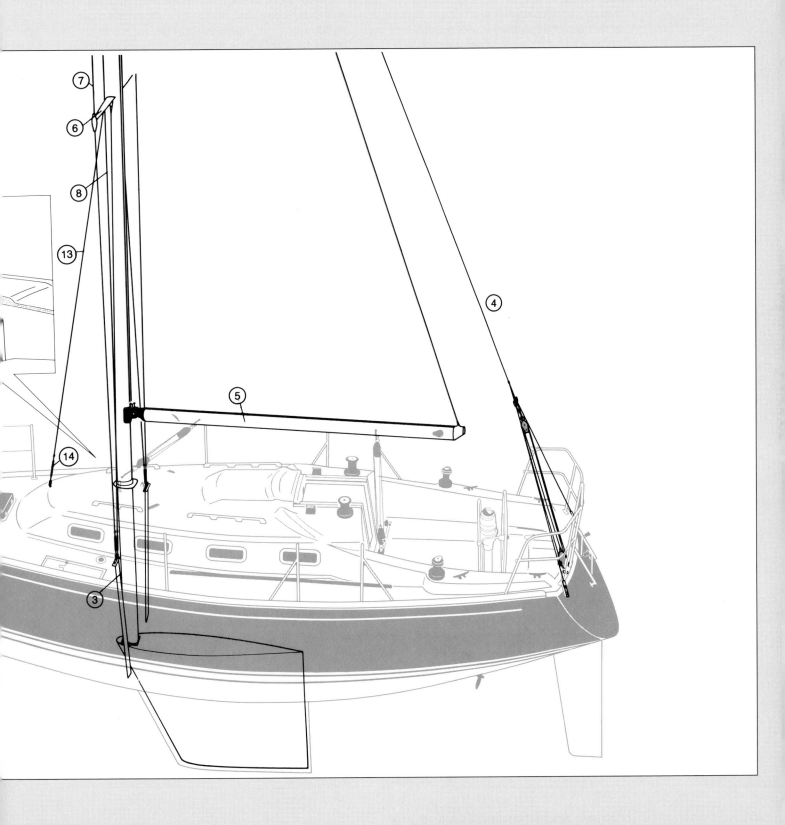

Wooden Spars and Spreaders

Wooden spars, especially when varnished, are a high-maintenance item. All masts, booms, and spreaders need regular close inspection for telltale signs of delamination and rot, and will need repainting or revarnishing at least every few years, probably every year if varnished and kept in the tropics.

Construction. In the days when labor was cheap, very fine round and oval spars were constructed. The procedure was to laminate a hexagon or octagon, and then round out the corners. Nowadays wooden spars are almost invariably a box section, which is much less labor intensive and far easier to clamp up. The occasional mast will incorporate a double-box section, with the outer box laminated to the inner one (Figure 15-2).

Since no planks will be long enough to run the complete length of a mast side, several planks must be joined together. The usual joint is a simple *scarf*, in which a taper is cut in both boards and the two glued together (Figure 15-3A). The taper should have a *ratio* of at least 1:8, i.e., with a board 1 inch (25 mm) thick the taper should extend over a length of 8 inches (20 cm). The feather edge of the taper is weak and susceptible to damage until it is glued up; sometimes it is squared off (Figure 15-3A), but this is a more difficult and time-consuming joint to execute properly and is not often done. In the finished box spar, the scarf joints in the four sides must be staggered up and down the length of the spar so that no two are in close proximity. The exterior tapers should be pointing down

so that water cannot work into the joint.

Some spars are hollow from top to bottom, with just a blocking piece at the head to keep water out of the masthead fittings. Such a spar tends to distribute loads evenly over its whole length. Many spars include additional internal reinforcement (blocking) at the spreader-attachment points and the base (Figure 15-3B). In any event, such blocking should always be tapered at top and bottom to eliminate *hard* spots that would tend to concentrate stresses. The blocking also must provide a free passage for water to drain out.

Plastic resin, resorcinol, and epoxy glues are all

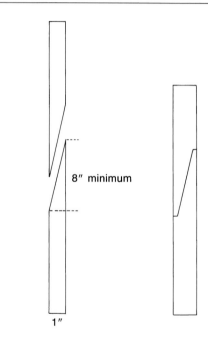

8″ minimum

1″

Figure 15-3A. (**Left**) Simple 1:8 scarf joint. (**Right**) Squared-off scarf joint.

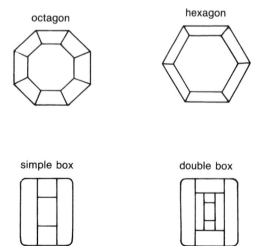

Figure 15-2. Wooden mast construction.

octagon

hexagon

simple box

double box

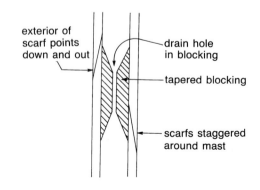

exterior of scarf points down and out

drain hole in blocking

tapered blocking

scarfs staggered around mast

Figure 15-3B. Details of proper wooden mast construction.

used. To be effective, the first two require very close fits in all the joints—they have no gap-filling properties. Epoxies are more tolerant. Resorcinol leaves an unsightly dark purple glue line at joints. For making repairs, a suitable epoxy (e.g., West System, System Three) is probably the best bet.

All wood spars should be treated internally with fungicide. While external rot can usually be found and repaired before a failure occurs, internal rot is an undetectable time bomb waiting to bring the rig down. If in doubt, the next time the mast is unstepped, pour a gallon of rot-proofing agent (e.g., Cuprinol) into it and slosh the fluid gently from end to end, rotating the spar periodically, until the wood is thoroughly saturated.

Paint or varnish. Varnished spars on a traditional boat look beautiful, but they do require a lot of work, especially in hotter climates. Even the most expensive varnishes with ultraviolet blockers will hold up no more than two years in the tropics, normally only one. The topsides of spreaders will *never* go more than a year, and are frequently cracking and peeling within a few months. This admits moisture, which is then trapped by the intact varnish on the undersides and inboard ends of the spreaders, causing rapid rotting. A strong case can be made for painting, rather than varnishing, the upper spreader surfaces.

Aside from looks, varnish does have one advantage over paint: Any water that penetrates the varnish is immediately apparent as a dark stain in the wood below. Failures with painted surfaces are far less obvious—the paint generally has to blister or the wood become spongy (in which case rot is well advanced) before problems are noticed. Painted spars will, however, hold up for as long as five years between coats, especially with many of the newer paints.

The main problem with varnish is the time required for its upkeep. We have developed a quick and dirty method for laying on a substantial thickness of varnish very quickly. The masts are unstepped and laid out horizontally. We wash them, lightly abrade them with a palm sander, put plastic bags on the winches, tape off other fittings, and then pick a *hot* day to varnish. I load up an airless sprayer and then shoot the whole length of the mast at walking speed, getting one half of the upper side at the same time. The airless sprayer really pumps out the varnish. There are runs and drips everywhere. Someone else walks behind with a large paintbrush, working out the runs and dribbles. Once I get to the end of the mast, I grab another brush and start at the beginning, working on the runs. We keep this up until the varnish tacks up (that's why we pick a hot day—it tacks up faster), and then spray the other side and the other half of the upper side. The next day we roll the mast and do the underside. *With just two coats we can lay on as much varnish as we used to in seven coats of hand brushing, and in a total time of around two hours!* It doesn't look quite as pretty close up, but from ten feet it looks the same, and it lasts two years (just) in the tropics.

Danger areas. The following are the most likely areas for rot to get started:

Fasteners. Any fastener, even when properly bedded but especially when improperly bedded, is a potential source of water ingress and thus rot. The loads that modern rigs impose on fittings, combined with undersized or insufficient fasteners, frequently will cause the fasteners to crush surrounding woodwork. The fastener loosens, bedding compounds pull free, and water wicks in (Figure 15-4). Loose hardware is a sure sign of trouble, but the wood surrounding even securely fastened hardware should be inspected closely, at least annually, for signs of deterioration.

Where problems are being experienced with excessive loads on the wood, the Gougeon Brothers (manufacturers of West System epoxies) have shown that an effective answer is to drill an oversized hole, fill this with epoxy, and set the fastener in this epoxy plug. The epoxy penetrates and bonds to the surrounding wood and, with a considerably larger surface area than the original fastener, dissipates the loads on the fastener over a much greater area.

Several years ago, after ripping a couple of cleats off our mast and an outhaul track off a boom, we rebedded all the hardware using the Gougeon Brothers' techniques and have had no more failures.

The specific procedure is as follows (see Figure 15-5):

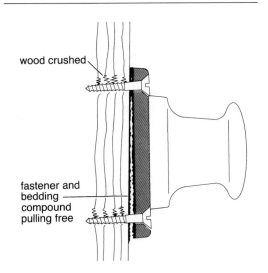

wood crushed

fastener and bedding compound pulling free

Figure 15-4. Fasteners subjected to excessive loads, such as those holding this halyard winch, can crush the wood surrounding them, allowing fasteners to loosen further and water to penetrate. *(Jim Sollers)*

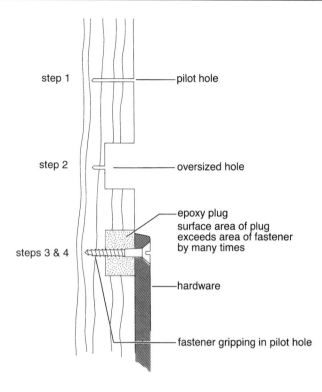

step 1 — pilot hole

step 2 — oversized hole

epoxy plug
surface area of plug
exceeds area of fastener
by many times

steps 3 & 4

hardware

fastener gripping in pilot hole

Figure 15-5. For longest life, fasteners subjected to high loads should be embedded in epoxy. Detailed instructions are in the text. *(Jim Sollers)*

1. Drill a pilot hole to the depth of the fastener.
2. Drill the oversized hole to a little *less* than the depth of the fastener.
3. Fill the hole with epoxy and top up as the wood soaks it up. On vertical surfaces, first wet out the hole (a pipe cleaner works well) and then thicken the epoxy with microballoons or talc—as much as is needed to stop the glue from draining out. In a pinch, talcum powder works well as a thickening agent.
4. Clean the fastener (acetone works well) and install it when the epoxy begins to gel. The section of fastener that runs down into the pilot hole (at the bottom of the oversized hole) should provide just enough grip to snug up the fastener until the glue sets.

Interestingly enough, the Gougeon Brothers also have shown convincingly that on most applications a stainless steel machine screw makes a much stronger fastener than either a regular wood screw or a self-tapping screw. Their book, *The Gougeon Brothers on Boat Construction*, is a gold mine of useful information for anyone with extensive woodwork.

Exit holes. Any exit holes for electric cables or halyards are likely to let in water sooner or later. The worst case is where a cable runs down into a mast, providing a perfect path for water to trickle in. All cables should have drip loops where they exit the mast, and the exit holes should be angled downward (see Figure 15-11).

Base of spreaders. As noted previously, the upper faces of wooden spreaders are notorious for letting in water, which drains down into the spreader bases (due to the angle of the spreaders) and becomes trapped. Another common source of spreader problems: the holes through the spreaders for mounting pins (Figure 15-6). As often as not the spreader hardware consists of a stainless steel plate fastened on the top and bottom sides with two clevis pins passing through both the plates and the spreader. Water can run down the pins and into the spreader.

This problem with spreader-mounting holes is easily cured in one of two ways: (1) Remove one of the plates, drill oversized holes in the spreader, fill with epoxy, and allow to set. Then replace the plate and drill through the epoxy plug for the clevis pins (Figure 15-7 top). (2) Design the spreader mounting bracket so that the wood does not protrude into the area of the clevis pins (Figure 15-7 bottom).

Base of the mast. With both deck-stepped and keel-stepped masts, the heel fitting is a notorious source of dampness and rot. It must be designed to allow any water running down either inside or outside the spar to drain away and also to provide a free flow of air around the heel. The heel fitting needs regular close inspection.

Mast partners. On keel-stepped masts, mast *partners* (the blocking where a mast passes through the deck) can be the source of problems for similar reasons as above—dampness and poor air circulation.

Masthead. Problems can develop on uncapped masts, or masts with improperly sealed head boxes. On many traditional rigs the stays and cap shrouds are looped around the masthead and supported by blocks of wood on the mast side (Figure 15-8). The masthead itself is bare. The end grain *must* be properly capped, a function traditionally served by sheet copper or a wooden disc. Even if the rest of the spar is varnished, paint the top few feet for added protection—it will look perfectly shipshape.

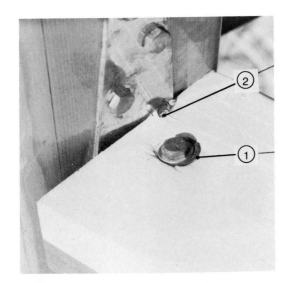

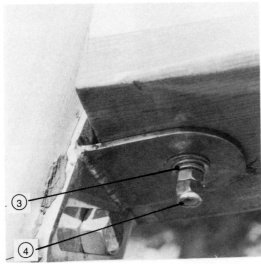

Figure 15-6. How *not* to install a spreader. These are top and bottom views of a spreader installation on a *brand new* mast. (**1**) No upper spreader plate. The wood is crushed already, and is sure to soak up water and rot. Any up-or-down loading on the spreader will bend the mounting bolt and crush the wood further. (**2**) The single bolt has allowed the spreader to rotate and crush its inner face. Note the split in the grain, already extending up the spreader. (**3**) As the bolt works against the upper spreader face, it will embed itself and loosen. The lock washer will exert no tension. (**4**) The nylon locking ring of the Nyloc nut engages no threads and therefore will not lock. This spreader is likely to fail before long, bringing the mast down with it.

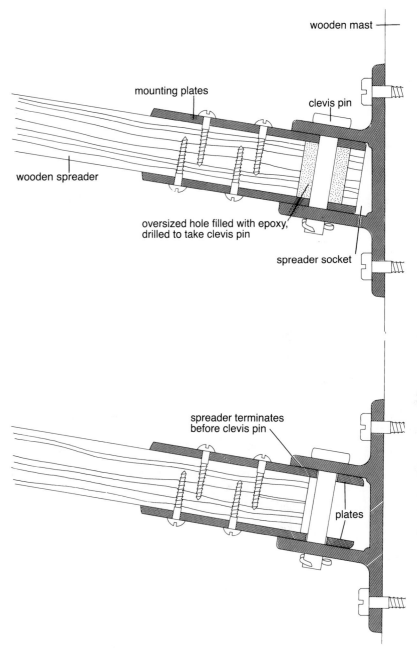

Figure 15-7. Two superior approaches to spreader base fittings. Contrast these with the example shown in Figure 15-6. (**Top**) A clevis pin mounted through an epoxy plug. (**Bottom**) Top and bottom spreader plates extended past wooden spreader. (*Jim Sollers*)

Spars   481

Figure 15-8. Traditional
masthead attachments.
(Jim Sollers)

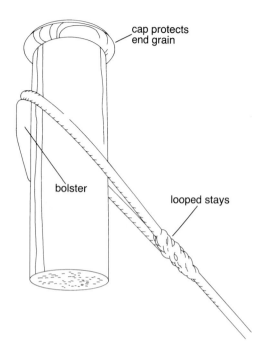

cap protects
end grain

bolster

looped stays

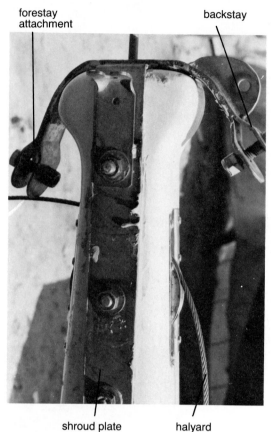

forestay
attachment

backstay

shroud plate

halyard

Figure 15-9. Wooden spar with external masthead
hardware.

Other spars have masthead boxes incorporating halyard sheaves and attachment points for stays and shrouds. Older designs tend to be let into and attached to the sides of the spar, leaving exposed woodwork (Figures 15-9 and 15-10). Newer spars sometimes have an all-purpose head box, which simply drops over the top of the mast (Figure 15-11). In the latter case, the head box must be sealed (i.e., welded shut with a plate) below the sheaves so that no water can ever make its way down into the spar. Electric cables that are run internally in the mast can exit the spar below the head box and run up its outside rather than upset its watertight integrity. For maintenance and overhaul of head boxes, see Masthead Boxes, later in this chapter.

Sprung seams. Over time the constant flexing of a mast as it works may weaken and eventually crack some of the glue lines. This is more likely if the mast is improperly tuned (excessive mast bend, slack rigging—see Tuning a Rig, at the end of this chapter). A lightning strike may also open up seams.

Bowsprits. These are prone to rotting in three distinct areas:

1. At the tip where the *cranse iron* (the bobstay and headstay hardware) attaches,

2. At the bow of the boat where there is generally another collar of sorts,

3. At the butt block or bits.

It is essential to remove all the hardware periodically (every few years) and closely inspect the wood beneath. The loss of a bowsprit endangers the whole rig; it is not worth taking chances.

Repairs. One of the principal advantages of wooden spars is that they can be repaired, generally being returned to as-good-as-new condition.

Anytime the protective paint or varnish layer is damaged, it should be patched up as soon as possible (as long as the underlying wood is dry). Lin and Larry Pardey, widely published cruising sailors, carry a fingernail polish jar (the kind with the brush attached to the underside of the lid) filled with varnish. Whenever they have a minor scratch, they can paint over it immediately, without the fuss of digging out varnish cans, brushes, and brush cleaner. Since the brush is kept in the jar, it doesn't need cleaning. An excellent idea.

Small areas of damage to spars are treated by chiseling out the affected area and cutting an insert to fit. Preferably the insert, or Dutchman, should be made of the same kind of wood with the grain running in the same direction.

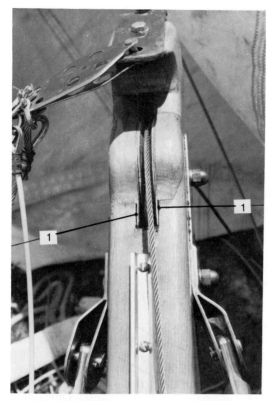

Figure 15-10. (**Above**) How *not* to fit masthead sheaves. This is the same mast shown in Figure 15-6. Note the gaps for rainwater entry (1), and the split-out grain (2).

Figure 15-11. Wooden spar with head box. *(Jim Sollers)*

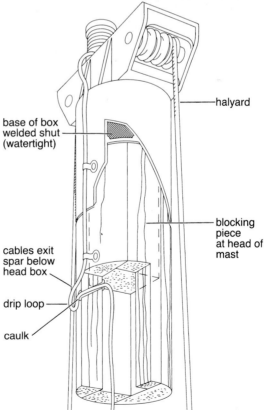

Large areas of rot or damage must be cut back to clean wood. Fresh planks then are fitted in. As often as not the hardest part of a major repair is finding an adequate bench to support the spar and enough clamps to fit the new pieces (which should be clamped at least every 12 inches).

The important steps to remember are:

1. Keep the scarf-joint ratios at or above 8:1.
2. Stagger the joints around the spar.
3. Have the outsides of joints pointing down.
4. Treat interior surfaces with an antirot solution.
5. Taper all internal blocking.
6. Find out what caused the problem in the first place and fix it!

Aluminum Spars and Spreaders

When set up right, modern aluminum spars are long lived and almost maintenance free. However, the failure to carry out the little maintenance required, or to spot and rectify danger signals from just one fixture, can result in the loss of a whole rig.

Construction. Aluminum spars are *extruded*—that is to say molten aluminum is pushed through a mold, cooling and gelling as it goes. The interior parts of the mold are held in place by metal rods attached to the exterior parts of the mold. The aluminum has to flow around these retaining rods and reform on the other side.

The extrusion is tempered, or hardened, in the process. (Tempering of metals, with the exception of copper, which behaves in reverse of most metals, is done by raising the metal to a high heat and then cooling it rapidly.) Then the upper section of most masts is progressively tapered. This is done by cutting a section out of the extrusion, bringing the halves together, and welding them back up. However, the welding process reheats the metal around the weld and then allows it to cool relatively slowly. This effectively undoes the tempering in the area of the weld, softening the metal. (This process is known as annealing.) The degree of softening, and its impact on spar strength, depends on a number of factors, including the kind of welding gun used (MIG welding requires less heat than other methods) and the amount of metal in the weld area (some walls are thickened on the sides and forward face to add strength); some quality spars are retempered *after* the tapering.

Many masts have various fixtures welded in place, such as the head box, spreader sockets, winch bases, and halyard exit boxes. This can make the mast soft in these areas, and so is not favored by some manufacturers, but on the other hand there are none of the corrosion problems that can develop around the fasteners on non-welded fittings. The mast is now *anodized* or painted.

Anodizing or painting. Aluminum is notoriously hard to coat. The surface oxidizes very rapidly (which gives it that typical gray appearance of untreated metal) and surface coatings will not adhere to the oxidized metal.

Once the initial oxidation has occurred, the surface becomes relatively stable. Apart from its unsightliness and the fact that it leaves gray deposits on sails and halyards, untreated aluminum works fine for spars (many European aluminum-boat builders leave their hulls bare). Surface coatings are therefore largely cosmetic.

Anodizing electrochemically builds up a hard protective coating both *within* the surface metal of the aluminum and on it (as opposed to paint, which only sits on the surface). With anodizing, the *inside* of the mast is also treated, though not to the same extent as the outside. Should an anodized surface become scratched or damaged it cannot be reanodized—the best thing to do is clean the bare metal and then polish it with a good-quality, liquid silicone polish (for cars or boats).

In order to get paint to key into aluminum, the surface must first be cleaned and microscopically roughened to improve the adhesion of the paint. This can be done with sanders but generally is done by treating with phosphoric acid, which eats into—*etches*—the surface of the metal, removing oxidation in the process. This acid is washed off and the bare metal is immediately treated with a zinc chromate primer, which inhibits fresh oxidation. The paint is applied as soon after as possible to seal the surface—generally a primer of two-part epoxy followed by one of the two-part linear polyurethane top coats (e.g., Awlgrip, Imron, Interthane Plus).

Damaged painted areas can be restored by the owner using the same steps. Various companies (e.g., the Gougeon Brothers, and Norseman Marine, Ft. Lauderdale, FL) market aluminum *prebonding kits* with the necessary acid for etching, zinc chromate primer, and instructions for use. Some of the linear polyurethanes also are available for application by brush. (Observe all safety warnings—these paints are hazardous!) The resulting touch-up job will not match an original sprayed finish, but can come close.

In any event, painted masts will need repainting sooner or later, whereas anodizing generally lasts for the life of the spar. Another advantage to anodizing is that it will show stress areas (the anodizing takes on a crazed pattern or goes dull white) more clearly than painted masts (Figure 15-12).

Danger areas. A periodic quick inspection will discover most problems before they get out of hand.

Welds. As stated, during the extrusion process aluminum spars are hardened. Any welding causes localized softening (annealing) of the extrusion. Vertical welds up and down a spar (e.g., for tapering) present no great problems, but any welds *around* the spar produce a weak section prone to buckling. Notable in this respect are welded spreader sockets, especially where the sockets wrap a good way around the spar.

Any clustering of welded fittings, winch bases, or the like around one area of the mast will pro-

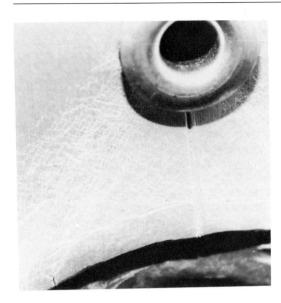

Figure 15-12. **Stress patterns show up clearly on an anodized aluminum mast.**

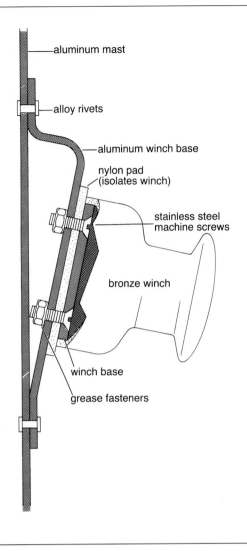

aluminum mast

alloy rivets

aluminum winch base

nylon pad
(isolates winch)

stainless steel
machine screws

bronze winch

winch base

grease fasteners

Figure 15-13. Dissimilar metals used to mount hardware can cause galvanic corrosion problems on aluminum masts. Grease fasteners well, and regrease annually. *(Jim Sollers)*

duce a weak section. Welding shroud tangs can soften the tangs: Flexing of the shrouds will lead to fatigue and failure. Excessive heat when welding head boxes will sometimes soften the metal where the forestay and backstay toggles attach, and thus lead to failure.

All welded fixtures should be inspected regularly and carefully for any signs of cracks around the welds or deformation of the fixture or mast wall.

Hardware and fasteners. Aluminum is fairly well down the list in the galvanic series table (Chapter 4). Most hardware and fasteners are well up (e.g., bronze and stainless steel). With a little salt water, these are excellent conditions for galvanic interaction!

Larger items of hardware *must* be insulated from the spar with a nylon or similarly electrically inert pad (Figure 15-13). Where this is impractical, a zinc chromate paste between the hardware and the mast wall will help protect the aluminum, serving the same function as a sacrificial zinc anode.

Fasteners present special problems. Aluminum alloy rivets are compatible with aluminum but will be eaten away rapidly if in contact with more noble metals. They work well for fastening aluminum spreader brackets, winch bases, exit boxes, and so on, but cannot be used on stainless or bronze hardware. These items are generally attached with Monel rivets or stainless steel self-tapping and machine screws.

Stainless steel fasteners should be coated with a corrosion inhibitor (such as Tefgel or Duralac), but essentially nothing will permanently stop corrosion. Sooner or later oxidized aluminum will build up around the fastener and freeze it in place—attempts to remove it will likely just shear off the head. Since aluminum oxide has a greater volume than the original aluminum, sometimes enough pressure is generated to break fasteners without any outside help!

If it is ever likely that the fittings held in place with stainless steel fasteners will need to be removed (e.g., boom ends with internal lines and fittings), the fasteners should be pulled annually and recoated with a corrosion inhibitor to prevent them from becoming locked in place.

Note: Walter Ivison of Norseman Marine tells me that they now use aluminum screws coated with *Duralac* (available from Norseman) for fastening hardware. When using stainless steel, Norseman uses only 316, which they electropolish and then hand-buff to create the maximum corrosion resistance.

Spars   485

Figure 15-14. Aluminum mast repairs. This boat fell over in the yard, crushing the mast at the spreaders. The ruined section of mast was cut out and a new section spliced in.

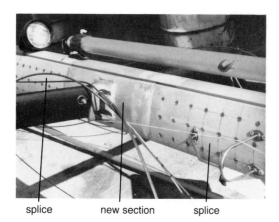

splice   new section   splice

Spreaders and spreader sockets. Spreaders are either round tubes or have an airfoil *(streamlined)* cross section. The former are designed for compression loads only and must not be forced backward and forward or up and down. The latter will take some fore-and-aft loading and are used where bends are induced in the mast to improve sailing performance, but once again they will take very little up-and-down loading.

Some spreaders (normally tubular ones) are *flexibly* mounted with a limited swing fore and aft to relieve stresses created by flexing masts and rigging. Most spreaders, however—particularly airfoil-section spreaders—are rigidly mounted. Unfair loads can be generated by excessive mast bend, the pumping action of slack lee-side rigging, or allowing a mainsail to bear against the spreaders when running downwind.

The most excessive fore-and-aft loads generally arise as a result of cranking down on a backstay adjuster, causing the mast to flex forward at the spreaders. The spreader sockets try to pull free of the mast wall on the forward edge and to compress the mast on the aft edge (Figure 15-15). Look for cracked welds or loose rivets on the front face, and dented mast walls to the rear. Any damage is going to require a specialist's attention.

Semiflexible tubular spreaders frequently bear on a hardened rubber pad in the base of the spreader socket. If excessive play is evident, check this pad and replace it if it is damaged or destroyed.

Newer masts usually have *spreader bars* that pass clean through the mast. The loads from opposing spreaders tend to cancel out, reducing the load on the mast wall.

Cutouts. Aluminum spars inevitably have a number of holes cut into them for various fittings (e.g., exit boxes) and access hatches. These holes

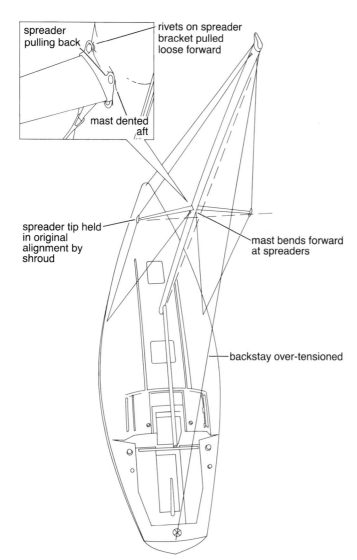

spreader pulling back

rivets on spreader bracket pulled loose forward

mast dented aft

spreader tip held in original alignment by shroud

mast bends forward at spreaders

backstay over-tensioned

Figure 15-15. Effect of excessive mast bend on spreaders. *(Jim Sollers)*

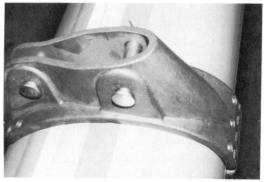

Figure 15-16. **This excellent type of spreader socket distributes the spreader's loads over a substantial area of the mast.**

Spars and Standing Rigging

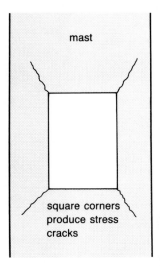
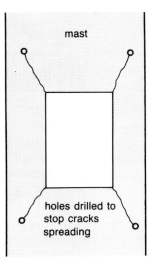
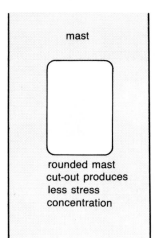

must never be concentrated in any one area or severe weakening of the spar will result. Most important is not to have exit holes horizontally opposed to one another. All cutouts should have rounded corners to reduce stress concentration. If cracks start to radiate out from corners, they can be halted temporarily by drilling a small hole (up to ¼ inch or 6 mm) at the point of the farthest extension of the crack (Figure 15-17). Keep loads on the rig down.

Mast heels. Mast heels are particularly susceptible to corrosion. Keel-stepped masts are down in the (generally damp) bilges, while deck-stepped masts are subject to constant saltwater spray. The mast step needs to be kept drained and ventilated (make sure the mast step has a drain—some don't—and that the drain is clear). Periodically washing off salt will slow down corrosion. Stainless fasteners should be pulled and treated with a corrosion inhibitor annually.

Maintenance and overhaul. Aluminum spars require very little attention.

Masthead boxes. Modern masthead boxes integrate halyard and topping-lift sheaves, masthead electrical equipment mounts, cap shroud tangs, and forestay and backstay attachment points into one neat and seaworthy package.

On aluminum spars the head box is open at its base to allow electric cables, halyards, and topping lifts to be run inside the mast. On wooden spars the box should be sealed below the sheaves to keep water out of the mast.

Head boxes are either welded in place or bolted (Figure 15-18).

If halyards become recalcitrant, it is important to go aloft and find out why as soon as possible. Salt crystals will plug masthead sheaves just as they will freeze up deck-level blocks. Attempts to free a sheave by dragging a halyard over it will only score the sheave and abrade the halyard.

head box assembly

head box installed

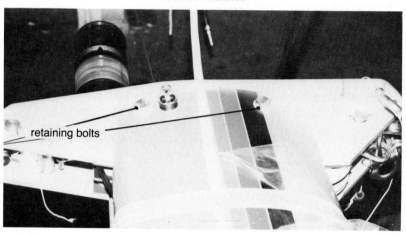

retaining bolts

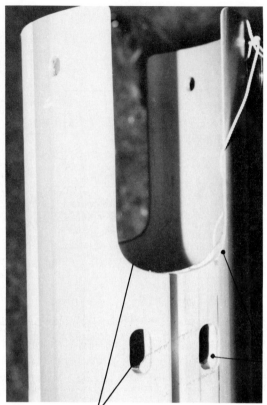

note well rounded cut-outs

Figure 15-18. Removable head box, which fits into the U-shaped cutout in the mast.

Slack off all the halyards. Once aloft, check all the sheaves for free movement. Flex the sheaves up and down; there should be no binding nor any undue play.

Removal of sheaves. This is straightforward enough, but there is always the risk of dropping parts down inside the mast. The first step, therefore, is to tape a piece of line to each sheave, turn the sheave until the line can be pulled out the other side, and then tie the sheave off securely. The sheaves are accessed by removing a plate from the top of the mast, which will allow them to be lifted out, or else by removing a couple of cotter pins, or small plates screwed to the box on either side (Figure 15-19). After these plates or cotter pins are removed, the sheave pin is driven out, using a punch and hammer if necessary. The sheaves can then be withdrawn with the lines already tied around them. Clean and inspect the sheaves and pins. Before replacing, lubricate with a light machine oil or penetrating oil (WD-40, etc.).

Replacing halyards. It is important to main-

tain a free fall inside the mast and not to tangle with other lines. First set up all other halyards tightly to hold them in their normal alignment; next attach a short length of light chain (bicycle chain works well) as a weight to a messenger line and feed it over the appropriate sheave at the masthead. Feed the messenger line down into the mast, and retrieve the chain at the base through the appropriate exit hole using a piece of bent coat hanger. Tie the messenger line to the halyard and use it to pull the halyard up through the mast. The same technique is used for running electric cables inside the internal conduit. Note: When not in use halyards should be secured so that they don't slap on the mast continually. Apart from the irritation of the noise, sooner or later this action will wear through anodizing or paint.

Spinnaker halyards. These are generally led through blocks suspended at the masthead. The blocks swivel to accommodate changing spinnaker positions but at the same time provide a constantly fair lead for the halyards to the masthead sheaves, thus eliminating undue friction.

However, on some excessively windage-conscious boats (e.g., racing boats), the suspended blocks are dispensed with and the spinnaker halyards run straight off the masthead sheaves. Fairing pads are fixed around the box exit. Whenever the pull of the spinnaker halyard is off to one side, it drags over these pads. This leads to wear of the pads and halyards, and considerable friction when raising and lowering the spinnaker. If this kind of rig is used, the fairing pads and halyards will need regular inspection.

Sail track and slides. Only nylon sail slides should be used on aluminum spars, since metal will score the track and generate galvanic corrosion. Periodically flush salt crystals out of the slides and track, which then can be lubricated with silicone car or boat polish (not grease). Masts with a luff groove (as opposed to a track) will accept either special sail slides or a boltrope.

If the sail slides are correctly matched to the track or groove and everything is clean and polished, but the sail tends to jam, the problem most likely lies in the method of attaching the slides to the sail rather than in the mast and slides (Figure 15-20).

End of season. When a mast is unstepped at the end of the sailing season, it and all its rigging should be washed free of salt crystals and the inside of the mast hosed out. Pay particular attention to hard-to-reach areas and the mast heel. Do not use detergents, since some can cause corrosion. (If detergents *are* used, be sure to rinse well.)

Check all moving parts for free operation or undue wear and lubricate lightly with a penetrat-

ing oil such as WD-40. Remove and treat with a corrosion inhibitor any stainless steel fasteners that must not be allowed to freeze up. Inspect all welds and fasteners for cracks and movement, particularly spreader sockets. Check the mast

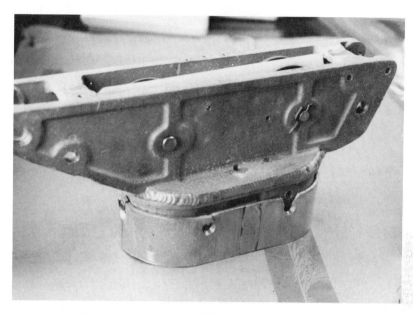

Figure 15-19. Removable head box. To remove sheaves, pull out the cotter key (split pin) and knock out the clevis pin. Be sure to tie a lanyard around the sheaves to prevent their falling into the mast. This mast got tangled up in a drawbridge as it was opening and was picked up by the masthead, which tore the head box from the mast. This is not a recommended method for removing the head box.

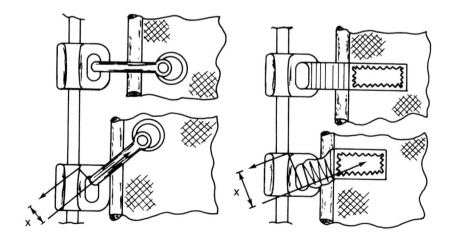

Figure 15-20. Attaching slides to the sail. Use a round shackle (left) that can move freely in the slide. Keep the distance marked X small; this will allow the slide to run freely. At right, the slide is attached by a fabric band; distance X is too great and the slide will jam. (*David Potter,* The Care of Alloy Spars and Rigging, *Adlard Coles Ltd.*)

Going Aloft

Having been at a masthead for several hours at a time on more than one occasion, let me tell you that comfort (or, at the least, minimizing discomfort) is a prime consideration. I would advise sailboat owners to get one of those deep-sided canvas bosun's chairs with lots of pockets all the way around. Just one point: The pockets tend to sag and do not retain tools securely—it is worth putting Velcro tape on the larger ones to close them off.

Safety

- Do *not* hook a bosun's chair to a snap shackle on the halyard. Use a screw shackle or a bowline.
- Do *not* use a wire halyard with a rope tail. If this must be done, first check the rope-to-wire splice *very closely*.
- Do *not* use a winch directly below the mast to go aloft—any tool dropped will land on the winch operator who will probably let go of the rope tail, and down you will come. Rig a block and take the line to a cockpit winch.
- Do *not* use electric winches—it is all too easy for the winch operator to run the bosun's chair up into the head box and tear the halyard loose from the bosun's chair.
- *Do* set up another external halyard or taut line so that you have something to hang onto and help pull yourself up. In the event of a riding turn on the winch (which can create quite a dangerous situation as it is unwrapped), you can take the weight off the hoisting line.
- *Do* place a safety line or strap around the mast as you go aloft. Should the hoisting line fail or come loose, the safety strap will hold you. It will have to be undone and reset at each spreader.
- *Do* tie off once up. This is a most basic safety precaution. It also frees up both hands for working. A good strong belt will be more comfortable than a piece of line. Have the winch operator *cleat off the hoisting line* even if using a self-tailing winch.

The most difficult work aloft is repairing things *on top of* the mast—for example, masthead lights. The bosun's chair most likely will not get you high enough. I take up a couple of short lengths of line and hang "stirrups" from the masthead, one higher than the other, such that the lower one puts my chest at masthead

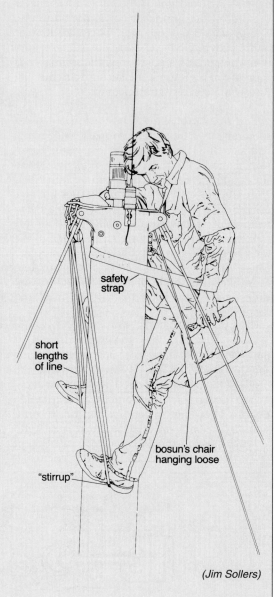

safety strap

short lengths of line

"stirrup"

bosun's chair hanging loose

(Jim Sollers)

level (with a straight leg), and the other (about a foot higher) allows me to push myself up a little more if necessary. I stay in the bosun's chair so that if I slip it will hold me, and strap myself off as high as possible. It's still a pretty nerve-wracking business. Do you have any better method?

wall around the spreader sockets and shroud tangs or *ball sockets* (see below) for distortion (Figure 15-21). Inspect the forestay and backstay-mounting holes in the head box for signs of elongation.

Before storing a mast, *dry it well*. It is excellent practice to apply a coat of silicone boat or car polish. Support the mast evenly at several points along its length so that no section is sagging. Don't store stainless steel rigging against aluminum spars, since corrosion is likely.

Downwind, Whisker, and Spinnaker Poles

All poles used for winging out sheets and sails are designed for *compression loading only*—that is to say, the poles must be set up so that all loads are transmitted directly along the length of the pole to the heel fitting (generally mounted on the mast). In this respect poles are very like spreaders—flexing loads (such as wrapping the pole around a shroud) are likely to cause a pole to buckle.

So far as possible a pole must be set up at a right angle to the mast. The more a pole deviates from a right angle, the more likely it is to be dri-

ven up or down the mast, suffering damage in the process.

There are dozens of different end fittings for poles. Almost all include an anodized aluminum casting together with some form of spring-loaded pin (a piston). Poles are subject to a lot of saltwater spray. Galvanic interaction between the stainless steel spring and piston and the aluminum housing is common, more so on poles that are rarely used. Since the pistons are a close fit in their housings, they frequently freeze up.

Telescoping poles and end fittings need frequent flushing with fresh water. Where excessive

Note the bulging.

Figure 15-21. Check for these trouble spots around the shroud socket area of a mast wall: (**Left**) Mast wall distorted by T-ball shroud socket; (**Right**) mast wall cracked by shroud socket.

Table 15-1. Spar Maintenance Checklist

Item or Aspect	Spar Material	
	Wood	Aluminum
Finish	Check for bare spots, blistering, peeling, cracking, and delaminating. Remove and replace all rotted areas. Refinish.	If spars are anodized, clean and polish any bare spots. If spars are painted, clean, acid-etch, and repaint bare spots.
Fasteners	Check for separation of wood and fastener, water ingress, and rot. Repair and rebed as necessary.	Check for stress patterns, looseness, cracks, and corrosion. Remove any fasteners that must come out periodically; clean, grease, and replace.
Spreaders	Pay particular attention to spreader tops and the attachment points to the mast.	Check spreader sockets for cracks (especially if welded), mast deformation, and loose rivets. Check any rubber pads in semiflexible spreader sockets.
Spreader angles	Make sure all spreaders bisect their shrouds.	Same as for wooden spars.
Heel fitting	Check for water and rot.	Check for corrosion.
Masthead	Check sheaves for free-spinning and wear; where sheaves are set in the mast, check for water ingress into the masthead.	Check sheaves for free-spinning and wear.
Mast track	Check all mast track for loose fasteners and misaligned joints.	Same as for wooden spars.
Storage	Wash off all salt, dry, and store in a cool, dry place with adequate support.	Same as for wooden spars. Keep all rigging out of contact with the spars.

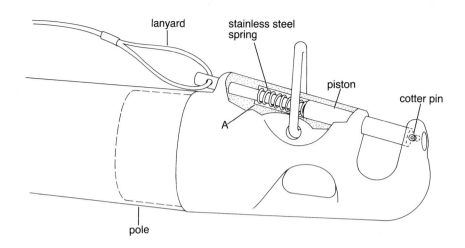

lanyard

stainless steel spring

piston

cotter pin

A

pole

salt builds up, white vinegar will dissolve it. Avoid using detergents; some attack anodized aluminum.

Even if not used, pole fittings should be *exercised* frequently. Lack of use is the biggest problem in the life of poles and end fittings. End fittings can be lubricated lightly with Teflon-based grease to inhibit corrosion.

Where an end fitting does freeze up, it can generally be easily restored to service, usually as shown in Figure 15-22.

The spring-loaded piston is held in place by a cotter pin. If this is removed, the piston and spring can be slid out of their cylinder (it will be necessary to remove the lanyard). If the piston is frozen up, hot water and vinegar will remove most deposits; then you can knock the piston out with a punch, hitting it at the end where the lanyard attaches. Be sure to get a good-sized punch

and hit it squarely—if the top of the piston gets burred over, it is not going to pass through the narrow part of the cylinder bore. In serious cases of corrosion, the spring and cylinder bore will be completely plugged with aluminum oxide, and quite a bit of force will be needed to free things up.

After repeated freeze-ups, several years ago we drilled out our cylinders by running an oversized drill in from the cotter pin end (we opened the cylinders up by an extra $\frac{1}{32}$ inch). We have never had a problem since. (Note: This will destroy any anodizing, but since it was completely corroded anyway we weren't worried.) *It is absolutely vital to drill no farther than point A in Figure 15-22—if the drill goes all the way through, the piston spring will have nothing to seat on and the fitting will be ruined.*

Standing Rigging

Wire Rope

Rod rigging (see Rod Rigging below) is slowly winning acceptance on cruising boats, but even so almost all rigging is still done with stainless steel wire rope. First, the terminology. The basic unit of construction is a *wire*. A straight length of wire is used as a *center wire*, and then a number of other wires are *laid up* around the center wire to form a *strand*. One strand is used as a *core cable* and other strands, or individual wires, are laid up around this core to form the finished cable, known as *wire rope* (see Figure 15-23).

When forming strands and cables, the individual wires or strands are *not* bent around their cen-

ter wires or cores: All of the individual wires are manufactured with the required bends already built in so that they naturally take up the right position without stressing (*preforming*). Depending on the direction in which the wires or strands are laid up in relation to their center wire or core, they are *right lay* or *left lay*. Under a load, a cable laid up in only one direction tends to unravel and stretch, therefore the outer layers of wire rope are laid up in a direction opposite to that of the inner layers—any tendencies to unravel or stretch cancel out. (Norseman has a line of wire rope called Dyform in which the strands are not only pre-

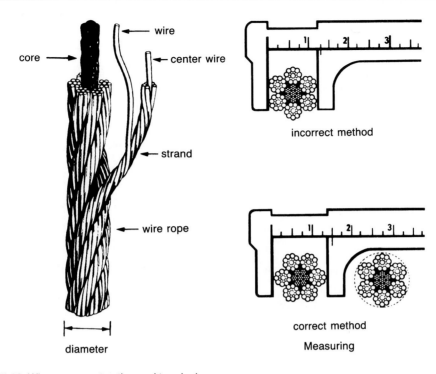

Figure 15-24. Norseman Dyform wire rope. (Norseman Marine)

incorrect method

correct method
Measuring

Figure 15-23. Wire rope construction and terminology. Wire rope is measured as shown at right. (Loos and Co.)

formed but also shaped to eliminate the air spaces that occur around circular strands—Figure 15-24. This results in a considerably stronger and slightly heavier rope for a given diameter, or, put another way, in a smaller and lighter rope for a given strength. To quote Norsemen: "the next best thing to rod, but with all the advantages of wire.")

The fewer the wires and strands in the construction of a cable, the greater its strength and the less its stretch, the ultimate being a cable of only one solid strand—rod rigging. However, the fewer the wires and strands, the less the flexibility and therefore the greater the tendency for the cable to fatigue and fail.

Almost all standing rigging uses 1 × 19 wire rope. This consists of an inner strand (the core) that has 6 preformed wires laid up around 1 straight center wire (giving a total of 7 wires). Twelve more individual preformed wires are laid up around this core. The designation "1 × 19" refers to the fact that there is one strand (the core) and a total of 19 individual wires (Figure 15-25).

Where greater flexibility is required, 7 × 7 and 7 × 19 cable is used. A 7 × 7 cable has 7 strands with 7 wires each (the strands are the same as the core in 1 × 19 wire rope); 7 × 19 wire has 7 strands with 19 wires each (each strand is the same as 1 × 19 wire rope). The 7 × 19 wire—the

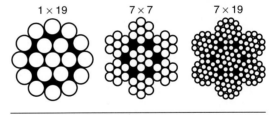

1 × 19   7 × 7   7 × 19

Figure 15-25. Strand arrangement of the most commonly seen types of wire rope. (Norseman)

most flexible—is commonly used for steering cables and halyards.

Wire rope is rated at a breaking strength, which is just that—the load under which it breaks. Industrial practice, where lives are frequently at stake, is to establish a *safe working load* of 20% to 25% of the breaking strength. In marine use a safe working load of up to 50% of the breaking strength is frequently used (it cuts cost as well as weight aloft). The argument is that the rigging is always in column (i.e., straight) and the rope is less likely to fatigue. This takes no account of the constant flexing that can rapidly build up a very high number of fatigue cycles. When rigging or rerigging a boat it is far better to use the safer industrial practice—establish a safe working load of no more than 25% of breaking strength (Table 15-2).

Stainless steel wire rope is made from many different grades of stainless steel. *Nothing but 316 should be used on boats.*

Table 15-2. Breaking Loads for Stainless Steel Wire Rope[1]

Nominal Diameter (strand size) MM	Inches	1 × 19 Minimum Breaking Load Pounds	Kilograms	7 × 7 Minimum Breaking Load Pounds	Kilograms	7 × 19 Minimum Breaking Load Pounds	Kilograms
2	—	704	320	532	242	—	—
2.5	—	1,100	500	—	—	—	—
3	1/8	1,584	720	1,199	545	1,122	510
4	5/32	2,816	1,280	2,130	968	2,134	970
4.76	3/16	3,960	1,800	—	—	2,827	1,285
5	—	4,400	2,000	3,322	1,510	3,124	1,420
5.56	7/32	5,295	2,470	—	—	3,857	1,753
6	—	6,336	2,880	4,796	2,180	4,488	2,040
6.35	1/4	7,084	3,220	—	—	5,031	2,287
7	9/32	7,810	3,550	6,534	2,970	6,116	2,780
8	5/16	10,208	4,640	8,514	3,870	7,986	3,630
9	—	12,914	5,870	—	—	—	—
9.53	3/8	14,476	6,580	—	—	11,330	5,150
10	—	15,950	7,250	13,310	6,050	12,474	5,670
11	7/16	19,294	8,770	—	—	—	—
12	—	22,880	10,400	19,162	8,710	17,952	8,160
12.7	1/2	25,630	11,650	—	—	20,123	9,147
14	9/16	31,196	14,180	26,180	11,900	24,420	11,100
16	5/8	40,832	18,560	—	—	—	—
19	3/4	47,564	21,620	—	—	—	—
22	7/8	63,954	29,070	—	—	—	—
26	1	89,320	40,600	—	—	—	—

1. The loads given are based on Norseman figures. Each company gives slightly different figures.

Fitting End Connections (Terminals) to Wire Rope

Eye terminals using thimbles. At one time, when galvanized wire rope was the norm, almost all rigging was formed into an eye around a thimble and then spliced back into itself. Today wire splices have been almost completely superseded by cable clamps and Nicopress (Talurit) sleeves.

Cable clamps (Crosby or Bulldog clamps) have a U-bolt and a *saddle*. The saddle is scored with grooves to match the lay of the external wires in the rope it goes around. When using cable clamps, *the saddle always goes over the standing (loaded) part of the cable* and the U-bolt over the bitter end, since the U-bolt tends to crush and weaken the rope (Figure 15-26).

Two, and preferably three, clamps should be used, spaced 2 to 3 inches (50 to 75mm) apart and snugged tight. Galvanized cable clamps in sizes below 3/8 inch (10 mm) have a tendency to shear off when tightened; stainless clamps are much stronger.

Nicopress (Talurit) fittings consist of a copper sleeve that is slid up the cable. The bitter end of the cable is wrapped around a thimble and fed back through the eye alongside the standing part. The sleeve is crimped (swaged) with a special tool. The finished eye splice is both strong and neat, but inevitably some deformation of the wire occurs, reducing its strength. A Nicopress kit (the swaging tool and a collection of different-size thimbles and sleeves) is a useful item in any emergency rigging kit.

All wire terminals using thimbles suffer from a number of problems:

1. Unless impractically large thimbles are used, 1 × 19 wire, especially in sizes over 1/4 inch (6mm), cannot be wrapped around a thimble without deforming the wire's lay (and therefore weakening the wire). Both 7 × 7 and 7 × 19 wire are more tolerant, and for this reason thimbles and cable clamps are used extensively as wire terminals in steering systems.

2. Almost all thimbles are relatively lightweight and open at the base. Under a load the thimbles tend to pinch, slacking the fit of the cable, or even collapse. It is preferable to use thimbles with the base welded shut or, best of all, thimbles machined from solid metal (hard to find and expensive—Edson International [New Bedford, Massachusetts] manufactures one or two sizes).

3. Cosmetically speaking, cables terminated in thimbles are nowhere near as attractive as most other terminations.

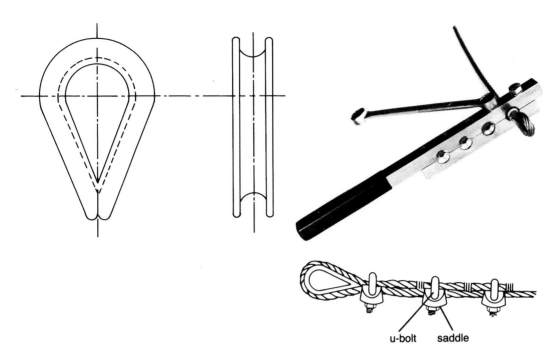

Figure 15-26. Although rigging eyes spliced in wire rope around thimbles are seldom seen these days, eyes retained by cable clamps or Nicopress (Talurit) sleeves are a common sight. They are just as secure as a splice, and far easier to make. Be sure to use the proper size thimble and the proper tool for crimping the sleeve, such as the portable Nicopress tool shown here. If using cable clamps, be sure the saddle rests on the *standing* part of the wire rope. *(Norseman)*

u-bolt   saddle

Swages. Swaged terminals are manufactured to make a close fit over the end of the wire rope for which they are designed (Figure 15-27). The section of the terminal around the rope is then passed through a set of rollers and subjected to enormous pressure. The metal of the terminal is squeezed down into the lay of the cable and effectively *cold welded* to the cable.

With the right equipment and skilled operators, swaging produces fast, neat, low-profile bonds exceeding the breaking strength of the wire rope, and is therefore popular with boat manufacturers and riggers alike. However, it must be done right.

All swaging tends to work-harden the metal involved. The use of incorrect swaging pressures and/or the repeated rolling of fittings will make the terminal brittle and prone to develop hairline cracks. It is not uncommon for improperly swaged fittings to fail within 2 years.

Unfortunately it is generally not possible to tell with a visual inspection whether swaging has been done correctly (unless a terminal is obviously banana-shaped, in which case it should be discarded immediately). If having swaging done, take it to a reputable rigging loft. (Check the swaging machine: The best swages are made by hydraulic one-time-pass-through TecNik machines; manual boatyard machines generally have twin rotary dies through which the fitting must be passed twice, which frequently results in a banana shape; the worst machines are rotary hammers, which will work-harden a terminal, resulting in premature failure.)

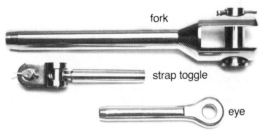

fork

strap toggle

eye

Figure 15-27. Swaged terminals look so nice when new, but unless done by skilled professionals, they have a relatively high rate of failure. *(Gibb)*

Compression fittings. There are a number of compression-type fittings on the market, the best known being those made by Norseman and Sta-Lok (Figures 15-28A and B). They all work on the same principle. A belled sleeve, tapered and threaded toward its lower end, is slid up the cable. The outer wires or strands of the cable are unlaid and a tapered wedge or cone is slid up over the core. The outer wires or strands are then reformed around the wedge or cone, the sleeve is slid down over the top, and the terminal itself is screwed into the sleeve. The individual wires or strands of the cable are sandwiched between the sleeve and the wedge or cone and held firmly (Figure 15-29). In all instances the bond is stronger than the cable itself. Castlok fittings are a variation on the same theme, but in this instance, epoxy glue is used in place of a metal cone (Figure 15-30). The glue sets up, forming a solid, incompressible plug, which serves much the same function as the cone (which is why I have included these terminals here).

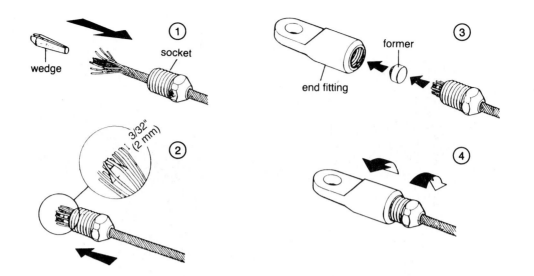

Figure 15-28. Alternatives to swaged terminals, such as the Sta-Lok, Norseman, or Castlok rigging terminals, are fully as secure as swages, and can be installed relatively easily by the boatowner—even at sea.

Figure 15-28A. Sta-Lok terminals are designed for use with preformed 1 x 19, 7 x 7, and 7 x 19 wire rope. The 1 x 19 wedge is plain, but the wedge for 7 x 7 and 7 x 19 rope has a castellated ring with six gates to take the strands. These are not interchangeable. (1) Cut the cable cleanly. (There should be no protruding wires.) Slip the socket over the end of the cable, and unlay the outer wires or strands to expose a section of the center core equal in length to the wedge. (2) Slip the wedge over the center core of the cable (narrow end first), leaving about 3⁄32 inch (2mm) of core and outer wires protruding beyond the wide end of the wedge. Re-lay the outer wires or strands around the wedge, taking care to retain the wedge in its correct position. Carefully pull the socket into position over the wedge to prevent the wires or strands from unlaying. Check the assembly to ensure that the outer wires are spaced evenly around the top of the wedge, and that none of the wires has slipped into the slot in the wedge. Each of the six outer strands of 7-strand ropes should lie in the "gates" provided (not illustrated). (3) Insert the *former* into the threaded hole in the end fitting. Screw the end fitting onto the already assembled unit and tighten with a wrench. Too much force can damage the threads; use no more than can be applied with one hand. (4) To waterproof the fitting, unscrew the two parts and insert a raisin-size blob of silicone caulking on the male thread, inside the bottom of the end fitting. Apply two or three drops of Loctite on the male thread of the socket; screw both parts together again, and tighten. The end fitting may be unscrewed whenever required for inspection or rewiring. When rewiring, cut off and discard the end of the cable and the old wedge. Always use a new wedge when rewiring. The remainder of the terminal parts may be reused a number of times if undamaged. (*Sta-Lok*)

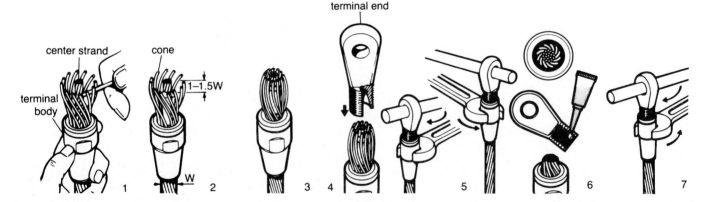

Figure 15-28B. To assemble Norseman terminal fittings: (1) Slide the terminal body over the wire rope, and unlay the outer strands from the center strands. (2) Slide the cone down over the center strand, leaving exposed a length equal to 1.5 times the full diameter of the rope. (3) Relay the outer wires or strands, spaced evenly around the cone. (4) Fit all the protruding wires into the blind recess of the terminal end fitting (eye, fork, stud, etc.), and start threading the body and end fitting together. (5) Complete the assembly, turning the appropriate component in the direction of the lay of the rope, as shown in the sketch. Tighten until the resistance indicates that the cone is being compressed into the body of the terminal. Do not overtighten; you may damage the threads. (6) Unscrew the fitting to inspect and ensure that the wires are evenly spaced and closed neatly over the cone. Apply a thread-locking adhesive, such as Loctite, to the threads. (7) Insert a blob of marine sealant, such as 3M 5200, into the end fitting's blind hole and retighten the assembly. Repeat if necessary until the sealant oozes from the body end. Wipe clean. (*Norseman*)

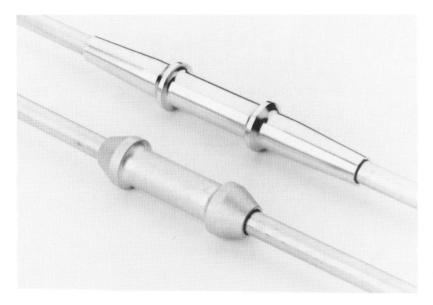

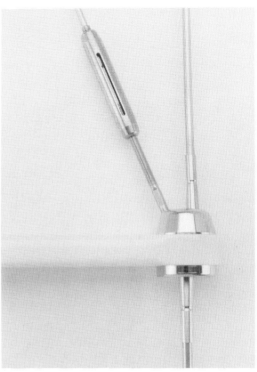

Figure 15-33. **Spreader bends, to relieve the stress of rod rigging where it bends around the tip of a spreader.** (*NavTec*)

Figure 15-34. **Discontinuous rod rigging, which eliminates altogether the bending stress at the spreader tip.** (*NavTec*)

rigging seems to boil down to a matter of cost. There is no question that rod is more expensive, quite a bit more so in many cases. However, rod rigging manufacturers claim that today's rod rigging will outlast a comparable wire rig. If an owner intends to keep a boat for many years, rod rigging may turn out to be the cheapest long-term option, with its performance benefits simply thrown in as an added bonus!

Fitting Rigging to a Boat

All boats use *chainplates* to fasten stays and shrouds to the boat (stays run in a fore-and-aft direction, shrouds athwartships). Chainplates are nothing more than heavy metal straps fastened securely to the hull, or else a U-bolt, which goes through the deck and is fastened from below with either a substantial backing plate or some means of spreading the load to the hull (generally a *tie bar* of some sort). A chain plate has a hole in its top to take a clevis pin. Unfortunately there is no international standardization of pin sizes, which often makes matching of chainplates, clevis pins, and end fittings a matter of trial and error.

Next come *turnbuckles* (rigging screws) to tension the rig (Figure 15-35). A turnbuckle is a hollow sleeve, threaded at both ends but with one thread being right-handed (normal) and the other left-handed (reverse thread). The right-handed thread should be uppermost. A threaded stud goes in each end, one right-handed, one left-handed. Turning the turnbuckle one way pulls both studs in, tightening the rig; turning it the other way pushes both studs out, loosening the rig.

Various means are used to make the connections from chainplates to turnbuckles, and from turnbuckles to wire rope or rod rigging terminals. The most common are solid toggles, strap toggles, forks, eyes, and straight-threaded terminals. However the connections are made, *the lower ends of all stays and shrouds must be free to flex in all directions* (Figure 15-36). This movement is generally provided by a strap toggle.

Where the upper ends of shrouds attach to a mast, by far the most common practice is to terminate the wire rope with an eye fitting, which slips between two metal plates (tangs) fastened to the mast. A clevis pin passing through the tangs and the eye is secured with a *cotter pin* (split pin). This allows fore-and-aft flexing but no athwartships play.

A second method of attaching shrouds, becoming increasingly popular on aluminum masts, is to fasten a slotted ball socket inside the

Figure 15-35. Turnbuckles come with a variety of end fittings to tailor them to different situations aboard. *(Gibb)*

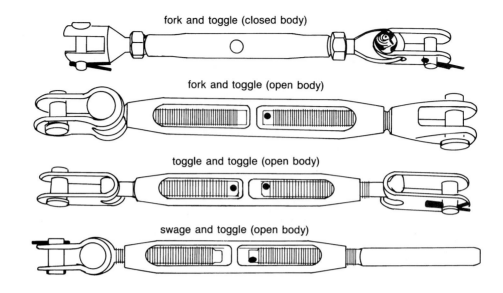

fork and toggle (closed body)

fork and toggle (open body)

toggle and toggle (open body)

swage and toggle (open body)

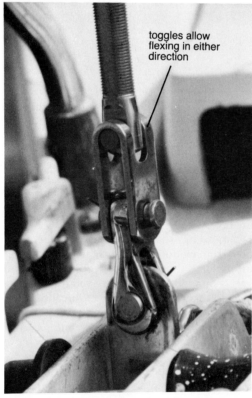

toggles allow flexing in either direction

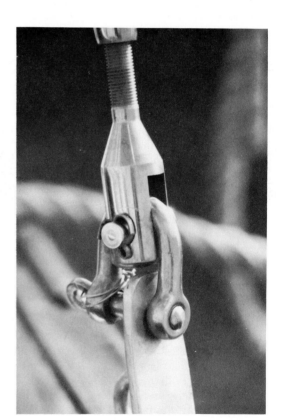

Figure 15-36. Stays are subject to considerable flexing and therefore must have toggles—top and bottom—to prevent early rigging failure. (**Left**) Toggles allow flexing in either direction. (**Right**) Use of a shackle as a temporary toggle. The shackle pin has been lashed correctly with seizing wire.

Spars and Standing Rigging

mast wall. The shroud is terminated in a T-terminal (Figure 15-37). With the shroud slack, the tee is held sideways, slipped into the slot, and then turned back to its proper position; the shroud is then tensioned. The curved face of the tee-end rests in the ball socket and is free to flex a limited amount in all directions.

Stays, especially headstays, are subjected to considerable flexing in all directions and *must have a toggle at the head as well as the foot.* A typical arrangement is to run a clevis pin between two plates welded to the head box. A strap toggle is hung from the clevis pin (Figure 15-38). Where the head box has a single, central mounting plate, a slotted strap toggle fits up either side of the plate. Otherwise the installation is the same.

Many newer spars have what is called a *stemball* fitting as the upper terminal on the stays and shrouds. Stemballs once again are free to flex a limited amount in all directions. When a stemball is used on a headstay, this flexing is adequate to handle the loads of a hanked-on sail, but it is not adequate to handle the additional flexing imposed by a roller-reefing headsail. Where a roller reefer is fitted, the stemball will need adapting so that it is fully toggled (Figure 15-39).

If a backstay is used as an antenna (aerial) for an SSB (single sideband) or ham radio, insulators are fitted at the top and bottom of the stay (though the bottom insulator is often not necessary—Chapter 7). For wire rope, these insulators come with both swaged and compression-type terminals. Many rigs also incorporate a backstay tension adjuster, which may be an arrangement of blocks with a tackle, an oversize turnbuckle with handles attached to the barrel, or a hydraulically operated cylinder.

Inspection and Maintenance

Wire rope. *Rigging is designed for direct in-line loading only.* Any flexing fatigues the wire rope. Without toggles the stress is concentrated at the exit points from the wire rope terminals; with toggles it is distributed through the cable as a whole. *The use of toggles is essential to reduce stress,* but eventually the *fatigue cycles* will still build up to the point at which the rigging fails.

Given the inevitability of failure, how soon should properly installed and maintained rigging be routinely replaced? Norseman recommends: after once around the world in the Whitbread race; after three heavy races such as the transatlantic or Round Britain; after 5 to 8 years of seasonal ocean racing; after 10 years around the buoys; and after possibly 12 to 15 years of summer cruising. In the meantime, rigging should be given a close annual inspection for

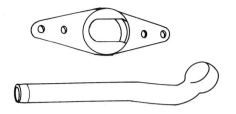

Figure 15-37. The ball-and-socket shroud terminal, increasingly popular on aluminum masts, allows a certain amount of flexing in all directions. *(Gibb)*

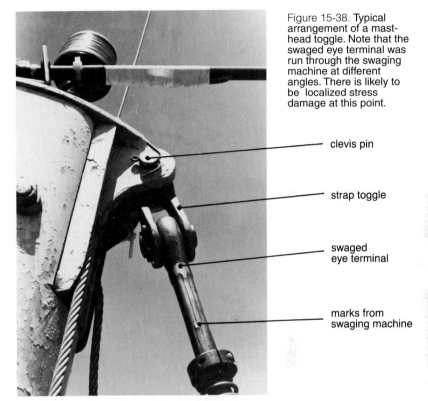

Figure 15-38. Typical arrangement of a mast-head toggle. Note that the swaged eye terminal was run through the swaging machine at different angles. There is likely to be localized stress damage at this point.

clevis pin

strap toggle

swaged eye terminal

marks from swaging machine

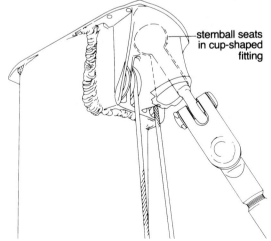

stemball seats in cup-shaped fitting

Figure 15-39. Stemball fittings, as fitted to Isomat spars, act much like a toggle. In this instance the forestay is fully toggled below the stemball in order to absorb the stresses of a roller-reefing rig. *(Jim Sollers)*

Table 15-3. Rigging Checklist

Part or Aspect	Procedure
Cable terminals	Check all clevis pins, toggles, forks and eyes for elongation, wear, and spreading of toggles or forks.
	Check all cables at terminal exits for signs of stranding.
Cable clamps	Make sure cables are wrapped tightly around thimbles.
	Check thimbles for distortion.
	Make sure that clamps are tight.
Swages	Discard any banana-shaped swages and swages with signs of cracking or repeated rolling.
Turnbuckles	Undo all turnbuckles; clean, regrease, and reinstall.
Ball-and-socket shroud terminals	Check the socket and mast for any signs of deformation.
Shroud tangs	Remove the mounting bolt and check for crevice corrosion.
Alignment	Check all chainplates and rigging terminals for alignment. Pay particular attention to the correct placement of toggles and to even loading on fork terminals.

any of the following danger signs:

Stranded wire rope. Wire rope rarely breaks without some warning. Usually before total failure, one or two individual wires fracture and stick out, forming nasty *fish hooks.* The most likely places are where the rope enters terminal fittings (Figure 15-40). *There is no acceptable number of broken wires in a rope.* Even if only *one* has failed, the cable has been severely overstressed and needs immediate replacement.

Deformed wire rope. When a wire rope is dragged through too sharp a turn (e.g., undersized sheaves, spinnaker halyards dragging around masthead fairing pads, or roller-reefing halyards wrapping around the forestay) the rope will be permanently deformed (it generally forms a spiral when not under tension). *It cannot be straightened again;* this would merely compound the problem by putting the rope through more severe stresses. It will fail sooner rather than later and needs replacing.

Stress points on hardware. Pay attention to the following:

1. Chainplates must be lined up exactly with the shroud or stay that they support.

2. If tangs or chainplates incorporate any bends or welds (most do), the bends and welds are the most likely points of failure (Figure 15-41). At the first sign of cracks or pinholes they should be replaced. A magnifying glass helps in inspection, but better yet is annual use of one of the proprietary crack-detection sets on the market (Spot-check, Magnaflux, etc. Cracks can also be detected by scrubbing a fitting with an iodine solution and bronze wool).

3. Stainless steel attachment bolts on external chainplates, and the through-deck bolts on U-bolt chainplates will eventually succumb to crevice corrosion. These should be withdrawn and inspected every few years, especially if there is *any* sign of moisture ingress via the fastener.

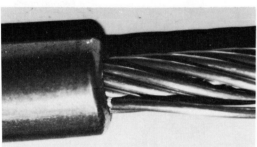

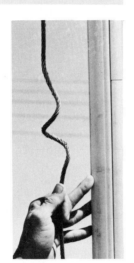

Figure 15-40. **(Top)** Stranded wire rope. **(Middle)** Fractured strands sticking out. Remember: "There is no acceptable number of broken wires in a rope." **(Bottom)** This deformed wire rope is the result of halyard wrap on a roller-reefing unit (see Chapter 16).

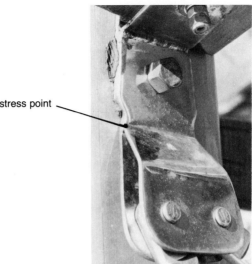

stress point

Figure 15-41. **(Top** and **bottom)** Stress points on hardware.

chain plate   stress point

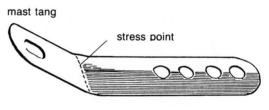

mast tang

stress point

4. Swages are especially prone to cracking down the body of the swage (Figure 15-42). Ideally, they should be crack-tested every year or two (see above). No cracks are acceptable! If a swage is at all curved (banana shaped), it also needs replacing—it has been improperly swaged and may fail without warning.

5. T-terminals on shrouds will develop small cracks on the inside of the radius as they fatigue. The mast-reinforcement plates may develop elongated slots or loose rivets, or distort the mast wall.

6. Thimbles will start to collapse (elongate), work loose in their cable eyes, and wear through at the point of pressure on the thim-ble. Cable clamps need retightening periodically.

7. If any fork terminal is unevenly stressed, sooner or later the loaded side is likely to crack and break off (Figure 15-43). Eye terminals are inherently stronger and alignment is not so critical.

8. Turnbuckles of *all*-stainless-steel construction have a bad habit of *galling*, a process of cold-welding that destroys the threads and makes it impossible to screw or unscrew them. *Almost always the cause is dirt in the threads.* If at any time a turnbuckle (or any other threaded fitting, for that matter) becomes hard to turn, *don't force it.* Spray it with penetrating oil, give the threads time to

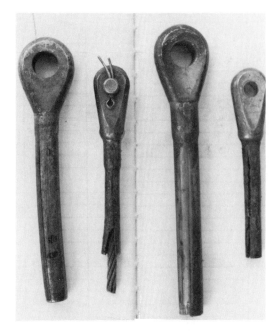

Figure 15-42. **Even professionally done swages are hard to check for hidden flaws. Corrosion in the socket is a particular problem. The swages on the left are banana shaped as well as cracked.**

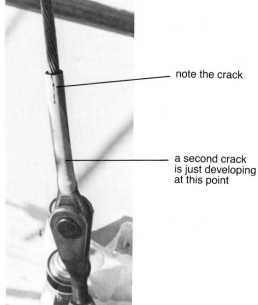

— note the crack

— a second crack is just developing at this point

Figure 15-43. **Broken fork terminal and cracked turnbuckle.**

cool down (a surprising amount of heat is generated), screw it back the other way, lubricate again, and then keep working it backward and forward and hope it frees up. Bronze, and stainless turnbuckles with bronze thread inserts or bronze studs, are far less prone to galling than all-stainless-steel ones. There are various proprietary lubricants (Tef-Gel, Duralac) that will also help to eliminate galling.

9. Every clevis pin should be withdrawn annually and inspected for wear on the pin itself and for elongation of the holes, or cracks around the holes through which it passes. Stainless steel will tolerate a certain amount of elongation without serious loss of strength, but *aluminum will not.* If the mounting holes in aluminum brackets are stretching, the bracket is being overloaded and failure is not far off.

10. Clevis pins, eyes, and strap toggles must be closely matched with only small clearances. Overly long clevis pins will allow toggles to spread and the pins to bend; undersized eyes will allow the clevis pin to bend. In both cases the pin is likely to fail (Figure 15-44).

11. Cotter pins (split pins) need to be opened out 20 to 30 degrees and should be taped to avoid snagging sheets and other lines.

12. Many shroud tangs (and some other items of hardware) are held with a bolt through the mast. These bolts can suffer from hidden crevice corrosion and should be withdrawn and inspected periodically. When replacing, be sure to securely lock the retaining nut either with a cotter pin or by peening over the threads on the end of the bolt. (If a Nyloc nut is used—one with a nylon insert that stops it from working loose—replace the nut.)

Corrosion. Stainless steel is corrosion resistant so long as it has a free flow of air (oxygen) over its surface. Remove this oxygen and add a little stagnant water and it can corrode quite rapidly (Chapter 4). *These are exactly the conditions found in many lower wire terminals and closed-body turnbuckles and around some clevis pins*

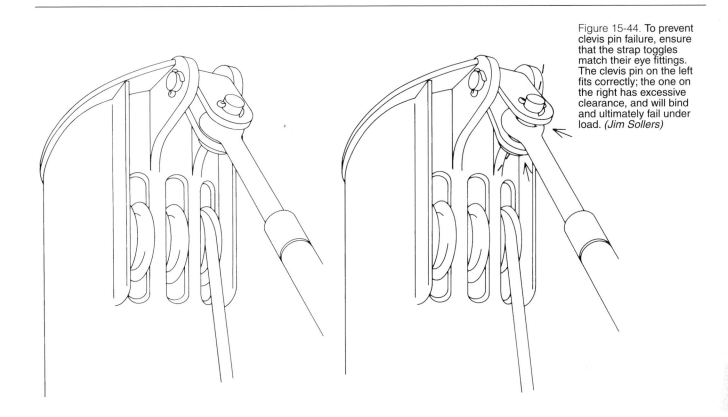

Figure 15-44. To prevent clevis pin failure, ensure that the strap toggles match their eye fittings. The clevis pin on the left fits correctly; the one on the right has excessive clearance, and will bind and ultimately fail under load. *(Jim Sollers)*

(particularly those passing through wooden spreaders) *and chainplate attachment bolts*; also where inboard chainplates pass through a deck. Crevice and pinhole corrosion in these fittings is often virtually undetectable and can lead to a serious rigging failure without warning (Figures 15-45A, B, C, and D).

Wherever possible all lower terminals should be filled with something to keep water out. Sta-Loks and Norsemans are made up with a sealant; Castloks are automatically filled with glue. Swages present a special problem and are notorious for sudden failure in the tropics. When terminals are new, and before their first soaking in salt water, lower swage terminals can be heated *gently* until beeswax or anhydrous lanolin flows down into the lay of the cable to fill any air spaces.

All turnbuckles and any other fittings with threaded studs should have any rigging tape removed, be completely undone, and have the body and threads checked for corrosion once a year. After a thorough cleaning they should be lightly greased or coated with a corrosion inhibitor before reassembly. Any chainplate or chainplate fastener that might get damp should be withdrawn and inspected every few years.

Annual maintenance. In addition to the above recommendations, the rigging should be washed of all dirt and salt before the winter layup. Boots or tapes on spreader tips should be removed for cleaning and inspection. If the rigging is left attached to aluminum spars, make sure the stainless wire is not resting on the aluminum; corrosion would be the likely result.

Tuning a Rig

Static tuning. Before stepping a mast it is useful to measure the *exact* length of the cap shrouds (the two shrouds coming from the masthead down to chainplates in line with each side of the mast). Next, check the chainplates to see that they are the same distance out from the base of the mast and the same height above the deck. Finally, measure from the centerline of the mast aperture in the deck, or the deck plate if deck-stepped, to each chainplate to make sure the mast is centered in the boat. The two measurements should be within an inch of each other.

The masthead is centered before any other tuning is done. Given equal-length cap shrouds and equally spaced chainplates, if the cap-shroud turnbuckles are set to the same length and tensioned equally when the mast is first stepped, the masthead must be centered in the

Figure 15-45. **An anatomy of a rigging failure:**

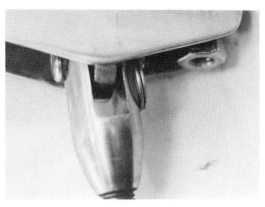

Figure 15-45A. The below-decks backing plate and tie-rod arrangement for a U-bolt chainplate. Note that although the hardware looks perfectly clean, the lock nuts are barely engaging the threads of the U-bolt.

Figure 15-45B. During the 10-year working life of this rig, water has found its way down the U-bolts into the main retaining nuts. Unseen crevice corrosion has weakened the nuts to the point at which some have cracked.

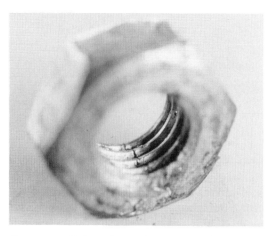

Figure 15-45C. In 15 knots of wind, and 3- to 4-foot swells, the main retaining nuts on a shroud chainplate broke up. The chainplate jerked up a half inch. The sudden shock load on the barely engaged lock nuts stripped the threads off the chainplate U-bolt, allowing it to pull out of the deck. With the loss of the shroud, the load transferred to the cap shroud. The retaining nuts burst on its chainplate, and the rig went over the side. The rig had to be cut loose and sank in 8,000 feet of water. It took a year and over $20,000 to replace it.

Figure 15-45D. Here's another fine mess! The stainless steel shackle has caused extensive galvanic corrosion of the iron centerboard; the shackle pin and shackle plate are both deformed with the pin about to pull out of the cheek plate; the thimble is deformed; and the wire rope is seriously abraded. The centerboard could let go at any time.

boat athwartships (Figure 15-46). Another method of checking this is to tie off a halyard so that its free end just reaches the top of one of the cap shroud chainplates. When moved across to the other side of the boat, it should just touch the other chainplate.

When tensioning any shroud, its spreader must be set up to *bisect the angle of the shroud it supports,* and then the spreader ends must be *locked in this position.* On double-spreader rigs where two shrouds pass over the lower spreader, that spreader must be set up to bisect the angle formed by the *intermediate* shroud. It is amazing how many boats violate this rule, risking a col-

lapsed spreader and the loss of the whole rig. If the spreader tips have no locking devices, cable clamps can be placed around the shrouds above and below the spreader. (Note: Some spreaders mounted on spreader bars are rigid enough to not need locking in place.)

The fore-and-aft masthead alignment is set up by adjusting the forestay and the backstay. (If the rig has twin backstays, these too should be measured before stepping the mast so that they can be adjusted equally.) Most masts are set up vertically, but some are raked aft a degree or two. None are raked forward. If the boat is sitting level in the water, a weighted line hung from the

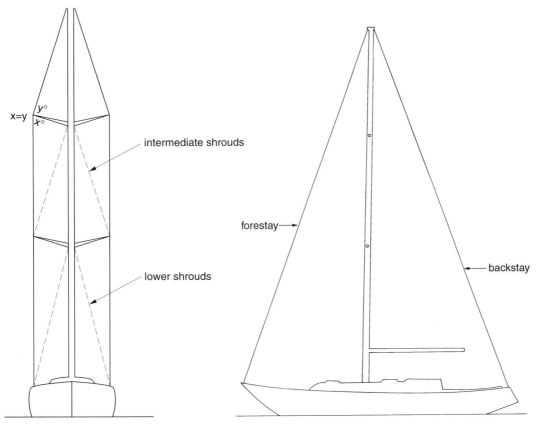

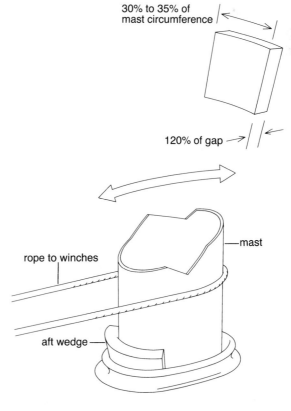

intermediate shrouds

lower shrouds

forestay

backstay

Figure 15-46. Static rig tensioning. (**Left**) Center the mast athwartships with the cap (upper) shrouds and set up tight. (**Right**) Set the *rake* with the fore-stays and backstay(s) and set up tight. Pull the mast into a straight column athwartships using first the intermediate, then the lower shrouds. Use little more than hand tension. *(Jim Sollers)*

30% to 35% of mast circumference

120% of gap

rope to winches

mast

aft wedge

Figure 15-47. For keel-stepped masts, set the fore-and-aft wedges in place. Compress the first pad by running a line passed around the mast to the sheet winches, then slip in the second pad. *(Jim Sollers)*

masthead (or set out far enough to compensate for taper) will act as a plumb bob, but generally the fore-and-aft angle can be eyeballed from dockside with more than enough precision.

In a modern boat, where the rig is set up relatively tightly, the cap shrouds are tensioned to around 15% of their breaking strain, or 10% of the boat's displacement. Because they are the longest shrouds, and therefore subject to the most stretch, they are set up tighter than intermediate (if fitted) and lower shrouds. A backstay is tensioned to around 20% of its breaking strain (which in turn tensions the forestay). There are a number of relatively cheap ($20) tension gauges on the market; one is a useful investment. Always take up on the cap-shroud turnbuckles an equal amount to keep the masthead centered athwartships.

With keel-stepped masts, wedges (*chocking*) are now installed at the partners (the reinforcement around the hole in the deck). Wood can be used on wood spars, but hard rubber is always used on aluminum—one pad in front and one to the rear (Figure 15-47). The total thickness of the pads should be 120% to 125% of the total

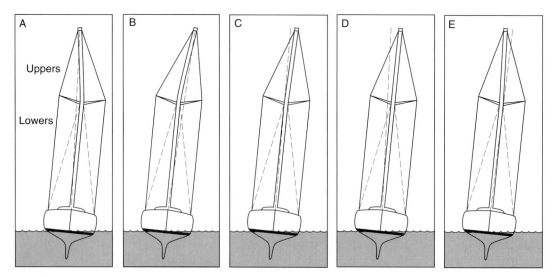

Figure 15-48A, B, C, D, E. Tuning under sail. The windward shrouds on the rig at (**A**) are too loose. The masthead is correctly positioned, but the spreaders are out of column. The rig at (**B**) has its windward lowers too tight. The masthead is correctly positioned, but the spreaders are out of column. The rig at (**C**) has its upper shrouds too slack. The spreaders are in column, but the masthead is sagging off. The rig at (**D**) has both its uppers and lowers too slack and the mast is sagging off along its entire length. The rig at (**E**) has its uppers too tight and the masthead is dragged off to windward.

gap between the mast and partners. The total length of the pads should add up to 30% to 40% of the total circumference of the mast. No pads are placed at the mast sides. The pads will be easier to slip in if soaked in dishwashing liquid.

The most inaccessible pad is slipped in first. A line is tied around the mast and led through suitable blocks to a cockpit winch so that the mast can be pulled forward or backward to compress the first pad and allow the second one to be forced in. The pads should be held to the mast with a large hose clamp (Jubilee clip) so that they do not work their way out when the boat is sailing.

Now sight up the mast track or luff groove and pull the mast into a straight column athwartships using first the intermediate (if fitted) shrouds and then the lower shrouds. Intermediate shrouds are set up a little less tight than upper shrouds; lowers, just a little more than hand tight. Where a rig has an inner forestay and/or double lower shrouds, it is preferable to induce a slight forward bow in the mast at this time. This helps to flatten the mainsail—in any case, when under sail the headsail tension on the forestay will tend to pull the masthead forward and so bring the mast back into a straight line.

Tuning under sail. It is time to go sailing (Figure 15-48). With the boat hard on the wind (Force 4 to 6; 11 to 27 knots), the lee-side rigging should not be slack (although it will lose some of its tension). If necessary, take up some more on the turnbuckles, but be sure to do this equally on both sides. The cap shrouds should need very little, if any, additional tensioning. Once they have been set up at the dock, final tuning should really be done using the lower shrouds to alter mast shape.

When you sight up the sail track, it is desirable that the mast should always remain straight in an athwartships direction. In strong winds the masthead almost always will sag off a little bit to leeward. If the masthead is curving up to *windward*, the windward lower shrouds are too slack; if it is sagging off excessively to *leeward*, the windward lower shrouds are probably too tight.

Under moderate sailing loads, the forward bend induced in the mast at dockside will tend to straighten out. Any tendency for the masthead to curve forward must be counteracted by tightening the backstay(s). It is almost impossible to overtighten backstays using just a spike or screwdriver through the turnbuckle—the tension achieved will not come close to that produced by a hydraulic backstay adjuster.

Sometimes, after repeatedly increasing the tension on various shrouds and stays, the rigging is still slack, especially under a load. In this case *there are serious structural problems that need resolving.* It is important not to keep tightening the turnbuckles—in certain instances it is possible to drive a mast through the cabin top (if deck-stepped), or to pull the ends of the boat into a banana shape (which will open plank seams on wooden boats and loosen bulkheads and joinery on fiberglass boats). A bowsprit butt block may be forced off the foredeck. Major structural alterations or reinforcements are urgently needed.

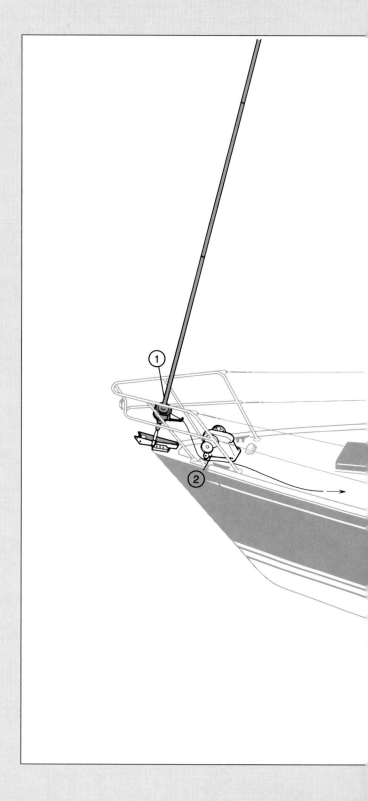

CHAPTER 16

Figure 16-1. These are other high-repair-cost items that can remain virtually troublefree through the application of proper maintenance procedures. *(Jim Sollers)*

(1) roller furling jib
(2) anchor windlass
(3) boom vang
(4) turning block
(5) line stopper
(6) backstay adjuster
(7) winch
(8) mainsheet
(9) topping lift
(10) genoa track

Running Rigging, Deck Hardware, and Roller Reefing

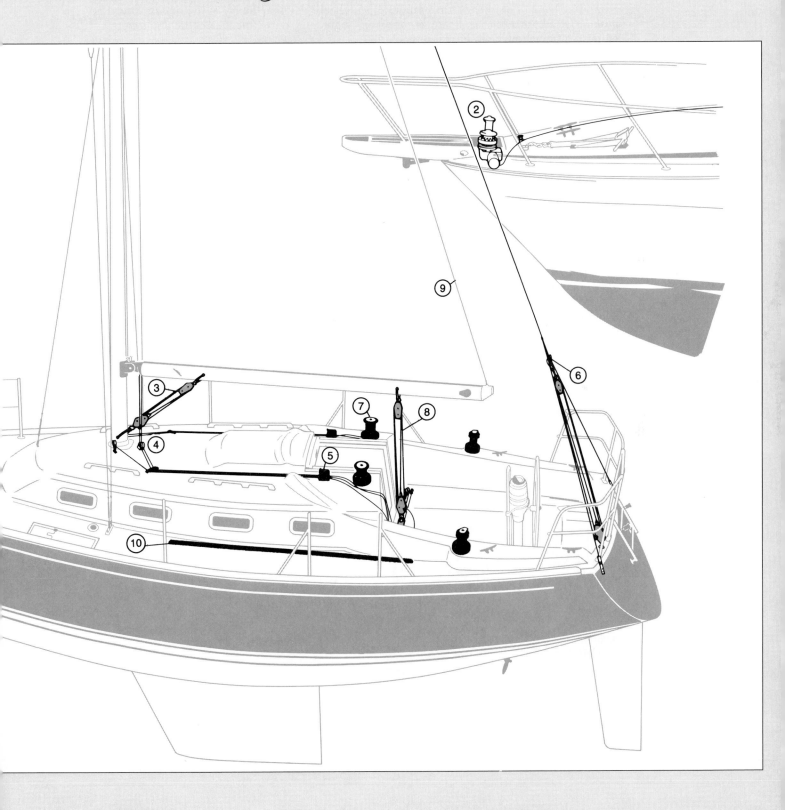

Terminology and Loading Factors

First, some nomenclature. The basic unit of running rigging is a *block*. The wire or rope is led around a *sheave*. This sheave turns on either a *bushing* (sleeve) or a *bearing*. Bearings consist of either a number of balls set in a machined groove (a *race*) or else *rollers* (pins set on end around a central shaft). On either side of the sheave is a *cheek plate (side plate* or *shell).* The cheek plates are reinforced by *straps* through which pass the central bearing shaft, fasteners to hold the block together, and the fastening for the block *head assembly*—the means by which it is attached to the boat (Figures 16-2A and B).

Sheaves may be either plastic or aluminum; bushings may be bronze or plastic; ball bearings are generally plastic. (I am using the term *plastic* to cover some widely varying materials.) Rollers are usually bronze or stainless steel. Cheek plates may be plastic, aluminum, or stainless steel. Straps are always stainless steel except in a few expensive racing blocks where titanium is used.

Sheave selection. Three factors are important in sheave selection: the overall diameter of the sheave, the shape of its groove, and the material from which it is constructed.

Diameter. Pulling any wire or rope around a sheave deforms the lay of the line or wire. The tighter the curve, the greater the distortion.

Groove shape. The groove in a sheave must match the shape of the line or wire passing over it if it is to provide maximum support and minimum distortion. A groove suitable for ½-inch (13-mm) Dacron line will provide poor support for ¼-inch (6-mm) 7 × 19 stainless steel wire rope. Even different kinds of line use different groove shapes—Kevlar likes a flatter groove than Dacron (Figure 16-3). Grooves for wire rope are frequently scored to match the lay of the outer strands of the rope.

Materials. Sheaves for synthetic line are generally plastic while those for wire rope are almost always aluminum in order to withstand the greater abrasion. Wire would soon tear up plastic sheaves.

Loading factors. Blocks are designed to take a direct pull on the sheave with only minimal side-

Figure 16-2A. **Modern block construction.** *(Schaefer Marine Products)*

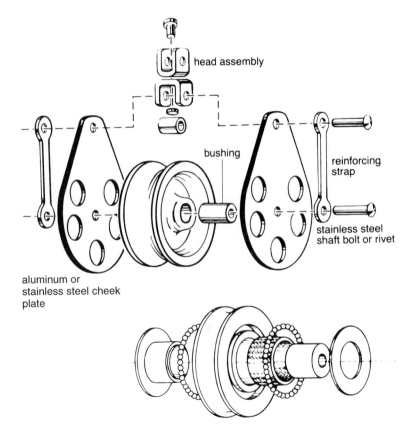

head assembly

bushing

reinforcing strap

stainless steel shaft bolt or rivet

aluminum or stainless steel cheek plate

Figure 16-2B. (**Below**) Bearing-type block construction. (**Right**) Use of bearings in a cam cleat and in the pedestal of a swivel block. *(Harken)*

cam cleat

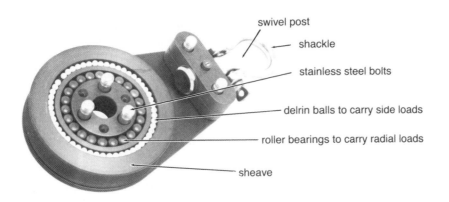

swivel post

shackle

stainless steel bolts

delrin balls to carry side loads

roller bearings to carry radial loads

sheave

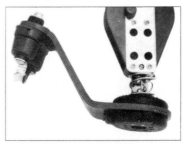

countersunk bolt

stainless steel strap

delrin sideplate
ball bearings

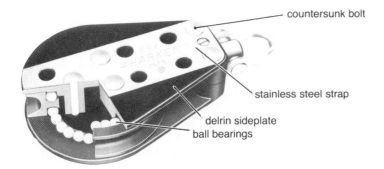

ways loading. Numerous head fittings are available to ensure the correct alignment of block and line (straight shackles, *upset* shackles, swiveling heads, spring-loaded bases, etc.). Blocks are rated at their *safe working load*, which is generally 50% of the breaking strength of the hardware.

Loads on blocks are directly related to the angle through which a line is turned. For example, a block that does not turn a line at all is subjected to no load, while one that turns a line through 180 degrees is subjected to a load of *double* the pull on the line. Figure 16-4 and Table 16-1 illustrate block loading factors.

If blocks are subjected to greater loads than they are designed for, or to more than minimal sideways loading through improper alignment, the sheaves, bushing, and/or bearing will deform and friction will build up rapidly. Even correctly rated blocks may start to deform if left permanently loaded (when you are not sailing, a block should be left in an unloaded state as far as is possible). Sometimes deformed plastic bearings and sheaves will recover their proper shape after

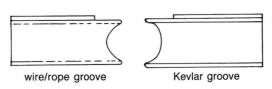

wire/rope groove   Kevlar groove

Figure 16-3. Block sheaves are available for use with different types of rope or wire. Use of the incorrect sheave can lead to early failure of rope. *(Harken)*

Table 16-1. Block Loading as a Function of Turning Angle

Turning Angle	Block Loading Factor	Block Load [Based on 100 lbs. (45kg) Line Tension]
0°	0	0 lb. (0kg)
30°	.518	51.8 lbs. (23.5kg)
45°	.767	76.7 lbs. (34.9kg)
60°	1.000	100.0 lbs. (45.45kg)
90°	1.414	141.4 lbs. (64.3kg)
120°	1.732	173.2 lbs. (78.7kg)
135°	1.846	184.6 lbs. (83.9kg)
150°	1.931	193.1 lbs. (87.8kg)
180°	2.000	200.0 lbs. (90.9kg)

a period of rest, but frequently damage is permanent. In cases of extreme overloading, blocks will *explode* (disintegrate) without warning, creating a serious safety hazard.

Maintenance

Cleaning. Every time a block gets wet and dries out, salt crystals are left behind. In time the accumulation of salt in the bearings increases friction. This in turn increases wear on the moving parts, or else freezes up the block completely—especially common with infrequently used blocks.

All blocks need flushing with fresh water several times a season to wash out salt crystals, dirt,

and any by-products of corrosion. Particularly stubborn deposits will generally succumb to *hot* water. If not, use plain white (clear) vinegar, but rinse after flushing. Detergents generally should not be used on anodized aluminum, since some contain chemicals (ammonia) that will attack anodizing. Stains on stainless steel can be removed with copper scouring pads or a bronze wire brush (not steel wire wool, since tiny flecks of steel left behind will rust and leave more stains).

Sheaves should be spun to ensure free turning without excessive play. No lubrication is needed, but a shot of WD-40 or some silicone spray will do no harm.

Combating corrosion. Almost all blocks incorporate two or more galvanically incompatible metals, so sooner or later corrosion is inevitable. Aluminum sheaves and cheek plates, being the least noble metal involved, get eaten away. Stainless steel shafts suffer from crevice corrosion. The buildup of aluminum oxides in a block, together with salt and dirt, helps to freeze it up. It should be noted that aluminum cheek plates are primarily a weight-saving measure intended for racing boats. Since the blocks will be replaced every few seasons, corrosion will be minimal. Unfortunately, these blocks have also been widely used by manufacturers of cruising boats. Here the blocks need to hold up for many years; corrosion frequently becomes a problem. *Cruising sailors should specify blocks with stainless steel or plastic cheek plates.*

Disassembly. Smaller, cheaper blocks are riveted together and cannot be disassembled. If cleaning and lubrication do not return a block to service it will have to be discarded. Larger and more expensive blocks are bolted together, and thus can be disassembled when necessary.

Frequently, through-bolts become corroded in place. Remove the nuts, flush with hot water and white vinegar, and spray with penetrating fluid. Grip the bolt head and try working it backward and forward to free it up. If this fails, put the nut back on and screw it down until just flush with the top of the threads on the bolt, support the block on the other side, and hit the nut smartly with a hammer (Figure 16-5). This should jar things loose. Then go back to twisting the bolt back and forth.

Sheaves that ride on bearings (as opposed to bushings) generally have a retaining plate to hold the balls or rollers in place. The bearings come out complete with the sheave, and are then accessible by removing the retaining plates. Inspect the bearing races for any indentations and the balls for flat spots. In either case, replace.

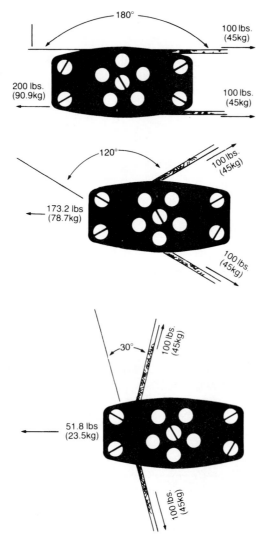

Figure 16-4. **Block loading factors.** The load on a block depends on the tension of the line passing through the block and the turning angle involved. *(Schaefer Marine Products)*

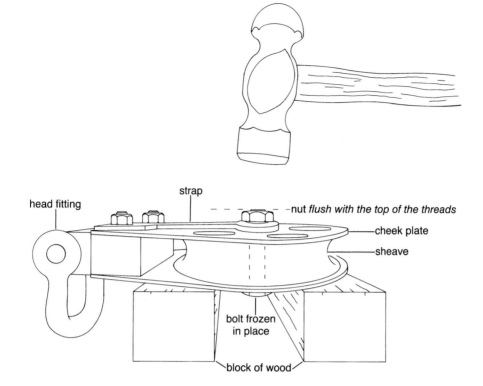

Figure 16-5. **Removing a corroded-in-place sheave bolt.** *(Jim Sollers)*

head fitting

strap

nut *flush with the top of the threads*

cheek plate

sheave

bolt frozen
in place

block of wood

Winches

Winches can be operated with a handle inserted in the top *(top-acting)* or the bottom *(bottom-acting)*. In the case of larger winches on racing boats, they may be set up with handles on both sides *(coffee grinders)*. Most are designed so that the drum turns in only one direction and locks in the other. The exception is halyard winches, which have a brake. When the brake is released the drum is free to rotate in reverse.

Regardless of individual differences the operating principles remain the same. There is a high degree of similarity among different types of winches and also among similar winches from one manufacturer to another. The following focuses on top-acting winches, since these constitute the overwhelming majority.

How They Work

If a handle is fitted to the outer rim of a winch drum, any turning force exerted on the handle will be the same as the pull of the winch (assuming no friction losses, etc.). But if the handle is lengthened until it is four times as long as the distance from the outer rim of the drum to its pivot point (center), the same force on the han-

dle will produce four times the pull at the winch (Figure 16-6). The trade-off is that the handle is now moving through four times the distance that it was before: If it is turned at the same speed as before, only one-quarter as much line will be pulled in in the same time—in effect, we have a 4:1 gear ratio.

This relationship between the distance of the winch handle and drum rim from the pivot point of the drum is what imparts power to small, simple winches. The actual mechanism is as follows:

The winch handle turns a shaft *(spindle)* with a gear on it (Figure 16-7). The body of the winch (the drum) contains hinged, spring-loaded metal pieces called *pawls*, which bear against this gear. When the spindle is turned in one direction the pawls engage the spindle gear, locking the drum to the spindle so that drum and spindle turn as one. When the spindle is turned in the other direction the pawls hinge inward against their springs and disengage the spindle gear, allowing the drum to remain stationary *(ratcheting* or *freewheeling)*.

At this point we have the ability to turn the drum, but when we let go of the winch handle there is nothing to stop the drum from spinning in reverse when under a load. Another set of

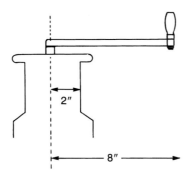

Figure 16-6. Winches: How they work. The line pull of the winch equals four times the turning force on the handle.

2"

8"

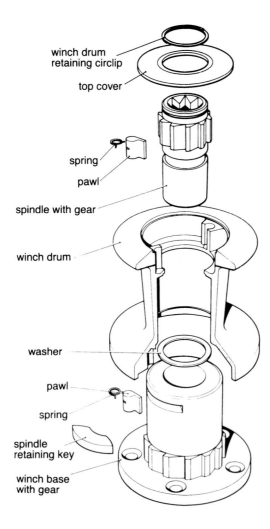

Figure 16-7. Single-speed, direct-drive, top-acting winch. *(Lewmar)*

winch drum retaining circlip

top cover

spring

pawl

spindle with gear

winch drum

washer

pawl

spring

spindle retaining key

winch base with gear

spring-loaded pawls in the drum, operating in the opposite direction to the first set, engages a second gear on the winch mounting plate (winch base). This gear is forever locked in one place. Cranking on the winch handle turns the drum, which ratchets around the baseplate gear. When the winch handle is released the second set of pawls engages the baseplate gear and prevents the drum from spinning in reverse.

What I have just described is a *single-speed, direct-drive, top-acting* winch: *single-speed* because there is always the same gear ratio between the spindle (i.e., winch handle) and the drum; *direct-drive* because the spindle directly engages the drum; and *top-acting* because the winch handle is inserted in the top.

Halyard winches. A *reel-type* halyard winch is essentially the same, with the exception that the baseplate gear is itself free to rotate but has a brake band around it, which is fastened to the baseplate (Figure 16-8). When the brake band is tightened, it locks the baseplate gear to the baseplate and the winch operates as above. When the brake band is loosened, the baseplate gear is free to rotate and the drum unwinds. But note that as it unwinds, the drum pawls engaging the spindle gear will lock the drum and spindle together and spin the spindle with the drum. Thus, if the winch handle is left in the winch, it too will spin, and herein lies the cause of many a broken finger and wrist. *Never release the brake on a halyard winch with the handle in place.* (Note that the same situation arises with a regular winch if the pawls engaging the baseplate gear fail for any reason—*never leave handles in winches!*)

Multiple-speed winches. When the winch handle is turned on a single-speed winch it engages the drum in only one direction and freewheels (ratchets) in the other. On a two-speed winch the handle also engages the drum in the second direction, but at a different gear ratio (i.e., given the same winch handle speed, the drum turns at a different speed). This is achieved as follows:

There is the usual single-speed gear machined onto the spindle. The spindle also fits inside a second gear. Pawls on the spindle ratchet inside this second gear when the winch handle is cranked in the first (single-speed) direction. The pawls engage the inside of this second gear when the winch handle is turned in reverse (the single-speed gear itself is ratcheting at this point). The spindle and second gear are now turning in reverse. Obviously, to be of any use the drum itself must continue to turn in the single-speed direction; otherwise it would just oscillate back-

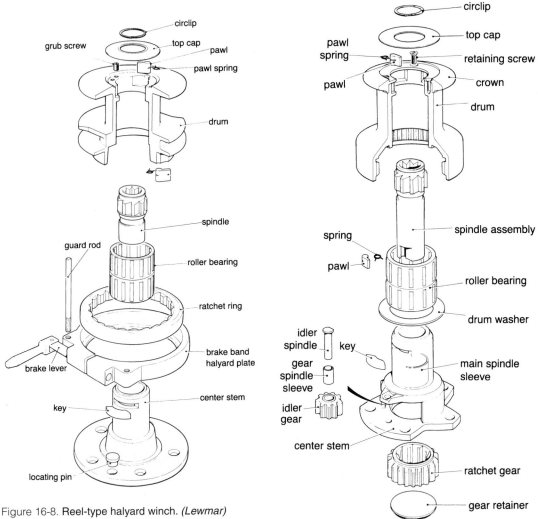

Figure 16-9. Two-speed winch. *(Lewmar)*

Figure 16-8. Reel-type halyard winch. *(Lewmar)*

ward and forward as the handle was cranked backward and forward. An *idler gear* is fitted between the second spindle gear and the drum; this converts the backward spindle movement into forward drum movement (Figure 16-9).

With this arrangement, although it is a little hard to visualize, any load on the drum (e.g., line pull) tries to turn the spindle in one direction via the first (single-speed) gear, and the opposite direction via the second gear. Since the spindle cannot rotate in two directions at once, the winch is effectively locked in place by these counterposed forces. When the drum is spun the other way (freewheeled) both gears ratchet, allowing it to turn.

In order to make a winch more powerful, the gear ratio between the handle and the drum must be increased. This could be done by increasing the length of the winch handle, but this is clearly impractical. Instead, what is done is to fit more gears into the winch and play with the relative gear sizes (Figure 16-10). The net result is that a large three-speed winch can look quite complicated, but the principles remain the same as for the simpler winches.

Servicing and Overhaul

Maintenance. All winches incorporate dissimilar metals, notably bronze, stainless steel, and, in many cases, aluminum. All are subject to salt-water spray to a greater or lesser extent, leading to the accumulation of salt crystals inside the winch over time. Here we have all the ingredients for galvanic interaction, especially between aluminum parts and stainless steel and bronze gears, shafts, and fasteners (Figure 16-11).

Almost all winches are lightly greased internally. In some environments there is quite a bit of dust and sand in the atmosphere. In any event, given time the grease will clog with dirt and salt, reducing its lubricating properties. The winch will stiffen up (this is most easily felt by

Winches   517

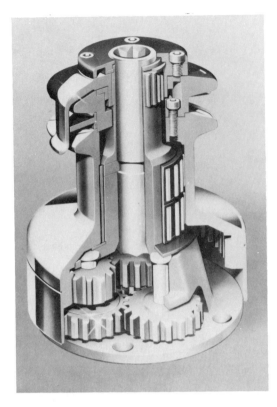

Figure 16-10. Larger winches, with higher gear ratios to handle higher loads, are more complex than simple winches. *(Lewmar)*

rotating the drum backward by hand with no load on it—it should be free-spinning) and wear will accelerate.

For these reasons winches need regular cleaning—Lewmar recommends a monthly hosing down and light oiling and greasing, a partial strip-down two or three times a season, and a complete strip-down once a year. With this kind of attention most winches will operate trouble-free for many years.

Given the ease and speed with which a winch can be serviced, *it is a shame that so many boatowners go from one year to the next without paying the slightest attention to their winches.* If servicing is left until a noticeable problem has developed (extreme stiffness, drum freewheels in both directions, etc.), the winch is likely to have suffered unnecessary and permanent damage.

Disassembly. The pawls and pawl springs are very small, easily lost, and absolutely indispensable to winch operation. *Before dismantling, clear the area around a winch and plug any nearby drains*—sometimes the pawls and springs hang up and fly out at unexpected moments. Even better, keep spares on board in case any do get lost or broken.

Figure 16-11. Galvanic corrosion around a stainless steel fastener in an aluminum self-tailing mechanism.

stainless steel fastener   aluminum self-tailer

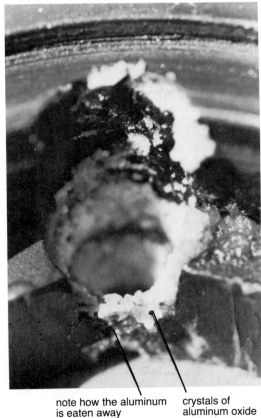

note how the aluminum is eaten away   crystals of aluminum oxide and salt

The top of the winch must first be removed (Figure 16-12A). On some the whole top unscrews; others are variously retained with machine screws, socket-head screws, or spring clips, often called *circlips* (Figure 16-12B). Beneath the top cover may be a couple of *collets* fitted into slots in the spindle (Figure 16-12C). Removal should be self-evident. If the winch has a self-tailing mechanism this comes off next. First *note the position of the stripper arm in relation to the boat so that it can be put back in the same place.* Some self-tailers have a number of springs—lift the top plate off carefully to prevent the springs from flying out. (Note that unless there is a specific reason to disassemble a self-tailing mechanism, it can normally be lifted off in one piece with the drum, in which case this step can be ignored.) The winch drum now can be lifted off (Figure 16-12E)—this is where care must be taken to watch out for loose pawls, especially any fitted in the base of the drum.

On all but the largest winches all of the bearings and gears are now accessible. The bearings should be retained in a *cage* and may be inside the drum or on the center stem. With the bearings removed, somewhere in the center stem will be a key or collets, which must be gently pried out to release the spindle (Figure 16-12F and G).

If any corrosion is present, the spindle itself may be a little hard to remove. A good spraying with penetrating oil will help, and a winch handle can be locked in place and used to work the spindle out. Any gears will be retained by shafts (also called spindles) that simply lift out (Figures 16-12H and I). Larger winches have replaceable sleeves around the gear shafts, or the gears themselves ride on small roller bearings.

Gear shafts, sleeves, and/or bearings should all go back in the same place. It is best to lay everything out on a clean work surface, with the various parts the right way up and in the correct relationship to each other.

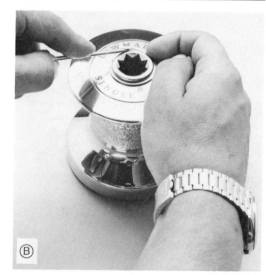

Figure 16-12. **Step-by-step winch disassembly for cleaning and maintenance.** Remove screws (**A**), circlip (**B**), or unscrew the winch top (not shown). If the winch is self-tailing, pull out retaining collets (**C**). On a halyard winch the halyard must be released from the drum, accomplished here by undoing the two "grub" (Allen) screws (**D**). (Note: sequence continues on next page.)

Figure 16-12 (*cont.*). Lift off the drum and bearings (**E**), and oil the top drum pawls (**F**). Remove the spindle. The plastic key, which fits into a groove in the spindle and is itself retained by the bearings fitted around the winch stem, holds the spindle in place (**G**). You can pry loose a spindle, or gear shaft (**H**). Finally, remove the gears (**I**). *(Lewmar)*

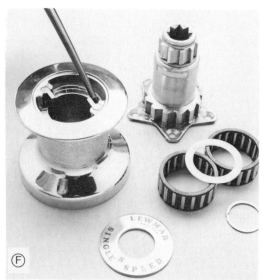

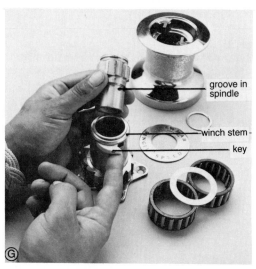

groove in spindle

winch stem

key

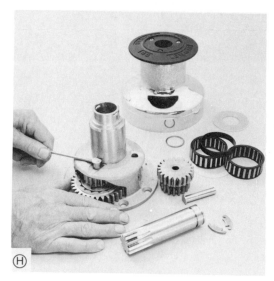

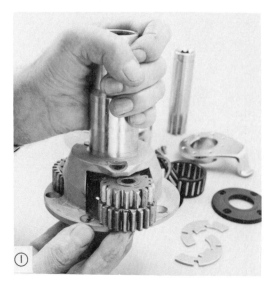

Thoroughly clean everything in kerosene (paraffin) and dry with a lint-free rag. Inspect the gears for worn, chipped, or stepped teeth; the stainless steel shafts for crevice corrosion; the bearings for corrosion or flat spots; the center stem and inside of the drum for corrosion; above all the pawls for any signs of wear or chipping; and the pawl springs for corrosion and loss of tension. Anodized aluminum self-tailing mechanisms retained by stainless steel fasteners are especially susceptible to corrosion around the fasteners. A little Tefgel, Duralac or the like on the fastener threads will help to keep this at bay.

Reassembly. Reassembly is the reverse of disassembly (Figure 16-13). Pay special attention to those all-important pawls and springs, which should be lightly oiled (3-In-One Oil, Marvel Mystery Oil). Make sure that ratchet gears are

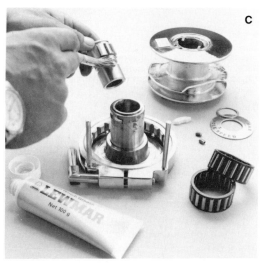

rightside up (Figure 16-13D) and the parts properly seated. *Do not grease* the pawls—the grease is likely to attract dirt and salt until eventually the pawls bind in their housings and fail to operate. Gears and bearings should be *lightly* greased, however, with a Teflon-based marine grease (Lubriplate, Marine Lube A, etc.).

No oil or grease should ever be applied to the brake band or mechanism on any halyard winch—doing so can create a serious safety hazard.

Note that gear shafts fit into holes in the baseplate. During cleaning operations particles of dirt are liable to fall into these holes. They must be scrupulously cleaned out or the shafts will not seat properly. The shafts themselves have odd-shaped heads fitting into machined recesses and *must be properly seated*. The spindle key fits into a machined groove in the spindle. If it won't go in, *don't force it* (in fact, *nothing* on a winch needs forcing). Raise or lower the spindle a fraction until the key is an easy fit.

Refitting a self-tailing mechanism. If it has a separate stripper ring (Figures 16-13F and 16-14) make sure to place it under the stripper arm (it fits in a slot) and to put the stripper arm back in the necessary relationship to the boat to make the

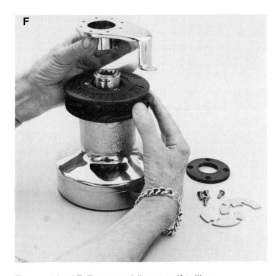

Figure 16-13F. Reassembling a self-tailing mechanism. Note the stripper arm being lined up to fit under the feeder arm.

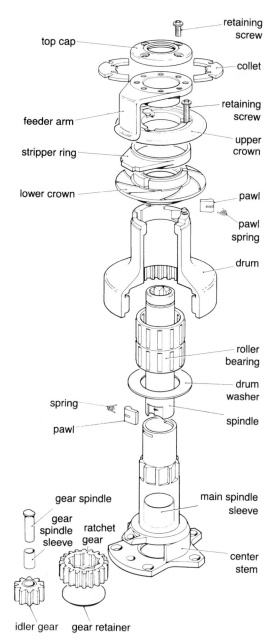

Figure 16-14. Self-tailing winch. *(Lewmar)*

retaining screw

top cap

collet

feeder arm

retaining screw

stripper ring

upper crown

lower crown

pawl

pawl spring

drum

roller bearing

drum washer

spring

pawl

spindle

gear spindle

gear spindle sleeve

ratchet gear

main spindle sleeve

center stem

idler gear

gear retainer

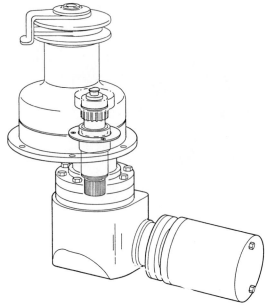

Figure 16-15. Electric-powered winch. The winch is essentially the same as a manual winch with the exception of some minor modifications to take the motor drive. *(Lewmar)*

sheet fall in the correct place. Any fasteners just need to be pinched up—don't overtighten, especially where plastic housings are involved.

Powered Winches

Powered winches are becoming more popular. Until recently almost all had electric motors, but now there is a trend toward some very sophisticated hydraulic systems (e.g., Lewmar's Commander system). In any event, the winch end of things is just the same as a manual winch, except for some minor modifications to the spindle to allow a motor to be geared in from below (Figure 16-15).

The motor end of a powered winch is the same as for a powered windlass—see Electric Windlasses later in this chapter. Some two- and three-speed winches are also being powered; here sensitive electronic equipment, linked into a central microprocessor, senses the load on a winch and reverses the motor at a certain point. This has the same effect as reversing the direction of cranking on a winch handle—it engages another gear. At higher loads an electromagnet is tripped to engage a third gear (where fitted).

If a two-speed winch operates only at one speed, try reversing the power leads *from* the control unit *to* the motor (*not* the power leads *to* the control unit—that would probably wreck the control unit).

Faced with a motor failure, run all the usual voltage tests (Chapter 3); jump the motor directly from the battery to make sure it really is at fault. Check the brushes, brush springs, and commutator; run the motor tests outlined in Chapter 6.

Anchor Windlasses

Anchor windlasses can be horizontal or vertical. In the former the drum (for rope) and *wildcat* (*gypsy*, for chain) stick out the sides; in the latter they are set one on top of the other. Windlasses are both manually operated and powered, the majority of the latter having electric motors, but some being hydraulically driven.

General Maintenance

Windlasses are generally low-maintenance, troublefree items. The most essential part of preventive maintenance is to keep the windlass covered when not in use, and occasionally to wash down the exterior surfaces with fresh water. Open-gear (nonlubricated) windlasses should be flushed out at the same time.

Most windlasses run in an oil or grease bath. Infrequent use causes the lubricant to settle out. In addition to maintaining oil levels, *periodically crank the windlass to distribute lubricant around the gears*. Many gears, sprockets, and chains are steel—a failure to turn the windlass over from time to time will lead to rusting and seizure. A sample should be taken annually from the base of the gearbox to check for salt water or emulsification. In either case the gearbox should be flushed and fresh lubricant added. (To clean out a grease-filled box the windlass must be unbolted and the baseplate removed.) Sometimes special greases are used that coat and adhere to the internal parts better than a normal grease. Refer to the manual.

Clutch cones and brake linings need annual lubrication; the manual will specify the type of lubricant. The clutch nut is undone and the wildcat slipped off to gain access to the clutch or brake pad. Where the windlass has a *plated steel* shaft (as opposed to bronze or stainless steel) be sure to remove the rope drum annually and grease the shaft or the two will seize together and be *impossible* to separate.

Problems Common to All Windlasses

Corrosion. Anchor windlasses occupy one of the most exposed positions on any boat, subject to constant saltwater drenchings. Since most incorporate dissimilar metals (notably aluminum, bronze, steel, and stainless steel), there is an obvious potential for galvanic interaction. Windlasses should therefore periodically be washed down with fresh water, and *should be kept covered*. Luckily, most *external* corrosion problems tend to be cosmetic or peripheral to the main functioning of the windlass (e.g., blistered paintwork on aluminum windlasses, and oxidizing of aluminum housings and baseplates around stainless steel fasteners; to reduce problems, all fasteners should be coated with a corrosion inhibitor). These problems can be irritating and make disassembly and overhaul difficult, but rarely interfere with the basic functioning of the windlass.

Far more damaging is *internal* corrosion, which leads to seizure. Corrosion from condensation alone can seize up an unused windlass. Windlasses in anchor wells, even though closed off and protected, are actually more prone to corrosion than those on foredecks—the anchor well produces a wonderfully warm and humid atmosphere! It is essential to turn windlasses over regularly, to maintain oil and grease levels, and to ensure that no water enters the windlass case.

Snubbing loads. The majority of operating problems arise from overloading a windlass through excessive snubbing loads. When an anchored boat is lying to an all-chain *rode* (anchor line) in choppy seas, the foredeck can pitch up and down through many feet, gaining considerable momentum in the process. If the anchor is well buried, as it should be, the anchor windlass is subjected to repeated shock-loading when the bow comes up, which may tear it loose from the foredeck or shear a shaft (Figure 16-16).

Anchor windlasses are just not designed to handle heavy snubbing loads, although from time to time some are inevitable and even necessary, particularly when breaking out a deeply buried anchor. In general, though, the windlass should always be protected against shock loads. This is done as follows:

1. Drop the anchor, pay out adequate scope (at least 4:1 on chain), and set the anchor (make sure it is dug in).
2. Attach a length of *nylon* line (the snubbing line) to the anchor chain at the bow roller, leave a few feet to dangle, and firmly cleat off the other end to a samson post or equivalent (Figure 16-17).
3. Pay out some more chain until the snubbing line is taking all the anchoring loads, and then feed out a foot or two more and lock off the windlass.

It is important to use nylon rope for a snubbing line, since it will stretch and act as a shock

Figure 16-16. Windlass shaft sheared by snubbing loads.

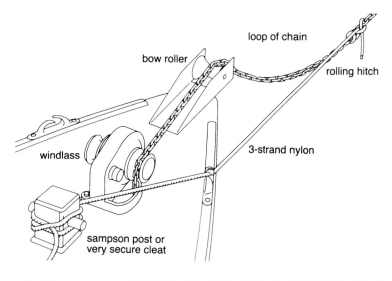

Figure 16-17. Relieve the load on windlasses with a snubbing line. On boats with bowsprits and bobstays, lead the snubbing line through the bulwark chock. The boat will lie slightly off the wind and the bobstay will not "saw" on the snubbing line and anchor chain. (Jim Sollers)

absorber. Three-strand nylon is better in this respect than plaited (braided) types. The size of the line will depend on the boat's weight and the sea conditions—too heavy a line will not stretch; too light will break. Three-eighths inch (10 mm) works well on most boats to around 25,000 pounds; ½-inch (13 mm) up to 40,000 pounds; ⅝ inch (16 mm) thereafter. Only a few feet is required—certainly no more than 15 feet (5 meters) need be let out in most conditions. The amount of chain left dangling (note loop in Figure 16-17) should be about one-quarter the length of the snubbing line. In a strong blow the line will stretch tight, allowing the chain and windlass to take some of the load. Nylon will tolerate repeated stretching to 125% of its original length without failure.

Many people use chain hooks to attach a snubbing line to the chain. Having lost several I

now use a rolling hitch and have never had a snubber either slip or prove too difficult to undo (Figure 16-17).

Should the snubbing line part, the windlass will be subjected to a sudden shock load which may break the shaft or simply cause the chain to jump up on the wildcat and start running out. Once a chain starts to do this, it very often will not reseat itself. *It is essential to have at least one more line of defense against loosing all the chain.* A very strong attachment point for the bitter end of the chain is obviously called for, but *it would be better to have an additional chain stopper on deck, or to place a loop of chain around a samson post.* If all the chain should run out, and the boat comes up short on its bitter-end attachment point, there may well be an enormous shock load that simply rips the bitter end loose.

Chain difficulties. Sometimes chain will jump off a wildcat. This can be the result of an improper match between the chain and the wildcat but can also arise through improper chain leads and twisted chains.

Chain sizing. The big difficulty in matching chain to a wildcat is that there are no universally accepted international standards for chain sizes. Although Europe is standardizing around International Standard ISO 4565, "Small Craft Anchor Chains," this is gaining no following in the USA (probably because all dimensions are

Table 16-2. Approximate Chain Dimensions (USA)[1]

Type of Chain	Trade Size in Inches	Wire Size in Inches	Working Load Limit in Pounds	Pitch	Nominal Inside Width in Inches	Maximum Length 100 Links in Inches	Links per Foot	Weight per 100 Feet in Pounds
BBB Chain	5/16	11/32	1,950	1.00	0.50	104	12	120
	3/8	13/32	2,750	1.09	0.62	113	11	173
	7/16	15/32	3,625	1.21	0.68	126	9¾	232
	1/2	17/32	4,750	1.34	0.75	139	9	307
Proof Coil Chain	5/16	11/32	1,900	1.10	0.50	114	11	106
	3/8	13/32	2,650	1.23	0.62	128	9¾	155
	7/16	15/32	3,500	1.37	0.75	142	8¾	217
	1/2	17/32	4,500	1.54	0.79	156	7¾	270
High-Test Chain	5/16	11/32	3,900	1.01	0.48	105	12¼	110
	3/8	13/32	5,400	1.15	0.58	121	10½	160
	7/16	15/32	7,200	1.29	0.67	134	9⅛	216
	1/2	17/32	9,200	1.43	0.76	148	8½	280

1. Working load must not be exceeded. European chain is measured in millimeters, but there are differences in measurements from one country to another.

given in millimeters!). Even within individual countries, chain manufacture still tends to be a small-shop operation, and variations in chain of nominally the same size are common. *The only sure way to match the chain and the wildcat is to take the wildcat to the chain.* Better still, order chain from the windlass manufacturer when you purchase the windlass.

The nominal size of chain is a measure of the diameter of the metal *(wire)* in the links. In Europe, nominal and actual diameters coincide, but in the USA it is customary to use wire that is 1/32 inch larger in diameter than the nominal size of the chain!

For any given chain size, there are three different link lengths (called *pitch*) in common use. These used to be called *BBB, proof-coil, and high-test,* but are now designated by a *grade system,* with the grade being related to the strength of the alloy used to manufacture the chain. BBB and proof-coil, sometimes referred to as G3 or *System-3,* are made from the same material, which is between grades 28 and 30 (the higher the number, the stronger the alloy). High-test *(G4 or System-4)* is made from material which is between grades 40 and 43. Table 16-2 summarizes chain statistics.

Typical *safe working loads* (now generally referred to as *working load limits,* or simply *working loads*) are normally (but not always—read the fine print) defined as 25% of the breaking load *under a straight, even pull* (Table 16-2 again—note that this will considerably overstate the actual breaking load in many service conditions, particularly when subjected to snubbing loads).

Chain lead. On a horizontal windlass the wildcat must be at least as high as the bow roller so that the chain feeds *at least horizontally and*

preferably up to the wildcat (Figure 16-18). This ensures proper engagement of the chain and wildcat. On the other side of the wildcat, the chain ideally should have a free fall of a foot or two so that its weight maintains a little pull on the wildcat. With vertical windlasses it is sometimes necessary to have someone tail the chain from below (i.e., maintain pressure on it). If this is not done, the chain can get jammed between the stripper and the deck opening.

Twisting of chain. If a boat repeatedly swings around its anchor, the chain can twist up. The same thing can happen when a combination three-strand nylon line and chain rode is put under a heavy load—the nylon may partially unlay and twist the chain. When the anchor is weighed, the chain has a tendency to sit on the surface of the wildcat rather than seat in it. The chain can then skip back out. Swivels fitted between the chain and the anchor will help to eliminate the twist in the chain, but having looked at a few and used one or two I suspect that most swivels form *the* weak link in an anchor system. It is a rare occasion indeed when

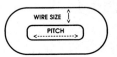

Note: Pitch and wire size can be used to determine the exact type of an unknown chain. They are always measured with calipers for accuracy.

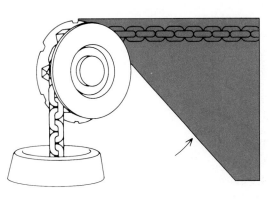

Figure 16-18. Chain must be horizontal or slope up to a wildcat (i.e., be within shaded area). *(Simpson Lawrence and Jim Sollers)*

twisted chain is anything more than a minor irritation, and I prefer to live with it.

Galvanizing. In time the galvanizing will strip off anchor chains. In certain instances this can happen quite rapidly, such as on a boat anchored on top of a steel wreck. Galvanic interaction can strip the zinc off the anchor chain in a matter of days! The chain should be turned end for end each year, and regalvanized when it starts to rust.

Turning the chain also ensures that all connections and links (shackles, swivels, chain-to-rope splices, and the fastening on the bitter end) get undone and inspected at least once a year. Be sure to properly seize all shackles with stainless steel wire after doing them back up.

Horizontal Manual Windlasses

How they work. The engineering problem that has to be overcome is how to convert back-and-forth (reciprocal) motion of the operating lever into a constant rotation at the main shaft. Two approaches are followed, which I call *spur gearing* and *ratchet gearing.*

Spur gearing. A gear (the *crank* gear) is keyed to the same shaft that the crank handle turns backward and forward. Two smaller gears (*spur*

Figure 16-19. **The spur-geared manual windlass revealed: the popular SL555 from Simpson Lawrence.** *(Simpson Lawrence and Jim Sollers)*

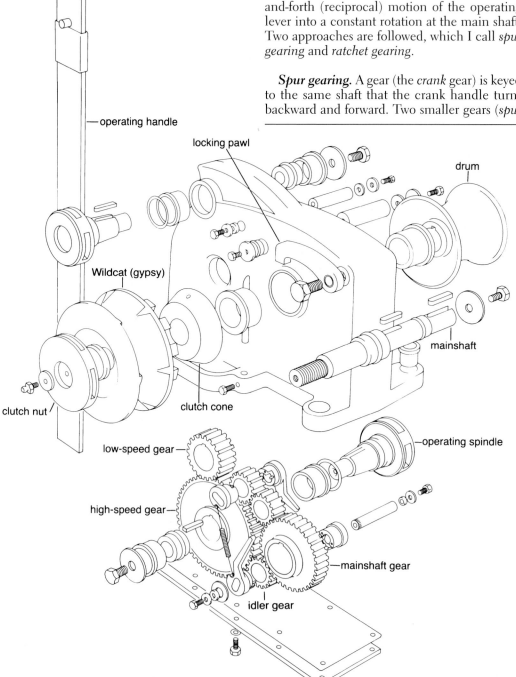

Running Rigging, Deck Hardware, and Roller Reefing

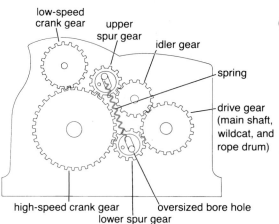

low-speed crank gear
upper spur gear
idler gear
spring
drive gear (main shaft, wildcat, and rope drum)
high-speed crank gear
lower spur gear
oversized bore hole

Figure 16-20. The operation of a spur-geared manual horizontal anchor windlass. Pulling back and pushing forward on the winch handle both rotate the wildcat and rope drum in the same direction (**A** and **B**). A load on the wildcat forces both spur gears against the crank gear, locking the windlass (**C**). *(Jim Sollers)*

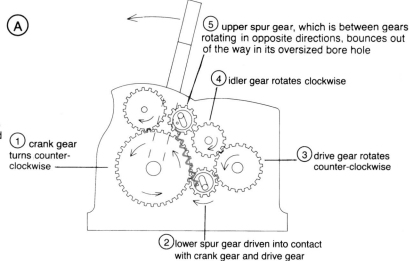

(A)

(5) upper spur gear, which is between gears rotating in opposite directions, bounces out of the way in its oversized bore hole

(4) idler gear rotates clockwise

(1) crank gear turns counter-clockwise

(3) drive gear rotates counter-clockwise

(2) lower spur gear driven into contact with crank gear and drive gear

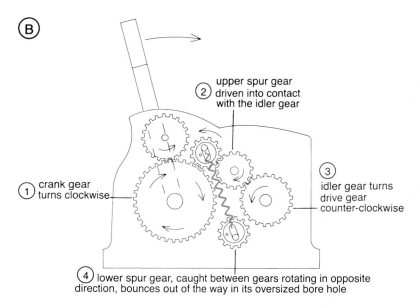

(B)

upper spur gear (2) driven into contact with the idler gear

(1) crank gear turns clockwise

(3) idler gear turns drive gear counter-clockwise

(4) lower spur gear, caught between gears rotating in opposite direction, bounces out of the way in its oversized bore hole

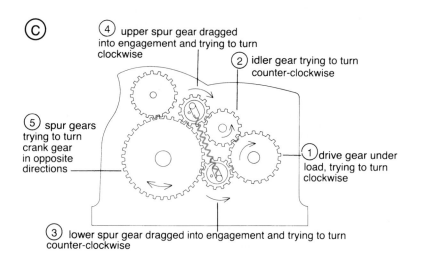

(C)

(4) upper spur gear dragged into engagement and trying to turn clockwise

(2) idler gear trying to turn counter-clockwise

(5) spur gears trying to turn crank gear in opposite directions

(1) drive gear under load, trying to turn clockwise

(3) lower spur gear dragged into engagement and trying to turn counter-clockwise

gears) are placed in contact with the crank gear. These spur gears have oversized bore holes that allow them to flop back out of contact with the crank gear. A spring between the two spur gears holds them up against the crank gear. One spur gear also contacts a gear (the drive gear) keyed to the output shaft, the other spur gear contacts an idler gear, which in turn is permanently engaged with the drive gear (Figure 16-19).

When the crank handle is moved in one direction (counterclockwise in Figure 16-20), the crank gear traps the lower spur gear between itself and the drive gear, turning the drive gear. The drive gear not only turns the main shaft and wildcat, but at the same time turns the idler gear. The second (upper) spur gear finds itself between the idler gear and the crank gear, which are turning in opposite directions. It is bounced out of the way against the spring pressure.

When the crank handle is moved in the other direction (clockwise) the crank gear traps the upper spur gear between itself and the idler gear. This turns the idler gear, which reverses the direction of rotation and so imparts the same rotation as before to the drive gear and the output shaft. The lower spur gear finds itself between the drive gear and the crank gear, which are moving in opposite directions. It is bounced out of the way against the spring pressure.

When the wildcat (gypsy) is under a load, both spur gears are forced down into contact with the crank gear, but in *opposite* directions of rotation. The counterposed forces lock the windlass up and prevent the wildcat from letting out chain. Some means is needed to release the wildcat in order to drop the anchor.

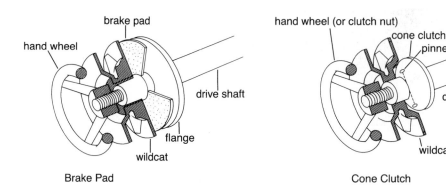

Figure 16-20D. Chain is veered by loosening the wildcat's cone clutch or brake pad. Tighten the hand wheel or clutch nut when you have sufficient scope. Careful; this is a good place to lose a finger.

brake pad

hand wheel

drive shaft

flange

wildcat

Brake Pad

hand wheel (or clutch nut)

cone clutch

pinned to shaft

drive shaft

wildcat (gypsy)

Cone Clutch

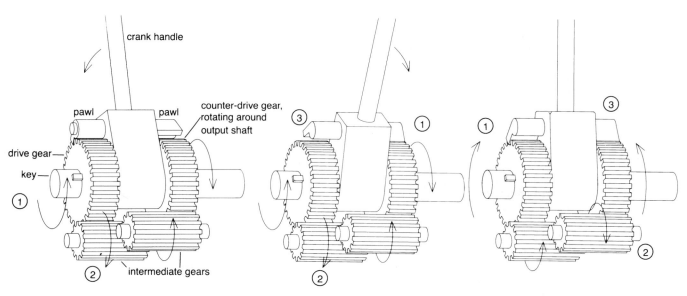

crank handle

pawl   pawl   counter-drive gear, rotating around output shaft

drive gear

key

intermediate gears

Figure 16-21. The operation of a ratchet-geared windlass. (**Left**) **1**. Handle cranked as shown; pawl engages drive gear and turns it counter-clockwise. **2**. Intermediate gears reverse rotation and counter drive gear freewheels around output shaft; pawl bounces out of engagement. (**Center**) **1**. Handle cranked as shown; pawl engages counter drive shaft and turns it clockwise. **2**. Intermediate gears turn drive gear counter-clockwise. **3**. Drive gear pawl bounces off the gear. (**Right**) **1**. A load on the windlass tries to turn the drive gear counter-clockwise, locking it into its pawl. **2**. The intermediate gears attempt to turn the counter drive gear counterclockwise, locking it into its pawl. **3**. The two gears, *locked in opposite directions*, lock up the windlass. (*Jim Sollers*)

The wildcat is not itself keyed to the drive shaft. Either it is tapered on its inner face and sits on a tapered friction pad (a *cone clutch*), the latter being locked to the shaft, or the wildcat is trapped between a flange on the drive shaft and a friction (brake) pad or lining. In both cases a handwheel or clutch nut, threaded to the end of the main shaft, can be tightened to trap the wildcat and lock it to the shaft, or loosened to let the wildcat freewheel (Figure 16-20D). Tension on the handwheel or clutch nut acts as a brake to control the rate of release of chain.

A second (low) speed is easily added to this windlass by placing another small (low-speed) crank gear in contact with the primary (high-speed) crank gear. When the operating lever is used to crank the low-speed gear backward and forward, this gear turns the high-speed gear, but at a greatly reduced rate. From there on everything is the same as above.

Ratchet gearing (Figure 16-21). The crank handle rotates around the output (wildcat) shaft

with a gear on either side of the handle. One gear (the *direct-drive* gear) is keyed to the output shaft; the other (the *counterdrive* gear) floats (i.e., is free to rotate around the shaft). On either side of the crank handle assembly are pawls, which are counterposed (i.e., face in opposite directions) to each other.

When the crank handle is moved one way, one pawl engages the direct-drive gear, turning it and therefore the output shaft. The other pawl bounces over the counterdrive gear. When the handle reverses, the direct-drive pawl bounces free while the counterdrive pawl engages and turns the counterdrive gear.

The counterdrive gear meshes with an intermediate gear. This in turn meshes with a second intermediate gear, which also engages the direct-drive gear. When the counterdrive gear turns one way, the direct-drive gear turns the other way (i.e., the same way as before).

When a load is applied to the wildcat, and through it to the direct-drive gear, the reverse rotation brings *both* the direct-drive and the

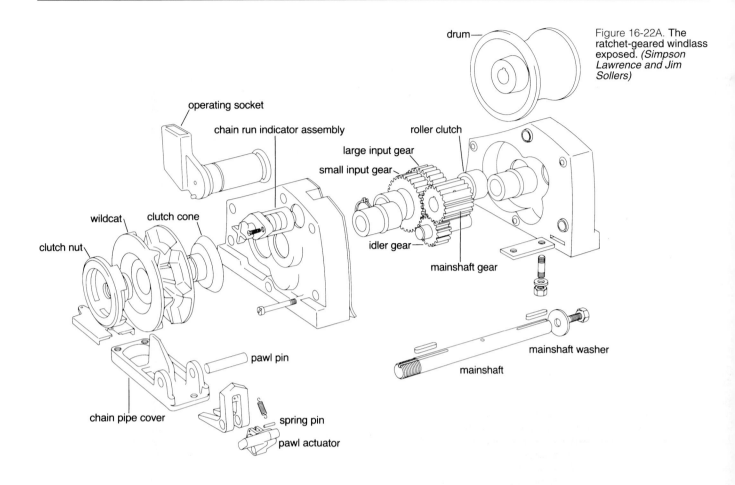

drum—

operating socket

chain run indicator assembly

roller clutch

large input gear

small input gear

wildcat   clutch cone

clutch nut

idler gear—

mainshaft gear

pawl pin

mainshaft washer

mainshaft

chain pipe cover

spring pin

pawl actuator

---

counterdrive gears up against their pawls but from opposite directions. The counterposed forces effectively lock up the windlass. The wildcat can be released only via a cone clutch or brake, just as on a spur-gear-type winch.

A variation on the same theme keys the crank handle to an auxiliary shaft with two gears on it (Figure 16-22A). Both gears are mounted on roller clutches such that they freewheel (ratchet) in one direction and grip in the other. The clutches are installed in opposite directions (i.e., one locks one way, the other the opposite way). One gear directly engages an output gear on the main shaft; while the other engages the output gear via an idler gear (on an idler shaft). Operation is then as in Figure 16-21.

Yet another variation on the same theme is the popular small Simpson Lawrence Hyspeed (510) windlass, which has two bicycle sprockets mounted on the main shaft on opposing ratchets (Figure 16-22B). The operating lever drives two chains backward and forward, turning the sprockets. One chain drives its sprocket directly; the other chain is fed around rollers to reverse the direction of drive. When the handle is cranked one way, one sprocket turns the shaft while the

other freewheels; cranking the other way engages the second sprocket while the first freewheels.

Dismantling and repair. While the windlass is still securely fastened to the foredeck remove the clutch nut or handwheel, and the rope-drum retaining bolt. Pull off the drum and the wildcat.

Wildcats will jam on clutch cones when ungreased and unused—loosen the clutch nut and then lever the wildcat free. (A stubborn wildcat can be broken loose by jamming the anchor against the stemhead, loosening the clutch nut, and operating the windlass.) Plated steel shafts will corrode to rope drums and may not come free, even with a 10-ton press! In that case the output shaft must be hacksawed through, obviously necessitating subsequent replacement.

Now remove the windlass from the foredeck (generally four bolts). Some windlasses use no lubrication and have an open base. Others are filled with oil or grease and have a plate that must be removed.

With the base open, tap out the main shaft—in some cases it may come out either side of the windlass, but if the holes in the sides of the windlass casing differ in size, it will have to come out

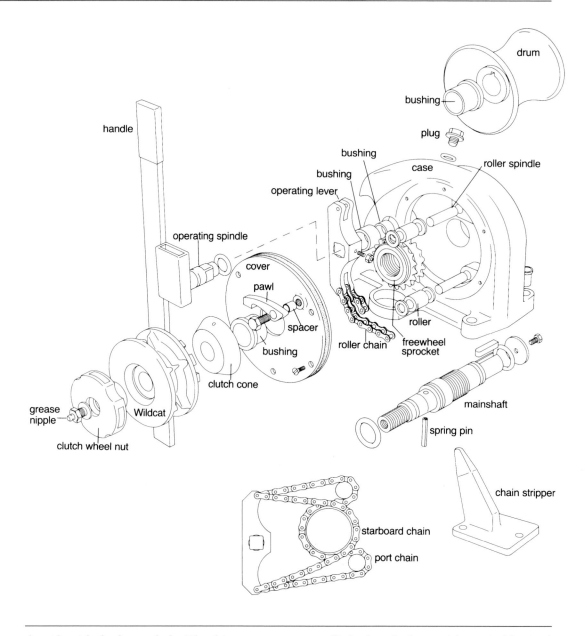

Figure 16-22B. Chain-drive ratchet-geared windlass. *(Simpson Lawrence and Jim Sollers)*

the side with the largest hole. The drive gear or sprockets, and any other gears and parts mounted on the shaft, will all come loose and can be retrieved through the base of the windlass. Watch out for keys locking gears to shafts—they are easily lost and hard to replace.

Any other gears are removed the same way. The various shafts will have retaining screws, seals, and/or plates; once these are undone the shaft is knocked out and the gear falls into the windlass.

Inspect the gears for broken or chipped teeth, or steps in the teeth; inspect the shafts for ridges; slide the gears back on their shafts and check for play; slip the shafts into the windlass housing and also check for play. Most shafts fit into removable bushings. If these need replacing, they can

generally be knocked out with a suitably sized *drift*; a socket with an outside diameter a little less than the diameter of the bushing works well. The important thing is to exert an even pressure over the whole bushing.

Fitting new bushings will be greatly facilitated if boiling water is poured over the housing to expand it. But first, warm the *entire* housing to avoid any sudden localized heating, which could cause castings to crack. Knock the new bushing in using a piece of hardwood as a drift.

Windlasses frequently use only a small portion of their gears. (For example, the main crank gear on a spur gear windlass generally moves back and forth through 90 degrees), and loads are concentrated on only one side of shafts and bushings. Faced with some breakdowns and no

Running Rigging, Deck Hardware, and Roller Reefing

spare parts, it may be possible to get by temporarily by turning bushings and gears through 90 or 180 degrees and reassembling.

Vertical Manual Windlasses

A vertical manual windlass has a winch handle socket in the top of its drum. A winch handle is used to turn the drum and the wildcat, winching in the anchor. Ratchets on the windlass pedestal engage the drum to keep it from unwinding. Between the drum and the wildcat is a friction pad or surface (Figure 16-23). Turning the winch handle in reverse unscrews a clutch nut, allowing the wildcat to freewheel and let out chain.

Unscrewing the clutch nut completely allows the drum and wildcat to be lifted off, exposing any clutch cones (friction pads) if fitted, as well as pawls and springs. Inspect the clutch cones (or friction surfaces between the drum, wildcat, and winch base if no clutch cones are fitted) for excessive wear or scoring. Pay particular attention to the pawls and pawl springs (see the relevant sections on winches earlier in this chapter).

Electric Windlasses

How they work. A large electric motor drives the windlass through a reduction gearbox. Three types of gearing are normally used: offset (spur) gears (Figure 16-24), worm gears (Figures 16-25A, B, and C), and epicyclic (planetary) gears. Motors are reversible by switching the power leads, although in many installations the motor is used only for hauling in the anchor; the anchor is then let out as in manual installations (i.e., by loosening the clutch nut). In all cases the wildcat and drum are ratcheted so that they can be operated manually, independently of the motor and gearing, in the event of windlass failure. However, manual operation is normally direct drive (no gearing) and therefore provides very little power.

Offset (spur) gears. These are far more efficient than worm gears, which typically absorb up to 45% of motor output, dissipating it as heat. Because of the efficiency of offset gearing, when a load is placed on the windlass the gears can spin the motor in reverse, allowing the windlass to let out chain or line. This type of electric windlass has to incorporate a braking device; typically a clutch locks the gears when the windlass is not in use, but is electrically released via a solenoid as soon as the motor is energized.

Worm gears. These provide a tremendous

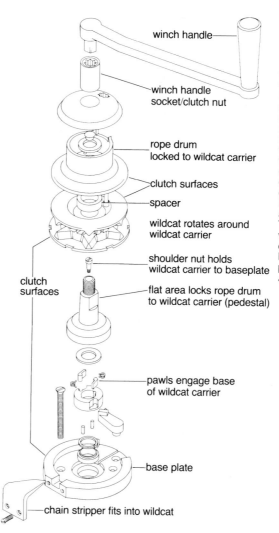

Figure 16-23. Vertical manual windlasses are gearless, the length of the winch handle providing the only leverage. Cranking tightens the clutch nut, trapping the wildcat between the clutch friction surfaces. Continued cranking rotates the drum, ratcheting in the anchor rode. The pawls prevent it from unwinding. Reversing the winch handle's direction loosens the clutch nut, and allows chain or warp to veer out. Note: the clutch surfaces are metal-to-metal. Trapped particles of dirt will lead to scoring. To compensate, some units have renewable friction pads. *(Simpson Lawrence and Jim Sollers)*

winch handle
winch handle socket/clutch nut
rope drum locked to wildcat carrier
clutch surfaces
spacer
wildcat rotates around wildcat carrier
shoulder nut holds wildcat carrier to baseplate
flat area locks rope drum to wildcat carrier (pedestal)
clutch surfaces
pawls engage base of wildcat carrier
base plate
chain stripper fits into wildcat

amount of resistance to being driven backward by a load on the windlass. No separate clutch/brake is needed. However, they are, as noted, very inefficient. The main rationale for their use is that they tend to be cheaper, and they enable a more compact installation to be made (the motor on most units is horizontal rather than vertical), which interferes less with headroom in the boat. There are, of course, fewer parts to break down, so reliability is higher. (Given the small amount of use that most windlasses see, reliability is probably more important than efficiency.)

Lewmar employs a very-fine-toothed modified worm gear (called a *spiroid gear*) in its powered winches and windlasses.

Epicyclic (planetary) gearing. This type operates on the same principles as a planetary actuator on an autopilot (Chapter 13).

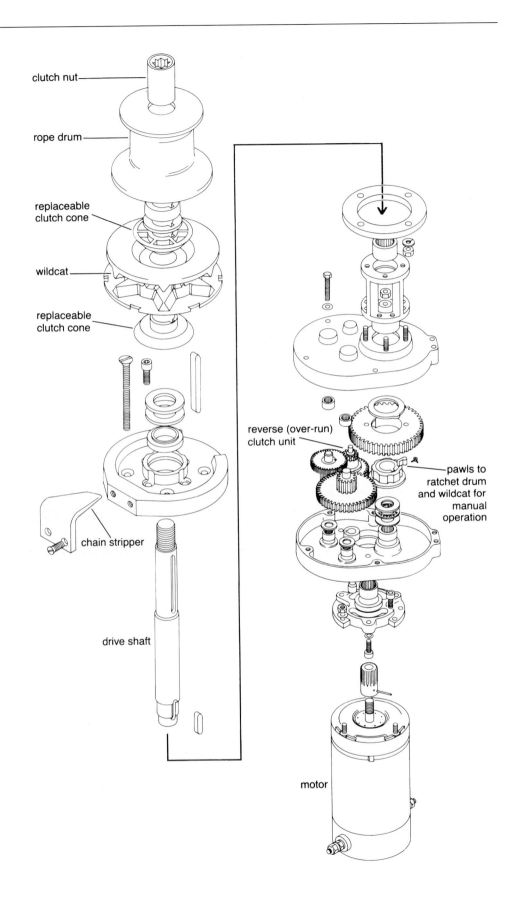

Figure 16-24. Electric
windlass with offset
gearing. *(Simpson
Lawrence and Jim Sollers)*

clutch nut

rope drum

replaceable
clutch cone

wildcat

replaceable
clutch cone

chain stripper

drive shaft

reverse (over-run)
clutch unit

pawls to
ratchet drum
and wildcat for
manual
operation

motor

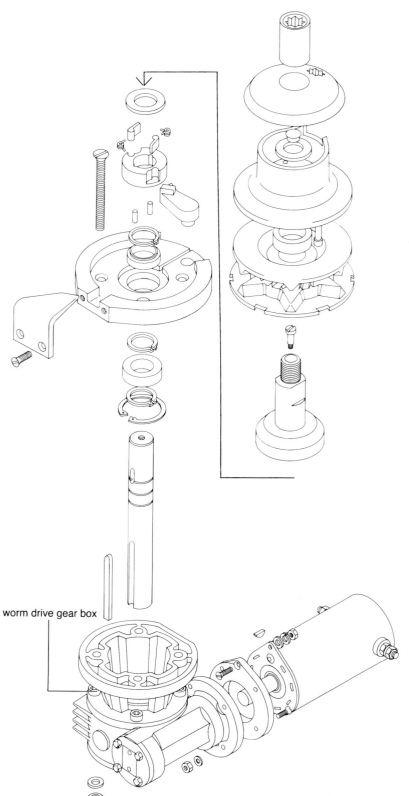

worm drive gear box

Figure 16-25A. Electric windlass with worm gearing.
(Simpson Lawrence and Jim Sollers)

Figure 16-25B. The arrangement of the gears in a vertical windlass. *(Maxwell)*

Figure 16-25C. Cutaway of a beautifully designed horizontal windlass. *(Lighthouse Manufacturing Co.)*

Installation. Troublefree operation of an electric windlass installation is largely dependent upon the quality of its installation.

Electrical considerations. A typical 12-volt windlass will draw from 60 to 100 amps at its *working load.* (*Working load* is an ill-defined concept that varies from manufacturer to manufacturer.) However, put that same windlass under a near stalling load, and *its current draw can easily jump to 300 to 400 amps* (Table 16-3).

A windlass will commonly have a 30- to 40-foot cable run between it and the batteries that are powering it. When pulling 300 amps, if voltage drop is to be limited to 10% over a 30-foot cable run (in each direction), a 3/0 cable (85 mm²) is needed (Table 16-4 and Chapter 3). At higher loads and over longer distances considerably larger cables are needed. These sizes of cable are, in most situations, impractically large—the upper size of cables in boat use is generally 2/0 (67 mm²). What this means is that *even with the largest practicable cable size, many windlasses suffer from a greater than 10% voltage drop when under maximum load.* This causes a loss of power when it is needed most, and a tendency to stall, which in turn can lead to overheating and burnout. Voltage-drop problems are greatly compounded if cables are sized for the *rated working load* rather than the *maximum load. Windlass cables should be sized on the basis of a 10% voltage drop at maximum load; if this produces an impractically large cable, at the least 2/0 cable should be used.*

It is sometimes suggested that long, heavy cable runs can be avoided by having a separate windlass battery in the forepeak with short connections to the windlass. But anytime this battery is well discharged, it will pull an alternator's full output. If the boat has a high-output alternator, this may amount to 100 amps or more, necessitating heavy charging cables, and bringing us back to where we started.

The positive cable to a windlass is generally fastened to the boat side of a battery isolation switch or to a positive distribution post or bus bar (Figure 16-26); the negative cable should be fastened to the boat's main negative bus bar (see Chapter 4). Note, however, that if a shunt-type ammeter is wired into the negative battery circuit (Chapter 1) between the common ground point and the battery negative(s), and if the stall load on the windlass *exceeds the rating of the shunt,* the windlass negative must be wired to the *battery* side of the shunt so that the windlass current does not flow through the shunt. Wired like this, the ammeter will not measure the current draw of the windlass, but since windlass use is infrequent and for short periods of time, its effect will not be significant in terms of the overall DC load.

A windlass must have some sort of overload protection as close to its batteries as possible. Should the windlass ever stall (locked rotor state) or get stuck "on" (which can happen with a defective

Table 16-3. Windlass Current Draw vs. Load[1]

Load (pounds)	Current Draw (amps)	Speed of Recovery (meters/minute)
500	110	8.6
1,000	170	7.2
1,500	230	5.8
2,000	290	4.3
2,500	350	2.9
3,000	410	1.5

1. These data are based on a Lewmar 2000 (12-volt), which takes a working load of 1,000 pounds and a maximum load of 2,000 pounds.

Table 16-4. Conductor Sizes for 10% Voltage Drop at 12 Volts

Current draw (amps)	Length of conductor from battery to windlass and back (Feet)					
	10	20	30	40	50	60
100	10	6	4	4	2	2
125	8	6	4	2	2	1
150	8	4	2	2	2	1
175	6	4	2	2	1	1/0
200	6	4	2	1	1/0	2/0
250	6	2	1	1/0	2/0	3/0
300	4	2	1/0	2/0	3/0	4/0
350	4	2	1/0	2/0	3/0	4/0
400	4	1/0	2/0	3/0	4/0	

Cable Size: AWG

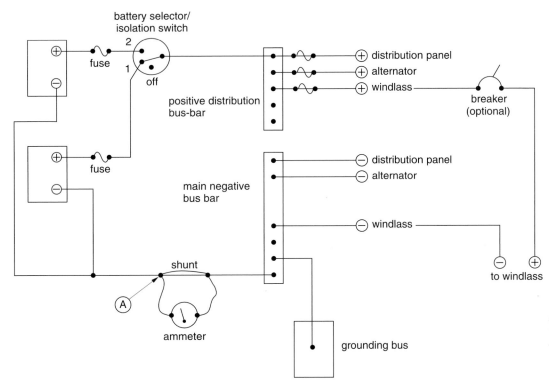

Figure 16-26. **Wiring a windlass into the boat's DC circuits. Note:** If the full-load current of the windlass (when combined with the other loads) exceeds the rating of the shunt, the windlass negative should be wired to point A.

switch), its current draw will rise sharply to the point at which it may melt down wiring (especially if the cables are undersized) and *start a fire.* Overload protection can take the form of either a suitably-sized fuse (relatively cheap) or a circuit breaker (expensive).

The circuit to a windlass is closed by a solenoid, which in turn is energized by another circuit which passes through a foot switch, or some other remotely operated switch. *Any such control circuit should have its own isolation switch that is kept in the "off" position except when the windlass is actually in use* (Figures 16-27A and B). This is a matter of basic safety. So long as this switch is "off," there is no chance that someone will accidentally activate the windlass (e.g., by inadvertently standing on a foot switch). Since the wiring in the control circuit is relatively lightweight (12 to 18 AWG) the switch need be no more than a simple toggle switch.

The main solenoid terminals carry the full operating current of a windlass. When a solenoid closes, and then when it opens once again, there is a tendency for arcing to occur across the points as the circuit is made and broken. *For a long, troublefree life the solenoids need to have a rating equal to the full-load draw of the windlass.* The solenoid must be in a dry location (not, for example, in an anchor well—if the drain plugs, and

the well floods, the solenoid will short out). If a solenoid does short, or stick in the "on" position, *the windlass will operate continuously and uncontrollably.* The only way to stop it will be to turn off the main isolation switch or to trip the main breaker.

Mechanical considerations. A windlass needs to be solidly mounted to an inflexible base. This is important for several reasons. First of all, the windlass mount must obviously be capable of withstanding all the loads that may be imposed on the windlass, including occasional severe snubbing loads. Second, *if the windlass flexes, the seal between the windlass base and the deck will open up, allowing water to find its way below, perhaps onto sensitive electrical components.* Third, an increasing number of electric windlasses are the type with a *vertical* capstan on which the motor is mounted below decks, with a spacer between the capstan and motor unit (Figure 16-28). The drive shaft runs from the motor, through the spacer unit, into the capstan. *Any flexing of the deck is likely to throw out the alignment between the motor and the capstan unit,* leading to increased friction, a loss of performance, premature bearing damage, and perhaps motor damage.

Below decks, the windlass motor and all asso-

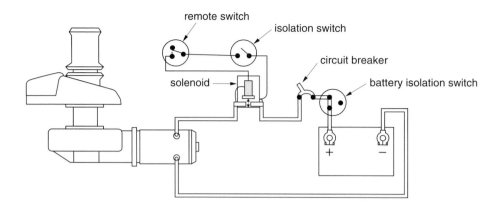

Figure 16-27A. Wiring diagram for a nonreversing electric windlass. *(Lewmar)*

remote switch
isolation switch
circuit breaker
battery isolation switch
solenoid

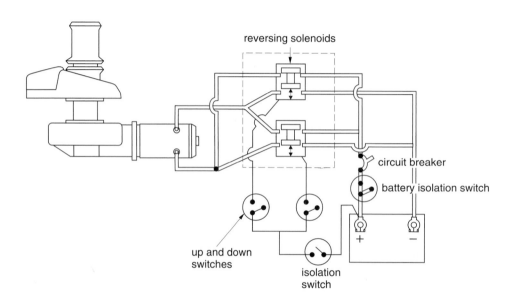

Figure 16-27B. Wiring diagram for a reversing electric windlass. Note that with this kind of arrangement, operating both switches simultaneously will put a dead short across the batteries. Some other reversing installations are protected against such an eventuality. *(Lewmar)*

reversing solenoids
circuit breaker
battery isolation switch
up and down switches
isolation switch

Figure 16-28. Vertical windlass with spacer. For troublefree operation the deck must be rigid enough to prevent flexing between the capstan and the belowdecks installation. *(Maxwell)*

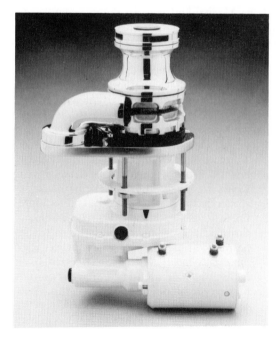

ciated wiring must be protected from any potential drips, and from the chain as it flays around in a seaway (Figure 16-29).

Operation. The majority of electric motors fitted to windlasses are modified starter motors with wound field coils (Chapter 6). These motors are designed for intermittent use only—in automotive use for no more than 30 seconds at a time. They do not incorporate cooling fins or fans of any kind. If run for longer periods of time, especially under heavy loads, they will rapidly heat up. Sustained high-load usage will cause the motor to burn up.

A correctly sized circuit breaker will provide limited protection from damage to the motor that might arise from an excessive current (amperage) draw or a short circuit. *It will not provide protection from excessive heat buildup as a result of prolonged operation or repeated high-load operation.* Even if the windlass has a sophisticated elec-

Running Rigging, Deck Hardware, and Roller Reefing

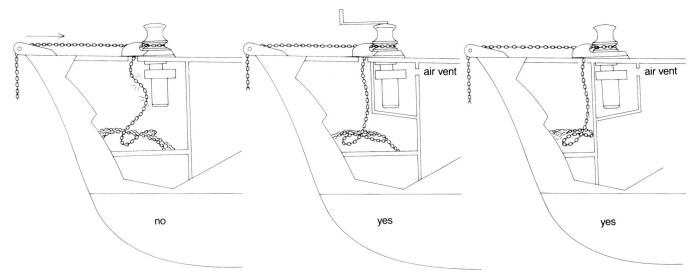

no   yes   yes

Figure 16-29. **Proper windlass installation.** The unprotected windlass motor (**left**) is subjected to salt corrosion, and can be shorted out by the chain. Enclosing the motor (**center**) solves both of these problems. The best solution is to mount the windlass assembly outside the chain locker (**right**). *(Simpson Lawrence and Jim Sollers)*

tronic Overload Protection Unit (OPU, or similar designation), *if the unit is repeatedly tripped and then reset, motor damage will result.* In the final analysis, regardless of protection devices, an operator without a sense of the limits of tolerance of a windlass motor can destroy just about any motor.

To protect the motor *a boat should be motored or sailed up to its anchor so that the windlass is basically just taking the weight of the rode and anchor.* Rather than using the windlass to break out a stubborn anchor, *the rode should be snubbed up to a samson post or cleat and the engine used.* Running the engine has the added advantage that the alternator will keep the battery voltage up, reducing the voltage drop at the windlass.

Maintenance and troubleshooting. At least once a year, inspect all terminals and connections, and if any corrosion is present, clean them. Then spray the terminals with an appropriate sealer, such as CRC 2043 Plasti-Coat, CRC 3013 Soft-Seal, or CRC 2049 Clear Urethane. If the windlass has seen much active service, the motor brushes need inspecting: Replace them if they are worn down to the point where they are flush with the tops of their holders. At this time, blow out any carbon dust, and wipe the surface of the *commutator* clean (Chapter 6), taking particular care to get the carbon out of the insulated grooves between the copper bars. If the commutator is seriously contaminated with carbon, it should be sprayed with an appropriate cleaner, such as CRC ElectroClean.

Safety. Before working on an electric windlass:

1. *Turn off the battery isolation switch before disconnecting the main cables from any part of a windlass circuit.* If a live cable is accidentally shorted to a ground, very high amperages will flow which can cause serious burns and damage.

2. Always isolate any circuits before working on them so that the windlass is not accidentally set in motion.

3. When performing tests on a windlass, remove the anchor chain from the gypsy beforehand so that the anchor is not accidentally dragged into the stemhead, stalling the windlass and perhaps damaging the stemhead. However, *always tie up an anchor before taking its chain off the gypsy!* This will stop the anchor from slipping overboard and the chain from running out uncontrollably.

Most problems with electric windlasses are electrical in nature. A typical unidirectional ("up" only) circuit is shown in Figure 16-30—it is basically the same as a starter-motor circuit; the same tests can be made (Chapter 6). (A circuit with both "up" and "down" functions is shown in Figure 16-27B.)

Failure to operate at all. Check for voltage at the inputs to the solenoids and foot switches (point 1, Figure 16-30). If no voltage is present, the battery isolation switch or control-circuit isolation switch is "off," the breaker (if fitted) is tripped, or a fuse is blown. If voltage is present,

Troubleshooting Chart 16-1. Electric Windlass—Failure to Operate

Warning: See important safety tips in the text

Is there voltage at the input terminals to the solenoids and foot switches? **YES**	**NO**	Check the battery isolation switch, circuit breaker, control-circuit isolation switch, and any fuses.
Press the foot switch or operate the remote switch. Is there voltage at the positive switch terminal on the solenoid? **YES**	**NO**	The foot switch, or remote switch (or its wiring), is defective.
Keep the foot or remote switch activated. Is there voltage at the main output terminal on the solenoid? **YES**	**NO**	Check the solenoid coil ground circuit. If OK, repair or replace the solenoid. (Note: double-check that it is the solenoid that is at fault by jumping out its two main terminals. If the windlass now operates, the solenoid is defective).
Check the motor ground circuit and the motor brushes.		

have someone operate a foot or other switch and test for voltage at the positive foot-switch terminal on the solenoid (point 2, Figure 16-30).

If no voltage is present, the foot switch is defective. If voltage is present, keep the switch depressed and check for voltage at the main solenoid output terminal or motor input terminal (point 3, Figure 16-30). If no voltage is present, check the solenoid coil ground circuit for a break—if it is intact, the solenoid is defective (refer to Chapter 6).

If voltage is present at the main output from the solenoid, the motor itself is open-circuited. Take a close look at the motor wiring and wiring connections, particularly those on the ground side. If any signs of corrosion are present on any terminals, remove the cables and clean the terminals. If the problem still can't be found, take a look at the brushes inside the motor to see if any are hung up in their brush holders. If the brushes are in good shape and making a firm contact with their commutator, the motor is likely burned up (open or short circuit).

Bellows switches. Lewmar uses *air bellows* in place of switches. A small air chamber with a diaphragm is connected, via PVC tubing, to

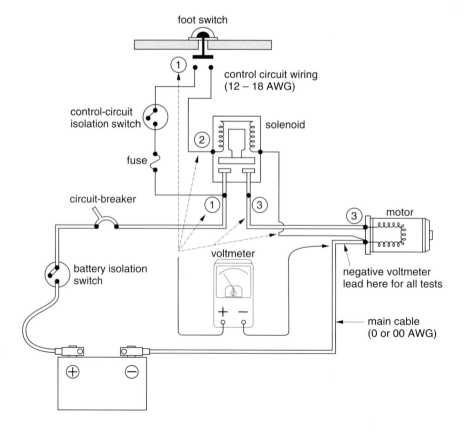

Figure 16-30.
Unidirectional ("up" only) windlass circuit, showing the position of the voltmeter leads for the various tests outlined in the text (1, 2, and 3).

another chamber and diaphragm attached to the solenoid switch. Depressing the first diaphragm causes air pressure to move the second diaphragm, which operates the switch. There are no external switches on deck likely to get wet and corrode.

If the air switch appears to have failed, jump out the main solenoid terminals. If the motor now runs, check for air leaks on the PVC tubing connections, collapsed or damaged tubing, or holes in the switch diaphragms.

Note that with older switches a potentially dangerous situation can arise with long tubing runs in hot areas (e.g., engine rooms, or under teak decks, which soak up the sun). The air in the tube can expand enough to trip the switch and set the motor off! If this should happen, bleed off some air pressure and see about shortening, or rerouting, the tubing (newer switches have a built-in safety bleed).

Breaker trips every time the battery isolation switch is turned on. There is a short in the circuit, most likely as a result of a burned-out motor. However, first check the entire circuit for other possibilities—a piece of equipment may have fallen against a hot terminal and shorted it to a ground; if any of the circuitry is exposed in the anchor well (it shouldn't be, but sometimes is) the drain may have plugged and the well flooded, shorting the cables. Note that if the anchor is up against the stemhead, and the "up" switch has shorted, whenever the battery isolation switch is turned on the windlass will kick into action under a stall load and trip its breaker. If it turns out to be the motor that is at fault, refer to Chapter 6.

Sluggish operation. *Do not continue using a windlass that operates sluggishly*—it may burn up. If the windlass is overloaded, ease the load (e.g, by motoring up to the anchor, or by tying off the rode and using the boat's engine to break the anchor out). Make sure the alternator is charging the batteries and that the voltage is well up.

If operation is still sluggish, check the voltage across the windlass motor terminals *while someone operates the windlass* (point 3, Figure 16-30). *There should be at least 11.0 volts* (on a 12-volt system). If the voltage is low, there is a severe voltage drop in the circuit—check for undersized cables, poor or corroded connections, or resistance across the battery isolation switch or solenoid (feel them to see if they are heating up). If voltage is above 11.0 volts, and the anchor is not fouled, the motor is seizing mechanically (check the alignment of the motor and the windlass on through-deck installations) or burning up.

Dismantling and repair. The top (above-decks) end is similar to a winch and generally simplicity itself to take apart. Motor removal is also very straightforward—the removal of two or three bolts should allow it to be pulled out.

Gearboxes must be tackled carefully with close attention to where *and which way around* everything goes. Note in particular that Lewmar's spiroid gearboxes are built to close tolerances. *Extreme precision* is required on reassembly to ensure correct meshing of the gears. It is best not to delve into gearboxes unless absolutely necessary.

Hydraulic Windlasses

A separate pump supplies hydraulic oil at high pressure (typically up to 2,000 psi) to a hydraulic motor on the base of the windlass. Reversing oil flow reverses winch operation. Cutting off oil flow locks the winch. As with all other windlasses, a manual clutch/wildcat release for letting out chain is provided, and the wildcat is ratcheted for manual operation in the event of motor failure. Oil pressure can be supplied by either an engine-driven pump or an electric pump (e.g., Lewmar Commander systems—Figure 16-31).

Problems. Hydraulic windlasses are generally very rugged and troublefree. Most difficulties arise as a result of one of the following:

Leaks. Leaks, as ever, are the bane of any hydraulic system. Leaks lead to air in the system, and then pumps can become air-bound. If the hydraulic pump is working but the windlass fails to work, check the oil level in the system; top up and purge (bleed) as necessary, and find out where the lost oil is going.

Dirt and moisture. The next most common causes of hydraulic problems—hydraulic systems must be *scrupulously* clean. Pumps and motors are built to *very close* tolerances. Valves will not seat with even a speck of dirt on them. Pistons and cylinders will score. When installing hydraulic hoses, be very careful not to get sawdust in them as they are pushed through holes in bulkheads, and watch out for dirt in quick-fit connectors. All units should have a filter on the return line to the hydraulic tank.

Moisture can arise from condensation in hydraulic oil tanks; periodically drain a sample of oil from the base of the tank and check for contamination. If not removed, moisture will cause rust on all kinds of sensitive parts and lead to expensive damage.

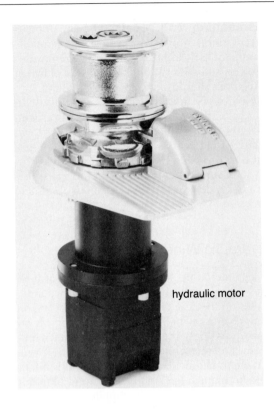

Figure 16-31. Hydraulic windlass (**right**), and an electric-powered hydraulic powerpack (**far right**). Solenoid-operated hydraulic control valves (upper right on the powerpack) direct oil to the winch through the connectors (two per winch; one each side). *(Lewmar)*

hydraulic connections, 2 per winch or windlass— one each side

12-volt motor

motor solenoid

hydraulic motor

hydraulic pump

oil reservoir

solenoid-operated hydraulic control valves direct the oil flow

Undersized hydraulic lines. Hydraulic lines that are too small for the system they are serving create pressure drops, overheated pumps, and loss of performance (just as undersized wiring causes voltage drop and overheated motors). Anchor windlasses, in particular, are frequently at the end of long hose runs, so make sure the hoses are adequate; keep bends to a minimum; and avoid tight radiuses. Hydraulic plumbing is covered in more detail in Chapter 11.

Electrical problems. Most hydraulic systems are operated via electric solenoid valves, remote switches, etc. These are the most likely source of problems—see the Maintenance and Trouble-shooting section on electric windlasses, and also the section on Starter Motors in Chapter 6.

Dismantling and repair. As with an electric windlass, the top (above-decks) end is similar to a winch, and generally simple to take apart. Below decks will be the motor and a reduction gearbox. Hydraulic motors and gearboxes are built to close tolerances and should be left alone (the more so as spare parts are most unlikely to be on board). About the only thing that might be done is to unbolt the motor to see if it is spinning when the windlass is turned on. If not, the problem lies in the pump, plumbing, or electrical circuits, and not in the motor itself. While the motor is out, try to operate the windlass manually, just to make sure it is not frozen up.

Roller Reefing and Furling

Almost all new sailboats are now fitted with *roller-reefing* headsails, and a good many with roller-reefing mains and mizzens. A high proportion of older boats are being retrofitted with roller-reefing headsails.

There are a number of potential mechanical problems with roller reefers. Headsail damage is also more common with roller reefers than with conventional hanked-on sails: roller-reefing headsail repairs are a meal ticket for some sailmakers around the cruising circuit. The following sections look at various roller-reefing failures, their causes, and means to reduce their probability.

How It Works

There are two principal types of roller reefing. The first (not very common now), more properly called *roller furling*, takes a headsail with a wire luff. A swivel drum is attached to the tack of the sail with the drum shaft fixed to the deck. The sail is tensioned as normal with the halyard. When the drum is turned (by means of a furling line) the sail is rolled up around its own luff wire (Figure 16-32A).

This is strictly a *furling* rig to be used when the sail is luffing (i.e., not filled with wind). Attempts to furl or reef a sail under load will twist the luff wire and sail (the tack of the sail will wrap up before its head). This is the major problem with these rigs; it can be avoided by use only under the proper conditions.

The principal advantage of this rig is that it is completely independent of the headstay and so forms no part of the standing rigging—failure does not jeopardize the mast. Sails also can be dropped and changed as easily as regular hanked-on headsails.

The second type of rig employs a *foil*—an aluminum extrusion into which the luff tape of a sail slides. This foil is fitted around the headstay. (On a few units, the foil *is* the headstay.) An upper swivel fits around the foil and attaches to the halyard and the head of the sail; a lower drum grips the foil (Figure 16-32B). When the drum is turned, the foil rotates and wraps the sail around itself. Since the foil is rigid and grips the sail along its whole length (more or less), the sail is rolled up evenly (there is no twist between the tack and the head). For this reason (and this

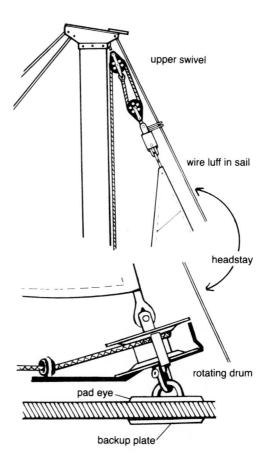

Figure 16-32A. Roller-furling headsails. Note that the headstay is independent of the furling mechanism. *(Schaefer Marine Products)*

upper swivel

wire luff in sail

headstay

rotating drum

pad eye

backup plate

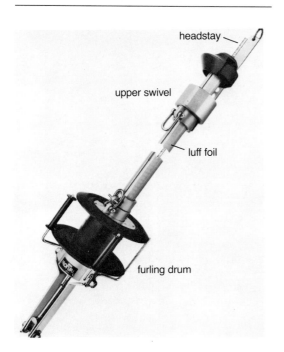

headstay

upper swivel

luff foil

furling drum

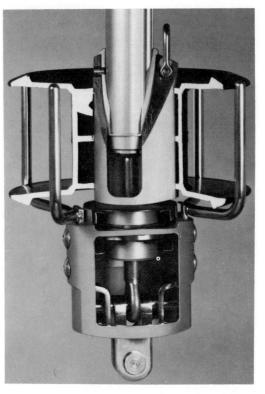

Figure 16-32B. Roller-reefing headsail. The headstay passes through the luff foil, making the furling unit part of the standing rigging. *(ProFurl)*

is their principal advantage) these rigs can be used for reefing and are commonly known as roller *reefers*.

The principal disadvantage of a roller reefer is that it is incorporated in the standing rigging. Failure can, in certain instances, lead to the loss of the headstay and so jeopardize the mast. Aside from this, the roller reefer cannot be put up and taken down without disconnecting the headstay. This means that many problems (for example, with a foil section) are just about irreparable at sea and may render the headsail unusable. Unless an auxiliary headstay is fitted (few are) and standby hanked-on headsails kept on board (this too is rare), the boat is left without its principal sail.

A secondary problem is the difficulty of making sail changes, for example, shortening sail in a blow. A conventional sail can be dropped and gasketed (tied off to make it manageable) and then unhanked. A roller reefer has to be pulled out of its luff groove in the foil. In order to do this the whole sail must be unfurled and the sheets eased. In any kind of a wind, the sail left in the foil will be flogging around while the loose sail will be building up on the foredeck and trying to take off.

Taking down roller-reefing headsails can be tough—but setting the new sail is even worse. It has to be fed into the luff groove just right, and eased on up with the halyard. The portion of sail set will be banging around; the sail still to be set will be billowing all over the deck. No matter what claims are made for various *prefeeders*, headsail changes on roller reefers are no fun, especially for the shorthanded!

Problems and Answers

The following focuses on roller reefers, but the section on bearings and swivels is applicable to roller furlers.

Headstay failure. Headstay failure is not common, but it is more common than on rigs without roller reefers. Since it is potentially so catastrophic, it deserves special attention.

A hanked-on headsail has its tack attached at the deck. A roller-reefed sail is tacked to the top of the furling drum. With a hanked-on sail, sideways loading (which generates headsail sag) is spread uniformly from the tack up through the stay; on a roller reefer there is a concentration of stress at the drum. *Whatever method is used to mount the drum, it must be properly toggled to relieve this stress.* Many are not. If the drum is fastened to the stemhead with metal straps, a toggle needs to be placed between the straps and the stemhead (Figures 16-33A and B).

Many roller-reefing drums are fastened to a turnbuckle (rigging screw) rather than the stemhead (Figure 16-33C). In this case, a specially

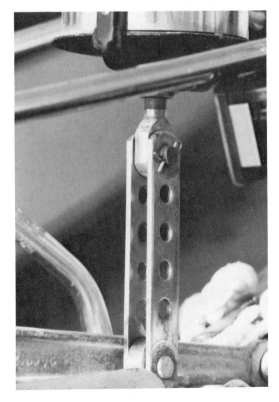

Figure 16-33A, B. Heading off problems with roller-reefing installations. The arrangement shown at right allows only sideways flexing, while that shown at far right permits only fore-and-aft flexing.

designed turnbuckle with a beefed-up lower stud is needed to carry the extra side loading.

Fastening the drum to a turnbuckle (rather than to the stemhead) has a couple of potential disadvantages. If the bearings become stiff, or when reefing and unfurling under a load, the sail can generate fairly high twisting (torsional) loads on the turnbuckle. These can undo the lower turnbuckle stud, or occasionally lead to a complete failure of the lower portion of the turnbuckle or its mounting hardware. Alternatively, the torsional stresses can *unlay the headstay*, leading to wire fatigue and failure. This is very hard to detect since the stay is completely covered by drum and foil.

If the turnbuckle fails, since the drum is not independently fastened to the deck in any way, the whole headstay, foil, sail, and drum assembly will break loose and start flogging around. The masthead is left with no support and the mast is in imminent danger of collapse. In order to get things back under control, the sail must be taken down, but to do this it must be taken out of its groove, and to do this *it must be completely unfurled*—compounding problems!

A variation on this disaster sometimes occurs when a turnbuckle-mounted drum is raised off the deck with a distance piece of some sort (Figure 16-34A). Such distance pieces must be designed to withstand high torsional loads—rod rigging and wire rope are out of the question. Heavy metal straps should be used, properly toggled.

Not only must a drum be properly mounted and toggled, it is also vital to *fully toggle the headstay at the masthead*. A hanked-on headsail is dropped when not in use; a roller-reefing headsail stays on the headstay. The combined weight of the foil, sail, and swivels is considerable. Anytime the boat is pounding or rolling (e.g., motoring into a head sea), the whole shooting match flexes all over the place. (Try placing a hand well up any rolled-up sail to see just how much it can be bounced around, no matter how tightly the rig is set up.) The headstay is subjected to severe additional flexing on top of normal sideways loading. *Masthead toggles are essential* (see page 501).

More and more boats have a stemball fitting on the forestay at the masthead (Figure 16-35). A *stemball will not provide adequate toggle action for a roller-reefing headsail*. An adapter and toggle should be set in place as shown in the illustration.

Bearings. Swivel and drum bearings have variously been made of carbon steel, stainless steel, plastic, or a combination of stainless steel and plastic. The multiplicity of bearing types (and manufacturers' claims that they have developed

Figure 16-33C. Correctly installed headstay and roller-reefing gear. The toggles allow flexing in either direction.

Figure 16-33D. Headsail roller-furling gear. This headstay has no toggle, but this is permissible because headsail sag affects only the headsail luff wire and mounting, which is adequately toggled.

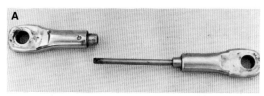

Figure 16-34. Roller reefing failures. (**A**) This piece was used to raise an expensive roller-reefing rig off the foredeck. As the rig was unwound and rewound, the rod twisted until it failed (after only a few months' use). The rig (sail, foil, and furling drum) came loose and flailed around, endangering life and limb. (**B**) Roller-reefing swivel unit. This is no way to treat a roller-reefing unit! Sand is certain to enter into the bearings, causing them to seize.

the perfect bearing!) is a reflection of the problems that have been experienced in the search for bearings that will hold up in roller-reefing applications. Today most bearings are made of an ultra-high-strength plastic called *Torlon*, which seems to hold up extremely well,

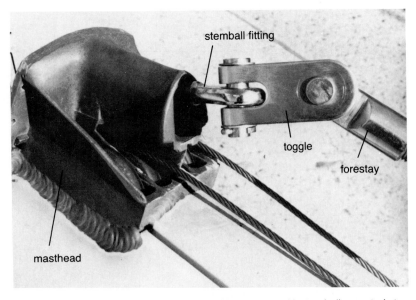

Figure 16-35. Isomat spar with stemball-mounted stay modified to include a toggle to protect against flexing caused by a roller-reefing rig.

although some (notably those in ProFurl units) are still carbon steel.

The loads on bearings can be high, especially if attempts are made to reef or furl a sail under tension, using a cockpit winch on the reefing line (something that most manufacturers say should *not* be done, but which is done routinely by many sailors, often with destructive results). These loads are not spread uniformly around a bearing since the tack and head of the sail, and the halyard, must all be attached off-center to clear the foil and headstay (Figure 16-36A). This generates point loading—pressure concentrated on only a small area of the bearings and bearing housings (races)—which tends to jam bearings. (This problem does not arise with roller-furling rigs since there is no foil or headstay to contend with and all attachments are made to the center of the various swivels.)

Furlex has tried to solve some of these problems by incorporating a patented *lash compensator* in its swivels. The lash compensator cancels out the off-center pull of the sail and halyard and reduces point loading (Figure 16-36B). Other manufacturers spread the bearings, which has the effect of spreading the load.

Carbon steel bearings are the hardest and will therefore consistently withstand abuse and unfair point loading better than stainless steel and plastic. But any kind of steel, of course, is terribly susceptible to rust in a salt atmosphere. Carbon steel bearings (earlier Schaefer roller-furling rigs, ProFurl) must be greased for life (special greases are used) and *sealed*. The bear-

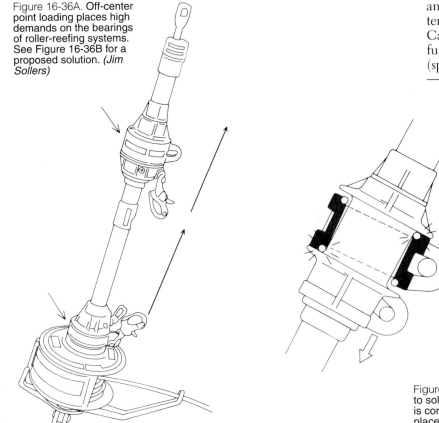

Figure 16-36A. Off-center point loading places high demands on the bearings of roller-reefing systems. See Figure 16-36B for a proposed solution. *(Jim Sollers)*

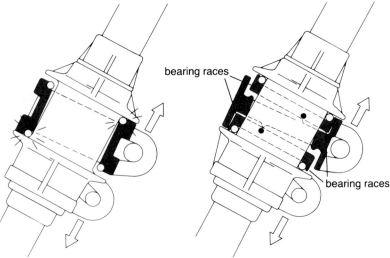

Figure 16-36B. The lash compensator from Furlex seeks to solve the problem in Figure 16-36A. The off-center load is concentrated at the two points marked, which are so placed that the bearing races spread the pressure evenly over the balls. *(Jim Sollers)*

ing seal is probably the most important part of the unit over the long run!

Because of problems with grease seals, for a time most roller reefers used stainless steel bearings. Stainless steel bearings have balls made of 316 stainless steel running in races of 304. In the presence of salt, corrosion between the two can occur. Even more likely is a galvanic interaction where the stainless races fit into their aluminum housings.

The bearings are almost always open so that they can periodically be flushed clean with fresh water. But very few owners flush the bearings more than once a season, and certainly no cruising sailor is going to pour a bucket of precious fresh water down the roller reefer after every sail! So inevitably, salt and dirt accumulate in the majority of units.

Another problem with these open stainless steel bearings is that stainless steel is hard, but not that hard. If the rig is left heavily loaded in one position for long periods of time, the balls can deform and the races indent, especially if corrosion occurs at the point of contact between the balls and the races. The bearing begins to run roughly, friction builds up, and all kinds of other problems develop, in the most extreme cases leading to *galling*, also called *cold-welding*—a process in which molecules on the surface of one part transfer to the surface of the other, rendering the bearing useless.

By alternating stainless and plastic ball bearings (the races are still stainless) the chances of galling can be significantly reduced, though not eliminated, and friction is lessened. Hood and Plastimo, among others, have used this approach. However, the plastic, being softer, carries very little of the bearing load, thus effectively reducing the load-bearing portion of the bearings.

Today, *all*-plastic *(Torlon)* balls are more commonly used, notably by Harken and in the newer Schaefer and Hood units. The balls run in an inner race of nickel-plated silicon bronze and an outer race of specially coated and hardened aluminum. In order to compensate for loss of hardness the bearings are increased in size and number, and are carefully engineered to spread the loads; otherwise ball deformation is inevitable.

Once friction begins to develop in any bearing, the drum-mounting shaft and the halyard swivel tend to turn with the foil during furling and unfurling operations, exerting torsional stresses on the drum-mounting hardware and pulling the halyard around the forestay. (Halyard wrap is probably *the* most common problem with roller reefers and is dealt with in Halyard Wrap and Riding Turns, below.) The greater the bearing friction, the more the torsional stresses. Sooner or later something will

give—the drum mount or turnbuckle, the halyard, or the headstay.

Because of potential bearing problems, almost all manufacturers recommend slacking the halyard before reefing or unfurling, as well as easing the sheets and allowing the sail to luff, though not to flog. These measures lessen friction and point loading on the bearings. However, many halyard winches and halyard cleats are mounted on the mainmast. One of the principal reasons for having a roller reefer in the first place is to avoid having to go forward when the wind begins to pipe up and it is time to shorten sail. In practice, very few sailors slacken the halyard from one month to the next, let alone every time they use the reefing gear. (Note that if a backstay is tensioned *after* the halyard has been tensioned, as the masthead moves aft the halyard is tensioned further, frequently putting excessive loads on roller-reefing bearings. First tension a backstay; only then tension a halyard.)

Regardless of your normal operating practices, if a roller reefer is becoming hard to operate, it should *never* be forced. The use of cockpit winches, and worse still electric winches (since these give no feel for what is going on), is a strict no-no! Go forward and find out what the problem is before something expensive gets broken.

Extrusions and extrusion bearings. The aluminum extrusions used for foils vary greatly in strength, shape, and the means used to join individual sections together. All are critical to a smoothly operating, long-lived roller reefer.

Since the reefing drum turns only the lower end of an extrusion, if a sail is rolled up under a load, the extrusion is subjected to strong torsional (twisting) forces. *Many lightweight extrusions cannot handle these stresses*—the extrusion buckles and/or the joints deform.

Foil extrusions come in numerous shapes (Figure 16-37). A round extrusion requires a uniform pressure to furl or unfurl the sail even when the sail is loaded and the extrusion sags off to leeward. It will turn smoothly and wrap tightly. In contrast, oval-shaped extrusions may work well at the dock, but under a load and the inevitable headstay sag, they tend to rotate unevenly and jerkily, increasing stresses on the extrusion and its joints. Inadequate headstay tension will exacerbate this situation.

Most joints are made with extruded sections (*splice pieces, sleeves*), which make a close fit inside the sections of foil being connected (Figure 16-38). Inside the splice a plastic bearing will be fitted around the headstay. This centers the foil on the headstay and reduces friction during furling and unfurling operations.

The foil sections and splice pieces are vari-

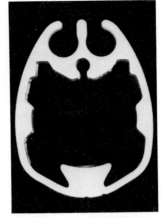
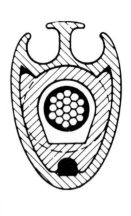

Figure 16-37. Roller-reefing extrusions. **Left**: A round extrusion turns smoothly and wraps tightly, but creates more windage. **Center**: More streamlined extrusion with twin luff grooves. **Right**: A streamlined oval extrusion with twin luff grooves—preferred for racing. *(ProFurl)*

Figure 16-38. Extrusion joints. *(ProFurl and Hood)*

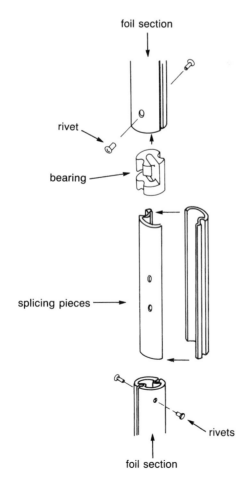

Hood's spring-loaded "Button-Lock" extrusion joint

foil section

rivet

bearing

splicing pieces

rivets

foil section

ously held together with pins, setscrews, spring-loaded buttons, pieces of wire, silicone caulking, and glue. In time, torsional stresses loosen all but the best joints. Loose joints lead to luff groove misalignment, and then the sail starts to hang up in the joints. Luff tapes jam, making it impossible to take sails up and down, and sails get torn. There is normally no solution to this problem short of new foils and connections.

One or two units incorporate full-length PVC inserts around the headstay, which act as a bearing and keep the stainless steel stay insulated from the aluminum foil. However, other manufacturers claim that when the headstay and foil sag under a load, this setup increases friction unacceptably. In any event, PVC absorbs chlorine, which attacks stainless steel.

Instead of a full-length headstay liner, most units have bearing inserts that are placed around the headstay at each joint in the foil. The idea is to use only as many inserts as are strictly necessary to keep the foil centered on the headstay (and out of contact with the stay itself) even

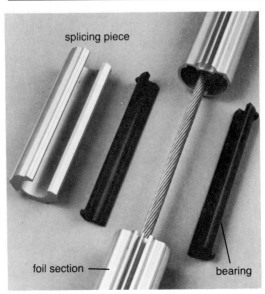

splicing piece

foil section

bearing

Figure 16-39. This wire halyard wrapped around the forestay, which sawed through it: Down came the sail. The disappointed owner (this was the second offense) complained that it had spoiled his day's sailing. He should look on the bright side. The halyard could just as easily have sawed through his forestay: Down comes the mast. For a look at what caused his problems, see Figure 16-40A.

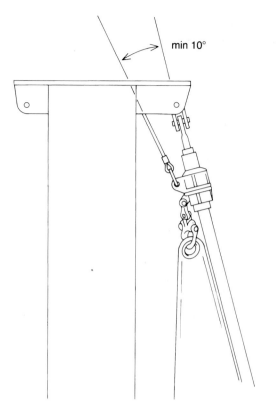

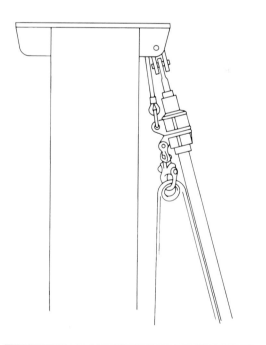

Figure 16-40A, B. Preventing halyard wrap. The angle shown at top is good. The halyard shown at bottom angles into the headstay and is sure to wrap sooner or later. (Jim Sollers)

under conditions of maximum headstay and foil sag. This reduces friction to a minimum while keeping the foil and the stay apart.

Halyard wrap and riding turns. Halyard wrap occurs when the upper half of the halyard swivel turns with the lower half, wrapping the halyard around the forestay. Wire halyards become permanently deformed and rope halyards can be seriously abraded and weakened. The foil may be damaged if the swivel is too low (see following paragraphs). If excessive pressure is applied (e.g., winching in the reefing line), the halyard will part (Figure 16-39), or the headstay or its end terminal and hardware may be damaged, endangering the mast.

By far the most common cause of halyard wrap is improper installation in the first place, even by factory-authorized rigging lofts. There are three common, and interrelated, faults:

1. The angle the halyard makes with the headstay is too small.

2. The swivel is too low.

3. The swivel is too high.

When a sail is hoisted, the halyard should angle away from the headstay by 10 to 30 degrees (Figure 16-40A). If the halyard runs parallel to—or worse still, angles into—the headstay, there is very little to stop it from wrapping around the stay (Figure 16-40B); the slightest friction in the upper swivel (such as is almost sure to develop over time) will cause halyard wrap. If necessary, the halyard must be led through a fairlead fastened to the front of the mast to provide the correct lead angle (Figure 16-40C and D).

One or two roller-reefing units incorporate specific antiwrap devices (Figure 16-41)—generally a *deflector ring* fitted around the headstay above the foil to hold halyards off the headstay. The ProFurl unit has a solid metal strap between the top of the upper swivel and the halyard. If the swivel turns, this strap comes up against a protrusion on the deflector ring (which ProFurl calls Multitop) and the swivel then turns no farther, thus providing a positive lock against halyard wrap. Harken has a mast-mounted sheave performing the same function as the fairlead in Figure 16-40C, but with less friction.

The lower the swivel on the foil, the longer the exposed length of halyard, the smaller the halyard angle, and the greater the chance of halyard wrap. When a sail is hoisted and winched up to its maximum halyard tension, the swivel should be almost at the top of the foil. *If not, a pendant must be fitted to either the head or the tack of the sail to allow the swivel to come up this far* (Figures 16-42A and B). If it is intended to use more than one sail on the same roller reefer, *each sail should be supplied with a pendant such that the upper swivel always hoists to the same position.*

However, it is equally important that no pendant allow the swivel to come even partially off the top of the foil. If this happens, the off-center loads on the swivel will cause it to cock to one side, jamming on and damaging the foil.

Most swivels slide up and down the foil on nylon pads (inserts or bushings). In time the off-center loads on the swivel cause these pads to wear down on opposite sides at the top and bottom (this problem is most likely with oval foils). The swivel cocks a little to one side (Figure 16-43A, B, and C). In some cases, as the foil turns in reefing and unreefing operations, it catches on the upper (halyard) half of the swivel, dragging the swivel around with it and wrapping the halyard around the headstay. New pads are needed.

Riding turns on the reefing drum. Another common problem. The causes are just the same as for riding turns on winches—inadequate ten-

Figure 16-40C, D. **A halyard fairlead can establish the correct angle (left), even when the swivel is too low (right).** *(Jim Sollers)*

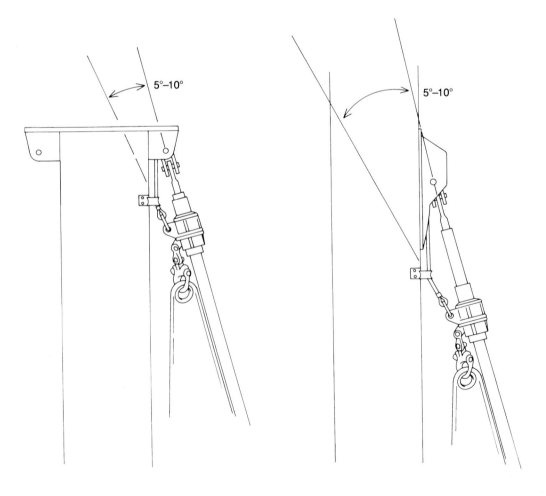

Running Rigging, Deck Hardware, and Roller Reefing

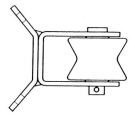

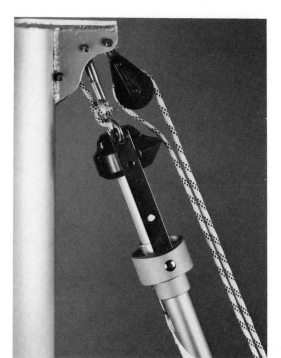

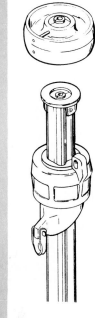

Figure 16-41. Halyard antiwrap devices. (**Above**) Harken's mast-mounted sheave. (**Center**) Two views of ProFurl's Multitop, which uses a halyard deflecting ring to prevent halyard wrap. (**Right**) Facnor/Merriman's halyard deflector ring. (*Harken, ProFurl, Merriman Yacht Specialties*)

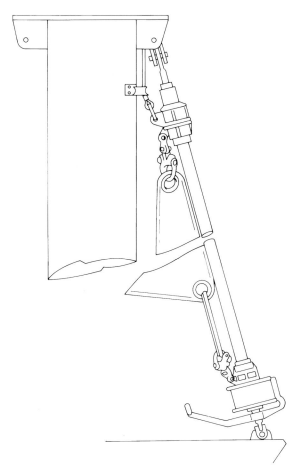

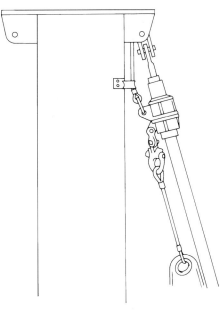

Figure 16-42A. A superior solution to the low swivel and fairlead is to add a pendant to the tack…

Figure 16-42B. …or the head of the sail. (*Jim Sollers*)

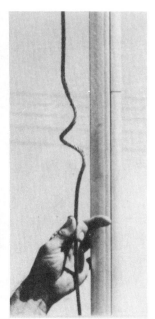

Figure 16-43A. (**Left**) The off-center loading of this rig wore the nylon bushing in the halyard swivel, causing it to hang up on the extrusion at the point shown. Note the excessively large clearance worn into the opposite side.

Figure 16-43B. The halyard then wrapped around and ultimately destroyed the extrusion (**left center**). Note that the swivel was mounted too low; it should have come almost to the top of the extrusion. (**Center right**) This is what happened to the halyard.

Figure 16-43C. (**Right**) Here's another rig with an incorrect halyard lead angle. Take a look around the anchorage; you'll see dozens!

sion and incorrect sheet lead angles. If the reefing drum does not include an integral sheet lead, a suitable pad eye or block must be set up on deck to ensure that the reefing line runs onto the drum *at an angle of 90 degrees to the headstay* (Figure 16-44). During reefing and unfurling operations always maintain a moderate tension on the reefing line to keep it from jumping around. In addition to maintaining a fair lead onto the drum for the reefing line, *the line must be lead back to the cockpit through a series of blocks that ensure minimal friction.* When the sail is partially reefed, the load on the sail will cause this line to work backward and forward. If the line is dragging across a hard surface at any point, sooner or later it will part, allowing the entire sail to unroll uncontrollably. Since the sail is only likely to be reefed in heavy conditions, this too will only occur in heavy conditions, which will make the situation very difficult to handle. If synthetic line (as opposed to wire rope) is used for the reefing line, the largest line size that will fit on the drum should be used. This will not only provide the maximum strength, but also make for the greatest ease of handling (in practice, ⅜-inch line is often the largest that can be accommodated; ½ inch, if it fits, is much easier on the hands).

Sail damage. Headsail damage is more prevalent with roller reefers than with hanked-on headsails. Generally the genoa is set up as the primary (and frequently the only) sail for the roller reefer. When the wind pipes up, either there is no smaller sail to set or, rather than setting it, the genoa is steadily reefed down. Sooner or later the

sail encounters wind strengths for which it was not designed and blows out. Correct sail design will help to alleviate stresses (generally radial or vertical panels), as will the use of heavier sailcloth in the panels closest to the leech—those still operational when the sail is reefed.

When reefing down, if the halyard and sheets are eased too far the sail rolls up loosely. In a gale of wind the poorly furled head of the sail will flog around and eventually tear up. Gentle pressure must be maintained on the sheets while reefing so that the sail rolls up tightly. Once the sail is completely rolled up, continue turning it a few more times to wrap the sheets around it.

Even when furled, the outer wraps of a sail are still exposed to the sun's ultraviolet (UV) rays. To prevent degradation of the sailcloth, a sacrificial strip of material must be sewed to the leach of the sail. All too often one sees roller reefing sails with torn and tattered UV covers—slowly and steadily sunlight will literally be eating up the outer wrap of the sail. The next time it is put to a test, it is likely to fail; once a tear starts, it is going to run clear across the sail.

Summary: Do's and Don'ts

Do:

• Install the unit properly with:

1. The halyard swivel at the top of the foil as close to the masthead sheave as possible.

2. The halyard angled away from the swivel by at least 10 degrees.

3. All the sails to be used fitted with suitable pendants to ensure that the swivel is hoisted to the same height with each one.

- Keep the headstay tight to avoid foil sag.
- Slack off the halyard, ease the sheets, and luff up when reefing.
- Retain *moderate* tension on sheets and reefing line at all times to avoid loose wraps and riding turns on the reefing drum.
- Flush stainless and plastic bearings at regular intervals with fresh water.
- Slack the halyard at all times when the sail is furled to avoid prolonged point loading on the bearings.
- Install adequate toggles at both ends of the headstay and on the drum mount (where appropriate).
- Check the lower turnbuckle terminal on turnbuckle-mounted units to make sure that it is not backing off.

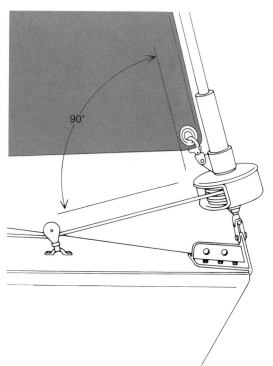

Figure 16-44. **To prevent riding turns on the drum, the furling line must enter the drum at right angles to the headstay. Moving the forward lead block fore-and-aft centers the line vertically in the opening.** *(Jim Sollers)*

Don't:

- Try to reef the sail against full sheet tension.
- Reef with a highly tensioned halyard.
- Tension the backstay after tensioning the halyard.
- Leave the halyard tensioned when the sail is not in use.
- Force the reefing line. If it jams or there is unusual resistance, *find out why*: Check for halyard wrap, a riding turn on the reefing drum, or rough bearings.
- Let the sail flog when reefing—uneven tension on the reefing line is likely to cause a riding turn.
- Force a sail up or down its luff groove.
- Use reefed sails in wind conditions stronger than the sailcloth is designed to tolerate.

Powered headsail reefers. Some larger rigs are driven by electric and hydraulic motors (Figure 16-45). Older hydraulic units tend to have a direct drive from the hydraulic motor, and rely on the motor check valves to maintain oil pressure and keep the sail in position. Any pump, check valve, or seal leaks result in creep and in the slow unwinding of the sail.

Some units also have adapted industrial hydraulic equipment with *steel* interiors. Water in the hydraulic oil (such as from condensation in oil reservoirs) leads to rusting of sensitive parts

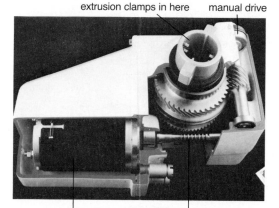

extrusion clamps in here   manual drive

electric motor   worm gear

Figure 16-45. **Worm gearing on an electrically powered headsail reefer.** *(ProFurl)*

and thus all kinds of problems. For other problem areas and troubleshooting see the earlier sections of this chapter on hydraulic windlasses.

Newer hydraulic drive units use worm gearing (which acts as an effective brake against the sail's unwinding) and all-stainless-steel construction. Electrically driven units are very similar (on the motor and control side) to electrically powered windlasses—refer to the relevant section for troubleshooting.

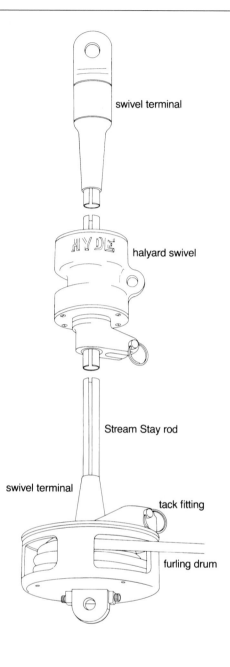

Figure 16-46A. The Hyde Stream Stay—at one time a popular option for retrofitted behind-the-mast roller reefing that also serves as a roller-reefing headsail unit. The Stream Stay has a solid aluminum extrusion, mounted on its own swivels, that replaces the existing headstay or behind-the-mast stay. *(Hyde and Jim Sollers)*

swivel terminal

halyard swivel

Stream Stay rod

swivel terminal

tack fitting

furling drum

Figure 16-46B. MetalMast Marine's Reefaway—a hybrid with all the features of behind-the-mast reefing, but placed inside a separate, open-backed mast extrusion. The Hyde Stream Stay also may be mounted in this fashion. *(MetalMast Marine and Jim Sollers)*

Maintenance

Some roller reefers are advertised as *maintenance free*. It would be a foolish owner who took this too literally! All roller reefers incorporate dissimilar metals in the drum assemblies, foil joints, and upper swivels. The drum assemblies in particular are subjected to a great deal of saltwater spray and therefore are prone to galvanic corrosion. At the very least this unit needs a thorough flushing with fresh water several times a season and before a winter layup.

If the drum and swivel have open bearings, they should be rotated while being flushed. This helps to wash out all the salt and dirt. Plastic and stainless steel bearings will benefit from a good shot of WD-40. At the end of the season, after stainless steel bearings have been thoroughly washed out, pump in a little Teflon-based waterproof grease and spin the units to spread the grease around the balls and races.

Before winter layup wash the foil. Detergents containing ammonia should not be used on anodized aluminum. After washing, rinse well and liberally coat all aluminum surfaces with a silicone car or boat polish.

In-Mast and Behind-the-Mast Reefing

How it works. The success of roller-reefing headsails resulted in the adaptation of the same hardware to furling and reefing applications for mainsails and mizzens. In almost all instances, existing headsail reefing equipment with minor modifications or no modifications is installed either inside a specially built mast or just behind the mast.

Exactly the same principles apply as for headsail reefing. The sail feeds into a slot in a foil. The head of the sail is attached to a swivel, which fits around the foil, and is hoisted by the sail halyard; the tack of the sail attaches to a furling drum or some other fitting attached to the foil. The foil is rotated to wind up the sail.

Now for some minor variations. The foil on a *behind-the-mast* reefer must be set up on the equivalent of a substitute headstay, and this stay must be kept tensioned to prevent sail sag (Figures 16-46A, B, and C). Generally a rod is fitted between a bracket at the masthead and a fixed gooseneck, then tensioned by tightening a nut on the underside of the gooseneck mount. The foil rotates around the rod.

In-mast reefers, which have a narrow slot in the mast, are not subject to sail sag—the slot in the mast provides support along the length of the sail (Figures 16-47A and B). As long as the *sail* is ten-

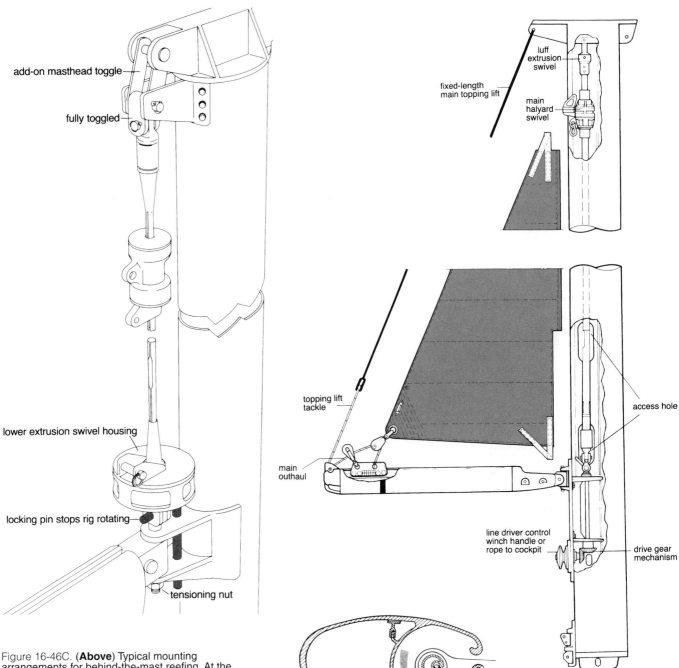

add-on masthead toggle

fully toggled

lower extrusion swivel housing

locking pin stops rig rotating

tensioning nut

Figure 16-46C. (**Above**) Typical mounting arrangements for behind-the-mast reefing. At the masthead…and at the tack. *(Jim Sollers)*

luff extrusion swivel

fixed-length main topping lift

main halyard swivel

topping lift tackle

access hole

main outhaul

line driver control winch handle or rope to cockpit

drive gear mechanism

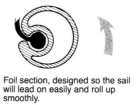

Foil section, designed so the sail will lead on easily and roll up smoothly.

Figure 16-47A. In-mast reefing arrangement.

Roller Reefing and Furling　　　553

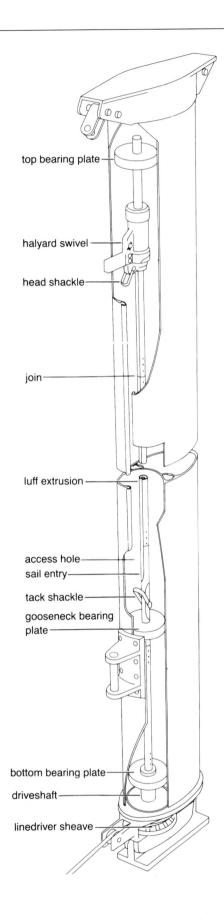

Figure 16-47B. In-mast reefing with an untensioned luff rod. The linedriver can be fitted as shown only on a deck-stepped mast. *(Jim Sollers)*

top bearing plate

halyard swivel

head shackle

join

luff extrusion

access hole

sail entry

tack shackle

gooseneck bearing plate

bottom bearing plate

driveshaft

linedriver sheave

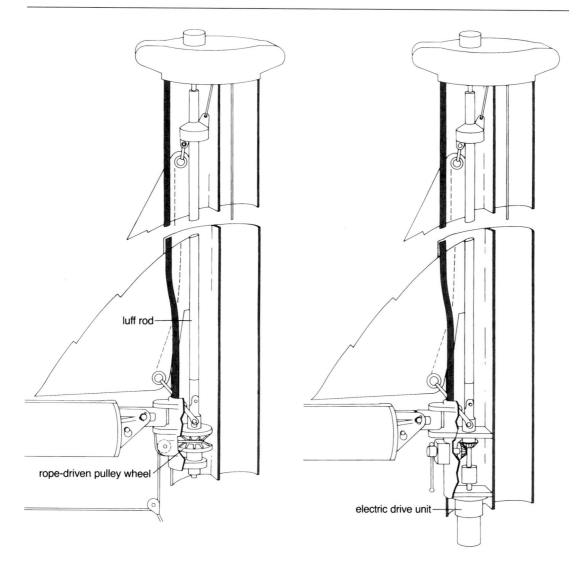

luff rod

rope-driven pulley wheel

electric drive unit

Figure 16-48. In-mast reefing drive options. Standard small-mast gooseneck features rope-driven pulley wheel set at right angles to the luff rod, with furling lines led aft (**left**). Electric-drive unit positions an electric motor and reduction gear and clutch under the bevel gears that drive the luff rod. Most manufacturers also produce hydraulic-drive units. *(Jim Sollers)*

sioned (via its halyard), there is no need for any tension on the foil or on any rod around which it rotates. In fact, there is not even a need for the rod at all—the foil can simply be set up in bearings attached to the inside of the mast. However, with wider mast slots, inadequate rod or foil tension *can* allow the foil to sag into the slot and jam.

Foils can be turned (Figure 16-48) by a conventional reefing drum, a line driver, a motor, or by cranking with a winch handle (in the event of motor failure). A line driver resembles the jaws on a self-tailing winch. An *endless* line (i.e., one big loop) feeds through the jaws, around various blocks, and back to a similar unit in the cockpit. A winch handle is used to turn the cockpit driver, cranking the sail in or out. Line drivers are either installed directly on a foil or set in the aft face of the mast, turning the foil via a set of bevel gears.

Problems and answers. Much of the information in the section on roller reefing is applicable, especially that relating to bearings, foil extrusions, halyard wrap, and maintenance. In addition, certain other points need noting.

Mast bend. In-mast reefers cannot accommodate mast bend—the foil extrusion and sail will hang up on the mast. Behind-the-mast reefers will suffer from changing rod tension with changes in mast shape. Note that *behind-the-mast reefers should be fully toggled at top and bottom to accommodate sail sag* (see the section on headsail reefing). Some retrofitted behind-the-mast reefers can impose severe bending stresses on masts (rather like the string on a bow—Figure 16-49) in which case *aft* lower shrouds are a necessity to keep the mast in column (straight)—*in-line* shrouds will not work. Running backstays

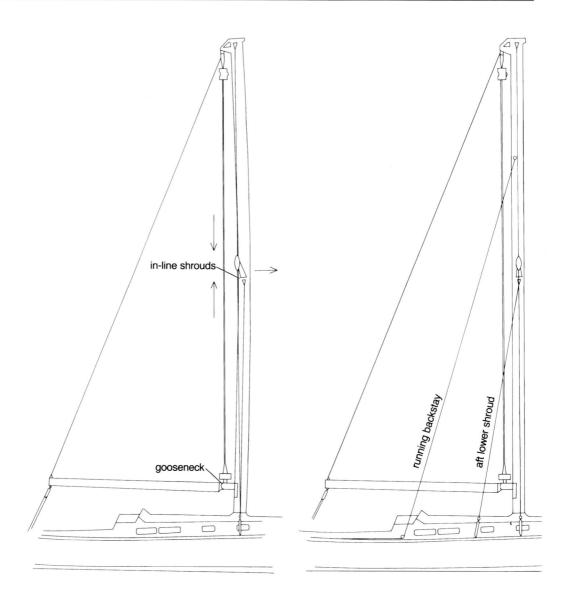

Figure 16-49. Behind-the-mast reefers impose severe strains on the mast, which must receive additional support (**right**). (Jim Sollers)

in-line shrouds

gooseneck

running backstay

aft lower shroud

may be needed to keep the mast from *pumping* in heavy seas. Some masts still may not be able to take the added strain. In-mast reefing does not suffer from the same problems since the mast loading is all in direct compression.

Tension. Moderate tension must be maintained at all times on the clew of the sail when reefing and unfurling. If this is not done, the sail will wrap and unwrap loosely, jamming inside the mast or mast slot. Some first-generation units jammed up so badly that the sails had to be cut out! This has been largely eliminated by improving the ratio of foil sizes to slots. Nevertheless it may still prove impossible to wind up a jammed sail and start again. The tack of the sail sometimes has to be disconnected, the halyard slacked, and the whole sail pulled down and reset.

In-mast rod tension. Where an *in-mast* foil is mounted on a rod, excessive tension on the rod will merely distort mounting brackets, damage bearings, and wear out bevel gears, etc. (Figure 16-50). As mentioned previously, tensioning *in-mast* mounting rods will do nothing to improve sail shape or performance.

Motor failures. See the relevant sections on powered windlasses—motor installations are very similar (both electric and hydraulic).

Fluting. Anytime a boat with a slotted mast is berthed, the sail is rolled up, and the wind

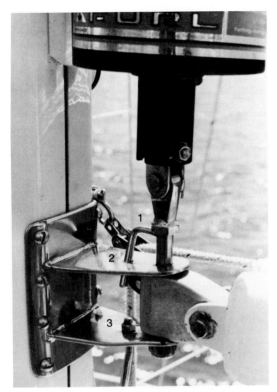

Figure 16-50. Inadequate mounting hardware on a custom-built (aftermarket) behind-the-mast reefer. The pin (**1**) is bending. Soon its weld will break and the whole rig will unwind uncontrollably. The two gooseneck retaining plates (**2** and **3**) are also flexing upward. In time these welds will crack and the whole boom and sail assembly will come adrift.

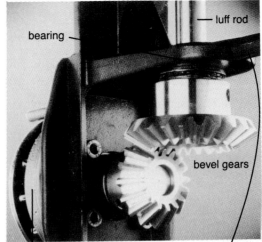

Figure 16-51. Excessive in-mast rod tension will distort the mounting bracket, potentially throwing out bearing alignment and gear engagement. *(Kemp Spars)*

moves aft of the beam, the wind will make a moaning noise as it blows across the slot (just like blowing across the top of a bottle). This is easily stopped by hoisting a strip of sailcloth (an antivibration strip or *flute stopper*) up the slot. The problem does not occur at anchor since the boat will stay head to wind.

Glossary

Accumulator—an air-filled tank used to smooth out pressure in a freshwater system; also a tank used in a refrigeration system to trap liquid refrigerant that might otherwise damage the compressor.

Aerial—see *antenna*.

Alignment—the bringing together of two coupling halves in near-perfect horizontal and vertical agreement.

Alternating current (AC)—an electrical current reversing its direction at regular intervals. Each repetition of these changes is a cycle and the number of cycles that take place in 1 second is the frequency.

Alternator—a machine for generating electricity by spinning a magnet inside a series of coils. The resulting power output is alternating current. In DC systems this output is rectified via silicon diodes.

Ambient conditions—the surrounding temperature or pressure, or both.

Ammeter—an instrument for measuring current flow.

Ampere (amp)—a measure of the rate of electric current flow.

Ampere-hour (Ah)—a measure of the amount of electricity stored in a battery.

Annealing—a process of softening metals.

Anode—the negative terminal of a battery or cell.

Antenna (aerial)—a conductor that radiates or collects radio waves.

Antenna gain—the measure of the effectiveness of an antenna.

Antisiphon valve—a valve that admits air to a line and prevents siphonic action.

Aqualift—an engine exhaust and silencing system in which cooling water is injected into the exhaust and carried out by the exhaust gases.

Area effect—the influence on the rate of corrosion of the relative areas of an anode and a cathode when connected in a galvanic cell.

Armature—the rotating windings in a generator (AC or DC).

Atmospheric pressure—the pressure of the air at the surface of the earth, conventionally taken to be 14.7 psi.

Atomizer—see *injector*.

Babbitt—a soft white metal alloy frequently used to line replaceable shell-type engine bearings; also used in the traversing nut on worm steering.

Back pressure—a buildup of pressure in an exhaust system.

Backstay—a wire rope or rod giving aft support to a mast.

Ball valve—either a valve with a spring-loaded ball or one with a ball rotating in a spherical seat.

Battery—*Automotive:* a lead-acid battery with many thin plates and low-density active material. *Deep-cycle:* a lead-acid battery with thicker, stronger plates and high-density active material. *Wet-type:* a conventional lead-acid battery with liquid electrolyte.

No-maintenance: either a sealed, conventional wet battery with excess electrolyte or a sealed gel-type battery. *Gel-type:* a lead-acid battery in which electrolyte is trapped in a gel.

Battery isolation switch—a switch installed next to the battery and carrying full battery output, used to isolate the battery from all circuits.

Battery sensed—a voltage regulator that senses system voltage at the battery (as opposed to at the alternator).

Bearing—a device for supporting a rotating shaft with minimum friction. It may take the form of a metal sleeve (a bushing), a set of ball bearings (a roller bearing), or a set of pins around the shaft (a needle bearing).

Bearing race—the outer cage within which a set of balls rotates in a roller bearing.

Bendix—the drive gear (pinion) arrangement on a starter motor.

Bevel gear—a means of transmitting drive through a 90-degree angle.

Binnacle—a housing for a compass.

Bleeding—the process of purging air from a fuel or hydraulic system.

Block—the general term for a rigging pulley.

Blocking diode—a diode used to permit charging of more than one battery from one power source without paralleling the battery outputs. Also known as a *battery isolation diode*.

Blow-by—the escape of gases past piston rings or closed valves.

Bobstay—a stay from the tip of a bowsprit to the waterline.

Bonding—the process of electrically tying together all major fixed metal items on a boat.

Bosun's chair (a corruption of *boatswain's* chair)—a canvas seat used for hoisting someone up a mast.

Bottle screw—see *turnbuckle*.

Bridge rectifier—an arrangement of diodes for converting alternating current (AC) to direct current (DC).

Brush—a carbon or carbon-composite spring-loaded rod used to conduct current to or from commutators or slip rings.

Btu (British thermal unit)—a unit used to measure quantities of heat.

Bulldog clamp—see *cable clamp*.

Bushing—see *bearing*.

Bus bar (busbar)—a heavy copper strap used in breaker boxes and circuit panel boxes for carrying high currents and making multiple connections.

Cable clamp—a U-shaped bolt with a saddle used to join or to make loops in wire rope.

Cam—an elliptical protrusion on a shaft.

Cam cleat—a cleat with two spring-loaded, toothed jaws that trap and hold a line.

Capacitor—a device for storing electric energy. A capacitor blocks the flow of DC but lets AC through (analogous to a flexible membrane that will oscillate but not allow flow through it).

Cap shroud—see *shroud*.

Cathode—the positive terminal of a cell or battery.

Caulking—various semiflexible compounds used to seal seams. Sometimes applied with less precision to sealing and bedding compounds.

Cell—a single unit that makes electricity through chemical energy. A group of cells makes a battery.

Centrifugal action—the process of imparting velocity to a liquid through a spinning impeller that drives the liquid from the center of a pump housing to its periphery.

Chainplates—the metal straps bolted to a hull to which standing rigging attaches.

Check valve—an electrical or mechanical valve that allows flow in only one direction.

Cheek plates—the plates that enclose the sheave on a block.

Choke—see *inductor*.

Circlip—see *snap ring*.

Circuit—the path of electric current.
A *closed* circuit has a complete path.
An *open* circuit has a broken or disconnected path.
A *short* circuit has an unintentional direct path bypassing the equipment (appliance, resistance) in the circuit.

Circuit breaker—a load-sensitive switch that trips (opens a circuit) if a threshold-exceeding current flows through it.

Clevis pin—a metal pin with a flattened head at one end and a hole for a cotter pin (split pin) at the other. It is used to fasten rigging together.

Clew—the lower, aft corner of a sail.

Clutch—a device used to couple and uncouple a power source from a piece of equipment. It may be manually, hydraulically, or electromagnetically operated.
A *cone* clutch forces a tapered seat onto a tapered friction pad.
A *brake-band* clutch tightens a friction band around a smooth face on a gear.
A *disc* clutch holds alternating metal and friction plates together.

CNG—compressed natural gas.

Coaxial cable—a cable enclosed in an insulating sleeve (or dielectric), then a metal braided sleeve, and finally another insulating sleeve.

Cold cranking amps (CCA)—the number of amps a battery at 0°F (–17.8°C) can deliver for 30 seconds and maintain a voltage of 1.2 volts per cell or more.

Cold plate—a refrigerator or freezer tank containing an evaporator coil and a solution with a freezing point below that of water.

Collet—a metal chip designed to hold winch spindles and engine valves in place.

Common ground point—a central stud, normally connected to the earth's ground via a through-hull fitting, to which are attached AC and DC grounding circuits, any bonding circuit, various radio and lightning grounds, and any cathodic protection system.

Commutator—the copper segments that are arranged around the end of an armature and on which the brushes ride.

Compression ratio—the volume of a combustion chamber with the piston at the top of its stroke as a proportion of the total volume of the cylinder with the piston at the bottom of its stroke.

Compressor—a device used to compress refrigeration gases.
A *reciprocal* compressor has two pistons attached to a rotating crankshaft as in a conventional engine.
A *swash-plate (wobble plate)* compressor has five or six pistons attached to a plate that oscillates, driven by a rotating cam.

Condenser—a unit designed to remove sufficient heat from a compressed refrigeration gas to make the gas condense into a liquid.

Conditioning—see *equalization*.

Conductance—a measure of the ability to conduct electricity.

Conduit—a pipe in which electric cables are run; also a reinforced sheathing used with steering and engine control cables.

Cone clutch—see *clutch*.

Constant-current voltage regulation—see *voltage regulation*.

Continuity—a complete path or circuit through which current can flow.

Corrosion—a process that leads to the destruction of two metals.
Galvanic corrosion arises when dissimilar, electrically connected metals are immersed in an electrolyte (e.g., salt water). A current is generated, leading to the destruction of the *anode* (*less noble* metal) and the protection of the *cathode* (*more noble* metal).
Pinhole and *crevice* corrosion are the results of galvanic corrosion occurring in just one piece of metal due to differences in the composition of the metal.
Stray-current corrosion is the result of external current leakage through metal fittings in contact with an electrolyte, such as salt water. Massive corrosion can occur where the current leaves a fitting. The term *electrolysis* refers to the passage of electricity through the electrolyte.

Cotter pin—a pin with two legs. With legs together the pin is placed through the hole in a clevis pin. The legs are then opened outward to prevent the cotter pin from backing out of the hole. The cotter pin, in turn, prevents the load-bearing clevis pin from backing out of its retaining hole.

Creep—the slow seepage of hydraulic fluid down the sides of a piston or ram, or through check valves, leading to gradual movement of the rudder or steering wheel.

Crosby clamp—see *cable clamp*.

Cup washer—a dished leather or neoprene washer fitted to the rod end in some piston-style pumps.

Current—the rate of flow of electricity (measured in amps).

Cutless bearing—a ribbed rubber sleeve in a metal tube, used to support a propeller shaft.

CVJ (constant velocity joint)—a type of propeller shaft coupling that permits considerable engine misalignment.

Cycles—see *alternating current*.

Deep-cycle battery—see *battery*.

Diaphragm—a reinforced rubber membrane that moves in and out in certain pumps.

Dielectric—an insulating material. See *coaxial cable*.

Diffusion—the process by which the acid in a battery electrolyte permeates the active material in the plates.

Diode—an electronic check valve.

Direct current (DC)—an electric current that flows in one direction only.

Disc-drive steering—see *radial-drive steering*.

Double-pole switch—a switch that makes or breaks two separate connections at the same time.

Dowel—a round metal or wooden pin.

Drier—a cylinder containing hygroscopic (water-absorbing) material used to remove moisture from refrigeration circuits.

Drift—any suitably sized round metal bar used to knock out bushings, clevis pins, and the like.

Drip loop—a deliberately induced low spot in a run of electrical cable designed to keep moisture out of terminal boxes, etc.

Drive ratio—the ratio between the radius of a driven pulley and the radius of the driving pulley.

Duckbill valve—a hemispherical rubber valve with a slit in it and with protruding rubber lips. Internal pressure forces the lips apart; external pressure closes the lips, sealing the valve.

Earth—the reference point (*ground potential*) for AC circuits.

Earth leak—see *ground fault*.

Electric motor—a device for converting electromagnetic force into rotary motion. *Universal* motors operate on both AC and DC. *Permanent-magnet* motors also run on both currents. *Induction* motors operate on AC only.

Electrolysis—see *corrosion*.

Electrolyte—the solution in a battery; a liquid conductor of electricity.

Electromagnet—a magnetic force induced by passing a direct current through a coil wrapped around an iron core (shoe).

Electromagnetic clutch—a cone clutch in which the driving and driven halves are pulled together by an electromagnet.

Equalization—the process of driving a liquid electrolyte (wet) lead-acid battery up to its highest natural voltage in order to reconvert sulphated plate material back into active material.

Eutectic—a particular level of a salt solution at which the whole solution freezes at one specific temperature (as opposed to progressively freezing through a process of ice crystallizing as temperatures lower).

Evaporator—the unit in which liquid refrigerant converts back into a gas, absorbing latent heat in the process.

Excitation—the initial magnetism induced in a field winding in order to initiate alternator or generator output.

Excitation windings—a separate set of coils built into the stator on brushless AC alternators, and used to induce field current in the rotor.

Expansion valve—a valve with a minute, adjustable orifice used to separate the high- and low-pressure sides of a refrigeration system, and through which the liquid refrigerant sprays into the evaporator.

Extrusion—a complex metal (normally aluminum) shape produced in continuous lengths.

Fail-safe diode—a diode set to block current flow at normal voltages but to open with abnormally high voltage. Used to protect alternator diodes against accidental open-circuiting.

Fast fuse—used to protect alternator diodes against accidental reverse polarity.

Feed pump—see *lift pump*.

Feeler gauge—thin strips of metal machined to precise thicknesses and used for measuring small gaps.

Fid—a softwood plug to hammer up and block off a through-hull fitting or hull opening below the waterline in the event of a failure of the through-hull.

Field windings—electromagnetic coils used to create magnetic fields in alternators, generators, and electric motors.

Filament—a very fine piece of high-resistance wire that glows red (or white) hot when a current is passed through it.

Filter—an electrical device for screening out unwanted interference; also a device for screening out impurities in fuel, air, or water.

Filter/drier—see *drier*.

Flap valve—a simple rubber flap, sometimes weighted. Fluid pressure opens it in one direction and closes it in the other.

Flashing the field—the use of an external DC source to supply momentary excitation to alternator or generator field coils.

Flax—a natural fiber used in packing.

Flexible-impeller pump—a pump with a rubber impeller and a cam on one side of the pump chamber. As the impeller passes the cam, its vanes are squeezed down, expelling fluids trapped between them. The vanes then spring back, sucking in more fluid.

Float charge—the current required to maintain a battery at full charge without overcharging.

Forestay—a wire rope, or rod giving forward support to a mast.

Frequency—see *alternating current*.

Fuse—a protective device designed to break a circuit by melting if the current goes above a certain level.

Galvanic corrosion—see *corrosion*.

Galvanic isolator—a device that blocks galvanic currents but closes a circuit when faced with higher voltages.

Gain—see *antenna gain*.

Galling—a process of "cold-welding" that can

completely seize up stainless steel fasteners, particularly when their threads are dirty or damaged.

Gasket—a piece of material placed between two parts to seal them against leaks.

Gassing—a process in which battery electrolyte breaks down, giving off hydrogen and oxygen.

Gate valve—a valve in which a flat metal plate (gate) screws down to block off flow.

Gauge set—a pair of gauges mounted on a manifold, which can be connected to a refrigeration unit to measure high and low pressures, and to vacuum down and charge the unit.

Gear ratio—the relative size of two gears. If the gears are in contact, their relative speed of rotation will be given by the gear ratio. Example: If the gear ratio is 8:1, the smaller gear will rotate eight times faster than the larger gear.

Generator—a machine for generating electricity by spinning a series of coils inside a magnet. The resulting power output is alternating current. In DC systems, this output is rectified via a commutator and brushes.

GFCI (ground-fault circuit interrupter)—a safety device that breaks an AC circuit anytime a short to ground occurs; also known as a residual current circuit breaker (RCCB).

Glow plug—a heating element installed in diesel engine precombustion chambers to aid in cold-starting.

Gooseneck—a swivel fitting that holds a boom to a mast.

Governor—a device for maintaining an engine or electric motor at a constant speed, regardless of load.

Grid—a lead-alloy framework that supports the active material of a battery plate and conducts current.

Ground—a connection between an electric circuit and the earth, or some conducting body serving in place of the earth.

Grounded conductor—a normally current-carrying AC conductor maintained at earth's potential (i.e., the neutral wire).

Grounding conductor—a normally non-current-carrying AC conductor maintained at the earth's potential (i.e., the ground wire). Also used to refer to bonding wires attached to DC equipment.

Ground fault—a current leak to ground bypassing proper circuits.

Ground point—see *common ground point*.

Gudgeon—one-half of a rudder hinge, the other half being the *pintle*.

Gypsy—a wheel on a windlass notched for chain (also called a *wildcat*).

Halyard—a wire rope or synthetic rope used to raise a sail.

Halyard wrap—the twisting of a headsail halyard around the forestay.

Head—a marine toilet.

Head box—the assembly of sheaves and wire rope attachments at the top of a mast.

Header tank—a small tank set above an engine on heat-exchanger-cooled systems. The header tank serves as an expansion chamber, coolant reservoir, and pressure regulator (via a pressure cap).

Heat exchanger—a vessel containing a number of small tubes through which cooling water is passed, while raw water is circulated around the outside of the tubes to carry off heat from the cooling water.

Heat-shrink tape and tubing—insulating tape that shrinks and melts when heated to form an effective seal. Also known as *self-amalgamating* tape.

Heat sink—a mounting for an electronic component designed to dissipate heat to the atmosphere.

Hemp—see *flax*.

Hertz (Hz)—the unit of frequency of an alternating current. One hertz equals one cycle per second.

Holdover plate—see *cold plate*.

Hose adapter—a standard plumbing fitting on one end with a suitable hose connection on the other.

Hose barb—a tapered and ridged fitting that slides up inside a hose.

Hose clamp—an adjustable stainless steel band for clamping hoses. Also known as a *Jubilee clip* in the UK.

Hunting—a rhythmical cycling up and down in speed of a governed engine.

Hydraulic steering—steering using a manual hydraulic pump driven by the steering wheel, and operating a hydraulic piston (ram), which turns the rudder via a tiller arm.

Hydrometer—a float-type instrument used to determine the state of charge of a battery by measuring the specific gravity of the electrolyte (i.e., the amount of sulphuric acid in the electrolyte).

Impedance—a kind of alternating current resistance; the ratio of voltage to current.

Impeller—the rotating fitting that imparts motion to a fluid in a rotating pump.

Impressed-current cathodic protection—a means of protecting underwater hardware by pushing controlled amounts of current into the water.

Incandescent light—a light with filaments.

Inches of mercury—a scale for measuring small pressure changes, particularly those below atmospheric pressure (vacuums).

Inductance—a property of a conductor or coil that determines how much voltage will be induced in it by a change of current.

Induction motor—an AC motor in which the stator coils generate a rotating magnetic field that drags the rotor around.

Inductor—a coil so designed that it filters out unwanted radio frequency noise.

In-mast reefing—roller reefing for mains and mizzens installed inside specially extruded masts.

Injection pump—a pump designed to meter out precisely controlled amounts of diesel fuel and then raise it to injection pressures at precisely controlled moments in an engine cycle.

Injector—a device for atomizing diesel fuel and spraying it into a cylinder.

Injector nut—the nut that holds a fuel line to an injector.

Insulated return—a circuit in which both the outgoing and returning conductors are insulated.

Interference—undesired radio wavelengths.

Inverter—a device for changing DC to AC.

Isolation transformer—a transformer that transfers power from one winding to another magnetically and without any direct connection.

Joker valve—see *duckbill valve*.

Jubilee clip—see *hose clamp*.

Kilo—1,000, as in *kilowatt* or *kilohertz*.

Latent heat—heat absorbed or given up during changes of state with no change of temperature.

Life cycles—the number of times a battery can be pulled down to a certain level of discharge and then recharged before the battery fails.

Lift pump—a low-pressure pump in a fuel-injection system supplying fuel from the tank to the injection pump.

Line driver—a winch with a set of jaws that grips an endless line (a continuous loop).

Lip-type seal—a seal, using automotive-style oil seals, that is used in place of a stuffing box.

Liquid slugging—liquid refrigerant entering a compressor as a result of excess refrigerant being fed into the evaporator.

Live—a circuit energized with electricity.

Loading coil—a coil placed in series with an antenna and used to tune it.

Load testing—the use of a high load for a short period of time to test a battery and check its ability to perform under actual engine starting conditions.

Lower shroud—see *shroud*.

LPG (liquefied petroleum gas)—petroleum gases, principally propane and butane, that liquefy at relatively low pressures (below 200 psi).

Macerator—a specially designed impeller for breaking up solids prior to pumping.

Machine screw—a countersunk, slotted screw with machined threads such as are found on bolts.

Machine sensed—a voltage regulator that senses system voltage at the alternator (as opposed to at the battery).

Main down conductor—the cable from a lightning rod to an immersed ground plate or ground (such as an external ballast keel).

Manifold—a pipe assembly, attached to an engine, that conducts air into the engine or conducts exhaust gases out of it; any pipe assembly with more than one fitting screwed into it, for example, a gauge set manifold.

Manometer—a U-shaped, water-filled tube used for measuring very low pressures (commonly from 0 to 1 psi).

Mechanical seal (*rotary seal; face seal*)—a spring-loaded seal used in place of a stuffing box on a propeller shaft.

Mega—1,000,000, as in *megawatt* and *megahertz*.

Microfarad (MFD or µF)—one-millionth of a farad; a measure of capacity.

Milliamp (millivolt)—one-thousandth of an amp (volt).

Mole wrench—Vise-Grips.

MOV (metal oxide varistor)—one kind of transient voltage suppressor. MOV's have an open circuit until hit by a high voltage (a voltage spike or surge) and then conduct to ground in order to short out the spike (surge).

Needle bearing—see *bearing*.

Noble metal—a metal high on the galvanic table. Noble metals are likely to form a cathode in any cases of galvanic corrosion and therefore are unlikely to corrode.

Noise—a general expression for electrical interference.

Offset gear—an arrangement of gears in which one gear engages another on the same plane (i.e., the gears are in line with one another).

Ohm—the standard unit of measurement of resistance.

Ohmmeter—an instrument for measuring resistance. Usually incorporated as one function of a multimeter.

Open circuit—see *circuit*.

Open-circuit voltage—the voltage of a rested battery that is not receiving or delivering power.

Orifice—a very fine opening in a nozzle.

Outhaul—a device for tensioning the foot of a main or mizzen sail.

Overcharging—forcing excessive current into a battery. The battery will heat up and start to gas.

Packing—square, grease-impregnated, natural fiber rope, usually hemp (flax), used to seal stuffing boxes.

Packing gland—see *stuffing box*.

Parallel connection—connecting battery positive terminals together and negative terminals together to increase system capacity without increasing voltage.

Parallel paths—paths to ground, other than that provided by the main down conductor, taken by a lightning strike.

Pawl—a spring-loaded metal piece used in winch ratchets.

Pedestal—the column on which a steering wheel and various engine controls are mounted; generally topped with a binnacle and compass.

Pilot light—a constantly burning small flame used to ignite main burners on a gas appliance.

Pinion—a small gear designed to mesh with a large gear (for example, a starter-motor drive gear).

Pintle—one-half of a rudder hinge, the other half being a *gudgeon*.

Pitch—the total distance a propeller would travel in one revolution, as determined by the amount of deflection of its blades, if there were no losses as it turned.

Planetary gears—an arrangement of small gears around a central drive gear, with a large ring gear around the outside of the small gears.

Points—the metal pieces that make and break the circuit in various switching devices, such as pressure switches, solenoids, circuit breakers, ordinary switches, etc.

Point loading—uneven loading on a bearing,

which throws all the pressure on one part of the bearing instead of distributing it evenly over the whole bearing.

Polarity—the distinction between positive and negative conductors in a DC system; the opposite magnetic poles in an alternator, a generator, or an electric motor.

Polarity indicating light—a test light on AC circuits to check that the neutral wire is the grounded conductor and not the hot wire.

Polarized circuit—an AC system in which the grounded (neutral) and ungrounded ("hot") conductors are connected in the same relationship to all terminals and loads.

Potentiometer—a variable resistance used for adjusting some voltage regulators.

Primary winding—the incoming side of a transformer.

PSI (pounds per square inch)—Pressure measurement. Psia (pounds per square inch absolute) measures actual pressure with no allowance for atmospheric pressure. Psig (pounds per square inch gauge) measures pressure with the gauge set to zero (0) at atmospheric pressure (14.7 psia). In other words psig = psia–14.7. Unless otherwise stated, psi always refers to psig.

Purging—the process of removing all air from a refrigeration gauge set before connecting to a refrigeration system. Also, bleeding a diesel engine fuel system or hydraulic system.

Pyrometer—a gauge for measuring exhaust temperatures.

Quadrant—a type of rudderhead fitting to which the steering cables are attached.

Quartz halogen—a special type of bulb element that gives off more light per watt consumed than conventional incandescent filaments.

Race—the inner and outer cases on a bearing between which the balls are trapped.

Rack-and-pinion steering—traditionally a geared quadrant attached to the rudderpost is driven by a small pinion on the steering wheel drive shaft. A more modern version has the steering wheel driving a beveled gear in the pedestal with the output transmitted by solid rods to a tiller arm attached to the rudderpost.

Radial-drive steering—a large pulley wheel attached to the rudderpost is turned via cables driven by the steering wheel.

Ratchet—a gear so designed that spring-loaded pawls lock it in one direction but allow it to rotate, or ratchet, in the other.

Raw water—the seawater side of cooling systems.

Reciprocal—up-and-down motion.

Rectifier—see *diode*. A *bridge rectifier* is an arrangement of diodes to convert AC to DC.

Refrigerant—the gas used in refrigeration and air-conditioning systems (formerly R-12 or R-22 in boat use; sometimes referred to as Freon-12 and Freon-22, which are trade names of the DuPont Company, but now also including HFC 134a and various "blends").

Relay—an electromechanical switch activated by a small current in its coil.

Reserve capacity—the time in minutes that a battery will deliver 25 amps before dying.

Residual magnetism—magnetism remaining in field winding shoes after all current has been cut off to the field windings.

Resistance—the opposition an appliance or wire offers to the flow of electric current, measured in ohms.

Reverse polarity—connecting a battery backward, i.e., connecting the positive terminal to the negative cable and the negative terminal to the positive cable.

RFD (receiver/filter/drier)—see *drier*.

Rheostat—a variable resistance.

Riding turn—the result of one turn on a winch "riding" up over another, effectively locking it up.

Rigging screw—see *turnbuckle*.

Ripple—undesired alternating current superimposed on a direct current power supply.

Roller bearings—see *bearings*.

Roller chain—bicycle-type chain, generally made of stainless steel, used primarily in steering systems, but also in some windlasses.

Roller furling—furling a sail by rolling it around its own luff wire. The sail can be used only fully unfurled. This is not a reefing system.

Roller reefing—furling a sail by rolling it around a solid luff extrusion. Sails can be used partially furled (i.e., reefed).

Rosin-core solder—a type of solder for electrical work with rosin-type flux set in a hollow tube.

Rotary seal—see *Mechanical seal*.

Rotor—the name given to the rotating field winding arrangement in an alternator.

Rudderpost, pipe, or stock—the metal post around which a rudder is constructed and to which a tiller arm or quadrant is attached.

Rudderstops—solid stops that limit the turning radius of a rudder. They must always stop the rudder before the limits of the steering system are reached.

Rudder tube—the hollow tube in which rudderpost bearings are set. It frequently terminates in a stuffing box.

Running backstays—intermediate backstays set up on quick-release levers.

Running rigging—rigging used to hoist and control sails.

Sacrificial anodes—anodes of a less noble metal (generally zinc) electrically connected to underwater hardware and designed to corrode, thereby protecting the rest of the hardware.

Samson post—a strong post in the foredeck.

Screening—the placing of electronic equipment in grounded metal boxes to reduce interference.

Secondary winding—the output winding of a transformer.

Self-amalgamating tape—see *heat-shrink tape*.

Self-discharge—the gradual loss of capacity by a battery when standing idle.

Self-limiting—a built-in feature of some stator windings that limits alternator output to a certain maximum regardless of speed of rotation.

Self-steering—an apparatus that holds a sailboat on a set course in relation to the wind.

Separators—the material used to divide one battery plate from another.

Series connection—a circuit with only one path for the current to flow. Batteries or appliances are connected one after another; in the case of batteries, negative to positive. Batteries in series deliver greater voltage but no greater capacity than a single battery.

Series-wound motors—a DC motor in which the field winding is connected in series with the armature. If unloaded, series-wound motors run away and can self-destruct.

Servopendulum—the principle underlying many self-steering devices.

Sheave—the pulley within a block.

Shielding—the placing of electric cables within grounded, braid-covered sheaths (or copper tubing) in order to reduce interference.

Shim—a specially cut piece of shim stock used as a spacer in specific applications, generally engine alignment.

Shim stock—very thin, accurately machined pieces of metal.

Short circuit—see *circuit*.

Shroud—wire rope or rod supporting a mast in an athwartships direction. *Cap* shrouds (*upper* shrouds) run to the masthead, *intermediate* shrouds to the upper spreaders (if fitted), and *lower* shrouds to the lower spreaders.

Shunt—a special low-resistance connection in a circuit enabling an ammeter to be connected in parallel with the circuit.

Shunt-wound motors—motors in which the field windings and armature are connected in parallel.

Sine wave—the wave made by alternating current when voltage is charted against time.

Siphon—the ability of a liquid to flow through a hose if one end is lower than the liquid level, even if the hose is looped above the liquid level.

Siphon break—see *antisiphon valve*.

Slinger—a washer on an electric pump shaft designed to deflect any leakage past the shaft seals away from the motor.

Slip rings—insulated metal discs on a rotor or armature shaft through which current is fed, via brushes, to or from armature or rotor windings.

Slow-blow fuse—a fuse with delayed action for use with motors with high starting loads.

Skeg—a small keel aft used to support a rudder.

Snap ring—a spring-tensioned ring that fits into a groove on the inside of a hollow shaft or around the outside of a shaft.

Snap-ring pliers—special pliers for installing and removing snap rings.

Snubber—see *fail-safe diode*.

SNR (signal-to-noise ratio)—the ratio of the desired signal to the background noise.

Solenoid—a powerful relay.

Spade rudder—a rudder with no support beneath the hull.

Spanner—a wrench.

Specific gravity—a measure of the density of the electrolyte in a battery, i.e., the strength of the acid and therefore the battery's state of charge.

Spike—a sudden high-voltage peak superimposed on a DC system.

Spindle—a shaft in a winch.

Spiroid gear—a particular type of worm gear.

Split charging—charging two or more batteries independently from one charging source.

Split pin—see *cotter pin*.

Spreader—a strut on a mast to improve the angle of shrouds and stiffen the mast panels.

Spreader socket—the means of attaching a spreader to a mast.

Spur gears—a variation of offset gears.

Standing rigging—permanently attached rigging supporting a mast.

Standpipe—a variation of an Aqualift exhaust.

Stator—the stationary armature on an alternator within which the rotor spins.

Stays—devices to provide fore-and-aft support for a mast.

Stray-current corrosion—see *corrosion*.

Stuffing box—a device for making a watertight seal around a propeller shaft at the point where it exits the boat.

Sulphation—the normal chemical transformation of battery plates when a battery discharges. If a battery is left in a discharged state, the sulphates crystallize, causing a permanent loss of capacity.

Sun gears—see *planetary gears*.

Supercharger—a blower mechanically driven by an engine and used to pressurize the inlet air.

Superheat—an adjustment of an expansion valve in a refrigeration system designed to produce maximum efficiency while providing a margin of safety against liquid slugging at the compressor.

Suppressor—a resistor put in series with a spark plug lead to reduce ignition-radiated interference.

Surge—see *spike*.

Surge protector—see *fail-safe diode*.

Swage (swedge)—a wire rope terminal in which the terminal is cold-welded to the rope by extreme pressure.

Swash plate—see *compressor*.

Tack—the lower forward corner of a sail.

Tailpiece—a hose adapter that screws onto a through-hull or seacock.

Tang—a fitting on a mast to which rigging attaches.

Thermistor—a resistor that changes in value with changes in temperature.

Thermocouple—a device containing two dissimilar metals, which generates a very small voltage when heated. It is used to open a solenoid on gas appliances; if the flame fails, the solenoid closes.

Thermostat—a heat-sensitive device used to control the flow of coolant through an engine; or a heat-sensitive switch used to turn a water-heating element off and on.

Thickness gauge—see *feeler gauge*.

Thimble—a grooved metal fitting around which loops in wire rope are formed.

Tinning—the process of getting solder to adhere to a soldering iron, wire end, or fitting.

Tiller arm—a short lever arm bolted to a rudder-post.

Toggle—a swivel joint used in rigging.

Topping lift—a line used to hold a boom off the deck.

Transformer—an AC device consisting of two or more coils used to magnetically couple one circuit to another. Depending on how the coils are wound, it can be used to lower or raise voltage. See also *isolation transformer*.

Transient voltage suppressor—see *fail-safe diode*.

Traversing nut—the nut that rides up and down the worm gear in worm steering.

Trickle charge—a continuous low-current charge.

Trim tab—a small rudder hinged to the trailing edge of a main or auxiliary rudder.

Turbocharger—a blower driven by engine exhaust gas and used to pressurize the inlet air.

Turnbuckle—an adjustable fitting used to tension standing rigging.

Two-pole switch (or breaker)—see *double-pole switch*.

Ty-wraps—plastic cable ties used for bundling up cables and/or fastening them to a hull side.

Ungrounded conductor—a current-carrying conductor in an AC circuit that is completely insulated from ground (a "hot" conductor).

Upper shroud—see *shroud*.

Vacuum—pressure below atmospheric pressure.

Vacuum pump—a pump to suck a refrigeration system into an almost complete vacuum.

Valve—a device to allow gases in and out of a cylinder at precise moments, or a means of controlling the flow of liquids, such as a ball valve, a gate valve, etc.

Valve clearance—the gap between a valve stem and its rocker arm when the valve is fully closed.

Valve cover—the housing of an engine bolted over the valve mechanism.

Vane pumps—pumps with hard plastic blades (vanes) slotted into a central rotating hub.

Variable-pitch propeller—one in which the pitch of the blades is adjustable.

Varistor—a resistor that changes in value with changes in voltage.

Vented loop—see *antisiphon valve*.

Vise-Grips—Mole wrench.

Volt—a unit of measurement of the "pressure" in an electrical system.

Voltage drop—the loss in "pressure" in wiring, switches, and connections due to unwanted resistance.

Voltage regulation—the process of controlling the output of an alternator or a generator. The output is normally matched to the battery's state of charge, tapering down as the battery comes up to full charge; this is *constant-potential* regulation. Alternatively, output can be maintained at a certain level regardless of state of charge; this is *constant-current* regulation.

Watt—a unit of electrical power.

Wavelength—the distance between successive crests of a wave (radio, sound, or water).

Wear plate—a replaceable plate found in some pumps.

Wildcat—see *gypsy*.

Windings—coils in a motor or transformer.

Worm gear—a particular type of high-reduction gear used to redirect a drive force or torque through a 90-degree angle.

Worm steering—the application of worm gearing to a steering unit.

Wrench—spanner.

Yaw—the characteristic of a boat, particularly a sailboat running downwind, to wander rhythmically either side of a course line.

Zone of security—the "protected" area beneath a lightning rod.

Appendix A: Checklist of Winterizing Procedures

It is far better to perform most routine maintenance at the end of the season when laying up rather than when recommissioning for the next season. Engines, in particular, will benefit from clean oil. Problem areas will be identified while you have plenty of time to fix them.

Note: Whenever using antifreeze, *remember that ethylene glycol (automotive antifreeze) is poisonous, so do not put it in freshwater systems. Use propylene glycol, which is nontoxic.*

Laying-Up

Engine and Gear Train

- Change the engine and transmission oil at the beginning of the winter. The old oil will contain all kinds of harmful acids and contaminants, which should not be left to work on the engine and transmission all winter long.
- Change the antifreeze on freshwater-cooled engines. The antifreeze itself does not wear out, but it has various corrosion-fighting additives that do.
- Drain the raw-water system, taking particular care to empty all low spots. Remove rubber pump impellers, lightly grease with petroleum jelly, and replace. Leave the pump cover screws loose so that the impellers won't stick in the pump housings. Run the engine for a *few seconds* to drive any remaining water out of the exhaust. Wash salt crystals out of any vented loops.
- Check the primary fuel filter and fuel tank for water and sediment; clean as necessary. Keeping the tank full will cut down on condensation.
- Squirt some oil into the inlet manifold and turn the engine over a few times (without starting) to spread the oil over the cylinder walls.
- Grease all grease points.
- Remove the inner wires of all engine control cables from their outer sheaths; clean, inspect, grease, and replace. Check the sheathing as outlined in Chapter 9.
- Seal all openings into the engine (e.g., air inlet, exhaust) and the fuel tank vent. *Put a conspicuous notice somewhere that you have done this so that you remember to unseal everything at the start of the next season.*
- Inspect all flexible feet and couplings for signs of softening (generally from oil and fuel leaks) and replace as necessary.
- Inspect all hoses for signs of softening, cracking, and/or bulging, especially hoses on the hot side of the cooling and exhaust systems.
- Check the propeller-shaft coupling setscrews or through-bolt.
- If hauling out: Check for propeller blade misalignment; flex the propeller and propeller shaft to check for Cutless bearing wear; tighten any strut mounting bolts; inspect a stainless steel propeller shaft for any signs of crevice corrosion and remove the propeller nut and check under it.

Batteries
Bring to a full charge. Equalize wet-type deep-cycle batteries. Top up. Clean the battery tops. Unless the batteries are being properly float-charged (via a solar panel or battery charger with *float* regulation) remove from the boat and store in a cool, dry place. Bring wet-type batteries to a full charge once a month.

Generators and Electric Motors
Clean and spray with a moisture-dispelling aerosol such as WD-40. Brush springs, in particular, will benefit from a shot of spray. Where generators have grease or oil fittings, give one shot or put in a drop. Pay particular attention to starter motor pinions.

Electrical Circuits
Clean corrosion off all terminals and connections and protect with petroleum jelly or a shot of WD-40 or other moisture-dispelling aerosol. Pay particular attention to all external outlets, especially the AC shore-power socket. Open up all coaxial connections if there is any possibility of water ingress; clean, repair as necessary, and reseal.

Electronic Equipment
Remove to a warm, dry place.

Refrigeration and Air-Conditioning Units
Drain any condenser raw-water circuits. If loops in the circuits make this impossible, pump 30% to 50% antifreeze solution through the unit. Spray a compressor clutch (with WD-40).

Toilets
Drain and/or pump a 30% to 50% antifreeze solution through the system. (Note: Specialized holding tanks, such as Raritan's ElectroSan, must be winterized according to the manufacturer's instructions.) Break loose the discharge hose and check for calcification. Wash out all vented loops.

Pumps
Drain and/or pump through a 30% to 50% antifreeze solution. Remove flexible impellers,

lightly grease (a Teflon-based grease), and put back. Leave pump covers loose; tighten down only when recommissioning. Inspect all vanes, impellers, etc., for wear, and check for shaft seal leaks. If wintering in the water, check the bilge pump float switch, wiring, switch, and the state of charge of the battery.

Freshwater Systems
Pump out the tanks and drain the system. Clean the tanks. If antifreeze is used in any pumps, make sure it is *propylene glycol*. Lightly oil connecting rod bearings (if fitted) on freshwater pumps.

Stuffing Boxes
If hauling out, repack. If wintering in the water, tighten down to stop any drip. *Be sure to loosen before reusing the propeller or the shaft will overheat* (post a note in a prominent place).

Seacocks
If hauling out, pull and grease all seacock plugs where this is possible. Dismantle and grease gate valves. If wintering in the water, close all seacocks (except cockpit drains) and make a close inspection of cockpit drain hoses and clamps.

Hydraulic Systems
Drain a little oil and check for water or contaminants. Top up as necessary. Check all seals and hoses for signs of leaks, and hoses for damage.

Water Heaters
Drain all water. *Leave a conspicuous notice somewhere so that you will be sure to refill before turning electric heaters back on.*

Stoves
Drain a little fuel from kerosene and/or alcohol tanks and check for any water or contaminants. Close LPG or CNG gas valves *at the cylinder*. It is a good idea to renew filaments on filament-type igniters at least every two years.

Steering
Lightly oil cables, and oil or grease sheave and pedestal bearings as called for. Pay particular attention to the worm gear (if fitted) and other steel parts that might seize up. Remove cables from conduits; clean, inspect, grease, and replace. Check all sheave mountings, bracing, and rudderstops. Check the rudderhead and tension the cables. With pedestal-type rack-and-pinion steering, remove the top plate and input socket screws; clean, grease, and replace.

Running Rigging
Wash all blocks. Disassemble and clean where possible. Use hot water and vinegar on stubborn

salt deposits. Lubricate and reassemble. Wash all synthetic lines in a warm detergent solution. Adding a little bleach will do no harm.

Spars and Standing Rigging

- *Wooden spars and spreaders:* Wash and inspect closely for any signs of rot (e.g., softening or discoloration), especially on spreaders and around fasteners and exit holes. Seal bare spots even if you are not varnishing or painting at this time.

- *Aluminum spars:* Wash and inspect for signs of corrosion, distortion of mast walls (especially around spreader sockets), crazing of anodizing, and hairline cracks (especially around welds and cutouts). Remove and grease any fasteners that must be prevented from freezing up. Wax the spar before storing.

- *All spars:* Withdraw mast tang bolts and check for crevice corrosion. Remove boots or covers from spreader tips. Remove head box sheaves and inspect shafts and sheaves. Lubricate and replace. Remove turnbuckle boots, tape, etc. Undo all turnbuckles; clean, inspect, and grease. Pay close attention to clevis pins; when replacing, tape over the ends of cotter pins (split pins). Inspect swages for hairline cracks. Wash all rigging. Do not store stainless against aluminum spars.

Winches, Windlasses, and Deck Hardware
Strip down, clean, grease, and oil all winches. Pay particular attention to pawls and pawl springs. Check the lubricant in windlasses for water and change as necessary. Crank windlasses over to spread lubricant around the internal parts. Remove the rope drum and wildcat (gypsy) and grease clutches and shafts. Check fasteners on all deck hardware; check carefully for flaws in the bedding (caulking) that might cause deck leaks.

Roller-Reefing Gear
Thoroughly flush all open bearings with warm fresh water. Regrease or lubricate as called for by the manufacturer, spinning the bearings to spread the lubricant around. Wash extrusions and apply wax. Pay close attention to all joints. Do not leave the sail up; it should be stowed for the winter.

Sacrificial Anodes
Inspect and change all zincs as necessary (hull, rudder, propeller shaft, engine cooling system, refrigeration condenser, etc.).

Recommissioning

1. Check the layup list and complete those jobs that weren't done.
2. *Observe and obey all conspicuous notes*, and envision areas that should have such notes but do not (plugged-off engine air inlets and exhausts, overtightened packing nut, empty hot water tank, etc.).
3. Check all hoses and through-hull connections (hose clamps: *undo the clamps a turn or two to check for corrosion of the band inside the screw housing*).
4. Check the refrigerant charge on refrigeration systems—engine driven compressor seals are especially prone to drying out and leaking during long periods of shutdown.
5. "Exercise" (i.e., switch on and off a few times) all switches—this helps to clean surface corrosion off terminals. Open and close seacocks; spin blocks and windlasses. Turn the steering wheel from side to side and check for any stiff spots or binding. Spin the drum and halyard swivels on roller reefers.
6. Tighten down all flexible-impeller pump covers; prime centrifugal pumps.
7. Once the boat is in the water, allow the hull to stabilize (this takes a few days on wooden hulls) and then check the engine alignment.

Appendix B: Freeing Frozen Parts and Fasteners

Problems with frozen fasteners are inevitable on boats. One or more of the following techniques may free things up.

Lubrication

- Clean everything with a wire brush (preferably one with brass bristles), douse liberally with penetrating oil, and wait. Find something else to do for an hour or two, overnight if possible, before having another go. Be patient.
- Clevis pins: After lubricating and waiting, grip the large end of the pin with Vise-Grips (Mole wrench) and turn the pin in its socket to free it. If the pin is the type with a cotter pin in both ends, remove one of the cotter pins, grip the clevis pin, and turn. Since the Vise-Grips will probably mar the surface of the pin, it should be knocked out from the other end.

Shock Treatment

An impact wrench is a handy tool to have around. These take a variety of end fittings (screwdriver bits, sockets) to match different fasteners. The wrench is hit hard with a hammer and hopefully jars the fastener loose. If an impact wrench is not available or does not work, other forms of shock must be applied with an acute sense of the breaking point of the fastener and adjacent engine castings, etc. Unfortunately this is generally acquired only after a lifetime of breaking things! Depending on the problem, shock treatment may take different forms:

- A bolt stuck in an engine block: Put a sizable punch squarely on the head of the bolt and give it a good knock into the block. Now try undoing it.
- A pulley on a tapered shaft, a propeller, or an outboard motor flywheel: Back out the retaining nut *until its face is flush with the end of the shaft* (this is important to avoid damage to the threads on the nut or shaft). Put pressure behind the pulley, propeller, or flywheel as if trying to pull it off, and hit the end of the retaining nut or shaft smartly. The shock will frequently break things loose without the need for a specialized puller.
- A large nut with limited room around it, or one on a shaft that wants to turn (for example, a crankshaft pulley nut): Put a short-handled wrench on the nut, hold the wrench to prevent it from jumping off, and hit it hard.
- If all else fails, use a cold chisel to cut a slot in the side of the offending nut or the head of the bolt, place a punch in the slot at a tangential angle to the nut or bolt, and hit it smartly.

Leverage

- Screws: With a square-bladed screwdriver, put a crescent (adjustable) wrench on the blade, bear down hard on the screw, and turn the screwdriver with the wrench. If the screwdriver has a round blade, clamp a pair of Vise-Grips to the base of the handle and do the same thing.
- Nuts and bolts: If using wrenches with one box end and one open end, put the box end of the appropriate wrench on the fastener and

hook the box end of the next size up into the free open end of the wrench to double the length of the handle and thus the leverage.

- Cheater pipe: Slip a length of pipe over the handle of the wrench to increase its leverage.

Heat

Heat expands metal, but for this treatment to be effective, frozen fasteners must frequently be raised to cherry-red temperatures. These temperatures will upset tempering in hardened steel, and uneven heating of surrounding castings may cause them to crack. Heat must be applied with circumspection.

Heat applied to a frozen nut will expand it outward, and it can then be broken loose. But equally, heat applied to the bolt will expand it within the nut, generating all kinds of pressure that helps to break the grip of rust, etc. When the fixture cools it will frequently come apart quite easily.

Broken Fasteners

- Rounded-off heads: Sometimes there is not enough head left on a fastener to grip with Vise-Grips or pipe (Stillson) wrenches, but there is enough to accept a slot made by a hacksaw. A screwdriver can then be inserted and turned as above.
- If a head breaks off it is often possible to remove whatever it was holding, thus exposing part of the shaft of the fastener, which can be lubricated, gripped with Vise-Grips, and backed out.
- Drilling out: It is very important to drill down the center of a broken fastener. Use a center punch and take some time putting an accurate "dimple" at this point before attempting to drill. Next, use a small drill to make a pilot hole to the desired depth. If Ezy-Outs or "screw extractors" (hardened, tapered steel screws with reversed threads, available from tool supply houses) are on hand, drill the correctly sized hole for the appropriate Ezy-Out and try extracting the stud. Otherwise drill out the stud *up to the insides of its threads but no farther*, or irreparable damage will be done to the threads in the casting. The remaining bits of fastener thread in the casting can be picked out with judicious use of a small screwdriver or some pointed instrument. If a tap is available to clean up the threads, so much the better.
- Pipe fittings: If a hacksaw blade can be gotten inside the relevant fittings (which can often be done using duct tape to make a handle on the blade), cut a slit in the fitting along its length, and then place a punch on the outside alongside the cut, hit it, and collapse it inward. Do the same on the other side of the cut. The fitting should now come out easily.

Miscellaneous

- Stainless steel: Stainless-to-stainless fasteners (for example, many turnbuckles) have a bad habit of "galling" when being done up or undone, especially if there is any dirt in the threads to cause friction. Galling (otherwise known as "cold-welding") is a process in which molecules on the surface of one part of the fastener transfer to the other part. Everything seizes up for good. Galled stainless fastenings cannot be salvaged—they almost always end up shearing off. When doing up or undoing a stainless fastener, if any sudden or unusual friction develops, *stop immediately*, let it cool off, lubricate thoroughly, work the fastener backward and forward to spread the lubrication around, go back the other way, clean the threads, and start again.
- Aluminum: Aluminum oxidizes to form a dense white powder. Aluminum oxide is more voluminous than the original aluminum and so generates a lot of pressure around any fasteners passing through aluminum fixtures—sometimes enough pressure to shear off the heads of fasteners. Once oxidation around a stainless or bronze fastener has reached a certain point it is virtually impossible to remove the fastener without breaking it. (A reader has written to say that if corroded aluminum parts are immersed in fresh water for 7 to 14 days, the aluminum oxide precipitates out, allowing fasteners to be undone.)
- Damaged threads: If all else fails, and a fastener has to be drilled out, the threads in the casting may be damaged. There are two options.
1. To drill and tap for the next-larger fastener.
2. To install a Heli-Coil insert. A Heli-Coil is a new thread. An oversized hole is drilled and tapped with a special tap, and the Heli-Coil insert (the new thread) is screwed into the hole with a special tool. You end up with the original size hole and threads. Any good machine shop will have the relevant tools and inserts.

Appendix C: Tools and Spare Parts

The following tool and spare parts list may cause some people to accuse me of letting my imagination run wild. Let me assure you we have had all of this and more (including oxyacetylene, rolls of copper tubing, and a complete variable-pitch propeller unit) on board at various times, and have used almost everything at one time or another on our boat or someone else's. (Note: When ordering spares, always include the model number *and the serial number* of the equipment the spares are for, in case there have been changes within a model range.)

Mechanic's Toolbox

Screwdrivers—Phillips head and slotted—a selection. Especially useful is a short-handled version of each for awkward corners.

Open end/box end wrench (spanner) set—¼" to 1" (or metric equivalent, or both if you have a mixture of American and metric nuts and bolts)

⅜" drive socket set, ¼" to 1" (or metric, as above). The ⅜" is much easier to handle in tight spaces than a ½" drive, but with the larger sized sockets (over ¾") will get severely stressed, so buy only top-quality ratchets and extensions.

6" and 10" crescent (adjustable) wrench

6" and 10" Vise-Grips (Mole wrench)

12" and 18" pipe wrench—preferably aluminum, which is much lighter and won't rust nearly as badly (although aluminum wrenches still have steel jaws)

Side-cutting needlenose pliers

Ballpeen hammer

Set of Allen wrenches (keys)

Set of feeler (thickness) gauges—inches or metric, as appropriate

Aligning punches—these taper to a reasonably fine head

Straight punches—for knocking out recalcitrant clevis pins, etc.

Cold chisels

Files—flat, half round, and round

Scrapers—for removing old gaskets

Brass-bristle wire brush—steel bristles leave flecks of rust

Emery cloth

Fine and medium grinding paste

Hacksaw and blades—buy one in which the end fittings are captured, i.e., cannot fall out when the blade breaks, or they are sure to get lost

Snap-ring (Circlip) pliers—both inside (internal) and outside (external)

Pulley puller—very useful on occasion

Set of taps and dies—American, metric, or both

Propane torch

Small vise—if it can be accommodated (some very neat ones clip into a standard winch socket)

Engine and Mechanical Supplies

Engine and gearbox oil

Oil filter (and sealing rings) and an oil-filter wrench

Fuel filters and a fuel-filter wrench (where needed)

Filter funnel for taking on fuel

Grease gun

Greases (Teflon, water pump)

Oil squirt can

Silicone spray

WD-40

Valve cover gasket

Injector sealing washers (if fitted)

Injector

Set of injector lines (injection pump to injectors)

Lift pump (feed pump) diaphragm

Pump overhaul kits for all cooling water pumps (impellers/diaphragms, seals, and bearings)

Gasket cement

Thermostat

Hoses (including oil cooler hoses)

O-ring kit (an assortment)

All belts

Packing

Wrench (spanner) for packing nut

Packing removal tool

¼", ⁵⁄₁₆", ⅜", and ½" stainless steel threaded rod

Stainless steel nuts and lock washers for the above

Length of ¼" and ⅜" keystock

Flare tubing kit (if there is any flared copper tubing on board)

Tubing cutters

Zincs (world cruisers might consider carrying a spare heat exchanger and oil cooler)

Electrical Tool Kit

Different sizes of multistranded and tinned copper cable

Wire strippers/crimpers

Appropriate crimp-on terminals

Heat-shrink (self-amalgamating) tape and tubing

Electrician's putty

Insulating (electrician's) tape

Soldering iron, solder, and flux (rosin type)

Spare coaxial end fittings and connectors

Hydrometer for battery testing

Battery terminal puller

Multimeter

Test light(s)

Amprobe for measuring AC amps (if the boat has a lot of AC equipment)

Ground fault tester for checking dockside power

Flashlight batteries

Fuses

Petroleum jelly—for greasing terminals

Spare alternator and voltage regulator

Lightbulbs (especially quartz halogen navigation bulbs—note that boats with higher voltage regulator settings will blow bulbs faster than those with lower settings)

Ballast units for fluorescent lights

Woodworking Tool Kit (choose to suit)

Crosscut saw

Chisels

Wood bits (drill bits)

Plug cutters

Set square

Framing square

Bar clamps

Doweling

Epoxy glue and thickeners

Plastic resin glue (e.g., Weldwood)

Tenon (back) saw

Mallet

Countersink

Tape measure

Bevel square

C-clamps

Plane

Sandpaper—wet-or-dry, #180 grit to #400

Power Tools (where appropriate)

Electric drill—½" chuck

Set of drill bits—$\frac{1}{16}$" to ½"

Set of holesaws—very useful, buy good quality

Jigsaw

Circular saw

Palm (block) sander

Router and bits

General Supplies

Paint, varnish, and brushes

Paint scrapers

Thinners

Acetone

Fiberglass cloth, mat, and disposable brushes

Fasteners—bronze threaded nails, bronze or stainless steel screws, stainless steel nuts and bolts

Duct tape

Masking tape

Teflon tape—very useful

Bedding (caulking)—polyurethane adhesive such as 3M 5200, polysulphide adhesive sealant such as Boatlife or Thiokol, silicone sealant

Old inner tube—when cut up in strips and wrapped tightly around ruptured hoses, it seals very effectively

Selection of all-stainless-steel hose clamps (Jubilee clips)—be sure to check the screws for nonmagnetism, indicating a 300-grade stainless steel

Copper pipe and fittings—where appropriate

PVC pipe, fittings, and glue—check the glue annually and replace as necessary; it may dry out

Sail repair kit

Selection of hoses and hose adapters (hose barbs, etc.)

Antifreeze—ethylene glycol for general purpose; *propylene glycol for freshwater systems*

Rigging kit

Length of cable as long as the longest stay on the boat—preferably 7 × 19, which is more flexible than 1 × 19 and can be used in steering repairs

End fittings for the above—StaLok, Norseman, or Castlok. If using 7 × 19 wire be sure to get the correct inserts if they differ from those used on 1 × 19 wire.

Turnbuckles, toggles, forks, and eyes—StaLok, Norseman, or Castlok

Bolt cutters

Nicopress (Talurit) kit

Cable clamps (Crosby clamps, bulldog clamps)—matched to cable sizes

Thimbles—matched to cable sizes

Shackles

Seizing wire

Complete chain and wire rope assembly for wheel steering

Selection of clevis pins and cotter pins (split pins)

One or two spare blocks

Specific Supplies

Pump overhaul kit—impeller/diaphragm/vanes/cup washers, seals, bearings, and any valves for every pump on board

Spare DC motors for electric pumps, especially vital ones (e.g., an electric toilet or refrigeration condenser pump)

Brushes for universal or permanent-magnet motors

Freshwater pump overhaul kit and pressure switch

Manual toilet overhaul kit—valves, piston cup washers or O-rings, piston rod seal (get extra spares)

Baby (mineral) oil

Muriatic acid

Winch pawls and springs

Generator brushes and capacitors

AC electric motor capacitors

Wind generator vanes (blades) and brushes—where appropriate

Self-steering wind vanes

Autopilot belts—where appropriate

Hydraulic oil if there are any hydraulic systems on board

Electric water heater element and thermostat

Gas stove and appliance thermocouples and/or optical sensors

Burner and pressure tank repair kit—kerosene or alcohol stove nipple (orifice) wrench, 10-mm wrench (spanner) for the valve stem packing, an eraser-tipped pencil (for removing cleaning needles), and cup washers for the fuel tank pump

Spare burners and burner parts (valve stems, cleaning needles, and nipples), sealing washers

Mantles for pressurized kerosene (white gas) lanterns or gas lanterns

Refrigeration supplies:

    Refrigerant—R-12, HFC-134a, and/or R-22

    Stem-type valve wrench

    Gauge set

    Leak detection kit—to fit the propane torch in the mechanic's tool kit

    Refrigeration oil

    Receiver/filter/drier (or filters and sight glass if the unit has individual components)

    Compressor clutch coil

    Special tools for removing the compressor pulley

Condenser water pump overhaul kit

Expansion valve

Sacrificial zinc anodes

Multifunction "key" for undoing fuel and water fill caps, and deck plates—very useful little item

Softwood fids—to fit all seacocks and hull openings below the waterline

One or two plywood blanks—to fit portholes, with some means of quickly securing them, in case a porthole gets stove in

Hydraulic systems:

    Length of hydraulic hose as long as the longest hose run on the boat

    Sufficient fittings to be able to use hose length to replace any hose run

    Hydraulic oil—a good reserve supply

    Spare filter

Appendix D: Useful Tables

Table D-1. Fraction, Decimal, and Metric Equivalents

Fractions	Decimal In.	Metric mm.	Fractions	Decimal In.	Metric mm.
1/64	.015625	.397	33/64	.515625	13.097
1/32	.03125	.794	17/32	.53125	13.494
3/64	.046875	1.191	35/64	.546875	13.891
1/16	.0625	1.588	9/16	.5625	14.288
5/64	.078125	1.984	37/64	.578125	14.684
3/32	.09375	2.381	19/32	.59375	15.081
7/64	.109375	2.778	39/64	.609375	15.478
1/8	.125	3.175	5/8	.625	15.875
9/64	.140625	3.572	41/64	.640625	16.272
5/32	.15625	3.969	21/32	.65625	16.669
11/64	.171875	4.366	43/64	.671875	17.066
3/16	.1875	4.763	11/16	.6875	17.463
13/64	.203125	5.159	45/64	.703125	17.859
7/32	.21875	5.556	23/32	.71875	18.256
15/64	.234375	5.953	47/64	.734375	18.653
1/4	.250	6.35	3/4	.750	19.05
17/64	.265625	6.747	49/64	.765625	19.447
9/32	.28125	7.144	25/32	.78125	19.844
19/64	.296875	7.54	51/64	.796875	20.241
5/16	.3125	7.938	13/16	.8125	20.638
21/64	.328125	8.334	53/64	.828125	21.034
11/32	.34375	8.731	27/32	.84375	21.431
23/64	.359375	9.128	55/64	.859375	21.828
3/8	.375	9.525	7/8	.875	22.225
25/64	.390625	9.922	57/64	.890625	22.622
13/32	.40625	10.319	29/32	.90625	23.019
27/64	.421875	10.716	59/64	.921875	23.416
7/16	.4375	11.113	15/16	.9375	23.813
29/64	.453125	11.509	61/64	.953125	24.209
15/32	.46875	11.906	31/32	.96875	24.606
31/64	.484375	12.303	63/64	.984375	25.003
1/2	.500	12.7	1	1.00	25.4

Table D-2. Inches to Millimeters Conversion Table

Inches	Millimeters	Inches	Millimeters	Inches	Millimeters
0.001	0.0254	0.010	0.2540	0.019	0.4826
0.002	0.0508	0.011	0.2794	0.020	0.5080
0.003	0.0762	0.012	0.3048	0.021	0.5334
0.004	0.1016	0.013	0.3302	0.022	0.5588
0.005	0.1270	0.014	0.3556	0.023	0.5842
0.006	0.1524	0.015	0.3810	0.024	0.6096
0.007	0.1778	0.016	0.4064	0.025	0.6350
0.008	0.2032	0.017	0.4318		
0.009	0.2286	0.018	0.4572		

Table D-3. Torque Conversion Table, Pound Feet to Newton Meters

Pound-Feet (lb.-ft.)	Newton Metres (Nm)	Newton Metres (Nm)	Pound-Feet (lb.-ft.)
1	1.356	1	0.7376
2	2.7	2	1.5
3	4.0	3	2.2
4	5.4	4	3.0
5	6.8	5	3.7
6	8.1	6	4.4
7	9.5	7	5.2
8	10.8	8	5.9
9	12.2	9	6.6
10	13.6	10	7.4
15	20.3	15	11.1
20	27.1	20	14.8
25	33.9	25	18.4
30	40.7	30	22.1
35	47.5	35	25.8
40	54.2	40	29.5
45	61.0	50	36.9
50	67.8	60	44.3
55	74.6	70	51.6
60	81.4	80	59.0
65	88.1	90	66.4
70	94.9	100	73.8
75	101.7	110	81.1
80	108.5	120	88.5
90	122.0	130	95.9
100	135.6	140	103.3
110	149.1	150	110.6
120	162.7	160	118.0
130	176.3	170	125.4
140	189.8	180	132.8
150	203.4	190	140.1
160	216.9	200	147.5
170	230.5	225	166.0
180	244.0	250	184.4

Table D-4. Feet to Meters Conversion Table

Feet – metres 1 foot = 0.3048 m			
ft.	met.	ft.	met.
1	0,305	31	9,449
2	0,610	32	9,754
3	0,914	33	10,058
4	1,219	34	10,363
5	1,524	35	10,668
6	1,829	36	10,973
7	2,134	37	11,278
8	2,438	38	11,582
9	2,743	39	11,887
10	3,048	40	12,192
11	3,353	41	12,497
12	3,658	42	12,802
13	3,962	43	13,106
14	4,267	44	13,441
15	4,572	45	13,716
16	4,877	46	14,021
17	5,182	47	14,326
18	5,486	48	14,630
19	5,791	49	14,935
20	6,096	50	15,240
21	6,401	51	15,545
22	6,706	52	15,850
23	7,010	53	16,154
24	7,315	54	16,459
25	7,620	55	16,764
26	7,925	56	17,069
27	8,230	57	17,374
28	8,534	58	17,678
29	8,839	59	17,983
30	9,144	60	18,288

Table D-5. Meters to Feet Conversion Table

Metres – Feet 1 metre = 3.2808 feet	
met.	feet
1	3,28
2	6,56
3	9,84
4	13,12
5	16,40
6	19,69
7	22,97
8	26,25
9	29,53
10	32,81
11	36,09
12	39,37
13	42,65
14	45,93
15	49,21
16	52,49
17	55,77
18	59,06
19	62,34
20	65,62

Table D-6. Inches to Centimeters Conversion Table

Inches – centimetres 1 inch = 2.54 cm	
inches	cm
1	2,54
2	5,08
3	7,62
4	10,16
5	12,70
6	15,24
7	17,78
8	20,32
9	22,86
10	25,40
11	27,94
12	30,48

Table D-7. Degrees Fahrenheit to Degrees Celsius/Centigrade Conversion Table

°F	°C	°F	°C	°F	°C	°F	°C	°F	°C	°F	°C	°F	°C	°F	°C
-454	-270	-31	-35	19.4	-7	70	21.1	120.2	49	171	77.2	225	107.2	660	348.9
-450	-268	-30	-34.4	20	-6.7	71	21.7	121	49.4	172	77.8	230	110	662	350
-440	-262	-29.2	-34	21	-6.1	71.6	22	122	50	172.4	78	235	112.8	670	354.4
-436	-260	-29	-33.9	21.2	-6	72	22.2	123	50.6	173	78.3	239	115	680	360
-430	-257	-28	-33.3	22	-5.6	73	22.8	123.8	51	174	78.9	240	115.6	690	365.6
-420	-251	-27.4	-33	23	-5	73.4	23	124	51.1	174.2	79	245	118.3	693	370
-418	-250	-27	-32.8	24	-4.4	74	23.3	125	51.7	175	79.4	248	120	700	371.1
-410	-246	-26	-32.2	24.8	-4	75	23.9	125.6	52	176	80	250	121.1	710	377
-400	-240	-25.6	-32	25	-3.9	75.2	24	126	52.2	177	80.6	255	123.9	716	380
-390	-234	-25	-31.7	26	-3.3	76	24.4	127	52.8	177.8	81	257	125	720	382
-382	-230	-24	-31.1	26.6	-3	77	25	127.4	53	178	81.1	260	125.7	730	388
-380	-229	-23.8	-31	27	-2.8	78	25.6	128	53.3	179	81.7	265	129.4	734	390
-370	-223	-23	-30.6	28	-2.2	78.8	26	129	53.9	179.6	82	266	130	740	393
-364	-220	-22	-30	28.4	-2	79	26.1	129.2	54	180	82.2	270	132.2	750	399
-360	-218	-21	-29.4	29	-1.7	80	26.7	130	54.4	181	82.8	275	135	752	400
-350	-212	-20.2	-29	30	-1.1	80.6	27	131	55	181.4	83	280	137.8	760	404
-346	-210	-20	-28.9	30.2	-1	81	27.2	132	55.6	182	83.3	284	140	770	410
-340	-207	-19	-28.3	31	-0.6	82	27.8	132.8	56	183	83.9	285	140.6	780	416
-330	-201	-18.4	-28	32	0	82.4	28	133	56.1	183.2	84	290	143.3	788	420
-328	-200	-18	-27.8	33	0.6	83	28.3	134	56.7	184	84.4	293	145	790	421
-320	-196	-17	-27.2	33.8	1	84	28.9	134.6	57	185	85	295	146.1	800	427
-310	-190	-16.6	-27	34	1.1	84.2	29	135	57.2	186	85.6	300	148.9	806	430
-300	-184	-16	-26.7	35	1.7	85	29.4	136	57.8	186.8	86	302	150	810	432
-292	-180	-15	-26.1	35.6	2	86	30	136.4	58	187	86.1	310	154.4	820	438
-290	-179	-14.8	-26	36	2.2	87	30.6	137	58.3	188	86.7	320	160	824	440
-280	-173	-14	-25.6	37	2.8	87.8	31	138	58.9	188.6	87	330	165.6	830	443
-274	-170	-13	-25	37.4	3	88	31.1	138.2	59	189	87.2	338	170	840	449
-270	-168	-12	-24.4	38	3.3	89	31.7	139	59.4	190	87.8	340	171.1	842	450
-260	-162	-11.2	-24	39	3.9	89.6	32	140	60	190.4	88	350	176.7	850	454
-256	-160	-11	-23.9	39.2	4	90	32.2	141	60.6	191	88.3	356	180	860	460
-250	-157	-10	-23.3	40	4.4	91	32.8	141.8	61	192	88.9	360	182.2	870	465
-240	-151	-9.4	-23	41	5	91.4	33	142	61.1	192.2	89	370	187.8	878	470
-238	-150	-9	-22.8	42	5.5	92	33.3	143	61.7	193	89.4	374	190	880	471
-230	-146	-8	-22.2	42.8	6	93	33.9	143.6	62	194	90	380	193.3	890	477
-220	-140	-7.6	-22	43	6.1	93.2	34	144	62.2	195	90.6	390	198.9	896	480
-210	-134	-7	-21.7	44	6.7	94	34.4	145	62.8	195.8	91	392	200	900	482
-202	-130	-6	-21.1	44.6	7	95	35	145.4	63	196	91.1	400	204.4	910	488
-200	-129	-5.8	-21	45	7.2	96	35.6	146	63.3	197	91.7	410	210	914	490
-190	-123	-5	-20.6	46	7.8	96.8	36	147	63.9	197.6	92	420	215.6	920	493
-184	-120	-4	-20	46.4	8	97	36.1	147.2	64	198	92.2	428	220	930	499
-180	-118	-3	-19.4	47	8.3	98	36.7	148	64.4	199	92.8	430	221.1	932	500
-170	-112	-2.2	-19	48	8.9	98.6	37	149	65	199.4	93	440	226.7	940	504
-166	-110	-2	-18.9	48.2	9	99	37.2	150	65.6	200	93.3	446	230	950	510
-160	-107	-1	-18.3	49	9.4	100	37.8	150.8	66	201	93.9	450	232.2	960	516
-150	-101	-0.4	-18	50	10	100.4	38	151	66.1	201.2	94	460	237.8	968	520
-148	-100	0	-17.8	51	10.6	101	38.3	152	66.7	202	94.4	464	240	970	521
-140	-96	1	-17.2	51.8	11	102	38.9	152.6	67	203	95	470	243.3	980	527
-130	-90	1.4	-17	52	11.1	102.2	39	153	67.2	204	95.6	480	248.9	986	530
-120	-84	2	-16.7	53	11.7	103	39.4	154	67.8	204.8	96	482	250	990	532
-112	-80	3	-16.1	53.6	12	104	40	154.4	68	205	96.1	490	254.4	1000	538
-110	-79	3.2	-16	54	12.2	105	40.6	155	68.3	206	96.7	500	260	1004	540
-100	-73.3	4	-15.6	55	12.8	105.8	41	156	68.9	206.6	97	510	265.6	1022	550
-94	-70	5	-15	55.4	13	106	41.1	156.2	69	207	97.2	518	270	1050	566
-90	-67.8	6	-14.4	56	13.3	107	41.7	157	69.4	208	97.8	520	271.1	1100	593
-80	-62.2	6.8	-14	57	13.9	107.6	42	158	70	208.4	98	530	276.7	1112	600
-76	-60	7	-13.9	57.2	14	108	42.2	159	70.6	209	98.3	536	280	1150	621
-70	-56.7	8	-13.3	58	14.4	109	42.8	159.8	71	210	98.9	540	282.2	1200	649
-60	-51.1	8.6	-13	59	15	109.4	43	160	71.1	210.2	99	550	287.8	1202	650
-58	-50	9	-12.8	60	15.6	110	43.3	161	71.7	211	99.4	554	290	1250	677
-50	-45.6	10	-12.2	60.8	16	111	43.9	161.6	72	212	100	560	293.3	1292	700
-40	-40	10.4	-12	61	16.1	111.2	44	162	72.2	213	100.6	570	298.9	1300	704
-39	-39.4	11	-11.7	62	16.7	112	44.4	163	72.8	213.8	101	572	300	1350	732
-38.2	-39	12	-11.1	62.6	17	113	45	163.4	73	214	101.1	580	304.4	1382	750
-38	-38.9	12.2	-11	63	17.2	114	45.6	164	73.3	215	101.7	590	310	1400	760
-37	-38.3	13	-10.6	64	17.8	114.8	46	165	73.9	215.6	102	600	315.6	1450	788
-36.4	-38	14	-10	64.4	18	115	46.1	165.2	74	216	102.2	608	320	1472	800
-36	-37.8	15	-9.4	65	18.3	116	46.7	166	74.4	217	102.8	610	321.0	1500	816
-35	-37.2	15.8	-9	66	18.9	116.6	47	167	75	217.4	103	620	326.7		
-34.6	-37	16	-8.9	66.2	19	117	47.2	168	75.6	218	103.3	626	330		
-34	-36.7	17	-8.3	67	19.4	118	47.8	168.8	76	219	103.9	630	332.2		
-33	-36.1	17.6	-8	68	20	118.4	48	169	76.1	219.2	104	640	337.8		
-32.8	-36	18	-7.8	69	20.6	119	48.3	170	76.7	220	104.4	644	340		
-32	-35.6	19	-7.2	69.8	21	120	48.9	170.6	77	221	105	650	343.3		

Table D-8. Nautical Miles to Kilometers Conversion Table

1 Nautical Mile = 1.8520 Kilometres
(identical conversion for Knots — Kilometres/hour)

nm	0	1	2	3	4	5	6	7	8	9	nm
0	0	1,85	3,70	5,56	7,41	9,26	11,11	12,96	14,82	16,67	0
10	18,52	20,37	22,22	24,08	25,93	27,78	29,63	31,48	33,34	35,19	10
20	37,04	38,89	40,74	42,60	44,45	46,30	48,15	50,00	51,86	53,71	20
30	55,56	57,41	59,26	61,12	62,97	64,82	66,67	68,52	70,38	72,23	30
40	74,08	75,93	77,78	79,64	81,49	83,34	85,19	87,04	88,90	90,75	40
50	92,60	94,45	96,30	98,16	100,01	101,86	103,71	105,56	107,42	109,27	50
60	111,12	112,97	114,82	116,68	118,53	120,38	122,23	124,08	125,94	127,79	60
70	129,64	131,49	133,34	135,20	137,05	138,90	140,75	142,60	144,46	146,31	70
80	148,16	150,01	151,86	153,72	155,57	157,42	159,27	161,12	162,98	164,83	80
90	166,68	168,53	170,38	172,24	174,09	175,94	177,79	179,64	181,50	183,35	90
100	185,20	187,05	188,90	190,76	192,61	194,46	196,31	198,16	200,02	201,87	100

Kilometres — Nautical Miles
1 Kilometre = 0.5400 Nautical Miles
(identical conversion for Kilometres/hour into Knots)

km	0	1	2	3	4	5	6	7	8	9	km
0	0	0,54	1,08	1,62	2,16	2,70	3,24	3,78	4,32	4,86	0
10	5,40	5,94	6,48	7,02	7,56	8,10	8,64	9,18	9,72	10,26	10
20	10,80	11,34	11,88	12,42	12,96	13,50	14,04	14,58	15,12	15,66	20
30	16,20	16,74	17,28	17,82	18,36	18,90	19,44	19,98	20,52	21,06	30
40	21,60	22,14	22,68	23,22	23,76	24,30	24,84	25,38	25,92	26,46	40
50	27,00	27,54	28,08	28,62	29,16	29,70	30,24	30,78	31,32	31,86	50
60	32,40	32,94	33,48	34,02	34,56	35,10	35,64	36,18	36,72	37,26	60
70	37,80	38,34	38,88	39,42	39,96	40,50	41,04	41,58	42,12	42,66	70
80	43,20	43,74	44,28	44,82	45,36	45,90	46,44	46,98	47,52	48,06	80
90	48,60	49,14	49,68	50,22	50,76	51,30	51,84	52,38	52,92	53,46	90
100	54,00	54,54	55,08	55,62	56,16	56,70	57,24	57,78	58,32	58,86	100

This is how it works!
Example 43 nm = ?? km
Go down the first column until you come to 40, then move across to 3.
The result is where the two rows meet (79.64 km)
For values of over 100, the decimal point should be adjusted.
Conversely: 43 km = ?? nm
43 km = 23.22 nm

Table D-9. Kilowatts to Horsepower Conversion Table

Kilowatts (kW) into Horsepower (HP)
1 kW = 1.3596 HP

kW	0	1	2	3	4	5	6	7	8	9	kW
0	0	1,3596	2,72	4,08	5,44	6,80	8,16	9,52	10,88	12,24	0
10	**13,60**	**14,96**	**16,32**	**17,67**	**19,03**	**20,39**	**21,75**	**23,11**	**24,47**	**25,83**	**10**
20	27,19	28,55	29,91	31,27	32,63	33,99	35,35	36,71	38,07	39,43	20
30	**40,79**	**42,15**	**43,51**	**44,87**	**46,23**	**47,59**	**48,95**	**50,31**	**51,66**	**53,02**	**30**
40	54,38	55,74	57,10	58,46	59,82	61,18	62,54	63,90	65,26	66,62	40
50	**67,98**	**69,34**	**70,70**	**72,06**	**73,42**	**74,78**	**76,14**	**77,50**	**78,86**	**80,22**	**50**
60	81,58	82,94	84,30	85,65	87,01	88,37	89,73	91,09	92,45	93,81	60
70	**95,17**	**96,53**	**97,89**	**99,25**	**100,61**	**101,97**	**103,33**	**104,69**	**106,05**	**107,41**	**70**
80	108,77	110,13	111,49	112,85	114,21	115,57	116,93	118,29	119,64	121,00	80
90	**122,36**	**123,72**	**125,08**	**126,44**	**127,80**	**129,16**	**130,52**	**131,88**	**133,24**	**134,60**	**90**
100	135,96	137,32	138,68	140,04	141,40	142,76	144,12	145,48	146,84	148,20	100

Horsepower (HP) into Kilowatts
1 HP = 0.7355 kW

HP	0	1	2	3	4	5	6	7	8	9	HP
0	0	0,7355	1,47	2,21	2,94	3,68	4,41	5,15	5,88	6,62	0
10	**7,36**	**8,09**	**8,83**	**9,56**	**10,30**	**11,03**	**11,77**	**12,50**	**13,24**	**13,97**	**10**
20	14,71	15,45	16,18	16,92	17,65	18,39	19,12	19,86	20,59	21,33	20
30	**22,07**	**22,80**	**23,54**	**24,27**	**25,01**	**25,74**	**26,48**	**27,21**	**27,95**	**28,68**	**30**
40	29,42	30,16	30,89	31,63	32,36	33,10	33,83	34,57	35,30	36,04	40
50	**36,78**	**37,51**	**38,25**	**38,98**	**39,72**	**40,45**	**41,19**	**41,92**	**42,66**	**43,39**	**50**
60	44,13	44,87	45,60	46,34	47,07	47,81	48,54	49,28	50,01	50,75	60
70	**51,49**	**52,22**	**52,96**	**53,69**	**54,43**	**55,16**	**55,90**	**56,63**	**57,37**	**58,10**	**70**
80	58,84	59,58	60,31	61,05	61,78	62,52	63,25	63,99	64,72	65,46	80
90	**66,20**	**66,93**	**67,67**	**68,40**	**69,14**	**69,87**	**70,61**	**71,34**	**72,08**	**72,81**	**90**
100	73,55	74,29	75,02	75,76	76,49	77,23	77,96	78,70	79,43	80,17	100

This table is very simple to use. Read off the tens in the vertical scale and the units in the horizontal scale. The answer is where the two lines meet.

Example (above): convert 63 kW into HP. Go down the first column until you find 60 and the across until you come to 3. The result is where the two rows join.
63 kW = 85.65 HP.
For values of over 100, the decimal point should be adjusted.

Example (below): Convert 65 HP into kW. Go down the first column until you find 60 and then across until you come to 3. The result is where the two rows join.
63 HP = 46.34 kW.
For values of over 100, the decimal point should be adjusted.

Table D-10. Pounds per Square Inch to Kilograms per Square Centimeter Conversion Table

lb. per sq. inch	0 kg per sq. cm	1 kg per sq. cm	2 kg per sq. cm	3 kg per sq. cm	4 kg per sq. cm	5 kg per sq. cm	6 kg per sq. cm	7 kg per sq. cm	8 kg per sq. cm	9 kg per sq. cm
0	..	0.0703	0.1406	0.2109	0.2812	0.3515	0.4218	0.4922	0.5625	0.6328
10	0.7031	0.7734	0.8437	0.9140	0.9843	1.0546	1.1249	1.1952	1.2655	1.3358
20	1.4061	1.4765	1.5468	1.6171	1.6874	1.7577	1.8280	1.8983	1.9686	2.0389
30	2.1092	2.1795	2.2498	2.3201	2.3904	2.4607	2.5311	2.6014	2.6717	2.7420
40	2.8123	2.8826	2.9529	3.0232	3.0935	3.1638	3.2341	3.3044	3.3747	3.4450
50	3.5154	3.5857	3.6560	3.7263	3.7966	3.8669	3.9372	4.0075	4.0778	4.1481
60	4.2184	4.2887	4.3590	4.4293	4.4997	4.5700	4.6403	4.7106	4.7809	4.8512
70	4.9215	4.9918	5.0621	5.1324	5.2027	5.2730	5.3433	5.4136	5.4839	5.5543
80	5.6246	5.6949	5.7652	5.8355	5.9058	5.9761	6.0464	6.1167	6.1870	6.2573
90	6.3276	6.3980	6.4682	6.5386	6.6089	6.6792	6.7495	6.8198	6.8901	6.9604
100	7.0307	7.1010	7.1713	7.2416	7.3120	7.3822	7.4525	7.5228	7.5932	7.6635

kg per sq. cm	0 lb. per sq. in.	1 lb. per sq. in.	2 lb. per sq. in.	3 lb. per sq. in.	4 lb. per sq. in.	5 lb. per sq. in.	6 lb. per sq. in.	7 lb. per sq. in.	8 lb. per sq. in.	9 lb. per sq. in.
0	..	14.22	28.45	42.67	56.89	71.12	85.34	99.56	113.79	128.01
10	142.23	156.46	170.68	184.90	199.13	213.35	227.57	241.80	256.02	270.24
20	284.47	298.69	312.91	327.14	341.36	355.58	369.81	384.03	398.25	412.48
30	426.70	440.92	455.15	469.37	483.59	497.82	512.04	526.26	540.49	554.71
40	568.93	583.16	597.38	611.60	625.83	640.05	654.27	668.50	682.72	696.94
50	711.17	725.39	739.61	753.84	768.06	782.28	796.51	810.73	824.95	839.18
60	853.40	867.62	881.85	896.07	910.29	924.52	938.74	952.96	967.19	981.41
70	995.63	1009.9	1024.1	1038.3	1052.5	1066.8	1081.0	1095.2	1109.4	1123.6
80	1137.9	1152.1	1166.3	1180.5	1194.8	1209.0	1223.2	1237.4	1251.7	1265.9
90	1280.1	1294.3	1308.6	1322.8	1337.0	1351.2	1365.4	1379.7	1393.9	1408.1
100	1422.3	1436.6	1450.8	1465.0	1479.2	1493.4	1507.7	1521.9	1536.1	1550.3

Table D-11. Pound Feet to Kilogram Meters Conversion Table

lb./ft.	0 kg metre	1 kg metre	2 kg metre	3 kg metre	4 kg metre	5 kg metre	6 kg metre	7 kg metre	8 kg metre	9 kg metre
0	..	0.138	0.277	0.415	0.553	0.691	0.830	0.968	1.106	1.244
10	1.383	1.521	1.659	1.797	1.936	2.074	2.212	2.350	2.489	2.627
20	2.765	2.903	3.041	3.180	3.318	3.456	3.595	3.733	3.871	4.009
30	4.148	4.286	4.424	4.562	4.701	4.839	4.977	5.115	5.254	5.392
40	5.530	5.669	5.807	5.945	6.083	6.222	6.360	6.498	6.636	6.775
50	6.913	7.051	7.189	7.328	7.466	7.604	7.742	7.881	8.019	8.157
60	8.295	8.434	8.572	8.710	8.848	8.987	9.125	9.263	9.401	9.540
70	9.678	9.816	9.954	10.093	10.231	10.369	10.507	10.646	10.784	10.922
80	11.060	11.199	11.337	11.475	11.613	11.752	11.890	12.028	12.166	12.305
90	12.443	12.581	12.719	12.858	12.996	13.134	13.272	13.411	13.549	13.687
100	13.826	13.964	14.102	14.240	14.379	14.517	14.655	14.793	14.932	15.070

kg/m	0 lb. ft.	1 lb. ft.	2 lb. ft.	3 lb. ft.	4 lb. ft.	5 lb. ft.	6 lb. ft.	7 lb. ft.	8 lb. ft.	9 lb. ft.
0	..	7.23	14.47	21.70	28.93	36.17	43.40	50.63	57.87	65.10
10	72.33	79.56	86.80	94.03	101.26	108.50	115.73	122.96	130.20	137.43
20	144.66	151.89	159.13	166.36	173.59	180.83	188.06	195.29	202.52	209.76
30	216.99	224.22	231.46	238.69	245.92	253.16	260.39	267.62	274.86	282.09
40	289.32	296.55	303.79	311.02	318.25	325.49	332.72	339.95	347.19	354.42
50	361.65	368.88	376.12	383.35	390.58	397.82	405.05	412.28	419.52	426.75
60	433.98	441.21	448.45	455.68	462.91	470.15	477.38	484.61	491.85	499.08
70	506.31	513.54	520.78	528.01	535.24	542.48	549.71	556.94	564.18	571.41
80	578.64	585.87	593.11	600.34	607.57	614.81	622.04	629.27	636.51	643.74
90	650.97	658.23	665.44	672.67	679.90	687.14	694.37	701.60	708.84	716.07
100	723.30	730.53	737.77	745.00	752.23	759.47	766.70	773.93	781.17	788.40

Table D-12. Coated Abrasive Grit Sizes

Grade	Garnet, Aluminum Oxide, or Silicon Carbide		Emery Cloth	Flint
Very fine	600, 500			
	400	10/0		
	360			
	320	9/0		
	280	8/0		
	240	7/0		
	220	6/0		Extra fine
Fine	180	5/0	3/0	
	150	4/0	2/0	
	120	3/0		Fine
Medium			0	
	100	2/0		
			1/2	
	80	0	1	Medium
			1 1/2	
	60	1/2		
Coarse			2	
	50	1		Coarse
			2 1/2	
	40	1 1/2		
	36	2		
Very coarse			3	
	30	2 1/2		Extra coarse
	24	3		
	20	3 1/2		
	16	4		
	12	4 1/2		

Table D-13. Comparative Sheet Metal Thicknesses

Gauge No.	Uncoated Steel and Stainless Steel*	Aluminum, Brass, and Copper
28	0.015″ (1/64″)	0.012″
26	0.018″	0.016″ (1/64″)
24	0.024″	0.020″
22	0.030″	0.025″
20	0.036″ (1/32″)	0.032″ (1/32″)
18	0.048″ (3/64″)	0.040″
16	0.060″ (1/16″)	0.051″
14	0.075″ (5/64″)	0.064″ (1/16″)
12	0.105″ (7/64″)	0.081″ (5/64″)

*Galvanized steel is slightly thicker than uncoated or stainless steel.

Table D-14. Equivalencies

Square Measure Equivalents

1 square yard = 0.836 square meter
1 square foot = 0.0929 square meter = 929 square centimeters
1 square inch = 6.452 square centimeters = 645.2 square millimeters

1 square meter = 10.764 square feet = 1.196 square yards
1 square centimeter = 0.155 square inch
1 square millimeter = 0.00155 square inch

Cubic Measure Equivalents

1 cubic inch = 16.38706 cubic centimeters
100 cubic inches = 1.64 liters
1 Imperial gallon = 4.546 liters
1 Imperial quart = 1.136 liters
1 US gallon = 3.785 liters
1 US quart = 0.946 liter

1 cubic centimeter = 0.061 cubic inch
1 liter (cubic decimeter) = 0.0353 cubic foot = 61.023 cubic inches
1 liter = 0.2642 US gallon = 1.0567 US quarts = 0.2200 Imperial gallon

Weight Equivalents

1 Imperial ton (UK) = 2240 pounds (long ton)
1 short ton (USA) = 2000 pounds
1 ton (of 2000 pounds) = 0.9072 metric ton
1 ton (of 2240 pounds) = 1.016 metric tons = 1016 kilograms
1 pound = 0.4536 kilogram = 453.6 grams

1 metric ton = 2204.6 pounds
1 kilogram = 2.2046 pounds

Miscellaneous Equivalents

1 Imperial gallon (UK) = 1.2 gallons (US)
1 h.p. = 2,544 Btus
1 kw = 3,413 Btus

Index

swages, 495, 503, 504, 564; thimbles, 494, 503, 565; wire, 494; wire rigging, 498. *See also* Fittings

Terminology: blocks, 512; rigging, 492; solar panels, 190–191

Testing: AC circuits, 108–111; armatures, 204–205, 216; auxiliary winding-type circuits, 207; batteries, 42–46; battery isolation diodes, 73; bonding circuits, 149; bridge rectifiers, 203, 204; brushes, 204–205; capacitors, 204, 217; capacitor-type circuits, 207; capacity, 45; coaxial cable, 235; commutators, 215; compressors, 348; DC motors, 214; diodes, 82–83, 205, 206; electrical circuits, 149; electric motors, 214–215, 377; exciter windings, 207–208; field windings, 203, 216; galvanic isolators, 102; gauges, 288–289; glow plugs, 262; ground faults, 91, 93, 94, 109; iceboxes, 332; isolation transformers, 166; load, 44–45, 562; LPG cylinders, 461–462; with multimeters, 262; with ohmmeters, 90–91; polarity, 109; for resistance, 86; rotors, 205, 206–207; sending units, 289; short circuits, 90–91; starter motors, 220–222; stators, 205–206; voltage, 73, 109; with voltmeters, 93; windings, 205

Test lights, 85
Thermal overload, 166, 216
Thermal runaway, 24
Thermistors, 167–168, 564
Thermocouples, 464, 564
Thermopure waste treatment systems, 378–380
Thermostatic expansion valve (TXV), 338
Thermostats, 472, 564; winding protection, 185
Thickness gauge. *See* Feeler gauge
Thimbles, 494, 503, 565
Threading: damaged, 569; hose, 363
Through-deck bolts, 502
Through-hulls, 380–385; fids, 385, 560; hose attachments, 385; installation, 384–385
Thrust bearings, 307, 312
Tie bars, 499
Tillers, 423, 446–447, 565; autopilots, 447; emergency, 441
Time delays, 419
Tinning, 234, 565
Toggles, 499, 500, 501, 504, 565
Toilets, 365–380; clogging, 369; discharge regulations, 365–366; double-acting piston, 370, 371, 372; electric, 374, 375–377; electrified, 369–375; installation, 366–367; Jet Head, 380; Lavacs, 375; laying-up, 566; maintenance,

367–368; manual, 369–375; problems, 368–369; pump failure, 374; repairing valves and pistons, 374–375; Royal Flush, 380; troubleshooting and repair, 368–380; VacuFlush, 380, 381; vented loops, 366; winterizing, 368

Tools, 570–572; electrical, 119–122, 570–571; mechanic's, 570; power, 571; for servicing Sanden compressors, 344; woodworking, 571
Topping lift, 565
Torque conversion table, 575
Traction batteries. *See* Deep-cycle batteries
Transfer switch, automatic, 179
Transformers, 162–163, 166, 565; isolation, 103, 166, 562; polarization, 103
Transient voltage suppressors. *See* Fail-safe diodes
Transistors, field effect, 170
Transmissions: clutch adjustments, 302–303; connecting, 309–312; control cables, 303–304, 305; how they work, 296–300; hydraulic units, 308; inboard/outboards, 299–300; maintenance, 300–301; manual units, 308–309; oil seal and output coupling, 306; operating principles, 302; operating problems, 305–306; output-shaft coupling, 307; overheating, 305; planetary, 296–297; preloaded thrust bearings, 307; remote controls, 304; troubleshooting, 301–307; two-shaft, 297, 298, 299; V-drives, 297–299, 300
Traversing nut, 427, 565
Triacs, 160
Trickle charge, 565
Trim tabs, 448–449, 565
Triple-diaphragm pumps, 413
T-terminals, 503
Tubing: breakaway, 453; capillary, 338, 348–349; copper, 358–361; fiberglass, 430–431; heat-shrink, 561; maintenance and troubleshooting, 428–431; propane flow, 462; refrigeration size, 460–461; resistance effect of, 391–392; rudder, 423, 563; securing runs, 461
Tubing cutters, 359
Turbochargers, 285, 565; testing, 284–290
Turbocharger wheels, cleaning, 285–286
Turnbuckles, 499, 500, 503, 504, 565
12-volt batteries, 24
12-volt electrical systems, 13, 34
TXV. *See* Thermostatic expansion valve
Ty-wraps, 565

UHMWPE. *See* Ultrahigh molecular-weight polyethylene

Ultimate switch, 418
Ultrahigh molecular-weight polyethylene (UHMWPE), 430
Unbond, 148–150
United Kingdom, cable-sizing formula, 117
Universal motors, 210–211, 560; electrical problems, 215–217; maintenance procedures, 216; operation, 211; permanent-magnet, 388; speed regulation, 213–214; wound-field-coil, 388
USA: cable-sizing formula, 116; liquefied petroleum gas cylinders, 458

VacuFlush toilets, 380, 381
Vacuum, 565
Vacuum pumps, 565
Valve clearance, 565
Valve cover, 565
Valves, 565; antisiphon, 558; ball, 383, 384, 558; check, 559; duckbill, 369, 560; expansion, 348–349, 560; flap, 560; gate, 382–383, 561; globe, 382–383; master shutoff, 460; repairing, 374–375; safety (relief), 472; service, 352–353; solenoid, 264–265; stem-type, 355; thermostatic expansion, 338
Vane pumps, 388, 404, 565; troubleshooting, 399
Variable-pitch propeller, 565
Variable-speed technology (VST), 208–210
Variable-speed technology generators, 209; troubleshooting, 210
Variable-volume impeller pumps, 388
Varistors, 167–168, 565; metal oxide, 153, 154, 562
Varnish, 479
V-belts, HP ratings for, 19
V-drives, 297–299, 300
Vented loops, 366–367, 558
Vent fittings, 363
Vent hoses, 362
Vertical windlasses, 531, 533, 536
VHF antennas: emergency, 235; gain and signal radiation patterns, 232; range in nautical miles, 231
Vibration, 51–52
Video display noise suppression, 243
Vise-Grips, 562, 565
Vmp. *See* Load voltage
Voltage, 3–4, 76; dockside testing, 109; electronic equipment problems, 228–230; ghost, 79; load, 191; measuring, 78, 81; natural, 132; open-circuit, 44, 51, 191, 562; peak inverse, 71–72; at peak power, 191; ripple, 59, 563; root mean square, 170; for solar panels, 191–192; testing, 214
Voltage drops, 76, 169, 565; conductor sizes for, 115, 534; measuring, 30; testing for, 73,

JAN - - 2012